THE FIFTIES

The Daily Telegraph

THE FIFTIES

A UNIQUE CHRONICLE OF THE DECADE

edited and introduced by
DAVID HOLLOWAY

researched by
DIANA HEFFER

foreword by
W.F. DEEDES

SIMON & SCHUSTER
London . Sydney . New York . Tokyo . Singapore . Toronto

First published in Great Britain by
SIMON & SCHUSTER LIMITED 1991

A Paramount Communications Company

Simon & Schuster Limited
West Garden Place
Kendal Street
London W2 2AQ

Simon & Schuster Sydney Australia Pty Limited

A CIP catalogue record for this book is available from The British Library
ISBN 0 – 671 – 71079 – 6

Phototypeset by Learning Curve
Printed and bound in Great Britain by Butler & Tanner, Frome and London.

CONTENTS

ACKNOWLEDGEMENTS

The creation of such a record as this is essentially a team effort. While I must take any blame there is for including what some may find the wrong items and excluding others that might be deemed essential, and while I am solely responsible for the final selection and the space given to each entry, much of the credit must go to Diana Heffer. Her researches through the files of *The Daily Telegraph* to find news stories and features that I half-remembered or had discovered through other sources led her to make exciting discoveries of her own, fascinating to someone who, unlike me, was coming to the 1950s from the, so to speak, wrong direction. Her ability with microfiche and photocopier has made this book come to fruition.

The marvels of modern printing have made it possible for the old issues of *The Daily Telegraph* to be "scanned" and reproduced in a more readable type, while Diana and Brian Coulon and his team in *The Daily Telegraph* picture library have performed wonders in tracking down the original illustrations, the ones on the pages of 40-odd-year-old issues being incapable of salvaging. At Simon & Schuster, Claudia Shaffer's enthusiasm, attention to detail and calm insistence on the importance of deadlines has been vital. And it was Fenella Smart's, and Learning Curve's Jo Beerts' skills that gave the book the elegance of design it possesses. Anyone who has ever handled newspaper cuttings will know their capacity for getting all over the place. With the cuttings of a decade to play with, I managed almost to submerge a whole house, to cover a dining-room table with gum and to leave trails of paper slivers everywhere. Only a wife, such as Sally, could have endured the discomfort, have succoured and counselled me while writing her own book at the same time.

My final and greatest debt is to the editors, sub-editors, staff reporters and correspondents (most of them anonymous in those days before by-lines were put at the top of even the shortest piece of copy) as well as the contributors who made *The Daily Telegraph* the supreme newspaper that it was then, and is today.

David Holloway, July 1991

The Daily Telegraph

FOREWORD

In this book there is something for everybody. If you are under 40, you will discover from these pages how backward and old-fashioned we were before the advent of chairpersons, trainers, Madonna and the Walkman. If you are over 60, you will come across ample evidence to show how sadly things have gone downhill here since your younger days. If you are somewhere between 40 and 60, you are free to reach whatever conclusions you please.

It was a decade of fresh hopes, old fears, lost faiths. Starting with shortages all round, it ended with the Prime Minister declaring to his Bradford audience, "Let us be frank about it. Most of our people have never had it so good." King George VI died and Queen Elizabeth II succeeded him. War, quenched in Europe, broke out in the Far East, in the Middle East and in Africa. The Treaty of Rome was signed. Europe drew together, our Colonial Empire drew apart. Amid the ruins of war the concrete jungle was born. Debutantes went out, by order of the Queen. The "teenagers" came in - with money to spend.

Lord Radcliffe, Reith lecturer of 1951, caught the tone as well as anyone by remarking prophetically: "The gulf between the present and the past, which gets wider and deeper with startling speed, marks the general inability which afflicts society not merely to agree with earlier beliefs about the place and purpose of human life in its temporal existence but even to have beliefs about the matter at all."

We entered the 1950s with a heavy overdraft. The second world war had mercifully cost us less in blood than the first, but the material cost had been calamitous. The yoke of the war-time controls still lay heavily upon us. Rationing of food was not ended until July 1954 when the people of London made a funeral pyre of their ration books in Trafalgar Square. This newspaper had raised my post-war wage of £18 a week to £21, which in the absence of anything much to buy in the shops seemed entirely adequate.

Much of Europe still lay in ruins. Rebuilding was slow. Countries like Poland and Greece had lost a fifth of their dwellings, Germany and Russia far more. We were relatively fortunate, losing only one in every 17 homes. Not until the end of 1954 was the Government able to end the war-time system of issuing licences to builders - a rich source of sharp practice, scandal and ill-feeling. Lord Montgomery, laden with military honours, lamented to me that his local council had refused him a licence to convert a Hampshire mill into the home of his dreams. Only 46% of British householders possessed bathrooms.

The mood was sombre, well symbolised by Carol Reed's film *The Third Man*, which had its London première early in 1950. Harry Lime in his grim surroundings seemed a significant fragment of our times. We went about humming or whistling his signature tune. George Orwell died of tuberculosis - too soon to reap the rewards of his uncannily accurate pessimism. *Animal Farm* and *Nineteen Eighty-Four* became essential reading.

Clem Attlee, whose Labour Government had been struggling in rough seas since 1945, called a general election in February 1950, a dreadful month for canvassing. Some 1,868 candidates presented themselves to the British electors. The campaign was memorable to me because it was my first, but carried few distinguishing marks. Dr. Hill, the Radio Doctor, moving effortlessly from digestive ailments to "ghost stories of the inter-war years" in an election broadcast, scored a resounding hit. Labour won narrowly in the closest finish for 100 years, Liberals lost 314 election deposits and those of us who won returned to seats in the House of Lords. The new House of Commons, replacing the chamber destroyed by fire bombs in 1941, was not ready for opening by the King until nine months later.

Although I had first joined the editorial staff of The Daily Telegraph in 1937, my own contributions to the following pages are mercifully obscure. On return from the war in 1945, I joined the Peterborough column and, subject to one or two short intervals, stayed with it until 1974. I can, however, recognise my hand in a paragraph reproduced from 1952: "Mr. James Callaghan, 40-year old Socialist M.P. for South Cardiff, will be worth watching when the struggle for the Socialist Executive between the forces of Mr. Attlee and Mr. Bevan develops at Morecambe ....To describe Mr. Callaghan as a dark horse would be inappropriate. In Opposition he has matched ambition with assiduity. Though only a junior Minister in the last Socialist Government, he has come right to the fore in recent months."

There were shafts of light amid the gloom as the decade opened. That enduring musical *South Pacific* won a Pulitzer prize. T.S. Eliot's play, *The Cocktail Party*, gave our dramatic critic W.A. Darlington "one of the most satisfying emotional experiences of my play going life". Winston Churchill's horse, Colonist II, won eight of his eleven races, the last six in succession, and took the Jockey Club Cup. Described as the bargain horse of the year, he was also - with another election in the offering - a strong electoral asset to his owner. The head of the National Hairdressers' Federation observed that men's hair was growing longer than their wives'.

Soap rationing ended before 1950 was out, and the 5s limit on meals in all hotels and restaurants, which had been in force since 1942, was abolished. Bon Viveur whetted appetites in our columns by describing a dinner partaken at Chinon, near Tours, which had cost her companion no more than £2 7s in English money. It comprised two dry Martinis, Les Escargots Maison (baked with garlic butter and parsley), L'Omelette Gargamella, Noisettes de Veau Tourangella à la Crême, Salade Verte, one bottle white Mon Cure 1947 (sec), one bottle Vin de Chinon 1947, two liqueurs, Marc des Prunes. Sainsbury's first self-service store opened at Croydon.

Radio flourished, but television was still in a primitive state of black and white. In 1953, Mr. Harold Macmillan, then Housing Minister, and Mr. Ernest Marples, his parliamentary secretary, were chosen to deliver for the Conservative party the first party political broadcast on television from Lime Grove. I was called upon to be anchorman. There being no video-recording, everything had to go out live; and there being no teleprompt, every line had to be learned by heart and rehearsed. On the day of transmission, Mrs. Grace Wyndham Goldie the producer kept Mr. Macmillan and myself at rehearsals for 10 hours. Marples, sensibly, took the afternoon off at the Cup Final.

The potentially most dangerous international event of the decade, still not fully resolved, was the invasion of South Korea. In June 1950 the forces of Communist-ruled North Korea crossed the 38th parallel and occupied all territory north of the Imjin river. President Truman ordered American forces to give support to troops of the Korean Republic. Mr. Attlee supported President Truman.

The Security Council approved a motion by seven votes to one authorising all members of the United Nations to go to the aid of South Korea. The Russians were still absent over the representation of China. For the U.N. it was a moment of rare post-war unanimity. "The decision they took," observed the editor of the Annual Register at the time, "may well alter the whole course of world history." General MacArthur took charge, Parliament voted another £100 million for defence expenditure, National Service was extended from 18 months to two years.

Another sign that the Cold War had shifted to the Far East came in October 1950 when a force of 3,500 French troops in north-east Tonkin was overwhelmed by a Viet-Minh rebel force. The French Government sent General Juin, France's leading expert on colonial warfare.

Our cultural revolution had not fully broken out. Manners were gentler. Nobody thought about Mrs. Whitehouse. An episode involving Noel Coward and the BBC is a guide to the way we thought in 1950. Certain lines in four lyrics of Coward's new musical play, *Ace of Clubs*, were considered unsuitable for broadcasting. One of the lyrics, sung as a duet between two cats, ran thus: "Love in the moonlight can be sublime/ Now's the time, Charlie, I'm / Bound to give in if you'll only climb over the garden wall." "Bound to give in", thought likely to arouse immoral ideas among listeners, was replaced by "waiting for you". Similarly, lines which ran "New Jersey Dames / Go up in flames / If someone mentions bed" were replaced by "In Tennessee, the BBC / Would blush to hear what's said." The BBC, Mr. Coward declared, had been courteous about it, and he saw their point of view.

Politically, it was the Conservatives' decade. Labour won the 1950 election by a whisker; but in truth their leading Ministers were worn out, and showed it. Sir Stafford Cripps, whose name was synonymous with austerity, left within five months of the election. Ernest Bevin died nine months later, in April 1951. In the same month, Attlee, who was in hospital nursing ulcers, had to accept the resignations of Nye Bevan and Harold Wilson, ostensibly because Cripps's successor at the Treasury, Hugh Gaitskell, had imposed health charges on false teeth and spectacles.

Throughout the decade, the newspaper's editor was Sir Colin Coote. He had spent five years in politics as a Liberal M.P. for the Isle of Ely (1917-22), was closely in touch with politicians, but not invariably sound in all his judgments. In the issue of 1955, there will be found a short article by Sir Colin written after Anthony Eden had at last succeeded Winston Churchill. "Part of the task of those who sit in the gallery of the House of Commons," wrote Coote, "is to discern budding Pitts and Hampdens among the back benchers. It is my boast that from the eyrie I discerned Anthony Eden in 1925, about two years after he had entered Parliament."

Coote's deputy at the time, Donald McLachlan, made considerably more impact six months later by writing a critical article about Eden, the relevant sentence of which ran like this: "There is a favourite gesture of the Prime Minister's which is sometimes recalled to illustrate this sense of disappointment. To emphasise a point he will clench one fist to smack the open palm of the other hand - but the smack is seldom heard. Most Conservatives and almost certainly some of the wiser trade union leaders are waiting to feel the smack of firm Government." Headed "Waiting for the Smack of Firm Government" this article attracted as much attention as anything which appeared in *The Daily Telegraph* throughout the decade.

Churchill had taken office in the autumn of 1951, survived a stroke in 1953, offered me junior office in his last reshuffle of 1954, and finally handed over to Anthony Eden, in the spring of 1955. Eden won a summer election, was felled by Suez and ill-health a year later. Harold Macmillan was preferred to R.A. Butler - in controversial circumstances which bode ill for the Conservative party. I left office, not out of disagreement over Suez (as one or two contemporaries did), but because a junior minister's salary of £1,500 a year could not sustain a young family. Ominously dubbed as Supermac, the Prime Minister won a third successive election for the Tories in 1959 more comfortably than either of his predecessors. From then on, the journey lay downhill. For Conservative Prime Ministers three is not a lucky number.

Perversely, it was also the Trade Unions' decade. How they relished Churchill's appointment of the emollient Walter Monckton as Minister of Labour in 1951! Post-war industrial labour was no longer the underdog. Railways, newspapers, buses, steel, docks, there were not many realms in which they failed to establish an ascendancy which prevailed until the early 1980s.

In the early hours of February 6, 1952, King George VI (who had undergone a lung operation four months earlier) died in his sleep at Sandringham House. He was only 56. His daughter and heir, Princess Elizabeth, learned of this in Kenya at a hunting lodge. There had been a picture, deeply poignant in retrospect, of a frail-looking King waving her good-bye as she left for Africa.

For reasons now difficult to explain Queen Elizabeth's Coronation in June of that year caught the public heart. A nation which had been struggling back to normality for almost a decade was beginning to feel its age. The aftermath of the war had been wearisome and in so many ways disappointing. This sombre stage was suddenly lit by a graceful figure declaring that, whether it be long or short, her life would be given to service of her country and the Commonwealth. She bore a great name. We speculated on a new Elizabethan Age. This was to be our New Frontier. As some of us sauntered round the Palace on the Coronation's eve, early editions of the newspapers were on sale, proclaiming that Hillary and Tensing had conquered Everest. It seemed a good omen.

From then to this day the Queen's heart has lain with the Commonwealth, and in that realm this was a decisive decade. With the granting of independence to India in 1947, a great cornerstone had been shifted. From then on the process of granting autonomy to Britain's colonial possessions was set in train. There were set-backs, some of them reported in these pages - turmoil in Cyprus, Mau Mau in Kenya, ill-starred federations in the West Indies and Central Africa. In 1959, I attended celebrations to mark self-government in Northern Nigeria. The Premier was Alhaji Sir Ahmadu Bello, an aristocrat and rare statesman. He was joined on this occasion by the Prime Minister of the Federation, Abubakar Tafawa Balewa. Both were men far above the ordinary, and within a year or so both of them had been murdered.

But there were also gains. In March 1952 Dr. Krame Nkrumah became the first African Prime Minister south of the Sahara. Sudan, Malaya and the West Indies won independence. Before the decade was out, Macmillan had appointed Iain Macleod to the Colonial Office, and the wind of change freshened.

It was a decade in which treachery became news, starting with the sentencing in 1950 of Dr. Fuchs at the Old Bailey to 14 years for passing to the Russians secrets of our atomic bomb. A year later, Donald Maclean and Guy Burgess vanished from the Foreign Office. They began a long trail of mystery, stretching through three decades, which was to become a national obsession. Harold Philby, then First Secretary at Washington Embassy, was challenged by a Labour M.P. late in 1955. Bland - and sometimes boring - to the last, he shrugged it off. Mr. Macmillan, then the Foreign Secretary, assured the Commons there was no reason to identify Philby with the "third man".

At the other end of the spectrum, Senator McCarthy began his long crusade of guilt by association against America's alleged Communists. His principal target was the State Department and the first line in his beguiling song was - "Any man may be a Communist." Notwithstanding a vote in the U.S. Senate at the end of 1954 which condemned him by 67 votes to 22, he lasted an intolerably long time.

Three murders in this country changed our history. In 1952 Christopher Craig and Derek Bentley were found guilty of murdering P.C. Sidney Miles. Bentley, 19, was hanged, Craig, 16 ½, whose hand was on the gun, was saved by his age and sent to prison.

In June 1953 John Christie, an £8 a week clerk, who lived at 10 Rillington Place was sentenced to death for the murder of his wife. Three years earlier Timothy Evans had been hanged for the murder of his baby daughter at the same address. A macabre tale was slowly to unfold.

In July 1955 Ruth Ellis was hanged for the murder of her lover, the last woman so to die in this country. These unconnected events gave a decisive impetus to the campaign to abolish capital punishment, a campaign which prevailed a decade later.

I have kept all the letters I received as an M.P. during the Suez crisis of June-December 1956. They remind me how deeply people were aroused by this event. It ended the political career of Anthony Eden who had succeeded Churchill not much more than a year earlier, and led to the most uncontrolled anger I ever witnessed in the House of Commons. The Home Secretary being perpetually in Cabinet at this time, his Parliamentary Under Secretary was saddled with additional duties; and I was called upon to persuade a sceptical House of Commons to pass the Homicide Bill, which aimed to restrict hanging for murder to armed gangsters. It bore a very short life.

Speaking with hindsight and the detachment of one who was a member of the Government and therefore away from our office at the time, I perceive from an editorial of November 2, 1956 that our judgment on the Suez affair had not fully grasped the truth of that engagement: "The purpose of our forces in action is not to make war but to stop it. This is police action, taken by France and the United Kingdom... Is it really shameful to stop fighting by force?" The same editorial carries also a splendidly rhetorical sentence, "As for our own people, who can yet judge?" Very much the style of the time. Again, the opening of a *Daily Telegraph* leader at the time of the Notting Hill riot in 1958 strikes one as odd: "Unlike most problems, that of coloured migrants to Britain grows smaller rather than larger the more closely it is examined."

This was the time when Commonwealth immigration, mainly from the West Indies, first became a matter for comment. Ministers took stock of it in 1956-57, during my time in the Home Office, persuaded themselves that an austere Budget had checked the main movement, and let the matter lie. A measure to regulate numbers was not brought forward until 1962, and this was largely ineffective until Labour became seriously alarmed in 1965.

There were portents of what lay ahead between those times and these. "Space travel is bilge," the Astronomer Royal said early in 1956. Undismayed, the Russians had sent Sputnik 1 and a little dog called Laika into space by the end of the next year, and the Americans had Explorer up by March 1958. Britain's motorway network was announced. The first stretch was ceremoniously opened by the Prime Minister in December 1958 - and closed by frost damage one month later. Life peers were introduced into public life. After three years' work, Wolfenden in 1957 opened a long and controversial chapter of social reform by calling for the decriminalisation of homosexuality between consenting adults. Figure-hugging jeans became fashionable.

Our cultural development was diverse. Bill Haley - "We're Going to Rock around the Clock" - arrived. *My Fair Lady* reached the stage. When the Archers marked their 800th episode early in 1954, they boasted an audience of 10 million. *Lolita* and *Lucky Jim* were published, the Goon Show introduced us to Harry Secombe, Peter Sellers and Spike Milligan, Olivier gave us his version of *The Entertainer* and *The Bridge Over the River Kwai* won three Oscars. At the close of the decade John Betjeman's collected poems were selling like hot cakes, indicating that we were ready again to laugh at ourselves. In May 1959 a Picasso was sold for £55,000, then a world record - which tells us as much about the value of our currency as of his pictures. In that final year the Mini was launched and Hugh Carleton Greene was made Director-General of the BBC - a portent of many things.

In sport the mixture was surprisingly like it is today - unexpected triumphs, sad disappointments and youthful prodigies. Among the highlights were Roger Bannister's four-minute mile (1954); Christine Truman's contribution to our first Wightman Cup victory for 28 years - she was only 17 (1958); and our first victory in the Ashes for 20 years (1953). Our first five batsmen then were Hutton, W.J. Edrich, P.B.H. May, Compton (D) and Graveney. Jim Laker took 19 wickets in a single match (9/37, 10/53) (1956). Matthews - "too-old-at-38" - was still Wizard of the Dribble in 1953. Sir Gordon Richards, 50, and champion jockey on 26 occasions quit the saddle (1954).

The decade left its mark in two particular respects. City skylines rose higher and teenagers established their own culture. We shape our institutions, Churchill once observed, and then we are shaped by them. High rise blocks rose like tombstones - which for some of their residents they were to become. Filing cabinets were designed for men and women to work in. Land was precious. Self-sufficiency in food was the aim. Thus the afflictions of today's inner city areas came into being.

For the young, new heroes arose in the West - James Dean, Marlon Brando, Bill Haley, Elvis Presley. The Beatles had not quite arrived, but they were just round the corner. The Teddy Boys introduced us to a new style of dress. What developed in the 1950s was a style of culture designed to be exclusive, to set young people apart from their elders, to sever the present from the past.

Lord Radcliffe shall have the last word. A revolution, he pointed out in a postscript to the Reith Lectures of 1951, is generally brought about by a revolutionary leader, who by temperament is unlikely to stand any nonsense from his own theories. Our own revolution possessed no such leader, and had no such control. "Which," concluded Lord Radcliffe, "leads me to think that the English revolution of the twentieth century may continue for a longer period of time and arrive in the end at a more complete break with the past than many other more dramatic social disturbances."

These pages help us to judge how far he was right.

W.F. Deedes

INTRODUCTION

It is very rare for a decade to provide any sort of exact framework for recording historical change. For instance, William the Conqueror did not choose to arrive in 1060 nor did Henry Tudor arrange for the Battle of Bosworth to occur in 1480. Only, among English kings, did George III conveniently choose to reign from 1760 to 1820. So it is only to be expected that, strictly speaking, the 1950s are an artificial division of time. You could say that the building of the post-war world began in 1945 and the Cold War that began operations immediately hostilities ceased was still clearly in evidence when the decade closed. So, the Fifties, which have never gathered an adjective in the way that the Swinging Sixties did, have no particular end or beginning but they do have a character of their own and this selection from the pages of *The Daily Telegraph* during that period is an attempt to capture in miniature the spirit of the age.

I must emphasise that this is not a history of the time nor even a formal narrative trying to tell the whole story but something far more like a tapestry, recording images from the period as they were presented in words and pictures in one newspaper. Some events like the Coronation of Queen Elizabeth II or great natural disasters like the earthquake at Agadir are complete in themselves. Others like the Mau Mau terrorism in Kenya or the troubles in Cyprus went on for years. It would have been easy to fill the tapestry with continuing accounts of long running events like the Korean War, the Arab/Israeli confrontation culminating in the dispute over the Suez Canal or the changing temperatures in the Cold War. What I have tried to do is to pick out one incident in these long-running dramas to characterise the event as a whole. Nothing, I think, does this better than the single dispatch from Budapest written at the height of the Hungarian uprising in the autumn of 1956. All the agonies of Hungary are there. So much of the action in the Korean War is represented by two reports from war correspondents. And in the obituary of Christopher Buckley, *The Daily Telegraph* war correspondent, who was killed in battle there.

The whole essence of this compilation is that it should represent the Fifties as they were seen in the pages of *The Daily Telegraph*. Nothing has been altered although, for reasons of space, many of the items have been shortened. Some of those whose views are recorded here and still survive may indeed regret, certainly, some of the statements that they made then, and many of the judgments confidently propounded at the time have in the event proved to be erroneous. What matters is that this is how people then were thinking. It is for the formal histories of the period to provide the necessary correctives, analyses and commentary.

The fact that it has only been possible to allot sixteen pages to each year has meant that much has of necessity been omitted. It would have been only too easy to crowd the pages with accounts of disasters, trade disputes and international disagreements. These must, of course, find some place. But one train crash or one strike is, however terrible or personally involving it may have been, very like another and my intention here has been to cover as much ground, and as many different sorts of ground, as possible. Some of the items chosen are there for they seem to typify particular sets of social circumstances or describe life as it was then. For instance, at the beginning of the decade, the British were allowed to spend only £50 a year on holiday travel abroad and, in consequence, needed guidance on how best to spend their tiny allowance. The ending of the five-shilling limit on the amount a restaurant might charge for a meal meant that many of those going out for a meal required help in finding their way through a menu, and were for the first time sampling exotic food which we take for granted today. The impact of television can only be hinted at, though it was one of the great influences of the decade. I can remember going out with a Gallup pollster to question people on the eve of the Queen's Coronation and returning to the office to report that it would seem likely that nearly half the population within reach of a television transmitter intended to watch the ceremony in Westminster Abbey, mostly in groups on receivers especially hired for the occasion. This was greeted with astonishment, yet it proved to be true. Today it is unlikely that any drama production could have the impact that the television transmission of a version of George Orwell's *Nineteen Eighty-four* did in the mid-50s. Other images in this tapestry record events, not all that important in themselves but which show what was thought at the time about them and some tell of the people who have subsequently become well known for one reason or another. *The Mousetrap* was thought quite good of its kind; young Messrs Greaves and Charlton were predicted to have futures as footballers; Dame Iris Murdoch could do better if she tried to be less clever.

For each year two representative front pages have been chosen. In order to fit the format of the book they have been pared slightly. The five other news pages allotted to each year have been constructed from the issues of the years and are not in chronological order. For reference, the actual date is printed under each entry. Two pages carry editorials and articles of general interest and there is a page devoted to the arts. Two pages are devoted to obituaries and three to the coverage of sports events. So far as the sports pages are concerned, there is no intention of giving a full list of results or a comprehensive account of the whole sporting scene. Here, rather, are reports of some outstanding performances — Roger Bannister's sub-four-minute mile; Stanley Matthews's first cupwinners medal, and Devon Loch's fatal stumble just before the finish of the Grand National. For the reader's amusement a crossword a year and its solution have been included but, and I must take the blame for having made the decision, *The Daily Telegraph's* favourite column, "The Way of the World" by Peter Simple, has been omitted, partly because it was only conceived in the middle of the 1950s and the odd snippet from it would not do justice to the wit and wisdom of the feature.

Much changed during the 1950s: the first rocket landed on the moon; jet airliners went into service; the hydrogen bomb exploded. Stalin and Einstein died. Much of the old order changed. Colonies won their independence. The "mini" was hailed as the "peoples car" and *Look Back in Anger* seemed to spell the end of drawing room comedy in the theatre, as clearly as *Lucky Jim* heralded a new sort of fiction. Values of many kinds changed. It is, by the way, almost impossible to give any sort of guide to the changes in monetary values since the 1950s, though the reader will see, from the advertisements and from the news stories giving account of spending on household goods or changes in the budget, what the average family might be earning and spending. The price of *The Daily Telegraph* remained constant throughout the decade at 2 ½ d, the equivalent of 1.25p. At the beginning of the decade, paper was rationed and the size and circulation of newspapers controlled by their pre-war levels. By the mid-1950s rationing was ended and the papers were allowed to find their own level and to put on extra pages. No longer would the reader find the obituaries sharing the same page as the racing results or the theatre notices alongside the police court reports. There was even a whole page devoted to book reviews.

For me, the 1950s were a rather special period. Quite by chance, my future wife and I joined the same paper, the *News Chronicle*, on the same day, January 1st, 1950. Two years later, I proposed to her as we both waited at the American Embassy in London, which was acting as a ship-to-shore link, for news whether the *Flying Enterprise* with its lone skipper, Captain Carlsen on board, would make harbour. At neat two-year intervals our three children were born in 1954, 1956 and 1958. And just after the decade ended, I joined *The Daily Telegraph*. I have tried to avoid choosing items simply because I was *there*. Equally, I am conscious that I may have caused distress by not including items when you, the reader, were there. All I can hope is that those who were around in the Fifties will find their memories jogged or, indeed, as I have done, find pleasure in re-discovering great events or minute household details that they had totally forgotten. And for those who never knew the Fifties, I hope that this tapestry in words and pictures will serve as an idiosyncratic introduction.

David Holloway

1950

For the first time the United Nations went to war. The North Korean forces had streamed southwards over the 38th parallel and an international force, under the command of General MacArthur, arrived to attempt to drive the invaders out. By the end of the year, it was far from certain that they would succeed. The formation of the international force was only possible because the Russians, who would certainly have used their veto to defeat the resolution, were boycotting United Nations meetings at the time. The sending of British troops to Korea meant that the period that National Servicemen would spend in uniform was raised from 18 months to two years.

In Europe, the first small beginnings of an economic community were made with the announcement of the Schuman Plan under which the coal and steel industries of those traditional enemies, France and Germany, would, if their governments agreed, be put under a single "high command." Winston Churchill, the leader of the Opposition in the House of Commons, called for European unity: "We Europeans should best preserve world peace and our own survival by standing together."

In Britain, the Labour Government, elected in the last days of the Second World War, was running out of steam and in the February General Election barely scraped home with a majority so small that it was, in the words of *The Daily Telegraph* editorial, "tantamount to a vote of censure". Klaus Fuchs, the atom scientist, was sentenced to 14 years', imprisonment for passing on secret information to the Russian Government.

The older order changed with the deaths of George Bernard Shaw, General Smuts, so long Prime Minister of South Africa and a member of the War Cabinet, and Lord Wavell, the British army commander in the Western Desert and Viceroy of India. George Orwell died just before the publication of his last book, *Nineteen Eighty Four*.

The wartime austerity continued with most foodstuffs still rationed but the ban on restaurants charging more than 5s for a meal or serving any customer with more than one "main course" was lifted. A new fabric called Terylene was announced by ICI.

The public thrilled to the to the music of *Carousel* on the London stage, marvelled at the adventures of Thor Heyerdahl as recorded in his book of his journey by balsa raft across the Pacific ocean, *Kon-Tiki*, and warmed to the success of the British film industry in producing *The Blue Lamp*. In cricket England succumbed to the spin-bowling skills of Ramhadin and Valentine, celebrated in the calypso record that rode high in the charts as "those two little friends of mine". The 14-year-old "jockey prodigy", Lester Pigott, was riding winners and, after coming second in the Cambridgeshire, was suspended from riding for the rest of the season.

As the year came to a cold end, there came the astonishing news that the Coronation Stone had been stolen from Westminster Abbey by a group of young Scottish nationalists determined that it should be returned to its original home at Scone.

CHURCHILL MEMOIRS – PAGE 4

The Daily Telegraph

and Morning Post

4 A.M.

No. 29,539 LONDON, THURSDAY, MARCH 2, 1950 Printed in LONDON and MANCHESTER Price 1½d

SOCIALISTS DECIDE THEIR TACTICS

GO-SLOW POLICY ON NATIONALISATION

MR. MORRISON SAYS 'NO REVOLTS'

CONSERVATIVES TO AWAIT THE KING'S SPEECH

By Our Political Correspondent

There seems little doubt that the Government intends to "go slow" with fresh nationalisation proposals in the new session of Parliament.

At yesterday's meeting of the Parliamentary Labour party, one Left-wing member, Mr. Michael Foot (Devonport) proposed that a start should be made immediately with the nationalisation plans contained in the Socialist election manifesto. These included the nationalisation of sugar, cement and water and the "mutualisation" of industrial assurance.

I understand that there was little response from the meeting. Mr. Attlee called for unity and Mr. Morrison gave a warning that there was no scope for indulgence in the luxury of revolts against the Government. He stressed that solidarity and regular attendance were vital.

Government quarters point out that, in any case, there will be little time for major legislation if the first session of the New Parliament is to end in July, as is generally expected. Finance will occupy most of the time.

What legislative proposals are contained in the King's Speech on Monday are not likely to be highly controversial. Several new Bills may be introduced into the House of Lords while the Commons press on with the essential business of dealing with the supplementary estimates.

The Conservative 1922 Committee, with Sir Arnold Gridley, M.P. for Stockport South, in the chair, also met after the House, which had assembled to elect the Speaker, rose. They were addressed by Mr. Churchill, who welcomed new members.

He told them of the conclusion of the Conservative Shadow Cabinet's deliberations on Tuesday, that no line of action could be laid down until after the Government's intentions were disclosed in the King's Speech.

MR. WEBB'S PROMISE

Food, Not Calories

After the Parliamentary Labour party meeting, which lasted two hours, Mr. Maurice Webb said of his job as Food Minister: "I will try not to use the word 'calories' at any time, but just talk about food."

Mr. Attlee said that the party was "in very good heart". "The Government," he added, "will be meeting the House and going forward in the firm determination to carry the country through in this difficult period. Let us go through together." A meeting of the National Executive of the Labour party followed the Parliamentary party meeting. It lasted less than half an hour, and afterwards Mr. Morgan Phillips, secretary of the party, said: "The National Executive made a brief review of the election results.

"It expressed congratulations to myself and the staff at Transport House for the work done in the course of the election. It deferred any further consideration of the detailed report on the campaign to be circulated later."

UNANIMOUS VOTE

Mr. Attlee As Leader

After the Parliamentary Labour party meeting this communiqué was issued:

A meeting of the Parliamentary Labour party took place at Church House, Westminster, this morning (Mr. Maurice Webb, M.P., in the chair).

On the motion of Mr. Herbert Morrison, M.P., seconded by Lord Addison, the Prime Minister was unanimously re-elected leader of the Labour party.

Mr. Attlee opened a general discussion on the work of the coming session and stated that the Government would do all that it felt necessary in the interests of the country.

Mr. Morrison replied to the discussion.

Members of the National Executive committee of the Labour party were present. Mr. Sam Watson, the chairman of the Executive, congratulated the party on the great increase in the Labour vote.

LIST OF JUNIOR MINISTERS MAY BE OUT TODAY

By Our Political Correspondent

The Prime Minister postponed last night the announcement of the changes among junior Ministers. These, it is expected, will be published to-day. Ten offices must be filled as a consequence either of election casualties or of the promotions to higher office announced on Tuesday. There are 39 junior Ministerial appointments.

The list of changes will probably be long as a considerable reshuffle may take place. Those which are definitely vacant, with the names of their holders before the election in brackets are:

Parliamentary and Financial Secretary, Admiralty (Mr. J. Dugdale, now Minister of State for Colonial Affairs);

Parliamentary Under - Secretary Colonies (Mr D. R. Reeswilliams, defeated in the election);

Parliamentary Under-Secretary Commonwealth Relations (Mr. P. C. Gordon-Walker, now Secretary for Commonwealth Relations);

Parliamentary Secretary Food (Dr. Summerskill, now Minister of National Insurance);

Parliamentary Under - Secretary Foreign Affairs (Mr. C. P. Mayhew, defeated in the election);

Parliamentary Under - Secretary Home Office (Mr. K.G. Younger, now Minister of State);

Parliamentary Secretary Labour, (Mr. Ness Edwards, now Post-Master-General);

Parliamentary Secretary National Insurance, (Mr. T. Steele, defeated in election);

Parliamentary Secretary, Town and Country Planning (Mr. E.M.King, defeated in election);

Parliamentary Secretary, Board of Trade (Mr. L.J.Edwards, defeated in election);

I understand that one probable appointment is that of Miss Margaret Herbison to be one of the Parliamentary Under-Secretaries for Scotland. This would involve the transfer of one of the existing Under-Secretaries, Mr. Fraser or Mr. Robinson.

Another possibility is the appointment of Mr. Douglas Jay as Parliamentary Secretary to the Board of Trade. His former Office, Economic Secretary to the Treasury, has been abolished with the appointment of Mr. Gaitskill as Minister for Economic Affairs.

SEXTUPLETS BORN

BRUSSELS, Wednesday.

A native woman in the Belgian Congo has given birth to sextuplets, four boys and two girls, according to a report received here and which is being checked by the Colonial Ministry.

CHANNEL MINE

A mine was seen in the Channel yesterday about 16 miles south-west of Beachy Head. It was exploded by the destroyer Finisterre sent from Portsmouth.

DR. K. E. J. FUCHS, who was yesterday sentenced to 14 years' imprisonment, for four offences under the Official Secrets Act.

MATRON OF 21 'TOO YOUNG'

PROTEST ON NURSERY APPOINTMENT

Daily Telegraph Reporter

A protest against the recent appointment of 21-year-old Miss Marjorie Julia Evans as matron of a day nursery in West Thurrock, Essex, is being made by the National Association of Nursery Matrons. Miss Evans, who was 21 last April, gained her diploma in 1945.

Mrs. Mace, secretary of the association, which is recognised by the Royal College of Nursing, said yesterday that she had written to Dr. W. T. G. Boul, medical officer for Thurrock, on the matter. She had not yet received a reply.

"I believe her appointment was made by the public health committee of the local authority," said Mrs. Mace. "I have heard that the matter is now being considered by the Ministries of Health and Education.

"Miss Evans's appointment is contrary to guidance given in a joint circular issued by the Ministries. This states that matrons should be not less than 25 years old and deputy matrons not less than 23.

"A matron should have had at least four years' nursery nursing after certification and she should normally have held a post as a deputy matron.

"Although any appointment will depend on the individual, and some exceptions may be reasonably made, we think that anyone of Miss Evans's age cannot possibly have had sufficient experience.

"EMOTIONAL MATURITY" NEED

"A degree of emotional maturity is necessary in a nursery matron. The job carries a large responsibillty in arranging meals and other details as well as just looking after the children.

"We believe the appointment of one so young is morally wrong. There is no quarrel over Miss Evans's academic qualifications.

"I have been told by Miss Neill, the nursery supervisor for Essex, that the appointment of Miss Evans was made against the supervisor's wishes."

An official of the National Society of Children's Nurseries said that the case had been brought to their notice. They were leaving action to the association of whose opinions they approved.

CORSETS TO BE DEARER

CLOTH PRICES UP

Most utility corsets are likely to be dearer after changes next week in manufacturers' permitted prices. In a few cases there have been reductions, but mostly there are increases of between one and five per cent.

These, states the Board of Trade, are "due to rises in the cost of cloth and accessories." The Order notifying the changes is to be followed in a few days by another extending their effect in some measure to retailers.

A corset manufacturer said yesterday: "We are very short of utility cloth at present. It does not pay the makers to produce it. Due to devaluation the makers say they lose 5d per yard."

14 YEARS FOR GIVING SECRETS TO RUSSIA

SOVIET WAS SAVED 5 YEARS IN COMPLETING ATOM BOMB

Daily Telegraph Reporter

The maximum penalty of 14 years' imprisonment was passed by the Lord Chief Justice, Lord Goddard, at the Old Bailey yesterday on KLAUS EMIL JULIUS FUCHS, 38, chief of the theoretical physics branch of the Government's secret atomic research establishment at Harwell, Berks. [Full Report—P7.]

He had admitted giving to Russian agents information about atomic research which in the words of the charge was calulated to be directly or indirectly useful to an enemy and prejudicial to the safety or interests of the State.

Dr Fuchs had for years been passing details of British and American atomic developments to Soviet agents in both this country and the United States. He was one of six men in Britain, the atomic mission sent to America, who knew one of the most vital secrets of the atomic bomb – how to explode it.

Nobody can prophesy what worldwide repercussions there may be from the information he gave Russia. But leading scientists are unanimous in believing that he showed the Russians enough short cuts in research to enable them to complete and explode their first atomic bomb probably five years earlier than they hoped.

The first news that an atomic explosion had taken place in Russia was given on Sept. 23 last year. A joint announcement was made by Britain and the United States.

SEVEN YEARS' ACCESS

Avoided Suspicion

As Fuchs left the dock to begin his long sentence one question was uppermost in everybody's mind in the overcrowded court. How did he contrive to avoid suspicion so successfully that he was never under observation until shortly before his trial?

Both the British and American security services knew he had been a fanatical Communist since his student days in Germany, knew of the Communist background of both his brother and sister.

They knew also that his name was mentioned several times in documents belonging to Dr. Alan Nunn May, 34, another atomic scientist, sentenced to 10 years' penal servitude in 1946 for betraying atomic secrets to Russia.

For seven years this young, white-faced ex-German had been allowed access to laboratories at Harwell, the British atomic establishment near Didcot, Berks, at universities in this country and the United States, at Oakridge, Aronne, Los Alamos and other American centres of atomic research and development.

SCIENTIST TOLD CRIME NEAR TO HIGH TREASON

Daily Telegraph Reporter

In passing sentence on Fuchs at the Old Bailey yesterday. Lord Goddard, the Lord Chief Justice, said: "You have betrayed the hospitality and protection given to you with the grossest treachery."

Regardless of his oath, he betrayed "secrets of vital import for the purpose of furthering a political creed held in abhorrence by the vast majority of this country." The judge enumerated four matters which seemed the gravest aspect of the crime:

1. Fuchs had imperilled the right of asylum which this country extended to political refugees.
2. He might have caused the gravest suspicion to fall on those he falsely treated as friends both in Britain and the United States, and who were misled into trusting him.
3. He might have imperilled Britain's good relations wlth the great American Republic.
4. He had done irreparable and incalculable harm both to this land and to the United States.

The Lord Chief Justice added: "Your crime is only thinly differentiated from high treason. But in this country we observe rigidly the rule of law and, as it is not, technically, high treason, you are not tried for that offence."

"PALE AND IMPASSIVE"

Fuchs stood upright as he was sentenced, his hands clenched at his side. His face was pale and impassive as it had been throughout the trial. Most of the time he seemed to be indifferent.

The case attracted world-wide interest. American and Dutch journalists flew to England specially for the hearing.

Spain, India, Bulgaria, Czechoslovakia, Russia and all the Dominions except South Africa had newspaper representatives present. Special telephones were installed for American newspapers and agencles.

In the section for distinguished visitors were the Duchess of Kent and Marshal of the R.A.F. Viscount Portal of Hungerford, war-time Chief of the Air Staff. There were diplomatic representatives from a number of countries.

"OTHER CRIMES"

Cmdr. Burt, head of the Special (Political) Branch at Scotland Yard and a senior officer of M.I.5 during the war, sat in the well of the crowded court with Det.-Insp. G. G. Smith, another Special Branch officer who took part in the invesgation, and United States Embassy officials.

Before being sentenced, Fuchs, who spoke with a pronounced German accent, said: "I have also committed some crimes other than the ones with which I am charged. When I asked my counsel to put certain facts before you I did so to atone for these crimes. I have had a fair trial."

INFORMATION ON SOVIET AGENTS

IDENTITIES KNOWN

Daily Telegraph Reporter

Repercussions are likely to follow quickly in this country and America as a result of information which I understand Fuchs has imparted to the British Secret Service chiefs. It concerns his association with Russian agents.

The identities of some suspected agents are already known to the British and American security officers. There is a possibility of special arrangements being made to enable Fuchs to carry on his scientific work while in prison.

The matter is likely to come before the prison commissioners for consideration after discussions with senior scientists when Fuchs has served a short period of his sentence. The first six months are likely to be served at Maidstone or Parkhurst.

He may afterwards be transferred to one of the new prisons without bars. There is even a possibility that by special arrangement with the Home Office, he may later be permitted to lecture on atomic research under escort to scientists outside the prison.

EIRE FACES ROAD AND RAIL STOPPAGE

Dublin Move To End Strike Fails

N.U.R. REJECTS PROPOSALS

From Our Own Correspondent

DUBLIN, Wednesday.

Eire is threatened with a stoppage of rail and road transport. This follows the rejection to-night by the National Union of Railwaymen of the Labour Court's proposals for a settlement of the 10-day-old strike which has left a large part of Dublin without buses.

The dispute is at present confined to the Clontarf bus depot. But the Irish Transport Union, which has a monopoly of membership in the Dublin bus transport services, may now spread the strike to all garages

This would paralyse all road transport. It is believed that if the Transport Union made such a move, the N.U.R., of which nearly all railway employees are members, would take similar strike action.

The strike began because a bus driver decided to transfer from the Irish Transport Union to the N.U.R. The remainder of the 310 men at the depot refused to work with him. Later a second driver followed the first in transferring to the N.U.R.

The N.U.R. maintained that the constitutional right of every man to freedom of association had been guaranteed by the courts. To force a man to belong to a particular union was against the individual right of every citizen.

The Labour Court proposals were that the two former members of the Transport Union should be re-admitted to that union. If they did not wish to adopt that course, the Transport Company, which is now nationalised, should find them alternative employment on other road services. The Transport Union adopted these proposals.

COUPLE FOUND DEAD IN FLAT

WOMAN STRANGLED

The bodies of Kingsley Stead, 68, and Jessie Stead, 69, were found in their flat at Ingram House, Park - road, Hampton Wick, Middlesex, yesterday.

Mrs. Stead was found in the bedroom, having apparently died from strangulation. Mr. Stead was in the scullery with cuts on the wrist. The gas oven was on and a Pekingese dog was found killed by two stab wounds.

Their son, Mr. Geoffrey Stead, 48, who lived with them at Ingram House, a large block of self-contained flats, returned home at 1 p.m. and was unable to get any answer. He called another tenant, Mr. O'Dare, and with the head porter, Mr. J. Tanner, forced the door, which had been bolted and chained.

Mr. Stead was a former director of customs, excise and trade in Palestine. He held this position for 14 years, retiring in 1938 when he left the Colonial Service.

He was created an O.B.E. in 1928 and C.B.E. in 1933.

FARM PRICE TALKS

Leaders of the three British farmers' unions yesterday went to the Ministry of Agriculture, for the start of the annual price review talks. Discussions are expected to last a fortnight and Cabinet approval is needed before the new rates become operative.

The Daily Telegraph

No. 29,548 LONDON, MONDAY, MARCH 13, 1950 — and Morning Post — Printed in LONDON and MANCHESTER Price 1½d

80 KILLED IN WELSH AIR CRASH

WORST DISASTER IN CIVIL AVIATION HISTORY

7 WOMEN DIE: 2 MEN IN TAIL ESCAPE

From Our Special Correspondents

SIGGINGSTON, Glam, Sunday.

A Tudor V airliner crashed here this afternoon, and 80 of its 83 occupants were killed. Only three passengers, three men, survived. The deathroll is higher than in any previous civil aviation disaster anywhere in the world.

The plane, with a crew of five, including an air hostess, was returning from Dublin to Llandow airport, about 15 miles to the west of Cardiff. It had been specially chartered to convey 78 passengers, including six women, to and from the Wales v Ireland international Rugby match at Belfast yesterday. The party had motored from Belfast to Dublin airport for the return trip.

According to eye-witnesses, the Tudor came in low towards the airport in fine, clear weather. Then it started to climb and its engines cut out. The aircraft immediately nose-dived into a field near the airport and broke into pieces.

The three survivors were taken to a farm a few hundred yards away. Two of them, who had travelled in the tail of the plane, escaped almost unhurt.

Sixty ambulances were called to the scene, and took bodies of the dead to the R.A.F. station at St. Athan, near here.

Among those who arrived this evening at the scene of the crash were Lord Pakenham, Minister for Civil Aviation, and Air Vice-Marshal D.C.T. Bennett, chairman of Fairflight Ltd., owners of the Tudor. A Ministry investigation team is also on its way from London.

LOAD IN ORDER

"Within Requirements"

Air Vice-Marshal Bennett said: "As far as we can see everything was in correct order. There was a total of 83 people on board, a load within the certificate of air-worthiness requirements." He expressed deep sympathy with the relatives of the dead crew and passengers.

He said the crashed aircraft had flown for over 1,400 hours and had been extensively engaged on the Berlin airlift. "In fact it holds the record for the best achievement of any aircraft on the Berlin airlift. It flew more hours than any other British or American machine."

The pilot, Capt. D. Parsons, a married man whose home was at Maidenhead, joined his firm after serving with the R.A.F. He had been flying Tudors for 17 months.

He was awarded the M.B.E. for work on the Berlin airlift in last year's Honours List. He was 25.

INQUIRY TO BE HELD

Minister's Sympathy

Lord Pakenham expressed a wish to meet the three survivors. He offered his deepest sympathy to relatives of those killed and intimated that there would be a court of inquiry.

It is believed that the pilot in crossing the farm field might have thought he was too low and tried to rise to clear the hedge and main road. While rising, the machine turned sideways and struck the ground.

One wing of the giant airliner was knocked off and the plane's body cut in two. The passengers were strapped in their seats. In crashing the seats probably gave way, which accounted for the severe head injuries sustained.

Seventy-one passengers were killed outright, 10 were severely injured and nine have since died. Two men who were the last to board the plane and sat in the tail, walked out of the wreck almost uninjured, apart from cuts, abrasions and shock.

The rear part of the fuselage seemed to be almost intact, but the front part was badly smashed. Petrol was streaming down the sides but there was no sign of any fire. One man who was badly cut over the forehead with blood streaming down his face, staggered out of the plane and said: "For God's sake, get some help."

"By this time practically everyone In the village had arrived on the scene and were crowding round, helping to get out bodies. Ambulances were arriving from Barry, Cowbridge, Bridgend and all the surrounding towns. R.A.F. men from the airfield were there too.

"We moved some of the debris and carried out three or four bodies. An R.A.F sergeant tried to get us to lift up the fuselage to see if anyone was still alive underneath, but we could not manage it."

PLANE NEAR HOUSE

Missed by 30ft

With Mr Newman were his two brothers, Vivian Andrew, 19, and Frederick Selwyn, aged 27, and their 62 year-old father, William Joseph Newman. Mrs Newman was ill in bed in a room in the house which stands on the roadside and which the plane missed by about 30 feet.

Police and R.A.F. had recovered all the bodies within an hour of the crash The three survivors are now in St. Athan R.A.F. hospital

The wings of the plane were broken off and pieces of the body were strewn over a distance of 50 yards. Parts of the engine were found at the tail of the plane.

Airmen were busy sorting out the wreckage and making lists of the personal property strewn alongside. It included a pearl necklace in a case, tins of fruit and other presents which the victims were bringing home as mementoes of their trip to the international.

The plane, which was 100ft long and had a wing-span of 115ft was a mass of tangled wreckage with the seats, attache cases and personal luggage strewn about. Many parts of the aircraft were reduced to matchwood.

72 PASSENGERS TUDOR'S NORMAL LOAD

ADJUSTMENT FOR EXTRA OCCUPANTS

By Air Cmdre. L.G.S.PAYNE, Daily Telegraph Air Correspondent

The Tudor V which crashed near Llandow was equipped to carry up to 72 passengers normally on short journeys.

At least nine versions of the Tudor airliner have been built. The original Tudor I was intended for the North Atlantic route and designed to carry 12 passengers, with sleeping berths.

Other versions had larger fuselages to accommodate more passengers. The Tudor V was another version of The Tudor II, the standard day type of which was designed to take up to about 60 passengers in seats, or about 40 with seats and bunks, and a crew of seven.

Eighty-three occupants seems an unusually large number for the plane to carry, but the carriage of more passengers than it was originally designed to take would not necessarily be dangerous if the fuel load was adjusted and runways of adequate length were used.

The Tudor V had an internal layout intended to meet the requirements of the British South American Airways Corporation. The only type which ever went into regular airline service was The Tudor IV, a cross between The Tudor I and Tudor II.

This type was finally withdrawn from passenger service after the loss of the Star Ariel between Bermuda and Jamaica in January 1949. Another, the Star Tiger, had been lost a year before between Azores and Bermuda. No trace of these planes was found.

USED ON AIR LIFT

Tudors were successfully used as freighters on the Berlin air lift. They included The Tudor II and The Tudor V of Fairflight Ltd., Air Vice-Marshal Bennett's company. A plan to adapt Tudor passenger airliners as freighters for use by B.O.A.C. was abandoned.

Chiefly to enable Fairflight Ltd. to use its Tudors on charter passenger services, Tudor IIs and Vs were given certificates of air-worthiness for such services last summer. This was after various US modifications had been made. In October, it was reported that most of the remaining Tudors other than those required for jet engine research were to be broken up.

Llandow is an R.A.F. airfield in South Wales west of Cardiff. Its use by civil aircraft is limited to planes operating on charter services and to those operating on scheduled services which may be diverted there in bad weather. It is not available for use at night.

The airfield has three tarmac runways. Two of them are 3,000ft long, which is on the short side for comparitively large four-engined types such as Tudor IIs or Vs. The other is 4,800ft long. The only high obstruction in the immediate vicinity is a water tower.

STAMPEDE FOR CUP TICKETS

WOMEN HURT

Daily Telegraph Reporter

Thousands of people, many of whom had waited all night, fought and jostled outside Highbury and Stamford Bridge Yesterday for tickets for next Saturday's F.A. Cup semi-final between Arsenal and Chelsea at Tottenham Hotspurs, ground.

There were 50,000 tickets available, 28,000 at Stamford Bridge and 22,000 at Highbury. Stampedes occurred at both grounds when late-comers arrived. Eventually the police restored order.

The most serious incident occurred at Highbury, where soon after the turnstiles opened, a small group of men broke from the 1,000-yard queue. This started a concerted rush for the gates.

Women and children screamed and were thrown into the roadway. Some women were taken in a fainting condition to houses where they received attention for cuts and bruises.

SCENE AT THE AIR CRASH, near Cardiff

KING FAROUK GREETS DUKE OF GLOUCESTER

TEA AT PALACE

From Our Own Correspondent

CAIRO, Sunday.

The Duke and Duchess of Gloucester, on their way to Kenya by air to attend celebrations on March 30 marking the elevation of Nairobi to city status, arrived in Cairo to-day from Malta. They will stay the night here.

They left London Airport yesterday in a Viking of the King's Flight. Last night they stayed at Malta as the guests of Sir Gerald Creasy, the Governor. British Navy ships fired a Royal salute as their plane took off this morning.

Abdel Latif Pasha, King Farouk's Grand Chamberlain, met them at Farouk Airport. He presented the Duchess of Gloucester with a bouquet. Sir Ronald Campbell, the British Ambassador, was also at the airport.

KING HON. BRITISH GENERAL

Shortly after their arrival, the Duke and Duchess had tea with King Farouk at Kubba Palace. A court circular said that while King Farouk received the Duke, Princess Fayza the King's sister, received the Duchess.

After tea, King Farouk presented the Duke with his portrait and the Duchess with the Grand Order of Al Kamal (perfection).

The court circular added that King Farouk had been informed that he had been appointed an honorary General in the British Army on the orders of King George.

The Duke and Duchess are spending the night at the Embassy as the guests of Sir Ronald Campbell. They will leave for Khartoum early to-morrow.

MAJ. GOTTLIEB: BRITISH PROTEST

CLUB'S TREATMENT

From Our Own Correspondent

Sir Victor Mallet, British Ambassador, to-day confirmed his resignation from membership of the Circolo Cassia club because he disliked the manner in which Maj. Gottlieb had been treated.

Maj. Gottlieb, a Vienna-born naturalised British subject, was found dead in his bath on Tuesday. His wrists were slashed.

Sir Victor said he had heard reports that the president of the club had his consent to Maj. Gottlieb's expulsion from the club. These reports were "absolutely untrue."

The expulsion issue arose over an application by an American Jew for membership. This started proposals for the exclusion of Jewish members.

The club committee says Maj. Gottlieb was excluded because of the obscurity of the source of his income. It is now established that his exclusion contributed to his depression before his suicide.

AMETHYST'S RETURN

After refitting at Devonport, the frigate Amethyst, 1,430 tons, damaged by Chinese Communist guns in the Yangtse, will be completed in April. She will sail later to rejoin the Far Eastern fleet on the North China patrol.

57 p.c. VOTE IN FAVOUR OF KING LEOPOLD'S RETURN

BELGIUM CALM FOR POLLING

From H.D. ZIMAN, Daily Telegraph Special Correspondent

BRUSSELS, Monday, 3 a.m.

Belgians have voted 57.68 in favour of King Leopold's return. This result of yesterday's poll to test the nation's opinion was announced by the Ministry of the Interior early this morning. Figures were:

TOTAL VOTE		5,236,740
BLANK AND SPOILT FORMS...	151,477	
VALID VOTES		5,085,263
FOR THE KING'S RETURN ...	2,933,382	
AGAINST		2,151,881

The King had given an undertaking that he would relinquish the throne if he received less than 55 per cent. of the country's vote.

Parliament is not bound to restore him on the strength of his gaining any definite percentage.

FLEMISH SUPPORT

In the four Flemish-speaking Provinces the King received majorities ranging from 68 per cent in Antwerp to 83 per cent in Limburg. The strongly Catholic Walloon (French-speaking) province of Belgian Luxembourg gave him a majority of over 65 per cent, and Namur, also Walloon, 53 per cent.

The Walloon provinces of Liege and the Hainault rated only 41.5 per cent.

In the province of Brabant, which includes Brussels, there was a bare majority in his favour. Brussels however, gave him a majority of only about 49 per cent. The figures were 387,914 for him and 417,400 against.

'COUNTRY'S VERDICT"

After announcing the results M. de Vleeschauwer, the Christian Social Minister of the Interior, stated "The country has pronounced its verdict. Twenty-one constituencies out of 30 have shown majorities for the King. Seven provinces out of nine have shown majorities."

WEATHER BEATS FORECAST

NORTH HAS 10 Hrs SUN

The weekend forecast of more wintry weather failed yesterday. Although temperatures were a little lower than on Saturday, the wintry conditions covered only northern and east Scotland and spread away south-east to the Continent.

The winds were lighter over England and Wales than had been expected. With the abundant sunshine the air was warmed on its journey south.

An absolute drought has developed over an area extending from Norfolk to Kent and westwards to East Devon. In London and at many other places the duration is now 16 days.

DUKE OF EDINBURGH

By Our Political Correspondent

CANNES, Sunday

The Duke of Edinburgh whose destroyer, the Chequers, is visiting San Remo, last night presided at a banquet in Cannes in aid of the Sunnybank Anglo-American Hospital. With the aid of the Aga Khan and the Begum he attended a gala dinner at the municipal casino to-night. While in Cannes he stayed with Nadejda, Marchioness of Milford Haven, his aunt.

T.U.C. PLEA ON LIVING COSTS

MEETING TO-NIGHT WITH CHANCELLOR

By Hugh Chevins

Sir Stafford Cripps will to-night meet members of the Special Economic Committee of the Trades Union Congress to give them the latest details about Britain's economic position.

He will hear from the union leaders proposals to offset the rising cost of living. It is unlikely that any move will be made heartening either to the Chancellor or to the committee.

He will be unable to promise concessions in the Budget, or otherwise, which will satisfy all or many of the trade unionists. The T.U.C., though anxious to avoid the creation of new difficulties for the Government, will be unable to guarantee firmer wage stabilisation in return for the concessions they seek.

Sir Stafford will see that the unions are divided not only on the basic issue of wages restraint. It will be apparent they have sharp differences over the order of priority which should be applied to various expedients for counteracting inevitable rises in the cost of living.

This division will prevent any expression of opinion from the T.U.C as a body. Individual members will be allowed to air their own views.

A group will raise the question of increasing family allowances. It seems certain that Sir Stafford, particularly in view of the inability of the T.U.C. to restrain unions from making wage demands, will not be amenable to any change.

EXTRA SUMMER PETROL AGAIN

By Our Political Correspondent

A double standard petrol ration for June, July and August, as last year, is stated in political quarters to be certain.

It is regarded as unlikely that the increase will be sanctioned by the Cabinet, who may consider the matter at their meeting to-day. The double ration for the three summer months will permit an additional 270 miles of motoring.

COMMUNISTS INVADE SOUTH KOREA

TANKS 12 MILES FROM CAPITAL: CALL FOR AID

U.S. ARMS REPORTED ON WAY FROM JAPAN

SECURITY COUNCIL CONDEMN ACT OF AGGRESSION

Soviet-dominated North Korea launched an attack at dawn yesterday on the southern half of the country. While troops and tanks crossed the frontier and invasion ships sailed down the east coast, planes attacked the airfield at Seoul, the southern capital.

Within a few hours the Northern army had stormed over the 38th parallel, the border between the two States, and had occupied all the territory north of the Imjin river. South Korea mobilised its troops and sent them by train, lorry, bus and car to meet the invaders.

Early to-day fierce fighting was reported north and north-east of Seoul. The Northern troops crossed the river with 90 tanks. The Korean Minister in Tokyo reported that they had reached a point 12 miles from the capital.

Further east the Southern defenders seized a town five miles north of the 38th parallel. Meanwhile attacks from the sea were reported on the east coast, and it was said that four beachheads had been established.

U.N. CALL FOR WITHDRAWAL

The United Nations Security Council was urgently summoned last night at Lake Success, New York. Russia was not present, as she is continuing her boycott while Nationalist China is represented.

The council adopted a United States resolution condeming the North Korean attack as an "act of aggression", and calling for a withdrawal to the 38th parallel.

(June 26)

U.S. ORDERS WARSHIPS, PLANES TO KOREA

MR. ATTLEE PLEDGES BRITISH SUPPORT

AMERICAN FIGHTERS ATTACK TANKS

President Truman yesterday ordered American air and naval forces to give cover and support to the troops of the Korean Republic in their fight against the invaders from Communist-ruled North Korea.

At the same time he ordered the 7th Fleet to forestall any attack on Formosa. American forces in the Philippines are to be strengthened and military aid to the Philippines and Indo-China speeded up.

Mr. Attlee in the House of Commons yesterday endorsed Mr. Truman's statement. He said that Britain supported the American resolution before the Security Council asking members of the United Nations to help the Korean Republic.

Gen. MacArthur, Supreme Allied Commander in Japan, has been placed in command of the American forces ordered into action. He has been given wide discretionary authority. A small advance American headquarters in Korea has already been set up.

ALREADY IN ACTION

President Rhee, of the Korean Republic, broadcast yesterday that American bombers and fighters were already attacking Communist tanks and naval elements were also reported to be in action.

News from the battle fronts was confused. The southerners claimed to have recaptured Uijongbu, 12 miles north of Seoul, the capital.

It was from Uijongbu that the main Communist break-through developed.

The President and his Cabinet were reported to be still in Seoul. A break in radio and telephone communications later revived fears that the northerners had again entered the city.

U.S. NOTE TO RUSSIA

The United States has sent a Note asking Russia to use its influence to halt the fighting. The Note is also regarded as a tacit warning to Russia against lending direct or indirect aid to the northern invaders.

The Security Council, by 7 votes to 1, approved a motion asking the Council to authorise all members of the United Nations to go to the aid of South Korea. It was submitted by Mr. Austin, the American delegate, who said the United Nations faced "the gravest crisis in its existence." Sir Terence Shone, the British delegate, had pledged support.

The Russians, continuing their boycott over the representation of China, did not attend the meeting. The Russian delegate had been expected to appear. He had attended a secret luncheon with an American representative and M Lie, Secretary-General.

(June 20)

CITY IN STATE OF SIEGE

STREETS BARRICADED

From Denis Warner
Daily Telegraph Special Correspondent
OUTSIDE SEOUL, Sunday.

Seoul is in a state of siege and its capture by American and South Korean Marines may be a costly and fairly long operation. Prisoners and the few civilians who have escaped from the city estimate the defenders at 17,000 to 18,000, compared with the 4,000 to 5,000 originally reported by American intelligence. The total includes everyone mobilised including newly activated 17th and 18th division cadets and a "home guard", organised from among Communist converts and sympathisers.

Since the Inchon landing, prisoners say, every main street has been barricaded and sandbag pillboxes dominate the main point sand buildings. The City Hall, goal and Capitol Building are strong-points on which the defence will be based.

A rigidly enforced curfew keeps residents at home under threat of death. No one is allowed to enter or leave the city unless on official Communist business.

ATTACK ON HILLS
Communists in Caves

A mile and a half across the ripening rice fields and two low-lying hills is Duk Soo Palace, administrative and physical centre of Seoul. From forward American posts the palace and other prominent city points are clearly identifiable, but the Communists are delaying closer inspection with determined resistance.

Outside the city the Americans this week-end maintained strong pressure and continued to encounter firm resistance. Marines entered the city boundaries, but they remain more than half a mile from the nearest built-up area in approximately the same position they occupied on Friday.

A new attack began early in the afternoon against the last low-lying hill line before Seoul. But initial opposition seemed to preclude any hope of an early break-through into the city itself. From caves dug into the last natural defensive positions Communists denied the advance all week-end.

Yesterday afternoon the Marines fired onto one hill 3,600 artillery rounds. Yet when riflemen began to move up its slopes they met heavy machine-gun and mortar fire.

South Korean Marines, who were the pivot of the attack earlier, were withdrawn after heavy casualties. Yesterday their place was taken by another American Marine unit, which immediately became heavily engaged.

"This is the best-directed mortar fire I've ever seen," a Marine colonel said. "They had nothing like this in the southern perimeter. It's better than anything the Japanese ever had."

Marines early to-day discovered one of the reasons why - a North Korean complacently sitting with a radio among their lines, acting as direct mortar and artillery observer. He was quickly despatched, but the Marines had no doubt that there were others among seemingly innocent civilians who suddenly appeared in their lines.

ENEMY RAID
Civilians Watch Battle

While the main attack continued this morning in co-ordination with a river crossing by a Marine force from Yongdungpo, a small enemy formation tried to cut the American supply route north of the river. Planes and South-Korean units contained it about half a mile from the supply route.

Civilians from recently liberated towns and villages watched this battle from their already fought-over homes with remarkable unconcern. One of these villages, not more than 30 small huts, boasts a little Christian church with a flimsy bell-steeple. In the middle of the battle the bell began to ring for the first time in weeks. Many people moved quietly from their hilltop view of the war and went into church to pray.

(September 25)

THE SMILING CROWD reading the official bulletin which was pinned to the gates outside Clarence House at midday yesterday.

PRINCESS ELIZABETH: A DAUGHTER

6lb. BABY BORN AT CLARENCE HOUSE

Daily Telegraph Reporter

A daughter was born to Princess Elizabeth at Clarence House shortly before noon yesterday. The baby weighed 6lb. Prince Charles, now 21 months old, weighed 7lb 6oz at birth.

A notice, handwritten in ink, was hung on the wrought-iron gates leading into the Mall at 12.54 p.m. It read:

Her Royal Highness the Princess Elizabeth, Duchess of Edinburgh, was safely delivered of a Princess at 11.50 a.m. to-day. Her Royal Highness and her daughter are both doing well.

(August 16)

FOUR NAMES FOR BABY PRINCESS

Anne Elizabeth Alice Louise

Daily Telegraph Reporter

The two-week-old daughter of Princess Elizabeth and the Duke of Edinburgh will be christened Anne Elizabeth Alice Louise. Her proper name and title will be her Royal Highness Princess Anne Elizabeth Alice Louise of Edinburgh.

She will not be known as "her Royal Highness The Princess Anne." The article "The" is reserved for the children of the Sovereign.

(August 30)

£80,000 OF NYLONS FOUND IN LINER

MOVES AGAINST BLACK MARKET

From Our Own Correspondents
LIVERPOOL, Friday.

Thousands of pairs of nylon stockings have been discovered by Customs officers in a five-day search of the Cunard White Star liner Franconia, 20,175 tons, at Liverpool. The stockings would have had a value of £80,000 in the black market.

They were of the finest quality and in fashionable shades. They were hidden in first-class cabins, in corners of the engine room and behind timber linings of the ship's inner hull. One hiding place contained 3,000 pairs.

Customs officers think that the ship has been used as a floating store. None of the stockings are damaged and the wrappings are unsoiled. Some had been hidden for several months.

The search began on Monday when the vessel tied up. Reinforcements from the Customs branch special department were sent to help when the searching squads reported that the liner was "stuffed with nylons."

BLACK MARKET DEALERS

They completed their search a few hours before the Franconia left dock to-night. She will anchor in mid-Mersey before berthing at Princes landing stage in the morning to take on passengers for New York.

Stockings have been smuggled ashore in small quantities when the Franconia has reached Liverpool once in three weeks on the completion of her 6,000-miles round voyage to New York. They have been disposed of to street pedlars in the city and posted to black market dealers all over Britain.

SEARCH ON RETURN

As a hiding place has been emptied of stockings, replacements have been brought on board during the week the ship was in New York. When she returns in May squads will again search her.

Statements have been taken from members of the crew. Black market dealers on Merseyside are known to the authorities. The prosecutions branch of the Customs believes that its action will break up the biggest nylon-smuggling ring in Britain.

(April 8)

SERETSE SAYS HE IS EXILED FOR FIVE YEARS

Daily Telegraph Reporter

Seretse Khama, 27, chief-designate of the Bamangwato tribe of Bechuanaland, said last night that he had been told by Mr. Gordon-Walker, Secretary for Commonwealth Relations, that he must not return to his country for five years without permission.

"I have been offered an annual allowance of £1,100 if I will live in England and relinquish my claim to the chieftainship," he said. "I have refused the offer.

"I consider the matter is not a personal one, but one on which my tribe, which accepted me, should be consulted. The Government, I was informed, thought that was impossible."

Seretse arrived in London on Feb. 14 for talks on the problems arising from his marriage to Miss Ruth Williams, 24, a London typist, and the question of his succession to the chieftainship. A commission inquired into the matter in Africa.

Its report has not yet been made public. Last night Seretse said that, though he had three times asked to see the report, he had always been refused.

LAWYERS AT TALK

His statement followed a meeting yesterday afternoon with Mr. Gordon-Walker and Viscount Addison, Lord Privy Seal.

Lord Rathcreedan, a barrister, and Mr. P. Fraenkel, a South African lawyer, accompanied Seretse. Since his arrival in England Seretse has had one meeting with Mr. Noel-Baker, the former Secretary, and two with Mr. Gordon-Walker.

Seretse said: "I was told yesterday that it was a Cabinet decision that I should not return. I was also informed that my wife could be excluded immediately from the territory, but for reasons of health they would not insist on my wife's return here for the time being.

"Mr. Gordon-Walker would give no reason why I should be excluded, except that it might cause disturbances if I were confirmed as chief of the Bamangwato. The Government proposes to introduce a direct government in the territory.

"My tribe has not rejected me. Without their consent I cannot give up the chieftainship. I was invited to come to this country for talks, with an assurance that I would be allowed to return home.

"I HAVE BEEN TRICKED"

"Now I am told that I will not be allowed to return. I consider that I have been tricked in a way that I would not have thought possible by a Government of Britain. I must discuss the development fully with my legal advisers."

KOREA : COMPOSITE BRITISH FORCE

INFANTRY, ARMOUR & ARTILLERY TO GO

EXTRA £100 MILLION FOR DEFENCE EXPENDITURE

By Our Own Representative

WESTMINSTER, Thursday Morning.

An effective British land force is to be sent to Korea as quickly as possible. This was one of the main points in the statement by Mr. Shinwell, Minister of Defence, in the House of Commons yesterday. [Report - P7.]

He said that the Government would place under the orders of the United Nations a self-contained force, which would include infantry, armour, artillery and engineers, as well as its own administrative unit. Mr. Shinwell also announced that:

The Navy was recalling a certain number of Naval and Marine officers on the retired and emergency list and men of the Royal Fleet Reserve and would retain in the Service some whose service was due to expire shortly;

Measures now being taken to strengthen the fighting forces would add another £100 million to the Defence Bill.

He also stated that Australia and New Zealand were sending a special combat unit for service in Korea.

(July 27)

BRITISH LEAD ADVANCE ON PYONGYANG

40-MILE DRIVE IN 24 HOURS

From Eric Downton
Daily Telegraph Special Correspondent

GEN. MACARTHUR'S H.Q., TOKYO, Wednesday Morning.

After a 40-mile advance northward in the past 24 hours the British Commonwealth Brigade is this morning reported to be nearing the outer defences of Pyongyang, capital of North Korea. It is spearheading the drive from the south.

Moving rapidly up the main road the Brigade yesterday overran Sariwon, an important road and rail junction, and messages from Eighth Army H.Q. received here early to-day placed them beyond Hwangju, about 20 miles from Pyongyang. The Argylls, riding on American tanks, are leading the force.

Across the hills to the north-east of the Brigade the South Korean First Division has passed Samdung and is only 16 miles from the capital. United Nations troops may well enter Pyongyang within the next 24 hours.

On the east coast other South Korean divisions are on the point of securing two secondary prizes. Last night they reached and began fighting for Hamhung and Hungnam. Both towns are over 60 miles north of the port of Wonsan.

Another thrust by South Korean units is moving westward along the Wonsan-Pyongyang road. Unconfirmed reports say that it has reached Changimni, 40 miles east of Pyongyang.

In mileage the greatest gains yesterday were made by the American 24th Division. It covered 50 miles in one day, turning north at Haeju and going up to Chaeryong, 10 miles south east of Sarlwon.

On all the major sectors it has been a gallop for the past two days. Opposition generally has been weak and sporadic with every indication of disorganisation in flight by Communist units.

A communiqué issued by Gen. MacArthur's H.Q. last night referred to "a day of spectacular gains."

Maj-Gen. Gay, commander of the American First Cavalry Division, to which the British Brigade is attached, returned from an inspection of the front yesterday and said: "You can get all the prisoners you want. I personally met a column of them down the road just now.

"I could not be bothered with them and directed them to go to Sinmak and surrender there."

The British Commonwealth Brigade ended their long spell of fulfilling frustrating minor roles at dawn yesterday. Then, on the orders of Maj-Gen. Gay, they passed through the leading elements of the first Cavalry Division and began their advance from positions in the Sohung-Sinmak area.

They found Sinmak, which was taken by the Seventh Cavalry Regiment of the First Division the previous day, a mass of ruins. Led by the Argylls the brigade advanced in lorries and Bren carriers and with infantrymen riding on the sides of American Sherman tanks.

Their road wound among hills intersected with narrow waterways. For some miles they moved unimpeded.

TRENCHES ABANDONED

Last accounts from observers with the Brigade told of a clash with a force of about 400 North Korean troops entrenched in an orchard several miles south of Sariwon. The Argylls in the leading lorries came under fire from the orchard soon after they resumed movement following a halt to clear a nearby hamlet of snipers.

Machine-guns were set up in a roadside ditch and mortar crews brought their weapons into action. Sherman tanks also shelled the orchard. A spotting plane directed fire.

Infantrymen crawled round on to the flanks of the enemy position and then several American Mustang fighter-bombers attacked. They used bombs and rockets.

Finally Maj. Wilson ordered a charge. His troops went across a rice field into the orchard. The Communists broke and ran in retreat up into the hills behind the orchard. Then the Argylls reformed and continued their advance.

(October 18)

REINFORCEMENTS FOR KOREA. Men of the Middlesex Regiment inside an R.A.F. Transport Command aircraft.

LONGER SERVICE AND MORE PAY

CALL-UP PERIOD TO BE TWO YEARS

By A Political Correspondent

The Government's plans for increasing the strength of the defence forces were announced by the Prime Minister in a broadcast last night. Amplified in two White Papers published to-day [full summary and new rates of pay - P7], the proposals fall into two parts.

1 Extension of the term of National Service from 18 months to two years.

2 Increased emoluments for Regulars and, in the last six months of their new two-year engagements, for National Servicemen from to-morrow.

The extra cost to be borne on the Service Estimates is calculated at £68½ million. Part of this will be recoverable by the Treasury in income-tax.

Basic pay increases, operating from to-morrow, range from 75 per cent., or 3s a day, for recruits to 10 per cent., or 8s a day, for officers of Brigadier level.

A recruit will now receive 49s a week instead of 28s and a staff sergeant can now draw up to £10 12s 6d a week, with marriage allowances.

Rates for higher officers will be announced later. Members of the women's services will receive increases of about three-quarters of those for corresponding male ranks.

The longer term of National Service will apply to men serving on Oct. 1 and to those called up after that. Their period of reserve service will be reduced by six months.

(August 31)

FRENCH 'OVERWHELMED' IN INDO-CHINA BATTLE

GEN. JUIN SENT TO REPORT

From Our Own Correspondent

PARIS, Tuesday.

Most of the 3,500 French troops who covered the evacuation of the Indo-China frontier post of Kaobang, in north-east Tonkin, have been lost, French Army headquarters in Saigon said to-day.

The force had been "overwhelmed" by Viet-Minh rebel forces estimated at 20,000. Only 500 French troops fought their way through.

The French Cabinet, concerned at these latest successes of the Communists, to-day decided to send out Gen. Juin, 61, France's leading expert on Colonial warfare. He is to report on the situation.

The army communiqué, issued in Saigon, said: "This is the first time we have met an enemy perfectly trained and equipped, having at his disposal an excellent radio network and knowing how to co-ordinate his actions."

Two groups of French troops tried in vain to get through to Thatkhe on Saturday night. "At last on Sunday after bloody fighting one part of the force opened the way.

"The remainder were encircled and assailed from all sides. They succumbed after inflicting extremely heavy losses."

RED CROSS MEETING

French representatives were going to-day to meet Viet-Minh representatives near Thatkhe to negotiate a Red Cross truce. It was stated that the Viet-Minh had told the French they would hand over some wounded and prisoners at this meeting.

(October 6)

700-MILE TRIP WITH LOBSTERS

Daily Telegraph Reporter

A lorry load of lobster and crab bought direct from Wick, Caithness, was standing outside Billingsgate when the market opened at 6 a.m. yesterday. The lorry had started its 700-miles journey on Saturday evening.

The driver was James Simpson, of Scarfskerry, near John O'Groats. He and his relief, W. Allan of Mill of Mey, were cooperating in an experiment by Penland Firth lobster fishermen who have found difficulty in getting lobsters to market in good condition by road and rail.

Simpson collected his load of lobsters and crabs fresh from the sea, some from St. Margaret's Hope, Orkney. They were alive when packed for transport south. He was in London by 3 p.m. Sunday, ahead of his own schedule to catch the Monday morning market. Both men were in high spirits after a night's rest at the end of their arduous trip.

LOSSES DURING TRAVEL

If profit results, the venture will mean much to Caithness lobster fishermen. They often suffer losses during the summer, when lobsters go bad on the long and slow rail journey and are condemned on arrival at market.

(June 27)

JUDY GARLAND NICKS THROAT WITH GLASS

'HYSTERICAL ACT', SAYS STUDIO

From Our Own Correspondent

NEW YORK Tuesday.

Judy Garland, 27, the film actress, made a "superficial laceration" on her throat with a broken drinking glass last night, the Metro-Goldwyn-Mayer studio disclosed to-day. It was described as an "impulsive, hysterical act."

Miss Garland did not arrive on Saturday for a rehearsal of her role in "Royal Wedding". The studio announced that she had been suspended and would be replaced.

Her husband, Mr. Vincent Minelli, the film director, had earlier denied reports that she had attempted to cut her throat. Two evening newspapers in Los Angeles alledged that Mr. Minelli took a knife from her before she could harm herself.

"There is no truth whatever in the report," he said. "The poor girl is very much upset, but this . . . No."

"BROKE DRINKING GLASS"

A statement issued by Mr. R. Wheelwright, a studio publicity official, said "Miss Garland was in conference last night at her Hollywood house with her husband, Mr. Carlton Aslop, her business manager and Myrtle Tully, her secretary. They were discussing her future."

The statement continued: "At one point in the discussion Miss Garland, who has been under a strain and ill, became very despondent and hysterical and rushed into the bathroom, locking the door behind her.

"She broke a drinking glass and with the broken glass made a superficial laceration on her throat. Minelli got her to open the door and she was immediately very repentant and weeping."

(June 21)

EGYPT'S DEMANDS TO BRITAIN

WITHDRAWAL AT ONCE FROM CANAL ZONE

By A Diplomatic Correspondent

Mr. Morrison announced in the House of Commons yesterday that Mr. Bevin expects to be able to make a statement next week on a demand by Egypt for the ending of the 1936 Anglo-Egyptian Treaty.

The demand was made in a speech by King Farouk, read at the opening of Parliament in Cairo yesterday by Nahas Pasha, the Prime Minister. The King stated that his Government demanded the "total and immediate" evacuation of British troops in the Suez Canal Zone.

It also demanded the unity of Egypt and the Sudan under the Egyptian Crown. Shortly after the speech the Egyptian Embassy in London telephoned the Foreign Office that Salah el Din Bey, the Foreign Minister, would be coming to Britain next Wednesday.

(November 17)

25,000 LONDON DRIVERS DECIDE TO STRIKE

IMMEDIATE STOPPAGE TO AID SMITHFIELD MEN

By An Industrial Correspondent

Delegates representing 25,000 van and lorry drivers in Greater London decided last night on an immediate stoppage of work in support of the Smithfield strikers. Hundreds of drivers began to stop work immediately after the decision had been taken.

The meeting was called by the unofficial Shop Stewards' Association of the Transport and General Workers' Union. The 250 delegates who attended said they had a mandate to vote for or against a strike.

The strike will affect all forms of road transport other than buses and trams. If the drivers of petrol lorries stop work, supplies to public transport services will be seriously affected and buses may stop.

A strike headquarters is being set up in the Smithfield canteen. There arrangements will be made to provide food and perishables to hospitals and other institutions.

Newsprint supplies will not be affected. Mr. H. A. Jones, the delegate representing drivers in this section, walked out of the meeting because, he said, it was acting unconstitutionally.

NOT UNANIMOUS

The vote was far from unanimous, but the effects of the decision cannot be underestimated.

The full effect of the strike will not be felt to day, but weekend meetings are being arranged to explain the implications of the decision.

Mr. J. Farquehar, a member of the executive of the Transport and General Workers' Union, who is also a member of the Smithfield Meat Trade Committee, said last night that he expected that other districts in the country would eventually be affected as long distance transport men would be involved in the strike.

The resolution expressed disgust at the response to approaches for an amicable settlement of the Smithfield dispute and for an undertaking "that the need for immediate wage increases for transport workers should be recognised and pressed by the union."

It called for an immediate stoppage of work and meetings of drivers of "C" licence vehicles to ensure that no van or lorry with a trade union driver "appears on the road on Monday."

COMMUNISTS BLAMED

Mr. Deakin, general secretary of the Transport and General Workers' Union, said later that "these people are completely irresponsible," and advised members to disregard the decision.

"They are acting very clearly with the support of active members of the Communist party who are out to create the utmost confusion at this time in the interests of a foreign Power," he said.

The Smithfield dispute started on June 23, when 1,400 meat van drivers stopped work because of alleged delays in negotiations over their pay claim for a weekly increase of 19s.

Meat Ration :

Last night the Ministry of Food announced that the Londoner's meat ration this week would be 1s 4d worth of carcase meat. In addition supplies of corned beef will be available.

(July 8)

THE CORONATION STONE STOLEN

CHRISTMAS DAY THEFT AT THE ABBEY

SCOTTISH COUPLE IN CAR HUNTED

WATCH ON ROADS AND PORTS

Daily Telegraph Reporters

The Coronation Stone was stolen early on Christmas morning from under the Coronation chair in Westminster Abbey, where it had rested for 650 years. Scottish nationalists are suspected.

The thieves apparently hid in the Abbey overnight, removed the stone - it is of sandstone, 26¾ in by 16¾ in by 10¾ in, and weighs 458lb (over 4cwt) - and forced their way out with a crowbar through the doors at Poets' Corner. They escaped by car or van.

Scotland Yard warned police chiefs throughout the country to watch for the stone and for a Ford Anglia driven by a woman, aged about 25. With her was a man of about 29.

The car had been seen near the Abbey by a policeman about the time of the theft. Both the man and woman in it spoke with Scottish accents.

Late last night Scotland Yard sent a special message to all airfields and seaports, British Road Transport services and British Railways. It asked them to keep watch for any heavy packages, particularly those labelled "geological specimens."

Police watched roads to the North. But at a late hour the Yard were still without a trace of the stone.

The King, who is spending Christmas with the Royal family at Sandringham, was informed of the theft the same morning.

PADLOCK FORCED

Coronation Chair Damaged

Removal of the stone, which is also known as the Stone of Scone and was brought from Scotland to London by Edward I in 1296, is believed to have been planned and carried out by Scottish nationalists. The door which they forced in Poets' Corner is a temporary door in place of one damaged by bombs during the war.

The padlock had been broken and the wood near the lock chipped. The coronation chair was moved from its place behind the High Altar. A large splinter was knocked from one leg when the stone was moved from it but the damage is not extensive.

The stone was then apparently partly carried and partly dragged, probably in or on a sack, through the south screen door, along the length of the altar, down four steps leading from the sanctuary, round the south transent, and then out through the door at Poets' Corner.

GLASS BROKEN

Grazes on the Floor

Total distance from the Coronation chair to the door is 140 ft. After leaving the Abbey the stone was probably dragged 150ft over the cobble-stoned footpath leading out to Old Palace Yard to be loaded into a car or van.

Besides the damage to the Coronation chair, the glass from the notice beside the chair was broken. Carpets in front of the altar and in the sanctuary were crumpled and woodwork on the way to the door scratched.

WRIST WATCH CLUE

Crowbar Found

A man's wristlet watch and a crowbar were found lying on the opposite side of the chair to the direction in which the stone was moved. The watch is round, with a brown or buff face and black strap.

It is thought the thieves put it on the floor to time themselves and possibly a meeting with a car outside the Abbey.

A police constable on patrol has given a description of the man and woman in the car. They were near the King George V statue opposite the Houses of Parliament when the constable first spoke to them.

They said they were on their way to Brighton for Christmas and had stopped to look at the statue on the way. Both had Scottish accents. He walked back with them to their car, which was parked in the road near the Poets' Corner entrance. The woman got into the driver's seat and the man next to her, and the car was driven away.

A conference between officials and Scotland Yard chiefs was held at the Abbey yesterday. A further conference will be held at the Yard to-day.

Additional staff at the Criminal Record Office were recalled to the Yard to help check the descriptions of the man and the woman with the records. The woman is about 25 with long dark hair, short pointed nose, dark eyes, fair complexion and thin lips. She was dressed in a green check coat with a big collar.

The man was aged about 26 to 29, fair complexion, slight snub nose, fair hair, uncombed and of medium height.

The Yard description of the stone issued to police forces throughout the country says two corners are cut off. Two iron lifting rings, each about 4in in diameter, are fitted at each end of the stone.

(December 27)

THE CORONATION CHAIR, enclosing the famous Stone of Scone in the Chapel of Edward the Confessor, Westminster Abbey.

290ft 'PENCIL' FOR FESTIVAL

WINNING DESIGN IN FEATURE CONTEST

Daily Telegraph Reporter

A structure shaped like a giant silver pencil and rising vertically to a height of 290ft is to be the dominating feature of the Festival of Britain. The Festival opens on the South Bank of the Thames next year.

The "pencil" will give the impression of floating perpendicularly over the exhibition as if in defiance of the laws of gravity.

The designers are three young London architects who have an office in Westminster. They are Michael Powell, Philip Powell, and Hidalgo Moya. For their effort they have won the first prize of £300 offered by the Festival authorities for a "striking and original feature".

The pencil, which at its widest part has a diameter of 14ft, is to be constructed of latticed aluminium. Shining brightly in the sunlight, it will be even more impressive in the dark when illuminated from inside.

(January 12)

A BLUE MOON IS SEEN IN LONDON

Daily Telegraph Reporter

The basis for the adage,"Once in a blue moon," was obvious to people all over London last night. They saw the harvest moon as a pale blue disc.

From the roof of THE DAILY TELEGRAPH building in Fleet-street it could be observed clearly. The shade of blue appeared to vary slightly, as though a coloured haze was passing across its face. Few stars were visible.

The phenomenon was also observed at places as far apart as Bristol and Bridlington, Yorks, and in Scotland, where, in the afternoon, the sun had appeared blue.

Following the phenomenon of the blue sun in Scotland the meteorological station at Renfrew learned that a R.A.F. plane had reported finding a thin layer of dust and sand at 43,000ft over the east of Scotland. At 20,000 to 30,000ft it found a layer of ice particles in the thin cirrhus cloud formation.

One expert said the dust cloud was almost certainly part of a great American sandstorm of a few days ago. The dust had been carried across the Atlantic.

An official at the Meteorological Office in London said last night: "We have had reports from meteorological stations in the north of England about the appearance of a blue moon, and we have seen it ourselves in London. It was definitely blue.

"Blue suns and blue moons, which are due to the same cause, are rare. It will need a large survey into meteorological records to say when they were last reported in this country - if at all.

"They have been reported in North Africa and North America."

HAZE LAYER

Red Colour Absorbed

Our METEOROLOGICAL CORRESPONDENT writes: Undoubtedly the bluish colour of the moon can be traced to the same cause as that which gave rise to the blue sun.

The haze layer encountered by the R.A.F. pilot may have been caused by a volcano eruption or an intense forest fire and carried a long distance from its source.

It has been demonstrated in the laboratory that with a certain size of dust particle the red end of the spectrum shown by a rainbow can be absorbed. The light absorbed will be bluish in colour.

(September 27)

FREEZE-UP ON ROADS WORST SINCE 1947

Further falls of snow and sharp frost, after the coldest night of the year, made road conditions in many parts of Britain last night the worst since the great freeze-up of early 1947. Motorists were warned by the Automobile Association to make only essential journeys.

The most dangerous roads were in the area south of a line from Lancaster to Darlington, extending roughly to a line from Chester to Derby and King's Lynn, where the snow was up to six inches deep. The average depth was just under a foot at Driffield, Yorks.

All forms of transport were dislocated. Thousands of tons of coal could not leave pits in Yorkshire and the East Midlands because empty wagons were unable to reach collieries. There will be no racing today, and the two rugby trials have been cancelled. (Details P3.)

The widespread snowfall was the heaviest in Britain in December since 1937. In several places snow ploughs failed to break through drifts several feet deep caused by high winds which isolated villages in Somerset, Yorkshire and Lincolnshire.

Air liners had to circle over London Airport from 1.45 p.m. until about 3.15 p.m. because runways were icebound. Electricity load-shedding for all areas began at 7.30 a.m. with cuts of up to 30 per cent in some areas.

(December 6)

WOMAN DRIVES FIRST GAS TURBINE CAR

85 M.P.H. IN TEST

From Our Special Correspondent

TOWCESTER, Northants, Thursday.

A woman drove the first car in the world propelled by a gas turbine engine in tests at Silverstone racing track, near here, to-day.

She was Mrs. Kathleen Wilks, 58, a grandmother and wife of Mr. Spencer Wilks, managing director of the Rover Company, of Solihull, near Birmingham.

Outwardly a modern, streamlined touring model, the car was described by its makers, the Rover Motor Company, as a "mobile test bed." The engine was housed in the rear seat compartment, but that would not be its normal position.

Controls have been reduced to two pedals-accelerator and brake. The makers claim that many of the major problems have been solved.

The engine runs on paraffin. Its fuel consumption is higher than the normal piston-type.

10 YEARS' RESEARCH

After testing the car yesterday the R.A.C. reported to-day that no attempt was made to obtain maximum speed but 85 m.p.h. was readily attained. Accelerating from a standstill the car smoothly reached 60 m.p.h. in 14 seconds.

"Although no provision for silencing the exhaust was observable, the volume of noise was not excessive or unpleasant," the report added. "It was naturally accentuated during acceleration."

Mr. Spencer Wilks, who has brought out this first gas turbine car following 10 years of research said: "It will be three or four years before the gas turbine car is in production."

(March 10)

SANDRINGHAM CROWDS GREET ROYAL FAMILY

From Our Special Correspondent

SANDRINGHAM, Tuesday.

The Royal Family spent Christmas here in the traditional homely atmosphere. When they went out they were greeted warmly by villagers and visitors, who also saw Prince Charles and Princess Anne out with their nurse.

On Christmas Eve 1,000 people greeted the King and Queen, Queen Mary, Princess Margaret and Prince William and Prince Richard, sons of the Duke of Gloucester, at West Newton village church, where there was a carol service. Torches lit the way along the church drive.

The church was filled, and even more people remained outside to listen to the singing. Among those who gave Bible readings at the service were Capt. W. Fellowes, the King's agent at Sandringham; Mr. C. H. Cook, the King's head gardener at Sandringham; Kenneth Basham, a choirboy, and Anne Crowe, a local schoolgirl.

On Christmas Day the King and Queen, Queen Mary, Princess Margaret, the Duke and Duchess of Gloucester and their two sons and members of the King's personal staff attended morning service and Communion at the church in Sandringham Park.

FAMILY HEARS BROADCAST

In the afternoon, after the traditional meal of Norfolk turkey, at which there were some guests, the family sat by a radio set in the drawing room while the King, from his study, broadcast his message to the Commonealth.

(December 27)

NEW ARK ROYAL LAUNCHED

THE QUEEN'S TRIBUTE TO FAMOUS NAME

From Nowell Hall.

Daily Telegraph Naval Correspondent

BIRKENHEAD, Wednesday.

With huge crowds lining the waterfront and thronging the decks of a host of beflagged ships in the Mersey, the Queen this afternoon launched the hull of the 36,800-ton carrier Ark Royal from the Birkenhead yard of Cammell Laird.

In the dockyard alone were 54,000 people. Among them were 400 specially invited naval guests - officers and men of the former 22,000-ton Ark Royal, sunk by the Germans in 1941.

As the new carrier entered the water she was greeted with a roar of cheering and a blare of ships' sirens. A few minutes later, with the waiting tugs closing in on her in mid-river, squadrons of naval aircraft, flying in close formation, passed low in salute.

The ship which had been seven years on the slips, will be one of the two biggest carriers in the Royal Navy. The other is her sister ship, the Eagle, launched by Princess Elizabeth in 1946 and expected to be in commission later this year.

Dressed overall to welcome the Ark Royal to the Royal Navy was the 23,000-ton carrier Illustrious, flagship of Adml. Sir Rhoderick McGrigor, C.-in-C. Plymouth. I was among 1,400 guests who watched the ceremony from her flight deck.

21-GUN SALUTE

On receiving a signal from the shore that the Queen was approaching, the Illustrious fired a salute of 21 guns. After the Queen had inspected the guard of honour we heard through the ship's radio the "still" sounded as her Majesty mounted the launching platform.

The ship's company lining the port side in the keen southerly wind removed their caps. They joined in the short broadcast service which followed.

Then we heard the Queen speak the traditional words: "I name this ship Ark Royal. May God protect her and bless all who sail in her." There was silence as the Queen pressed the button to set in motion the mechanism which released the ship.

For a few moments the 800ft long hull appeared stationary. Then the ship passed slowly down the slipway between the tall cranes, some of which were cleared with less than a foot to spare.

The launching of the longest ship ever built on Merseyside went without a hitch. The Ark Royal settled quietly into the water and passed stern first out into the river, leaving behind her a trail of flotsam.

After visiting the company's shipbuilding and engine shops the Queen walked to the quayside.

Later, when she lunched with guests at the shipyard, the Queen accepted from Sir Robert Johnson, chairman of the shipbuilders, a souvenir diamond brooch in the shape of two flowers. She removed the larger brooch she had been wearing and pinned the new one to her dress.

Sir Robert said: "The New Ark Royal has been planned to be the most perfect aircraft carrier in the world. She is going to be ahead of anything afloat."

(May 4)

EUROPEAN COAL AND STEEL POOL

FRENCH PROPOSAL TO OTHER POWERS

JOINT PRODUCTION WITH GERMANY

M. SCHUMAN 'FIRST STEP TO FEDERATION'

From Our Own Correspondent
PARIS, Tuesday.

M. Schuman, French Foreign Minister, announced to-night that the French Government is to propose that the whole of the French and German coal and steel production should be placed under common "High Authority."

This organisation would be open to all other countries in Europe and to Russia. Details of the plan had been sent to-day to Britain, Belgium, Holland, Luxembourg, Italy and the High Commissioners in Germany.

M. Schuman said he had mentioned the proposal to Mr. Acheson, American Secretary of State, yesterday. It was not on the agenda of Thursday's three-Power meeting in London, but it "might come up for discussion."

The decision had been reached in an effort to eliminate the centuries-old opposition of France and Germany, and as a first step towards European Federation.

It would change the destiny of regions long devoted to the manufacture of armaments.

"World peace," he said, "cannot be safeguarded without creative efforts measuring up to the dangers that menace it.

"A united Europe will not be created in a moment, nor all at once. It will be created by concrete accomplishments which build, first of all, a factual basis for solidarity." The French plan was for immediate action on a limited but decisive point

FRENCH AIMS
Identical Conditions

M. Schuman said that France was ready to open negotiations on the following points:
1-The common High Authority should ensure with the least possible delay the modernisation of production and improvement of quality.
2- Coal and steel should be supplied to the German and French markets and to the market of any participating nations under identical conditions.
3-Exports to other countries should be from a common pool of production.
4-Conditions of labour in the industries participating should be equalised.

Shipment of coal and steel between the member countries should be free of Customs duty. A unified transport tariff wuld be necessary.

HIGH AUTHORITY
U.N. Representative

The proposed High Authority would consist of delegates chosen by Governments on an equal basis and a president chosen by the same Governments. Any dispute would be settled by an arbitrator, who would be appointed by all concerned.

M. Schuman said that the proposal in no way prejudiced the right of ownership in the various enterprises. He denied that it would constitute a cartel since the organisation would assure the fusion of markets and the expansion of production.

RUHR AND SAAR
Position of Germany

The proposal did not affect the powers conferred on the International Authority of the Ruhr or any obligations imposed on Germany as long as they remained in force.

Any eventual German participation would have to be approved by the three High Commissioners. The Saar, as part of the French economic union, would be included in the proposal, he added.

Asked if German steel output under the proposal would remain within its present limitations, he replied that it would be increased if the High Authority decided that there was sufficient demand.

"The solidarity of production which this scheme would assure would not

only make all war between France and Germany unthinkable but materially impossible," M. Schuman declared.

"The establishment of this powerful production union, which is open to all countries who want to participate, would result in furnishing to all these countries the raw materials of industrial production fundamental to their economy and security,"

M. Schuman was closely questioned about the possible British reaction to his proposals. At first he refused to comment, then said that he would not have put the proposal forward if he had expected a rebuff.

(May 10)

UNITY CALL TO EUROPE BY MR. CHURCHILL

'PRESERVING OUR OWN SURVIVAL'

Daily Telegraph Reporter

Mr. Churchill roused a great audience of nearly 7,000 people to cheering when, at a meeting of the United Europe Movement at the Albert Hall last night, he made a powerful plea for unity among European countries.

He spoke of the "vehement hostility" of the Communist party in every country to steps towards European unity. "The more we have progressed, the more bitter has become the Communist campaign of vilification." He also said:—

"We Europeans should best preserve world peace and our own survival by standing together and bringing all the force of a steadily and swiftly uniting Continent to the aid of the world organisation in the perils and problems with which it is confronted. Once again the path of duty is the path alike of safety and of honour."

There was no doubt, he declared, that the tide of Communism in Europe, which "only two years ago engulfed Czechoslovakia," had for the moment been halted by the economic integration of the peoples of Europe.

He referred to "the armed might of the Kremlin oligarchy" which, while frothing words of peace, had maintained larger armed forces than almost all the countries in the world put together.

The battle of Korea was as much the battle of Europe as if it were being fought in our own towns and countryside.

The great audience had risen to its feet when Mr. Churchill, with Mrs. Churchill, walked on to the platform followed by two former Prime Ministers of France. They were M. Reynaud and M. Ramadier. Also on the platform was Dr. Bucerius, a member of the Federal German Parliament.

(July 22)

PRESIDENT TRUMAN

ATTEMPT TO KILL MR. TRUMAN

PUERTO RICANS' GUN-FIGHT AT PRESIDENT'S HOME

From Our Own Correspondent
WASHINGTON, Wednesday.

Two Puerto Rican revolutionaries to-day made what Secret Service men called a "maniacal" attempt to assassinate President Truman in Blair House, his temporary residence. One was killed and one of the President's guards died in hospital

Mr. Truman, who was resting upstairs when gunfight between the Puerto Ricans and his guards broke out on the stairs to the house, was unhurt. The second assailant and two other guards were seriously wounded.

Both gunmen were identified by the Secret Service as members of the Puerto Rican Nationalist party. Last week the party staged an uprising to demand independence for Puerto Rico, an American possession in the West Indies.

A White House announcement said that the Puerto Ricans tried to force their way in "with the express purpose of shooting the President."

Firing pistols, they tried to enter a few minutes before Mr. Truman was due to leave for Arlington Cemetery. He was to speak at the unveiling of a memorial to Field-Marshal Sir John Dill, head of the wartime British Military Mission in Washington.

The assailants were identified as Griselio Torresola (dead), a young man, of Ward Drive, New York, and Oscar Collazo, 37, of Brook-avenue, the Bronx, New York.

Apparently unperturbed, Mr. Truman left by a back door a few minutes after the shooting. His guards carried sub-machine guns.

His appearance at the cemetery was calm and unruffled. After speaking briefly he went directly to his office in The White House. Extra servicemen were hurriedly detailed to guard his route and mingle with those who were

present at the unveiling ceremony.

Blair House, normally used as a house for distinguished visitors is being used as the President's residence while the White House is being renovated. The houses are almost opposite one another on Pennsylvania-avenue.

STAIRCASE BATTLE
Covering Fire

The policeman who died was Leslie Coffelt, 40, North Wayne-boulevard, Arlington, Virginia. The wounded are Joseph Downs, Silver Spring, Maryland, whose condition is critical, and Donald Birdzell, whose condition is fair. The shooting was at 2.30 p.m. Washington time. The men were shot on two different sets of stairs leading to Blair House, which is composed of two houses converted into one—Blair House and Blair Lee House.

(November 2)

A GREAT NEW PRESSURIZED SPEEDBIRD
...THE **HERMES**

Yes, the new Hermes Speedbirds are pressurized for swift smooth "over-the-weather" flying between London and West Africa. (Accra, Lagos and Kano). You sit – or lie back–in the world's most relaxing adjustable aircraft seats and enjoy traditionally fine Speedbird service all the way. Complimentary meals ... no tips.

B.O.A.C. TAKES GOOD CARE OF YOU

Free advice and information available on request from your local B.O.A.C. Appointed Agent or B.O.A.C., Airway's Terminal, Buckingham Palace Road, London SW1. Telephone: VICtoria 2323 Early reservations essential.

FLY B·O·A·C

BRITISH OVERSEAS AIRWAYS CORPORATION

HOPE ABANDONED FOR SUBMARINE MEN

10 DEAD: 55 OTHERS STILL MISSING

MANY ESCAPED BUT DROWNED IN THE TIDE

Daily Telegraph Reporter

The Admiralty announced last night that no hope could now be entertained of further survivors from the submarine Truculent, sunk in collision in the Thames Estuary on Thursday night. It is feared that 65 are dead. Ten bodies have already been recovered.

There were 80 on board—six officers, 56 ratings and 18 dockyard technicians. Four ratings joined just before sailing.

Only fifteen were rescued, four of them were officers, nine ratings and two technicians.

Survivors said that two-thirds of the submarine was flooded. The vessel was fitted with three escape hatches, of which two were used.

It is believed that 40 men got through the escape hatches but many were swept away by the tide in the dark. Some of the Davis escape gear was in flooded compartments and could not be reached. A number of the men had to hold their breath while escaping through the hatches.

SIGNALS BY GRENADES

From daybreak to nightfall yesterday divers and frogmen tried to get in touch with any men remaining alive in the submarine. Hand grenades were exploded around the Truculent as a signal. The divers tapped the hull, but no answer was given. Attempts to fix an air line failed.

Diving ceased at dusk. H. M. S. Moorfowl, a wreck-lifting vessel, anchored over the Truculent for the night. Today at 8 a.m. slack water, full-scale salvage operations will begin, despite deteriorating weather.

SURVIVORS 'BOBBED UP LIKE CORKS'

SOME MEN HAD NO ESCAPE GEAR

From Our Special Correspondent
CHATHAM, Friday.

Dressed in duffle coats and wearing old shirts and trousers, 10 survivors of the lost submarine Truculent were brought ashore in the frigate Cowdray here this evening. They described how they had escaped "bobbing up to the surface like corks."

All escaped through the engine-room hatch. One man said that two-thirds of the submarine was flooded.

Some said they did not have an opportunity of getting their escape gear which was in other compartments.

When the Cowdray came into No. 3 basin, ships in the dockyard sounded a welcome on their sirens. The survivors were transferred to a launch and brought ashore. Three bodies, draped in White Ensigns, were brought ashore in another launch.

HIT SEA BED
Bulkhead Shut

Seated round a table in one of the rooms in the barracks the survivors gave brief accounts of their experiences.

Petty Officer R. C. FRY, 35, of Upper-close, Forest Row, Sussex said: "When the crash happened the submarine hit the sea bed before any of us could escape. We shut the bulkhead door and the stokers' mess deck door and remained in the engine room until our escape."

2nd Class Engine Room Artificer EDWARD CHARLES BUCKINGHAM, 38, of St. David's-road, Southsea, said the collision occurred at 7.5 p.m. "We started flooding up in the engine room to increase the pressure at 7.45 p.m., and we were ready at about 8.10 p.m. to start getting away.

'I was second from the last, Chief E.R.A. Hine folowed me. We swam together for a little while, and then I lost him."

(January 14)

LT. BOWERS GUILTY OF HAZARDING TRUCULENT

SEVERELY REPRIMANDED

From Nowell Hall
Daily Telegraph Naval Correspondent
R.N. BARRACKS, CHATHAM, Thursday.

With his sword pointing towards him on the president's table, Lt. Charles Philip Bowers, 28, commander of the submarine Truculent, to-night heard Capt. A.P. Atwill, Deputy Judge-Advocate of the Fleet, announce that he had been found guilty of negligently or by default hazarding his ship.

He was sentenced to be severely reprimanded. The court-martial found that a charge of negligently or by default losing his ship was not proved, and he was acquitted on this charge.

Lt. Bowers pleaded not guilty to both charges. The verdict was announced after the court-martial had been sitting all day [Report P.3] and after the president and members had deliberated in private for an hour and 25 minutes.

With tense features and standing to attention two paces in front of the Provost Marshal, who carried a drawn sword, Lt. Bowers was severely reprimanded. Then, while everybody was still standing, he saluted and left the court.

WIFE INFORMED
Wait at Friend's House

This evening the news was broken to his wife by telephone. With their two young children she had been awaiting the verdict all day at a friend's house near Chatham.

The court-martial followed a Naval Board of Inquiry into the loss of the Truculent, of which Lt. Bowers assumed command last October. The submarine was sunk with the loss of 64 lives, after being in collision with the Swedish tanker Divina in the Thames Estuary on the night of Jan. 12.

(February 10)

SOCIALISTS 314: BARE MAJORITY CERTAIN

LEAD OF 10 WITH 6 RESULTS TO COME

CONSERVATIVES AND ALLIES 294

LIBERALS 8: CABINET WILL CONSIDER POSITION TO-DAY

At a late hour last night, with results announced for 619 constituencies, the Socialists, holding 314, had a lead of 10 over all other parties.

They were thus assured of an absolute majority of four in a House of Commons of 624 members (625 including the speaker). The state of the parties was:

	At Dissolution	
Labour and allies	390 ...	**314**
Conservatives and allies ...	219 ...	**294**
Liberals	10 ...	**8**
Others	21 ...	**2**

[These figures do not include the Speaker.]

This situation came at the end of a day in which the prospects of the parties had fluctuated minute to minute. Just before 5 p.m. the Opposition parties drew level with Labour four times. Overnight, the Socialists had a lead of 60.

GAINS AND LOSSES

Owing to the redistribution of seats, results in only 434 divisions can be compared with those of the previous Parliament. Gains and losses in these constituencies as they affect the main parties were:

	Gains	Losses
Labour and allies	10	50
Conservatives and allies	56	5
Liberals	1	3
Others	0	9

(February 25)

PETROL NINEPENCE UP: RATION DOUBLED

FEW MAJOR CHANGES IN THE BUDGET

Sir Stafford Cripps, Chancellor of the Exchequer, in his Budget statement yesterday [Report—Pages 8 and 9], announced only two important changes in taxation. These were:

PETROL.—Tax raised by 9d a gallon from 6 p.m. last night, making the price 3s. The Chancellor did not think there would be many applications for increases in fares, although bus companies' costs will be about 5 per cent higher.

Standard ration will be doubled for 12 months from June 1, instead of for only three months. This will give 180 miles a month instead of 90. Farmers using vehicles operated on taxable oil will receive an annual grant at a cost of £2 million to £3 million a year.

INCOME-TAX.—Rate on first £50 on which tax is chargeable reduced from 3s to 2s 6d in the pound and on the next £200 from 6s to 5s. This will mean lower tax on overtime for most workers.

The rate of tax on earnings, including overtime, after the usual allowances, works out in many cases at a maximum of 4s 10d in the £, Sir Stafford said. This will be reduced to 4s. Where the average rate is 2s 5d, it will be cut to 2s. Maximum benefit under the lower rates will be £115s a year, or 4s 4d a week.

(April 19)

RESIGNATION OF SIR STAFFORD CRIPPS

By Our Political Correspondent

The resignation of Sir Stafford Cripps, Chancellor of the Exchequer, for reasons of health was announced last night. He is 61. He is succeeded by Mr Gaitskell, 44, Minister of State for Economic Affairs since March 1. The salary for each post is £5,000 a year.

Mr. Gaitskell has been deputising for the Chancellor over the whole field of financial and economic business since he took his present office. He takes over all the responsibilities previously held by Sir Stafford for the coordination of economic policy.

His appointment to one of the greatest offices of State at such an early age, after only five years as an M.P., is already causing intense speculation among politicians.

(October 20)

CHANCELLOR'S SCHOOLMASTER TALK FOR M.P.s

SIR S. CRIPPS THE ONLY ENTHUSIAST

By Our Own Representative

WESTMINSTER, Tuesday.

Nothing but the expectation that to-day's was a pre-election Budget saved the occasion from being the dullest Budget day for many years. The event was as impressively staged as ever.

Crowded galleries, thronged benches, members standing beyond the Bar, cheers for Sir STAFFORD CRIPPS, the Chancellor of the Exchequer, as he placed his battered despatch case on the table, curiosity over the glass of fruit juice placed beside it- all contributed to the authentic atmosphere.

The question hour ended. The speaker left the chair to give way to the Chairman of Ways and Means. The Serjeant-at-Arms removed the Mace, and just after 3.30 Sir Stafford stepped to the dispatch box.

The house settled back in anticipation of new and possibly exciting pronouncements. Two and a half hours later, when the Chancellor sat down, all but the new members must have been thinking: "This is where we came in a year ago."

For the tax changes he had announced left the general situation practically unaltered.

HEADS BOWED

Sir Stafford appeared in the character of a schoolmaster. This impression was heightened when about midway through his speech all heads were bowed over copies of the financial Blue Paper from which he quoted.

(April 19)

MR. ERNEST BEVIN

MR. BEVIN'S CHALLENGE AND OFFER TO RUSSIA

From Hugh Chevins, Daily Telegraph Industrial Correspondent

MARGATE, Thursday.

Mr. Bevin, bearing the marks of the strain of the last five years and speaking in a voice which sometimes almost failed, vigorously challenged and made a big offer to Russia at the Labour party conference here to-day. [Report—P7.]

He said, amid a storm of cheers from most of the 1,500 delegates: "Russia can sit down with us at the table tomorrow and we will forget the past. But—and I ask you for your support—we have a right to be treated as honest people."

The Foreign Secretary who returned from the United States yesterday, scored an even bigger triumph for his policy than he did here three years ago when he made his famous "stab in the back" speech.

On a card vote a resolution implying criticism of Mr. Bevin's policy was defeated. The figures were 4,861,000 to 881,000.

(October 6)

2 BRITONS WIN NOBEL PEACE PRIZE

EARL RUSSELL AND PROF. C.F. POWELL

From Our Own Correspondent

STOCKHOLM, Friday.

Two Britons were to-day awarded prizes worth over £11,000 by the Nobel Foundation Prize Committee. They are:

EARL RUSSELL (Bertrand Russell, the Philosopher) 78, who was awarded the 1950 literature prize "in recognition of his many-sided and important work in which he has constantly stood forth as a champion of humanity and freedom of thought", and

Prof. C.P. POWELL, 46, professor of physics at Bristol University, who received the 1950 physics prize for his discovery of the method of photographing the atom at the moment of fission and his discoveries concerning the mesons formed by this process.

The 1949 literary prize, which was withheld last year, was given to Mr. WILLIAM FAULKNER, 53, the American novelist, for his "forceful and independent artistic contributions to modern American Fiction".

Lord Russell who returned in September from a 33,000-mile lecture tour of Australia, is now lecturing in the United states.

Prof. Powell is a vice-president of the Bristol Peace Committee and a member of the branch. He said at Bristol on Tuesday:"I am not a Communist and have no political affiliations whatever."

(November 11)

I.C.I. TO MAKE NEW FIBRE

YORKSHIRE FACTORY

A factory costing several million pounds, is to be built at Wilton, near Redcar, Yorks, for the manufacture of a synthetic textile fibre known as Terylene, Imperial Chemical Industries announced yesterday. The fibre promises to compete in price and use with cotton, silk and wool.

The announcement was the first indication on either side of the Atlantic that Terylene was ready for production on a commercial scale. Its basis is ethylene glycol, known to most motorists as anti-freeze mixture.

Terylene is chemically different from other synthetic fibres. it was discovered in 1940 by two chemists of the Calico Printer's Association, Mr. John Whinfield and Dr. J. T. Dickson.

It is said to be very strong, unaffected by moth, easy to launder and unshrinkable. The manufacturers claim that silks made from it drape well and are pleasant and soft to the touch.

(November 11)

RIVIERA WEDDING OF ERROL FLYNN

From Our Own Correspondent

PARIS, Monday.

Errol Flynn, 41, the film actor was married for the third time to-day at Monaco and Nice. His wife, Patricia Wymore, 23, comes from Salina, Kansas.

The civil ceremony at Monaco Town Hall was followed by a religious ceremony at the Lutheran Church of the Transfiguration, at Nice. Prince Troubetskoy, husband of the former Miss Barbara Hutton, was one of the ushers.

(October 24)

U.S. WILL MAKE HYDROGEN BOMB

MR. TRUMAN ISSUES 'GO AHEAD' ORDER

From Our Own Correspondent

WASHINGTON, Tuesday.

President Truman to-day gave the order for the United States to proceed with the project for making the hydrogen atomic bomb. Such a weapon, it is claimed, might prove to be 1,000 times more destructive than the atomic bombs dropped on Japan.

The President thus ended a controversy which has raged for several months over the merits of the project and its possible cost estimated at £700 million. He announced his decsion in the following statement:

"It is part of my responsibility as Commander-in-Chief of the armed forces to see to it that our country is able to defend itself against any possible aggressor. Accordingly, I have directed the Atomic Energy Commission to continue its work on all forms of atomic energy weapons, including the so-called hydrogen or super-bomb. Like all other work in the field of atomic weapons, it is being, and will be, carried forward on a basis consistent with the overall objectives of our programme for peace and security."

(February 1)

TRAPPED MINERS FREED AT 1 A.M.

RESCUERS DRILLED HOLE FROM OLD PIT

WAIT UNDERGROUND FOR GAS TO CLEAR

From Our Special Correspondent

NEW CUMMOCK, Ayrshire, Saturday Morning.

A hundred and sixteen of the 128 miners who were trapped 720ft below ground in the Knochshinnoch Castle Colliery here were rescued at 1 a.m. to-day. They escaped through a hole drilled in a 30ft-thick seam of coal into a neighbouring disused working.

The remaining 12, who became separated from the main party after the landslide, are not accounted for. Fears for their safety are growing.

The 116 were kept down the pit for 90 minutes until all gas, which had hampered rescue work, had been cleared from the escape passageway. All were medically examined before walking the two miles from the seam to the surface.

A bore-hole was drilled through the seam at 10.30 last night and the air found to be clear. The hole was then enlarged with picks and the men, who had been working on their side, were able to talk to their rescuers.

Just before midnight squads went down with bottles of beer and sandwiches for the 116, who had had no food for about 24 hours. They were fed as they made their way through the hole.

The weary miners had been underground since Thursday afternoon. At 10.30 that night almost an entire field, sodden by torrential rain, subsided into the workings, sealed the road with mud and trapped them.

Amazingly one telephone line to the surface remained "live". Over that they were told where rescuers were tunnelling towards them.

At 12.30 a.m. a crowd of several thousand people stood in the Bank pit yard awaiting the arrival of the trapped men at the surface. From the time the news of the breakthrough was heard the people stood expectantly in almost complete silence under the glare of the lights in the pit yard.

First news of the breakthrough was received by Mr. H. Brown, foreman of the early shift, who stood by the telephone communicating with the trapped men at the Castle Colliery office. Answering the telephone was Andrew Houston, 55, of New Cumnock, foreman in charge of the back shift.

600ft WALL OF GAS

Fans Used To Disperse It

During the day the rescuers had first to get rid of a 600ft wall of 'black

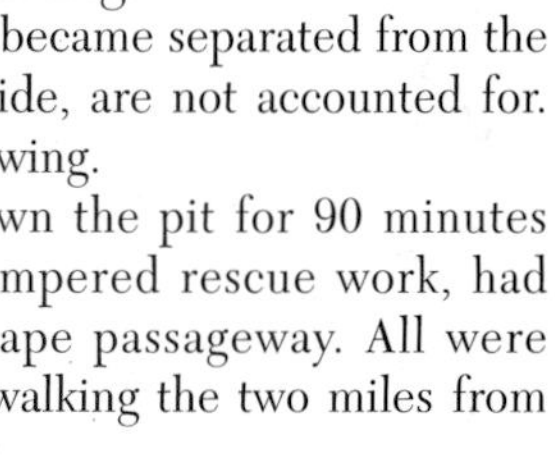

damp', a colourless, odourless poison gas. Fans and outside canvas hoses were used to disperse it.

Fresh air was reaching the men through a gap of about six inches over the mound of mud which blocked the road. There were also apertures in the debris above the gallery.

Towards evening there was a crowd of about a thousand people. Prayer meetings were held at the pit head with women, miners and rescue workers taking part.

(September 9)

First Night

A POET'S NEW COMEDY

BRILLIANT OLIVIER PRODUCTION

By W. A. Darlington

Is it the bleak, regimented life that we live now that makes a play like Christopher Fry's "Venus Observed" seem somehow a glimpse of a lost enchantment, or is it the poet's power to make us conscious for a time of a melancholy beauty existing only in his imagination?

This is a rhetorical question, for I cannot answer it. I only know that at the James's Theatre last night while my intellect was bewilderedly chasing the will-of-the-wisp of Mr. Fry's meaning, my spirit was at rest, lulled by the beauty of the sounds and sights offered to it.

WIT AND ODDITIES

It is Mr. Fry's way to dispense with story, and to make his effects by cunningly woven traceries of words, by flashes of wit, by oddities of character, by individual strokes of "theatre." Since he has control of all the weapons he uses, the fact that he has thrown away one of the strongest does not finally matter. We knuckle under without ado.

His central figure this time is a duke of our own time who, wishing to choose a duchess from among his three old loves, cares so little which he is to take that he leaves the choice to his son, who, like Paris, is to present an apple to the winning goddess. Meanwhile the Duke is more interested in observing the heavens through his telescope.

But a fourth lady, daughter of the Duke's eccentric and dishonest old agent, arrives from America and—for some reason not even yet very clear to me—draws a small pistol and shoots the apple out of the Duke's hand, after which her own hand becomes the object of rivalry between father and son.

FIRE AND PHILOSOPHY

Later the ducal mansion is set on fire by one of the ladies, the one who loves the Duke most deeply; and when she has given herself up to the police the rest of the house-party, with shawls and quilts over their evening dress, spend the night philosophising in a ruined temple in the garden.

Laurence Olivier, whose venture this is, produces the play impeccably and plays the Duke with his special gift of clear-cut precision and with infinite charm.

LADY FOR BURNING

Valerie Taylor, as the lady who is for burning, Brenda de Banzie and Rachel Kempson play the three goddesses quite beautifully, George Relph produces much comedy and a touch of pathos as the agent, and Denholm Elliott does very well as the son.

Heather Stannard, a newcomer of real promise, has a fine personal success as the girl with the gun; but may I implore her to learn to use that warm velvety voice of hers more distinctly. At present she is the least clear of a notably well-spoken company.

Roger Furse's decor is a real delight in itself.

(January 19)

MARGARET LOCKWOOD as "Peter Pan", at the Scala.

'PETER PAN'

MISS LOCKWOOD AGAIN

Margaret Lockwood, playing Peter Pan at the Scala for the second year, has a new straight wig, which adds something to her boyishness. Her attack is firmer, but she smiles too much and there is still the occasional suggestion of a musical comedy heroine. I have seen better Peters, and many worse.

Alan Judd had the traditional double of Mr. Darling and Capt. Hook. He has the advantage of a fine sonorous voice and has realised the importance of giving full value to the words in Hook's part.

The Wendy of Shirley Lorimer is the best I have seen for years She has a grave youthful charm and is at once the child and the Barrie woman. It is good to see Jane Welsh again as Mrs. Darling, and Russell Thorndike is completely satisfying as Smee, the non-conformist pirate.

(December 21)

'X' CERTIFICATE FOR FILMS

UNDER 16s EXCLUDED

By Our Film Correspondent

"X" certificates are to be issued by local authorities to exclude children under 16 from films considered unsuitable even if accompanied by parents. This was staged at a meeting in London yesterday of the Association of Municipal Corporations.

It was reported that the British Board of Film Censors had recommended local authorities to take steps without waiting for Government action.

Under present law, children under 16 are forbidden to see "A" (Adult) films unless accompanied by parent or guardian, and "H" (Horrific) films in any circumstances. The proposed "X" certificate will be granted to films "wholly adult in conception and treatment," to which the "H" certificate is inappropriate.

Writers and producers feel that the new category will enable them to treat sex and other subjects with a freedom enjoyed by Continental film-makers.

(July 14)

MUSICAL PLAY ON NEW LINES

FINE CHORUS IN 'CAROUSEL'

By George W. Bishop

Don't go to "Carousel" at Drury Lane expecting to see another "Oklahoma."' The author and composer, Oscar Hammerstein II and Richard Rogers, are the same, and there is again the brilliant choreography by Agnes de Mille, but "Carousel" is quite different from any other musical play

The story based very roughly on Molnar's "Liliom" is about Billy Bigelow, a handsome young barker in a New England fairground who falls in love with a dewy-eyed innocent named Julie Jordan. Whether they marry is not clear. Very likely not, for he is a bad lad.

They have a child, and one of the grand moments of the evening is the eight-minute soliloqy to his unborn son.

That the son turns out to be a daughter he does not discover until he is "up-there", a sort of circus heaven, for Billy Bigelow is killed in the act of robbery, and most of the second act of the play takes place after his death.

He is given one day on earth, where he has the satisfaction of seeing his daughter launching herself on her own feet. It is possible to enjoy a great deal of "Carousel" without taking the story too profoundly. The best thing about it is the music. There is a great deal of it, and although there are such magnificent tunes as "June is Bustin'" and "When I marry Mr. Snow", much of it is a finely orchestrated background to the action.

EXCELLENT CHORUS

The chorus singing is better than anything heard in a musical for a long time, and it is sung by an English chorus–the best, according to the composer, that any production of "Carousel" has ever had. The dancing is enchanting, and Billy Bigelow is splendidly acted by Stephen Douglass. He has a good voice and a fine braggart presence. Iva Withers plays the innocent heroine with extraordinary charm. Of the others in a long cast special praise should go to Margot Moser, Bambi Lynn, Eric Mattson, Jack Melford, Morgan Davies and Marjorie Mars.

(June 8)

'THE COCKTAIL PARTY'

EARTHIER TONE IN ELIOT PLAY

By W. A. Darlington

T. S. Eliot's "The Cocktail Party," when first produced at the Edinburgh Festival last year, gave me one of the most satisfying emotional experiences of my playgoing life. On the material plane it was puzzling at many points, but that somehow did not matter.

Few of the questions which were then raised are answered in the London production, which came to the New Theatre last night. Alec Guinness made the psychiatrist, who is the play's central character, a dedicated, possibly supernatural, being and passages in Eliot's text seemed to bear him out. The piece seemed then to be something like a modern style "Pilgrim's Progress," in which Harley Street and Mayfair characters conspired to help the soul along the hard way to Heaven.

There is no such suggestion in Rex Harrison's earthy playing of the Unknown Guest. He is no more than an eccentric scientist who has formed certain members of his London acquaintance into a sort of underground movement for bringing unhappy people out of their troubles.

Which is right? Both readings will have their devotees, no doubt; but I am very certain that mine is, as they say, a Guinness.

TECHNICAL TRIUMPH

The measure of the play's quality, anyhow, is that neither interpretation shakes one's faith in it. Whether it is a "great" play only the operation of time can show—but we need not wait for the future to tell us that it has greatness in it. And its technical skill, as a piece of dramatic verse writing of a pattern now carried beyond the stage of experiment, is a thing to marvel at.

In a play where style in the acting matters so much, some comparison between the original company— most of whom are now sharing in the play's great success in New York—is inevitable.

Margaret Leighton gives an excellent performance as Celia Coplestone, and comes nearer than I had expected to the sense of vocation which Irene Worth gave to the part. Gladys Boot lacks Cathleen Nesbitt's shimmer and sparkle as the enigmatic Julia, but substitutes something authentic and valuable of her own.

Ian Hunter's much more suitably cast as Edward Chamberlayne than Robert Flemyng—who is anyhow too young for the part. Alison Leggatt can hardly be bettered as Lavinia.

Donald Houston, the only player to be seen both in Edinburgh and in London, is the least impressive member of the cast because the least audible.

Such criticisms, however, are merely incidental to the main fact that this is a play which nobody should miss.

(May 4)

PICASSO SHUNS HIS ART SHOW

PROTEST AT BRITISH 'REPRESSIVE ACTION'

Daily Telegraph Reporter

Pablo Picasso, the Spanish artist, declined to attend the private view yesterday of an exhibition of his work at the New Burlington Galleries. He did so in protest against "the British Government's repressive action towards the second world peace congress."

The exhibition, of work done by Picasso at Provence during the last four years, opens to-day. "It will definitely go on and will continue till Dec. 16," said an official of the Arts Council, which arranged it. Admission costs 1s.

The exhibition is on loan and Picasso receives no fee. But all the 83 works are for sale. The top price is £1,500 for an oil painted in 1947 entitled "A Skull and Sea Urchins." Other oils are prized at £1,000.

PICASSO'S NOTE

Picasso's decision not to attend the exhibition was conveyed to the Arts Council in a typed note handed to Mr. Gabriel White, assistant art director, in the crowded gallery. If stated:

"I understand that the exhibition of my work, organised by your council, is in effect an exhibition held under Government auspices. In view of the British Government's repressive action towards the second world peace congress and its conduct towards so many of my friends and colleagues, I have decided to cancel my acceptance of your invitation."

(November 15)

A DISCONCERTING SANDWICH

FLIPPANT WAR PLAY

By W. A. Darlington

Last night at the St. James's I found Denis Cannan's new play, "Captain Carvallo," a rather disconcerting sandwich, a thick slab of flippancy between two thinner slabs of seriousness.

By this, I mean that the play has serious overtones, because Mr. Cannan has something to say. It is flippant in dialogue and characterisation, because he is desperately anxious to get laughs. It is serious at bottom, because war is an inescapably serious affair.

Captain Carvallo is a charming young invader who finds himself billeted on a household of partisans who have orders to bump him off. But he has made love to Smilja, his beautiful hostess, made friends with her guest, Professor Winke, and excited the missionary zeal of her husband. None of them wants to kill him.

So Smilja attracts him to her bedroom, where they read Victor Hugo together, while the two men blow up his billet in the stables. And there is a good deal of essentially serious discussion of motives and emotions, in which I could take hardly any interest because of the author's determination to make me laugh. I hardly laughed at all, though others in the audience were more fortunate.

Richard Goolden got what there was to be got out of the foolish husband, and Peter Finch made quite a nice piece of work as the professor. The play had also the advantage of one of Tanya Moiseiwitch's pleasing settings and of Laurence Olivier's direction.

(August 10)

B.B.C. CHANGE NOEL COWARD SONGS

AUTHOR CRITICAL

Daily Telegraph Reporter

Because the B.B.C. does not consider that certain lines in four lyrics of Mr. Noel Coward's new musical play, "Ace Of Clubs," are "suitable for broadcasting," the author has rewritten them.

A recording of the show, which opened last Tuesday at the Palace Theatre, Manchester, is to be made by the B.B.C. at Hulme Hippodrome, Manchester, next Sunday. Mr. Coward said, in Manchester yesterday, that the lyrics were "Josephine," "Some thing about a sailor," "Chase me, Charlie," and "I like America."

Alteration was required in the following verse from "Chase Me, Charlie," which is sung "as a duet by two cats":

Love in the moonlight can be sublime
Nows the time, Charlie, I'm
Bound to give in if you'll only climb
over the garden wall.

In the amended version, "waiting for you" is substituted for "bound to give in".

Mr. Coward commented "I think it is very, very silly. Apparently the B.B.C. think that the idea of a cat saying, 'I'm bound to give in', awakens immoral ideas among the listeners."

"NEW JERSEY DAMES"

Another alteration is in the following lines in "I like America":

New Jersey Dames,
Go up in flames
If someone mentions bed.

That has been changed to:

In Tennessee, the B.B.C.
Would blush to hear what's said.

Mr. Coward added: "It isn't anything worth making a fuss about. The alteration of the lines has not made much difference. The B.B.C. have been very courteous about it and I can see their point of view."

A friend of Mr. Coward said. "What might be understood and appreciated by an adult audience might not be suitable for everyone in the wide range of the radio audience. The B.B.C. apparently felt that rather than provoke criticism from a minority of its listeners the lines could quite easily be altered."

(May 22)

A NEW NOEL COWARD PLAY

ROMANCE IN A NIGHT CLUB

By W. A. Darlington

Noel Coward has not lost his hold over his public, or his popularity with first-nighters, or his skill with words and music. Getting into the Cambridge Theatre last night to see his new musical play "Ace of Clubs" was not merely hard work, but an ordeal, so dense and tense was the crowd of sightseers outside. And the author took his seat in his box to an ovation of royal dimensions. Then the show turned out to be a pretty good one, and all was well.

SAILOR WINS

A night-club queen, but a very nice girl really, is loved by a sailor and desired by a big bad man of the underworld. After a good deal of rough-and-tumble the sailor gets the girl and the police get the bad man.

This gives Mr. Coward all the chances he needs for a characteristic mixture of toughness and sentimentality; and if some of the tough characters turn sentimental at rather surprisingly short notice when they hear Mantovani's orchestra strike up, that is all in this rather silly but entertaining game.

Several of the sentimental ditties, in particular those sung by Sylvia Cecil as the owner of the club, were encored; but for my part I very much preferred an arbitrarily inserted number in which three juvenile delinquents told us what a delightful life they have under our grandmotherly laws. This was Coward at his acid best.

A VERY BAD MAN

Pat Kirkwood, whom one must always admire for the authority with which she puts her songs over, is the heroine. Graham Payn makes a nimble and likeable sailor. Elwyn Brook-Jones gives the Bad Man a really remarkable nastiness.

The show had a uniformly warm reception from its first audience.

(May 4)

BRITISH ATOM FILM AT FESTIVAL

From Campbell Dixon

VENICE, Sunday.

Even if this isn't quite a vintage year, Britain has already made a creditable showing at the International Film Festival here. "The Blue Lamp" has been liked in Venice as everywhere, and it will be interesting to see how the foreign critics, whose palates generally respond only to dishes highly seasoned with sex and sadism, will react to the simple heroism of "Morning Departure."

"State Secret" went very well with the public, not so well with some of the critics. Sidney Gilliat's picture of a dicatorship, with its ruthless and cynical opportunism, was too uncomfortably near the truth to suit zealots o the left and right.

Just as brilliant and perhaps even more topical is the Boulting Brothers' "Seven Days to Noon," completed just in time for the Festival. Although the treatment is distinguished by lively characterisation and witty incident, the theme could hardly be more urgent

A British atomic scientist (Barry Jones) writes to the Prime Minister announcing that if all work on armaments is not abandoned within one week, he will destroy London. Scotland Yard's Special Branch goes into action, led impressively by André Morell, and tension mounts steadily as the days pass and the missing scientist still eludes capture. At last the population is evacuated, and troops, searching methodically, move through a City eerily silent and deserted except for prowling cats.

(September 4)

PACIFIC JOURNEY

In "The Kon-Tiki Expedition" Mr. Thor Heyerdahl describes an astonishing journey which he and five fellow-Scandinavians made by raft from the coast of Peru to the Pacific Islands. The raft was made of balsa logs bound together with rope, and as far as possible modelled on copies of ancient vessels in Peru and Equador: and the idea was to demonstrate that the Polynesians could have migrated by such means across the Pacific Ocean.

To set forth in so frail and dubious a craft required immense courage. If anything had gone wrong they would all assuredly have been drowned; on their long journey which took them from April 28 to Aug. 7. Whatever may be the anthropological value of "The Kon-Tiki Expedition," it provides a fascinating account of a bizarre and adventurous enterprise excitingly and modestly recounted.

(November 31)

MAX MILLER LOST JOKE BOOKS

ROYAL VARIETY INCIDENT EXPLAINED

An incident at the Royal Variety Performance at the Palladium on Monday evening was explained last night. The call to Max Miller to "come off" heard by many of the audience, was made after he had exceeded his time.

Mr. Julius Darewski, Mr. Miller's manager and agent, said last night: "It appears that Mr. Val Parnell, organiser of the show, was annoyed because Max put on an unrehearsed act. This had caused him to exceed his time.

"It had been arranged for Max to put on the 'Blue book and white book' act, producing the books and asking the audience which one they wanted their jokes from. The rehearsed jokes had been noted in both books

"When he appeared on the stage he felt for the books and found that they had disappeared. It was a terrible ordeal for him especially on that occasion, and he had to act quickly.

"GIVE ME A CHANCE"

"He decided to put over the act he has been doing for the past few weeks. This went over the allotted time, but he had to complete it, or it would have been a failure.

"When he heard someone shouting to him to 'come off,' he was naturally distressed. He replied something about 'the others have had their chance, let me have mine.'

"It was all a storm in a tea-cup, and Mr. Miller is extremely sorry for any inconvenience that may have been caused." The two books were still missing. "They may have been taken by some practical joker."

(November 15)

THE DAILY TELEGRAPH
AND
MORNING POST
DAILY TELEGRAPH - June 29, 1855
MORNING POST - November 2, 1772
[Amalgamated October 1, 1937]
135 Fleet Street, London, E.C.4
Telephone: Central 4242

MAJORITY, BUT NO MANDATE

WHAT was one of the quietest elections of modern times has proved in its final stage the most exciting in our history. Not since 1852 has there been a closer finish, and never has fortune swayed more dramatically between the parties during the count. Victory, if that is the name for it, has gone to the Socialists, but they can have little cause to rejoice, for it gives them no moral authority to do more than carry on as caretakers. They have secured not a vestige of a "mandate" to execute any of their major projects, including notably the nationalisation of half a dozen more industries. A majority reduced from 180 to the neighbourhood of 18 is tantamount to a vote of censure which they cannot ignore. Their success, such as it is, they owe entirely to the reckless intrusion of the Liberal party, whose tale of forfeited deposits reflects incisively the country's opinion of its conduct. It can be estimated that if the votes cast for Liberals in seats won by the Socialists on a minority poll had gone to the Conservatives, as in general they almost certainly would, the Conservatives would have gained between 40 and 50 more seats. The effect would have been to give them a substantial and workable majority.

★ ★ ★

The Conservatives, though naturally disappointed at their failure to defeat the Socialists outright, have good ground for consolation, especially in view of the handicap imposed by the Liberals, which is hardly likely to be repeated at another election. To have all but wiped out a two-to-one majority is no mean achievement. Though it would be an exaggeration to speak of a landslide, since the turnover of seats was much greater than the turnover of votes, the revulsion against the Socialists is placed beyond argument.

(February 25)

LIBERATION LONG OVERDUE

MOTORISTS had scarcely dared to hope for any early inclusion among the beneficiaries of those "experiments in freedom" in which the Government have lately been indulging. How, indeed, could it be supposed that Ministers would enact in May what they had scorned as fantastic in February? The unbridled abuse which was poured by leading Socialists on Mr. CHURCHILL for his suggestion that more petrol might be made available is still fresh in the memory. "Irresponsible" was the epithet applied by Sir STAFFORD CRIPPS, to which Mr. ROBENS, the Parliamentary Secretary to the Ministry of Fuel and Power, added "dishonest." Mr. BEVAN and Mr. SHINWELL both called it "bribery". MR. NESS EDWARDS, now Postmaster General, declared that it was "playing with the economic recovery of the nation to win electoral advantages." According to Mr. ATTLEE, it was "quite easy to see that Mr. CHURCHILL had not given one moment's thought to the sub."

The new Australian Government, when it announced the abolition of petrol rationing, received intimations of the displeasure of Downing Street in a somewhat tart communiqué concluding with the pronouncement that " the United Kingdom Government reiterate the continued urgent need for economy in dollar expenditure and the consequent need for continuing economy in the use of all petroleum products, both here and throughout the sterling area."

In the sequel it has turned out that Mr. CHURCHILL despite the strictures of Mr. ATTLEE, had given a good deal more thought to the subject than the Government.

(May 2)

FAMILY GATHERING

PARLIAMENTARY tradition was reshaped yesterday in the dedication of the new House of Commons. Often enough in the past half century statesmen from overseas have been welcomed in the precincts of Parliament and given places of honour in the Gallery of the House. Never before, however, have the presiding officers and other representatives of the legislatures of distant members of the Commonwealth been directly associated with its proceedings. In the House itself they were yesterday privileged to share the domestic prayers of its Members, from which "strangers" are normally excluded. They stayed to hear the first motion in the New Chamber passed with acclamation - a motion in honour of the peoples and countries from which they came. Even more significant, they themselves joined in the Speaker's procession which filed solemnly into Westminster Hall, where the KING was to receive Addresses from both Lords and Commons.

Thus on this unique occasion - rightly recorded for posterity - the Parliaments of Commonwealth and Empire were collectively associated with the proceedings of the two Houses at Westminster on which all these younger bodies are patterned. The presence of the KING and the Royal family in Westminster Hall symbolised the constitutional link which binds the self-governing peoples of the Commonwealth. But the tenor of his Majesty's speech, no less than that of the Prime Minister, made it clear that Dominion and Colonial legislatures were represented not in virtue of some legal tie but as members of a family gathering. Three separate reasons could indeed be given for inviting them to the Commons' housewarming - their comradeship in the days when the old Chamber was destroyed, their splendid gifts to adorn the new Chamber and their close resemblance in character and procedure with our own House of Commons. All these independent reasons for welcome, however, are aspects of brotherhood in that common "faith in freedom" to which his Majesty alluded.

(October 27)

QUEEN MARY'S GIFT

WITH a "characteristically" gracious gesture, Queen MARY has presented to the nation a carpet of her own making, begun in the dark days of 1941 and now almost complete. Equally characteristic of her Majesty is her intention that the nation shall reap a practical reward from her many hours of patient work. For the carpet is to adorn not one of the great museums of this country, but some public collection across the Atlantic, whose payment may help to lessen the Exchequer's dollar weakness.

Patronage of the arts has been a royal tradition in this country for many centuries, but members of the Royal House have seldom possessed the knowledge of the true connoisseur or been themselves creators. Many a museum curator can bear witness that Queen MARY is an exception, possessing the detailed acquaintance with art history which combines with natural taste to form aesthetic judgment. A keen collector of things of beauty, her Majesty has now added with her needle a fresh treasure to delight others' eyes.

MR. WEBB ABOLISHES 5s MEAL LIMIT

RESTRICTION OF COURSES ENDS: AID TO TOURISM

Daily Telegraph Reporter

From to-day the 5s limit on meals in all hotels, restaurants and catering establishments is abolished. It has been in force since June, 1942.

Mr. Webb, Minister of Food, announced the abolition in the House of Commons yesterday. The announcement means that there will be:

1.—No restriction on the number of courses served;
2.—No restriction on what may be served as a " main dish;"
3.—No restriction on the prices which may be charged for a meal.

A Ministry spokesman said last night:" House charges allowed under the 1942 Order are now abolished. But there is nothing to prevent a hotel or restaurant imposing its own cover charge."

The Minister said the decision would be reviewed in the autumn to see whether it should be permanent.

MORE DOLLARS

"Watch for Abuses"

The announcement was made in a written reply to Mr. John Lewis (Soc., Bolton). It said:" I hope as a result of this step that the tourist and catering industries will now be able to make a bigger contribution to our dollar balance of payments, which is, of course, the most urgent of our economic problems.

" The catering industry have agreed to keep the situation closely under review themselves and will watch for any evidence of possible abuses in the matter of prices and diversion of supplies.

"I might also say that I have been assisted in arriving at this decision by evidence that this restriction no longer has any substantial merit as an instrument of equity in the consumption of food supplies."

HOTELS SURPRISED

More Varied Menus

Mr. Webb also announced that he intends to revoke the Meals Service at Social Functions Order. The Order limits the number who may be served with meals at one function.

The abolition of the 5s limit came as a surprise to many of the leading hotels in the West End, although the catering trade has pressed for it since the end of the war.

Although price restrictions are completely removed it is not expected that the smaller restaurants and public houses catering for thousands of city workers will increase their prices. Menus, however, will be more varied.

CLARIDGES, THE SAVOY and the BERKELEY will be offering a wider choice of menus. It is not known what changes, if any, will made in prices.

(May 2)

SHOPS FOR THE FULLER FIGURE

AN American friend of mine flew in from New York a few days ago. Here for a fortnight, her ambition is to take back cashmere sweaters as presents for her friends and a really good black tailor-made suit for herself.

Cashmere sweaters for export are certainly good dollar earners. My friend ordered a superb black suit, which is being made to order in two weeks with three fittings. As she was about to leave the fitting room she remarked, rather sadly: "London mirrors are very fattening," adding after a moment, "I think my new suit rates a brand-new foundation." And so we visited the corset department.

Away With Bulges

As I told her, unless you know exactly how to try on a foundation garment for a correct fitting, you may make the wrong choice.

Girdles and corsets should come two inches below the "tail" bulge. There should be no bulges below the garment - try slipping three fingers under the suspender end to make sure there is room enough. When you try on a corset or girdle, it is very important to sit down, because when sitting you expand considerably. If you bulge over the waistline, then you need a size larger. If the garment is too narrow it will ride up.

In trying on a corselette you need to be even more careful to get the correct fit. One very important point to watch: there must be enough length from the brassière cup to the waist and between the waist and the widest part of the hips. Otherwise the garment will drag and be harmful. One of the most satisfactory corselettes my friend was shown is called the Controlette.

Sit For A Fit

Very few women think of sitting down while they are trying on a brassiere to test the fitting. But it is important to do so because your diaphragm expands then. Incidentally, while we were looking at brassières I came across a charming little strapless bra made from rayon satin in white, peach or black, for the modest price of 9s 11d.

(March 13)

Revolution In The Kitchen: Radar Cooking

To get a 3-course dinner will take the housewife of the future 5 minutes instead of 2 or 3 hours.

THE prophet of future leisure for housewives is Mr. Owen Webber, American business man, president of the electrical-engineering firm over there that is making the revolutionary electronic cookers. These work on a similar principle to the radar equipment developed during the war.

For the benefit of DAILY TELEGRAPH women readers, he has air-mailed to this feature his conception of the shape of things to come in the home.

Shopping. Instead of going from shop to shop to acquire a bagload of raw foods which require time to prepare and cook, she will select a 3-course dinner from a "library" of pre-cooked deep frozen (or sealed and lightly frozen) dishes.

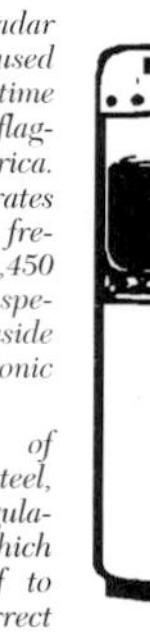

The radar cooker was used for the first time in the U.S. flagship America. Cooker operates on its own frequency 2,450 megacycles - specially set aside for electronic cooking.

Oven is of stainless steel, has clock regulator at top which enables chef to select correct cooking times.

Preparation of Meal. Will consist of putting her packages from the local store's deep freeze into the deep freeze container of her own "frig." and, five minutes before she wishes to serve the food, taking it out of her "frig" (combined as a unit with radar cooker), putting it on a plate in the electronic oven and getting it piping hot in a matter of seconds.

Deep freezing and radar cooking are regarded by Mr. Webber as the big developments in the food industry that will practically drive the housewife out of her own kitchen. They mean the end of home cookery - as we have known it in the past and as a home creative art.

Meat, poultry, vegetables and puddings will be prepared and pre-cooked by big commercial kitchens under leading chefs, and go from these kitchens to be packaged and deep frozen for sale over the counter as separate dishes or complete meals. This is already happening on a big scale in America and to a lesser extent here.

Closely connected with this development will be the new radar cooker, which heats foods with such incredible rapidity as to be ideal for use with these already-cooked meals, though it is, of course, equally effective for cooking raw foods.

(January 10)

TAKING THE CAR ABROAD

Tips For Women Drivers

MANY people are taking their cars abroad for the first time this year.

Among the novices a high proportion are women travelling together, while, with the family parties, often a wife, sister or daughter are co-drivers.

Here are a few tips for women from one who has driven thousands of kilometres on the Continent.

How To Pack

If you are spending one or more nights on your journey have an overnight bag with washing and sleeping things and arrange your bulk luggage so that it need not be touched until you reach your destination. In the car take a pack of tissues and well-corked bottles of cleansing milk and eau de cologne. Keep them within reach, for they are the best refreshers on a long journey.

What To Wear

A printed suit or dress in an uncrushable fabric is the best choice. Print is less likely to show oil or dust marks than a plain fabric. You may prefer the suit for restaurant meals on the way, but if you think a dress cooler, have one of the tailored, button-through type, which would enable you to do without a dressing-gown in the overnight bag. For the boat you will want a top coat. It may not be needed once you land, but do not throw it at the back of the car - it will get filthy. Keep it in an old pillow-case. You will want comfortable shoes, broad enough to keep on the pedals for two or three hours at a stretch. Sling-back sandals are cool, but not really sensible because you will dirty your heel. I am assuming you will wear stockings, and if you have a pair of fish-net nylons never will you be more pleased with them than on a long car journey.

Driving And The Car

"Tenez le droit" you know, but I find that after reversing I am apt to put the car on to my more usual left.

(July 27)

LONDON DAY BY DAY

More Stars for Gen. MacArthur
Sibelius Enjoys his Birthday

GEN. MARSHALL, America's Defence Secretary, has sent a message of congratulations to Gen. MacArthur. Characteristically, Gen. MacArthur's reply begins: "Thanks, George, for your fine message."

MacArthur is 70 and Marshall will be in December. I can think of no combination of this age in any recent war.

The President has also sent his congratulations. He may well be considering what honour America can find to mark MacArthur's latest success. The General has accumulated most of them.

Like Eisenhower and Marshall, he is a General of the Army, a five-star rank: There is only one rank higher, and only one man, Gen. Pershing, has ever held it.

On the Box

TRAINING speakers in the subtleties of microphone manner has been an important activity at Conservative headquarters for about three years. The results ought to be apparent in the election broadcasts.

Broadcasting liaison officer to the party is Mr. Jack Profumo, the candidate at Stratford-on-Avon, who was on General Alexander's staff in Italy and became a Brigadier at 29. He is assisted by another officer of that rank, Brigadier J. W. Hinchcliffe.

Leaders who broadcast will be wholly responsible for writing their own scripts, but have sought advice on the art of broadcasting, which is really talking to a family fireside group. Speakers have been able to make records and hear themselves afterwards to correct faults. Lord Woolton has probably spent more time and trouble on his radio technique than anybody else but the average preparation time is an hour for every minute of the broadcast.

85th Birthday

SIBELIUS is 85 to-day. I offer my congratulations to the greatest living composer.

In a recent picture of him he looks hale and hearty. Two British musicians are connected with it. Gordon Bryan, the pianist and composer, snapped it in the master's garden at his house outside Helsinki.

The print I reproduce Sibelius autographed in May this year for another friend, Basil Cameron.

Both know Sibelius well and have done much to popularise his music here. Mr. Cameron tells me that Sibelius is still working away at his eighth symphony, for which the world has been waiting over 20 years.

Eiffel Tower Film

ENGLISH cameramen, my Paris correspondent tells me, have been climbing over the Eiffel Tower making preliminary shots for a film to be called "The Lavender Hill Mob." Alec Guinness and Stanley Holloway will star in the picture.

Revenue and publicity from film-making will help to swell the tower's already handsome profits. The 500-franc shares issued by Eiffel when he founded the company which runs it are now quoted on the Bourse at around 20,000 francs. Last year 21m francs were distributed in dividends to the 200 shareholders, and 48m francs were put in reserve.

Reserves have to meet a heavy call every seven or eight years when the tower needs a complete repainting. This takes nearly 30 tons of paint.

Not to Stand Again

THERE will be regret over the muddle in South-West Wolverhampton which has led Mr. Enoch Powell, M.P., to decline to stand again at the next election.

A vote of censure by a ward committee was repudiated by the Conservative divisional executive, but Mr. Powell thought he could not co-operate with those who passed the vote.

He entered the Commons only in February and came with a remarkable background. A Fellow of Trinity, Cambridge, and a former Professor of Greek at Sydney University, he has a new translation of Herodotus to his credit.

Private to Brigadier

In the war - when he wrote some of his translation - he rose from private to brigadier. After the war the Conservative put him in charge of Home Affairs in their research department.

Still only 38, Mr. Powell has the kind of intellect that burns more fuel than a frail frame can contain. He has been burning it fast since February.

It might be best for him and Wolverhampton if he turned for a while to one of two recreations - fox hunting and writing poetry.

PETERBOROUGH

THE LINE OF FASHION—1. DAY CLOTHES

PARIS IN DETAIL

By Winefride Jackson

1 2 3

SKETCHES BY HARTLAND

PARIS detail sketches show that we are back to the "New Look" with a difference—the shorter skirt, just touching the calf, and the change in detail. This, at least, is the way Dior sees autumn fashions, and for many women it will be just a little matter of "turning up the hem".

This time Dior uses an oblique line. Draperies, panels, yokes and collar all cross from side to side, the oblique effect emphasised with panels of uneven length, or a single panel breaking the jacket hemline.

Just to remind you of the autumn colours: Black, silver, slate grey, tobacco or walnut brown with black, bottle green with black or wine. More vivid: Peacock blue, sapphire blue, geranium red.

Jacques Fath (1) Calls his silhouette "svelt," the atmosphere created by his autumn dressing, "high toned." Judge this for yourself from the two piece ensemble sketched—slim dress "skinned" thighs, knee flare with duck's-tail kick, all released from stitched pleats. Fitted jacket has long revers and cuffs of black seal.

Essential requirement of "high-toned" wearer—the smallest of small posteriors!

Balmain (2) Leading advocate last spring of the tube silhouette, Balmain has repented and designed a beautiful collection for autumn with the waist in the right; place and a certain amount of Eastern atmosphere. Here you see his afternoon tunic dress with slim skirt subtly draped to one hip and the arum-lily tunic. Skirt is in jersey, bodice and tunic in black velvet.

Eastern note—pointed cap in leopard fur matched by barrel muff.

Dior (3): Significantly named Favori, the three-piece ensemble in silver grey flannel will probably be one of Dior's most successful models. Note cross-over panel carried over bust like a scarf collar, tucked under belt and allowed to hang below jacket hem. Jutting pocket is placed on opposite side to panel. Flat beret is in nutria, the season's fur.

(September 4)

JANE GORDON describes

New Make-Up For Older Women

WHEN there is so much specialised beauty service for the older women, there is no excuse for the over-fifties to let their looks go. This is particularly true of Englishwomen, who so often can be better looking as they grow older and their hair turns grey or white.

It then needs very careful handling. When permanent waves are given professionally the operator bakes the white hair for a much shorter duration than when dealing with coloured hair. For home perms, the test curl on white hair must be timed with the greatest care in order to get the best results. Personally, I dislike blue or mauve rinses for white hair, because I think they are unbecoming to the older complexion.

THE woman with the yellow white hair usually has an ivory skin, and the blue or mauve rinse makes her complexion look sallow, whereas the iron-grey woman often has a florid complexion, which the blue rinse in my opinion, only accentuates.

However the fact remains that blue rinses are very popular, and the most effective blue rinse for grey or white hair is a concentrated liquid, price 5s 6d. This is colourless in the bottle, but two or three drops will tint the rinsing water to the shade required. You can also get packets of blue rinse powder for 3 ½ d from most chemists.

THIS season's shades of make-up are most becoming to blondes and older women. The newest lipstick is called Pretty Pink and is perfect for the teen-ager, the blonde or the white-haired woman. The price is 6s 6d. One of the most intriguing novelties although its weight is a disadvantage, is the double day-and-night lipstick. The gilt case actually holds two lipsticks and is priced at 8s 4d, each refill costs 2s 11d. The range includes ten pairs of lipsticks.

For the white-haired women with green, brown or hazel eyes the night and day shades are Pink-Ice for day, which is a coral rose shade, and Dangerous Red for evening. For the grey-haired woman with blue or grey eyes, the lipstick container holds Pink Orchid for day and Pink Purple for evening.

THE latest powder foundation is called Beauty Base. It is a tinted cream and has certain advantages which make it particularly suitable for older women, especially those with a florid complexion. The cream is not only nourishing but it is capable of covering little surface veins and holding the powder well. The price is 3s 9d, and it is perfumed to harmonise with all good toilet waters and essences.

The delicate ivory type of complexion usually needs a lightly tinted foundation cream of the vanishing type. One of the best I have found lately is priced 4s 2d. This does not colour the skin at all but holds the powder well. The same firm makes an excellent cleansing milk which is suitable for the super-sensitive, slightly dry skin which often goes with white hair.

THERE are any number of special beauty treatments to be found in London for the older woman, and, if you know where to find them, it is not necessary to pay exorbitant prices. For instance, you can get a double-chin treatment 10s 6d and a tired-eye treatment for the same price. Radio-active mud pack with massage also costs 10s 6d and an oil treatment for dry or lined skins is 12s 6d.

(January 12)

Nature Notes

CABBAGE WHITE BUTTERFLIES

Cabbage white butterflies are the gardener's curse. There are two kinds, the Large and the Small Cabbage White, the latter being almost a small replica of the former.

But their caterpillars differ widely. That of the Small White is green and is found scattered singly over the cabbage.

The caterpillars of the Large White are a greyish-yellow mottled with black, are found in groups, and have a faintly obnoxious smell which enables them to keep together by following the scent trail of their fellows.

It is the Large White that in certain summers migrate in large numbers across the Channel and up across Southern and Eastern England.

(July 24)

THE CHILDREN'S PARTY

Discussed by Actress-Mother And West End Chef

WELL KNOWN actress RACHEL KEMPSON (below), in private life, Mrs. Michael Redgrave and mother of Vanessa 14, Corin 11 and Lynn 7, is giving two children's parties – a supper-dance for the two elder and an afternoon tea-party for Lynn and cousin Juliet.

Miss Kempson (now appearing in "Top of the Ladder" at St. James Theatre) has decided views on what to serve on these occasions. In quite a few things she disagrees with West End chef de cuisine M. CONIL, whose controversial views on the Englishwomans cooking have appeared in this feature. As the father of two children, this authority on haute cuisine inevitably has strong ideas on the choice of party fare for the young.

***MRS. MOON'S CAKE**

5oz sugar, 5oz S.R.flour, 3 eggs, 3oz margarine

Beat sugar and egg yolks, then add softened margarine. Beat well. Add flour gradually.

Whip whites of egg until stiff and add last. Separate into three portions, colour one with cochineal, another with one dessertspoonful sweetened chocolate powder, leave third plain.

Bake each about 20 minutes. Stick layers together with jam or butter icing, use water icing for top, and decorate.

M. Conil: As a chef I could not help mentally criticising the mistakes made at a recent party at which my children were guests.

The mother of the little hostess had made a royal spread. Everything was there — trifles, ice cream, chocolates, cream cakes, lemonade and biscuits. Of course the children sampled them all! And the memory of a gay party was impaired by the discomfort of the aftermath. I blame the failure of that party on two things - cream and too much fondant icing. I would remind mothers that it is not always the best children's party that has the richest cream cakes and sweets.

Miss Kempson: I agree with M. Conil that children should not be given over-rich food. I never serve cakes that are covered with too much cream. I find that the plainer foods actually go better than very fancy kinds.

But I disagree with austerity. I believe you can have a royal spread without overdoing it. One of our family specialities is a *three-coloured iced layer cake. Mrs. Moon (the Redgraves cook) makes it.

M. Conil: I would make a sponge cake, and with the aid of a knife and fancy cutter, fashion from it dainty little cakes no bigger than a mouthful similar to petits fours. By decorating and garnishing them sufficiently I would make them attractive enough to amuse and entice the children to eat as many as they wanted. Never give them chocolate to eat. Instead coat your gateau with it and you will find they appreciate it more.

Miss Kempson: There will be biscuits— including chocolate ones— for the younger children's party, and a variety of small cakes. I shall also give them tomato, honey and jam sandwiches, all made with wholemeal bread (they never eat white bread).

Ice Cream, But Not With Fruit!

M. Conil: If you must give the child ice-cream, don't give it them with fruit, but serve it with plain dry cakes.

Miss Kempson: Not plain dry cakes! Children love ice-cream and jelly but they want something exciting with it. I give them fruit salad and ice cream. You have to consider their tastes as well as their tummies!

M. Conil: Mixing the wrong kind of foods is bad. Don't mix pastries and cakes, for instance stick to one dry thing and one light fruit and custard. You will find this is sufficient, and no one will be ill afterwards.

RACHEL KEMPSON

Miss Kempson: I do believe in as much variety as possible. For the 25 older children at my supper-dance, I shall have a menu which could almost be used for a grown-up party. A buffet table will be laid in front of the bow window of the studio *(attached to the Redgraves' 17th century Thames-side home)*. On it will be chipolata sausages and small rolls of ham on sticks, savoury sandwiches made with wholemeal bread, tiny iced and decorated sponge cakes, Shrewsbury biscuits, Madeleines and cream-topped fruit baskets. As the guests leave, I shall offer them steaming hot soup.

M. Conil: Don't give them lemonade, it upsets their tummies. Serve tea instead or a squeeze of orange or lemon juice in water. Remember that cold milk also has a bad effect with sweets.

Miss Kempson: I agree about drinks I never serve fizzy ones. I give the smaller children fruit quashes. The older ones have cider cup, made almost the same as for grown-up parties but without an alcoholic effect, and tea, if they want it.

Do readers agree with M. Conil's list of don'ts, or do they like Miss Kempson, consider their children's tastes as well? One guinea for letter published.

(December 27)

TRAVELLER'S QUEST

By *Bon Viveur*

Artist Biro and I are on holiday in France searching along our chosen route for small hotels where food, wine and accommodation are outstanding, yet the prices compare favourably with the inns and hotels of England.

Chinon, Near Tours

WE disembarked at Le Havre in the morning, and that evening 200 miles on our journey, we stopped at the Hostellerie Gargantua at Chinon. This small hotel with its winding central stone staircase, was first built as a private residence for the French King's Governor nearly 500 years ago. Above us, graceful, tremendous, swept the ramparts of the Chateau de Chinon where the Dauphin received Joan of Arc.

Below us in the Rue Voltaire was the house where Richard Coeur de Lion is said to have died. Over the cobbles shook the frame of an incredibly minute cart and pony bells jangled in rhythm with the thinly distant echo of the Harry Lime Theme! Chinon was still en fête after the July 14th celebrations, and we danced till dawn in the village square—free, of course.

Breakfast On The Terrace

We dined, explored the wine cellars of the Hostellerie and tasted wines as their guests, we slept in most excellent beds and woke to coffee, croissants, a giant wedge of butter and a large bowl of fresh cream, all laid out for us under a canopy of vine and wisteria on the small terrace. For all this, and dinner, we paid 2,240 francs for two people, £2 7s 0d in English money.

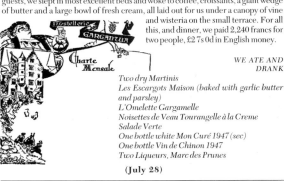

WE ATE AND DRANK

Two dry Martinis
Les Escargots Maison (baked with garlic butter and parsley)
L'Omelette Gargamelle
Noisettes de Veau Tourangelle à la Creme
Salade Verte
One bottle white Mon Curé 1947 (sec)
One bottle Vin de Chinon 1947
Two Liqueurs, Marc des Prunes

(July 28)

Bon Viveur In Pre-Christmas London

WHERE THE YOUNG DANCE AND DINE

SEARCHING London for places where our young can dine and dance at reasonable prices, where they can go alone and leave us parents unworried by the fire. I have made some Interesting discoveries.

I have found that jive is eminently respectable and favoured (1) by royalty and (2) by students. I have found chaperones in force at a West End teenagers' club. I saw little drinking of spirits, much Coca-Cola being served, and a resurgence of interest in formal clothes among the youthful clienteles.

Evening Dress By Choice

Day dress is frowned upon at some places. At the 20th Century Group of the Overseas Club, members change from choice not ruling, to dance for 3s 6d. Student's subscription costs 1gn. Young members throng a marble staircase dance in a ballroom panelled with the arms of the Colonial territories. The buffet provides sandwiches, salads, ice creams, low-priced drinks.

At the dances for the young members group of the English Speaking Union, white gloves are sometimes worn! Day frocks are rare, short dresses rarer still. Full skirts swing out as dancers twirl to the three beat of old-fashioned waltz music. Membership costs 2gns for under 25's, dancing with running buffet, 4 to 5s.

I visited the London Jazz Club for their regular Saturday night Jive session (3s and 2s 6d membership). I went in to disapprove. I came out chastened. This is the reverse of a glamorous pastime, but if ever I saw a harmless one, healthily indulged, it was here. The proceedings are solemn, strenuous, and as respectable as a Victorian social. But, oh, the noise!

Sambas, But Edwardian Elegance

I took my headache to the Bryanston Club and stood beneath the Edwardian lighting thoughtfully. The ghostly echoes of Almack's 18th century subscription dances are here, even though the members in faultless evening dress dance sambas and Scottish reels to Geraldo's band. Tickets cost 15s 6d, guests 18s 6d, subscription 1gn. A running buffet supplies soups, hot sausages, sandwiches, sweets and savourics.

Here, youth has chosen to be elegant and will not tolerate infringement of its standard.

The conga, the samba, the rhumba and the old-fashioned waltz were favourites at the Blue Pool Restaurant, where a Saturday night dinner-dance costs 8s 6d. Boys and girls in suits, in short frocks thronged the floor, some in evening dress but not many.

They ate their dinner with interest and it was a good one but concentrated on the dance floor, commenting upon the excellent time of the band. These boys and girls are connoisseurs of dance time, and woe betide the band that does not meet with their requirements.

The Harry Lime Theme wins their approval at the Celebrité. Time and again they ask for it, and sit and listen. I saw more youth than maturity in this restaurant where 15s 6d is charged for dinner and continuous dancing to two bands from 7p.m. to 1am.

Candlelight And Sophistication

On went my quest until at cabaret time I entered some of the more expensive restaurants.

I found youth at the Colony and the Society, sipping their drinks supping, very poised. I thought they looked a different type, more sophisticated, more aware of their surroundings, which were delightful. I like to think the candlelight, the cabarets and film stars seemed most romantic to them–but I was never sure, suspecting that the older visitors were having the greater fun with the impressive menus, the fine wine lists and the slick cabaret turns.

I found myself returning in thought to the American Teenagers' Club which holds dances at Winfield House in Regent's Park. This club was started by Mrs. Lewis Douglas. Sharman is missed there now, but her mother's scheme flourishes as 13 to 20-year-olds under the benignant, watchful eye of official chaperones. Mothers send cookies, cakes, sandwiches to swell the buffet, the youngest wear their party frocks, the most mature, dress clothes and evening dress. These are charming parties.

(December 15)

Obituary

SIR HARRY LAUDER

EARNED £2,500 A WEEK

Sir Harry Lauder, who has died aged 79, delighted millions for more than a generation with his pawky jokes and lilting songs, his swinging kilt and crooked walking-stick, his ebullient joviality and wistful tenderness.

He was essentially a Scottish comedian. But he captivated the Sassenach, and went on to conquer the English-speaking world. Few artists have ever evoked such spontaneous enthusiasm from all kinds of audiences.

At the height of his career he was earning £2,500 a week. During an American tour he received £3,000 for broadcasting three songs. Yet at one time he had been glad to accept 35s a week.

Harry Lauder was born on Aug. 4, 1870, at Portobello, near Edinburgh. His father died young, and the family had a hard struggle. As a "half-timer" —combining work with schooling—Harry made 2s a week in a flax mill. Starting as a pit-head boy, he worked for 10 years as a miner in Hamilton.

Popularity as an amateur singer tempted him to leave the mine for the stage, and he toured Scotland with concert parties. As the result of an early long-term contract with the Royal Theatre, Birkenhead, he continued to appear there for 5s a week years after he achieved wealth and fame. In the intervening years he learned to drive many hard bargains.

MADE NAME IN LONDON

In 1900 Lauder came to London. The agents were discouraging, but December brought him a stroke of luck. Another artist had dropped out of the bill at Gatti's Music-hall, in Westminster Bridge-road. Lauder was hurried on as an extra turn, He came off with his name made.

With the Irish song "Calligan, Call Again!" he scored a sensational success. At the Royal Holborn, and later at the Oxford, he consolidated his reputation. Triumphs in London were repeated all over the provinces and then in tour after tour of the United States—22 in all—of Canada, South Africa, Australia and New Zealand.

Those who heard him will never forget such songs as "I Love A Lassie," "Stop Yer Ticklin' Jock," "Just a Wee Deoch-an'-Doris," and — perhaps best-known of all "Roamin' in the Gloamin'." To a large extent he was his own author and composer.

During the wars of 1914-18 and 1939-45 he worked hard to entertain the services and to raise money for war funds. His only son was killed in action in 1917, while Lauder was playing at the Shaftesbury in the revue "Three Cheers."

SANG FOR ENSA

He was knighted in 1919. His stage appearances had become rare in the years preceding the war but he sang for the troops at Ensa concerts and made several war-time broadcasts. Only two years ago he was approached with a view to visiting Hollywood to sup.rvise and act in a film of his own life in which Danny Kaye was to appear as the young Lauder.

He married, in 1890, Annie Vallance daughter of a Hamilton mine manager. She died in 1927.

G. W. B. writes: The obvious secret of Harry Lauder's great popularity was his rich baritone voice. He chose his songs to suit his audience, and the simple ballads of the "I Love a Lassie type" made an immediate appeal. No variety artist ever brought such a lovable personality on to the stage.

The real secret was that Lauder was a wonderful showman: he was a little man, and he put himself and his stumpy walk over with the perfect art that disguises any semblance of art. Lauder himself was far greater than his songs and his amusing and homely patter.

(February 27)

G.B.S. The Most Remarkable Literary Man Of Our Time

By W. A. Darlington

GEORGE BERNARD SHAW (1856-1950)

THE death of George Bernard Shaw, in his 95th year, removes from among us the most remarkable literary man of our time and one of our quaintest characters.

"Remarkable" is indeed the right word for in both senses it is apt. It means "noticeable" as well as "distinguished," and it was the essence of Shaw's individuality that, knowing himself to be the latter, he sometimes went to unnecessary lengths to make himself the former.

Born into a generation which liked its distunguished men to take themselves and each other seriously and with a becoming reverence, he declined to do either the one or the other. Whenever he saw a nose that seemed to him to need tweaking, he tweaked it without bothering to inquire very closely to whom it might happen to belong.

Since nose-tweaking is an amusement which entails considerable loss of dignity in both parties concerned, Shaw very soon managed to make himself the object of a great deal of dislike. and of the quite genuine contempt of many well-meaning folk.

The Popular View

ACCORDINGLY, for many years his name was anathema to the general public, which thought of him vaguely as a wrong headed Irishman with a violent red beard and subversive political notions to match, who wore curious clothes, ate vegetables. wrote queer plays which were not real plays at all, and had publicly announced himself to be a better playwright than Shakespeare.

YET, in spite of the fact that it was Shaw's foible to exhibit himself publicly as a man of genius, a man of genius he was. He could stimulate affection as well as irritation. He was an original thinker, with a forceful method of exposition, and even if he had never written for the theatre at all he would have been prominent in the worlds of literature, politics and journalism. It is for his work in and about the theatre, however, that his name will go down to posterity.

He came late in life to the theatre —he was nearly 30 when he began to write dramatic criticism, and 36 before he saw his first play staged— but from the first he was magnificently at ease in it. His mastery of technique was supreme, and it was just because of this mastery that he was able to put the theatre to uses for which, said the shocked up-holders of theatrical convention, it was never designed. Yet Shaw revolutionised our stage—not by supplying new models, but by tearing down outworn conventions

His long continued obscurity was due to the fact that he was ahead of his time and had to wait for the world to catch up with him. Throughout his youth – almost from the cradle, if we are to believe his own account—he was a rebel against accepted conventions.

Born in Dublin on July 26, 1856, he was the son of an Irish Protestant gentleman with, he says, " no money, no education no profession, no manual skill, no qualification of any sort for any definite social function. But he had been brought up to believe that there was an inborn virtue of gentility in all Shaws, since they revolved impecuniously in a sort of vague second cousinship round a baronetcy."

Arriving in London at the age of 20, he plunged into furious activity, political and literary. He was one of the first members of the Fabian Society and a tireless expounder of Socialist doctrine. Also, though he declared that he " never wanted to write", he produced five novels between 1880 and 1883. None was successful.

Start in Journalism

IN 1885, when he was 29, he was given a post on the staff of the Pall Mall Gazette, and soon after became art critic of the World, under Edmund Yates. Then when T. P. O'Connor started the Star he engaged Shaw to write short subsidiary leading articles at £2 l0s a week.

But Shaw denounced the Liberals. He was hastily transferred to a less dangerous sphere of operations, and wrote musical criticism under the name of Corno di Bassetto.

These articles quickly attracted attention by their originality and wit, and in 1890 he went to the World as music critic. He held this post for four years. In 1895 he was appointed dramatic critic of the Saturday Review.

Brilliant Critic

HOW brilliantly he filled that position is a matter of literary history. His volumes of collected criticisms are still among the best things he ever wrote. These articles, contributed over a period of three years, established Shaw as a man to be reckoned with. Indeed, until he began to make real headway as a dramatist, they were his chief claim to fame.

Shaw's fourth play in the order of writing was "Arms and the Man," and it was the first of his plays to be '.given a production in an ordinary West End theatre. It was not a success. Its unromantic picture of war, which hundreds of thousands of Englishmen were to discover 20 years later to be a true picture, did not suit the ideas of 1894.

The play ran for six weeks. In the next 10 years new plays poured from his pen; but London knew them only by going to Stage Society performances or by reading them in printed form with their provocative prefaces. To this period belong "Candida," " You Never Can Tell," " The Devil's Disciple," and Caesar and Cleopatra."

Not until the Vedrenne-Barker managenent had featured his plays at the Court Theatre in 1904-6 did he begin to enjoy a kind of topsy-turvy popularity. His plays were still thought odd and rather dreadful, but people went to see them. "Fanny's First Play" was considered an excellent jest, and "Pygmalion," with its deft introduction of a Fearful Adjective, a still better one. Shaw was now, in fact, a chartered libertine whom only a few highbrows took seriously.

Prophet and Portent

AFTER the 1914-18 war, to his own great astonishment, he ceased to be considered a mere jester and became a prophet, a portent and a popular dramatist. "Heartbreak House" was greeted with a chorus of praise; "Back to Methuselah", though its enormous length was too much for all but a tough-fibred minority of playgoers, was received with universal respect; while "Saint Joan" was hailed as a masterpiece, and had an enormous run.

Finally he achieved apotheosis at Malvern, where, in 1929, Sir Barry Jackson held a Shaw Festival, which culminated with the production of another fine play, "The Apple Cart", before an audience mainly consisting of devout pilgrims from London.

New Play at 93

FOR ten years thereafter he contributed plays to this festival, though none which ranked with his best work. In 1949, again at Malvern, his last full-length play, "Buoyant Billions", proved that his mind was still alert even at the age of 93.

Apart from plays and dramatic criticism he wrote a number of political books and pamphlets. He married, in 1898, Miss Charlotte Frances Payne-Townsend, who died in 1943. In 1925 he was awarded the Nobel Prize for Literature.

(November 3)

MR. MACKENZIE KING

PREMIER OF CANADA FOR OVER 21 YEARS

Mr. W. L. Mackenzie King, former Prime Minister of Canada, who died on Saturday at the age of 75, had a record of service unique among British statesmen.

He was Prime Minister for 21 years, 157 days surpassing Walpole's record of 20 years, 326 days —previously the longest period of Premiership in the history of the British Commonwealth and Empire. His tenure of office was twice broken by a spell in Opposition.

He held public office under five Sovereigns. and he was Prime Minister during the terms of six Governors-General. When, in August, 1948, he resigned the leadership of the Canadian Liberal party, he had held it for 29 years.

His place in history is secure. Assuming the mantle of the great Laurier he led Canada to Dominion status and, beyond that, to a new world status.

Studious by training and frugal by habit, a bachelor and a Presbyterian, he evoked respect rather than affection. But he was a shrewd judge of men and a resourceful tactician.

WORLD LEADERS' TRIBUTES

Tributes paid yesterday to Mr. Mackenzie King's work included the following:

Mr. ATTLEE: He served his country with devotion and high distinction in peace and war. He rendered eminent service not only to Canada but to the British Commonwealth.

Mr. CHURCHILL: He was a great Statesman whose friendship I enjoyed for many years and whose services to Canada and the British Empire will long be remembered.

President TRUMAN: He brought his country to a new stature of greatness. In recurring international conferences growing out of two world wars he exercised an ever-increasing influence. In him freedom-loving peoples and democratic institutions found an unwavering champion.

Mr. DOUGLAS, United States Ambassador: The world has lost a statesman whose influence has always been for the betterment of mankind. He exerted a cementing influence between Canada, the United States and the Commonwealth.

(July 24)

KING GUSTAV OF SWEDEN DIES AT 92

PEACEFUL END IN HIS SLEEP

From Our Own Correspondent

STOCKHOLM, Sunday.

King Gustav V of Sweden died in Drottningholm Palace at 8.35 a.m. [7.35 G.M.T.] to-day. He was 92 and would have completed the 43rd year of his reign in December.

Princess Sibylla, widow of Prince Gustav Adolf, eldest son of the Crown Prince, was the only member of the Royal family present at his deathbed. Her four-year-old son, Prince Carl Gustav, becomes the new heir-presumptive.

As the flags sank to half-mast over the Palace a last bulletin issued by the King's three doctors stated:

The King's powers of resistance declined steadily throughout the night. His Majesty sank deeper and deeper into unconsciousness and passed away peacefully at 8.35 without any sign of a death struggle.

King Gustav was taken ill after a cabinet meeting on Friday. The death certificate gave the cause of death as " chronic bronchial catarrh and changes in the organs of circulation owing to old age."

THE NEW KING

The King is succeeded by his eldest son, Crown Prince Gustav Adolf, who will be 68 on Nov. 11 His accession to the throne as King Gustav VI will be proclaimed tomorrow afternoon.

(October 30)

E. J. MOERAN DEAD IN RIVER

GIFTED COMPOSER

Ernest John Moeran, the gifted composer, was found dead yesterday in the River Kenmare, near Kenmare, in Co. Kerry. He was 55.

He was in the habit of going for long walks with a notebook while working at his music. He was wounded in the leg in the 1914-18 war. An inquest is expected to be held to-day at Kenmare.

Ernest John Moeran, the composer died yesterday at Kenmare, Co. Kerry. He was 55. He was almost self-taught in music, but joined the Royal College of Music in 1913 for a few months before serving in the Army throughout the first world war.

The Halle Orchestra gave a performance of his first Rhapsody in 1924. Recent works are Concerto 1945, Sinfonietta for Orchestra, 1945, Oboe Quartet, 1946, and Cello Bonata 1947.

Our Music Critic writes: Moeran was among the most gifted of the young composers who 30 years ago found inspiration in folk-song and the poetry of country life.

(December 2)

GEN. SMUTS DIES AT HIS HOME, AGED 80

The Daily Telegraph announces with regret that Gen. Smuts, the South-African war leader, died at his home at Irene near Pretoria, yesterday. He was 80.

An official bulletin stated that his death occurred peacefully. He had been reported to be fatigued after the influenza which attacked him when he had nearly recovered from pneumonia.

The following bulletin was issued by his doctors at 9.15 B.S.T. last night:

"We regret to announce that Gen. Smuts passed away peacefully this evening after a sudden heart collapse.

"He had spent a happy day with Mrs. Smuts and his family in the open country which he loved so well and which, during his convalescence from his recent illness, he had expressed the desire to see.

"Soon after his evening meal he rose from the table, walked to his room and collapsed on his bed and in the presence of 'Ouma' ("Granny" as Mrs. Smuts was affectionately known throughout South Africa) and members of the family, passed quietly on.

"PERSONAL LOSS"

The King's Tribute

The following telegram was sent by the King last night from Balmoral to Mrs. Smuts:

"The Queen and I have heard the news of the death of Field-Marshall Smuts with great sorrow and a deep sense of personal loss.

"We send our heartfelt sympathy to you and to your family. In peace or in war, his counsel and his friendship were of inestimable value both to my father and to myself, while the force of his intellect has enriched the wisdom of the whole human race.- (Signed) GEORGE R.

Radio Silence

The B.B.C. interrupted the Light Programme at nine o' clock to make a special announcement of Gen. Smuts's death. Afterwards a minute's silence was observed. The home news at nine o' clock began with announcement and was followed by a 15 sec. silence.

(September 12)

VASLAV NIJINSKY

Vaslav Nijinsky, the ballet dancer, who died in London, aged 59, was born in Kiev, Russia to parents who were both dancers. He began dancing at the age of three and when he was 10 he entered the Russian Imperial School of Dancing.

At 18 he was dancing leading roles opposite Pavlova and Karavina. A quarrel with a Russian Grand Duke led to his suspension with the Imperial ballet.

He then joined the Ballet Russe, formed by Diaghilev, and became its star. The company rapidly gained fame and in 1911 he left Russia with it. During the next eight years the beauty and originality of his dancing was acclaimed in all parts of the world. While the company was in South America, he married a Hungarian society girl, Romoia de Pulski.

In 1919 Nijinsky became seriously ill and retired from the stage. He was declared an incurable victim of schizophrenia but his wife made every effort to find a cure for him. When he came to live in this country in 1947 he was partly cured. He had recently been living at Virginia Water, Surrey, with his wife.

(April 10)

LORD NORMAN

24 YEARS GOVERNOR OF BANK OF ENGLAND

Lord Norman, who died in London on Saturday, aged 78, was, as Montagu Norman, Governor of the Bank of England for 24 momentous years until he retired, because of ill-health, in 1944. He was created a baron in the same year.

He played an outstanding role in domestic and international economic and financial affairs during the troubled inter-war years, and was inevitably the subject of controversy, of praise and of blame.

The first Governor to recognise the importance of close collaboration between the Treasury and the Bank, he yet took care to preserve the individuality of the latter. He also extended the international dealings of the Bank, realising that the stabilisation of currencies could play an important part in the world's recovery.

Montagu Collet Norman, who was born in 1871, came of banking stock. His father was a partner in a well-known banking firm, and his mother's father, Sir Mark Wilks Collet, was himself a former Governor of the Bank of England. Educated at Eton and at King's College, Cambridge, where he achieved no great distinction, Montagu Norman entered the banking firm of Brown, Shipley and Co. in 1900.

DIRECTOR IN 1907

A trip to America, on which he acquired much knowledge and many friends, was followed by service with the Bedfordshire Regiment in the South African war, in which he won the D.S.O. He became a director of the Bank of England in 1907, and on the outbreak of the 1914-18 war became a whole-time assistant to the Governor.

Deputy-Governor in 1918, he was appointed Governor two years later. He proceeded to develop relations with the American Government and the Federal Reserve Banking system, and with Central Banking Institutions in Europe and within the Empire. At home he set up the Bankers' Industrial Development Corporation, which financed reorganisation schemes in the post-war years.

GOLD STANDARD ISSUE

The parts he played in the return to the Gold Standard in this country in 1925, and in the crisis of 1931, are still matters of controversy. In the subsequent years he earned many tributes for the energy and foresight with which he tackled Britain's problems, and he undoubtedly left an ineffaceable mark on the Bank and on the City.

The outbreak of the 1939-45 war found his energy undiminished, and his intellect undimmed. The extraordinary stability of this country's finances during the most expensive war in history was due in no small measure to his ability and labour. Early in 1944, however, he suffered a severe illness which necessitated complete rest. Since then he had lived in retirement in Campden Hill, Kensington.

(February 6)

MONTY BANKS

Monty Banks, the film-director husband of Miss Gracie Fields, died in a train near Sempioni, Italy. He was 52, and by birth an Italian, his real name being Mario Bianchi.

By 1937 he had established his reputation in America as a film producer. In that year he was appointed associate producer for pictures Miss Fields was making, partly in this country, for Twentieth Century-Fox. In March, 1940, they were married at Hollywood. Their arrival in this country soon afterwards and their return to America led to questions in Parliament concerning Mr. Banks's alleged pro-Italian sympathies. Later the same year he was granted American citizenship.

Monty Banks did not return to this country until 1947. Under American law Miss Fields remained a British subject. Among the productions he made in England were "Not So quiet on the Western Front," "Almost a Honeymoon," "My Wife's Family" and "We're Going to be Rich." One of his most recent pictures was "A Bell for Adano."

(January 9)

GENERAL SIR ARCHIBALD WAVELL (right) with General Claude Auchinleck.

NATION'S LAST TRIBUTE TO LORD WAVELL

Daily Telegraph Reporter

As the solemn cadences of "Nimrod" from Elgar's "Enigma Variations" softened and died, Field-Marshal Earl Wavell was borne yesterday by N.C.O.s and other ranks of his own regiment, the Black Watch, into the pillared quiet of Westminster Abbey.

Gathered to pay their last tribute to the soldier, statesman, poet were the highest and the humblest both of this country and of the territories over the seas where Earl Wavell served.

There were bemedalled men in mufti with tell-tale empty sleeves, dignitaries from the Middle East in flowing robes and head-dresses touched with gold, officers of the Indian and Pakistani forces who served under the field-marshal in the east.

There were Egyptians in national uniform, and, in embroidered and jewelled saris, the wives of Indian statesmen assembled to honour one whom they remembered both as a courageous soldier and a wise man in their own country's turbulent affairs.

TRAFFIC STILLED

In the Abbey the band of the Scots Guards played before the service Mackenzie's "Benedictus," the "Judex" excerpt from Gounod's "Mors et Vita", the measured intermezzo from Bizet's "Maid of Arles" and finally "Nimrod", from Elgar's "Enigma Variations."

In the silence which followed, with London's traffic stilled, the progress of the cortège as it approached the great West Door of the Abbey from Westminster Pier could be traced by the staccato commands as each detachment of troops presented arms, and by the steady approaching of the lamenting notes of "Flowers of the Forest" as pipers of the Black Watch led the procession to the door, where a trumpeter of the Household Cavalry sounded a General Salute.

The vast congregation rose as the coffin was borne through the West Door. Above the coffin was draped a Union Jack and on the Union Jack were the field-marshal's white-plumed hat, his baton, his pipe banner, and his ivory-handled sword.

Behind in the slow procession to the High Altar, came officers carrying the field-marshal's decorations and orders on cushioned salvers, and the pall-bearers—Admiral of the Fleet Viscount Cunningham, Field-Marshal Viscount Alanbrooke, Field-Marshal Viscount Montgomery and Field-Marshal Sir Claude Auchinleck, Gen. Sir James Steele, Gen. Sir George Giffard, Gen. Sir Alan Cunningham, and Gen. Sir William Platt, Lt.-Gen. Sir Arthur Smith and Air Chief-Marshal Sir John Slessor.

The slow, plaintive tolling of the Abbey bell mingled with the deep boom of Big Ben as the congregation waited with bowed heads until the opening sentences of the burial service were heard, sung by the choir in a 17th century setting by William Croft.

WORDS BY BUNYAN

There was no funeral oration. Instead Dr. Don, Dean of Westminster, read the last words of Mr. Valiant-for-Truth from Bunyan's "The Pilgrim's Progress."

"My Sword I give to him that shall succeed me in my pilgrimmage, and my Courage and Skill to him that can get it. My Marks and Scars I carry with me, to be a witness for me that I have fought his battles, who will now be my rewarder. So he passed over and all the trumpets sounded for him on the other side."

After the blessing the pipers played "Lochaber No More" and "After the Battle." Last Post and Reveille echoed and re-echoed in the high arches of the Abbey where the soldier-poet was carried past Poets' Corner on the last stage of his last journey.

(June 8)

PROF. HAROLD LASKI

Prof. Harold J. Laski who has died, aged 56, had been a member of the National Executive Committee of the Labour party since 1936, and was chairman in 1945-6. He wielded immense power in the party. Prof. Laski was the author, in October 1949, of a programme which urged large reductions in military expenditure, great increases in East-West trade, including Russia, a capital levy and capital gains tax, and no reduction of expenditure on social services. His writings on Socialism were voluminous.

He was born at Manchester and educated at Manchester Grammar School and New College, Oxford. His connection with the London School of Economics (London University) began in 1920. In 1926 he became Professor of Political Science at the school.

In November, 1946, Prof. Laski figured in the most widely discussed political libel action for many years — which he brought against a newspaper and lost. He claimed damages for alleged libel from the Newark Advertiser and South Notts Gazette, and its editor.

He complained of a report in that paper on June 20, 1945, of a meeting in Newark Market-place on June 16, during the General Election, alleging that it inaccurately stated that he said: "We shall have to use violence even if it means revolution." The jury found that the report was fair and accurate. They also found that the matter was one of public concern and judgement was entered for the defendants with costs.

The exact figure of the costs was not stated, but was put as high as £15,000. A subscription launched by Mr. Morgan Phillips, secretary of the Labour party, to defray the costs raised more than £13,000.

(March 25)

SIR H. BARKER

MADE MEDICAL HISTORY

Daily Telegraph Reporter

Sir Herbert Atkinson Barker, dominant figure in one of the most sustained controversies in medical history, died yesterday in Lancaster Infirmary at the age of 81.

A man of remarkable gifts, he specialised in manipulative surgery. Because he did not possess a degree he roused the antagonism of practically the whole medical profession for 25 years.

His claim was that the results he was achieving with patients proved that bloodless methods of operating made many surgical operations and orthopaedic appliances unnecessary. Subjected to attacks that were often bitter and abusive, he also knew that he was being regarded as a "quack."

With the greatest determination however, he went on with his work obtaining many spectacular successes with patients who in numerous instances were well-known people. The attacks on him led to a reversion of public feeling.

Famous men like George Bernard Shaw, H. G. Wells and W. T. Stead rallied to his support. Later they were to be joined by some eminent medical men. Finally, he triumphed over all the animosity. He was knighted in 1992.

TRAINED AS BONE-SETTER

At 18, he underwent training as a bone-setter and two years later set up practice in Manchester.

By curing a professional runner of an ankle injury that had apparently incapacitated him, he soon had a constant stream of damaged footballers and other players visiting him for treatment.

Shortly after coming to London in 1904 he thought that a good method of lessening medical animosity would be to get doctors to see for themselves the technique he was practising so successfully. Choosing names at random from a medical directory he issued invitations.

Dr. F. W. Axham was one of the doctors who accepted, and he was so impressed that he decided to help in the work. "But you will be struck off the Register if you do," warned Barker. "I can't help that," said Axham. "You must have an anaesthetist."

Barker's warning was justified. Axham was struck off the General Medical Council for "infamous conduct" in a professional sense. He died 21 years later — some said of a broken heart, for the G.M.C. had refused to relent. Only the Royal College of Physicians, Edinburgh, belatedly reinstated him.

PRIMATE PETITIONED

Meanwhile many attempts had been made to secure adequate recognition for Barker. Three hundred M.P.s and ex-M.P.s petitioned the Archbishop of Canterbury in 1920 to exercise an ancient power and grant him a "Lambeth degree". When this failed there was an equally fruitless plea to the House of Commons, but a year later came the knighthood.

In 1936 distinguished surgeons attended and admired a demonstration by Sir Herbert. In 1939 the British Medical Journal announced that films designed to perpetrate his technique had been made at St. Thomas's Hospital.

Sir Herbert commented: "My life's work is now fully justified. I am luckier than most pioneers."

(July 22)

CHRISTOPHER BUCKLEY KILLED IN KOREA

JEEP HITS MINE ON VISIT TO FRONT

From Denis Warner
Daily Telegraph Special Correspondent
TAEGU, Korea, Sunday.

Christopher Buckley, Chief Correspondent of THE DAILY TELEGRAPH in Korea, and Ian Morrison, Far Eastern Correspondent of the Times, were killed yesterday. The United Nations Jeep in which they were travelling hit a landmine in the South Korean lines north of Waegwan.

Ian Morrison, Col. M. K. Unni Nayar, Indian alternate member and observer with the United Nations Commission in Korea, and a South Korean lieutenant, who were also in the vehicle, were killed instantly. (Obituaries P3.)

Christopher Buckley died in the American army hospital at Taegu about 7.15 last evening. American doctors said it was improbable that he regained consciousness after the mine had exploded.

The party left Taegu early in the afternoon in the Jeep driven by Col. Nayar. At the headquarters of the 1st South Korean Division, which had been holding the Naktong River line immediately north of the 1st American Cavalry Division, they picked up a Korean engineer lieutenant as a guide.

LAST ROW OF MINES

The Jeep successfully negotiated five rows of mines. It then struck one in the sixth and last row and was destroyed.

MILITARY HONOURS

Christopher Buckley and Ian Morrison were buried with military honours in adjoining graves in a little tree-shaded cemetery attached to the Presbyterian mission at Taegu at six o'clock this evening.

Dr. Edward Adams and Dr. Archibald Campbell of the Presbyterian mission and Lt.-Col. Over-street, Episcopalian chaplain of the 1st Cavalry Division, conducted the service. Pallbearers included British, Australian, American, Chinese and French friends of the two correspondents, and Australian United Nations observers with whom both had worked during the campaign.

Those who met them for the first time in Korea liked and respected them as two of the hardest working and most courageous men in the field. Buckley, in appalling conditions, often worked, tireless, for 18 hours a day.

He was a daily visitor to the front. He based his despatches on observation and information under fire.

Ian Morrison, acknowledged to be the ablest and most distinguished of the correspondents permanently covering the Far East, did not lag behind Christopher Buckley in front-line coverage. Alone among correspondents covering the war, he had an uninterrupted tour of more than five weeks at the front.

Of 12 correspondents who have lost their lives or been reported missing in the Korean campaign, the bodies of only Buckley and Morrison have been recovered for burial.

(August 14)

From Field Marshal Viscount Montgomery
To the Editor of The Daily Telegraph

SIR—I have heard with deep regret of the death of Christopher Buckley. I knew him well, and indeed he was my comrade during many miles of the long journey from Alamein to Berlin.

A Commander-in-Chief in the field gets to know some war correspondents better than others, and this happened in the case of Christopher. I saw him often and was always glad to do so. He never abused my confidence and he never let me down; he could easily have done both any time he liked, but his integrity was of the highest order. I trusted him absolutely.

I saw him last in Germany during the first winter after the war was over. I was in bed with a bad attack of pneumonia, and he came to see me and have a quiet talk over post-war troubles. I have always remembered that visit. He wanted certain information, and I gave it to him knowing that I could safely do so. Yours faithfully.

MONTGOMERY OF ALAMEIN
Milly, Seine-et-Oise, France

(August 16)

GEORGE ORWELL

ERIC BLAIR, better known as George Orwell, whose death from tuberculosis is announced, had spent the last two years in hospital and sanatoria. He was to have left next Wednesday by air for Montana in Switzerland.

His interest in life never flagged, and though he detested being an invalid he never lost heart. He kept his fishing rods in a corner of the room and even last week was busy gathering material about Conrad, for whose novels, particularly "Under Western Eyes," he had a profound admiration.

In politics he belonged to the Left but he was far too honest and sincere to fall in with any current ideology. His lively allegory, "Animal Farm" - the best since "Gulliver's Travels" - illustrates the fallacy of revolution.

His last novel, "Nineteen Eighty-Four," develops the same theme less poetically and with more particular reference to the Soviet régime, which he increasingly loathed.

Misplaced Romanticism

He was a gentle, mildly eccentric character, in some respects reminiscent of Cervantes' Knight of the Rueful Countenance. Like Don Quixote he was deeply romantic and was resolved to apply his romanticism in an alien world.

Thus he tried, as it were, to write Fabian Tracts in the spirit of Kipling, to make D'Artagnan a backbench Labour M.P. It would not work, of course, but those who knew him will never forget the lovable, if curious effect produced.

(January 23)

AL JOLSON LEFT £1,750,000

From Our Own Correspondent
NEW YORK, Wednesday.

Al Jolson, the black-faced comedian and singer, who died suddenly of a heart attack at San Francisco yesterday, left nearly £1,750,000.

His lawyers confirmed to-day that he had left nearly £357,000 each to New York City College, Columbia University and New York University. He asked that the money should be used largely to help needy students "regardless of race, colour or religion."

(October 25)

TELEVISION OF 100 SPORTS EVENTS A YEAR

GATE NOW OPEN, SAYS MINISTER

By A Radio Correspondent

B.B.C. officials and representatives of nearly 100 sporting organisations agreed yesterday after a meeting with Mr. NESS EDWARDS, the Postmaster General, to the televising of 100 sporting events a year. It is expected that 20 will be major events.

Mr. Ness Edwards, announcing the agreement in London, said that he had set up a committee, to be known as the Sport Television Advisory Committee, with Earl Beatty as chairman. It would consist of representatives of sporting associations, interested parties, and the public.

The committee would ascertain the effects on the general national life and on individual interests of the televising of any events. From time to time it would report its conclusions.

The Association for the Protection of Copyright in Sport, which originally called for the ban on the television of sporting broadcasts, were prepared to postpone any question of a ban and to co-operate with the advisory committee. They had also agreed that arrangements would still be the subject of negotiations between the B.B.C. and the promoters.

"OPENED THE GATES"

Mr. Edwards said: "This has opened the gates of television as they have never been opened before. Those whose financial interests may be imperilled by this development must re-orientate their activities otherwise the tide of television will overwhelm them."

There was no doubt that television was going to play as big a part in the last half of this century as the cinema played in the first.

"I can see no form of social cultural or educational activity that it cannot invade. It can help us with our economic problems. I would say you cannot stop this thing. It is going on and I hope with ever-increasing speed and in an ever-widening field.

"Our television is far ahead of anything in Europe. The general progress we have made puts us in the forefront of all countries in the world. The home is going to have a new significance. It is going to alter the fundamental habits of our people."

(May 24)

MISS MORGAN'S BEST EVER

BEATS MISS CURRY IN SQUASH FINAL

By JOHN OLLIFF

Miss Janet Morgan, runner-up to Miss Joan Curry in the women's squash rackets championship last year and in 1948, won the title at last when she defeated the holder, 9-4, 9-3, 9-0, in the final at the Lansdowne Club, London, on Saturday.

It was the first time Miss Curry had been beaten since she took up the game competitively at the end of the war. Last year Miss Curry won 2-9, 9-3, 10-8, 9-0. The final in 1948 when Miss Curry survived match ball against Miss Morgan before winning 9-5, 9-0, 9-10, 6-9,10-8, was even closer.

Miss Curry's greatest assets have always been her fleetness of foot and fine match temperament. Her only really dangerous stroke is a forehand drop shot which, played from the left of the court away from her body dies away in the right-hand front corner.

For some inexplicable reason she did not use this valuable weapon on Saturday. It may have been that Miss Morgan's decisive killing of the ball in the forecourt prompted her to try to pin her opponent to the back of the court.

Miss Morgan now holds both the British and American titles, and must be considered with Miss Susan Noel, Miss Margot Lumb and Miss Curry as one of the four greatest players of the game.

EXHAUSTING WEEK

Miss Morgan is a games mistress at a school in South-East London and as the championship is held during term she has had a most exhausting week.

(February 27)

COLONIST II BRINGS HIS 1950 WINNINGS TO £7,202

Slams French Pair to Win 6th In a Row

From Hotspur

NEWMARKET, Thursday.

FROM the jockey prodigy Lester Piggott and the gallant filly Zina, so narrowly beaten in the Cambridgeshire yesterday, the scene shifted this afternoon to Mr. Churchill, another of racing's "new boys" and his equally gallant grey Colonist II, who set the seal on a memorable 1950 record by winning the Jockey Club Cup from his two French-trained rivals Pas de Calais and Miel Rosa

Colonist II and Mr. Churchill will go down in racing history as a unique partnership. Mr. Churchill had never owned a racehorse in his life until 15 months ago, when Colonist II, bred in France, was bought for him.

No one took the Venture very seriously, but this remarkable colt Started by winning a small race in Mr. Churchill's colours at Salisbury in August last year and has only occasionally stopped winning

He wound up 1949 with three wins worth in aggregate stakes £1,243. This year Colonist II has won eight of his 11 races — the last six in succession.

BARGAIN HORSE INDEED

The bargain horse of the year was how I heard Colonist II described after his triumph today. I would go further than that and say Mr. Churchill secured the bargain of 10 years when he became the owner of this horse who has taken on Brown Jack's mantle and is just as popular that grand stayer of the 1930's.

Mr. Churchill has enjoyed the thrill of watching Colonist II win nearly all his races. He flew in from Northolt this afternoon just in time to see his horse saddled. The race for the Jockey Club Cup is run over the full Cesarewitch Course of 2 ¼ miles and it's not until the field has turned well into the straight, a mile out, that the colours can be picked up.

Gordon Richards, on Baron Guy de Rothschild's Miel Rosa, who was receiving 12lb from Colonist II, was making the running on the outside when my glasses picked up the three starters. It was one of the rare occasions when Colonist II was being waited with by his jockey, Gosling, and for a moment I sensed danger from the other Frenchman, Pas de Calais, who was tracking the favourite.

But more than a quarter of a mile from home Gosling let Colonist II go and once again we had the gripping spectacle of this grey and gallant horse, flaxen tail flowing in the wind, plugging along in front. He finished a length and a half in ahead of Pas de Calais with Miel Rosa eight lengths behind the second.

(October 27)

SUSPENDED BOY JOCKEY LOSES IN PHOTO-FINISH

THOUGHT HE HAD WON CAMBRIDGESHIRE

From Hotspur

NEWMARKET, Wednesday.

Only a few hours after learning that he had been suspended by the Stewards of the Jockey Club from riding for the remainder of the season, LESTER PIGGOTT, the 14-year-old jockey, was involved in a most exciting finish to the Cambridgeshire to-day.

He had passed the winning post on Zina neck and neck with D. Smith on Kelling and K. Gethin on Valdesco. The crowd waited for the result. After consulting the photograph the judge awarded the race to Kelling by a neck, placed Zina second and Valdesco, a further head away, third.

Meanwhile, Piggott, thinking he had won, rode Zina into the winners enclosure. Even Mr. CHRIS JAVIS owner of Kelling—who was taken into the enclosure reserved for the second horse—thought that Zina had won.

"THOUGHT I HAD WON"

Lady Isabel Guinness, owner of Zina, who had come forward to congratulate Piggott, threw her hands in the air when the decision was announced, exclaiming: "Oh! how disappointing."

Piggott said: "I thought I had won. Zina had to race by herself. Had there been something alongside me she would have pulled out a bit more."

At his home at Lambourn he said "When I was going down the straight I thought the race was in my pocket."

Piggott's suspension follows the disqualification of Barnacle, on whom he finished first in the Manton Handicap at Newbury on Friday. An objection was lodged to Barnacle for crossing and boring and the race was awarded to Royal Oak IV who had finished second.

Piggott was given permission by the stewards of the Jockey Club to ride Zina and two other mounts to-day.

KEITH PIGGOTT, his father, and a trainer at Lambourn, said "Lester has taken this suspension in the right spirit." His mother said: "It will give my boy more time to concentrate on his lessons. He has a private tutor and settles down to French and arithmetic textbooks when the day's racing is over."

Lester Piggott, who will not be fifteen until Nov. 5, has been the most successful apprentice jockey since Frank Wootton, the boy prodigy of 40 years ago, who was champion jockey four times before he was 19. Piggott has already ridden 59 winners. Wootton had ridden 201 before his 19th birthday.

(October 26)

ALMOST A JOCKEY. L. Piggott winning the Orvieto Stakes on Sun Flame at Kempton Park for his 39th success. After one more win this 14-year-old rider will not be able to claim the Apprentice's allowance.

MANICOU EASY WINNER IN THE QUEEN'S COLOURS

POSSIBLE BEATEN BY EIGHT LENGTHS

From Hotspur

KEMPTON PARK, Friday.

Very happy racing history was made here this afternoon when the Queen's colours-blue, buff stripes, blue sleeves, black cap and gold tassel-were successful for the first time. Her Majesty and Princess Elizabeth were present to see the five-year-old chaser Manicou win the Wimbledon Handicap Chase by eight lengths from the Duchess of Norfolk's Possible and other rivals.

Fortunately visibility was nearly perfect and the Royal party were able to follow every incident of the three-mile race.

Manicou jumped faultlessly and though Grantham, his rider, did not take the lead until less than half a mile from home, he never had a moment's anxiety about the outcome.

Cheering, increasing in volume, began when Manicou went to the front entering the straight, to which point Possible, winner of the Molyneux Chase at Aintree a fortnight ago, had made the running. These two were well clear of the rest of the field and Manicou jumped slightly ahead at the last fence.

Taking this in his stride, the Queen's horse sprinted away on the flat to win handsomely. It was a first class performance. Not only did Manicou fence perfectly, but he showed plainly his ability to stay. He should win many more races in the Royal colours.

(November 25)

TRIUMPH FOR BRITISH SHOW JUMPING

By Our Hunting Correspondent

The final result of the Toronto Horse Show puts Britain first with five wins and one shared with five others, Mexico second with three, Canada two, the United States one, Chile and Eire nil.

One result has not been clarified, the President of the United States of Mexico Trophy, but it would appear that this went to Canada.

Coming at the end of an exhausting tour preceeded by a rough Atlantic crossing, this result is a triumph for Lt.-Col. H. Llewellyn, his team, and for British show jumping.

(December 2)

NARROW ESCAPE OF THE DERBY FAVOURITE

From Hotspur

EPSOM, Friday.

Prince Simon, favourite for to-morrow's Derby, his trainer, Capt. Cecil Boyd-Rochfort, and his jockey, W. Carr, had a narrow escape this morning when a runaway hack galloped out of hand into Epsom's paddock.

An onlooker, describing the scene, said: "We were going over to look at Prince Simon grazing quietly in the paddock when a runaway hack, ridden by an apprentice, appeared on the scene.

"It galloped straight towards Prince Simon, his trainer and the jockey, and it seemed certain that one of them would be sent flying. The hack missed Prince Simon and Capt. Boyd-Rochfort by three or four feet, galloped on towards the paddock fence, when the apprentice threw himself."

Prince Simon's owner is Mr. William Woodward, formerly chairman of The New York Jockey Club, who has not come over from the United States for the race as he is in bad health. The colt is American bred.

W.H. Carr, the favourite's rider, rode his first winner on the Epsom course yesterday. C. Elliott (Welsh View) is the only jockey in to-morrow's Classic to have ridden three Derby winners.

Gordon Richards, on Napoleon Bonaparte, will be having his 25th ride in the Derby. This is the only important race he has never won.

RICHEST RACE

The King and Queen, Queen Mary, Princess Elizabeth and Princess Margaret will watch the race, the richest ever to be run in England.

Owner of the winner will receive £17,010 and a gold cup valued £250. Second prize is £1,913 and third £906.

(May 28)

FADING GALCADOR HANGS ON TO WIN BY A HEAD

M. Boussac Lands Oaks-Derby Double

By Hotspur

For the first time since the Italian Chevalier E. Ginistrelli won both the Derby and the Oaks with his filly Signorinetta 42 years ago, the same owner, trainer and jockey have brought off the double at Epsom. M. M. Boussac, who won the Oaks with Asmena, landed the Derby with Galcador, ridden by Asmena's jockey, Johnstone, and trained by Semblat in France. Galcador beat the favourite, Prince Simon, by a head.

The defeat of Mr. Woodward's colt was a great disappointment to many. I had hoped to be able to say to-day that Prince Simon was probably a great horse. He is not. He is a very good one but no more. He had his race as good as won at 10 furlongs and again 10ft past the post-but not at the place which mattered. There seemed no excuse for him. After a furlong Carr had him well placed, he was second to Pewter Platter at the top of the hill, took the lead on the way down to Tattenham Corner, came round the Corner on the rails almost as handily as a polo pony, and then made the best of his way home.

With three furlongs to go I thought Prince Simon had his race won. He was out clear with at least a three lengths' lead, L'Amiral was beaten, Khorassan and Castle Rock were in trouble.

Two furlongs from home Galcador loomed up as the only danger to the favourite, and Carr, either because he sensed it or because he felt Prince Simon beginning to fade, asked his colt to quicken.

Prince Simon could not do so and at the foot of the hill Galcador was up with him and had gone into a lead of over half a length.

The race looked as good as over, but as Prince Simon met the rise he began to run on gallantly. In the last 100 yards he gained steadily on the fading Galcador, but the post-alas!-came just too soon.

(May 29)

SUSSEX JUST WIN IN POLO FINAL

Princess Elizabeth saw Sussex beat Oxfordshire by 5 goals to 4 in the final of the Open Polo Cup at Roehampton on Saturday and presented the Cup to the winning team.

Play moved at a fast pace from end to end as first one side and then the other attacked and the result was in doubt until the end.

Oxfordshire led for most of the game. They were 1 ½ goals up at the end of the second chukka and though Lakin scored a fine goal for Sussex, Walsh replied to keep Oxford half a goal ahead.

The fifth chukka, with the result hanging in the balance, was fought with great determination, Sussex just gaining the day by another Lakin goal

Sussex were represented by A. Gibbs, Col. P. Dollar, Col. G. Phipps-Hornby and J. Lakin, and Oxfordshire by Maj. A. David, Lt-Col. Horsbrugh-Porter, Col. H. Guiness and W. Walsh.

Earl Mountbatten earlier played well for Hampshire, who lost to Hertfordshire.

(July 17)

GREY SKIES AT ASCOT OPENING

HEAVY BETTING IN NEW ENCLOSURES

From Our Special Correspondent

ASCOT, Tuesday.

A grudging sun came too late from the grey clouds to give its entire blessing to the first day of Royal Ascot.

The sky was still overcast when just before the first race the royal party from Windsor Castle changed from cars to open landaus to make the traditional drive from Duke's Windsor Forest on the New Mile course along the stands.

In the first landau drawn by four Windsor greys were the King and Queen, the Duke of Gloucester and the Duke of Beaufort. In the second were Princess Margaret, the Princess Royal, the Marquess of Hartington and the Earl of Dalkeith.

It was the first free-petrol Royal Ascot day for 10 years. The Royal Automobile Club had on duty 120 men to control car parks for more than 12,000 vehicles but not all the spaces were used.

Queues were no longer a feature of the restaurants on the course. Grandstand visitors had a choice of Scotch salmon mayonnaise or lobster, roast chicken, turkey, duckling, lamb or beef or pressed brisket of beef or veal, ham and egg pie. Champagne was 50s a bottle.

(June 10)

AN ASCOT OF PICTURE HATS

The women made yesterday an Ascot of picture hats, with larger irregular shaped brims and sheer dresses made of filmy fabric, such as chiffon and net. Skirts were calf-length or shorter, and there were few traditional flowered prints.

Princess Margaret led the fashion for sheers with a filmy white dress which had a bolero in turquoise with a big sash of the same shade. She chose the Ascot rival to the picture hat-a small white one. The Duchess of Kent also had a small white flowered hat.

Navy blue was the most fashionable colour in dresses. Next came white, then black and dark brown. Favourite material apart from sheers were Shantung stiff, silken fabrics and broderie anglaise. Slim near-tubular lines were favoured and both vertical and horizontal pleats.

(June 14)

ENGLAND OUT OF WORLD CUP

SPAIN WIN WAY TO FINAL POOL

RIO DE JANEIRO, Sunday.

England are out of the World Soccer Cup Competition. They went down fighting here to-day when Spain beat them by the only goal of a splendid match.

Spain have won all their games in Pool B and go forward to the final Pool, having beaten England, Chile and the United States. The other finalists in the series are Brazil, Sweden, and Uruguay. Final placings in Pool B are:

	P.	W.	D.	L.	Goals For	Goals Agst	Pts
Spain	3	3	0	0	6	1	6
England	3	1	0	2	2	2	2
United States	3	1	0	2	4	6	2
Chile	3	1	0	2	3	6	2

Spain won to-day because they were the better co-ordinated side. because their forward line was more agile, and because their defence—the key to their victory—was firmer than that of the England team

England played well all through the first half and held their own on merit. From the moment that the Spanish centre forward Zarra beat Williams in the 48th minute they became nervous and unsettled.

The Spaniards, on the other hand, increased the pace and pressed their attacks even more vigorously. Zarra was the real man of the match, leading their offensives brilliantly and shooting and passing with precision.

England had no really outstanding player. The forward line was better than that which played against the United States, but none shone. The half backs were sound and the backs also played a good game. Williams could not be blamed for the only goal scored.

FAST AND EXCITING

Play was fast and exciting in the first half and the highest standard yet seen in the championship. Milburn, Mortenson and Baily played well together and at times gave the Spanish defence a lot of trouble.

In the 13th minute England netted when Milburn headed the ball past Ramaletts from a pass by Finney, but the Newcastle man was clearly off-side.

The best English scoring effort before half time came from Baily, who put in a sizzling drive which just missed the upright.

After Zarras's goal early in the second half, Finney was badly fouled in the penalty area, but the Italian referee seemed quite oblivious of the incident. There were other occasions when the referee failed to penalise the Spaniards. English officials were all of the opinion that England should have had all three penalties awarded to them.

(July 3)

URUGUAY DEFEAT BRAZIL

WORLD CUP SURPRISE

RIO DE JANEIRO, Sunday.

Uruguay sprang the biggest surprise of the competition when defeating hot favourites Brazil by two goals to one here to-day to win the World Soccer Cup for the second time in the short history of the championship.

The Brazilian team, who had expected to obtain gold medals and thousands of pounds for a win bonus, walked slowly off the field, heads bowed low, before the crowd of nearly 200,000. Few had given Uruguay a chance against them.

Brazil took second place in the tournament. Sweden, who beat Spain 3-1 in Sao Paulo to-day, filled third place, and Spain fourth.

(July 18)

(Solution No. 7531)

MISS TUCKEY BEATEN IN FINAL

From Our Own Correspondent

LAUSANNE, Sunday.

British women lawn tennis players reached the finals of the singles and doubles in the Swiss championships here this week-end, but were defeated in both in straight sets.

Miss K. L. A. Tuckey, after beating Miss Rosenquest (U.S.) 6-1, 6-2, lost to Wimbledon champion, Miss L. Brough (U.S.) 4-6, 2-6. Miss J. Curry and Miss Tuckey lost to Miss Brough and Mrs. T. Long (Australia) 4-6, 5-7, after defeating Miss J. Quertier (G.B.) and Miss N. Morrison (U.S.) 6-2, 6-4.

E. W. Sturgess (S. Africa) won the men's singles final, defeating Selxas by 6-4, 7-5, 3-6, 6-2, and partnered by Selxas, defeated Amphon (Philippines) and Misra (India) 7-5, 6-4 in the doubles.

Sturgess completed a hat-trick by taking the mixed title with Mrs. Long. They beat Selxas and Miss Rosenquest 7-5, 6-4.

(July 17)

FREEBOOTER'S RIDER KEPT HIS HEAD

PLENTY OF TIME FOR RECOVERY

By Hotspur

For the first time in the long history of the Grand National, Yorkshire-trained horses filled the first three places at Aintree on Saturday. Freebooter, the winner, is trained by R. Renton, near Ripon; Wot No Sun (second) by N. Crump, at Middleham; Acthon Major (third) by W.Easterby near Tadcaster.

Behind these came Rowland Roy and Monaveen. The Queen and Princess, in glorious weather, watched their chaser struggle into fifth place in a field of 49 runners. Only seven of which finished.

Crump won the National two years ago with Sheila's Cottage and Easterby came near to winning it with the gallant mare Melleray's Belle, but it was the first time Renton had had a fancied runner in the race.

The Royal party were given a great run by Montaveen, who jumped superbly in the lead to the fence before the Chair, where he blundered.

He was going well again at Beecher's second time round but made a bad mistake at the next fence when his winning chance finally went.

His jockey, Grantham, made a marvellous recovery when the horse first blundered. For a few strides Grantham, to use his own words, "was hanging on around Monaveen's ears".

The sunshine, the good visibility and the presence of the Royal family made this the most noteworthy Grand National since the war. But it was a great pity that Cloncarrig fell two fences from home when racing neck-and-neck with Freebooter with the race between them. Freebooter was left to win the race easily from Wot No Sun and in doing so became the first favourite to win since the victory of Sprig in 1927.

(March 27)

BUDGE PATTY holds his tongue between taut lips as he makes a powerful return.

PATTY IS NEW CHAMPION

WIMBLEDON TRAINING ON STEAKS DIET

Weather forecast for Wimbledon: Fine with considerable sunny periods; warm.

Daily Telegraph Reporter

Budge Patty, 26-year-old American living in Paris, is the new Wimbledon men's singles champion. He was not included in the United States ranking list for its Davis Cup team.

He received the Cup from the Earl of Athlone in the Centre Court Royal box yesterday after beating the Australian, Frank Sedgman. who is 22, by 6-l, 8-l0, 6-2, 6-3.

On Thursday Patty and his men's doubles partner, T. Trabert, played the longest set and match ever known at Wimbledon. They beat Frank Sedgman and K. McGregor (Australia) by ,6-4, 31-29,7-9, 6-2, the second set lasting for 2 hours.

Patty has played at every Wimbledon since the war. He has failed hitherto through lack of stamina.

Seven weeks ago he gave up smoking and went on a diet of beefsteaks. He had steaks for lunch and dinner every day

"Now I plan a rest in Paris with everything I fancy to eat except steak. And has anyone got a cigarette?"

After his rest Patty, who won the French championship about four weeks ago, will again become a non-smoker and steak eater. He will then tackle the American championship

Sedgman, who leaves with the Australian Davis Cup team for Canada this week-end, said his strained wrist had not handicapped him in the final.

(July 8)

CUP-TIE GAME ABANDONED

PLAYERS COLLAPSE

From Our Own Correspondent

DORCHESTER, Thursday.

The replayed F.A. cup-tie between Alton and Dorchester was abandoned here this afternoon after 52 minutes' play. Three Alton players were in the dressing-room receiving attention for exhaustion and three others had collapsed on the field.

The game was played in appalling weather with driving rain and heavy squalls. In the first half Alton had the wind behind them. After leading 2-0 they fought hard to keep Dorchester out.

But their right full-back was the first to collapse under the strain and was carried off the field. At half-time Dorchester led 3-2. Dorchester players were taking the field for the second half when a broadcast appeal was made for a doctor to go to the Alton dressing room.

Five minutes later eight Alton men came out, but play went on for only seven minutes. Ransom, the other full-back, headed out a certain goal and then, dropped to the ground. Soon afterwards two more players collapsed and Mr. W.N. Holman, the referee, abandoned the game.

(November 3)

LEAGUE TABLES TO DATE

DIVISION I Goals

	P	W	D	L	F	A	Pts
Sunderland	37	19	10	8	73	52	48
Manchester U	38	17	13	8	65	40	47
Liverpool	38	17	13	8	60	47	47
Blackpool	36	17	12	7	45	29	46
Portsmouth	37	18	9	10	64	34	45
W'hampton W	36	16	12	8	59	44	44
Newcastle Utd	37	15	12	10	65	48	42
Arsenal	37	15	11	11	62	48	41
Middlesboro	37	17	6	14	51	44	40
Derby County	37	15	9	13	60	56	39
Aston Villa	37	14	10	13	54	52	38
Chelsea	37	12	14	11	56	57	38
Burnley	38	13	12	13	34	37	38
Fulham	37	10	13	14	39	46	33
West Brom A	37	11	10	16	44	53	32
Huddersfield T	38	12	8	18	45	68	32
Bolton Wdrs	37	9	13	15	42	48	31
Stoke City	37	10	11	16	41	61	31
Everton	37	-8	13	16	35	58	29
Charlton Ath	38	11	5	22	48	62	27
Birmingham C	37	7	11	19	28	57	35
Manchester C	36	6	11	19	29	58	23

DIVISION II Goals

	P	W	D	L	F	A	Pts
Tottenham H	37	27	6	4	79	29	60
Sheffield Utd	38	16	14	8	59	46	46
Sheffield Wed	36	16	13	7	59	44	45
Southampton	36	15	12	9	53	42	42
Hull City	37	16	9	12	61	63	41
Leeds Utd	37	14	12	11	45	39	40
Brentford	38	14	12	12	40	44	40
Preston NE	38	15	9	14	31	47	39
Swansea Town	37	14	9	14	48	43	37
Cardiff City	36	15	7	14	37	37	37
Leicester City	38	11	15	12	50	36	37
Bury	37	14	8	15	57	34	36
West Ham Utd	36	12	11	13	48	47	35
Grimsby Town	36	13	8	15	63	62	34
Chesterfield	38	13	8	17	37	43	34
Barnsley	37	11	11	15	57	61	33
Blackburn Rvrs	37	12	9	16	47	52	33
Luton Town	37	8	16	13	35	47	32
Coventry City	36	9	11	16	42	51	29
Bradford	37	9	11	17	47	66	29
Queen's P R	38	9	11	18	35	54	29
Plymouth Arg	37	6	14	17	38	59	26

(April 10)

LOCKE SHOULD WIN OPEN AGAIN

CHAMPIONSHIP STARTS TO-DAY

From Leonard Crawley

TROON, Sunday.

To-morrow and on Tuesday a large field of rather more than 240 golfers set out to qualify for' the Open Golf Championship over the Old Troon and Loch-green courses here. After a round on each the first hundred will play for the championship over Old Troon on Wednesday, Thursday and Friday.

It is 27 years since the Open was last played here, and then Arthur Havers won a notable victory from the mighty Walter Hagen who chased him to the 72nd hole.

It was in that championship too that little Gene Sarazen, destined to become one of America's greatest players, failed to qualify in a violent storm of wind and rain. Everyone will be sorry to hear that this ever-popular figure has been kept at home by urgent business and will not be here to erase the memory of the most humiliating experience of his distinguished career.

Troon, 6,500 yards in length, is one of the finest seaside courses in the land. Perhaps on a calm day it lacks the big second shots of Hoylake and Carnoustie, but with the small and closely guarded greens and heavy rough accuracy is essential.

LOCKE A GREAT PUTTER

After a prolonged drought with only some 10 hours', rain in the last two months the fairways are in poor shape, and we must expect lots of hard luck stories of bad lies during the coming week, but the putting greens are in first-class order.

Taking the field as a whole, it would appear to lack the quality of years gone by since at the moment one cannot see more than a handful of players with a chance of winning. Bobby Locke, of South Africa, the holder will start one of the hottest favourites for any Championship that I can remember.

His golf in the last two months has been magnificent and he is as ever a great competitor. When Cotton was in his prime he was as near to being mechanically perfect as anyone that ever lived but there was always the question of his putting to worry his supporters.

Though Locke has never attained the mechanical perfection of Cotton between tee and green the Americans regard him day in and day out as one of the greatest putters of all time. It is therefore my opinion that he is going to win again this week.

In some ways I believe Roberto de Vincenzo of Argentina, a superb hitter of the ball, is possibly Locke's most dangerous rival. Though I have see him putt well he never inspires real confidence on the green, especially if he starts badly. His chances are entirely dependent on his putting touch in the next few days.

STRANAHAN AND McHALE

The two American amateurs, Stranahan and McHale, are highly accomplished golfers and Stranahan came mighty close to tieing with Daley at Hoylake three years ago. There is also Johnny Bulla, the American professional, a monumental figure of a man and a glorious hitter of the ball. He has already been second on two occasions in the British championship.

(July 3)

2,000 GREET BING CROSBY

GAY PRACTICE ROUND AT ST. ANDREWS

Bing Crosby, the American singer and film actor, yesterday played his first and only practice round at St. Andrews over the Eden course in preparation for the amateur golf championship, which begins to-day. He was followed by a crowd of 2,000.

Most of the spectators were young boys and girls. Many of them asked him to sign their autograph books; others tried to speak to him or even touch his clothing.

He wore a canary coloured pullover, a brown cardigan and over that a second maroon coloured pullover; and brown crocodile leather shoes. On his head was an unconventional knitted bonnet of white and black

Unaware of his plans, the authorities had provided no crowd control arrangements. His admirers crowded around him so closely that he had to clear a way for himself and his two partners to play from the first tee.

The partners were the two French entrants in the amateur championship—M. Baglieno and the Vicomte de St. Sauveur, husband of the British women's golf champion, who won the title last week at Newcastle, Co. Down.

WISECRACKS TO CROWD

Though hemmed in on all sides and scarcely able to take a step Bing Crosby remained cool and good natured. He chatted to the young people about their schools and kept everybody in good humour with his wisecracks.

Girls crowded and jostled one another to walk along beside the singer between shots. Some of the spectators had obviously never seen a golf course before and walked through carefully raked bunkers and over greens.

On one occasion when the Vicomte asked, "Shall I take wood?" Crosby replied, " Hit it with a whole tree." The atmosphere was one of gaiety.

Bing Crosby, to give the crowd their full measure of entertainment and golf, did a high-step dance before playing his last shot to the 18th. He laid the ball three yards from the pin, holing out in a birdie three.

A questioner asked him: "You don't think you are going to win?"

He replied: "Oh no. Not unless Mr. Wilson, my opponent, is a very bad golfer."

(May 22)

EMERGENCY AFTER FOOTBALL MATCH

NATIONS IN DISPUTE

From Our Own Correspondent

NEW YORK, Friday.

Diplomatic relations between the two Central American republics of Guatemala and Salvador have almost reached breaking-point, according to reports reaching here, as a result of tension caused by a football match between the two countries. The match ended in a fight which police stopped with firehoses.

In an anti-Guatemalan riot shortly afterwards in San Salvador, capital of Salvador, two persons were killed. The Finance Minister of Guatemala has now asked the Guatemalan Congress for immediate action on a Bill to facilitate the repatriation of all Salvador subjects, describing the problem as a "national emergency."

(May 25)

ENGLAND OUT FOR 151 RUNS ON TRUE WICKET

Memorable Bowling by Ramadhin

By E. W. Swanton

LORD'S, Monday.

THERE have been some sad days to describe in these last few years for those who tell the story of England's performances in Test matches. Only one more utterly dark and sinister than to-day comes to mind. It was the last at Leeds two summers ago, when Australia, by a weary combination of English limitations, snatched victory out of the jaws of defeat by making 404 in the fourth innings on a dusty, helpful wicket.

England were bowled out to-day at Lord's by West Indies on a wicket that was true and blameless, for 151, which left them 175 behind. With more than three days to go, West Indies took the clearest possible course in batting again and, by the close, the first pair had put their side in a position all but impregnable by increasing the lead to 220.

The first name to be mentioned must be that of Ramadhin. Whatever the future holds for this lithe, agile little man he may never have Test batsmen at his mercy so completely as he had in to-day's excellent spell of spin bowling.

England's first wicket fell at quarter past one with the score at 62. When the ninth man was out at quarter to five they had struggled by methods that were a strain and embarrassment to watch to 122, and Ramadhin in 33.3 overs had taken five for 34.

His analysis suffered somewhat at this unexpected juncture for Wardle did what many have been doing in impotent anguish with their umbrellas and walking sticks. He hit out, sometimes agriculturally, but often with orthodox, handsome strokes.

WENT DOWN PITCH

He even took a step or two out of his ground to hit the ball on the half-volley. But what came naturally to a bowler with little to lose was not to be achieved so easily by the batsman who came in to disturb the moral balance against an attack that was already very much on top.

Once again it is the batting that has failed, but the deeper cause is the generality of county bowling which has not the solid foundation of good length to keep the best batsmen tightly attuned.

Hutton, after a decently-composed start and a partnership of 62 with Washbrook that seemed as though it might build up to something massive, was stumped from a wide ball that he seemed to decide to chase before it was out of Valentine's hand. There was, of course, no Compton and Edrich, for all his many virtues, is not a substitute.

When Doggart arrived at No. 4, Washbrook having been drawn out by Ramadhin, he had to confront an attack that had settled into a steady rhythm of maidens, each more ominous than the last, with four or five fielders almost on the bat. Ramadhin indeed bowled 10 maidens in a row, most of them to Edrich, who plainly did not know which way the spin was going to work.

After Doggart had chosen the wrong ball to sweep, Parkhouse arrived into an environment even more overwhelming. He played quite nicely for a quarter of an hour and then thinking he saw a loose ball at last, hooked, head in the air, and was dreadfully bowled.

Edrich gave a stumping chance off Ramadhin that Walcott missed, but was shortly caught from a leg-break that Ramadhin turned up the hill, having been pinned down to only four scoring strokes in an hour an a half.

Evans, the Centurian of Old Trafford, hit two fours off Ramadhin and was then bowled off his pads by a short ball that he aimed to hook. Valentine's part at the nursery end had been less spectacular than Ramadhin's, though he kept a perfectly steady length and turned the ball slightly down the hill.

But now Yardley, after he had watched Jenkins toiling desperately for a while and had made a good punch or two, was bowled by a ball from Valentine that came with his arm. There was now no real prospect of a prolonged challenge, but at last came Wardle's spell of hard hitting which needed Jones and Worrell with the new ball to cut short.

(June 27)

The Scoreboard

WEST INDIES-First Innings

A.F.Rae, c & b Jenkin	106
J.B.Stollmeyer, lbw,b Wardle	20
F.M.Worrell, b Bedser	52
E. Weekes, b Bedser	63
C.L.Walcott, st Evans, b Jenkins	14
G.E.Gomez, st Evans, b Jenkins	1
R.J.Christiani, b Bedser	33
J.D.Goddard, b, Wardle	14
P.E.Jones, c Evans, b Jenkins	0
S.Ramadhin, not out	1
A.Valentine, c Hutton, b Jenkins	5
Extras (b 10, lb 5, w1, nb 1)	17
Total	**326**

Fall of wickets: 1-37, 2-128, 3-233, 4-262, 5-273, 6-274, 7-320, 8-320, 9-320.

BOWLING: Bedser 40-14-60-3; Edrich: 16-4-30-0; Jenkins: 35.2-6-116-5; Wardle 17-6-46-2; Berry: 19-7-45-0; Yardley: 4-1-12-0

Second Innings

A.F. Rae, not out	16
J.B.Stollmeyer, not out	29
Total (no wkt.)	**45**

Bowling: (to date): Bedser: 10-2-16-0; Edrich: 5-2-8-0; Jenkins: 9-4-17-0; Wardle: 5-2-4-0

ENGLAND -First Innings

Hutton, st Walcott, b Valentine	35
Washbrook, st Walcott, b Ramadhin	36
W.J.Edrich, c Walcott, b Ramadhin	8
G.H.G.Doggart, lbw, b Ramadhin	0
Parkhouse, b Valentine	0
N.W.D.Yardley, b Valentine	16
Evans, b Ramadhin	8
Jenkins, (R.O.), c Walcott, b Valentine	4
Wardle, not out	33
Bedser, (A.V.), b Ramadhin	5
Berry (R), c Goddard, b Jones	2
Extras (b 2, lb 1, w1)	4
Total	**151**

Fall of Wickets: 1-62, 2-74, 3-74, 4-75, 5-86, 6-102, 7-110, 8-113, 9-122.

Bowling: Jones 8.4-2-13-1; Worrell 10-4-20-0; Valentine: 45-28-48-4; Ramadhin: 43-27-66-5.

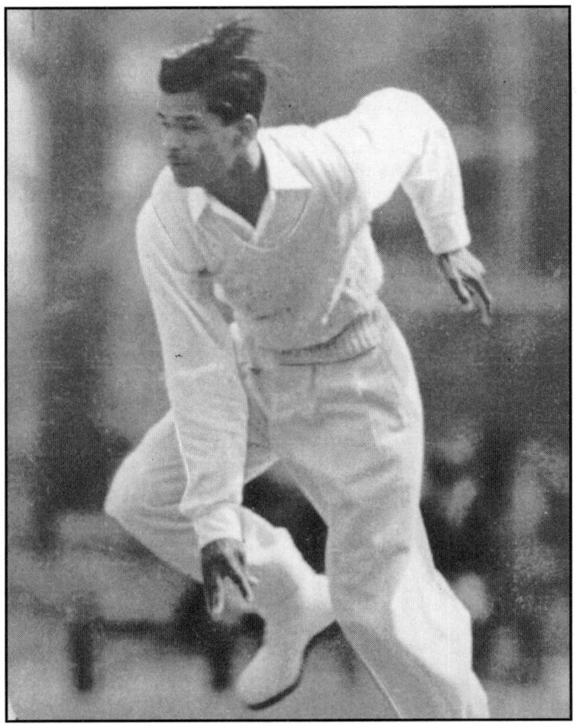

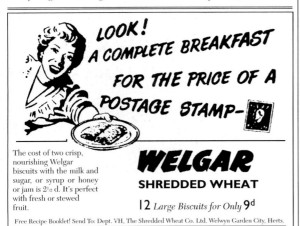

RAMADHIN, WRECKER-IN-CHIEF

<u>*Empire Games*</u>

EYRE BEATEN ON RUN IN IN GAMES MILE

LEWIS SECOND IN 440 YARDS

AUCKLAND, N.Z., Saturday.

Leslie Lewis, of England, finished second in the Empire Games 440 yards final, which was won as expected by E. W. Carr, of Australia here to-day.

Carr's time of 47.9sec equalled the Games record made by W. Roberts, of England, in 1938. Lewis returned 48 sec and Derek Pugh, the other English finalist, was fourth.

With his first throw Duncan Clark, of Scotland, broke the Games hammer record with a throw of 163ft 2in.

Another capacity crowd of 40,000 packed the Eden Park ground for the final day's track and field events. They saw 17 competitors start out from the stadium on the marathon run this afternoon.

Tom Richards, of Wales, the Olympic runner-up, wore a sun hat. They ran half a lap of the track before leaving the stadium on this first stage of the 26 miles 385 yards gruelling course.

Three New Zealanders, L. Fox, W. Bromley and J. Clark were first out with Jack Holden, England's hope, and his Welsh rival in the rear of the field.

The runners had covered only half a mile when a tropical shower drenched them to the skin. The rain was so severe that track events temporarily had to be abandoned.

When running was possible again Len Eyre, Yorkshire winner of the Three Miles, was second in the Mile. He led until 12 yards from the finish, where he was caught by Bill Parnell, of Canada, who won by four yards in 4min 11.0sec. Eyre's time was 4min 11.8 sec. Another Englishmen, Tom White (Lincoln Wellington A.C.), was fourth.

After Australia's almost complete eclipse of the opposition in Thursday's athletics it was good to see Britain come into her own yesterday by winning 15 medals—nine of them gold, in the swimming, diving, boxing and fencing events.

ENGLAND'S SEVEN FIRSTS

Seven first places were gained by England—three boxing, two fencing and two swimming,—and two, both in the boxing, by Scotland. England are now runners-up to Australia in the number of gold medals won with a total of 16 against Australia's 27.

In pouring rain, which continued all day, Miss Edna Child, of Middlesex, followed up her victory in Wednesday's springboard diving by winning the high diving and then announcing her intention to retire from big-time competition.

" I am getting too old for this sport," she said. "I don't think I will try for the Olympics in 1952." She is England's first double gold medallist and represented Britain in the 1936 Olympics in Berlin.

(February 11)

MAJESTIC LAP BY BANNISTER

OXFORD SPORTS TRIUMPH

By A Special Correspondent

Surprises, never absent from the University athletics match, were in unusual abundance at the White City on Saturday, when Oxford defeated Cambridge by 7 points to 50.

A strong wind dead against them severely handicapped the sprinters and precluded any chances they had of setting up records, but records for the meeting were established in the mile and the pole vault, both going to Oxford.

Bannister's mile was, in fact, the highlight of the afternoon. In gaining his fourth victory in successive years, he was content at first to allow Morgan, his team-mate, to set a good but comfortable pace and not until the last lap did Bannister appear to be at all concerned with running really fast. Then he lengthened out and strode round majestically for a 58.2 sec final lap to win as he liked in 4 min 14.8 sec, 1.4 sec better than the record which he established 12 months ago.

The wide margin of Oxford's success was based on the field events, where they had a clear superiority and where they gained their second record, Burger, of South Africa, pole vaulting 13 ft.

(March 20)

ENGLAND EIGHT WELL BEATEN BY AUSTRALIA

AUCKLAND, N.Z., Monday.

England's crew, short of practice in their own shell through the mislaying of their outriggers, were well beaten in the Eights, the first of five events comprising the Empire Games regatta which was begun on Lake Karapiro here to-day.

Captained by R. D. Burnell in the No. 4 thwart, they finished third and last, three lengths behind New Zealand, who in a tremendously close finish were beaten by a foot by Australia.

Conditions were ideal when the crews took the water, with England in the outside station. With only a gentle breeze blowing dead across the course positions made little difference, and Australia, on the inside, got away to a good start and were half a length in front after a little over half a mile had been covered.

At the mile New Zealand put in a tremendous burst to draw level, but the Australian stroke called for a fresh effort which carried his crew into a canvas lead. For the final quarter the crews rowed stroke for stroke with never more than a canvas in it while England battled hard, three lengths in the rear.

In an all-out finish Australia just held on to win a great race by mere inches. The England crew finished tired, but none was in a state of collapse. Jack Beresford, their coach, said afterwards, " Under the circumstances they rowed very well."

(February 6)

LANCASHIRE WIN EPIC GAME AGAINST YORKSHIRE

Yardley's Gallant Bid Just Fails

From E. W. Swanton

SHEFFIELD, Tuesday.

Lancashire beat Yorkshire here this afternoon by 14 runs after a day of agonising excitement which, many a year from now, will set tingling the blood of all those – and there were some 16,000 of us – who were lucky enough to be present at Bramall-lane.

After the Yorkshire innings this afternoon had gone through many palpitating changes of fortune, Wardle, at number nine, came in to join his captain Yardley, with only 125 on the board of the 182

The wicket was spasmodically spiteful still, though scarcely the venomous treacherous thing on which Lancashire had been bowled out for 117 in the morning.

The odds seemed long, but Yardley was playing most admirably, and whatever impious critics might say of certain technical limitations on faster wickets, he is ,as he has always been, an excellent batsman when the turf is taking the spin. No one who saw his partnership with Hammond on that evil day at Brisbane in the first test in 1946 could doubt that.

The mood of the whole day's cricket had been to "get at him before he gets at you." Only Hutton with his superb method had been above and beyond the necessity of chancing his arm. Wardle was the last man to close up at such a moment, and in hardly more than a quarter of an hour 27 more came for the eight-wicket, mostly runs truly made against bowling that remained steady and fielding that took inspiration from the occasion.

This was a moment, almost the only one in the match, when Yorkshire seemed really on top. And then, when another four or two would have counted beyond price, Wardle drove Berry hard off the meat of the bat straight back.

POETIC JUSTICE

Berry clung safely to the ball, and in that there was poetic justice since the game from its beginning had developed largely into a duel between these two left - arm bowlers and the Lancastrian had proved a clear and worthy winner.

With 30 needed Brennan took Wardle's place and began with a fine snick for four past the wicket-keeper to a roar that must have been heard far away in the heart of the city.

Yardley now monopolised the situation, drawing everything off his stumps with an easy dexterity that made it all look almost safe. His 50 arrived to a crescendo of cheering and then Brennan swung at an off-break and Wharton held a good, hard hit chest-high at short mid-wicket.

Now it was simply Yardley or no one. He declined single runs from each of the first three balls of Berry's next over, tried for the last time to flick the fourth of his wicket round the corner and so get the next over, and the ball, lifting, lobbed gently in the air to within reach of any of three men round the bat.

Thus it ended and Lancashire had beaten their ancient enemies for the first time since on this same ground Iddon's fine bowling had won the day 13 years before.

Since the war all the eight matches before this had been drawn, but in the late thirties Yorkshire had usually won with conclusive emphasis, and in recent times Lancashire has a long leeway to make up.

TRAGEDY FOR YORKSHIRE

This has not been a happy match for young Close, but he had his brief moments of glory, pulling his first ball, from outside the off stump, for a thrilling six to square-leg, sending Berry whistling over extra cover to the boundary, and giving his captain cause to hope that the improbable might after all be brought to pass.

The manner of his end was a tragedy for Yorkshire. Yardley declined a youthfully optimistic call for a second run. Close turned, and could no doubt have made his ground, but slipped up badly (was he properly studded?) and a quick pick up by Berry, followed by the slickest of returns, ran him out.

In a match of this kind there are always many "might-have-beens," and it seems hard after such a struggle that either side should have to lose, but tolerably composed afterthoughts emphasise that justice was certainly done in the result.

(May 31)

No. 7531 ACROSS

1 Common subject for a picture, not yet extinct (5,4)
9 Does this shrub tend to clean the land it grows on? (5)
10 Fifty-one act rage for bone (9)
11 "That —— and perfidious bark built in th'eclipse" (Milton) (5)
12 Though no lever it raises a lot (5)
14 It's in the Turnham Green/Acton district (5)
16 Business establishment in a strong position (4)
19 Without brain, or merely prosaic? (7)
21 Suitable vegetable at a B.M.A. dinner? (5)
22 "And like another —– fired another Troy" (Dryden) (5)
23 A change for the caterer (7)
24 " Under an alien sky comfort it is to say, 'Of no mean —— am I.'" (Kipling) (4)
25 A preliminary to the destruction of Troy (5)
27 Expression of regret for the shortage (5)
30 It takes many to make up this game of chance (5)
32 Like the catch dropped by the fielder, no longer in his control (3,2,4)
33 Describes the Thames up to Teddington (5)
34 Part of the Chassis for one's descendants (9)

DOWN

2 Business exchange (5)
3 One flower abroad but much with us (5)
4 Musical sound upset in 1 ac. (4)
5 Dickensian villain (5)
6 A sailor astern is astern (5)
7 But these heights must be higher than this (9)
8 The utensils to fulfil a promise (9)
13 The bad old Baron of old who lived in it should have had a pull over his neighbours (5)
14 Authorise (to enter the House of Lords?) (7)
15 It is mean to state how old one is ! (7)
17 Ponder how to gamble (9)
18 There's nothing new or strange in this saying (9)
20 Land of an early graduate (5)
25 One of Napoleon's Marshals (5)
26 Doesn't necessarily describe the bark of a husky (5)
28 Composer of music with a four down (5)
29 He has a stall of his own (5)
31 When this is up it is an even chance (4)

(January 2)

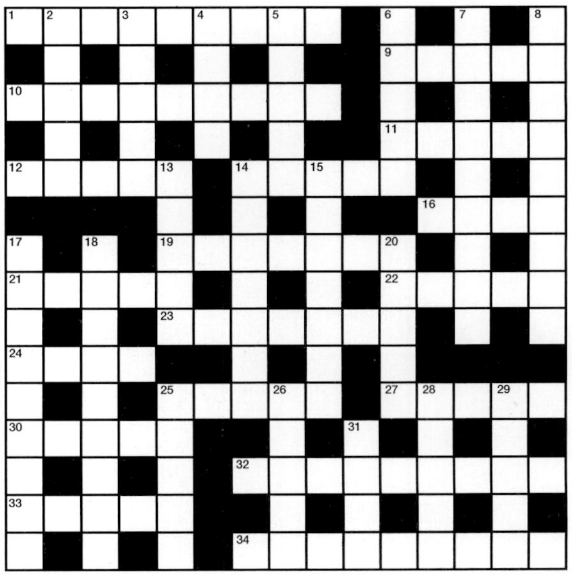

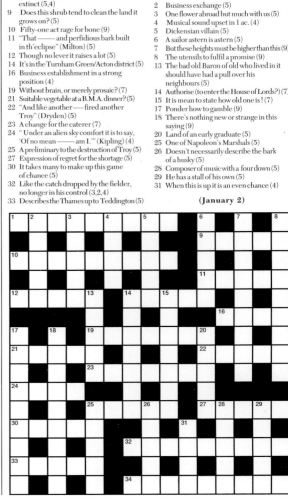

1951

The Korean War dragged on and became more desperate as the Chinese forces came to the aid of the North Koreans, though by July the long process of peace negotiations was begun. General MacArthur's desire to take the war into China led to his surprising dismissal by President Truman. The "Glorious Glosters" made their brave and desperate four-day stand against overwhelming forces on the Imjin River.

In Britain, the Labour Government was forced to cut the meat ration to its lowest level ever, the equivalent of 4 ozs of steak per person per week. The introduction by Hugh Gaitskell in the Budget of payments for medicine, dental treatment and for spectacles, previously provided free by the National Health Service, caused Aneurin Bevan, the Minister of Health, and others, including the future Prime Minister, Harold Wilson, to resign from the Government. The announcement that the Government had been forced to write off a loss of £36 million after the failure of a scheme to grow groundnuts in Africa also damaged its reputation. In the autumn a General Election saw the defeat of the Labour Government and the re-installation of Winston Churchill as Prime Minister.

Despite the continuance of austerity, King George VI opened the gaudy splendours of the Festival of Britain which served as a showcase for post-war British achievement, its new architects showing their inventiveness in the Dome of Discovery and the seemingly unsupported pillar of light, the Skylon, which dominated the London skyline at night. The Festival Gardens at Battersea Park provided London with a fun-fair. The design for the new Coventry Cathedral drawn up by Basil Spence was the centre of controversy.

The whole Western World was rocked by the disappearance of two British diplomats, Guy Burgess and Donald Maclean, who eventually turned up in Moscow and who proved to have been Soviet agents for many years, recruited when they were undergraduates at Cambridge. In the United States, Julius and Ethel Rosenburg were sentenced to death for passing on nuclear secrets to the Russians.

Political assassins caused the deaths of King Abdullah of Jordan and Liaquat Ali Khan of Pakistan. Ernest Bevin, veteran Trades Union leader, Minister of Labour in Churchill's war-time coalition government and foreign secretary in the post-war Labour administration died, in the fortress where he had been confined since the end of the war, as did, Marshal Pétain, the head of the French Government which collaborated with the Germans.

Oxford sank within yards of the start of the university boat race and lost the re-run by a record margin. Randolph Turpin briefly became a world boxing champion and Len Hutton scored his hundredth hundred in first-class cricket.

The illness of King George VI led to Princess Elizabeth, the Colonel of the Grenadier Guards, riding at the head of his troops and taking the salute on his behalf at the ceremony of Trooping the Colour.

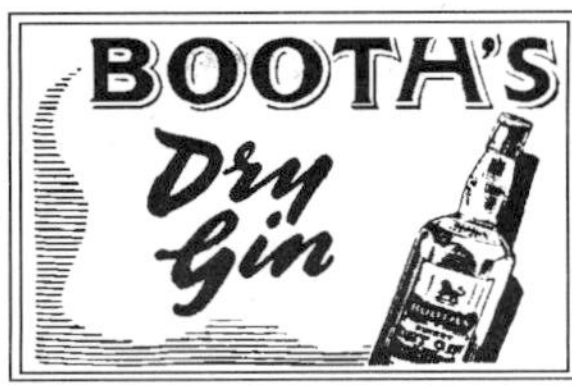

The Daily Telegraph

No. 29,933 LONDON, JUNE 9, 1951 and Morning Post Printed in LONDON and MANCHESTER Price 2d.

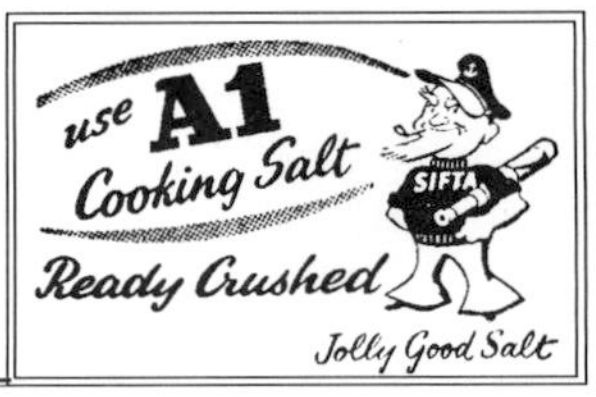

KOREA VISIT BY GEN. MARSHALL

'STALEMATE IS NOT INEVITABLE'

MORE NATIONS ARE TO SEND TROOPS FOR ALLIED ARMY

From Eric Downton,
Daily Telegraph Special Correspondent

U.N. COMMAND H.Q., TOKYO, Saturday Morning.

Gen. Marshall, the United States Defence Secretary, arrived in Tokyo last night after a day's tour of the Korean front, accompanied by Gen. Ridgway, Allied Supreme Commander in the Far East. He declared: "A stalemate in Korea is not inevitable."

After an 8,000-mile flight from America, the Defence Secretary has just held a 3 ½ -hour conference with Allied Commanders just behind the United Nations lines. The visit, which was a closely kept secret, caused a wave of speculation here on the possibility of it being connected with truce negotiations. This he categorically denied.

Asked if he had brought a new directive to Gen. Ridgway, he replied flatly, "I did not." It is recalled, however, that Gen. Collins, the American Army Chief of Staff, told the Senate last month that "definite new directive" for the Korean campaign was being developed.

"The Army," Gen. Marshall said, "is going to be handled in the most effective way. The 38th parallel is merely a figure of speech." The United Nations advance was "a question of the military deployment of forces." More United Nations members would contribute fresh troops to the Allied effort, he added.

The General insisted his Korea trip was "a purely military mission" to see the Eighth Army and to congratulate its leaders. They had achieved a "military classic" in defeating the Communist offensive.

Questioned on the possibilities of a cease-fire, he answered: "I really do not know. I think you ought to ask Chou En-lai and Mao Tse-tung."

TALKS IN TENT

Tight Security Measures

A special airstrip was prepared near a divisional command post to enable Gen. Marshall's plane to land. The post, close to the 38th parallel, is within sound of the front-line guns.

All United Nations commanders had been summoned to meet the Defence Secretary. Alighting from his military plane, which was the one used by Gen. MacArthur under the name "Bataan", he drove at once to a camouflaged tent for the secret conference.

In addition to Gen. Ridgway, he was accompanied by a personal doctor. Gen. Marshall, who is 70, showed signs of fatigue from his hurried flight.

Stringent security precautions were taken. The whole area had been roped off, and military police prevented war correspondents approaching the tent closer than 100 yards. On the way from the conference Gen. Marshall waved to cameramen and reporters, but he did not stop.

COMMANDERS CALLED

British at Conference

Other aircraft and Jeeps arrived with senior officers to join in the talks. With the Defence Secretary were Gen. Ridgway and Gen. Van Fleet, Eighth Army Commander. The United Nations Commanders included three British Commonwealth brigadiers.

These were: Brig. Brodie, British 29th brigade; Brig. Taylor, British 28th brigade; and Brig. Ruckingham, Canadian 25th brigade. Commanders of the Turkish, Greek, Siamese and Philippine contingents, and American divisional and corps commanders in the area were also assembled.

On his quick tour of the Eighth Army positions, Gen. Marshall conferred with Gen. Van Fleet, visited the headquarters of the First, Ninth and Tenth Corps and of the American First Cavalry Division.

In conversation with officers, he recalled that the last time that he was in Korea was during the Russo-Japanese war in 1904. Then he was an American observer at the battles of the Yalu river and in Manchuria.

U.N. DICUSSING PEACE PLAN, SAYS M. LIE

From Our Own Correspondent

NEW YORK, Friday.

M. Lie, United Nations Secretary-General, said to-day that member states were consulting about the next steps to be taken towards achieving peace in Korea. He was addressing a luncheon given by United Nations correspondents.

He had been "very pleased" he observed, with the response from delegates and many other sources to his proposal to end the conflict around the 38th parallel.

"But, of course, a cease-fire cannot be brought about unilaterally. We do not know what is in the minds of the North-Koreans and their supporters. We do not yet know whether they would welcome or reject a cease-fire.

M. Lie recalled that in Ottawa last week he said that if a cease-fire could be arranged approximately along the 38th parallel, the main purpose of the relevant Security Council resolutions would have been fulfilled, "provided that it was followed by negotiations leading to the restoration of peace and security.

"We must never forget that the objective of the United Nations forces in Korea is to win something much more important than a war. It is to win a collective security against future wars."

"In these circumstances the question arises as to what further steps, if any, the United Nations might take now towards bringing the fighting to an end.

"This is, of course, a matter for the member Governments to decide. I know they are consulting about the situation and I have had a number of talks with delegates about it, too."

13 HOURS' SUN ON COAST

DRY AGAIN TO-DAY

By Our Weather Correspondent

Some rain fell again yesterday in the Channel Islands and from South Cornwall to the Scilly Isles. In other parts of the British Isles it was dry, with sunshine in many areas.

At several south coast resorts and in western districts there were more than 13 hours of sunshine. Littlehampton had 15.3 hours, Ross-on-Wye 15.1 and Worthing 15.

Dry weather will continue to-day and tomorrow with sunshine in many districts.

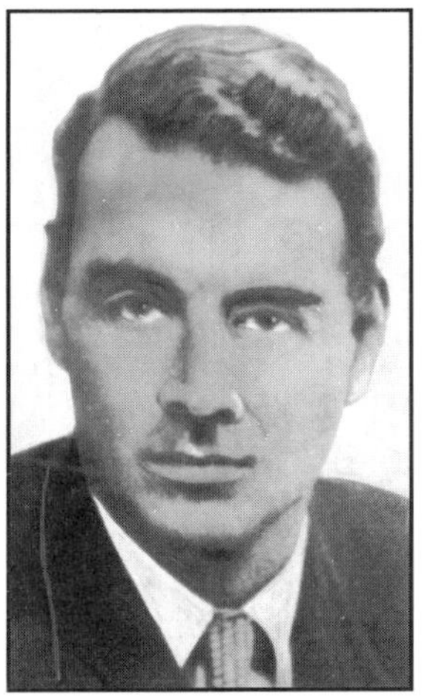

MR. GUY BURGESS

£1M. PLAN FOR GUY'S HOSPITAL

MINISTRY SANCTION FOR REBUILDING

A scheme to spend £1 million on rebuilding a large part of Guy's Hospital, London Bridge, was announced by Mr. Marquand, Minister of Health, at a dinner in London attended by governors of Guy's and members of the medical staff.

Guy's is the first hospital of its kind to be given permission to rebuild on so large a scale. Half the cost is understood to be coming from funds built up by donations from Lord Nuffield.

Plans include new premises and wards on the site of the wing destroyed by bombs in the war. Attacks reduced it to a 300-bed hospital.

Mr. W. D. Doherty, superintendent of Guy's, last night said the Ministry's sanction for them to go ahead with the rebuilding was a great relief. Now there were 575 beds in Guy's as against 620 before the war. They were aiming at an 800-bed hospital—the maximum allowed by the Ministry.

LONG-TERM POLICY

"The rebuilding of the whole of Guy's is a long-term policy going over possibly 50 years from now."

They now had permission to put up one block of the new building, in which it was hoped to house 350 beds.

"The two main buildings of the hospital are Guy's House and Hunt's House. We have long been greatly concerned about Guy's House. It had been thought that it would be necessary to pull Guy's House down, as the house has been in use constantly since 1724, when it was erected."

War damage to Hunt's House, built in 1851, was now being repaired.

"We are very anxious to keep the Guy's building for reasons of affection, sentiment and tradition. It is a feature on the South Bank and one of the few examples of 18th-century architecture there.

"The changes in the hospital will not in any way alter the character of Guy's as a great general hospital with an important medical teaching school."

FESTIVAL VISITORS

Attendance at the South Bank Exhibition yesterday totalled 51,118, compared with 54,258 on Thursday. A the Battersea Pleasure Gardens and Funfair visitors totalled 43,031 compared with 40,268 on Thursday. The Fun-fair had its millionth visitor yesterday, Mrs. M. Whiteman, of Routh-road, Wandsworth.

POLICE STOP CARS

Police stopped motorists in Baldock, Herts, early to-day and asked them. "Were you on this road between 11.30 p.m. and 12.30 a.m. on the night of June 6 to 7?" The inquiry concerned a complaint that an attack had been made on a woman travelling in a car.

JETS CRASH: FOUR DIE

From Our Own Correspondent

NEW YORK, Friday.

At least four pilots of eight jet fighters which crashed during a thunderstorm in Indiana to-day were killed, according to Richmond, Indiana, police. The planes were part of a formation of 35. Two pilots are known to have parachuted to safety.

MEDITERRANEAN CLUE TO MISSING BRITONS

GOING ON 'LONG HOLIDAY,' SAID TELEGRAM

Daily Telegraph Reporter

One of three telegrams received in England from the two missing Foreign Office officials provided last night the first definite indication of the nature of their disappearance on May 25. It spoke of a " Mediterranean holiday."

The telegram was sent in the name of Mr. Guy Burgess, and was received on Thursday by his mother, Mrs. J. R. Bassett, wife of Lt.-Col. Bassett, of Arlington street, Piccadilly. The text released by the Foreign Office, said:

Terribly sorry for my silence. Am embarking on a long Mediterranean holiday. Do forgive. GUY.

The French counter-espionage service released in Paris yesterday the text of two telegrams supposedly sent by Mr. Donald Maclean, the other missing man, to his wife and mother, Lady Maclean.

PARIS MESSAGES

"Do Not Worry"

They were handed in at the general post office in the Rue du Louvre, Paris, on Wednesday night, possibly by a woman. The one to his wife read:

Had to leave unexpectedly possibly. Sorry. Darling I love you. Please do not stop loving me- Donald

No explanation was given for the use of the word "possibly." To his mother the message was:

I am quite all right- Do not worry. Love to all, Maclean.

The mystery surrounding the messages was increased by the manner of their release. The text of the two messages apparently from Mr. Maclean was not released by the Foreign Office, but in Paris. The Foreign Office thereupon released the text of the telegram purporting to come from Mr. Burgess. There were grounds in London last night for thinking that the Burgess message was sent from Rome. The Foreign Office would not confirm this early this morning, apparently on security grounds, and Italian police said they had received no request to look out for the men.

TELEGRAM "CENSORED"

Only Part Released

It was learned in Paris last night that the text released there of the telegram sent to Mr. Maclean's wife is an abbreviated version. The full text contained 82 words. The French authorities, however, declined to explain why they omitted the missing words.

Sûreté Nationale inspectors believe that neither the telegram sent to Mr. Maclean's wife nor that sent to his mother were written by Mr. Maclean. They say that the 82-word telegram contained grammatical errors which an Englishman would not make.

They are trying to trace a " third man" believed to be an Englishman resident in Paris, whom Mr. Maclean, but not Mr. Burgess, is understood to have met twice in Paris last week-end.

Supt. L. E. Wilkinson of the Special Branch, Scotland Yard, left for France yesterday. It is believed he will take part in the inquiries into the missing men.

TWO MEN MAY NOW BE OUT OF FRANCE

From Our Special Correspondent

PARIS, Friday.

Late to-night high French police officials expressed the fear that Mr. Maclean and Mr. Burgess, the two missing British diplomats, might already have crossed the French frontier. They are, however, still continuing their search.

But they make no secret of the fact that their task would have been easier if they had been informed earlier by the British authorities of the two men's disappearance. They say that it was eight days after the men disappeared before they were informed. The belief here is that the telegrams received in England, purporting to come from the missing men, were sent by a woman who was a friend of Mr. Maclean in Egypt when he was a member of the Cairo Embassy.

FRIENDS IN CAIRO

Mr. Maclean was a friend of Sir Walter Smart and Lady Smart. Sir Walter for many years was Oriental Secretary to the British Embassy in Cairo.

Lady Smart has a villa at Pacy- sur-Eure, between Paris and Deauville. Mr. Maclean has frequently stayed at the villa, often by himself, but he was not there this afternoon.

The housekeeper at Lady Smart's house at Pacy-sur-Eure said that neither Mr. Maclean not Mr. Burgess had been to the house since their disappearance. "I remember Mr. Maclean well," she said. "If he had called here I should certainly have recognised him."

The proprietor of Pacy's riverside hotel said that he knew Mr. Maclean, but had not seen him recently. He added, however, that an Englishman had inquired for him at the hotel about a week ago.

"DRIVE FAST" ORDER

It was confirmed at the Sûreté to-day that the two men, after arriving at St. Malo, left by car for Rennes.

STAFF CHIEFS MEET

By A Diplomatic Correspondent

Gen. Bradley, Chairman of the United States Chiefs of Staff Committee, yesterday attended a meeting of the British Chiefs of Staff. Later he had a talk with Mr. Shinwell, Minister of Defence.

Gen. Bradley had lunch with Field-Marshal Sir William Slim, Chief of the Imperial General Staff.

CENSURE MOTION BY 70 M.P.S

MIDDLE EAST POLICY

Led by Brig. Fitzroy Maclean, Conservative M.P. for Lancaster, about 70 Conservative Back Bench M.P.s have tabled a censure motion on the Government for its handling of Middle East affairs. The motion reads:

"That this House regrets that the Government, by their lack of any firm or coherent policy in the Middle East during the past five years, and their failure to provide for its effective defence, have seriously increased the general risk of war and gravely endangered British interest throughout that area, notably in Persia.

"It deplores, in particular, the weakness shown by the Government in their dealings with Egypt over the Suez Canal; and urges them to take immediate steps to establish, after consultation with the Commonwealth, the United States and France, and in co-operation with the Governments of Greece and Turkey, an effective Middle Eastern defence system, designed to ensure the maintenance of peace in the area."

17,000 TONS OF FOOD HELD UP AT DOCKS

GROWING MENACE FROM STRIKE

MEAT CARGOES AT QUAYSIDE

By An Industrial Correspondent

Food supplies will be seriously affected if the unofficial strike of 1,403 London dock tally clerks is not settled within the next few days.

Last night, at the end of its fifth day, there was no sign of a break in the stoppage. More than 8,000 dockers and stevedores have been thrown idle, and the loading and discharging of nearly half the ships in the port have been stopped.

The number of ships idle yesterday increased to 87, compared with 79 on Thursday. Four were undermanned and 9 were working normally.

About 17,000 tons of food are held up. Work has stopped on three ships with cargoes of meat totalling 8,000 tons.

In addition, five ships, with 8,000 tons of raw sugar, are idle, and cargoes of pears, apples, butter, tinned fruit, dried fruit, rabbits and tea are held up. In all 16 food ships are affected.

A spokesman of the National Federation of Fruit and Potato Trades said that supplies of fruit to London Markets were dwindling. Prices were rising because of the strike.

The strike, which stared in the Royal Group on Monday, is in protest against the recruitment of a additional tally clerks by the London Dock Labour Board.

BOARD'S DENIAL

The men on strike have repeatedly claimed that the recruitment is a move by the employers to create a surplus of labour. The object, they say, is so that older men can be discharged and more shift work introduced for the younger men.

This was denied in a statement issued by the London Dock Labour Board yesterday. The Board proposes to increase the labour force in the port by 1,500 men, of whom 80 would be tally clerks.

A statement issued yesterday by the Transport and General Workers' Union, to which the majority of the men belong, called for an immediate resumption of work. It condemned those responsible for the strike for "reckless and irresponsible" action.

NOURSE MAY BE OUT OF TEST

THUMB TREATMENT

From E. W .Swanton

NOTTINGHAM, Friday.

A. D. Nourse, the South African cricket captain, who scored 208 against England in the first Test match at Trent Bridge to-day, will travel to Bristol tomorrow where the surgeon who inserted a metal pin into his fractured thumb will make a further inspection. Nourse's further part in the match is problematical.

He broke his thumb at Bristol three weeks ago. The injury was aggravated today.

His innings of 208, made in 9 hours, is the highest score by any South African in Tests against England. He was run out.

After declaring the South African innings closed at 483 for 9, Nourse did not field for the two overs during which England lost Ikin's wicket for four runs.

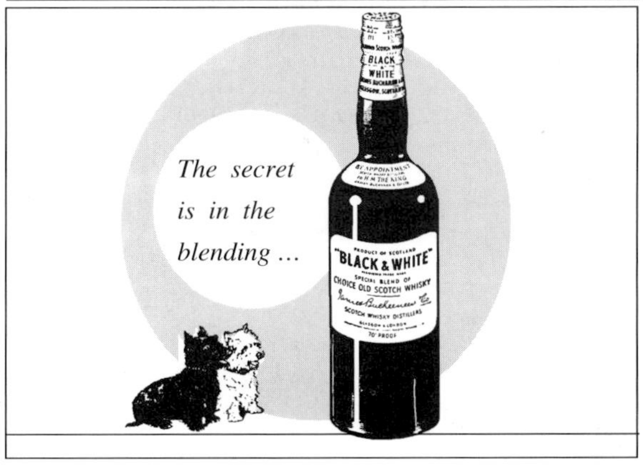

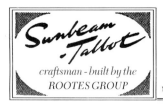

The Daily Telegraph
and Morning Post
No. 30,053 LONDON, OCTOBER 27, 1951
Printed in LONDON and MANCHESTER Price 2d.

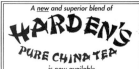

MR. CHURCHILL PRIME MINISTER

VISIT TO PALACE: MR. ATTLEE RESIGNS

CONSERVATIVE LEAD OF 18 OVER ALL

NAMES OF NEW CABINET EARLY NEXT WEEK

Mr. Attlee yesterday tendered his resignation as Prime Minister to the King, who received him at 5 p.m. The King then sent for Mr. Churchill and asked him to form a new Administration. Mr. Churchill accepted.

With results from 620 constituencies the Conservatives this morning had a lead of 18 over all other parties following Thursday's General Election Five results are still to be declared.[Full results to date are given in a special supplement with to-day's issue.]

Names of Ministers will be submitted to the King early next week. Mr. Churchill is expected to decide on the composition of his first peace-time Government during the week-end. The Conservative leaders are meeting to-day.

Mr. Attlee told the staff at Transport House last night: "I do not think there is any reason to dispute that our loss of seats has been due to the fact that, when it came to the point, more Liberals voted Conservative than Labour.

"Apart from that we would still be in office and I would still be Prime Minister, which I ceased to be a short time ago."

Mr. and Mrs. Attlee motored from 10, Downing Street to Chequers, where they proposed to stay until to-morrow evening.

The 620 results received so far include four unopposed returns and the aggregate votes cast were distributed as follows:

	1951	1950
Labour	**13,871,922**	**13,295,736**
Conservatives & Associates ...	**13,665,95**	**12,501,983**
Liberals	**710,934**	**2,621,489**
Others	**198,149**	**350,269**

Of the total, Labour obtained 48.8 per cent, Conservatives 48.1 per cent and Liberals 2.5 per cent. The total vote was 82.70 per cent of the electorate .

CONSERVATIVES LOSE ONLY ONE

The only seat lost by Conservatives was that of an Ulster Unionist to an Irish Socialist. They gained 24, including 21 from Socialists, and two from Liberals. The Liberals won one from Labour. Socialists captured two from the Liberals.

All members of the Front benches of both parties were returned. In addition to Mr. Hardman, Parliamentary Secretary, Ministry of Education, who lost his seat on Friday night, Mr. Crawley, Under-Secretary for Air, was defeated. He failed at Buckingham to a Conservative by 54 after a recount.

Mr. Churchill's majority at Woodford was slightly more than in 1950, and both his Independent and Communist opponents lost their deposits. Mr. Eden also increased his lead at Warwick.

Among the Socialist Ministers who were returned with smaller majorities were: Mr. Gaitskell at Leeds South, 1,000 down, Mr. Dalton at Bishop Auckland, 2,384 down, and Mr. Strachey at Dundee West, 1,395 down.

Sir Lynn Ungoed-Thomas, Solicitor-General, at North-East Leicester, increased his lead by 3,596 over the figure in the by-election in September last year.

LADY MEGAN LLOYD GEORGE OUT

Mr. Clement Davies, Parliamentary leader of the Liberal Party, easily retained Montgomery, but Lady Megan Lloyd George was defeated by 595 votes at Anglesey, which she had represented since 1929. The seat was captured by a Socialist in a three-cornered contest. Merioneth, another Liberal seat, also fell to Labour.

Lady Violet Bonham-Carter, who stood as a Liberal with Conservative support at Colne Valley, was beaten by Mr. Glenvil Hall, former Socialist Minister, by 2,189 votes. Another Liberal victim was Mr. Granville, member for Eye, Suffolk, since 1929. This was a Conservative gain.

All Mr. Bevan's supporters were returned. His wife, Mrs. Jennie Lee, held Cannock, although her majority was down by 1,000, and Mr. Driberg was returned for Maldon and Mr. Harold Davies for Leek, Staffs.

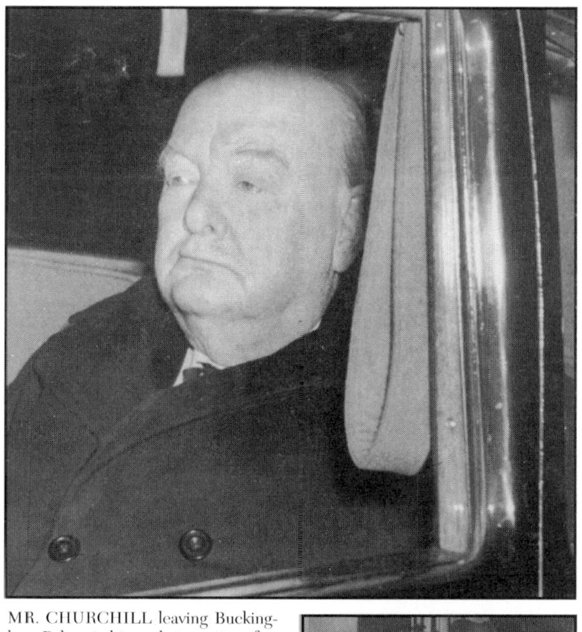

MR. CHURCHILL leaving Buckingham Palace in his car last evening after having had an audience with the King.

State of the Parties

The state of the parties last night with results announced by 620 of the 625 constituencies was:

	At Dissolution	NOW
Labour	315	293
Conservatives & Associates	299	319
Liberals	9	5
Irish Nationalists	2	2
Independent	0	1

DEFEAT WILL WIDEN LABOUR PARTY SPLIT

BEVANITE QUARREL

By Hugh Chevins
Daily Telegraph Industrial Correspondent

Bitter exchanges over their defeat at the polls and a resumption of the suspended quarrel between the orthodox Socialist leaders and the Bevanites will, it appears inevitable, mark the next meeting of the Labour party national executive committee.

The recriminations and the revival of the row, over which a make-believe front of unity was erected for electioneering purposes, are interlocked.

Whether the election was won or lost, incensed trade union members of the party executive determined, when they agreed to a truce a month ago, to have a later show-down with the Bevanites for the onslaught on them in the Tribune pamphlet "Going Our Way."

PAMPHLET ATTACK

The pamphlet appeared 24 hours after Mr. Attlee announced the date of the General Election. It was alleged that "most of the 12 trade union members of the national executive have been casting their votes against the wishes of the people who elected them."

Epithets of an unusually uncomradely character were hurled at the trade unionists. They included Mr. S. Watson, National Union of Mineworkers; Mr. W. T. Potter, National Union of Railwaymen; Mr. A. E. Tiffen, Transport and General Workers Union; and Capt. M. Hewitson, National Union of General and Municipal Workers.

It was only after much heartsearching that the trade unionists decided at a hurriedly called private meeting in Transport House to defer their reply.

They had persisted in the pamphlet, in their attacks on Mr. Gaitskell's Budget, and on the Government generally, for its "excessive defence programme" and for the Health Service charges on spectacles and dentures.

"NO REPENTANCE"

The Bevanites show no sign of repentance. Fortified by the success of his followers in the recent contest for places on the party executive and by the return of his associates in the General Election, Mr. Bevan is not likely to shrink from the fight.

The next meeting of the executive is due to be held late in November. A special meeting, however, may be called earlier.

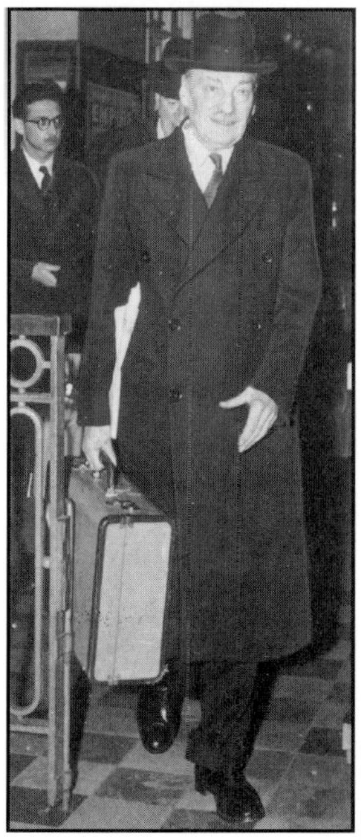

MR. ATTLEE RESIGNS.
Mr. Attlee on his way to the meeting of the Parliamentary party at the House of Commons, where he announced his resignation as Leader of the Labour party. He has held the office since October, 1935.

LIBERALS LOSE £9,900 DEPOSITS

NO INSURANCE

Daily Telegraph Reporter

The Liberals, in spite of their narrow front fight, have lost more deposits than the other parties combined. Of the 109 Liberal candidates only 43 can reclaim the £150 each put down.

The other 66 failed to secure the necessary eighth of the votes. Among them was Mr. Philip Fothergill, the party president.

Last year, the Liberals forfeited 311 deposits, involving £46,650. But, they were covered at Lloyd's for 183 fortfeits, so their actual loss was £19,200. This time Liberals were not insured and the loss was £9,900.

Three Conservatives lost their £150 this time. Other lost deposits included all 10 Communist candidates and I.L.P. three, Independents seven, Irish Nationalist one and Welsh Nationalists four.

29 YEARS' RECORD

589 Deposits Lost

The fortunes of the Liberal party during the last 29 years are shown in the following table, analysing their position in the last nine General Elections. The table is of Liberals fighting without any other party label.

	No. candidates	Seats Secured.	Deposits Lost.	Votes Obtained
1922...	339	53	24	2,516,287
1923...	454	159	8	4,311,147
1924...	343	40	38	2,928,747
1929...	512	59	25	5,308,510
1931...	112	33	5	1,403,102
1935...	161	20	40	1,422,116
1945...	307	12	64	2,245,319
1950...	475	9	319	2,621,489
1951...	109	5	66	710,934

WAR SCARE CAMPAIGN ON DOORSTEP

Ruse to Obscure Living Cost Issue

By Special Correspondents who conducted the recent DAILY TELEGRAPH *survey in the constituencies.*

Reports from almost every constituency in the British Isles confirm that the Socialist campaign cry of "Tory warmongers" penetrated even into the most remote hamlets of the country.

After the first indication at the Labour party conference at Scarborough on Oct. 1 that a " war scare" would make a good election stunt there was an apparent lull during which no public charges were made.

Socialist canvassers, however, started to use variations on the theme at the start and soon Conservative agents were reporting that an insidious canvassing campaign was being conducted.

It was not until a few days before polling that the campaign came to a sudden climax, typified by the headline: "Whose finger on the trigger?"

The smear-cry was repeated in every form from the blatant to the most subtle, in candidates' addresses, in special messages, in speeches, in organised heckling of Conservative speakers, and by word of mouth at the voters' doorstep.

ADVICE AT CONFERENCE

After the opening day of the Scarborough conference, THE DAILY TELEGRAPH Political Correspondent reported. that Socialist M.P.s and candidates had been advised to press insistently throughout the campaign the charge that the return of the Conservatives would increase the risk of war. It was being openly said by responsible party members, including Ministers, that by polling day the fear of war would obscure the cost of living as the main issue. Mr.Morrison was understood to hold this view.

UNDEMOCRATIC SAYS TASS

POLLING PICTURE

The keen interest of Russia and Iron Curtain countries in the British elections was evidenced in various forms. The Soviet News Agency Tass circulated during the night to all provincial newspapers a despatch from the Agency's London correspondent.

This gave a picture of the "undemocratic polling" by quoting the number of candidates standing for each party. It rounded up the report by stating that the British Communists were supporting Labour in all the constituencies where there was no Communist candidate "to prevent the Tories from winning."

Budapest Radio told its listeners that voting "was certainly very heavy." Moscow radio at midnight (Soviet time) told the Russian people of the result, and that Mr. Churchill was forming a Government. No comment was added.

'NO COALITION ' DEMAND

SOCIALIST MOTION

Liverpool Exchange Socialists' party divisional executive committee met last night, and sent a letter to Mr. Morgan Phillips, secretary of the Labour party, urging that in no circumstances must the national party consider a coalition. Liverpool Exchange had returned its Socialist M.P., Mrs. Braddock, with an increased majority.

The letter, accompanying a resolution for consideration by the National Executive, said it was being forwarded in anticipation of "early overtures from the Conservative party arising from the narrow majority in the new House."

The resolution reads: "Having read Mr. Churchill's statement following the result of his election the Exchange Labour party expresses its opinion that under no circumstances must the Labour party consider a coalition, knowing that a coalition cannot in any way be in the best interests of the workers of the country, whose only salvation lies in the application of the policy of the Labour party."

MR. TRUMAN CABLES TO MR. CHURCHILL

HOPE IN U.S. OF CLOSER LINKS

WASHINGTON VISIT EXPECTED

From Our Own Correspondent,
WASHINGTON, Friday.

President Truman to-night cabled his congratulations to Mr. Churchill on his election victory. White House officials declined to give out the text of the message though they said that Mr. Truman would not object if Mr. Churchill did so.

Mr. Truman similarly congratulated Mr. Attlee when he first became Prime Minister in 1945.

"We are glad Winston Churchill has won the British election," was the opening sentence in a leading editorial carried in papers of the Scripps-Howard chain to-day. Both the sentiment and the way in which it was expressed were typical of general American feeling.

Americans do not like Socialism, and they do like Mr. Churchill. Those two facts should provide a more propitious atmosphere for Anglo-American co-operation in diplomatic and economic fields.

All that officials permit themselves to say, however, is first, that they are glad the election is over and the period of uncertainty which had been delaying work on a number of foreign policy problems, particularly in the Middle East, has ended.

They also point out that it would have been extremely awkward if the election campaign had been later and if there had been no British Government with the necessary moral authority to deal with the renewed truce talks in Korea and problems which will arise at the United Nations Assembly in Paris.

PERSONAL DIPLOMACY

Closer Understanding

Secondly, there is official satisfaction that a Government will now be in office which at least has a more workable majority than its predecesor. But it is not too hard to guess that officials also share the general satisfaction that Mr. Churchill's voice will once again be at the service of the Western world and the general belief that an era of closer Anglo-American understanding will be inaugurated.

There was immediate speculation that Mr. Churchill might visit Washington, possibly just before Christmas, but more likely early next Year.

NEWS 'PHONED TO FRONT LINE

KOREA INTEREST

From Our Special Correspondent
With 1st. Commonwealth Division,
KOREA, Friday.

British troops sat up late to-night to hear election results. The broadcast returns were picked up at divisional brigade and battalion H.Q.'s and telephoned to front-line positions.

In forward sectors men were huddling close around campfires; a cold snap hit us to-day and winter clothing is not yet fully distributed. They waited for the buzz of field telephones to announce the latest result.

From tents and trenches on the hills, looking out toward the Communist positions, came discussions on the parties' chances. Judging by the comment I have heard most of the men fighting here wanted a Conservative victory.

They had not been impressed with the Socialists' handling of the Army. In tents which serve as officers' messes cheers greeting the Conservative successes were eloquent of the officers' feelings.

The Daily Telegraph

INQUIRY BUREAU

1,000 POLL QUERIES

The intense public interest throughout yesterday in the minute-to-minute results of the election is shown by the demands of THE DAILY TELEGRAPH Information Bureau.

In spite of the fact that the B.B.C. gave the state of the parties every quarter of an hour and that there was a continuous election programme on television, more than 10,000 calls were made to the Information Bureau in London.

HEAVY BRITISH LOSSES IN KOREA

GLOUCESTERS HARD HIT IN 4-DAY BATTLE

CHINESE DRIVE FOR SEOUL ON 2 ROADS: 10 MILES TO GO

From Denis Warner
Daily Telegraph Special Correspondent

U.N. COMMAND H.Q., TOKYO, Saturday morning.

Detailed accounts are now available of the four-day stand on the Imjin River front in West Korea by troops of the British 29th Brigade. They were given by survivors of the Gloucester battalion who have been trickling back to the United Nations line.

The Gloucesters' losses in the engagement, the most desperate fought by British troops in Korea, are officially described as very heavy. Less than a company have so far returned, but hope is still held for a good many of the remainder.

The British stand to upset the Chinese timetable, but last night the Communists were reported about 10 miles from Seoul. One enemy column was fighting round Uijongbu, and the second south of Munsan - both on direct roads to the capital.

Capt. M.G. Harvey, of Portsmouth, led the first detachment of 50 of the Gloucesters to safety late on Thursday. With ammunition spent and equipment discarded, his dust-stained group of men brought only their rifles, which they had refused to throw away.

The Gloucesters' ordeal began on Sunday night, when Communist bugle-calls on the west bank of the Imjin River announced the beginning of the spring offensive. Forward patrols on the east bank watched the Chinese form up.

Artillery temporarily broke the Communist formations. Survivors said it was moonlight and they could watch the shells falling, but the Communists reformed and began to wade the river in hundreds.

Many died in the river from the small-arms fire of the forward patrols, who withdrew only when their ammunition was spent. On the high ground overlooking the river the battalion awaited the attack.

BRITISH HOLD FIRE

Chinese Withdraw

The men held their fire until the Communists were moving up slopes, then let go with mortars, heavy and light machine-guns, rifles, sub-machine-guns and grenades. In face of this concentrated and sustained fire the enemy swung to the flanks.

In the darkness before dawn the Chinese consolidated in preparation for a daylight attack. It came at dawn, but the Gloucesters, as they were to do many times in the succeeding days, held their ground.

By nine o'clock it was almost victory. The Chinese withdrew, leaving hundreds of dead behind. During the afternoon, however, infiltrators moved deep into 29th Brigade territory and cut the Gloucesters' lines of communications. Machine-gun posts, reinforced by platoons of infantry, stopped all movement along the road to the rear.

At night came the second major attack. It came from both left and right flanks, and the Gloucesters moved to a hill where they formed a tight all-round perimeter, which was now attacked from all sides.

SUPPLIES LOW

Planes Drop Ammunition

Daylight enemy attacks continued all Tuesday, but supplies had become low. That night low-flying American planes parachuted to the heroic battalion which desperately needed small-arms ammunition, but only enough food for one can of rations to each man.

(April 28)

GEN. MACARTHUR RETURNING TO U.S.

1 A.M. DISMISSAL: GEN.RIDGWAY TAKES OVER

From Our Own Correspondent

WASHINGTON, Wednesday.

President Truman to-day dismissed Gen. MacArthur, 71, from all his commands in the Far East, including that of C.-in-C. United Nations Command. He is succeeded by Lt.-Gen. Matthew B. Ridgway, 56, Commander of the Eighth Army in Korea and formerly Deputy Army Chief of Staff.

The dismissal was announced by the President at 1 a.m. local time (6 a.m. G.M.T.). Soon afterwards the White House published a series of documents which showed that Gen. MacArthur had ignored repeated warnings by the President about making political pronouncements.

Gen. MacArthur said later in a telephone conversation with Mr. Martin, Republican leader in the House of Representatives, that he would return to the United States in about three weeks. This will be his first visit for 15 years.

President Truman broadcasting to the nation at 10.30 to-night (3.30 a.m. G.M.T.) on American Far East policy said that the cause of world peace is more important than the individual.

"We will not engage in appeasement," he said. "We are only interested in real peace." The three factors for peace were:

Fighting must stop;

Concrete steps must be taken to ensure that fighting will not break out again; and

There must be an end to aggression.

(April 12)

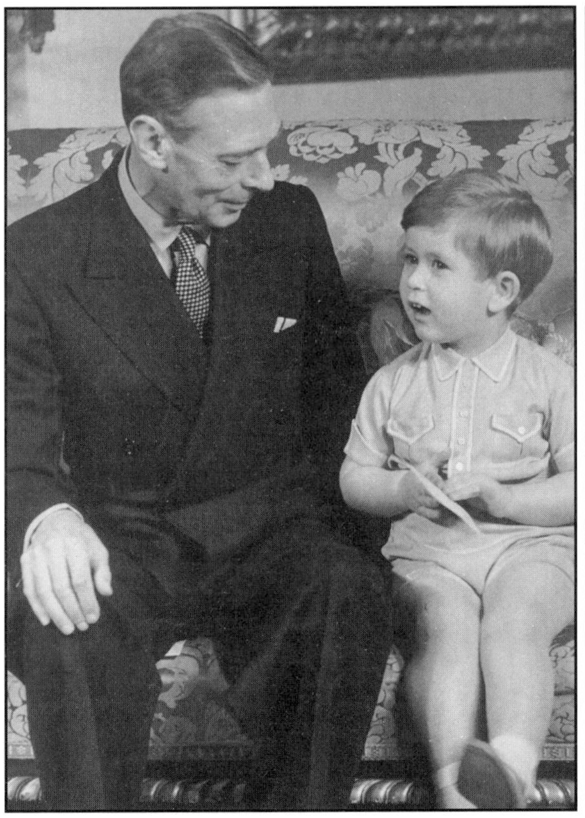

THE KING AND HIS GRANDSON. The first picture of his Majesty since his operation on September 23rd. It was taken at Buckingham Palace yesterday, when Prince Charles celebrated his third birthday and visited his grandparents.

THE KING HAS A LUNG OPERATION

CONTINUING ANXIETY FOR SOME DAYS

An operation on the King for his lung condition was performed at Buckingham Palace yesterday morning. A bulletin issued shortly before 4.30 p.m. stated:

The King underwent an operation for lung resection this morning. Whilst anxiety must remain for some days, his Majesty's immediate post-operative condition is satisfactory.

Signed:		
	DANIEL DAVIES	GEOFFREY MARSHALL
	THOMAS DUNHILL	C. PRICE THOMAS
	HORACE EVANS	JOHN WEIR
	R. MACHRAY	ROBERT A. YOUNG

A second bulletin issued at 9.15 last night stated:

The King's condition continues to be as satisfactory as can be expected.

It was signed by Daniel Davies, Horace Evans, Geoffrey Marshall, C. Price Thomas and John Weir.

Lung resection is the term used for removal by surgical means of the whole of one lung or part of the lung.

Mr Price Thomas, 57, surgeon at Westminster Hospital, performed the operation, which is believed to have occupied about two hours. It began about 10 a.m. in a specially-prepared room in the north wing of the Palace.

The Queen was the first to receive a report on how the King withstood the operation. Some of the doctors in attendance remained at the Palace for the second night in succession.

(September 24)

PRINCESS TAKES SALUTE AT COLOUR TROOPING

Daily Telegraph Reporter

Princess Elizabeth, who is Colonel of the Grenadier Guards, took the salute at the Trooping the Colour ceremony on Horse Guards Parade yesterday in honour of the King's official birthday. She wore a scarlet tunic, dark blue riding skirt and a tricorne replica of the hat worn by a Colonel of the Grenadiers more than 200 years ago.

From Buckingham Palace along the Mall to the parade ground she rode side-saddle on Winston, a light chestnut police horse. She won the admiration of the large crowds for the worthy manner in which she represented the King, who has been ordered a month's complete rest.

For just over an hour, with one white gloved hand relaxed - and occasionally patting her mount in time with the martial music, she watched the intricate, coloured pageantry of traditional march and counter-march.

Pinned to her tunic above the blue sash of the Order of the Garter were the Defence Medal and General Service Medal awarded to the Princess for wartime services in the A.T.S., the Jubilee and Coronation medals and the medal of the Star of India.

Her progress from the Palace was easily followed because of the crescendo of cheers and clapping. As she led the Household Cavalry to the arch of Horse Guards she saluted the Queen, Queen Mary, King Haakon of Norway, the Duchess of Kent and the Duchess of Gloucester, who had balcony seats with Princess Margaret and Prince Charles.

PRINCE CHARLES'S QUESTIONS

This was the signal for a torrent of eager questions from the young Prince to the Queen. Already she had been seen to laugh and flourish an explanatory finger during his persistent cross-examination as their open coach crossed the parade ground to Horse Guards Arch.

Throughout the ceremony Princess Elizabeth, who was escorted by the Duke of Gloucester, had effortless control of her mount. The chestnut hardly moved as the Guards' bands, drums and fifes played and the orders echoed back from the Admiralty building.

(June 7)

CANBERRA FLIES ATLANTIC IN 4hr. 40min.

ALL SPEED RECORDS BROKEN

From Our Special Correspondent

GANDER, Newfoundland, Wednesday.

The Canberra, Britain's first jet bomber, to-day broke all transatlantic air speed records with a 2,100-mile flight in 4hr 40min, an average speed of 439.64 m.p.h. It left Aldergrove, Northern Ireland, at 12.43 p.m. G.M.T. and arrived here at 5.23 p.m. G.M.T. (1.53 p.m. local time).

The flight was the first by a jet plane across the Atlantic without refuelling. The pilot was Sqdn.-Ldr. A. E. Callard, of Manchester. His crew was Flt. Lt. E. A. J. Haskett, of Portsmouth, and Flt. Lt. A. J. R. Robson, of Barry, Glam.

The Canberra's departure had been delayed a day because a seagull damaged the plane in a collision between Lancashire and Northern Ireland. Mechanics worked during the night to repair the damage.

It is expected it will stay overnight at Gander. To-morrow it will go to Andrews Field, near Washington, for tests before American experts.

The Canberra flew at between 40,000ft and 48,000ft. Before leaving Aldergrove, Sqdn. Ldr. Callard was told that he might have 90 m.p.h. winds against him. "Those conditions are acceptable." he said. "We will go."

During the crossing he and his crew wore special uniforms which were coupled to their oxygen supply, and breathing was done through the waistcoats. They provide a steady pressure round the lungs when inflated.

PERFECT FLIGHT

Sqdn.-Ldr. Callard said after landing: "The flight was perfect from start to finish. It would be hard for anybody to convince us that they had had a more pleasant trip than we did. Please tell my wife in Manchester that we arrived safely and had a very good trip."

(February 22)

NEW DEVICE TO FIGHT CRIME

MOTOR-CYCLE FLEET WITH RADIO PHONES

Daily Telegraph Reporter

Five Scotland Yard motor-cycle patrols equipped with two-way radio telephones went on duty for the first time yesterday.

They are part of a proposed fleet, first reported in THE DAILY TELEGRAPH on Jan. 6. 1949, of 35 wireless-equipped motor-cycle patrols which will eventually play a big part in the campaign against crime in London.

It is expected that the complete fleet will be operating by the end of the year. The two-way speech system with which the motor-cycles are fitted was perfected after three years of experiment.

The sets are believed to be the first fitted to police motor-cycles in Europe. Eventually it is hoped to cover most of the police divisions in the Metropolitan area with radio-equipped motor-cycle patrols. The number in use will operate more in the outlying divisions so as to augment the foot police.

(February 6)

BRITAIN ENDS STATE OF WAR WITH GERMANY

By A Diplomatic Correspondent

The formal state of war between Great Britain and Germany was officially ended at 4 p.m. yesterday by a notice in the London Gazette approved by the Privy Council. The war had lasted 11 years, 10 months and six days. It began at 11 a.m. Sept. 3, 1939, when the time limit on the British ultimatum to Germany expired unanswered.

Mr Morrison made a statement in the House of Commons on the British action. In reply to a question he said the ending of hostilities applied to Western Germany alone.

SUCCESSOR TO OLD REGIME

Britain, however, considers that the Federal Government at Bonn is the successor to the former régime for the whole of Germany.

Similar action was initiated yesterday by the Government of the United States and France, Australia, New Zealand and South Africa also announced that official hostilities with Germany had ceased.

The Israeli Foreign Office, however, announced that they did not consider "Germany's war against the Jewish People" had ended.

(July 10)

SHOP LIGHTING BAN STARTS ON MONDAY

TRADERS TO APPEAL

Daily Telegraph Reporter

The ban on the use of electricity for shop window and advertisement lighting, first imposed in the 1949-50 winter and continued last winter, will be reintroduced on Monday.

From then until Oct. 19 it will apply between 7 a.m. and 1 p.m., and from Oct. 22 to April 4 from 7 a.m. to 7 p.m.

Announcement of the ban was made yesterday by Mr. Noel-Baker, Minister of Fuel, in the Licence laid before Parliament under the Electric Lighting (Restriction) Order, 1949. The reduced period in the first fortnight repeats the modification made last year.

The use of private generating plant, candles or other such forms of illumination will not be restricted. These were banned for a period during the fuel crisis early this year. In England and Wales Christmas Day and Boxing Day are exempted from the Order, and Christmas Day and New Year's Day in Scotland.

Representations may be made today to the Minister by the Nations Chamber of Trade to allow further modification of the ban. A similar appeal made last year was rejected.

(October 5)

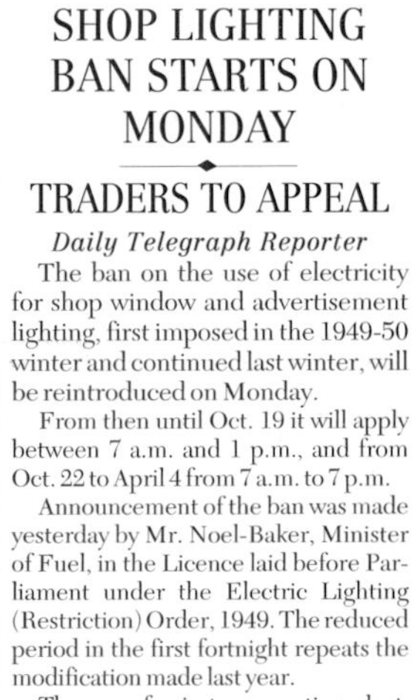

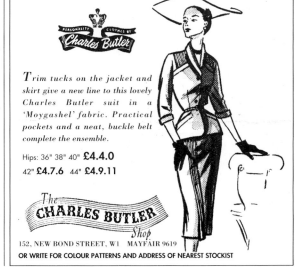

CABINET GIVES UP GROUNDNUT PLAN

AIMS 'INCAPABLE OF FULFILMENT'

£36,500,000 DEBT WILL BE WRITTEN OFF

By Our Political Correspondent

Failure of the Government's East African groundnut plan was officially admitted last night. Its original aims "have proved incapable of fulfilment," a White Paper said.

A new and drastically limited scheme will take its place. Supervision will be transferred from the Ministry of Food to the Colonial Office.

In place of the original aim to clear 3,210,000 acres by 1953 and the revised plan announced last November for the clearance of 600,000 acres by 1954, it is now proposed to confine operations to a total of 210,000 acres-with the possibility of some extension after review in 1954-over the next seven years.

The £36,500,000 which it is estimated has been expended on the scheme is to be written off. This will be authorised in a Bill which will be introduced shortly giving effect to the transfer.

The changes will result in nearly 40 per cent of the European staff now employed in East Africa losing their jobs in the next 12 months.

"Great disappointment and much personal hardship" will be involved, the White Paper says. Compensation at the rate of six or four months' salary plus the earned leave due, whichever is the greater, will be offered.

On wider grounds the White Paper says: "The revised programme submitted by the Overseas Food Corporation involves a radical change in the whole conception of the scheme. The original aim was to increase production of oils and fats to meet a world shortage which was and still is expected to persist.

"It was hoped that within a comparatively short time the scheme would make a substantial contribution to world supplies. This hope has not been fulfilled.

"The scheme must now be regarded as a scheme of large-scale experimental development to establish the economics of clearing and mechanised or partially mechanised agriculture under tropical conditions." This "cannot in itself contribute significantly towards Britain's food supplies."

(January 10)

MEAT RATION CUT TO 8d, LOWEST EVER

LESS FOR SAUSAGES AND PIES: HOPE OF MORE BACON

Daily Telegraph Reporter

The fresh meat ration will be cut from 10d to 8d a week from to-morrow week. The supplementary issue of 2d of corned beef will continue. This was announced by Mr. Webb, Minister of Food, in the House of Commons yesterday. [Report-P3.]

The manufacturing meat allowance will be reduced by about one-third, which will mean fewer sausages and pies. The decision follows the deadlock reached last week in the negotiations for a new meat agreement between Britain and the Argentine.

The ration, which has fallen in a few weeks from 1s 6d worth, is already the lowest ever in weight. Only once before-in March, 1949, when meat was 4d a lb cheaper, has it been at this price level.

This latest cut, the second in little over a month and the third since Dec. 10, was foreshadowed in THE DAILY TELEGRAPH on Dec. 23 and again on Tuesday.

FUTURE CHANGE UPWARDS

Mr. Webb was hopeful that the ration had now reached its lowest level and that future changes would be upwards. He also hoped soon to give a little more bacon.

He said he was adopting a policy of waiting to see if prices would fall before deciding whether to reimpose price control on poultry, rabbits and fish. He had been warned by the trade that controls would mean a black market in rabbits.

Mr. E. J. Baldwin, former president of the National Federation of Meat Traders, last night estimated that the weight of the average ration would now be reduced to about 5½ ounces. Three ration books would be necessary to secure a pound of meat, and an ordinary leg of lamb would take 13 books.

For the person with one ration book, the cut means that a fifth will be lopped off the medium-sized chop to which he was entitled.

Other examples of the weight of meat housewives can obtain when the cut comes into operation are:

English rump steak (2s 8d a lb) 4 oz
Top side steak (1s 10d to 2s 2d) 5½ oz
English mutton chops (2s 4d) 4½ oz
Imported lamb chops (2s) .... 5 oz
Imported ewe mutton, boneless (1s 8d) .... 6½ oz

(January 27)

114 HURRICANE DEATHS

WARSHIPS SENT TO JAMAICA

KINGSTON, Jamaica, Monday.

The death-roll in the hurricane which swept Jamaica on Friday night has now risen to 114. Two British frigates were on their way to the island to-day to give assistance.

They are the 1,430-ton Sparrow, which sailed from Bermuda, and the 1,600-ton Bigbury Bay, which has left Barbados. They have extra medical officers and supplies on board.

The hurricane, which [as reported in THE DAILY TELEGRAPH yesterday] caused damage estimated to total £20 million, was the worst in the West Indian island's history. The food situation is acute. Debris blocking the street of Kingston, the capital, is being cleared, and traffic is beginning to move again.

Telephone and telegraph services are still dead, but the electricity supply has been partially restored. About a fifth of the houses have been destroyed or damaged.

At Port Royal, which was practically wiped out, the hunt for 70 escaped prisoners is still going on. Rescue parties continue to dig for missing people.

SUGAR LOSS

Morant Bay, an important seaport, has been levelled. The United Fruit Co.'s central sugar factory has been wrecked and thousands of bags of sugar have been lost. Seventy to 80 per cent of the banana crop and about a third of other crops has been destroyed.

(August 21)

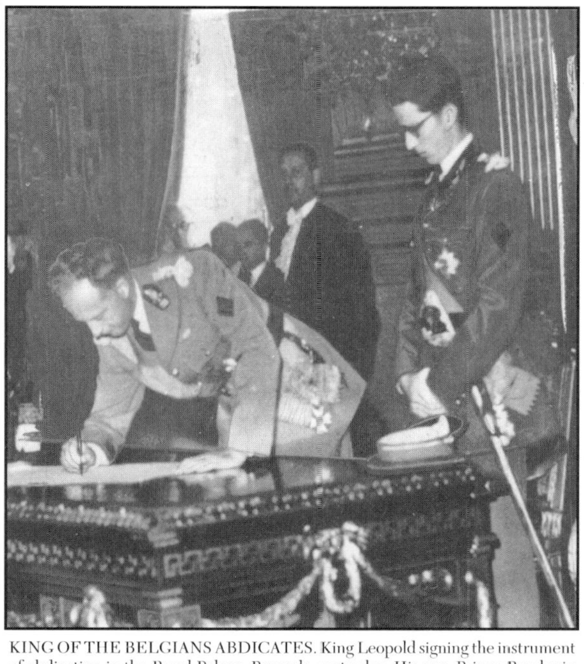

KING OF THE BELGIANS ABDICATES. King Leopold signing the instrument of abdication in the Royal Palace, Brussels, yesterday. His son, Prince Baudouin (right), will take the oath as King to-day.

MORRIS & AUSTIN FIRMS TO MERGE

CAR COMBINE WILL BE LARGEST IN BRITAIN

By W. A. McKenzie,
Daily Telegraph Motoring Correspondent

Proposals for a complete financial merger of Morris Motors and the Austin Motor Co. were announced last night. The assets of the combined companies will amount to nearly £66 million, making a new concern the largest in the British motor trade.

A joint statement by the boards of the two companies said that unified control would lead to more efficient and economical production and would further the export drive. It would be particularly beneficial to manufacturing and assembly abroad. The two companies will retain their separate identities and Austin and Morris vehicles will be produced as before.

The amalgamation will be carried out by the formation of a holding company with an authorised capital of £5 million. This will ask present share-holders to exchange their holdings for an equivalent number of its own 5s shares.

Lord Nuffield, 74, chairman of Morris Motors, will be the first chairman of the new concern. Mr L.P. Lord, 54, chairman and managing director of Austins, will be deputy chairman and managing director.

The new holding company will control the production and marketing of nearly 50 per cent of all the private cars made in the United Kingdom. The rate of production will be about a quarter-million units a year with exports of around 200,000 cars a year.

The combined labour force will be more than 42,000-just under half the labour strength of the six leading manufacturers.

In this move, big economies in production can be made and output increased. A spare part and maintenance service can be offered abroad highly competitive with that developed by American motor manufacturers.

The amalgamation is the more surprising, since in October, 1948, a close working arrangement was tried out. There was to be an interchange of information on production methods, costs, design, research and sales. The object was to achieve maximum standardisation and make the best use of the joint factory resources. Yet only nine months later this arrangement ended.

It was officially declared that the working arrangement would cease and that "no merger of any kind" would take place. I understand, however, that talks on a possible merger were never dropped.

(November 24)

MISS BANKHEAD TOASTS BRITAIN

CHAMPAGNE IN SHOE

Tallulah Bankhead, the American actress, who is visiting England for the first time since 1935, held a Press conference at the Ritz Hotel, Piccadilly, last night. It had an unconventional opening.

After an interval of 35 minutes, during which a 4,000-word resumé of Miss Bankhead's biography was handed round, she entered the room wearing a dress of black embossed satin, with a gold link chain and gold bracelet.

After welcoming her guests, Miss Bankhead climbed on a chair, removed her shoe and poured a glass of champagne into it. "To Britain, God bless her," she said raising her shoe.

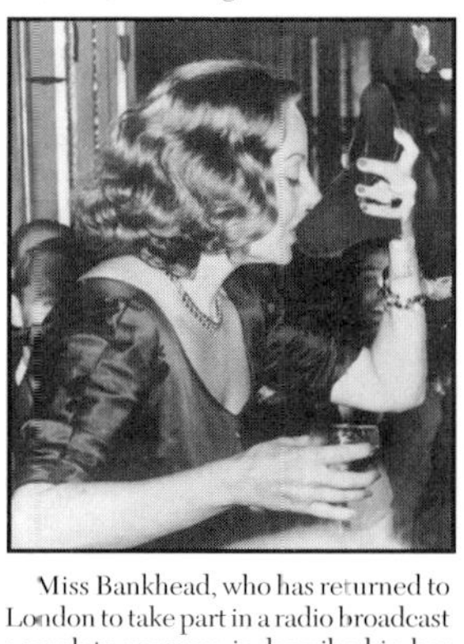

Miss Bankhead, who has returned to London to take part in a radio broadcast a week to-morrow, is described in her biography as primarily a phenomenon of nature. Her ability to talk "both on and off the stage is nearly legendary.

(August 8)

HOTEL PRICES UP TO-DAY

Two of London's largest "average price" hotels are raising their bed-and-breakfast charges to-day. The new increase makes hotel charges nearly 50 per cent higher than they were three years ago.

The price of single rooms at the Regent Palace and Strand Palace Hotels is to go up from 20s 6d to 22s, and double rooms from 31s 6d to 34s.

(September 3)

KING LEOPOLD SIGNS ACT OF ABDICATION

From Our Special Correspondent

BRUSSELS, Monday.

In the vast chandelier-hung Throne Room on the first floor of the Royal Palace here King Leopold III of the Belgians, who is 49 to-day, renounced his throne in favour of his son, Prince Baudouin, and signed the Act of Abdication before State dignitaries. Prince Baudouin is 20.

As a church clock struck noon Leopoldists in the crowd outside in the Place des Palais began a rhythmic chant of "Leopold," but they were hissed into silence. No sound reached the Throne Room, where the nation's leaders stood in a semi-circle facing the dais.

Their formal attire was relieved by the scarlet robes of Cardinal Van Roey, Archbishop of Malines, Primate of Belgium, the red robes of the Judiciary, and the tricolour sashes of the delegations from the Senate and the House of Representatives.

A minute before noon the double doors of the ante-room were flung open. Two ushers in black livery and knee breeches, followed by the court Chamberlain, heralded the King and his son.

Both wore the uniform of Lieutenant-Generals, with the crimson sash of the Grand Cordon of the Order of Leopold, and carried cap and white gloves in hand. King Leopold's wife, the Princesse de Rethy, was not present.

Both the King and Prince also wore a black patch on the left sleeve, in mourning for M. Baels, the father of Princess de Rethy, who died a few weeks ago. King Leopold married the Princess, then Mlle. Lilian Baels, in 1941.

The King and the Prince bowed stiffly to the right and left. King Leopold, showing signs of emotion, and Prince Baudouin, pale and self-controlled, went to the red chairs on the dais. On the table before them lay the Act of Abdication. Behind stood a white bust of Leopold I.

In slow, clear tones the King read his speech of abdication, first in Flemish, then in French. It took 18 minutes and was broadcast.

Prince Baudouin, who is to take the oath as King to-morrow, briefly acknowledged his readiness to accept his father's role. "I promise to do everything to show myself worthy of being your son" he said.

The King signed and then embraced his son. The Act of Abdication was witnessed by the Minister of Justice, M. Moeyersoen, and the Prime Minister, M. Pholien.

In his last message to the nation, King Leopold recalled that to restore order in the country, he agreed on July 31 last year that his powers should be conferred on his son. His intention was to renounce the throne finally if Belgians rallied to Prince Baudouin. This had been done. There were prolonged cheers of "Vive le Roi" and "Leopold", until King Leopold took his son by the shoulder and the two figures turned slowly from sight.

King Leopold, whose reign began in 1934 is the first of his dynasty to abdicate since Belgium became an independent monarchy in 1830. He will keep the courtesy title of King and has a civil list pension of £43,000 a year.

(July 17)

SCHUMAN PLAN INITIALLED

HOPE OF NEW CO-OPERATION

From Our Own Correspondent

PARIS, Monday.

Hopes of a new era for co-operation within a unified Europe were expressed when the agreement on the Schuman plan for pooling coal and steel resources was initialled at the foreign Ministry to-day.

M. Monnet, co-author of the plan, and the heads of the delegations of experts of Germany, Belgium, Italy, Holland and Luxembourg, the five other participating countries, took part in the ceremony. It was also attended by M. Schuman, the foreign Minister.

M. Monnet said that the plan had three essential points involving a basic transformation in Western Europe. These were:

1 – The supra-national character of the proposed community. "For the first time six countries have come together, not to seek a provisional compromise among national interests, but to take a concerted view of their common interests. This single view is expressed in a limited delegation of sovereignty to common institutions."

CREATING SINGLE MARKET

2 – The creation of a single market of 150 million consumers without customs duties or quantitative restrictions to hamper the movement of coal and steel within the territory formed by the six countries.

3 – The elimination of restrictive cartel practices and of excessive concentrations of economic power. Freedom and initiative are at the very basis of the projected organisation. The enterprises will have complete responsibility for their own management.

Prof. Hailstein, leader of the German delegation, on behalf of all the foreign delegations, said it was right that the plan should "eternally bear the name of M. Schuman."

The draft agreement will be published to-morrow. There are still a number of questions to be settled by the Foreign Ministers of the six Powers before they sign the final agreement, which will be in force for 50 years.

(March 20)

6d. ON INCOME TAX: 4d. A GALLON ON PETROL

PENSIONS, MARRIAGE & CHILD ALLOWANCES UP

SPECTACLES AND FALSE TEETH: 50p.c. CHARGE

Mr. Gaitskell, Chancellor of the Exchequer, introducing his first Budget in the House of Commons yesterday, said he knew it would not be popular, but claimed it was honest. In a speech lasting 2hr 12min [Report-Pp. 6 and 7] he proposed to "spread the burden widely and therefore thinly" as follows:

INCOME TAX: Sixpence on all three rates, raising the 2s 6d rate to 3s, the 5s rate to 5s 6d and the standard rate to 9s 6d.

MARRIAGE & CHILD ALLOWANCES: Each raised £10, from £180 to £190 for married couples, from £60 to £70 for a child.

PETROL TAX: Raised by 4 ½ d a gallon, making the basic retail price 3s 6d a gallon at garages from midnight last night. The increase also applies to other road fuel oils.

MOTOR-CARS: Purchase tax doubled, from 33 ⅓ per cent to 66 ⅔ per cent.

HOME APPLIANCES: Purchase tax similarly increased from 33 ⅓ per cent to 66 ⅔ per cent on wireless and television sets and valves and on gas and electrically-operated domestic appliances, applying to goods delivered to-day.

Certain "necessary" household articles like pastry boards, rolling pins, pot scourers, dusters, wash towels and ironing boards, hot water bottles, school satchels and shoe laces to be exempted from purchase tax.

OLD AGE PENSIONS: From Oct. 1, standard rate increased from 26s to 30s a week for single persons and from 42s to 50s a week for married couples, for men over 70 and women over 65.

Pensions remain unchanged for men retiring between 65 and 70 and women retiring between 60 and 65. Workers who postponed retirement would have the increment of their pension increased from 2s to 3s a week for each extra year they stayed at work.

The amount per week which pensioners would be allowed to earn without reduction of pension would be increased from 20s to 40s. Increases of benefits to widows with children and other children's benefits will be announced in a White Paper to-day.

INDUSTRY TO PAY MORE

PROFITS TAX: Increase from 30 per cent to 50 per cent in tax on distributed profits, as from Jan. 1 this year. Ten per cent. tax on undistributed profits is unchanged. Certain public utilities, mainly bus and water undertakings, at present exempt, to pay 10 per cent profits tax, also from Jan. 1, 1951.

The Chancellor gave notice to industry that from April 6 next year the 40 per cent initial allowances on expenditure on buildings, machinery, plant, mines and oil wells would be suspended. This is estimated to produce £170 million in a full year.

DIRECTORS' FEES: The amount allowable for directors' remuneration in director-controlled companies is raised from £2,500 to £3,500 a year where there are two full-time directors and to £4,500 where there are three or more.

NOTHING ON BEER OR SURTAX

UNCHANGED: Taxes on beer, spirits, wines and tobacco unaltered. No increase in the food subsidies.

(April 11)

BRITISH CONTROL SUEZ CANAL

MAIN TOWNS OCCUPIED

From Colin Reid,
Daily Telegraph Special Correspondent

PORT SAID, Thursday.

The British Army on the Suez Canal has occupied all main strategic centres on both banks between Port Said and Suez. This was the momentous news in Port Said to-day.

A British spokesman said that British forces forcibly took over all means of crossing the Suez Canal to the eastern bank, and seized the ferry between Suez and Sinai. Bridges and public utility services in the Canal Zone were also occupied.

Port Said remained in full rail, road and wire communications with Cairo and Egyptian towns.

Places where the British have taken control along the hundred miles length of canal and the lakes include Ismailia, from which there was later a partial withdrawal, the Canal railway crossing north of Ismailia at El Ferdan, and El Kantara, where there is a road bridge, and all points south of Ismailia as far as Kubry ferry, five miles north of Suez.

EGYPTIANS ISOLATED

No Newspapers

Egyptian forces established on the western side of the Canal and in Palestine are apparently isolated. Reports of all this were widely known in Port Said.

No newspapers reached Port Said from Cairo to-day. They had been seized at Ismailia by the British authorities in control.

Later a communiqué issued by General Headquarters, British Middle East Land Forces, said: "Due to a misinterpretation of orders it is regretted that newspapers from Cairo were prevented from entering the Canal Zone to-day. This will not occur again so far as the British military authorities are concerned."

What was happening further south was obscure. With Egyptians refusing permit landing or loading of British military stores here and in Suez an acute situation was developing.

Port Said has no Egyptian garrison of any consequence. The town is controlled by the police.

(October 19)

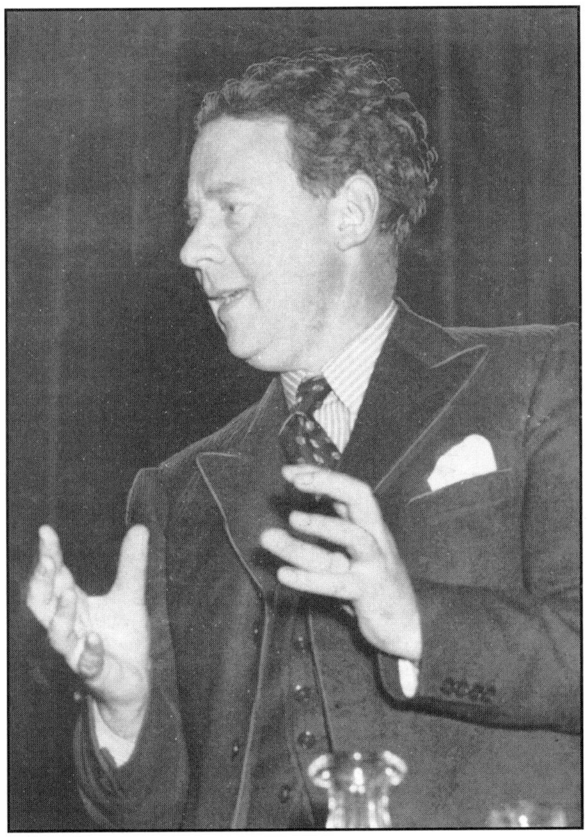

MR. GAITSKELL, Chancellor of the Exchequer.

TEST OF BRITISH ATOM BOMB SOON

AUSTRALIAN DESERT EXPLOSION

By Our Political Correspondent

Preparations are well advanced, I understand, for the first test in Australia of an atomic bomb of British manufacture. The test is likely to take place in the near future.

The first of a series of Canberra jet bombers is being flown to Australia to-day by Wing Cdr. D.R. Cuming, chief test pilot of the Royal Australian Air Force.

It will take off at dawn from Lyneham, Wilts. The despatch of the bomber may be connected with the projected experiment.

It is generally accepted that British knowledge of the techniques of production is well beyond the point at which the making of a successful bomb is possible. Further advance is understood to require knowledge which can only be derived from an experimental explosion.

The central desert of Australia was long ago selected as the testing ground for such an experiment.

A range for experimental work on guided missiles and rockets has been established there, at Woomera. The firing point in this desert area is about 350 miles north of Adelaide.

The range can be extended for 1,200 miles over land to the coast. Defensive and offensive weapons already tested there include guided missiles and bombs, proximity fuses and pilotless aircraft.

As long ago as Feb. 15 Mr. Attlee declared in the House of Commons that there was successful development of an atomic bomb in Britain.

On Feb. 17 THE DAILY TELEGRAPH Science Correspondent reported that the production of a bomb was only held up by shortage of fissile material.

It was confirmed on March 5 by Mr. Strauss, Minister of Supply, in a written Parliamentary answer, that Britain had the technical knowledge to produce a bomb.

(August 1)

FLYING ANTS IN LONDON

SUBURBS 'INVADED'

Thousands of flying ants "invaded" several London suburbs yesterday. Windows and doors had to be closed against them.

For over three hours the ants harassed shoppers and pedestrians in Ilford. They swarmed so thickly that motorists had to stop to wipe them from their windscreens.

In East Ham housewives tried to clear them with boiling water. In some places they formed a large moving heap on the footpath. Swarms were also reported in Cricklewood, Sidcup and Whitton, Middlesex.

Mating Flight

OUR NATURE CORRESPONDENT writes: At this time of year ant queens and drones come out for the mating flight, being restrained by the workers until the right moment arrives. This moment is believed to be determined by the weather.

After swarming, the queens, having mated, come back to earth, and get rid of their wings by biting them or rubbing them off with their legs or against solid objects such as stones or sticks. The pavement often becomes littered with hundreds of wings.

(August 12)

SPRING-CLEAN TO COST MORE THIS YEAR

Daily Telegraph Reporter

Spring-cleaning and repainting the home will cost more this year. Prices of domestic cleaning materials, paints, hardware and the handyman's tools have all risen since the autumn.

"The market has gone mad," said one dealer in domestic hardware yesterday as he illustrated how prices have increased. All items in tins, such as paint and polishes, are particulary affected.

Tinplate is getting scarcer and dearer each week, according to manufacturers, Examples of recent increases are:

	Last yr s	Last yr d	This yr s	This yr d
Washleathers	5	0	12	6
Floor stain	2	6	2	8
Enamel buckets	5	11	7	3
Chromium-plated "hearth set"	41	3	57	3
Brass polish		10	11	0
Gal.. enamel paint	55	0	60	0
Gal. flat interior	48	0	54	0
Pair pliers	3	1	4	3

Most tools have increased in price by 10 per cent since the autumn. Articles which have purchase tax are doubly increased since the purchase tax rises with the cost of the article.

(February 21)

MR. BEVAN RESIGNS: ASSAULT ON BUDGET

MR. ATTLEE ON A WIDE DISAGREEMENT

By Our Political Correspondent

Mr. Bevan, 53, Minister of Labour and National Service, has resigned from the Government. The King has accepted the resignation.

In his letter of resignation to Mr. Attlee, published to-day, Mr. Bevan expresses "objections to many features of the Budget" and launches a general assault on them. His objections to the charges for false teeth and spectacles in the National Health scheme, on which his fight was originally founded, are not specifically mentioned.

He declares that the Budget fails to apportion fairly the burden between different social classes and is based on a scale of military expenditure which is physically unattainable this year, regards rising prices as a means of reducing civilian consumption, and is the beginning of the destruction of the social services.

Replying, Mr. Attlee comments on this change of ground. "I note that you have extended the area of disagreement with your colleagues a long way beyond the specific matter to which, as I understood, you had taken objection."

Mr. Bevan has now made into an open split the chronic feud he has waged with his colleagues, in particular Mr. Morrison, Foreign Secretary, on major policy.

The great question now is the amount of support he will receive not only in the Parliamentary Labour party but in the Labour movement as a whole.

MR. WILSON'S POSITION

Decision To-day

Mr. Wilson, President of the Board of Trade, is considering his position and will decide what course he will take to-day. He accompanied Mr. Bevan to see Mr. Attlee on Budget Day, April 10, and was associated with him in protesting against the Health Service charges.

Mr. Wilson yesterday paid a visit to Mr. Attlee, who is in St. Mary's Hospital, Paddington. Upon leaving, Mr. Wilson declined to say anything. After the interview, many of his friends thought it likely that he would resign to-day.

Mr. Strachey, Secretary for War, who was also associated with Mr. Bevan's stand on the Health Service charges, is also believed to be considering his position. Last night he declined to make any comment.

STATEMENT TO-DAY

Party's Election Fears

Mr. Bevan, whose salary was £5,000, will make a resignation statement to the House of Commons to-day. The reaction to this may reveal the extent of the cleavage in Socialist ranks.

But for the fear of a split precipitating a General Election which the Socialists would be likely to lose, at least a large minority of the Parliamentary Labour party would be with Mr. Bevan. In present circumstances, the pressure of the party machine in the hands of Mr. Attlee and Mr. Morrison may reduce his following to comparatively small numbers.

It is evident from the course of events that Mr. Attlee and his senior Cabinet colleagues decided on Friday to force the Minister of Labour's hand. Their decision followed a fierce attack on Mr. Gaitskell, Chancellor of the Exchequer, in the Socialist fortnightly, Tribune.

(April 23)

7,000 LONDON DOCK MEN JOIN STRIKE

By Hugh Chevins,
Daily Telegraph Industrial Correspondent

Nearly 7,000 of 28,000 London dockers stayed away from work yesterday in protest against the arrest of seven men accused at Bow-street of conspiring to incite dockers to join an illegal strike. The seven, including three from Liverpool, were remanded on bail of £100 each until Tuesday week. [Report P5.]

In the other troubled areas the number of strikers fell, on Merseyside by 432 and in Manchester by 182. The total on strike at the three ports was 17,819.

Before the arrests on Thursday night 450 dockers in London had been on strike for two days in support of the unofficial Merseyside stoppage against the Transport and General Workers' Union acceptance of an 11s a week wage increase. The London strikers had already voted to resume work yesterday.

Instead, many stayed at home when they heard news of the arrests. Others stopped work after attending dock-gate meetings called by the unofficial London Port Workers' Committee.

More dock-gate meetings are to be held at all the London docks this morning.

A mass meeting "to consider a positive policy" for the strike has been called for Victoria Park, Bethnal Green, on Monday morning. Strike news from the ports last night was:

MERSEYSIDE: On strike, 9,001; at work, 7,070. Ships idle, 64; undermanned, 33; working, 22.

MANCHESTER: On strike, 2,097; at work 350. Ships idle, 18; undermanned, 5.

LONDON: On strike, 6,721; at work 19,190. Ships idle, 70; undermanned, 5; working, 81. About 2,000 absent from sickness, injuries and other causes.

(February 10)

PRINCESS GUEST AT TEA WITH GEN. EISENHOWER

SONGS AT PARTY

From Our Own Correspondent

PARIS, Saturday Morning.

Princess Margaret, through no fault of her own, kept Gen. Eisenhower waiting for 20 minutes yesterday standing in the entrance hall of SHAPE, where he had invited her to an informal tea. The driver of her car was directed off the arterial road from Paris to Marly by a mobile guard shortly before the party approached Versailles, and had to make a long detour.

As the Royal car drew up Gen. Eisenhower walked down the steps to welcome the Princess, who was accompanied by Lady Jean Rankin and Capt. Oliver Dawnay, the Queen's secretary. Gen. Eisenhower shook hands warmly with the Princess, saying, "Your Royal Highness, how nice to see you."

Princess Margaret was wearing a black tailored skirt and a yellow blouse, with a mink coat and a cloche hat. In the officers' lounge she met Mrs. Eisenhower and members of Gen. Eisenhower's staff.

After tea Gen. Eisenhower showed the Princess round the H.Q. She signed the distinguished visitors' book.

EVENING AT MAXIM'S

In the evening the Princess went to Maxim's, the favourite Paris restaurant of King Edward VII. She was the guest of Prince Paul of Jugoslavia.

The Princess, wearing a white satin evening dress and a white three-quarter length fur cape, arrived with the Duchess of Kent and the Duchess's sister, Princess Olga, wife of Prince Paul. The Duchess was in beach satin, with large mother-of-pearl buttons.

Others in the party were M. Charles de Beistegui, who gave what was described as "the ball of the century" in his Venice mansion in September, Baron and Baroness Cabrol, and Mme. Rally, a friend of the Duchess of Kent.

(November 24)

COMMUNISTS WILL JOIN TRUCE TALK

REPLY BY KOREAN AND CHINESE C.'S-IN-C.

TOWN 2 MILES SOUTH OF PARALLEL NAMED

From Eric Downton, Daily Telegraph Special Correspondent

EIGHTH ARMY H.Q., KOREA, Monday.

The Chinese and North Korean Communists last night announced their readiness to meet United Nations representatives for truce talks. They broadcast a message in reply to the proposal made on Friday by Gen. Ridgway, United Nations Supreme Commander in the Far East.

Their acceptance contained the counter-proposal that the meeting place should be Kaesong, a war-shattered town in South Korea, two miles south of the 38th parallel, instead of in the Danish hospital ship Jutlandia in the North Korean harbour of Wonsan, as suggested by Gen. Ridgway.

The earliest date proposed by the Communists is a week to-morrow. No comment on their reply was available at Gen. Ridgway's headquarters or those of Lt.-Gen. Van Fleet, Eighth Army Commander, as the official version was still awaited.

The Communist reply was broadcast in Mandarin and English from Peking and from Pyongyang, the North Korean capital.

It was issued by Marshal Kim Ir-sen, C.-in-C. of the Korean "People's Army," and Gen. Pen Teh-huai, described as "Commander of the lst Field Army and the Volunteers in Korea and Deputy C.-in-C. of the Chinese Communist Army."

They stated: "Your statement of June 30 this year concerning peace talks has been received. We are authorised to inform you that we agree to meet your representatives for conducting talks concerning cessation of military action and establishment of peace.

"We propose that the place of the meeting be in the area of Kaesong on the 38th parallel. If you agree, our representatives are prepared to meet your representatives between July 10 and 15, 1951."

This was the first time Gen. Peng Teh-huai had been named as commander of the Chinese volunteers in Korea. This post was previously believed to be held by the one-eyed Gen. Lin Piao. Gen. Peng became prominent as conqueror of the north-west in the Chinese Civil War.

(July 2)

MR. MORRISON BECOMES FOREIGN SECRETARY

By Our Political Correspondent

Mr. Bevin has left the foreign Office. He is succeeded as Foreign Secretary by Mr. Morrison. Yesterday was Mr. Bevin's 70th birthday. The Downing Street announcement said:

"Mr Bevin is laying down the heavy burden he has carried at the Foreign Office since the formation of the Labour Government in 1945. He has held departmental office uninterruptedly since he became Minister of Labour and National Service in the war-time Coalition Government in May, 1940.

"Those have been very strenuous offices. His new responsibilities will not entail the same amount of departmental work, but at the same time, as a senior member of the Cabinet, "He will undertake specific duties that are now being arranged."

Mr. Morrison was responsible for the Festival of Britain, the Central Office of Information, the Department of Scientific and Industrial Research and for general co-ordination of Government departments' activities. Which of these tasks will now fall to Mr. Bevin and which to Lord Addison is still unsettled.

He has still to discuss with the National Executive of the Labour Party and Transport House the question of who will discharge his functions as general director of the party organisation. It is unlikely that these will be compatible with his new duties as Foreign Secretary.

(March 10)

FIRST FLIGHT BY NEW JET

'DESIGN OF FUTURE,' SAYS TEST PILOT

The Avro Delta 707A jet plane, the latest development of the company's triangular wing "Flying Dart," has made its first flight at Boscombe Down, Wilts, it is announced to-day. Performance details, like those of its predecessor, the Delta 707B, remain secret.

Mr. R. J. Falk, the Avro test pilot specialising in research, was at the controls of the new plane. He said: "It handles beautifully, every bit as easily as the 707B. This is certainly the design of the future."

Sir Roy Dobson, Avro's managing director and a director of the Hawker-Siddeley Group, commented in London: "The Delta configuration is the logical conclusion of our search for an aircraft with the lowest possible drag and a high degree of manoeuvrability at altitude. We now believe we have it."

(July 23)

TV OFFER FOR ELECTION

STUDY BY PARTIES

By Our Radio Correspondent

The B.B.C. has offered television facilities to the political parties for the General Election campaign, and the matter is being considered by the party leaders. At the last election when there were only 285,000 licences, largely confined to the London area, the parties decided against using television.

Now the number of sets exceeds a million. The audience, which extends to all parts of the Midlands, will be expanded farther north when Holme Moss, near Huddersfield, opens on Oct. 12.

Party leaders will discuss how the medium could be used. The B.B.C. would probably prefer discussions on the lines of the "In the News" series, rather than individual addresses like those in the sound programmes. There would also be opportunities for using mobile units to televise from public halls and open-air meetings.

(September 25)

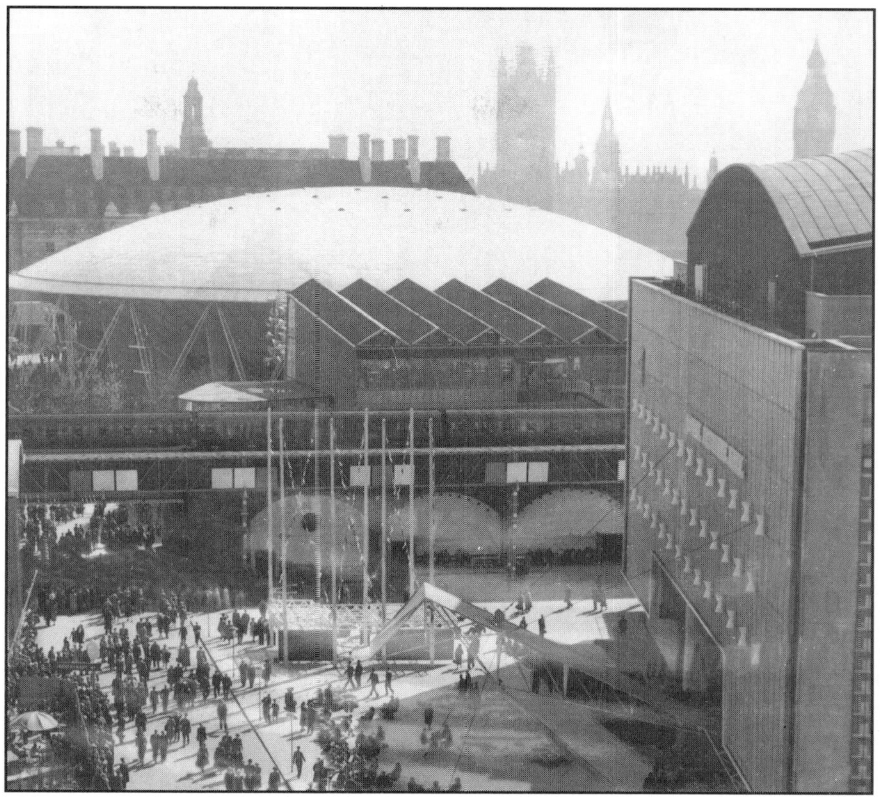

SUNSHINE AND SHADOW are seen in this general view of the South Bank Exhibition. Some of the thousands of people who flooded through the turnstiles are also well in evidence. The Dome of Discovery glints in the sunshine (centre background) with the Skylon towering above all (right).

98,000 VISIT SOUTH BANK EXHIBITION

CAFE PRICE CUTS AFTER PROTESTS

Daily Telegraph Reporter

A total of more than 98,000 people saw the Festival of Britain South Bank Exhibition during the weekend. The figures were:

SATURDAY............59,214
SUNDAY................38,857

The large number of visitors yesterday was despite the fact that the gates were opened two hours later than on Saturday. Earliest arrivals yesterday began to queue soon after 9 a.m.

They dispersed when reminded by the police that opening time was 12.30. By then, 1,500 people were awaiting admission.

After complaints of high prices for meals and drinks on Saturday there was a bigger supply of cheese and tomato sandwiches at 1s a round yesterday. The charge for afternoon tea in some restaurants was changed from 5s to 3s for lighter fare.

These concessions to the public were made after Mr. Gerald Barry, the director-general, and Mr. J. H. Polfrey, the catering manager had investigated complaints.

FEW FOR LUNCH

Lunchtime business was slow yesterday, partly because of prices, the 12.30 opening and partly because many visitors brought their own food. One result was that in the Royal Festival Hall restaurant a staff of between 350 and 400 served only 200 lunches at 7s 6d.

This restaurant, which charges 10s 6d for dinner and dancing in elegant surroundings, with a view of the exhibition and the Thames, will also start serving afternoon tea at 3s to-day. Charges here compare favourably with any good-class West End restaurant.

For concert-goers there are foyer bars where tea-shop and ordinary public-house prices will rule.

DISPLAY CANCELLED

Ten members of the London centre of the Women's League of Health and Beauty, who went to give two displays of exercises to music in the Exhibition Sports Arena, left after giving only one. The second display was cancelled.

Barefooted and barelegged, they found that the hard tarmac surface of the arena, strewn with small green gravel, bruised and cut their feet and knees. The 10 women, housewives and business girls of an average age of 32, wore white satin blouses and black satin shorts.

(May 7)

S. AFRICA VOTES BILL DECISION

SENATE'S POWER CONFIRMED

From Douglas Brown, Daily Telegraph Special Correspondent

CAPE TOWN, Thursday.

Mr. Van Niekerk, President of the South African Senate, to-day announced his decision that the Senate is competent to consider the Government's Bill to place the Coloured (mixed race) voters of Cape Province on a separate register. It can pass it by a simple majority, he said.

The entrenched clauses of the Constitution (under which a two-thirds majority of both Houses sitting together is necessary to deprive people of voting rights on the grounds of race) were "no longer of full force and effect."

From to-morrow, when the debate on the second reading begins, Opposition Senators will oppose the Bill in all its stages in the same way as their colleagues have already opposed it in the Assembly. Since they are in a minority, there is little doubt that it will become law before the end of the present session.

Whether after that it can be challenged in the courts is still a matter of hot dispute.

TORCHLIGHT DEMONSTRATION

Ex-Servicemen from all over the country and carrying torches have begun to converge on Cape Town. They are to stage a torchlight procession to Parliament on Monday night under the slogan: "Defend the Constitution."

Group Capt. "Sailor" Malan, a Battle of Britain pilot, who is a member of a motorised contingent from Johannesburg, said before leaving: "We will no longer stand for a Government, which, in the last war, openly supported our enemies."

Other ex-Servicemen attended a service in St. George's Cathedral, Cape Town, to mark Empire Day.

Afterwards a small group of school children and old soldiers gathered in the rain. They watched representatives of various patriotic organisations lay wreaths on the statue of Queen Victoria in the gardens of the Houses of Parliament.

The day was observed as usual as a public holiday, but there were few outward indications of its character. Dr. Malan, the Prime Minister, informed Parliament earlier this session that he intends next year to introduce legislation to abolish Empire Day as a holiday.

(May 25)

PHONE BOX CALLS TO COST 3D.

M.P.'S DISMAY AT INCREASES

By Our Own Representative

WESTMINSTER, Wednesday.

Higher charges for six Post Office services were announced in the House of Commons to-day by Mr. Ness Edwards, Postmaster-General. They were necessary, he said, to meet the steep rise in costs in practically all directions. The increases are:

INLAND TELEGRAMS, from 1s for nine words with 1d for each additional word, to 1s 6d for 12 words, with 1½d for each additional word, from July 1.

PHONE CALL-BOX FEES, From 2d to 3d for local calls, probably from Oct. 1.

INLAND MONEY ORDERS, poundage, including that on telegraph money orders, to be raised by 4d for sums up to £3, and by 2d for each succeeding step up to £10, with a minimum of 8d, from July 1.

C.O.D. FEES to be 10d instead of 4d on amounts up to 10s, with increases of 4d at each step up to £5, from July 1.

OVERSEAS PARCELS postage rates to be increased by about 50 per cent as soon as possible after June 1.

INLAND PRINTED PAPER postage to cost 1½d for the first 4oz from June 1, instead of 1d for the first 2oz.

(April 5)

STONE RESTORED TO WESTMINSTER ABBEY

ALL-NIGHT GUARD AFTER RETURN BY POLICE

Daily Telegraph Reporter

The Coronation Stone was restored to Westminster Abbey at 8.19 last night. Its return came 109 days after it was stolen from its place under the Coronation Chair in the early hours of Christmas Day. Guards kept watch on it in the Abbey throughout the night.

It came back to London as unobtrusively as it left. Apart from police, plain-clothes detectives and Abbey officials, only a few passers-by saw the historic 4cwt block of reddish-grey sandstone arriving. Among them were three singing Scotsmen in Tam o'Shanters, evidently in London for to-day's Association Football international.

Shortly after eight-o'clock two cars coming down from Millbank turned towards the barred side-entrance of the Abbey. The headlights of the leading car flashed on and off; figures ran from the shadows, and a number of police closed around the two vehicles.

The heavy iron gate to the Abbey was unbarred and in another second the two cars had moved into the lee of the south transept. Their 15-hour journey from Glasgow ended outside the Abbey doorway leading to the south transept, Poets' Corner and the high altar.

NOT IN ITS PLACE
"Further Notice" Awaited

The Dean of Westminster, Dr. Don, was at the door to receive the Stone. With him were Mr. T. Hebron, the Abbey Registrar, and Mr. W. Bishop, the Clerk of Works. Dr. Don left London by train later for St. Andrews. He is to preach there to-morrow.

Mr. Hebron said: "The Stone will not be placed in its proper resting place beneath the Coronation Chair until further notice."

No one was allowed inside the Abbey. Chief Insp. Osborne, who was in charge of police arrangements, said: "This is private property. No outsiders are allowed. You must leave the Abbey."

The decision to return the Stone immediately to the abbey was made by Scotland Yard after consultation with Sir Theobald Mathew, Director of Public Prosecutions. This decision probably means that the Director has decided not to proceed with any prosecutions concerning the actual theft.

He can, however, issue instructions to Scotland Yard to apply to the Bow-street magistrates' court for warrants for the arrest of suspects who are believed to have forced the door of the abbey at Poets' Corner when the Stone was stolen. They can be charged with breaking out of the Abbey.

Chief Det.-Ins. McGrath, who was in charge of the Stone, telephoned Scotland Yard for instructions when he was within 25 miles of London. He was told to take it to the Abbey and return it to the Dean.

(April 14)

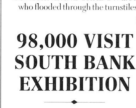

BUS MOWS DOWN CADETS: 23 DEAD

19 INJURED OUTSIDE CHATHAM BARRACKS

BOYS AGED 10 TO 13 HIT ON NIGHT MARCH

DRIVER WAS TO HAVE HAD SAFETY MEDAL TO-DAY

From Our Special Correspondent,

CHATHAM, Wednesday.

A double-decker bus ran into the rear of a company of 52 Royal Marine Chatham cadets marching along Dock-road here just before 6 o'clock last evening. In a statement issued late last night Mr. K. A. Horwood, Assistant Chief Constable of Kent, said that 23 boys were killed and 19 injured.

The youngest was 10 and the oldest 13. Only 10 of those in the front escaped unharmed. They were going from their headquarters at Melville Barracks to the Royal Naval Barracks to watch a boxing tournament between their members and the Sea Cadets.

When within 100 yards of the barrack gates in Pembroke-road a Chatham and District Traction Company bus ploughed into them. The accident occurred on a slight downward gradient between a high brick wall on the party's left and the embankment of the Gillingham road on the right.

The boys were marching on the left of the road in double-file under a regular Marine officer. Some cadets, those at the front, wore dark blue naval uniform with white belts, but a group at the rear were in civilian clothes.

The road was dry and the sky was overcast. Dock-road has its own system of single lamps 10ft high, but they are overshadowed by the more brilliant lights on the Gillingham road, which reflect over the tunnel-like appearance of the lower road. This gives Dock-road a shadowed effect.

FEW PASSENGERS

Driver's Long Service

The driver of the bus, John William George Samson, 57, of Albany-road, Chatham, was to have gone to the company's headquarters at Maidstone to-morrow to receive a medal for 25 years' safe driving. He has been with the bus company for about 40 years.

The bus, which had few passengers, was one in the quarter-hour service between Chatham and Pembroke-gate. There was a conductress aboard, believed to be named Dunster.

The assistant chief constable said that an inquest would not be held before Friday.

Mr Thomas W. Bowman, Mayor of Gillingham, in whose area the accident happened, was to-night considering raising a relief fund.

AREA CORDONED OFF

An emergency call was received at the Police station from a sailor, A.B. Krack, at 6.40 p.m. All available police officers were sent to the scene. As Krack was telephoning from the barrack gates, naval authorities sent four ambulances and three doctors to the stretch of roadway which resembled a battlefield.

Ambulances were also sent from St. Bartholomew's Hospital, Rochester. When the bodies had been removed to the R.N. hospital police cordoned off the area with red lamps, the bus standing derelict in the middle. A front mudguard was damaged by striking a lampost before the bus stopped.

Fire appliances and crew were also quickly on the scene and at a late hour were still assisting police to mark out the road. A 45-yard long strip of road, the length occupied by the marching boys was roped off and completely covered with a long roll of shining tarpaulin.

First people on the scene to give first-aid were men from the barracks. All available ambulances wre sent to the scene from all hospitals in the Medway towns. Police squads arrived in cars from several surrounding stations.

WITNESSED TRAGEDY

Boys Spread Over Road

Two petty officers and an able seaman were waiting for a bus 30 yards away when the accident happened.

One of them, Petty Officer John Williams 33, said "I was standing with another petty officer and an A.B. about 30 yards away. It was dark and suddenly I heard many screams. It made me go cold because it was the high-pitched screams of children.

"For a moment it was bedlam and I heard the squeal of heavy brakes. It sounded horrible. I saw a bus screeching to a stop and the three of us ran blindly up the road towards it.

"We saw all the boys. They were spread out from one side of the road to the other. I counted about 18 bodies lying pointing in every direction from one pavement to the other.

"I picked up two of the boys, but there was so little I could do. I stood there in the middle of the road and cried. I went all through the last war and have seen men killed, but these were boys.

"First assistance on the scene was the naval ambulance from the barracks 200 yards away. They were there within five minutes. No one could have sent for them in the time and I think they must have heard the accident in the barracks.

"Then men from the barrack gates arrived and within 10 minutes were rigging up lights all around the scene. I do not know what happened to the bus driver because I was looking at the boys.

Injured boys were calling for their parents. One little boy beside me, who was hurt, repeatedly called for his mother.

"There was one woman in the bus. She said to me ' The bus was running down the hill when I heard some bumps. Then I saw the children and did not know what to do.'

"I saw the bus standing empty at the side of the road. It was lit and had its lights on."

(December 5)

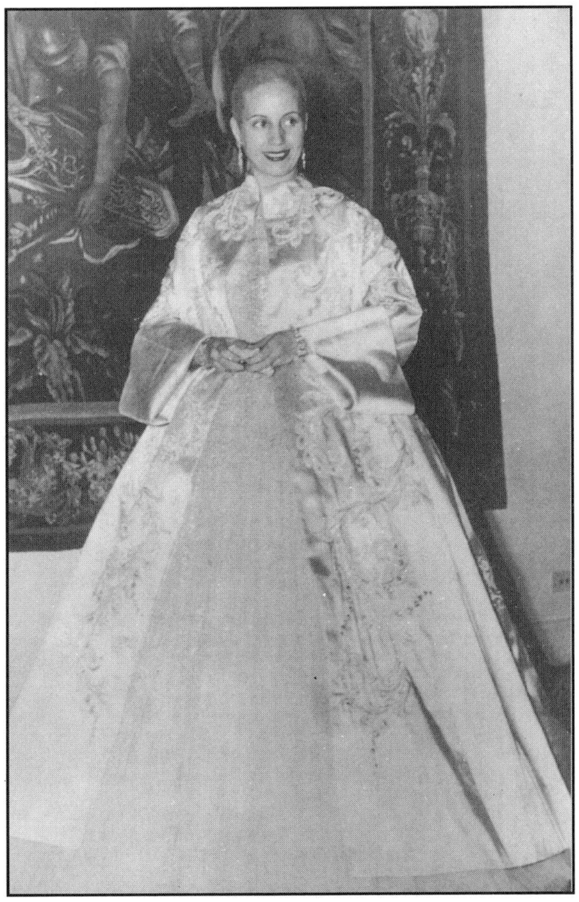

MME. EVA PERON

IRON CURTAIN'S 'CHRISTMAS FOR STALIN'

RED STAR ON TREES

From Our Own Correspondent

VIENNA, Thursday.

The Communist campaign to obliterate the Christian basis of Christmas and substitute a form of political festival has reached new heights this year. The so-called "Christmas" begins everywhere behind the Iron Curtain to-morrow, with gigantic celebrations for M. Stalin's birthday. He is 72 tomorrow.

The ideological offensive will continue unbroken until New Year's Day in an attempt to blur the significance of the two Christmas holidays. To fit this policy, the traditional Christmas-tree is being replaced wherever possible by the "winter-tree" or "New Year's tree."

In Rumania "winter-tree festivals" are being organised between Dec. 26 and Jan. 2. The Communist trade unions are supervising the programme, which features approved cultural entertainment without a religious background.

Hungary has kept its Christmas-tree. But it must now be dedicated to the republic, and the Star of Bethlehem on the top has been replaced by the red star of Russia.

SANTA CLAUSE ABDICATES

Father Christmas has had to abdicate throughout the Cominform countries in favour of "Father Frost". This is a Russian-type character representing winter in general.

(December 21)

MME. PERON IN HOSPITAL

OPERATION LIKELY

From Our Own Correspondent

BUENOS AIRES, Sunday.

Mme. Peron was in hospital to-day awaiting an operation for an unspecified ailment. Although recent bulletins have spoken of anaemia and mentioned the possibility of surgery, the removal to the President Peron Polyclinic at 10.30 p.m. yesterday took most observers by surprise.

A bulletin issued after her admission said that the final decision about an operation would be taken "within 24 hours." It added: "The general state of her health is good, and it is expected that she will undergo the surgical risks successfully." Dr. Finochietto, one of Mme. Peron's physicians and a leading Argentine cancer specialist, is in charge at the hospital.

Following the news that Mme. Peron has been admitted to hospital, all Peronista organisations have suspended campaigning for the elections, to be held on Sunday.

But another announcement added that Gen. Peron would broadcast on Monday, Wednesday and Friday.

It was also announced to-day that the Radical party's campaign in the province of Entre Rois, where Senor Santander, a deputy, was badly beaten a fortnight ago, and where Senor Rodolfo Ghioldi, the Communist Presidential candidate, was shot on Wednesday, would be completely suspended.

(November 5)

FOURTH ATOMIC BLAST SHAKES NEVADA CITY

GLARE SEEN 400 MILES FROM TESTING RANGE

From Our Own Correspondent

NEW YORK, Friday.

Another atomic explosion, the fourth in six days, occurred shortly before dawn to-day at the testing ground of the Atomic Energy Commission in the desert of Nevada. It was the biggest of the series.

It caused a concussion which struck the city of Las Vegas, 75 miles away, with the force of a minor earthquake. It was also the first to cause any damage there, shattering a big glass window in a shop.

Some high buildings swayed slightly. The flash of the explosion was described by distant observers as lighting the pre-dawn sky brilliantly. An orange-coloured ball of fire like a setting sun appeared over the area of the range.

Then came three distinct blasts - first a minor one and then two sharp jolting ones. All echoed and rumbled in the mountains of the Sierra Nevada.

The glare was seen more than 400 miles from the range. It was clearly observed in the area of San Francisco and Oakland, up to 425 miles away, about the distance from London to Glasgow.

RADIOACTIVE SNOW

At the same time as the news of the atomic explosion reached New York there were strong but officially unconfirmed reports that snow which fell this week in Rochester, New York State, was "measurably radioactive".

Rochester is about 170 air miles from New York City and 500 from Nevada. Radioactive dust has also been reported in Canada.

A.E.C. officials issued a statement today that "there is no possibility of harm to humans or animals" in the snow or dust. It added: "The University of Rochester is co-operating in investigation."

(February 3)

BRITONS PLAN EVEREST CLIMB

SPRING EXPEDITION

Daily Telegraph Reporter

A British expedition will make a new attempt to climb Everest in the spring it was learned yesterday.

The expedition will be lead by Mr. Eric Shipton, 44, who recently led an attempt to find a south-west route to the 29,000ft peak. He is expected to take the same team for the spring attempt: Mr. W.H.Murray, Dr. Michael Ward and Mr. T. Bourdillon of Britain, and two New Zealanders, Mr. H.E.Riddiford and Mr. E.P.Hilary.

There is believed to be a practicable way to the summit from the south-west once the cascading ice-fall of the Western Cwm., which blocked the Shipton reconnaissance expedition, has been negotiated.

Mr. Shipton has informed the Nepalese Embassy that he plans an expedition in the spring. A Swiss group has also applied to the Nepalese Government for permission to make the ascent in March or April.

(December 5)

U.S. COUPLE TO DIE FOR ATOM SPYING

Altered Course of History, says Judge

From Our Own Correspondent

NEW YORK, Thursday.

Sentence of death was passed here to-day on an American and his wife who were convicted last week of giving atom secrets in war-time to Russia. They were: Julius Rosenberg, 32, an electrical engineer, and Ethel Rosenberg, 35.

Both are residents of New York. They have two children and are the first American citizens ever to be sentenced to death for espionage in peace or war.

A third defendant, Morton Sobell, 34, a radar expert, was sentenced to 30 years' imprisonment. Judge Kaufman said he was convinced of Sobell's guilt, but added that it was of a lesser degree.

Ordering the Rosenbergs to be executed during the week beginning May 21, he declared: "Plain, deliberate murder is dwarfed by your acts. I have searched the records and my conscience for some reason for mercy, but I am convinced I would violate the trust placed in me if I showed any leniency.

"By your betrayal you undoubtedly have altered the course of history to the disadvantage of our country. I believe your conduct in putting into the hands of the Russians the atom bomb before our best scientists predicted Russia would perfect the bomb has already caused Communist aggression in Korea, with resultant casualties exceeding 50,000 Americans, and who knows but that millions more innocent people may pay the price of your treason."

CALL TO CONGRESS

Judge Kaufman also called on Congress to review the present penalties for peace-time espionage. He said the law as it stood meant that should any person be convicted now of transmitting secrets about the new type atom or hydrogen bombs the maximum penalty that could be imposed was 20 years.

The trial had indicated quite clearly that an "enemy" nation was "employing secret as well as out-spoken forces among our people."

The chief witness against the Rosenbergs had been David Greenglass, 29, who is Mrs. Rosenberg's brother. He has already pleaded guilty to war-time espionage and is to be sentenced to-morrow.

It was shown in evidence that the Rosenbergs had relayed to a Soviet spy ring such secrets as the drawings of the atom bomb dropped on Nagasaki, Japan, in 1945.

Spies to whom they gave information were said to be members of the international ring with which Klaus Fuchs, the German-born atom spy, was connected. Fuchs was gaoled in Britain in March last year.

A Soviet Vice-Consul in New York, Anatoll Yakovlav, was indicted at the same time as the Rosenbergs. But it was later stated he had escaped arrest by going to Russia.

The Rosenbergs showed no emotion to-day as the death sentence was passed on them. Their counsel and Sobell's announced afterwards that appeals would be lodged.

(April 1)

FAMILIES WELCOME THE GLOUCESTERS HOME

From Our Special Correspondent

SOUTHAMPTON, Thursday.

The Gloucesters are home. About 700 officers and men of the 1st Battalion arrived here this evening from Korea, in the troopship Empire Fowey, 19,121 tons, to the deafening cheers of relatives and friends of the regiment.

They had waited some hours to welcome back a unit of the British Army of which Gen. Ridgway, C.-in-C., United Nations Command, Far East, said: "I am extremely proud to have had it as a unit in the United Nations Command and I personally commend it for its brilliant record."

Fourteen months ago I saw the battalion leave here 900 strong under the command of Lt.-Col. J. P. Carne, whose name was given in the list of prisoners of war handed over by the Communists. Just 16 of the cheery men he took out that day came back to-night.

They were among the first ashore and had to face a large number of correspondents and photographers. They and the rest of the battalion who had relatives, or friends, waiting ashore were allowed to come down the gangway in batches for an "elastic" half-hour of reunion.

(December 21)

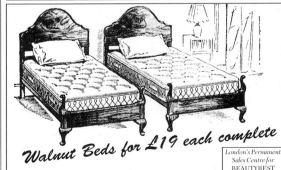

THE QUEEN LAYS STONE OF NATIONAL THEATRE

'A NEW PARTNERSHIP OF THE NATION AND STAGE'

Daily Telegraph Reporter

In the presence of many representatives of the world of British drama, the Queen yesterday laid the foundation stone of the National Theatre which is to rise, a memorial to Shakespeare, between the Royal Festival Hall and Waterloo Bridge on the South Bank of the Thames. Princess Elizabeth accompanied her.

Thousands of visitors in the exhibition grounds also witnessed the outdoor part of the ceremony. They cheered the Royal party's arrival, which was heralded by a fanfare by six State trumpeters.

The Queen was dressed in deep lavender, with fur dyed to tone trimming her shoulder cape. Princess Elizabeth wore a floral silk dress under a fitted coat of old gold, with white hat, bag, and elbow-length gloves.

They were conducted to the upper foyer of the Royal Festival Hall, where actors and actresses, dramatists and critics, and supporters of the theatre awaited them. The Queen was welcomed by Mr. Oliver Lyttelton, M.P., chairman of the Joint Council of the National Theatre and the Old Vic.

PREMIER AT CEREMONY

Those present at the short ceremony which followed included Dr. Fisher, Archbishop of Canterbury, and Mrs. Fisher, Viscount Jowitt, the Lord Chancellor, and Viscountess Jowitt, Mr. and Mrs. Attlee, Sir Denys Lowson, Lord Mayor of London, and Lady Lowson, Mr. J.W. Bowen, chairman of the London County Council, and Mrs. Bowen.

Bouquets were presented to the Queen and Princess Elizabeth by Carolyn Clare Meyer, 8, and Ashley Meyer, 6, great-grandchildren of Sir Carl Meyer. Sir Carl died in 1922. He was a supporter of the Shakespeare National Memorial Theatre, towards which he gave £70,000 in 1909. The Queen's bouquet contained all the flowers mentioned in Shakespeare's plays.

The Queen was performing the ceremony in the absence of the King, who is still convalescent. She conveyed his message of regret that he was unable to be present.

She recalled the early days when the English theatre won Royal recognition and protection, an alliance which the passing years brought to an end. "But now a new partnership of the nation and the stage is signified by the agreement of Parliament to build, largely at common cost, a theatre national in name and purpose.

"It is my hope that when this National Theatre is built it will fulfil two purposes. The first is to provide by the contributions of all and for the enjoyment of all, a playhouse worthy of the plays and players on whom success must depend."

(July 14)

NICHOLAS
MONSARRAT
writes the novel
of the year

The Cruel Sea

BOOK SOCIETY CHOICE
EVENING STANDARD
BOOK OF THE MONTH

'BILLY BUDD' AT COVENT GARDEN

MANY FELICITIES IN BRITTEN'S SCORE

By Richard Capell

Benjamin Britten's fifth opera, "Billy Budd", an opera of life in the Royal Navy soon after the Nore Mutiny, was given its first performance at Covent Garden on Saturday, conducted by the composer.

For the best part of two hours "Billy Budd" seems episodical and almost purposeless, despite the extraordinary resource and aptness of Britten's musical illustrations. Then the climax comes, and it is harrowing in its pathos. No one can fail to be moved, any more than admiration can be grudged for the vivacity of the score. But the long piece is pathetic rather than truly tragic, and the attempt made to draw a universal significance from the hero's doom is not brought home.

The subject comes from a painful story - a kind of elaborate anecdote - by Herman Melvill. Billy, a cheerful young foretopman in H.M.S. Indomitable, excites the insane animosity of the saturnine Iago-like master-at-arms, Claggart, who hatches a plot to bring against him a charge of mutiny. Faced with his accuser in the captain's cabin, Billy strikes him, and the master-at-arms falls dead. Billy is hanged.

This action has been dramatised for Britten by E.M. Forster and Eric Crozier - more or less dramatised, a phrase that means rather less than more. The fact is that neither of the chief characters, the inexplicable or, at least, unexplained Claggart and the enigmatic Captain Vere, is fully realised. The difference between life and art is that art must not be inexplicable, whatever life may be.

In Act II Claggart sings a counterpart of Iago's "Credo in un Dio," but we do not really know why. As for Vere, he stands by like a waxwork while Billy, at the court martial, is accused of murder, though knowing perfectly well that the act was mere manslaughter.

Yet it is Vere who, at the end, is "redeemed" by Billy or by his memory of Billy's sterling qualities. He is, in fact, the Amfortas to Billy's Parsifal. But all this is obscurely, and not dramatically, suggested.

UNIQUE SETTING

Britten's score cannot be called much of a structure, but the incidental felicities are innumerable, and many things are in his best vein - the lower-deck songs and dances, the brilliant ensemble of the battle scene and Billy's affecting farewell to life in the condemned cell. There is matter for study in the variety and certainty of the orchestral effects.

Scenically the opera is unique in its setting on board an 18th-century warship, and the admirable Covent Garden production interests the eye. The general scheme is a fiercely lighted foreground amid inspissated blackness.

The part of the victimised Billy is very happily entrusted to a personable young American baritone, Theodor Uppman. If Vere (Peter Pears) and Claggart (the gloomy Hagen-voiced Frederick Dalberg), are both rather stiff, there are many lively, well-characterised and well-sung minor performances, among others by Bryan Drake, William McAlpine, Hervey Alan, Anthony Marlowe and Inia Te Wiata. The audience voted "Billy Budd" a triumph.

(December 3)

PATRICIA MORRISON

First Night

A BEGUILING ACTRESS

SUCCESS OF 'KISS ME, KATE'

By W. A. Darlington

In New York 18 months ago I found it an article of popular religious belief that "South Pacific" was the best musical ever written. I said I liked "Kiss Me, Kate" just as much, and people looked at me with shocked eyes. On the voyage home a man solemnly congratulated me on my courage in stating openly a belief so contrary to dogma.

Well "Kiss Me, Kate" has now arrived in London, with Patricia Morrison still in the lead; and all I ask is that you should go to the Coliseum when you can get in - and judge for yourselves whether anybody need ask to see a more lively musical or beguiling actress.

The outstanding merit of the piece, both in regard to Sam and Bella Spewack's book and Cole Porter's lyrics and music, is its ingenuity.

There is quite a good story, about a leading actor and actress who a year after their divorce, come together as Petruchio and Katherine in a musical version of "The Taming of the Shrew" and conduct a blazing private row which gets tangled with the one they are conducting in the play.

To all this Cole Porter brings his gift for haunting, elusive music and for neat rhymes. I find his share of the entertainment even more delightful at a second hearing.

As for Miss Morrison, she was obviously added last night to the list of London favourites. She has amazing good looks, she can sing and she can hold the stage; the comic force she gets into her song "I Hate Men" is alone worth a visit to the Coliseum.

Bill Johnson makes a very satisfactory sparring partner for her, and has a fine voice. Julie Wilson as a Bianca far more sophisticated than the one Shakespeare drew, has a personal success.

(March 9)

A FEAST OF GOOD ACTING

By W. A. Darlington

In ancient days there used to be a play called "The Rival Queens" in which London used to delight to watch the great ladies of the playhouse trying to act one another off the boards.

To-day, stage methods are gentler. But still, those who go to the Haymarket to see N.C.Hunter's "Waters of the Moon" will capture something of the old-time thrill as they watch Dame Sybil Thorndike and Dame Edith Evans share the honours of a finely acted play.

Dame Sybil plays Mrs. Whyte, an ageing lady who has lost her home, her husband, her son and most of her money, and is living in a dreary private hotel on Dartmoor in a mood of resignation. Dame Edith plays Mrs. Lancaster,

---

ALEC GUINNESS AS HAMLET

INTELLIGENT AND SARDONIC

By W. A. Darlington

Alec Guinness gave us a deeply interesting Hamlet at the New Theatre last night.

It was cram-full of intelligence, it was beautifully spoken and, since Mr. Guinness is co-director of the play, it was obviously the exact Hamlet that his very well - graced actor wanted to present. I am not, therefore, being derogatory when I say that it does not rank with the great Hamlets. It was not conceived on that scale.

Mr. Guinness deliberately avoids purple patches, and discards many shades of stress and emphasis which have become traditional with present-day Hamlets. He speaks the plain text without flourish, and loses thereby all romantic colour and much emotional force.

On the other hand, he achieves an admirable sardonic quality which underlies and lights up everything that he does, giving the performance as a whole the unmistakable stamp of individuality.

TRICKS WITH LIGHTING

It is unfortunate that the style of the production, which plays strange and largely ineffective tricks with the lighting, should be out of key with the acting. In the play scene, for instance, all the lights were suddenly faded out except a spot directed on Claudius's face, and I felt as disconcerted as if I had heard somebody in the audience utter a loud yell.

All the more, because Walter Fitzgerald was doing far too well as Claudius to need this kind of interference. He makes the king the very type of the able, successful vulgarian wearing his crown as a black marketeer might wear a too-shiny topper.

Another very successful performance is that of Alan Webb as Polonius—a Polonius seen, for once, not through Hamlet's prejudiced eyes as a tedious old fool, but as he must have been—an administrator of proved quality still in harness but beginning to be too old for his work.

(May 18)

rich, confident and barely middle-aged, who thinks that everybody ought to agree with her that life is wonderful.

GLITTER AND GENTLENESS

In a three-day stay, enforced by ice-bound roads, Mrs. Lancaster upsets the dull monotony of life in the hotel, and infects all its inhabitants except Mrs. Whyte, with a longing for more spacious existence. Then she departs, and the spurious brightness fades.

Dame Edith's part is all vitality and glitter, and she achieves in it an easy coruscation. But the prize, if there were one, would go to Dame Sybi for the certainty of her gentle touch. Incidentally she is one of the few actresses who can carry off a piano-playing scene with the keyboard facing the audience.

The play is throughout a feast of good acting. Wendy Hiller and Leo Bieber have fine moments as the two people most affected by the visitation. Kathleen Harrison as the least refined of the hotels inmates is as delightful as ever.

(April 20)

BRITISH COMEDY SEEN AT ITS BEST

By Campbell Dixon

BRITISH films are still literary in inspiration, which explains why we make first-rate imaginative and semi-satirical thrillers, like "The Third Man," "State Secret" and "Seven Days to Noon," but never a realistic thriller comparable with "Boomerang" or "Double Indemnity."

Fantasy alone is not our long suit; we have yet to produce a "Pinocchio" or a "Wizard of Oz." But there is a sort of hybrid, a combination of thriller and fantasy, that our people now do better than any others.

THE LAVENDER HILL MOB (Odeon, Marble Arch) is a charming example. Hunting, the enthusiast said, gives us the image of war without its guilt and only five-and-twenty per cent of its danger. The new Ealing comedy gives us all the fun of safebreaking without any sense of guilt and no danger at all

The likeable scallywag has been a favourite in English fiction from Nashe's Jack Wilton to Hornung's Raffles. Here he plots to steal a cool million (if a million is ever cool), while we watch with serene assurance that nobody will be hurt and that if somebody must be robbed - well, who can afford it better than the Mint? We applaud his ingenuity, we laugh when plans go wrong, we feel a little pang of regret when - but I mustn't give away the end.

The setting (though outwardly the familiar London of the City and genteel boarding houses and Hendon Police College) is a Cloudcuckooland where the writ of the Public Prosecutor does not run. Losing contact with reality, we are as indifferent to our heroes' honesty as Charles Lamb was to the Restoration heroine's virtue. It is difficult to feel moral indignation at the backslidings of a figment. Alec Guinness's clerk, middle-aged and humble and underpaid, is not one clerk suffering from poverty and indigestion and the importunities of wife and children: he is an abstraction, the sum total (except for flesh and blood) of all the clerks who ever handled fabulous wealth in the course of the day's work and then went home to Surbiton on the 6.15.

Stanley Holloway, as the artist who helps him smuggle the gold out of the country in the form of models of the Eiffel Tower, is the epitome of all the romantics who ever dreamed of acquiring sudden wealth by one great gorgeous coup. Both Mr. Guinness and Mr. Holloway are at the top of their form.

(July 2)

'GAY'S THE WORD' APTLY NAMED

CICELY COURTNEIDGE

No musical show could be more aptly named than Ivor Novello's "Gay's the Word," presented at the Saville last night. The plot—a back-stage affair—was efficient rather than inspired and the lyrics by Alan Melville no more than neat. But for Mr. Novello's music, Jack Hulbert's production and Cicely Courtneidge's performances—gay really was the word

Miss Courtneidge was playing the part of a renowned musical comedy actress. She rose completely to this casting, and to her stage name as well, which was inevitably "Gay." Sentiment, burlesque, pathos or comedy a song or a dance—she can do it all.

The show started brilliantly with a witty parody on one of Mr. Novello's own Ruritanian romances. It then left the provincial stage, on which Gay Daventry had been performing, for his academy of acting —an establishment which gave every opportunity for students (and principals) to perform for us attractively; in song, dance and theatrical burlesque.

Finances cause a little trouble, the love between two pupils some diversion, and the excuse for some songs, sentimental and exuberant, very effectively sung in their different styles by Thorley Walters and Lizbeth Webb, with her attractive double-toned voice,

(February 17)

POIGNANT NEW OPERA

A new opera, " The Consul," by the American composer Gian-Carlo Menotti, worked powerfully on the nerves of the audience at the Cambridge Theatre last night.

It is a Kafka-like nightmare rendered poignant by the fact that the miseries of the woebegone folk seeking a visa for a better land have been, and still are, the actual experience of multitudes in our time.

As an opera the work is non-traditional. It derives rather from the cinema, and the music—terse, aptly illustrative and in its way resourceful—is like clever film music.

The effect owes much to the extraordinarily vivid characterisation achieved by the company. There was unrestrained applause for Marie Powers's singing of the grandmother's lullaby in the first act: for Norman Kelly's conjuring tricks in the Consul's waiting-room (a curiously bizarre effect): and above all for the protagonist, Patricia Neway, the desperate wife of a heroic outlaw, caught and strangled in the net of circumstance.

(February 8)

New Fiction

Tough Sea Story

By John Betjeman

The Cruel Sea. By Nicholas Monsarrat. (Cassell. 12s 6d.)

The Catcher in the Rye. By J.D. Salinger (Hamish Hamilton. 10s 6d.)

"The Cruel Sea" has the hallmarks of best-sellerdom. Book Society Choice, Book of the Month in America, all editions sold out before the book is written, highly commended by public libraries, such boosting is no recommendation to an envious cynic like your reviewer.

There is a surprising lack of reticence about sex in "The Cruel Sea". Indeed, the author seems deliberately to set out to shock his readers with the shore life of some sailors and with gruesome details of killing, as this about a depth-charge exploded among drowning men:

"Men floated high on the surface like dead goldfish in a film of blood. Most of them were disintegrated, or pulped out of human shape. But half a dozen of them, who must have been on the edge of the explosion, had come to a tidier end: split open from chin to crutch, they had been as neatly gutted as any herring. Some seagulls were already busy on the scene, screaming with excitement and delight. Nothing else stirred."

Strong and tough stuff, no doubt. This author's contempt for all except physical action, his admiration of human ferocity, and his dislike of those who speak and write make one wonder why he was so inconsistent as to write a book himself. But the wonder is soon dispelled by appreciation.

He wrote this book out of a deep affection for his fellow officers in corvettes and frigates. It is this affection which carries one through the 400 pages of grey and closely printed text. He is at his best when describing convoys and action against U-boats. His two chief characters, Ericson, the commander and hero, Lockhart, his No.1 and the hero-worshipper, are too good to be true. But his subsidiary characters, the officers who are more briefly sketched and whose backgrounds, whether Birmingham or Birkenhead, are so swiftly and touchingly portrayed - these come to life.

(August 31)

★ ★ ★

The narrator of "THE CATCHER IN THE RYE", by J.D.Salinger, is an American boy of 16, child of rich parents, and just sent away from his fourth school for refusing to work.

The manner of telling is conversational and full of American slang. But the boy himself, through all his strangeness and his chronic indolence, is somehow sane and charming. The book carries its reader along through the force of the narrator's personality and outlook.

(August 10)

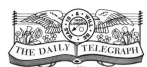

THE DAILY TELEGRAPH
AND
MORNING POST
DAILY TELEGRAPH - JUNE 29, 1855
MORNING POST - NOVEMBER 2, 1772
[Amalgamated October 1, 1937]
135 Fleet Street, London, E.C.4.
Telephone: 4242

PEACE PROSPECTS IN KOREA

COMMUNIST acceptance of Gen. RIDGWAY's offer of a meeting between military commanders in Korea has been announced in a manner which will do nothing to lessen the caution with which hopes of a cease-fire and armistice must still be held. Postponement of the proposed meeting for at least 10 days and the suggestion that it should be held on the only speck of territory south of the 38th parallel not occupied by the United Nations forces may be merely face-saving manoeuvres. But they may equally foreshadow Communist insistence upon terms (about the position of a demilitarised zone, for instance) which the United Nations could not possibly accept. Nevertheless, the fact that the Communists are ready for talks is in itself evidence that they now recognise the failure of their aggression, and to that extent, encourages hope of an early truce.

From cease-fire to armistice and from armistice to final settlement are two successive steps, the first of which may well be difficult, and the second both difficult and lengthy. What is of immediate importance is that the United Nations should agree, and stand unshakably, upon the minimum conditions for an armistice. Their unanimous desire to bring the slaughter to an end must not lead to acceptance of terms which might allow it to break out again when the aggressors think they have a better chance of success. The issue is one of common sense rather than principle. The 16 nations engaged in Korea are reported to have drawn up an armistice plan for submission to the enemy. Some of the points may be open to bargaining, but upon one of them there ought to be no compromise. This is the stipulation that an international commission, with facilities for inspection, be set up to see that the armistice terms are being carried out.

That observers should be able to travel freely in North Korea, or at the very least to make aerial reconnaissance, is a crucial provision. Without it an armistice would be valueless and precarious. Merely to suspend hostilities and establish a demilitarised zone, without controlling what went on north of it, would be to allow a breathing space from which the enemy, in his present situation, would benefit immeasurably more than the United Nations. Mutual pledges to bring no fresh forces into Korea would be useless unless it could be seen that they were being honoured; and since North Korea has a land frontier with Manchuria, actual inspection by representatives of the commission would be the only means of ensuring this.

Inclusion in the armistice-terms of provision for international supervision would, at the present stage, represent the one tangible gain from 12 months' fighting. North Korea, into which the Communists refused to admit the United Nations commission charged with unifying the country, would at least be opened to an international body, even if its purpose were limited to seeing that the armistice was observed. Other less palpable achievements could also be claimed for a peace based on such terms as those adumbrated in Washington. To bring the war to an end through the military worsting of the aggressors (which is the only reason why they are ready to talk at all) would enhance the prestige of the United Nations everywhere, and would make other potential aggressors pause.

(July 2)

NO ROAST BEEF IN OLD ENGLAND

HOUSEWIVES as they ruefully survey their eightpenny meat rations will find little to solace them in Mr. MAURICE WEBB's laborious apologia in the House of Commons yesterday. The Minister of Food based his excuses, such as they were, on adverse terms of trade. Like a fisherman explaining away a poor catch, everything was at fault - the weather, the current, the line, the hook - except his own angling. In fact, his failure has been truly lamentable. As Capt. CROOKSHANK pointed out in a pungent and telling speech, the meat ration to-day is considerably lower than it was in the most critical years of the war and compares unfavourably in quantity and quality with that provided to workhouse inmates in the much maligned pre-Welfare State days.

Everyone agrees that trading conditions have been difficult. There is less meat, available for purchase than there was before the war: the Argentine Government has used this shortage to drive tough, if not unscrupulous, bargains; prices have been rising, and look like soaring. All this is admitted, but in no wise excuses the Government for its total lack of foresight, for its belated and expensive improvisations (like suddenly deciding to buy non-carcase meat in France at a vastly higher price than the Argentine Government was asking for carcase meat) for its failure to foresee the trends of world trade and to act accordingly. It has bulk purchased and planned us into unprecedented scarcity, and landed itself in a situation in which it is paying out to the butchers as compensation for the meat they cannot sell about as much as it would cost to provide them with stock to make the compensation unnecessary. Not even on the flying island of Laputa (where "planning" was also highly regarded) did such a nonsensical state of affairs arise.

(February 9)

NATIONAL THEATRE

OUR National Theatre, for so long a dream of the few, is now fast becoming an actuality for the many. The laying of the foundation-stone by the QUEEN yesterday marked the close of 50 years of struggle and, we hope heralded a new era of achievement. The project originated in the minds of GRANVILLE-BARKER and WILLIAM ARCHER, but the movement they initiated seemed for many years to belie its name. True, it moved sideways to absorb the movement which proposed to erect a memorial to Shakespeare: it moved upwards, too, in public interest and esteem, borne aloft on the shoulders of many voluble supporters and on the strength of one magnificent benefaction from Sir CARL MEYER. But of forward movement it seemed incapable, until at last in 1937 it suddenly acquired an unsuitable site in Cromwell Gardens. The site, however, swallowed half of the available funds and further progress was out of the question. As SHAW remarked on behalf of other supporters, "The subject is not exhausted: but we are."

Now it really seems that all we have left to consider is what rôle the National Theatre should play in our national life. While there was no prospect of anything being achieved, aims and objects could be left vague and multifarious. But now we have to decide. It has been suggested that the new theatre could best serve the living drama by experimenting wherever possible with new material. But many will feel that the living drama is best served not by experiment but by the performance of plays of proven worth, recalling our great traditions and warning us of what great rivals we had in previous generations.

(July 14)

COVENTRY CATHEDRAL TO BE SIMPLE AND MODERN

WINNING DESIGN: ZIG-ZAG WALLS AND GLASS ENTRANCE

From Our Own Correspondent

COVENTRY, Wednesday.

The competition to find a new design for Coventry Cathedral, most of which was destroyed by bombing on Nov. 14, 1940, has been won by Mr. BASIL SPENCE, 44, of Moray-place, Edinburgh, it was announced to-day. He wins the first prize of £2,000.

Second prize of £1,500 goes to Mr. W.P. HUNT, 33, of Scroope-terrace, Cambridge. Third prize of £1,000 goes to Maj. A.D. KIRBY, 40, of Victoria-road, Swindon, Wilts.

Mr Spence said to-day that he did the winning design as a hobby, while working at the Festival Exhibition. The new cathedral could be described as a modern one.

His lifelong ambition was to design a cathedral. He was one of the architects who won Festival awards for housing last month.

"OUTSTANDING EXCELLENCE"

The 219 entries were judged by Sir PERCY THOMAS, Mr. EDWARD MAUFE, and Mr. HOWARD ROBERTSON, nominated by the Royal Institute of British Architects. Announcing their decision they stated: "We consider the general level of designs is disappointing, but the selected design is of outstanding excellence.

"The shape of the new cathedral is simple, the existing tower being an essential part of the design. The ruins of the old cathedral are retained but divided from the new simple rectangular building by a great porch and a huge glazed screen, which can be lowered into the ground so that the cathedral is open.

"The author's idea is that on such occasions there would be no physical obstruction between the whole population of Coventry and the altar. [The altar will be in the middle of the building.]

Structurally, the building is planned on simple lines.

CONCRETE VAULT

"A reinforced concrete vault, designed as lightly as possible, is supported by tall, elegant columns of steel cased in concrete, or post-stressed concrete units. Walls are of solid stone construction, pierced with windows.

"The floor is concrete with a finished surface of patterned stone, and the foundation is of concrete. The roofing is of copper laid on roofing felt. Built inside and out in local pink-grey stone, the new cathedral will harmonise with the old when weathered.

"The walls are of zig-zag pattern with all windows shining towards the altar. The nave accommodates seating for 1,374."

The report added that Mr. Spence stressed the beauty of the ruined cathedral as an eloquent memorial to the courage of Coventry people. He said that the major part of it should be allowed to stand as a garden of rest, treating it as an atrium to the new cathedral.

Dr. GORTON, Bishop of Coventry, said of the design: "I am delighted. The glass entrance will allow anyone to see right along the cathedral to the altar."

(August 16)

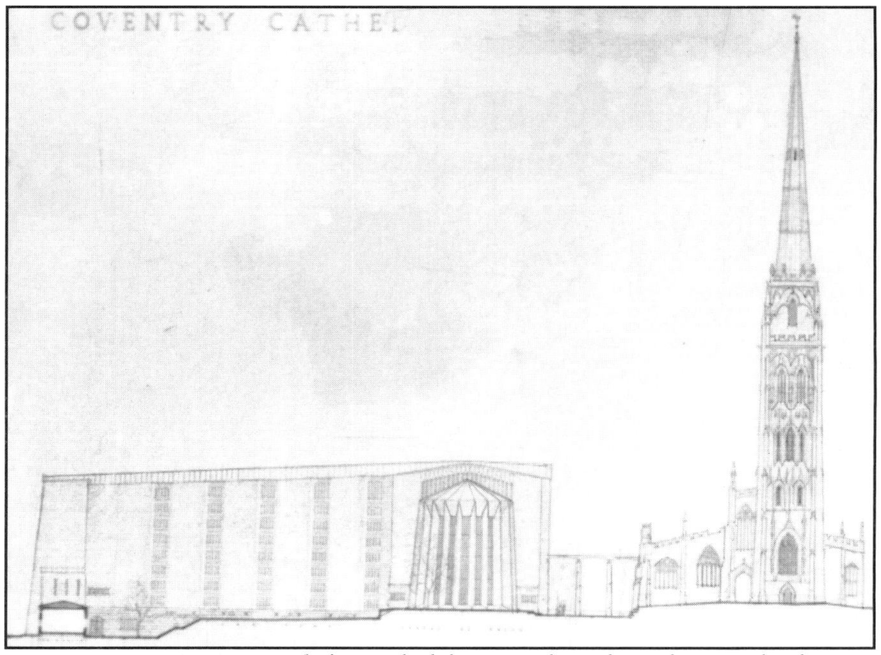

THE PRIZEWINNING DESIGN for the new catherdral at Coventry, showing the west elevation. On the right is a drawing of the old cathedral with the existing tower and ruins. The architect is Mr. Basil Spence, F.R.I.B.A.

DINING-OUT IN THE WEST END

The "Mayfair touch," implicit, I hope of restrained elegance and gastronomic skill, should not be peculiar to Mayfair. The Coronet Restaurant in Soho-street confirms my point. Here M. Michele supervises the service of his own creations - soufflé de sole Michèle (12s 6d for two persons), mousse de jambon de Courcy with pâté de foie gras (8s 6d) and crêpes Kinsale (5s). This latter, his outstanding achievement so far, is a simple sweet which will, I prophesy, win the approval of those who ordinarily avoid sweet sweets and turn for final solace to the cheeses. This 20-year-old restaurateur shows great promise both for his own future and our pleasures at the table.

The lovers of shellfish would do well to visit Wheeler's in Old Compton-street. Here Jack, once a wrestler, has a tremendous following as star oyster opener. The medium size oysters, when in season, cost 10s 6d per dozen, a lobster salad 7s 6d and half a good-sized lobster from 8s 6d. There is always fresh salmon in its season, 8s 6d. The coffee is also commendable.

At The Restaurant Tyrol, Dean-street, ask for M. Charles. He will serve you with some typical Austrian dishes. Wiener Backhuhn 5s, Tiroler Knoedel 3s 6d, Apfel-Strudel 2s. A three-course meal of consommé viennois, Frankfurter m. Sauerkraut and a Strudel will cost you 7s 3d. The setting is Tyrolean, designed by Ewald Guth with murals by Hubert Gurschner. Benches, panelling, doors, screens and bar-counter are the work of Tyrolean craftsmen.

I found it all charming, clean and crisp.

BON VIVEUR

(June 6)

THE KING OPENS THE FESTIVAL

SPLENDOUR AT ST. PAUL'S

By Guy Ramsey

With high splendour, with fittingly festal pageantry, the King yesterday inaugurated to the world the Festival of Britain.

Beside him on the steps of St. Paul's stood, shoulder to shoulder, all differences forgotten, the great ones of the country: before him, in thousand upon thronged thousand, his people; above him, crowning the majestic mass of the dome, the gilt cross gleaming in the fitful spring sun.

Slim, elegant, his Admiral of the Fleet's uniform slashed with the brighter blue of the Garter, the King spoke, the single microphone catching his words and radiating them to a crown grown suddenly silent. "One hundred years ago," he said, and spoke of the sanguine hopes of that vanished world.

Above loomed the Cathedral that had seen the Victorian dream shattered: around the desolate ruins that testified to the "March of Progress." But, here and there, the broken stones were ablaze with blossom: no flowers on a grave, but harbingers of the English spring, spiritual as well as seasonal emblems of renewal.

"We have not proved unworthy of our past," said the King - and before him were ranked the Yeomen with their Tudor halberds, the pikemen in their Stuart steel. "We can do better in the years ahead" -and the multitude kindled at the words.

WELCOME TO VISITORS

Britain Shows the World

"Let us welcome to our shores the many members of our British Commonwealth, and all the visitors from other lands who have come to see what this old country can do." All sorts and conditions of foreign visitors were in the crowd. They saw, in the magnificence of the official opening one small evidence of what this old country - blitzed and battered, its belt tightened, threatened but unshaken - still can do.

Many hours the crowd had waited, some of them since the grey and misty dawn broke over Ludgate Hill: waiting on the pavement, drinking from vacuum flasks, munching sandwiches grown stale; filling windows - a Latin American Legation occupying a barber's shop: lining roofs: perched precariously on rubble and bomb-splintered walls. Many hours the patient police had harried them with good humour, keeping clear the route.

Incongruity abounded: sixteenth- and seventeenth-century figures pouring out of gleaming buses: an ambulance shrilling down Ave Marialane: a couple of terriers gambolling ahead of the brilliant cavalcade of the Life Guards: spectators running across the road to snap the Household Cavalry, helmets doffed for the relayed service of dedication....

For more than an hour the forecourt was choked with gleaming limousines, with, here and there, a chugging taxi. The sporadic cheering rose to a roar as bent upon his walking-stick, Mr. Churchill made his way up the Cathedral steps.

PATTERN OF SOUND

Bells and Aircraft

Joyously the bells wove their intricate pattern of sound, their jangling beauty interspersed with cheers and shouting and, just twice symbolically, if one so cared to think - the scream of an aircraft as it sped across the sky.

The spasmodic cheering was suddenly sustained as, with jingle of steel and clatter of hooves, the Sovereign's escort cantered up the slope and, drawn by the Windsor greys, the carriages swept to the steps.

The Queen in lavender-blue; Princess Elizabeth in dark green; Princess Margaret in grey with a pink hat; the Duke of Edinburgh, like the King, in naval uniform with the Garter diagonal across his breast; the Duke of Gloucester and Duchess, in blue; the Duchess of Kent in champagne and brown, the Princess Royal in pink, the young Princes and Princesses of the Royal House.

The Lord Mayor, in his sable and gold, the pearl-handled sword upright in his hands - and far on the skyline on the Old Bailey, Justice, her sword, too, pointing to the sky. The tension rose, then relaxed as the glittering array vanished within the great portals.

The Guard of Honour grounded its arms; the H.A.C. laid down its pikes and filed away; we shifted, aware again of aching backs and weary feet. The nurses, male and female, of the St. John Ambulance, in the words of one Cockney spectator, "did a roaring trade in fainting women."

THE ENGLISH SCENE

Grey, Silver, Green

How English it was. The grey sky shot with silver, the grey mass of the Cathedral, the grey mist through which loomed the unbroken spires of the City; the green spaces of the distant park where were ranged the guns now not for defence but for ceremonial and deathless changes; the throng of those who had jeered at the Festival, shrugged at the Festival, derided the Festival but who were English enough to rejoice at it when it was come and, above all, to cheer the Royal Family, "God bless 'em."

The prayers within were relayed to the waiting throng. From my distant perch I saw one tiny child kneel on the kerb when the rhythm of the Lord's Prayer struck a familiar note. More than one voice from the road joined in shamefacedly, almost, as "Jerusalem" welled out from the choir.

A cheer for Mr. Attlee, a louder one for Mr. Churchill: the quiff of the Foreign Secretary, the grey head of the Home Secretary were identified with short bursts of applause.

(May 4)

THE BRIGHTER THE BETTER

For Winter Sports Fashions

Cables Winefride Jackson

From St. Moritz

Swiss faces are smiling here in St. Moritz. Hotels have been full for Christmas and the New Year. Many more people seem to be trying out a winter sports holiday, including the not-so-young.

It is too early in the season to know how much the English may contribute to Swiss coffers now that we are allowed to spend £100. For personal economic reasons many people may not want to take advantage of this amount, but at least we can hold our heads high.

The Swiss are also making concessions - to keep their visitors from straying to resorts in Austria, Italy and France, where prices are reputedly cheaper, particularly incidentals such as drinks and the odd shopping. After a stay of at least 14 days in Switzerland (it must be continuous in the same hotel) the visitor is given a grant of 50 francs - just over £4 - in cash, or it can be credited to the bill.

Ski-ing lessons are cheaper. Three two-hour sessions cost 17s 6d, against 25s last year, 12 lessons, £2. 10s, against £4. While most visitors buy or hire a ski outfit in London, the actual skis, including sticks, can be hired at the resorts. Here in St. Moritz, for 10 days this costs just under £2.

For fashion, this centre continues to lead the winter resorts. Smartest ski trousers are black. Jackets and sweaters on the other hand run to colour. Nothing is too bright, nothing too exotic - not even the wondrous hood I saw made of black monkey fur, the fur pointing upwards into a high peak. It nearly, but not quite, shook the local people, who normally are inured to fashion eccentricities.

Some of the French women wear a magpie effect of black and white - black ski suits, black caps and a short duffle-style jacket of white. The effect is strikingly smart.

PEACOCK-TRAIN SHORT EVENING DRESS

For gala dinners and dances over Christmas and the New Year women brought their smartest evening dresses. At the Palace Hotel some guests wore short tubular and strapless evening dresses of satin, ballerina dresses in layers of contrasting coloured tulle, the peacock-train short dress and the classic long dress.

Male sartorial note: Jacques Fath enlivening the dance floor in a dinner jacket of Stewart tartan. Some of his Paris mannequins also arrived to present his mid-season collection - mainly evening dresses and after-ski clothes. All after-ski slacks are now tapered into a bootee. The straight loose style is rarely seen.

Apart from these gala occasions, evening dress is not essential at even the larger hotels in St. Moritz, although the standard of cocktail and sports clothes is high.

Continental and American women have a flair for dressing up sweaters and slacks with colour in scarves and belts that extract the maximum smartness and femininity from sports clothes. It is a flair we might acquire with profit.

The newcomer to St. Moritz will find sophisticated life at the Palace and the Kulm (prices are high), traditional Swiss life at Steffani's with its celebrated Grotto Bar (from 25s a day) and dignified comfort at the Schweizerhof (from 2gns a day). These prices include room, food, taxes and tips.

(January 1)

Week-End Food

REINDEER MEAT

Daily Telegraph Woman Reporter

Reindeer meat at 4s 6d lb was displayed in several butchers' shops in Central London yesterday. There were cheaper cuts at 2s but they had more bone and gristle. A small chop cost 1s 6d and a joint for a family of four cost almost as much as a chicken.

For rationed meat choice may be made between beef and lamb. Many housewives are buying at the rate of 1s 4d for each adult, having held over last week's eightpennyworth.

No offal is available, but an increased variety of tinned meat is in butchers as well as grocers' shops. Packs of Czechoslovak luncheon roll made from veal and ham, pork sausages from South Africa (3s lb) and Scotch grouse from Midlothian (15s a tin) are new arrivals. Whole roast chickens, boned, are 17s 6d a tin. In addition cold roast chicken, ready for carving, is offered at 12s lb in the West End.

(February 16)

DOG-SKIN LININGS FOR FOOTWEAR

LEATHER SHORTAGE

Dog skins are being processed for lining footwear because of the high price and shortage of leather. Dog skins were first used commercially during the war-time evacuation of London when many people had their pets destroyed.

Some 50,000 skins came on to the market and these were used mainly in the manufacture of gloves. It is understood that present supplies come mainly from dog homes.

(January 11)

GOAT MEAT NOW

Daily Telegraph Woman Reporter

GOATS have joined reindeers to provide off-the-ration meat. Yesterday legs of goat cost 4s lb - 6d cheaper than reindeer. Stewing goat was 1s 6d lb and stewing reindeer, 2s. Goat, it was said, has a flavour resembling lamb. In colour, the flesh is much darker.

(February 26)

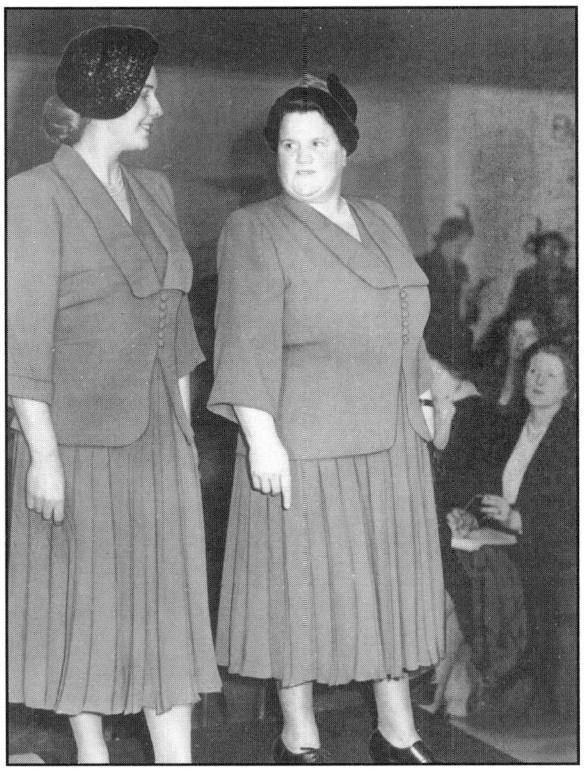

MANNEQUIN M.P. Mrs. Bessie Braddock, Socialist Member for Liverpool Exchange, displaying a turquoise marocain model at a parade of outsize fashions at the Dorchester yesterday. On the left is a professional mannequin, wearing an identical model in a smaller size.

PRINCESS MARGARET'S 21st BIRTHDAY

'Zodiac' Cake at Party To-night

From our Special Correspondent

BALLATER, Monday.

Princess Margaret comes of age to-morrow. Her 21st birthday cake, packed in a rope-bound wooden box, labelled "Fragile, with care, this side up," was delivered at Balmoral Castle to-day in readiness for to-morrow night's party.

The cake, single-tiered and two feet in diameter, weighs 30lb. Made by a London firm of caterers, it was brought overnight from King's Cross by Mr. S.E. Jacobs, of Thornton Heath, who decorated it.

It has 12 sides, on each of which is a sign of the Zodiac, worked in cream marzipan. Leo, the Princess's sign, is on the main panel. On the top is outlined in icing the Princess's personal standard.

Among the decorations are 21 silver candles, silver roses and thistles. Mr. Jacobs decorated one of the wedding cakes presented to Princess Elizabeth and the Duke of Edinburgh.

MR. W. WALLACE A GUEST

Travelling by the same train were Miss Jennifer Bevan, Princess Margaret's Lady in Waiting, and Mr. William Wallace, who will attend the party.

Because the King and Queen desire privacy, there are to be no official celebrations in Deeside towns for the birthday. There will be no dances or organised lighting of bonfires on the slopes overlooking the castle.

In the evening the King and Queen will give a small dance for the Princess. This will be attended by Princess Elizabeth and the Duke of Edinburgh, who are at Birkhall, a few friends who are staying at the castle, and others who will drive from houses in the district.

The only glimpse the sightseers caught of any member of the Royal family was in the afternoon, when Princess Margaret went for a drive with Group Capt. Townsend, Equerry to the King.

(August 21)

TEA UP ½d A CUP IN SOME CAFES

Customers at Lyons, Express Dairy and A.B.C. teashops and cafés yesterday found that their cup of tea cost 3d instead of 2½d.

The increase raises the price ½d above that of 1939. During the war the price went down to 2d, but was restored to 2½d last year. The further rise, made necessary by the general increase in costs, was decided on after consultation between the three firms.

(November 22)

MRS. BRADDOCK MANNEQUIN

CHAMPION OF THE OUTSIZES

Daily Telegraph Reporter

Mrs. Bessie Braddock, M.P., made her debut as a full-scale model yesterday in a mannequin parade of outsize gowns at the Dorchester, Park-lane. Her aim was to show that dress designers and manufacturers could mass-produce creations for stout women with slender purses.

The Socialist member for the Exchange Division of Liverpool made a speech. Then she crossed, re-crossed and sidled along a floodlit stage after the sleek professional mannequins.

Mrs. Braddock lent weight to her argument to the accompaniment of coffee early on and sherry and cocktails later. She modelled a turquoise-blue satin-backed marocain two-piece, presented to her by the manufacturers. On her head was a tiny black confection with a turquoise-blue cluster of small feathers.

Alongside her, similarly clad, was Miss Elizabeth Fry, a West End mannequin of praiseworthy proportions.

LENDING HER NAME

Mrs Braddock said: "I would not lend my name and publicity to something with which I was not satisfied." She had examined every one of the dresses and blouses in Norman Linton's collection of 34, all to be mass-produced at utility prices.

"I have been interested in outsize clothing ever since I was outsize; and that is ever since I was born.

"I have a sister as slim as I am stout. It angers me when I go shopping with her and see how she can pick a dress off the peg. Working women outside stock sizes can seldom find a dress suitable to them and within their means."

Mrs. Braddock's two-piece choice, according to technical data furnished by Mr. Linton, involved a semi-fitting jacket with horseshoe rolled collar, crystal-pleated bodice and multi-pleated skirt.

DIMENSIONS

As to dimensions, long the subject of conjecture in usually well-informed circles at St. Stephen's, Mr. Linton matched estimates with reality. Mrs. Braddock's two-piece, which became her, was for a women 5ft 2 in tall and for a 50in bust, 40in waist and 50in hips.

At £7 12s 5d her two-piece was the costliest item in the collection. Mrs. Braddock proved her point that slim-looking, youthful garments can be made cheaply for women of "homely" build.

Dresses costing from £3 14s 6d for women with hips more than 48in were paraded. There were blouses at £1 14s 6d for women with busts 42in to 48in.

(December 7)

AUSTIN SEVEN IS 8.3 h.p.

PRICE OF NEW CAR KEPT SECRET

By W.A MacKenzie,
Daily Telegraph Motoring Correspondent

Details of the re-born Austin Seven can be revealed to-day - 24 hours after the car, shrouded in dust sheets, had been wheeled into place at Earl's Court.

Britain's best kept Motor Show secret was, in fact, one of the earliest cars to reach the exhibition, where thousands of carpenters, electricians, painters and cleaners prepared yesterday for the opening by Mr. Strauss, Minister of Supply, to-morrow morning.

Every few minutes workmen took a surreptitious peep beneath the dust sheets. The one thing they could not see was the price, which will remain a secret for another 24 hours.

The betting is that it will be lower than the £280 basic price of the cheapest car at the moment.

30 BRAKE H.P.

The most surprising thing about the Austin Seven is that it is an "eight". It is rated at 8.3 h.p., with a cylinder capacity of 800 c.c., and develops 30 brake horsepower.

Even so, it is the smallest-engined car in quantity-production. Only the 919 c.c. Morris Minor and the 933 c.c. Ford Anglia are in anything like the same class.

The original Austin Seven was of 750 c.c. and developed 17 brake horsepower. But the new car is said to have an economy in petrol consumption greater than the 40 miles per gallon of its smaller-powered predecessor.

In appearance it bears no relation at all to the older "Seven". It is considerably larger, for it follows modern styling in placing the radiator and engine well forward in the chassis and in extending the body width to the outer edge line of the now discarded running boards.

GREATER LEG ROOM

Consequently, the interior width and leg room is far greater than before. There is also a capacious built-in luggage boot.

The car has the shape and the character of the bigger cars in the Austin range. It has a bulbous, grilled front, wings flared into bonnet and body sides, built-in head lamps, one-piece windscreen and a four-door, four-light steel body.

Mechanically the car is equally modern. Independent front wheel suspension, using coil springs, semi-elliptic rear springs; a four-speed synchromesh gear-box, with short control lever on the floor; and hydraulic brakes are all fitted. The car is 11ft 4 in in length and turns the scales at 13 cwt.

Another new car will be seen for the first time at the show. It is a three-litre Alvis-engined Healey sports three-seater. Modelled on the lines of the Nash-engined Healey, which is built at Warwick for export only, this new car, employing all British units, will be available for sale in the United Kingdom.

(October 16)

ROOTES GROUP PUT UP PRICES

£30-£80 INCREASES

Daily Telegraph Reporter

Increases ranging from £30-£80 in the price of its cars were announced yesterday by the Rootes Group, which comprises Hillman, Humber and Sunbeam Talbot cars.

The Group stated that up to now rising manufacturing costs had been offset by greater efficiency. But in the face of further material increases and a cut in total production, higher retail prices were inevitable. Increases, with old prices, are:

	Old Price	Purchase Tax			New Price	Purchase Tax		
	£	£.	s.	d.	£	£.	s.	d.
Hillman Minx Sln	395	110	09	05	425	118	16	1
Hillman Minx Coupe	470	131	06	01	505	141	00	7
Hillman Estate Car	465	129	18	04	495	138	05	0
Humber Hawk Sln	625	174	07	03	665	185	09	5
Humber S.Snipe Sln	895	249	07	03	945	263	05	0
S.Snipe Touring Lim	970	270	03	11	1,020	284	01	8
Humber Pullman Lim	1,395	388	05	00	1,475	410	09	5
Humber Imperl Sln	1,395	388	05	00	1,475	410	09	5
Sunbeam Talbot 90 Sln	775	216	00	07	820	228	10	7
Sunbeam Talbot 90 Cpe	825	220	18	04	875	243	16	1

The statement added: "It is particularly unfortunate that the comparatively modest increases which the Group has had to make are accentuated by the inflationary effect of purchase tax."

(February 2)

FOOD FOR ELECTION NIGHT

By Marguerite Patten

Last General Election we had no intention of sitting up all night, but as the results came through and we watched the reaction of the crowds on the TV screen, we found ourselves so keyed up that we just couldn't go to bed. We were unprepared for our sojourn then, but this year we're planning well ahead. Comfort above all else, plenty of cushions and blankets, food to keep us going, so that we shall feel fortified to accept depressing or encouraging results, as the case may be.

I toyed with the idea of a camp bed in front of the set, but don't think that will be possible. We live in an area where reception is poor; few people, therefore, have television, and we're already hearing from several friends who would like to watch with us. We can't provide beds for them all, but we certainly can feed them.

This is an occasion when I don't want to be in the kitchen, so all preparations are to be made beforehand, and the fare will consist of dishes that are soothing at that hour in the morning. I plan to have a large pan of good home-made MINESTRONE SOUP, a few small SAVOURY CUSTARD TARTS (I'm afraid I shan't have enough eggs to make many), and INDIVIDUAL HADDOCK PIES with creamy potato on top. These will keep beautifully and not become dry if I leave them in a very low oven. I can't imagine that we shall want elaborate sweets in the early hours of the morning, so we'll have fruit drinks, and some fingers of CARAMEL CAKE.

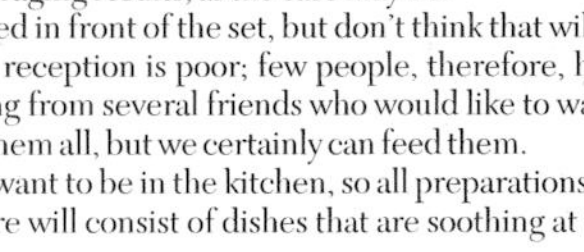

... in a very low oven.

I can't send the poor things home without any breakfast, so unless my grocer bequeaths me a few extra eggs - which is quite unlikely - I shall use part of a tin of kidneys and give my guests DEVILLED SAUSAGES and KIDNEYS ON TOAST.

I heard this morning from an old friend who says that once again she'll be doing a considerable amount of canvassing. With the long country runs, packed food is essential, and when I reply to her letter, "some ideas, please!" I know she'll not have much time for cooking, so suggest HAM AND TOMATO FINGERS AND FISH PUDDING (sent by a kind sister in Norway - the recipe, not the pudding), which is delicious as a filling in rolls, and a very good CURRIED GALANTINE.

(October 20)

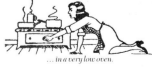

Obituary

IVOR NOVELLO

VERSATILE MAN OF THE THEATRE

Ivor Novello, who has died aged 58, was an actor-manager, playwright and composer whose talents found their fullest expression in spectacular musical romances. These invariably introduced melodies which established him as one of the most popular British song-writers.

Born in Cardiff, he was the son of Mr. David Davies, a Civil Servant, and Mme. Clara Novello Davies, the singer and choral conductor. To her faith, guidance and determination he declared in later life, he owed, more than anything, his success.

She continued to exercise a powerful influence on his career until her death in 1943. A choral scholarship took him to Magdalen College School, Oxford, and he later studied composition.

SUCCESS AT 21

In 1914, when he was 21, he wrote "Keep the Home Fires Burning," This song rivalled "Tipperary" in popularity with the Services and civilians alike during the 1914-18 War, in which Novello served in the R.N.A.S.

He made his stage debut in 1921, and three years later he began actor-management in London with "The Rat," which established him as a matinee idol. There followed "The Truth Game," "I Lived With You," "Fresh Fields" and "Murder in Mayfair."

The first of his musical successes with a Ruritanian background was "Glamourous Night," presented at Drury Lane in 1935. "Careless Rapture" and "Crest of the Wave" followed in 1936 and 1937 respectively.

"The Dancing Years" 1939 was withdrawn on the outbreak of the war, but reopened at the Adelphi in 1942. It then ran for nearly 1,000 performances.

His next success was "Perchance to Dream," 1945, "King's Rhapsody," from the cast of which he withdrew for several weeks at the turn of the year because of ill-health, opened at the Palace in September, 1949.

(March 7)

MR. SINCLAIR LEWIS

The work of Sinclair Lewis, the American author who has died, was remarkable for incisiveness and for characterisation, which was instantly recognisable. He was 65.

He wrote 21 novels. One of them, "Babbitt," won him the Nobel Prize for Literature in 1930.

He was impatient of humbug and of smugness. His "Main Street", which made him famous in 1920, was a savage assault on American small-town complacency and hypocrisy.

"Babbitt" lashed out in similar fashion at the over-standardisation of existence among American business-men, while "Elmer Gantry" portrayed a self-indulgent clergyman.

Mr. Lewis was born in a Minnesota town which was generally believed to have provided him with the background for "Main Street."

BACKGROUND FOR BOOK

While at Yale he did free-lance journalism, and continued in newspaper work after graduating. He held posts in New York and in San Francisco before the publication of "Our Mr. Wren," his first novel, in 1914.

Once established, he maintained a steady stream of controversial but eminently readable works. "Martin Arrowsmith," in 1925, told of a young doctor whose devotion to medical science triumphed over the prejudices of his colleagues.

Mr. Lewis was awarded the Pulitzer Prize for this novel, but declined it because he disapproved of the conditions under which the award was made. "It Can't Happen Here" was an indictment of Fascism, and "Kingsblood Royal" an attack on racial prejudice. "The Godseeker" appeared last year and his last novel, "World So Wide", is due for publication in March.

(January 11)

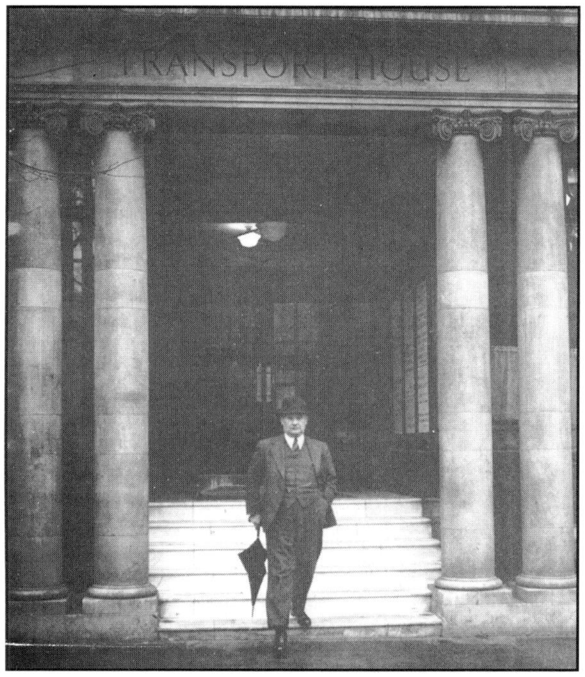

MR. ERNEST BEVIN

MR. ERNEST BEVIN

by Hugh Chevins

By the passing of Ernest Bevin the world has lost a true internationalist, the nation a sturdy patriot and the working-class movement a wise and courageous leader.

It is too early to assess the full merits or measure the success of his 5 ½ years work at the Foreign Office which ended with his resignation on his 70th birthday last month, and his appointment as Lord Privy Seal. At first his unorthodox diplomatic language, his drive, his handling of the state problems, his straight talking to other big Powers captured the imagination of the British public – and the Civil Servants.

Towards the end it became obvious to everyone that he was extremely ill. He aged rapidly, he looked tired and worn, his speeches lacked their customary fire, his doctor travelled everywhere with him. He battled on, but his friends would have been wise had they persuaded him earlier to retire and seek rest, for his policy became hesitant and stumbling.

RUGGED STATESMAN

At the height of his career Ernest Bevin's rough manners, his strident voice and his ragged speeches often belied to the outsider his breadth of vision, his prophetic far-sightedness., his calculating thought and his warm humanity. Behind the rugged – to some people, repelling – exterior there was the mind of a statesman.

He was a Socialist, but not a rigid Marxist theoretician. He could drive a fierce bargain, but he compromised. He could fight relentlessly, but his word was his bond.

He was a merciless, devastating debater who spared neither the feelings, nor the susceptibilities of his victims. He flayed friend and foe alike with scorn and contumely.

BIGGEST UNION

His dominant personality and his speeches at union conferences brought him to the notice of Ben Tillett, another West Countryman and dockers' leader, Tillett invited him to London. He was appointed national organiser of the union in 1910. Not many years had elapsed before he had superseded his old chief and effected the largest trade union merger of all time.

He moulded into one unit dockers, lightermen, stevedores, coal tippers and trimmers, grain weighers, taxi-cab drivers, motormen, lorry drivers, tramcar and omnibus drivers and conductors, carters, steel benders and fixers, farm workers, engineers, fishermen, clerks and administrative workers and general labourers.

From 1920 his power and influence in the trade union movement became unrivalled. The building of Transport House, in Smith Square, Westminster, which houses not only the headquarters of its own union but those of the T.U.C., the Socialist party and half a dozen other organisations, was Bevin's idea. He became the landlord of the Socialist and trade union movement and in 1937, chairman of the T.U.C. From 1925 to 1940 he was a member of the T.U.C. General Council.

MR. CHURCHILL'S CALL

Shrewd assessor of party politics though he was, Bevin was long content to remain aloof from the House of Commons. It was his rôle, he argued to emancipate the workers by industrial negotiation. But in May, 1940, when England's fortunes were at their lowest ebb, he received a call at Bournemouth from Winston Churchill to join the Cabinet as Labour Minister.

He accepted and gave his Department the insurance and dynamism for which Britain's most able Civil Servants had been longing. Often he shocked and bewildered the Civil Servants by dropping on their desks ruled foolscap sheets bearing in his own bold handwriting not only the framework but the complete structure for enlisting new hands for the war effort.

His mobilisation of 22 million fighting men and workers out of a population of 46 million had no parallel in history. Much of the remarkable network of consultative and advisory organisations he made for winning the war are being used in peace, though needing some reconstruction in the light of changed conditions.

It is no secret that, with other Socialist leaders, he had misgivings about the break-up of the National Government. His heart was set on unwinding, as he put it, the mobilisation scheme which he had wound up. He believed after VE-Day, however, that the mood of the rank and file was for a return to party warfare, and Bevin was loyal to the will of his followers.

When the Socialist Government was returned he had his eye on the Treasury, for, typically he felt the office of Chancellor of the Exchequer was the key post. The Prime Minister, however, wanted him for the Foreign Office. Again, out of loyalty Bevin subordinated his own desires.

TUSSLES WITH MOLOTOV

His tasks, including wearying trips to the Moscow, New York and Paris conferences, constant tussles with Molotov and Vyshinsky, solving the problems of Spain, Greece, Berlin, Palestine and Indonesia, and his part in the Brussels Pact and the Altantic Treaty were not made lighter by the querulous criticism of back-bench members of his own party and the Communists. They accused him of an anti-Soviet bias, of relying on the career diplomat.

He had no anti-Soviet bias, though a prejudice against the Communists would have been understandable after all the years of their wrecking activities within his union. All he asked of Russia was "cards on the table, face upwards."

He is survived by his wife and by a daughter. Mrs. Bevin took no active part in politics, but was a constant source of comfort and encouragement to him and acted as hostess at many diplomatic gatherings during his tenure of the foreign secretaryship.

(April 15)

PAKISTAN PREMIER ASSASSINATED

TWO SHOTS AT MEETING: CROWN LYNCH MURDERER

From Our Own Correspondent

KARACHI, Tuesday.

Mr. Liaquat Ali Khan, Prime Minister of Pakistan since it became a separate Dominion in 1947, died at Rawalpindi to-night shortly after being shot at a Moslem League meeting.

Two revolver shots were fired at close quarters, and the Prime Minister collapsed on the dais. The crowd pounced upon the assassin and beat him to death.

According to an unconfirmed report the man, named Syed Akbar, was a member of the Khaksar organisation. This is a semi-military Nationalist movement.

Akbar hailed from the Hazara district of the North-West Frontier Province. It is recalled that in 1943 a Khaksar tried to stab Mr. Jinnah, founder of Pakistan, in Bombay.

The leader of the Khaksars, Allama Mashriqi, who was educated at Cambridge, has been detained in gaol for several months. Khaksars have recently been agitating for his release.

Mr. Liaquat Ali Khan, who was 56, was rushed to hospital. He was given a blood transfusion, but succumbed to his injuries without regaining consciousness.

FUNERAL TO-DAY

To-night his body was flown to Karachi, where the burial will take place to-morrow with full military honours near the grave of Mr. Jinnah. Mr. Liaquat Ali Khan had left Karachi for Rawalpindi this morning.

The Cabinet met as soon as news of the assassination was received. Forty days' mourning has been ordered and all Government offices will remain closed for two days.

In Karachi grief is writ large on every face. It is generally acknowledged that Mr. Liaquat Ali Khan's death at the present juncture is a national calamity.

While no decision has been taken so far, it is believed in political circles that Sardar Abdur Rab Nishtar, Governor of the Punjab, will be appointed Prime Minister.

PLOT RECALLED

The Prime Minister's assassination came seven months after he had announced the discovery of a plot aimed "to create commotion in the country by violent means and in furtherance of that purpose to subvert the loyalty of the Pakistan defence forces."

Fourteen people were arrested, including the secretary of the Pakistan Communist party and senior officers of the Armed Services. They were all placed on trial.

(October 7)

DEATH OF MR. W. R. HEARST

5 SONS AT BEDSIDE

NEW YORK, Tuesday.

Mr William Randolph Hearst, the American newspaper publisher, died at 9.50 a.m. to-day at Beverly Hills, California. He was 88.

In the last few years Mr. Hearst had rallied many times from bouts of illness to confound reports that he was on the point of death. He was a man with great reserves of physical strength.

Despite his failing health, he maintained a close interest in the activities and progress of his many newspapers throughout the United States.

He leaves a widow and five sons, the eldest is Mr. William Randolph Hearst, junior. The sons and the chief executives of the Hearst Corporation were at his bedside when he died.

His doctor said to-day that Mr. Hearst had suffered several minor strokes during the past four years. He had recently spent much of his time in a wheelchair in his bedroom.

Mr. Impelliteri, Mayor of New York, has ordered that all flags on city buildings should be flown at half-mast tomorrow. A eulogistic tribute was paid to-night by Mr. H.S. Mackay, personal adviser to Mr. Hearst.

He disclosed that "as will be shown by Mr. Hearst's last will and testament when it is filed for probate, he leaves the bulk of his estate for the benefit of his fellow-Americans, for charitable, religious, educational, literary, scientific and public purposes." The size of the estate is not known, but it is expected to run into many millions of dollars.

(August 15)

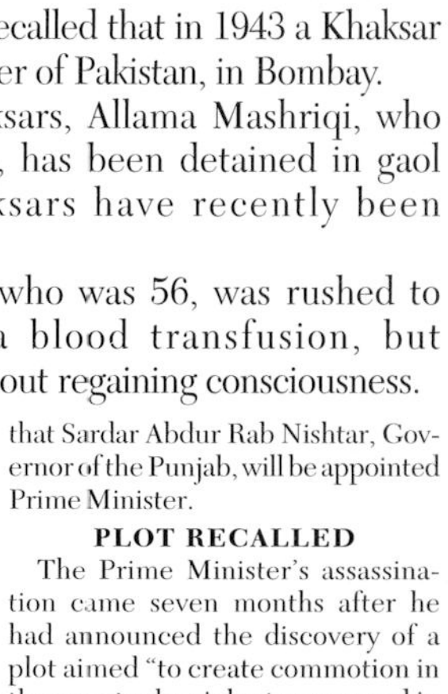

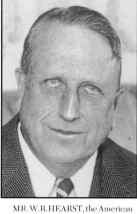

MR. W.R. HEARST, the American newspaper magnate.

MARSHAL PETAIN

1916 HERO LED APPEASEMENT

Marshal Henry Philippe Pétain, who has died at the age of 95, was born in 1856 in the Pas de Calais.

The first half of his career was undistinguished. He graduated from the military academy of St. Cyr and began the long climb of the promotion ladder in the normal way.

On the outbreak of the 1914-1918 war he was 58, a colonel commanding a brigade and due shortly for retirement. He had become an expert in fire power, although he had yet to fire a shot in anger. His pupils at Ecole Supérieure de Guerre included Francisco, later General Franco, and a young officer named Charles de Gaulle.

With the German invasion of Belgium and France his promotion was meteoric. Within two months he was a general, commanding an army corps. Within a year he was leading the Second Army in Champagne. Then followed Verdun, where his rallying cry "Ils ne passeront pas. Courage ! On les aura." made him the hero of France, and command of the Army Group of the Centre. Finally, in 1917, he succeeded Nivelle as French C.-in-C.

His steadfast and judicious blend of reforms and punishments prevented the spread of mutiny which had already broken out in many units, demoralised by many defeats. But, in March, 1918, when Ludendorff launched his supreme effort, Pétain's nerve showed signs of cracking. Lloyd George referred to his care and caution, and Poincaré described him in his diary as "defeatist." The end of the war, however, found his reputation unassailable.

MAGINOT LINE PLANNER

In 1925 he led the joint French-Spanish forces which suppressed the revolt of Abd-el-Krim in Morocco, and later worked on the plans of the Maginot Line. He was Minister of War in 1934, and was appointed Ambassador to Spain in March 1939. In May 1940, he joined the Reynauld Cabinet as Deputy Prime Minister and in June succeeded M. Reynauld as head of the French Government with the object of appeasing the aggressor.

Arrested in September, 1944, and taken to Germany, he returned voluntarily to France six months later to face his trial. He was found guilty on Aug. 15, 1945,on counts of treason and of conspiring to overthrow the Republic, and after the death sentence had been commuted by Gen. de Gaulle, taken to the Isle of Yeu, off the Atlantic coast, to serve his imprisonment. His lawyers had recently petitioned the Council of Ministers for a retrial.

Last November the National Assembly in Paris defeated by 466 votes to 98 a motion inviting the Government to end the imprisonment of Marshal Pétain and to "allot him a residence and conditions of existence which would satisfy both feelings of humanity and the requirements of public order."

GEN. FRANCO'S OFFER

In February of this year, on the 35th anniversary of the Battle of Verdun, Gen. Franco paid tribute to the character of the Marshal and to the part played by him in 1939-40 when he was Ambassador to Spain in improving relations between the two countries, and declared that he would willingly offer him asylum on Spanish soil.

(July 24)

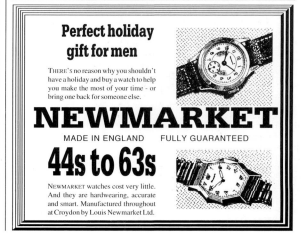

KING ABDULLAH ASSASSINATED

HIDDEN GUNMAN AT JERUSALEM MOSQUE

KILLER SHOT DEAD BY BODYGUARD

ALL-JORDAN EMERGENCY: YOUNGER SON REGENT

From Our Own Correspondent

JERUSALEM, Friday.

King Abdullah of Jordan, 69, was to-day assassinated in the Old City of Jerusalem within a few score yards of the Mosque of Omar, one of Islam's holiest shrines. His killer was immediately shot dead by the King's bodyguard.

The assassin was Mustafa Shakir, 21, a Jerusalem tailor, believed to be an Arab terrorist formerly employed by the ex-Mufti of Jerusalem. He hid behind a gate through which King Abdullah entered to attend noonday prayers at the Aksa Mosque, within the same compound as the Mosque of Omar.

The King had passed the outer door of the Mosque precincts and was approaching the Mosque itself when the murderer sprang from behind a gate and shot him in the back at close range. The King died instantaneously in view of the horrified onlookers. Two high officers with him were wounded.

A state of emergency was proclaimed throughout Jordan and the Old City administration put under control of the Arab Legion, the force commanded by the British officer, Glubb Pasha. The Old City is in Jordan territory, the western boundary forming part of the frontier with Israel.

A curfew was imposed, road blocks set up and searches started in the clustered, huddled street. The frontier was closed, including the Mandelbaum Gate, the only exit to Israeli Jerusalem.

King Abdullah's younger son, the Emir Naif, 36, was proclaimed Regent. The elder son, the Emir Talal, 42, is at present in Beirut undergoing treatment for a nervous breakdown.

This is the second assassination of a pro-British statesmen in the Middle East within a week. On Monday Riad el Solh, former Lebanese Prime Minister, was shot in Amman, capital of Jordan.

Incomparable Host

As a man, King Abdullah was an incomparable host. Widely read in Arabic literature, he always had an apposite quotation for any situation, grave or gay.

Possibly, he liked best to be among the Bedouin - for a tent to him was a palace. He loved to recount details of his early life in the Hejaz among the tribesmen. He had every custom in Bedouin lore at his finger tips.

MR. CHURCHILL'S REGRET

Mr. Churchill said at his Westerham, Kent, home; "I deeply regret the murder of this wise and faithful Arab ruler, who never deserted the cause of Britain and held out the hand of reconciliation to Israel. This is a tragic event."

A TRIBUTE

The Arab world can never be the same again without the rich, versatile, and solid character of King Abdullah of Jordan.

He was a man whose stature in statesmanship seemed ever to increase. Though he did not always see eye to eye with other leading Arabs, his prestige remained unassailable, however much denigration he suffered.

His loyal friendship to Great Britain was never questioned. It was the main plank in his foreign policy. Time and again he proved his steadfastness - most notably, perhaps, in 1941, when he sent his Arab Legion to Irak to help quell the rebellion of Rashid Ali.

To his own people beyond the Jordan he was a father, though among the Palestinians subsequently incorporated into his kingdom he had his critics. There were also Arabs outside Jordan who objected to his "Greater Syria" scheme.

(July 21)

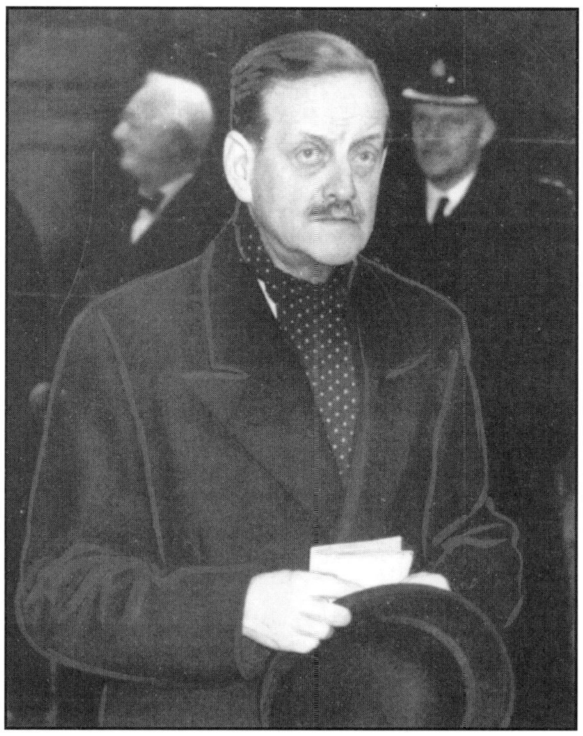

LORD BIRDWOOD, senior Field-Marshal of the British Army.

ANDRE GIDE

Andre Gide, who has died aged 81, had been for many years one of France's leading men of letters. In 1947 he was awarded the Nobel Prize for Literature. Some five months earlier Oxford University had conferred upon him the honorary Degree of Doctor of Literature, an act of homage which was condemned in the Moscow paper "Culture and Life" as "a blatant demonstration of the British reactionary spirit."

English readers have been made familiar with his great novels such as "The Immoralist" and "The Counterfeiters" through the translations of Dorothy Bushy, who also translated his autobiography. Gide himself was an enthusiastic translator of old and new masterpieces into French. Notably he was a translator of Shakespeare, and in 1948 Jean-Louis Barrault, the French actor, who had originally appeared in Gide's translation of "Anthony and Cleopatra," and later in his translation of "Hamlet," produced the latter play at the Lyceum Theatre, Edinburgh.

(February 20)

SIR CHARLES COCHRAN DEAD

A WEEK'S ILLNESS

Sir Charles Cochran, the theatrical producer, died yesterday in Westminster Hospital. He was 78. He was admitted eight days ago suffering from severe scalds received while he was having a bath at his home.

Lord Vivian, his partner, announced shortly after his death that the production of Miss Clemence Dane's new play, "The Lion and the Unicorn," scheduled for April, would be postponed indefinitely.

"The company feel that it is impossible at this moment to put out the ship without the captain," said Lord Vivian.

The funeral will be at Golders Green Crematorium at 4.15 p.m. on Monday.

(February 1)

LONDON DAY BY DAY

"Here we lay a stone"
A Chateau for the Windsors

When the Queen "well and truly" laid the foundation-stone of the National Theatre yesterday there was a sigh of relief at my side. "At last," said my companion. I could understand his feelings.

The project has been talked about, written about, appealed for and collected for since 1904, when William Archer and Granville-Barker put out the first detailed plan.

They have gone. So have such other supporters as Henry Irving, Barrie, Pinero and Shaw. Sir Laurence Olivier, present yesterday as a leader of his profession, was not born when the idea was first mooted. Sir Ralph Richardson, also present, was only two years old at the time.

Mr. Masefield's Verses

But there were links. Mr. S.R. Littlewood, the doyen of dramatic critics, is still happily with us to see the first stone of the theatre for which he was working in 1908.

Mr. Oliver Lyttelton was there to recall the enthusiasm of his mother, Mrs. Alfred Lyttelton, who as long as she lived worked for the project.

I will not say how old Dame Sybil Thorndike was in 1904, for her art is ageless. She came along yesterday to speak the verses which Mr. Masefield, the Poet Laureate, had written for the occasion:

"Here we lay stone, that, at a future time,
May bear a House, wherein, in days to be,
Tier above tier, delighted crowds may see
Men's passions made a play-thing, and sublime."

New Home

The Duke and Duchess of Windsor, I hear, are negotiating to rent the chateau at Louveciennes, near Versailles, which Louis XV gave to Mme. du Barry and where she lived until her execution.

A year ago they wished to buy the property, but the owner, M. Greyfie de Bellecombe, was unwilling to sell it. Now they have proposed to rent it on an 18-year lease.

The house of about 15 rooms, known as the Château du Barry, was built by Louis XIV and was entirely redecorated by Louis XV, who frequently stayed there. It stands in about 40 acres of beautiful grounds with ornamental ponds.

There is an old wives' tale that Mme. du Barry's jewels are buried in the grounds.

Sailor Author

At lunch yesterday I met Nicholas Monsarrat, one of the few younger authors who need have little apprehension about the reception of a book. His next novel, "Cruel Sea" - a story of the Battle of the Atlantic, which will be published on Friday - has a first printing in this country of 120,000 copies.

The first American edition of 35,000 copies was sold out within three weeks, and 300,000 copies are being produced for the American Book of the Month Club.

One of his earlier novels, "This is the Schoolroom", had poor reviews. It was cryptically dismissed by THE DAILY TELEGRAPH with the words: "Older people will not take it quite so seriously as the author does."

Since then, however, THE DAILY TELEGRAPH serialisation during the war of his "H.M. Corvette" and "East Coast Corvette" has presented him to a wider and more appreciative audience.

Dowdy English Women

Norman Hartnell is now in New York persuading American women of the English women's chic. His efforts are not helped by Nancy Mitford. Fresh from the success of her latest novel in the United States, she launches a little attack in the Atlantic Monthly on the way our English women dress. Here are two of her shafts:

"Contrary to what is sometimes supposed, their sports and country clothes are deplorable. They are of tweed, thick and hard as a board, in various shades of porridge, and made to last for ever.

"The women in London streets give a general appearance of tidy dreariness."

French women, in her opinion, are no better dressed:

"The fact is that elegance in Paris is confined to a small group of women who are seldom seen in public and never on the streets."

She allows her own country-women, however, one compliment:

"Our women seen at a ball are a surprise and a delight, for it is in the evening that English women excel."

Now it is Mr Hartnell's turn.

Eating Sparingly

Princess Elizabeth has been trying to avoid adding extra pounds during the Royal tour of Canada by eating sparingly.

This has taken a good deal of restraint since Canadian chefs have been outdoing themselves in attempts to please.

When she merely picked at her food during an elaborate luncheon in Ottowa, Mr. Coulter, the City Controller, chided her on her small appetite.

Princess Elizabeth replied with a smile,"Why if I ate meals like this I would have to get a new wardrobe."

PETERBOROUGH

LORD BIRDWOOD DIES AT 85

ORGANISED GALLIPOLI EVACUATION

Lord Birdwood, who has died aged 85, was the senior Field-Marshal of the British Army

In the Gallipoli campaign of the 1914-18 war he first commanded the Australian and New Zealand Army Corps, and was subsequently appointed C-in-C., Mediterranean Expeditionary Force. He commanded the Dardanelles Army during the evacuation.

Considering the dificulties of the terrain it was a brilliant achievement. Practically without a casualty, he brought away from the beaches 120,000 men, 300 guns and 9,000 horses. The entire operation was a model of its kind.

Later Birdwood and his Anzacs went to France. They fought well on the Somme and at Bullecourt in the Battle of Arras. During the last six months of the war Birdwood commanded the reconstituted Fifth Army.

POST WITH KITCHENER

Much of his career was spent in India, where he was born. William Riddell Birdwood was educated at Clifton and at Sandhurst, and served in the Hazara, Isazi and Tirah expeditions. He was Military Secretary to Kitchener in South Africa and again in India.

Later he was appointed Q.M.G. and then Secretary to the Government of India in the Army Department. In 1919 he was created a baronet.

Returning to India in 1920, he became G.O.C.-in-C. Northern Army. In 1925 he was promoted Field-Marshal and succeeded Rawlinson as C.-in-C., India. Five years later he was back in England.

In 1931 though never an under-graduate, he was elected Master of Peterhouse, Cambridge. He retired in 1938 and was created a baron.

He was appointed Captain of Deal Castle in 1935 and took up residence there. The castle suffered bomb damage during the war and he had to leave it. For a time he helped some friends by working as a farm labourer. Since 1943 he had lived at Hampton Court Palace in apartments given him by the King.

His wife, formerly Miss Jeanette Hope, died in 1947. A son and two daughters survive. The new baron, Lt.-Col. the Hon. Christopher Birdwood, will be 52 next Tuesday. He married, in 1931, Miss Vere Ogilvie. They have a son and a daughter.

Leaders' Tributes

Mr. Menzies, the Australian Prime Minister, said in Sydney yesterday: "Lord Birdwood's name will live as long as the tradition of the Australian Army." Other tributes were:

Sir THOMAS BLAMEY, the first Australian to reach the rank of Field-Marshal: Few commanders gave more of themselves to the men in the ranks.

Mr. CASEY, Australian Minister for External Affairs: A great human has passed on.

Field-Marshal Sir WILLIAM SLIM, C.I.G.S.: The Army has lost a man to whom it owed much.

(May 18)

CONSTANT LAMBERT

Constant Lambert, the composer and conductor, who has died in London, aged 45, was for 15 years musical director of the Sadler's Wells Ballet until 1947. In 1948 he rejoined the company as musical adviser.

His wife, formerly Mrs. Isabel Delmer, whom he married in 1947, created the scenery for his last ballet "Tiresias," produced last month at Covent Garden. By his previous marriage to Miss Florence Chuter, a film actress, in 1931, he had one son.

RICHARD CAPELL writes: Constant Lambert's early death leaves a severe sense of loss and unfulfilled promise. He was one of the most richly gifted English musicians of his generation.

When only 20 he won a European name by his music for a ballet, "Romeo and Juliet," commissioned by Diaghilev in 1926. It was the first time Diaghilev had accepted an English score, and its grace, assurance and wit promised great things.

Before long the young man achieved a brilliant success in the concert room with his "Rio Grande," but conducting encroached on his creative work.

Recently he had decided to conduct less and compose more, and his 1951 ballet "Tiresias" was welcomed as the first proof of a new phase. His book "Music Ho!" abounds in wit.

Wrote for Diaghilev

Constant Lambert's death makes a sorry gap in London's musical world. Ill-health had dogged him for some years and kept him much away from creative effort.

But when he conducted "Tiresias" at Covent Garden on July 9, apparently with his usual force, there was no doubt of his popularity with the ballet public.

This was well deserved, for he belonged to the old imperial guard of ballet, having actually written a ballet for the great Diaghilev.

In the middle 1920's Constant Lambert's promise was great. He and Sir William Walton, who was slightly his senior, formed with the Sitwells and maybe John Piper a commando force to shock the public into artistic sensibility.

(September 6)

LORD INVERCHAPEL

Lord Inverchapel, who died yesterday aged 69, was British Ambassador to China, Russia and the United States during the momentous years 1938-48.

He succeeded Sir Stafford Cripps in Moscow in 1942 and followed the Earl of Halifax in Washington four years later. Formerly Sir Archibald Clark Kerr, he was created a baron in 1946. Informal to the point of unorthodoxy, he scored an outstanding success in Russia but was less successful in the United States. In both countries he was admired for his personal qualities as much as he was respected for his tolerance and shrewdness. As a mediator he proved eminently successful. He persuaded M. Stalin, whom he first met during an air-raid on Moscow, to dine at the British Embassy.

He entered the Diplomatic Service in 1906. In the 1914-18 war he was a private in the Scots Guards. He was made a K.C.M.G. in 1935 and in the same year was appointed Ambassador in Baghdad, the youngest at that time.

(July 6)

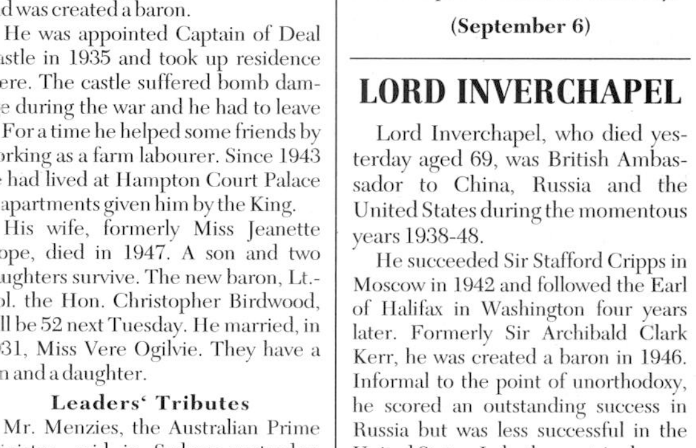

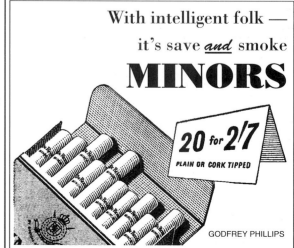

MODERATE WIND FOR BOAT RACE TO-DAY

PRACTICE IN MORNING

Boat Race weather forecast:- Light westerly wind, slowly increasing in the afternoon, sunny periods, rather cold.

Daily Telegraph Reporter

The Oxford and Cambridge Boat Race, called off on Saturday after the Oxford boat had sunk, will be rowed at 2-30 this afternoon.

The umpire, the Bishop of Willesden, Dr. Ellison, said last night that if the weather conditions again proved to be very bad he would consult the two presidents before making a final decision.

The tide will be in flood at the time the race is due to start. If the weather deteriorates and a high wind whips up the waters coming down, conditions might be even worse than on Saturday, stated Mr. W.T. Robbins, the Tideboard Inspector.

Land water from the higher reaches of the Thames continues to feed the swollen river. At Teddington lock yesterday it flowed at the same rate as on Saturday.

Because of the "no race" declaration on Saturday it is understood that there will again be a toss for position to-day. On Saturday Oxford won the toss and took the Surrey side.

(March 26)

CREWS RELAX AFTER RACE

OXFORD AT THEATRE

Daily Telegraph Reporter

The boat race crews relaxed last night. Oxford saw "Kiss Me Kate" at the Coliseum before dining at a London club. They went on to a party at the Hurlingham Club, where they have been staying.

The crew arrived at the Coliseum where they sat with friends in the centre box and during the interval were taken backstage and introduced to the leading players.

Cambridge went to a cocktail party at the Royal Automobile Club, after which they were entertained to dinner there by a party of Old Blues. Later they visited the Empress Club, Dover-street, for dancing, a cabaret show and supper.

As they entered the dining-room Harry Roy and his band played: "Can I canoe you up the river?" On the table was a special cake 18in long, in the shape of a boat with eight oarsmen and a light blue flag flying at the stern.

(March 27)

CHELSEA ENTER ROUND FOUR

By a Special Correspondent

Rochdale..........2 Chelsea..........3

Chelsea won their postponed Third Round F.A. Cup game against Rochdale yesterday, but they must have been an extremely relieved side at the finish.

There was little difference between the standard of play of either side. Third Division Rochdale were at their peak. First Division Chelsea well below normal. Chelsea in fact owed their success to Rochdale's slow start and to a second-half blunder by the young Rochdale goalkeeper, Lomas, who allowed a slow Bentley shot to bounce off his arm into the net.

There was plenty of action in the first half. Billington's third-minute goal, followed 16 minutes later by a good one from Bentley, made it look as if things were going to be very one-sided, but shortly before the interval Connor, a tireless Rochdale forward, reduced the deficit.

In the second half Chelsea, often hard-pressed, were relieved by Lomas's mishap, but Rochdale were far from being a spent force and four minutes from the end, in a goal-mouth scramble, Arthur scored.

In a desperate last-minute attempt to equalise Connor cut his way through but was brought down from behind. The referee decided, however, that the incident did not merit a penalty and that was that.

(June 10)

CAMBRIDGE ROW AWAY WITH BOAT RACE

12 Lengths Victory Was a Procession

By B.C. Johnstone

Cambridge dominated the re-rowed Boat Race from the start at Putney to the finish at Mortlake yesterday. They rowed steadily away from their Oxford rivals, whose sinking had caused the abandonment of the race on Saturday, and beat them by 12 lengths in 20 minutes 50 seconds.

The time in existing conditions could never have been a fast one. There can, however, be no question that Cambridge possessed speed. They were not as heavy as Oxford, yet the power they applied was infinitely greater. It was obtained by leg and body work being precisely timed.

It was not only in this respect that they were good, for throughout all their training they had been taught to work as a crew and not as individuals. This gave them the polish which made them so attractive to watch. They looked fast and they were fast.

All praise to the Cambridge coaches for the admirable way they had gained and timed the preparation of their crew, bringing it to its peak at the right moment. A week ago it seemed possible they had overshot this peak point, but by the judicious handling of Mr. Harold Rickett, this was overcome and he brought them to the post at the height of their efficiency.

Oxford rowed with great effort but it did not produce commensurable results. They worked hard and were game, but there was no life or spirit in it. They could not have beaten Cambridge except for an accident.

LUCK OF THE TOSS AGAIN

As on Saturday Oxford won the toss and they again chose the Surrey station. This time, however, the action was comparatively easy.

In taking this side they would have hoped to hold Cambridge sufficiently over the first five minutes to enable themselves to have the advantage of the long bend at Hammersmith. The river was smooth with a slight cross following wind. The tide was pretty poor.

The race started before the best of the flood. In any case the tide would not have been much stronger as the flood water coming down was considerable.

Both crews got out punctually and were at their stake boats by 2.20. Each made a good getaway, Cambridge at Oxford 9, 18 and 37 in the first minute. Cambridge moved their boat with the greater effect and at once went ahead. Perhaps after half a minute, but only for a stroke or two, the relative positions seemed to remain, Cambridge then continuing to forge ahead again.

At the end of the second minute Cambridge were a full length up. Between here and the mile it looked as if both coxswains were across the tide, and it was a little time before they had straightened up.

At the Mile Post (4.9 sec) Cambridge's lead was 2 lengths. They were rowing at 29 with great ease and powerful action, and their ship had a splendid run, Jennens giving them time and excellent length. There could be no doubt he had stamped his own clean and effective way of rowing on his crew.

QUITE OUTCLASSED

Coming up to Hammersmith, in spite of their lead, they made no attempt to take advantage of the long bend, and in fact were almost too much on the Middlesex side. It was here that Oxford needed to make their effort if they were to make any impression.

Davidge spurted, but it was clear by now the race was in Cambridge's hands.

At Hammersmith Bridge, which Cambridge shot in 7min 35sec, they were 12sec up on Oxford, and from then on it was a procession. Slight mist almost blurred the Cambridge crew, and as we in the Press launch kept with Oxford, we were unable to get a close up, but it was evident they were at the top of their form. They passed Chiswick Steps in 12min 28sec and Barnes Bridge in 17min 13sec.

Oxford fought gamely on, but they were quite outclassed. Davidge endeavoured to force up his stroke, and though he was well backed up by Turner at 6, it was obviously a forlorn hope. Cambridge had been able to keep at a steady rate of 28 to 29 strokes over the course, whereas Davidge had often raised it to 32.

(March 27)

BARBARIAN XV IN FORM

BACKS TOO GOOD FOR SWANSEA

By J.P.Jordan

Swansea ...9 Barbarians ...17

Fielding 14 internationals, the Barbarians defeated Swansea by a goal, a penalty goal and three tries to three tries in a splendid game, played in the worst possible conditions with pools of water lying on the St. Helen's ground.

There was not much in it between the packs. The Swansea forwards, with R.C.C. Thomas, W.D.Johnson and W.O.Williams at their head, were remarkably quick on the ball, and the Barbarians were finely served by R.C.Taylor, J.E.Nelson and until he had to retire with a damaged wrist, V.G.Roberts.

Behind the scrum the Barbarians held a pronounced superiority. D.W.Shuttleworth got through an enormous amount of work in the mud and soon settled down with his partner, M.C.Thomas. D.M.Scott and Lewis Jones made a resourceful pair of centres.

On the right wing J.V.Smith electrified the crowd with his superb burst of speed in scoring the last try, a spectacular effort on a par with J.D. Robins's stupendous kick that brought the penalty goal.

R. Sutton did a number of clever things at scrum-half for Swansea, but as an attacking force the home backs did not impress. Full marks must be given to the ready opportunism of B. Edwards.

SCOTT BREAKS THROUGH

After Lewis Jones (twice) and L.Davies had failed to land penalty goals for their sides, Scott broke through splendidly to score for the Barbarians. Five minutes later Taylor dribbled away with the ball under perfect control and scored a try that Lewis Jones converted.

Sutton slipped away to send Johnson across for Swansea, but before half-time Robins kicked a magnificent penalty goal from 50 yards out to give the Barbarians an 11-3 lead.

Ten minutes afterwards a dribble by Taylor and a pass by Nelson led to a try by Roberts. Swansea then scored two trys in quick succession, Barbarian fumbling giving Edwards the chance each time. Finally came Smith's try, the result of a long kick over the line and a thrilling sprint for the touch down.

(March 27)

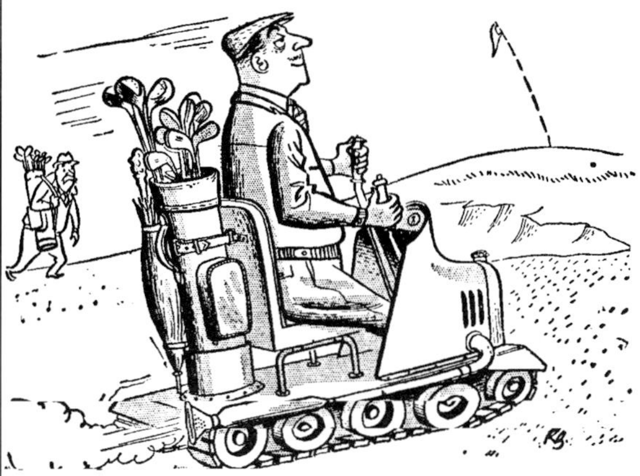

MOTOR HOW YOU WILL...

Mr. Mercury will give you more miles per gallon!

NATIONAL BENZOLE MIXTURE

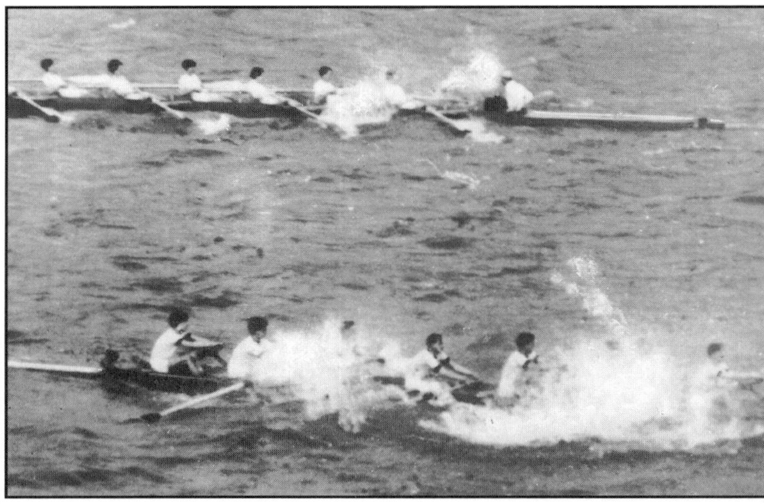

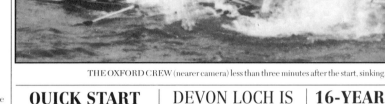

THE OXFORD CREW (nearer camera) less than three minutes after the start, sinking.

QUICK START UPSET JOCKEYS IN NATIONAL

FIRST FENCE RUSH.

From Hotspur

LIVERPOOL, Sunday.

Only three of the 36 runners in the Grand National at Aintree yesterday completed the course. Only the winner, the nine-year-old mare Nickel Coin, and the runner-up Royal Tan did not fall.

Many who saw the race were inclined to put part of the blame on the starter, Mr. L.L. Firth. He caught most of the jockeys by surprise when he set off the field sooner than is his habit in the National.

Half the jockeys were faced with the predicament of having to put their horses at the first fence faster than was advisable or finding themselves with much ground to make up as the race proceeded.

Several jockeys lost their heads rushing their mounts at the first fence.

EARLY FALLS

There were 11 falls at the first fence and three more at the next fence. After Valentine's ninth fence first time round, only seven horses were standing.

Loose horses were responsible for bringing down a number of runners. Among them were the well-fancied Freebooter, Arctic Gold and Concarrig.

I discussed the race with Mr. Firth. He is the senior starter for the Jockey Club, and officiates at all the famous races, including the Derby.

The starting gate at Aintree for the National is an old-fashioned type. Yesterday when Mr. Firth pressed the starting handle there was the usual time-lag of a couple of seconds before the gate was released. In that time two or three horses had turned round and were not facing the gate.

STARTER NOT TO BLAME

This was bad luck on the riders, but the starter was not really to blame. One jockey said: "Few of us were balanced and collected, and we were definitely caught by surprise."

(April 9)

DEVON LOCH IS 'CHASER IN THE MAKING

From Hotspur

KEMPTON PARK, Wednesday.

The Queen has a promising 'chaser in the making in her five-year-old Devon Loch, who, though still a bit backward, finished second to the more experienced Rahshas in the Vauxhall Novices' Hurdle here to-day.

Devon Loch has the stamp of a 'chaser rather than a hurdler, and it is at steeplechasing that he should shine.

The running in to-day's race was made by the grey Rahshas, who in last seasons Imperial Cup started favourite with a light weight - a useful type of horse to be still qualified for a maiden hurdle. Grantham, on Devon Loch, was lying second with Nital, the well-bred Flos Solis and Cent Francs close up.

On the far side of the course, with a mile to go there was little to choose between Rahshas and Devon Loch, with Flos Solis and Nital also going well.

Flos Solis made a mistake at the next hurdle, and at the bottom end of the course Rahshas and Devon Loch had drawn clear, with the race between them. Rahshas is not a stout finisher, but as they came to the last hurdle he was several lengths ahead of Devon Loch, with the Queen's horse tiring.

Devon Loch could not quicken in the run-in, and Rahshas won decisively by eight lengths, with Nital third, just in front of Red Rube and Flos Solis.

Devon Loch should be the better for the experience of to-day's race and it will be disappointing if he does not win a hurdle race for the Queen shortly.

(November 22)

Hockey

ENGLAND KEEP UP ATTACK

By a Special Correspondent

England...........4 Wales...........0

England, having won their first match in the international hockey series against Wales at Bournemouth, have made one change in their team for the game against Ireland at Birmingham on April 15.

The Hawks player P.D.R. Smith comes in at right back. D.J Carnill, of Oxford, reverting back to his normal position of left-back and W.H.R. Jones standing down.

England were so much the better side that Wales only occasionally penetrated the English 25-yards area and then not with sufficient force or momentum to be really dangerous, except once, when P. Dolan with a slashing first-time shot, hit the goal-post. For the rest, the game was one long duel between England's attack, in which the half-backs played a strong supporting rôle, and the Welsh defence. The honours were not all on one side.

The Welsh backs and wing-halves and especially their goal-keeper, G.B. Dadds, resisted with the utmost tenacity, and the English forwards, though they could weave patterns and make openings, often failed to hit a goal when they had the chance. J.C.G. Stocks scored three times and A.W. Wootton scored England's fourth goal.

Stocks's second goal was far and away the best. It was the reward of a dribble and swerve to the right, followed by a stinging cross-shot rather in the manner of Bobby Whitlock.

(March 27)

16-YEAR-OLD IS WORLD'S BEST WOMAN PLAYER

MISS CONNOLLY WINS U.S. TENNIS

FOREST HILLS (N.Y.), Wednesday.

For Miss Maureen Connolly, a 16-year-old Californian schoolgirl, a dream came true here to-day. She defeated the Wimbledon runner-up Miss Shirley Fry 6-3, 1-6, 6-4 in the final of the United States women's singles lawn tennis championship to become the youngest-ever holder of the title.

Miss Connolly, who defeated the Wimbledon champion, Miss Doris Hart, in her semi-final yesterday, has thus reached the pinnacle of American - and in fact world - lawn tennis, and she will not be 17 until Friday week. Previous youngest holder of the title was Miss Helen Wills, who took it at the age of 17 in 1923.

Miss Connolly looked as though she was beaten when she lost her control and permitted her 24-year-old opponent to run off six straight games for the second set. But she came again to wear down Miss Fry in a long and exhausting third set.

When Miss Fry hit the final point just beyond the baseline. Miss Connolly let out a yell that was heard throughout the stadium. Then she ran with arms outstretched to meet Miss Fry at the net and exchange hugs.

The final set, full of long baseline rallies, lasted 34 minutes, compared to 22 for each of the first two. The deciding game went to deuce three times and had the crowd sitting on the edges of their seats, cheering nearly every point.

(September 6)

LONDON HELD BY BERLIN

BELOW CLUB-FORM DISPLAY

Berlin.........1 London.........1

BERLIN, Wednesday.

The first soccer match between representative English and German sides in Germany since 1938 ended in a disappointing draw in the Olympic Stadium here to-day.

Much good constructive work by the half-backs of both sides came to naught forward and often bought catcalls and jeers from sections of the crowd of over 60,000. Twice local officials protested over the loudspeakers at the crowd's behaviour.

Gray (Chelsea) on the right-wing was prominent in a London attack which never really got going, though centre-forward Holton (Arsenal) showed fine opportunism in giving his side the lead with a first-time shot after 15 minutes.

Towards the end of the first half and for long periods in the second, the Berlin forwards stormed the London goal. Time and again they forced their way through an uncertain defence, but it was not until 11 minutes from time that they equalised, Kolmannsperger beating Brown with a stinging low drive.

(March 22)

IVERSON AGAIN MASTER OF ENGLAND BATSMEN

Australia Win Third Test & The Ashes

From E. W. Swanton

SYDNEY, Tuesday.

England have lost not only this Third Test but the rubber, suddenly and disappointingly, in an afternoon's cricket which emphasised once again the chief weakness of contemporary English batsmanship and also brought to light an Australian spin-bowler in the tradition of the great ones of the past. The margin of their defeat was an innings and 13 runs.

It was impossible not to feel utterly downcast by the showing of the English batsmen against Iverson to-day. There was a technical weakness, mostly concerned with footwork, or rather the lack of it, and there was, it must be confessed, a timidity of approach of which this batting was the expression.

On this matter I hope to have the opportunity to elaborate when these events can be seen in better perspective. For the moment I will try to express the feeling current among English critics and cricketers who have followed this series by quoting two observations made in the agony of watching England's second innings in these last two Tests.

It was at Melbourne when England were striving with such desperate care to make the 179 they needed to win that one old player observed: "Oh for half an hour of Owen-Smith."

And this evening another who himself might have dealt with Iverson more effectively almost than any Englishman on the ground, remarked that the old Scottish battlecry on the football field might be adapted to inspire our batsmen: "Feet, England! Feet!"

AUSTRALIA'S MERIT

But enough! This is the moment to congratulate Australia on having won the honours of the match by staunch, sturdy cricket. The merit behind their victory at Melbourne went largely unrecognised because of the general disappointment at England's defeat.

Similarly, at Sydney the injuries to Bailey and Wright have inevitably taken much of the gilt off Australia's gingerbread. Yet Hassett and his team may well feel that they were unlucky in not having the chance of gaining a victory fair and square without any alibis.

The game was a great triumph for Miller, the cricketing hero of Sydney, who, besides making 145 not out, made the catch in a hundred that began England's troubles on the first day and, looking back, virtually won the match in an over on the first afternoon.

It emphasised too, the more stolid all-round excellence of Johnson as well as bringing Iverson into the forefront.

Among the English players Brown himself achieved a memorable performance and Bedser heightened the esteem in which he is held here as a bowler. His contemporaries always said that Tate was relatively a greater bowler in Australia than at home, and I am sure the same is true of his successor.

Until the anti-climax at the end it was a fine game, watched under the blazing sun by some 18,000 people and followed with beating hearts by how many million others all over the world.

JOHNSON CAUTIOUS

No game of cricket in any close detail follows logical prediction and this morning's play was no exception. The new ball and Bedser were England's main hopes when play was continued. After the polish so to speak had worn off both the way looked open for Miller, aided by the Australian tail.

What happened was that for three-quarters of an hour Bedser did almost everything but take a wicket and that all four remaining wickets toppled within 20 minutes after he came off to rest.

As soon as Miller had gone from 96 to his second hundred in Tests against England he was almost yorked by Bedser, who soon afterwards was within an inch of bowling Johnson. It was a cautious matter-of-fact Johnson to-day. Incidentally, playing rather like a golfer in a medal round when he has grown a little scared of his score.

Warr, who shared the new ball bowling into the wind, strove away with great pluck and persistence, but he had to be content with some moral successes to reward his efforts. Brown at length gave Warr the wind and slipped into the old groove with his leg-spinners at the other end.

PARTNERSHIP OF 150 BROKEN

It was the captain who bowled Johnson with a googly, possibly via his pads or the edge of his bat. That was the end of a partnership of 150 runs which had lifted the Australian score from relative poverty to affluence. Almost from its beginning it had seemed to be marking the turning-point.

What now? Lindwall is a considerable batsman at such a stage, and Miller was playing easily and safely. But in Brown's same over Lindwall elected to sweep airily at a ball which so the umpire judged pitched on the wicket, and with Johnston's arrival one really could begin to see the end of the Australian innings.

As it happened, numbers 10 and 11 were both run out in the effort to keep Miller with the strike. It was a slick pick-up and return by Parkhouse which defeated Johnston's best turn of speed, while Iverson, who is built distinctly for comfort, found Miller unco-operative and just failed to re-make his ground.

Thus Miller was left unbeaten for 145 runs, quietly made, almost completely unspectacular and therefore out of character. But they were runs of some pedigree that saved the looks of the Australian innings.

So it was with a load of 136 runs on their backs that Hutton and Washbrook went to the wicket after lunch. As on the first day, their beginning against fast bowling was assured and admirable – and, as before, the partnership foundered on the advance of spin.

Iverson dropped his first ball on a length and in the absence of anyone prepared to bring footwork into the battle he never shifted from it. His direction generally is on the middle stump and the usual bias is from the off.

In the nature of things the ball is always hitting the pads either from the batsmen's design or because the degree of spin has defeated the stroke. This constant striking of the pads combined with a good deal of appealing – Australians have never been shy about asking questions – heightens the tension to a pitch where one feels that if runs do not come wickets must.

There had been several very nervous moments before Hutton pushed forward and edged the ball off the top shoulder high behind Tallon, the wicketkeeper, Johnson overbalanced sideways in attempting the catch but managed to keep the ball aloft and Tallon continued to spin round and grasp it by throwing himself full length.

WASHBROOK BOWLED

It is probably eloquent of English feelings at this early stage that one sighed for a touch of inspiration by Brown that might have sent Evans in next to nudge Iverson firmly through or over the infielders.

But I suppose Test matches must take their prosaic course. Simpson lasted for 10 minutes, then felt and touched a ball passing behind his legs.

Compton and Washbrook: here was perhaps a stable front. Compton, though he needed a quarter of an hour to avoid his second nought, middled the ball and Washbrook seemed not unduly uncomfortable, at least when he was not facing Iverson.

(January 10)

(Solution No. 7974)

	E	L	D	E	R	B	E	R	R	Y				
	A		O		E		X		H		D	R	A	W
	R	E	V	O	L	U	T	I	O	N		E		E
	S		E		A		R		D		O	P	A	L
T		S		R	I	P	E	N	E	D		R		L
R	E	P	A	I	D		M		S	O	L	E	N	T
A		A		G			E			R		S		E
F	A	C	T	O	R	Y	P	R	E	M	I	S	E	S
F		E		U			R			A		I		T
I	N	S	E	R	T		E		S	N	O	O	Z	E
C		H		S	U	N	S	P	O	T		N		D
J	O	I	N		R		S		U		S		S	
A		P		S	T	O	U	T	S	T	I	C	K	
M	O	S	S		L		R		E		G		Y	
				D	E	P	E	N	D	E	N	C	E	

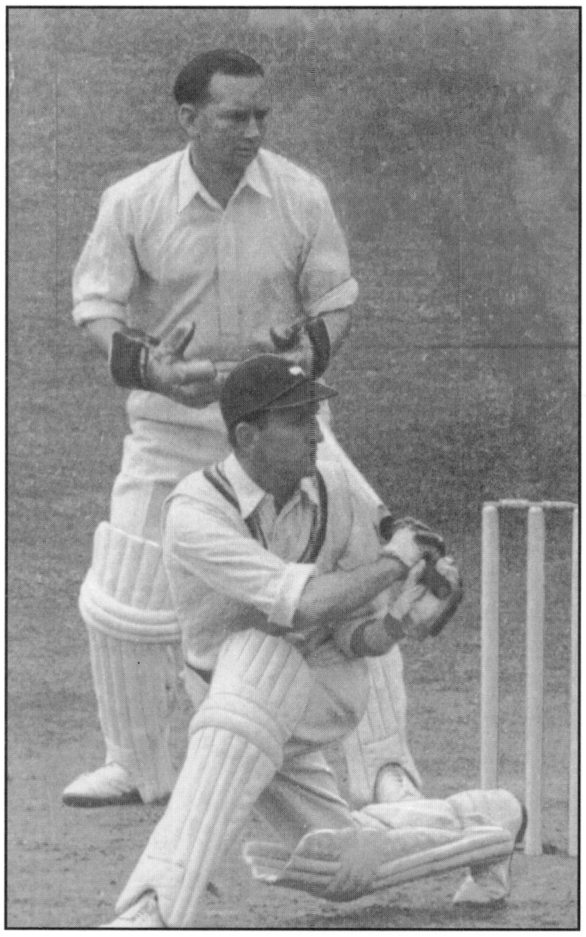

HOW IT'S DONE. Ken Hutton, who completed his century at the Oval, sweeping a ball from lock to the boundary in typical fashion.

ENGLAND WIN LAST TEST BY EIGHT WICKETS

Bedser, Hutton and Simpson the Heroes

From E. W. Swanton

MELBOURNE, Wednesday.

At last! England's victory by eight wickets in the fifth Test here this evening has altered the whole aspect of the tour as it will be remembered by the players taking part and by those both at home and in Australia who have been following the fortunes of the series.

Each reverse in the three series since the war has made it harder for the English side to break through. Now the reproach is past, and when the comedy of a last over by Hassett, and three premature stump-grabbings by the players, had culminated in Hutton making the winning stroke, one sensed much emotion of relief and pleasure among the spectators.

As England's captain observed, it would have been even nicer if this had been the match that had decided the Ashes. But at least the manner of victory made it clear that if things had run differently it could have been, for England won inside four days of playing time on a wicket that played true from first to last and, which is the crux of the matter, after losing the toss.

SURGE OF PESSIMISM

I confess that when Australia won choice of innings last Friday I felt a surge of pessimism which there was no point in passing on to those at home. Since M.C.C. sent their first team to Australia under P.F. Warner in 1903 Australia had failed only twice to win the fifth Test in 1912 and 1933.

Normally a touring side is at its peak, as Brown's team was, about the second and third Tests. But this apart, it is hard to visualise the present batting side, dependent as it has been on one man with only occasional and uncertain outside help, making a sizable score in the last innings.

Thanks to Simpson, England gained a three-figure lead yesterday after all, and thanks to Hutton, though the runs had to be fought for, there was no breathless, palpitating struggle this afternoon for the 95 which were needed to win.

When Bedser got the last Australian wicket to-day he brought his number for the series up to 30. If the bare fact does not sound impressive it should be enough to quote that Richardson took 32 wickets in an Australian Test series in 1894-5.

(March 1)

Final Scoreboard

AUSTRALIA - First Innings

J Burke, c Tattersall, b Bedser	11
A.R. Morris, lbw, b Brown	50
A.L. Hassett, c Hutton, b Brown	92
R.N. Harvey, c Evans, b Brown	1
K.R. Miller, c and b Brown	7
G. Hole, b Bedser	18
I W. Johnson, lbw, b Bedser	1
R.R. Lindwall, c Compton, b Bedser	21
D. Tallon, c Hutton, b Bedser	1
W.A. Johnston, not out	12
J Iverson, c Washbrook, b Brown	0
Extras (b-2, 1-lb)	3
Total	**217**

Second Innings

A. Morris, lbw, b Bedser	4
Burke, c Hutton, b Bedser	1
L. Hassett, b Wright	48
N. Harvey, lbw, b Wright	52
K. Miller, b c and b Brown	0
G. Hole, b Bailey	63
I W. Johnson, c Brown, b Wright	0
R.R. Lindwall, b Bedser	14
D. Tallon, not out	2
W.A. Johnston, b Bedser	1
J Iverson, c Compton, b Bedser	0
Extras (b-2, lb-8, w-1, nb-1)	12
Total	**197**

ENGLAND - First Innings

Hutton, b Hole	79
Washbrook, c Tallon, b Miller	27
F.T. Simpson, not out	156
Compton, c Miller, b Lindwall	11
D.S. Sheppard, c Tallon, b Miller	1
F.R. Brown, b Lindwall	6
Evans, b Miller	1
Bedser, b Lindwall	11
T.E. Bailey, c Johnson, b Iverson	5
Wright, lbw, b Iverson	3
Tattersall, b Miller	10
Extras (b-9, lb-1)	10
Total	**320**

Second Innings

Hutton, not out	60
Washbrook, c Lindwall, b Johnston	7
F.T. Simpson, run out	15
Compton, not out	2
Extras (lb-2)	2
Total	**93**

HUTTON GETS HIS 100TH HUNDRED

YORKS PILE UP RUNS AT OVAL

By Michael Melford

The crowd of near Test match proportions, which gathered at the Oval yesterday morning in the hope of witnessing a historic event, was not disappointed in its assumption that Hutton had chosen this ground of many previous triumphs as the scene of his hundredth hundred.

It also watched Yorks gaining a stranglehold over Surrey, who are 247 behind with nine second innings wickets standing, but there are occasions when the game may bow in importance to the individual, and this was one of them.

The 39 which Hutton required for his century when play began were made in 70 minutes, and with the ball scarcely turning at all and the great man clearly in form, there never seemed any likelihood of his failing.

When at last the deed was done, fittingly with a classic drive past cover-point, he had joined that illustrious 12, Hobbs, Hendren, Hammond, Mead, Sutcliffe, Woolley, Grace, Bradman, Sandham, Hayward, E. Tyldesley and Ames.

Though he was the master throughout, Hutton was taking no risks against some accurate bowling and was 3hrs 25 min reaching his century.

Afterwards, he drove with all majesty through the covers, pulled Lock most elegantly from a good length outside the off-stump to the mid-wicket boundary, and made another 51 in 70 minutes before being bowled while some way down the pitch attempting a prodigious drive.

LOWSON PLEASES

Lowson, with whom Hutton shared in a first-wicket stand of 197, bore the brunt of Bedser's attack with the second new ball when Hutton was in the eighties, and left memories of many graceful and perfectly timed strokes.

He was engaged in a delightful bout of driving when Parker had him playing a little too soon and took a good left-handed return catch.

Wilson's century, which occupied 3hr 5min, was a mixture of solid defence, powerful driving which brought him three 6's, and some surprisingly delicate cuts.

He was dropped at cover at 59, and gave one chance of stumping, both off E. A. Bedser, but otherwise seemed no more likely to get out on this perfect wicket than did anyone else.

Keighley played a number of good strokes to the on in a stay of two hours. He did not survive the third new ball after tea, but Wilson and Watson went on chasing the weary bowling until Yardley's declaration with a lead of 275 left Surrey 55 minutes to bat.

It did not seem inconsistent with Eric Bedser's previous fortune that he should soon be caught at the wicket through the ball lodging in the wicket-keeper's pads. The wicket, however, remained so amiable that, unless Surrey bat very badly to-day, Yorkshire may be hard-pressed to bowl them out a second time.

SURREY.-First Innings: 156 (Clark 47; Yardley 3-28; Truman 3-52, Appleyard 3-53).

Second Innings: 28-1 (M.R. Barton 7 nt; Bedser (E.A.), c Brennan, b Leadbeater, 8; Constable 12 nt; Ex. 1)

(July 17)

LIVELY INNINGS BY COWDREY

TAKES CENTURY OFF PLAYERS

From Michael Melford

SCARBOROUGH, Wednesday.

Seldom in its 65 years has the Scarborough Festival been uneventful, but it cannot often have seen an 18-year-old batsman, and an English one at that, take a century off a bowling side of near Test standard.

M.C. Cowdrey's innings against the Players to-day lasted 3 ¼ hours. When it ended he had with vigorous assistance from W.H. Sutcliffe, taken the Gentlemen out of early difficulties towards a score of 318 and had probably caused the pessimists to reconsider their views on the future of English cricket.

It was by no means a faultless innings - the easiest of three chances he gave to the slips was off the second ball he received - but the comfortable application and the amazing mature technique were there for all to see.

The bad ball was despatched with a force that discouraged interception, his square-cuts were superbly executed and skilfully placed and his on-side play could scarcely have been bettered.

This morning Bedser and Pritchard-bowled well on a damp wicket and removed two of the senior Gentlemen with only 14 on the board. Edrich was splendidly stumped falling forward to Bedser who in the next over launched himself high and wide to hold a magnificent catch in the gully from Simpson at the full extent of the right arm.

For the next 70 minutes until Tattersall came on May delighted everyone with an innings of considerable form.

(September 6)

JAKEMAN'S 258 BEST OF SEASON

A RIOT OF HITTING

Jakeman, the Northants' left-hander, established a new record for his county when he scored 258 not out against Essex, who are 125 behind with nine wickets in hand. This beat the previous highest score of 257 jointly held by Bakewell and Brookes and is the highest individual score of the season.

Batting for 320 minutes, Jakeman hit four 6s and 35 fours in a display of fierce hitting that will long be remembered by the holiday crowd. He was missed at 99 and at 237, but otherwise did not make a false stroke. It was Jakeman's fourth century of the season and his second against Essex.

It was a remarkable day's cricket. Northants lost three wickets for 38, all taken by Preston in his first 15 deliveries at a personal cost of six runs.

(July 17)

REES ROUND IN 6 UNDER PAR

CANBERRA, Monday.

D.J.Rees, British match-play golf champion to-day broke his own one-day-old record on the Royal Canberra course and then saw his new mark beaten by the Sydney professional, K.Nagle two hours later.

(March 27)

TURPIN WINS WORLD TITLE FOR BRITAIN

ROBINSON DEFEATED ON POINTS

Daily Telegraph Reporter

Randolph Turpin, 23, the coloured boxer from Leamington Spa, at Earl's Court last night brought the world middle-weight championship back to Britain for the first time since Bob Fitzsimmons won it at the end of the last century. He defeated the American coloured holder, "Sugar" Ray Robinson, 31, on points over 15 rounds.

Robinson who up to last night had lost only one out of 131 fights, was completely outfought in the biggest boxing upset for years. Turpin, who had lost twice in 43 bouts, dominated the contest from the start and took at least nine rounds.

The crowd of 18,600 gave the victor a tremendous ovation. He looked completely unmarked. He said: "Certainly Robinson hit me hard. He is a great puncher to the body and is a very cagey man to fight.

"I was completely confident from the start that I would win. My idea was gradually to weaken him with my hooks and then, if necessary knock him out. Unfortunately I couldn't catch him quite right."

"I HAVE NO EXCUSES"

Robinson said: "I have no excuses to make, Turpin won on his merits and proved himself the better man tonight. I am now going to take a holiday on the Riviera."

Mr. George Middleton, Turpin's manager, said: "Turpin promised before the fight that he would give Robinson a return in the United States, and we shall fulfill the promise." While about a thous and people waited at the main entrance for him Turpin slipped out of the building just before midnight through a rear door.

At the ringside were celebrities in all walks of life, society, politics, the stage, the turf, and all other sporting spheres. Outside Earl's Court, as the decision was announced, a cheer rose from about 1,000 people clustered in groups around cars with radios tuned in to the broadcast of the fight.

£25 FOR £5 TICKETS

Nine radio traffic cars, 16 motorcycle policemen, 30 traffic officers, some with radio, and more than 50 mounted and foot police controlled the crowds and traffic. Ticket "touts" were selling £5 tickets for £25 two hours before the fight.

Robinson received nearly £30,000 as his end of the purse. Turpin, as challenger, expected to get between £10,000 and £12,000. Robinson's purse is the biggest ever paid to a boxer in Britain, and the capacity crowd for Earl's Court paid more than £80,000 for admission.

(July 11)

DON COCKRELL'S NEXT FIGHT

MEETS LOW RANKED AMERICAN ON DEC. 4

By Lainson Wood

Important announcements were made yesterday in a disjointed effort to hold the decaying fort of British boxing.

Since the light-heavyweight champion, Don Cockrell, is the main prop in the crumbling edifice, perhaps the most important of them was the detailing of Cockrell's opponent at Harringay on Dec. 4, when Mr. Solomons, the leading London promoter, puts on a show for the fund of the National Playing Fields Association.

Mr. Solomons claims for his choice–Jim Slade, a 25-year-old Virginia "picaninny"– that he is the fifth best light-heavyweight in the world. Slade must have come on immensely in the last month, for in the latest ratings of the Ring, New York's boxing bible, he is not in the first ten.

Understandably, too stiff opposition for Cockrell has not been sought this time. He has a world title match with Joey Maxim in March.

(November 22)

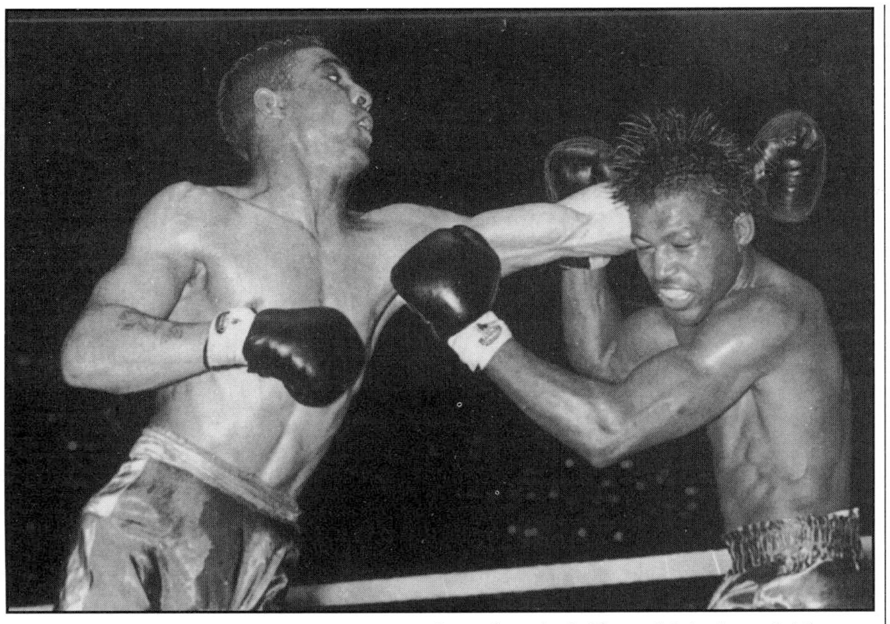

PUNCHING FROM HIS TOES. - Turpin rises and comes forward with all his weight behind a straight left that grazes Robinson's right ear.

TURPIN BEATEN IN TENTH ROUND

CHAMPION DAZED ON ROPES AS REFEREE STOPS FIGHT

From Lainson Wood

NEW YORK, Wednesday.

Randolph Turpin, 23-year-old coloured boxer from Leamington, lost his world middle-weight championship after a 64 days' tenure at the Polo Grounds here to-night as a result of one of the most sensational rounds of brilliant punching by the former champion, Sugar Ray Robinson, that I have even seen.

The end came when in the 10th round of a contest which had begun much in Robinson's favour, but which was beginning to swing ominously as Turpin stood up to all that Robinson had to give him, the referee stopped the fight. Robinson was, in fact, beginning to tire from his own efforts to set too hot a pace for the Englishman.

Moreover, at the start of the 10th round, Robinson's left eyebrow, cut in their first fight at Earl's Court, suddenly began to gush blood when their heads collided. It seemed that the turning point had arrived and maybe Robinson, a great tactician, realised that his last chance of beating Turpin was now or never.

He suddenly lashed out with a flurry of punches and landed a perfect right hook flush on the champion's jaw. Turpin sagged at the knees and was prevented from falling only by hanging on to Robinson's trunks. Robinson rained punches to Turpin's head until he was made to release his grip and fall in a heap on the canvas.

JUST BEAT THE COUNT

To his credit, Turpin beat the count by a whisker, and, shaking his head to clear away the mists of haziness before his eyes, he came out for a moment to trade blows with his opponent. Robinson, however, was not to be robbed of his prey this time.

His "killer instinct" now thoroughly aroused he drove Turpin back on the ropes, where the Englishman could only hang and take it. Miraculously, though he twice forced himself off them, he did not go down. But it was clear that he was out to the world, mercifully unconscious of the battering to which his head and body were being subjected.

No referee with a spark of humanity could have allowed such slaughter to continue. Mr. Ruby Goldstein, America's best, stepped in as Turpin fell like an empty sack, restrained Robinson and directed him to his corner.

(September 13)

ENGLISH RUGBY IN CLASS BELOW WALES

By J.P. Jordan

Wales.........**23**pts England.........**5**pts

Giving a magnificent display of Rugby football at its best and brightest, Wales outclassed England at Swansea by four goals and a try to a goal, their widest margin of victory since 'Hiddlestone's match' in the mud at Cardiff Arms Park in 1922.

The Welsh brilliance not only sent every Welshman home in a transport of delight but met with the warmest appreciation and admiration of every Englishman present.

Their forwards gave their backs no more of the ball from the scrums than did Robertsand his pack. Indeed, in the second half, England secured possession slightly more often. But what a contrast when the backs had it!

Slow heeling could not be blamed for the many dropped passes, the lack of resource and the absence of combination behind the English scrum. The plain fact was that in every art of Rugby England were a class below their scarlet-jerseyed opponents.

The Welsh forwards, or should I say John and Gwilliam, obtained an absolute mastery at the line-outs that must have been a shock to the English selectors.

England with 10 new caps were deficient in the super-skill of experienced Wales, with 13 of last year's Triple Crown team. Time and again the Welshmen were allowed to throw or knock the ball back to their outsides without a finger laid on them. Two of the tries were initiated this way.

LIKE BEST TOURING TEAM

G. Davies, Matthews and L. Jones revelled in their opportunities, and carried out passing movements among themselves and their wings so swiftly and so deftly that the English defence was wholly confounded. Irresolution in midfield tackling and waiting for the ball to pass were the chief weaknesses.

(January 22)

SAVITT WINS WIMBLEDON AT THE FIRST ATTEMPT

McGregor Beaten in Straight Sets

From Lainson Wood

WIMBLEDON, Friday.

Yet another Wimbledon champion has been reeled off the American production line. Richard Savitt, 24-year-old Cornell University graduate, triumphant at the first attempt, defeated Kenneth McGregor of Australia, 6-4, 6-4, 6-4, in the men's singles championship final here to-day.

Savitt is of the pattern to which we have become accustomed. That we can find no mass production method in turning them out like it may be slightly exasperating. The ingredients of the pattern are: force, firm control and unremitting efficiency.

All credit to him for succeeding in a task that seemed somehow not to have come quite naturally to him. Most of his strokes are awkardly produced and I could not help thinking, while watching the effort required to put them across, that a man with his torso and trunk and the singleness of purpose with which he must have set out on the Wimbledon road might have won the world heavyweight championship had he been otherwise minded.

It is the strokes and the way they are employed, not the way you fashion them, that win championships, and Savitt did distinguish himself from the ranks of the mass-produced at times by his better generalship in the important rallies, and his unfailing nerve.

IMMATURE McGREGOR

For all his great ease and fluency of stroke and execution, and his more athletic appearance generally, McGregor's immaturity as a tactician and a match player was all to obvious.

A man of wider experience might have seen that there was a harvest to be garnered from pressure brought to bear on the American's awkwardly produced backhand, especially if the pressure was deep and forceful, but McGregor played all too rarely on that wing.

Too often the stroke preceding the incursion was short and McGregor was passed or forced to volley up, which was equally fatal. His only reliable stroke on which to advance was his powerful first service, and once in command at the net he was not easily robbed of the point.

He was able to hold his service gains in the first set with the exception of the 5th when he fluffed a couple of volleys. He could not break Savitt's service, and so it was 6-4 to the American.

(July 7)

MILBURN GOALS WON CUP FOR NEWCASTLE

Blackpool Caught In Their Own Trap

By Frank Coles

Newcastle Utd.......................... **2** Blackpool..................... **0**

Newcastle are F.A. Cup-holders for the fourth time in a glittering career. In defeating Blackpool in Saturday's not so distinguished Final they completed a hat-trick in Wembley wins - 1924, 1932 and 1951 - and the latest triumph will always be known as Milburn's match.

This tall strapping young Tynesider is the fastest centre-forward I have set eyes on. He won the game in the first 10 minutes of the second half with two fine opportunist goals, would have had more but for Farm's sound anticipation between the Blackpool posts, and convinced every selector that he is the man to lead England against Argentina on the same ground on May 9.

Milburn's first goal at the fiftieth minute was against the run of play, as inspired by the brilliance of Matthews, Blackpool had done most of the attacking in the first half. That they were not able to turn any of Matthews streamlined centres to account was due to Brennan's complete bottling up of Mortensen and the sure tackling of the wing-halves, Harvey and Crowe.

The great winger shouldered the burden gallantly by doing two men's work. He was head and shoulders above every other in laying on scoring chances. If only Matthews had been blessed with shooting power he must have won the match off his own boots. Four times he tried his luck and was never on target.

FATAL TACTICS

All through the first half Milburn was a victim of Blackpool's offside tactics As often happens, however, this dangerous trap recoiled on those who set it. Indeed it was the direct cause of Blackpool's downfall.

At the fifth minute after the interval Blackpool had eight men up in an all out attack. A long clearance went straight upfield to Milburn only a few yards inside the Blackpool half and he was away clear in a flash. Most of the crowd expected the whistle for offside but a linesman ideally placed to judge signalled not offside. Milburn raced ahead, drew the goalkeeper out and fired a low shot into the net.

A finer goal has never been seen at Wembley. Little Taylor put the defenders off-balance with a back heeler to Milburn and from 25 yards the Newcastle leader let fly with his left foot. The ball was in the roof of the net before Farm could move.

BRENNAN'S STOUT DEFENCE

A two-goal lead gave Newcastle all the confidence they wanted.

The winners' strength lay in Brennan's stout defence and Milburn's thrust. Outside-left Mitchell was not the force I thought he would be for the simple reason that he spent much time falling back to tackle Matthews. Robledo was the constructive workman and Taylor full of tricky moves.

(April 30)

No. 7974

ACROSS

1 Not one of the younger fruits (10)
6 The prophecy of it involves a cross (4)
9 Does this involve a country's turnover, in a roundabout way? (10)
10 A present that might appeal to a friend (4)
13 I write in colour in quite a mature fashion (7)
15 Given back with material assistance (6)
16 Something dear to yachtsmen that might be stolen (6)
17 Labour is all important here, but a conservative basis of argument is included (7,8)
18 Inters differently just to put in (6)
20 Do it while listening-in and you may miss the sound of it beheaded!(6)
21 We all warm to the idea of a second part, but this leaves the the non-astronomer cold (3, 4)
22 How to give additional strength to any society (4)
25 A help towards support and defence afforded by one of the smaller branches (5, 5)
26 In time this is almost sure to go to the wall (4)
27 This is associated with a colony, but not a dominion (10)

DOWN

1 With hay about it's what comes to them, and not evidence (4)
2 It would be cynical to offer scraps to this bird (4)
3 Put down again so as to upset a fellow telephoning? (6)
4 If this is exceeded something is sure to burst! (7, 8)
5 Hordes came to him, and he helped to fashion a nation (6)
7 "Person rises" (anag.) (and who does the holding down?) (10)
8 Thoroughly tried to see if the water supply was all right? (4, 6)
11 The fruits of past neglect of our road system help to make it (7, 8)
12 It will be some other world spies chaps coming out of them! (5, 5)
13 For severe conditions others fit their ships accordingly, and we this (7)
14 Changed from this inactive state it could become biting (7)
19 One cannot but associate it with one of the hard cases of the sea (6)
20 Wet enough to employ in the turf (6)
23 One can hardly do it and remain anonymous (4)
24 A bunch of keys will open insular delight to you (4)

(June 7)

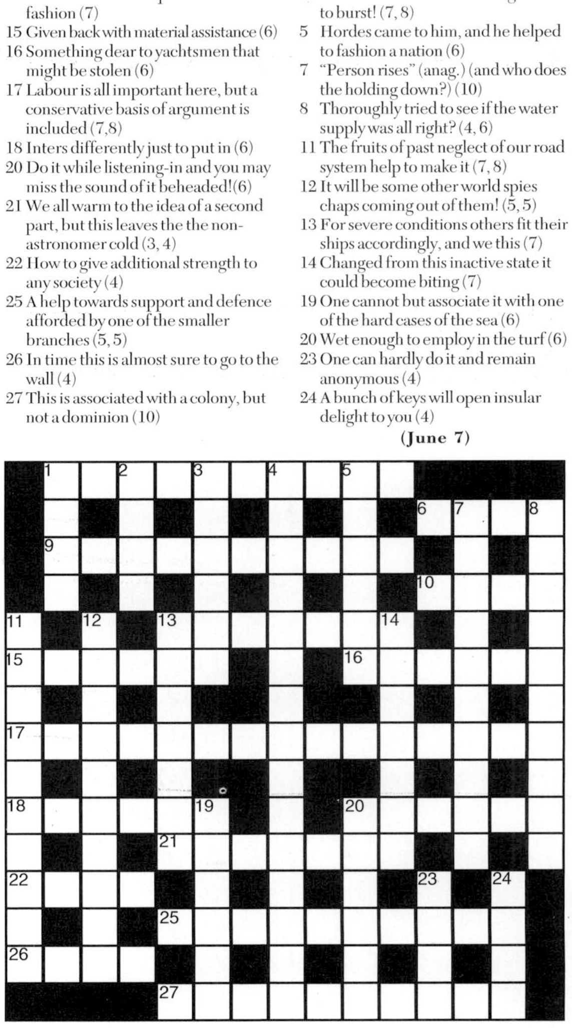

1952

A year of endings - and of beginnings. King George VI, who had led his people through many changes of fortune, died. King Farouk of Egypt, the ultimate sybarite, was unceremoniously booted off his throne, to be replaced by a military dictatorship whose growing power and intense nationalism was to become one of the dominant forces later in the decade. Chaim Weitzmann, the founding father of Israel died. Trygve Lie, the Norwegian who, as its Secretary General, had guided the United Nations from its outset, resigned. Charlie Chaplin, a victim of the McCarthy witchhunt, left America for the last time. The Utility mark, which had dictated standards for items like clothing and furniture during wartime and the years of austerity that followed, was abolished. The last London tram rattled and banged its way through the metropolis's streets. The identity cards that had been so reluctantly carried by the British people were abolished although ration books still remained.

A new Queen was on the throne of England, the news of her succession being brought to her while she and her husband were on a tour of Kenya. Africa had its first black Prime Minister. The ill-fated Comet introduced the first regular passenger service by a jet aircraft. General Eisenhower resigned his command to campaign successfully to become President of the United States. Agatha Christie's *The Mousetrap* began its run at the Ambassadors Theatre. Maria Callas made her debut at Covent Garden.

The trial of Christopher Craig and Derek Bentley for the murder of a policeman raised many questions. There was no doubt that Craig, a 16-year-old, had fired the fatal shot. His age prevented him being sentenced to death. Bentley was, in fact, already in police custody when the murder took place. Evidence was given that he had shouted encouragement to Craig and on those grounds he was sentenced to death. A portent of scandals to come was given when Richard Nixon, General Eisenhower's running mate for the Presidency of the United States was the centre of controversy over secret financial support given to him by rich Californian businessmen.

The world watched as Captain Carlsen stayed alone, until he was joined by a tug's mate, in a valiant effort to keep the badly damaged *Flying Enterprise* afloat in the January Atlantic storms. One terrible night of rain almost washed away the North Devon town of Lynmouth. The Mau Mau atrocities in Kenya necessitated the despatch of British troops while General Templer arrived in Malaya to add steel to the efforts to suppress the terror there. Moussadeq, the tragi-comical Prime Minister of Iran, much given to public weeping, precipitated an oil crisis by renouncing Britain's treaty of friendship with his country. And a bare quarter of an hour before the closing of the Olympic Games at Helsinki, Great Britain won its solitary gold medal. The Olympic Games had been dominated by the Czech runner Emil Zatopek who, already the winner of gold medals for the 5,000 and 10,000 metres races, ran a marathon for the first time in his life, and won, calmly asking the British leader of the race at 19 km, whether he could run any faster. Sad to say, he couldn't.

The Daily Telegraph
and Morning Post

No. 30,139 LONDON, THURSDAY, FEBRUARY 7, 1952

Printed in LONDON and MANCHESTER Price 2d.

DEATH OF KING GEORGE VI

PEACEFULLY IN SLEEP AT SANDRINGHAM

LAST WALK IN GROUNDS ON PREVIOUS EVENING

NEW QUEEN FLYING HOME: IN LONDON TO-DAY

PROCLAMATION TO-MORROW: PRIME MINISTER ON RADIO TO-NIGHT

HIS MAJESTY KING GEORGE VI DIED IN HIS SLEEP AT SANDRINGHAM HOUSE IN THE EARLY HOURS OF YESTERDAY MORNING. A SERVANT FOUND HIM DEAD IN BED AT 7.30 A.M. AN ANNOUNCEMENT FROM SANDRINGHAM, REPEATED IN A SPECIAL ISSUE OF THE LONDON GAZETTE LAST NIGHT, SAID:

The King, who retired last night in his usual health, passed peacefully away in his sleep early this morning.

Princess Elizabeth, who immediately became Queen, was informed of her father's death while she was at the Royal hunting lodge near Nyeri in Kenya. A thunderstorm delayed for two hours the departure of the plane which is to bring her to London, where she is expected at 2.30 p.m. to-day.

The Accession Council, which consists of members of the Privy Council summoned with other "notables of the Realm" such as the Lord Mayor of London, to act on the demise of the Crown, met at 5 p.m. yesterday to decide on the accession proclamation. This will be read at 11 a.m. to-morrow at St. James's Palace, at Temple Bar and on the steps of the Royal Exchange in the City.

The Queen, who is 25, is expected to take the Royal oath before a second meeting of the Council to-day. She was proclaimed Queen Elizabeth II of Canada in Ottawa yesterday. Prince Charles automatically becomes Duke of Cornwall.

Mr. Churchill will broadcast on all B.B.C. wavelengths at 9 o'clock to-night for 15 minutes.

OUT SHOOTING ON PREVIOUS DAY

The King, who was 56 and in the 16th year of his reign, was born at Sandringham. During what proved to be his last stay there he was out shooting on Tuesday morning and afternoon, and appeared to be in good health. In the evening he walked in the grounds.

The Queen-Mother and Princess Margaret accompanied him when he went to Sandringham last Friday. On the previous day he had gone to London Airport to see his elder daughter and the Duke of Edinburgh leave for Nairobi.

Queen Mary was informed at Marlborough House of her son's death. The Duke of Gloucester, who was at his home at Barnwell Manor, Northants, went to Sandringham on hearing the news. The Princess Royal was told at St. James's Palace. The Duchess of Kent returned from Germany last night, and the Duke of Windsor leaves New York in the Queen Mary to-day.

The Prime Minister and Sir David Maxwell Fyfe, Home Secretary, were given the news by telephone. A Cabinet meeting was held. The House of Commons and the House of Lords met formally for two minutes and adjourned until after the Accession Council, when M.P.s and Peers began to take the Oath of Allegiance to the new monarch. The two chambers are expected to meet on Monday for addresses of condolence and then adjourn until Feb. 19.

Subject to the wishes of the new Queen the body of King George will lie in state in Westminster Hall from Monday until the funeral, the date for which has not yet been fixed. Carpenters at Sandringham finished making the coffin of oak from the estate last night.

CINEMAS AND THEATRES CLOSED

The effect of the news from Sandringham was felt immediately throughout the nation. All cinemas were closed and the Lord Chamberlain directed that theatres should be shut for the day and also on the day of the funeral of the King. B.B.C. programmes were cancelled except for news bulletins. There will be a restricted programme from to-day until after the funeral. The Stock exchange and Lloyd's closed, courts adjourned and a number of public dinners and other functions were postponed. Flags in every town were at half-mast.

A RECENT PORTRAIT OF HIS MAJESTY KING GEORGE VI

LYING-IN-STATE ON MONDAY

PARLIAMENT TO SEND CONDOLENCES

By Our Political Correspondent

Parliament is expected to meet on Monday for addresses of condolence to Queen Elizabeth and the Royal family on the death of King George VI to be moved in both houses. Lords and Commons will then adjourn until Tuesday week, Feb. 19.

The body of the King will lie in state in Westminster Hall from Monday until the day fixed for the funeral. These arrangements are provisional until the Queen's wishes regarding her father's funeral are made known on her return.

Meanwhile, members of the House of Commons will take the oath to the Queen.

GOVERNMENTS CARRY ON

The Government and the Governments of Commonwealth countries all continue in office under the Demise of the Crown Act, 1901. This laid down that the position of all who held office under the Crown would not be affected by the Monarch's death.

No seals will be surrendered or letters patent cancelled. But Ministers will kiss hands and take the oath to the new Sovereign.

RETURN OF QUEEN: PREMIER'S PLEA

The following announcement was issued from 10, Downing Street last night:

"The Prime Minister feels that it would be in accordance with the wishes of the public that the return of the Queen to London should be as quiet as possible and that her Majesty should be met only by those whose official positions make it appropriate for them to be present at the airport.

"It is accordingly hoped that there will be no public gathering at London Airport to-morrow afternoon."

7.30 a.m. DISCOVERY BY SANDRINGHAM SERVANT

From Our Special Correspondent

SANDRINGHAM, Wednesday.

The King was found dead in his bed at Sandringham House at 7.30 this morning. He had died as he slept peacefully during the night.

A short while before he retired after a family dinner party last night the King took a last walk in the grounds. He admired the calm and quiet of the evening and was looking forward to a day's shooting to-day.

A servant who carried in his usual morning cup of tea could not rouse him. Immediately but quietly help was summoned.

Her Majesty was told. A message was sent calling for Dr. Ansell in the village of Wolferton, three miles away.

The village doctor drove along the road that winds through the Royal estate, flanked on either side by the brown withered ferns through which less that 24 hours earlier the King had himself walked. He was taken to the King's room. There was nothing he could do.

NO BLINDS DRAWN

No blinds were drawn over the windows of this favourite home of the King. The smoke from the first fires hung limp in the still morning air. No announcement was posted on the wrought iron gates at the end of the main drive.

ROYAL FAMILY CANCEL PLANS

DUCHESS FLIES HOME

The news was conveyed to Queen Mary at Marlborough House some time before the official announcement was made. "It came as a great shock to her," said a member of her staff.

It is understood that Queen Mary will remain in her own home. She will not undertake the journey to Sandringham.

The Princess Royal, in her apartments in St. James's Palace, was told by telephone from Buckingham Palace. Her visit to Switzerland, which she had planned following an attack of fibrositis, has been cancelled.

MEDICAL VIEWS ON CAUSE OF DEATH

By Our Medical Correspondent

Comfort must be taken by the Royal family and nation that his Majesty died in his sleep without pain.

Lumbar sympathectomy, performed three years ago for circulatory failure in his leg, gave evidence of arterial disease, and it is probable that the main artery of the body, the aorta, and the branches it gives to the heart called the coronary arteries, were also thickened, hardened and narrowed.

This condition can cause clotting, known as coronary thrombosis, which stops the heart. Death in these cases is sometimes immediate and painless.

Looking back, we also have the unrelenting course of the King's lung trouble, which resulted in resection. The same structural changes, probably a malignant growth, reported as being in the lung can occur in the brain as a secondary complication. Such changes are often without symptom until a fatal haemorrhage or clotting reveals their presence.

OTHER POSSIBILITY

It is possible that such a trouble may have been the actual cause of death. Another possible cause is clotting in the pulmonary circulation, a complication of resection more usually met in the immediate post-operative period.

All these conditions are sudden and though recognised, the date of the fact that they will occur cannot be foreseen.

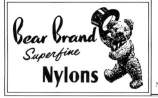

The Daily Telegraph and Morning Post
4 A.M.
No. 30,282 LONDON, THURSDAY, JULY 24, 1952 Printed in LONDON and MANCHESTER Price 2d.

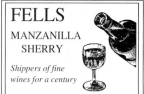

EGYPTIAN ARMY SEIZES POWER

GEN. NEGUIB NEW C.-IN-C. AFTER HEADING COUP

KING FAROUK ACCEPTS MAN HE REJECTED

ANTI-CORRUPTION DRIVE: MAHER PASHA AS PREMIER

From Eric Downton, Daily Telegraph Special Correspondent

CAIRO, Wednesday.

Egyptian armed forces, led by Maj.-Gen. Mohammed Neguib Bey, 51, former Cairo area commander, took control of Cairo, Alexandria and other cities early to-day without bloodshed. By to-night the coup had led to the return of Aly Maher Pasha as Prime Minister in place of Hilaly Pasha, whose Cabinet was sworn in only yesterday.

Army sources said King Farouk had asked Maher Pasha to form a new Cabinet this afternoon after the Army's "request" that the change of Governments be made "before 1800 hours to-day". Gen. Neguib had earlier proclaimed himself Commander-in-Chief of the Armed Forces and was confirmed in the appointment by King Farouk to-night. His predecessor as C.-in-C., Marshal Mohammed Haider, and other senior officers were put under arrest.

Gen. Neguib said the object of the coup was "to force a return to constitutional life and to purge the Army of corrupt elements". Maher Pasha, whom he described as "the only man suitable for this task", became Prime Minister after the Jan. 26 riots, on the fall of the Wafd Government.

King Farouk's attitude is an important unknown quantity in the new situation. He has accepted as C.-in-C. the general whom he refused to have as War Minister in the Cabinet of Sirry Pasha, Hilaly Pasha's predecessor in office.

There has been a good deal of criticism of the King in the Army. The dissidents no doubt hope to-day's demonstration will force him to clean up Egyptian political life.

Maher Pasha told reporters the situation was critical, but might clarify itself in a day or two. Gen. Neguib has said that the Army has no intention of interfering in the country's political affairs. He conferred with Maher Pasha for two hours to-day.

Some reports to-night say Maher Pasha will himself act as Minister of War and the Interior in a Cabinet composed mainly of independents. He might also hold the post of Foreign Minister, at least for a time. He leaves for Alexandria to-morrow to see King Farouk.

CAIRO'S SURPRISE

Planes Demonstrate

Tanks and troops patrolled the streets of Cairo and Alexandria throughout the day, but there was no disorder.

The coup was made at 3 o'clock this morning, when tanks, armoured cars and truck-loads of troops in full battle equipment took control of the main buildings, streets and squares in Cairo, Alexandria and other principal towns. In Cairo the radio buildings and telegraphic offices were among the first objectives.

A surprised city was awakened by fighter-bombers of the Egyptian Air Force roaring low over the city's roofs in demonstration.

Maraghy Pasha, Minister of the Interior, flew to Cairo from Alexandria to meet the dissidents. Gen. Neguib sent messages to foreign embassies in Alexandria and Cairo warning them not to "interfere" in Egyptian internal affairs.

Maraghy Pasha was to-night received in audience by King Farouk at the summer palace near Alexandria. He was understood to have acquainted the King with the results of his talks with the leaders of the coup.

Hilaly Pasha's day-old Cabinet had held an emergency meeting early this morning and his resignation as Prime Minister was received this afternoon. Then came the invitation from King Farouk to Maher Pasha.

DEFEAT FOR KING FAROUK

STORM RISING ROUND THRONE

By Our Diplomatic Correspondent

King Farouk's confirmation of Gen. Neguib as Egyptian C.-in-C. after the general's coup d'etat may indicate that the King intends, for the time being at least, to ride out the storm which is rising round his throne.

None the less his acceptance of the general whom he had a few days earlier vetoed as War Minister is an undisguised defeat.

Gen. Neguib's action yesterday was clearly precipitated by the appointment on Tuesday of Col. Sherine Bey, King Farouk's brother-in-law, as War Minister in the Hilaly Cabinet. A condition of Sherine Bey's appointment, no doubt agreed between the King and Hilaly Pasha, was almost certainly that Gen. Neguib would be posted to some remote spot.

Gen. Neguib evidently considered that, if he was to maintain his leadership of those parts of the Army which violently resented the corruption which was weakening its effectiveness, he must act at once. From his own point of view, he has been singularly successful.

He can now insist on the exposure and punishment of those concerned with supplying faulty equipment to the Army. What is not clear is the extent to which Maher Pasha, the Prime Minister, will pursue inquiries into civilian corruption.

ONE DRINK FOR GUESTS

The corks of champagne bottles popped at the George Hotel, Nottingham, at midnight last night, but only one drink was served to each guest attending a coming-of-age party.

This was due to an undertaking given by the Nottingham City Coroner, Mr. A. Rothera. He applied earlier in the day to Nottingham magistrates for an extension of the normal licensing hours from midnight last night to 12.30 a.m.

He explained that guests at the party wished to drink the health of Miss Jean Graham, of Nottingham, who was born at midnight on July 23, 1931.

At first Sir Jardine, chairman of the magistrates, regretted that the application could not be granted. Mr. Rothera then said: "I must confess to having a personal interest. I am proposing the toast and it is only a question of one drink of champagne."

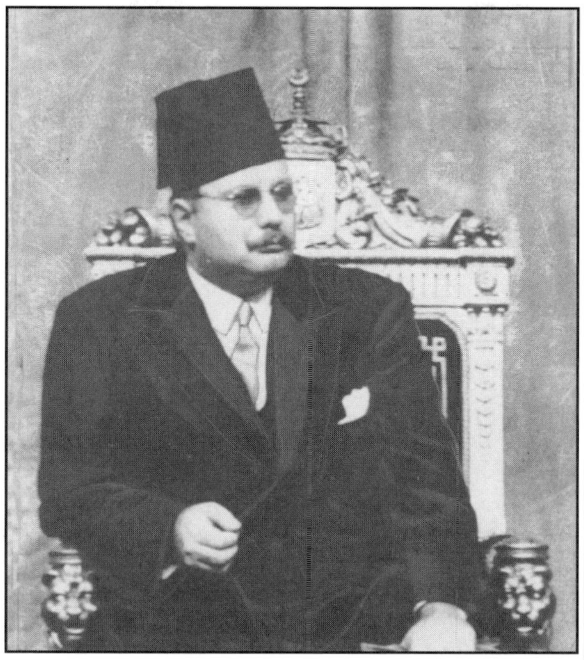

KING FAROUK OF EGYPT

M. QAVAM ESCAPES AFTER ARREST

Confiscation of Property Urged

From Our Own Correspondent

TEHERAN, Wednesday.

Qavam es-Sultaneh, whose four-day Premiership ended on Monday, has been arrested. He was taken into custody by the gendarmerie in Qom, a town about 60 miles south of Teheran.

The Qom gendarmes were instructed from Teheran to hold him pending further orders. It was later announced, however, that he had eluded his guards this afternoon and fled. The Teheran Government has told border posts to keep a close watch for him and arrest him on sight.

Several hundred demonstrators here were reported to have decided to go to Qom to drag "Qavam back to Teheran for trial". About 30 National Front Deputies have called for a special session of Parliament to-morrow to pass a resolution that all M. Qavam's property be confiscated and the proceeds distributed among the relatives of those killed in Monday's riots.

DAY OF MOURNING

To-morrow has been proclaimed a day of national mourning for Monday's victims, but Teheran is illuminated to-night to celebrate Persia's "victory" at The Hague. The Shah to-day in a message congratulated the nation and Dr. Mossadeq for The Hague result which is a "further step towards the nation's achievements of its goals".

Dr. Mossadeq to-day dismissed the Army Chief of Staff and the Gendarmerie Chief and appointed his own men. Last night he dismissed the Chief of Police.

NEW POLICE CHIEF

Kazem Sheibani, former Governor General of Khuzistan, South Persia, in which Abadan is situated, was to-night named Teheran's new chief of police. M. Qavam, during his four days of power, had summoned Sheibani to explain his complicity in demonstrations against the Qavam Cabinet.

The Majlis Committee which was set up to look into the riots has stated that they believe that Gen. Garzan, Chief of the Army General Staff, and Gen. Moghadan, the Teheran military commander, were responsible for the shooting. They recommended that they be tried and if possible executed.

THREAT TO BRITISH NURSES

Two British nurses in Teheran were threatened to-day by about 400 hospital employees, who accused the nurses of responsibility for the death of two wounded demonstrators. The nurses, who fled to the British Embassy, are identified as Sister Watt and Sister Kennedy.

The "National Iranian Oil Company" is holding a reception to-night to mark the "victory" at The Hague.

Mr. Churchill's Statement - P7

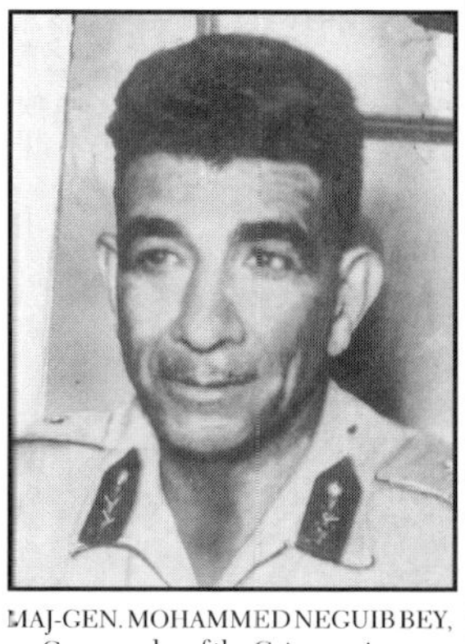

MAJ-GEN. MOHAMMED NEGUIB BEY, Commander of the Cairo garrison, who took over the city.

BETTER RIFLE FOR N.A.T.O.

280 BEING ADAPTED FOR BIGGER BULLET

By Lt.-Gen H. G. Martin
Daily Telegraph Military Correspondent.

Mr. Birch, Parliamentary Secretary, Ministry of Defence, announced in the House of Commons yesterday that experiments were proceeding for the development of an improved type of small arms ammunition and the weapons to fire it. Agreement on its characteristics had been reached between the North Atlantic Treaty Organisation Powers.

No round yet produced had fulfilled all the specifications. Experimental work was likely to be completed in the next 12 months.

The resulting round and weapon will then be accepted as standard by all N.A.T.O. countries. The rifle thus chosen may be the British 280. This is still being developed to take the round of greater hitting power that is now an accepted requirement.

It is clear from Mr. Birch's remarks that, in framing the specifications, the American experts have had their way. They have always favoured a higher velocity than that of the 0.280 rifle, and have maintained that nothing less than a 0.30 bullet could give a knock-out blow.

'HEAVY TAX' ON GOLF PRIZES

VON NIDA'S CRITICISM

By Leonard Crawley

Norman von Nida, the Australian professional, who has been outstandingly successful in British golf tournaments since the war, said yesterday at Harrogate that heavy taxation of prize money did not make it worth while for overseas players to come to this country any more. He did not think he would be competing here again.

Other overseas players, he stated, felt the same way. In his view the distribution of prize money was too wide, meaning presumably that those at the top of the list were not adequately paid and those further down the list had too much.

PROTEST VOTE BY DIXIECRATS

RENEWED THREAT OF DEMOCRATIC SPLIT

BALLOT MAY BE DELAYED

From Denys Smith and Alex Faulkner, Daily Telegraph Special Correspondents

CHICAGO, Wednesday.

A Dixiecrat revolt over the adoption by the Democratic party convention here of a rule requiring delegates to give loyalty pledges flared up again to-night. South Carolina delegates voted to boycott the convention.

The protest move was announced by Mr. Edgar Brown, the State's Democratic chairman. But later Mr. Byrnes, Governor of South Carolina and a former Secretary of State, said he wanted the delegation to attend to-night's session.

When the convention resumed South Carolina's delegation were in their seats. Mr. Byrnes, who was in conference with leaders of the Virginia and Louisiana delegations, said he had not known of the protest vote.

South Carolina, Virginia and Louisiana had held out against giving the pledge, even though it had been modified overnight. It was feared that if a walk-out did not materialise, at least there would be "fireworks" at the convention.

It had been hoped that a Presidential candidate would be nominated by to-morrow night or at any rate early Friday morning. The renewal of the southern "revolt" following dispute over rival delegations and the party platform may delay the ballot.

Mr. McKinney, the national committee chairman, stated that President Truman, who would not come to Chicago until after a candidate had been chosen, would introduce the nominee on Friday night if the programme were adhered to.

STEEL CALL BY MR. TRUMAN

ENDING STRIKE

From Our Own Correspondent

WASHINGTON, Wednesday.

Mr. Truman took the initiative in person to-night in an effort to end the 52-day steel strike. He summoned Mr. Benjamin Fairless representing the employers, and Mr. Philip Murray, of the United Steelworkers Union, to the White House to-morrow for a conference with him.

An announcement from the White House indicated that Dr. John Steel, acting Defence Mobiliser, will also be there. Mr. Fairless is chairman of the board and President of the United States Steel, one of the big six companies.

When a member of Mr. Truman's staff telephoned them, Mr. Fairless in New York and Mr. Murray in Pittsburgh, both accepted the summons at once. This is taken as boding well for the prospects of settlement.

A spokesman at the White House said to-night that one of the matters being studied by the President was the possible partial seizure of steel mills to ensure a renewed flow of armaments for Korea.

MORE DIE IN U.S. HEATWAVE

95DEG IN NEW YORK

From Our Own Correspondent

NEW YORK, Wednesday.

New Yorkers to-day had the 13th day of the longest heatwave in the 81-year history of the local weather bureau. Weather forecasters said that there was no relief in sight.

In 8 of the past 12 days temperatures have been above 90deg. and in the other four days above 85deg. To-day the temperature was 92deg at 11 a.m.

By 3 p.m. it had risen to 95 and was still climbing. The previous record for July 23 was 91.7 in 1918.

The heat has caused numerous deaths and countless cases of prostration throughout the eastern coast line. Nine people died from heat to-day and six yesterday in Baltimore alone.

CABINET MAY DISCUSS HIGHER COAL EXPORTS

ECONOMIC DEBATE BROUGHT FORWARD

By Our Political Correspondent

The Cabinet continued its review of the economic situation yesterday and is likely to finish it to-day in readiness for the two-day debate next week. This debate will now take place on Tuesday and Wednesday, instead of later in the week as planned originally.

The new arrangement will give Mr. Eden, who is recovering from jaundice, more time to prepare for the two-day debate on Germany, also planned for next week.

Non-Cabinet Ministers who attended yesterday's Cabinet were: Viscount Swinton, Chancellor of the Duchy of Lancaster and Minister of Materials: Mr. Selwyn Lloyd, Minister of State, deputising for Mr. Eden: Mr. Sandys, Minister of Supply: Mr. Eccles, Minister of Works: Mr. Head, Secretary for War: Mr. Thomas, First Lord of the Admiralty, and Lord De L'Isle and Dudley, Secretary for Air.

The housing programme and the possibility of deferring the National Service of apprentices in the engineering industry may have been discussed.

NEAR SAFETY LEVEL

I understand that the possibility of increasing coal exports above the 12 million tons already planned may be considered to-day. Coal stocks are already near the 17 million tons, the minimum safety level for entering the coal winter on Nov. 1.

On the other hand there is still some shortage of large coal for domestic use, which is also the type of coal principally required for export. Mr. Lloyd, Minister of Fuel and Power, is known to take a cautious view of the coal position and would like to begin the winter with at least 19 million tons in stock.

Mr. Churchill may speak on the second day of the economic debate, which will be opened by Mr. Butler, Chancellor of the Exchequer, with a general statement on the situation. Sir Walter Monckton, Minister of Labour, will also speak and probably Mr. Thorneycroft, President of the Board of Trade.

BANK HOLIDAY DEBATE THREAT

WARNING TO M.P.S

By Our Political Correspondent

Plans to adjourn the House of Commons before August Bank Holiday may have to be abandoned if delaying tactics by a group of Socialist M.P.s are sustained.

Mr. Crookshank, Leader of the House, stated yesterday that these tactics might involve sitting on Bank Holiday and perhaps beyond. If the opposition continues, the Government will, I understand, postpone the debate on the ratification of the contracts with the West German Republic now planned for Thursday and Friday, until the Bank Holiday, and possibly the following Tuesday.

There is considerable anger on the Government side at the apparent inability of the Opposition Front Bench to control the activities of their back-benchers. In the House yesterday a Government motion to take the third reading of the Civil List Bill immediately after the report stage, which had been agreed between the Whips, was opposed by Socialist back-benchers. In the division, which followed Opposition leaders voted against the motion in spite of the previous arrangement.

The Socialists claim that what is happening is no more than a repetition of the so-called "harrying" tactics by some Conservative back-benchers in the last Parliament. On those occasions, the Conservatives prolonged debate by tabling series of prayers. They did not attempt to hold up essential Government business.

RECTOR AND BOY DROWNED

From Our Own Correspondent

BARNSTAPLE, Wednesday.

The Rev. J.R.M. Etherington, 36, Rector of Withypool, Somerset, and one of his altar servers, Norman Hustable, 15, of Riverside Cottages, Withypool, were drowned while bathing at Instow, North Devon, to-day. They were on a village outing.

RESCUE TUG GETS TO CAPT. CARLSEN

MASTER 'DETERMINED TO STAY ON BOARD'

3-WAY RADIO TALK ON TOWING PLANS

'IMPOSSIBLE TO CONNECT BECAUSE OF LIST'

Daily Telegraph Reporters

The British salvage tug Turmoil, 1,136 tons, late last night reached the American freighter Flying Enterprise, 6,711 tons, which had been drifting in the Atlantic for six days and nights with only her master, Capt. Kurt Carlsen, aboard. The tug will try to tow the ship to a British port.

Capt. Parker, of the tug Turmoil, in a radio-telephone message to London at 3 a.m. to-day, said it was impossible to connect with Flying Enterprise "owing to the list and lurching of the ship.

"At daylight, if possible, will put men aboard and connect. Ship appears to have buoyancy." The gale has dropped to a gentle breeze.

The United States Naval H.Q. in London reported at 2.45 a.m. to-day the following message from the destroyer John W. Weeks, which was standing by in position 47deg 46min N. 11deg 53min W.: "Salvage tug Turmoil has arrived on scene and preparations are under way for taking Flying Enterprise in tow in accordance with plans formulated during three-way conversation among Capt. Carlsen, Capt. Parker, of tug, and Capt. Thompson, of destroyer.

"Flying Enterprise still listing 60 to 65deg to port and down slightly by the head. Rudder and screw clear of water and rudder swinging free. Ship will be towed by stern to prevent further flooding.

"Capt. Carlsen very cheerful and grateful for food, cigarettes and magazines passed to him earlier by the Weeks."

(January 4)

TUG MATE LEAPS TO LISTING FREIGHTER

7 EFFORTS AT TOW FAIL: NEW ATTEMPT TO-DAY

Daily Telegraph Reporter

After efforts to get a towing line to the American freighter Flying Enterprise, 6,711 tons, drifting in the Atlantic, had been suspended yesterday because of bad weather, a message last night said that conditions were improving again. It was expected that operations would be resumed early to-day, possibly before daylight.

The lonely wait of Capt. Carlsen, master of the freighter, ended in the afternoon when the first mate of the British salvage tug Turmoil, 1,136 tons, which reached the scene on Thursday night, struggled aboard. Capt. Carlsen had spent nearly a week alone in the ship, which was wallowing with a cracked deck and a 70deg list in the Atlantic swells.

The mate, Mr. Kenneth Roger Dancy, 27, whose home is at Hook Green, Kent, was staying aboard last night with Capt. Carlsen.

Capt. Parker, captain of the Turmoil, had to manoeuvre the tug slowly astern in a rough sea until it was possible for Dancy to leap on to the stern of the other ship.

It was reported from Brest last night that the 440-ton French sea-going tug Abeille 25 was on her way to join the Turmoil in aiding the Flying Enterprise. She sailed early yesterday morning.

During the day, seven attempts to get a line to the ship failed and work was suspended when a wind approaching gale force sprang up.

TALK TO DESTROYER

Commander's Description

I was given details of the rescue efforts by radio-telephone by Cmdr. W.L. Thompson, 35, captain of the United States naval destroyer John W. Weeks, 2200 tons, which for three days and nights has been standing by the freighter.

Over circuit through Land's End G.P.O. radio station, which was badly affected by fading, Cmdr. Thompson, from the wireless cabin of his ship, said:

"We were standing by while the Turmoil made seven attempts to get lines aboard the Enterprise. After trying to get lines to the bows the tug went around to the stern. Two more shots were made, but each time the wire parted.

"Eventually the captain of the Turmoil decided he would have to break off operations. The sea was getting up and the wind increasing as dark was falling and nothing more could be done for the time being.

"We have been in close touch, visually and by signal, throughout the day. The tug has been making desperate attempts to get the freighter secured. I think they are going to succeed and get the Enterprise back to port.

(January 5)

CARLSEN & DANCY SAFE IN FALMOUTH

SIRENS SOUND END OF FLYING ENTERPRISE

From Our Special Correspondents
FALMOUTH, Thursday.

At 4.10 this afternoon the Flying Enterprise sank within 41 ½ miles of her goal. Her master, Capt. Carlsen, stood at the rail of the tug Turmoil and watched her sinking slowly.

As he turned away and the tug headed for port, the wailing of ships' sirens signalled that the freighter's 15-day battle with storms had ended with her defeat. Flares washed from the decks ignited as they touched the water and lighted the final scene.

Capt. Carlsen and Mr. Kenneth Dancy, mate of the tug Turmoil, had stayed on board the stricken vessel until the heavy seas were pouring into her. Then they jumped from the funnel into the foaming water. They were picked up by the tug at 3.30, unhurt.

They were brought to-night in the Turmoil to Falmouth, and are staying on board the ship for the night. To-morrow they will be given a civic welcome by the town.

Capt. Carlsen had resisted several appeals to him earlier in the day to leave the ship. A helicopter which was to attempt to take him off had to turn back because of the weather.

In the last few hours, with gales increasing in fury, hopes of getting a new tow-line aboard had been abandoned.

(January 11)

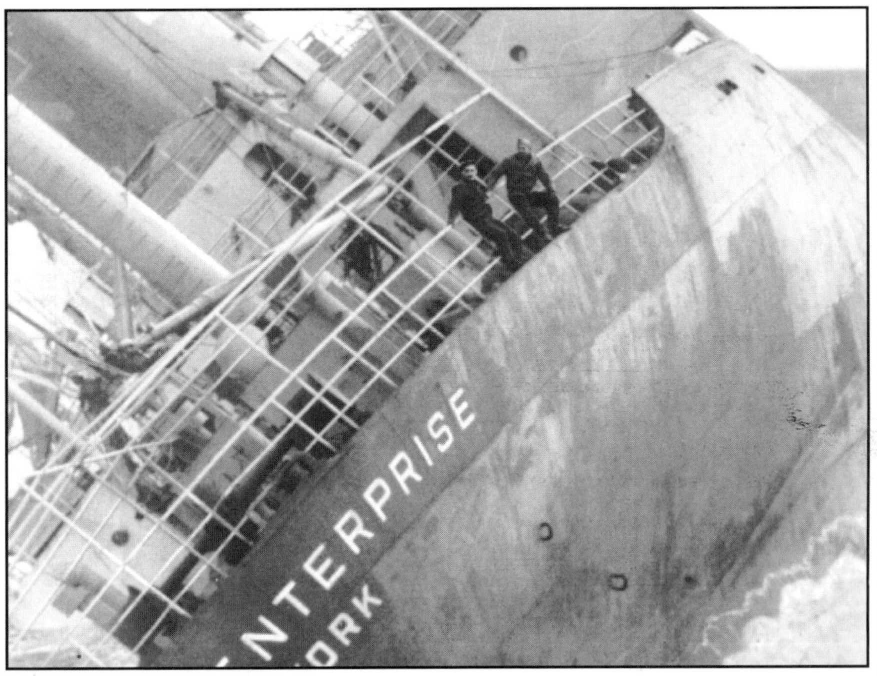

ONE OF THE LAST PICTURES of the Flying Enterprise, taken from sea level less than 24 hours before she sank 41 miles off the Lizard. Capt. Carlsen (Right) and Mr. Dancy were standing on the rails.

M.P.S VOTE FOR EQUAL PAY

WOMEN'S TRIUMPH

By Our Own Representative
WESTMINSTER, Friday.

The House of Commons to-day asked the Government to "name the day" when equal pay for equal work would be applied to women in the Civil Service, teaching and local Government service. That was the effect of a motion which was carried without a division. [Report - P7.]

It was a triumph for women - the hundreds who crowded the galleries throughout a five-hour debate, and the eight women Members who intervened in the debate. Only one speech against the motion was heard - from a man.

But it does not mean immediate equal pay. For the Government, Mr. Boyd-Carpenter, Financial Secretary to the Treasury, said that that was ruled out by the country's grave economic position.

He added, however, that the Government was now examining various schemes for introducing this reform by stages. It was keen to get on with it as soon as was practicable.

The motion was moved by Mr. Pannell (Soc. Leeds,W.) in a speech of wit and pointedness, which led inevitably to a debate of high order.

Pressure on Chancellor

OUR POLITICAL CORRESPONDENT writes: The acceptance without a division of the motion on equal pay for women in the public service will increase the pressure on the Chancellor of the Exchequer to implement this principle. The consequence will certainly be continual questions to Mr. Butler to "name the day".

The debate yesterday was the occasion for a pressure campaign of unusual intensity to persuade M.P.s to support the motion. Col. Schofield (C. Rochdale) referred to "the avalanche of postcards" which he had received.

(May 17)

AUTOMATIC DIP FOR CAR LIGHTS

DEVICE EXPECTED TO BE USED IN BRITAIN

By W. A. McKenzie
Daily Telegraph Motoring Correspondent

Automatically dipping headlights will be seen at the Earls Court motor show which opens to-morrow week. They will be fitted to two American cars built by General Motors. They are operated by a photo electric cell.

Whenever the beam of an approaching light strikes this light-sensitive cell a tiny electric current, boosted by an amplifier, works the dimming or dipping mechanism.

Dr. J.H.Nelson, chief engineer Joseph Lucas, Birmingham, said he had been carrying out tests. He considers it a major contribution to the solution of the dazzle problem.

(October 14)

DEAN REPEATS GERM CHARGES IN PULPIT

AMERICANS WALK OUT OF CATHEDRAL

From Our Own Correspondent
CANTERBURY, *Sunday.*

Most of the large congregation at Canterbury Cathedral this evening left in an indignant mood after the Dean, Dr. Hewlett Johnson, had used the pulpit there for 40 minutes to talk of nothing but China. He was preaching there for the first time since his recent visit to China.

When he quoted from documents which he said had been given to him by Chinese Christian leaders accusing "American aggressors" of bacteriological warfare, a number of Americans in the congregation got up from their seats and walked out.

I spoke later to three angry American women. They were visiting Canterbury from New York. One of them said:

"What that man said is all lies. I wonder he was not struck dead in the pulpit. I always thought that a cathedral was a place where they talked about God. Why is this man allowed to talk like this? I had to keep reading my Prayer Book to stop myself from shouting at him."

WOMAN BARS WAY

As the Dean walked towards the pulpit a grey-haired woman left her seat and barred his way. She said: "I defy you to go into that pulpit." The Dean pushed past her and she was led away by two vergers.

The woman was Mrs. Marie Cox, who refused to give her address. She said she had sat by the pulpit purposely to make that personal protest.

Dr. Johnson began with a glorification of the new China, compared with the China he visited in 1932, and quoted at length from documents. Frequently he banged his fist on the pulpit.

He said: "I was most emphatic in my statement to the Press and, I said it again and again and as carefully as I could, but it was ignored, that I was conveying the message of the Christian churches of the East to the Christian churches of the West and that it was their evidence and not mine."

Having spoken of charges made to him in China, he continued: "Time will prove it and I am willing to leave it to the British people and to history."

Referring to a Press united against him, he said:"It at least shows that the British people repudiate germ warfare. They say: 'The Americans could not possibly do that. The United Nations could not possibly do that. We can't be partners in germ warfare.'

"I thank God with all my heart for what the Press has unwittingly done for the salvation of the people of China from the appalling menace of germ warfare."

He quoted from a letter of welcome which he said had been addressed to Mrs. Johnson and himself on their arrival in China. The letter said: "We Christians of China would like to report to you the inhuman anti-Christian use by the American aggressors of bacteriological warfare launched against the Chinese and Korean peoples."

(July 21)

DEATH PENALTY ON U.S. ATOM SPIES TO STAND

HUSBAND AND WIFE

From Our Own Correspondent
NEW YORK, Monday.

The United States Court of Appeals to-day unanimously confirmed sentence of death passed last March on Julius Rosenberg, 34, engineer, and his wife, Ethel, 36, who were found guilty of passing wartime atomic bomb secrets to Russia.

They had appealed on the ground that the penalty was "cruel and unusual punishment". When they were sentenced in the Federal Court it was the first time the death penalty had been imposed for espionage in a United States civilian court in peace-time.

In its decision the court declared it was immaterial whether Russia was an ally or friendly nation during the period of espionage. The defendants had indicated at their trial that they preferred the Russian social and economic system to that of the United States.

CAUSE OF WAR

When Judge Kaufman sentenced the Rosenbergs in the Federal Court last April he said he believed their deeds had caused the Communists to start the war in Korea by enabling the Russians to obtain the atom bomb much sooner than they otherwise would.

"By your betrayal you undoubtedly have altered the course of history to the disadvantage of our country," he added.

Since conviction, the Rosenbergs, who have two small sons, have been in condemned cells at Sing-Sing. They have now only one chance of avoiding death, an appeal to the Supreme Court.

Greenglass was sentenced to 15 years' imprisonment, and a fourth defendant, Morton Sobell, 34, radar and electronics expert, was sentenced to 30 years.

(February 26)

GENERAL TEMPLER GETS MALAYA POST

HIGH COMMISSIONER AND MILITARY CHIEF

By Our Political Correspondent

The King has approved the appointment of Gen. Sir Gerald Templer, 53, as High Commissioner for the Federation of Malaya, the Colonial Office announced yesterday. The appointment was exclusively forecast in THE DAILY TELEGRAPH on Saturday.

The announcement, issued simultaneously in London and Malaya, said that "the High Commissioner in addition to the normal civil responsibilities of his office will direct all military and police operations and is being charged with full and direct responsibility for them."

The situation in Malaya "must be cleared up at once", Gen. Sir Gerald Templer, Britain's newly-appointed High Commissioner for Malaya, said at a Press conference in New York to-day.

He arrived this morning from Ottawa, where he had a discussion with Mr. Churchill. He was due to leave by plane later to-day for London with Mr. Eden.

Asked if he had talked with Mr. Churchill, Gen. Templer replied: "I know I shall get the fullest support." Invited to amplify the statement, he added: "I mean the fullest support in every way."

A reporter said: "In view of the fact that your predecessor, Sir Henry Gurney, was murdered last October, do you have any apprehensions about your personal safety?"

"None whatsoever," was the brusque reply. "That's my job."

POST'S IMPORTANCE

He added: "I fully realise the implications of the job and the importance of it, not only from the political and military, but also from the economic viewpoint. I shall do my best to do the job."

(January 16)

IDENTITY CARDS GO : SAVING OF £500,000

Daily Telegraph Reporter

The end of the identity card system was announced in the House of Commons yesterday by Mr. Crookshank, Minister of Health. It is now unnecessary to possess or produce the card, he said.

Notification of changes of address for national registration purposes would also no longer be needed. The old national registration numbers would be retained by health service patients as a means of identification and to avoid swelling doctors' lists.

He warned the public to await the official report before disposing of their cards. It was estimated that the abolition of cards would save about 1,500 people in staff and some £500,000 in cost.

(February 22)

FUNERAL OF KING GEORGE VI

SPLENDOUR AND GRIEF IN LONDON & WINDSOR

MOVING LAST RITES IN ST. GEORGE'S CHAPEL

FAMILY, FRIENDS & NATIONS TAKE THEIR FAREWELL

From Norman Riley,
Daily Telegraph Special Correspondent

WINDSOR, Friday.

The Most High, Most Mighty and Most Excellent Monarch, George VI, was gathered to the honourable company of his forbears in St. George's Chapel within the walls of Windsor Castle to-day after London had paid its tribute as he made his final progress through the streets.

He was committed to the Royal tomb beneath the banners of the Knights of the Garter whose plight it was to serve him as he had served his people.

As the Archbishop of Canterbury, Dr. Fisher, read the committal service, a small silver bowl was handed to the Queen. Throughout the service, it had stood on a small dark oak Jacobean stool, covered with a handkerchief of fine lawn, at the foot of the tomb of King Henry VI.

In the bowl was a handful of red earth. The Queen took between her fingers a few grains of the earth.

The Lord Chamberlain, the Earl of Clarendon, standing at the foot of the coffin, then held his stick of office out at arm's length and broke it into two parts. Eyes downcast, he reverently placed the two portions on the coffin. Nothing more final could symbolise the ending of his services to the King.

GUARDS' COLOUR ON COFFIN

Next came the commanding officer of the Grenadier Guards, Col. G.C.Gordon-Lennox, who proffered to the Queen the Colour of the King's Company of the regiment. This, too, was laid on the coffin - another of the unalterable privileges that go with the service.

Slowly the coffin began to sink beneath the tessellated cover. The Queen just as slowly let the grains of earth scatter down on the one simple wreath which remained.

For a while, in well-nigh unbearable silence, the whole assembly, with heads bowed, stared at the purple-hued void in the marble pavement.

Already the words of the Service - "Forasmuch as hath pleased Almighty God of His great mercy to take unto Himself the soul of our dear brother here departed" - seemed to belong remotely to the uncompromising past.

LAST HOMECOMING

And so the King came home for the last time to his own family church where he worshipped in rare week-end hours snatched from the burden of State affairs. Outside were left all the panoply and martial ceremony of public grief.

Within the chapel's grey-white walls King George VI was laid to rest in the presence of his own family and his dearest friends and retainers. The last rites were a fitting tribute to one who wore the mantle of high office through troubled years with such modesty and grace.

"God Save the Queen!" cried Garter King of Arms, George-Bellew, as it neared its close. And the Queen, white-faced beneath her veil, but steadfast and sure beyond her years, left the chapel to carry on, without consideration for self, the tradition for which her father had deemed no sacrifice too great.

(February 16)

NEWS BROKEN BY DUKE

QUEEN'S FORTITUDE

From Frank Harvey,
Daily Telegraph Special Correspondent
NYERI, Kenya, Wednesday.

News that she had become Queen came to Princess Elizabeth at Sagana Lodge, the wedding gift house here in which she and her husband were spending a brief holiday.

The news of the King's death was broken to her by the Duke of Edinburgh. She stood it bravely "like a Queen," it was stated.

First news of the death came from Mr. Granville Roberts, correspondent of the East African Standard. He was at lunch in the Outspan Hotel here when the telephoned message reached him from his Nairobi office.

He informed Lt.-Col. Charteris, the Princess's secretary, and then telephoned the news to Lt.-Cmdr. Parker, the Duke of Edinburgh's equerry at the Lodge. Lt.-Col. Charteris suggested that confirmation be obtained before the Princess was told.

From Government House a priority radio-telephone call to Buckingham Palace was put in. Confirmation came through shortly afterwards and the Duke then broke the news to his wife.

Press correspondents at the Outspan Hotel were summoned to a conference in the lounge, where Lt.-Col. Charteris, dressed in blue jeans and khaki shirt, said that "The lady we now refer to as Queen" would go straight home by air.

At Nyeri post office the postmaster cleared the lines to the 15,902-ton liner Gothic at Mombasa. The message gave the first news of the King's death to Lt.-Gen. Sir Frederick Browning, Comptroller of the Queen's Household.

He and other members of the party who were to have joined the Royal couple for the tour to Australia and New Zealand had flown from London Airport on Monday to Mombasa.

The Royal car left at 5.30 p.m. local time for Nanyuki, where the Queen and the Duke were to board a Dakota of East African Airways to fly to Entebbe, Uganda, where the B.O.A.C. airliner was waiting.

SILENT CROWDS

They arrived at Nanyuki at 6.47 driving through streets lined with silent crowds. All the Union Jacks which had been decorating the streets in readiness for to-morrow's big Army review had been taken down.

From one building a solitary Union Jack flew at half-mast.

On arrival the Queen and the Duke were met by Lt.-Gen. A. Cameron, G.O.C., East Africa Command, who presented to them the District commissioner, Mr. Glen Lockhart, the Director of Civil Aviation, Mr. Stacey Coles and the crew of the aircraft.

It was dusk when the Royal plane took off 10 minutes later.

(February 7)

CAUSE OF KING'S DEATH

DUE TO THROMBOSIS

By Our Medical Correspondent

It was learned at Sandringham yesterday that the cause of the King's death was coronary thrombosis. This is the name given to the formation of a clot in the coronary arteries - the vessels which supply the heart with blood.

When the flow of blood is stagnated by narrowing of the vessels due to arteriosclerosis or to contact with diseased tissue in the vessel walls, clotting occurs.

It has long been known that the King's arterial system was extensively diseased. The sympathectomy performed in 1949 was done to improve the defective circulation.

The King did not spare himself. It is true to say that his constant service was a factor in causing the disease that was the immediate cause of his death.

(February 8)

THE GUN CARRIAGE leaving Hyde Park at Marble Arch as the procession inclines left into Edgware Road. Behind the Queen's coach come the Royal Dukes, the Officers in Waiting and the Heads of State and members of British and foreign Royal families.

MR. CHURCHILL TO BROADCAST TO-NIGHT

B.B.C. CANCELLATIONS

By Our Radio Correspondent

Mr. Churchill will broadcast on all B.B.C. wavelengths at 9 p.m. to-day for 15 minutes. At least one American network, the Mutual, will relay the broadcast from coast to coast.

All B.B.C. programmes were cancelled yesterday except for the usual news bulletins, shipping and weather forecasts and gale warnings.

A single programme with suitable music and certain regular features such as the news bulletins and Children's Hour will be continued to-day and every day until after the funeral.

The first broadcast announcement was made yesterday by Mr. John Snagge at 11.15 a.m. Normal programmes including "Music and Movement" for the schools and "Mrs Dales Diary" on the Light were interrupted.

TELEVISION CHANGES

The television programme, which included a newsreel film of the King at London Airport, continued until 1.43 a.m. Television was closed down except at the times when programmes normally begin, namely 3 p.m., 5.30 and 8, when the announcement of the King's death was shown on the screen.

All variety and light entertainment will be eliminated from the television programmes until after the funeral. Regular items, such as children's and women's programmes will be given.

(February 72)

The Queen's Broadcast

'WE MUST KEEP ALIVE THE SPIRIT OF ADVENTURE'

Coronation Promises: Call to Prayer 'For Wisdom and Strength'

The Queen, in her Christmas Day broadcast to her people throughout the Commonwealth, said:

Each Christmas, at this time, my beloved father broadcast a message to his people in all parts of the world. To-day I am doing this to you, who are now my people.

Most of you to whom I am speaking will be in your own homes, but I have a special thought for those who are serving their country in distant lands far from their families. Wherever you are, either at home or away in snow or in sunshine, I give you my affectionate greetings, with every good wish for Christmas and the New Year.

At Christmas our thoughts are always full of our homes and our families. This is the day when members of the same family try to come together, or if separated by distance or events, meet in spirit and affection by exchanging greetings.

But we belong, you and I, to a far larger family. We belong, all of us, to the British Commonwealth and Empire, that immense union of nations, with their homes set in all the four corners of the earth. Like our own families, it can be great power for good, a force which I believe can be of immeasurable benefit to all humanity.

My father, and my grandfather before him, worked all their lives to unite our peoples ever more closely, and to maintain its ideals, which were so near to their hearts. I shall strive to carry on their work.

Many grave problems and difficulties confront us all, but with a new faith in the old and splendid beliefs given us by our forefathers, and the strength to venture beyond the safeties of the past. I know we shall be worthy of our duty.

Above all, we must keep alive that courageous spirit of adventure that is the finest quality of youth; and by youth I do not just mean those who are young in years: I mean, too, all those who are young in heart, no matter how old they may be. That spirit still flourishes in this old country and in all the younger countries of our Commonwealth.

On this broad foundation let us set out to build a truer knowledge of ourselves and our fellow men, to work for tolerance and understanding among the nations and to use the tremendous forces of science and learning for the betterment of man's lot upon this earth.

If we can do these three things with courage, with generosity and with humility, then surely we shall achieve that "peace on earth, goodwill toward men" which is the eternal message of Christmas, and the desire of us all.

At my Coronation next June, I shall dedicate myself anew to your service. I shall do so in the presence of a great congregation, drawn from every part of the Commonwealth and Empire, while millions outside Westminster Abbey will hear the promises and the prayers being offered up within its walls, and see much of the ancient ceremony in which Kings and Queens before me have taken part through century upon century.

I want to ask you all, whatever your religion may be, to pray for me on that day, to pray that God may give me wisdom and strength to carry out the solemn promises I shall be making, and that I may faithfully serve Him and you, all the days of my life.

May God bless and guide you all through the coming year.

(December 27)

16 DEAD IN FLOOD: 31 STILL MISSING

2 A.M. ANNOUNCEMENT ON DEVON DISASTER

PLEDGE OF HELP BY MINISTER

TROOPS SEARCH MUD-BURIED HOMES: DEBRIS BLASTED

By 2 a.m. to-day 12 bodies had been recovered and 31 people were missing at Lynmouth, the North Devon resort which was overwhelmed in a flood disaster on Friday night. Twenty-four of the missing are presumed dead, according to latest figures issued by the police.

The death roll is brought to 16 by the drowning of three Boy Scouts when their camp was swamped at Filleigh, south of Lynton, and the drowning of a postman at Parracombe. Troops, police and firemen worked unsparingly yesterday to restore life to Lynmouth, while relief workers helped hundreds of homeless people, some of whom escaped with only the clothes they wore.

Already there has been a big response locally to the relief effort. A steady stream of clothing poured in, mobile columns toured the area, and a missing persons bureau was established. The Red Cross in London is supplementing the supplies.

The disaster occurred when the West Lyn river, swollen by torrential rain, dashed down the valley, changing its course and sweeping all before it. Houses were smashed and some totally submerged beneath mud, rocks and debris. The town was evacuated.

PHENOMENAL RAINFALL

The primary cause of the sudden flooding was a phenomenal rainfall of 9in in a day on the high ground south of Lynmouth. In all, the floods struck an area of North Devon and Somerset from Dunster to Tiverton, South Molton and Lynton, embracing more than 250 square miles. A large part is impassable to traffic and those roads open are reserved for people working on evacuation and repair.

It will be six months before the West Lyn river can be re-directed to its proper course and roads and bridges restored. Troops are putting up temporary bridges.

Mr. Macmillan, Minister of Housing, is expected to visit the stricken town to-day. He has sent a message to Earl Fortescue, Lord Lieutenant of Devon, saying, "Please assure all concerned that we will do what we can to help." Prayers were said for the victims last night in West country churches.

A nation-wide relief fund has been started by Lord Fortescue and Lord Hylton, Lord Lieutenant of Somerset. They say in their appeal that "in the darkness of a single night part of Lynmouth has disappeared for ever," and that the damage is far beyond the resources of those in the stricken valleys.

WATERS SUBSIDE IN TOWN

From Our Special Correspondents

LYNTON, Devon, Sunday.

As the foaming brown flood waters of the East and West Lyn Rivers, which destroyed Lynmouth on Friday night, subsided here to-day, hundreds of homeless people were clothed, fed and given sleeping quarters in church halls and other buildings in Lynton and surrounding districts.

The Army, police, welfare and nursing services and the local council are co-operating to direct operations from Lynton Town Hall. Lynmouth has been evacuated.

The bodies of 12 people have now been found, three having been recovered to-day at Minehead, about 16 miles from Lynton. The figure of missing fluctuates as people are located.

Two of the missing are girl hikers who are known only by their Christian names of Gwen and Joyce. The girls called at the cottage of Mr. and Mrs. Ridd at Barbrook to shelter from the rain. The cottage was swept away and Mrs. Ridd is also missing but her husband is safe.

NO FRESH WATER

Police Get Gale Warning

There is no light, fresh water or telephone communication in Lynmouth. Only the police, other officials or people searching for their belongings were allowed in the town to-day.

To add to the difficulties of the searchers news of an impending gale, with estimated gusts of wind at 41 m.p.h. in the Lynmouth area, was sent to the special police on duty at Lynton.

R.S.P.C.A. officers rescued a number of cats, dogs and other pets which had sought refuge in the upper rooms of the torn and broken buildings and were still alive to-day.

All water in the Lynton area which is drawn from pipes has to be boiled for fear of contamination from broken sewage pipes. Loudspeaker vans toured the area to warn people. Army tankers brought supplies of fresh drinking water.

Contractors employed by the council to-day have been blasting away the boulders and rocks which were swept down by the torrent of water from the hills. This torrent caused the West Lyn River to change its course and flood through the centre of the town.

Roads are non-existent. Whole houses and shops in some cases are completely buried under tons of rocks and mud. It is believed that some of the missing people may be buried under this mass of rubble.

ON OLD COURSE

River Diversion

People here say that many years ago the West Lyn was diverted artificially from its natural course. In the flooding of Friday night it resumed its old course.

The town looks as if it had been hit by a V 2 rocket. As I walked down the steep hill from Lynton, residents and visitors who had crowded the town before the disaster were coming up in ones and twos with little bundles of their belongings which they had dragged from broken homes and hotels.

(August 18)

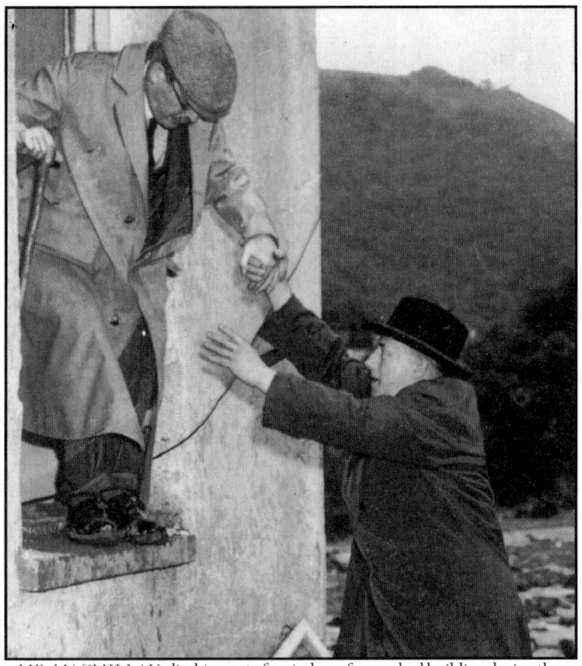

MR. MACMILLAN climbing out of a window of a wrecked building during the tour of inspection at Lynmouth yesterday.

'LIKE THE ROAD TO YPRES'

From Our Special Correspondents

Mr. Macmillan, Minister of Housing and Local Government, after a tour of the stricken holiday village of Lynmouth to-day likened the damage to that on the road to Ypres in the 1914-18 war. He spent more than an hour and a half among the debris and later discussed measures to be taken with the local urban district council.

Field-Marshal Sir William Slim, Chief of the Imperial General Staff, who arrived and left by helicopter, also inspected the damage to see if the Army could give further assistance.

Mr. Macmillan spoke to all sorts of people. Sometimes he had to shout or use sign language because of the heavy clatter of pneumatic drills blasting the displaced boulders.

He saw the bodies of two people, a man and a woman, which had been washed up on the shore carried through the village by ambulance men and police. Amid the rubble lay a cherry-wood pipe, a burst box of chocolates and a partly submerged car.

Once Mr. Macmillan stopped to read a poster, still hanging beside a ruined cottage. It pictured the beauties of the glen. "So this is what it was like once," he said. "It is unbelievable."

In what was once the post office he looked at picture postcards of Lynmouth, trying to identify the wrecked houses and hotels around him.

MEETING WITH COUNCIL

Government Sympathy

He made his comparison with the 1914-18 war at a Press conference, which preceded a private 75-minute meeting in the town hall here. At the private meeting, Mr. Macmillan expressed the Government's sympathy with the people of Devon in the disaster that had fallen upon "one of their most treasured beauty spots."

(August 20)

DR. NKRUMAH IS VOTED PREMIER

ACCRA, Gold Coast, Friday.

The Gold Coast Legislative Assembly to-day elected Dr. Kwame Nkrumah, 42, leader of the Convention People's party, as the Colony's first African Prime Minister. The voting was 45 to 31.

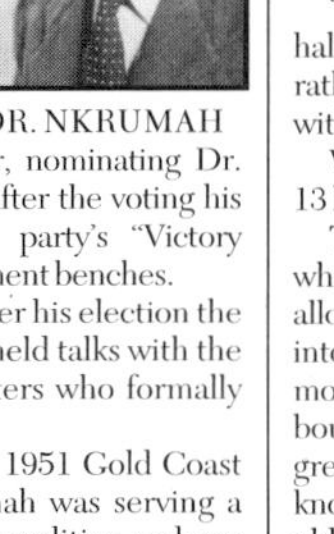

DR. NKRUMAH

Inside the Assembly Hall the gallery was crowded with Europeans and Africans when a letter from Sir Charles Arden Clarke, the Governor, nominating Dr. Nkrumah was read. After the voting his supporters sang the party's "Victory Song" on the Government benches.

Ninety minutes after his election the new Prime Minister held talks with the Governor and Ministers who formally resigned last night.

At the time of the 1951 Gold Coast elections Dr. Nkrumah was serving a two-year sentence for sedition and was released "as an act of grace" when his party was returned. - Reuter.

(March 22)

NEW U.S. LINER GAINS RECORD BY 10 HOURS

Daily Telegraph Shipping Correspondent

ON BOARD S.S. UNITED STATES, LE HAVRE, Monday.

A French jet fighter's victory roll this morning well above our giant funnels was the first tribute from the outside world to what must be the fastest liner ever built. Only an hour or two earlier I had stood on the bridge and heard Cmdre. Manning say, as we rounded Bishop Rock in a moderate gale: "We've done it."

At 6.16 a.m. B.S.T. we had made a 2,942 miles passage from Ambrose Light to Bishop Rock in 3 days 10 hr 40min at an average speed of 35.59 knots. This is 10hr 2min faster than the Queen Mary's record of 1938 and nearly four knots faster than that ship.

We were eight miles off the Rock when we passed and it was just visible in driving spray intensified by the fact that we were steaming at more than 36 knots at the time with a 45 m.p.h. wind on our beam.

Many passengers had danced all night to rousing Anglo-American tunes by a tireless ship's orchestra when they were suddenly warned by the ship's loud hailer that Cmdre. Manning estimated passing Bishop Rock at about six o'clock. Passengers were invited on deck.

ORCHESTRA ON DECK

The scenes were unforgettable as the record was broken. The orchestra, which had braved the elements to play on the sports deck, mustered on the enclosed promenade deck.

There, with champagne in hand, scores of passengers danced, sang and cheered, only pausing in their stride to join in singing the British National Anthem, the "Marseillaise" and "The Star Spangled Banner".

Up on the bridge Cmdre. Manning said: "Thank you. I am a proud man, but I have much in my favour.

"Radar picked up Bishop Rock light half an hour before we passed it. I would rather be without my right arm than be without radar. I have a wonderful ship."

We entered the port at half past five, 13 hours ahead of schedule.

This morning the Queen Elizabeth, which had altered schedule 24 hours to allow Cmdre. Manning to take his ship into Southampton's Ocean Terminal to-morrow, left her home port New York bound. Cmdre. Cove, her master, sent greetings to Cmdre. Manning, whom he knows, saying: "Welcome back to sea, old friend. Your magnificent vessel is another ocean greyhound. May she always sail in the piping times of peace."

(July 8)

MR. TRYGVE LIE RESIGNS U.N. POST

SURPRISE STATEMENT TO ASSEMBLY

COMMUNISTS COULD ENSURE KOREA TRUCE

NEWCOMER 'MAY BE MORE HELPFUL THAN I CAN BE'

From Our Own Correspondent

UNITED NATIONS H.Q., NEW YORK, Monday.

In a surprise statement to a plenary session of the General Assembly, Mr. Trygve Lie to-day announced his resignation as Secretary-General of the United Nations. Mr. Lie, who is 56, and who has held the post since the Organisation was founded in 1946, said his decision had been taken for personal reasons.

No hint of his impending resignation had previously reached the lobbies of the United Nations building. Mr. Lie disclosed that he had, in fact, first made known his intention to Mr. Pearson (Canada), president of the General Assembly, on Sept. 11.

Mr. Lie has drawn violent opposition from the Russians and is not recognised by them. Referring to this Communist hostility, he said there could be a Korean truce if Russia, China and North Korea were sincere in wanting peace.

If they were sincere, "a new Secretary-General, who is the unanimous choice of the five Great Powers, the Security Council and the General Assembly, may be more helpful than I can be." He did not want to stand

Mr. Lie, whose statement was received in complete silence, asked that his successor be appointed immediately. He said he had waited till the Foreign Ministers of all five Great Powers were present before making his announcement.

It would thus be easier to secure the necessary unanimous agreement among the five to appoint a successor, he explained. Mr. Acheson, United States, M. Schuman, France, and Mr. Vyshinsky, Russia, were in the crowded chamber when Mr. Lie made his speech, but Mr. Eden did not arrive until it was over.

Potential candidates for Mr. Lie's post mentioned to-night are Mr. Pearson, Gen. Carlos Romulo (Philippines), Dr. Padilla Nervo (Mexico) and Mr. Entezam (Persia).

(November 11)

COMET AHEAD OF SHEDULE

BEIRUT IN 5HR. 47MIN. FLYING TIME

Daily Telegraph Reporter

The jet era for passenger travel began at 3.12 p.m. yesterday when British Overseas Airways Corporation's Comet jet airliner left London Airport for Johannesburg. It carried 36 passengers.

Early to-day the Comet was on the third stage of its journey after leaving Beirut, Lebanon, at 11.16 p.m. for Khartoum. It was then five minutes ahead of schedule.

Flying time to Beirut was 5hrs 47mins. The time-table of the journey was:

		P.M. (B.S.T.)
LONDON AIRPORT ...	left	3.12
ROME	arrived	5.46
	left	6.42
BEIRUT, Lebanon ...	arrived	9.55
	left	11.16

There was a slight delay on the first stage, due to strong headwinds, and Rome was reached nine minutes late, in 2hrs 34mins. After just under an hour the Comet took off again for Beirut, seven minutes behind schedule. In this stage it regained the lost minutes and went ahead of its time-table.

The other stages after Khartoum were to be Entebbe, Uganda, and Livingstone, Northern Rhodesia. At each point an hour's stay was to be made.

MUSIC COMPOSED

One of the two women passengers sketched out during the flight to Rome the first music ever written in and for a jet liner, reported Reuter. "It is the Comet Prelude," explained Miss Avril Coleridge-Taylor, daughter of Samuel Coleridge-Taylor, composer of the music of "Hiawatha," who died in 1912.

The distinction of being the world's first fare-paying jet passenger went to Mr. A Henshaw, of Mablethorpe, Lincs. A collector of "first flights," he booked a seat 18 months ago. His son, Mr. Alex Henshaw, a well-known test pilot, holds the record for the London-Cape Town-London flight, which he made in 1939 at an average speed of 152 m.p.h.

The pilot is Capt. A.M. Majendie who has been flying the Comet for two years.

(May 3)

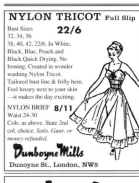

GEN. EISENHOWER STATES HIS AIMS

'LOGIC, NOT FEAR' IN FOREIGN POLICY

From Our Special Correspondent

ABILENE, Kansas, Wednesday.

Gen. Eisenhower came home to Abilene to-day as a civilian and was given a rapturous welcome, from the moment of his arrival in the morning to the end of his first campaign speech to-night for nomination as Republican candidate for the Presidency.

The speech, made in the open air and broadcast and televised throughout the United States, took the middle course of touching broadly on major issues without joining in controversies which could give ammunition to his critics. Both the General's matter and his platform manner have greatly pleased his backers.

On foreign policy, he said American military and other needs must be determined by "cold logic, not senseless fear." An America cut off from sources of raw materials would be like "a magnificent tractor in the field, with no fuel to power it."

Nevertheless he thought American spending on foreign aid had reached its peak. No factor in this calculation was more important than Europe's growing realisation that it must unite or sink further into difficulty.

On the home front he said one party had been entrenched in power too long. When that happened "the almost inevitable consequence is graft and incompetence." There were four dangers in the present situation.

These were disunity, inflation, excessive taxation and the spread of bureaucracy, all "dangerous lapses from the American way." There was "an increasing trend towards unreasonable antagonism between economic elements of our country."

"It is an indulgence in the fantastic notion that any major part of our society can long prosper unless the whole enjoys prosperity. This is a danger far easier to intensify than reduce by depending exclusively on legislation."

(July 5)

MR. EISENHOWER IS NEW U.S. PRESIDENT

MR. STEVENSON ADMITS DEFEAT AT 6.45 A.M.

From Alex Faulkner,
Daily Telegraph Correspondent
(BY TRANSATLANTIC TELEPHONE)

NEW YORK, Wednesday.

At 6.45 a.m. today Mr. Stevenson, Democratic candidate in yesterday's Presidential election conceded victory to Mr. Eisenhower, his Republican opponent.

By 6 o'clock Mr. Eisenhower held a lead of 1,857,208 over Mr. Stevenson. Popular vote totals at that point were:

EISENHOWER	**14,124,782**
STEVENSON	**12,267,574**

One of Mr. Stevenson's assistants said at 12.35 a.m., New York time (5.35 a.m., G.M.T.): "It's all over now. There is no doubt about that. There is no point in making a concession except for the formality of the thing."

From midnight onwards it was an Eisenhower parade. As millions of Americans sitting in front of television sets watched the mounting returns tabulated they saw a new political pattern emerging.

The Republicans were breaking into the South, which the Democrats normally take for granted. Big cities like New York, Chicago, Boston and Philadelphia were failing to give the Democrats the big leads needed to overcome Republican majorities in rural areas.

The Democratic coalition which has ruled the United States for 20 years gave every evidence of having fallen apart. The Democrats still hoped that later returns might alter the picture.

(November 1)

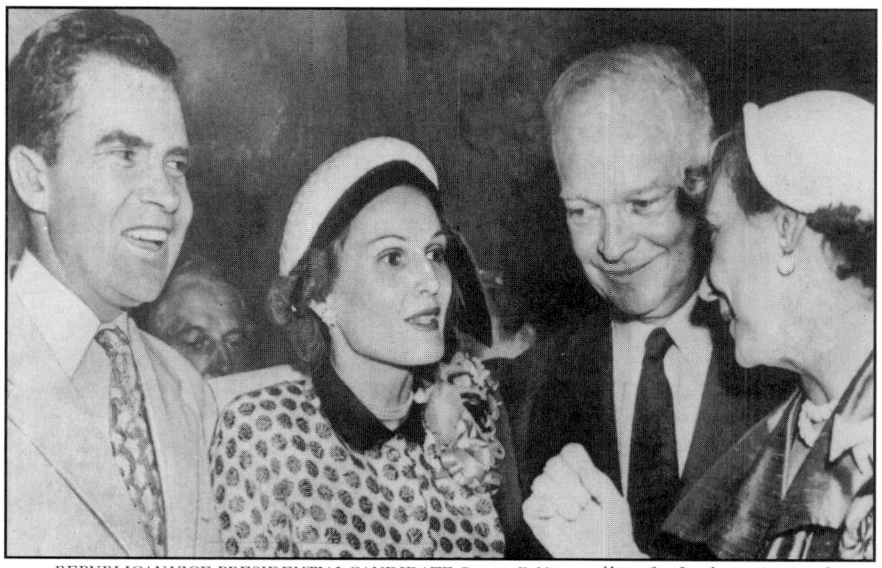

REPUBLICAN VICE-PRESIDENTIAL CANDIDATE, Senator R. Nixon and his wife, after the nomination of Gen. Eisenhower (2nd. right) as Republican Presidential Candidate.

U.S. STORM OVER GIFTS TO REPUBLICAN

CHARGE AGAINST MR. NIXON

PHONE CALL BY MR. EISENHOWER

From Denys Smith,
Daily Telegraph Special Correspondent

ABOARD MR. EISENHOWER'S TRAIN, Friday.

The publicity given to Senator Nixon's acceptance of financial assistance from wealthy Californian friends has cast a shadow over Mr. Eisenhower's otherwise extremely successful campaign swing through the mid-West, which started last Monday.

Mr. Eisenhower, in a formal statement issued earlier from the train, took the only attitude immediately possible, namely, that any man (even one's political associates) should be assumed innocent till proved guilty.

He asserted his present belief in Mr. Nixon's honesty, but made it clear that he had not yet spoken to him. Thus the door was left open for taking the unprecedented action of asking for Mr. Nixon's withdrawal if his explanations were not regarded as satisfactory.

NO PRECEDENT

There is no precedent for any vice-presidential, or for that matter, for a presidential candidate resigning in mid-campaign. There have, however, been some cases in which the National Committee of a party have picked a new vice-presidential candidate because the man nominated at the National Convention had died.

In the train opinion varied between the belief Mr. Nixon would resign and the belief that the whole episode would prove to be a storm in a teacup. One which seemed certain, however, is that if the agitation does not die down a great deal of dirty Congressional linen of both parties is going to be hung on the line.

It appears quite certain that Mr. Eisenhower would not have accepted Mr. Nixon as his partner had he known that there was anything embarrassing in his political past.

(September 20)

COMPLETELY VINDICATED, SAYS MR. EISENHOWER

Mr. Eisenhower has affirmed his full confidence in Senator Nixon as Republican Vice-Presidential candidate. He considers that the Senator stands completely vindicated on charges that he had used part of the political fund set up by Californian businessmen for his own use.

He announced this to an audience of 7,000 at Wheeling last night. His view was confirmed to-night by Mr. Arthur Summerfield, chairman of the Republican party. Of the 138 members of the party's national committee, the 112 with whom he had been able to get in touch had all upheld Senator Nixon.

(September 26)

TROOPS TO FLY TO KENYA

TERROR THREAT TO SOCIAL STRUCTURE OF COLONY

From Douglas Brown,
Daily Telegraph Special Correspondent

NAIROBI, Sunday.

It is now obvious that no consideration must be allowed to stand in the way of the complete eradication of the Mau Mau terror in Kenya. Anything less could lead to the collapse of the whole social structure of the colony.

This would leave its small European community in helpless isolation. The terror is not to be measured by the amount of violence reported over any given period.

This last week has been comparatively free from incidents. But the sense of danger has been increasing all the time.

The secret society has now emerged in Africa as a political weapon of devastating effectiveness. Neither riots, sabotage, strikes nor passive resistance can deal such paralysing blows at the confidence upon which all social organisation depends.

SUSPECTED TRIBE

Success of Terrorists

The Mau Mau success is to be measured, not by the number of horrible crimes it has committed, but by the fact that it has turned the whole of the leading Kenya tribe, the Kikuyu into suspected or potential terrorists. No one knows how many Kikuyu are in fact members of the society.

But everybody knows that the number is continually growing through an irresistible process of intimidation. This will only cease when the movement is destroyed at the source.

In effect, this means that in Nairobi and the farming area to the north there is hardly a faithful domestic servant, valued farm retainer or peaceable peasant who is not now necessarily regarded with fear and suspicion.

The consequences to the daily lives of both Europeans and Africans are catastrophic.

HORROR ON FARMS

Lonely White Settlers

Much has been written about the horror that has descended upon every lonely farm where the white settler and his wife and children live surrounded by Kikuyu squatters, many miles perhaps from telephone, police station or metalled road.

Even when they have not yet been attacked, threatened or had their cattle maimed, they report an ominous surliness among the farm workers with whom they used to live so serenely.

Moreover, they have all read of the Mau Mau's mysterious command to its members. "When the reed horn blows you will leave the farm, but not before the murders have been done." This may be mere mumbo-jumbo, but it is decidedly unpleasant.

NAIROBI AFFECTED

Home Guard Call

Now the terror has spread to Nairobi itself. The police this weekend called upon all available able-bodied European men to form sections of a home guard for night patrolling of the streets and gardens of the quarters where they live.

I was present at the inaugural meeting of one such section in a suburban drawing room six miles from the centre of the city.

There was a chilling unreality in the spectacle of 50 or so mild-looking Englishmen, office workers mainly, and of an average age of about 50, calmly counting their firearms and planning their roster for patrolling the trim lawns, orchards and tennis courts outside.

One shuddered to hear a charming piece of woodland, like a little bit of Surrey, described as the danger spot where natives armed with knives were in the habit of entering this residential area at night.

(October 20)

CHEAPER AIR FARES START

NEW ATLANTIC SERVICE

The International Airport at Idlewild, New York, had one of its busiest days for years to-day following the inauguration at a minute past midnight of tourist class transatlantic flights. Airlines said they had about 50,000 advance bookings.

The 11 airlines, including B.O.A.C., in the scheme are to provide 39 round trips to Europe weekly during the early summer. This figure will probably be increased to 71 by August 1.

The International Air Transport Association has estimated that the lower-priced flights will almost double the number of transatlantic air travellers this year from last year's record of 340,000 passengers.

The single tourist fare from New York to London is £96 9s compared with £141 2s. The return tourist fare is £173 13s: the standard return fare is £254.

(May 2)

NEW EDITOR OF THE TIMES

SIR WILLIAM HALEY

Sir William Haley, 51, Director General of the B.B.C. since 1944, has, it was announced last night, been appointed editor of the Times. He succeeds Mr. W.F. Casey, 68, who has held the post for the past four years and is shortly resigning after 39 years with the paper.

An announcement of Sir William's resignation from the B.B.C. said he will take up his new appointment before the end of the year.

Born at St. Helier, Jersey, Sir William was educated at Victoria College, leaving when he was 16. After two years as a wireless operator on a tramp steamer, he became a junior reporter in Jersey, later joining the Times as a telephonist.

Subsequently he went to Manchester as a reporter and later became editor of the Manchester Evening News and a joint managing director of the Manchester Guardian and Evening News Ltd.

(June 6)

LONDON CHEERS FOR MR. EDEN AND HIS BRIDE

Daily Telegraph Reporter

A big crowd cheered Mr. Eden the Foreign Secretary, and Miss Clarissa Churchill, niece of the Prime Minister, after their marriage at Caxton Hall register office, Westminster, yesterday.

Mr. and Mrs. Eden will fly to Portugal to-day for a brief honeymoon.

A crowd had assembled outside Caxton Hall well over an hour before the ceremony was due to start. Some people stood on walls to get better vantage points. They saw Sir Timothy Eden, Mr. Eden's elder brother, and Mr. Gilbert King, Mr. Eden's solicitor, arrive first, about 20 minutes before the ceremony.

Mr. Eden, wearing a dark-blue suit, drove up with the Earl of Warwick and Lord Warwick's son, Lord Brooke, about eight minutes before the ceremony. Lord Warwick, who is Mr. Eden's nephew, returned from holiday in Venice to be present. Lord Brooke obtained special leave from the National Service unit with which he is serving at Aldershot.

Before entering the hall Mr. Eden stood on the red-carpeted steps for a few minutes waving to the crowd.

PREMIER WELCOMED

Shortly afterwards the Prime Minister and Mrs. Churchill arrived, accompanied by motor-cycle outriders. They were given a vociferous welcome.

Miss Churchill was married from Downing Street. She arrived with her brother, Mr. John Churchill, on the stroke of 11.45, the time appointed for the ceremony.

She was wearing a mushroom pink shantung dress with a flared skirt and a corsage spray of white orchids. Her close-fitting hat was the same colour as her dress.

The dress was not made by any famous dressmaker, but by the traditional "little woman round the corner."

As the bride entered the room where the guests were waiting, Mr. J.D. Holiday, the Superintendent Registrar, who wore morning dress with a red carnation, took his place behind a table. Warm sunshine streamed through curtainless windows overlooking Caxton-street.

On the registrar's table was a letter which had been delivered earlier. It was addressed to the Rt. Hon. and Mrs. Anthony Eden.

As the newly-married couple left and walked, smiling, up the passage, Mr. Eden was on the left of his bride. After a few yards he turned to her, asking: "Am I on the right side?" She was not certain, so Mr. Eden said: "We'll ask Winston."

POINT OF ETIQUETTE

Mr. Churchill, who was just behind, also was momentarily uncertain on this point of etiquette. But in a few seconds he gave the answer: "On the right, so that you have your sword arm free."

Mr. Eden duly changed over, and when the couple emerged the crowd gave them a tremendous welcome. Police had difficulty in keeping the spectators back.

(August 15)

CYCLE POLICE CHASE RAIDERS

RADIO CAR LINK WITH PATROLS

Daily Telegraph Reporter

Squads of police on bicycles operating from stationary wireless cars, immobilised by fog but placed at key points throughout London, made a number of arrests during the week-end.

Thieves took full advantage of the fog cover and there were several attacks. It is believed that most of the incidents reported were the work of petty thieves.

As soon as a call was sent from Scotland Yard's information room to a car instructions were passed to the cycle patrols.

One smash-and-grab raider knocked himself out with the brick he threw at the window of a jeweller's shop in the Mile End Road, Stepney. The glass splintered, but the brick bounced back from a metal grille and struck him on the head.

He fell forward on to broken glass. A man arrested later was taken to the London Hospital suffering from severe cuts. It is expected that he will be in hospital for some time.

(December 8)

CRAIG'S AGE SAVED HIM FROM GALLOWS

GANG'S GUNS WERE STOLEN OR BOUGHT ILLEGALLY

Daily Telegraph Reporters

Christopher Craig, 16 ½, was sentenced by the Lord Chief Justice, Lord Goddard, at the Old Bailey yesterday to be detained during Her Majesty's pleasure. Derek William Bentley, 19 ½, was sentenced to death, with a recommendation to mercy. [Full report - P11]

Both had been found guilty of murder of P.C. Sidney Miles, 42, shot by Craig on top of a Croydon warehouse on the night of Nov 2. The jury took 77 minutes to reach their verdict.

Craig, described as one of the most dangerous criminals ever to stand in the dock, was saved from the gallows by his age. No murderer under 18 can be hanged.

Bentley's father, with tears in his eyes, said after the trial, "We will appeal. We will go through every court and to the Queen if necessary." Craig was taken to Wormwood Scrubs and Bentley to Wandsworth Prison.

BOYS' FIREARMS

School Warning

The ease with which Craig and his friends obtained firearms and ammunition has alarmed many parents. The 300 boys at Norbury Manor school, where Craig was a pupil, have been warned that anyone found with a gun will be severely punished.

Police inquiries have established that there is no centre at Croydon where arms are sold, but it is known that they can be bought in London. Some of Craig's weapons were given to him by friends of his brother Niven, 26, sentenced at the Old Bailey six weeks ago to 12 years' imprisonment for armed robbery.

The gun that killed P.C. Miles had been stolen from a Purley house. Its loss was not reported because the owner had no permit.

Craig's story in the witness-box that the ammunition found at his home had been picked up from shooting ranges was closely investigated by the police. They found nothing to support it.

Police believe that some of it had been bought illegally and that the rest had been stolen and passed on to Craig. Other boys in the gang had guns originally obtained from people who had not handed in war souvenirs.

MANY DIFFERENT GUNS

Greatest Interest In Life

A 15-year-old pupil from Craig's old school said, "I do not know how many guns I saw him with. They seemed to be his greatest interest in life."

"He mostly had 0.22 calibre pistols but I have known him to bring starting pistols and all sorts of guns. There was an old French revolver of which he was especially proud."

"He seemed to change and became moody after leaving school and starting work. He often came round to my house in the evenings, and we all noticed that he seemed to be getting more and more miserable. When his brother Niven was sentenced it seemed to finish him completely."

The youngest of eight children, three boys and five girls, Craig was born in Norbury. He lived at home with his parents in a seven-roomed terrace house in Norbury Court Road. At home he was not unduly troublesome but was naturally lazy.

He had a flair for engineering work and repairing wireless sets. Soon after leaving school he went to work as a petrol attendant in a Croydon garage. It was here that the "ragging" referred to at the trial took place. He carried a gun to work because "it made him feel big".

BENTLEY'S WEAKNESS

Injured In Bombing Raids

It was during this period that he renewed his association with Bentley, whom he had met some years before. Bentley, lonely because he thought everybody knew of his year at an approved school for stealing tools, encouraged the friendship.

Bentley was always physically and mentally weak. When only a few hours old he had an operation which left a permanent chest weakness. Twice during the war he was buried under the debris of his home in Southwark during the bombing raids. He received head injuries.

He was convicted of shopbreaking and in 1948 was again in trouble with the police and was sent to an approved school at Bristol. He returned home in 1950 and was so ill that he was unable to keep a job. His father, an electrician, took him on as an assistant.

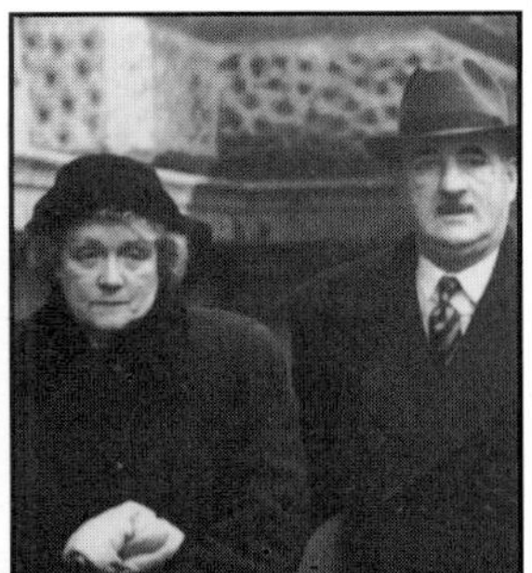

MR. AND MRS. CRAIG

Mrs. Craig referred to by counsel at the trial as "England's most tragic mother" has been interested in the work of the approved schools and once gave a broadcast talk. Her subject was "War and the Young Offender."

(December 12)

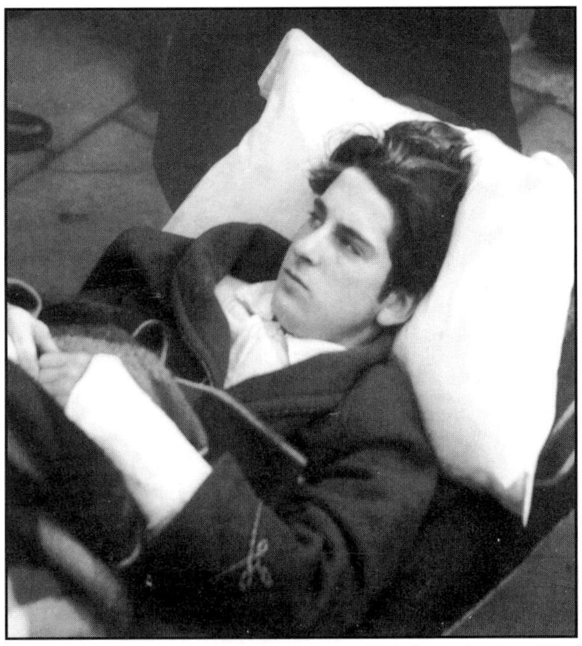

ACCUSED YOUTH ON STRETCHER IN COURT; Christopher Craig, 16, leaving Croydon Magistrates' Court yesterday on a stretcher after he had been accused of being concerned with Derek William Bentley, 19, in the murder of P.C. Sidney Miles on Nov. 2.

TIME TO RECONSIDER BAN ON FLOGGING

Daily Telegraph Reporter

Lord Goddard, the Lord Chief Justice, last night condemned "the great and disturbing increase of crime which is disgracing this country at present, and more especially the crimes of violence which are so prevalent." He was speaking at the Lord Mayor of London's banquet to her Majesty's Judges.

He suggested that the discontinuance of flogging and birching had led thugs to believe that violence was worthwhile. If gangsterism were continuing the remedy was to restore corporal punishment" and to extend it, and not limit it."

The Lord Chief Justice discounted the theory that the crime wave was an aftermath of the war. Such a theory, he said, ignored the old-age motives of greed, the desire for easy money, lust and cruelty.

There was a widespread breakdown of discipline. One reason why criminals wre not detected quickly was the shortage of police, who were being overworked to a distressing degree.

Lord Goddard who was replying to the toast of "Her Majesty's Judges," proposed by Sir Leslie Boyce, the Lord Mayor, said the reader seldom opened a newspaper without seeing a description of some shocking crime or great robbery.

This culminated in "that outrageous robbery of Her Majesty's mails," when not only was the mail stolen but the servants of the Post Office were left battered, bruised and bleeding in the street by the thugs who carried it out.

REASONS FOR CRIMES

No Single Cause

"It is very easy to find excuses for the increase in crime. But I believe it is no longer possible to put it all down to the outcome of the war, which, after all, has been over for a good many years.

Still less can we find comfort to ourselves by believing that the so-called policy of full employment would relieve the incitement to crime. There is a widespread breakdown of discipline throughout the country, and there is no single cause which can be found to account for it.

(July 3)

MOSSADEQ DENOUNCES TREATY WITH BRITAIN

CONSULATES SHUT TO-DAY: PERSIAN 'FESTIVITIES'

From Eric Downton,
Daily Telegraph Special Correspondent

TEHERAN, Sunday.

Persia to-day denounced her 1857 friendship treaty with Britain as outmoded. She also renewed the demand, made a week ago, for the immediate closure of British Consulates.

Arrangements have already been made for the closure to-morrow of British Consulates throughout Persia. This step was mainly demanded on the ground of interference by British officials in Persian internal affairs.

Several of Dr. Mossadeq's most violently anti-British supporters, including M. Makki, Secretary General of the National Front, who played a prominent part in oil nationalisation, and Ayatolla Kashani, the powerful Moslem leader, have called on the nation to celebrate to-morrow as a "national festival."

The Treaty denunciation was contained in a Note handed over at the British Embassy in reply to the British Note last Wednesday which protested against the proposal to close the consulates and denied interference in Persian internal affairs.

Britain contended that Persian refusal to allow a British Consulate to be maintained in any place where any Power maintained a consulate was a clear breach of the 1857 Treaty.

Apparently the Persian Note handed over to-day did not abrogate the 1857 Treaty outright. British Embassy officials began studying it for clearer understanding of the contents.

Immediately after broadcasting an appeal by Ayatollah Kashani for support for the Government demonstration in Teheran to-morrow, Teheran radio last night played the tune "Pennies From Heaven." This juxtaposition although doubtless unintentional, was remarkably apt.

The Mossadeq régime, despite its efficacious appeals to mob emotions, is rapidly driving the country into a major financial crisis. It is difficult to see how anything short of supernatural aid can now save the country from severe financial difficulties.

But the imminence and extent of political repercussions to the financial crisis should not be exaggerated. The primitive nature of the Persian economy will cushion and dissipate the effects of the financial troubles, which will hit mainly the middle class, Civil Servants and, to a lesser extent, the Army. These classes represent only a small segment of the population.

(January 21)

JORDAN DEPOSES KING TALAL

From Our Own Correspondent

AMMAN, Jordan, Monday.

Prince Hussein, 17-year-old Harrow schoolboy, was to-day proclaimed King of the Hashemite Kingdom of Jordan, in succession to his father, King Talal, 43, who was found by Parliament to be mentally unfit to continue to rule.

The Senate and Lower House met jointly in private to consider medical reports and the Government's recommendation that King Talal's reign should end. Prince Hussein's accession to the throne was announced 5 ½ hours later, at 3.30 this afternoon, after three doctors had been questioned about King Talal's health by a Parliamentary committee.

An official statement said the two Houses reached their decision to depose King Talal "with the greatest sorrow," and they wished him a speedy recovery. A Regency Council will govern for the new King until he is 18 next year. The date will fall in mid-April or on May 2, depending on interpretation of the Constitution on the use of the Moslem calender.

King Hussein is at present spending the school holidays with his mother, Queen Zeine, at Lausanne, Switzerland. When King Talal was in Switzerland in June the Queen let it be known that she did not want him to visit her until his mental condition improved.

(August 12)

88 DEAD, 170 HURT, IN 3-TRAIN CRASH

ENGINES PLUNGE OVER STATION PLATFORM

Daily Telegraph Reporters

Under the glare of arc lights and search-lights, rescue squads were still hacking their way early to-day through the wreckage of three trains, two of them expresses, which at 8.20 a.m. yesterday crashed on the main London-Scotland line at Harrow and Wealdstone Station, Middlesex. Latest casualty figures showed 88 dead and 170 injured in hospital. [List on P9]

It was feared that the death-roll would be even higher, in this the worst British train disaster in 37 years. At 3 a.m. to-day a number of bodies were known to be still in the tangled wreckage. It was unlikely that two or three coaches underneath could be explored before dawn.

The 8.15 p.m. sleeper express from Perth to Euston, travelling along the two-mile straight at nearly 70 miles per hour and 95 minutes late, smashed into the rear coaches of the 7.31 rush-hour local train from Tring to Euston in which were about 600 passengers.

Then the 8 a.m. businessmen's express from Euston to Manchester, travelling at 45 m.p.h., hit the wrecked engine and coaches thrown in its path. The two 120-ton engines of the Manchester express sliced through the carriages, plunged 50ft across the platform and, rearing up, overturned on the parallel Bakerloo Line.

The Manchester express was five minutes late at leaving Euston because of brake trouble. It ran into the wreckage one minute after the first collision. If it had left Euston on time it would have been clear of the station before the crash.

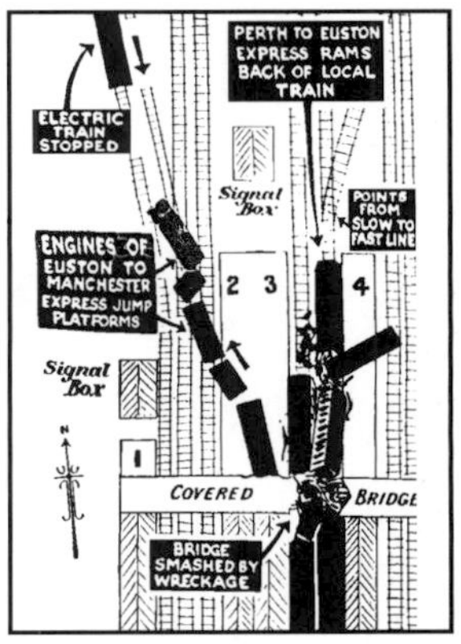

One coach of the Manchester-bound train, piled high on top of the wrecked carriages, hit the 40ft high glass-panelled footbridge and tore a hole through it.

Most of the casualties were in the local train. Of the dead, 19 had not been identified.

Early to-day rescue squads tunnelling under the debris were temporarily withdrawn while a giant crane lifted a whole coach from the top of the pile. Soon afterwards another body was brought out.

(October 9)

M. GROMYKO ARRIVES IN LONDON

Daily Telegraph Reporter

M. Gromyko, new Soviet Ambassador, arrived in London last night. He was welcomed at Victoria Station by members of the staffs of the Russian and Eastern European Embassies in London.

He was accompanied by Mr. Celokvostikov, Chargé d'Affaires in London, who met him in Dover. Mr. Mohler, head of the Northern department of the Foreign Office, and Mr. Shuckburgh, principal private secretary to Mr. Eden, were present as representatives of the Queen and the Foreign Office.

M. Gromyko said "I am very glad to be in this country. I would like to see a strengthening of the understanding between the British people and the people of the Soviet Union, especially now when there are many important international problems which must be solved.

UNDERSTANDING NEEDED

"I would like to see not only the maintenance of the understanding which existed between our peoples during the last war when both countries fought against a common enemy, but the strengthening of such understanding.

"Good normal relations between our countries would be a contribution towards solving the problems still unsolved as well as a strengthening of international peace."

As he walked towards his car pamphlets headed "Russia threatens war," and beneath it "Korea To-day - Britain To-morrow?" were scattered on the pavement. Police were seen to grapple with a young man, and a voice was heard to cry: "Go home, Gromyko, we don't want Communism here."

(July 29)

U.S. INQUIRY ON MR. CHAPLIN

RE-ENTRY PERMIT 'IS NO GUARANTEE'

From Our Own Correspondent

WASHINGTON, Sunday.

Although Charlie Chaplin applied for and was given a re-entry permit into the United States it is understood here that it makes no difference to the course dictated by Mr. McGranery, Attorney General, when Mr. Chaplin returns.

McGranery last Friday ordered the immigration service to hold Mr. Chaplin - probably on Ellis Island - and to conduct a hearing to see whether he was a fit person to be allowed to enter the United States.

It is not yet known whether the Deparment of Justice is acting because of Mr. Chaplin's political leanings. The Department yesterday said that it had "plenty of information" about Mr Chaplin which had caused its action.

IDENTITY PURPOSE

It presumably thinks it has something comparatively new as Mr. Chaplin was cleared in 1948 by both the immigration service and the Department of Justice of any subversive activity.

The Department had this comment to make on Mr. Chaplin's re-entry permit, which is usable until July next year: "It is no guarantee of anything. It is merely to identify him to the United States immigration people at the port of entry."

The American committee for Cultural Freedom, an organisation opposed to Communism, yesterday denounced Mr. McGranery's action as "a sordid and childish manoeuvre."

(September 22)

AN EIGHTIETH BIRTHDAY SALUTATION

R.V.W. AND ENGLISH MUSIC

By Richard Capell

In a Gloucestershire rectory, 80 years ago to-morrow, was born one who was to enrich the English heritage in a measure for which generations to come will still be giving thanks, as do we whose privilege it is to be contemporaries, whose hearts and minds he has uplifted and refreshed.

In that same Gloucestershire there had, 24 years before, been born Hubert Parry, who was to be Ralph Vaughan Williams's teacher; and 15 years before, in neighbouring Worcestershire, Edward Elgar. The time had come when once again, English music could stand up and look English poetry in the eyes.

Of these three great English musicians, the latest born, Vaughan Williams's, is the most racy; the one most devoted to our native traditions and most conscious of the influence of homeland sources, the one who has deliberately set out to derive his music from the glories of our past - the prose of the Prayer Book, the Authorised Version and "Pilgrim's Progress," the verse of Chaucer, Shakespeare, Herbert and many another of the incomparable roll of our poets, and moreover Blake's majestic art.

He is the one, also, who has most deliberately set out to make music for all possible occasions in the nation's life; not for the grandiose festival only, but also for the bands of schoolchildren with fiddlers only to be trusted in the first position; for the opera house and also for the cinema theatre; for the symphony concert and for congregational hymn-singing in the least of country churches.

Let me be excused a little rememoration. There long ago existed a magazine, edited by I know not whom, called " The Vocalist " and in its pages Vaughan Williams's song "Linden Lea" first saw the light.

For the schoolboy I was this was an introduction to the composer whose name - soon to be celebrated as the musical editor of the new "English Hymnal" - I had never heard. It was a song that, once known, could never be forgotten, a song to fall in love with.

" Linden Lea " tells us a good deal about the young V.W. Here was someone who could write a lovely tune : and here was an English voice. But no one could have dreamed at that time of the mighty growths that were to come of such a sapling.

The " Pastoral Symphony", which I hold to be one of the most beautiful musical compositions of our times, while recognising the peculiarities which make it a rather rare visitant to our concert rooms, is compact of folk-songlike melody, although there is no quotation of actual folk-song.

So strange a symphony it is, one unlike any other, a symphony with three slow movements, a symphony that has never seemed altogether at home in a London hall. Like other compositions by V.W., it sounds at its best in one of the cathedrals of the Three Choirs, on a September afternoon, far from the hurly-burly.

(October 11)

Concrete Lamp-Standards In Old Town Settings

By John Betjeman,
Daily Telegraph Architectural Correspondent

No one will deny the need for good street lighting. But there is growing concern about the ugly concrete lamp-standards which are being introduced into our old streets and country towns.

The Minister of Transport requires lights along trunk roads to be over a certain distance apart. What type of standard is used is left to the local authorities, but the Minister pays a percentage of the cost if the local authorities use a design which has been passed by the Royal Fine Art Commission.

The Council's surveyor will produce a sheaf of catalogues with which he has been supplied. On some of these the concrete firms supplying the designs put "Passed by the Royal Fine Art Commission."

It is not until the standards are up that bewildered citizens and possibly members of the street lighting committee itself realise that the Royal Fine Art Commission could not possibly have approved of these towering, sick serpents which have wholly altered the skyline and scale and look of the town. And they will be right, for the Royal Fine Art Commission does

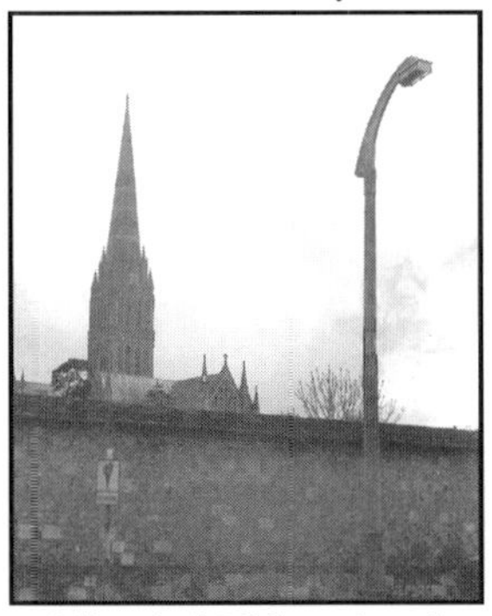

A skyline ruined: Salisbury spire and one of its many concrete neighbours.

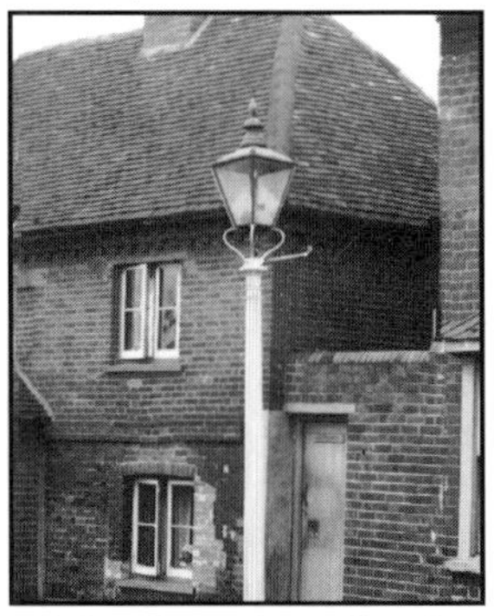

Dignity and proportion: An old cast-iron lamp-post in Church street, Theale, Berks.

not approve of the placing of these concrete standards in old towns.

In August, 1950, Lord Crawford, the chairman of the Royal Fine Art Commission, stated the position of the Commission.

The standards now being erected throughout the country have caused the Commission much concern. Of the many designs submitted for them, few have met with their approval.....The Commission has confined its activities to "passing" those which avoided the worst faults.

"But even if standards are well designed for trunk roads, they well may look grotesque in different surroundings. The siting material and size of new standards are as important as their design ... Far more consideration should be given to the matter, especially when it is essential to provide new installations in old settings."

The Commission could not have approved of the examples illustrated here, nor of other such schemes all over the country of which Banbury, Abingdon, Devizes, Crewkerne, Wantage, Lincoln, Corsham, Carlisle and Wokingham are only some horrible examples known to me personally.

At the present moment Marlborough's famous High Street is threatened with a line of concrete standards down either side and another row down the middle. It is a pity that the Royal Fine Art Commission ever allowed itself to get into the position where its name could be used to encourage such brutalisation.

If you start to look at old iron lamp-posts in side streets, especially those which have not been altered by "swan-necks" in the place of their original glass lanterns, you will see how gracefully they fit into any street. Their proportions date from late Georgian times. They vary from district to district, as does everything good and traditional in England.

Concrete standards never vary except in brutality. They lack proportion in themselves and to their surroundings. A very thick column generally of a lumpy shape with a giant's match-strike at its base rears up to bend over and carry, one would expect, a very large corpse. Instead, all this effort goes into hanging a tiny bubble of a light or else a thing like a carpet sweeper.

Concrete will never weather; it will only streak and crack. It is too thick at its base for the narrow pavements of the old towns, too unyielding in its texture beside the infinite and delicate varieties of building materials all over England, too coarse in its detail and outline beside the subtle mouldings and carvings which survive in almost every English town.

The chief argument in its favour is that it is cheap and easily obtainable. But we should not sacrifice the priceless heritage of our modest and easily damaged town architecture to such a penny wise, pound foolish policy.

There are alternatives. Where the houses are tall enough - and that is in most towns- Newbury's example can be followed. Here simple iron brackets have been fixed to the upper storeys of the houses.

In daytime they lose themselves in the hanging signs of the main street. At night they shed ample white light. Bath has similar lighting. There is no compulsion to have that blue or orange light which drains the colour from old brick and the blood from our faces.

Where the surrounding houses are too low, iron standards, as at Swindon

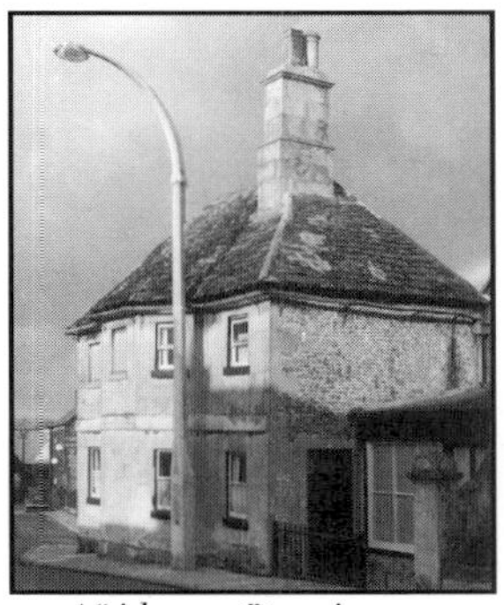

A "sick serpent" towering over a Georgian stone-tiled toll house at Chippenham, Wilts.

and Oxford, are preferable. And if the shortage of steel is so great now that not even for such beautiful places as, let us say, Ludlow, Louth, Oundle, Stratford-on-Avon, Cheltenham, Bristol, Newcastle, Wells, Kings Lynn or Reepham is steel permissible, then even wooden poles will do as a temporary measure.

Every lighting authority will be doing England a service if before embarking on a scheme it consults the local representative of a body like the Council for the Preservation of Rural England. This can be arranged by direct contact with the London headquarters of the C.P.R.E. And in the big towns the local Arts or Architecture Society could give advice.

A town may be beautified by a well thought out lighting scheme. England's beauty is in its variety and it is ours to protect. Each place is a different problem.

(February 23)

VIVIEN LEIGH WINS OSCAR

PERFORMANCE IN 'STREETCAR'

From Our Own Correspondent

NEW YORK, Friday.

Vivien Leigh heard over a portable wireless set in her dressing-room at the Ziegfeld Theatre, New York, last night that she had won the Motion Picture Academy's Oscar award to the best actress of 1951 for her performance in "A Streetcar Named Desire." She is appearing here with her husband, Sir Laurence Olivier, in the two Cleopatra plays.

This is her second Oscar. The first was for her performance as Scarlett O'Hara in "Gone With The Wind", in 1939. Humphrey Bogart, who once wrote in a magazine article that Oscars were nonsense, was named the best actor of 1951 for his performance as the river boat captain in "The African Queen".

"Streetcar" also won Oscars for Kim Hunter and Karl Malden as supporting players. This is the first time one film has won more than two Oscars for its acting.

Another British success was the choice of "Seven Days to Noon" as having the most original story, written by Paul Dehn and James Bernard.

The choice of "An American in Paris", based on the music of George Gershwin, as the best picture of the year was a big surprise.

The Gershwin film also won awards for screen play, score, photography, art direction and costume design. Its producer, Arthur Freed, was given the meritorious achievement award in honour of the late Irving Thalberg.

(March 22)

Film Notes

MR. HUSTON MAKES A COMIC EPIC

By Campbell Dixon

THE AFRICAN QUEEN (Warner) is not, as some might suppose, another epic of roaring lions, and black-mambas in the beds, and the savages with an untamed white queen oddly resembling one of the shapelier Hollywood blondes.

This British (or Anglo-American) production is based on one of C.S.Forester's novels, which in turn was inspired by a little-known chapter in the East-African campaign of 1915. In that year two armed motor-launches were shipped from London to Cape Town and carried 2,500 miles north by rail, thence 500 miles north by jungle track and river and rail again to the shore of Tanganyika. There they made short work of the German vessels that had been impeding operations.

The true story has everything that makes for entertainment, except love. Mr. Forester, that master craftsman, soon took care of that. The two new motor-launches become one disreputable river steamer, "The African Queen". Instead of several smart young officers of the Royal Navy we have the drunken, unshaven Cockney who is the old tub's whole crew, and an English spinster whose missionary brother dies of injuries and grief after a German raid on his village.

The Cockney (become a Canadian to suit Mr. Bogart's accent) arrives just in time to bury the missionary and take his sister down river. The rest is the strange love story of the angular spinster and the grubby engineer, and the revelation in both of the capacity for heroism often lying unsuspected in quite ordinary people.

As in all Mr. Forester's stories, the treatment is factual and vivid. Is the lake commanded by a German vessel? Well, the lady points out, "The African Queen" is carrying oxygen tubes and explosives, and a German explorer has descended the unknown river in a canoe. If "The African Queen" could also by some miracle pass the rapids and waterfall, and if the oxygen tubes could be filled with explosives, then they would have torpedoes : and with torpedoes—

I shall not spoil your fun by describing their hazards and heart-breaking set-backs or the skill with which Mr. Huston has realised them on the screen. I simply beg you to see this original and entertaining production for yourself.

(January 7)

'NORMA' SUNG WITH SPIRIT

BRILLIANT SOPRANO AT COVENT GARDEN

By Richard Capell

Bellini's "Norma", long absent from Covent Garden, won a warm-hearted welcome at the Italian performance given there on Saturday, and the principal singers - all splendidly spirited, even though not ideally accomplished - received ovations, especially after the big B flat trio, which is now transplanted into the second act.

The famous old opera has a noble subject; and though Bellini's Muse paid him intermittent visits – the music of the Druidical processions is that of the Sunday afternoon band on the Piazza - there are certain pages of everlasting beauty.

But only the presence of a very exceptional singer justifies a revival. One who can perform the title part is the greatest of rarities. A new Greek soprano, Maria Callas, now undertakes it. She turned out to be a brilliant, not a perfect, artist. We had to wait until the second act to discover how good she could be.

This means that she did not pass the great test, namely, the cavatina "Casta Diva", one of the loveliest of soprano songs and perhaps the most difficult of all. This was a disappointment. The flaws were a broken, aspirated performance of the gruppetti at the beginning of the melody, and later on an occasional loss of roundness – not to say a shrillness – on high notes.

VIVID CHARACTER

The fact remains that the newcomer is extraordinarily gifted, both vocally and temperamentally. She excelled in excited tempi, and no one will forget this offended Druidess's fury when she rounded on the faithless Pro-consul, her two-faced lover.

(November 10)

A PROBLEM PICTURE BY SIR A. MUNNINGS

STIR CREATED AT ACADEMY EXHIBITION

Daily Telegraph Reporter

Sir Alfred Munnings, 73, past President of the Royal Academy, has once again created something of a stir at the Academy Summer Exhibition which opens to-day. He has painted a problem picture.

Sir Alfred has called it, with a typical gesture, "In the Room. A problem picture. " But it has created something of a problem for his admirers.

Within an hour of the beginning of yesterday's private view almost all of his typical works had been bought. But no-one had ventured forth with the £1,000 to spend on this graphic work which may well be " The Picture of the Year. "

Indeed many passed it by. One woman dismissed it from afar. " There seems to be a large crowd around that one; I can't see why, " she said.

NOTHING STARTLING

In the overheated atmosphere of private view, crowds almost reminiscent of the homeward-bound hour politely jostled their way around. They had no forewarning of what to expect as no Academy banquet had been held the previous night owing to Court mourning. They found, however, nothing really to startle or shock.

Sir Frank Brangwyn's " The Prodigal Son " marks his own return to exhibiting at the Academy after a long absence. It was, I understand, Sir Gerald Kelly, the President, who persuaded the 84-year-old Academician to submit this year. This picture attracted much interest.

(May 3)

First Nights

NEW CHRISTIE THRILLER

A STRONG CAST

By W.A. Darlington

Agatha Christie is an author whose plays I almost invariably enjoy; but writing notices about them is completely unrewarding. Take this latest effort of hers, " The Mousetrap", at the Ambassadors. Two murders happen in it, one just before the rise of the curtain, and one during a blackout.

Eight characters are gathered in a snow-bound guest-house- host, hostess, five guests, and a detective sergeant. One of them is known to be a killer, and shortly proves it by doing in the least attractive guest.

That is very nearly all I can safely tell you, except that the guests are rather a peculiar lot, and that an authoress of Mrs Christie's experience can be relied on to provide them all with guilty pasts, or suspicious movements, or false names so that none are ever quite certainly not "The One" until the time comes for the final show-down.

Sheila Sun is charming as the hostess and has a nice massive husband in John Paul. Richard Attenborough has a busy time as the detective and Allan McClelland plays an odd young man with wicked skill. Mignon O'Doharty, Aubrey Dexter, Jessica Spencer and Martin Miller complete the very strong cast which is directed with skill by Peter Cotes.

(November 26)

UPSETS IN TV PROGRAMME

GILBERT HARDING INCIDENTS

By L. Marsland Gander,
Daily Telegraph Radio Correspondent

There was a fog in the television programme "What's My Line?" last night. In this quiz, a panel of four, under the chairmanship of Eamon Andrews, try to guess the occupation of various challengers.

The first incident occurred at the beginning, when the white line that normally unfolds under the opening caption came on as a short dash. Then it stuck due to a film break.

Finally, at the end of the programme, the roller caption which announces the names of the panel appeared crookedly on the screen.

Mr Gilbert Harding was often heard mumbling when out of the picture. He seemed to be tired and abstracted.

Mr Graeme Muir, the producer in charge, said to me afterwards: " Gilbert Harding had bad asthma and the fog had affected him badly. He telephoned to me in the morning, saying that he did not want to come, but agreed to do so. "

MR. HARDING EXPLAINS

"Tiddly Reference"

Mr Harding said later: "Asthma aided by the fog - I may have overfortified myself against it. If I appeared a bit tiddly then viewers were not wrong in thinking I was a bit tiddly."

A B.B.C. spokesman said: "We noticed a difference in Mr. Harding's manner and intend to make inquiries to-morrow."

(December 8)

New Fiction

IN LONDON, S.W.1

By John Betjeman

Excellent Women,
By Barbara Pym.
(Cape 12s 6d)

Barbara Pym is a splendid humorous writer. She knows her limits and stays within them. She writes about the world which is much bigger than people suppose, of professional men - clergymen, doctors' widows, the higher but not the top grades of the Civil Service, naval officers and their wives, gentlewomen who are not yet quite distressed.

There are those who may find "EXCELLENT WOMEN" tame, with its fussing over church bazaars, "high" and "low" churchmanship, a boiled egg for lunch and a cup of tea before going to bed, but to me it is a perfect book. The setting is London S.W.1, neither the smart nor the slummy part of it. The narrator, Mildred, is a vicar's daughter of about 30, not bad-looking but very dim, and still unmarried.

We leave the book happily wondering whether Mildred will marry her high church vicar or an inarticulate anthropologist who has asked to meet her mother. Miss Pym's chief characters and her lesser ones are all carefully observed and wittily described. She is not sarcastic but always dry and caustic.

"Excellent Women" is England, and, thank goodness, it is full of them.

(June 25)

Daily Telegraph and Morning Post, 1952

THE DAILY TELEGRAPH
AND
MORNING POST
DAILY TELEGRAPH - JUNE 29, 1855
MORNING POST - NOVEMBER 2, 1772
[Amalgamated October 1, 1937]

135, Fleet Street, London, E.C.4.
Telephone: Central 4242

A SELF-INFLICTED EXILE

KING FAROUK, who joins the ever-growing company of exiled monarchs, can blame no one but himself for that fate. When he succeeded his father, KING FAUD, in 1936, he was young, handsome and popular. He enjoyed the prestige that came from being the first fully independent King of Egypt in modern times. He inherited an ample private fortune from his father. His country was safe from external attack behind the shield of the British forces under a treaty negotiated between equals. In the lands of his exile he may still be able to place his hands on substantial material assets which will permit him to continue to enjoy the luxurious mode of life for which he earned notoriety as a ruling sovereign; but the rest of his splendid inheritance he has dissipated with a profligate hand. His departure from Egypt on Saturday was forlorn and unlamented. TACITUS's judgement on GALBA rises to the mind - Omnium consensu capax imperii nisi imperasset, if he had not been King, no one would have doubted his ability to rule.

Some excuse for his failure may be found in his upbringing. His father's household was far from edifying. He was never sent to school, and while studying under tutors in England he was kept secluded from all contact with the life of his times.

As in the case of other monarchs in history, the failure of his first wife to provide him with an heir coarsened his character and brought out his latent dictatorial tendencies; and not only Western nations were shocked when a diplomatist's engagement was terminated to provide him with a second bride.

Though his high stakes at the gaming tables caused scandal in a land where bitter poverty presses upon the great masses of the fellaheen, he might have remained on his Throne if the habits of his private life had not infected the conduct of public affairs. Wiser counsellors tended to get eliminated, and sycophants who led the young king along the path of self-indulgence and self-assertion took their place. KING FAROUK had neither the training nor the character to resist such persuasion, and the luxury, profligacy and intrigues that have undermined so many Oriental courts proved to be his undoing also. The prophecy of Isiah seemed again to be fulfilled: "The Egyptians I will give over into the hand of a cruel lord; and a fierce king shall rule over them."

The rampant corruption in high places roused deep resentment among the Egyptian patriots in all classes. As far back as two years ago reports began to arrive that the King's Throne was insecure. For a time the King succeeded in diverting the public wrath from himself to Great Britain by lending his support to the demands for the evacuation of British troops from the Canal Zone and the unification of the Nile Valley. It was never more than a transparent dodge, and the events of the present year have shown how wise successive British governments have been to rest upon our rights under the 1936 treaty and to insist that the future of the Sudan is for the Sudanese themselves to decide. The immediate occasion of KING FAROUK's fall has been his refusal to have Gen NEGUIB as Minister of War and his appointment to the post: but this is only the culminating point of a *malaise* that goes back for years. It is not for

Great Britain to express any wish on the form the Egyptian Government should take; that is a matter for the Egyptians alone. But it will be the universal hope of the British people that out of the present troubles Egypt will rise purified and strengthened, so that we may continue to work together in ensuring the peace of the Middle East.

(July 28)

YOUNG CRIMINALS

IT is not the circumstances of their crime, but their youth, which has focused horrified public interest on the trial of CHRISTOPHER CRAIG and DEREK BENTLEY. Murder by deliberate shooting was committed by a boy of 16, and his guilt is shared by a companion of 19. As defending counsel said of Craig, they are a symbol of wayward youth, and the nation's anxiety about the state of youth has become fixed on them. There is all too serious reason for such anxiety. Murder by juveniles is rare, but violent robbery is not, and convictions for lesser crimes are being recorded at the staggering rate of more than 1,240 a week. How many of the 64,800 young people who were found guilty of indictable offences last year have set their feet on a path which - if we do not find the right deterrents and remedies - may lead them to the dock where CRAIG and BENTLEY stood?

The analphabetic CRAIG confessing to the possession of 40 to 50 firearms since the age of 11 might be dismissed as exceptional case of "mania", but for his statement that he used to "swop" guns with his school-fellows and that "five, maybe more" of them also had such weapons. This lurid light on the state of affairs at one school suggests that there must be a very widespread breakdown of parental authority. Nor, when a young offender is brought before the courts, can we be assured that they have the right remedies or use them rightly. BENTLEY, also illiterate, had committed a previous crime, for which he had been sent to an approved school; he came out, unreformed, to become a murderer.

Concern about the problem of crime too often begins and ends with the offender and his "treatment". But the law and those who administer it - and the public opinion which makes and changes it - must never lose sight of the paramount duty of protecting society.

(December 12)

L'AFFAIRE CHAPLIN

Mr. CHAPLIN has spent 40 years in California, earning a large fortune and world-wide fame. During that time he has refused to apply for his American citizenship. He has also shown a quite marked lack of enthusiasm for throwing in his lot with the native land, which is Britain.

There can be no question that the U.S. Attorney-General is fulfilling the law of his country, whatever may be thought of the Attorney-General's choice of a moment to define it. Nor can there be any question of individual vindictive persecution. By deliberate and almost life-long choice, Mr. CHAPLIN is classed as a would-be re-entrant. The fact that he is a comedian of genius is of no relevance to the question of human rights. Mr. CHAPLIN has no unquestionable right to live in the country where he has so long chosen to be a permanent stranger. If he is barred from return, he may well feel aggrieved, and his admirers may well disapprove of the decision. But his misfortune should still be regarded as a highly modified tragedy, even if it happens to be him. Mr. CHAPLIN has often been called "a citizen of the world". Even if he is turned away by the country of his non-adoption, most of the world is still open to him, and he has the means to make himself comfortable wherever he should choose to go.

(September 23)

SALUTE TO THE LONDON TRAMS
A Great Transport Era Passes into History

BY LORD LATHAM, Chairman of London Transport

The era of the London tram, which will draw to a close at midnight on Saturday, July 5, when the last 200 of them pass from the London scene forever, will rank as one of the most interesting in transport history. In both its horse and electrified phases, the tram has been serving Londoners from the time of the American Civil War until the present day.

History will see it as one of the greatest impulses which London has had to social advancement, to freedom of movement, and to wider fields of employment, cultural and social intercourse.

It was in 1861, at the height of Victorian prosperity and expansion, that London received its first tram at the hands of George Francis Train, an American. Train, who had built the first British "street railway" at Birkenhead the year before, following methods already popular in the United States, laid raised tracks along the Bayswater-road from Marble Arch to Porchester-terrace.

"The People's Carriage"

Like many other pioneers of the Victorian age, he was aware of the revolutionary social implications of the enterprise he was urging forward. He counted, he said, on support for his tramways from those millions who could "have at my expense the use of a pair of greys and an elegant carriage large enough for their entire family for twopence each... I cannot think that anyone would wish to throw an impediment in the way of introducing so great a luxury as the people's carriage."

Unhappily for him in his latter statement he proved to be wrong. The rails he had laid down in 1861 inconvenienced other road users, and within a few months he was told to remove them.

But the need for improved facilities in the capital was too great for tram enterprise to be daunted for long. Within eight years three more tramways were sanctioned - the Metropolitan Street Tramway in Kennington; the Pimlico, Peckham and Greenwich Tramway; and the North Metropolitan Tramway in the East End.

A Vast Expansion

Municipal enterprises had so far played no part, but this was foreshadowed in the Tramways Act of 1870, which empowered local authorities to permit tramways to be established in their areas, with option to purchase

after 21 years. There followed a vast expansion of trams comparable to the railway boom of the 1840s.

In 1876 the first western suburban lines were laid down from Acton to Shepherd's Bush. In 1879 the tram reached Croydon; in 1880 Bermondsey; in 1881 Tottenham and Edmonton.

By 1881 three pioneer companies, London Tramways, London Street Tramways and North Metropolitan Tramways, had 500 cars on 30 routes and carried 65 million passengers a year. And by 1891 thirteen tram companies were carrying over 130 million passengers.

This great expansion of the horse tram in London evokes many interesting reflections. Although the tram was late in the field compared with the horse bus, which had been running since 1829, it met an instant need in the ever-expanding capital, and swiftly outdistanced its non-railed rival.

It was in the old and new working-class and middle-class areas that the tram blazed its trail. Although promoters optimistically proposed tramlines in Piccadilly itself, the authorities of the wealthier areas invariably vetoed such plans. In this they differed from those in many other European capitals. Thus the tram never appeared in the West End's wider thoroughfares, while the City Corporation resolutely excluded it from their own narrow streets.

Help to Housing

Elsewhere the tram was the standard-bearer of progress. Opportunities of employment further afield were opened up by it. Workers were aided to leave the congested central area (it was stated at that time that property values in Battersea were raised 40 per cent by the tram).

It is an intriguing reflection that after nearly half a century of steam railway there should have been a new transport boom based on the old-age motive power of the horse.

By the late 1880's some of London's trams were running by no fewer than four mechanical systems - steam at Edmonton and Stamford Hill; steam cable on Highgate Hill (the first of its kind in Europe) and Brixton; compressed air in Caledonian Road; and battery vehicles along Barking Road. But not one of these achieved permanency, and as late as the time of King Edward VII's accession (1901) the horse tram was still supreme in London.

Enter the L.C.C.

It is worth noting how far at this date the popular horse tram had triumphed over the horse bus. In 1901 horse trams were carrying 341 million passengers annually, as compared with 270 million who travelled by bus. These figures compare with London Transport's present 4,000 million by road passengers.

By this time the London County Council, which was to become one of the world's largest operators of trams, had entered the scene. The Council set up in 1889, early decided to achieve tram co-ordination in its area. Powers to operate were granted in 1896 and, to anticipate for a moment, the Council had by 1909 acquired 113 miles of tramway from 13 undertakings, constituting virtually all the tramways in its area.

During the period when the L.C.C. was consolidating its system, the mechanisers of tram had at last evolved a successful electric vehicle utilising current carried from a central supply.

Blocking the Traffic

The L.C.C. obtained powers to electricity in 1901, but the distinction of having London's first electric service in operation escaped it. This was achieved by the London United Tramways by a man who, 40 years before, had been office boy to George Francis Train - Clifton Robinson (later Sir Clifton Robinson). He ran electric trams from Shepherd's Bush to Acton, Hammersmith and Kew Bridge in 1901, anticipating the L.C.C. by two years.

The electrified tram entered its era in a blaze of glory. The infant motor-bus was noisy, smelly and unreliable, and the L.C.C. tram received a covered top in 1904, over 20 years earlier than any bus.

To most Edwardians the supremacy of the tram seemed permanent. Sir Clifton Robinson suggested in 1905 that the motor-bus would have a wide field of usefulness as a feeder to trams, for in respect of speed and intensive traffic, he said, "the road carriage must prove inferior to the railbourne vehicle."

The Royal Commission of London Traffic of 1903 foresaw four lines of trams on wide new avenues, and considered that they would "continue to be the most efficient and cheapest means of transport". Their expectations at first seemed to be well founded, although even in 1905 certain disadvantages inherent in trams were beginning to be realised, and critics were pointing out

that they were "blocking the very traffic they ought to relieve"

For some years trams continued to go ahead. Between 1903 and 1915 the L.C.C. carried out a great feat in electrifying 144.½ miles of routes. Apart from the local authorities two private companies, the London United Tramways and the Metropolitan Electric Tramways, created a system extending jointly over 100 miles.

The Conquering Bus

By 1911 the victorious tram was carrying two-thirds of the road passengers of the Greater London area.

But in the next decade there came a turn in the tide. The motor-bus greatly improved technically, and with more flexibility and lower capital costs, began to gain ground rapidly.

By 1921 the tram's share of London traffic had dropped to a half. Three years later the L.C.C., after incurring its first tram deficit in 25 years, was discussing "a rail-less tram or omni-bus" for future development. By 1927 tram passengers had dropped to a third of the total.

The M.E.T. and L.U.T. companies made a last attempt to turn back the tide with their radically improved Feltham trams of 1931, but after 1932 no more trams were built for London.

When in 1933 the London Passenger Transport Board took over 327 miles of tram routes, a policy of complete replacement of trams by trolleybuses was decided on, and most routes north of the Thames were converted by 1940.

After 91 Years

After the war the balance between the trolleybus and the greatly improved oil-engine bus changed, and it was decided to replace the remaining trams by buses. That vast and complex operation has changed the transport face of much of London, involving over 100 miles of routes and over 800 vehicles. It has been completed in 21 months, three months ahead of schedule.

And so the trams, with their virtues and their shortcomings, disappear from the London scene after 91 years. Their replacement by more manoeuvrable and more flexible types of transport has been long foreseen as inevitable, but we may salute them as they pass into history for the notable part in which they have played over nearly a century in the developing and changing life of London and in the daily journeyings of its people.

(June 25)

A ROOM OF ONE'S OWN
on a undergraduate's budget

"Don't forget to offer your visitors coffee in the morning, tea in the afternoon and sherry in the evening before Hall."

This advice comes from the 1951 "Varsity Handbook".

Of course, hours are given daily to study, but the time that seems to count most is that spent in entertaining, not for the sake of the food and the drink, but for the endless opportunity that it gives of talking... talking... everybody usually talking at once.

What do undergraduates talk about? What do they think of? Religion plays an important part in Cambridge and Oxford life to-day. Before the last war, Freud's name cropped up in most informal discussions. To-day there seems little interest in psychology.

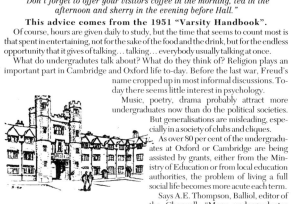

Music, poetry, drama probably attract more undergraduates now than do the political societies. But generalisations are misleading, especially in a society of clubs and cliques.

As over 80 per cent of the undergraduates at Oxford or Cambridge are being assisted by grants, either from the Ministry of Education or from local education authorities, the problem of living a full social life becomes more acute each term.

Says A.E. Thompson, Balliol, editor of the *Cherwell*: "Many undergraduates have overdrafts." And Greville Janner, Trinity Hall, ex-president of the Union at Cambridge: "Most men depending entirely on grants or scholarships need to do paid work in the vacations to make both ends meet."

Here is a typical term's budget from a Oxford woman undergraduate who is at Lady Margaret Hall.

	£	s	d
Junior Common Room subscription	1	0	0
Art fund		5	0
Club subscriptions		13	6
Books		30	0
Logs for bed sitting room fire (winter)		10	0
Laundry		10	0
Repairs to nylon stockings		15	0
Paper for study		10	0
Food and drink for entertaining	4	0	0
Eating out	2	16	0
Flowers, notepaper, cosmetics, hairdresser etc.	4	0	0
	£18	9	6

College fees and tuition charges cost the women less than the men. Probably £47 would cover board and lodging at a women's college per term, with tuition fees £28. Vida Russell, who is a student at Lady Margaret Hall, manages on £10 a term pocket money. Enterprising Newnhamites give a dinner party in their rooms to 6 young men before the Christmas Ball. Cost of the dinner, plus wine, was 35s for two people.

(April 15)

'KITE' MARK WILL REPLACE UTILITY SIGN

Daily Telegraph Reporter

CC41, the utility mark on cloth, clothing, household textiles, footwear and bedding, is to be abolished on Monday. In its place will be "The Kite Mark", issued by the British Standards Institution.

Monday is the day for the introduction of the proposals of the Douglas Committee on purchase tax, which marks the end of the utility scheme. The utility mark has been in use for 10 years.

When any goods are in the shops after Monday bearing the utility mark, it will mean they are made in accordance with former utility requirements and were in stock before March 17, or that they were made after March 17 on contracts placed before that date.

Mr. Thorneycroft, President of the Board of Trade, gave details of the new scheme in the House of Commons yesterday (report p7). Questions and answers on the scheme are:

What guarantee of quality shall we get?

Most of the trades and industries will use "The Kite Mark" to signify that a certain standard of quality has been reached. This mark is already used for a number of household commodities and bedding. There will be no compulsion on manufacturers to use the mark.

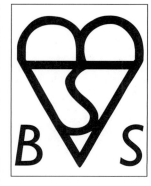

THE NEW "KITE" MARK

QUALITY MAINTAINED

How shall we know that the quality of goods is maintained?

All goods bearing the mark will be subject to a certain measure of surveillance from time to time to make sure that the requirements are being kept up.

Why has furniture not been included in the new scheme?

It has received special treatment because the opinion of the Douglas Committee was that the utility scheme provided some guarantee, in contrast to the general effect elsewhere, against inferior and ill-made articles.

The Committee considered that because of the high cost of furniture and the ease with which serious constructional defects could be concealed, the consumer was in need of special protection.

(March 14)

38 p.c. OF HOUSEWIVES COOK THREE MEALS DAILY

SURVEY REPORT SHOWS LUNCH AS MOST ELABORATE

Daily Telegraph Reporter

Secrets of the cooking stove, if not of the tin opener, are revealed in a new Mass-Observation Survey, "Cooking for the family." The disclosures followed the earlier ones which showed that housewives spent about four hours each day preparing meals.

Weekend meals are not included in the present review for which 200 London housewives were the "guinea pigs". The survey ruled out hot drinks from under the the heading of "cooking", but admitted breakfast toast.

It shows that of the women questioned, 38 per cent had cooked three meals the previous day. Only seven per cent had made no overnight plans at all for such meals.

Thirty-eight per cent also cooked breakfast, lunch and an evening meal. Nine per cent cooked for breakfast and lunch. Lunch, with fewer members of the family to cater for, was usually the most elaborate meal.

"WARMED-UP MEAT & GRAVY"

Potatoes proved to be the most popular single ingredient of a cooked meal. The observers' panel emphasises the presence of the depressing items of "warmed-up meat and gravy".

There is praise for the enterprise of a research chemist's wife who prepared for herself and five children "Stewed steak, onions, carrots, pearl barley, peas and mashed potatoes followed by a trifle with old port wine", and a lunch prepared by the wine importer's 35-year-old wife.

(December 30)

THE CASUAL LOOK

SHORT HAIR AGAIN

BUT THE FRINGE COMES BACK

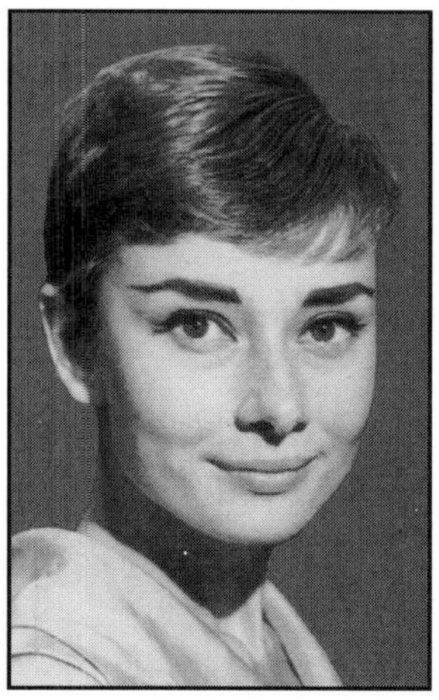

After another season of short hair, there seems to be no prospect for longer styles for autumn. Mannequins are still having their hair cropped, the poodle and short duck-tails proving the most popular.

Ever since the urchin cut swept the country in 1949 and 1950, we have been keeping our hair "short back and sides", preferring frequent trims to complicated manoeuvres with curlers.

The fringe is on its way back for autumn, not so much for the poodle cuts that have all their interest at the back, but to with with the styles that have straight back hair.

Here Audrey Hepburn, young British actress who has been having great success on Broadway, wears her hair in a casual style with a fringe and brushed-back sides falling into straight back hair.

The effect is very similar to the urchin cut, except that most "urchins" had their hair falling over their ears (and sometimes their eyes as well!).

For Your Beauty Bag

One powder compact can last a lifetime, so unless manufacturers produce from time to time novel ones which you feel you must have, their sales are limited to one per head of the female population. Latest novelty is a musical box compact now tinkling away in an Oxford-street store. You pay heavily for the originality and the exquisite craftsmanship of the Swiss makers - between 7 and 8gns according to the amount of engraving on the lid. This makes it a buy for a special occasion - a 21st birthday, a wedding present or an anniversary.

You have the choice of five tunes. They include the Harry Lime theme, La Vie en Rose *and Brahms's Lullaby. Fortunately you can switch off the tune, for it might be disconcerting to have the music drawing attention to you when titivating in public.*

(August 6)

THE AMERICAN CAREER WOMAN TAKES OVER

Chic
Brilliant
Feminist

The motion picture world would have you believe that the American Career Woman is a combination of Rosalind Russell, Mme. de Pompadour and Emmeline Pankhurst. With a mere wave of her lacquered fingers she reorganises international cartels, dupes foreign Governments, invents revolutionary machines and quixotically crushes all who oppose her, especially M-E-N, to pulpy subservience.

THIS IS PRACTICALLY TRUE.

To-day's career woman has to combine the chic of a film star with the brilliant connivance of a Pompadour, and while she will condescend to recognise M-E-N as a contributing force, she is basically the staunch feminist. Where she differs most from her British counterpart is that, instead of hiding her skirts behind a male outlook, she amiably turns the liability of being a woman in a man's world into an enviable asset.

To show you a specific type, take a New York woman advertising executive who earns in the neighbourhood of 15,000 dollars (£5,000) a year, is 32-years-old, a college graduate, lives in a small but well-furnished mid-Manhattan flat. Her day begins by 9.30 a.m. she has read her mail, seen the early newspapers, left instructions for dinner. Her chief exercise is walking to her office and playing early morning tennis during the summer.

To maintain her position, she considers it good business to spend about one-fifth of her income on grooming and clothes. She has her hair done once a week, nails twice, facials bi-monthly. Her favourite shops keep her size and clothes preferences on file and call her when they have something special. You won't find her copying the fashion magazines but, like the Duchess of Kent and other fashion leaders, she prefers to get inspiration from the latest trends and go off on her own hook.

The cut-throat atmosphere of the business world demands constant vigilance, although it is this very insecurity which spurs the career woman on to bigger and better things. There is pure incentive in the thought of eight other equally-qualified women eyeing your job.

In New York alone, women in the top income bracket include a newspaper publisher, radio station owner, department store director, food magnate, engineering consultant and leaders in every field of endeavour.

(September 14)

Playtime Moves To Balmoral For Royal Youngsters

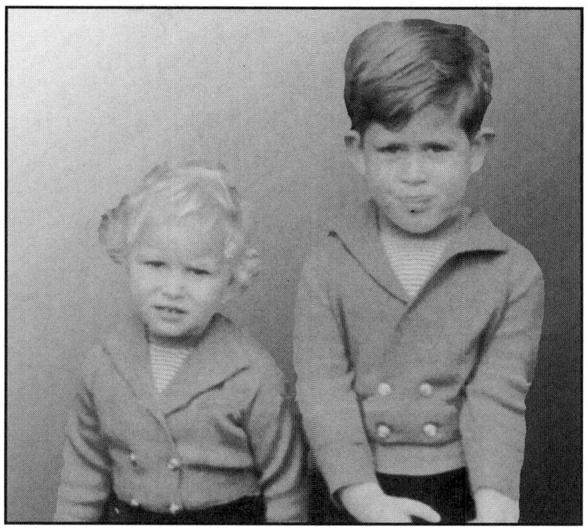

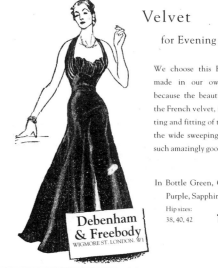

A CLOSE-UP OF THE LITTLE DUKE, who is four in November, and his sister, two, in their woollen jackets and corduroy trousers.

When Prince Charles, Duke of Cornwall, steps off the train at Ballater station next Thursday with Princess Anne, you can be sure he will persuade the genial stationmaster, Mr. Charles Milne, to show him the engine by asking, after he has shaken hands, "Where's the driver?" The Prince has displayed an interest in things mechanical for some time.

Once installed on the Deeside, the small Prince does his best to imitate his parent's sports. So far his own fishing has been confined to the ornamental pond in front of Balmoral, where his "guddling" attempts had to be restrained on an important occasion by his Aunt Margaret.

He is very proud that his mother is a sportswoman. When Her Majesty landed a salmon from the River Dee on her last visit, he delightedly informed everyone he met, "My Mamma has caught a big fish."

One of the best features of the Deeside vacation is that royal parents have time to romp with their children on the lawns, and introduce them to distinguished guests.

FIFTY-MILE DRIVE TO MEET GRANDMAMMA

Prince Charles is particularly attentive to the Queen Mother, a favourite nursery visitor. Indeed, on her first visit to Balmoral after the King's death, the chatty companionship helped greatly to relieve her Majesty from some of the poignant memories which Balmoral holds for her. So anxious is Prince Charles to greet his Grandmother on her arrival that he drives almost 50 miles with his nurse to welcome her with a kiss at Dyce airport, Aberdeen. On the last occasion he was so interested in Grandmamma that he forgot the sweets and biscuits that he had taken with him. "Just wait there a minute," he told her Majesty, and proceeded to climb back in the plane in which he had embraced her. He met Nurse Lightbody coming out of the place with the precious parcel.

It is Grandmamma who accompanies the children on their favourite picnic to the Wendy Hut at Birkhall Estate - where they lived for their holiday until their mother became Queen. The picturesque little hut, given to Princess Margaret on her fifth birthday by Aberdeen businessmen, had just been discovered by the royal children when they had to leave Birkhall.

To the little Duke and Princess the hut is what the baby bear's chair is to Goldilocks - "just the right size." Here they have a Peter Pan and Wendy existence.

They have tea at a tiny rustic table in the 10ft-high room so different from the spacious rooms of palaces and castles to which they are accustomed, and push out little lattice windows to make sure Grandmamma is enjoying herself too.

On ordinary days - when neither parents nor grandmother would have something planned for them - the children start the day by playing in the castle grounds. Prince Charles pulls his red metal battlewagon around with his cuddly dog and teddy-bear as passengers, while Princess Anne tries to steal a ride for her cuddly toys, and assistant nurse Agnes Couper or her colleague keeps a watchful eye on proceedings.

(August 5)

Women Decide On Black Accessories

While awaiting the new Queen's return to this country to-day and her decision on the subject of Court mourning, relatives and friends of the Royal family anticipated her wishes and by the evening most of them were in black.

"Court mourning is a personal matter and everything depends on the wishes of the Sovereign who decides its extent and the length of the period," stated the Lord Chamberlain's Office. On the last occasion, Court mourning for King George V, in 1936, consisted of six months' full mourning and three months' half mourning.

A member of one of the Royal households said from to-day she will wear a black dress, coat, hat, gloves and black or grey shoes, but probably not, as for old-time Court mourning, black stockings.

Wives of foreign diplomats in this country are also waiting for the Royal ruling. At India house it was stated that Indian ladies of the diplomatic circle in London will probably wear black, for though white is the mourning colour in their country, it is not practical here.

FASHION SHOWS CANCELLED

Chief Royal dressmaker, Hartnell, cancelled the afternoon showing of his spring collection, as did Hardy Amies, who made some clothes for Princess Elizabeth's Canadian and proposed Australian tours. Stiebel, who has designed clothes for Princess Margaret, had intended not to show his collection during the afternoon, but buyers turned up and the show went on as usual.

Almost without exception the women who watched the spring collection at Worths were in black or had on a black dress under a fur coat. Black hats were almost universal headgear.

By noon, West End stores were already changing their fashion displays in the windows. Some of them draped bands of black crêpe paper across until the windows could be cleared. Others took out the gay spring clothes which they had put there at the beginning of the week and substituted clothes in black, white and grey. Even children's displays were replaced in grey.

WEST END STORES GET THE NEWS

Shop assistants in most stores were first to hear the news through the stores' intercommunications systems. They passed it on to their customers, who went on their way with grave faces.

By early afternoon, well-dressed women were ordering plainly tailored black suits (few dresses and coats were asked for) and buying black hats, which millinery departments had hurriedly stripped of all trimmings except black veiling and velvet. In Bond-street, a steady flow of people was going into one shop and buying the small black item - hat, glove, belt, jersey, just to show a touch of black for mourning.

(February 7)

RENAISSANCE OF SOHO

BON VIVEUR REVISITS THIS COLOURFUL DISTRICT

I have been re-exploring Soho - that little London colony of food and foreign tongues. The tantalising fragrance of newly-ground coffee, the colourful, clustered windows of comestibles, the pastas, cheeses, spices, herbs and wine are all gathered closely together in an area which is roughly enclosed by Charing Cross-road, Oxford-street, Regent-street and Coventry-street.

You must come by day as well as by night, bearing a roomy shopping bag - your passport to the daily pageant - for you'll discover goods you'll not find elsewhere in England: the cheeses from the foreign produce merchants in Old Compton-street, the rare fruits the continental fruit stores sell, the wine shop which stocks the one and only Vermouth of Chambery, the astonishing grocery stores of King Bomba, who is almost a Royal figure among Soho shopkeepers, and the French bookshop which stocks the best of cook books, including the modern chef's bible, "Le Répertoire de la Cuisine".

Restaurateurs' Association

In between these shops the little restaurants swing their countless signs wooing you into family celebrations when shopping is over. A hit or miss choice, this restaurant business among such a multitude, for not all of them are good.

Interesting news, therefore, is that 12 of them have formed the nucleus of a Soho restaurateurs' association. In February the association will be launched with a gala month, members vying with each other to produce unusual dishes from Europe, intriguing wines, singers and entertainers, all with no price increase, so they explain.

By opening membership to striving newcomers and launching a campaign to recapture the Montmartre atmosphere, this new association can do much to raise the general standard and make Soho the Mecca it once was.

I discovered one little Mecca in the area when I made the acquaintance of Mr. Weisz, at his Hungarian Csarda Restaurant in Dean-street. I settled down in the simplest of unpretentious rooms to most excellent Hungarian fare, as authentic as that served in Budapest - szekely goulash with sauerkraut, 5s, and hot pancakes stuffed with cream cheese.

These hot, special sweets are as notable a feature for their welcome difference as is the tremendous variety of wines which include an unusually wide range of Tokays. Dishes on the table d'hôte, wonderful value for 7s 6d, are chiefly French, and I especially recommend their mousse de foie gras de volaille, demi printemps aux champignons, and riz au petit pois.

Problem of Chinese Food

You have been writing to me bewailing the complexities of choosing Chinese fare even when the dishes are defined in English. Says a reader, "I mix the wrong things together, I'm sure." With this is mind, I spent an evening with Mr. Young at his Hong Kong restaurant is Shaftesbury-avenue. Together we chose a well-balanced, inexpensive Chinese meal for two. Try one portion of special chop suey, 2s 9d, a half portion of chicken and mushroom in gravy, 3s, and one portion of special fried rice, 2s 6d. Finish with lichees in syrup, 2s for two persons, jasmine tea, 1s for two, and you'll have spent 13s 3d altogether and spent it well. Do try chopsticks, they're very easy really.

When you are feeling festive and inclined to widen your spending arc, I recommend chicken and corn soup and mixed Chinese vegetables with water chestnuts, bamboo shoots and Hong Kong seaweed to accompany fried pork, fried rice and chop suey. By the way, eggs buried in the hot soil of China are an intriguing hors-d'oeuvre with Chinese pickles. Be daring, try them for 3s 6d. I did.

(January 18)

Katharine Hepburn Tries Our Dress And Beauty Quiz

"No one cares what you wear nowadays so long as you are good-natured"– Hollywood actress Katharine Hepburn speaking.

Happy-go-lucky Miss Hepburn, here to act in Shaw's "The Millionairess", let me try out on her our new Dress and Beauty Quiz. So I learnt the only make-up she wears is vivid lipstick – "cosmetic firms would go bankrupt if they relied on me."

Freckles stand out on her sun-tanned face like spots on a leopard. She scrapes greying red hair on to the top of her head, bath-time fashion; never wears perfume, believing it is good enough if you "smell clean". She has two hats, but carries instead of wearing them.

Her favourite outfit – "it saves so much bother" – is a cream linen jacket, white-cotton T-shirt, beige gaberdine slacks, crêpe soled shoes.

Life must be singularly uncomplicated... but only Miss Hepburn could get away with it!

W.F.C.

(April 5)

Obituary

MME. PERON'S RISE TO POWER

INFLUENCE AMONG WORKERS

Few dictators' wives have played so prominent a part in Eva Peron, wife of the Argentine President, who died at the Buenos Aires on Saturday aged 33.

She wielded at least as much power in Argentina as her husband. Her popularity with the masses probably exceeded his.

Her own Cinderella-like rise to affluence and fame contributed as much as anything to her influence over the workers. Her beauty and the warm, vibrant voice which had made her a radio favourite, could transport crowds and blind them to the incongruity of a woman in diamonds and mink glibly identifying herself with them as "We, the shirtless."

Generous and sympathetic by nature, she was also shrewd enough to realise the propaganda value of making the welfare of the poor her immediate concern.

DISPENSED MILLIONS

The Eva Peron Foundation dispensed millions of pesos, subscribed in the main by business men and the trade unions in aiding the destitute, maintaining hospitals and homes for the aged and providing parks and schools. Every year millions of Christmas parcels were despatched to working-class homes labelled "From Eva Peron."

Born in the village of Los Toldos on May 7, 1919, Maria Evita Duarte, was the daughter of a farm labourer who died during her infancy. Her mother, a coachman's daughter, opened a boarding house after her bereavement.

At 15 Eva went to Buenos Aires determined to become an actress. Several years of laborious effort resulted only in small parts, but culminated early in the 1939-45 war, in a radio début that was an immediate success. She became known as "Senorita Radio."

In 1944 Gen. (then Col.) Peron, who had assisted in a coup d'état which overthrew the Ramirez administration and installed President Farrel, met Eva and asked her to broadcast an appeal for victims of an earthquake. Their friendship ripened not only into courtship but into a stronger political alliance. They were married secretly in 1945.

EUROPEAN TOUR

In the following year Peron became President; his wife, it was soon clear, meant to share his responsibilities and authority. She toured Europe in 1947, but cancelled a scheduled visit to Britain. It was reported that she considered inadequate the arrangements made for her reception and entertainment.

In August last year she aroused hostility in the Army by announcing that she would offer herself for the Vice-Presidency in the November elections. So strong was the pressure brought to bear against her that she subsequently withdrew.

Considerable speculation abroad followed an abortive "revolt" by Army officers in September. Some American critics considered that the rebellion was engineered by Peronistas to provide an opportunity for retribution against the Army.

Mme. Peron's health, however, was by then giving such serious cause for anxiety that she was unable, in any capacity, to take any part in the elections which returned her husband as President for a second term.

A few days after his victory at the polls she had to undergo a major operation. She never fully regained her health.

(July 28)

MAHARAJA OF JODHPUR

The Maharaja of Jodhpur, who was killed in an aircraft crash on Saturday, aged 28, was reputed to be one of the wealthiest men in the world. He succeeded to the title in June 1947. In 1948 he married Miss Alexandra McBride, a girl born in India, who had been a nurse in India. He had previously married Princess Sri Krishna Kunwecha Sahaba, and their four-year-old son is heir to the title.

(January 29)

THE PASSING OF OUR BELOVED KING

IN MEMORIAM KING GEORGE VI
BY ALFRED NOYES

Quietly once again the moving hand
Has turned a page of history. Everywhere
The imminent sense of death is on the land,
That democratic doom which all men share.

Faithful, and good and true, he played his part
With steadfast courage and unshaken will.
Even when the blade of death was at his heart
He served his country and he serves her still.

Could we but share that simple love of truth,
Burying the hates that cripple and enslave,
Like Milton's eagle in her mighty youth
His Commonwealth would tower above his grave;

Deathless, O not in glory or renown,
But in that love which still outlasts the years—
There is no splendour in a monarch's crown
Can match the splendour of his people's tears—

Deathless, by simple following of the right,
That supreme law which was his life and light.

Deep and sudden sorrow has come upon the nation: the King is dead. Throughout many lands the passing of the Head of the Commonwealth is being mourned. But among his own people in the United Kingdom, and elsewhere as well, thoughts have turned first to the character and personality of the man who most recently upheld it.

★ ★ ★

When he was called unexpectantly to the Throne over 15 years ago, KING GEORGE VI proclaimed his resolve "to work" before all else for the welfare of the British Commonwealth of Nations. No resolution was ever more consistently fulfilled. The affection and respect which his Majesty earned were the reward not of mere endeavour, but of a full achievement implicit in his own qualities. A wide understanding and a lofty conscience, personal dignity and personal simplicity, directness of mind and imperturbability of mien: these are some of the essential traits which go to the making of a successful Constitutional Monarch. All the Royal attributes were outstanding in King George VI. He possessed as well two natural gifts perhaps more rare: a capacity for affairs inestimable in dealing with his Ministers and a talent for happy family life treasured by his people.

★ ★ ★

There are other British Monarchs of recent times who have enjoyed a comparable popularity, but they have not always enjoyed it to the same degree throughout their reigns. It was as they reached or outlived the common span of mankind that the full richness of their countrymen's regard flooded around them as an added grace. KING GEORGE VI did not attain old age; grief for his loss is heightened by the knowledge that it was the strain of duties cheerfully sustained in a time of unrelenting stress which first undermined his health.

Heavily as public business weighs upon the physical stamina of statesmen they have at least their comparative relief while out of the office. Upon the King the pressure was unceasing for more than 15 years. Nor did he allow himself substantial remission from those minor but exhausting ceremonial and social exactions which the traditions of quieter times have laid upon the Head of State. With less readiness for self-sacrifice the reign now ended might perhaps have been doubled in length, but decades could have added little to a popularity so immediate from the moment of his accession and so unwaveringly sustained.

★ ★ ★

The confident regard for the nation for its Sovereign took strong root in the realisation that the King was so genuinely and actively interested in all sides of national life. It had been his privilege and remained his pride to have served as a naval officer in action at the Battle of Jutland, and later to have qualified as a pilot of the Royal Air Force. It might be natural for the Head of the Armed Forces to take pleasure in the ceremonial inspection of men of the Services. But there was no mistaking the eagerness with which his Majesty, in a second world war, visited units not merely all over the Kingdom, but in every Western theatre of active operations. And it was no mere ceremonial of which the KING was disappointed when he was led to reconsider his intention to watch from the cruiser the D-Day landing in Normandy.

Equally persistent was his Majesty's close attention to the civilian and industrial aspects of Britain. The many war time tours of factories and bombed areas were the sequel to his presidency, when the Duke of York, of the Industrial Welfare Society. It was he himself, too, who had created an annual camp to bring together youths from industry and from public schools for a common holiday, in which the Royal camp leader participated.

★ ★ ★

In peace the KING had shown by his personal example that we are one nation with one destiny. Even more significant was his example in war. Bomb-smitten Londoners were proudly aware that through the heaviest raids the KING and QUEEN, at Buckingham Palace, were sharing their perils – though few realised at the time that the Palace was hit. An even greater instance of his Majesty's steadfastness-requiring moral and not simply physical courage-was his refusal in the dark days of 1940 to send the Princesses to safety in Canada-they stayed as other young people in Britain stayed.

★ ★ ★

There were, however, things which the KING could not share with the mass of his subjects: his Ministers and commanders gave him, at his wish, a constant and close acquaintance with the operational and political anxieties. Mr. CHURCHILL has been permitted to include in his War Memoirs a number of illustrative letters which passed between the Prime Minister and his Sovereign. It was against the background of these anxieties that the KING conducted in such outward good heart those wearing tours of industrial areas or military headquarters which he never allowed to appear a routine.

Few beyond his successive Prime Ministers can estimate the responsibilities which fell to the KING for decision or advice during his reign. On the other hand, it is not difficult for any ordinary citizen of imagination to realise on reflection the burden simply of audiences and investitures, of public speeches and ceremonial tours which his late Majesty sustained. For one who had many years a slight handicap in utterance it must have required superb endurance even to broadcast from time to time.

★ ★ ★

His Majesty's resistance to the tension was strengthened by two influences perhaps more important in forming his character even than his unusual will-power and sense of public duty. One was the firm religious faith which the King held and so often exhibited on days of thanksgiving or intercession. The other was the support afforded to him by an ideal marriage. It is indeed impossible to dissociate either the public activities of the KING or the warmth of national feeling which encompassed him from the glowing personality of his Consort.

In mourning a noble KING we acknowledge our debt and offer our sympathy to his QUEEN whose presence blended with his not merely to attract the loving loyalty of his subjects but the admiration of other nations. It was not only in their native land or in the Dominions to which they travelled, but on visits to France and the United States that the very appearance of the KING and QUEEN together drew to them friendly affection.

★ ★ ★

In this country the group was usually a large one, including Queen MARY-who saw her son so consummately inherit the strong conscience of his parents-and the two Princesses, fortunate enough in having passed their youth in so united a family. It is to the elder Princess, now our Queen-regnant, that the nation and the Commonwealth henceforth owe allegiance, in full faith that an equally high sense of responsibility and an equally devoted family life may prove the foundation of a reign as illustrious as that of KING GEORGE, and (we must pray) less arduous.

(February 7)

DEATH OF SIR STAFFORD CRIPPS

PEACEFUL PASSING IN SWISS CLINIC

From Our Own Correspondent

ZURICH, Monday.

Sir Stafford Cripps, former Socialist Chancellor of the Exchequer, died in the Bircher-Benner clinic here to-night. He would have been 63 on Thursday.

His death was announced in a statement issued by Dr. Dagmar Liechti, his physician, on behalf of Lady Cripps, who was at her husband's bedside until he died. This said "Sir Stafford Cripps passed away peacefully at 11 o'clock to-night."

The cause of death was not specified. It is believed that Sir Stafford never recovered from the "state of deep and painless unconsciousness" which was announced in a bulletin issued this morning.

This afternoon he rallied for a short period, but had a relapse soon afterwards. It is believed that his remains will be taken to Britain for burial.

CABLE FOR SON

Lady Cripps sent a cable to her son John in England asking him to come over as quickly as possible. He was due here on Wednesday. Her daughter, Miss Peggy Cripps, will arrive in Zurich to-morrow morning.

Last month a bulletin stated that Sir Stafford was responding well to treatment for the localised recurrence of his spinal tubercular infection.

He had a bone infection, spondylitis, which obliged him to remain on his back for months encased in plaster. It was later announced that he was also suffering from a "rare and dangerous disease."

An Enigma to All

What a tangled skein awaits Sir Stafford Cripps's biographer! Politicians have died in this century an enigma to the public. Sir Stafford was an enigma to his colleagues and even to his intimates.

I have heard some of them "explaining" him. No two ever gave the same explanation. There are, however, facts about him which are beyond argument. He drove himself terribly hard. Stories of his rising before dawn to begin work were true. From subordinates he exacted a like devotion to duty.

A man at one time responsible for drafting Sir Stafford's speeches told me the most miserable moment of his career. It was the first occasion on which, having submitted a draft to his master, he received the whole speech back-rewritten in Sir Stafford's own hand and red ink.

Astringent Wit

His austerity was widely misunderstood. It was less the self-denial of an ascetic than the habits of a man with a bad digestion. His last months were full of pain, borne with characteristic courage.

It was part of his creed to draw from himself the last ounce. He submitted to a mode of living which he believed achieved it.

His diet of nuts seemed to him no more eccentric than Mr. Churchill's war-time habit of going to bed after lunch in order to filch the most working hours from the twenty-four.

Sir Stafford was not a popular House of Commons man. He did not try to mask his intellectual superiority. There was a frigidity of manner which chilled his supporters and annoyed his opponents.

His wit, when it came, was astringent. Making a conventional afternoon dinner speech left him, and his audience, quite cold. He had not a uniformly high opinion of his Parliamentary colleagues and that he did not always try to conceal.

Last Words in the House

His powers of exposition were unrivalled. Sir Stafford had no tricks, making no attempt to attract his audience except by the power of remorseless logic. In private conversation this power was cogent enough to convince many against their will.

Sir Stafford Cripps's last speech to the Commons, in July, 1950, contained this sentence: "Do not let us ever forget that in our generosity it is not our money we are giving away, but that of somebody else."

There, perhaps, is a glimpse of the inner struggle of the man who, though he remained a thorough-going Socialist to the last, may in the end have come to argue with himself: "Socialism is not enough."

(April 22)

DR. MONTESSORI

FOUNDER OF NEW TEACHING THEORY

Dr. Maria Montessori, whose kindergarden system of education, founded in Italy in 1908, subsequently gained favour in many parts of the world, has died, aged 81.

The first woman to secure a medical degree from the University of Rome, she was concerned at the beginning of her career with the care of mentally defective children. Her experiences at this work convinced her that the normal child would develop more quickly if allowed a great deal of freedom in the classroom.

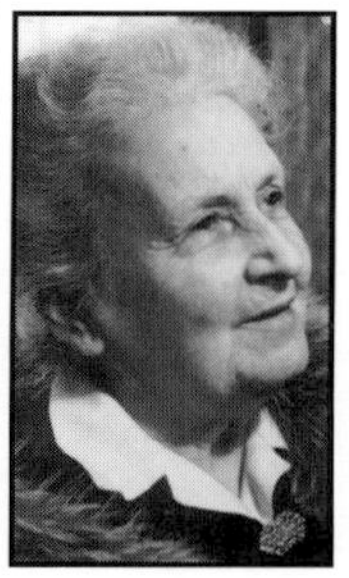

DR. MONTESSORI

She was repelled by the sight of children kept immobile behind their desks "like butterflies transfixed with a pin". This, she declared, "annihilated" the children instead of disciplining them. She introduced small, comfortable desks and chairs, and low windows from which the children could see the world outside.

Her small pupils enjoyed a liberty of choice in the subjects they were to study which shocked contemporary educationists. Children, she argued, learn first with their hands. She gave them knots to untie and stoppers to fit into bottlenecks; they learned the alphabet by feeling cardboard letters as much as by seeing them, and when they tired of a subject it was dropped.

INNOVATIONS DISPUTED

Some of her innovations are still the subject of dispute. Attention was drawn to the perils inherent in their application to all children without regard to important factors. Punishments and rewards were alike banished and fairy-stories had no part in the curriculum; these were replaced by true stories of mankind and of the animal world.

Children, she decided, could assimilate knowledge, much more quickly than had generally been supposed, provided that the dividing line between work and play was eliminated. Consequently she taught arithmetic at three-and -a -half, and algebra at five. Extension of some of these principles by inexperienced and over-enthusiastic disciples has, in the opinion of some authorities, done more harm than good.

Dr. Montessori's theories, however, gained ground in the face of objections. "Childrens Houses" were opened all over the continent, and spread to England and America. There are now 300 in Britain alone and countless other schools have adopted her principles in part.

MATHEMATICAL PRODIGY

Born near Ancona on Aug. 30, 1870, Maria Montessori was a "progressive" from early youth. She shocked contemporaries in Rome by dispensing with a chaperone, and was something of a mathematical prodigy. She was diverted from her original intention of becoming an engineer by the sight of a maimed and bleeding beggar in the street.

Mussolini was not slow to realise the value of the Montessori schools with a view to the training of future Fascists, but Dr. Montessori was hardly less quick in realising the dangers of his sponsorship. She left Italy in 1932 and four years later her schools there were banned. In India when war broke out, she was interned as an enemy alien, but allowed to continue her activities.

Dr. Montessori was the author of several books which described her methods. She was unmarried.

(May 7)

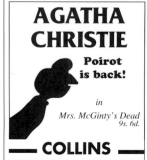

THE FOUNDER OF ISRAEL

Dr. Weizmann's Unique Achievement

By Malcom Muggeridge

Dr. CHAIM WEIZMANN, who has died in his 78th year, was more than any other single individual responsible for the creation, first of a Jewish National Home in Palestine, and then of the State of Israel. Thanks largely to his efforts Jewish nationhood has been restored after 2,000 years. The threads of history were picked up again, and the race which had existed for centuries as strangers in strange lands acquired a country and became a nation.

It was a unique achievement. In the Russian ghetto in which Dr. Weizmann was born the idea of an independent Jewish state would have seemed infinitely remote. Yet no doubt it would have seemed equally so to the Children of Israel in captivity in Egypt.

The visionary is rarely wholly satisfied with the realisation of his vision. Promised lands are better seen from afar than near at hand. It may be doubted whether Dr. Weizmann found in the turbulence of present-day Israel the precise fulfilment of the Zionist hopes which had buoyed him up through so many difficult years.

Palestine the Only Goal

In any case, he latterly took little part in Israel's affairs. He became a remote and honoured figure, whose loss, even so, will be deeply felt, but more for what he symbolised than for the functions he performed as President.

In his interesting autobiography, "Trial and Error," he has described how he was first drawn into the Zionist Movement, and how he came to devote himself wholly to its service.

For a time he was closely associated with Theodore Herzl, the first great Western protagonist of Zionism; but he it was who transformed a vague aspiration into a particular objective. He wanted more than just the resettlement of Jews in some available territory like Uganda. Zionism was, for him, "in a sense Jewishness itself, set in motion for the recreation of a Jewish homeland."

The homeland, as far as he was concerned, could only be Palestine. In his first conversation with Balfour, in 1906, the Uganda project was mentioned. "Supposing I were to offer you Paris instead of London, would you take it?" he asked.

Balfour, he writes, "sat up, looked at me, and answered: 'But, Dr. Weizmann, we have London,'" to which he replied: "That is true. But we had Jerusalem when London was a marsh."

Signal Service to Britain

He first came to England in 1904, and subsequently for 40 years had a British passport, which he only relinquished in favour of the first one ever to be issued in Tel Aviv. This country he held in deep affection, which not even the last unhappy days of the Mandate could wholly efface.

At first he worked in Manchester as a research chemist, and then, in the 1914-18 war, was able to perform a signal service for the British Government by discovering a new process for making acetone for cordite.

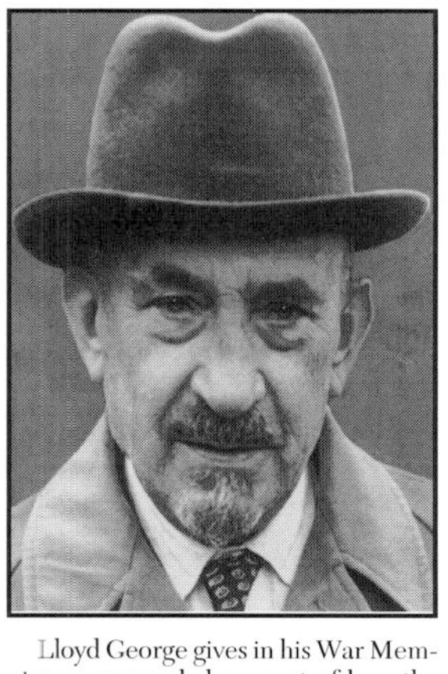

Lloyd George gives in his War Memoirs an apocryphal account of how the Balfour Declaration was the only recompence Dr. Weizmann asked for this service. "I almost wish," he writes, with one of his rare touches of bitterness, "that it had been as simple as that, and that I had never known the heartbreak, the drudgery and the uncertainties which proceeded the Declaration."

What is certainly true is that he declined all rewards and honours, and after the war threw himself with renewed fervour into working for the National Home. His character combined by a remarkable degree the visionary and the practical man of affairs. If his interests were limited, as he said himself, to chemistry and Zionism, he pursued both with unflagging energy and singleness of purpose.

None who ever encountered him will forget the immense dignity, the sense of personal disinterestedness and far-sightedness which his presence conveyed. His face was like a fine parchment, on which both the tragedies and glories were written.

The Long View

Looking back now on the Balfour Declaration and all that flowed from it, in the light of the present melancholy situation in the Middle East, its wisdom may seem questionable. To a world tormented by nationalism has been added one more nation; where one set of refugees have been accommodated, others have been created and sit now in hopeless camps looking despairingly across at the lands of which they have been dispossessed.

Yet Dr. Weizmann, if he might have admitted as much, would still have looked to more distant consequences. Jewish history, which the English-speaking West knows through the splen dour of the Authorised Version of the Bible, provided the dynamic of Zionism, and its fulfilment belong to the same enduring traditions.

Israel exists, Dr. Weizmann would have contended, and will continue, whatever mistakes may have been made, and limitations imposed by virtue of the troubled circumstances of its birth; therein lies the justification of all his efforts.

Even, too, from the narrower view of British or Western interests, matters have not gone so awry as at one time seemed the case. Balfour was not solely actuated by humane considerations fortified by Dr. Weizmann's skilful persuasion. He and other Conservative statesmen, like Mr. Amery and Mr. Churchill, saw the advantages of a Westward-looking, economically advanced State in the vacuum left by the collapse of Turkish power.

If their successors, though committed to larger promises, lost sight of this consideration and became captivaed by the fantasy of Arab power and friendliness, such a State as Balfour envisaged has, in fact, come to pass.

The advantage it offers, with the whole Arab world turning hysterically against the West, are beginning again to be apparent. By a circuitous, humiliating and bloody route we are returning to where Dr. Weizmann and Balfour began.

Zionism and Marxism

As is pointed out in "Trial and Error", the Soviet Government has consistently put down Zionism with a heavy hand; and the immigrants who have arrived in Israel from behind the Iron Curtain are for the most part frantically anti-Stalinist.

Thus, far from the trend in Israel being, as was feared, towards Communism, the present tendency is all the other way. There, of all the countries in the world, a full awareness exists of what a Stalinist dictatorship is really like.

A Modern Prophet

British institutions and way of life never lost their place in his regard, and in the Second World War, as in the First, his scientific skill was placed unreservedly at the disposal of the British Government. Both his sons served with the British forces and one of them, Michael, an R.A.F. flight lieutenant, was reported missing in 1942.

His domestic life was particularly serene. Of his wife, Vera, he has written that she "so organised as to give me a stable and tolerably safe background: if I have been able to carry on, to give my whole mind to my work, without taking much thought for financial or other practical matters, it has been entirely due to her forethought, her devotion and her savoir faire."

(November 10)

EVA PERON

MADAME PERON, who died yesterday after a long illness, was a woman much loved, much hated, greatly envied and, in her last days, greatly to be pitied. Like the Byzantine Empress THEODORA, she rose from the stage to be the equal consort of a dictator, and she always retained a flamboyant beauty and seductive manner of speech which made the common man, whether part of audience or mob, her slave. Her ambition was as boundless as her loyalty to her husband; in good times and in bad alike she never lost faith in his star and always declared herself his "humble collaborator".

For all her apparent emancipation, she remained in all her things obstinately feminine. Her approach to problems was practical, capricious and arbitary. Did the poor lack money? They must be given more. Did society sneer at her? It must be humiliated. Did newspapers criticise the régime? They must be suppressed. For theory and principle she had a profound contempt. Her political outlook was fashioned out of little more than bitter hatred of hereditary wealth and privilege and an ostentatious sympathy for the oppressed. This was enough to ensure her power: but it was not good enough to give Argentina good government.

(July 28)

MR. ROOSEVELT'S DOG DIES

COMPANION 5 YEARS

From Our Own Correspondent

NEW YORK, Sunday.

One of the most famous dogs in history, President Roosevelt's black Scottish terrier, Fala, who died in his sleep yesterday, two days before his twelth birthday was buried to-day in the rose garden at Hyde Park, near the grave of his master. He was President Roosevelt's constant companion for five years.

Fala's original name was Big Boy. The President re-named him in memory of one of his Scottish ancestors, who was known as "Murray, the outlaw of Fala Hill".

He was aboard the United States batleship Augusta, in which Mr. Roosevelt and Mr. Churchill drafted the Atlantic Charter in August 1941. In the 1944 Presidential Election campaign the Republicans asserted that a destroyer had been sent to pick him up after he had got left behind in the Aleutian Islands. Denying this, Mr. Roosevelt said: "They are even trying to make war on Fala."

In 1946 he was again prominently in the news when Mrs. Roosevelt was visiting Maine and a Portland hotel refused to let her take him to her room. She thereupon cancelled her reservation and stayed with Fala in a tourist cabin.

(April 7)

ELLA SHIELDS DIES AT 72

MADE 'BURLINGTON BERTIE' FAMOUS

Miss Ella Shields, the male impersonater, died in Lancaster Royal Infirmary yesterday, aged 72. She was identified most of her career with "Burlington Bertie", the tragi-comic, seedy "swell" she created and made famous on the music-halls of the English-speaking world.

She was taken to hospital unconcious on Monday night from a holiday camp near Morecambe, Lancs. She collapsed there on Sunday after singing "Burlington Bertie" to 3,000 holiday makers and never regained conciousness.

She introduced the song in England in 1914; since then, dressed invariably in superbly-cut but out-at-elbow male evening clothes, she had popularised it in America and throught the Commonwealth.

Her audience rarely permitted her to bring her act to a close until they had heard the familiar but well-loved lines: *"I'm Bert, Bert, I haven't a shirt. But my people are well-off, you know. Nearly everyone knows me, From Smith to Lord Rosebery. I'm Burlington Bertie from Bow!"*

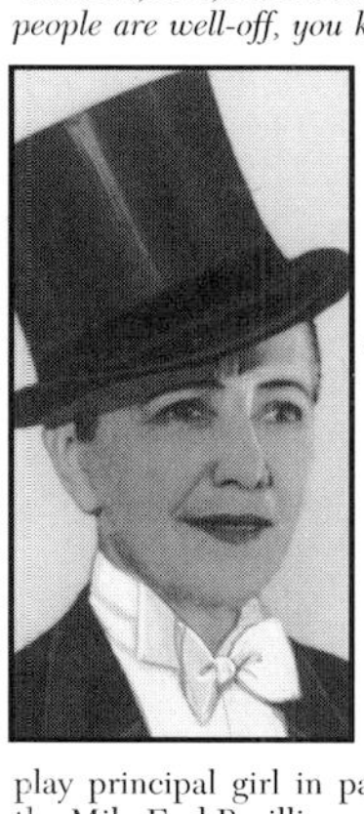

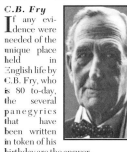

American-born, of Irish parentage, Ella Shields made her first stage appearance in 1898.

In 1904, booked to play principal girl in pantomime at the Mile End Pavillion, she also sang ballards and coon songs at Forester's and other London music-halls.

She was initially persuaded to appear as a male impersonator by a producer who had watched her imitating an old soldier at a private party. An immediate success, she featured on the bill at the opening night of the London Palladium in 1910: in 1948 she appeared at the same theatre in the Royal Variety performance.

She never tired of singing "Bertie" she said. Another song she made popular was "Show Me the Way to go Home".

Miss Shields announced her "retirement" in 1929, but had since made several tours with the old-time music-hall star show "Thanks for the Memory". She had also appeared on television.

(August 6)

MISS GERTRUDE LAWRENCE DIES

BURIAL IN U.S.

From Our Own Correspondent

NEW YORK, Sunday.

Gertrude Lawrence, the actress, whose performances charmed two continents for more than 25 years, died in the New York Hospital yesterday at the age of 54. After a post-mortem examination, it was stated that she had died of "acute disorder of the liver".

Her husband, Mr Richard Aldrich, the producer, was at her bedside. After she had entered hospital on Aug. 16 her indisposition was attributed to the after-effects of treatment she had received for a rash caused by poison ivy.

Miss Lawrence had been leading in "The King and I", the musical version of Margaret Landon's novel "Anna and the King of Siam". Following theatrical tradition, the matinee and evening performances continued yesterday, and it is understood that there is no intention of taking the play off.

Constance Carpenter, who has played the rôle during Miss Lawrence's absence, has taken her place. Slips announcing Miss Lawrence's death were placed inside programmes and a notice was put up in the foyer.

There will be no performance on Tuesday when the funeral takes place at Upton, Massaschusetts. Miss Lawrence will be interned in the Aldrich family plot where eight generations of her husband's family are buried. She will be buried in the white satin gown she wore in the ballroom scene of "The King and I".

The funeral service will also take place on Tuesday at Fifth-avenue Presbyterian Church, New York. Her body will lie in state in New York so the public will be able to file past the bier to-morrow.

42 Years an Actress

Anyone who had met Gertrude Lawrence on or off the stage in the post-World War II era found it difficult to credit the span of her career. Counting childhood appearances, it covered 42 of her 54 years.

She first appear as a leading lady 31 years ago. That was in Charlot's "A to Z" with Jack Buchanan.

Even her better remembered triumph with Noel Coward in "Private Lives" was 22 years ago. She had taken over Beatrice Lillie's leading part in "Tabs" before the Armistice in 1918.

She had a quality, something much more vivid than commonplace vitality, which confused all the landmarks by which most of us measure the passage of time.

(September 8)

COUNTESS OF DUDLEY

GAIETY STAR

Gertie Millar - in private life, Gertrude, Countess of Dudley - died yesterday at her home in Chiddingfold, Surrey, aged 73. The best known of what might be called the "royal line" of Gaiety girls who, after delighting Edwardian audiences, married into the peerage, she was the widow of the second Earl, who died in 1932.

Her rise to stardom was Cinderella-like. That a Bradford mill-worker's daughter should become one of the most scintillating figures of the West End stage and be the nightly toast of the "bloods" of the town, endeared her to audiences as much as her prettiness and all-round air of delicate charm.

That her singing voice was hardly worthy of mention, and that she was seldom called upon to demonstrate the slightest histrionic ability made no difference to the adulation she nightly aroused. She radiated personality in everything she said and did on the stage, and her daintiness made her the darling of stalls and gallery alike.

Her first appearance was in a Manchester pantomime as the girl babe in "Babes in the Wood" at the age of 13. In 1899 she played at the Grand Theatre, Fulham, as Dandini in "Cinderella" at £3 a week.

In 1901 she first stepped onto the Gaiety stage. A tiny part as a flower-girl had been interpolated for her in "The Toreador", and she sang a song, "Keep Off the Grass" which had been written specially by Lionel Monckton, the composer, who later became her first husband. Her success was immediate and quite overwhelming.

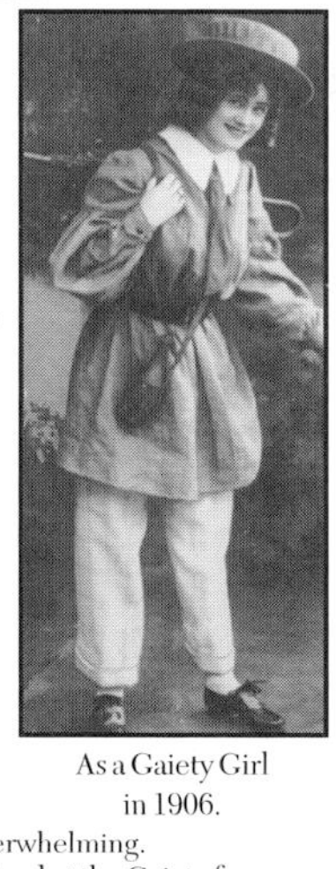

As a Gaiety Girl in 1906.

She remained at the Gaiety for seven years. One of her greatest successes there was "The Orchid", in 1903: other shows were "The Spring Chicken", 1905; "The New Aladdin", 1906; and "The Girls of Gottenberg", 1907, in which she later appeared in New York.

Her every movement and spoken line was instinctive with grace and sweetness.

(April 26)

LONDON DAY BY DAY

Flying Admiral

T.S.Eliot's Modesty

Vice-Adml. Lord Mountbatten, who takes over his duties as C-in-C, Mediterranean, next Thursday, will leave for London Airport to-morrow in one of the Vikings of the Queen's Flight.

The few days remaining before the relief of Adml. Sir John Edelsten will be filled. To-morrow night Adml. Mountbatten will be in Naples, where he is to be the guest of Adml. Carney.

The two have known one another for many years. Early next week he intends to go to Fayid to meet Gen. Sir Brian Robertson, C-in-C of the Middle East Land Forces.

Twice an Admiral

In taking charge of the Mediterranean command as an acting admiral – the post carried the rank of admiral - Lord Mountbatten will be so promoted for the second time in his naval career.

Unique Library

Despite a temperature of 83 degrees the London Library was crowded yesterday afternoon to welcome its new president, Mr. T.S.Eliot.

His speech, which lasted for more than half an hour, described how he joined the library during "my modest career as a financier".

Particularly graceful was his hope that the London Library should be considered as the private library of each of its members.

If it disappeared, he said, it would be a disaster to the world of letters. No other collection could fill the vacancy.

C.B. Fry

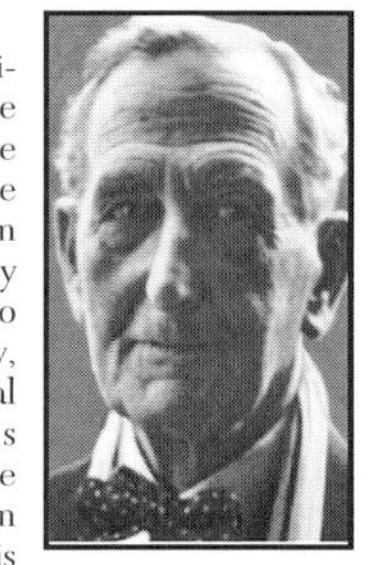

If any evidence were needed of the unique place held in English life by C.B. Fry, who is 80 to-day, the several panegyrics that have been written in token of his birthday are the answer.

All paid tribute to the fertility and versatility of his intellect. Apart from his eminence as a cricketer, a footballer and an athlete, he has touched life at so many points.

In recent years his extraordinary vitality has given place to a mood of philosophic calm. He is still to be seen at Lord's, but no longer as the focus of a crowd, demonstrating strokes with his walking stick in the Long Room.

Sitwell Pilgrimage

Yesterday the Sitwells made a pilgrimage. Sir Osbert, with his sister Edith, travelled from Renishaw to Scarborough for an official inspection of their old family home, Woodend.

It's described as official since the event caused a susceptible stir in Scarborough's social and municipal life. Since last year Woodend has been the Corporation's property as a flourishing natural history museum and vivarium.

To a Vivarium

After lunch the expedition was made. It was the first time the Sitwells had seen their old home in its present form.

After looking round his old home in its new guise, Sir Osbert commented: "It makes us feel historic. I have a living terror of being stuffed and put into a museum."

During a visit to the room which had been set aside as "The Sitwell room", for which the family have lent portraits, the talk turned to painting. Sir Osbert recalled an occasion when he had been asked his opinion of Mr. Churchill's painting, and his reply: "It is better than Hitler's."

Rising Anti-Bevanite

Mr. JAMES CALLAHAN, 40-year-old Socialist M.P. for South Cardiff, will be worth watching when the struggle for the Socialist Executive between the forces of Mr. Attlee and Mr. Bevan develops at Morecambe. He is on Mr. Attlee's side, and he is standing for the Executive.

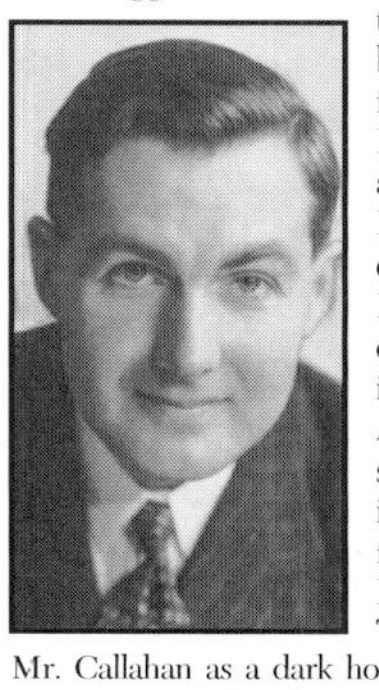

To describe Mr. Callahan as a dark horse would be inappropriate. In Opposition he has matched ambition with assiduity. Though only a junior Minister in the last Socialist Government, he has come right to the fore in recent months.

While Mr. Barnes, late Minister of Transport, spoke from a back bench, Mr. Callahan shared the Opposition lead with Mr. Morrison in transport debates. He intervenes, with cool insolence but good humour, on any topic that takes his fancy.

"We'll Call Her Susan"

Susan increased its lead in 1951 as the most popular name for girls. It heads the list in the birth notices of THE DAILY TELEGRAPH with 115.

This is the same number as in 1950, but Elizabeth, though still runner-up has dropped from 96 to 73. Jane, previously third, now ties with Elizabeth for second place.

Sarah has risen from a sixth to fifth place. If classed together, Sarah and its pet form Sally, are second on the list. Such popular Victorian names as Phyliss, Alice and Evelyn score only five between them. Amongst the picturesque girls' names now little used are Cressida, Viola, Athene, Imogen and Cassandra.

"What About David?"

David - 148 - is still top of the boys, but losing ground to Michael, Peter, John and Christopher. The once popular William - 38 - comes low, bracketed 19th with Jeremy. There are but four Georges and a single Arthur.

PETERBOROUGH

DEFEATED ARSENAL LIVED THEIR FINEST HOUR

Newcastle Equal 61-Year-Old Record

By Frank Coles

Newcastle United .... 1 Arsenal 0

For gripping drama and thrills, and the sight of a magnificent losing fight against odds, I have known nothing in Wembley's 29 years' Cup Final history to equal Saturday's match in which Newcastle United defeated Arsenal by 1-0 and so became the first team since 1891 to win the Cup two years in succession.

I have seen all the Wembley Finals and have not felt so stirred as I was by the courage of Arsenal's 10-men team. Disorganised by an injury to right-back Barnes, they held out against one of the most redoubtable attacks of modern times until within five minutes of the imminent half-hour.

Arsenal lost and lived their finest hour. In a team of heroes 38-year-old left-half Joseph Mercer shone like a beacon. There can never have been a more masterful display in a big match.

Spindle-legged Mercer inspired his side. At the 25th minute poor Barnes, who had not missed a match all the season through injury and had been Arsenal's Rock of Gibraltar in defence, limped off helplessly crippled. From that moment Mercer wore the mantle of Captain Courageous and his colleagues rose nobly to the leader's unquenchable spirit.

And Mercer and his men were not in any mood to buckle under the cruel blow. Sorely handicapped though they were with outside-left Roper at right-back, centre-forward Holton out of his element altogether on the left-wing and right-winger Cox for ever eager to burst through the Brennan barrier. Arsenal came back in an unforgettable second half not to accept defeat as inevitable but to challenge Newcastle's right to keep the Cup. And how narrowly they missed a famous victory!

TERRIFIC DYING EFFORT

Though visibly weakening under the terrific strain Arsenal hurled themselves at the Newcastle goal in a last minute dying effort to save the game, and the 100,000 crowd, long since drenched in thrills, saw three Arsenal and three Newcastle players finish flat on their backs in the Newcastle goalmouth with the ball just outside the net.

George Robledo's winning goal at the 85th minute was merciful relief to friend and foe. For by now Arsenal players were falling like nine-pins or reeling like punch-drunk boxers from sheer physical exhaustion, and with time running out there was the not-at-all-pleasing prospect of an extra half-hour.

Robledo ended the tension by heading into the net, the ball hitting the foot of the post on its way. The opening was made by Mitchell, but before his centre arrived from the left wing, Roper lay in a heap in the penalty area-completely knocked out.

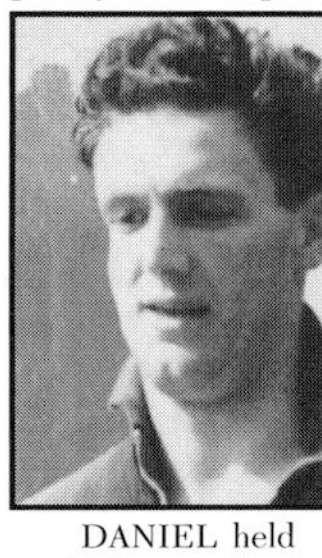

DANIEL held Milburn in check.

Newcastle deserved to win but their form was most disappointing to anyone who saw them touch the heights against Spurs and Portsmouth in January. For a side of such repute they made a surprisingly slow and unconvincing start and might have been a goal down in less than five minutes when Lishman tried an overhead speculative shot from 10 yards. The ball seemed to be heading straight for the unguarded right-hand corner of the net but it missed the tantalising target by a few inches.

In the short spell they were at full strength Arsenal were much more enterprising and effective in attack, and their skilful ball control, feinting and swerving and the on-the-ground passes of Logie and Lishman surpassed anything Newcastle produced.

DANIEL'S GALLANT ROLE

Milburn was the danger man right enough. Down the middle or out on the wings he tried everything he knew to unbalance Arsenal's defenders, but young Daniel, his injured arm in a light plastic cast, met the challenge manfully. Indeed, Forbes gave a great-hearted non-stop display in defence and attack. Daniel and Mercer reduced the quality of Newcastle's forward play to a low level.

(May 5)

Ups And Downs In The League

DIVISION I- Champions: Manchester United. Runners-up: Tottenham Hotspur. Relegated: Fulham and Huddersfield Town.

DIVISON II- Champions: Sheffield Wednesday. Runners-up: Cardiff City. Relegated: Rangers and Coventry City.

DIVISON III (S)- Champions: Plymouth Argyle. Runners-up: Reading. For re-election: Walsall and Exeter City.

DIVISON III (N)- Champions: Lincoln City. Runners-up: Grimsby Town. For re-election: Workington Town and Darlington.

DERBY SECOND THROWS JOCKEY AFTER FINISH

LATE WEIGH-IN

From our Special Correspondent

EPSOM, Wednesday.

Lester Piggott, the 16-year-old jockey, was the central figure in a thrilling end to the Derby at Epsom today. The race was won by the Aga Khan's Tulyar, with Piggott, on Mrs J.V. Rank's, Gay Time, three-quarters of a length behind.

Just past the finishing post, Gay Time threw Piggott, who returned to the weighing room on foot with the intention of objecting to Tulyar for interference in the race. Mr. Noel Cannon, trainer of Gay Time, was questioned by the Stewards, but stated he did not wish to object and no objection was laid.

Gay Time was caught by a stable head lad a mile away, and brought back to the unsaddling enclosure. Piggott, who had already passed the scales without his saddle, was weighed in a second time.

The Stewards issued a statement to say that "as soon as the horse was caught Piggott weighed in as second. The delay was unavoidable."

CHAPTER OF ACCIDENTS

Mrs Rank said: "It was a chapter of accidents. Gay Time spread a plate in the paddock and was late out. He was knocked at the start and again in the race the jockey told me. Piggott thought he had grounds for an objection, but we decided we would not object."

A sudden rush of money on Tuylar brought down his odds until he started favourite at 11-2. The horse was responsible for one of the biggest betting gambles in the history of the race.

Tuylar was led in by Aly Khan. It was the third Derby win for the jockey, C. Smirke. The race was worth £20,487 to the winner-the biggest prize in Derby history.

(May 21)

ITALIAN FOOTBALL STAR KIDNAPPED

BOUND IN LIGHTHOUSE

From Our Own Correspondent

ROME, Friday.

Luigi Scarabelli, the Italian football international, who was kidnapped at Leghorn last Sunday night, was found yesterday by four Communist journalists in an abandoned lighthouse on the coast near Leghorn. He was tied up and in a state of exhaustion.

The journalists had received an anonymous phone call telling them where to find the footballer. The police have ruled out the possibility that it was a publicity stunt for the footballer or for his wife Lillia Silvi, a film star.

Scarabelli was brought back to Rome with his wife last night under strong police escort.

The footballer was detained all night for questioning and this morning was taken away by police to an unknown destination.

(April 12)

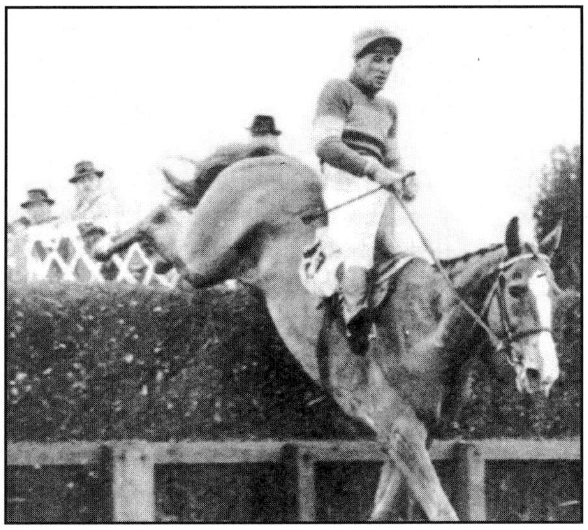

MONT TREMBLANT, well riden by Dave Dick.

MONT TREMBLANT SLAMS GOLD CUP RIVALS

Freebooter Falls: Shaef Unlucky

From Hotspur

CHELTENHAM, Thursday.

Miss Dorothy Paget won her seventh Cheltenham Gold Cup to-day with her six-year-old Mont Tremblant. The finish was tame, but it would certainly not have been so had not Knock Hard fallen two fences from home when lying second and going, in my opinion, better than the winner.

A race which had looked reasonably certain to end in a close finish failed to do so through various incidents. Shaef finished second in spite of almost losing his bridle at the water first time round.

Freebooter fell on the first circuit on his unlucky course. E.S.B. was lying second but a beaten horse when he came down at the last fence., but there was no excuse for Silver Fame, who, on the soggy ground, ran like a light of former days.

Both the Champion Hurdle and the Gold Cup have been won for the first time in the same season by horses bred in France. Mont Tremblant is the third French-bred to win the Gold Cup following Medoc II and Fortina.

Mont Tremblant was bought in France as a four-year-old for Miss Paget by Mr. Stacpoole, formerly leading amateur rider on the Continent. In France the horse won once on the flat and twice over hurdles.

Out of a mare who had good jumping form, Mont Tremblant was bought primarily as a 'chaser though he ran over the hurdles in England last season.

GREENOGUE WELL AWAY

To describe the race. Greenogue soon was out in front and passing the stands was leading from E.S.B. with Shaef and Silver Fame well placed. Shaef made a mistake at the water, almost lost his bridle and for the rest of the way apparently had his bit in his teeth. After the water Freebooter and Cushendun improved and at the bottom end of the course Greenogue led from E.S.B. and Freebooter with the field bunched close together.

At the fence after turning for home Freebooter took off to soon and came down. Greenogue still led at the half-way with Silver Fame, Knock Hard, E.S.B. and Mont Tremblant all going well. As they went away from the stands for the second time Mont Tremblant began to move up, followed by Knock Hard. Greenogue was beaten at the fence after the water and old Silver Fame began to weaken at the bottom end of the course.

When they turned for home for the last time the race seemed to lie between Mont Tremblant, E.S.B., Knock Hard and Shaef. Three fences out Mont Tremblant was leading from E.S.B. and Knock Hard. Two fences from home Mont Tremblant was still nearly two lengths in front of Knock Hard, who was steadily catching Miss Paget's 6-year-old.

KNOCK HARD COMES DOWN

I thought then that Knock Hard's speed would prove decisive in the run-in as on more than one occasion it had done with stable companion Cottage Rake. It was not to be. Knock Hard got too close to the fence and came down, leaving Mont Tremblant clear of the tiring E.S.B.

As Mont Tremblant came to the last he had his race won barring a fall.

(March 7)

MISS ALTWEGG IS CHAMPION

GAINS GOLD MEDAL IN FIGURE SKATING

OSLO, Wednesday.

Miss Jeanette Altwegg, 21-year-old world, European and British champion, gained Britain's first Gold Medal in the Sixth Winter Olympic Games here to-night by winning the women's figure skating title.

She won by a margin of over two points from the 16-year-old American, Miss Tenley Albright, with Mdlle Jacqueline du Bief (France) third.

Britain last won this event in 1908, when Mrs E. Syers was successful, but Miss E. Muckolt, was second in 1924. Miss Cecilia Colledge also runner-up in 1936 and Miss Altwegg third in 1948.

DIFFICULT PIROUETTES

Though Miss Altwegg's free-skating did not equal that of either Miss Albright or Mdlle du Bief, she gave a very beautiful performance. She took no chances, seemed to be very calm and went through a series of difficult pirouettes and loops without any mishaps.

When the Union Jack slowly ascended the prize-winner's flagpole, " God Save The Queen " was played for the first time ever in a Winter Olympics.

Next week Miss Altwegg goes to Paris to defend her world title. Whether she retains it or not she is expected to retire from active competition afterwards.

Other events decided were the cross-country ski race, in which Britain was not represented, and the women's slalom. Mrs Andrea Mead Lawrence (U.S.) completed a Gold Medal double by winning the slalom for which, after all, two British women competed. Results:

WOMEN'S FIGURE SKATING: J. Altwegg (G.B.) 161.76pts, 1; **E.T.Albright** (U.S.) 159.13, 2; **J du Bief** (France) 158.00, 3; **Other British Placings: B.Wyatt** 148.37, 7; **V.Osborn** 144.76, 9; **P.Devries** 132.81, 17;

WOMEN'S SLALOM (aggregate times for 2 runs): **A.M.Lawrence** (U.S.) 2m 10.6s, 1; **O.Reichert** (Germany) 2m 11.4s, 2; **A.M.Buchner** (Germany) 2m 13.3s, 3; **British Placings: H.Laing** 2m 27.9s, 23; **S.Mackintosh** 2m 29.4s, 27.

CROSS-COUNTRY SKI RACE (50 kilos): **V.Hakullinen** (Finland) 3h 33m 33s, 1; **E.Kolchmainen** (Finland) 3h 38m 11s, 2; **M.Oestenstad** (Norway) 3h 38m 28s, 3-Reuter.

(February 21)

SPRINGBOKS FINISH WITH 14 POINTS IN 12 MINUTES

Barbarians Lack Reliable Goal-Kicker

By E.W. Swanton

Barbarians .... 3pts South Africans 17

The Springbok tour, so far as the British Isles is concerned, ended on an appropriately satisfying note at Cardiff on Saturday, for in their last match before they cross to France the South Africans beat the Barbarians convincingly.

The score of a goal, three penalty goals and a try to a try could mean much or little. I would say that it disguises the truth in that the Barbarians had quite a share of the play; while it discloses the very important fact that whereas the Springboks had a competent goal-kicker the Barbarians palpably lacked one.

Considering that two such outstanding members of their representative side as J.D. Brewis and J. Buchler were unfit to play, the Springboks were probably well content with their performance against a team of such lustre as the Barbarians fielded against them.

In the first half they seemed to be missing greatly the thrust and purpose that Brewis has generally given to their attack. Up to the point, 18 minutes after half-time, when Keevy celebrated his promotion to stand-off by putting them ahead with the first of the penalties, little had been seen of the positional skill and mutual support which normally distinguish their football.

Most of the marks had gone to their forwards, among whom Dinkelmann, in all phases, and Muller and Van Wyk, in the open, played conspicuously well. But from then onwards the Springbok movements gradually regained their habitual sweep and stride, and the Barbarians, for all their determined endeavours to keep the ball moving, soon found themselves fighting a progressively more forlorn battle.

In fact, though in this period they only once crossed the Barbarian line, the Springboks scored 14 points in 12 minutes. That was that, and the proceedings thereafter were mainly of academic appeal. Cardiff being Cardiff, the 50,000 spectators to a man remained until the last whistle, and they were rewarded by some of the best football.

MISSED PENALTIES

From the Barbarian standpoint the game was something of a disappointment. The Springboks used the exceptional speed and fitness of their wing forwards to dislocate the Barbarian attacks. In this harassing, and at the line-out in their endeavours to kick the ball away from the towering John, the Springboks frequently offended.

But though three of the 10 penalties given against them in the first half might have been converted, the Barbarians missed them all. The goal kick from Elliot's try was also missed, and when Rees Stephens, improving considerably on one previous effort by himself, two by Elliot, and one by Woodward, almost shaved the post after half an hour's play, it was a reasonable estimate that the Barbarians should have been 11 points up instead of three.

If they had been, probably they could have pulled out sufficient reserves of energy and resource to hold their lead. As it was, several players could not wholly shake off a reaction from the previous Saturday's rigorous international at Twickenham.

Nor, it must be added, were the Barbarians helped by the difficulties experienced by Cannell and Woodward in fitting in with an otherwise Welsh set of backs. Cannell's hands clutched uncertainly at the crisp, short passes of B.L. Williams and Morgan.

Kendall-Carpenter and Stirling upheld the credit of English forward play, and Elliot, the lone Scotsman, was in excellent form. But it was inevitably largely a Welsh effort wherein the more prominent players were Morgan, B.L. Williams, and of course, John.

DELIGHTFUL JINK

The Barbarian try was begun by one of these delightful jinks of B.L. Williams to which no defenders seem to find the counter. Morgan took his pass and had almost reached the line when he threw a high overhead pass to Woodward. A South African diverted the ball out of Woodward's reach, but Elliot came diving up and was awarded the touch-down.

The lead was held for 10 minutes before Marais punted into the left corner, where Ochse took the ball on the bound, making Woodward look somewhat ponderous in the process, and 3-3 was the score at half-time.

Afterwards the Springbok pressure increased, and whereas all the penalty kicks had been awarded against them, now they had quite a spate. Keevy's first goal came after the Barbarians had been penalised apparently for collapsing the scrum. His second followed a sadly heedless piece of offside play, I am sorry to say, by the Barbarian captain, Nelson.

Almost from the kick-off a run by Ochse on the left prepared the way for a try by Van Wyk, and, as someone observed, it seemed appropriate that the last Springbok try should be scored by this brilliant loose forward. Keevy kicked the goal from this, and when Willis was offside on the fringe of the scrum, it was Johnstone's turn to prove himself a place-kicker.

There the scoring ended, and the green jerseys filed off at the final whistle to applause appropriately fervent and prolonged. Teams:

BARBARIANS: G.Williams (Wales); J.E.Woodward (England); B.L.Williams (Wales); L.B.Cannell (England); K.Jones (Wales); C.Morgan (Wales); W.R.Willis (Wales); J Kendall-Carpenter (England); D.M.Davies (Wales); R.V.Stirling (England); E.R.John (Wales); J.E.Nelson (Ireland) (capt.); V.G.Roberts (England); R.G.Stephens (Wales); W.I.D.Elliot (Scotland).

SOUTH AFRICANS: A.C.Keevy; F.P.Marais; M.T.Lategan; R.Van Scheer; J.K.Osche; P.Johnstone; P.A.du Toit; F.E.Van der Ryet; W.Delport; H.Bekker; S.P.Fry; E.Dinkelmann; J.du Rand; C.J.Van Wyk; M.Muller (capt.).

(January 28)

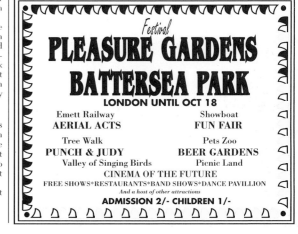

ENGLAND NEED 37 TO WIN SECOND TEST

From E.W.Swanton

LORD'S, Monday.

England virtually won the second test here this evening after a day's play made memorable by the Queen's first visit of her reign. The teams were presented to her Majesty in front of the pavilion at the tea interval, as they had been to her father and her grandfather, and by a happy coincidence the cricket she saw comprised a gay, indeed hilarious, expiring batting effort for India by Ramchand, who scored 42 runs from the 42 balls bowled to him.

Previous to his coming in, Trueman had bowled out Umrigar almost before the Queen had settled into her seat in the committee room window, and so here, too, tradition was followed in the swift capture of what has become known as a Royal wicket.

Once more the major honours were annexed by Mankad in what has been a game of extraordinary and often unaccountable contrast. Since Thursday morning brilliance has been followed by futility, timidity by aggression.

One cannot readily recall a Test match which divided itself more naturally into separate chapters each distinct from the last. This pattern was faithfully followed to-day.

CLASSIC INNINGS

First came the continuation of the defiant partnership of Mankad and Hazare which had taken the score from 59 to 137 on Saturday evening. These two repelled the English bowlers to-day until half-past two. Hazare defending while Mankad built up an innings that will take its place among the classics.

When at last Mankad was beaten, all but 32 of India's arrears of 302 had been obliterated.

The next chapter, making allowance for an estimable piece of bowling by Laker, tells the story of India's un-expectantly-granted-opportunity being utterly squandered. Within an hour and a half the six wickets that mattered had all fallen for 53 runs and the bright hope had faded to the merest glimmer.

Once more the scene changed with the suddenness of a magic lantern show. Ramchand swung his bat in a death-or-glory innings which after all enabled India to set England 77 runs to win.

The last chapter, as different again as could be imagined, contained the struggle for this handful of runs which was induced by some very fine spin bowling by Mankad and Ghulam Ahmed.

A PERFECT INNINGS

The merit of Mankad's batting strains the vocabulary. His eye is the basis of it - eye, one could say, and heart. His philosophy is a profoundly simple one that the ball is "maun to be hit" and if the bowler beats him, as happened a few times with Laker to-day, this reaction consists of a determination to contrive an attacking stroke off the next.

He is not going to be dominated. Not the least important thing about his innings was his speed between wickets and perfect judgment of a run. To this the phlegmatic Hazare so responded as to become unrecognisable in this respect.

It is just that innings like Mankad's do not normally happen in the solemn run of county cricket, and the bowlers were taken out of their element just as thoroughly as the batsmen when, as happens annually now, there arrive two spin-bowlers from overseas who confine them by flight and good length.

HAZARE A BARN DOOR

At one o'clock Mankad had scored 84 more runs this morning in an hour and a half, bringing his score to 170. Whether by luck or the cunning of Hazare, who may well have feared that at this rate his partner must surely encompass his own destruction, he received only 17 balls in the period remaining to luncheon, and so, surprisingly he failed to add a further 100 to his score by the interval. Hazare, who has plenty of strokes when he thinks fit to use them, had played the part of the obdurate barn door.

(Solution No. 8311)

The Scoreboard

INDIA–First Innings:

233 (V.Mankad 72, V.S.Hazare 69 not out, Trueman 4-72; Watkins 3-37)

Second Innings

V.Mankad, b Laker	184
P.Roy, b Bedser	0
H.R.Adhikari, b Trueman	16
V.S.Hazare, c Laker, b Bedser	49
V.L.Manjrefar, b Laker	1
D.G.Phadkar, b Laker	16
P.R.Umrigar, b Trueman	14
M.K.Mantri, c Compton, b Laker	5
G.S.Ramchand, b Trueman	42
S.G.Shinde, c Hutton, b Trueman	14
Ghulam Ahmed, not out	1
Extras (b 29, lb 3, nb 4)	36
Total	**378**

ENGLAND–First Innings:

537 (Hutton 150, Evans 104, P.B.H.May 74, Graveney 73, R.T.Simpson 53; Mankad 5-196, Gulam Ahmed 3-106).

Second Innings

Hutton, not out	27
R.T.Simpson, run out	2
P.B.H.May, not out	8
Extras (lb)	3
Total (1 wkt)	**40**

At half past two Mankad was bowled at last by Laker, driving over a long half-volley. How he missed it I can not wholly understand, and if he had not I assume he would still have been batting, unless he had run out of partners.

LAKER'S STEADY BOWLING

Laker got a little more turn out of the wicket this afternoon, bowling surprisingly enough, from the Nursery end, and so spinning up the hill.

He was on from now until the end of the innings, and in spite of some agricultural treatment from Ramchand, bowled in this period 22 overs for 50 runs and four wickets.

The complexion of affairs changed utterly with Mankad's departure. Hazare, whose contribution is hard to imagine at by the score sheet, was nicely caught low down at second slip from a leg-cutter that went up the hill and Manjrekar, after struggling awhile, was bowled playing outside a good length off-break.

India's fortunes now rested very much with Phadkar and Umrigar, but the feverish manner in which they approached the situation did not bode well for their chances. There were, however, some strong hits, and once Umrigar, striking Laker ferociously with the spin, came mighty near doing a serious injury to Hutton, fielding at short square leg.

Not for nothing is that position called suicide corner and it was a relief to see that Hutton demoted himself, thereupon, and left it untenanted. Phadkar and Umrigar both left soon after India had their noses in front, whereupon Ramchand put up his performance.

England's effort to make the 77 needed in the hour and 20 minutes remaining found a crowd, who had been somewhat spoilt by the earlier heroics, severely critical. In fact, India in the evening phase had held all the psychological tricks.

They rubbed the new ball in the dust and set Mankad and Ghulam Ahmed to spin it straight away, and with much accuracy and some guile they proceeded to do so. Simpson on his own call was run out by a quick throw by Roy from short third man that hit the wickets. Hutton for awhile found himself pinned and May was 25 minutes getting off the mark.

(June 24)

TRUEMAN just after delivering the ball.

TRUEMAN FIRST ENGLAND FAST BOWLER TO TAKE 8

All Fourteen Catches Were Accepted

By E. W. Swanton

England won the third Test and the rubber, to be precise, at 20 minutes past five on Saturday, but India's defeat was as certain as anything could be the moment the Manchester weather changed for the worst the night before the match.

The 1902 Test at Old Trafford which Australia won by three runs, was not only the last Test that England lost on this ground it was the last that England lost anywhere on a wicket wet from the first ball to the last.. The handicap is too great for visiting sides from sunny countries, whether Indians or South Africans, New Zealanders, West Indians - yes, or Australians.

I would say, taking the wicket, the bowling and the fielding into consideration, that while 347 would nearly always be a winning score, a reputable Test batting side should have been capable of a much longer and more productive resistance in the first innings.

HAZARE IN THE BREACH

The second innings was inevitably much less significant. When a side follows on 289 behind, having been bowled out for 58, and there are 2.5 days to go, the only prospect of a prolonged counter-effort depends on a successful start.

Once again India's first two wickets fell before the board showed double figures, and though the faithful Hazare, with his vice-captain Adhikari, stood in the breach for an hour, Hazare was dislodged at last. Thereafter the last offences crumbled and dissolved.

The irresistible pressure of events submerged the Indians so swiftly that they were bowled out a second time in the day, an indignity that has not happened to a Test side since the 'nineties.

That was only one of a fistful of facts and figures that zealous mathematical experts unearthed while the slaughter was going on.

The scope of international conflict at all games is so greatly enlarged that most 'modern' records become entirely irrelevant. The mention of them is agreeable chiefly because it revives memories of the giants of old.

FIRST SINCE VERITY

Thus, no England bowler has taken eight wickets in an innings, as Trueman did, since Verity bowled out Australia at Lord's on the sticky dog.

The Scoreboard

ENGLAND–First Innings

Hutton, c Sen, b Divecha	10
D.S. Sheppard, lbw, b Ramchand	34
Ikin, c Divecha, b Ghulam Ahmed	29
P.B.H. May, c Sen, b Mankad	69
Graveney, lbw, b Divecha	14
Watkins, c Phadkar, b Mankad	4
Evans, c & b Ghulam Armed	71
Laker, c Sen, b Divecha	0
Bedser (A.V.) c Phadkar, b G Armed	17
Lock, not out	1
Extras (b 2, lb 2)	4
Total (9 wkts. dec.)	**347**

Did not bat: Trueman.

India - First Innings

V. Mankad, c Lock, b Bedser	4
P. Roy, c Hutton, b Trueman	0
H.R. Adhikari, c Graveney, b Trueman	0
V.S. Hazare, b Bedsar	16
P.R. Umrigar, b Trueman	4
D.G. Phadkar, c Sheppard, b Trueman	0
V.L. Manjrekar, c Ikin, b Trueman	22
R.V. Divecha, b Trueman	4
G.S. Ramchand, c Graveney, b Trueman	2
P. Sen, c Lock, b Trueman	4
Ghulam Armed, not out	1
Extras (lb 1)	1
Total	**82**

Second Innings

V. Mankad, lbw, b Bedser	6
P. Roy, c Laker, b Trueman	0
H.R. Adhikari, c May, b Lock	27
V.S. Hazare, c Ikin, b Lock	16
P.R. Umrigar, c Watkins, b Bedser	3
D.G. Phadkar, b Bedser	5
V.L. Manjrekar, c Evans, b Bedser	0
R.V. Divecha, b Bedser	1
G.S. Ramchand, c Watkins, b Lock	1
P. Sen, not out	13
Ghulam Armed, c Ikin, b Lock	0
Extras (b 8, lb 1)	9
Total	**82**

(July 21)

"Pity! It appears the Hope of the Side must now retrace his steps — leaden-hearted, moist-eyed and dry-throated … Hawkins! Burn my batting average and pour out the Rose's! When fully refreshed I will challenge you to a desperate game of noughts and crosses!"

ROSE'S LIME JUICE

makes thirst worth while

COMPTON HITS HIS 100TH FIRST-CLASS CENTURY

Northants Make Him Fight For Runs

From E.W.Swanton

LORD'S, Wednesday.

Middlesex and Northamptonshire, both at present leading contenders for the Championship, fought a tense and interesting battle for the initiative here this afternoon, and as a further relish to the occasion Denis Compton reached his century of centuries.

As was appropiate it was made for the county which brought him forth before the world just 16 years ago, and as was likewise appropriate, Northants required him to fight hard for his 100 from 0 to 99.

At this point F.R.Brown, remembering perhaps how a certain E.A.Nepean on this ground proffered a slow long-hop to "W.G." when the great man needed but four runs for his thousand in May, and having mercy, maybe, both on the principal performer and on the nerves of his admirers, also sent down a long-hop which Compton duly hooked to the Mound boundary.

(June 12)

LEANDER CLIP 6sec OFF HENLEY RECORD

By B.C.Johnstone

Leander enhanced their already high reputation and rather boosted British hopes for Helsinki when winning the Grand Challenge Cup at Henley on Saturday in 6min 38sec, the fastest time ever and six seconds better than their record-equalling performance on Friday.

Other outstanding performances were put up by the Pembroke College, Cambridge, who beat Trinity College, Oxford, in the Visitors' Cup in 6 mins 14secs, four seconds faster than any previous time; M.T.Wood (Australia), who took the Diamonds; the University of Pennsylvania (U.S.) who retained the Thames Cup, and the fast Belgian pair, R.George and J.van Stichel, who won the Double Sculls.

On each day of Henley this year an exceptionally strong wind was blowing up the course, conducive to fast times but also a danger to crews in the rough water, especially along the enclosure where it had some repercussions.

The opening race of the last day - the semi-final of the Thames Cup between University College of London and Christ's College, Cambridge - was a foretaste of the close racing we were to witness in subsequent events.

It was, however, the battle between Leander and Sydney RC of Australia that was awaited with the keenest interest of all. It was appreciated, both were of high quality in oarsmanship and racing.

EXCITING TUSSLE

Leander went off at 41 to Sydney's 43. The crews kept level for a short time but at the quarter-mile signal Leander were half a length up and had managed to increase their lead to a length at the half-mile. To do so they had had to keep at 36 to Australia's 33.

The latter reduced the gap by raising to 36 and more from here on while Leander were a fraction lower. At the mile post there was only a third of a length between them and in the final spurt Leander got home by half a length.

Both crews gave a fine example of rowing, the Australians, splendid watermen and with fine physique, seemed not quite so long in their stroke as Leander, but their ability to move their boat fast was undoubted.

Leander had their foundation on the three stern oars. It was in these same positions they had rowed in the Cambridge crew who had won in America. Jennens at stroke has rowed in and won many fine races. In his judgment and racing quality on Saturday he was at his best.

Windham and Brian Lloyd, behind him at seven and six, made up a perfect combination. Their fast time is a worthy reflection of their length and the terrific power they exercise when rowing. It puts them in the highest class.

(July 7)

WARWICK TIE WITH SUSSEX

HOLLIES GETS LAST MAN OUT L.B.W.

If the County Championship programme continues to produce fortunes as took place during the match between Sussex and Warwickshire at Hove, which ended in a tie, cricket's future should be assured.

After some three hours of tense play, the Sussex last pair, James and Webb, came together with their side wanting 12 to defeat the champions.

Scorning the presence of fieldsmen crouching a few yards from the wicket, they gradually took the total nearer to 132, which would give their side the match. Each run was loudly cheered by the excited crowd, many of whom had hurried to the ground on hearing that Sussex were engaged in a tense struggle.

The cheers were renewed when, at last, the scores became level. Everything now depended upon Hollies.

In a hushed atmosphere he ran up to bowl. The ball sped on its way and struck Webb on the pads. Umpire Hills said, "No" to a concerted appeal. With the next ball Hollies again rapped the pad. A triumphant appeal followed almost instantaneously. Umpire Hills raised his finger, and the match was tied.

WORCESTER HOLD OUT

There was another exciting finish at Worcester where the county's fast bowlers, Perks and Flavell, were the heroes of a race-against-the-clock victory over Somerset. The pair came together with nine minutes left for play requiring nine runs to win.

Gallantly they held out against the spin attack of Robinson and Hazell, and when, with three still wanted, Perks went down the pitch and drove Hazell to the sight-screen, Worcestershire were home by one wicket.

ESSEX, after taking two days to gain the initiative at Chelmsford, hung on to it and defeated Derbyshire by nine wickets. The last three Derbyshire wickets fell at 127, Ray Smith (five for 33) bringing his match figures to 10 for 116.

(May 14)

MILLWARD GETS HOME ON THE LAST GREEN

By Leonard Crawley

E.B.Millward, of the Ferndown Club, Dorset, won the England Amateur Golf Championship at Burnham and Berrow on Saturday, beating T.J.Shorrock, of North Manchester, on the last green in the 36-hole final.

Millward, who is not a stylish player, has had his ups and downs, in the post-war golf, but has kept himself fit, practised assiduously and thoroughly deserves his success.

He has, as near as one could imagine, the perfect build of a golfer, being strong and sturdy, with a fine pair of hands. He swings the club quickly and, unlike the copy-book players, the head of the club makes the initial movement on his backswing.

With his eye in he is long and straight, but it is on and around the greens where he is most gifted. Throughout the championship he putted smoothly and confidently.

GOLFER OF HIGH PROMISE

Shorrock, who is left-handed, has played well in several boys' championships since the war and at 22 is a golfer of undoubted promise. His slow and rhythmic swing is agreeable to watch and full of hidden power.

To pay him a high compliment I do not think he is anything like as good as he will be in a few years time, which may be some slight consolation for his defeat on Saturday.

(May 5)

MISS CONNOLLY, SUPREME & CONFIDENT, WINS THROUGH

Sedgman Well Worthy Of Triple Crown

By Lance Tingay

To win the Lawn Tennis Championship at the first attempt is remarkable. To do so when only 17 is memorable, though not unique, and Miss Maureen Connolly, who accomplished that feat, will have a distinct niche in the game even if she never comes back to Wimbledon.

"Little Mo" in fact intends to do so, and this being the case, there seems every reason why this chirpy and irresistible Californian will go on winning the women's singles for a great number of years. She should get even better and her game, based on solidity of driving strength, is of the type that endures.

The greatest player at the 66th Wimbledon meeting was Frank Sedgman. He was unbeaten in three events, a feat not lightly achieved. Yet despite his might the Wimbledon that ended on Saturday belongs more to Miss Connolly.

Her concluding triumph, executed in one of the best women's finals seen for years, came after much adversity. An injured shoulder was in itself a physical handicap. The concomitant fuss, the difference of opinion with her coach, who for the best of motives wanted her to scratch, was an even greater mental one.

CHAMPION'S FLAIR

Though Miss Connolly wavered in the early rounds - wavered indeed to almost defeat against Miss Susan Partridge - she never lacked her champion's flair. She got better in the later stages and against Miss Louise Brough, thrice holder of the title, she was supreme and confident.

Miss Brough also played her best lawn tennis of the championship. She used her wide variety of stroke, her strength of service and power of volley, in fact all the equipment of the complete player she is. She exploited, too, Miss Connolly's weakness, with a slow mid-court ball on her forehand, though in this respect the 17-year-old was less vulnerable than she had been earlier.

Against this Miss Connolly replied with some network that was relatively indecisive. Her volleying would not have taken her far against Miss Brough. It was the withering precision of her ground strokes, more especially on the backhand that brought Miss Brough to defeat. These ground strokes, nimbly taken on the run and full of venom and accurate pace, were the instruments with which Miss Connolly gained her title.

Miss Brough led 5-4 in the first set. The match so tough up to that stage was decided in the 10th game. Deuce was called three times before Miss Connolly won it, though Miss Brough, who was serving, never got within a point of set.

MISS BROUGH TIRES

From that stage Miss Brough's game was passed. She wearied, almost faltered and though her zest flickered anew at the end when she saved four match points in the second set, it was merely delaying what was bound to come. Indeed, had Miss Brough after all won the first set I think Miss Connolly would still have taken the match.

GREAT DAY FOR SEDGMAN

Saturday was a great day for Sedgman. It may not be exciting when the favourite canters home, but his qualities should be appreciated. His doubles win with Ken McGregor was simply taken. Victor Seixas and Eric Sturgess were quite outplayed and the final was never very good.

The Australians were so obviously to be the victors that it seemed of no importance when the losers led 3-1 in both first and third sets. They did not win either.

Yet as a match it was a remarkable tour de force by Sedgman: McGregor did not do well. He fumbled much. Sedgman played like a man and a half. He seemed unable to miss and had that spark of inspiration when he could return as winners even short smashes directed at his feet. Fred Perry years ago used to display the same flair in singles matches.

WONDERFUL RECORD

Sedgman's doubles record is, I think, unique. It began in the late summer of 1950 in the United States when he and John Bromwich won the American National Title. Since then Sedgman has not been beaten in a major doubles contest. He has won the American title twice, the Australian title twice, the French title twice and now the Wimbledon title twice.

The Champions

MEN'S SINGLES

F.A.Sedgman (Australia) bt J.Drobny (Egypt): 4-6, 6-2, 6-3, 6-2

WOMEN'S SINGLES

Miss M. Connolly (U.S.) bt Miss L. Brough (U.S.): 7-5, 6-3

MEN'S DOUBLES

K. McGregor & F.A. Sedgman bt V.Seixas & E.W. Sturgess 6-3, 7-5

WOMEN'S DOUBLES

Miss S. Fry & Miss D.Hart bt Miss L. Brough & Miss M. Connolly 8-6, 6-3

MIXED DOUBLES

F.A.Sedgman & Miss D. Hart bt E.Morea & Mrs T.D.Long 4-6, 6-3, 6-4

Include two Davis Cup Challenge rounds and there are 10 vital doubles that have been won. Bromwich partnered him for the first two, McGregor for the next eight. How much longer will he keep it up? Presumably until his young colleagues Lew Hoad and Ken Rosewall draw level with his skill.

WORTHY DOUBLES CHAMPIONS

Miss Doris Hart and Miss Shirley Fry are women's doubles champions for the second time.

Miss Brough and Miss Connolly held them for the first set only. Afterwards they were outplayed. Miss Connolly is not yet in the same class in doubles as in singles. She has the pace of shot, but when it comes to those adroit angles which mean so much on the bigger court, Miss Hart is twice as good.

NO EASY TRIUMPH

When it came to the last final Sedgman did not gain his triple crown without travail. He and Miss Hart lost the first set before coming through. With their success they won their second Wimbledon title together. They have already won that of France twice and that of America once.

Sedgman, therefore, was unbeaten at Wimbledon just as he was in the United States Championships in 1951. His supremacy in singles on grass and as a doubles exponent on any surface is beyond dispute.

(July 7)

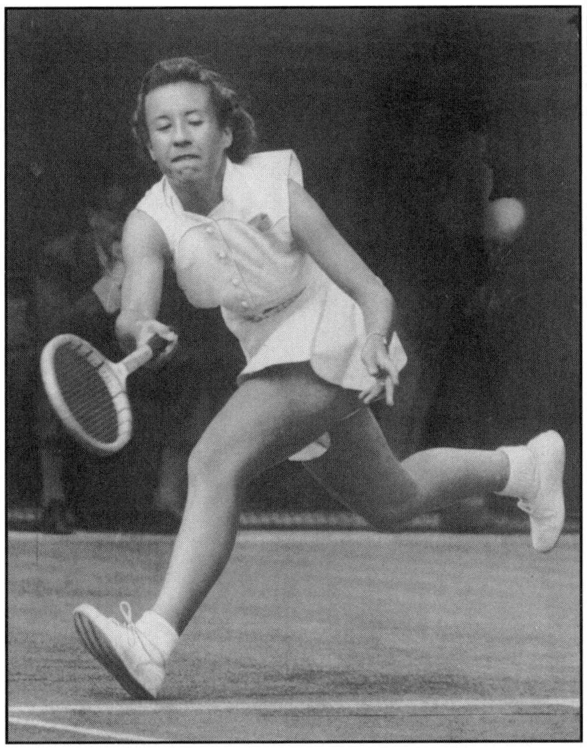

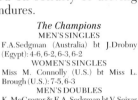

MISS MAUREEN CONNOLLY, playing her first singles with easy grace.

DROBNY LANDS HARD COURT HAT-TRICK

By Lance Tingay

Jaroslav Drobny (Egypt) and Miss Doris Hart (U.S.) each won two titles when the British Hard Court lawn tennis championships ended at Bournemouth on Saturday. Britain had the solace of G.L.Paish and Mrs I.Rinkel taking the mixed doubles.

Drobny's defeat of Frank Sedgman will surely rank among the memorable events of the season. There were happenings in it - notably Drobny's mistrust of his own powers in the last few games and Sedgman's forehand failings and lack of service strength - that rule it out as a great combat, but few such stirring tussles have been seen on Bournemouth's centre court.

SHOTS OF INTENSE FURY

Had the match continued as it began it would have rated as one of the best of all time. On a slow moist court in a dead, damp atmosphere, conducive it seemed mainly to defensive play, both projected from masters' weapons shots of intense fury.

The most striking aspect of this match was the speed on either side. It lasted only an hour and a half as Drobny used pace and dexterity against the pressure of the Australian who, staunch as an oak, tried to hammer out a victory from the net.

(May 6)

FOUR RECORDS IN OLYMPICS

BRITISH HOPE FAILS IN 10,000 METRES

From Our Special Correspondent

HELSINKI, Sunday.

Four new Olympic records were set up in Helsinki to-day, the first day of the Olympic Games competitions. The 15th Olympiad was formally opened yesterday by M.Paasikivi, the Finnish President.

The climax of to-day's events was the 10,000 metres race, won by the Czech, Emil Zatopek, in 29min 17sec. This was 42.6sec better than his Olympic time four years ago in London, but 14.4sec slower than his own world record in 1950.

Britain's hope, Gordon Pirie (South London Harriers), found the pace too hot and finished seventh. His compatriot, F.Sando, was fifth.

Other record breakers were:
N.Romaschkova, Russia, 168ft 8 ¾ in the women's discus
Charles Moore, United States, 50.8sec in 400 metres hurdles, second round.
Walter Davies, United States, 6ft 8 ⅜ in in high jump.

In the first round of the Olympic Soccer tournament Jugoslavia drew 5-5 with Russia after leading 5-1 15 minutes from the end of normal time. Extra time was played without addition to the score. There was a British referee, Mr. Arthur Ellis, who refereed last season's F.A. Cup Final. The tie will be replayed on Tuesday.

GERMAN "PEACE ANGEL"

Girl Sent Home

Barbara Rotraut-Pleyer, 23, the West German girl who staged a demonstration as an "angel of peace" at yesterday's opening ceremony, was put on a plane for Hamburg to-day.

The girl, a law student, had told the Finnish police that she came to Helsinki to plead for international unity because she thought the Games an appropriate occasion for such an appeal. Getting no help from the West German Olympic attaché, she tried to approach President Paasikivi.

(July 21)

AUREOLE'S DEBUT

QUEEN'S HORSE WINS

From Hotspur

YORK, Tuesday.

The Queen's two-year-old colt Aureole, of which much is expected, made a winning debut in the £1,500 Acomb Stakes here to-day. The colt was an outsider and the victory was unexpected as it was backward and running against experienced opponents.

Capt. Charles Moore, the Queen's racing manager, sent a telegram to her Majesty after the race informing her of the victory. Capt. Moore thinks the Queen has a high-class colt in Aureole, which was bred at Sandringham.

(August 20)

ZATOPEK WINS MARATHON

OLYMPIC RECORD BEATEN EASILY

From Frank Coles,
Daily Telegraph Special Correspondent

HELSINKI, Sunday.

The Duke of Edinburgh and the Duke of Kent to-day saw Emil Zatopek, 31, the Czech runner, set up an Olympic record which will probably stand for all time. He crowned his earlier victories in the 5,000 and 10,000 metres by a great triumph in the marathon.

No other long distance runner has won such a hat-trick since the Games were started in 1896. He finished the 26-mile course in 2hr 23min 3.25sec. The previous Olympic record was 2hr 29min 19.2sec. J.Peters the fancied British competitor, retired with cramps after 20 miles. G.Icen, London tailor, finished ninth.

Describing the race Peters said: "I soon got into the rhythm of my running and was quite satisfied with myself at 19 kilometres when Zatopek closed up the gap and turned to me as we ran shoulder to shoulder and said: "Can't you go any faster?"

ZATOPEK FORGES AHEAD

"I told him that I could although my legs were beginning to pain me considerably. Zatopek shrugged his shoulders and then forged 20 yards ahead and looked round to see if I was following. I kept going, but my legs suddenly gave way."

Britain gained her highest honour of the Games to-day when Mrs Sheila Lerwill, 32, a housewife from Swanley, Kent won a silver medal for the second place in the women's high jump.

(July 28)

TEXT-BOOK ANGELO IS TOO NEGATIVE

JABS WAY TO EASY WIN

No fighter has demonstrated more painfully, than did George Angelo, the South African middleweight champion, at the Seymour Hall, London, last night that the right way to box is the anchor to academic ignominy, writes **Lainson Wood.**

Angelo, who was to have been Randolph Turpin's comeback trial-horse in January, easily outpointed Jimmy Davis, of Bethnal Green. Davis a knowledgeable boxer, will wear the scars of Angelo's jabs for some days.

Lewis Carroll wrote about the "jabberwock, with eyes of flame." Angelo last night was the jabber with dulled eyes and dull enterprise. The way he tucked in his elbows and shot out his punches was text-book stuff but I could not help thinking that against such a flamboyant puncher as Turpin he must be torn to ribbons despite his considerable defensive qualities.

(March 7)

BRITAIN'S FIRST GOLD MEDAL

JUMPING SUCCESS ON LAST DAY OF GAMES

From Our Special Correspondent

HELSINKI, Sunday.

Fifteen minutes before the closing ceremony of the XVth Olympic Games here to-day the National Anthem greeted Britain's only victory of the Games. Britain's gold medal was won by three riders and their horses in the team section of the Prix des Nations.

The Duke of Edinburgh watched throughout as Britain's team, Col. H.M.Llewellyn on Foxhunter, Lt-Col. D.N.Stewart on Aherlow, and W.White on Nizefella, gained an exciting triumph.

Moreover, White failed only narrowly to win the individual section. He tied with four other competitors, but failed in a jump-off and was placed fifth.

Foxhunter was Britain's hero. After a bad first round and jumping last of the British team, he gave a magnificent performance in the second to record a faultless round.

40 MEDALS FOR U.S.

The British team won with 40 ¾ faults. Chile were second with 45 ¾ faults and the United States third with 52 ¼. During the Games the United States won 40 gold medals and Russia 22. The United States also came out top on the unofficial points count, scoring 615 to Russia's 555 ½. Britain finished ninth with 117.

(August 4)

G.RICHARDS THROWN

Gordon Richards, the champion jockey, was thrown in front of the stands before the start of the Great Metropolitan Handicap here to-day. He was giving the top weight Approval a preliminary canter.

Approval apparently shied and jinked at a roll of a coconut matting by the side of the course and used to protect it at pedestrian crossings. An ambulance went to get Richards, but he was able to get up and limp into it.

Richards remounted and cantered back to the start. Approval ran well and led round Tattenham Corner, but in the end was beaten by its big weight.

(August 23)

HALIBURTON HAS AMAZING ROUND OF 61

LOWEST EVER IN BRITISH GOLF

From Leonard Crawley

WORTHING, Wednesday.

There is nothing quite like a day on the Downs in mid-summer, and those who came to Worthing to watch the first round of the Spalding golf tournament were rewarded by sunshine and a clear blue sky, a cool breeze, and last but by no means least an outstanding round of 61 by T.B.Haliburton, the 37-year-old Scottish-born Wentworth professional.

His score, an all-time record in British golf, is likely to stand for years to come in spite of the modern ball, equipment and all that venerable old age will say about it. The previous best was 62 last year by Australian Peter Thomson.

HOLED TWO CHIP SHOTS

Haliburton holed two chip shots in the course of his amazing round and required only 23 putts. Here are the details of his round:

First hole (341 yds): A drive, a pitch and two putts, 4; **2nd.** (455): A drive, a five iron through the green, and he holed the chip back from 15 yards for a 3. **3rd.** (190): Four iron, ten yard putt, 2. **4th.** (370); A hooked drive into deep rough, a lost ball for four minutes, a 3 iron to the edge of the green, and two putts, 4. **5th.** (418); Drive, pitch, one putt of four yards, 3. **6th.** (523); Drive, spoon, pitch, putt of two yards,4. **7th.** (161); Sixth iron, two putts, 3. **8th.** (457); Drive, hooked spoon, holed 25-yard chip for a 3. **9th.** (140); Eight iron from the tee, missed 6ft putt for 2; and consequently out for 29.

10th. (363); Drive, short chip, holed the putt for a 3. **11th.** (255); Drive to the edge of the green, chip, one putt, 3. **12th.** (455); Pushed drive, three iron 20 yards short of green, chipped up, holed two-yard putt, 4. **13th.** (400); Drive, pitch, two putts, 4. **14th.** (172); Four iron from tee, two putts, 3. **15th.** (429); Drive, brassie, chip, one putt of two yards, 4. **16th.** (483); Drive, brassie, chip, one putt, 4. **17th.** (394); Drive, pitch-and-run, two putts, 4. **18th.** (370); Drive, pitch, 3-yard putt, 3. - Total 61.

(June 12)

No 8311

ACROSS

1 Seems a bright boy but was dreaded in the main (5,5)
6 A play that many people haven't seen (4)
8 The priest came to get something from a warm-blooded mammal (10)
10 Colourful water (4)
12 Revision of a mite (4)
13 The Duke of Norfolk is head of this College (7)
16 Sounds like a bit quiet (5)
17 Colin's not available 100 times and more but don't reject him in cold weather (5)
18 Part of 14 down (3)
19 Palindromic play (3)
20 The bar kind are worth picking up (5)
21 The last word at the Gare du Nord? (5)
22 Much the same as ampersand C (3)
23 Noticed an axiom (3)
24 Novel sounding letter in the post (5)
25 A horse-laugh from that ass next door? (5)
26 You get to it over the hills and just beyond (7)
30 Love's near relation (4)
32 There's sufficient here to get one back if curtailed (4)
34 His job is to find a dwelling for a small gentle man (5-5)
35 A bodiless voice, perhaps (4)
36 Each summer provided the old-time smoker with one (10)

DOWN

1 Some cheek this! (4)
2 Naturally someone must in every competition (4)
3 Partly tree and partly verandah (5)
4 A bad mark in a University exam. paper (5)
5 One spot in the middle got a move on (5)
6 Some people make a lot of this (4)
7 A set of early history books (10)
9 A boy may dislike being kept in by this, but…(10)
11 …if wise, he will this his master (4,2,4)
13 What a flesher may become (7)
14 A written character that won't help you to a fresh job (5)
15 Raw-boned and raw-hearted (7)
16 A hidden source of ham which people know little about (3,2,1,4)
19 If farmers didn't do it, worse might come of it (5)
27 Where the darkiest employer comes back from? (5)
28 A ground from which to cast yourself down (5)
29 A gambles, B takes part in chaotic teas (5)
31 Reduplicated toy (2-2)
32 A scratch man can't necessarily do it (4)
33 Just fancy! (4)

(July 8)

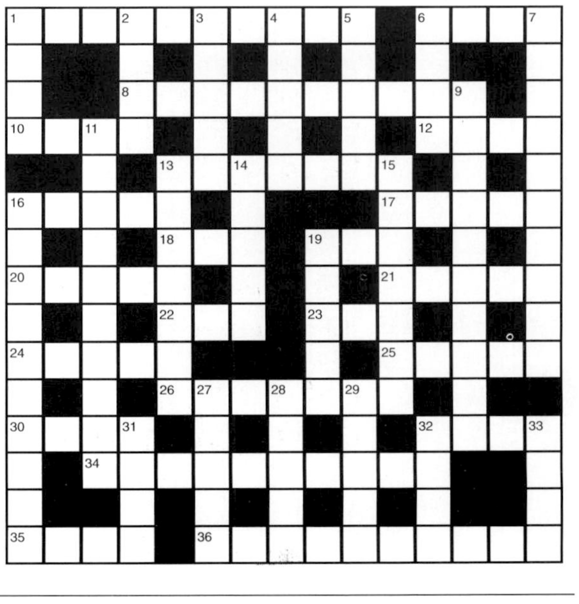

1953

The dawn, they said, of a new Elizabethan Age. On the coldest June day this century, the shivering crowds, who had spent the night sleeping on the pavements in their eagerness to see the young queen ride by on her way to her Coronation, learnt that Everest had been climbed. The auguries were good. The end of rationing was announced. After months of negotiation a truce was signed to end the war in Korea.

The mood of celebration was echoed by the fact that in the sporting field Gordon Richards, so long the champion jockey, at last, at his 28th attempt, rode his first Derby winner on Pinza, though there was disappointment that the Queen's horse Aureole was beaten into second place. At 38, Stanley Matthews, "the Wizard of Dribble", achieved his first FA cup winner medal. And England under the captaincy of Len Hutton, were the victors in the Test series against Australia.

The death of Stalin or to quote *The Daily Telegraph* headline of the time, "Mr. Stalin", foreshadowed the end of his terror campaign, a fact that was underlined by the execution later in the year of his hatchet man, Beria, the Minister of Internal Affairs. The cracks in the united Comminzern front showed when President Tito of Yugoslavia (still called "Jugoslavia") visited London and received a royal welcome. On the other hand, the Committee on Un-American Activities, under the chairmanship of Senator Joseph McCarthy, was gaining in power and operating almost as a rival to President Eisenhower's administration.

Although it was not announced at the time, the Prime Minister, Winston Churchill, suffered a stroke in the autumn. But it was a full year of honour for him. The Queen made him a Knight of the Garter and he was awarded the Nobel Prize for Literature. Dr. Albert Schweitzer was honoured with the Nobel Peace Prize.

The year saw, too the burgeoning of the Television Age. A Gallup Poll showed that nearly half the population within range of TV transmitters watched the Coronation Ceremony at Westminster Abbey grouped round 10 or 14 inch television screens, many specially hired for the occasion. Before the year was out plans for a commercial TV network were announced. The cinema rather desperately responded with gimmicks like 3-D which required the audience to wear special glasses in order to appreciate the sensational effects on the big screen. A further threat to the cinema's long reign was evident when colour television was demonstrated in New York.

The question of capital punishment was much in the news. Early in the year, despite the jury's recommendation of mercy, Derek Bentley was hanged for the murder of a policeman when the gun was fired by his companion in crime and he himself was already in police custody. Later, John Reginald Halliday Christie was hanged for a horrific series of murders where the bodies were concealed in his home in Rillington Place. Controversy was later to arise over the fact that Christie's lodger, Timothy Evans, had already suffered the death penalty for a murder that had possibly been also committed by Christie.

The natural disasters included floods that swept in from the North Sea to submerge part of the English east coast and to breach the dikes in Holland and to put one-sixth of the land area of that country under water. An earthquake struck the Ionian Islands off the west coast of Greece and caused more than a thousand deaths.

The British people were saddened by the death of Queen Mary whose upright figure and elaborate toque hats had so long been a symbol of majesty to the nation.

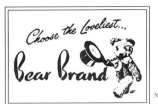

FULL PROGRAMME–16-PAGE SUPPLEMENT

The Daily Telegraph

4 A.M.

and Morning Post

No. 30,547 LONDON, TUESDAY, JUNE 2, 1953

Printed in LONDON and MANCHESTER Price 2d.

THOUSANDS WAIT TO ACCLAIM THE QUEEN

POLICE CLEAR CARS AT 1 a.m.: GATES CLOSED

MANY SLEEP IN COLD ON PROCESSION ROUTE

50,000 IN TRAFALGAR SQUARE AT 4 a.m.: MALL BRAZIER FIRE

TO-DAY'S WEATHER. - Showery but with sunny intervals; during the afternoon, some showers will be heavy, with hail and thunder. Temperatures will not rise to 60 degrees except in a few places.

Today, in Westminster Abbey, in the presence of 23 Princes and Princesses from foreign lands, eight Colonial rulers, 11 Commonwealth Prime Ministers and 8,000 leading citizens of Britain, the Empire and the world, Elizabeth II will be crowned Queen of the United Kingdom of Great Britain and Northern Ireland and of her other Realms and Territories, Head of the Commonwealth, Defender of the Faith.

By midnight, more than 10 hours before she drives from Buckingham Palace with the Duke of Edinburgh for the historic ceremony, hundreds of thousands of her subjects had already "camped out" along the gaily decorated route, waiting to acclaim her. More were arriving every minute to seek vantage points.

The principal times of the Queen's procession are:

10.26 a.m.: Her Majesty leaves Buckingham Palace.
11 a.m.: Arrival at Abbey.
2.50 p.m.: The Queen leaves the abbey.
4.30 p.m.: State Coach reaches Palace.

[Full details of the processions are given in to-day's DAILY TELEGRAPH Coronation Supplement.]

The length of the return procession can be judged from the fact that when the Queen enters her State coach at the Abbey, the first troops will be nearly at Marble Arch.

SLEEPING ON PAVEMENTS

There were unprecedented scenes along the route last night. Pavements in the Mall, in Trafalgar Square and along Whitehall had become crammed with men, women and children of all ages and from all quarters of the world. By midnight almost every inch of space was occupied.

In the cold night, with a temperature of only 45 deg at 1 a.m., many tried to sleep huddled under rugs and raincoats, while others were sitting patiently waiting for the morning. Some used tarpaulins for protection. At one spot in the Mall, wastepaper was lit in a brazier. A constant stream of newcomers trampled around them seeking a vacant place for the night. Trafalgar Square was a surging throng of singing people. More than 50,000 were there at 4 a.m. Half an hour earlier light rain began to fall.

There were cheers as the news spread that Everest had been conquered. There was a solid mass in Whitehall by 10 p.m. and the Mall became impassable even earlier. Pedestrians were forced into the road and traffic halted.

Prince Bernhard of the Netherlands, who is representing Queen Juliana at the Coronation, had to complete his journey on foot down the Mall to York House, St. James's Palace, after his car had been brought to a standstill.

Shortly before 1 a.m. police began diverting motor traffic from the route. Gradually, the masses of people took possession of all available space within the crowd barriers. The big gates across the Strand were closed at 12.35 a.m. The side gates remained open for pedestrians.

50,000 AT PALACE

"Sleeping out" was banned near the Palace, where only a few dozen people strolled by after midnight. But a crowd which numbered 50,000 at times filled the pavements and most of the roadway during the day.

Earlier, those waiting had long-range glimpses of the Duke of Cornwall, who was seen waving from a window on the second floor several times. Queen Elizabeth the Queen Mother and Princess Margaret were given a great reception when they drove to the Palace to attend a luncheon for Commonwealth representatives. It was repeated when they left in the afternoon and again when they returned in the evening. Their car was halted repeatedly by the crowds which broke the police cordon.

Thousands more who had gathered around the Abbey were rewarded in the afternoon when Princess Margaret arrived to see the arrangements inside. Police had difficulty in clearing a way for her car. The Duke of Gloucester, with his sons, Prince William and Prince Richard, also visited the Abbey.

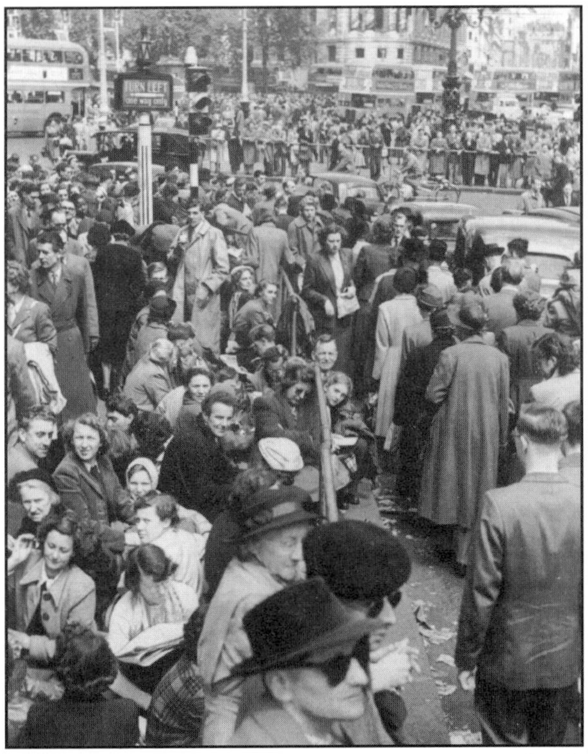

READY AND WAITING. Part of the crowd packing Trafalgar Square, through which the Queen will pass three times tomorrow.

ROUTE CROWDS SHELTER UNDER BLANKETS

LATECOMERS FIND CAMPERS 10 DEEP

Daily Telegraph Reporter

The Coronation Procession route became a vast dormitory last evening. In intermittent rain thousands of spectators prepared to camp out for the night.

Some of the more enterprising rigged up shelters. They tied blankets to bus stop railings on the kerbside. Others tied tarpaulins to trees and decorated them with red, white and blue.

The great invasion, launched at dawn yesterday, made the crowd scenes of the previous days look like "small-scale dress rehearsals." By midnight the pavements all along the route were a solid mass of humanity.

People were camping 10 deep round the whole of Trafalgar Square, where the procession passes three times.

The Daily Telegraph

TO-MORROW

To-morrow THE DAILY TELEGRAPH, *which will be devoted almost entirely to a description of Coronation Day in word and picture, will consist of 12 pages plus a 24 page (half size) free supplement.*

This will be the largest issue of THE DAILY TELEGRAPH *since 1939.*

Thousands milled round the Square and buses could move only at a crawl. High-spirited youths exploded fireworks at the foot of Nelson's Column.

ZERO HOUR PASSED

Though midnight was zero hour for closing the Square traffic was still going through and also through Whitehall at 12.15 this morning. Police began to control Trafalgar Square onlookers at midnight to make room for barriers on the route boundaries. People changed their positions in the hope of being immediately behind the barriers.

More people were sleeping along the pavements in Cockspur Street. Pedestrians had to walk in the road to avoid them. There were queues all down Haymarket and about 50 people were stretched on the pavement under Her Majesty's Theatre.

Thousands flocked down Whitehall, sometimes stumbling over people already seated along the pavements. All the time, from railway stations, buses and taxis, a constant stream of others arrived to seek a vantage point. All traffic in the Mall was stopped at 10 p.m. Vehicles were jammed solid, three deep, the whole length of Whitehall from Parliament Square to Trafalgar Square.

(Continued on P.10, Col 6)

MORE POUR IN BY ROAD, RAIL AND PLANE

TRIPS FROM PARIS

By road, rail and air many thousands of people hurried into London yesterday from all parts of the country and from abroad.

RAIL: By the early hours of to-day nearly 6,000 ordinary relief and special main-line trains had arrived. There were lively scenes as relatives and friends waited for visitors.

Travel to London was easy. But then difficulties began. The influx threw a strain on all available forms of transport. Queues waited for taxis, and those waiting in vain joined the thousands going by Underground. The Tubes carried particularly heavy traffic from the northwest suburbs.

Early to-day four late excursions arrived at Victoria from Paris, Brussels and Dieppe, bringing about 2,500 short-stay Continental visitors, including 800 American Servicemen. Since Whit Monday 35,000 Continental visitors are estimated to have arrived.

70 SOUTHERN SPECIALS

About 70 long-distance special trains running into Southern Region main line stations brought about 35,000 from the South and West Coasts. Traffic from Scotland and the North-East was particularly heavy; 26 additional trains were put on bringing by the early hours 10,000 to 12,000 people, in addition to those travelling by ordinary services.

Many more thousands from the Midlands and North-West came into Euston and St. Pancras in about 30 specials. Another 10,000 travelled in West Country specials.

MALTA PREMIER IN OWN COACH

Dr. Olivier, Prime Minister of Malta, and Mrs. Olivier, will have their own carriage in the Coronation procession of Commonwealth Prime Ministers, it was learned yesterday. Under previous arrangements, they were to ride in the same carriage as Viscount Brookeborough, Prime Minister of Northern Ireland, and Viscountess Brookeborough.

THE QUEEN'S DRESS

Details of one of the best-kept Coronation secrets the Queen's gown that she will wear under her robes, are released this morning.

It is one of the most beautifully jewelled dresses ever made. National emblems of every country in the Commonwealth have been incorporated as jewelled motifs.

A large number of people have worked on the dress and everything that has gone into its making and into the making of the robes, is British.

EVEREST CLIMBED BY BRITISH EXPEDITION

NEW ZEALANDER & SHERPA REACH THE SUMMIT

QUEEN TOLD OF CONQUEST

From Colin Reed
Daily Telegraph Special Correspondent

KHATMANDU, Monday.

Everest has been conquered by the British expedition. The climbers to reach the summit of the 29,002ft peak were E.P. Hillary, the New Zealander, and Tensing, the Sherpa.

The news of the success was conveyed in a message from the leader of the expedition, Col. Hunt. The feat was carried out on Friday.

MESSAGE TO PALACE

U.S. Radio Spreads News

News of the conquest of Everest was communicated to the Queen at Buckingham Palace last night. In America announcers broke into radio and television programmes to give the news.

Messages reaching Khatmandu from the Khumbu Glacier base camp stated that an unsuccessful assault on Everest was made by the expedition on May 25. This attempt should have taken place on May 23, but it was thrown off schedule by the delay in carving a traverse route to the South Col across the face of Lhotse, 27,890ft.

Camp 7 was unfortunately established above the wind/swept South Col above 26,000ft on May 22, these reports said. The first assault group was reported to have set out on May 24 from Camp 6, and it had plans to establish Camp 8 on the final ridge in case it failed to reach the summit the following day.

VICTORY AFTER 32 YEARS

Special Equipment

Planning for this year's attempt on Everest was carried out with scientific thoroughness. In this the expedition had the benefit of the accumulated experience of previous unsuccessful attempts during the last 32 years.

It was recognised that the chief factor in the achievement of success would be the state of the weather. Given a calm interlude between the dying down of winter winds and the onset of the monsoon, Col. Hunt felt that with the great advantage of its latest improved equipment, the expedition was more likely to be successful than any previous party.

For months before the expedition started out every item of the equipment to be used was given close consideration. Special equipment included new lightweight oxygen breathing apparatus for use particularly on the last stages of the long slow climb through rarefied air.

Improved high altitude clothing to defeat cold included nylon smocks and trousers and down suits. Light-weight boots, insulated and rubbersoled, were specially designed by scientists for the final 6,000 feet of the assault on the peak.

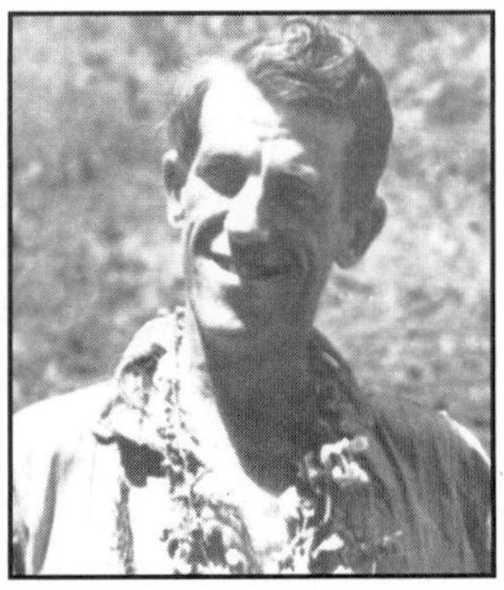

EDMUND HILLARY

SWISS NEAR SUMMIT

The Swiss expedition of last spring narrowly failed to reach the summit on May 28, achieving the record height of about 28,200ft.

This great climb was made by Lambert and Tensing. Without sleeping bags or a stove to melt snow for drinking water, they spent the night of the final climb on the open mountain at 27,500ft.

The second Swiss expedition, in the late summer of last year, made the only attempt that has been made to climb Everest after the monsoon.

CAREFUL TIMING

The Last Struggle

Members of the British Everest Expedition, sponsored jointly by the Royal Geographical Society and the Alpine Club, sailed from Tilbury on February 12, with equipment for their attempt. Col. Hunt left London by air a fortnight later.

May 15 had originally been planned as D-day for the beginning of the final assault on the summit. By careful timing from the base camp, stage by stage up the mountain, the expedition calculated to have the assault party poised within striking distance of the summit at exactly the right moment.

Seven of the team, Ward, Bourdillon, Hillary, Evans, Lowe, Pugh and Gregory, were already experienced in Everest climbing.

(Continued on P. 10, Col. 6)

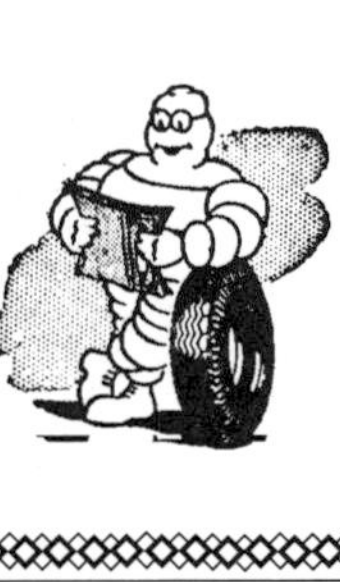

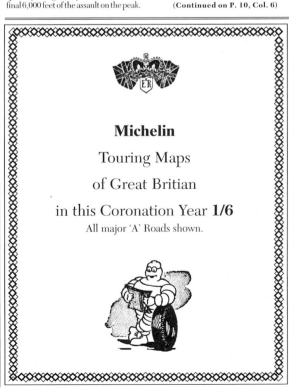

The Daily Telegraph and Morning Post
No. 30,682 LONDON, FRIDAY, NOVEMBER 6, 1953
Printed in LONDON and MANCHESTER Price 2d.
4 A.M.

CHURCHILL MEMOIRS–PAGE 6

ALL RATIONING TO END NEXT YEAR

MEAT TRADE BACK TO PRIVATE ENTERPRISE

FARMERS TO GET NEW PRICE GUARANTEES

MARKETING BOARDS SEEN AS LONG-TERM SOLUTION

By Our Agricultural Correspondent

All food rationing is to end next year. This is made clear in a White Paper published yesterday announcing the Government's plans for marketing farm produce and restoring the meat trade to private enterprise.

Proposals are made for continuing guarantees to farmers under the Agriculture Act, 1947. They include a new method of guaranteeing fatstock prices when meat rationing ends next summer.

Farmers will be free to sell their cattle, sheep and pork pigs to whom they wish and will be given a two-fold guarantee, on individual and collective prices. Bacon pigs will be sold by grade and deadweight.

The plan, it is stated, "does not exclude the possibility of a producers' Marketing Board for meat as a long-term solution." Every facility would be given for the immediate setting up of a board to develop voluntary marketing of fatstock.

Retail prices of meat and bacon, under the new system, will cease to be controlled. No general increase in average prices is expected.

MILK MARKETING

Full Powers for Boards

Other proposals are:

Milk: Full marketing powers can be restored to the Milk Marketing Boards in 1954, subject to safeguards for the Exchequer, the consumer and other interests.

Eggs: The farmers' views have been invited on permanent marketing arrangements.

Potatoes: The Government has put to the farmers proposals for restoring the Potato Marketing Board in time for the 1955 harvest.

Wool: The Wool Marketing Board will continue and will be used to implement the price guarantee.

Sugar Beet: The existing system will continue subject to administrative arrangements when Ministry of Food control ceases.

Discussing meat, the White Paper says the annual turnover is more than £300 million home-produced and more than £200 million imported.

"When control was imposed at the outbreak of war it was clearly understood that the private traders would have their businesses returned when the need for control had passed: and this obligation must be honoured."

TWO-FOLD GUARANTEE

Scheme Explained

The two-fold price guarantee for all fatstock, other than pigs for bacon curing, will work as follows:

After each annual price review for the classes of stock covered the Government will determine guaranteed individual prices according to grade, and standard prices.

If an individual farmer gets less than the guaranteed price for his fat animal on auction the Government will bring what he gets up to that price.

If the price which farmers as a whole have been paid for fatstock over 12 months falls below the standard the difference will be the collective guarantee payment.

The White Paper gives the following example in terms of fat cattle:

Standard price is 130s a cwt: the individual price guarantee, 120s per live cwt: average market realisation price, 125s. Then

(a) If the individual producer sells his beast in the market for 128s a cwt he will get that plus 5s, the difference between the standard price and the average market realisation price, a total of 133s.

(b) If he sells for 123s he will get the 5s difference between the standard and average market price, a total of 128s.

(c) If he sells for 112s he will get 8s to bring this up to the individual guarantee of 120s, plus the 5s difference between standard and average market price, a total of 125s.

MR. BEVAN GOES UP IN SHADOW CABINET LIST

SAME 12 CHOSEN

By Our Political Correspondent

There is no change in the composition of the Parliamentary Committee of the Labour party, the Socialist Shadow Cabinet. The result of the ballot for it was declared yesterday.

Mr. Bevan has improved his position to ninth in the list of the 12 elected, as compared with twelfth last year. The most notable advance has been that of Sir Frank Soskice, the former Attorney-General. Last year he was elected on the second ballot. this year he is third in the list.

The second ballot device was introduced last year to prevent "plumping" for Bevanite candidates. It altered the relative positions of the second six elected, but had no effect on the final composition of the Parliamentary Committee. The first ballot secured the same result.

The question of voting procedure was raised at a party meeting later. It was decided that a single ballot should in future be used.

The following is the full list, with the votes obtained this year. Last year's vote on the first ballot is given in brackets:

Mr. GRIFFITHS, 180 (194): Mr. GAITSKELL, 176 (179): Sir F. SOSKICE, 168 (111): Mr. CALLAGHAN, 160 (137): Mr. DALTON, 159 (140): Mr. EDE, 134 (189): Mr. ROBENS, 133 (148): Dr. SUMMERSKILL, 129 (130): Mr. BEVAN, 126 (108): Mr. NOEL-BAKER, 118 (121): Mr. SHINWELL, 108 (124): Mr. GLENVIL HALL, 106 (113).

MR. EDE LOSES VOTES

Mr. Ede has dropped a substantial number of votes and Mr. Robens has lost some ground. Mr. Callaghan has improved his position to fourth from sixth. Mr. Griffiths has lost some votes, although he still heads the list, while Mr. Gaitskell has gone up one place owing to the displacement of Mr. Ede.

The full Shadow Cabinet will now consist of the above 12 together with Mr. Attlee, Leader: Mr. Morrison, Deputy Leader: Mr. Whiteley, Chief Whip: Earl Jowitt, Leader of the Socialist peers: Lord Shepherd, Chief Whip of the Socialist peers: and Lord Henderson, elected representative of the Socialist peers.

SIR D. MAXWELL FYFE

Sir David Maxwell Fyfe, Home Secretary, was last night adopted as prospective Conservative candidate for Epsom, where Mr. McCorquodale, the sitting member, is not seeking re-election. Sir David announced in August that he would not recontest the West Derby division of Liverpool. Ministerial duties made frequent visits to Liverpool difficult.

STILL READY FOR TALKS SAYS MR. EDEN

'ANY TIME, WITHOUT CONDITIONS'

By Our Own Representative

WESTMINSTER, Thursday.

General cheers greeted a declaration by Mr. Eden in the House of Commons to-day that despite the latest Russian Note, Britain was prepared to discuss Germany and Austria with her "at any time, at any place and without any conditions."

He ended a wide survey of the international scene by saying: "If others choose to slam their doors, to barricade them, ours remain open.

"Talks at any level remain our objective. Our work is a work for peace, which we shall not abandon."

But he had been concerned on the multiplicity of problems. It was hard to find any sign that fundamental Russian hostility had been modified.

GERMANY ALTERNATIVE

Speaking of the European Defence community he reiterated that our partnership would be as close as anything we could devise short of actual membership.

The alternative to bringing Germany into discussions on European defence was to see Germany as a vacuum at the centre of Europe with a national army, perhaps giving herself to the highest bidder. Mr. Eden made these other points:

Egypt - Negotiations are in a state of suspended animation. A satisfactory agreement is still possible. We are content to wait.

Sudan - We are not satisfied with the way the Egyptian Government has carried out the agreement that the election should be conducted in a free and neutral atmosphere. There have been persistent efforts to arouse anti-British prejudice.

Israel-Jordan - The Government is deeply concerned. The United Nations truce supervisory organisation must be strengthened and the problem of Arab refugees solved.

U.S. "IMPEDIMENT"

From the Opposition Front Bench Mr. McNeil criticised the allied approach to a meeting with Russia as conditional and qualified. He suspected the first impediment was in Washington, not in Moscow.

Disquiet about the Anglo-Egyptian negotiations was expressed by Mr. Powell (C. Wolverhampton S.W.). Referring to reports that complete evacuation of the Canal Zone by British forces was being discussed he said gravely that he could not support or assent to such a fatal step.

There was an angry outcry of agreement and dissent when he suggested that a factor in this matter was the attitude of the United States.

Mr. Nutting, Under-Secretary for Foreign Affairs, said the imputation against the Americans was quite untrue. They were in full agreement with us on Egypt and other problems in the area.

Report of debate - P11

TALK ON REPLY TO RUSSIA

By Our Diplomatic Correspondent

British, French and American officials are expected to discuss shortly in Paris whether a reply is to be sent to the Russian Note.

The longer-term aspects of Western policy will be discussed by Mr. Eden, Mr. Dulles, American Secretary of State, and M. Bidault, French Foreign Minister, when they are in Paris next month for the meeting of the North Atlantic Council.

Mr. Eden said in his Commons speech yesterday that five of seven questions affecting Anglo-Soviet relations, which had been outstanding for years, had been resolved since April. The five matters were:

1.- Settlement in the case of a Soviet ship which fouled a buoy in the Tyne.
2.- Mrs. Hall, the Russian wife of a British subject, was allowed to leave Russia to rejoin her husband.
3.- Mr. George Bundock, who had had to remain inside the British Embassy, where he was employed, to avoid arrest, was allowed to leave the country.
4.- Certain areas were reopened to travel by foreigners already in Russia.
5.- Anglo-Russian fishing agreement extension.

The two unresolved matters are not disclosed.

ROYAL CORGI ON NEW SEAL.

The obverse side of the new seal for the County Palatine of Lancaster, which, with another seal for the Duchy of Lancaster, has been completed by the Royal Mint. It shows the Queen in uniform, mounted on the police horse Winston, with one of her Corgis running beside the horse's foreleg.

The designer, Mr. E Carter Preston, of Liverpool, said last evening that he had taken some liberties in his design. For instance, although the Queen is dressed as for Trooping the Colour, she carries the sceptre in her right hand. The background is composed of rose bushes, and the Lancastrian badge, a rose surmounted by a crown, is shown.

On the new Duchy of Lancaster seal, the Queen is seated in the Chair of Accession in the House of Lords, and the Coronation robes are shown in a classic, stylised form.

ENGINEERS' 15 p.c. WAGES CLAIM REJECTED

MARCH BROKEN UP BY POLICE

By Hugh Chevins
Daily Telegraph Industrial Correspondent

Engineering employers yesterday firmly refused to bow to intimidatory strikes and mass demonstrations and rejected the unions' claim for a 15 per cent wages increase for more than 2,500,000 workers in Britain's key export industry.

Although the intimidation was unofficial and Communist-led, the Confederation of Shipbuilding and Engineering Unions, when presented the demand, made no apparent attempt to disown it.

For more than two hours before the meeting between representatives of the Engineering and Allied Employers' National Federation and the leaders of 39 unions affiliated to the confederation, crowds of workers who had staged short strikes streamed along Tothill Street, Westminster.

COMMUNISTS WATCHING

Carrying banners and chanting "We want 15 per cent," they included men from London, the Clyde and other centres in the North. Watching from a distance were well-known Communist figures.

When the milling crowds grew to about 3,000, mounted and foot police began to clear the street. It is well within the area where demonstrations are forbidden when Parliament is sitting.

The police acted with patience and good humour, amid some resistance, taunts and the flinging of fireworks. One arrest was made for obstruction.

POLICE GUARD DOORWAY

Eight policemen stood guard at the doorway to the employers' headquarters and allowed only the negotiators to enter. Some of the union leaders commented angrily on the demonstration. One said: "The employers are fully entitled to break off all negotiations in view of this row."

Standing alone, opposite the spot where the police and the crowd jostled, was Mr. C Berridge, Communist North London organiser of the amalgamated Engineering Union, and secretary of the London district of the confederation. This unit of the confederation, without authority, called the London strike and the demonstration.

LADY ABERGAVENNY

The Marchioness of Abergavenny died at her home, Eridge Castle, Tunbridge Wells, Kent, yesterday.

BUS COMPANIES SEEK 7S 6d A WEEK PAY CUT

By An Industrial Correspondent

Representatives of the privately-operated bus companies in the provinces and of the Transport and General Workers' Union last night discussed the wages of 90,000 bus workers. The union leaders claimed a substantial increase.

The employers sought a 7s 6d a week reduction because of the proposal to reduce the permitted number of standing passengers from eight to five. The employers' demand will go before the industry's conciliation committee. The union's application will probably go to arbitration.

The union applied for higher wages on the grounds of higher living costs in July. Negotiations were in progress when the employers learned that the union had approached the Ministry of Transport for a revision of the Order of 1949, laying down the maximum number of standing passengers to be carried. Then the employers made a counter-claim for a pay cut.

They said that to reduce the number of standing passengers would seriously effect many companies' financial positions. Representatives of the municipal transport undertakings will meet the union on Thursday to discuss the proposal on standing passengers.

TOSCANINI ILL

From Our Own Correspondent

NEW YORK, Thursday.

Toscanini, 86, the conductor, is suffering from "a light attack of flu" it was announced to-day. He will be unable to make his first scheduled appearance as conductor of the National Broadcasting Company symphony orchestra on Sunday. His place will be taken by Pierre Monteux.

PUBLIC INQUIRY INTO GATWICK AIRPORT PLAN

Daily Telegraph Reporter

A full inquiry into the proposed extension of Gatwick Airport as an alternative landing ground to London Airport is to be held, probably in February. This was announced by Mr. Lennox-Boyd, Minister of Transport and Civil Aviation, at a Gatwick meeting last night.

He attended the meeting, which was spirited and sometimes rowdy, in response to requests by a local protest committee. He explained the proposals and answered critics in the audience of 500.

As well as representatives of local councils and organisations, Sir Miles Thomas, chairman of British Overseas Airways Corporation, and Mr. Peter Masefield, chief executive of British European Airways Corporation, were present. Sir Gordon Touche, Conservative M.P. for Dorking, presided.

The terms of reference for the inquiry, given by Mr. Lennox-Boyd, state that the objections to be heard meant objections relating to the suitability of the site, or to the effect of the proposed developments on local interests.

OBJECTORS' LIMITS

The inquiry would be open to objectors to suggest detailed modifications of the scheme as now proposed. It would not be open to question the need to provide a major airport to serve as an alternative to London Airport or to make proposals as to how that need should be met.

Mr. Lennox-Boyd said this would enable objectors to claim such points as Gatwick being fogbound, that drainage problems are insoluble, and that Gatwick is a "crowded industrial area or unspoilt rural area or both."

He said that the figure of £20 million which had been suggested as the cost of the scheme was "quite ludicrous." The cost of stage one would be £6 million.

ATOM TEST BY U.S. IN SPRING

H-BOMB MAY BE USED

From Our Own Correspondent

WASHINGTON, Thursday.

New American atomic tests, it was unofficially reported to-day, will take place next spring at Eniwetok or Bikini, the proving grounds in the Pacific. It is expected that they will further the development of the authentic hydrogen bomb.

The Eniwetok tests in 1951 proved that the ordinary atom or fission bomb could hold a high temperature long enough to fuse hydrogen or its compounds.

Last year the tests were believed to have included a small amount of tritium. It was demonstrated that this had fused and so increased to explosive force. But this experiment was conducted with a "device," not an actual bomb.

Next spring's test may be of an actual deliverable bomb composed of the ordinary atom bomb "trigger" surrounded by an appreciable quantity of tritium.

ELIZABETH II IS CROWNED

WITH THE SPLENDOUR AND SOLEMNITY OF AN HISTORIC RITUAL INSIDE WESTMINSTER ABBEY, WITH TRADITIONAL POMP AND COLOUR AND PAGEANTRY ALONG THE ROYAL ROUTE OUTSIDE, ELIZABETH II WAS YESTERDAY CROWNED QUEEN AMID THE AFFECTIONATE ACCLAIM OF MILLIONS OF HER PEOPLE IN THIS COUNTRY AND THROUGHOUT HER GREAT COMMONWEALTH OF NATIONS.

The assembly of nearly 8,000 in the Abbey, Princes and premiers, peers and commoners, heard her in a clear, sweet voice take the Coronation Oath which binds her to the service of her peoples and to the maintenance of the laws of God; saw her, clad in a robe of gold, receive from the Archbishop of Canterbury, Dr. Fisher, the Crown of St. Edward: and joined in the heartfelt cry, oft-repeated, of "God Save the Queen." For the first time, through the agency of television, millions of people in their homes were spectators of the impressive rites.

The Duke of Edinburgh, first after the Archbishop to kneel and place his hands between those of her Majesty in the act of homage, was at her side during the Communion.

At the end of the long ceremony the Queen, invested with a robe of purple velvet, wearing the Imperial State Crown, and carrying the Orb and Sceptre, drove in a 2 ½ -mile-long cavalcade back to Buckingham Palace. The streets were lined by nearly three million people, many thousands of whom had waited all night in rain and cold. The coolness of the showery weather seemed to emphasise the warmth of their welcome as roar after roar of thunderous applause surged round the Royal coach.

With the bells of London pealing joyously and the vast multitude cheering itself hoarse, the radiant Queen neared the Palace. Here there was one of the greatest demonstrations of popular enthusiasm ever witnessed in the capital.

It was repeated and increased when at 5.42 p.m. her Majesty came out on the balcony to acknowledge the tumultuous loyalty of the crowd - the first of six appearances during the evening. With her were the Duke of Edinburgh, the Duke of Cornwall, Princess Anne, Queen Elizabeth the Queen Mother and Princess Margaret.

The rain had stopped and the sun was struggling through the clouds as three minutes later jet fighters of the R.A.F. flew over to salute the newly crowned Sovereign.

In a moving and intimate broadcast last evening to the Commonwealth, the Queen pledged herself again to the service of her peoples "as so many of you are pledged to mine. Throughout all my life and with all my heart I shall strive to be worthy of your trust."

(June 3)

THE STATE PROCESSION down the nave of the Abbey after the Coronation ceremony. The crowned Sovereign, carrying the Orb and Sceptre, is escorted by (left) the Bishop of Durham, Rt. Rev. H. W. Bradfield. Her Majesty's train is borne by (left: front to back) Lady Mary Baillie-Hamilton, Lady Jane Heathcote-Drummond Willoughby, Lady Rosemary Spencer-Churchill, and (right) Lady Jane Vane-Tempest Stewart, Lady Anne Coke and Lady Moyra Hamilton. Behind them is the Mistress of the Robes, the Duchess Dowager of Devonshire. She is followed by the Groom of the Robes and the Ladies and Women of the Bedchamber.

MR. CHURCHILL MADE A K.G.

Daily Telegraph Reporter

The Queen at Windsor Castle last evening made the Prime Minister a Knight of the Garter and invested him with the insignia of the Order.

Sir Winston Churchill, who was accompanied by Lady Churchill, dined with the Queen and stayed the night at the Castle. This morning they go to Chequers for the week-end.

The ceremony took place in the Green Drawing Room. There the 78-year-old Prime Minister knelt before the young Queen who, taking a sword, touched him first on the right shoulder and then on the left. The Duke of Edinburgh and Princess Margaret were present.

At that moment Mr. Churchill became Sir Winston and his full formal title "The Right Honourable Sir Winston Churchill, K.G., O.M., C.H., M.P." Her Majesty then handed him the insignia.

The Prime Minister is the sixth commoner to receive the honour this century. The others were Sir Edward Grey, Mr. Balfour, Mr. Asquith, Sir Austen Chamberlain and Mr. Baldwin. All except Sir Austen were elevated to the Peerage.

The late King George VI offered Sir Winston this distinction in July, 1945, but he asked leave to decline.

At that time the Order was a political award conferred on the recommendation of the Prime Minister of the day. This was changed the following year.

On Dec 4, 1946, it was announced that the Garter, like the Order of Merit, would be within the sole prerogative of the Sovereign. This removed it entirely from the sphere of politics.

The founder of the Churchill family was Sir Winston Churchill (1620-1688) who was knighted by Charles II in 1663. He was father of John Churchill, first Duke of Marlborough, victor of Blenheim.

(April 25)

QUEEN DENIES BALMORAL SALE REPORTS

From Our Special Correspondent

BALLATER, Wednesday.

Reports that the Queen was considering selling Balmoral Castle were quashed to-day, on her authority. The Marquess of Aberdeen made public her denial at the rail terminus here, after welcoming the Royal family for their annual holiday at Balmoral.

He expressed concern at the reports and asked the Queen if she could deny that she intended disposing of the castle. "Most certainly," she replied.

"The Queen's assurance is good news for Deeside and for Scotland," Lord Aberdeen said to me. "The Royal family get great relaxation at Balmoral, and I hope that everybody will co-operate in ensuring that there is no intrusion on their privacy this year."

WELCOME FROM 3,000

About 3,000 people welcomed the Queen, who was accompanied by the Duke of Cornwall and Princess Anne.

(August 6)

QUEEN NAMES ROYAL YACHT BRITANNIA

SHIP 'A NECESSITY': TRIBUTE TO THE LATE KING

From Our Own Correspondent

CLYDEBANK, Thursday.

The 4,000-ton Royal yacht, being built at John Brown's Yard, Clydebank, was launched here to-day by the Queen, who named the ship Britannia, during the first visit of her reign to Clydeside. A bottle of Empire wine was used in the naming ceremony.

After the launching the Queen, who was accompanied by the Duke of Edinburgh, boarded the new P. and O. liner Arcadia to watch the yacht being manoeuvred into its fitting-out basin. The Arcadia is due to be launched in four weeks.

The Queen and the Duke were taken by lift to the top deck of the Arcadia. With Sir William Currie, chairman of the P. and O. Company as guide, they watched the tugs gently nosing the handsome new yacht out of the main stream into the basin.

"SEA NO BARRIER"

Presentation of Glasses

Speaking afterwards in the model room of the yard the Queen told Lord Aberconway, chairman of John Brown's, that she felt, as did the late king, her father, that the building of a yacht was a necessity and not a luxury for the Head of our great British Commonwealth.

Between the countries of the Commonwealth the sea was no barrier, but the natural and indestructible byway. She was speaking in reply to a presentation to her by Lord Aberconway, on behalf of the builders, of a set of old glasses.

The glasses had been engraved by Mr. Laurence Whistler, a brother of the late Mr. Rex Whistler. The Queen said she was sure that all present would realise how much the building of the Britannia had meant to the late King.

With the wise advice of the Admiralty and that of the builders, he laid the plans for the vessel which should wear the Royal Standard in days of peace and which in the event of war should serve the cause of humanity as a hospital ship.

(April 17)

FINAL PLAN FOR AFRICAN FEDERATION

By A Diplomatic Correspondent

Details of the final plan for federation of Southern Rhodesia, Northern Rhodesia, and Nyasaland, were published yesterday in two White Papers.

In its final shape the scheme is the result of the work of last month's London conference of representatives of the British Government and the governments of the three territories. Their task was to consider amendments and agree to revision of a scheme outlined in a White Paper in June.

One of the new provisions is that, to give the Federal State time to establish itself, there should be no change in the division of powers for 10 years without the consent of all three territorial Legislatures.

The white Paper report of the conference states that the African Affairs Board would have the same powers as under the original scheme to refer to the British Government legislation discriminating against Africans. But it was now brought within the framework of the Federal Parliament instead of being a body outside it.

AFRICANS' SHARE

"Marked Improvement"

It would have two members from each territory, one European and one African, drawn from those members of the Federal Legislature who had been specially elected or appointed to represent African interests. The Board would take its place in the constitution as a Standing Committee of the Legislature.

Adoption of the scheme, described as "sound and fair," is urged in the interests "of all the inhabitants". Its acceptance now depends on the result of a referendum in Southern Rhodesia, and debates in the Legislatures of Northern Rhodesia and Nyasaland and in Parliament.

(February 6)

EVEREST CLIMBED BY BRITISH EXPEDITION

THYANGBOCHE, NEPAL, June 5 (delayed).

Col. Hunt, leader of the Everest team [on whom the Queen has bestowed a Knighthood], said to-day of the successful climb, "Hillary and Tensing made the summit with a safe margin of time, oxygen and effort."

It was a full day before he got the news. "Sleeping bags laid on the snow were to be the success signal. But after a fine day mist obscured the higher camps. It was not until the following afternoon that the assault party and support group came down the face of Lhotse and we got the tremendous news that they had reached the top. We can hardly yet believe it is true."

British members of the expedition did Sherpa porters' work and carried 50lb and 60lb loads to Camp 9 at 27,900ft "the highest ever placed. The Sherpa Ang Nima went to this height and Da Namgyl to 27,350ft. Several of the team spent three nights on the Col, and George Lowe four nights."

ACCLIMATISATION

"Tremendous Dividends"

Col. Hunt gave this history of the expedition: "We started with two big periods of acclimatisation, which paid tremendous dividends.

"At the beginning of May I myself and Charles Evans, Tom Bourdillon, Charles Wylie and Michael Ward made a reconnaissance of the Lhotse face to decide on our plan and to test the oxygen equipment. The plan was for two assaults: the first with closed-circuit oxygen equipment to give it an opportunity of proving itself. The second was with the usual open-circuit type.

"The first assault was also a reconnaissance for the second. I selected Evans and Bourdillon for the first, while for the second Hillary and Tensing stood far above everyone in fitness.

Each party had a support group: myself and two Sherpas for the first and Alfred Gregory and three Sherpas for the second. Their job was to be at the South Col and to aid the men making the assault. Ingredients for the camp on the south-east ridge were to be carried by support groups.

"On May 25 the first big party of Sherpas started for Camp 7. On the way the 'coolies' would not go further, and Wilfred Noyce went on alone with one Sherpa. We could see this from the West Cwm. I decided the build-up must go on and sent Hillary and Tensing up to boost the Sherpas. It worked. We saw the whole party move to the South Col with food, tents, fuel and equipment.

"The weather was good, and the first assault party went to Camp 5 on May 22 and moved to the South Col in the evening. This assault was delayed 24 hours because of a bad wind and tiredness after the heavy climb. The second assault party was 48 hours behind.

"On May 26 the first assault went up. Evans and Bourdillon had instructions to go for the south peak and, if the oxygen was working well and the route good, to make for the top. With the Sherpa Da Nagyl I carried loads to 27,350ft and left a dump for the second support group. As the first assault group came down the second party went up to the Col.

"On May 27 the night was all hell let loose. There is no place on earth so inhospitable as the South Col, and the second party, too, was delayed 24 hours.

"On the 28th the morning was lovely. Hillary, Tensing and the support group went up. One Sherpa, Ang Nima, went to the south-east ridge at 27,900ft. The party carried the rest of the equipment and picked up what I had left at the dump.

THEY "MADE IT"

Hillary and Tensing

"On the 29th Hillary and Tensing went for the summit and made it. This was tremendously exciting. It had been a big effort.

"We had had a steady build-up and because of acclimatisation and diet the expedition enjoyed remarkable health."

(June 5)

CHRISTIE SENTENCED TO DEATH

INSANITY PLEA FAILS

JURY'S VERDICT AFTER 1 ½ HOURS

Daily Telegraph Reporter

JOHN REGINALD HALLIDAY CHRISTIE, 55, the £8 a week clerk who is the self-confessed murderer of at least seven women, was sentenced to death at the Old Bailey last night. He had been found guilty of the murder of his wife, Ethel, 54, at their home in 10, Rillington Place, Notting Hill.

It took the jury 84 minutes to reach their verdict. They found that Christie was sane when he strangled his wife and buried her under the floor-boards in the front room.

Throughout the day counsel had made their final speeches. The Judge, Mr. JUSTICE FINNEMORE, had spent 2 hours 34 minutes summing up the evidence. He had described the case as "a horrible one and a horrifying one."

"I do not know whether any jury before in this country or perhaps in the world," he said, "has seen and heard a man charged with murder go into the witness box and say to the jury: 'Yes, I did kill this victim. I killed six others as well over a period of 10 years.'"

JURY RETIRES

The Attorney-General, Sir LIONEL HEALD, had likened the jury to "travellers in some strange country." They might almost wonder whether the whole thing was not a dream.

The jury of nine men and three women filed out of court to consider what they had heard in the past four days. It was 4.30 p.m. Judge and counsel left the court. Christie was led out of the dock.

For an hour and 24 minutes there was talk and gossip in the corridors, and then the news that the jury was returning. Slowly they filed back into the box and sat down. It was 5.27 p.m.

SMILE AND BOW

Christie re-entered the dock. He smiled wanly at the Judge and bowed slightly. His hands trembled as he gripped the dock rail.

He watched and waited, as did the hushed and stilled court. The foreman said just one word. "Guilty." There was no addition of the two words "but insane" which would have saved his life.

Christie licked his lips. "Have you anything to say why sentence of death should not be passed?" he was asked. A vigorous shake of the head as his mouth formed an inaudible "No."

At 5.30 Mr. Justice Finnemore began to pronounce sentence. As he did so all eyes were on the dock. There the balding, bespectacled Christie shifted his weight from one foot to another.

He looked up at the wall above the judge: he looked up at the ceiling: he closed his eyes. At the end of the sentence two warders gripped him firmly and hustled him away to the cells and later to Pentonville.

Evans Case Review Sought

Relatives of Timothy John Evans, 25, who was hanged in 1950 for the murder of his baby daughter Geraldine, 14 months, at 10, Rillington Place, have written to Sir David Maxwell Fyfe, Home Secretary, asking him to review the case. At the trial Evans blamed Christie for the death of his wife, Mrs. Evans. After his arrest Christie stated that he had strangled Mrs. Evans.

(June 26)

SCHOOL MEAL PRICE UP

2d MORE IN MARCH

Daily Telegraph Reporter

The charge to parents for school meals will be increased from 7d to 9d, from March 1. Announcing this in the House of Commons yesterday, Miss Horsbrugh, Minister of Education, said that the present cost per meal was 1s 5½d.

The cost would have been 1s 6½d but arrangements had been made for economies in overhead charges. A similar increase in Scotland was announced by Mr. Stuart, Secretary for Scotland.

(June 23)

TWICE COMMENDED FOR HIS POLICE WORK

NEW CHECK ON MISSING WOMEN

Daily Telegraph Reporter

He was a meek and mild little man, this John Christie, a man who, in his own words never wanted to hurt anyone. He had been happily married for 24 years. The one question is: "Why did he kill seven women, some of whom he had scarcely known?"

The solution will never be known. No one, counsel for the defence, counsel for the prosecution or psychiatrists could supply the true answer, an answer, as the Judge said, "maybe locked-up in his own heart."

Christie admired pretty girls, but his physical disability, slight build and almost apologetic demeanour did not attract them. Yet he was vain, taking pride in his appearance and collecting scores of snapshots of himself.

Was his method of gassing his victims before assaulting and strangling them a psychological way of gaining the power he desired over women? After his confession that he did not know how many women he had killed, police are checking lists of missing women in the cities where he had lived.

TWISTED MENTALITY

They believe that somewhere in these cities lies the solution to the problem that the court hearing did not answer. What twisted the mind of Christie to such an extent that he changed from the well-brought-up son of a respectable family to a sex murderer?

The twisted mentality of the man is illustrated by his love for a kitten. He found the animal in pain and called a veterinary surgeon. The man who had already strangled three women and buried two of the bodies in his garden left the room sobbing because he could not bear to see the kitten receive an injection.

A few months later he had murdered his wife. The polite little man who raised his hat to neighbours and smiled as he passed the time of day will be remembered as the British "Bluebeard."

The home-made "death-mask" with which Christie gassed his victims after he had lured them to his flat and talked about his knowledge gained with the St. John Ambulance Brigade and while a policeman, has been reconstructed in Scotland Yard's Black Museum.

LETTERS LOST

But for the complaints of neighbours, his murders might not have been discovered even yet. they complained of the bad smells. He used disinfectant, but the nuisance persisted. Then he heard that a complaint was going to be made to the local authorities, so he prepared to run away.

He sold his furniture in such a hurry that the dealer who bought it found the drawers full of photographs and papers. Among them were his police notebooks and diaries covering several years.

In these may well have been recorded the real number of his victims, but they were all destroyed by the dealer when he could not trace Christie.

Christie's life started in a comfortable semi-detached house in Chester Road, Boothtown, Halifax, where he was born on April 8 1899, one of seven children of Mr. and Mrs. Ernest John Christie.

"RATHER SHY"

His father was the first superintendent of the local St. John Ambulance Brigade. He was founder of both the Conservative Association and Primrose League branches and was associated with the Boy Scouts' Association.

At a local school, where he was classed as above average intelligence, Christie had many friends. He joined the Wolf Cubs and eventually became a King's Scout. At 14 he joined the St. John Ambulance Brigade. The study of anatomy interested him so much that he wanted to be a doctor.

He left school and took several jobs, some of them clerical. Then came his war service. The partial dumbness and loss of sight he suffered resulted from wounds at Ypres and gassing at the battle of the River Yser.

NATURE CHANGING

The man's nature was changing. He went home to Halifax after his discharge with a good war record and took a job as a clerk.

The following year was eventful. His father found him a clerical post in a wool factory. While training as a shorthand-typist at evening classes he met Ethel Simpson.

Both were ambitious and they met often to help each other with their studies. They fell in love and were married at Halifax Register Office.

Christie became a temporary postman in 1921, while living in rooms in Brunswick Street. During the year he was commended for efficiency on his round in the Northowram district. But people began complaining that letters they were expecting had not been delivered.

TERMS IN PRISON

Changes of Employment

G.P.O. investigators found that the "efficient" postman had been opening letters and destroying them after extracting postal orders. Christie was convicted at Halifax on two charges and sent to prison for three months.

When he came out of Armley Prison, Leeds, he got a job as a clerk. His wife tried to help him but in 1923 he was again in trouble and was put on probation for attempted false pretences.

He drifted to London, found employment as a clerk but within a year he was imprisoned again for stealing money and goods while living in Uxbridge. He thought he had learned his lesson and for five years he worked hard as a clerk in transport firms, an attendant in cinemas and attended St. John Ambulance lectures in his spare time.

ATTACK ON LANDLADY

Then he had trouble about rent with his landlady at Uxbridge and struck her on the head with a cricket bat. He was sentenced to six months' imprisonment for malicious wounding.

When he left prison a Roman Catholic priest offered him a job as handyman-chauffeur. He offered Christie's wife a job as cook-housekeeper so that they could be together. Mrs. Christie joined her husband in London.

The priest was called abroad and Christie went with him while his wife remained in London. When Christie returned he repaid his benefactor by stealing his car. He was sentenced to three months' imprisonment.

They were dismissed from their employment and found lodgings in the flat at 10, Rillington Place, paying 10s a week rent. Christie worked in a cinema and his wife found a part-time job.

To neighbours the couple seemed ideally happy. On a long holiday they visited resorts as far apart as Blackpool and Brighton and stayed with Mrs. Christie's aunt, Mrs. Legge, in Sheffield.

They returned to London, where Christie got another clerical job until he joined the Police War Reserve when the 1939-45 war started. He served satisfactorily until December 1943, when he was released to take up work in essential industry.

For a while he was an aide to the C.I.D. and worked with senior detectives, learning much about criminals and their haunts. His two commendations were for "efficient detection of crime."

He started spending hours alone and then the "polite, little man" the neighbours knew became moody and morose.

EVANS MURDERS

The Evans murders had been discovered. Although he had considerable experience as a policeman, Christie was upset at being called as the Crown's chief witness. Residents in Rillington Place found it difficult to understand.

At the trial of Timothy Evans, the defence counsel, cross-examining Christie, brought out his record of five offences. The neighbours thought that it was the answer to his obvious distress.

NEW LEASE OF LIFE

With the Evans trial over Christie and his wife went to Sheffield and stayed with Mrs. Legge. After about three weeks he seemed suddenly to take on a new lease of life. Evans's appeal had been dismissed. Christie began to take an interest in the garden.

With his wife he returned to Rillington Place, where two of his victims were at that time buried in the garden. Then his health started to fail. He became a clerk at a British Road Services depot.

He left and drew unemployment pay. Then a few months later in December, 1952, his wife disappeared. To hide her death he started weaving the fabric of lies and deceptions which was so devastatingly used against him by the Attorney-General.

(June 24)

J.R.H. CHRISTIE, who was sentenced to death at the Old Bailey for the murder of his wife Ethel last December.

GAOL CLASH AS BENTLEY DIES

EXECUTION NOTICE BOARD DAMAGED

Daily Telegraph Reporter

Police and demonstrators clashed and two men were arrested when Derek Bentley, 19 ½ was executed at Wandsworth Prison yesterday. He died for his part, with Christopher Craig, in the murder of P.c. Sidney Miles at Croydon on Nov. 2.

There were angry scenes when the execution notices were hung outside the prison gates. A crowd of more than 500 people shouted and booed.

Coins, apple cores and other missiles were flung at the prison officer who posted the notices and at the police. Repeated efforts were made to tear down the notices. The glass of the black-framed board in which they were pinned was smashed. Extra police were brought up.

INQUEST JURY WARNED

At an inquest at the prison a verdict of death by judicial hanging was returned. The deputy coroner for Battersea, Mr. C.W. Robertson, said to the jury: "You are in no way involved in the controversy which rages in this case."

Bentley's home in Fairview Road, Norbury, was quiet after the recent activity there. The only caller was a postman with another 200 letters.

At 8.40 a.m., 20 minutes before Bentley was due to die, Mrs. Van Der Elst, the campaigner against capital punishment, arrived at the prison.

"AN INNOCENT MAN"

Mrs. Van Der Elst hammered on the gate with its massive iron knocker. "I must see the governor," she shouted. There were cries of "Freedom," "They are hanging an innocent man," and "Let her talk."

At 9 a.m. by the prison clock the crowd, which had grown to more than 500, stood silently. Men removed their hats. Mrs. Van Der Elst led the singing of "Abide with me" and the 23rd Psalm, "The Lord is my Shepherd."

(January 29)

CRASH HELMET PLEA FAILS

By Our Own Representative

WESTMINSTER, Wednesday.

The Earl of Birkenhead, Lord-in-Waiting, in the House of Lords this evening warned motor-cyclists that every time they went on the road they courted death more often than any other road user. He begged them, in their own interests, to wear crash helmets.

Nevertheless he declared against making their use compulsory. Speaking for the Government, he said that, in the opinion of the police, such a law would be quite unenforceable.

"If we can secure a really good-looking and safe crash helmet and secure the co-operation of the motor-cycle clubs, we could get a large proportion of motor-cyclists to wear them without compulsion."

(January 29)

CHAPLIN UNABLE TO WORK IN U.S.

Daily Telegraph Reporter

Charlie Chaplin arrived in London from Geneva last night. He issued this statement on why he would never return to the United States: "It is not easy to uproot myself and my family from a country where I have lived for 40 years without a feeling of sadness.

"But since the end of the last world war I have been the object of lies and vicious propaganda by powerful reactionary groups who, by their influence and by aid of America's yellow Press, have created an unhealthy atmosphere in which liberal-minded individuals can be singled out and persecuted.

"Under these conditions I find it virtually impossible, therefore, to continue my motion picture work, and I have given up my residence in the United States."

The 64-year old British-born film star, who was accompanied by his wife Oona, recently went to live at Vevey, Switzerland, overlooking Lake Geneva. His children are attending school there.

He handed over his United States reentry permit last week. Earlier the American immigration authorities said they might not let him return on political and moral grounds. He has been accused of Communist sympathies.

(April 18)

LONDON COUPLE MARRY ON PIE CRUST TV SHOW

3m. SEE COMMERCIALS

NEW YORK, Wednesday.

Three million people watched a London couple, Eunice Gayson, 22, an actress, and Donald Hunter, 31, a writer, married today before television cameras here. Before and after the ceremony there were sponsored items.

The couple were worried at first because of the commercialism involved. But they said later that they thought their wedding had been handled beautifully.

Miss Gayson, of Prince Edward Mansions, Bayswater, had been appearing in the London stage show "Over the Moon." Her husband, of Green Street, Mayfair, writes under the name of Leigh Vance.

They were guests on a programme called "Bride and Groom." The marriage ceremony, on a television stage arranged as a chapel, was conducted by the Rev. Claudius Kulow, of the English Lutheran Church of St. Albans, New York State.

EXPENSES AND GIFTS

The couple had their travelling expenses paid. They were also given gifts valued at between £280 and £350 and a film of the entire wedding.

The 15-minute programme, transmitted from 48 stations, opened with the bride and bridegroom being questioned in a living room setting. The scene switched to the chapel for the wedding and back to the living room, where the couple saw their gifts. They will be guests of the show organisers at a hotel until they leave by plane on Friday.

BISCUIT-MAKING HINTS

During the commercial scenes a cooking expert showed viewers how to make biscuits from "Betty Crocker Pie Crust Mix," a product of the programme's chief sponsor. The scene went like this:

Master of Ceremonies: "Have you ever seen an English newspaper? Well, the British cram an awful lot of news in a mighty little space. But I bet they can't do any better than we can do right here." *(M.C. holds up box)*

"You know ... I'll bet you've never seen 12 recipes take up so little space as these right here on the box." *(M.C. picks out recipe.)*

"Well, look...look here...cookies...that's all the directions there are. And do you know why...? *(While master of ceremonies is talking, camera shifts to hand of cook, sifting flour into a bowl, adding salt, etc....)*.

"... Because this recipe here doesn't start out by saying to measure and sift so much flour ... and some baking powder and salt ... blend in shortening." *(Camera returns to M.C.)*

"Nope. These directions here say, to take two cups of - *(name of product)* ... What I'm getting at is there just aren't any shorter, simpler recipes than *(name of product)*."

(July 2)

WAR ENDS IN KOREA

CEASE-FIRE FLARES GO UP

From John Ridley
Daily Telegraph Special Correspondent

SEOUL, Monday.

With the last chime of 10 o'clock to-night a hush came over the battlefront of Korea for the first time in more than three years. The armistice signed at 10 o'clock this morning to go into operation 12 hours later became suddenly and almost startlingly effective.

Guns which had showered steel on to the enemy and mortar barrels which had become on occasions red-hot from constant firing were silenced. Eyes which had strained at night across no-man's land relaxed.

At last after weary months of wrangling the truce had become a reality, at any rate for the time being. On the stroke of 10 p.m., cascades of flares rose from both front lines as Allies and Communists celebrated the armistice.

DEFENCES BLOWN UP

Withdrawal Preparations

Only one battalion of the British Commonwealth Division really rose to the occasion. That was the King's Regiment which at 10 p.m. had a bugler on a hill position playing the "Cease Fire."

Toasts to the Queen were drunk, but there was little celebrating among the Commonwealth forces. Front-line troops have already begun to blow up defences before obeying the order to withdraw.

Both sides have to retire 2,000 yards to leave a 2 ½ -mile demilitarised zone. On the Allied side South Korean reserves were the first to draw back to the south of the zone.

TRUCE SIGNING

"HALL OF PEACE"

The truce signing at Panmunjom this morning, attended by Gen. Harrison, chief Allied delegate, and Gen Nam II, his Communist opposite number, was a strange unemotional ceremony. It was held in the enormous "Hall of Peace," built by the Communists in three days.

The gigantic wooden building looks like a cross between a large village hall and a pagoda. Shortly before 10 o'clock we trooped into it and took our seats.

Facing us across the hall were the Chinese and North Korean representatives. They all looked stern and angry.

On our side of the room we had, in addition to representatives of the Press of the free world, the divisional commanders of most of the units fighting in Korea. Gen. West, the Commonwealth Division's commander carrying a long shepherd stick, sat in the front row.

With so many languages to be heard Panmunjom to-day resembled the Tower of Babel. Surrounding the Hall of Peace, from which all the Picasso doves had been eliminated, were soldiers of all the nations fighting in Korea. At one entrance stood Gnr. Colin Hughes representing Britain.

Precisely at 10 o'clock Generals Harrison and Nam II strode into the hall, one from the south door and the other from the northern entrance. They marched briskly to their appointed seats and without looking at each other began signing documents put before them by aides.

As they completed their signatures the blue cloth-covered documents of the Allies were laid beside the red leather-covered documents of the Communists. There was no sound except the whirr of movie cameras.

Each delegate signed in a purposeful, businesslike way. It was all over in 10 minutes. Without even a glance at one another Gen. Harrison and Gen. Nam II walked towards their separate entrances.

(July 28)

5 SPIRITUALISTS ROBBED

'WE FELT NOTHING'

Five spiritualists, including a medium, were undisturbed when thieves ransacked rooms below them at Holland Park during Saturday night. The theft was at the headquarters of the Greater World Christian Spiritualist League in Lansdowne Road.

On the second and third floors were Mr. Henry Bendall, 67, president of the League, and Miss Winifred Moyes, 60, a medium. They and the three others live on the premises.

The thieves threw things about and smashed open a cash box. They took £18 and Mr. Bendall's new hat.

Mr. Bendall said yesterday: "We neither heard the thieves nor felt their presence. Perhaps the reason we felt nothing was that they were poor unfortunates who needed the money more than we did."

(April 13)

P.o.W.s SAIL FOR HOME FROM JAPAN

TOKYO, Tuesday.

The first contingent of British prisoners of war from Korea to leave for home since the armistice was signed on July 27, sailed to-day from Japan in the troopship Asturias, which will arrive at Southampton on Sept. 17.

Ex-prisoners have again reported that the Communists are holding some prisoners who refused to accept Communist indoctrination. One report says that 40 prisoners are being held back at Camp No. 1.

Fus. Derek Kinne, Royal Northumberland Fusiliers yesterday gave an account of Communist brutality in a broadcast over the American Armed Forces Far East network.

STRUNG FROM CEILING

He said that at one stage of his captivity he was strung from the ceiling with a rope around his neck, and one foot touching the ground. His captors told him that when he became exhausted he would hang himself and "be responsible for your own death."

He said he was also punished for openly decrying propaganda in the London Daily Worker.

He said his worst experience came after he had been accused of killing a guard. "The guard had taken me out into the yard and was beating me with a crease-gun (American-type submachine-gun). Suddenly the gun went off, shooting him through the head.

"I was taken to a room and made to stand to attention while other guards beat me. Then they strung me to the ceiling and beat me again.

"For a month I sat cross-legged for 17 hours a day, seven days a week. I was not allowed to wash, and there was no medical treatment."-Reuter and B.U.P.

(August 18)

MR. CHURCHILL, shaking hands with Marshal Tito, President of Yugoslavia, at 10 Downing Street yesterday.

LONDON GREETS MARSHAL TITO

Marshal Tito was welcomed in London yesterday by the Duke of Edinburgh, Mr. Churchill and Mr. Eden. His arrival for a five-day visit, during which he will have important talks, was marked by elaborate security precautions.

Spectators were kept well away from Westminster pier, where he landed from the Port of London Authority launch Nore. He had transferred to the launch from his ship Galeb at Greenwich. All the bridges under which he passed were cleared of people and guarded by police.

An escort of the Royal Navy patrol boats accompanied the Marshal up river. Then, in the shadow of Big Ben, he stepped, bronzed and smiling, to the pier, gripped the Duke of Edinburgh warmly by the hand and said in English: "I am very glad to see you."

After handshakes with Mr. Churchill, Mr. Eden and Viscount Waverley, chairman of the Port of London Authority, the Marshal stepped forward on a red carpet to a microphone to read a greeting. Speaking in English, he said:

"I wish to assure the people of Britain that they should consider the people of my country as their staunch allies, because the people of the new Jugoslavia are striving towards the same ends as the people of Britain."

A large crowd gathered at Greenwich to watch Marshal Tito transfer to a Port of London Authority launch. Coasters at the mouth of Deptford Creek were dressed overall, their crews lining the rails.

As the Galeb and her escort of naval patrol boats approached, 90 minutes late, the Marshal could be seen on the upper bridge. Mr. Velebit, Jugoslav Ambassador, went aboard to greet his President. They went into the Marshal's suite for a conference lasting half an hour.

Marshal Tito, in his blue uniform as Supreme Commander of the Jugoslav armed forces, walked down the gangway and entered the launch, which sped up-stream with its escort of naval craft and police launches.

BRIDGES CLEARED

Sightseers Kept Off Wall

All bridges over the river were sealed and guarded before he passed beneath them to Westminster. River police launches kept constant patrol at Westminster Bridge.

Hours before Marshal Tito's arrival at 4.18 p.m. the bridge was crowded with sightseers, but all were moved away shortly before the launch came in sight.

The launch reached Westminster Pier, which had been transformed with blue and white striped canopies and red carpets, at 4.18 p.m. Mr. Churchill, top-hatted and smoking a cigar, had been waiting then for four minutes.

The Duke of Edinburgh, wearing for the first time the uniform of Admiral of the Fleet, stood beside them. Stock and suntanned, his blue eyes twinkling, Marshal Tito leapt from the launch before tying-up was completed.

He grasped the Duke by the hand, saying: "I am very glad to see you." In turn, he greeted Mr. Churchill, Mr. Eden and Lord Waverley.

Then he stepped to a microphone to read his greeting to England. None of the public could hear the speech. The nearest spectators were crowed on the Embankment steps outside County hall on the opposite side of the river.

(March 17)

COMMERCIAL TV TO HIRE TIME

ADVERTISERS' 6 MINS. IN THE HOUR

FIRST STATIONS IN LONDON, BIRMINGHAM & MANCHESTER

By Our Political Correspondent

A new public corporation to provide a television service from its own transmitters in competition with the B.B.C. will be set up under the Government's plans, announced in a White Paper yesterday. It is hoped to establish the Corporation by June, 1954.

The programmes will be supplied by commercial companies, who will hire facilities from the Corporation, and draw their revenue from advertisements. The contents of the programmes will be under the strict control of the Corporation.

They will not be "sponsored." Advertisers will have no control and advertising and programme material will be kept separate. About three, four or six minutes' advertising will be allowed in each hour's broadcasting.

Assuming Parliamentary approval of the necessary legislation, commercial programmes could be on the air possibly by Christmas, 1954, and certainly by mid-1955. Cost of adaptation of sets to receive an alternative programme would vary in relation to the distance from the transmitter. It will be from £6 to £15.

The Corporation will begin with stations in London and possibly two other large centres of population. These will probably be Birmingham and Manchester.

The Postmaster-General, Earl De La Warr, is discussing with the B.B.C. an increase in the amount of the television licence fee to put the Corporation in a better position to compete. The fee, at present £2, may be increased to £3.

The White Paper stresses that the new system will be alternative to the B.B.C., which will continue as the main instrument for broadcasting.

Extension of its activities already authorised will give the B.B.C. the highest density of television coverage in the world. More than 90 per cent of the population will be within range of its television services.

(November 14)

WHITE BREAD BACK IN SHOPS NEXT WEEK

SMALL LOAF WILL BE 1 ½ d DEARER

Daily Telegraph Reporter

Government control of the milling industry ends at midnight to-night. From next week white bread will be back in the shops after 13 years.

The National Association of Master Bakers announced yesterday that the recommended price for the new 14oz white loaf was 5 ½ d in London and 6d in most other parts of the country.

A spokesman for the association said that no general price recommendation had been made for the 1 ¾ lb white loaf "because most bakers are going to feel their way by producing the small loaf first." The National loaf of similar size costs 4 ¼ d.

Small sliced and wrapped white loaves will be 6 ½ d in London and 6 ½ d and 6 ¾ d in other parts of the country.

NO SUBSIDY

The spokesman added that the increased price of the white loaf was due to there being no Government subsidy on white flour. In addition it cost the baker 5s a sack more than National flour. Bakers must still make the subsidised National loaf.

Yesterday I sampled the whiter bread, but could detect little or no difference in taste compared with the National loaf. The extraction rate for the new loaf will be 72 per cent, compared with that of the National loaf of around 80 per cent.

(August 29)

LONDON AIRPORT WILL BE 'FINEST IN WORLD'

3 ¼ m. PASSENGERS A YEAR

London Airport development, due to be completed by 1960, will make it the "finest in the world," said Mr. Lennox-Boyd, Minister of Transport and Civil Aviation, yesterday.

He estimated that by the time the new buildings were completed at a cost of £6,700,000, the airport would handle 3,250,000 passengers a year. If Britain did not proceed with the scheme, people would go elsewhere.

Apart from lounges, restaurants and bars, there will be shops and hairdressing saloons. There will also be a roof garden "waving base" where passengers friends can watch departures.

Mr. Lennox-Boyd recalled that the development scheme was bound up with the decision to reduce the number of airports serving London from seven to three. Northolt, Bovingdon and Croydon would cease to be operational, leaving London airport, Gatwick and Blackbushe as operational with Stansted as a reserve.

London airport would be required to handle more than twice the number of its present aircraft movements and more than twice the number of passengers by the end of 1955. The total development scheme would cost £26 million and of that £14 million represented expenditure on initial development.

"STREAMLINING MOVEMENT"

One of the aims of the new buildings was to streamline the movement of the passengers. They would be directed rapidly through customs, immigration and other necessary formalities.

There would be 10 parallel channels for passengers to their aircraft and luggage would follow along another route. These 10 channels were expected to be in operation by the end of 1955.

The development plans published yesterday show that the central terminal area will be reached by a main access tunnel from the Bath road 86ft wide and nearly a mile long. It will contain two separate 20ft-wide carriage ways separate cycle tracks and two pedestrian paths.

PANORAMIC VIEW

The central terminal area will be diamond-shaped. The main concourse occupies the heart of the building at first and second floor levels. The "waving base" will be directly off the lounge bar. Spectators will have a panoramic view of the terminal apron and the whole airfield.

Replying to a question about the use of helicopters for passengers from London to the airport, Mr. Lennox-Boyd said that at the moment no helicopters large enough to bring passengers to the airport were in production. There was ample space for the landing of helicopters at the airport if this should come about.

He paid a tribute to the architect of the new buildings, Mr. Frederick Gibberd.

(September 17)

OVER 280 DIE IN EAST COAST FLOODS

HURRICANE SMASHES SEA DEFENCES

35,000 EVACUATED FROM HOMES

CANVEY ISLAND SWAMPED: 500 PEOPLE MISSING

More than 280 people lost their lives and many hundreds are missing through floods which ravaged the East coast of Britain early yesterday. Thousands were made homeless when the sea, whipped by a hurricane, smashed coast defences, and a wall of water, in some cases 8ft high, poured inland.

The death-roll in the floods, the worst of the century, will, it is feared, prove even higher. The disaster came swiftly after the loss of the motor vessel Princess Victoria, which foundered in a storm in the Irish Sea on Saturday with the loss of 128 lives.

At Canvey Island, Essex, police estimated that 153 people were drowned. Five hundred were still missing there late last night. Some bodies were found in trees.

Scarcely a place on the coast from the Orkneys to the Thames Estuary escaped damage. Several villages were devastated. Damage already calculated runs into millions of pounds.

Relief services were in progress last night. It was estimated that about 35,000 people have been evacuated and many more have still to be rescued.

FAMILIES DEFY NEW DANGER

The worst-affected areas are:

ESSEX: Canvey Island was swamped by a sudden flood which trapped hundreds in their homes. More than 150 people were taken to hospital. About 13,000 were evacuated, but some families last night refused to leave, despite a further threat through high tides.

Chalets were under 12ft of water at Jaywick Sands, near Clacton. Some people clinging to roof-tops awaiting help fell into floods through exhaustion.

An urgent call went out for amphibious craft to rescue 300 people cut off by extensive floods on Foulness Island.

12 AMERICANS LOST

NORFOLK: There were heavy casualties on the shores of North Norfolk, where the death-roll is believed to be about 60. Twelve American Servicemen were drowned near Hunstanton and a number of others are missing. The villages of Cley and Salthouse were almost devastated. The sea rushed five miles inland in this area.

KENT: The submarine Sirdar sank in dry dock at Sheerness, and the frigate Berkeley Castle capsized. There were no casualties.

SUFFOLK: Felixstowe was flooded until it resembled a lake. An estate of prefabricated houses was overwhelmed, with a death-roll of 21. Boats were rowed into a Lowestoft church to rescue 40 children sheltering there.

LINCOLNSHIRE: Mablethorpe and Sutton-on-Sea were evacuated as far as possible, but hundreds were still awaiting rescue last night. About 20 lives were lost in the Skegness area. Floods were 20ft deep in parts.

(February 2)

MRS. MACLEAN AND CHILDREN VANISH

Mrs. Donald Maclean, wife of the missing British diplomat, has disappeared from Geneva, the British Consulate there announced yesterday. With her three children, she left on Friday to spend the week-end in the Montreux area with friends and did not return.

Yesterday a telegram purporting to be from Mrs. Maclean was received in Geneva by Mrs. Melinda Dunbar, her mother. It was from Territet, near Montreux, and, after referring to "unforeseeable circumstances," said: "Shall remain here longer than I thought. We are all in good health."

(September 17)

AMERICAN, 22, WINS GEORGE MEDAL

QUEEN'S INTEREST IN HIS FLOOD RESCUES

Daily Telegraph Reporter

The George Medal has been awarded to Airman Reis Leming, 22, 67th Air Rescue Squadron, United States Air Force, who saved 27 people trapped during the East Coast flooding on the night of Jan. 31.

Leming made three difficult trips with a rubber raft and succeeded where other craft failed. He was in the water

four hours. It was disclosed afterwards that he cannot swim.

The Foreign Office stated yesterday: "As a consequence of the Queen's visit to the flooded areas, her Majesty has been pleased to award the George Medal to Airman Reis Leming, of the United States Air Force, in recognition of his extreme gallantry on several occasions in rescuing people who had been trapped in their houses near Hunstanton."

PROMPT AWARD

The Queen has taken a personal interest in Leming's bravery. It is understood that the promptness of the award is due to her close attention.

Airman Leming is now on a radio and television tour of the United States to raise money for British flood victims. He left by air last week to tell of his experiences. His home is at Toppenish, Washington State.

Leming is 6ft 3in, and it was his height which enabled him to push the rubber raft through the flood waters to isolated homes. During his struggles the exposure suit he wore was badly ripped, making him more vulnerable to the ice-cold water.

LAUNCH DRIVEN BACK

He set off with the raft after an Air Force "Weasel" had been swamped and a motor launch driven back by the gale. Without a word to anyone, he waded into the floods, pushing the raft.

The third trip took him more than an hour and when he returned with nine more people he was moving very slowly. Another five minutes in the water might have proved fatal a doctor stated.

(February 20)

AMONG THE MANY HOMES that Her Majesty visited was that of Mr. and Mrs. Benton, Feenhams Highway, Tilbury, which she is seen leaving. An R.A.F. hot pump is being used to dry out the house.

KENYATTA SENTENCED TO SEVEN YEARS

'MASTER-MIND' OF MAU MAU NEW TERROR EXPECTED

From Eric Downton
Daily Telegraph Special Correspondent

NAIROBI, Wednesday.

In a heavily guarded school-house courtroom at Kepenguria to-night Jomo Kenyatta and five other African leaders were found guilty on all charges against them of organising the Mau Mau terrorist movement. They were given the maximum sentences.

Kenyatta, 59, central figure in the trial, was sentenced to seven years' hard labour for managing Mau Mau and three years' hard labour for being a member, the sentences to run concurrently. The others were each sentenced to seven years' hard labour for assisting and three years for being members, the sentences to run concurrently.

The magistrate, Mr. Thacker, described Kenyatta as the master mind behind a plan to drive the Europeans from Kenya. He had persuaded his people to murder and commit atrocities.

He recommended to the Governor, Sir Evelyn Baring, that all the six be restricted in residence. This means, if the Governor concurs, that they will be confined to live within the closed Northern Frontier Province for the rest of their lives, or until the order is rescinded.

Notice of intention to appeal was given by defence counsel. Mr. Somerhough, the public prosecutor, said that all six had 14 days to lodge an appeal and none would be required to begin to serve his sentence until the verdict was confirmed by the Supreme Court.

NAIROBI GUARD
Most Anxious Night

Kenya is tense to-night as news of the sentences spread. Acts of terrorism by Mau Mau as a demonstration against the judgment are expected. All security forces, military, Home Guard and police, throughout the colony are on the alert.

Special precautions are being taken in Nairobi, where the possibility that Mau Mau may make this a signal for launching a campaign of terrorism against Europeans and loyal Africans cannot be ruled out.

All available security forces in the Nairobi area, including troops of the Lancashire Fusiliers and The Buffs, are standing by. Armoured cars are patrolling African areas.

Police reserves and Home Guards are out in force, many armed with sten guns. This is probably Nairobi's most anxious night since the emergency started.

EIGHT-HOUR JUDGMENT
Lightning Flashes

In a darkening courtroom lit by two paraffin lamps, with lightning flashing in the sky, Mr. R.S. Thacker, Q.C., a retired Supreme Court judge, took nearly eight hours to deliver his judgment after a trial lasting 58 days.

(April 9)

COOLING PLANT AND FUEL GAUGES FAIL

URGENT REPLACEMENTS FOR ANOTHER FLIGHT TO-DAY

From John Chappell
Daily Telegraph Special Correspondent

CASTEL IDRIS, Libya, Friday.

In what he called a "practice run" over the Libyan Desert course Lt.-Cmdr. Michael Lithgow to-day flew his Vickers Supermarine Swift F4 jet fighter at an average speed of 737.6 m.p.h., setting up a world airspeed record. The announcement was made by Royal Aero Club observers.

He easily beat the 727.6 m.p.h. claimed for the Hawker Hunter jet flown by Sqdn. Ldr. Neville Duke on Sept. 7 on the Sussex Coast. The speed achieved was more than the one per cent. necessary to establish a new record. Over four runs the Swift flew at 743.6, 729.5, 745.3 and 730.7 m.p.h.

Conditions were by no means ideal. Lt.-Cmdr. Lithgow, who is 33, was not satisfied, and before he knew the result of his runs he said he would make another flight to-morrow whatever to-day's speed might be.

Among other handicaps Lt.-Cmdr. Lithgow had to overcome were a fault in the fuel gauge and partial failure of the refrigeration in the cockpit which nearly stopped him breathing.

Because he did not know how much fuel he had he could not make full use of the reheat system which provides extra power. He switched on this "boost" five miles from the start of each of his four runs instead of 10 miles away.

Replacement gauges were flown out from Blackbushe Airport, Hants. They should reach here about noon to-morrow. A spokesman said they would not claim the record until they had seen the results of to-morrow's flights.

The regulations provide that a claim for a record must be lodged.

(September 26)

DUTCH FLOOD DEATHS NOW 605: WATER 40FT DEEP

WOULD-BE RESCUERS KILLED

From Our Own Correspondent

THE HAGUE, Monday.

The Netherlands News Agency put the dead in the Dutch floods at 605 late to-night, and there may be many people still missing. One-sixth of the country's land surface is under water, which is 40ft deep in some areas. Rubber boats and food parcels have been dropped in Zeeland and Brabant.

Dr. Drees, the Prime Minister, said in a broadcast to-night that the whole west coast from Texel to Dutch Flanders, about 140 miles, had been afflicted by the "disastrous" floods. "Unfortunately the losses in human lives are great.

"The full extent is not yet known, but certainly hundreds have died, including many attempting to rescue others. We commemorate them with deep respect, and our sympathy goes out to the relatives."

A Dutch Government spokesman said: "Like the British in the Dunkirk evacuation, we have called on owners of little ships to marshal at central points from which they are being redirected to the worst areas. Holland's entire fishing fleet is being mobilised to help."

BRITISH HELICOPTERS

Britain has sent Holland four helicopters to help the rescuers and this evening six more were arriving. Holland is using 16,000 troops.

The Rhine Squadron of 13 British tank-landing craft and three motor launches are reported to be sailing down the Rhine from Dusseldorf to aid Rotterdam.

QUEEN JULIANA'S TOUR

Queen Juliana returned to the Palace to-night to rest after spending 12 hours in the flooded areas. Wearing rubber boots, she waded to the town hall of Middleharnis, on Goere Island, to receive reports. At Numansdorp she sat in a café to talk with evacuees.

(February 3)

MAU MAU TRY TO BURN DOWN ROYAL LODGE

What was suspected to have been an attempt by Mau Mau terrorists to raid and burn down the Royal Lodge at Sagana, near Nyeri, was foiled last night. It was here that the news of King George VI's death was broken last year to the Queen.

Patrolling near the Lodge Inspector Trafford disturbed a gang, which fired several shots at him but missed. They then escaped into the forest.

About the same time a sentry guarding the Lodge raised the alarm when he detected several men lurking in a bush. Sentries opened fire and the gangsters fled.

The Royal Lodge, a wedding present to Princess Elizabeth, as she was then, from the people of Kenya, is on the wooded slopes of Mount Kenya, north of Nairobi. It has been empty for a year except for a European caretaker, who lives in a small house in the grounds.

(April 4)

OXFORD MAN'S POEM CAUSES BAN ON GRANTA

Daily Telegraph Reporter

The Proctors of Cambridge University have banned the undergraduate magazine Granta because of the publication in the issue for May 2 of a poem said to be blasphemous. It is entitled "Aubade" and is addressed to the Deity.

The author is Anthony de Hoghton, 34, son of Sir Cuthbert Hoghton, of Hoghton Tower, Preston, Lancs. He is a graduate of Magdelen College, Oxford.

Mr. J.C. Dickinson, Junior Proctor at Cambridge, said last night: "All junior members of the University are banned from working on Granta, either from the business point of view or by contribution, until the end of December.

"We took action in such a way as to show that we disapproved of the publication of the poem, which was offensive and uncomplimentary to God and highly crude. The question of penalty for Mark Boxer, the editor of Granta, is under consideration by the authorities."

No disciplinary action was taken, he said, until he and the Senior Proctor, Mr. A.R. Prest, had consulted the Vice-Chancellor, Sir Lionel Whitby, and the Proctorial Syndicate.

(May 20)

BERIA SHOT WITH SIX OTHERS

EXECUTION FOLLOWS SECRET TRIAL

By David Floyd
Daily Telegraph Special Correspondent on Communist Affairs

Moscow announced at 10.30 last night that Lavrenti Beria, 54, former Russian Minister of Internal Affairs and head of the secret police, was shot yesterday. Six others accused of high treason with him were also executed by a firing squad.

A Supreme Court statement, published on page two of Russian newspapers to-day, said that a special secret session of the court, presided over by Marshal Koniev, sat between Wednesday of last week and yesterday. A supplementary announcement said:

"Sentence on L.P. Beria, V.N. Merkulov, V.G. Dekanozov, B.S. Kobolov, S.A. Goglidze, P.Y. Meshik and L.E. Vlodzimirsky, to the highest criminal penalty, to be shot, with the confiscation of their personal property and the stripping of their military titles and awards. The sentence is final and there is no appeal."

Beria, said the announcement, betrayed the motherland, acting in the interests of foreign capitalists, and setting up a treacherous group of conspirators. The group consisted of the six others.

The main charges against Beria were:

1 That he tried to seize power for himself.
2 That he tried to set his police organisation above the Communist Party and the Government.
3 That he had sabotaged industrial and agricultural production, and
4 That he tried to "restore capitalism."

Beria was accused of being connected with foreign intelligence services in the Civil War. In 1919 in Baku, he was a counter-revolutionary agent under the control of British Intelligence.

Becoming, in March 1953, Minister of Internal Affairs he had prepared to seize power. He promoted more and more conspirators to leading posts in the Secret Police.

He was also accused, with the aim of creating food difficulties, of sabotaging measures to raise the economy of collective farms and State farms. He carried out "terrorist acts" against those who, he was afraid, would expose him.

Although all seven are stated to have been at the trial and to have confessed the world will never know whether they actually confessed or whether they had an opportunity to defend themselves.

LAVRENTI BERIA

(December 24)

FIRE AFTER EARTH QUAKE. An aerial view of the island of Zakinthos, off the mainland of Greece, which burned fiercely after earthquake shocks along the coast. Five more shocks were reported yesterday.

1,000 FEARED DEAD IN GREEK 'QUAKE

'I SAW A MOUNTAIN SLIDE INTO THE SEA'

RESCUE EFFORTS BY ROYAL NAVY SHIPS

WATER SUPPLIES BEING SENT: HELICOPTERS ON WAY

From Our Special Correspondent
ATHENS, Thursday.

The death-roll in the earthquakes that struck the Ionian Islands, off the west coast of Greece, was to-night estimated at more than 1,000. The number of injured is more than 2,000. More earth tremors were reported late to-night.

British and American warship crews are working with Greek troops and rescue teams among the smoke and ruins of the devastated towns and villages. Three British warships, the cruiser Gambia, 8,000 tons, destroyer Daring, 2,610 tons, and frigate Wrangler, 1,710 tons, arrived at the islands to-day, the fourth day of the earthquake.

Adml. Earl Mountbatten, C.-in-C. Mediterranean Fleet, flew from Malta to the Greek islands. His wife, Countess Mountbatten, who is Superintendent-in-Chief of Nursing Services of the St. John Ambulance Brigade, went with him. He arranged for water supplies to be sent into the area by the Navy.

Mr. John Asher, of the Mutual Security Agency (a post-Marshall Plan body), broadcasting to-night from Argostoli Harbour, said: "Ten minutes ago we had a terrible shock. I saw a mountain sliding into the sea.

"From Argostoli and Lixouri alone 400 dead have been counted. Everything is in confusion. Water is needed desperately.

"We do not yet know what it is like in the hills. The number of dead cannot yet be assessed accurately since the clearing of debris has not yet begun."

CAPITALS DESTROYED

Havoc on Islands

In the past 24 hours 34 shocks were registered at Athens Observatory. All towns and villages on the island of Cephalonia have been destroyed.

Vathy, capital of Ithaca, and Zakinthos, capital of Zante, have been devasted by tidal waves and fire. A village in Cephalonia is reported to have disappeared. There are cracks and crevasses all along the shore.

All observers stressed that what is most needed in the islands at present is water, since the waterworks were completely destroyed and the wells were filled with mud.

American aid to the islands is gathering momentum in the arrival at Cephalonia of the United States cruiser Salem and with the announcement by Gen. Hart of the United States Military Mission, that the Army will replace all stores used by the Greek Army in the stricken area.

KING PAUL ON WAY

Visiting Stricken Area

King Paul of the Hellenes and Queen Frederika left Athens this afternoon aboard the corvette Propolitis with supplies for the earthquake area. The Greek Government denied reports that the islands were sinking. It stated: "Landslides may occur, but no sinking of the islands is expected."

Late to-night 30 fires were still burning in the port of Zakinthos. Although rescue ships have reconnoitred the main coastal towns, nobody has been able to penetrate inland because of a complete breakdown in communications.

(August 14)

CLERGY TO GET £550 MINIMUM

By Our Ecclesiastical Correspondent

Every beneficed clergyman of the Church of England is to have a minimum stipend of £550 a year immediately and a house free of rates and dilapidation charges. The Church Commissioners decided this at a special general meeting yesterday.

Dr. Fisher, Archbishop of Canterbury, announced the decision at a Press conference. He said it was due largely to the laity's magnificent response to the "Archbishop's challenge" in 1947.

(June 23)

SIR WINSTON ACCEPTS NOBEL LITERARY PRIZE

By Our Political Correspondent

Sir Winston Churchill was officially informed by Mr. Gunner Hagglof, the Swedish Ambassador, yesterday afternoon that he had been awarded the Nobel Prize for Literature. The Ambassador called on the Prime Minister at 10, Downing Street and was photographed with him on leaving.

The Prime Minister formally accepted the award and indicated that he would like to go to Sweden to receive it, if his duties allowed.

The prize, which is worth £12,000, is the highest literary award in the world. Sir Winston is the first statesman and the seventh Briton to be honoured with it.

(October 16)

NOBEL PEACE PRIZE FOR DR. SCHWEITZER

Daily Telegraph Reporter

Dr. Albert Schweitzer, 78, who 48 years ago sacrificed a brilliant career as a philosopher, scientist, theologian and musician to become a medical missionary in the French Congo, has been awarded the 1952 Nobel Peace Prize.

The announcement and that of the 1953 award to General Marshall, former American Secretary of State, was made last night by the Nobel Committee of the Norwegian Parliament.

By the age of 30 Dr. Schweitzer, son of an Alsatian pastor, had achieved more than many eminent men have done in a lifetime. He had secured doctorates of philosophy, theology and music.

Eight years later, after obtaining medical degrees, he was working with native labour in a jungle clearing on building a hospital. He acted as his own architect and often as a carpenter.

This was the beginning of the settlement at Lambaréné which later became almost a missionary work legend. Since then, he and his wife have laboured increasingly to relieve the distress and sufferings of the natives and to teach the Gospel.

BUILDING LEPER VILLAGE

Now, like all his income, the £12,000 prize money of the award is expected to be devoted to the mission. His niece, Marie Wyott, said in Strasbourg last night that he would probably use it to build a new leper village in Africa.

(October 31)

145,304 HOMES IN SIX MONTHS

In the first six months of the year 145,304 permanent houses were built in Britain. Since completions in 1952 and 1951 increased during the second part of the year, by about 10 per cent and 16 per cent, the Government's target of 300,000 houses is likely to be reached in 1953.

The total for the first half of the year is 34,340 more than in the 1952 corresponding period. In June 26,598 houses or flats were built, over 6,000 more than in June, 1952 and about 2,000 fewer than the record month of March, 1953.

(August 6)

DEADLOCK ON FISHING BAN

NEXT MOVE MUST COME FROM ICELAND

Efforts to reach an agreement with the Icelandic Government on the fishing dispute have failed and the British Government is unable to offer any further suggestions for a settlement.

Britain suggested on Jan. 20 that one clear-cut issue capable of quick decision, namely the baseline drawn across Faxa Bay, should be referred to the International Court at The Hague.

Iceland replied that it was ready to consider the proposal only on condition that it received a definite guarantee that the British fishing industry would lift the ban on landings of Icelandic fish in this country as soon as agreement on the terms of reference to the Court had been reached.

No Further Suggestions

The British fishing industry refused to give such an undertaking and insisted that the matter should be settled by the Permanent Commission set up by the Overfishing Convention. In a further Note of April 24, the Icelandic Government felt unable to add anything to its previous reply.

"The British Government can only regard this as equivalent to a refusal of its proposal and has so informed the Icelandic Government. It has further been made clear to them that the British Government regrets that it is unable to offer any further suggestions for a settlement of the dispute.

"It is willing to consider any constructive proposals put forward by the Icelandic Government to resolve a situation which threatens to impair the traditional friendly relations between the two countries."

(May 21)

ACTRESS AND TWO MEN GUILTY OF LARCENY

From Our Special Correspondent
BLACKPOOL, Monday.

DIANA MARY GITTINS (DIANA DORS, the actress), 21, was found guilty of larceny and given an absolute discharge at Blackpool magistrates' court to-day. Her husband, DENNIS HAMILTON GITTINS, 28, and JAMES FREDERICK MARKALL, 52, were each fined £10. Notice of appeal was given in all three cases.

An earlier charge of burglariously breaking out of the home of Frank Rogers at Kingsley Court, Park Road, Blackpool, and stealing liquor valued at £4 7s 6d, was reduced to larceny. Mr. L. Robinson, defending, had submitted that there was no prima facie case to answer.

The small court was crowded for the hearing, which lasted nearly five hours. Crowds assembled outside the court-house to catch a glimpse of Miss Dors.

(July 28)

SWEETS ARE OFF THE RATION TO-DAY

AMPLE STOCKS: CONTROL OF PRICES LIFTED

Daily Telegraph Reporter

The immediate end of rationing and price control of sweets was announced in the House of Commons yesterday by Major Lloyd-George, Minister of Food. Purchases can be made to-day without coupons. The announcement took the trade by surprise. A spokesman of the Cocoa Chocolate and Confectionery Alliance said last night, "We are very glad about it. We will do all we can to make it work."

Major Lloyd-George said he had no doubt that stocks were sufficient to meet all possible demands. This view is shared by the manufacturers, though they say there may be a temporary shortage of some varieties.

Some price increases are likely. Manufacturers say a revision of distributors' margins is overdue.

The trade says present prices are unreal. Adjustments are likely, with some prices going up and others down. The higher price increases will probably be about 2d a lb.

The sweet ration has stood at 6oz a week since Dec. 30, 1951. According to the Ministry, the public has bought an average of 5 oz.

STAFF SAVING

Sweets have been accumulating in the shops for months. Stocks are not likely to be exhausted by a run on shops similar to that in April, 1949. Rationing was then lifted on a 4oz a week ration, only to be reimposed again four months later.

Rationing began on July 26, 1942, with 8oz a month. It reached 20oz a month on Aug. 17, 1947, but fell to 16oz the following October. It fluctuated, reaching its highest level of 26oz in July, 1951, until December, 1951.

Major Lloyd-George, in a written reply yesterday, said there was no possibility at present of buying enough non-dollar sugar to end rationing, much as he would like to.

(February 5)

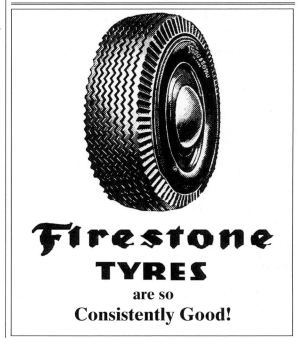

SIR WINSTON DISCUSSES MODERN ART

Views on Unknown Prisoner

Daily Telegraph Reporter

Sir Winston Churchill gave Royal Academicians an insight into his views of the controversial sculpture of the "Unknown Political Prisoner" exhibited at the Tate Gallery when he attended the Coronation dinner of the Royal Academy of Arts in Burlington House last night.

He was the principal guest, and for the first time in public since he was made a Knight of the Garter by the Queen at Windsor last week he wore the star and dark blue sash of the Order.

"This afternoon," he said, "I visited the Tate Gallery and I looked particularly at the "Unknown Political Prisoner." I understand that it is to be erected, or some suggested that it is to be erected, 300ft high on the cliffs of Dover.

"I am not going to attempt, even as an honorary member extraordinary of the Royal Academy, to pronounce upon the artistic merits or otherwise of this work.

"But if it is to be erected 300ft high on the cliffs of Dover, I feel that my duties as Lord Warden of the Cinque Ports might well force me to give it a very direct measure of attention." (Laughter and applause.)

CHEERS IN THE RAIN

Unit Inspected

Although he is an Honorary Academician Extraordinary, and has five pictures in this year's exhibition, Sir Winston attended in his capacity as Prime Minister.

Before going in to dinner, in accordance with tradition he inspected a detachment of the 21st Special Air Service (Artists) T.A., successors to the Artists Rifles. Although it was raining at the time, Sir Winston, in overcoat and top hat, walked round the ranks, which were drawn up in the courtyard of Burlington House.

A big crowd, some of whom had waited for more than an hour in the rain, gave him three hearty cheers as he walked into the Academy to be greeted by the President, Sir Gerald Kelly.

In the large Number 3 gallery, where the dinner was held, the scene was one of impressive tradition, with the distinguished company including diplomats, politicians and Service leaders.

Around the walls hung many of the works entered in this year's exhibition. Some were portraits of people present. Sir Gerald Kelly presided.

(May 1)

SIR A. BLISS MASTER OF THE QUEEN'S MUSIC

Sir Arthur Bliss has been appointed Master of the Queen's Music in succession to the late Sir Arnold Bax, said an announcement in the London Gazette last night. Sir Arthur is 62.

Sir Arnold Bax died on Oct. 3, aged 69. He had held the office since 1942.

During the Coronation service the Queen's entry into Westminster Abbey was made to a new work by Sir Arthur. He was knighted three years ago.

His musical career was interrupted by the 1914-18 war. He was wounded on the Somme and gassed at Cambrai.

His "Madam Noy," for voice and six instruments, first heard in 1920, was described by one writer as "a rather weird composition." It showed the young returned officer as something of a musical rebel.

By 1928 a mature touch appeared with his choral work, "Lie Strewn the White Flocks." Two years later came "Morning Heroes," which was dedicated to his brother "and all other comrades killed in battle."

The field of his work covers ballet, opera and chamber music. He was a pioneer in writing music for films.

(November 18)

SIR LAURENCE OLIVIER AND VIVIEN LEIGH have changed their plans for their return to the theatre this summer. Instead of appearing for a limited Coronation season in a revival of Barrie's play, "The Admirable Crichton", they will be seen in Terence Rattigan's new play, "The Sleeping Prince."

The production is to be directed by Alfred Lunt, with settings by Roger Furse and will open at the St. James's Theatre at the end of May under the joint management of H.M. Tennent Ltd. and Laurence Olivier Productions Ltd. Vivien Leigh will return from Hollywood early in April. Sir Laurence leaves on Tuesday for a holiday abroad. Rehearsals start on April 20.

EXCELLENT FILM IN THE YEAR OF 3-D

By Campbell Dixon

This has been a year of excitement and experiment, gambles on new processes, two or three colossal hits, and ten or a dozen artistic successes of quite a different kind.

The box-office sensations have been 3-D thrillers or gigantic widescreen spectacles. Never before has a film taken £585,000 at one cinema, as "The Robe" has just done in New York. The artistic films, on the other hand, have nearly all been small.

This, I think, is profoundly significant. I am not decrying showmanship. Most producers are in the business to entertain the public and, in doing so, make money. That is an honest ambition supported, if it needs support, by authorities from Dr. Johnson onward.

To sneer at "The Robe" because it is gigantic or fabulously profitable is silly: such a film gives millions of excellent people much harmless excitement and pleasure, and that is precisely what the showman is for. To praise it, just because it is gigantic and fabulously profitable, would be equally silly.

Not, of course, that size and quality are wholly incompatible. "Julius Caesar," despite some miscasting, shows that Shakespeare is not outside the range of a Hollywood director as brilliant as Joseph L. Mankiewicz; and in "Roman Holiday", "The Man Between, "Moulin Rouge," "The Beggar's Opera," "Gilbert and Sullivan" and "Young Bess" we had great talent working on a big or biggish canvas.

Two Small Masterpieces

Let me just start picking my Ten Best Films of the Year - not necessarily your Ten Best, of course - and the gulf between artistic values and "production values" will be seen widening every minute.

"Julius Caesar"? By all means. "The Robe," "The House of Wax."" "The Sword and the Rose." "Rob Roy"? No. Such films, however effective in their way touch life only at second or third hand. They shed no light on experience, they reveal nothing of human nature, they fail even to remind us of what we already know.

At the other end of the scale, at the top among the little things, are two masterly studies of children. Rene Clement's "Forbidden Games" was so intensely imaginative, and conveyed so poignantly, the silent griefs and fears and longings of the very young, that one thinks of it, nearly a year later, still with something of a pang. This film will always be remembered, I think, with the classics of the screen. The other film, "The Kidnappers," is very British in its freedom from morbidity, its humour and its happy ending. It, too, must rank high.

Two unusually modest Hollywood films, "Come Back, Little Sheba" and "The Actress," were notable for close observation, a sympathy warm but never mawkish, and fine acting. In one, Shirley Booth was the epitome of all the ordinary, unsuccessful middle-aged women whose dowdy and slightly absurd exterior conceals a good and tender heart.

In the other Jean Simmons played brilliantly that always appealing figure - the girl in an obscure prosaic setting, dreaming radiant dreams of fame. As she was also extremely good in "Androcles and the Lion," "Young Bess" and "The Robe" this might be called Miss Simmons's year.

French Contribution

From France came that wistfully funny trifle, Jacques Tati's "M. Hulot's Holiday," and René Clair's much bigger and more exuberant "Les Belles de Nuit." Though neither showed its director quite at the top of his form, either would have made a lesser director's name.

Donald Swanson's "The Magic Garden," though previously exhibited here and there in England was not shown in the West End or to the critics before this year, so qualifies for consideration. Made in South Africa, with the smallest possible resources, this delightful little comedy has poetry, fun and that sense of wonder which most of us lose as adolescence hardens into maturity.

(December 23)

'LUCKY BOY' RUN FINISHES

3 PERFORMANCES

Daily Telegraph Reporter

The musical play "Lucky Boy," which was booed on its opening night, has closed at the Winter Garden Theatre, Drury Lane, after only three performances. Although the cast and orchestra turned up there was no performance last night.

Shortly before curtain up at 7.30 p.m. a letter from the author, Mr. Ian Douglas, who was backing the West End run, was pinned to the stage door notice board. It said he could not meet commitments because of lack of funds.

Doris Hare, the leading lady, said the cast were distressed because they had worked hard to make the show succeed.

"We had hoped to pull off a good British musical comedy at the Winter Garden, the home of musical comedy," she said. "The music was lovely and it would have been a change after all the American productions."

(September 26)

Strange Beauty of Lowry's Own Lancashire

By T. W. Earp

The stay-at-home regional painter, who resists the lure of the conventional picturesque and finds his material in his native surroundings, is now a comparative rarity. But L.S. Lowry, who shows his recent works at the Lefevre Gallery, Bruton Street, has made the industrial area of northern England as surely his own domain in art as were the Five Towns that of Arnold Bennett in fiction.

With the vision of a Primitive he has discovered pictorial qualities in a scene where others might find only desolation. He has created a beauty poignant and strange, yet never swerving from fidelity, in the far-reaching spectacle of factories and mean streets, as with "Industrial Landscape" and "Ashton-under-Lyne." In the smouldering glow of tint and clarity of line, the scene takes on a new reality by the very candour of its presentation.

But there is further interest in the artist's way of peopling his landscape. His small well-defined figures, as in "The Steps" or "The Second-hand Shop," are never mere adjuncts to the composition: they have their own individuality and purpose in action. Such paintings as "An Open Space" or "Industrial Panorama" not only portray the setting, but fill it with human significance.

AYRTON AND SUTHERLAND

It is the same sense of life which gives their vividness to the paintings by Michael Ayrton shown at the Redfern Gallery, Cork Street. His elders and children, as in "Figures in a Red Room" and "Blind Girl with Sculpture" leave the impression of being much more than studio studies. They have an arresting depth of characterisation which rises to mastery in the portrait, "Constant Lambert."

At the same gallery the gouaches by Graham Sutherland again reveal his gift for transposing natural forms into new creations of pattern and rich colour, as in the red "Stone in Estuary," and the green "Thorn Tree". Bryan Winter's abstractions are happiest when they still keep a share of representation, as in "Newlyn Harbour," while those of Michael Rothenstein expand into resonant harmonies of colour from their basis of railway signals and fireworks.

(October 9)

ONE ACT IN ROYAL VARIETY SHOW CHANGED

Daily Telegraph Reporter

Only one act in the programme for the Royal Variety performance at the London Coliseum to-night has been changed. It is the mission hall scene from the American musical "Guys and Dolls," which the Queen, the Duke of Edinburgh, Princess Margaret and the Duchess of Kent have seen during its London run.

All references to religion have been deleted from the scene. In the original the setting is the "Save-a-Soul mission" in New York, and the players are a group of Broadway gamblers and uniformed missionaries. To-night, the missionaries will not wear their uniforms.

The words "brother" and "sister" have been changed to "Mister" and "Miss." In the song "Sit Down, You're Rocking the Boat," references to heaven and the devil have been changed. The "boat to heaven" will become the "boat to judgment."

A spokesman for the theatre said last night: "These are not last-minute changes. It was never intended to include the original mission scene in the royal show. We have made the alterations so that there could be no possibility of offending any religious group."

(November 2)

BOB HOPE AT THE LONDON PALLADIUM

Bob Hope and humour returned to the Palladium last night. He was in good form, and the drinking scene he plays with Gloria De Haven was extremely funny. Miss De Haven, here for the first time, also appeared on her own with a variety of songs.

(September 15)

First Night

BRILLIANT CAST AT HAYMARKET

FEAST OF ACTING IN STATIC PLAY

By W.A. Darlington

A pleased atmosphere in the Haymarket Theatre throughout the evening, and a most enthusiastic reception after curtain-fall, showed that N.C. Hunter's "A Day by the Sea" will rank among the major successes of this season.

And well it may. London play-goers are notoriously more interested in acting than in plays, and here is a positive feast of acting provided by a cast which glitters with titles and high talent.

Though I enjoyed it continuously, I do not rank "A Day By The Sea" as high as his "Waters Of The Moon," which was itself no very satisfactory piece of dramaturgy.

Do I hear somebody mention Chekov, of whom Mr. Hunter is obviously an earnest disciple? Then let this point be made quite clear. Beneath each play of Chekov runs a powerful current, whose force can be gauged by the eddies which appear on the surface. Beneath Mr. Hunter's surface there flows only a gentle trickle.

THE ONLY DEVELOPMENT

Only one of Mr. Hunter's 10 admirably-drawn characters changes or develops during the play under notice. That is the diplomat of 40 played by John Gielgud who learns that his habit of taking his job too seriously is a mistake both professionally and personally. He tries to be on again with an old love, Irene Worth, who, however, holds that what's done cannot be undone.

As for the diplomat's mother and aged uncle David they only exist to enable Sybil Thorndike to be deliciously irascible and Lewis Casson to dodder with brilliance. There is also a charming eccentric for Frederick Piper to play.

Yes, a feast of acting - skilfully produced too, by John Gielgud - except that in the picnic scene the number of people unsuitably dressed for the beach is excessive.

(November 22)

NO CENSORS' CUTS IN 'LES BELLES DE NUIT'

By Campbell Dixon

Despite much talk about possible cuts, the British Board of Film Censors has not only passed René Clair's "Les Belles de Nuit" intact, but given it a U certificate. This liberality has surprised even some of the film's backers.

When it was presented in Italy last year M. Clair was asked to accept four cuts. He insisted that his production be accepted or rejected as it stood.

It was expected that the British Board of Film Censors would at least object to the scene in which Gina Lollobrigida is seen nude by a distant admirer as she steps into a bath.

The British decision was no doubt influenced by the fact that M. Clair, as always, has avoided the least suggestion of sensuality. So gay and charming is the film that no one was surprised when the Queen and the Duke of Edinburgh chose it as the attraction they specially wished to see.

They will attend a private showing at the Rialto Theatre to-morrow night. The public showing will be on Thursday.

(February 10)

ROLAND PETIT'S 'CARMEN'

"Carmen," the high spot of their 1949 season, was given again by Roland Petit's Ballets de Paris at the Stoll Theatre last night. With Clavé's enchanting decor and Bizet's music, it is still Petit's most vital and exciting work. Colette Marchang, by turns fierce and seductive but always the embodiment of grace, is an able successor to Renée Jeanmaire, who created the role.

Petit's Don José is a masterpiece of portraiture, and his solo in the tavern scene almost as enthralling as Massine's Miller's Dance used to be. The bedroom scene pas de deux is fascinatingly beautiful.

(September 1)

First Night

U.S. MUSICAL ON NEW LINES

CHARM OF 'THE KING AND I'

By W.A. Darlington

In their attempts to raise the standard and status of the musical play by breaking away from the old worn-out forms, Richard Rodgers and Oscar Hammerstein have never hit on anything more original -or, I dare say, more successful - than "The King and I."

It opened in London to enormous applause last night at Drury Lane, and if anything is certain in this world it is that the directors of that theatre will not have to look for another play for a matter of years.

Yet how unlikely a theme for a musical must this appear to traditionalists! The story of the English governess who taught the Royal family of Siam nearly a century ago lacks almost all the ingredients once thought indispensable. Instead, we have a romance hinted rather than stated and doomed anyway to frustration, an evening of melancholy charm and no comedy at all except the quaintness which arises from the contrast between East and West.

How far Anna Leonowens corresponds to the historical lady, or to the heroine of Margaret Landon's novel from which the piece is adapted I am in no position to say. At Drury Lane, in the person of Valerie Hobson, she is a woman of sweetness, dignity and charm.

Miss Hobson acts with sincerity, and sings well enough, and is to be congratulated on her first appearance on the musical stage.

A KING IN CONFLICT

Herbert Lom brings off a fine piece of acting as the King, torn between his character as a despot and his desire to be considered an enlightened reformer. He, too, is equal to the needs of the music - which, by the way, has all Mr. Rodgers's famous haunting quality.

Much of the evening's enchantment is due to its atmosphere, the impressive settings (by Jo Mielziner, as usual) of the King's palace, and the hordes of little dusky princesses, in their quaint clothes, who are Anna's pupils. Quaint, again, is the word for the elaborate ballet, a Siamese version of "Uncle Tom's Cabin."

(October 9)

MORE MELLOW HAMLET

IMPRESSIVE FACADE AT OLD VIC

By W.A. Darlington

After the bleak bare platform of the Assembly Hall at Edinburgh it is a relief and a comfort to see Michael Benthall's production of "Hamlet" done before the impressive faççade with which James Bailey has decorated the Old Vic stage.

This is not now a "picture" stage, since all the significant action of the play takes place in front of the proscenium arch. For the purpose of procuring the greatest sense of intimacy for the greatest number of spectators, this seems to me superior to the platform, which is all very well for occasional experiments but should be kept for them.

Richard Burton's playing of the name-part seems to me to have mellowed a little since the first Edinburgh performance. I no longer get the impression of frantic haste which then spoilt my enjoyment.

On the other hand, I still have to report that this Hamlet leaves me emotionally unshaken except at rare intervals.

ARTIFICIAL DELIVERY

Partly this is due to a traceable cause - the monotony of the actor's delivery. He has a trick of going slowly up the scale in recitative which not only sounds artificial in itself but defeats his otherwise admirable ability to keep his audience intent on the sense of what he is saying.

Possibly this is an effect of his Welsh blood; but I am sure he will have to discard it before he will be able to render Shakespeare's poetry with the moving force which one suspects is latent in him.

Michael Hordern's Polonius improves on further acquaintance, and so in its orotund way does Laurence Hardy's Claudius.

(September 15)

THE DAILY TELEGRAPH
AND
MORNING POST
DAILY TELEGRAPH - June 29, 1855
MORNING POST - November 2, 1772
[Amalgamated October 1, 1937.]
135, Fleet Street, London E.C.4.
Telephone: Central 4242.

MASSACRE IN KENYA

YESTERDAY'S massacre at Uplands, only about 25 miles from Nairobi, was horrifying in itself. Equally horrifying is the insight afforded into the general situation in Kikuyu reserve. It is significant that both the massacre itself and the accompanying raid on the police station at Naivasha bore evidence of having been carefully planned and co-ordinated. Yet we are often told that the head of Mau Mau has been cut off. No mere headless body could conduct operations on such a scale. It is significant, too, that these operations must have been planned and executed almost under the very noses of the police. More than a hundred posts have recently been built in the Kikuyu reserve. If none of these was aware that anything was afoot, contact with the local population must still leave something to be desired.

Apart from increasing tension throughout the Colony, the massacre is certain to have other grave results. Those butchered were loyal Kikuyu - members of the home guard, Government servants and the like - their wives and children. It has not been easy for little people of this kind to maintain their decency under the continual pressure of "persuasion" and open threats. The fact that the Government cannot even repay them with security for their lives has now been forcibly demonstrated. What will their wavering fellow-tribesmen think now, when they see the terrible price of loyalty? A courageous few will be confirmed in their conviction that Mau Mau must be eradicated: among these one can count for certain those heroic Kikuyu Christians who in adversity still proclaim their faith. The majority, however, are more likely to be confirmed in their terror of a gang whose arm seems longer than that of the law.

The Kikuyu reserve is in a very dangerous condition - certainly no part of it can in future be regarded as "quiet." It was overcrowded before the emergency began. It is even more overcrowded now, as tens of thousands of Kikuyu stream in from their former homes in the White Highlands or wait in transit camps en route. Many others have been evicted by their employers, who are justifiably doubtful of Kikuyu loyalty. The Kenya Government has done its best - though with little effect - to check this exodus. Meanwhile food and work are short in the reserve, and Mau Mau propagandists find willing listeners among the hungry and idle.

Influential Europeans and Asians, awake to the dangers of such a state of affairs, have been urging the Kenya Government to create employment by initiating a large-scale programme of public works. It must be said, however, that this is easier said than done. Kenya's resources are not limitless, and to inflict upon them at the moment the additional burden of hastily planned schemes of dubious economic value might prove the last straw. The direct cost of the emergency is at least £200,000 a month. The Kenya Government's first task is to bring protection to the unprotected, to ensure that yesterday's dreadful scenes are never repeated.

(May 28)

NEITHER DYING NOR LIVING

IT is an astonishing tribute to preventive medicine that in 1951 the number of deaths from diphtheria should have been only one-third of the number of persons known to be suffering from leprosy. Hardly less impressive is the fall of nearly 40 per cent in five years in deaths from tuberculosis. The Ministry of Health, whose Report has just been issued, may justly take some pride in such achievements, but there is another and darker side to the story. Though some diseases such as scarlet fever, have become comparatively mild and rare, others, such as measles have become both more common and more deadly. In five years, notified cases of dysentery have multiplied by nearly eight times for no evident reason.

Lung diseases, principally cancer, are now fatal for nearly six times as many males as 20 years ago, and nearly three times as many females. On this difficult and disturbing issue, the Ministry has some sober words to say: "Excessive cigarette smoking may possibly be one of the factors concerned, but it cannot be the only factor because cancer of the lung is known to occur in persons who have never smoked tobacco in any form." It is to be hoped that these cautionary remarks are duly noted by the authors and sponsors of a gravely ill-advised television programme which encouraged retrospective panic, with no evident advantage to anyone.

(April 14)

REDOUBLED OUTRAGE

A GRAVE view cannot fail to be taken of the shooting down of a British aircraft on its lawful occasions within the international air corridor. It is all the graver in that it follows within two days of the attack on an American aircraft well within the American zone. One such incident might possibly be explained as due to an error in location or an excess of zeal on the part of the crew. But it is improbable that any Soviet or satellite crew would embark on so dangerous a course except in obedience to higher authority.

The two outrages accord ill with the professions of peaceful intentions so recently made by the new Soviet leaders over the bier of STALIN.

Whatever the explanation, there cannot be a shred of justification for these wanton and criminal violations of international order. In former days such things could not have taken place without instant retaliation. In these days, when we live in a state that is neither peace nor war, nothing satisfactory - or even true - can be obtained from the Communist Government concerned. The only answer is to equip the Western Air Forces with the most modern machines and provide that they have both the authority and the power to defend themselves.

(March 13)

Senator McCarthy and the Shade of Huey Long

From Denys Smith

WASHINGTON.

The chief opposition to the Eisenhower Administration has not been provided by the Democratic Party but by a small group of Republican extremists who accept the leadership of Senator McCarthy of Wisconsin. Mr. McCarthy, who was recently accused in the Senate of perjury and deceit, has been consistently engaged in anti-Communist activities, directed particularly against the State Department.

SEN. McCARTHY

In action, the Senator is disappointing. A little below average height, blackhaired and swarthy, with a chin which always looks in need of a shave, he gazes at the ground most of the time he is speaking.

His delivery is soft-voiced and conversational, with no oratorical tricks. The style well suits his stock-in-trade of the innuendo, the half-truth and the statement wrenched out of its context. Since there is no exaggeration in his manner of speaking his listeners are not led to expect exaggeration in the substance of his speech. He has a keen sense for assertions which will be startling enough to capture public attention and newspaper headlines.

When proved wrong he does more than withdraw his previous statement: he behaves as though he had never made it, and will be saying something quite different next day, with equal assurance.

Exploiting Fear

His relationship to President Eisenhower is very like that of Senator Huey Long of Louisiana to Roosevelt. In Huey Long's day the public were concerned about the depression which brought unemployment, low wages and low farm prices. To-day the public is concerned about the external and internal threat of communism.

In both cases the voters rejected the previous Administration at the polls because they did not think it aware enough of the dangers which the country faced, or active enough in meeting them. Senator McCarthy believes, as Senator Long believed, in riding the trend of the times. Long played on people's hopes: "Every man a king" was his slogan. Mr. McCarthy plays on people's fears - "Any man may be a Communist."

There is little doubt that Mr. McCarthy, like Long, sees the White House at the end of his ride. Had Long lived he might have come very near his goal. But Mr. McCarthy is less of a threat.

For one thing, he has not been able to make Wisconsin his pocket borough as Long made Louisiana. For another, he is mainly a threat by sufferance.

The Bohlen Vote

People began to wonder at what point the Administration would decide that conciliation had gone far enough. That point came when Mr. McCarthy attacked the nomination of Mr. Charles Bohlen as Ambassador to Russia. He was now attacking an action which had originated with Republican Administration, not a condition which it had inherited from its Democratic predecessor.

Mr. Bohlen was the personal choice and personal friend of President Eisenhower himself, and Mr. McCarthy lost his fight by a vote of 74 to 13.

The Bohlen episode was significant, not so much because it showed Mr. McCarthy could be decisively checked but because it showed clearly that he was prepared to use the same tactics against President Eisenhower and Mr. Dulles as he had used against President Truman and Mr. Acheson.

Further proof was provided when, to offset this rebuff, Mr. McCarthy announced with great flourish that he had negotiated an agreement with certain Greek shipowners not to trade with Iron Curtain countries. The impression he tried to create was that the poor old floundering State Department had fallen down on the job again.

The was against Mar. McCarthy has not yet been won; but the Administration has shown that it is ready, if necessary, to give battle.

(April 16)

FILM ACTRESS'S JEWELS STOLEN

NEW YORK, Wednesday.

Jewellery valued at about £3,000 belonging to Elizabeth Taylor, the British-born film actress, and her parents, was reported stolen to-day from a hotel room here.

Mr. Francis Taylor, the actress's father, said the lock of a chest in which the jewellery box was kept had been forced. Among other valuables a brooch, a clip and a pair of ear-rings belonging to his daughter were missing. - Reuter.

(July 2)

SMOKE COSTS £3 A HEAD

CALL TO ACTION

By Our Science Correspondent

Filthy, smoke-laden air was costing Britain £150 million a year, or £3 a head, said Mr. Arnold Marsh, general secretary of the National Smoke Abatement Society, in Nottingham yesterday. In smoky towns the figure would be considerably higher.

But even those who lived in the cleaner countryside paid indirectly for smoke by increased prices and taxes. "No-one would stand for such private and public expense if it were suddenly imposed on us."

At Nottingham the estate at Clifton, where use of smokeless fuel is a condition of tenancy, was the largest smokeless area planned in Britain. The first smokeless zone experiment in the centre of Manchester had proved so successful that a proposal to double its area was now being condsidered.

(August 18)

HUNT FOR HOUNDS

ENTIRE PACK VANISH

A foxhunt became a hunt for the hounds in the Quorn country near Markfield. Leicestershire, following the disappearance in the fog of the £1,000 Atherstone pack. They outran the field and vanished in full cry after a meet at Market Bosworth.

The hunt had drawn a fox in the Carlton woods in their own territory and a perfect scenting day set them off on what looked like being a record run. The hunt covered 10 miles with the fox well in the lead and the field lying a poor third.

Soon after the followers abandoned the chase fog came down. The pack of 18 ½ couples dispersed, it is believed, following a kill. The hounds were spread over many square miles.

The greater part of the pack had been retrieved when the hunt servants concluded their chase.

(March 4)

TV AND RADIO SETS IMPROVE THEIR LOOKS

LARGEST TELEVISION TUBE.— One of the sets with a 27in. direct screen to be seen at the Radio Show opening at Earl's Court to-day. The popular size for a screen is 12 in.

Radio and TV sets are becoming more and more efficient. But their appearance matters just as much as their performance to the woman who likes her home to be well furnished, and too many of them are uncompromisingly box-like in shape.

One auto-radiogram that has broken away from the usual design is displayed at the Earl's Court Radio Show. With its neat lines and contemporary "stick" legs, it would look very much at home in a modern room.

For husbands interested in technical details, it is a five-valve, all-wave, three-speed model for A.C. mains and plays both standard and long-playing records.

Hair-Drier Interferes

Another attractive piece of furniture is the new TV set shown above. The surround of the 15in screen juts out and is shaped like a picture frame. Special suppressor circuits deal with both sound and vision interference.

Talking of radio and TV interference, there is a stand at the exhibition showing the devastating effect unsuppressed electrical household gadgets can have on programmes. Chief offender is the hair-drier, which is mostly in use just when the family is settling down to the evening's programme.

As it costs 17s 6d to fit an effective TV and sound interference suppressor, it is understandable why few hair-driers, or electric irons and vacuum cleaners for that matter, have them. Especially so if the owners of the offending gadgets do not possess a TV set themselves.

(September 8)

PUBLIC VOTE ON FURNITURE

CONTRAST OF STYLES ON VIEW

Daily Telegraph Reporter

An exhibition of two identical living rooms, furnished in contrasting styles at the same total cost, opens to-day in the Exhibition Hall of Charing Cross Underground Station. The public will be asked to vote in secret for the room it prefers.

Arranged by the Design and Industries Association, the exhibition will be opened by Lord Latham, retiring chairman of the London Transport Executive. It is called "Register Your Choice."

(February 25)

The Truth About The Hemline

Paris Designers Agree to Differ

At last, on this official day of Paris fashion picture and sketch releases, we can show you what the Dior short skirt report really means. The two sketches on the extreme right are both from his collection. You notice the length of his autumn line - 17in from the ground.

But not every smart woman in Paris, London and New York will wear the short skirts of M. Dior. Far from it! Some will adopt the longer-then-before graceful skirtlines of M. Pierre Balmain, whose autumn dictate, "11in from the ground," covers another 6in of leg!

Fashion Badges

There was a series of "Noes" when I rang through yesterday to Pierre Balmain's salon in Paris.

"Will M. Balmain shorten his new line in view of all the fuss about short skirts?" I asked.

"No. NO. *NO*. Certainly not," I was told.

"So M. Dior will have no influence on M. Balmain's styles," I inquired. "NONE AT ALL," was the firm reply.

This autumn you will have fun identifying which fashion dictators smart women follow. For skirt lengths have become the badges of rival couturiers.

By Winefride Jackson

SKETCHES BY HARTLAND

Russian Influence

Melon sleeves are quite a feature of Paris. Givenchy uses a slim one which looks like a leg o'chicken sleeve, compared with the Edwardian leg o'mutton.

Jacques Fath's suit on right shows a larger melon sleeve. The Persian lamb polo collar and the toque give the first touch of Russian inspiration in fashion we have seen for a long time.

One word of warning: the women who adopt the short skirt will need to worry about straight stocking seams far more than the others.

Not So Startling Now

As for the new Dior hemline, is it so startling? Not perhaps after our minds, if not our eyes, have become attuned to the shorter length. But it was a great surprise at the time, when I went to his collection direct from Pierre Balmain's.

Balmain's autumn dress in grey wool with the hip-to-bodice tab-belts, is on the extreme left above. It shows the skirt hemline 11in from the ground, compared with Dior's 17in. These measurements are based on the mannequins' figures.

To compare the London hemline, about which I wrote yesterday, I show you a suit from Hardy Amies (second sketch) in orange and lemon black-flecked tweed. The hemline is 13 ¼ in from the ground, a little shorter than mid-calf.

The 1953 "Flapper"

With Dior's new short skirt, the accent is on youthful simplicity in styles. However, I don't agree that it revives the hard, perpendicular line of the mid-1920's "flapper" style. If a mere young-looking trend in fashion can be called "flapper," then the 1953 "flapper" with her fitted waistline is a more graceful, several-times removed cousin of the 1920's.

In fact there is very little in Dior's autumn line to link it with this period except perhaps for his hip-banded jacket (second from right). This hip-band motif is repeated, without confining the hips, throughout his collection.

The glove-fitting dress under this jacket has a closely defined natural waist, with the diaphragm smoothly elongated to a full bustline.

Your Waist Is Still There

In other words, the real dress waistline is still small, and in its natural place. This particular tow-piece is in black and white flecked tweed, following the trend for thick tweeds in suits, dresses and jackets.

On the far right is the cupola or dome line in skirts, where pleats almost bounce out over the hips from a tiny waist. Even in this full, grey wood dress you see the hips indicated with a band.

(August 18)

NEW FORDS ARE DEARER

AUSTERITY TYPE ABANDONED

By W.A. McKenzie
Daily Telegraph Motoring Correspondent

Fords have reversed their policy, as old as the T Model Ford, of austerity motoring at the minimum cost.

Sir Patrick Hennessy, deputy chairman and managing director of the Ford Motor Co., surprised the prophets yesterday when he revealed details of the new Anglia and Prefect models.

Instead of an "Eight" and a "Ten" shorn of all unnecessary equipment and trimmings, selling at a record low price of post-war cars, as had been predicted, the new models are:

Powered by an 11 h.p. 1.172 cc engine.

Identical in chassis and bodywork save that the Anglia has two doors, the Prefect four:

Furnished with every accessory and refinement considered desirable for the overseas markets:

Dearer than the old Anglia and Prefect, and the new Standard Eight and Austin A30.

The new Anglia will cost £360, plus £151 tax, a total of £511, compared with the old price of £445 (£313 + £132 tax). The new Prefect will be £560 (£395 + £165) compared with £526 (£370 + £156).

STANDARD CHEAPEST

Next is the Austin A30 at £540. The Morris Minor two-door model is £529 and the four-door £574.

Since the Anglia has left the 8 h.p. class price comparisons with the smallest engined rivals are illogical. But they serve to show that Fords are concerned more with performance than with any war on price.

At their price the Anglia and Prefect will be regarded as setting a new standard in value for money. Comparative acceleration and maximum speed figures show that they will provide something new in family car motoring up to an initial cost of at any rate £600.

In styling the new Fords are similar to the Consul and Zephyr models of the same factory. Overall length is 12ft 7½ in compared with 13ft 8in for the Consul. Yet the proportions are so similar that it is difficult to distinguish the smaller cars from the larger ones at a distance.

(September 29)

COLOUR TV HAS BRILLIANT NEW YORK TEST

From L. Marsland Gander
Daily Telegraph Radio Correspondent

NEW YORK, Thursday.

B.B.C. observers watched the most striking and spectacular demonstration of colour TV yet given here to-day. They are seeking ways of adapting the system to British standards.

The main difficulty is that the present British wave-length channels are too narrow and will not carry as much colour information. The essential feature of the American system is "compatibility", which means that coloured pictures will be received as black and white on ordinary receivers.

The B.B.C. intends to put colour on the existing channels, though overcoming technical difficulties may take some years. To-day was historic because it will probably be seen in future as the official birthday of Colour TV.

In the Starlight roof-room of the Waldorf Astoria Hotel 13 types of receiver, each made by a different manufacturer, were shown working on three different methods of transmission. Members of the Federal Communications Commission looked on to decide whether the standards could be approved and permission be given to start a public service.

BLACK AND WHITE DOOMED

After the conspicuous success of the demonstration there can be little doubt of the Commission's approval. Most of the sets were using a tube developed by the Radio Corporation of America or variations of it.

Subtle shades of colour, from vivid reds and greens to delicate pastel hues including realistic flesh tints, made a delightful impression on the eye. It spells the ultimate doom of black and white TV in America.

There was tension and excitement among the 300 or 400 experts, including 40 Press representatives, when the first transmission by the National Broadcasting Company from the Empire State Building began.

(October 16)

HOW MUCH FREEDOM?

Mary Carpenter Investigates The Restrictions On Women Undergraduates

How stringent are the regulations governing women undergraduates and students? This question has been raised again recently by the expulsion from a Welsh university of a girl student - an action upheld by the university committee in its recent report.

Inquiries to various universities in England and Wales show that women have as much latitude as possible, and that they have equal freedom with men.

Women's colleges at Oxford may appear somewhat sterner than those at Cambridge ... at the former, undergraduates must be in by 11.15 unless they have special permission to stay out until midnight; at both Girton and Newnham they may stay out until midnight without permission.

Men Visitors And Drinking

Students at London's Bedford College must be in their rooms by 10.30 normally and by midnight in any case; in Glasgow the hour is 11.15 (later by permission). Leeds insists that its students are in by 10, but they may arrange for another student to wait up for them on promise of arriving an hour later.

In Durham the women are in by 10.30 except on Saturdays, when it is 11. Southampton, our youngest university, sets the time at 11 and midnight on Saturdays.

Although drinking is not encouraged anywhere, most universities have a list of licensed premises which are not objected to. Leeds frowns on visits to public-houses, other North Country universities neither encourage nor bar students from drinking. Most principals find that freedom to drink is not abused in any way.

The fact that large numbers of students cannot take incoming telephone calls in their halls of residence and hostels is a criticism often voiced ... but calling them to take personal messages could so easily become a full-time job. And there are plenty of call-boxes for outgoing calls.

Leeds wardens make a point of taking messages until 7.30 in the evening, after which a student goes on duty for the others. In Scotland and the North students have facilities for message-taking.

"A Grave Responsibility"

Miss E.M. Scott, Principal of St. Aidan's, Durham, sums up this question on freedom - from the College point of view: "We feel strongly about the moral welfare of students who, after all, are with us to study rather than to live a social life. Regulations are easier to-day than ever before, but we still have a grave responsibility."

(July 22)

INTELLIGENCE TESTS A 'FAD'

Criticism of the "fad" of intelligence tests in schools which were being carried out at the expense of more essential subjects was made by Miss Jennie Lee (Soc., Cannock) in the House of Commons at question-time yesterday.

Her remark was greeted with applause from both sides of the House.

She remarked that excessive training for these tests, "a passing fad now being discredited", was making the task of the teachers more difficult. She advocated a return to more time being devoted to essential subjects like reading and writing.

Miss HORSBRUGH, Minister of Education: I am fully in agreement with what you have said, as I think are the enormous majority of teachers. I believe there has been too great a swing of the pendulum from children sitting in rows of desks. I think we may now achieve a better balance.

(January 30)

Make a List

Coronation Day will be exciting - but exhausting. There may be glorious sunshine and soaring temperatures - and discomfort. It may rain and there'll still be - discomfort. ***But not if you're prepared for either contingency.***

Whether you've a seat in a stand, or whether you'll be staking a claim to a square foot of pavement on the route - you've got to remember **EVERYTHING**. *So make a list.*

What about make-up? *Those who climb into seats at 7 a.m. will need a lasting one. To achieve this ... strip face of any grease before making up ... lightly press powder into the foundation, brush off surplus.*

MAKE-UP FOR ABBEY

For the abbey, wear ... a foundation that reflects a maximum of light, advises a leading cosmetician. (It should be lighter and brighter than the skin.) ... a pastel shade of rouge, without a tinge of blue ... a brilliant lipstick. When you have made up, pat over the face with a sponge moistened with skin freshener but wrung out almost dry - this will make the skin glow in the dim lighting.

Notes For Your List: THE BENCHERS *must remember ... a non-crushable dress (seersucker won't show the creases) ... a cushion (you can buy a shopping bag which will inflate into a cushion, about 4s 3d) ... something to do to while away the hours ... and something to eat.*

THE ALL-NIGHTERS *must remember ... a dark dress and an old (repeat, old) coat ... a shoulder bag, not a handbag ... that air-cushion bag ... something to do ... and eat. Warning - you cannot take a stool to the scene of your vigil. The police may confiscate it. Nothing can be taken that obstructs the view of others.*

BOTH MUST REMEMBER ... *a damped flannel in a plastic box for cooling-off and cleansing ... paper tissues ... malt tablets for sustaining power ... glucose sweets for pepping-up nerves ... a cardboard mug and spoon ... and a bottle of sparkling glucose drink (there's one used by convalescents) rather than a vacuum flask ... a solid eau-de-Cologne stick.*

ADVICE FROM THE EXPERTS

ABOUT YOUR FEET. *Carry out eau-de-Cologne and foot powder drill for a few days before Coronation Day ... wear lace-up shoes ... take a self-adhesive foot pad (10d and 1s) or two in your bag to appease blisters. Wear silk stockings rather than nylons, which are non-absorbent.*

A leading optician has advice FOR TVIEWERS. *You need the room dark, but not blacked out. Have a shaft of light at your back but the screen must be in darkness ... have some ventilation ... move away from the set occasionally and get some fresh air.*

(May 30)

To Wear Or Not To Wear Gloves For Evening?

By Winefride Jackson

The Englishwoman while flouting fashion conventions during the day, preferring what is comfortable to what is smart, is a stickler for "the right thing" when it comes to evening dress.

With the start of winter evening parties, the latest spate of inquiries I have received concerns gloves for evening. There are no rigid rules of etiquette to-day, but for those who are a little hazy on this subject here is a guide to help you:

For a formal evening reception, when the men will be wearing white ties and decorations, you should have long, above-the-elbow gloves in white or pastel shades.

If the reception includes dinner, then the gloves should be unfastened, your hand slipped out and that part of the glove tucked under at the wrist, so see there are buttons on your gloves to enable you to do this. If you are taking a cocktail before dinner, just please yourself whether or not you free your hand.

The important thing is to feel comfortable and relaxed if you are to contribute to the enjoyment of the evening. If you feel still happier carrying your gloves, then do so.

For The Gala Performance

For dancing, please yourself. On or off is correct, but if you easily get hot hands, it is pleasanter for your partner if you keep your gloves on.

When the Queen, Queen Elizabeth the Queen Mother and Princess Margaret attended a gala theatre performance the other evening, I noticed that 75 per cent of the women in the audience, like the Royal family, wore long gloves. It certainly added to the beauty and graciousness of the occasion.

Sometimes members of the Royal Family do carry their gloves instead of wearing them.

If the evening occasion is an informal theatre visit, differ or dance, most women, if they are wearing evening dress, prefer to have elbow length gloves with them. They can be of any colour, dark or light.

Women are also puzzled about what sort of gloves to wear with short evening dress. For the older women, ordinary elbow length: for the young the wrist-length glove specially designed for evening can be very attractive. In fact young people are wearing shorties a lot for evening nowadays, and very gay they look, too.

(November 2)

MISS KATHLEEN FERRIER

SINGER'S CAREER CUT SHORT AT 41

Daily Telegraph Reporter

Miss Kathleen Ferrier, who in a brief period had become world-famous as a contralto, died in London yesterday, aged 41, after a painful illness.

Her international reputation was rapidly achieved after her first singing lesson in 1940. She toured Europe, Canada and America, and sang at every Edinburgh Festival except this year's.

The news of her death brought sadness to many friends. Behind it was a story of suffering courageously borne.

Their consolation was that she died peacefully. She learned two years ago that there was little hope of recovery, but the crisis did not come until last February.

She was then appearing with the Covent Garden Opera Company for the first time, in Gluck's "Orfeo," and it was also to be her last. Because of her illness the last two performances were cancelled.

In her final appearance her artistry captivated the audience, but it was seen that she was limping and was being assisted by other members of the cast. When the curtain fell she could hardly walk from the stage.

She was taken to University College Hospital. In midsummer she left hospital but remained too crippled to walk and presently had to return there from her Hampstead home.

The daughter of a Blackburn headmaster, she went to work in Blackburn Post Office at the age of 14. She was a telephone operator there and in Blackpool.

By paying other girls to take over part of her duties, she continued her piano studies. The prize of a piano in a national competition enabled her to give lessons.

CHALLENGED TO SING

In 1937 she entered as a pianist for a local competitive music festival. On the "dare" of a girl friend she also entered as a singer, and won first prize in both sections in addition to a special award for the best singer in all classes.

For her first professional engagement, at a harvest festival, she was paid a guinea. Sir Malcolm Sargent, who heard her sing in Manchester, advised her to go to London.

With her father and sister, she lived in Hampstead and studies under Mr. Roy Henderson. In 1943 she made her London debut in the "Messiah" at Westminster Abbey.

Three years later she won acclaim at Glyndebourne. She was appointed a C.B.E. in the New Year Honours. In June she was awarded the Royal Philharmonic Society's gold medal for her services to music.

A LOVELY VOICE

Unforgettable Roles

RICHARD CAPELL writes: Kathleen Ferrier was a beautiful and noble-hearted singer, and her stricken state this year, when her artistic powers had seemed to promise ever greater achievements, was felt as a personal sorrow by many outside her immediate circle.

Along with a lovely voice went uncommon musicianship and a deeply-feeling nature. Her singing of the alto solos in the "St. Matthew Passion" will never be forgotten by those who heard it, and she also excelled all her contemporaries in Mahler's alto music.

(October 9)

QUEENSHIP EXALTED THROUGH MANY TROUBLED YEARS

By Guy Ramsey

In the room above Queen Victoria's nursery in Kensington Palace, on May 26, 1867, there was born to the Duke and Duchess of Teck a daughter christened, in the elaborate fashion of Royalty, with the names of her most eminent relations: Victoria Mary Augusta Louise Olga Pauline Claudine Agnes.

For the first 20 years of her life she was known by none of them, but as Princess May; for the last 40 at Queen Mary.

She was a great-granddaughter of George III, a cousin of Queen Victoria; through her grandfather, the Duke of Wuerttemberg, and her other, Princess Mary Adelaide of Cambridge, she was related to almost every Royal house, past and present, in Europe; even to the luckless Stuarts and the ancient Hungarian dynasty of Arpad.

Many influences went to form, what became the strongest character of Britain's 20th-century Royalty; a charming, feckless, extravagant mother, who was to rely on a daughter, still in her teens to produce order out of the chaos of her household bills and her engagement diary; her august, imposing, rather frightening cousin, Queen Victoria, who regarded her as a potential successor; a radical Alsatian governess, "Bricka," who was a passionate intellectual at a time when women were not encouraged to scholarship.

Her position demanded considerable state, but the family income was slender: and, when Princess May was 16, Florence was selected as a residence combining economy with amenity.

A steady diet of serious books was at once enjoined on her to fill a leisure lacking the normal pastimes of her class; suited to her temperament, which was intensely practical: and blessed refuge to a girl whose shyness and silence in conversation made most social contacts a torture. To those who but yesterday regarded Queen Mary as the very epitome of self-possession, of dignity, gracious serenity, it seems inconceivable that she ever lacked the presence and poise that came to be her very hallmark. Yet, for the last half of her public life shyness was a torment conquered only by a ruthless perseverance and a sense of duty to her position that made all personal considerations secondary.

On her return to England Princess May became, inevitably, something of a society figure: but it was not until 1891 that she really impinged upon the public consciousness.

Her engagement was announced to the Duke of Clarence, the tall, good-looking, eldest son of Edward, Prince of Wales. That marriage was, quite realistically in the nineteenth century: an "arranged" marriage, arranged by the old Queen who subordinated all personalities to the interests of the State. After the Duke's death, she married his younger brother, the Duke of York. The Duchess of York was a devoted mother, who, whenever possible, had her children "downstairs" to tea. She set aside one day every week to care for them herself, bathing them, putting them to bed. Upon her the burden of the Royal round of duties lay heavy, and though much of it was distasteful she never shirked.

Like all scions of a Royal house her memory was trained on an already good natural base. Punctuality, "the courtesy of Kings" - her father-in-law, King Edward VII, coined the phrase - was her watchword.

But those who resigned themselves to "just another Royal visit" found, instead of the superficial glance, the formal congratulation they expected, someone whose genuine interest caused her to search to scan and, where necessary, to correct.

When, as Queen, she visited one settlement which had spent most of its funds on premises for the committee, leaving the people for whom it was designed in penurious tenements, she demanded: "Take me over them. No house which houses my subject is too mean for me to enter."

At the end of the tour she declared: "They are a degradation: if something is not done immediately, my name will be removed from your list of patrons." In two months the houses were rebuilt.

It was the outbreak of the 1914-18 war that brought out the depth of her sense of duty.

At home and, once, in the deepest secrecy, abroad, the Queen's hand was perceptible in all relief work.

No man was so badly hurt, so hideously disfigured that she shrank from a meeting; no hospital so frightful that she shirked a visit.

She went to France with a single lady in waiting for a fortnight, touring both the dressing-stations and the base hospitals. Her needlework Guild was so enthusiastic that the Queen herself was compelled to check their activity lest it should press overhardly on those who must sew for their living.When the newly formed W.A.A.C. lay under the unjust reproach of their freedom, she accepted the titular command: stilling at a stroke the jests and libels and setting an example the newest recruit strove to emulate.

The very Court itself assumed a new tone once Queen Mary was its dominant figure. Edward VII had encouraged reaction against the solemnity of Victorian modes: but the new Queen said: "My daughter will grow up at Court: I want her surroundings to be suitable and I intend that every mother whose girls come to Court shall feel that they are so."

The Court became, as it has remained, what the people expect and want it to be.

To the end of his life the Queen was at her husband's side. On the announcement of his imminent death by Lord Dawson of Penn, his Majesty's doctor, and its publication authorised by her Majesty, the nation prepared for the passing of an upright, much-loved and conscientious Sovereign. In the days of mourning the sympathies of millions were silently extended to his life's companion and helpmate.

Queen Mary was 70 when, after the heartbreak of the Abdication, her second son was crowned in 1937. It marked her sense of public fitness that, on the balcony of Buckingham Palace she, the great star who had shone undimmed for a quarter of a century, gladly yielded to the newcomers her pre-eminence: urging them forward as she herself stepped back. It marked, too, the quintessence of Royal technique, for Kings are made as well as born.

Neither physical age nor personal sorrow could quench the inexhaustible vitality of the woman who became, not, as was usual, "the Queen Mother," but, individually, Queen Mary - so to remain when other sad events pressed upon her in her last years.

When the skies of Europe were again ablaze with the lethal stars of war there came to her again the routine of hospitals, maternity homes, girls' hostels. In Badminton, the Gloucestershire home of the Duke of Beaufort, she spent the years of the second world war: silver-haired, riding in the high old-fashioned Daimler.

When peace came again there she was still: the embodiment of the indomitable, the eyes still clear, lorgnetted in society, smoke-glassed at Wimbledon: dressed in the style that had become a signature - the flowered toque, the inevitable long parasol or umbrella, the stately carriage, the shrews appraisal, the gracious word, the rare smile, prized for its very rarity.

She saw her children, and her grandchildren, stamped with the tenacious features of the Tecks: fair-haired, high-coloured, handsome, robust: saw her granddaughter married to yet another kinsman.

"Thank God," she said back in 1923, "Elizabeth is not one of these modern girls." For Queen Mary's view of womanhood was inevitably and unchangeably cast in the Victorian mould of her birth. "I am still old fashioned enough to regard maternity as women's highest achievement," was one of her dicta.

Almost the last achievement that stands to her name was typical of her: her carpet. For eight years the keen Royal eyes, the deft Royal fingers had wrought this remarkable rug in grospoint needlework. She gave it to, and as the then Prime Minister Mr. Attlee accepted it on behalf of the nation: she wished that it might bring dollars to the country.

(March 25)

DEATH OF EUGENE O'NEILL

MOST CHALLENGING OF U.S. DRAMATISTS

Eugene O'Neill, the famous American dramatist, died yesterday, aged 65, at Boston, Mass., where he had lived for the past two and a half years. He had been suffering from bronchial pneumonia. His wife, doctor and nurse were at his bedside when he died.

In 1936 he was awarded the Nobel Prize for literature. He won the Pulitzer drama prize three times, in 1920, 1922 and 1928.

His plays were mostly unorthodox and challenging: he was frequently accused of morbidity, lewdness and profanity. But his diversified talents made probably a greater impact on the theatre than any of his American contemporaries.

Two of his plays, "Strange Interlude," first produced in England in 1931, and "The Iceman Cometh," not yet seen in this country, take more than four hours in running time.

The first is remarkable for the lengthy soliloquies which hold up the action of the play for several minutes at a time. The second is a typical study by O'Neill of social dereliction, set in a New York saloon. It created a deep impression on its production in New York in 1946.

The presentation of "Mourning Becomes Electra" in London in 1937 was hailed by many as a theatrical event of the first magnitude. O'Neill invested this modern tragedy on a Greek theme with immense power and vigour, and lightened its horrific nature with touches of genuine sublimity.

EARLIER SUCCESSES

Among the earlier successes which had established his reputation were "The Emperor Jones" and "Anna Christie." "Desire Under the Elms incurred the Lord Chamberlain's ban, and although written in 1924, was not seen in London until 16 years later. "Ah, Wilderness!" which appeared in 1932 was an unusually - for O'Neill - homely comedy.

The son of an American actor of distinction, Eugene O-Neill was born in New York in 1888. After Princeton and Harvard he went on a gold prospecting trip to British Honduras.

Several voyages in sailing-ships and in steamers - in one of which he tended mules from Buenos Aires to Durban - were followed by a spell as a newspaper reporter. Then his health broke down, and while in a sanatorium he began to write plays. In 1949 he was afflicted with Parkinson's disease, a form of palsy, and had since lived in seclusion.

He was married three times. His widow was formerly Miss Carlotta Monterey. One of his two sons by his former marriages was found dead in his New York home in September last year. Mr. O'Neill's only daughter, Oona, is married to Mr. Charles Chaplin.

(November 28)

DYLAN THOMAS

Dylan Thomas, the poet, broadcaster and storywriter, who has died in New York, aged 39, was regarded by many as the most promising present-day poet in Britain. His reputation in the United States was as great as in this country.

For a contemporary poet, his sales were regarded by his publishers as exceptional. His "Collected Poems, 1934-1952," which won him the William Foyle Poetry Prize last January, has already sold more than 9,000 copies. Born in Swansea, son of a schoolmaster, his first interest was journalism, but he left it when he found he could not master shorthand.

Edith Sitwell was one of the first to recognise Dylan Thomas's talent. In a review of his second published work, "Twenty-five Poems," in 1936, she wrote: "The work of this very young man (he was then 22) is on a huge scale, both in theme and structurally - his themes are the mystery and holiness of all forms and aspects of life."

In 1940 he published a book of autobiographical sketches, "Portrait of the Artist as a Young Dog." "The World I Breathe" appeared in 1940 and "Deaths and Entrances" in 1945. Since the war he had broadcast often on the Third Programme and had made several successful lecture tours in America.

(November 10)

ICE STAR DIES BEFORE AUDIENCE

OPENING NIGHT

MUNICH, Thursday.

Mrs. Rene Fensom, 26, British ice-skating star, had a heart attack and fell dead on the ice before the audience at a Munich ice show. Doctors believe that extreme heat may have been the cause.

Mrs. Fensom was dancing to the music of "Blue Moon" on the opening night of the show. Spectators thought she had merely tripped. Her death was not announced.

Mrs. Fensom's husband was also in the show.

(September 4)

RAOUL DUFY

M. Raoul Dufy, the French painter, who has died at his home in Forcalquiers, near Digne, South-East France, aged 76, had suffered in recent years from arthritis. During the winter he had had lung trouble.

T.W. EARP writes:

It was the aim of his painting frankly to give pleasure and to the end it retained echoes of his early days as one of the so-called Fauvists, or Wild Men of Art, in association with Matisse and Derain.

Driving straight to the essentials of form he hardly carried his subject beyond the stage of a sketch, but the effect of swiftness and ease holds a fine quality of rhythm. It is reinforced with the freshest and gayest of colour.

His themes are pared down to their decorative elements with a true French lucidity and much thought went to evolve a manner which gives in paint the impression of an unpremeditated lyric. Northern France, Paris, the Riviera, the circus and the racecourse were favourite scenes.

(March 24)

TOM SHARKEY DIES AT 79

Tom Sharkey, probably the finest heavyweight boxer never to hold a title and the last link with the great fighters of the 1890's, died in San Francisco yesterday, aged 79. He had been in hospital with heart trouble since last August.

During 11 years in the ring he won 35 of his 54 fights by knockouts and earned about 250,000 dollars, but he died penniless. In recent years he had been cared for by friends.

Many of his opponents have become almost legendary figures, including John L. Sullivan, James J. Corbett and the original Jack Dempsey, known as "the Nonpareil." Only one man knocked him out, the Cornishman, Bob Fitzsimmons, the only Briton to win the world heavyweight title.

Sharkey, an Irishman, was careful with his prize-money and opened a bar in New York, but he was a poor businessman. He betted heavily and invested unwisely.

(April 18)

EX-KING CAROL DIES

HEART ATTACK

LISBON, Saturday.

Ex-King Carol of Rumania has died at Estoril near here at age of 59, it was announced early this morning.

Marshal Urdarianu, formerly a Minister of the Rumanian Court, stated that the ex-King died of a heart attack at 12.30 a.m. to-day.

Princess Helena of Rumania (formerly Mme. Lupescu) was at his bedside when he died.

Marshal Urdarianu said the ex-King felt quite well until half an hour before midnight when he was suddenly taken ill. A doctor was called, but despite his utmost efforts, he could not save ex-King Carol's life.

The Marshal said no arrangments for the funeral could yet be announced.

Ex-King Carol had lived at Estoril, a fashionable seaside resort about 15 miles from Lisbon, since October, 1947. - Reuter.

(April 4)

KING IBN SAUD DEAD

CAIRO, Monday.

King Ibn Saud, who moulded the wastes of Arabia into a kingdom and pacified its tribes, died at 4.30 a.m. to-day at the Royal home at Riadh, Saudi Arabia. He was 74.

Spanned Two Eras

KING IBN SAUD'S long and romantic reign spanned the era of the Arabia of camels and date palms and that of cars, planes and oil. Our long tradition of friendship with the Moslem world has rather caused us to regard him as the dashing feudal chief who carved a great empire for himself with the sword.

The Americans take a different view. To them the King appeared as the leading exponent of Arab nationalism. How true that view may be is a matter for debate.

It is certain, however, that in the last troubled 10 years in the Middle East Ibn Saud threw his influence on the side of moderation.

(November 10)

Obituary

HILAIRE BELLOC

PROLIFIC AND GIFTED WRITING

England loses one of her most gifted, versatile and prolific writers by the death of Hilaire Belloc. He would have been 83 on July 27.

A literary jack-of-all-trades who was master of several, he wrote over 100 books between 1895 and 1942.

He was essayist, publicist and historian: biographer, poet and nonsense-rhymer: novelist, topographer and satirist. He was also wit, politician, lecturer, and a connoisseur of wine and lover of beer.

Rumbustious, bellicose and dogmatic, he tilted at windmills with staggering self-assurance. But while few authors could be more stimulating or provocative, he could express his love of the English countryside with an exquisite tenderness. It is probable that his less forceful works will prove the more enduring.

Joseph Hilaire Pierre Belloc was born at St. Cloud, near Paris, the son of a French barrister.

FRENCH ARMY SERVICE

Belloc, an only son, was educated under Newman at the Oratory School, Edgbaston. Before he went up to Balliol he had completed his term of military service as a driver in the 8th Regiment of French Artillery.

He became a naturalised British subject in 1902. From 1906 to 1910 he was M.P. for South Salford, first as a Liberal and later as an Independent.

As an orator he occasionally startled the Commons with his volcanic turbulence, but he found the atmosphere at Westminster uncongenial. He was unamenable to party discipline, and abhorred the intricacies of party politics.

In the meantime he had published some first-rate nonsense rhymes, lambasted the Jingoists in merciless satirical verses, and won a widening public by "The Path to Rome," which described a journey he made on foot across Europe. In "The Four Men" he had begun to sing the praises of Sussex, where, at Horsham, he was to make his permanent home.

MILITARY CRITIC

During the 1914-18 war he became a military critic and wrote many brilliant commentaries which events disproved. Between the wars he sailed his yacht Nona in home waters and roamed near and far in quest of material for his books.

His later works included a four-volume history of England and biographies of Richelieu, Napoleon, Charles I, Cromwell and Milton.

A staunch Roman Catholic, he never abandoned his thesis that the evils of our time were derived from the Reformation and that the only hope for the world was a return to the Faith of Rome. In 1934 he and Chesterton received the Knight Commandership, with Star, of the Order of St. Gregory the Great.

(July 17)

MR. STALIN IS DEAD

Mr. Stalin, ruler of Russia for 28 years, died in the Kremlin last night at 9.50. Moscow time (6.50 p.m. G.M.T.), Moscow Radio announced this morning. His doctors gave the final cause of death as heart failure.

The news of the 73-year-old Prime Minister's death was given in this way: "The heart of the comrade and inspired continuer of Lenin's will, the wise leader and teacher of the Communist party and the Soviet people, Joseph Vissarionovitch Stalin, has stopped beating."

Mr. Stalin apparently died in his four-room flat, where he had been lying comatose since he became ill on Sunday. The Moscow announcement gave no indication of who would succeed him.

THE LATE JOSEPH STALIN

LATEST OF THE TSARS

JOSEPH STALIN, like LENIN before him, has died in his bed. The mortal end of dictators does not always come so calmly, but STALIN knew the hazards of his profession as well as anyone and took exceptional care to avoid them. His end may well create something like panic among the Communist stooges abroad, who may be thought by his successor to be on the wrong foot. It may rouse hope among the many millions living in perpetual panic under communist regimes. To the stooges we may be indifferent. To the victims, a profound sympathy dictates the advice not to seek a swift and useless martyrdom by revealing their hopes.

It was his greatest achievement to have brought the Bolshevik revolution into the main current of Russian life. His character remains enigmatic, but TROTSKY'S splenetic dismissal of him as a man of the utmost insignificance is certainly wide of the mark. While professing complete fidelity to the Bolshevik Revolution, he turned it inside-out, or perhaps we should say outside-in. Whereas the events in Petrograd in 1917 had been for TROTSKY only the first stage in a world overthrow of capitalism, STALIN directed his main energies to the consolidation of "Socialism in one country," which the party theoreticians had declared to be impossible. It may be that he never renounced the secret aim of world revolution and that, if he had lived, he would have given another decisive twist to Soviet policy; but he has not lived.

His nationalistic outlook, strange in a Georgian, was indispensably helped by the patriotic surge that followed the German invasion in 1941. The old Russian love of the fatherland that had defeated NAPOLEON again came to the rescue of STALIN. Pride in the army, and a host of other characteristics of the old regime, came back, and, strangest of all, the persecuted Orthodox church became again the ally of the State. Russia had in many ways reverted to type. The Secretary-General of the Communist Party had taken the place of the Tsar of All the Russias, but in his queer way – the way, it is said, of GEORGE ORWELL'S "Big Brother" – he still sought to be "the little father." His personal share in these doings is beyond dispute. When he and ROOSEVELT and Mr. CHURCHILL conferred during the war, it was a meeting of Titans. Now Mr. CHURCHILL alone remains. He was bearing great responsibilities while STALIN was an unknown revolutionary and ROOSEVELT an untried figure, and he is still at the helm. It is to be hoped that posterity will not pass upon STALIN the verdict which Mr. CHURCHILL passed on LENIN: "The Russian people's worst misfortune was his birth, their next worst - his death."

(March 6)

PROKOFIEV THE JESTER

A SAD ENDING

By Richard Capell

SERGEI PROKOVIEV had long been suffering from an impaired heart when he died in Russia last month, and he was absent from the famous musical conference at Moscow in 1948, when the most considerable composers in Russia were hauled over the coals by the formidable Andrei Zhdanov, the Kremlin's "arbiter of the arts." After the conference he wrote to recant and to confess the errors of his ways, but not in quite such abject terms as others did.

Poor Prokofiev, the playboy of the musical world of the 1920s! The West knows little about his last phase, but enough has come to light to suggest that the jester's end was pathetic.

Only to remember the description Nicolas Nabokov has given us of the composer as he appeared on his last visit to America, in 1938, betraying his "profound and terrible sense of insecurity," is to feel a pang; for Prokofiev, though not a very likeable character, was a gifted creature who has earned a niche in the history of 20th-century music.

It is generally assumed that homesickness sent him back to live in Russia after he had made a name and fortune in the West. This is probably to overrate the emotional capacity of his nature. It is much more likely that his decision was the outcome of the lionising he enjoyed on his first return to his native land, in 1925.

In the West he was, after all, only one of a good many bright lads; he saw himself ruling the roast at home. The pressure that was to be brought on him to alter his style in the interests of the Russian cabman's wife was something he cannot have foreseen.

There was a star danced, and under that was Prokofiev, like Beatrice, born. A whim of chance, as well as his native talent, earned him notoriety when he was a very young man. Leonid Sabaniev, a pundit of the Moscow Press, was so misguided as to give the composer's "Scythian Suite" a terrible wigging without having heard the work.

The suite had been announced in the programme of a Koussevitzky concert, but had had to be withdrawn: a scathing notice nevertheless appeared in the Moscow "News of the Season." Prokofiev's name was made. His fellow-composer Nabokov, who has given us the liveliest account that exists of Prokofiev the man, has explained why his music met, in his early years, with such surprising disparagement - music so friendly and amusing. The clue is to be found in Prokofiev's bearish manners.

Nabokov calls him 'a kind of big baby who must tell the truth on all occasions". It was characteristic than when a French composer introduced himself, saying what a pleasure it was to meet him, the Russian "stared at the man with cross bull eyes," and said: "On my part there is no pleasure."

Nabokov gives him credit for such frankness; but there was a vein of brutality in it. It is painful to read of the dog's life he led his luckless Spanish wife Lina. In Russia he at last abandoned her and her children, to take up with a young woman related to Kaganovitch, Stalin's associate.

Nabokov says that Stalin personally intervened to save Prokofiev - suddenly become suspect because of his Western connections - at the time of the "purges."

Those who in the 1920s regarded Prokofiev as a kind of precocious schoolboy with a facility for playing the piano in a mechanical way were not aware of the clever head he had for non-musical activities - for chess, for instance, in which he had a victory over Alekhin to his credit.

A curious thing about his career is the popularity won - the greatest won by anything he wrote - by a composition quite uncharacteristic of him. This was the so-called "Classical Symphony."

Nabokov tells us that the "Classical Symphony" was purely an exercise. Prokofiev had always had the habit of composing at the piano, and to test his power of dispensing with an instrument he wrote this little symphony with its conventional harmonies.

Alexander Werth, to whom we are indebted for an intimidating account of Zhdanov's 1948 conference, and who greatly admires Prokofiev, calls this piece "a delicious pastiche of Mozart." Its resemblance to Mozart is that of chalk to cheese, or that of a Dutch doll to a living girl.

(April 4)

'IRISH JOAN OF ARC' DIES

Mrs Maud Gonne MacBride, the Irish patriot whose followers called her the "Irish Joan of Arc," died in Dublin last night, aged 88. The daughter of a British Army officer, she was an avowed enemy of the British Empire, which she once described as "a symbol of evil."

Her husband, Major John MacBride, was executed in 1916, following the Easter week rebellion. She was the mother of Mr. Sean MacBride, former Fife Minister for External Affairs.

She went to Ireland at the age of 19, and then her life changed. In the west of Ireland she saw poor tenants being evicted in the Land League "war." From that time dated her vehement hatred of Britain. When Queen Victoria made a State visit to Dublin Maud Gonne protested against her "taking the shamrock in her withered hand."

OFFERED HELP

When her father died some time later, she determined to work for Ireland and offered to join Michael Davitt, then opposing the evictions.

Davitt would not have a young girl associated with his land campaign, nor would the Fenians. Eventually she formed her own organisation known as the "Daughters of Ireland" and agitated throughout England against the evictions.

She was in France when the Great War broke out and remained there until the Irish rising and her husband's execution in 1916, when she determined to get back to Dublin.

She travelled dressed as a tramp. When she got to Dublin she was arrested and taken to Holloway gaol. Later she was released because of bad health.

She went on with her work and was arrested many times for her activities. In 1929 she was accused of seditious libel. She was expelled from Northern Ireland in 1933 when she attempted to attend a demonstration in Belfast.

Mrs. MacBride was a close friend of W.B. Yeats, who wrote the play "Cathleen of Houlihan" for her.

(April 28)

MABEL LOVE DIES AT 78

GAIETY GIRL AND FAMOUS BEAUTY

Miss Mabel Love, the musical comedy star of Victorian and Edwardian days, died yesterday at Weybridge. She was 78.

She was one of the original "picture postcard" beauties: at the height of her career hundreds of thousands of copies of her photograph were sold.

Among artists with whom she appeared were William Terriss, Beerbohm Tree, Dan Leno, Lewis Waller, Arthur Bourchier and Robert Loraine.

NEW YORK VISIT

Her graceful dancing attracted attention when she appeared at the Lyric in 1890 in "La Cigale". She also became a favourite at the Gaiety.

Engagements at Covent Garden and at Drury Lane were followed by successful visits to Paris and New York. Bluebell in "Bluebell in Fairyland" was one of her most popular roles.

On retiring from the stage in 1912 Miss Love taught dancing and elocution. She returned to the stage in 1938 after a 26 years' absence to play in "Profit and Loss" at the Embassy Theatre.

(March 16)

LONDON DAY BY DAY

Abbey Lottery
Cricketing Knight

By last night most peers had received their letter from the Earl Marshal saying whether or not they had been successful in the Abbey ballot.

Over the week-end I have spoken to a number of them. Though the Earl Marshal's office refuses to give any figures, my impression is that about 20 per cent of those applying have been excluded.

There is no doubt of considerable resentment at the ballot, even among the successful.

Treated Like Tennis

As one peer put it to me:

"The Coronation is being treated as if it were Wimbledon tennis. The peers do not attend as mere spectators. They have a part to play in the ceremony and accordingly own a duty as well as a right to be there."

There was also a strong feeling that the obvious solution had been shirked. Why were wives, not attending of their own right, to be admitted when those with a constitutional position were to be kept out?

Hobbs a Knight

A C.H. goes to Mr. Benjamin Britten, one of several honours to music. Sir Arnold Bax becomes a K.C.V.O. and Dr. William McKie, of Westminster Abbey, a knight.

Jack Hobbs and Gordon Richards, with knighthoods, bring to their respective fields honours without precedent.

It is true that there is Sir Donald Bradman, but Hobbs in his 71st year becomes the first professional cricketer to receive the honour.

Both names have, on occasion, been cited by those who desire to see "more imaginative Honours Lists."

Colette at 80

Colette, the novelist, has just celebrated her 80th birthday by heading the table at a lunch of the Académie Goncourt, of which she is president. The other 11 members of the Academy, all distinguished writers, helped her to blow out the eight candles on her birthday cake.

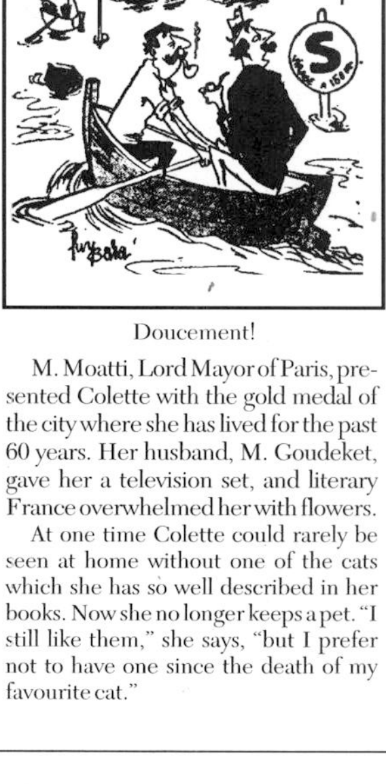

Doucement!

M. Moatti, Lord Mayor of Paris, presented Colette with the gold medal of the city where she has lived for the past 60 years. Her husband, M. Goudeket, gave her a television set, and literary France overwhelmed her with flowers.

At one time Colette could rarely be seen at home without one of the cats which she has so well described in her books. Now she no longer keeps a pet. "I still like them," she says, "but I prefer not to have one since the death of my favourite cat."

Antartica, Antarctica

When Vaughan Williams's seventh symphony is performed for the first time to-morrow in the Free Trade Hall, Manchester, readers of the Hallé Society's souvenir programme will notice that the title of the work is "Sinfonia Antartica." The composer's manuscript and the band parts spell it Antarctica.

The Oxford University Press told the Hallé last week that it had been decided to spell Antartica with one c. This is correct Italian. The other would be the modern Latin form.

Mr. Peter Scott, the artist and director of the Severn Wildfowl Trust, will be at the performance. The symphony commemorates the last expedition in 1911-12 of his father, the explorer.

Vaughan Williams used some of the themes for the film "Scott of the Antarctic." One movement is headed by a quotation from Scott's last journal.

Off the Beam

Sir Compton Mackenzie, I see, has suggested that there should be "sharper discrimination" in selecting voices for the Third Programme.

It seems that the B.B.C. is already well aware of the problem. I recently heard some B.B.C. men discussing whether a critic should be invited to take part in a certain programme.

The discussion ended when one of the men said firmly: "Really, you know, his voice is not quite Home Service."

PETERBOROUGH

FARMS, SMALLHOLDINGS

(12/- per line)

WOODCOCKS

30, ST. GEORGE'S STREET, W.1. (MAY.5411.)

25 minutes from Charles Cross

RESIDENTIAL FARM WITH GOOD PROFITS. 74 acres market garden land, lovely house, up-to-date pig buildings, cottages. Highly recommended at £14,750. Retail business optional.

DELIGHTFUL SITUATION GOOD INCOME LOW TAXATION ISLE OF MAN. Location 2 hours by air. 44-acre mixed holding with charming Residence 4 beds, main electricity. Excellent dairy, pig and poultry buildings. Strongly recommended from inspection at £5,750 Freehold

DAIRY FARM for sale, near Colchester. Possession Michaelmas, 124 acres, attested buildings for 40 cows, modern compact farmhouse with modern conveniences and cottages. Good situation on bus route, outskirts of small market town. Freehold price, £12,000. Substantial mortgage available to approved purchaser - Apply to Owners, Kensal House, 553-579 Harrow Road, London, W.10. Tel: Ladbroke 1071.

GLORIOUS HARBOUR & SEA VIEWS, overlooking popular Pembs Holiday Village. School & bus. FREEHOLD FARM 40 acres, average milk cheque £80 monthly. Cosy house, modernised, mains E.L., piped water all buildings. Attested cowshed, piggeries, everything stocks crops, milking machine, tractor and implements, £4,500: no offers. Owner willing to teach the right people. Or without stock £3,500. Write G.H. 2126. Daily Telegraph.

(June 23)

HORSE THAT WON AT 10-1 FOUND

ANOTHER ALSO TAKEN AWAY: BETS FIRM NAMED

Daily Telegraph Reporter

There were three developments yesterday in the investigations into the attempted betting coup at Bath races on Thursday, when the telephone cable to the racecourse was cut, "isolating" it for half an hour before the first race.

The first was that Francasal, 10-1 French winner of the Spa Selling Plate, was traced to Carters Barn, Sonning Common, near Henley-on-Thames, Oxon. Scotland Yard officers there supervised the loading of it and another horse of similar colour and markings into a horse box. Both were taken to Epsom.

At Carters Barn Francasal was in the care of Mr. Zicky G. Webster, a horse carrier. Mr. Webster was out for the day, but his wife said that he had received a telephone call asking if he would look after two horses for a day or two. They arrived on Saturday.

Meanwhile Mr. A Harrison Ford, secretary of the National Turf Protection Society, named a firm of bookmakers which, he said, had placed "a substantial commission for the horse."

Thirdly, a man who may be able to help the police to their inquiries was questioned at Bracknell police station, Berks, late last night about the betting coup.

It is now thought that there may have been a "switch" without the knowledge of the owner, trainer or jockey. On Friday Francasal was driven back to a farm at Burnham and collected from there early on Saturday morning.

The former owner of Francasal, M. Chatain a Frenchman, said yesterday that he sold it a fortnight ago for £300. It was good for nothing as a racer.

SEARCH FOR LORRY

Advice to Bookmakers

Police throughout Britain were on the look-out yesterday for a lorry bearing three registration letters and the numbers 478.

The lorry is believed to have been in Weston Lane, near the racecourse, when the cable was cut, probably with an oxy-acetylene burner. This effectively prevented bookmakers from contacting the course to lay off the bets, which would have reduced Francasal's price.

The general public is not deeply involved. But the attempted coup threatens to cost bookmakers thousands of pounds.

The National Sporting League advised its members who accepted large bets on the horse shortly before the race to send covering cheques to the League. It will hold the money until inquiries are ended.

TWO MEN WITH HORSE

Farmer's Report

Mr. A.J. Layton, farmer, of Cabbage Hill Farm, Binfield Bracknell, said yesterday that on the night of July 12 a horse-box arrived with the horse. Besides the driver there were two men, "a big man and a small one." They put the horse in the stables and left after feeding it.

About six o'clock the next morning the driver returned and took the horse away. The day after the race the horse was again brought back by the driver and "the big man," whose age Mr. Layton put at about 50. On Saturday morning the same driver collected the horse at 8 a.m. and drove off.

Widespread inquiries in the case are being made by Scotland Yard. Undercover men mingled with racegoers at Ascot on Saturday.

"SMALL GANG" THEORY

Many Suspects

Investigations have revealed that a large number of bets were placed on Francasal in London after the cable had been cut. Some of the police inquiries are being made in Hampstead and other North London areas.

It is believed that the coup was planned and carried out by a small London gang with minor agents in many parts of the country and directed by someone operating from London.

(July 20)

FINE ROWING TAKES LIGHT BLUES TO VICTORY

By B. C. Johnstone

One bright spot in the dull monotony of Saturday's disappointing Boat Race was the fine rowing and racing spirit of the Cambridge crew in beating Oxford by eight lengths in 19min 54sec over the famous Putney to Mortlake course. Alas, Cambridge were too soon too far in front of Oxford and therefore of the Press launch for the beauty of their rowing to be fully appreciated.

During the morning pipe-openers Cambridge were held up and almost swamped by the wash of a launch. Most of them were frenched, but the mishap had no dampening effect on their morale.

Going to the start about two hours later - after winning the toss and choosing the Surrey side - their paddling down gave the impression at once of alertness and complete confidence. In marked contrast Oxford looked almost tired. All we were to see a few minutes hence was portended in those launching minutes.

The Bishop of Willesden (Dr. Ellison), starter and umpire, got the crews quickly away. For a few strokes they were level, but Hall, striking 37 in the first minute, soon had Cambridge a quarter of a length up. At Craven Steps it was a length and by the Mile Post it was 1½, Cambridge then striking 30 to Oxford's 28.

FOUNDATION OF SUCCESS

Even at this early stage Cambridge's ascendancy was all too obvious. Their rowing was really good and they set off in the proper racing spirit, going all out to establish an early lead regardless of the distance they had to travel.

To me, it was a reminder of the dash and will to dominate of Douglas Stuart, who stroked the Light Blues in my years in 1906 and 1907. Stuart maintained that a lead in the first stages was the truest foundation of victory.

Oxford's rowing was strangely lifeless and hurried and as Cambridge moved on towards Hammersmith Bridge no doubt was left in the minds of following onlookers about the issue.

Through the Chiswick Reach there was rougher water and a stronger headwind. To Cambridge it made no difference, for they rowed through it with ease and fine watermanship. Oxford looked more uncomfortable than ever, and with the pace of their ship deteriorating they were five lengths the bad at Chiswick Steps, Cambridge then striking 27 to Oxford's 28.

McCAGG OUTSTANDING

Along Duke's Meadows Cambridge increased their lead, but from the Press launch we could still see their excellent cohesion and easy and effective power.

The outstanding oarsman was McCagg, of Harvard University. He showed great versatility in the way he adopted the English style.

His perfection in it was in itself a proof of its quality. He was a great pillar of strength in the middle of the boat.

Oxford had shown such promising training that it is difficult to account for their poor showing in the race. They lost, it seemed, all their good points when it came to the test.

(March 30)

GORDON RICHARDS on Derby winner Pinza.

QUEEN PRAISES G. RICHARDS

FIRST DERBY WIN

By Hotspur

To the intense disappointment of an immense crowd, the Queen's colt Aureole was beaten into second place in the Derby on Saturday. But Aureole's defeat was tempered because the winner was Sir Victor Sassoon's Pinza, ridden by Gordon Richards, to whom a knighthood was awarded in the Coronation Honours.

It was Richards' first Derby victory and the 28th in which he has ridden. Though there are no definite plans, I should not be surprised if Richards, now in his 50th year, retires from the saddle, having at last won the greatest of all races. After the race, the Queen sent for him to congratulate him.

Pinza was bred by Fred Darling, who was not well enough to be at Epsom. Darling taught N. Bertie, Pinza's trainer, his knowledge of training.

Richards spent about six hours yesterday at his Marlborough home looking at congratulatory messages.

(June 8)

FOXHUNTER WINS THIRD GOLD CUP

WHITE CITY RECORD

From Our Hunting Correspondent

WHITE CITY, Wednesday.

The Queen and the Duke of Edinburgh saw Lt.-Col. Harry Llewellyn on Foxhunter win the King George V Cup for the third time at the International Horse Show here tonight. Foxhunter is the only horse ever to have done so.

Col. Llewellyn was greeted with tumultuous applause. Still mounted on Foxhunter, he bared his head while the National Anthem was played and then, with Miss Marie Delfosse, winner of the Queen Elizabeth II Cup, went to the Royal Box, where the Queen presented both cups.

After receiving their trophies Miss Delfosse and Col. Llewellyn rode round the arena to cheers from the 24,000 spectators.

In the final round of the cup Capt. Tubridy, of Ireland, on Red Castle, made eight faults over a course raised to 5ft 6in. In a silence that could be heard, Col. Llewellyn and Foxhunter went round with only four faults. Third was Lt. D'Inzio, of Italy, on Merano.

(July 23)

MISS SMYTHE IS CHAMPION OF U.S. HORSE SHOW

FOXHUNTER FAILS

From Our Special Correspondent

HARRISBURG, Pennsylvania, Thursday.

Miss Pat Smythe, 24, of Britain, has become Individual International jumping champion of the Pennsylvania National Horse Show. She won the title last night by beating the best riders of four countries, including Lt.-Col. Llewellyn, Britain's Olympic gold medallist.

Miss Smythe, riding Prince Hal, was 10th of the 12 riders to answer the call of the ring-master's bugle. The crowd of 6,000 cheered as she soared over the course, easily taking jumps which had confounded several of the others.

Col. Llewellyn was eliminated when Foxhunter refused the fourth jump three times. He said afterwards he lost a stirrup and could not control his horse.

Miss Shirley Thomas, 18, of Canada, followed Miss Smythe on White Sable. She too turned in a faultless performance.

The jumps were then raised or widened. The British girl rode first and all was well until the eighth jump, which Prince Hal refused, crashing into the barrier, registering three faults.

But he held his footing and Miss Smythe remained in the saddle. She cleared it on the second attempt.

Miss Thomas cleared two barriers. But she knocked over the third, registering four faults and making Miss Smythe the winner.

Her victory gave Britain five out of the seven international blue ribbons and trophies which have so far been awarded. Ireland has won two.

SECOND IRISH WIN

Ireland won its second blue ribbon when Capt. Michael Tubridy, riding Ballynonte, took the Pennsylvania State Police Trophy.

(October 30)

WRONG HOLE IN ONE

A golfer who holed in one yesterday did not celebrate the feat. Mr. A Brown, of Osborne, winner of the Jacob's handicap cup at the Isle of Wight alliance meeting at the Needles, hooked his drive at the seventh. The ball swerved and dropped into the sixth hole.

(May 4)

MARSHALL WAS SUPERB ON EARLY MIST

National a Triumph for the Irish

By Hotspur

EARLY MIST, bought by Mr. J.V. Rank as a yearling with the object of winning the Grand National and sold to Mr. J.H. Griffin, of Dublin, for 5,300 guineas at the Rank dispersal sales, was the easiest winner of this famous steeplechase since the war.

His victory by 20 lengths from the courageous Mont Tremblant was a complete triumph for his owner, who came near to winning the race two seasons ago with Royal Tan, his brilliant young trainer, Vincent O'Brien, and his jockey, Bryan Marshall.

O'Brien, who trains in Co. Tipperary, is in his middle thirties, and has easily the most outstanding record of any National Hunt trainer in these islands.

In the last six years he has saddled the winners of four Cheltenham Gold Cups, three Champion Hurdles, and now the supreme triumph - the National. Indeed an amazing record and deserving of every credit.

Of Marshall, another Irishman in the top rank of his profession, one can only say that no man since the war has been more deserving of the highest honours. He has had some terrible falls in the past two seasons, yet his nerve remains unshaken. His riding and judgment on Saturday were beyond praise.

The Irish cannot claim the National as a total Irish success, however, for Early Mist, though Irish owned, trained and ridden, was bred in England. His breeder was Mr. D.J. Wrinch, of Shotley Hall, near Ipswich, who bought Early Mist's dam, Sudden Dawn, for only 27 guineas in 1938.

ILL-FATED CARDINAL ERROR

The race was run in a fairly good light, but unfortunately nowhere near as good as on the two previous days. Quite Naturally, the subject of a last-minute sale, fell at the first fence when leading, but there was only one other casualty here and it was not until the fifth fence that the first really well-fancied horse went out.

This was Cardinal Error who for the last time paid the penalty of clouting a fence too hard. He got too close to it and, sad to say, this good 'chaser broke his back.

At Becher's first time round, Ordnance was in front with Little Yid, Mont Tremblant, Parasol II and Early Mist among those close up.

Ordnance bowled merrily along in front taking his fences in his stride and at the Canal Turn had quite a long lead.

There was plenty of grief here. Parasol II, lying second, came down and was, unfortunately, killed. She brought down Whispering Steel who, according to his rider, had been jumping superbly.

There was still more grief, and when the field came on to the racecourse for the first time Ordnance held a clear lead of Mont Tremblant, Little Yid, Armoured Knight and Early Mist.

Ordnance dragged his hind legs through the Chair fence but got over and passing the stands was well clear of Mont Tremblant, Little Yid, Early Mist and Armoured Knight.

The five were so far in front on the remainder that even at this stage it looked as if one of them was reasonably certain to win - a fairly unusual occurrence half-way through a National.

Among the rest, who were fairly strung out, were Witty, Senlac Hill, Cloncarrig, Overshadow and Irish Lizard.

At the second last fence Early Mist was clearly going the better and although making a slight mistake here he had his race won at the last and came right away in the long run-in to win unchallenged.

Mont Tremblant ran on to finish second, four lengths in front of Irish Lizard, who made up a considerable amount of ground after being badly baulked. It did not affect the result.

GALLANT MONT TREMBLANT

I had thought that Mont Tremblant might not be courageous, but no horse could have shown more courage than the top weight on Saturday. He was absolutely stone cold after the race, and how he came to jump that last fence so cleanly and well is something worth remembering.

Witty unseated his rider at Becher's second time round when fifth or sixth, the sure-footed Larry Finn was brought down by Glen Fire and Hierba fell at the Canal Turn when well placed.

Cloncarrig came down at the last fence before coming on the racecourse for the second time, when well in front of Irish Lizard. Overshadow made no bad mistakes but was just not fast enough.

Senlac Hill, to the surprise of many, got round but jumped too deliberately and thus took too much out of himself. Wait and See was brought down.

Lucky Dome, to the amusement of many, jumped a piece of paper in front of the grandstand on his way to the post - and that is about all! As our Irish racing correspondent foreshadowed the Aintree fences were too much for him.

(March 30)

BRITISH WIN AT LE MANS

From W.A. McKenzie
Daily Telegraph Motoring Correspondent

LE MANS, Sunday.

A cosmopolitan crowd of 800,000 at Le Mans to-day gave an unprecedented welcome to Britain's greatest motor-race triumph of all time. Four Jaguars finished first, second, fourth and ninth in the 24-hour Grand Prix d'Endurance.

The winning Jaguar, driven by Tony Rolt and Duncan Hamilton, covered 2,540 miles in the 24 hours at an average speed of 105.6 m.p.h. This was almost 9 m.p.h. better than the previous record of 96.67 m.p.h. set by the winning Mercedes-Benz last year.

Other British cars finished high among the survivors. A Nash-Healey, driven by Leslie Johnson and Bert Hadley, took 11th place: an Austin-Healey driven by Gatsonides and Johnnie Lockett was 12th: a Frazer Nash, driven by Ken Wharton and P. Mitchell was 13th: and the Austin-Healey driven by Becquart and Gordon Wilkins took 14th place.

With eight British cars finishing in the first 14, it was unquestionably Britain's day, for only 26 cars of an entry of 60 finished at all. In a dozen languages round the course I was told: "Before the Coronation you have Everest. Afterwards, you have Le Mans."

(June 15)

MATTHEWS LAUGHS AT AGE AND SELECTORS

Cup Hero May Go on S. American Tour

By Frank Coles

Blackpool...4 Bolton Wanderers...3

CORONATION YEAR Cup Final will be remembered for all time as the match Stanley Matthews won, and in doing so gave the answer to the England selectors, who omitted him from the team against Scotland a fortnight ago and from the party which leaves for South America on Thursday.

On the second issue there is time for amends to be made. The too-old-at-38 cry was stifled for all time by Matthews himself in the grandstand finish he staged against Bolton. If, as I understand, Matthews is invited to make the tour all the football world will be delighted.

I have watched his climb to the heights since the day he started 22 years ago. One of the fittest men in football he should in five years' time still be selling his dummies and laughing at age.

Quite apart from the Matthews masterpiece, there has never been a Wembley Final to match this one. It began with the drama of Lofthouse's first-minute goal and ended with Perry's last-minute match-winner for Blackpool.

HERO'S GOAL BY BELL

Then there was the tragedy of Farm's two goalkeeping blunders and the sight of hopping Bell, Bolton's half-cripple, heading a hero's goal.

Just one of these incidents would have been enough to feature the story of any normal big match. On this never-to-be-forgotten afternoon there were half-a-dozen other thrills and in nearly all of them Matthews drew the 100,000 crowd to him like a magnet.

Matthews the maestro. Matthews the Wizard of Dribble. Old Man Matthews thrown into the discard by the selectors - the captions have been used over and over again. Now it was Matthews, the complete footballer in the flesh, who inspired the greatest rally Wembley has known in 30 years.

When, 10 minutes after the interval, Bell headed home Holden's ideal cross from the right wing to put Bolton 3-1 up Blackpool's stock stood at zero and it was as plain as anything could be that Garrett, Robinson (playing his first Cup-tie) and Perry, the whole of the team's left flank, were rapidly losing touch.

None but a player of genius could have saved this critical situation. Matthews saw his opportunity, seized it with both feet and without any exaggeration played Bolton out of the match in the gripping climax.

MORTENSEN SCORES

Blackpool's rally which was to end in glorious triumph began with 23 minutes to go. Matthews, in full cry, placed the ball from the right away over towards the far post where goalkeeper Hanson seemed to have it covered. But a scramble and a scuffle developed and the next thing we saw was Mortensen and the ball in the net.

Bolton were shaken and about to be shattered. The handicap of having their left-half Bell, who pulled a leg muscle early in the game, a passenger at outside-left, was doubled when Banks, the left-back, was also injured and Blackpool at once took full strategic advantage of their luck.

Pulling Perry across from the left wing they attacked mercilessly down the right flank with Tom Thumb Taylor for ever drawing the defence before sending Matthews away to torment his pursuers.

Matthews has never had a better service, and in this final phase he played the game of his life with the fascinated crowd swaying this way and that in harmony with his bewildering body swerves and pattern weaving.

(May 4)

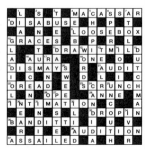

CHAMPIONS FOR SEVENTH TIME

By A Special Correspondent

Arsenal...3 Burnley...2

Twelve minutes of frantic, triumphant and inspired teamwork which cut through and battered down their last obstacle won for Arsenal their seventh championship - a Football League record - by the most slender margin since they first established their jealously guarded supremacy in 1930.

Not in the 23 years they have endured and survived could they have had to fight so fiercely as they did at Highbury last night against Burnley on a pitch more typical of the hazards of November than of the first day of May.

The 51,586 crowd roared from start to finish as Arsenal fought the game they had to win and as Burnley took on the challenge they scorned to foresake.

It was something of an anti-climax when, with the sky red in its setting, police took up their touchline guard of honour to allow the champions to stagger from the field. For Arsenal had won the title merely by a goal average only .099 better than Preston's.

FOUGHT TO THE END

And they nearly did not win at all, for twice Burnley came near to drawing level in the closing minutes. Firstly when Holden was felled in a tackle in the penalty area which must have called for a close decision, and secondly when Adamson's skidding shot was just held by Swindin.

Indeed Burnley, storming to recovery from a score of 1-3 at half-time, kept Arsenal desperately defending for the last 40 minutes.

How then did Arsenal manage it, especially as Burnley had taken the lead only eight minutes from the start through Stephenson? It was a typical Arsenal response of spirit.

(May 2)

MERCER'S LAST GAME

Standing on the steps of Highbury Stadium last night, less than half an hour after leading the club to their Championship triumph, Joe Mercer, the Arsenal captain and left-half, told thousands of cheering fans:

"Thank you all. This has been the most splendid day of my life but I am sorry to have to tell you it has been my last game for Arsenal. I am retiring from football."

MISS HARDING'S FINE MILE

By A Special Correspondent

Holders successfully defended their titles in only five of the 12 events in the Women's A.A.A. championships at the White City on Saturday, the all-round standard being notably high.

Miss Enid Harding, changing over from the half-mile to the mile, set up a new British record with 5min 9.8sec; Miss Ann Pashley equalled the British Native 100 yards record in 11sec: and Miss Jean Desforges, finding better form than on the previous evening, took the 80 metres hurdles in 11.5 sec and the long jump with 17ft 11¼in.

The final of the 100 yards was a real thriller, Miss Pashley running a splendid race to win by inches from S. Burgess with J. Scrivens third and the holder, Heather Armitage, fifth.

(July 6)

(Solution No. 8,514)

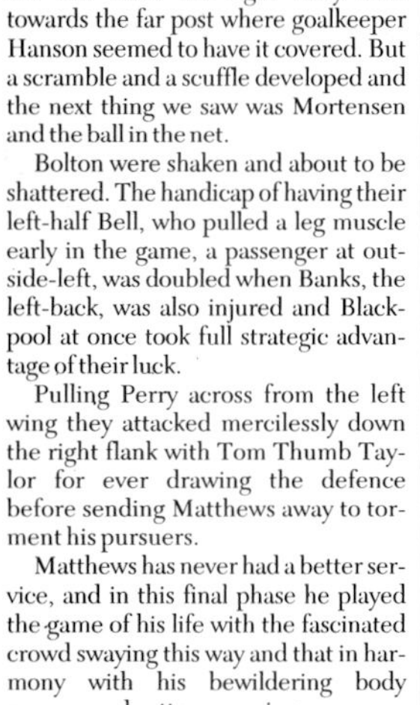

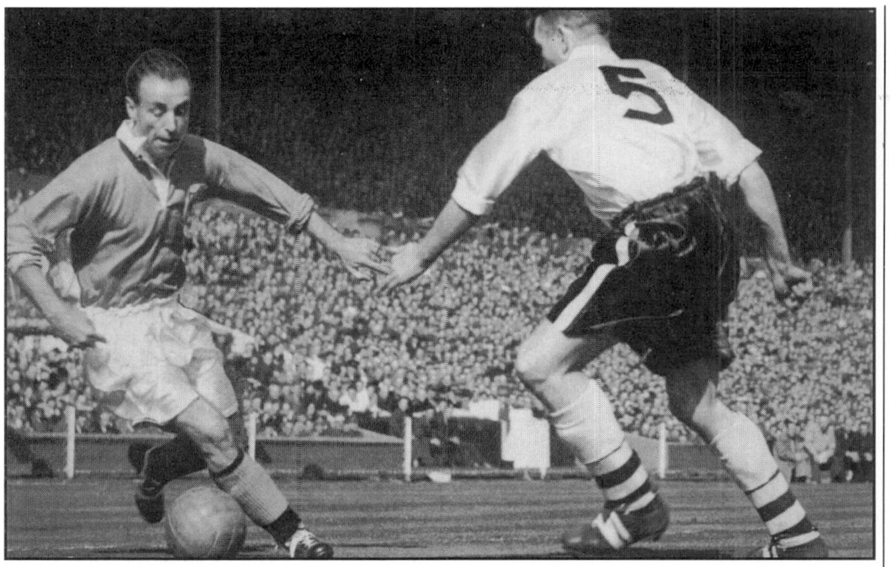

HOW IT'S DONE. With this typical touch by the Wizard of Dribble, Matthews had Barrass going the wrong way.

BRILLIANT HUNGARIANS ROUT ENGLAND

Winners Were the Complete Team

From Frank Coles

England.................... 3 Hungary.................... 6

ENGLAND'S proud record of never striking the home flag to a team from the Continent was shattered here this afternoon after standing the test of half a century. The immense consolation in defeat is that the spell was broken by a Hungarian side playing English-style football at its choicest. For the first time a major match at Wembley produced nine goals and six is the highest number scored against England for 72 years.

It was, indeed, a famous victory achieved by the most brilliant display of football ever seen in this country. The Hungarians flashed before our eyes as fit and as fast as a track team.

The mantle of masters rests gracefully on their shoulders. In scientific ball control of the highest degree, in speed and, above all, in shooting ability they outmatched England. From goalkeeper to outside-left they held the whip hand.

Centre-forward Hidegkuti, whose hat-trick performance will make him a national hero, not only carries a shot in his boots as powerful as Lawton or Lofthouse or any other England leader present or past, but he is as light as a feather when running into position to shoot.

The most complete forward, however, was Puskas, inside-left and captain. He scored a fantastic goal and was the architect of Hungary's most dangerous attacks which flowed with the sweet rhythm of a team fashioned in all the arts and crafts of the game.

AGGRESSIVE MATTHEWS

Not Enough Support

Add the remarkable speed of the wingers, Budai and Czibor, the solid worth of Bozsik as an attacking wing-half, the perfect example of stopper centre-half play by Lorant and the picture is complete.

England, well and truly conquered before half-time, fought on grimly making the best of a thankless job. They did splendidly in the circumstances to score three goals, but I am sorry to write that the latest forward formation was little if any improvement on those fielded against Ireland and the Rest of Europe.

The most disturbing shock was the failure of Taylor to give Matthews the support he was entitled to expect on the right wing. Robb also had a poor match. Matthews, as usual, was the most aggressive raider when he could be released, and Mortensen and Sewell worked tremendously hard to inject some method and understanding into the line.

The answer of the forwards as a whole might well be that they received little support from the wing-halves. Wright and Dickinson were too busy attempting to stem the incoming tide which threatened to overwhelm them.

And, further behind, the slowness of Ramsey, Eckersley and Johnston was a painful reminder that England must start to build anew if she is to avoid a repeated humiliation in next year's World Cup matches in Switzerland.

GOAL IN 90 SECONDS

Hidegkuti Sells The Dummy

The crowd was given an immediate glance at the shape of things to come when 90 seconds after the kick-off the amazing Hidegkuti scored a goal which left English defenders and onlookers in open-mouth astonishment at the suddenness yet simplicity of it all.

The pattern of the Hungarian attack was the wingers stationed well up and Hidegkuti playing hide and seek behind his inside forwards. In the 21st minute he stole from the debris of the English defence left by Puskas, Czibor and Kocsis and it was Hungary 2, England 1.

Then began 20 minutes of spellbinding football by the Hungarians, in which Merrick was continuously in action. In the 27th minute Czibor and Budal, the two wingers, caressed the ball along the right wing. Puskas was there for the final pass of a movement in which no English player got near the ball, and he shot brilliantly into the goal after juggling the ball on to his left foot - 3-1.

Five minutes later it was 4-1, but this time the goal was a lucky one. Bozsik took a free kick and as Puskas and Wright leapt for the ball it was deflected into the net by Puskas.

ENGLAND ON ATTACK

It was only in the last quarter of an hour before the interval that England were able to develop attacks. Matthews, receiving his first pass for nearly 20 minutes, gave Robb a heading chance, but Grosics saved brilliantly.

Five minutes from half-time Robb put the ball through to Mortensen, who squeezed a way past two Hungarians to shoot England's second goal, but 4-2 was a formidable score with which to start the second half.

After seven minutes Bozsik, emphasising that the Hungarians have long lost the continental weakness in shooting, drove into the goal a shot from 25 yards.

Four minutes later the Hungarians scored their sixth goal. It was Hidegkuti again, and again it was that body swerve quickly followed by a powerful shot which enabled him to score.

(November 26)

MARCIANO WINS IN FIRST ROUND

WALCOTT PROTESTS AT 'FAST COUNT'

From Our Own Correspondent

CHICAGO, Friday.

Rocky Marciano knocked out Jersey Joe Walcott in the first round here to-night to retain the heavyweight boxing championship.

Marciano wrested the title from Walcott by a knock-out in the 13th round last September. To-night he retained it in 2 minutes 25 seconds.

Walcott seemed to lose the fight more by accident than anything else. Marciano caught Walcott with a left hook which didn't seem to have a great deal of power behind it. But it was sufficient to send Walcott down. He immediately rose to his knees and sat listening to the count. He seemed slightly bewildered and that might have accounted for the fact that instead of getting up at the count of nine he was late.

TOUCH AND GO

It was touch and go whether he was actually on his feet again before the count of ten. The referee ruled he was not and declared Marciano the winner.

Boos broke out as the referee pointed to Marciano as the winner and Walcott, with an astonished expression on his face, looked around.

A moment later he was protesting to the referee at what he claimed was a fast count. His seconds joined in the protest, but the referee waved them aside.

Walcott showed his sportsmanship when he went to his corner. Marciano came over to commiserate with him and Walcott's face burst into a wide smile as he accepted Marciano's proffered hand.

(May 16)

DROBNY WINS WIMBLEDON'S LONGEST SINGLE

93 GAMES WITH PATTY

By Lance Tingay

The longest singles match ever played in the lawn tennis championships at Wimbledon took place yesterday between Jaroslav Drobny, 31, the former Czech, now an Egyptian, and Budge Patty, 29, the American resident in Paris and title winner in 1950.

Drobny beat Patty in their third round contest which began at 4.45 and ended in fading light at 9 o'clock. Ninety-three games were played in all.

Towards the closing stages of this exhausting match both men were attacked by cramp.

At 10 games-all in the fifth set the Referee of the Championships, Col. John Legg, came on to court to make a decision about the failing light. He instructed the umpire to stop the match at 11 games-all.

Instead, Drobny took the set 12-10 to win the most exhausting contest the Championship has seen.

Throughout, the match was played at a stirring pace. Patty was three times within a stroke of winning in the fourth set and three times again in the final set.

The score - 3-6, 16-18, 3-6, 8-6, 12-10.

(June 30)

MISS CONNOLLY'S RECORD BEST FOR 21 YEARS

Three Strange Wimbledon Facts

By Lance Tingay

The Wimbledon Lawn Tennis Championships that ended on Saturday will not have had their day-to-day happenings so closely recorded as some other years, but the historian of the game will, on three points, write of them as unique. One will be the memorable third round singles between J. Drobny and B. Patty on Thursday, June 25, when for 93 games and for four hours and a quarter, two fine players contested Wimbledon's longest match.

That is a matter of fact. Second, he will write of the final of the women's doubles, in which Miss Hart and Miss Shirley Fry beat Miss Connolly (yes, the fabulous Miss Connolly) and Miss Julie Sampson, as the briefest ever. 6-0, 6-0 was the score, the only time a pair of spectacles has appeared on Wimbledon's final records.

Miss Connolly is women's singles champion for the second time. Her international tally is now Wimbledon 2, United States 2, France 1 and Australia 1, six major singles titles gained since the autumn of 1951 - and she only 18 years old.

Her Wimbledon win, which everyone took for granted and only doubted momentarily in the stirring exchanges of Saturday's final, was devastatingly achieved.

Despite the two long, wonderful sets against Miss Hart, sets that were a joy to watch, Miss Connolly retained her title for the loss of only 19 games in all.

NOW SHE MUST PRACTICE

Miss Connolly has weaknesses. She is not yet the perfect lawn tennis machine. Her service could be strengthened, for were not the two double faults she served in the ninth game of the first set an admission of relative failure? (Here Miss Hart was superior. Her two doubles were divided between the sets.)

Her volleying could be made more certain. It is irrelevant, in this context, to proclaim her present volleying skill as adequate because she invariably has an open court in which to put the ball, such being the power of her ground strokes. Doubtless, too, her footwork could improve. As with the four-minute mile in athletics there is always something for which to strive.

And, who knows, another woman may come along who can belt the ball with the pace, accuracy and consistency of Miss Connolly, who can thump as backhand winners what any other player might achieve twice out of ten attempts as "blinders."

So Miss Connolly will continue to work four or five hours, every one of six days out of seven, practising, practising and practising. She is to defend her title next year. It would be as well to back her now while any odds are offered.

The Champions

MEN'S SINGLES

V.Selxas (U.S.) bt K.Nielsen (Denmark), 9-7, 6-3, 6-4.

WOMEN'S SINGLES

Miss M.Connolly (U.S.) bt Miss D.Hart (U.S.), 8-6, 7-5.

MEN'S DOUBLES

L.A.Hoad & K.R.Rosewall bt R.Hartwig & M.G.Rose, 6-4, 7-5, 4-6.

WOMEN'S DOUBLES

Miss S.Fry & Miss D.Hart bt Miss M.Connolly & Miss J.Sampson, 6-0, 6-0.

MIXED DOUBLES

V.Selxas & Miss D.Hart bt E.Morea & Miss S.Fry, 9-7, 7-5.

ALL ENGLAND PLATE - Men: G.L.Paish (G.B.) bt J.W.Ager (U.S.), 4-6, 6-0, 7-5.

Women: Miss M.P.Harrison (G.B.) bt Miss E.P.Lombard (Ireland), 1-6, 6-3, 6-3.

JUNIOR INVITATION TOURNAMENT - Boys: W.A.Knight (G.B.) bt R.Krishman (India) 7-5, 6-4. Girls: Miss D.Killan (S.A.) bt Miss V.A.Pitt (G.B.), 6-4, 4-6, 6-1.

(July 6)

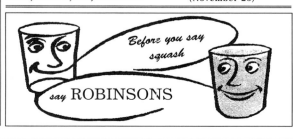

CRICKET SUPREMACY HAS PASSED TO ENGLAND

'Elusive Victory' After Twenty Years

From E. W. Swanton

OVAL, Wednesday.

THE Fifth Test, which had seemed to turn so sharply England's way when Australia were battling against the spin bowlers yesterday, duly ended in victory here shortly before 3 o'clock this afternoon: that elusive victory which has been awaited ever since D.R. Jardine's side won the Ashes 20 years ago.

The margin of eight wickets was conclusive enough, but the result was not gained without a fight to the last ball as between Edrich, May and Compton on the one hand, and Johnston, Lindwall and Miller, supported magnificently as ever in the field on the other.

Johnston bowled to-day without respite until Hassett came on as at Melbourne on a similar occasion in '51, to bowl a final comedy over at his end.

Lindwall, likewise, from the pavilion end kept up a ceaseless, fast and accurate attack apart from five overs from Miller, until he gave the ball finally to Morris, off whom Compton hit the last four needed.

It took two hours and 40 minutes of resolute batsmanship to make the final 94 runs. May's wicket being the Australians' only reward.

BLEND OF AGES

It all took one back 27 years to the August evening when for the first time since the first war Australia's colours were lowered in a Test rubber, and the crowd let themselves go as though a reproach had been wiped away. Then, as now, England's side was a blend of the ages, from the youthful Chapman and Larwood to the grizzled Rhodes, and Strudwick playing, too, in his last match against Australia.

It cannot be said that any of Hutton's present team are anywhere near the end of their tethers but certainly several are, or should be, at the beginnings of fine achievements. One thinks of the four in this team who were not born when Bobbs and Sutcliffe were fashioning that former victory on an Oval sticky-dog: Graveney, May, Trueman and Lock. The performance of the latter three over these last few days was rich in promise.

In 1926 it was universally said that the change in the tide would be all for the good of cricket in Australia. They had won three rubbers, with consummate ease, and the keen edge of competition was worn blunt. Exactly the same situation exists, so our Australian friends assure us, in their country to-day.

Three rubbers have been won against England, and now, after the warning jolt of the drawn series against Cheetham's admirable young South Africans in the last Australian summer, it is established that the supremacy has passed to other hands.

It will prove to be the spur that has been needed in Melbourne, Sydney and Adelaide, and one can almost savour the unholy relish with which the next M.C.C. side will be received at Perth in October next year.

FINE AUSTRALIAN SIDE

The fielding of this side has scarcely ever been surpassed, and if the form of some of the more experienced batsmen has been erratic and unreliable is it not proper to give the chief credit to the English bowlers. Against the run of our county sides Morris, Miller, Hole and the others have looked fine enough batsmen: and Harvey, with 10 centuries already, has been absolutely devastating.

Bedser must take the palm, but the honours of the series have not been monopolised by the captain and his foremost bowler. Everyone of to-day's XI has played a part at one time or another, along with several not called upon in this match: Watson, Wardle, Tattersall, Statham, Simpson, and not least, Brown.

Bailey's unique contribution will not quickly be forgotten, while in support of all the bowling Evans has been, as usual, quite admirable.

On Hutton has been the greatest strain. Anyone who has seen all five Tests, and who has realised how he has upheld the batting and appreciated the difficulties he has encountered in the field, three times with only four bowlers, almost always irked by the presence of a left-handed batsman and with several fieldsmen of limited mobility, will give him a high degree of praise for his efforts.

(August 20)

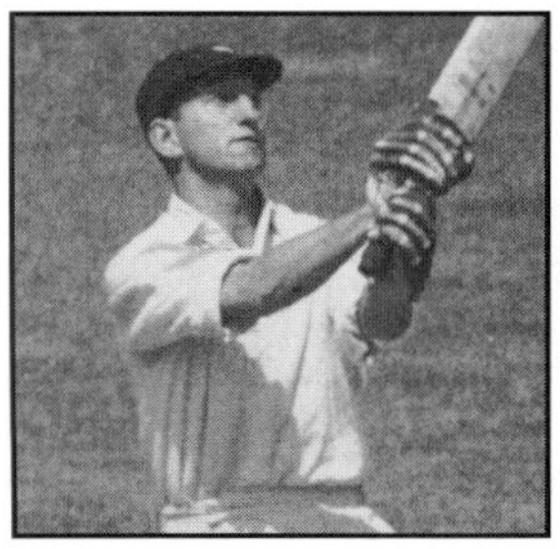

LEN HUTTON

The Scoreboard

***AUSTRALIA*-First Innings**

A.L.Hassett, c Evans, b Bedser	53
A.R.Morris, lbw, b Bedser	16
K.R.Miller, lbw, b Bailey	1
R.N.Harvey, c Hutton, b Trueman	36
G.B.Hole, c Evans, b Trueman	37
J.H.de Courcy, c Evans, b Trueman	62
R.G.Archer, c and b Bedser	10
A.K.Davidson, c Edrich, b Laker	22
R.R.Lindwall, c Evans, b Trueman	5
G.R.Langley, c Edrich, b Lock	18
W.A.Johnston, not out	9
Extras (b 4, nb2)	6
Total	**275**

Fall of wickets: 1-38, 2-41, 3-107, 4-107, 5-118, 6-160, 7-160, 8-207, 9-245.

Second Innings

A.L.Hassett, lbw. b Laker	10
A.R.Morris, lbw, b Lock	26
G.B.Hole, lbw, b Laker	17
R.N.Harvey, b Lock	1
K.R.Miller, c Trueman, b Laker	0
J.H.de Courcy, run out	4
R.G.Archer, c Edrich, b Lock	49
A.K.Davidson, b Lock	21
R.R.Lindwall, c Compton, b Laker	12
G.R.Langley, c Trueman, b Lock	2
W.A.Johnston, not out	6
Extras (b 11, lb 3)	14
Total	**162**

Fall of wickets: 1-23, 2-59, 3-60, 4-61, 5-61, 6-85, 7-135, 8-140, 9-144.

ENGLAND-First Innings

Hutton, b Johnston	82
W.J.Edrich, lbw, b Lindwall	21
P.B.H.May, c Archer, b Johnston	39
Compton (D), c Langley, b Lindwall	16
Graveney, c Miller, b Lindwall	4
T.E.Bailey, b Archer	64
Evans, run out	28
Laker, c Langley, b Miller	1
Lock, c Davidson, b Lindwall	4
Trueman, b Johnston	10
Bedser (A.V.), not out	22
Extras (b 9, lb 5, w 1)	15
Total	**306**

Fall of wickets: 1-37, 2-137, 3-154, 4-167, 5-170, 6-210, 7-225, 8-237, 9-262.

Second Innings

Hutton, run out	17
W.J.Edrich, not out	55
P.B.H.May, c Davidson, b Mille	37
Compton (D.) not out	22
Extra (lb 1)	1
Total (2 wkts.)	**132**

Fall of wickets: 1-24, 2-88.

2 LEANDER AND R.A.F. VICTORIES

BRITAIN KEEP EIGHT HENLEY TROPHIES

By B. C. Johnstone

The oarsmanship at Henley Royal Regatta last week gave a fine picture of the healthy state of English rowing. It is a long time since the standard at Henley has been so consistently high and the struggle so keen.

The exemplary display of racing and style of Leander, when beating the French crew, Metropolitaine des Transports, and winning the Grand Challenge Cup for the second year in succession, was worthy of the famous English clubs they were representing.

From the start to the finish there was never any doubt of Leander's superiority. At a lower stroke than their opponents they went ahead from the start improving their position all the time. As they moved along the enclosure they seemed to attain the acme of the art of rowing.

(July 6)

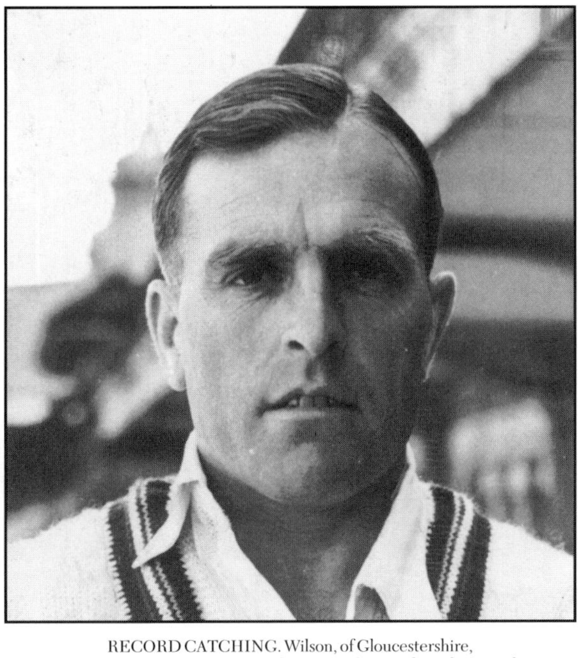

RECORD CATCHING. Wilson, of Gloucestershire, the only wicket-keeper to have taken 10 catches in a first-class match.

WILSON TAKES 10 CATCHES: SETS WORLD RECORD

From E. W. Swanton

PORTSMOUTH, Friday.

WHEN Shackleton propelled himself wearily to the wicket here this evening a few seconds before the clock struck five the Gloucestershire score read 103 for seven. Three wickets in the last over was surely altogether too rich?

But facing Shackleton was Cook, who after coming in last for Gloucester all his days now finds himself promoted to No. 9 in front of two young batsmen reputedly of highly eccentric technique, Wells and McHugh.

Hampshire, so felt all who were in the know, had a chance yet. Cook played so late to the first ball that he seemed to trap it inches from the stumps, miraculously without knocking the wicket over. He narrowly averted disaster from the second ball and the third and was bowled behind his legs with the fourth.

Now only a hat-trick would do, and Wells, stopping the fifth ball, celebrated his success by hoicking the last for a single.

TWO BOWLERS BARRED WAY

Gloucestershire in the last innings needed to make 149 in a minute or two over two hours. Two men Shackleton and Cannings, plus the Hampshire fielding, stood between them. It did not seem an unduly tall order, though the pace in the wicket added to the somehow uneven height to which the ball came up meant that the runs would need working for.

These bowlers, as it turned out, lasted unchanged, and their length and stamina not only kept Gloucester at arm's length from victory but came very near to snatching it for Hampshire.

This morning Hampshire did very well to add 139 to the overnight score of 57 for three, losing only two wickets in the process. Thus at lunch they were 131 on with five wickets in hand and a possible two and three-quarter hours' cricket left.

Their thoughts began to turn towards some quick runs afterwards, and the setting of a task to Gloucestershire. The latter, however, had kept back the new ball, and before any aggressive Hampshire ideas could materialise the attack was coming from Lambert.

LAMBERT AT HIS BEST

With the old ball Lambert in an hour and a quarter's spell before lunch had taken the wickets of Harrison and Rayment. By taking four for 12 in this phase he made his analysis seven for 73, which arithmetically and possibly also in fact is his best effort for Gloucestershire.

But records of wider moments coincided with Lambert's performance, for in this short period after lunch Wilson brought the number of his catches in the match to 10. Only one cricketer in history has previously taken 10 catches in a match, the prince of modern Gloucester players, Hammond, who a quarter of a century ago caught 10 Surrey batsmen at Cheltenham and incidentally, made 100 in each innings.

WILSON MAKES IT 500

No wicket-keeper has ever caught 10, although two, Don Tallon of Australia, and Pooley in the dark ages have taken 12 wickets. Finally to begin his benefit season Wilson to-day brought the number of his victims to 500. Among present-day English wicket-keepers only Evans and Yarnold have more.

(May 9)

BRITISH CAR WINS AT MONTE CARLO RALLY

By W. A. McKenzie
Daily Telegraph Motoring Correspondent

MONTE CARLO, Sunday.

For the second year running Britain was the winner of the Monte Carlo Rally, which ended here today. Maurice Gatsonides, of Haarlem, Holland, driving professionally in a team of Ford Zephyr cars from Dagenham, Essex, snatched the victory from a field of 100 drivers who entered, on level terms, in the final eliminating test.

Second was another British entry, Ian Appleyard, in a Jaguar. Ian who, as usual, was accompanied by his wife, Pat, is Britain's leading rally driver and the only Alpine Trial gold cup winner.

Third and fourth were the Frenchmen, R. Marion (Citroen) and M. Grosgogeat (Panhard). Fifth came C. Vard, the Irish driver of a British Jaguar, who was "placed" two years ago. He was accompanied by A.R. Jolley.

BEST BRITISH EFFORT

Although British cars have won three times before, this result is the best British effort yet in the Rally. The 100 surviving drivers had their last test today in the mountains above Monaco.

The aim was to drive to a precise time schedule round a 50-mile course of tortuous roads. In contrast to conditions last year, the course was dry except for a snowy five-mile stretch.

A British woman just missed by bad luck the Ladies' Cup, the Coupe des Dames, which has not been won by a British driver since 1932. She was Sheila Van Damm, daughter of Mr. Vivian Van Damm, the Windmill Theatre owner.

TWO WOMEN FINALISTS

She and a Frenchwoman were the only women to qualify for the eliminating trial. It was therefore a duel between her and Mlle. M. Pochon, driving a small Renault.

Miss Van Damm, in her Sunbeam-Talbot, was putting up a performance which must have won her the cup. But just before the finish she suffered a puncture which lost her three minutes.

Last year's winner, Sidney Allard, made the best time of the day in the accelerate-stop-accelerate test, held on arrival here, in which drivers had to qualify for entry in to-day's final test. His time was 21 8-10sec.

(January 26)

'UNBEATABLE' HOGAN WINS OPEN BY FOUR STROKES

New Champion Has No Equal

From Leonard Crawley

CARNOUSTIE, Friday.

BEN HOGAN, of the United States, won the Open Golf Championship here this evening with the wonderful total of 282. Peter Thomson, of Australia; Frank Stranahan, the American Walker Cup player; D.J. Rees; and A. Cerda, of the Argentine, tied for second place with 286, and R. de Vicenzo came next, one stroke further behind.

Hogan had rounds of 70 and 68 to-day and I think we are all agreed that if he did not bring this great course quite to its knees his marvellous golf has at least humbled it and his winning score will be unbeaten here for generations.

Hogan, who won his fourth American Open earlier this year, thus becomes the third American ever to have held the two major championships of the world at the same time.

It will be seen from Hogan's four rounds of 73, 71, 70 and 68 that he gradually warmed up in preparation for his final triumph. He is undoubtedly the best golfer in the world to-day, and who shall say he is not the best of all time?

He seems to have the indefinable quality of being able to bring himself to his supreme peak when the pressure is greatest. His great predecessor Walter Hagen was much the same, but whereas he was a genius at improvisation and would play a number of bad shots, Hogan is the nearest thing we have seen to the perfect golfing machine.

To-day he made two mistakes, which included a disaster this morning at the 17th, and this afternoon he did not quite hit his second shot to the 14th right out of the middle of the club.

Mercifully he has not putted well or anything like his best this week, and his chipping might also have been better. Otherwise his winning score would have been fantastic.

STRANAHAN FALTERS

Of those in the hunt, Stranahan was out first and went very well, though at a deplorably slow step for 13 holes.

At the 14th he hit a shocking tee shot into a copse and took six, which made a heavy load on his back. A grand three at the 18th put him round in 73 for 217, but he had obviously lost ground.

Vicenzo came next. He was out in 37, which did not seem quite good enough and fives at the 12th and 14th, where he took three gratuitous putts, looked serious. But he came back and he finished gloriously in 4 3 3 4 for 71 for a total of 214.

Rees, behind him, began with 12 fours in a row. Whereas he got a four at the sixth, he dropped a shot at the short eighth, where he failed to get down in a chip and a putt.

A three and a four at the 13th and 14th holes created visions of a 70 - only visions, for he finished disappointingly in 5 4 5 4, three shots more than one had dared to hope. Thus with 73 he stood at 215 with a round to go.

Thomson's golf was well nigh faultless, and apart from the 15th, where he took five, he did every hole in par. His 71 was a lovely exhibition and brought him in to second place with Rees at 215.

Brown began with a three and was out in 35, only to drop three shots in the next four holes, and 75 was the best he could do.

(July 11)

No. 8514

ACROSS

4 The anti-type was often seen in Victorian Drawing rooms (8)
8 Diana's sailor practice? … Sorry to undeceive you (8)
9 Free fight a horse may find himself in (5-3)
10 There are three of them. One for each meal in the day? (6)
11 Advice to the man at the bar who told tall stories (4, 2, 4)
16 Petrarch's lady has lost her head but what an air she has! (4)
18 Just "a" clue (3)
19 May in a Norfolk town? Causes consternation, certainly (7)
21 The part of 36 across of occasional interest to a treasurer (5)
22 Nymph's entreaty to those who would learn? (5)
23 What a dog may do to a bone (7)
26 What Edgar Allan might become (3)
28 You may find her with ten in the extra building (4)
29 Hint (10)
33 Pay an unexpected visit to the baths? (4,2)
35 It sounds as if the robbers forbid a song (8)
36 A prelude to a broadcast, maybe (8)
37 Attacked when the poor mug was ill (8)

DOWN

1 Peculiar without the makings of colour (4)
2 Can and must be involved in study (7)
3 Its child is full of grace (7)
4 A peach of a singer! (5)
5 Not the composer to cut out obviously (6)
6 A valuable kind of whale (5)
7 A suitable tax for a Pacific island (5)
10 Happy-headed flowers (8)
12 The compiler's raw materials (5)
13 Eat and run to get the vessel for drink (3-3)
14 An antiseptic, that is with a god in (6)
15 He flies in legend but does not find it restful (8)
16 Fragrant climb? (6)
17 If you aim at this, the chances of success are very small (6)
20 Small in a short street. Charming! (5)
24 Plainly speaking a Shavian play (7)
25 Not polished and unusual to begin with even in Scotland (7)
27 A staple mixture for preparing woad, perhaps (6)
30 Gets "warm" … (5)
31 … and here lots of people get very warm most of the time (5)
32 This is all Greek to us even if it is poetry (5)
34 Curtail a valuable tooth to get boy's name (4)

(March 4)

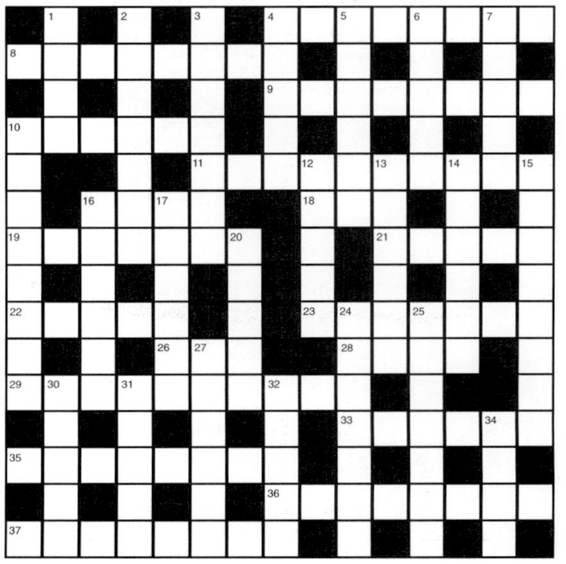

1954

In the splendour of Westminster Hall both Houses of Parliament gathered to pay tribute to Sir Winston Churchill on the occasion of his 80th birthday. He was presented with his portrait painted by Graham Sutherland. At the time he made it evident that he did not like the picture which he said, privately, made him look as if he was sitting on the lavatory. Many years later, it was learnt that Lady Churchill had destroyed the picture.

The long struggle between the French army and the Vietnamese people was ended after 75 days of talks in Geneva masterminded by Anthony Eden, the British Foreign Secretary. Further east the tension rose as the Chinese Communist government looked as if it might invade Formosa, the last bastion of the Chinese Nationalist forces under Chiang Kai-shek. Long-range artillery duels were fired.

It was a year of adventure and tragedy in the air. The "Flying Bedstead" test aircraft accomplished the first vertical take off. New air routes were flown over the North Pole. The de Havilland Comet, the first jet airliner in regular passenger service, suffered a series of misadventures. An enquiry into the loss of a Comet which crashed into the sea shortly after taking off from Rome airport found that the aircraft had been suffering from metal fatigue. The first American atom-powered submarine was launched.

Londoners queued in their thousands when a Roman temple was discovered during building work near the Mansion House in the city. Two boys, by chance, unearthed its greatest treasure, a complete head of the Roman god Mithras. Britain was exposed to a new form of evangelism when Dr. Billy Graham brought American-style religious fervour across the Atlantic. 180,000 people attended Dr. Graham's final rally at Wembley Stadium.

In February, Jogn Betjeman declared he had never laughed so much since he had read Evelyn Waugh's Decline and Fall. He had been reading Kingsley Amis's Lucky Jim. He thought less well of Iris Murdoch's first try at fiction, Under the Net: "There is a little too much farce and fantasy for the good of the novel." The production of a television version of George Orwell's 1984 caused what a BBC spokesman called, "a great many complaints". Others thought that the event showed that television drama had come of age. The complaints were probably happier with the first British television "soap", The Grove Family, which started its run in April.

One of the great barriers in sport came down when Roger Bannister ran the mile at Oxford in under four minutes. Later in the year he confirmed his supremacy by beating the Australian Jogn Landy to win the Empire Games title, again in under four minutes. At Wimbledon Jaroslav Drobny, the Czech-born player, won the men's single title, beating the 19-year-old Ken Rosewall in a five-set final that lasted 2 hours 36 minutes, then the longest finals in Wimbledon's history. The hundredth University Boat Race was won by Oxford, the Dark Blues' first win of the decade.

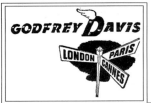

The Daily Telegraph

and Morning Post
No. 30,943 LONDON, FRIDAY, SEPTEMBER 10, 1954 Printed in LONDON and MANCHESTER Price 2d.

1,100 DIE IN 12-SEC. EARTHQUAKE

TOWN SHATTERED IN ALGERIA: 5,000 INJURED

VILLAGES & FARMS IN WIDE AREA WIPED OUT

THOUSANDS HOMELESS: ARMY MOBILISED FOR RESCUE WORK

From Our Special Correspondent

ALGIERS, Thursday.

More than 1,100 people, it is estimated, were killed in a 12-second earthquake that shattered the Algerian town of Orleansville and wiped out villages and farmsteads in the surrounding area early to-day. Five thousand people were injured.

Many more thousands are homeless. So wide-spread was the devastation that all means of communication with the area were cut for a time. No official casualty figure is expected for at least a further 24 hours.

Troops have been mobilised from all parts of the North African territory to help dig out the dead and injured beneath the piles of crumbled masonry. Early to-night 450 bodies had been recovered.

The first shock, just after 1 a.m., destroyed the town's hospital, prefecture of police, the prison, railway station, three hotels and numerous apartment houses. Wide fissures opened in the streets and a block of flats collapsed. Then the old cathedral, which dates from Roman times, and a new Roman Catholic church fell in ruins.

Men, women and children rushed screaming from their beds. They scrambled through the littered streets, trying to reach the safety of the open fields outside the city's walls.

Old women were seen scrabbling at the rubble in vain attempts to reach their families trapped beneath. A nine-year-old girl sat wailing outside the ruins of her house. She still clutched a ragged cloth doll.

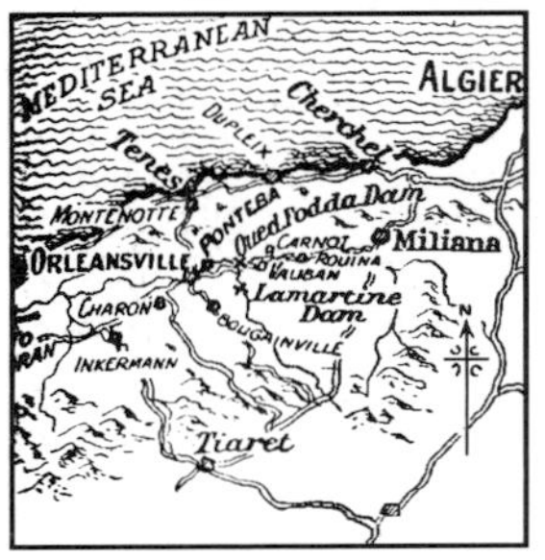

Flames licking the devastated buildings, the rumble of collapsing masonry and the anguished cries of the fleeing population turned the night into a Dantesque inferno. The public services, deprived of their operating centres, were unable to function for some time.

AIRLIFT FROM AREA

Injured Flown Out

As dawn broke over the devastation, the first Army lorries bringing aid from outside reached the town. Most of the population, Algerian and French alike, were camped in miserable huddles on the outskirts.

An emergency field hospital was set up in an open field to replace the destroyed town hospital. All day hundreds of injured were taken in for treatment. Many of the more seriously injured were evacuated to Algiers.

Every available Air Force plane was pressed into service to operate an airlift from the stricken town to Algiers. A plane took off every 30 minutes with injured.

Between 600 and 800 have already been admitted to Algiers hospitals. By to-night almost the whole population had left the town and the Army was in control.

NO SIGN OF LONE SWIMMER

TUBE & MAST SEEN IN CHANNEL

Daily Telegraph Reporter

A rubber inner tube with small mast attached, similar to one being towed by Edward May, 44, in his attempt to swim the Channel unescorted, was reported at Boulogne yesterday to have been sighted by a French trawler skipper Edouard Boulogne. He said it was mid-way between Dover and Calais.

Boulogne, whose trawler is the Les Boleines, said two bottles were on the raft but there was no sign of any man in the water. He tried to recover it but the trawler was moving to quickly.

May, a steel worker at Scunthorpe, Lincs., entered the water at Cape Gris Nez at 4.45 a.m. on Wednesday and despite searches by aircraft, life boats and other vessels has not been seen since. Earlier yesterday the search was called off and Dover police announced last night that he had been officially reported missing.

"OWN RESPONSIBILTY"

Mr. Louis Scott, a Scunthorpe jeweller and May's manager, said at Dover that a note was given to him by May. This stated:

"I am undertaking at my own responsibility, to swim the English Channel from Cap Gris Nez to Dover without escort of a boat, towing an inflated tube carrying my own provisions to sustain myself whilst swimming. This is an ambition I have wanted to achieve for a number of years."

Mrs. Florence May, the swimmer's wife, who is the mother of nine children, said: "I am still hoping. My husband said when we were first married 25 years ago that he would swim the Channel."

GIRL OF 16 BEATS MISS CHADWICK

TORONTO, Thursday.

Marilyn Bell, 16-year-old Toronto choir girl, touched the Canadian shore of Lake Ontario to-night after a 32-mile swim from the American side. Florence Chadwick, who has swum the Channel both ways, abandoned her attempt to swim the lake after competing 15 miles.

Miss Bell was 21 hours in the water. She was pulled from the water into a boat. - B.U.P.

SIR W. CHURCHILL

By Our Political Correspondent

Sir Winston Churchill leaves his own home, Chartwell, near Westerham, to-day to spend a few days at Chequers, the official country house of the Prime Minister. On the way he will call at 10, Downing Street.

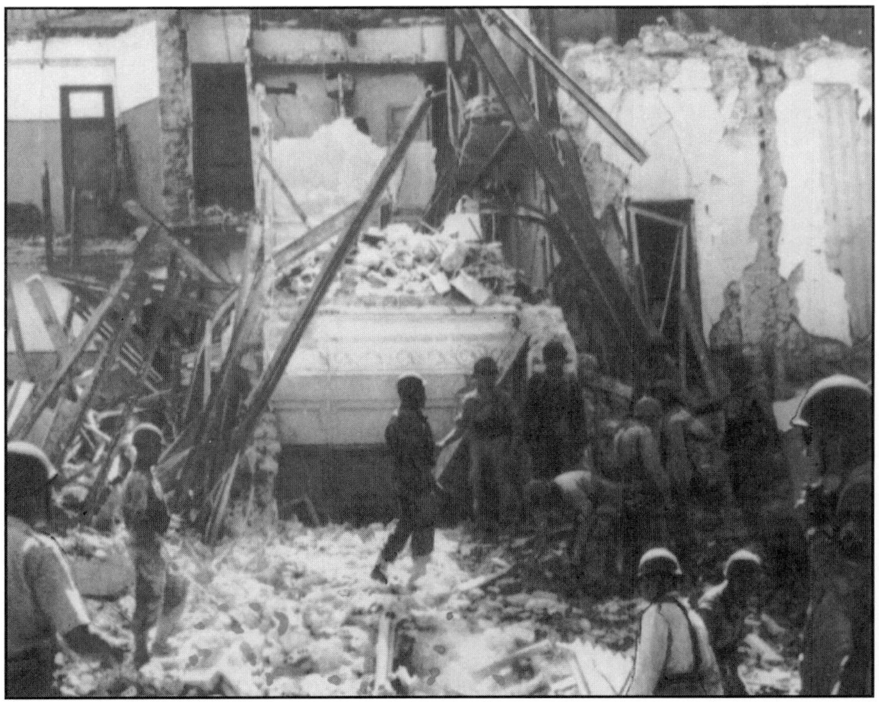

ALGERIAN EARTHQUAKE DEVASTATION. Rescue workers moving among shattered buildings in Orleansville after the 12 sec. earthquake yesterday. A radio picture early to-day.

'HOLIDAY' FOR MAJ. SALEM

POLITE EGYPTIAN DISMISSAL

From Our Own Correspondent

CAIRO, Thursday.

Major Salah Salem, Minister of National Guidance, was to-day granted a holiday by the Egyptian Council of Ministers. Lt.-Col. Hussein el Shafei, Minister of Social Affairs, will act on his behalf.

The bare announcement that Major Salem, the recently much-publicised travelling "ambassador" had been, granted leave is believed in Cairo to be a polite way of indicating his dismissal from power.

Such a move, though rumoured recently after a reported dispute between Major Salem and Lt.-Col. Nasser, Prime Minister, comes as a surprise. It had appeared that their personal quarrel had been patched up.

Since then Major Salem has been on another official visit - this time to Jordan - returning on Monday after what appeared to be another triumph of integrating of policies of Arab State with that of Egypt.

STRANGE JUNCTURE

In political and diplomatic circles here it is thought strange that a Minister of Major Salem's standing should be given leave at such a time. The Government is dealing with the final negotiations of the Anglo-Egyptian treaty, discussions on American aid and the execution of a large-scale economic development projects at home.

Differences between Major Salem and some members of the Revolution Command Council are said to have come to a head on his return from Irak more than a fortnight ago. There was a rumpus in Arab circles about statements he made which were taken to imply that agreement had been reached on the question of the unity of Irak and Syria.

NAUTILUS IN U.S. NAVY SOON

ATOMIC SUBMARINE

From Our Own Correspondent

WASHINGTON, Thursday.

The Nautilus, the world's first atom-powered submarine, will officially join the United States Navy on Sept. 30, it was announced to-day. The commissioning ceremony will take place at Groton, Connecticut, where she was constructed.

Sea trials are expected to follow in a few months. The Nautilus has an underwater speed of 25 knots. She has a displacement of 2,800 tons, and is 300ft long. The only limit to her range will be the crew's endurance and the submarine's capacity to store food and oxygen for the crew. She need never refuel.

The Nautilus will be commanded by Cdr. Eugene Wilkinson, with a crew of 10 officers and 85 men. They have been undergoing training for nearly three years.

COMMUNIST THREAT IN FORMOSA STRAIT GROWS

From Denis Warner
Daily Telegraph Correspondent

MANILLA, Thursday.

Although the prospect of an all-out Communist offensive against Formosa is widely discounted by Western intelligence agencies in the Pacific, the situation in Formosa Strait is expected to become progressively more serious.

The Communists have accumulated a force estimated at about 150,000 men along the Fukien coast, with the apparent intention of seizing many of the Nationalist-held islands near the mainland. Quemoy, only 4,000 yards from the coast, is the first of these.

American intelligence reports indicate that the island could be held against a determined Communist attack only by securing a beachhead on the mainland. This is obviously impracticable, and the loss of Quemoy therefore appears certain.

The United States Seventh Fleet, it may be taken for granted, will not be committed in any extremely hazardous operation along the China coastline. But the danger of much more serious incidents will certainly increase if the Communists attempt to seize other islands closer to Formosa.

NATIONALIST ISLANDS

Two Other Main Groups

Quemoy, at the mouth of the Communist-held Amoy Harbour, has been a listening-post for Chiang Kai-shek's forces for the last three years. It has been used as a jumping-off base for Nationalist spies. From it Nationalists have harassed the mainland and enforced their blockade.

With an area of about 70 square miles, it has a population of 50,000 and a garrison of 40,000. An attack by Communists in 1950 was successfully beaten off.

Apart from this post the Nationalist hold other islands along the Chinese coastline and in the 100-mile strait between the mainland and Formosa. Many of these are so small that they could not be easily defended against a serious assault.

These Nationalist bases include the Tachen group, about 200-miles north of Formosa, Whit Dog Island and Matsu Island. Close to Formosa, 25 miles from its western edge, are the Pescadores, a group of about 63 small islands. Those are mainly flat, nowhere more than 300ft above sea level. The area of the biggest is about 24 square miles.

1,000 TROOPS

U.S. Guarantee

Although the Nationalists have 1,000 troops in the Tachen group, the loss of about 40 of these islands is accepted as inevitable against a full-scale Communist attack.

MR. DULLES HAS FORMOSA TALK WITH CHIANG

TAIPEH, Formosa, Thursday.

Mr. Dulles, United States Secretary of State, to-day paid a brief visit to Formosa, where he met Chiang Kai-shek, the Chinese Nationalist leader. Mr. Dulles declined to say what they discussed, but it was believed to have included the air and artillery duels round Amoy.

He said on arrival that the United States was standing by Nationalist China against aggression. "Red China is now intensifying its military and propaganda against free China," he said.

"But we shall not be intimidated. The United States is proud to stand with those who, having passed through so many years of crises, are yet courageously sustained by faith that will not be subdued."

Mr. Dulles flew on to Tokyo after only a few hours in Formosa.

GONZALES OUT OF T.T.

Froilan Gonzales, the Argentine driver who leads the Ferrari team will not be fit to drive in the International Tourist Trophy race at Belfast to-morrow.

ARREST OF AN M.P. IN SANITORIUM

Capt. Peter Baker In Court To-day

CHARGES OF FORGERY

Daily Telegraph Reporter

Capt. Peter Arthur David Baker, 33, publisher and Conservative M.P. for Norfolk South, was arrested at Virginia Water, Surrey, yesterday afternoon on a charge of uttering forged documents.

The warrant alleged seven similar offences. He will appear at Bow Street this morning.

Capt. Baker has been a voluntary patient in Holloway sanatorium, a mental hospital at Virginia Water, since April. His health had begun to deteriorate a few months earlier.

He was arrested at the sanatorium by Chief Detective Supt. R. Stevens, head of the Yard's fraud squad, who is in charge of the case. Capt. Baker was taken by police car to West End Central police station where he was charged. He was kept in custody last night.

Within a few weeks of his entering the sanatorium in June, his group of companies, which included publishers, printers, consulting engineers, whiskey blenders and an organisation for packing books for export, began to fail.

£1 MILLION GROUP

Baker started as a publisher in 1945 when he formed Falcon Press with £900. Within seven years he has built his interest into a group with assets estimated to be worth nearly £1 million. Prominent businessmen and several politicians joined his companies.

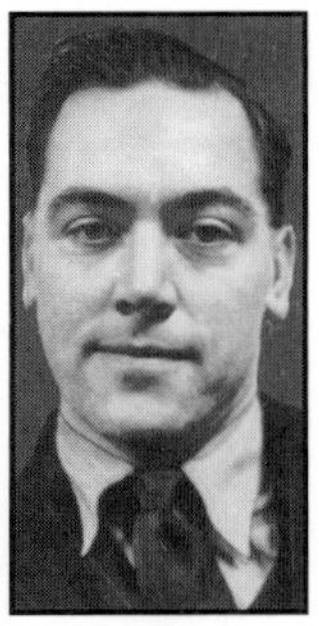

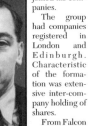

The group had companies registered in London and Edinburgh. Characteristic of the formation was extensive inter-company holding of shares.

From Falcon Press developed the Peregrin Press Ltd., Grey Walls Press Ltd. and the Dunstead Trust, an investment company which became the parent company of several of those in the Baker group. It is these four which are being wound up.

A few weeks before the winding-up orders were made there were several resignations from the board of the Trust.

Capt. Baker has represented Norfolk South since 1950, when he had a majority of 2,429 over his Socialist opponent, Mr. Christopher Mayhew. In 1951 he increased the majority to 3,239 in a straight fight with another Labour candidate.

The energy he expended on his Parliamentary and business interests, coupled with his war-time experiences, led to his health failing. Early this year he decided not to stand again for Parliament.

THE AGA KHAN

The Aga Khan, who is 77, was making a swift recovery from his attack of bronchitis and had got up yesterday, said the Begum Aga Khan at Cannes last night. Prof. de Vienes, a French physician, who flew to Paris on Wednesday, would probably leave to-day. - Reuter.

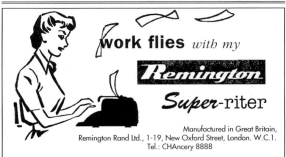

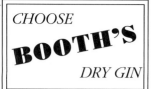

The Daily Telegraph

No.30,967 LONDON, FRIDAY, OCTOBER 8, 1954
and Morning Post
Printed in LONDON and MANCHESTER Price 2d.

PORT OF LONDON NEAR STANDSTILL

4,000 JOIN STRIKERS: 130 SHIPS IDLE

MORE CARGOS SENT TO CONTINENT

MOTOR EXPORT HIT: 11,000 TONS OF SUGAR HELD UP

By An Industrial Correspondent

Following a further serious spread of the strikes yesterday, London docks, apart from Tilbury and one private wharf, were at a standstill. There were 130 ships idle last night, compared with 90 on Wednesday.

Four thousand more men joined the strikes, bringing the total of dockers and stevedores out to 17,000. In addition 8,000 men employed in Thames-side ship repair yards are idle.

British Railways announced that with one or two minor exceptions, no further consignments of goods for London docks would be accepted. British Road Services have applied a similar ban.

Exporters who use their own transport to the docks are being asked to get in touch with individual sheds to see whether storage room is available. More ships are being diverted to discharge cargos at Continental ports.

At Cardiff, the Katha, 4,875 tons, with a cargo of cotton, ground-nuts, timber and tomatoes was boycotted by dockers who were told she was originally bound for Tilbury. She sailed last night for an unknown destination.

The motor car industry will be one of the worst hit by the closing of the port. About half of Britain's car exports go through London's docks. Manufacturers are trying to divert traffic to other ports.

FOOD POSISTION

Meat for Three Weeks

Food suppliers are not likely to be affected for some time, because stocks are plentiful. An official of the meat trade said there was ample of home-killed meat and stocks for at least three weeks.

An official of Tate and Lyle, the sugar refiners, said no sugar exports have left London because of the strike. The position was becoming increasingly serious.

"Our export ships have all had to leave the dock empty, and there will have to be a drastic revision of our shipping schedule." There were more than 11,000 tons of refined sugar waiting in dock warehouses to be shipped abroad.

Victor Marney, of the Transport and General Workers' Union, an unofficial strike leader, gave a hint yesterday of a possible further extension of the dispute. At a meeting at London's West India dock he said that mass meetings "might be held all over the country until the empire of the employers crumbles".

ASIANS WITHDRAWN

Agreement with Employers

The disastrous spread of the strikes followed charges made on Wednesday by unofficial and official leaders. They asserted that the employers had introduced Indian seamen from other ships to the docks to handle baggage and mail.

The night it was announced by the London port employers that Asian labour imported to the docks was being withdrawn. This followed negotiations between the employers and Mr. Deakin, general secretary to the T. and G.W.U.

The ship involved was the P. and O. liner Chusan, 24.215 tons. The employers said last night that after the withdrawal of the Asians the only work done would be carried out by the actual crew of the vessel. They would handle only personal baggage and stores for the forthcoming voyage.

JAPAN READY FOR TALKS ON CASH FOR PoWs

From Our Own Correspondent
TOKYO, Thursday.

Direct negotiations on the payment of compensation to Allied prisoners of war and their dependants under the San Francisco Peace Treaty will begin in Tokyo next week, it was learned here to-night.

The Japanese Government has agreed to this procedure as a result of an approach by British, Dutch and Pakistani representatives in Japan. They acted as a local committee of the Allied Beneficiary Powers,

Sir Norman Roberts, until recently a British Commercial Minister in Japan, is expected to arrive in Tokyo on Tuesday. He will conduct the talks as chief representative of the executive committee of the Beneficiary Powers.

A high Government source here revealed that Mr. Yoshida, the Japanese Prime Minister, gave instructions that before he left for Europe that these funds, if released, were to be used for the payment of indemnities to prisoners of war.

COMETS 'READY IN A YEAR'

REASON IS KNOWN

NEW YORK, Thursday.

Mr. Frank Hearle, of the De Havilland Aircraft Co., sailing from New York to-night to Britain in the Mauretania, said the Comet airliners should be ready to enter service again within a year.

The reason for the grounding was clear. "A little reconstruction will be required, but they are badly wanted," he said.

The question of the return of the Comets depends upon the inquiry into the Comet incidents.

BAIL OFFER FOR CAPT. BAKER, M.P.

APPLICATION TO-DAY

Daily Telegraph Reporter

Application for bail for Capt. Peter Baker, publisher and Conservative M.P. for Norfolk South, who faces seven charges of uttering forged documents, will be made at Bow-street to-day. Sureties will be offered by his mother-in-law, Mrs. Olga Scott, of Bridge House, Marden, Kent, and his father, Major Reginald Baker.

Capt. Baker was remanded in custody on Monday after one of his two sureties for bail, Sir Michael Balcon, the film producer, withdrew.

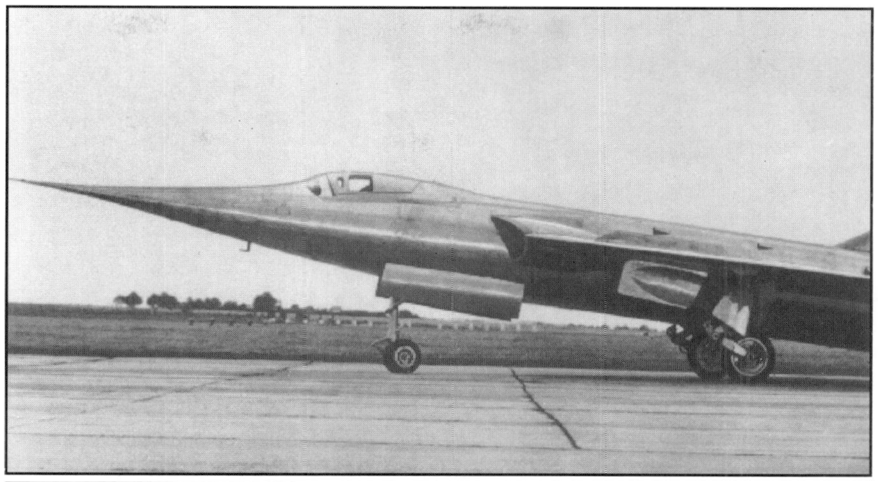

THE FIRST PHOTOGRAPH issued of the Fairey Delta 2 supersonic research aircraft. It may prove to be the fastest jet-propelled aircraft that has yet flown, and will show that no disturbance is felt when passing through the sound barrier in level flight, provided this is done at sufficient speed.

TRIUMPH FOR DR. ADENAUER

BIG MAJORITY BACKS LONDON DECISIONS

From Our Own Correspondent
BONN, Thursday.

The Adenauer Coalition Government's resolution approving the principals of the London agreements on Germany was accepted by a show of hands in the Bundestag to-night after a non-stop debate of nearly 12 hours. The majority appeared to be over two-thirds.

All the Coalition parties voted solidly in favour. The Social Democratics Opposition voted against, and there were no abstentions.

As I forecast yesterday the debate was a triumph for Dr. Adenauer, the 78-year-old Chancellor. With unflagging energy he dominated the debate, not leaving the Government bench. He made a long speech, and on five occasions engaged in long and lively exchanges.

The resolution approved, advocated European unity and the security and freedom of the German people in the community of free nations as the preconditions for the early reunification of Germany. It endorsed a German defence contribution as "onerous but necessary"

There was special reference for the desire to create "a lasting basis for the friendly, neighbourly existence of France and Germany." The resolution left openings for the Opposition concessions to a bi-partisan policy, but they adhere rigidly to their demand for talks with Russia on reunification as their first step.

MRS. WHEELER VERDICT TO-DAY

SUMMING-UP BEGUN

Daily Telegraph Reporter.

A verdict will be given to-day at the trial at Wiltshire Assizes at Salisbury of Mrs. Mavis Wheeler, 39, accused of shooting at Lord Vivian. The court adjourned last night 20 minutes after Mr. Justice Byrne began his summing up to the jury of nine men and three women.

Mrs. Wheeler, who was in the witness-box for three hours, gave her version before a crowded court of the events at her cottage at Potterne on the night of July 30, when Lord Vivian was wounded. She testified in a firm voice.

Before Mrs. Wheeler resumed her evidence, Lady Vivian, who had been listening, left the court. She had heard Mrs. Vivian say that Lord Vivian had told her that his marriage wasn't very happy.

QUEEN TO GO TO ARTIST'S STUDIO

PORTRAIT SITTINGS

Signor Pietro Annigoni, the Italian portrait painter, who is to paint a portrait of the Queen said last night, "Her Majesty has expressed a preference to attending at the studio placed at my disposal at Kensington, rather than that should go to Buckingham Palace."

It is understood that she shall wear formal robes for the portrait, which is hoped to be completed this year for Fishmongers' Company. The price is stated to be £2,000.

CONSERVATIVES' DEBATE ON EMPIRE TRADE

G.A.T.T. REVISION OPPOSED

From Our Political Correspondent
BLACKPOOL, Thursday.

A demand for the revision of the "no new preference" clause on the General Agreement on Tariff and Trade was decisively rejected by the Conservative party conference here to-day.

Mr. Thorneycroft, President of the Board of Trade, said that in Washington Mr. Butler, Chancellor of the Exchequer, had asked the Commonwealth Finance Ministers for their views. Not one would pledge support for an attack on the rule against new preferences. The Ministers emphatically supported continued membership of the G.A.T.T.

This revelation decided the matter for the conference, though an amendment calling for freedom of action on Imperial preference was vigorously pressed by Sir Victor Ralkes, M.P. for Garston, and Mr. Leopold Amery.

Sir Victor refused to withdraw his amendment when requested to do so by Mr. Thorneycroft. On a show of hands it was overwhelmingly defeated.

Mr. Thorneycroft pointed out that under the Government's present policy United Kingdom imports from the Commonwealth were 54 per cent of total imports, against 39 per cent before the war. Exports to the Commonwealth with 53 per cent, against 49 per cent, before the war. We did not remain in G.A.T.T. for sentimental reasons, he said, but because it paid us to be in.

In defeating the G.A.T.T. amendment, the platform prevailed over the only serious attack of the day on Government policy. Mr. Eden was received with greater enthusiasm than ever. No criticism was made against his foreign policy speech.

SUEZ CRITIC'S SUPPORT

Mr. Julian Amery, M.P. for Preston North, one of the leaders on the attack of the Suez agreement supported the proposals of the nine power conference for a German defence contribution and the pledge to retain British forces on the Continent.

Mr. Eden was loudly applauded when he said that what was different about this pledge was that it was given "to prevent a war and not to win a war."

FUTURE OF MR. EDEN

NO DECISION MADE

From Our Political Correspondent
BLACKPOOL, Thursday.

There is some discussion on whether Mr. Eden's speech to-day may be his last as Foreign Secretary. Many Conservatives now urge that he should take non-departmental office as Deputy Prime Minister and Leader of the House of Commons with some general responsibility over the whole field of policy.

This project is undoubtedly under consideration but no declaration has been reached. Should Mr. Eden leave the Foreign Office, he would be succeeded by Mr. Macmillan, Minister of Housing and Local Government. It would be the occasion of a major Government reshuffle.

TV TEST OF STATEMEN

GOOD PERFORMANCE FROM BLACKPOOL

By Campbell Dixon

Watching the Conservative Conference, the first ever televised, English viewers saw last night why TV technique is important - why, indeed, it may soon help to decide who governs nations.

In future it will not be enough that a man should be a good statesman. He must look and sound statesman-like. He must be a good performer.

Last night's show wasn't too exacting, for it had first been filmed and we saw selected passages. This doesn't mean that the speakers had the advantage of the film star.

Politicians may repeat themselves, but they cannot expect a re-take. An unfortunate mannerism, or a halting delivery, was always a handicap. On "live" TV it may be fatal.

BRILLIANCE DISTRUSTED

Politicians are less fortunate than actors again in that they must provide their own dialogue. This, however, is not such a handicap as it seems. Burke was probably too eloquent for high office: Sheridan was too witty. There is nothing the British public distrusts so much as brilliance, which accounts for many a success and makes Sir Winston's almost inexplicable.

Bearing this in mind, last night's performers may be congratulated. Any latent tendencies to brilliance were firmly suppressed, and Mr. Eden's speech and informal comments were delivered with just the right blend of gravity and charm.

PRODUCER NEEDED

Among the others, Mr. Julian Amery was quick and vehement, Mr. Ian Harvey assured, Mr. Peake resonant. But the show badly needed a producer. Mr. Peake looked anywhere but at the millions watching him. The light was poor, the sound uneven.

BULL CHARMED BY BEETHOVEN

From Our Own Correspondent
PARIS, Thursday.

An angry bull which broke loose on its way to the slaughterhouse at Dijon today charged into a concert hall, where the Conservatoire Orchestra was playing. In alarm the musicians stopped playing.

As the animal appeared restive the conductor induced them to begin a Beethoven Symphony. The bull appeared to like this. It stood in quiet contemplation until police arrived and led it away. The concert continued.

FIRST FLIGHT OF SUPERSONIC RESEARCH JET

FAIREY DELTA 2

By Air Cmdre. L.G.S. PAYNE
Daily Telegraph Air Correspondent

The Fairey Delta 2 supersonic research aircraft made its first flight at Boscombe Down, Salisbury Plain, on Wednesday, piloted by Mr. Peter Twiss, a test pilot of the Fairey Aviation Company. It was released from the secret list yesterday.

The plane, which is powered by a Rolls Royce Avon jet engine, has been built under the Ministry of Supply research programme.

It will be used to investigate flight and control characteristics at transonic and supersonic speeds in level flight. Data thus obtained will be invaluable for the design in supersonic military aircraft and perhaps future civil airliners.

The Fairey Delta 1 research plane which first flew in March, 1951, and has been seen at Farnborough air displays, was not designed for supersonic speeds. The Fairey Delta 2 was originally intended for research at speeds close to that of sound (760 m.p.h. at sea level).

A "DRAWBRIDGE" NOSE

During its design and development it became clear that this expectation would be exceeded. The makers said yesterday that it will "provide for research connected with the sound barrier and beyond".

It is a single-seater, mid-wing delta design of all-metal construction. Two interesting features, externally evident, are the wings and the nose. Though the wing curve is exceptionally thin, the main wheels of the tricycle undercarriage have been designed to retract fully into the wings.

In flight or on the ground the pilot can lower the whole of the nose section; like a drawbridge. This secures a good forward view of take-off and landing. It should be particularly useful for landings, as delta-wing aircraft usually touch down with their noses high in the air and then tip forward on to their nose wheels.

KUBELIK FOR COVENT GARDEN

MUSICAL DIRECTOR

Rafael Kubelik, 40, the Czech-born conductor, has accepted an invitation to become the musical director of the Covent Garden Opera Company. His duties will start in a year's time, but he will be guest conductor at Covent Garden next April.

Martin Cooper writes: Rafael Kubelik's appointment will give Covent Garden its first permanent musical director since Dr. Karl Rankl left in 1951. Kubelik is well known in Britain and his recent conducting of his countryman Janacek's opera "Katya Kabanova" at Sadler's Wells was generally acclaimed.

Since the war Kubelik has worked much in America where he conducted the Chicago Symphony Orchestra from 1950-1953, but he has paid many visits to Europe, and conducted at the Edinburgh Festival in 1948 and 1949. He has recently been conducting in the Dutch Concertgebouw Orchestra.

INDUSTRY TEMPO SPEEDING UP

MORE EMPLOYMENT

By An Industrial Correspondent

Indications of increasing tempo in the manufacturing industries are given to-day by the Ministry of Labour in its summary of the manpower situation. Fewer workers are on short time and more are working overtime.

The hard core of unemployed, those without a job for two months or more, is getting smaller. At the end of August, the number in employment of all kinds was 22,620,000, an increase during the month of 100,000, mainly school leavers. There was a similar trend last year.

Unemployed were fewer by 4,000 between August 9 and September 13. Total registered unemployed on September 13 was 236,000 representing 1.1 per cent of the working population.

35 FEARED DEAD IN COMET CRASH

DIVE IN SEA OFF ELBA ON LONDON FLIGHT

10 CHILDREN AMONG THE PASSENGERS

ITALIAN FISHING BOATS PICK UP 15 BODIES

From Our Own Correspondent

ROME, Sunday.

A Comet Airliner of the British Overseas Airways Corporation, flying from London to Rome on the last lap of a trip from Singapore, crashed in the Mediterranean, 10 miles south of Elba, to-day. There were 35 on board and it is feared that there are no survivors.

Ten of the 29 passengers were children, most of them returning to school after holidays with their parents in the East. Adults on board included Mr. Chester Wilmot, war correspondent and author, and Capt. R.V. Wolfson, general manager of B.O.A.C.'s subsidiaries overseas.

The 36-seater plane, known to pilots all over the world as "Yoke Peter" from the last two of its identification letters, G-ALYP, was the one which started the world's first scheduled jet liner passenger service on May 2, 1952 - a weekly return from London to Johannesburg. The pilot was Alan Gibson.

Two Italian fishing vessels recovered 15 bodies. A minesweeper is reported to have found a piece of fuselage, with the identification number, and five bodies near by, south of Calamity Point, southernmost tip of Elba.

(January 11)

RABBITS MAY BECOME RARE IN MANY AREAS

KILLING DISEASE HAS SPREAD TO 16 COUNTIES

By Our Agricultural Correspondent

Myxomatosis, the rabbit-killing virus disease, has now taken such a firm hold over a large part of the country that by the end of the summer rabbits may become a rarity in many counties. Already 16 counties are affected.

Reports from Devon, Cornwall, Sussex and Kent state that rabbits are dying in thousands. Some farmers believe that the casualty rate on their land is more than 90 per cent. So far 68 outbreaks have been notified.

Kent, where the disease originated last autumn, has had 14. Essex seven, and Sussex, Cornwall and Gloucester six.

Other counties affected are Suffolk, Isle of Wight, Randor, Bedford, Norfolk, Anglesey, Pembroke, Cardigan, Buckingham and Oxford.

EFFECT OF COLD WEATHER

The spread would have been even more rapid but for the cold, we weather, which meant fewer than usual of the blood-sucking insects which carry the disease.

Though the Myxamotosis Advisory Committee recommended in a recent report that no attempt should be made to introduce myxamotosis into unaffected areas, some farmers have obtained infected animals and released them on their farms.

An R.S.P.C.A. inspector said last night that while the Society deprecated the spreading to the spreading of the disease artificially it had no power to take legal action. Wild rabbits are not covered by the Protection of Animals Act.

"We have told our inspectors that if they come across rabbits suffering they should take steps to see that they are painfully destroyed as quickly as possible."

The Ministry of Agriculture accepted the Committee's report but it has no power to stop the farmers spreading the disease. A Ministry spokesman said: "We are naturally anxious to take advantage of this disease to get rid of the rabbits."

KILLING SURVIVORS

"As soon as it has swept through an area we will make a concerted attack with local farmers to kill off survivors. If some rabbits develop immunity we could soon be infested again."

The spectacle of hundreds of rabbits dying near popular walks over the Sussex Downs has disturbed many people. The Society of Sussex Downsmen and the R.S.P.C.A. has appealed for mercy patrols to exterminate infected animals.

(July 1)

EASY QUESTIONS BAFFLE YOUTHS

EMPLOYERS' REPORT

Questions such as "How many 2.5d stamps can be brought for half a crown?" and "What does H.R.H. stand for?" were put to boys and girls after they had left secondary modern schools by a South London firm, and 30 per cent of them could not answer.

This is one of the statements in a report about educational standards from a cross-section of manufacturers in Greater London, Surrey, Sussex and Kent.. The London and South-Eastern Regional Board for industry decided yesterday to send it to the educational authorities in the region.

Fifty-six per cent of the employers were dissatisfied with the educational standards achieved by the secondary modern school system.

(February 4)

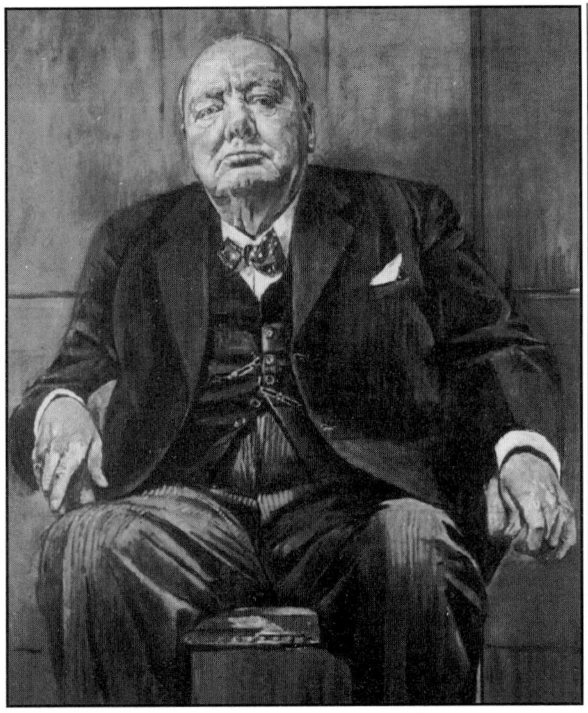

SIR WINSTON'S BIRTHDAY PORTRAIT.
Graham Sutherland's portrait of Sir Winston Churchill which is to be presented to the Prime Minister in Westminster Hall to-day. It is the birthday gift from both Houses of Parliament. This is the photograph of the portrait preferred by the artist.

SIR WINSTON 80 TO-DAY: PARLIAMENT'S TRIBUTE

Daily Telegraph Reporter

Sir Winston Churchill will awake this morning on his 80th birthday to begin one of the most crowded and colourful days of his life.

It will be a day of presentations, speeches and of congratulations from all over the world, unprecedented in the history of British Prime Ministers.

From the quiet homely atmosphere of gifts and good wishes from his family and staff at 10, Downing Street, he will go out to the State opening of Parliament at 11 a.m. At noon the M.P.s and other distinguished guests; numbering about 3,000, will crowd into the historic Westminster Hall.

There Sir Winston will receive Parliament's tribute, an illuminating address signed by M.P.s and the portrait of himself painted by Mr. Graham Sutherland. [Picture above.]

VISIT TO PALACE

Final Engagement

The Prime Minister's final engagement of the day will be an audience of the Queen at Buckingham Palace at 7 p.m. After that he will return home for a quiet dinner with Lady Churchill.

Throughout yesterday gifts and greetings arrived in hundreds at No. 10. Bags of letters, cards and packages arrived from all over the world.

They were the tangible expressions of esteem in which Sir Winston is held in every country, among peoples of every colour and surprisingly varied political beliefs. Although Parliament was not in session, Ministry of Works officials were busy at the Palace of Westminster with last-minute preparations for to-day's presentation ceremony.

Electrically heated green leather chairs, decorated with the gilt of portcullis of Westminster, were arranged in Westminster Hall. Millions will be able to watch the historic moment on television to-day.

PORTRAIT GIFT

Cigar Missing

The portrait, joint gift from the Lords and Commons, will be presented by Mr. Attlee. It will be framed in gold. As will be seen from the picture, it shows the Prime Minster seated in a wooden armchair, wearing a black coat, striped trousers and a spotted bow tie.

There is no cigar. After painting the familiar Churchill emblem, with a wisp of blue smoke rising from it, Mr. Sutherland abandoned the idea because he felt it was not in keeping with the State character of the portrait.

90LB CAKES

Decorations Tell Story

Later Sir Winston will go to the Royal Gallery of the House of Lords to receive a pair of antique silver jugs. These will be presented to him on behalf of past and present Conservative, Unionist and National Liberal members of both Houses.

At lunch he will preside over a family gathering of about 14, including some of his grandchildren. Two cakes, each 90lbs before being iced, were delivered yesterday.

Each measured a yard across. This allowed only about 1.5 inches clearance on either side through the door of No. 10.

Decorations on the cakes tell the story of Sir Winston's life. One, iced in pale amber, has eight big candles and badges depicting milestones in his career.

In words of gold is the phrase adapted from one of Sir Winston's war-time remarks: "A thousand years hence free people will say this was our finest man." Another is Sir Winston's own prescription for a statesman's conduct: "In war, resolution; in defeat, defiance; in victory, magnanimity; in peace, goodwill."

The second cake, in pink and white sugar, has 80 candles. Lady Churchill will choose one to remain at No. 10 for Sir Winston's private party. The other will be cut after the presentation in Westminster Hall.

(November 30)

£20 PEDESTRIAN FINE PROPOSED IN BILL

COMPULSORY TESTS OF CAR ROADWORTHINESS

TRIAL FOR PARKING METERS

By W. A. McKenzie
Daily Telegraph Motoring Correspondent

Fines on pedestrians are introduced in the Government's Road Traffic Bill, designed to improve safety on the roads, which was published yesterday.

Pedestrians who fail to comply with the traffic directions given by police will be liable for a fine up to £20. Maximum penalties for driving offences increase under the Bill. Some are doubled. The other main proposals are:

Roadworthiness. - Powers to enforce examination of vehicles. The Ministry will provide testing stations and also may delegate the work, under safeguards to private garages.

Disqualification. - Those disqualified for reckless, dangerous or careless driving or driving under the influence of drink will have to pass the driving test before they can regain their licences.

Parking. - Local authorities will be able to charge for parking on the roads and install meters for this purpose. The police will have the power to remove vehicles causing obstruction.

Cyclists will be liable to penalties up to £30 for reckless, dangerous or careless riding.

"L" Drivers. - There will be power to withdraw a provisional licence from a driver who abuses a provisional licence arrangement.

FIRST TEST STATION

Free to Motorists

Mr. Boyd-Carpenter, Minister of Transport, will not wait until the measure becomes law before opening an experimental station for testing vehicle's roadworthiness. It will be in the London area.

He said yesterday that motorists will be able to submit vehicles to the "pilot station" for testing without charge.

Asked about the regulations for pedestrians, the Minister said that these did not render them liable to a fine if they ignored traffic lights, but only for failing to comply with the directions given by a policeman. "I think we have to proceed rather gently with this first substantial application of the law to pedestrians," he added.

The schemes for charging for parking on the road and installing parking meters will be confined at first to the London area, and be experimental. Hitherto it has not been legal for charging on the public highway.

Local authorities must keep parking accounts. Any surplus will be available only for providing alternative parking space off the road.

DRIVING BAN PENALY

Scope Increased

The scope of disqualification for serious driving offences is to be increased. Some examples of increased maximum penalties, with the existing ones in brackets, are:

SPEEDING: £30 first conviction (£20); £50 subsequently (£50).

CARELESS DRIVING: £40 first (£20); subsequently £80 or three months or both (£50 or three months).

RECKLESS OR DANGEROUS DRIVING: £100 or four months, or both subsequently £100 or six months or both (£100 or four months or both). The maximum on indictment, two years or a fine or both, remains unchanged.

DRIVING UNDER THE INFLUENCE OF DRINK OR DRUGS. - £100 or four months or both (£50 or four months); subsequently £100 or six months or both (£100 or four months or both). On indictment two years or a fine or both (six months or a fine or both).

(December 9)

NEARLY HALF OF COUNTRY'S DOCK MEN ON STRIKE

ALL WORK STOPS AT BIRKENHEAD

By Hugh Chevins
Daily Telegraph Industrial Correspondent

Nearly 35,000 dockers were on strike in London, Liverpool and Birkenhead last night out of a national total of 76,000. The London stoppage, now in its third week, is in protest against "compulsory" overtime.

The Merseyside total was not as high as that hoped for by the Communist and fellow-traveller agitators. All the 2,000 Birkenhead dockers stopped work, but not more than 7,000 of the 15,500 at Liverpool joined the strikers.

Meanwhile the members of the court appointed by Sir Walter Monckton, Minister of Labour, to inquire into the causes and circumstances of the dispute held a preliminary meeting yesterday. They will have their first formal meeting in public to-morrow at Seymour Hall, Marylebone.

The inquiry will then decide whether other meetings should be in public. Members of the Court are, Sir Raymond Evershed, Master of the Rolls, Sir Godfrey Mitchell, Chairman of George Whimpy and Co., the contractors, and Mr. J. Crawford, President of the National Union of Boot and Shop Operatives

R. Barrett, secretary of the National Amalgamated Stevedores and Dockers, again expressed concern at the appointment of Mr. Crawford, a moderate-minded union leader to the Court. There is, however, no question of the stevedores boycotting the inquiry because of Mr. Crawford's appointment.

(October 19)

TREND TOWARDS EASY LIVING

'SPOON-FED PEOPLE' THROUGH PLANNING

A warning against the danger of producing a "spoon-fed" population viewing life through rosy spectacles was given in London last night by Sir Henry Self. He was speaking at the opening of the annual conference of the Modern Churchmen's Union, of which he is President.

Sir Henry, who is Deputy Chairman (Administration) of the British Electrical Authority, said that the virtues of the welfare state so clearly outweighed its vices that everybody welcomed it. But that did not mean that we should not be on guard against some aspects of its development.

It would be impracticable to have an ordered society with full employment and a right standard of living without planning. A planning policy brought "a tendency towards easy living and the parallel, yet misguided assertion of individual rights to maximum benefits."

It is probably true to say that overall planning for the lives within an ordered society must tend to level downwards to a common average. "We must seek ways and means within the welfare state of preserving adventurous living and creative enterprise."

(September 7)

RUSSIAN MURDER GANG SURRENDER

ASSASINATION PLOT IN GERMANY REVEALED

EX-ENVOY IS HEAD OF TERROR SECTION

CIGARETTE CASE PISTOLS TO FIRE CYANIDE BULLETS

From Our Own Correspondent

BONN, Tuesday.

A staff officer of the Russian M.V.D. (secret police) and two East German Communist assistants, who were sent to Frankfurt to assassinate the leader of the Russian emigré resistance organisation, have surrendered to the Americans. They have been granted asylum and protection.

The Russian Capt. Nikolai Kholov, who, with the two Germans, gave himself up in February, appeared at a press conference at the headquarters of the American High Commission at Mehlem to-day. He gave a full account of his mission.

The weapons to be used were four silent pistols firing dum-dum bullets loaded with potassium cyanide. Two of them were concealed in cigarette cases which discharged their missiles through the tips of dummy cigarettes.

All four pistols, with their ammunition, were exhibited at the Press conference. The method of operation was explained by an American ballistics expert.

An American official said the information given by Capt. Khokhlov and the Germans had been subjected to "a careful world-wide checking by high security officers."

He added that "only after they were satisfied on all points was it decided to make the matter public."

SECRETS OF M.V.D.

Role of Ex-Envoy to U.S.

Capt. Khokhlov, who has worked for the M.V.D. in Rumania, Austria, Germany and West European countries, has given the American authorities a full description of the activities and methods of the organisation.

The terrorist section he worked for was under the control of the second chief directorate of the M.V.D. The head of this is Mr. Alexander Panyushkin, who was Soviet Ambassador to the United States from 1947 until 1952.

INTENDED VICTIM

Anti-Communist Leader

The intended victim was Mr. Georgi Okolovitch, head of the N.T.S. organisation in Frankfurt. This is the Russian anti-Communist emigré organisation, whose West Berlin leader, Dr. Truschnovitch, was kidnapped and taken to East Berlin last week.

There is reason to believe that the M.V.D. organised this kidnapping to find out why the assassination of Mr. Okolovitch in Frankfurt had not taken place, and what had happened to the agents. The East German authorities claim that Dr. Truschnovitch went over to them voluntarily.

(April 23)

TERROR GROUPS REVEALED

TRAINING OF AGENTS

The information on the working of the M.V.D. given by the three agents affords a remarkably clear picture of the extent to which the organisation was affected by both the "Jewish purges" in 1951 and the liquidation of Beria in 1953.

Some astonishing details were also revealed of the vast ramifications of the "terror" organisation and its earlier "liquidation" operations.

The 9th Otdel, an abbreviation meaning "The 9th Section for Terror and Diversion," was the group under which the agents were trained and operated. It is responsible for "special action tasks," primarily such activities as sabotage, assassination and kidnapping.

The Otdel was originally designed for a long-range programme intended to support and direct partisan activities behind enemy lines in the event of a future attack on Russia. Its officers are in the notorious Lubianka Prison in Moscow.

(April 23)

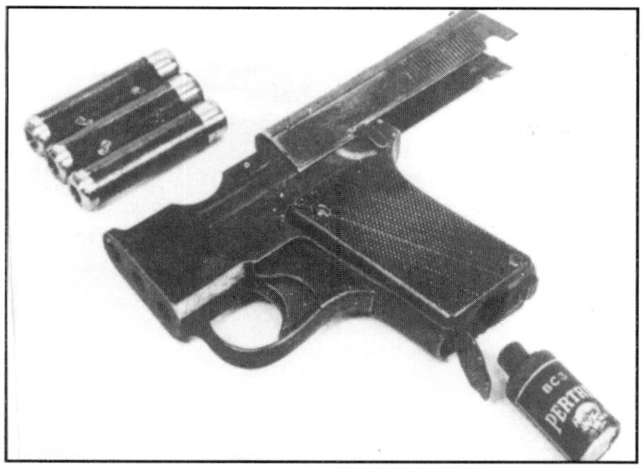

ASSASSINATION WEAPONS produced by the K.G.B. laboratory in Moscow for use by Captain Nikolai Khokhlov. Above: The battery-powered pistol given to Captain Khokhlov. It fired both poisoned and dumdum bullets.
Below: A cigarette case which, dismantled, yields an electric pistol designed to fire poisoned bullets noiselessly.

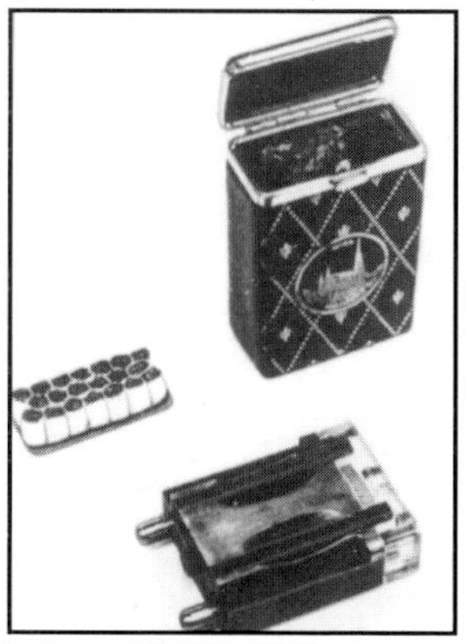

U.S. LAUNCHES ATOM-POWERED SUBMARINE

From Our Special Correspondent

GROTON, Connecticut, Thursday.

The world's first atomic-powered submarine, the Nautilus, was launched to-day by Mrs. Eisenhower at groton, Connecticut. Wet fog shrouding the shipyard rolled away five minutes before the launching, and the Nautilus went down the slipway in sunshine, cheered by 20,000 spectators.

Cdr.Wilkinson, the submarine's prospective captain, was on the bridge with several of his officers and men. A number of shipyard workers had also been accorded the honour of being aboard at the launching ceremony.

ALTERNATIVE ENGINE

The Nautilus, whose power plant could furnish enough electricity to, meet the needs of a small city, will be fitted with an atomic boiler using Uranium 235 to create steam to drive a turbine. As an alternative power plant she will have a diesel-electric engine.

She will be able to cross the Atlantic submerged and at a speed of more than 20 knots. Technically, she will be able to go round the world submerged, the need to surface arising not from the demands of the vessel but from those of her crew.

Her cost, excluding the cost of the nuclear power system, was more than £10 million. The keel was laidin June 1952. She was built at Groton by the General Dynamics Corporation and much of her nuclear power plant was constructed in the Idaho desert by the Westinghouse Electric Corporation.

(January 22)

GIRL RUSTICATED AT OXFORD

LATE AFTER DANCE

Daily Telegraph Reporter

Winifred Valerie Maud Thomas, 23, an undergraduate of Lady Margaret Hall, Oxford, has been rusticated for three weeks and gated for the rest of term because she attended a dance without permission and returned late to college. The dance was the Oxford Union Society's ball on the last night of last term. Miss Thomas's absence from college was noticed when there were two telephone calls for her from Switzerland. At present she is in Lausanne.

(January 14)

LONDON GOLD MARKET TO REOPEN

STEP ON MONDAY

By Our City Editor

The London gold market, closed since the outbreak of war in 1939, is to reopen open Monday. The decision to allow the market to resume business on a restricted basis was announced by the Treasury last night.

The price on the London market will be determined by demand and supply.On Monday morning at 10.30 the first gold "fixing" will take place.

Representatives of the four firms of bullion brokers and of Rothschilds and Johnson Mathey, refiners, will meet in Rothschilds' offices at New Court, St. Swithins Lane. On the basis of the buying and selling orders to hand, the price of gold will be announced to the public.

The unit for dealings will be a bar of 400oz, worth about £5,000 at the current quotation. Russian gold will be accepted as good delivery.

TRADE OPPORTUNITY

The Government's decision is in line with general market policy of freeing commodity markets and creating greater opportunities for British traders, merchants and bankers to make their full contribution to increasing our supplies of foreign currencies.

The new arrangements aim at restoring the London market to its pre-war position and enabling people who have hitherto bought and sold gold in terms of dollars to deal in the metal in sterling.

It is hoped that a substantial part of the British Commonwealth's gold production will in future be sold through the London market.

TRANSFERABLE STERLING

Side-by-side with the reopening of the gold market, the Treasury also announces a new move towards freer dealings in sterling in the foreign exchange market. Although no changes are proposed in restrictions on convertibility of pounds into dollars, concessions are granted to residents of non-sterling countries.

Whereas, until now, pounds owned by such non-residents could only be freely transferred to another resident of the same country, or to a resident of the sterling area, they will become spendable, from Monday, anywhere in the world, except in the dollar area.

(March 20)

LINK BETWEEN SMOKING AND CANCER

A relationship between smoking and cancer of the lung "must be regarded as established" on statistical and other evidence, the Standing Advisory Committee on Cancer and Radiotherapy has reported to Mr. Macleod, Minister of Health. The commitee has been investigating the matter for three years.

It considers that the risk increase with the amount smoked, particularly of cigarettes. The committee adds, however, that the presence in tobacco smoke of an agent causing lung cancer is not certain.Other factors such as atmospheric pollution and occupational risks contribute to the increase in the disease.

Mr. Mcleod, who gave details of the report, said yesterday that no reliable, factual estimate could be made on the precise effect of smoking. He gave a warning against "uninformed and alarmist conclusions," and assured the public of further vigorous research.

Britain's leading tobacco manufacturers had already decided to provide a £250,000 fund over the next seven years to further research into the effects of smoking on lung cancer. In a joint statement yesterday they stated that there was no proof that smoking caused the disease.

LONG CONTROVERSY

Variation in Incidence

Our Medical Correspondent writes: The definite assertion that there is a relationship between cancer of the lung and smoking disposes partly of an argument which has persisted even longer than these three years of preliminary investigations. But the mention by the Minister of differences in the incidence of the disease between urban and rural areas indicates that research must be made into smoke from factory chimneys and vehicles' exhausts.

Share Prices Lower

Our City Editor writes: On the Stock Exchange prices of leading tobacco shares were marked down sharply following the Minister of Health's statement.

(February 13)

700 MORE ARRIVE FROM JAMAICA

A further 700 Jamaicans arrived at Plymouth yesterday in the Italian liner Auriga, 10,856 tons. Most travelled in two special boat trains to London and the Birmingham area.

In their light summer clothing, they huddled together shivering on the liner's deck in the rain. A 22-year-old painter said: "We will be alright. There are plenty of good jobs." A waiter added: "They say that while we're looking for work we can draw £3 or £4 a week for doing nothing."

Inspired by reports of high pay, all had borrowed or used savings to pay at least £70 fare. Many had only a few pounds when they landed and some had difficulty in buying rail tickets.

(September 7)

CHINESE NATIONALISTS BOMB AMOY BASES

100 COMMUNIST JUNKS SUNK, ATTACKERS CLAIM

From Our Own Correspondent

HONG KONG, Tuesday.

Chinese Nationalist bombers, warships, and artillery to-day made a heavy attack against the mainland of Communist China. More than 100 Communist junks were destroyed, according to an official report from nationalist H.Q. at Taipeh, Formosa.

The Nationalist Defence Ministry said its air force and navy also sank a small Communist warship and several big motor junks. Shells and bombs caused explosions and fires in Communist ammunition dumps.

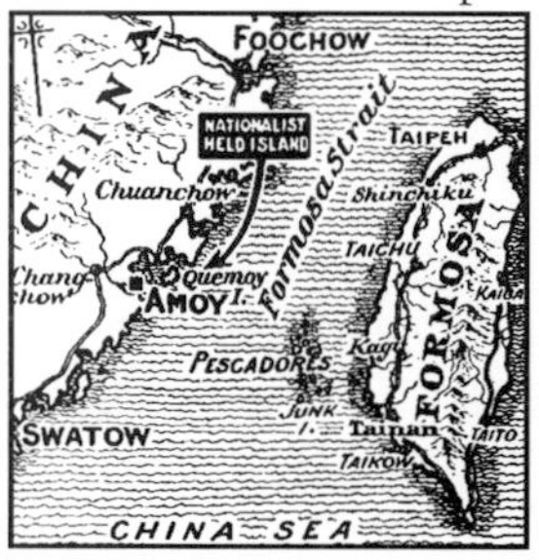

The main target was Amoy, mainland port only three miles from the Nationalist-held island of Quemoy, which had been shelled for three days by the Chinese Communists.

Nationalist artillery on Quemoy opened fire on Amoy at dawn. Then the bombers and warships went in, including two destroyers recently handed over to the Nationalists by the United States.

More than 100 planes in 150 sorties bombed and attacked Communist positions on the mainland and in nearby islands. The Nationalist communiqué reported a "satisfactory result."

A Peking radio report claimed that Communist anti-aircraft units shot down three Nationalist planes and damaged 20 others. The radio also said Nationalist planes attacked Hsien Yu and Lin Cheun.

JUNK CONCENTRATIONS

Diplomatic Aim Theory

Junk concentrations reported along the coast close to Quemoy have heightened speculation about the imminence of a Communist attack on the Nationalist-held island. A foreign diplomat in Taipeh said such an attack was expected.

Its main purpose, it is believed in Hongkong, would be diplomatic. It would be aimed at forcing the United Nations to discuss Formosa as a "danger-spot."

In this way the Peking leaders hope to win support for their claim to Formosa. They would probably count it a victory if they succeeded even in having the issue debated.

The recent arrival of American equipment for the Chinese Nationalist Navy and Air Force has greatly strengthened defences in Formosa.

(September 8)

ALGER HISS IS RELEASED

CHARGES FALSE, HE CLAIMS

From Our Own Correspondent

NEW YORK, Sunday.

Protesting his "complete innocence" and declaring that he would now devote himself to dispelling "the deception that has been foisted on the American people," Alger Hiss was released from gaol at Lewisburg.

He had served 44 months of a five years' sentence he received after being found guilty of perjury in denying that as director of the office of Special Political Affairs in the State Department he transmitted Government secrets to a Communist spy ring.

Now 50 years old, he was met at the prison gate by his wife Priscilla, who works in a New York store, and their son Tony.

"A MYTH DEVELOPED"

After emphasising his determination to prove the falseness of the charges made against him by Whittaker Chambers, a former magazine writer who later confessed that he had acted as a courier for a Soviet espionage group, Hiss said:"I have had to wait in silence while in my absence a myth has been developed."

(November 29)

POWERS SOUGHT ON IMMIGRANTS

By Our Political Correspondent

The Government is considering the problem of immigration from Commonwealth countries. Proposals are being discussed that powers be introduced to restrict immigration or to deport citizens of Commonwealth countries, who are automatically British subjects.

The issue has been raised, in particular, by immigration from Jamaica. Mr. Lloyd-George, the Home Secretary, is likely to make a statement on the matter soon, but he is unlikely to be able yet to give a Government decision.Two major problems are raised:

1.-It would be a major departure from practice to restrict the entry of British subjects to this country.

2.-The Government would not contemplate any legislation which applied discriminatory restrictions on grounds such as colour.

On the other hand, most countries of the Commonwealth, including colonial territories, have restrictions on immigration both from Britain and other Commonwealth countries. A solution may be found by legislating on a reciprocal principle.

Restrictions would be applied to immigrants on the same basis as countries applied restrictions to the immigration of people from Britain.

INFLUX FROM COLONIES

Now 800 a Month

Between Jan. 1 and Nov. 30, 8,500 immigrants from the Colonies entered this country, mostly from the British West Indies. It is thought that coloured immigrants in Britain now number 65,000. More are coming at the rate of 800 a month.

In the first six months of this year 3,200 immigrants entered the country from Canada, 6,700 from Australia, 5,800 from India and Pakistan, 4,000 from Malaya and 2,400 from South Africa.

(December 6)

QUEEN'S ARTIST ROBBED OF £303

RAID ON STUDIO

Daily Telegraph Reporter

Signor Pietro Annigoni, 44, the Italian painter, who will start a portrait of the Queen next month, was left with only £5 yesterday to buy materials for it. A thief raided his studio in South Edwardes Square, Kensington, and stole £300 in £5 notes and 3,000 francs (£3).

"Fortunately, I have already arranged about the canvas for the Queen's portrait," he said yesterday. "It was made up in Italy before I came to London and cost nearly £30".

(October 20)

BRITISH JET TAKES OFF VERTICALLY

'FLYING BEDSTEAD' TEST SUCCESSFUL

Daily Telegraph Reporter

Britain has made an aircraft with no wings or rotors which will take off vertically from a horizontal position. It has been nicknamed "The Flying Bedstead."

Mr. Sandys, Minister of Supply, who gave the first news of it last night, described it as "really no more than an aero engine with a pilot mounted on top." It weighs three and a half tons.

"A few weeks ago," the Minister added, "this strange contraption successfully lifted itself into the air without the aid of wings or rotors of any kind. It then proceeded to circle around under complete control for about 10 minutes and landed again without trouble.

"It may well be that these new and exciting experiments will in due course lead to a revolution in aeronautical development every bit as important as that which has resulted from the introduction of the jet engine."

The machine, which was experimental, was being constructed by Rolls-Royce in conjunction with the Ministry of Supply.

The Minister made the disclosure at the dinner of the Society of British Aircraft Constructors in London to mark the Farnborough air display. Until he spoke the machine had been "top secret" said a leading aircraft designer.

It was learned later that "The Flying Bedstead" made its maiden flight at Hucknall airfield, Notts, on Aug. 3. The man at the controls was Capt. R.T. Shepherd, 58, the Rolls-Royce chief test pilot for 16 years until 1951. He volunteered to handle Britain's first wingless VTO [Vertical Take-Off] aircraft.

TWO JET ENGINES

Exploring Lift Problems

He said last night "It is rather difficult to describe. There is practically nothing to it except two jet engines, a frame and a platform on top for the pilot, controls, etc.

"It is the most unorthodox-looking device you have ever seen, and at the moment it is only a device for exploring the problems of lift and of controlling an aircraft of that type. Eventually you apply all the principals to a proper aircraft."

Capt. Shepherd said the machine is not a flying saucer or anything like one. There was no pretence at stream-lining and no cowling. "It's a real open-work job with no protection for the pilot." It was about 20ft in diameter.

Since he had first flown it "The Flying Bedstead" had been taken up several times by Mr. Harry Bailey, the firm's chief test pilot, and by Sqn. Ldr. Harvey of the R.A.F. Farnborough. Each flight lasted about 10 minutes because that was the limit of the plane's fuel supply.

DOWNWARDS JETS

Thrust Varied

The tubular rectangled shaped "Flying Bedstead" is fitted with four small wheels. It has two jet engines fitted horizontally and the jet pipes leading off point downwards.

The machine was built to prove that a heavier than air machine could rise and remain still in the air in a stabilised condition. It has at present no forward propulsion but the pilot can tilt the machine so that it drifts under control at slow speed.

The machine is balanced in the air by the pilot using a stability control worked by a system of small jets. He can vary the thrust on the jets.

Planning began about two years ago. When first tested it was held on balance by ropes. It has now been off the ground, under its own control, in short flights up to a height of nearly 30ft.

It t cannot take off from an ordinary field because the heat from the jets is too intense. A concrete take-off base is necessary.

Capt. Shepherd has been flying for 38 years. After he relinquished the position of chief test pilot for Rolls-Royce he became the company's flying consultant.

He flight-tested such famous engines as the Kestrel, the Buzzard, the Merlin and jet engines which Rolls-Royce produced. In November, 1946, he flew from Paris to London in 41 minutes in the Lancastrian Nene, the first jet-propelled airliner.

(September 7)

ATTEMPT TO KILL EGYPT'S PREMIER FAILS

SHOTS HIT TWO ON BALCONY

From Our Own Correspondent

ALEXANDRIA, Tuesday.

Shots were fired as Lt. Col. Gamal Nasser, Prime Minister, was addressing a mass-rally held here to-night to celebrate the signing of the Anglo-Egyptian agreement on the Suez Zone.

The Prime Minister was not harmed. Standing on a balcony looking over Manshia Square, he and members of his party sheltered behind the rostrum as the fusillade broke out. But two of the party were wounded.

Mr. Mirghany Hamza, Sudanese Minister of Education, Irrigation and Agriculture who stretched out a hand to save Col. Nasser, was hit in the palm. Maitre Ahmed Badr, Alexandria Secretary of the Government-sponsored Liberation Rally, was injured in one shoulder.

Police seized the would-be assassin. They said he was Mahmoud Abdel Latif, 20, a Cairo tinsman. On him was found a membership card of the fanatical Moslem Brotherhood, which campaigned for the immediate evacuation of British troops and opposed the recent agreement.

CONFESSION CLAIM

With three other arrested men he was questioned by the Chief Public Prosecutor at Mustapha Barracks. He is stated to have said he fired eight shots.

According to police sources he confessed to the attack at the instigation of Brotherhood leaders, naming Abdul Kader Auda, an Executive Council member.

Crowds estimated to number 250,000 filled the Square and the adjacent roads for what was intended to be a climax to a day of lionising Col. Nasser. The would-be assassin was only a few yards from the balcony.

SHOTS RECORDED

Recordings of the speech were later broadcast. After shots had spattered the balcony Col. Nasser could be heard shouting: "Catch that man. Gamal Abdul Nasser is safe. My blood is for you."

For several minutes he continued shouting, becoming more and more hoarse and excited. Then he ended with half a sob, crying: "I will die for you. Others will carry on. Let him kill me. Let him kill me."

When he resumed his speech the crowd cheered, shouting: "Yehia Gamal," meaning "Hail Gamal."

Later he was guest at a dinner given by Alexandria lawyers. Mayor Salem, speaking at the dinner, said: "If Col. Nasser died the revolution would go on."

(October 27)

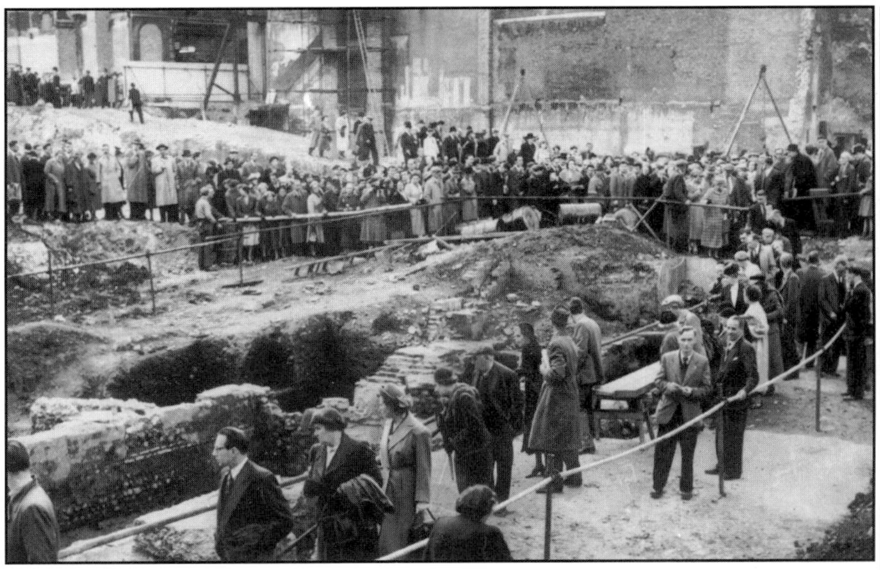

PUBLIC SEE ROMAN TEMPLE REMAINS.
A long queue filing yesterday past the remains of a Roman temple uncovered on a building site near the Mansion House.

SECRETS BAN ON LEADING U.S. ATOM MAN

From Our Own Correspondent

WASHINGTON, Tuesday.

Dr. J. Robert Oppenheimer, 49, America's foremost atomic scientist, has been barred from all secret atomic information while a new investigation is made of his supposed links with Communism. He was the war-time director of the Los Alamos plant where the first atom bomb was made.

The Atomic Energy Commission announced that Dr. Oppenheimer had been suspended from the post of adviser on atomic matters to the commission. A board would investigate and advise whether the suspension should be made permanent.

The Commission's statement said: "The President in consultation with the Secretary of Defence and the Director of Office of Defence Mobilisation, directed that pending a security review of material in the file a blank wall will be placed between Dr. Oppenheimer and any secret data."

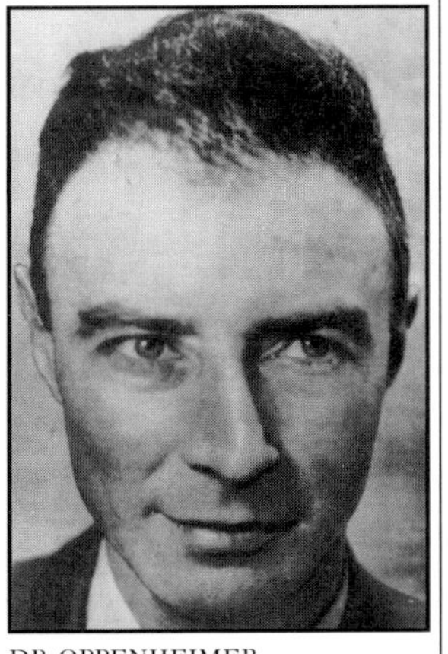

DR. OPPENHEIMER.
He is said to be one of the greatest theoretical physicists in the world.

The three-man board was set up and was now sitting under the chairmanship of Mr. Gordon Gray, former Secretary of the Army, and now President of North Carolina University. The other members were Mr. Thomas A. Morgan, former President of the Sperry Corporation, and Dr. Ward V. Evans, Professor of Chemistry, Loyola University Chicago.

SCIENTISTS' DISMAY

Biggest Security Case Yet

In formally questioning the veracity, conduct and even loyalty of the man who knows more about nuclear physics than anyone else in the United States, the Eisenhower Administration has thrown the scientific world into dismay. It has started a security inquiry which easily overshadows any case yet undertaken.

Its revival of charges, investigated and dismissed in the late 1940s, was decided upon last December under the stricter security code established in the previous April. There is a strong suspicion that the Government's action was prompted by a desire to forestall action by Senator McCarthy's Senate Investigating sub-committee.

(April 14)

15,000 QUEUE TO SEE TEMPLE

MORE DISCOVERIES ON CITY SITE

Daily Telegraph Reporter

For the second day in succession large crowds gathered in the City yesterday to view the remains of the Roman Temple discovered near the Mansion House. Last night's estimate of the crowd was 15,000 compared to 10,000 on Tuesday.

At dusk, when the site was closed, between 3,000 and 4,000 people were turned away. Queues for admission began forming in the afternoon and became 800 yards long.

They grew by thousands in a few hours as City workers left their offices and stopped on the way home. Before the site opened a line of people six deep encircled it.

To prevent congestion, subsidiary queues were formed by the police in adjoining streets and the scene resembled that outside some large sports stadium. Spectators allowed through 100 at a time, were controlled by a police loudspeaker which exhorted them to keep moving.

QUEUES IGNORED ADVICE

As the evening wore on the loudspeaker was directed towards the thousands still waiting outside warning them that they had no chance of getting in. But the crowd remained despite appeals by the police officers and Mr. Grimes, director of the excavations, who toured the queue advising people to go home.

Once in, the spectators moved briskly around the roped-off 60ft by 20ft site of the temple. They paused only to read the labels fixed to its most significant features by the archaeologists.

Many people carried copies of last Saturday's issue of The Daily Telegraph, in which a tabulated picture of the temple was published. Using this as a guide they were able to identify the apse, altar, the tiled inner walls bearing the impression of the colonnades and the original mortar floor.

EASTERN WALL UNCOVERED

The archaeologists, working against time, uncovered the eastern wall yesterday afternoon. This ensures that they can make a plan of the complete layout before the site is demolished to make way for the foundations of Bucklersby House.

The entrance to the temple, on the eastern side, has to be identified. It is also possible that the foundations of an annexe exist outside the wall.

Despite extensive digging no trace of a crypt has been discovered. The archaeologists believe that the temple did not contain one.

Many important finds are still coming to light. Last night a stone bowl about 18in in diameter was discovered against a corner of the east wall. It is believed to have had a ritual use.

The excavations are likely to be discussed at a meeting of the Court of Common Council to-day.

Mr. Grimes said last night that he was well satisfied with the progress of the work. It had been directed mainly towards discovering and recording the complete layout.

(September 23)

ALL BRITAIN SEES THE ECLIPSE

Daily Telegraph Man's Plane Trip

By Leonard Bertin

Daily Telegraph Science Correspondent

Astronomers from almost every civilised country converged yesterday on the narrow strip of the northern hemisphere 8,000 miles long, the only part from which they could see the total eclipse of the sun by the moon. This belt stretched from Nebraska in North America to Jodhpur in India.

I saw the spectacle myself from what was probably the highest position at which an eclipse has ever been observed. In a three-seater Canberra jet bomber flying at nearly 50,000ft., we were above all clouds and with nearly 90 per cent of the earth's atmosphere below us.

In Sweden, parties of astronomers from 12 countries had mixed viewings. They did not all see the same phases of the eclipse, but many expressed confidence that when the various data were added together and photographic material analysed they would have a fairly comprehensive picture.

A partial eclipse was visible clearly from almost all areas of Britain, for at least part of its duration. A layer of thin cloud which reduced the intensity of the sunlight assisted the observers by making darkened glasses unnecessary.

THOUSANDS WATCH

In London the sky became dull, but not dark. With the intermittent cloud the change in light was hardly noticeable, but thousands of office workers who took an early lunch to crowd the parks and office roofs obtained a good view.

(July 1)

SCHOOL TO HAVE 3-DAY OPENING

FIRST OF 1,700 GIRLS START TODAY

Daily Telegraph Reporter

Kidbrooke School, the London Country Council's first specially built comprehensive school, will be opened "by instalments" this week. To facilitate the opening the arrival of the 1,700 girls will spread over three days.

To-day three forms, the fourth, fifth and sixth, will start work. The second and third forms will join the school to-morrow and the first form, who are new entrants to secondary education, will arrive on Thursday.

The whole school will assemble together for the first time on Friday morning. They will be addressed by their headmistress, Miss M.G. Green, former headmistress of Colston Girls' School, Bristol, who is 41.

Miss Green, chosen for this £1,600-a-year post from 29 applicants, was busy yesterday with the final preparations for to-day's opening. She had discussions with her 16 heads of departments and gave final instructions to her teaching staff of 80.

ADVICE TO PREFECTS

In the afternoon she received the prefects, for each of whom she had a word of advice. The prefects were appointed by the schools which were being incorporated into Kidbrooke.

These are Charlton Secondary, Manor Park Secondary, part of the London Technical College and part of the Woolwich Polytechnic. All of the children from the junior schools, who will make up the first form have passed the Common Entrance examination.

The six schools will be split into 65 classes, of which the first form pupils will account for 15. The decision as to which group each child will join will be based on interviews and reports from previous schools.

While the syllabus will be the same for all, the time taken on each subject will vary according to the group. Children who show signs of quicker development may be transferred to another group.

SUBJECT OF CONTROVERSY

The school occupies about 10 acres with 16 acres of playing fields and cost £560,000 to build, with a further £55,000 for equipment. It has been the subject for bitter controversy. There was strong opposition from the L.C.C. Conservative minority, while education experts have expressed divergent views on the advisability of creating schools of such a size.

(September 14)

POWERS ENDORSE INDO-CHINA PACT

MR. EDEN: BEST WE COULD DEVISE

The final session of the nine-nation Geneva conference gave its formal assent yesterday afternoon to the Indo-Chinese cease-fire agreements. Reached on the 75th day of the talks, they end a war which has lasted nearly eight years.

The first two pacts, covering two of the three associated states, Viet-nam and Laos, were signed before dawn yesterday [as reported in later edition of Daily Telegraph]. The one for the third state, Cambodia, was delayed until after noon by Cambodian objections.

At the final session eight of the nine nations subscribed to a declaration which said that they would consult on matters referred to them by the commission which is to supervise the armistice. The ninth nation, the United States, issued a separate statement, saying she would view with grave concern any violation of the pacts. [Text of declarations - P.9.]

Mr. Eden described the settlement as "the best that our hands could devise." Chou En-lai, Chinese Prime Minister, who thought it "regrettable" that the United States did not subscribe to the declaration, said the success of the conference was "tremendous".

AMERICAN ASSURANCE

President Eisenhower said at his press conference that there were some features of the agreement, including partition, which the United States did not like. But she would not use force to upset it.

In a broadcast from Geneva, M. Mendès-France, French Prime Minister, said that the terms were the best that could be hoped for in the circumstances. Reports from Hanoi indicated that it might be several days before the armistice became completely effective.

(July 22)

FRENCH LOSE TWO STRONGPOINTS

SAIGON, Monday.

There is no longer any doubt that the Viet Minh, disregarding appalling casualties, including thousands of dead, are determined to make this the decisive battle of the Indo-Chinese war. Half their total regular Army forces are committed.

One defensive position has fallen to the Viet Minh and two others are under continuous violent attack. A High Command spokesman to-night said they were still "stubbornly resisting."

The first position, a group of defence posts embracing a battalion area defending the north-eastern approaches to Dien Bien Phu, fell after 10 hours' savage fighting early yesterday morning. The survivors, who faced forces estimated at six battalions, later linked up with another defensive position.

Meanwhile the north-western defensive position, of similar size, came under heavy attack. Bright weather soon after dawn allowed fighters and bombers to come in on low-level attacks.

COUNTER-ATTACK

"Magnificent Morale"

In the north-western area the Viet Minh attackers were in turn assailed by the French. In a tangled mass of wire and broken bunkers the defenders regained some ground lost earlier in desperate fighting.

Twelve miles away, at the southern extremity of the Dien Bien Phu bowl, a third of defensive position also threw back attack after attack. Again a combination of artillery, Air Force support and a first-class mobile reserve served the French well.

In a radio message to his C-in-C., Gen. Navarre, Col. De Castries, the Dien Bien Phu Commander, said: "I am full of confidence in the victorious issue of the battle, thanks to the magnificent morale of troops".

RADIO CALL

Truce Message

There were now new French troops in the fight. They parachuted down from flying "boxcars" in the dusk last evening ready for immediate action. To-day weapons, food, ammunition and medical supplies were sent in by the same method.

During the morning the Viet Minh sent out a radio call for a truce to allow them to collect their wounded. It was the first such request yet made, according to French sources.

A wounded French officer who had been captured crossed the lines with written confirmation of the request. The defenders agreed and for four hours the fighting ceased.

At this stage the French were hurriedly repairing the airstrips, which had been put out of commission by the heavy Communist gunfire. During the truce French transport planes landed unmolested to fly out wounded.

REBEL STRENGTH

Half Forces Committed

The question now is how long Gen. Vo Nguyen Giap, Viet Minh commander, can maintain full pressure. He probably can draw upon 29 or 30 infantry battalions, and by a conservative estimate at least half of these must have been already committed and in many cases badly mauled.

(March 16)

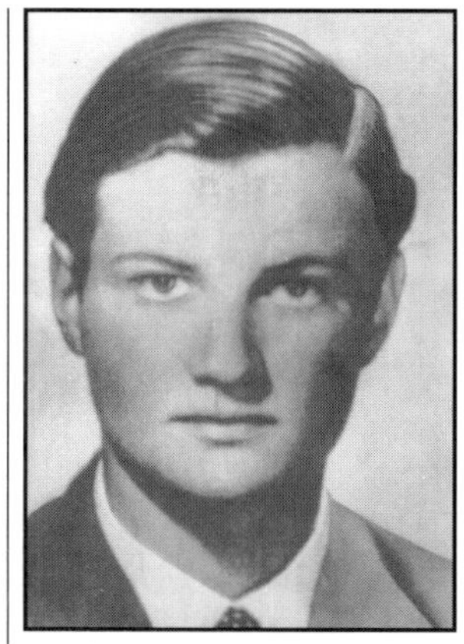

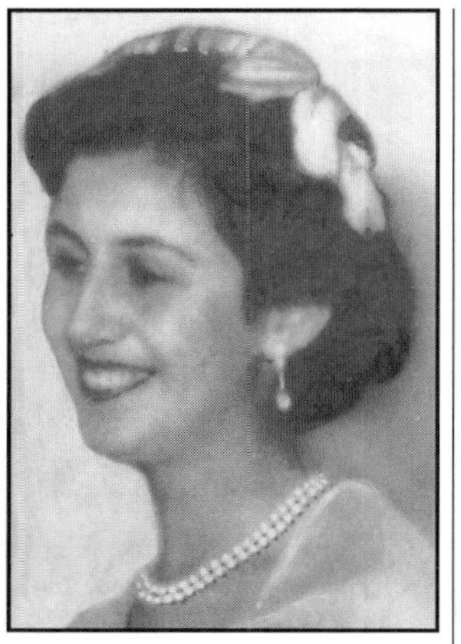

WEDDING OPPOSED BY PARENTS. Mr. James Goldsmith, son of a Savoy Hotel director, whose marriage to Maria Isabella Patino (right) has been opposed by her father Senor Antenor Patino, former Bolivian Minister to Great Britain.

180,000 ATTEND GRAHAM FINALE

'MOST THRILLING 12 WEEKS'

Daily Telegraph Reporter

Mr. Billy Graham, the American evangelist, convinced that a religious revival is already on its way among intellectuals, preached last night in St. Aldgate's, Oxford, to dons and undergraduates. The service was relayed to the Wesley Memorial Church and St. Peter's Hall. All three churches were full.

On Saturday, the last day of his three-month Greater London crusade, he addressed audiences totalling 180,000 at White City and the Empire Stadium, Wembley.

The final meeting of the campaign in the evening at Wembley ended with at least 10,000 out of 120,000 present filing from the terraces over 15 specially built bridges across the greyhound track on to the football pitch. They stood in silence before the rostrum as a declaration that they had accepted Christ.

RESPONSE BIGGER THAN U.S.

It was, said Mr. Graham, "bigger than anything the United States can do, and that includes Texas." He added:

"I have one request before I leave. The past 12 weeks have been the most wonderful and thrilling weeks I have ever known in my life. I am going to ask you to promise to be in church to-morrow morning and evening.

"Let's fill our churches to-morrow. Let's make it the greatest occasion the Church has known in years. I may be saying farewell, but in thousands of churches to-morrow the real crusade begins."

At the end of the Wembley meeting the Archbishop of Canterbury, Dr. Fisher, pronounced the Benediction and offered a short prayer for what had been "planned and thought, attempted and done through the work of this mission".

Thousands of people went straight from the afternoon White City meeting to the Wembley finale.

The Cup Final limit of 100,000 spectators had been waived. About 10,000 people stood on the pitch throughout the two-and- a-half hour rally in rain and cold wind which Mr. Graham said would clear any American stadium in five minutes.

UNDERGRADUATES QUEUE

A queue formed an hour before the Oxford meeting began. Undergraduates stood six deep in St. Aldgate's aisles. Afterwards about 200 remained behind in person to Mr. Graham's call to "give themselves to Christ".

(May 24)

FIVE ILL FROM 'ATOMIC DUST'

JAPANESE FISHERMEN

TOKYO, Wednesday.

Twenty-one members of the crew of the Japanese fishing boat Fukuryu Maru 5 are under observation in hospital at Yaizu, about 150 miles southwest of Tokyo, to-day. Five are reported to be seriously ill.

The boat was found to be covered with white atomic dust when it entered harbour on Sunday. The radioactive dust came from an American atomic explosion in Bikini island on March 1. - Reuter.

(March 14)

BRITISH TROOPS SAIL FROM EGYPT

MARINES FOR MALTA

PORT SAID, TUESDAY.

About 2,300 British troops from the Suez Canal Zone embarked here to-day as Egypt announced that Anglo-Egyptian committees have nearly completed work on an evacuation agreement.

The first troops to leave in the early hours to-day were 450 men of Royal Marine commando units, called to Egypt at the peak of the Canal Zone dispute. They left for Malta in the cruiser Glasgow.

About 1,450 men of the 1st Bn. the South Lancashire Regt., 2nd Bn. the Parachute Regiment, and attached troops embarked for Britain. They are being replaced by men of the Royal Warwickshire Regt. from Korea. - Reuter.

(August 18)

BOLIVIAN GIRL AND FIANCE NOT TRACED

Daily Telegraph Reporter

Late last night Mr. James Goldsmith, 20, son of a Savoy Hotel director, and Maria Isabella Patino, 18, daughter of Senor Antenor Patinio, former Bolivian Minister to Britain, who are planning to marry, had still not been traced. Maria's parents are opposed to the marriage.

From to-morrow the couple, who gave notice of their intended marriage in Edinburgh on Dec. 29, can be married anywhere in Scotland. Mr. W.S.Cockburn, registrar at the office at which the marriage notice was posted, confirmed this yesterday.

He said that a certificate to that effect was valid for three months. It could not be handed to anyone except the couple concerned or their officially appointed representative. He was precluded by law from handing it to the parents without the couple's consent but their parents could have a copy.

DAUGHTER "TOO YOUNG"

Senor Patino, who was Bolivian Minister to Britain from 1938 to 1944, inherited from his father a fortune from the tin mines of Bolivia. He believes that his daughter is too young to marry.

He went to Edinburgh two days ago with his lawyer, in the hope of stopping the marriage. If he can find his daughter he may still be able to persuade her against the marriage, but by Scottish law persons over the age of 16 can marry without their parents' consent.

Mr. Frank Goldsmith, who has large hotel interests in both Britain and France, said in Cannes yesterday: "In our family, the son doesn't need to ask the father for permission to marry. But I do think he is too young and so is she".

He described how his eldest son, Theodore, 24, a cadet at the Officers' Training School, Eaton Hall, Cheshire, told him of his forthcoming wedding. "Teddy said, 'I have three weeks' leave. I'm going to use them to get married,' and that's how I learned about it."

(January 5)

PREMIERS FLY OVER ARCTIC

NEW ROUTE OPENED

The new "Arctic short cut" route from Europe to California was opened yesterday by two Scandinavian Airlines DC-6B airliners. One set off from Copenhagen for Los Angeles and the other in the opposite direction from Los Angeles.

Among the 33 passengers in the Helge Viking from Copenhagen was Prince Axel of Denmark and the Prime Ministers of Denmark, Sweden and Norway, Mr. Hedtoft, Mr. Erlander and Mr. Torp.

This plane was expected to pass the Royal Viking, which took off in the morning from Los Angeles, over the inland ice of Greenland, at about 2 a.m. G.M.T. The Royal Viking landed in Greenland at 11.32 p.m. and left at 1.01 a.m. First stop for the Helge Viking is at Southern Stroemfiord, Greenland, after a six hours' flight. The other stop is at Winnipeg.

About 535 miles are saved compared with the usual transatlantic route via New York. The Arctic "short cut" is about 5,800 miles.

(November 16)

9 POWERS AGREE ON GERMAN ARMS

By Our Diplomatic Correspondent

The nine-power London conference ended yesterday with agreement on methods to be adopted for bringing Germany into Western defence and increasing European unity. A Final Act published by the conference (full text - P11), said it dealt with "the most important issues facing the Western world."

These it defined as "security and European integration within the framework of a developing Atlantic Community dedicated to peace and freedom." Germany has agreed to important restrictions on armament production, including absolute prohibition of atomic, chemical and biological weapons.

In addition Dr. Adenauer, the Chancellor, has declared that the Federal Republic "undertakes never to have recourse to force to achieve the reunification of Germany or the modification of the present boundaries of the German Federal Republic."

Germany will enter the North Atlantic Treaty Organisation, and, with Italy, will adhere to the Brussels Treaty. The Brussels Treaty Organisation will exercise important controls over armaments of its member countries on the Continent.

It is understood that Belgium, Holland and Luxembourg also announced their intention to ban production of atomic, biological and chemical weapons. No mention of this was made in the Final Act.

The earliest time the agreements announced yesterday are likely to come into effect is towards the end of the year. It is hoped that full texts embodying the agreements will be signed at meetings to be held in Paris from Oct. 20 to 23.

The chief hurdle after that will be ratification in Paris. M. Mendès-France, French Prime Minister, has made it clear he will not place the agreements before his Assembly unless he can also lay at the same time a Franco-German agreement on the Saar.

ENDING OCCUPATION

Allied Declaration

The London agreements, with the Franco-German Saar agreement still to be negotiated, will be presented to the Assembly by M. Mendès-France as "one package", designed to form the basis for a new French foreign policy.

Other main provisions of the Final Act are a declaration by Britain, France and the United States that they intend to end the occupation régime "as soon as possible", and important provisions for strengthening the control powers of Gen. Gruenther, N.A.T.O.'s Supreme Commander in Europe.

In the speeches that preceded the signing ceremony at Lancaster House Mr. Eden said it was his belief that they had built well for the future of Europe. "We all pray that the result of our work will be shown in greater confidence and a more enduring peace throughout the world."

MR. EDEN PRAISED

"Momentous Role"

Mr. Dulles, American Secretary of State, paid a striking tribute to Mr. Eden. He said they were deeply appreciative of his leadership, not only as chairman but in the convening of the conference and the preliminary work.

"The contribution which you have made in that capacity, to-gether with the contribution which, through you, your Government has made has been indispensable and historically momentous. I believe it will mean that this conference will go down in history as one of the greatest conferences of all time".

(October 4)

MAU MAU GANG CHIEF GIVES HIMSELF UP

From Our Special Correspondent

NAIROBI, Sunday.

"Gen. Tanganyika," one of the principal lieutenants of "Gen. China" in the Mount Kenya area, last night became the first Mau Mau gang leader to give himself up after reading China's surrender letters. In the same area another wounded gang leader, "Gen. Katanga," was captured.

Tanganyika gave himself up to a Kikuyu Home Guard post in the South Nyeri reserve. The choice of surrender site was peculiar as the Home Guard is less well disciplined than regular security forces and might have killed him on sight in revenge for atrocities on their families.

Unofficial reports say that he was, indeed, beaten before making his identity and purpose plain. But there is no doubt that he intended to surrender.

Yesterday morning there was a hastily arranged meeting between special branch police officers and Tanganyika's representatives in the Kikuyu reserve. For this meeting the head of the security branch, Assistant Commissioner Gribble, flew hurriedly from Nairobi to Nyeri.

"PERSONAL GESTURE"

Reason for Surrender

The officers were told that the terrorist intended to surrender as a "personal gesture in aid of China's plan." This intention was confirmed in a letter to China.

Tanganyika, who commanded a "battalion", surrendered without any of his gang. He is now detained at Karatina police station. His real name is Miqiuki Kamutho.

Vigorous action taken to-day by the Home Guard does not bear out the frequently made contention that the morale of the loyal Africans would be shattered by China's reprieve. In the Kiambu area they killed six terrorists and captured nine weapons. They also inflicted casualties in the Mount Kenya area.

10,000 FINED £1

New Policy Launched

To-day the Kenya Government launched the new policy of acting against ordinary residents of the Kikuyu reserve, which was foreshadowed in China's surrender letter. They imposed a fine of £1 on each of the 10,000 adults in the Kangema division of the Fort Hall district, where a District Officer, Mr. J.H.Chandler, was murdered at the week-end.

The fine was levied under a new emergency regulation which empowers a District Officer, subject to the Governor's prior approval, to fine summarily each inhabitant of an "affected area." An "affected area" is broadly defined as one in which the inhabitants are active in furthering Mau Mau.

While there is no hunger in the reserves, the fine will hit the Kikuyu hard, as the terrorists have cut down cash crops in many areas. Other non-punitive measures against non-co-operators are being considered.

LAND FORFEITURE

Act in Force Soon

The Royal Assent has just been received for the Kenya Government Act authorising the forfeiture of land held in the reserves by Mau Mau leaders. It is to be gazetted in Nairobi quickly and will considerably increase the Government's powers.

The seven-page Act allows the forfeiture of lands held by those imprisoned for seven years or more, or those who the Governor is satisfied have "led or organised armed or violent resistance against the forces of law and order whether or not the suspect has been apprehended, charged or convicted."

(March 8)

MR. EISENHOWER SUPPORTS ARMY AGAINST McCARTHY

ANGER OVER 'SURRENDER' VIEW

From Our Own Correspondent

WASHINGTON, Thursday.

President Eisenhower to-night came out in full support of Mr. Stevens, United States Secretary of the Army, in his dispute with Senator McCarthy, who has accused the Army of "coddling Communists."

Mr. Stevens issued a statement declaring that he would "never accede to the abuse of Army personnel under any circumstances, including committee hearings." After a White House conference, Mr. Hegerty, Presidential Press Secretary, said the President had seen Mr. Stevens's statement and "approves and endorses it 100 per cent."

The Army Secretary said he received assurances that Senator McCarthy and the Senate Investigating sub-committee would not permit any future abuses of army officers called to give evidence.

"ASSURANCES GIVEN"

Protection of Witnesses

"If it were not for those assurances I would never have entered into any agreement whatsoever," declared the Secretary. "I want to make it perfectly clear that should such abuses occur in the future I shall once again take all steps at my disposal to protect the rights of individuals."

The strong declaration of principles embodied in Mr. Stevens's statement appeared to nullify the impression created by him yesterday in his "memorandum of agreement" with Mr. McCarthy and Republican members of his committee.

Mr. Stevens is known to have been greatly incensed at the interpretation placed on this memorandum. This was that he had capitulated ignominiously. He denied reports that he was going to resign.

Senator McCarthy to-night accused Mr. Stevens of making a completely false statement. "I very carefully explained to Mr. Stevens at our meeting on Wednesday that he was Secretary of the Army and not running the committee," he said.

"Absolutely no concession was made that any witness was abused. We made it very clear that any witness from the Army or anywhere else, if he is not frank or truthful, will be vigorously examined to get the truth about Communist activiies."

Shortly before he had stated: "As far as I am concerned the incident is closed. We all make occasional errors of judgment. Bob Stevens and I have differed on this, but I think on the whole he is doing a very good job."

"PEACE PACT"

Project Abandoned

Mr. Stevens to-day refused to subscribe to a "peace pact" which Senator Dirksen and other Republican members of the McCarthy committee attempted to draw up. In this Mr. McCarthy and the Army Secretary were to have professed identity of views in the treatment to be accorded to members of the Army.

The statement, however, never materialised. It was, learnt to-night that one obstacle was Mr. McCarthy's objection to a demand by Mr. Stevens that it should guarantee no more "abuse" of Army witnesses.

(February 26)

MR. McCARTHY CONDEMNED BY STATE

From Our Own Correspondent

WASHINGTON, Thursday.

For the fourth time in its history the United States Senate to-night voted to censure one of its members. Senator McCarthy was condemned by a 67 vote to 22 on two counts. These said:

1. He abused and flouted the authority of the Elections Sub-committee three years ago.
2. He abused the special committee under the chairmanship of Senator Watkins, of Utah, which recommended that he be censured.

The vote on the second count was 64 to 24. The vote on the first count, which took place last night, was 67 to 20.

The word "censure" did not actually appear in the resolution, but even the McCarthy supporters derived no solace from this. Senator Welker remarked that "condemn" was a more severe term, since a judge did not censure a prisoner, he condemned him.

ZWICKER ISSUE DROPPED

Senator McCarthy's abuse of Gen. Zwicker was squeezed out of the censure resolution during the course of the day, when opposition to its inclusion developed from the Democratic side as well as from the anti-McCarthy wing of the Republican party.

Early this year Gen. Zwicker, in accordance with the instructions of his superiors, had declined to answer Senator McCarthy's questions about who promoted Major Peress, a dentist suspected of Communism.

Mr. McCarthy lost his temper and told Gen. Zwicker, among other things, that he was not fit to wear his uniform. The Zwicker affair raised the issue of the respective constitutional rights of Congress and the executive branch of Government.

A total of 22 Republicans, 44 Democrats and Senator Morse, Independent, voted to condemn Senator McCarthy's conduct. The 22 opposing votes were all Republican.

Senator McCarthy was absent during most of the debate. But he appeared before the final vote, answering "present" when his name was called.

(December 23)

6 MONTHS' GAOL FOR DR. JAGAN

Dr. Jagan, leader of the People's Progressive party and deposed Prime Minister of British Guiana, was sentenced to six months' imprisonment to-day for violating the Governor's order restricting his movements to Georgetown. He was arrested on April 3 at Mahalcony village, 38 miles away.

Dr. Jagan, who did not plead and did not give evidence, made it clear that he had no intention of observing the emergency regulations, which he described as "Fascist."

He called upon his followers in a political speech to the magistrate, Mr. Sharples, to violate the regulations similarity and to wear a mourning band at the Queen's birthday celebrations in the colony.

He said he was not afraid of prison as the whole colony was one big gaol under the emergency regulations. The law was Fascist and its framers, Sir Alfred Savage, and Mr. Lyttelton, Colonial Secretary, were also Fascists and should be before the court instead of him.

(April 3)

MARRIAGE OF MISS MARILYN MONROE

Marilyn Monroe, 27, the film actress, and Joe DiMaggio, 37, former baseball star, were married today in San Francisco. Their names had been linked for many months and the marriage came as no surprise.

Reports that it was to take place were intensified during the past week after the Twentieth Century Fox film company suspended Miss Monroe for not reporting for work on a film. This afternoon she telephoned the studio and said: "I am marrying Joe to-day."

News of the marriage spread rapidly, and there was a crowd of about 400 in the judge's chambers where the ceremony was due to be performed.

Miss Monroe was hatless and was wearing a dark brown broadcloth suit with a white mink collar. She was carrying a bridal bouquet of three white orchids.

"We are both very happy," she announced. The best man was Mr. Barsacchani, Mrs Barsacchani was matron of honour.

(January 15)

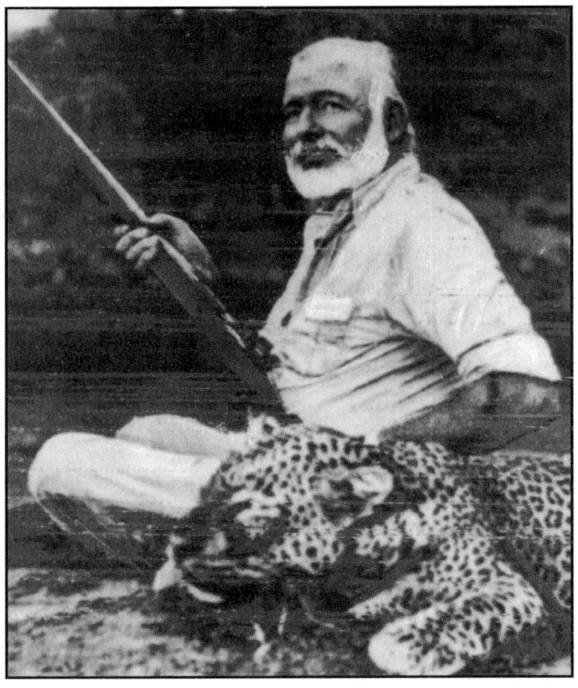

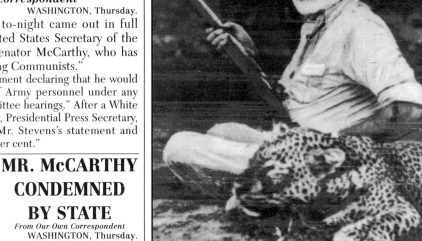

AUTHOR MISSING. Mr. Ernest Hemingway, the American writer, kneeling beside a leopard he had killed during the African safari he was on when his chartered plane made a forced landing in Uganda on Saturday.

HEMINGWAYS' PLANE SPOTTED IN JUNGLE

NOVELIST & WIFE MAY BE SAFE, SAYS B.O.A.C. PILOT

From Our Own Correspondent

KAMPALA, Uganda, Sunday.

A plane missing since yesterday with Mr. Ernest Hemingway, 55, the American novelist, and his wife aboard is lying damaged in the Uganda jungle near Lake Albert, a British Overseas Airways captain reported to-day.

The Hemingways' plane, chartered at Nairobi yesterday for a visit to Murchison Falls, failed to arrive later at Masindi, a refuelling point 40 miles away. The B.O.A.C. Argonaut, flying from Entebbe to Khartoum, was diverted 80 to 100 miles to help in a search.

Capt. R.C. Jude, of Horsham, Sussex, captain of the airliner, stated that the plane appeared to be little damaged. A police rescue party is on its way from Butiaba, on the shores of Lake Albert, to the scene of what appears to have been a forced landing.

The area is one of the least accessible in Uganda, teeming with crocodile, elephant, buffalo, lion and other big game. According to reports the plane came down three miles from Murchison Falls.

At the Falls the River Nile drops 400ft through a narrow rock and jungle gorge and flows on to Lake Albert. The pilot was the only other person on board the chartered plane.

Unconfirmed reports say that a spotter plane made contact with a motor launch on the River Nile. It was possible that the motor launch was carrying the survivors.

"NEAT LANDING JOB"

Plane Spotted in Scrub

Capt. Jude said he sighted the aircraft on the south bank of the Nile. There were no signs of life.

"It looked as if the chap made a neat job of landing. The plane plopped right into scrub trees growing about 20 feet high along the river valley."

He doubted if Mr. Hemingway and others aboard were killed in the crash. "You can't tell about these things. One wheel of the undercarriage was broken, but otherwise the plane appeared little damaged.

"I would think the passengers climbed out and made for the river, which is only 300 yards away.

"It is really wild-looking country below the gorge of Murchison Falls. We circled as low as 200ft and saw several elephants and buffaloes roaming among the trees on the other side of the river."

(January 25)

NOBEL PRIZE DEFENDED

From Our Own Correspondent

STOCKHOLM, Friday.

The award of the £12,500 Nobel prize for literature to Ernest Hemingway, the American author, for his novel, "The Old Man and the Sea," was de-fended here to-day by Marshal Ekeberg, President of the Nobel Foundation, and by Dr. Oester-Ling, President of the Swedish Academy.

The choice had given rise to some controversy. Mr. Hemingway, who is 55, was not well enough to travel from his home in Cuba, so Mr. Cabot, American Ambassador here, received the award on his behalf from King Gustav.

Dr. Oesterling, defending Mr. Hemingway against charges of callousness, said: "It may be true that Hemingway's earlier writings display brutal, cynical and callous sides which may be considered at variance with the Nobel Prize's requirements for a work of an ideal tendency.

(December 11)

END OF RATIONING

Food rationing in Britain ends today, 14 years after its war-time introduction. Meat, the last rationed commodity, will be freed at midnight. Celebrating housewives will gather in Trafalgar Square to sing "The Roast Beef of Old England."

(July 3)

SIR K. CLARK HEAD OF RIVAL TV

FIRST TASK TO PICK 3 TRANSMITTER SITES

From L.Marsland Garner
Daily Telegraph Radio Correspondent

The Postmaster-General has appointed Sir Kenneth Clark, 51, to be chairman of the Independent Television Authority. He is chairman of the Arts Council.

The Authority is set up under the Television Act, which received Royal Assent last Friday. It will provide 10 years' commercial broadcasting services additional to the B.B.C. services.

Two women are among the other eight members of the Authority. They are Miss Margaret Popham, former Principal of Cheltenham Ladies' College, and Miss Dilys Powell, 53, the film critic.

The Television Act laid down that the Authority would pay to each of its members, according to office, "such renumeration, whether by way of salary or fees, and such allowances as the Postmaster-General may, with the approval of the Treasury, determine." No announcement has yet been made on salaries.

Sir Charles Colston, 62, former chairman and managing director of Hoover, will be deputy chairman of the Authority. Other members will be:
Lord Aberdare, 58, chairman of the National Association of Boys Clubs;
Lt.-Col. Arthur Chichester, chairman of Moygashel, whose special interest will be in Northern Ireland;
Sir Henry Hinchcliffe, 61, director of Barclays Bank;
Dr. T.J.Honeyman, 63, director of Glasgow Art Gallery and Rector of Glasgow University, who will make Scottish interests his special care.

(August 4)

ITALY OPENS TV SERVICE

A regular television service was begun in Italy to-day. This morning television studios and transmitters were officially inaugurated in Rome, Milan and Turin. They will provide six hour programmes on week-days, and 12-hour programmes on Sundays.

The Pope addressed a message to the bishops of Italy on television. It might become a danger "owing to the abuses and profanations to which it might be carried." He ordered the bishop of each diocese where there was a transmitter to detail a priest to watch the programmes and to take action against any considered unsuitable.

Television in Italy is a monopoly of the State-controlled Italian broadcasting corporation. A large part of the transmitting equipment was supplied by British manufacturers.

(January 4)

VALERIE HOBSON TO MARRY M.P.

Valerie Hobson, 38, leading lady in the Drury Lane musical "The King and I," is to marry Mr. John Profumo, 39, Parliamentary Secretary to the Ministry of Transport and Civil Aviation. The engagement is announced on page six. The wedding is expected to take place early in January.

Miss Hobson was formerly married to Mr. Anthony Havelock-Allan, the film producer.

(October 21)

ATOMIC PLANT WILL BE IN STEEL DOME

'POWERFUL PROJECT' SAYS MINISTER

By Our Own Representative

WESTMINSTER, Monday.

The new plant for the production of energy, to be built at Dounreay, Caithness, was described in the House of Commons to-night as "the most powerful and dramatic project of its kind so far conceived."

This was one of many telling phrases used by Sir David Eccles, Minister of Works, in describing the future of atomic energy for industrial purposes.

He was moving the second reading of the Atomic Energy Authority Bill, which was given a second reading after a Socialist amendment had been defeated by 244 votes to 226, a Government majority of 18. The Bill transfers research and management from the Ministry of Supply to a Board of six to 10 men.

The choice of Dounreay, near Thurso, for the new atomic power station was exclusively forecast in the Daily Telegraph last November. It will be of the fast "breeder-reactor" type. This means that it will produce more secondary atomic fuel than it burns of primary fuel.

"DOME OF DISCOVERY"

These are some of the things Sir David had to say about the new station:

It will occupy some hundreds of acres on the coast, and will provide employment for 600 people;

For safety's sake, it will be housed in a large spherical steel shell -a real Dome of Discovery;

It should show the way to remarkable economies in the consumption of uranium.

Sir David hoped that within 10 years nuclear reactors would be paying their way. The new source of power would come just in time for Britain. Her coal supplies were running out, she had little water-power and almost no oil.

On the subject of atom bombs Sir David revealed that many, more powerful than those dropped on Japan, were now in store. There were many new devices for delivering them. These reserves of atomic weapons could do for mankind what poison gas failed to do-make the next war too terrifying to start.

(March 2)

MORE WATCH TV: FEWER LISTEN IN

By A Radio Correspondent

An increase in the popularity of television programmes and a corresponding drop in sound features is shown in a report for the September quarter published yesterday by the B.B.C. There was an average of 10 million adult viewers against eight million in the same quarter last year.

An estimated 26 million listened in compared with 28 million. In the year about a million families bought television sets.

(October 23)

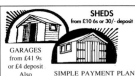

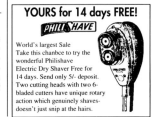

'THE DECAMERON' IS NOT OBSCENE, SAYS COURT

SHOP WINS APPEAL AGAINST DESTRUCTION ORDER

Daily Telegraph Reporter

Without calling the author, last heard of at Certaldo in Italy in 1375, the Wiltshire County Appeals Committee at Trowbridge yesterday decided that Boccaccio's "The Decameron" is not obscene.

The decision reverses an order made by Swindon magistrates in July for the destruction of a two-volume, three-guinea, illustrated edition of "The Decameron," along with works by a Mr. Hank Janson. These and other recent titles such as "Dames Fry Too" were among 348 books seized by the police from the shop of Mrs. Elsie Fould, in Commercial Road, Swindon.

Of these, 87 were returned to Mrs. Fould; 64 were not deemed obscene by the bench; and 197, under about 50 titles, were ordered to be destroyed, Boccaccio's classic among them.

Yesterday Mrs. Fould successfully appealed against the order. After a two and three-quarter hours' legal argument by counsel and a five-minute adjournment by the committee, the chairman, Mr. A.W. NORTHEY, said: "The committee are not satisfied the book in question is obscene. The appeal is allowed with costs."

"REVOLTING" THEMES

Shop for "Dirty Books"

Mr. J.T. MOLONY, for the Director of Public Prosecutions, said some of the tales in "The Decameron" seemed revolting in their themes. It was important to remember the setting in which the books were displayed.

They were offered for sale at a shop where newspapers and periodicals were available in conjunction with a variety of books, the titles of which were certainly calculated to appeal to those looking for literature undesirable by ordinary decent standards. Those wanting dirty books would satisfy themselves from the titles on show that they had found the right place.

For those who wish to study early Italian literature or wish to discover what an Italian novelist poured from his pen in the 14th century there are places where 'The Decameron' should be available and no doubt is."

Mr. NORTHEY: Would you say that a copy of this book in the Swindon public library is a proper thing?

Mr. MOLONY: That is perfectly proper, I gather the literary merits of this book are considerable. It is perfectly right that students of Italian social history should have access to it.

NOT HOLIDAY READING

Reply to Chairman

He continued: "When it is found in a setting of literature calculated to attract minds that are susceptible to be corrupted then it is calculated to attract those who would only get a pornographic satisfaction from it" calculated to give the idea that all a woman wanted was to get a man.

"The Decameron" might instil that idea in a young mind. The idea was not generally true of women in this country. "To suggest that women may be susceptible to these overwhelming urges which only need touching off is obscene according to our ideas."

VARIETY ON SALE

30 Titles in Window

Det. Sgt. J. PEARE said there were about 30 titles of obscene books in the window of Mrs. Fould's shop with "The Decameron." Cross-examined by Mr. STEPHENSON, Counsel for Mrs. Fould, he said that children's books, detective and cowboy stories were also on sale.

Mr. STEPHENSON, submitting his case, added: "Is there anything in this book which would suggest to prospective purchasers in Swindon in 1954 thoughts and desires which would otherwise not have occurred to their minds?"

Quoting a number of legal authorities dating back to the reign of Queen Victoria, he said there was extraordinarily little reference to sexual aberration in "The Decameron" compared with what could be found in more modern works for which orders for destruction had not been made in this case.

"Is it a work of sheer filth? Has it a tendency to corrupt and deprave the minds of people?" he asked.

SWINDON'S BLUSHES

14th Century Comparison

It was more to be compared with the works of Rabelais, Chaucer, and Shakespeare. It poked fun at the Church, at friars and monks, in a way which was a little unpleasant but as far from being obscene as was possible.

It was a series of stories which would cause fewer blushes in 14th century Italy than in 20th century Swindon.

There is a danger that Shakespeare might be held to be destructible. If his Pericles, Prince of Tyre, were taken out and sold in paper covers in this shop for half a crown would the justices be justified in ordering its destruction as obscene?"

(September 16)

1953 'OSCAR' FOR AUDREY HEPBURN

BEST FILM ACTRESS

From Our Own Correspondent

NEW YORK, Friday

The British actress Audrey Hepburn, 24, was voted the best film actress of 1953 last night by the Academy of Motion Picture Arts and Sciences for her performance in the film "Roman Holiday."

She received the "Oscar" at a television gathering in the Centre Theatre, New York. She was hurried there by car with a motor-cycle police escort from the theatre in 46th Street where she is starring as a waternymph in the play "Ondine."

Other awards included:

William Holden: Year's best film actor for performance in "Stalag 17."

"From Here to Eternity": Year's best film, and seven other "Oscars," equalling record of "Gone With The Wind."

Walt Disney: Four "Oscars" for cartoons and documentaries, increasing his total to 22.

George Stevens, director: Irving Thalberg award for distinguished accomplishment. The Western film "Shane" helped to win this.

(March 27)

A GAY FROLIC FROM BRISTOL

By W.A. Darlington

There are some shows which defy solemn criticism, and "Salad Days" at the Vaudeville is one of them.

If I had not been carried away last night by its lunatic gaiety, if I had not been made to laugh, if I had not enjoyed its first half hugely and its second half quite a good deal, I could assemble a number of good academic reasons why it should not have been worth importing to London, even after its happy reception at the Bristol Old Vic.

But you can't argue academically about a frolic like this. The only test is whether you enjoy it. If my reactions are anything to go by you will.

It is a loose-knit musical fantasy about a boy and a girl who leave college to face the world, and come into possession (never mind how) of a magic piano.

A ramshackle affair, in fact. Then why is it so attractive? Well, it has youth and freshness and gusto: and it has Denis Carey's light touch as director.

Eleanor Drew as the girl acts and sings pleasantly; John Warner as the boy is a nimble dancer. Newton Blick has a gloriously funny little interlude as a bishop forced to dance to the magic music.

(August 6)

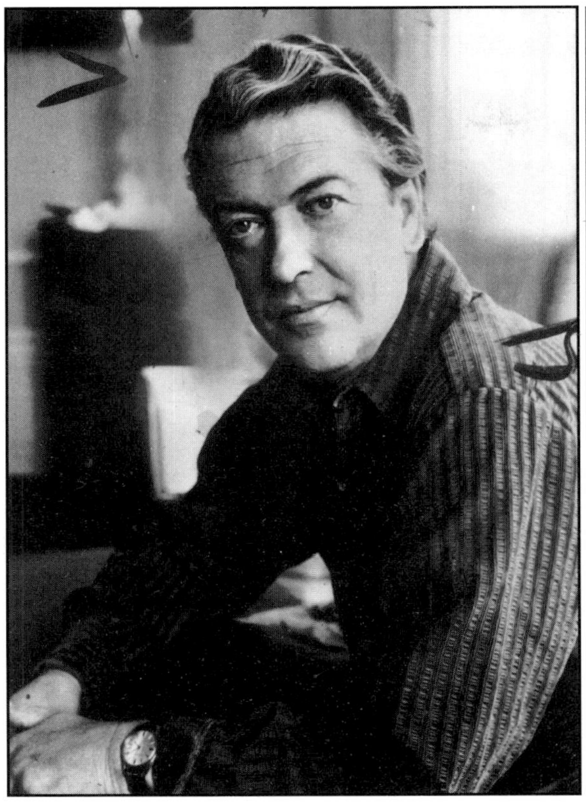

KINGSLEY AMIS

New Fiction

Amusing Story of Life at a Provincial University

By John Betjeman

Lucky Jim. By Kingsley Amis (Gollancz. 12s 6d)
Lord of the Flies. By William Golding. (Faber, 12s 6d) Oct 15
Under the Net. By Iris Murdoch (Chatto & Windus. 12s 6d) June 11

I do not remember to have laughed so much at a new funny book as I have done at "LUCKY JIM," by Kingsley Amis, since when I first read Evelyn Waugh's "Decline and Fall" - and that was in 1928. The scene is a provincial university, an exam-passing, self-important, mercenary world where a good memory was mistaken for learning, where futile essays were written each with "its funereal parade of yawn-enforcing facts, the pseudo-light it threw on non-problems."

A good deal of such nonsense goes on at Oxford and Cambridge too in the name of "research" into history, literature and art. For me, the most refreshing feature of Mr. Amis's book is his tolerant contempt for the whole set-up which keeps the reader giggling throughout the book.

His hero, James Dixon, is a lecturer on history, newly arrived and not secure in his position. He is in his probationary first year of teaching and already one of the nastier of his pupils delights in showing up his tutor's ignorance. Chiefly poor Dixon has to keep in with his Professor, a mad mediaevalist who is very musical and gives madrigal concerts with oboes and recorders.

A Madrigal Party

Dixon having disgraced himself at a madrigal party by not being able to sing in tune, escaped from the house where he was staying with his Professor as host and came back drunk. He went to the bathroom to eat toothpaste and try to feel better.

When he woke up next morning he found he had burned huge holes in his bedclothes with a cigarette. He tried to repair the damage by sawing away the burnt fringe with a razor and only made matters worse.

These and similar situations carry one through a book which is itself a good story, full of suspense and with a most satisfying happy ending. Every character is distinct - the lady don with thick spectacles who is in love with Dixon and always making scenes with him; the footling Professor:

"There was a small golden emblem on his tie resembling some heraldic device or other, but proving on close scrutiny to be congealed egg-yoke. Substantial traces of the same nutritive was to be seen round his mouth, which was now ajar."

There is the Professor's formidable wife, his two ghastly sons and a variety of comic characters, none hated and all life-like. The one adverse criticism I can make is that there is a certain amount of over-writing but this is wholly out-weighed by the merits of the comedy. Indeed, it is a Harold Lloyd film or a Buster Keaton film in prose, lacking the pathos of Chaplin.

(February 5)

Let no one suppose that, because it is about a party of boys dropped on a deserted, tropic island, "LORD OF THE FLIES" by William Golding is anything like "Coral Island." I think it will make entertaining reading for boys, even though the beasts which lurk in the jungle and haunt the lonely starlit nights of the imaginations of the younger boys of the party. But the entertainment that boys and adults will have in this readable and blood-curdling book will be derived from that rather unpalatable thing, the moral which it teaches.

The boys elect as their chief the one among their number who is most sensible and adult and who realises that if they want to be rescued they must keep a smoky fire going. Soon the school bully among them founds his own tribe of hunters and institutes a reign of terror and deposes the elected chief. He works his tribe up to mass blood lust and two of the weaker and more individualistic boys are murdered.

The child is father to the man, if I may be scarcely original. What these boys do to one another is what we as adults do to one another. If we refuse to think of the common good, reverence nothing and obey only our senses.

(October 15)

★ ★ ★

"UNDER THE NET," by Iris Murdoch, is a first novel of that London life which features intellectuals, washouts and seedy characters in general. The hero, Jake Donaghue, who knocks up a living by hack translations, is a weak but decent fellow who enmeshes himself in a series of fantastic adventures. Miss Murdoch relates these farcical episodes with great gusto and feeling, but there is a little too much farce and fantasy for the good of the novel.

The tension of the story is not sustained. The other characters are adequately drawn, but it is rather the personality of the author than the reality of her people which impresses me.

(June 11)

STORM OVER ORWELL PLAY

TORTURE SCENES

By L. Marsland Gander
Daily Telegraph Radio Correspondent

Three storms of public protest broke over the B.B.C. television service during the week-end. The third and most violent occurred during the transmission of the George Orwell play "Nineteen Eighty-Four" last night.

The other two were when Max Wall, the comedian, was cut off in the middle of his act on Saturday and earlier in the evening last night when Gilbert Harding was unusually irritable during "What's My Line?" (Report - P9)

Warnings had been put out twice by the B.B.C. before the Orwell play pointing out that it was unsuitable for children or sensitive people. By the interval many telephone complaints had been made.

Many people rang up THE DAILY TELEGRAPH complaining particularly of the scenes of mental torture, including one in which Peter Cushing was threatened with torment by rats. A B.B.C. spokesman said there had been "a great many complaints."

VIVID IMPACT

It is difficult to imagine a novel being more faithfully, or effectively, adapted for television than was George Orwell's fantasy "Nineteen Eighty-four" last night. The performance was one of the drama department's most polished achievements.

Orwell's frightening forecast of life in an all-too-possible future under a totalitarian regime contained little dialogue but much description. Credit must be given to the adaptor, Nigel Kneale, for organising the story in dramatic form without any sacrifice of its impact on the imagination.

All the essentials of the original were there to build up a hideous picture of a rule based on hate in which thought, truth or love are forbidden, and the movements of every person watched day and night by means of television cameras in every home. The final scenes depicting the "brain washing" of a diversionist by torture, both physical and psychological achieved an almost unbearable reality.

As the revolutionary, Winston Smith, who longs for the freedom of the forgotten past, and commits the crime of love, Peter Cushing gave a remarkable performance, being especially convincing in his portrayal of fear. Yvonne Mitchell caught the mood of the girl he loves, and the cold imperturbability of the Inner Party member who administers the torture was perfectly suggested by André Morell.

(December 13)

MOORE TORSO REJECTED

Daily Telegraph Reporter

The proposed purchase by Manchester Art Galleries Committee of Henry Moore's bronze figure "Draped Torso" was rejected yesterday by the City Council.

Opponents of the purchase plan applauded the vote of 34 in favour and 56 against. The proposed price was £760.

The work has been on view for members of the council. But Councillor FITZSIMMONS, chairman of the Art Galleries Committee, said that only 61 of the council's 139 members had inspected it.

Opposing the purchase, Councillor STOCKDALE described the figure as ugly. He felt that it was "an expression or creation of a mind that was unusual or in a peculiar state."

(April 8)

BURNING BRANDY FADES TV PICTURE

By A Radio Correspondent

Too much light from burning brandy on Philip Harben's Christmas pudding caused the picture to "peel" last night in the television programme "Your Christmas dinner." Viewers saw the picture turn white and darken at the centre.

Mr. Harben, demonstrating how to warm the pudding, poured a liberal quantity of spirit over it. When he struck a match flames blanked out the screen. The picture returned immediately to show him toasting viewers over the still burning pudding and hoping that their christmas would be "a flaming success."

(December 21)

TOSCANINI CONDUCTS LAST U.S. CONCERT

RETIREMENT AT THE AGE OF 87

From Our Own Correspondent

NEW YORK, Sunday.

The retirement of Arturo Toscanini, generally regarded as the greatest symphony orchestra conductor in the world, was announced to-night. He was 87 last month.

The announcement came from Brig.-Gen. David Sarnoff, chairman of the board of the Radio Corporation of America and the National Broadcasting Company. It was timed to coincide with the last concert of the winter season of the N.B.C. symphony orchestra conducted by the maestro.

Gen. Sarnoff released copies of a letter from Toscanini written on his birthday on March 25. In this he said," Now the sad time has come when I must reluctantly lay aside my baton and say goodbye to my orchestra."

He would carry with him "rich memories of these years of music making." The letter gave no specific reason for his decision to leave the orchestra.

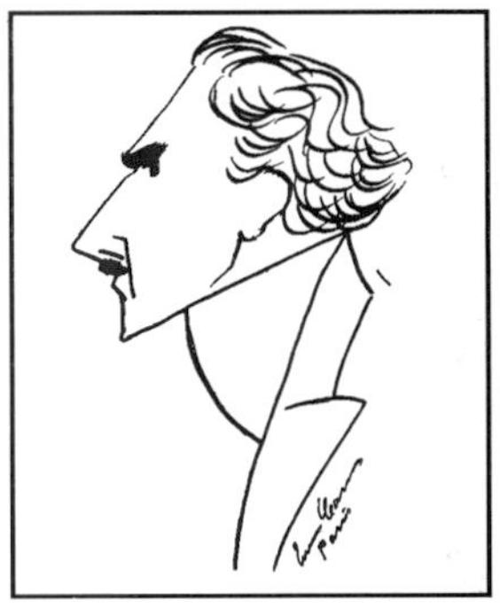

CARICATURE OF TOSCANINI by Enrico Caruso. The two made music together at La Scala in Buenos Aires and at the Metroploitan.

"ENNOBLED OUR LIVES"

In reply, Gen. Sarnoff wrote, "I realise that after more than 65 years of absolute dedication to the art of music you have fully earned the right to lay down your baton. Yet I am saddened, along with millions of people in America, indeed all over the civilised world, at the thought that we shall no longer be privileged to look forward to your broadcasts and concerts, which for so many years ennobled our lives.

"That you have made your decision at a time that finds you at the very height of your artistic powers only adds poignancy to our deprivation."

Signor Toscanini's letter, addressed to "My very dear David," began with a reminiscence about the invitation 17 years ago "to become the musical director of an orchestra to be created specially for me." It continued:

"You will remember how reluctant I was to accept the invitation because I felt at that time I was too old to start a new venture. However, you persuaded me, and all of my doubts were dispelled as I began rehearsing for the first broadcast of Christmas night in 1937 with the group of fine musicians whom you had chosen.

"A JOY FOR ME"

"Year after year it has been a joy for me to know that the music played by the N.B.C. symphony orchestra has been acclaimed by the vast radio audiences all over the United States and abroad...."

(April 5)

TV INTRODUCES 'GROVE FAMILY'

"The Grove Family," which began its television life last night, is born of certain fictional conventions. One is that a querulous senile grandmother is amusing and not pathetic. Another that the average English suburban family cannot pronounce the Queen's English properly.

Yet another that "Mum" must badger Father to buy carpets and refrigerators. The youngest son ought also to be a perky, imaginative little liar.

If you accept all this and it arouses the warmth of fellow feeling, then author Michael Pertwee will succeed. Personally, I do not yet find the family particularly endearing but there will be plenty of time in a two months' run.

(April 10)

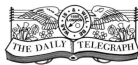

THE DAILY TELEGRAPH
AND
MORNING POST
DAILY TELEGRAPH - June 29, 1855
MORNING POST - November 2, 1772
[Amalgamated October 1, 1937.]
135, Fleet Street, London E.C.4.
Telephone: Central 4242.

CRUCIAL BATTLE IN INDO-CHINA

SEVEN years of fighting in Indo-China have now reached a climax in the desperate battle raging at Dien Bien Phu. For both sides immense issues hang upon the outcome. After a long period of guerrilla tactics and jungle fighting, it may seem surprising to find such large forces committed in a "set-piece" battle. The reason is probably that both sides see in it a chance of winning the war quickly. It mat be assumed that the war of attrition has created problems for the Viet Minh no less than for the French.

The fact that such a battle is now taking place is a triumph for the tactical ideas of Gen. NAVARRE. Though an important cross-roads, Dien Bien Phu is not otherwise of great military significance. Gen. NAVARRE'S action in concentrating 14 battalions in the town and strongly fortifying it was no doubt deliberately intended to be a trailing of his coat. From this point he was able to harass the Viet Minh columns on their way to northern Laos, and in this way the town had a nuisance value. But its real significance has been to invite a full-scale attack from the Viet Minh; and the Viet Minh commander has fallen into the trap or seized his opportunity - at this moment it is still uncertain which phrase should be employed.

Three of the best Viet Minh regular divisions are being used in the assault, and used in such a manner that they are exposed to withering artillery fire. Their losses are heavy, and are such as to encourage the hope that France may gain in this fortress a decisive victory such as she could never win in the jungle. But the stakes are high. If the Viet Minh forces should prevail - and they have only to gain control of the airstrip for victory to be in their grasp - the effect on the French military position in Indo-China would be calamitous.

A decisive victory would strengthen the hands of the French in the discussions with the Viet Nam representatives now taking place in Paris. The object of the Viet Nam delegation appears to be to obtain the independence of their country while assuring themselves of continued French support against any attack. The French are naturally reluctant to shoulder all the burdens that would be obtained by Viet Nam membership of the French Union and none of the advantages. Many concessions have been made since the Emperor BAO DAI was recognised as head of the State: but, as we have discovered in our own dependent territories, nationalistic claims are an auction in which every concession is soon outbid. If Gen. NAVARRE'S policy at Dien Bien Phu should be successful it will also be reflected in the Five-Power Conference to be held at Geneva. It is much to be hoped that no more will be heard of giving greater help to France in Indo-China in return for ratification of E.D.C. The fate of Indo-China for the Western world is far too serious to be made the subject of bargaining of this character. This is no mere colonial war, but Indo-China is the place deliberately selected by international Communism for its challenge to the Western world.

(March 16)

PARTY LINE

FEW men in recorded history have enjoyed a triumph of such quality as that of M. DIOR this week. After the display of his new "H-line" fashions, the assembled worshippers burst into a storm of acclamation which made the welkin (or the cash registers) ring. It is said that women buyers kissed him in transports of admiration and moist gratitude. This is indeed a feat, for when it comes to bargaining over clothes, men are not a patch on women. M. DIOR did it by parading a series of young females dressed in the style in which all young, and not so young females will shortly be dressed.

Seen from the side these young females have the solidity and depth of a playing card. Seen from the front they looked like an hour-glass suffering from middle-age spread. That is to say, there is a very slight indentation at the waistline or thereabouts, just enough to prove that women are not cut out in sections from a larger piece of material, as by a circular saw. In another collection shown the day after M. DIOR'S, M. FATH exhibited a young lady in a space suit, complete with a space visor. The idea was ingenious and attractive, but it was unavailing. M. FATH'S far-reaching mind no doubt concocted this notion many months ago. How was he to know that the day before he introduced his space suit to the world, M. DIOR would have abolished female depth? But that is what happened. It creates a serious problem for Hollywood female stars that, just as films are becoming three-dimensional, they must shrink into two dimensions.

(July 3)

FLYING SAUCERY

ANOTHER outbreak of flying saucery brings stories ranging from the plausible to the childish. That mysterious aircraft of eccentric shape may have been seen is not disputed. There are secret lists, and not all of those who suggest spaceships are necessarily irresponsible. Nor are circular aircraft without precedent. There was an American disc-winged aeroplane, and over forty years ago Capazza designed a lenticular airship which would have qualified as either a saucer or a cigar, according to one's viewpoint.

All down the centuries people have reported prodigies in the sky. They usually have been what they expected, or feared, to see - devils, murdered emperors, departed relatives, unpleasant animals, and, under threat of war, embattled armies among the clouds. Nowadays people still fear war and dread curious flying machines for what they may bring. Without denying the possibility that various odd aircraft exist, unknown to millions and undescribed in technical papers, it is fair to assume that most stories of flying saucers, dishes, beer bottles, cigars and "luminous engines" are the ghost stories of to-day.

(October 4)

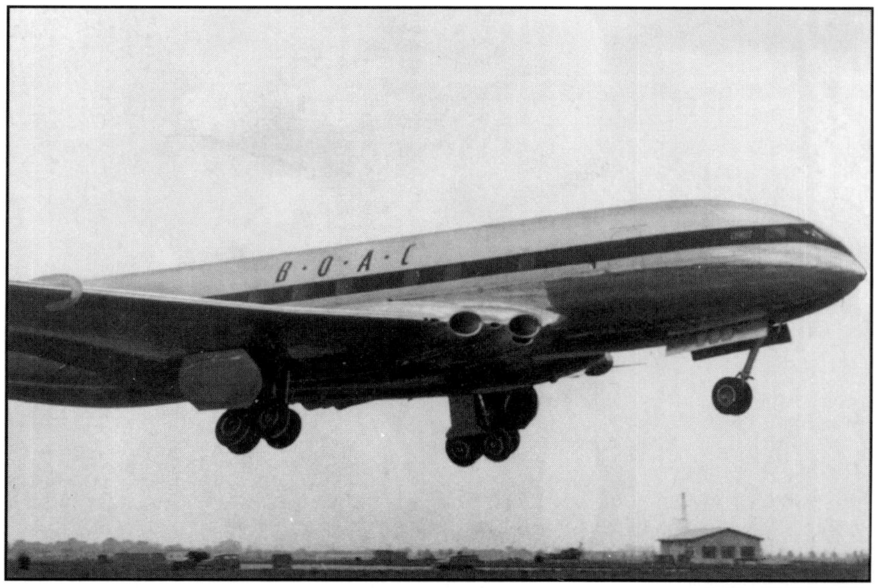

THE B.O.A.C. COMET jet airliner which crashed in the sea yesterday between the islands of Elba and Monte Cristo. The comet is seen taking off from London Airport for Johannesburg on May 2, 1952, to inaugurate the world's first jet plane passenger service.

METAL FATIGUE BROKE COMET, SAY EXPERTS

CABIN 'ACHILLES HEEL' IN ELBA DISASTER

Daily Telegraph Reporter

Metal fatigue at the "Achilles Heel," a panel containing a radio direction-finding aerial in the roof of the pressurised cabin, is believed to have caused the disaster to the Comet airliner LG-ALYP. The plane crashed into the sea off Elba on Jan. 10 with the loss of 35 lives.

This conclusion of the technical investigation was presented by Sir Lionel Heald, Q.C., for the Crown, at the opening in London yesterday of the Court of Inquiry into the crash and that of the Comet G-ALYY off Naples on April 8. Lord Cohen presided.

Quoting from the report of Sir Arnold Hall, Director of the Royal Aircraft Establishment at Farnborough, Hants, where the technical "investigation" was carried out, Sir LIONEL read:

"We have formed the opinion that the accident at Elba was caused by structural failure of the pressure cabin. The low fatigue-resistance of the cabin has been demonstrated." Tests showed that at the age of the plane at the time of the accident there was a distinct risk of fatigue failure arising.

Wreckage indicated that the failure was of the same basic type as that produced during tests. This explanation seemed to be consistent with all the circumstantial evidence.

MAXIMUM STRESS
2 to 1 Safety Factor

Sir Lionel said the Air Registration Board seemed to have been satisfied that the maximum stress concentration at any one point under operating conditions would be only about 40 or 50 per cent of the ultimate stress of the material. This would give a safety factor of two to one.

"They all thought they were proceeding on the basis of two to one. By the end of 1952 it appears to have been appreciated that fatigue would be a serious factor in aircraft like the Comet. Before, it was not considered so serious."

During tests carried out on another Comet, G-ALYU, in a water tank at Farnborough, points were found around the aerial "window" (a section of non-metallic material in the fuselage necessary to avoid the electrical screening of the aerial) and the passenger cabin windows with stress as much as 70 per cent of the ultimate.

Discussing ways to prevent a recurrence of such disasters, he said: "It does seem quite clear that the Sir Registration Board requirements should be amended."

Sir LIONEL described the technical investigation as "one of the most remarkable pieces of scientific detective work ever done." Sir Arnold had started by forming the view that the Elba plane broke up at about 30,000ft, and came down in a series of clearly defined parts.

The Elba Comet had flown for 3,681 hours before the crash and the Naples Comet for 2,784 hours.

As parts of the wreckage had become available he had then been able to build up a remarkably informative picture of the accident. All other evidence, including that from Italian witnesses on the island of Elba, supported the conclusion.

The great care taken by the Navy in salvaging 80 per cent of the plane from the sea bed allowed deductions to be made from marks on metal and paint. It had been not only possible to arrive at a positive conclusion, but the sequence of events had been deduced.

In addition to the plane subjected to pressure tests in the water tank at Farnborough, another Comet, G-ALAV, was flown by Royal Aircraft Establishment test pilots at Farnborough. More than 20 scientists went up with them. The plane carried about 100 pieces of test apparatus.

"We should recognise these brave people, including one woman, who took off on experimental flights designed to produce the actual conditions at the time of the crash when no one knew what had really happened or what danger there was."

[The woman is Mrs. Anne Burns, 38, of Church Crookham, Hants, an Oxford graduate in engineering science. In 1940 she joined the Farnborough Establishment, where she and her husband, Mr. Dennis Burns, are employed on research work.]

Events before the accident, including the take-off from Rome airport, were normal. The last message from the pilot was heard by an Argonaut pilot, but was not considered unusual, although it stopped or was interrupted by another plane.

PASSENGERS THROWN
Emptying of Cabin

It seemed that the passengers were thrown suddenly and violently forward and upward. Within about one-third of a second of the occurrence the cabin was empty.

The sequence was:

1. Violent disruption of the centre part of the passenger cabin.
2. Fuselage and nose and outer part of the port wing fell away.
3. Main part of wing, then separated, caught fire.
4. Fuselage aft of rear spar, with the tail still attached, fell into the sea.
5. Main part of wing still on fire, hit the water in an inverted position.

Although it was clear that there had been fire, this started after the plane had begun to break up. The main proof of this was found in two pieces of material which formed an integral part but were torn apart.

One was badly burned but the other piece bore no trace of burning. Had the fire occurred before disintegration, traces of the fire would have shown on both pieces.

FUEL CAUGHT FIRE
Engine "Clean Health Bill"

The pressure cabin showed no signs of burning. The engines had been burned by the fuel catching fire. The fire had taken some minutes to develop and continued for about the period it would have taken for the pieces to fall to the sea.

The engines could be given a "clean bill of health." There was nothing to indicate that they were connected with the cause of the accident.

Sir Lionel held up a model of a Comet from which he indicated that parts could be removed in the order in which the plane was believed to have broken up. He said that a model of one-tenth scale had been made to reproduce what was believed to have happened. A film was available of this model.

"The fact is that all this is accounted for, and can only be accounted for, by a sudden disruption of the pressure cabin and that is something which is 'a priori' most likely of all when the aircraft is reaching its maximum height and when the greatest strain and stresses are being imposed on the pressure cabin.

"It is a matter on which Sir Arnold will satisfy you. I do not believe anyone can have any real doubt on the matter after hearing Sir Arnold's explanation.

CAPTAIN'S CLOCK
Impact Put Hands Back

"One interesting point showing the care of the investigation relates to the captain's clock. It was found stopped at 09.50 hours. This appeared to be wrong because there was actually a message to the base after that time.

"Careful examination and experiments showed that there was really no doubt that the cause was almost certainly the fact that the impact caused the hands to go back to 10 minutes to 10, where they stuck."

There was absolutely no ground for supposing the accident was due to a failure on the part of the pilot or the crew. And having eliminated all other possibilities, Sir Arnold would say there was only one thing left, metal fatigue.

This was an accurate technical term and scientists did not like it. It meant that a structure which had an ample reserve of strength when it was new might fail in its normal working after a certain length of time.

AUTHOR'S DESCRIPTION
"Not a Bit Overdone"

Sir Lionel referred to Nevil Shute's book, "No Highway," and the film of this story. In it a scientist predicted that a plane would suffer from fatigue.

The captain of the plane made an examination with a torch, but the scientist told him this method of inspection was no good because nothing could be seen until the failure occurred. This dramatic description was "not in the least bit overdone."

(October 20)

GERMANY'S WHEELS OF FORTUNE

From Alistair Horne

WOLFSBURG, near Brunswick.

WITHOUT doubt the most staggering single accomplishment of the German post-war industrial recovery has been at the Volkswagen car works here, which now claims to be the fourth biggest car manufacturer in the world.

With the most modern automatic machinery, much of which was obtained from America under the European Recovery Programme, Volkswagen are leaving the assembly lines at a rate of one every 80 seconds.

Of the 180,047 cars sold last year, 111,921 - more than 61 per cent - were exported. Three thousand of these were sold in England. Australia recently granted the first licences for the sale of 3,500 cars. Assembly works have been set up in Canada, South Africa, Belgium and Ireland, and similar plants are planned for Brazil, Australia and New Zealand.

By British standards the car may seem austere to the point of crudity. It reacts sharply to every bump in the road, there is little room for rear passengers and even less for luggage.

But the secret behind the universal attraction of the Volkswagen, apart from its robustness, lies in the servicing that goes with it, which makes British car owners in Germany deeply envious. The firm boasts that it has a repair depot on an average of every 20 miles throughout Europe. Each customer gets a list of standard charges for all repairs.

Dozens of bright young "customer consultants" are sent round the world to advise dealers: they are subjected to intensive psychological training and equipped with a manual which breaks down the human race into 41 basic types.

These include "the brute," "the know-all," "the credit-no-good," "the ingenu" and "the hesitator." The manual explains in high seriousness, with detailed illustrations, how best to break down the sales resistance of each category.

Investors Case

There has been much speculation in Germany recently as to the outcome of the "Volkswagen Investors" case. About 336,000 Germans were duped by the Nazis to invest £80 each to finance construction of the plant in return for a "people's car".

In January a German court ruled that Volkswagen had been party to the contract, and the company may now have to give free cars to all the surviving investors, or else a sum of money. The firm says it is not unduly disturbed at this.

The company, which was restarted after the war by the British authorities, has no shareholders, so dividends can be put to reserve. It is understood to have made profits totalling nearly £45m. in the past five and a half years.

(April 2)

FIRST DIESEL CAR GOES INTO PRODUCTION

By Our Motoring Correspondent

Britain's first post-war production model Diesel car, announced by the Standard Motor Co., will, it is claimed, cut travelling costs by 50 per cent. Deliveries will start in April.

Judging from London taxicabs running on the Standard 2.1-litre Diesel engine, a motorist travelling 20,000 miles a year will save £125 in fuel costs alone, compared with a petrol-engined vehicle of similar capacity. The 2.1-litre engine has now been put in a modified Vanguard chassis, and is available in all Vanguard models.

In Britain petrol costs about 10 per cent more than Diesel fuel. The estimated fuel consumption of the Diesel Standard is 40-45 miles per gallon. The fuel tank capacity is 15 gallons, so that it will have a range without refuelling of between 600 and 675 miles.

List prices, with purchase tax, are as follows:

	Price £	Tax £	Total £
Vynide Trim	735	307	1,042
(with heater)	747	312	1,060
(with heater and radio)	774	323	1,097
Leather Trim	750	313	1,068
(with heater)	762	318	1,081
(with heater and radio)	789	329	1,118

Prices of the Vanguard with petrol engine remain unchanged.

(February 6)

FAMILY LIFE STOOD WAR STRAIN WELL

HISTORIANS' VIEW

The effect on family life of the strains and stresses of total war, with fathers away in the Services and mothers working in factories, is described in the latest volume of the official history of the Second World War. The book is entitled "Studies in the Social Services."

The authors' verdict is that the family as an institution fared better than could have been expected. According to some of the evidence it flourished.

Marriage became more popular than ever before. There was a great increase in the number of people marrying under the age of 21.

The popularity of marriage "was matched by the popularity of having babies." But the war was "an even more powerful stimulus to divorce." Petitions filed in England and Wales rose from 9,970 in 1938 to 24,857 in 1945, with a post-war peak of 47041 in 1947.

2 ½. m HUSBANDS AWAY

At the peak of the war effort there were 2 ½ million husbands living away from their wives and families.Immediately before D-Day the number of overseas troops in Britain had risen to nearly 11/2 million.

Between the outbreak of war and the end of 1945 there were 60 million changes of address in a civilian population of about 38 million.

In contrast to the First World War there was a great increase in illegitimate births. About 102,000 additional illegitimate births were registered. The rate rose by 1945 to nearly three times the pre-war level.

The percentage of "irregularly conceived maternities" later regularised by marriage fell from 70 per cent. before the war to 37 per cent. in 1945.

RESTRAINTS LOOSENED

The explanation in part was that progressive recruitment of young men into the forces made immediate marriage difficult or impossible. There was also the general loosening of social restraints.

Among mothers under the age of 25 the percentage of irregularly conceived maternities during the whole of the war was actually lower than in 1938-39. What was nearly as astonishing was the substantial rise in them among older women.

The authors conclude that the habits of society proved more stable than could reasonably have been expected but that the effects of the war on the family would take many years to work themselves out.

("Studies in the Social Services," Stationery Office 22s 6d.)

(April 26)

THE STRUGGLE FOR FASHION LEADERSHIP

By Winefride Jackson

The biggest battle for fashion leadership for years is now waging between Dior and Fath. Dior says no bust and the long torso line that all but makes you look like a beanpole.

Jacques Fath says curves and the "S" silhouette that gives a gentle roundness to the figure. Judging by the two suit pictures released to-day, who do you think is going to win fashion leadership?

I'm all for making clothes as comfortable as possible. If you tend to be flat-chested and would like to ease your waistline, then be smart and follow Dior.

If you have a rounded figure and prefer to keep a grip on your waist, then you can still be smart by wearing just such a suit as that of Jacques Fath, in dark grey wool.

(April 27)

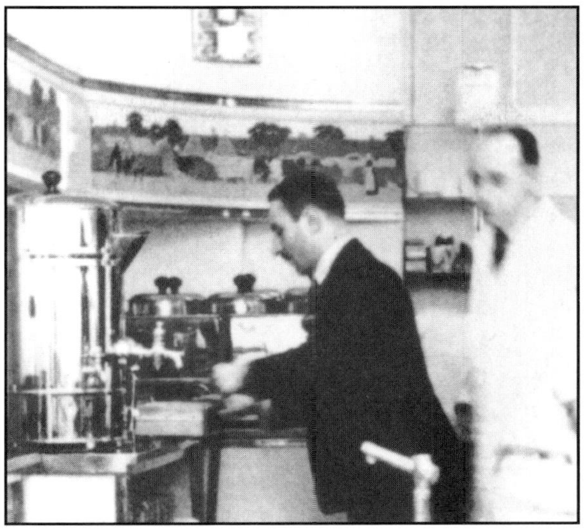

MR. FORTE working in his first milk bar.

MR. FORTE JOINS BOARD OF CAFE ROYAL

ASSOCIATES CO-OPTED

Daily Telegraph Reporter

Mr. Charles Forte, 44, head of the catering firm, Forte's and Co., which runs restaurants and milk bars in London, has been co-opted, with some of his associates, to the board of the Café Royal, the famous Regent Street restaurant.

A spokesman for the restaurant confirmed the appointments last night. He would not make any further comment.

The directors held a meeting at the premises during the evening and discussed the position. It is not yet known whether there will be any substantial changes in its running.

It owes its existence to a penniless Burgundian peasant, Daniel Nicolas Theyenon, who, as Daniel Nicols founded it in 1865 with £5 borrowed from a money-lender. It became one of the world's most famous restaurants and was a resort of bohemians for many years.

When Regent Street was rebuilt in the late twenties, the premises were modernised, but in 1929 the business was bankrupt with liabilities of £418,000.

£200,000 PURCHASE

About 18 months later it was bought for £200,000 by Sir Bracewell Smith, chairman of the Ritz Hotel and a former Lord Mayor of London, and Mr. George Harvey, of the Connaught Rooms.

(April 6)

NUDISTS FORM A NEW GROUP

Because of a dispute with the British Sunbathing Association, 35 leaders of the Nudist movement decided to form a new organisation at a meeting in London yesterday.The 6 ½ hour meeting was held in the centrally-heated smoking room of a Bloomsbury hotel.

(April 26)

SHORTHAND AND TYPING WILL GET YOU ABROAD

By Winifred Carr

Opportunity to travel is the biggest lure for girls who are job-hunting today. Prospects of getting to the top and high salaries are taking second and third place.

To-day, a girl whose work takes her abroad is the envy of her friends. And whenever such a post becomes vacant it is rarely advertised; there is invariably a waiting list of applicants for it.

The Queen's Commonwealth Tour, Princess Alexandra's recent visit to Canada and the United States, and Princess Margaret's intended tour of the Caribbean have all added fire to this urge to see the world.

Join The Services

Air hostesses, ships' stewardesses and nannies are the obvious jobs to help you get abroad. But there are others, and the way to land most of them, say the girls who are in them, is to know shorthand and typing.

When Princess Margaret visits Jamaica, she will probably see three girls there who are the envy of the entire Women's Royal Army Corps. Two of them are N.C.O. shorthand-typists. The third is the officer in charge of the Company, which consists largely of locally enlisted girls.

One of the conditions which all Service women have to agree to on joining up is that they will serve anywhere in the world. And they certainly do. There are members of the W.R.A.C. and the W.R.A.F. in Germany, Austria, Cyprus, Gibraltar and Singapore, working as administration officers, cipher experts, photographers, typists, telephonists, cooks, parachute packers, medical orderlies, radiographers and physiotherapists.

A girl who typed her way across America three years ago, when she was only 22, is Dilys Morgan. Last year, too, she travelled 10,000 miles, visiting Denmark six times, Jugoslavia and Paris twice, and Sweden once. She is personal-secretary to the director of an airline, and in her free time is joint honorary secretary of a newly formed travel club, intended for women who work in the travel business.

Take The Plunge

"Learn shorthand and typing, save up your fare, go abroad, and then look for a job; that's the best way of seeing the world," advises Miss Morgan. "Or, if you want to work in the tourist business, join a large travel agency as a shorthand-typist, learn at least one language and take every opportunity you can."

Men are given most of the best travel jobs in tourist firms and agencies, it is true, but there are also some opportunities for women. One coach service which covers Europe has as many women couriers as men. These girls in their smart pale blue uniforms get a basic rate of about 30s a day during the season, from Easter to the end of September, with tips on top of that. "In winter, they usually take jobs as nannies or shorthand-typists," said one of the firm's officials.

(October 13)

HOUSES WILL HAVE COLOURFUL ROOFS AND RED CEILINGS

This year will see great strides made in housing. One of the newest developments is to plan the house around the kitchen. The housing expert, C.H. Kitchin, says we are learning, at long last, that this is the most important room. So the 1954 kitchen will be roomy, easy to clean and planned to save unnecessary movement and labour.

Another major principle of new houses is to achieve the maximum warmth from the minimum of fuel. So fuel economy is now a primary consideration instead of an afterthought. The wasteful open grate is doomed. Open fires will be the continuous burning type. They will be fitted with back boilers to heat the water or to run radiators in other rooms.

Fuel Saving Pays The Cost

More houses, too, will be planned to keep the heat indoors. The cost of properly insulating new houses can be saved in fuel in three years. Timber is now off ration, so we may see more softwood floors and less flimsy joinery. Solid floors are usually cheaper and help retain the heat, and there is plenty of variety in attractive finishes.

Mr. Kitchin doubts if any new material will replace traditional brick for house building. But coloured roof tiles and varies renderings will save us from monotony of appearance.

What about your rooms in 1954? Terra-cotta ceilings (a harking back to the late 18th century, when Etruscan red was fashionable for interior decoration) and warm grey for drawing room walls will be a perfect foil for books and paintings.

Plain, fitted carpets will date you. Young couples are putting back the clock by choosing patterned floor coverings. But designs much be less assertive than in Victorian times. To-day's modest patterns are made of such things as thin lines.

Mr. Paul Reilly, of the council of Industrial Design, who makes this forecast, believes that people with rooms with high ceilings will be more experimental in having them re-decorated in deep colours this spring. In the formal, square room, the vogue for having two walls in one colour and two in another will disappear and will be reserved for rooms of awkward shape.

Contemporary furniture will grow in popularity, but will mellow in line, becoming less angular and more comfortable.

(January 1)

THE MERMAIDS OF CLEETHORPES

VISITORS COMPLAIN

Daily Telegraph Reporter

Four mermaids, draped with seaweed which have been placed around a fountain and lily ponds on the promenade at Cleethorpes, Lincs, may be "censored" by the council. This follows complaints by holiday-makers that they are "rude" and unsuitable for children to see. The mermaids are floodlit at night.

Mr. Arthur Ingham, the resort's entertainments manager, said yesterday that he had had a number of letters of protest, mainly anonymous. Councillor A. Baden Winters, the deputy mayor, declared: "I cannot see anything disgusting about the mermaids. I think they are just naughty."

To-night a deputation of councillors will examine them. "If necessary they will be censored," said Mr. Ingham, but did not explain how. "The examination is being made at night, because that is when they are supposed to look their rudest."

The mermaids are part of this year's new illuminations. They were made by the town's lighting staff and painted by a local artist.

(August 19)

'DISNEYLAND' PLAN

LOS ANGELES PLAYGROUND

Walt Disney has announced plans to spend more than £3 million on building an amusement centre and Museum of Americana outside Los Angeles to be called "Disneyland." The centre will resemble a gigantic film set.

(May 3)

SCHOOLS BAN BOYS' FANCY HAIR STYLES

5s TO £2 COSTS

Daily Telegraph Reporter

Hair styles adopted by "Edwardian" youths are finding favour among boys attending secondary schools. Boys in various parts of Britain have presented themselves for the autumn term wearing frizzy mops or lengthy locks curled at the ends.

For these, they, or their parents, paid anything from 5s to £2 a head. But in most cases, headmasters say: "Go home and have your hair cut."

Mr. Frederick Stanley Watkins, 34, newly appointed headmaster of Canvey Island Boys Secondary School, found a number of his senior pupils, aged 14 to 15, wearing their hair in a "peculiar style." He has asked parents to see that by next Monday their boys come to school with their hair cut in a "more English manner."

He said yesterday that he looked to the senior boys to set a good example to the juniors. He hoped parents would co-operate.

NOT TOLERATED

In a North London secondary school, the headmaster has not even asked the parents to co-operate. He said to me: "I have just told them that I will not tolerate it.

"I think it is degrading. The boys look silly. Some have tried it on, but I have told them that if they wanted to wear their hair in that way they would have to go elsewhere.

Headmasters in other parts of London and the Home Counties, with few exceptions, said they had had boys coming to school with unorthodox hair styles.

Mr. W.J.L. George, of the National Hairdresser's Federation, said there were now dozens of British hair styles for men, with "sculpted" styles finding more favour. Charges for styling varies from 3s to £2.

He said that a new style, known as the "Long Arcade," would be introduced at a competition at Nottingham to-day, when a team would be selected to represent Britain in an international competition at Brighton next month. The length of the hair in the new style would be about 2 ½ in.

This will be the first time that the international hairdressing competition includes men's hairdressing.

(September 9)

HYPNOSIS USED IN TV TOOTH EXTRACTION

3 TAPS, THEN TRANCE

By L. Marsland Gander
Daily Telegraph Radio Correspondent

Television showed a 19-year-old dental nurse having a wisdom tooth extracted under hypnosis in a Lime Grove studio last night. The patient was Sylvia Langley, of Westcliff-on-sea, and there were three unnamed dentists in the studio.

The one who made the extraction explained that Miss Langley had been conditioned to put therself to sleep. "To-night," he said, "We want to put her into a deep enough trance to anaesthetise the jaw.

I am going to tap three times and she will fall into a trance." Miss Langley, a pretty brunette, was seated in an ordinary dentist's chair. When the hypnotist tapped with a metal object her head fell limply back and her eyes closed.

A shadowgraph was then shown of the tooth to be removed, the dentist explaining tha it was necessary to cut away the gum. Viewers saw a close-up inside Miss Langley's gaping mouth while the dentist probed about.

While another nurse stood by and a second dentist gave a commentary the hypnotist was seen swiftly wrenching out the tooth, which he held up to the camera.

(May 27)

LORD SIMON

POLITICS & LAW: HELD SIX OFFICES

With the death of Viscount Simon there has passed away one who seemed to have every qualification to reach the top of the political tree, but who had to rest content with pre-eminence in the legal profession. No abler man has ever failed to win the affection of his fellow-country-men and the confidence of his colleagues.

He was superb at obtaining judgment for his clients; but his own judgment was singularly faulty. Capable of deep feeling himself - his little monograph on his mother is a delicate literary gem - he was quite incapable of inspiring it in others.

While still in his forties he refused the Lord Chancellorship; and during the First World War he was almost alone among the leading figures of the day in refusing to acquiesce in conscription. Such actions which, in another, might have greatly enhanced his political status, in his case failed to do so for no apparent reason.

All had, nevertheless, to bow to his magnificent mental endowment, which earned him £50,000 a year at the Bar and a succession of high offices.

He had his great moments, such as those when, in three devastating speeches, he did more to cause the collapse of the General Strike of 1926 than any other single man: or when, as chairman of the Indian Statutory Commission of 1927-30, he produced the report on constitutional reform which remains the model of a State document.

On the other hand, his tenure of the Foreign Office from 1931-35 was little short of disastrous, though, of course, it coincided with a period in which any Foreign Secretary might have failed. Nor was his tenure of the Exchequer from 1937 - 40 in any way inspired. It is fair to say that, in view of his quite outstanding talents, his career was probably a disappointment to many, including himself.

MINISTER'S SON

John Allsebrook Simon was born on Feb. 28, 1873, the son of a Welsh Congregational Minister. He was educated at Fettes, and Wadham College, Oxford, where he was President of the Union in 1896. In the following year he was made a Fellow of All Souls.

After establishing himself, with immense success, at the Bar, he turned to his deepest love - politics; and entered Parliament on the crest of the Liberal flood in 1906. When Asquith formed his second Government in 1910, he became Solicitor-General, and three years later, Attorney-General.

His first purely political post was Home Secretary, but, owing to his attitude towards conscription, he held it only for a year. Thus excluded from the Lloyd-Georgian ranks, he lost his seat in 1918, and, in the subsequent suicidal squabbles within the Liberal party, ranked naturally as an Asquithian.

He re-entered Parliament in this guise in 1922, and for a time was chairman of the so-called Independent Liberals in the House of Commons.

14 YEARS OF OFFICE

Gradually, however, he came to incline towards that section of Liberals to whom co-operation with the newer kind of Tory was not repugnant, and for 14 years, from 1931 to 1945, he held high office in successive National Governments, ending with a five-year period as Lord Chancellor. This, like his other legal posts, obviously suited him better than any more political appointment.

His main diversion throughout his career was golf, and his tall, slightly bowed figure, with its curiously jerky walk, was a familiar feature of Walton Heath for many years. Courteous, benign, erudite and upright, there yet always seemed to be a streak of fundamental coldness in him which precluded any feeling of warm intimacy and made him seem a strangely solitary figure.

By his marriage with his first wife, who died in 1902, he had one son and two daughters. In 1917 he married again - Mrs. Kathleen Manning, a widow, who survives him. The heir to the viscountcy is the son, the Hon. John Gilbert Simon, born on Sept. 2 1902. He married in 1930 Miss J. Christie Hunt. They have one son and one daughter.

(January 12)

DUFF COOPER: AN APPRECIATION

By Colin R. Coote

Though the life of Duff Cooper - how much more familiar to his friends than "Lord Norwich"! - was all to short, it was, in a certain sense, singularly complete.

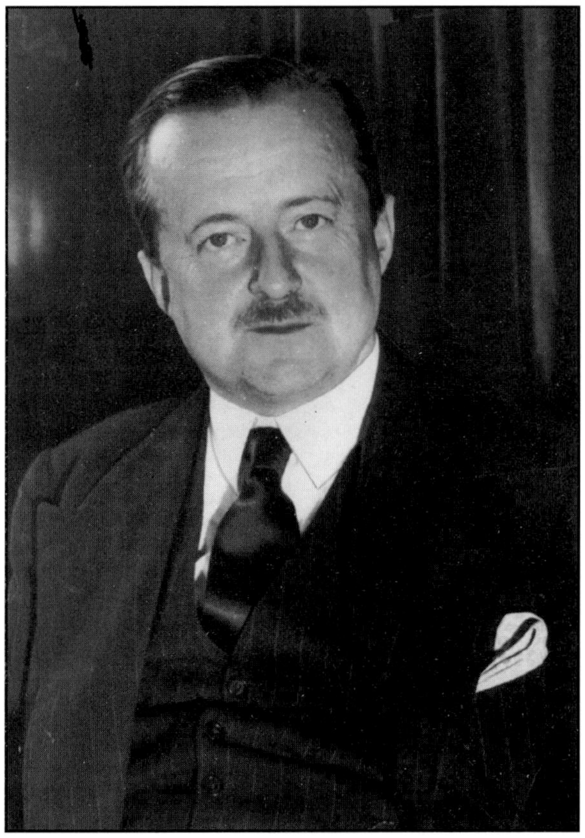

He saw, little more than a year ago, his only son married. He had just published a brilliantly graceful autobiography. He had only recently received a viscountcy. He had, indeed, wound up both a political and a literary career, and definitely established in both a place high in the second rank, with not infrequent incursions into the first.

What he had not ended at all was the grace and verve which he brought to conversation and contact with a large circle of friends. He had indeed "warmed both hands before the fire of life" and brought from the experience a stimulating warmth into any assembly where he was present.

A certain truculence and dogmatism in his make-up was a reflection not of inhumanity but of a stout adherence to principle. He said things bluntly and boldly, because he felt them deeply.

He was born in 1890, one of a coruscating generation whose sparks, alas, were so largely extinguished in the First World War. In him and his like there was not only intellectual brilliance but a capacity for enjoyment and an appetite for duty which produced a natural aptitude for leadership.

His father was a well-known surgeon and his mother a sister of the first Duke of Fife, so that, in those days, he started with certain social advantages. But he made his career for himself by never hesitating to risk it.

The outbreak of war in 1914 happened to find him in the Foreign Office. His restiveness in this shelter gradually grew, until he discarded it in 1917 to join the Grenadier Guards. It was as a platoon commander in that famous regiment that he won the D.S.O.; and D.S.O.'s were not showered on subalterns.

Military courage was easily translated into political courage and loyalty to superior officers into loyalty to political chiefs. He entered Parliament in 1924 for Oldham - also the political nursery of his close and reciprocally loyal friend Sir Winston Churchill. But he really made his first big mark by rallying to the support of Mr. Baldwin - then suffering from one of his rare sags in popularity - in the famous by-election of 1929 in St. George's.

In the next decade the Treasury, the War Office, and the Admiralty gave varied scope to his talents. As an observer in the Press Gallery, I loved the vivacity and the spontaneity of his speeches. Like a very few other good Parliamentarians - Sir Robert Horne and Mr. Bonar Law, for example - he spoke without or with only the barest of notes. The practice lends life and thrill to debate as nothing else can.

Loyalty to Mr. Baldwin was naturally transferred to Mr. Neville Chamberlain, but could not sit so easily on so ardent a spirit. Though he long suffered in reticence, those who were with him when the Munich terms became known perceived he was stricken to the heart. He resigned his office; and his speech of resignation was not unworthy of a place in our Parliamentary annals.

I have ruined, perhaps, my political career (he said). But that is of little matter. I have retained something which to me is of greater value. I can still walk about the world with my head erect.

A House, frenzied with relief from the fear of war, was made to feel it "possible that they were mistaken."

Having thus joined Sir Winston Churchill and Mr. Eden as a target of Hitler's anathemas, he was marked for high responsibility in time of war. But he found nothing really congenial until after the liberation of France, when he became Ambassador in Paris for nearly four years.

Though sometimes accused of an undue predilection for Gen. De Gaulle, he was not in fact the dyed-in-the-wool Francophile which some thought. Certainly the spacious life and sharp tongue of France (where he lived after his retirement) appealed to him. Certainly he believed that Western civilisation, and perhaps Western safety, was bound up with France. But all he strove to do was to make the best use of such instruments as France offered for cementing Anglo-French friendships. He was a bigot in nothing save personal affections.

In a lesser but still notable sphere, his career had some striking resemblances with that of Sir Winston Churchill himself. He too could wield the pen as well as the tongue - and wield it best as a biographer. His "Talleyrand" is a real work of art and of fact. In one respect he was even superior to Sir Winston. His only novel, "Operation Heartbreak," is a classic compared with Sir Winston's only novel "Savrola."

As his autobiography so tenderly and endearingly reveals, he would never have walked the path of life with so firm a tread without his wife. It was she who "taught the torches to burn bright" for him. As Lady Diana Manners, she had been the reigning beauty of the second decade of the century, and she never ceased to reign over his heart.

Now that he has gone, so suddenly and tragically, his friends can measure her loss, which is England's loss too.

(January 2)

M. JACQUES FATH DIES AT 42

CREATOR OF 'S'-LINE

Daily Telegraph Reporter

Jacques Fath, the Parisian dress designer, who has died aged 42, opened his dress shop shortly after his marriage in 1937. It was a small shop, and was run almost single-handed by Fath.

The firm prospered, but it was not until after the war that Fath became world-famous. Among the styles he introduced were the "urchin" haircut and the "S" line.

He and his wife were famous for their parties and receptions, to which Paris society were invited. His August collection was hailed by critics as the best of his career.

One of the "Giants"

WINEFRIDE JACKSON writes: Paris can ill afford to lose Jacques Fath, for with Christian Dior and Balenciaga he was one of the "giants" in the dress-designing world.

The gay summer parties at his country chateau were reported all over the world. He personally produced the cabaret and was at his happiest when taking part.

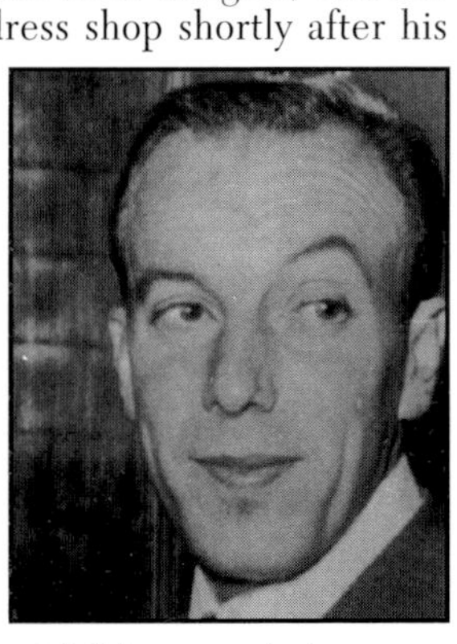

I shall always remember his imitation of Maurice Chevalier a few summers ago. It was superb. Had he not chosen to be a designer he might well have made a name for himself on the stage in burlesque.

(November 15)

MR. S. ROWNTREE

Mr. Seebohm Rowntree, the former chairman of the York cocoa and chocolate concern, who has died aged 84, was a Quaker, who for more than half a century made a speciality of the study of poverty and of the effects of gambling.

A son of the late Joseph E Rowntree, he became a partner in the firm at the age of 20, and quickly established a reputation as an enlightened, humane employer. He came to prominence in 1899 with the publication of "Poverty; A Study of Town Life," the first of three elaborate surveys of social conditions in York. The others were "Poverty and Progress," 1941, and "Poverty and the Welfare State," written in collaboration with Mr. G.R. Lavers and published in 1951.

Chairman of Rowntree's from 1925 until 1941, he was president of the Outward Bound Trust, whose school he helped to found, and vice-president of the Churches' Committee on Gambling. He was credited with the invention of flag days.

He was made a Companion of Honour in 1931. His wife, formerly Miss Lydia Potter, died in 1944; four sons and a daughter survive.

(October 8)

HENRI MATISSE

Henri Matisse, doyen of French painters, who has died aged 84, studied in his youth for the Bar. In later years he became one of the most controversial of modern artists.

Born on the last day of 1869 at Le Cateau, Northern France, he abandoned his legal studies after enrolling as a student at the Ecole des Beaux Arts in Paris. For a time his talent developed on orthodox lines. Many of his early works were copies of Old Masters, and some examples were purchased by the French Department of Fine Arts.

He came gradually under the influence of the Impressionists, and finally became a leader of "Les Fauves," an extremist group who painted in every style but the traditional. Matisse was described as "the most persistent of the experimentalists." By 1909, however, when he opened his own atelier, he had adopted rather more conventional methods.

On his first visit to Nice in 1916 he was so struck by the luminous atmosphere that he made his permanent home there. He spent two years working in Morocco. Bedridden by rheumatism in recent years, he had worked chiefly in chalks. In August he was nearing the completion of his biggest work in ceramics, weighing 2½ tons.

PRINCIPALLY A COLOURIST

T.W. EARP writes: Matisse was above all a colourist, and one of painting's lyric poets. At a time when other pioneers of the modern Paris School were engaged in carrying yet further Cezanne's new treatment of form, he pursued a serenely independent course.

He believed, and on several occasions asserted, that the object of paintings is to give pleasure, and such intellectual complications of art as the cubism practised by Picasso had no attraction for him. He preferred to evolve exquisite modulations of radiant colour, based on a tenuous but elastic design which was the final summary of his themes' pictorial qualities.

Using a kind of linear shorthand in supple arabesque, he netted the essentials of form with an extreme economy of means. There are affinities with Persian painting in the free gesture and rhythmic sweep of his brushwork. His series of "Odalisques" is a proclamation of this kinship.

The coast of Normandy and, later the neighbourhood of Nice furnished most of his subjects in landscape, while characteristic figure studies depicted women seated by a window overlooking the sea.

Much of his recent activity was devoted to the decoration of a chapel near Nice. the most important exhibition of his work in this country took place at the Victoria and Albert Museum in December, 1945.

(November 5)

Obituary

MME. COLETTE

Mme. Colette, the best-known and most distinguished French woman novelist since George Sand, died yesterday at the age of 81.

Although she had been a notable Parisian figure for more than half a century, only in old age was she accorded an appropriate, dignified status by her fellow-countrymen. Author, or part-author, of more than 50 works, among the best-known of which were the "Chéri" and "Claudine" series, she wrote with exquisite precision, but shocked an earlier generation by her choice and treatment of subjects.

Sidonie Gabrielle Colette was born at Saint-Sauveur en Puisaye, in Burgundy, the daughter of a retired Army officer. At the age of 19 she made a surprising marriage with a M. Willy, a novelist and critic, who was outstandingly picturesque even in a Paris remarkable for such striking contemporary personalities as Toulouse-Lautrec, Debussy and Zola.

Together, Colette and Willy - his real name was Henri Gauthier-Villars - wrote the Claudine books; subsequently it was appreciated that Willy contributed little else than his name to the works. After their divorce she danced in the music halls; this phase of her career provided her with material for several novels.

Subsequently, in addition to consolidating her success as an author, she worked as a dramatic critic, a literary editor and a fashion writer. She again essayed the stage, this time as a straight actress, before marrying the late M. Henry de Jouvenel, the French politician. M. Willy, her first husband, died, forgotten and in penury in 1931.

Colette was president of the Académie Goncourt, to which she had earlier been elected as the first woman member.

(August 4)

MR. CHESTER WILMOT

Mr. Chester Wilmot, the Australian author and broadcaster, who has died in the Comet disaster, was 42. An incisive commentator on world affairs, he will be best remembered for his masterly book "The Struggle for Europe," published in 1952. It is widely regarded as a classic of contemporary history.

As a B.B.C. commentator in 1944 he glided in with the Sixth Airborne Division on D-Day.

He was the narrator in "The Queen's Journey," the Christmas Day broadcast which preceded the Queen's message from New Zealand.

Mr. Wilmot had been military correspondent of the Observer since 1952. He was killed on his way home from a 25,000-mile survey of the Far East on behalf of the B.B.C.

(January 11)

DEATH OF VISCOUNT CAMROSE

Editor-in-Chief of 'The Daily Telegraph'

THE DAILY TELEGRAPH announces with deep regret the death of Viscount Camrose, Chairman and Editor-in-Chief of this newspaper.

He died yesterday at the Royal South Hants Hospital, Southampton, of a sudden heart attack. He had been recuperating there from a gastric complaint and had been expected to return to his home, Hackwood Park, Basingstoke, in a few days. He would have been 75 next week.

Lord Camrose, in partnership with Lord Kemsley and Lord Iliffe, acquired THE DAILY TELEGRAPH from the late Lord Burnham in 1928. In 1937 he bought out his partners and became sole proprietor.

When he assumed control the circulation of THE DAILY TELEGRAPH was 84,000 copies daily. To-day, twenty-six years later, it is well over one million. This phenomenal growth was attained solely by journalistic merit without alteration of the character of the paper.

To all great organisations there come moments of ordeal and sorrow when one of the human strands of which they are woven is snapped by the hands of Fate. Such a moment occurs to-day in the history of THE DAILY TELEGRAPH. By the death of Lord CAMROSE, it has lost the man who gave it new life and over a quarter of a century of inspiration. As the Prime Minister, a close friend for a generation, has declared, "Patriotism and an earnest desire for a stable yet progressive society were his unswerving guides."

But the work of such men does not die with them. In their lifetime they establish professional standards and modes of thought which endure long after they have passed away. The buildings of great architects mellow with time, but do not change their shape. Lord CAMROSE devoted the best of his years and of his powers - and they were fine years and great powers - to the establishment and advancement of quality journalism. THE DAILY TELEGRAPH is his memorial; and those whom he has left behind will strive to keep it worthy of him.

(June 16)

SIR G. ROBEY DIES WITH CANE IN HAND

ILL SIX MONTHS

Daily Telegraph Reporter

Sir George Robey, pre-eminent on the British stage for more than 50 years as the "Prime Minister of Mirth," died early yesterday at his home at Saltdean, Sussex, aged 85. He was holding the small brown cane that he had twirled on hundreds of stages.

He was a great clown whose warmth of manner defied even the most austere to resist him. He was long in the front rank of the world's great entertainers.

To millions of people the comic bowler hat, the large mobile eyebrows and the famous cane were the symbols, as well as the props, of his genius, for inspiring laughter.

Sir George had been seriously ill for six months and had been confined to bed for nearly three weeks. For some days before his death he was in a semi-coma. He died in his wife's arms.

ARTISTS' TRIBUTES

There was a flow of tributes to him yesterday from people in all walks of life. Bransby Williams, the character actor, who is 88, expressed the sentiments of many when he said: "George was a great humorist and a great character." They first met at the Tivoli in 1896.

Violet Loraine, who appeared with him in his first revue, that famous war-time success, "The Bing Boys are Here," at the old Alhambra in 1916, described him as "the greatest comedian the world has ever known or ever will know. He was the most vital and alert character I ever met."

Sir George Robey, whose real name was George Edward Wade, was trained as an engineer. After studying at Cambridge for a time he joined a Birmingham firm and worked for four years in a machine shop.

At 21, having made some reputation as an amateur entertainer, he drifted into a professional engagement at the Aquarium Theatre, Westminster. In June, 1891, he was given a trial in a matinée at the Oxford

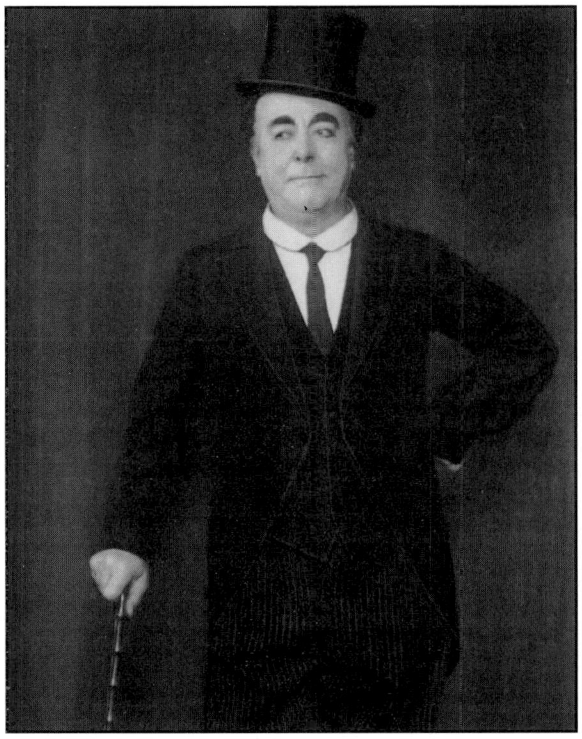

GEORGE ROBEY in his original part of Lucifer Bing in the revival of the world famous musical comedy revue "The Bing Boys Are Here."

Music Hall, Oxford Street. He was an immediate success and obtained a 12 months' contract.

Later engagements were at the Trocadero, Standard, Paragon, Metropolitan, London Pavilion and Tivoli. Tours in the Dominions followed, and soon he was established as one of the most popular comedians on the variety stage.

SHAKESPEAREAN SUCCESS

In 1935, with some trepidation, he played Falstaff. He scored a triumph.

He was made a C.B.E. for services in the 1914-18 war, when he became an officer in the Motor Volunteer Corps, and also raised £500,000 for war charities.

Sir George continued to delight audiences at an age when most men would have sought retirement. He celebrated his 79th birthday in 1947 by performing at the Nottingham Empire. In the same year he appeared at the R.A.F. Association Festival of Reunion, sponsored by THE DAILY TELEGRAPH, at the Albert Hall.

In 1949 he entertained garrison troops in Austria. In addition to more recent music-hall tours and B.B.C. broadcasts, he played Tony Weller in the film version of "The Pickwick Papers" in 1952.

KNIGHTED IN WHEELCHAIR

His knighthood was conferred in the last New Year Honours; he received the accolade, seated in a wheelchair, from Queen Elizabeth the Queen Mother at Buckingham Palace in February.

A fine athlete in his day, Sir George played both football and cricket in first-class company. He had a passion for collecting stamps and china. His love for the violin led him to learn not merely to play the instrument but also to make it.

In addition to publishing a number of books, mostly autobiographical, Sir George was also a painter. He exhibited at the Royal Academy and at the Institute of Painters in Water Colours.

He married, in 1898, Miss Ethel Haydon, the Australian musical comedy actress. The marriage was dissolved and, in 1938, he married his manager, Miss Blanche Littler, the theatrical proprietor and producer, who survives him.

Sir George's son by his first marriage is Mr. Edward George Robey, the London Metropolitan magistrate. The funeral is at the Downs Crematorium, Brighton, to-morrow at 2 p.m.

GIFT OF AUTHORITY

Commanded Audience

W.A. DARLINGTON writes: Sir George Robey's greatest gift as an artist was his authority. From the moment of his entry the audience was his to command. He had just those qualities on which our race likes to pride itself, and just those defects which it is apt to forgive in itself most easily.

He was courageous and kind-hearted, and he played games well. He was intelligent but not intellectual - obstinate, proud and modest in just the right degree. He liked honest vulgarity and was genuinely shocked by clever suggestiveness.

As a comedian, he was inimitable, but future generations will not find it easy to understand wherein his genius lay. His get-up and his catch-words were not funny in themselves. Yet with these he made the whole British Commonwealth laugh. How he did it is a secret which has died with him.

(November 30)

FRANCIS BRETT YOUNG

Francis Brett Young, who has died aged 70, was an author and poet of distinction who wrote with dignity and grace equally of humble English country folk and pioneers in Africa.

His best-selling novel, "The House Under the Water," described the effects on a village community of inundation to provide a reservoir: "The City of Gold," in contrast, told in glowing terms the story of the growth of Johannesburg. His best known book of poems, "The Island," was an ambitious, epic work in which he expressed his love for, and admiration of England.

Like several other distinguished authors, Francis Brett Young started his career as a doctor. The son of a doctor, he was born near Birmingham and educated at Epsom College and at Birmingham University.

As a ship's surgeon he travelled extensively in the East, and later practised in the coal-mining districts of the Midlands and among the fisherfolk of Devon. All these experiences provided him with material for his novels, the first of which "Undergrowth", written in collaboration with his brother, appeared in 1913.

After service in the R.A.M.C. in East Africa during the 1914-18 war he produced a crop of eminently readable novels such as "Black Diamond", "The Young Physician," "Portrait of Claire" - awarded the James Tall Black Prize - and "My Brother Jonathan". These all had the Midlands as background.

There followed, among others, "Portrait of a Village," "Dr. Bradley Remembers" and "A Man About the House" which ran as a play and like several others of his books was filmed.

(March 29)

GEN. GUDERIAN

Gen. Heinz Guderian, who has died aged 65, was Hitler's last Chief of Staff. A Panzer specialist, he organised and executed the armoured penetrations into Poland in 1939 and France in 1940; he was responsible for the break-through at Sedan Twice he figured in disputes with Hitler which threatened his career.

(May 17)

ANDRE DERAIN

André Derain, who has died aged 74, had been long established as one of the most talented and versatile French painters.

He joined in his youth the Montmartre group which included Picasso and Matisse, but later broke away to form, with Vlaminck and Rouault, the "Fauve" group, which was influenced by Van Gogh and Gauguin. Despite his absorption of ideas from many masters, he remained an individualist; in later life he greatly simplified his technique.

During his Fauve period, in 1905, he painted a number of studies of the Thames: one of them, "Pool of London", was purchased in 1951 by the Royal Academy under the Chantrey Bequest for £1,500. His scenery and costume designs for such ballets as "La Boutique Fantasque," "Epreuve d'Amour" and "Harlequin in the Street" won high praise.

In July of this year, after a dispute with his wife, the Versailles court granted her an order of attachment on his paintings in his studio. He appealed to the Paris court.

(September 11)

MARQUESS OF QUEENSBERRY

SOLDIER, AUTHOR AND SPORTSMAN

The Marquess of Queensberry died at Folkestone yesterday aged 58. Like his grandfather the author of the Queensberry rules of boxing, he had wide sporting interests.

Francis Archibald Kelhead Douglas was the eleventh holder of the title. He wrote a book giving an account of his family under the title "The Sporting Queensburys."

Educated at Harrow he went to Sandhurst and joined the Black Watch, and in the 1914-18 war was twice wounded.

(April 28)

LONDON DAY BY DAY

Sir Winston's Pigs
Somerset Maugham Honoured

SIR WINSTON CHURCHILL has taken decisive action in the controversy which recently centred on the Landrace pig. He has started a pedigree herd of his own at Chartwell.

One boar and three maiden gilts have gone to him from Mr. Patrick Dolan, who has one of the leading herds at Little Hadham.

The Landrace pig, imported chiefly from Sweden, has had an uphill career in this country. The pioneers in this field in the late 1940s saw in the Landrace a breed which would help match the uniform quality of Danish bacon pigs.

Expanding Breed

They were not popular in all quarters. Early this summer the disease atrophic rhinitis was confirmed among the breed and imports were strictly controlled - they still come from Sweden.

The British Landrace Pig Society in Malton, Yorkshire, tell me, however, that they are now self-supporting. They will shortly have 350 registered owners - they had just 200 only five months ago.

Over a thousand pigs are registered in the herd book, with another 3,000 (under 10 weeks) notified.

Some believe that notwithstanding earlier vicissitudes the Landrace is destined to become our premier breed. The Prime Minister evidently supports this view.

Honoured

Out of a thin Birthday Honours List Mr. Somerset Maugham's C.H. will probably attract the most attention and receive the widest approval.

It marks the year of his 80th birthday. I have observed before on the curious fact that he has hitherto been unhonoured by this country though he is a Commander of the Legion of Honour.

Dr. Edith Sitwell's D.B.E. will also give pleasure and may even cause a faint stir on the West coast of America.

The only member of a famous family triumvirate to receive an honour, she is described inadequately as a poet.

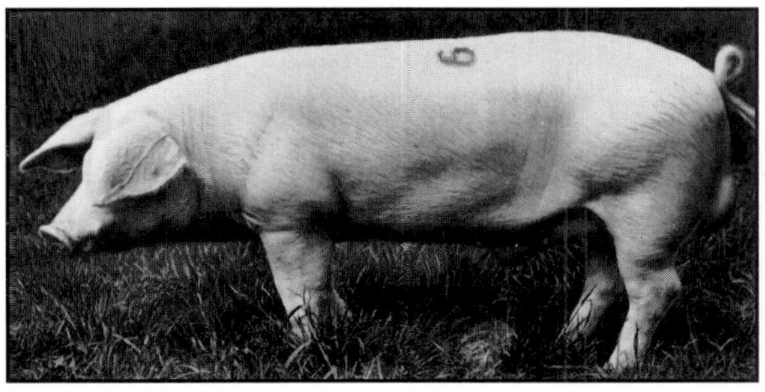

Against the Philistine

Some may prefer the citation which appears under the particulars Sir Osbert Sitwell gives of himself:

"For the past 30 years has conducted, in conjunction with his brother and sister, a series of skirmishes and hand-to-hand battles against the Philistine."

A third mark for literature is the Knighthood for Mr. Arthur Bryant, the historian, who does not skirmish with the Philistines but lures them to the lending libraries.

None of the top honours will cause much political ripple. Lord Soulbury becomes the ninth Viscount to be created by Sir Winston's administration.

U.K. Baronies for Lord Cooper and the Earl of Dundee mean that two former Conservative or Unionist M.P.s will augment the Government benches in the House of Lords.

Mr. Deakin's Feat

As Mr. Scrymgeour-Wedderburn, the Earl of Dundee sat in the Commons from 1931 until 1945 and held office. So did Lord Cooper, as Lord Advocate for Scotland, from 1935 until 1941.

Mr. Arthur Deakin received a Companionate of Honour from the Socialist administration, becomes a Privy Councillor under a Conservative one, yet contrives to remain "Mr. Deakin" to members of the T.G.W.U.

This is a triple achievement of unsurpassed delicacy.

MR. WEDGWOOD BENN'S request for permission to introduce a personal Bill into the House of Lords to renounce his father's title recalls a similar intent on the part of the late Lord Selborne.

For 10 years before his succession to the earldom of Selborne in 1895, Lord Wolmer, as he then was, had sat happily in the House of Commons.

As the prospect of going to the Lords did not appeal to him, he decided to remain in the Commons, and for a few days after his father's death refused to give up his seat.

He was supported by various other eldest sons of peers.

Lady Rhondda's Petition

Unfortunately Lord Wolmer had irritated the Irish Nationalist Members by accusing some of personal corruption. They led the attack on him and he was forced to give up his seat.

Mr. Wedgwood Benn may be comforted to know that after his forced translation Lord Selborne had a distinguished Ministerial career.

By way of contrast, just 27 years later, Lady Rhondda had her petition to sit and vote in the House of Lords rejected by the Committee of Privileges.

In March the Committee reported in favour of her claim. When the petition was referred back to them they turned it down by 20 votes to 4.

Victorianism -

There is a connection between two violently contrasted picture shows now on in London. At the Leighton House Art Gallery are the paintings and drawings of that gifted Victorian amateur, the ninth Earl of Carlisle.

They are admirably suited to the quiet Victorian atmosphere of Lord Leighton's studio and well deserve a visit.

The link between this and the exhibition at the Leicester Galleries is Winifred Nicholson, one of the three exhibitors. A grand-daughter of Lord Carlisle, she helped to organise this show of his.

While Mrs Nicholson's work belongs essentially to this present age it is Henry Moore's sculpture that is providing the sensation for the crowded rooms at the Leicester Galleries.

- And Modernism

I have been there twice recently. Each time Moore's imaginative conceptions were having an almost hypnotic effect on the viewers. These are of all ages, with the young perhaps in a majority.

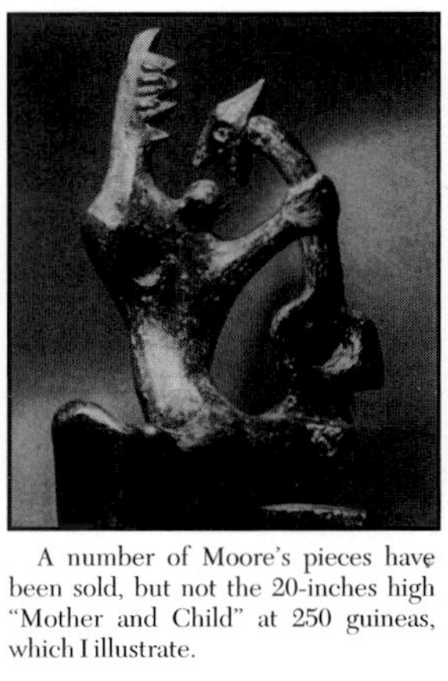

A number of Moore's pieces have been sold, but not the 20-inches high "Mother and Child" at 250 guineas, which I illustrate.

PETERBOROUGH

THOMSON IS NEW CHAMPION: COMPLETE GOLFER AT 24

Locke, Rees and Scott Tie Second

From Leonard Crawley

SOUTHPORT, Friday.

Peter Thomson, of Australia, who has twice finished second, won the Open Golf Championship here this evening with the grand score of 283. His four rounds were 72, 71, 69 and 71, a model of consistency.

D.J. Rees, South Herts, Sydney Scott of Carlisle City, and A.D. Locke, of South Africa, tied for second place with 284, and J. Adams, A. Cerda and J. Turnesa came next two strokes behind. P. Toogood was first amateur with 291, and this wound up a real Australian year.

Australia won the international matches, and D.W. Bachli won the Amateur Championship for them. They have also won the Formby Hare, the Prince of Wales Cup, the Royal St George's Gold Vase and the Golf Illustrated Gold Vase.

To-day we had one of the most exciting championships of the last quarter of a century and up till the very last moment no one could feel sure that Thomson had won.

The crowds were enormous and by noon the turnstiles showed that all records had been broken. They were admirably handled by a highly competent body of members of the Royal Birkdale Club.

Thomson is a splendid hitter of a golf ball and at 24 he must have many more successes before him. He is armed to the teeth, and with his great power and athletic figure he is well nigh the complete golfer. Moreover he has the most delightful demeanour and we wish him a successful reign as champion.

VITAL THIRD ROUND

Scott's Good Start

The vital third round began as the clocks across the sandhills in nearby Southport were chiming their morning argument as to the exact moment of 8 a.m. The sun was up, and until well on into the afternoon the huge car park glistened ever brighter and grew like the shimmering waters of a flood.

One of the most important men this morning was Sydney Scott, of Carlisle City. He got off to a good start and held it. He reached the turn in 33, and then, just to show his mettle, he got a grand 3 at the 10th and the question was could he last? Though he got his 3 at the short 13th, two regulation 5's at the 14th and 16th left him with par for a 69.

His second to the home hole was lucky. Having pitched in the bunker his ball bounced out to the edge of the green and the cheers of the throng around the clubhouse rang up to heaven. His total for three rounds was now 212 and likely to give him a lead.

SPENCE SLIPS BACK

Yesterday's leader, the gallant Bill Spence, although out in 34, had 6's at each of the 12th and 14th holes and the best he could do was 74 for a total of 215. If he was on the lucky side going out his putting deserted him on the long trek home.

Alliss was playing with him and looking rather fierce and determined after early adventures, finished bravely in 71 for 217.

Cerda had to work desperately hard after a modest start, and only a long putt for a 2 at the 13th put him back at level 4's. On the face of it his 71 with a total of 215 was a brave effort.

REES IN FORM

Unlucky To Take 69

Rees, in great form, was out in 34 and from the great scoreboard and walkie-talkie experts perched faithfully on the tops of strategic sandhills, news came that he was holding on and playing right well.

His last five holes in 5, 4, 3, 3, 4, in no sort of way did him justice, since at the 14th he missed from two feet, and after a terrific 3 at the 16th, he missed from seven feet for a 2 at the 17th. Though 69 was mighty good it might also have been better, and he went to lunch bracketed with Scott up to this time.

There was now every indication that only two more counted, Thomson, of Australia, out in 34, Locke, of South Africa, out in the same figure, and both playing beautifully.

Thomson, playing with Stranahan and playing magnificent golf, finished in 69 to join Scott and Rees in the lead at 212.

KING OUT OF IT

Alas! poor Sam King, who went off last and must have felt like young Jack Hearne years ago who, having had his pads on for a day and a half while Hobbs and Rhodes were doing their deadly work against the Australians at Melbourne, went in at last and got out first ball. King took 7 at the first hole and was virtually gone for good.

Then the picture of the final scene began to stand out through the haze and the heat. The names of Rees, Thomson and Scott were quite clear, but Locke's had to be added, for with one of the final benders from the right to left he had put his second to the home hole stone dead for a 3 and a score of 69. The old apparition of the mighty man had reappeared to haunt the three leaders from a distance of two strokes throughout their last and final round.

Almost before the proceedings of the morning had had time to sink in the fourth round had begun. The crowd was now vast and moved like an army about the majestic scene.

Scott played really well. Every approach putt finished past the hole or went firmly in. His tee shot to the short 13th was not good. From the edge of the sloping green he finished 10ft past the pin and his next failed to drop. A vital stroke had gone.

His putt for a 2 at the 17th from 12ft was distinctly unlucky to stay above the ground, but with a brave 4 at the home hole he was round in 72 for 284 - a splendid score that would, taking all in all, be unlucky not to win.

DASHING REES

Rees behind him was playing well and ever giving the hole a chance. After 13 he required 5, 4, 5, 3, 4, to tie. With a brilliant 3 up the hill at the 16th he had one in hand for a win and, after missing the green at the short 17th, he chipped up and sank the putt to hold on.

With typical dash he hit hard and straight and just over the 18th green. His ball lay 3ft up the bank eight yards from the hole. As he came through the immense gathering they gave him a warming cheer as he plodded over the turf to examine his chip shot.

His mind was soon made up, but his head did not stay down and his ball squirted away six or seven feet to the right of the hole. He missed the next and a golden opportunity had gone. He was 284 after all and level with the gallant Syd Scott.

EXCITED CROWD

Guess New Champion

Great men were behind him and playing well. Thomson was out in 35 and when three-quarters of an hour later, he came round the sandhills into full view on the 13th tee, followed by an exciting, panting mob, there was that old feeling that the commonsense of a British crowd had buttoned themselves to the new champion.

(July 10)

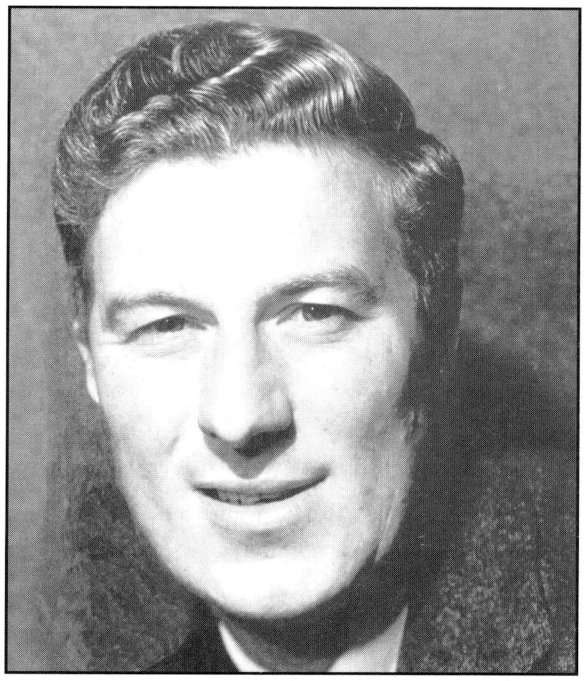

PETER THOMSON, winner of the Open Golf Championship.

THE QUEEN HAS 2 WINNERS ON LAST DAY OF ASCOT

Daily Telegraph Reporter

Two of the Queen's horses won at Ascot yesterday, the last day of the meeting.The third of her three runners was second.

In the morning the Queen and the Duke of Edinburgh went with a riding party to the course. While galloping towards the winning post the Duke, who was leading, saw a double wire stretched across the course. He shouted a warning and ducked under the wires, which were about eight feet from the ground.

The Queen and the other members of the party were able to slow down and get under the wires. They were seen to laugh and joke about the incident.

Maj. R.C.Bulteel, clerk of the course, said later: "I understand from the Post Office that it was a wire which had been put up a day or two ago over the course and had sagged. It is a temporary one."

"Apparently the posts or something had loosened, causing the wire to sag. But it could be seen quite easily about a quarter of a mile away."

"NO REAL DANGER"

The Duke of Norfolk, who was on the course at the time, said he understood that there was "no real danger" to the Queen and the Duke as they rode under the wires.

An Ascot official said it was the first time the Queen or the Duke had ridden there. The Queen rode astride. She wore jodhpurs, a hacking jacket and a silk scarf.

An onlooker said the party included the Duke and Duchess of Gloucester, Princess Alexandra, the Duchess of Norfolk, the Duke and Duchess of Beaufort and Lord Porchester.

In the afternoon the Queen saw her horse Landau, ridden by Sir Gordon Richards, win the first race, the Rous Memorial Stakes. Her Aureole was victorious in a photo finish with M.Marcel Boussac's Janitor in the Hardwicke Stakes.

Wearing a dress of caramel coloured silk with a little caramel straw hat to match and a mink cape, the Queen visited the paddock three times during the afternoon with other members of the Royal family. She went twice to the unsaddling enclosure to see her winners.

At the beginning of the meeting the Queen made her traditional drive from the Golden Gates.

BANQUET AT WINDSOR

In the evening the Queen gave the Waterloo banquet in the Waterloo chamber at Windsor Castle. It was the last of the Ascot Week dinner parties there.

To mark the end of Ascot Week the Queen gave a dance in the Waterloo Chamber. At midnight there was a surprise fireworks display on the East Terrace.

(June 19)

COCKELL'S 'NO' TO £8,000 OFFER

Don Cockell, British and Empire heavyweight champion, is "not interested" in an offer of £8,928 from America to meet Tommy Jackson, the 22-year-old New York Negro, in the United States in June.

Mr. J.Solomons, the London promoter, who had been informed of the offer, said yesterday: "I have had a long talk with Mr. J.Simpson, Cockell's manager, and he said that in view of other commitments which he was not prepared to disclose at the moment he would not accept it."

Mr.Simpson later said: "We have had all sorts of offers for Cockell, some bigger than the one to meet Jackson. Our immediate object is Rocky Marciano and the world title. Cockell, by beating La Starza, has earned the right to a title fight."

(April 2)

PIGGOTT LOSES LICENCE FOR SIX MONTHS

By Hotspur

Lester Piggott, 18, the apprentice who won the Derby on Never Say Die, will not ride under Jockey Club rules again this season. The Stewards of the Jockey Club yesterday decided to withdraw his licence to ride.

The Stewards, Maj.-Gen. Sir Randle Feilden and Lord Willoughby de Trafford (acting for the Duke of Norfolk), made their decision before racing began as a result of a report by the Ascot Stewards on the King Edward VII Stakes on Thursday when Piggott rode Never Say Die.

At the moment Piggott is attached to his father's stable at Lambourn, Berks, and lives at home. I understand that Piggott is now required to attach himself to another stable.

MISSING ST LEGER

There is no question of him being allowed to ride again for six months after new arrangements have been made. He will miss the St Leger at Doncaster in September at which he was to have ridden Never Say Die.

I understand the offence for which Piggott has been suspended took place before the scrimmaging between Rashleigh, Garter and Never Say Die. In evidence, Piggott, I believe said, that he had been unable to prevent Never Say Die hanging to the left at one period.

It is this proneness to hang which caused J.Lawson, trainer of Never Say Die, and Mr. Gerald McElligott, English racing manager of Mr.R.S.Clark, to advise Mr. Clark at one time against running Never Say Die in the Derby.

LEFT-HANDED CORNER

Epsom is a left-handed course and it was realised that Never Say Die would probably be suited to it, but was apprehensive whether the colt would be all right at Ascot which is right-handed.

The televised recording of the King Edward VII Stakes showed Rashleigh, the mount of Sir Gordon Richards, veeringsharply to the right soon after entering the straight. The offence for which Piggott has had his licence withdrawn apparently happened just before this incident.

(June 19)

U.S. OWNER DID NOT WANT TO RUN DERBY RUNNER

BOY JOCKEY'S TRIUMPH

Daily Telegraph Reporter

For the first time for 73 years an American-bred horse, Never Say Die, won the Derby yesterday. Not since 1881, when Iroquois won, has this happened.

The race was watched by the Queen, the Duke of Edinburgh and other members of the Royal family.

They saw Never Say Die, a 33-1 chance, ridden by 18-year-old Lester Piggott, pass the post two lengths in front of Arabian Night with Darius third. A photograph called for by the judge showed that Arabian Night gained second place by a neck. The Queen's horse, Landau, was eighth.

For the past 20 years, Mr. Robert Sterling Clark, the owner of Never Say Die, has raced his horses in England and France. After a dispute with the American authorities he said he would never again race his horses in the United States.

Mr. Clark, who is 78, is a retired financier. He lives in New York but has his stud at Upperville, Virginia, where Never Say Die was foaled.

Only once has he seen his colours carried to victory in England. That was when his filly, Javotte, of the same female line as Never Say Die, won at Newmarket four years ago.

VISITS TO ENGLAND

He usually makes one trip a year to England but has been to busy to travel so far this year. His wife is French-born. His brother, Mr. Ambrose Clark, is also a well-known American breeder.

There is no particular significance about the fact that yesterday's winner is called Never Say Die.

In New York yesterday his secretary said: "It is extremely hard to keep finding names for race-horses. Never Say Die was chosen at random." Mr. Clark takes a particular interest in naming his horses personally.

According to our New York Correspondent, Mr. H.S. Finney, a close associate of Mr. Clark in bloodstock raising said: "Mr. Clark did not think the colt had much of a chance for the Derby and did not want to run him."

"But Mr. George McElligott, of the British Bloodstock Agency, his manager in England, said he was sure the horse had a very good chance and ought to be run. So he was sent to Joe Lawson (the trainer) with yesterday's happy consequences." He wanted all the credit for the triumph to go to Mr. McElligott.

Mr. Clark himself said the success of Never Say Die had "completely flabbergasted" him. "It is the crowning glory of my career of 35 years as a breeder but I never expected it."

One of his first acts on hearing the news was to send a cable to the Earl of Rosebery, saying: "Good families live long." This was said to be a complimentary reference to the fact that Never Say Die's third dam Galaday was a member of one of Lord Rosebery's famous families.

Mr. Clark said he would have been "tickled to death" to have had his colt finish even among the leaders and had no idea of ever winning the race.

NEVER BACKS OWN HORSES

Mr. Finney said: "He didn't have a bet on Never Say Die. He never backs his own horses. He doesn't like to jinx them."

For the first time in my memory the Derby winner was led in not by the owner or a relation of the owner, but the lad who "does" the horse - and "on top" was Lester Piggott, unperturbed, a pale young man of 18, and I think the first apprentice to win the Derby in the 20th century.

Piggott is bred to be a top class jockey. His father, Keith Piggott, was a well-known steeplechase rider, his grandfather, Ernest Piggott, won the Grand National on Jerry M in 1912, and on Poethlyn in 1918 and 1919. Lester's mother was a Rickaby.

BED AT 9 P.M.

Two of his great-grandfathers, M. Cannon and K. Cannon, won the Derby and a great-great-grandfather, T. Cannon, also won the race.

On the eve of the race Lester, as usual, went to bed punctually at 9 p.m., but before he did so, he and his father, who now trains at Lambourn discussed the race.

(June 3)

DROBNY WINS WIMBLEDON AT 11th ATTEMPT

LONGEST FINAL

WIMBLEDON WEATHER FORECAST: *Cloudy early in the day with little rain; sunny periods during morning, but probably showers in afternoon; rather cool N.W. wind.*

Daily Telegraph Reporter

Jaroslav Drobny, 32, the man with the reputation as the world's unluckiest lawn tennis player, became Men's Singles champion at Wimbledon yesterday when he beat Ken Rosewall, the 19-year-old Australian.

King Gustav of Sweden, Princess Margaret, and the Duchess of Kent were among the capacity crowd of 14,600 who saw Drobny win the most exciting final for years by 13-11, 4-6, 6-2, 9-7. It lasted 2hr 36min and was the longest singles final in the history of the Championships.

Drobny was given a terrific ovation as one of the most popular winners for many years. He refused an order to return to Czechoslovakia in 1949 and later took up Egyptian nationality. Last year he married the former British lawn tennis international, Miss Rita Jarvis.

She watched every stroke of his long match from the front row of the competitors' stands and Drobny's first action after winning was to look towards her and hold out his arms. They are expecting a baby in the autumn.

FIRST APPEARANCE IN 1938

Drobny first played at Wimbledon in 1938. This was his 11th attempt there, and he was the No 11 seeded player. Twice before he has reached the final.

In 1949 he lost to the American, F.R. Schroeder, and went down in 1952 to F.A. Sedgman, of Australia.

He is the first left-hander to be champion for 40 years. The last one was Sir Norman Brookes in 1914. Drobny won the French Championship in 1951 and 1952 but has long been regarded in the lawn tennis world as the man who won all matches but the last.

He said afterwards: "I'm delighted to have won. It has been my ambition for many years. I shall defend my title next year but I doubt if I shall make a really serious attempt to retain it. I have no desire to turn professional."

"I HAD TO WIN"

"I felt I had to win this year at all costs. In a way I'm sorry Rosewall, who is a fine player, had to lose but he is young and will be able to win in the next ten years."

"I shall have no special celebration. I shall just go home and relax." Relaxation is perhaps the secret of Drobny's success this year. On recent mornings he has spent his time in fishing.

Drobny recently started an export business in Paris. At present he is living with his father-in-law, the managing director of a firm of fountain-pen manufacturers, on a farm at Dormans Park in Surrey.

The lawn tennis championships end to-day. In the women's singles final, Miss M. Connolly is attempting to win for the third successive year. She plays a fellow American, Miss L. Brough. The three doubles finals will also be played.

(July 3)

ROGER BANNISTER BREAKS FOUR-MINUTE MILE

Time of 3min 59.4sec is Triply Checked

From Jack Crump

OXFORD, Thursday

The first four-minute mile in the history of athletics was accomplished here to-day by Roger Gilbert Bannister, 25-year-old medical student, who was timed officially to run the distance in 3min 59.4sec. This was two seconds faster than the world record of Gundar Haegg, of Sweden, made in 1945.

This great triumph by an English athlete on an English track - Bannister ran on the Iffley Road ground, where he learned his running as an undergraduate - took the sporting world by surprise. It came at the start of an athletic season in America and in Europe, where several runners, notably John Landy (Australia), Joseph Barthel (Luxemburg), who beat Bannister in the 1952 Olympic Games, and Wes. Santee (U.S.) planned final assaults on the "even time" mile. Landy, who has done 4min 2sec, is soon to make an attempt in Finland.

When Bannister ran a mile in 4min 2sec at Motspur Park last year it was disallowed as an official record in this country because of technical non-compliance with the required conditions.

There is no danger, however, of his time this evening failing to be ratified by the International Amateur Athletic Federation.

Three official timekeepers certified the time and the race, which was run in a properly constituted match between the A.A.A. and Oxford University, was on a track which measured half an inch more than the required 440 yards.

The world record application form has been completed by officials of the British Amateur Athletic Board, who will formally submit the performance for ratification without delay.

POOR CONDITIONS

Bannister's historic run was all the more remarkable because it was his first public race this season, and the chilly and blustering wind, varying between 15 and 25 m.p.h., made conditions far from ideal for record breaking.

HOW RACE WAS RUN

Brasher Sets Pace

Luckily the weather improved, and it was learned when the six runners in the race went to the starting line that Bannister and his great friend, C.J. Chataway, were to attempt to run a "really fast mile."

The competitors, in addition to Bannister and Chataway, were the Olympic steeplechaser, C.W. Brasher, W.T. Hulatt of Alfreton, the Northern Counties champion, and two Oxford runners, G.P. Dole and A.D. Gordon.

From the start it was Brasher who went out in front, followed by Bannister and Chataway, and it was obvious that the pace was correct if a new world record were to be achieved. Brasher was leading slightly at the end of the first quarter-mile in 57.4sec., with Bannister a yard behind in 57.5sec. and Chataway in third position in 57.6sec.

Brasher nobly assumed the role of pacemaker, and at the half-mile stage led in 1min 58sec, with Bannister clocked at 1min 58.2sec. with Chataway in third place 1/5th of a second slower.

After two and a half laps Brasher, having done his self-allotted task splendidly, faltered, but immediately Chataway sprang forward to take over the lead. At the bell, with three-quarters of a mile covered, Chataway was one yard ahead of Bannister in 3min 0.4sec. Bannister's official time being 3min 0.5sec.

At once the cheering crowd realised that the historic four-minute mile was an exciting probability. All round the last lap the crowd roared encouragement to the runners, and when Chataway slowed with 250 yards to go, Bannister strode into the lead, quickly opened a gap and, appearing not even to be strained, sprinted to the tape in fine style and broke it to win in 3min 59.4sec.

He was exhausted as he stumbled from the track, but quickly recovered on learning that he had achieved the world's first four-minute mile. He had also established a new world, British Empire, British national, British all-comers, European, English native and a whole string of other records.

Chataway finished in second place in 4min 7.2sec and Hulatt third in 4min 16sec. Once again Chataway had unselfishly run a magnificent race in support.

RAN AS PLANNED

1,500 Metre Prospects

I spoke to Roger Bannister soon after the race and he told me that the intermediate lap times of 57.5sec, the half-mile in 1min 58.2sec and the three-quarter mile in 3min 0.5sec were almost exactly what he had hoped.

He expressed the greatest delight, not merely on being the first man to achieve the coveted distinction, but also of having performed this feat on the track of the University where he was athletic president.

Bannister's time was taken at the 1,500 metres mark by one watch and was returned at 3min 43sec, which is equal to the world record time standing to the credit of the Swedish runners, Gundar Haegg and Lennart Strand, and the German, Werner Lueg. But since there were not the recognised number of timekeepers specifically timing at this intermediate distance, it cannot go forward as equalling the world record.

Unquestionably in my view a new 1,500 metres record is something which Bannister confidently may look forward to achieving this season - an important season in view of the Empire and European Games later in the summer.

(May 7)

HAEGG AND BANNISTER LAP BY LAP

This is how the world record miles of Bannister (3min 59.4sec) and Gundar Haegg of Sweden (4min 1.4sec in 1945) compare:

	Bannister	Haegg
1st lap	57.5sec	56.6sec
2nd lap	60.7sec	61.9sec
	(1min 58.2)	(1min 58.5)
3rd lap	62.3sec	61.2sec
4th lap	58.9sec	61.7sec

This was Bannister's progress: 220 yds, 28.7sec, 440 yds 57.5sec. 660 yds 1min 27.5sec, 880 yds 1min 58.2sec, 1,100 yds, 2min 29.6sec, 1,320 yds 3min 0.5sec. 1,540 yds, 3min 30.4sec.

PAT SMYTHE'S RECORD JUMP

BRUSSELS SUCCESS

From Our Own Correspondent

BRUSSELS, Monday.

Miss Pat Smythe on Prince Hal beat her own world high jump record for women by 10 centimetres (3.9in) in clearing 2.2 metres (7.218 feet) in the final event of the five-day Brussels International Horse Show tonight.

After following closely the Golden Sash holder, Mlle. Yvonne de Laissardiere (France), throughout the show, Miss Smythe ended first and took over the Golden Sash with a three-point lead. Prince Hal was given the Golden Cockade for being the best throughout the show.

Miss Smythe's record jump was made at the first attempt. Mr. Alan Oliver, riding Red Admiral, took second place with the same height. He conceded victory to Miss Smythe because he considered his mount could not make a higher jump.

(November 23)

(Solution PRIZE COMPETITION of January 9 – No. 8778)

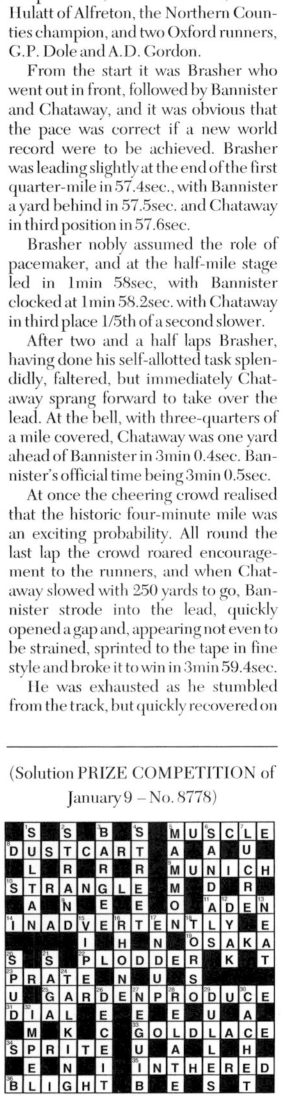

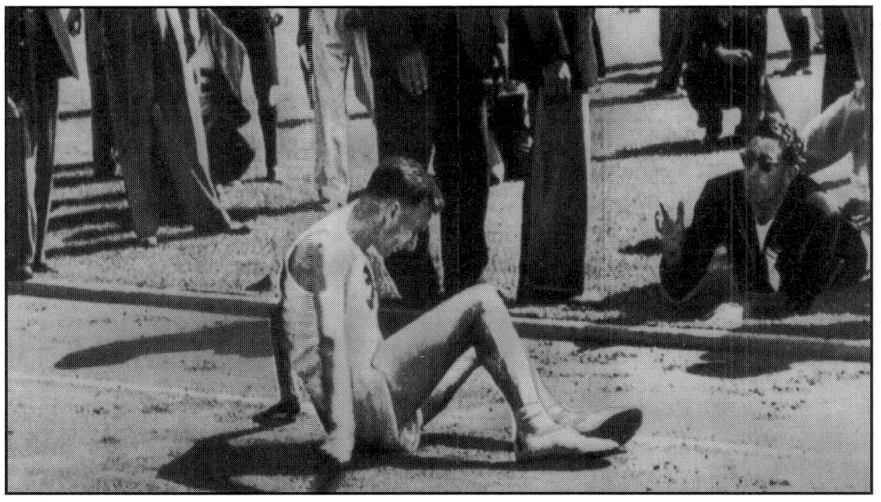

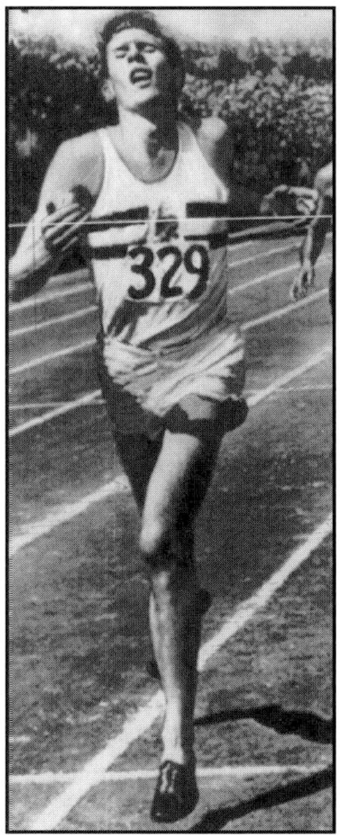

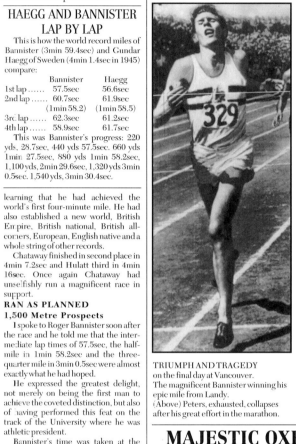

TRIUMPH AND TRAGEDY on the final day at Vancouver.
The magnificent Bannister winning his epic mile from Landy.
(Above) Peters, exhausted, collapses after his great effort in the marathon.

BANNISTER WINS GREATEST MILE OF ALL

Peters' Sensational Marathon Collapse

From A Special Correspondent

VANCOUVER, Sunday.

TRIUMPH - the complete and utter triumph of Roger Bannister in the greatest mile race ever run - and DISASTER - the collapse of Jim Peters, the 35-year-old English marathon runner, within sight of the tape - these "two impostors" stalked the running track almost side by side at the close of the British Empire and Commonwealth Games here yesterday.

No more emotional turn of events could have been staged than the scene of Peters's misfortune following so quickly on the mile thrill.

In this Bannister, his fair hair falling over his eyes, his features contorted with the all-out effort of his shole body, held up his final burst and only streaked past his great Australian rival, John Landy, in the last 100 yards to win the third under-four-minute mile ever achieved - all of them in the past three months.

Peters entered the stadium for two laps of the track to the winning post fully a quarter of an hour ahead of the rest of the field. An ovation such as Bannister received greeted him but the crowd was quickly hushed by the realisation that Peters was in considerable distress. He sprawled on the track, almost insensible, but obeying some instinct he dragged himself to his feet and struggled on.

He stumbled, fell again, rose and blundered blindly from side to side of the track. Eventually the English trainer, Mick Mayes, mistaking the finishing line, went to the assistance of Peters, who was consequently disqualified 220 yards from the winning-post.

The great little runner was given oxygen on the track and rushed in an ambulance to hospital suffering from exhaustion. To-day he was stated to be recovering sufficiently quickly for there to be hopes that he may yet be fit to run in the European Marathon at Berne on Aug. 25.

PETERS GAVE HIS ALL

TRIBUTE TO GREAT ATHLETE

By Jack Crump

No one except the great runner Jim Peters is, would have given every ounce of energy in an endeavour to bring honour to his country in his poignant failure.

It requires a man of rare physical courage to run himself into a state of utter and complete exhaustion, and it is of little account that in forcing the pace so relentlessly - and taking an unnecessarily long lead - he may have been the victim of an error of judgment.

Peters is unable to run his big races in any other way. He trains hard and conscientiously for a race and once in it, gives of his all. This attitude towards his sport has brought Peters well earned fame and the distinction of being the world's fastest-ever marathon runner.

I have had the privilege of being with him as his team manager on several occasions, the last in April of this year when he ran a find race to finish second in the Boston Marathon. A more genuine sportsman I have never known, certainly no one with finer team spirit and physical and mental courage.

British athletes everywhere will share this sympathetic tribute to him.

DISTRIBUTION OF MEDALS

		Gold	Silver	Bronze
England	...	23	24	20
Australia	...	20	11	18
Canada	...	9	20	14
South Africa	...	16	7	12
New Zealand	...	7	7	5
Scotland	...	6	2	5
N. Rhodesia	...	1	4	4
Wales	...	1	1	6
Nigeria	...	1	3	3
Pakistan	...	1	3	2
S. Rhodesia	...	2	2	1
Trinidad	...	2	2	0
N. Ireland	...	2	1	0
Jamaica	...	1	0	0
Hongkong	...	0	1	0
Uganda	...	1	1	0
Barbados	...	0	1	0
Brit. Guiana	...	0	0	1

(August 9)

MAJESTIC OXFORD ROWING IN ROUGH WATER

By B.C. Johnstone

OXFORD put up a really fine performance in the 100th Boat Race on Saturday, when beating Cambridge by 4 lengths in 20 minutes 23 seconds over the 4 ¼ miles from Putney to Mortlake. They had the race won from the time they ran into rough water just above Hammersmith Bridge. There they took a commanding lead and settled down to row firmly to the finish while they watched the efforts of Cambridge to cope with the waves.

On rounding into the weather opposite the Doves Cambridge momentarily wallowed. For a second or so they seemed to be battling against seas too heavy for them. At the same time Oxford forged ahead, cutting their way with fast, clean assurance.

Nothing Cambridge could do, and they never gave up experimenting or trying, could put them in the race again.

Oxford, having passed the worst patch, left the shelter of the bank and rowed superbly in the mid-stream turbulence. Unperturbed, serene, every man from bow to stroke plying his oar with majestic ease, Oxford took their calm, unruffled way to the finishing post.

TOSS NOT DECISIVE

Oxford on Better Side

Winning the toss Oxford correctly chose the Surrey side, giving Cambridge the worse water. But the toss was not a deciding factor, for the roughness of Corney Reach would always have been the undoing of Cambridge.

Oxford got away with great speed striking 20 strokes in the first half minute and 38 in the minute, to 36 by Cambridge. Both eights settled down well. After two minutes they were level, as they were also at the Mile (4 minutes dead), and there could never have been more than a few feet in it either way.

CAMBRIDGE LURCH

Up to Hammersmith (7m 13s) the water was fairly smooth and the race followed my expectation.

At the Doves, just short of two miles, came the unpredictable, for they ran into conditions they had not encountered in training. Wind against the stream had stirred up the water.

Rating 34, Oxford sailed into it with complete confidence, control of their boat and rode well through it. Cambridge, at three strokes less, lurched badly, lost pace, the boat became unsteady and cohesion went.

The Light Blue cox, to help his men, came right into the Surrey shore, even inside Oxford's course, lost distance rapidly and as a race all was over.

At Chiswick Steps (12m 5s) the Dark Blues were 11 seconds up. While Oxford now made light of the heavy going in midstream Cambridge crept under the Middlesex bank, sacrificing tide and distance. Soon they had to alter course sharply to pass under the central arch of Barnes Bridge (Oxford 16m 48s, Cambridge 17m).

LONGER THAN TRIAL

Oxford finished with triumphant assurance, but their 20m 23s was 1m 20s more than they took in their first trial, a striking comment on the conditions over the second half of the course.

(April 5)

SIR GORDON RICHARDS QUITS THE SADDLE

PLAN TO TRAIN AT BECKHAMPTON

By Hotspur

Sir Gordon Richards, 50, champion jockey on 26 occasions, has retired from the saddle. He will train at Beckhampton, Wilts, at a 30-horse stable built by the late Fred Darling.

He announced his retirement last night at his bungalow at Worthing, Sussex, where he is recuperating from his accident at Sandown Park on July 10. A bone in his pelvis was fractured when the Queen's filly Abergeldie unseated him and rolled on him.

"I have talked the matter over with Mr. Noel Murless, the trainer and all concerned and everything is now settled," he stated. "I shall not ride again in public.

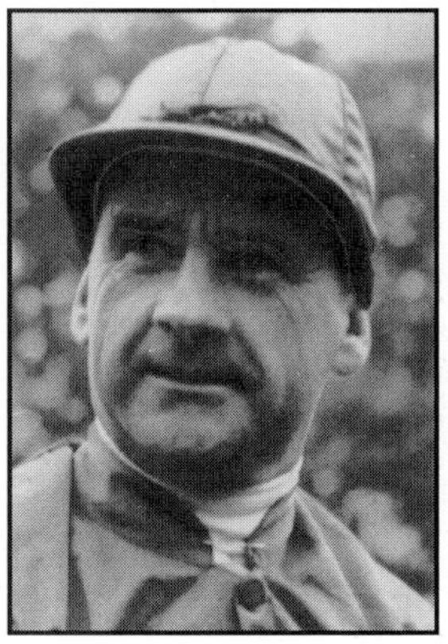

SIR GORDON RICHARDS

"After 34 years as a jockey, every minute of which I have enjoyed, it is naturally with no little regret that I make this announcement. I wish I could see the season out, for I shall miss the familiar racing scene and the thrills a jockey gets when a vast and enthusiastic racing public shares his triumphs."

"My last accident has ended my riding career sooner than I had planned. I have made a good recovery and my doctors say I shall be walking about normally in two to three weeks. But I could not hope to be fit to ride in races until mid-October at the earliest. There would be no point in striving to do that because the principal owners for whom I ride have by that time retired their best horses for the year."

Before his accident Sir Gordon had made plans to retire at the end of the present flat racing season and become a trainer at Beckhampton, near his home at Marlborough. He was for many years first jockey to Fred Darling, who trained at Beckhampton like his father before him.

ARCHER'S RECORD BEATEN

He won practically all the principal flat races. In 1933 he passed Fred Archer's season's record of winners with a total of 259, and in 1947 broke his own record with 269. Archer's total of 2,749 winners was eclipsed by Sir Gordon in 1943. His riding record is 21,834 mounts, 4,870 winners.

In the days of Steve Donoghue the most popular racecourse cry was "Come on, Steve." In Gordon Richards's day it has been "Come on, Gordon," and it has been shouted now with immense fervour by a large number of Englishmen for close on a quarter of a century.

It is difficult to prophesy who will succeed him because he has so overshadowed his contemporary jockeys. It has been, in fact, Gordon first and the rest nowhere in most racing seasons.

(August 11)

CUP FINAL IN FULL ON TV

By Our Radio Correspondent

The B.B.C. is to broadcast both in sound and on television the whole Cup Final from Wembley Stadium on May 1. The Corporation has paid £1,500 for the television transmission, a record fee for football.

No seperate payment is made for the sound commentary. This is included in a £2,000 agreement with the Football Association and the Football League, by which a match is broadcast every Saturday.

(January 12)

CUP FINAL THRILLS BUT LITTLE SKILL

Finney Fades While Barlow Shines

By Frank Coles

West Bromwich Albion .... 3 Preston North End 2

A FIVE-GOAL Cup final with the match-winner scored only two minutes from time automatically ranks high in the long catalogue of thrilling Wembleys. But I wish West Bromwich Albion's 3-2 victory over Preston could have been gained in the grand manner the 100,000 crowd had come to expect of the best team of the season.

In a long experience from the first Wembley Final 31 years ago, I assess the 1954 contest in the low class - a spoiling duel in which dour, dominant defence on both sides exposed the poverty of England's present-day forward craft.

Not until late in the second half could Albion find the delightful rhythm which made them the most talked of side in the country a few weeks ago.

And Preston, who came to the Final on the crest of the wave, were obvious victims of Wembley nerves. As North End failed altogether to get to grips with themselves and produce normal form, they had no alibis in defeat.

Preston's biggest disappointment was Tom Finney. Hailed as probable match-winner, he was naturally the target of close tackling by Millard and Barlow, with outside-left Lee joining in the "fun". But a strangely stereotyped Finney held steadfastly to touchline raiding, which played straight into the enemy's hands.

WHERE FINNEY WENT WRONG

When Finney found himself locked out by numbers he should have upset Albion's plan by doing some unorthodox wandering into the middle in the Matthews style. As it was, he had one glorious scoring chance just before half-time, but from 15 yards and unmarked he fired high and wide.

Preston were tactically wrong in failing to use outside-left Morrison more often when they saw how soundly Finney was held and also realised the poor support Foster was giving him. Baxter at inside-left, tried hard, but a high bouncing windblown ball severely handicapped little Wayman, who was mastered in the air by Dugdale.

The soundest section of Preston's team was their half-back line. Powerfully-built Marston commanded the middle for most of the time, and right half Docherty shared the honours of the day with Albion's left-half, Barlow. Firm in the tackle, Docherty is a most accurate user of the ball, with a highly developed sense of the urgency of attack.

Both Cunningham and Walton, the backs, made dangerous mistakes, and goalkeeper Thompson showed plainly in the number of times he fumbled the ball that Wembley atmosphere had him bothered and bewildered.

PANICKY KEEPING

Griffin Sees Chance

But there had rarely been a Wembley play without stage fright. Last year it was Farm, the Blackpool goalkeeper. On Saturday it was Thompson. Twice he dropped the ball when chased by eager Albion forwards and there was an impression of panicky misjudgment in positioning which gave Griffin, the Albion right-winger, a chance to shoot the winning goal from so near the dead ball line that the slenderest chance of the match was to provide the glorious victory.

Yet Thompson showed no nervousness in a great but vain effort to save the goal on which the game turned - the penalty goal which made the score 2-2 for Albion 27 minutes from the end.

Barlow, suddenly taking command of the play in a majestic spell of 15 minutes, had dribbled the ball inside the Preston penalty area and was closing in to shoot. Only the fast tough Docherty could reach him and his tackle was from the side. Barlow hurtled over his thigh, and no one doubted that it was a foul which had prevented a goal.

HOLE IN PENALTY SPOT

Then an unprecedented incident happened. Allen could not put the ball on a Wembley penalty spot because of a deep heel mark. There were protests when he placed the ball just behind and had to stamp the spot into shape before he could take his shot. The Stadium was hushed during this critical moment.

Allen hit the ball right-footed and Thompson anticipated his intention with a dive which brought his right hand to the ball without being able to turn it round the post. It was a brilliant attempt to save Preston's Cup-winning lead.

ALLEN EXPECTED IT

Move That Made Goal

Mr. Luty had given the right decision then, but he appeared at fault on other occasions - and, important occasions, too. In the first few minutes Millard tackled and felled Finney with unheeding desperation and the second tackle might well have brought a penalty if the game had emerged from a cold start in which reactions were still slow.

Finney's lack of variety and Barlow's subdued play repressed the spirit of the match until between the 21st and 22nd minutes, first Albion then Preston scored. Nicholls charged down a Cunningham clearance and the ball ran to Lee. He made for the Preston goal with a curving run and shot hard for the far post. Allen, knowing the move, raced up just in time to sidestep the ball into the net with his right foot. His tremendous speed off the mark alone made this goal.

(May 3)

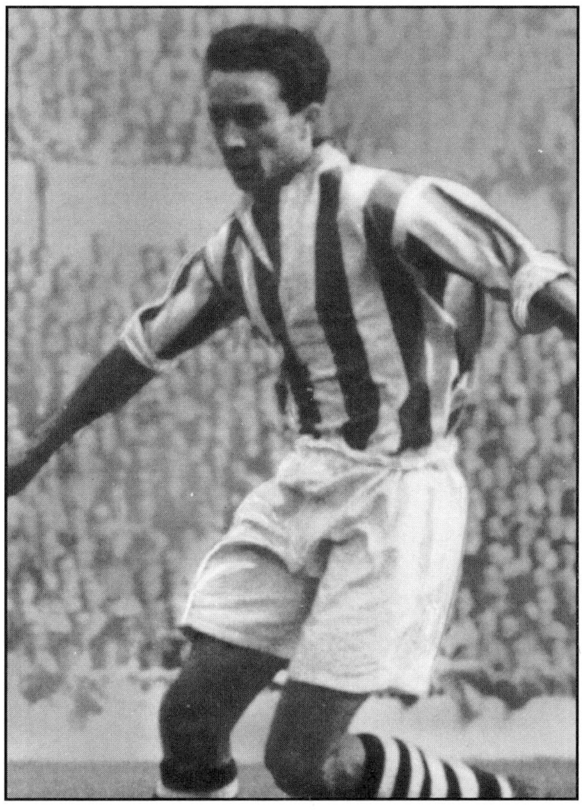

RONNIE ALLEN, West Bromwich Albion centre-forward.

MASTERLY 205 BY HUTTON: ENGLAND ALL OUT 414

Weary W. Indies Attack Punished

From E.W. Swanton

KINGSTON, Jamaica, Thursday.

ENGLAND in the indomitable person of Hutton thrust home the advantage they had gained on the first two days of the fifth Test. West Indies went in again at five o'clock this evening 275 runs to the bad and it would seem that only some exceptional batting over these next two days can save the game for them.

One has been watching Hutton now for the best part of 20 years and in that time he has built a record of achievement second only to Sir Donald Bradman's. Whatever he does, he has almost lost the capacity to surprise us. Yet from the viewpoint of physical stamina and mental concentration this latest innings is a thing apart, at any rate so far as the post-war years are concerned.

In his youth he once stayed in 13 hours 20 minutes against Australia, but it was in English summer weather after his captain had won the toss and there was a Sunday break intervening. In this match he batted a few minutes short of nine hours in tropical heat. When he was finally got out after the tea interval he had been on the field continuously for the best part of three days. This, moreover, was the hottest of the three.

As to the technical side of the job, need more be said than that he gave only one extremely difficult chance (immediately after reaching his 100) and that one could count on the fingers of the hands the number of times he was beaten.

By this afternoon he had forced his opponents to their knees and one will long retain the picture of the West Indies trailing wearily into their tea preceded by a figure pale and with a slight stoop of the shoulders but walking briskly as though anxious to get the interval done with so that he could continue to chase them.

As it happened he made no more, but if Hutton's innings has not won the match, the West Indies will either have to bat superlatively well or England will have to bowl and field indifferently ill.

The pre-match predictions as to the wicket have been quite falsified and in fact it is the fastest the M.C.C. have played on since the first colony match against Jamaica. This fact made the loss of King's services today all the more unfortunate for West Indies.

EVANS RESTRAINED

Hutton In No Hurry

The early play this morning went entirely according to the English plan. King, who strained a thigh muscle last evening, did not appear and the West Indies bowling without him lacked its sharp edge, well though Atkinson bowled.

Hutton accumulated in a leisurely way the six he needed for his 100, a monumental effort that had so far lasted five hours and 40 minutes.

At the other end Evans held himself in with conscious restraint, prepared apparently to try and repeat his stonewall effort at Adelaide just after the war when, of course, his reputation as a batsman was inconsiderable.

Soon after noon Hutton had what in the case of a less illustrious person could only be described as a rush of blood to the head. As happened when Sobers was bowling yesterday, he suddenly, and for no apparently logical reason, lashed out. This time it was Ramadhin whom he pulled savagely two balls running. The first was a horribly difficult chance to Gomez high overhead at deep mid-on, the second time the ball was hit cleanly wide of Gomez to the boundary.

The mood swiftly passed and the captain, defying time and the heat, schooled himself once more to circumspection.

Today was stiflingly hot, for the breeze which usually makes things bearable was scarcely enough to rustle the flags above the pavilion. The West Indians were obviously feeling it as Ramadhin walked languidly back to his mark.

(April 2)

The Scoreboard

WEST INDIES - First Innings

139 (C.L. Walcott 50, Bailey 7-31)

Second Innings

J.B. Stollmeyer, not out	12
J.K. Hold, not out	7
Extra	1
Total (no wkt)	**20**

BOWLING

	O	M	R	W
Bailey	4	2	5	0
Trueman 4	1	14	0	.

ENGLAND - First Innings

Hutton, c McWatt, b Walcott	205
T.E.Bailey, c Sobers, b McWatt	23
P.B.H. May, c sub, b.Ramadhin	30
Compton, hit wkt. b King	31
W. Watson, c McWatt, b King	4
Graveney, lbw, b Atkinson	11
Evans, c Worrell, b Ramadhin	28
Wardle, c Holt, b Sobers	66
Lock b Sobers	4
Laker, b Sobers	9
Trueman, not out	0
Extras	3
Total	**414**

SURREY RUSH WORCESTER OUT FOR 25 RUNS

Half Share in Championship Now Sure

From Michael Melford

THE OVAL, Wednesday.

SURREY'S advance along the last leg of their journey to the championship reached a more precipitous pace here to-day than even they have achieved before.

They put Worcestershire in, bowled them out for 25, declared at 92 for three themselves and took two second-innings wickets for 13, all between two o'clock and half-past six. A half share in the championship has thus already been won. The other half must surely follow early tomorrow.

Worcestershire's total of 25 is only one run more than the lowest in their history, and is the lowest in first-class cricket since Somerset were bowled out by Gloucestershire for the same figure in 1947. The last eight wickets fell for only five runs.

These events would suggest a pitch of almost unparalleled wickedness, but that is an exaggeration. Bedser certainly had the important wicket of Richardson early on with a ball that lifted and Lock and Laker subsequently turned the ball varying amounts at varying paces; but everything could not be blamed on the pitch which was no better when Worcestershire batted again.

The ingredients of Surrey's success therefore were yet another superb piece of spin bowling by Lock and Laker, some singularly inept batting and all the luck that was going. Catches went to hand every time and were held with customary certainty.

FIVE WICKETS FOR TWO

The feats of Lock and Laker have been eulogised often enough recently. It need only be said here that it is hard to imagine any other bowlers in the world making more out of this wicket than they did and that to-day Lock, with his pace through the air and bite off the wicket, was the senior partner. His five wickets for two runs were taken in only 32 balls.

The Worcestershire batsmen doubtless found the amiable tracts of Worcester poor practice ground for a wicket like this. Their confidence, moreover, was undermined from the first over of the day in which Richardson was caught low down at first slip off a ball that lifted sharply to find his glove.

For 45 minutes afterwards, however, Kenyon and Outschoorn went warily and not too perilously against Bedser and Loader until Kenyon was caught at second slip.

Laker then came on, followed three overs later by Lock and they swept through the later batsmen, taking seven of the last eight wickets in 35 minutes. The other wicket was a run-out, for which the honours were divided between Barrington, the thrower, and Laker, the bowler. The innings lasted 105 minutes.

(August 26)

PRIZE COMPETITION - No. 8778

Three prizes of books to a value of thirty shillings, to be selected by the winners from advertisements in THE DAILY TELEGRAPH on Fridays, will be awarded to the senders of the first three correct solution opened.

ACROSS

5 It moves men to action (6)
8 Refuse to go? Then send for this (8)
9 Foreign city with a good deal to turn in in (6)
10 To kill thus is uncommon about fifty (8)
11 Some think being stationed in this place is a beast of a job (4)
14 "Lad very intent" (anag.) (but he did not mean to be) (13)
19 A Japanese city (5)
22 He has a curious heart, but manages to get along steadily (7)
23 So to talk needs mostly speed (5)
25 Excellent stuff for vegetarians (6, 7)
31 It is usually looked at for a time (4)
33 This makes its contribution to general trimmings (4,4)
34 The elf of an extended spar (6)
35 Short of 7 down, by all accounts (2, 3, 3)
36 Plant disease, usually fungoid (6)

DOWN

1 Ruler of a sporting association in what its sport needs (6)
2 Londoners' way to put one's ship in peril (6)
3 His language is proverbial, but would he veto an Americanism? (6)
4 Describes a well known 2 down (6)
5 A god who receives miserly respect? (6)
6 Young Sarah's about and can cover a couple of feet (7)
7 The kind of asset that could be cruel (5)
12 Many who have met him have lost their heads (4)
13 It is not only bovine, but quite in order (4)
15 Starts off as a "somebody," but has not a leg to stand on (5)
16 A runner between banks in France (5)
17 Finish in a reversed position?
18 Height thus shown has its human part (5)
20 Small spade - for digging potatoes? (4)
21 The yarn that upset a state of fluid (4)
24 A habit that is taking about middle age? (7)
26 Crooked practice taking only a short month to tie up (6)
27 Where there are pyramids, he's at the top (6)
28 To get the bishop to tell, behead him! (6)
29 An American statesman with many overseas interests (6)
30 The seal that had a pain in its middle (6)
32 A mischievous 34 across starts to drive (5)

(January 9)

Name .... No. 8778

Address ....

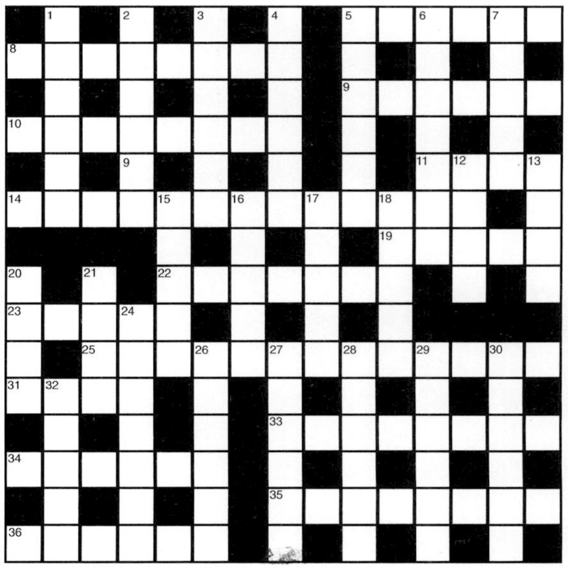

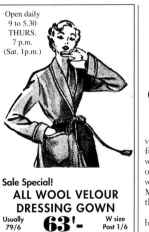

'IT'S NOT SKI-ING' SAY RUSSIANS

CHAIR-LIFT SHUNNED

GRINDELWALD, Switzerland, Sunday.

The first Russian ski-ing team to visit Switzerland to-day shunned the funiculars and chair-lifts at Grindelwald. "Up by chairlift, down by force of gravity - what has that got to do with honest physical culture?" said Mr. Constantin Sorokin, leader of the 10-man team.

"Ski-lifts and the like would not be approved in Russia. Sport without toil and sweat, without the satisfaction of self-denial and self-conquest, is nothing more than an amusement."

The Russians, whose average age is 20, are all national or regional champions. They include six women cross-country skiers. They are training for international competitions this week. B.U.P.

(January 4)

1955

By one of those sad accidents of history, one of the biggest stories of the year went unreported by London based newspapers because they were, for the first time since 1926, on strike. During the 26 days of the strike by engineers and electricians, Sir Winston Churchill announced his retirement. He was succeeded by his Foreign Secretary, Anthony Eden, who immediately went to the country and was returned with a slightly increased majority. Because of the newspaper strike, The Daily Telegraph issued a special supplement to cover the period in which it did not appear. One of the pages reproduced here is that of the supplement that was published on April 21.

Sir Winston relinquished office voluntarily. In Russia, Malenkov, Stalin's somewhat inconspicuous successor, was pushed aside to make way for the more flamboyant Bulganin and Krushchev. Juan Peron was forced from the Presidency of Argentina into exile.

In Britain, the emphasis was on reconstruction, Green belts round the major cities were announced, as was a considerable programme for the building of new roads including, for the first time, motorways. The plans to build a dozen nuclear power stations were tabled, and the housing programme showed a considerable increase over the previous year. Independent television made its debut and the British were introduced to the doubtful pleasures of a toothpaste commercial. And a further sign of the times: the MCC admitted a professional cricketer to its membership. Not unnaturally, the first to be elected was Len Hutton, the recently retired captain of the English cricket team. His place as the head of the side had been taken by P.B.H. May, the youngest captain ever to have led an English side through a series.

Although the offer of an amnesty to Mau Mau rebels in Kenya brought hope of future quiet, troubles in Cyprus were brewing and reinforcements of British troops were sent to the island. In North Africa, there were widespread insurrections against the French Colonial administration. The American Supreme Court ordered the Southern States to end the segregation by colour of their schools.

The world of science lost its most illustrious name when the death of Albert Einstein was announced. Alexander Fleming, the discoverer of penicillin, had died a month earlier.

The discussion over the death penalty achieved a new sharpness when the Home Secretary refused a reprieve to Ruth Ellis who had been found guilty of shooting her lover. She would, in fact, prove to be the last woman hanged in Britain. An American serviceman who had gone berserk killed three men before hi-jacking a car and firing indiscriminately at people on a Kentish beach. When cornered he killed himself.

After much speculation and a great deal of public discussion, some of it of a sensational sort, an announcement came from Buckingham Palace that Princess Margaret had decided not to marry the divorced Group Captain Peter Townsend. *The Daily Telegraph* condemned the sensationalism and wished the Princess future happiness.

The Daily Telegraph

SUMMARY OF THE MAIN EVENTS AT HOME AND ABROAD DURING THE NATIONAL NEWSPAPER STRIKE

SIR WINSTON CHURCHILL

By

Lady Violet Bonham Carter

★

The author, a daughter of the late Earl of Oxford and Asquith, has been a close friend of Sir Winston ever since he was a member of the Liberal Government of 1906.

THE blow has fallen - a blow for which our minds had been prepared but not our hearts. By his own choice and in his own time Sir Winston Churchill had laid down his leadership and a chapter has closed - as glorious in achievement and romance as any in our history.

His going has brought a deep sense of irrevocable loss, not only to the nation and the Commonwealth, but to Europe, to our transatlantic Allies, to the Free World he saved and of which he is to-day the greatest citizen.

Yet while he lives he cannot but remain the Counsellor of the nation - the touchstone of its constancy to the greatest purpose he served. His vision will still light the way ahead, his pulse "like a cannon" beat through fainter hearts.

Nor in assessing him need we await the verdict of history. "with its flickering lamp." Time cannot touch or tarnish his imperishable record. In his own life he has taken a place among the Immortals. He stands with Pitt and Chatham as the one who from the fire of mortal peril forged his country's "finest hour". All that the world then owed to Britain in salvation Britain owes to him.

In 1940 Sir Winston Churchill was 66. Like Chatham he had to wait for power through years of drift, dishonour and disaster.

Power came to him, not as a load but a release. When on the night of May 10, 1940 he became Prime Minister, he wrote: "As I went to bed at 3 a.m. I was conscious of a profound sense of relief. At last I had the authority to give directions over the whole scene. I felt as though I were walking with destiny and though all my past life had been but a preparation for this hour and for this trial... I thought I knew a good deal about it and I knew I should not fail." And in this fearless certainty he never faulted.

★

MANY, now and hereafter, will attempt to gauge, define and analyse the elements which combined to make him perhaps the greatest war leader in our history.

Some will be recognised by all; the Promethean, spirit which defied and hurled back every challenge, the flame of courage which turned our darkest night to day, the impetus of purpose which swept into service every resource of mind, heart, nerve and fibre in the nation, his faith in his fellow countrymen - "the island people united and unconquerable" - his sense of the greatness of the English spirit and tradition, and his determination to preserve "its message and its glory."

Yet all these might have been to no avail had he not possessed as well that rare gift of strategic thinking and grasp of detail which he himself calls "an acute military perception of what would help and what would hurt, of what would cure and what would kill" - and without which modern armies cannot win.

Above and beyond this mastery of the art of war he has a capacity for sustained and solitary thought, an elemental power of intellectual and emotional concentration on one aim. He understands what Napoleon describes as "the value of being able to focus objects in the mind for a long time without being tired."

The qualities of action, counsel and speech are distinct and they have rarely been so perfectly united in one man. To him thought, action and expression have always been a combined operation.

No politician has ever spent less time or found less ease in an armchair. His life has been a cavalry charge from start to finish. Irresolution is to him a vice unknown. He has never hesitated to take drastic and immediate actions at the supreme moment.

His decision in August, 1940, to send our only available armoured division round the Cape to Egypt while this country stood in imminent danger of invasion was - in his words - at once "awful and right." His offer, during the agony of France, of an indissoluble union between our two countries was a generous and imaginative act of statesmanship. His instant declaration of full support of Soviet Russia proved his single-minded dedication to one aim.

A CONVERSATION is recorded to have taken place in the presence of Pitt as to the quality most needed in a Prime Minister. While one said Eloquence and another Knowledge and another Toil, Pitt said "Patience."

Patience was not one of nature's gifts to Winston Churchill, but to his infinite credit he acquired it. When in our hour of direst need we were refused the right to the Irish ports, he showed a measure of patience and forbearance of which in youth he might have fallen short.

Reading the story of his dealing with the Kremlin, of their grasping and graceless demands, reproaches and suspicion, one marvels at the "patience in the face of ceaseless affront" with which he managed to endure them.

But his last ordeal was surely the hardest. When victory was assured though not yet won, Sir Winston thought and saw beyond it. He recognised that Soviet Russia had become "a mortal danger to the free world" and that a new front must be created against her onward sweep. He pleaded that, above all, a settlement must be reached between East and West "before the armies of democracy melted."

His words fell on deaf ears. He was "no longer fully heard" by Roosevelt, his trusted friend and colleague, and Gen. Eisenhower believed Berlin to be "devoid of military and political importance."

Thus Soviet Russia was established in the heart of Europe, the Iron Curtain fell and "in the moment our best and what might have proved our last chance of durable world peace was allowed composedly to fade away."

★

THE late Lord Rosebery once wrote that "the English love a statesman whom they can understand - or at least think they can understand." The English people took a long time to understand Sir Winston Churchill. One recalls the well-worn clichés used about him in the past - "unstable," "erratic," "not a safe man." Until 15 years ago he had no organised body of support behind him either in Parliament or the country. His warnings against the Nazi peril were unheeded both by the Government and by the nation. He was left to rust unused on a back bench.

How came it that a man who had never been the leader of any political party in the state was acclaimed by all as the unchallenged leader of the nation - its voice, its will, its soul?

Sir Winston himself has given one answer to this question when he said that "to hold the leadership of a party or nation with dignity and authority requires that the leader's qualities and message should meet not only the need, but the mood of both." Not only did he then meet the nation's need, but he became the inspired expression of its mood and purpose.

There are moments in the life of nations when those who lead them are unmasked by circumstance. Those who seem great in small days in great days prove infinitely small. Just such a challenge of Fate at long last enabled Winston Churchill's fellow-countrymen to see him plain. The greatness of the hour revealed his own.

"Your mood," he wrote to Lord Lothian in Washington, "should be bland and phlegmatic. No one is downhearted here." And it was true; for he had made us feel with him that "this was a time when it was equally good to live or die."

And he brought not only fortitude but gaiety to its grimness. "We are awaiting the long-promised invasion. So are the fishes." Thus he broadcast to the French people from a basement amid the crashes of an air-raid. Hearing his chuckle we ignored the bombs and laughed with him.

He shared our tears. When he saw the gallant Londoners sticking up "little pathetic Union Jacks" among the ruins of their homes he was "completely undermined and wept." An old woman said: "You see he really cares - he's crying"

We recognised a human being - vulnerable to the simplest emotions - who shared our common clay and had invested it with a new glory. At last he was not only understood, but loved - as few Prime Ministers have ever been - (though still not by the Tadpoles and the Tapers, the pack of "little dogs and all" that yelp at greatness). He was in tune with the hour, with what he called the "tragic simplicity and grandeur of the times" - with the epic battle between freedom and tyranny, good and evil, life and death.

★

THOUGH a natural partisan, he had never been wholly at ease in party politics. In order to extend himself he needs a national, or better still, an international setting. He could never squeeze himself into the narrow mould of any party creed. Hence his strong preference even in times of peace for Coalition - a paradox in one so combative.

The Tory party seemed his natural home. But despite his historic sense of tradition he is untrammelled by convention. Despite his romantic feeling for the aristocracy his broad humanity has always carried him beyond the bounds of class. His adventurous, incalculable mind, forever on the move, could never be "contained" by the Conservatives and its questing, restless brilliance has often filled them with an unconcealed disquiet.

The Liberals in their great days gave him more scope and a better run. But though a democrat to the bone, a passionate libertarian with a strong sense of human rights and social justice, he was never quite a Liberal. He never shared the Liberal inhibition from invoking force to solve a problem. And although he revels in discussion he is, by temperament an intellectual autocrat.

In his fundamental outlook he has shown throughout his life a rare consistency. In changing from one party to another he has never sacrificed a principle (except perhaps once when, as a member of Mr. Baldwin's Government, he swallowed tariffs).

If he has not seen eye to eye with his contemporaries it is because so often he has seen further ahead than they did. All his great flashes of prophetic vision were at the time either denounced, derided or ignored. Yet every one of them has since been vindicated by events. He may well claim that his claim at Fulton gave birth to the North Atlantic Treaty Organisation and his appeal at Zurich to the Council of Europe and to the European Defence Community.

His great speech to the House of Commons on May 11, 1953, proposed a meeting at the highest level between the Great Powers was a brave bid for peace - "peace - the last prize I have left to win" - and the one he desired above all the others. Again he alarmed those (and there are many) who dare not take the risk of hope, and confounded others who had hurled him at the odious calumny of war-monger.

★

PERHAPS the most precious legacy of his statesmanship is the Anglo-American Alliance. He has always believed in the "yoked destiny" of the British and American peoples. "A child of both worlds" he became the great interpreter between his father's and his mother's countries.

The merging of friendly and like-minded nations into larger units has been a recurrent theme in his political thought. Hence his dream of an United Europe, his proposal for a ....

(Continued on P. 2. Col. 2)

THE NEW PRIME MINISTER

By

Colin R. Coote

PART of the task of those who sit in the gallery of the House of Commons is to discern budding Pitts and Hampdens among the back benchers. It is my boast that from the eyrie I discerned Anthony Eden in 1925, about two years after he first entered Parliamnet.

For so young a man - anyone in his twenties is reckoned a political baby at Westminster - he had both poise and presence. For one so temporamentally on edge, and so oratically commonplace he gave a remarkable impression of quietude and quality.

Parliament in those days had a large leaven of young men of Ministerial calibre. Here was one who matured as expected.

★ ★ ★

HIS success was, nevertheless, in some respects surprising. He never thrilled an audience in his life. He produced his effects in private by that elusive and indefinable quality called "charm" - which generally means giving an interlocutor the impression of being tremendously interested in what is being said.

In public, he scored because his every sentiment was felt to be fundamentally sincere. He convinced of his sincerity not only his own countrymen, but also foreigners.

His claim to be the next leader of the Conservative party after Sir Winston has long been unchallenged. This is the more remarkable because we are often told that the British electorate is far more widely concerned with bread-and-butter politics than with foreign affairs: and yet they undoubtedly liked and trusted one who fitted the Foreign Office like a glove.

The explanation is probably that Sir Anthony Eden has had that measure of luck which must often be joined to merit if a man is to rise to the top. It was his luck that two world wars had taught the British people that they must take an interest in foreign affairs. It was his luck that the interest concentrated on hopes of achieving peace through international organisations.

It was his luck to be young enough to enshrine the hopes of the younger generation and old enough to know at first hand the experiences of the older. So in the eyes of millions he became the bright young figurehead on the ship which successive British Governments were, slightly arthritically, trying to steer towards peace.

Nevertheless, he might have remained just another Minister if he had failed to possess ideas of his own about how peace was to be attained. His political stature was made by his resignation in 1938 from the post of Foreign Secretary in Chamberlain's Government.

It was not an easy decision for an ambitious young man to take - and Wolsey's advice to cast away ambition is one of the biggest pieces of political nonsense in history. The real reason was that the Prime Minister himself had virtually taken over the conduct of foreign affairs.

That was intolerably humiliating to a Foreign Secretary.

★ ★ ★

SO he went into the political wilderness with decision - though also with discretion. For though the comments of his Under-Secretary (the present Lord Salisbury, who resigned with him) on Munich may well be remembered to this day, I don't think anyone recalls what Eden said about that disastrous episode. But the resignation set the seal on his reputation for sincerity; and, in due course, gave him the reputation for having seen clear. It also cemented an already established harmony with Sir Winston. From that time forward it was a case of "Who touches Count Hannibal, touches Tavannes" - Sir Winston would never hear a disparaging word about him. Indeed, it is said that the only condition he made about taking office on the outbreak of war was that Eden should take office too.

Of course he had, and has, his critics. There are some that think his metal, though true, is light. There are others who recall that, on the rare occasions when he was not concerned with foreign affairs - at the War Office in 1940 and as Leader of the House - he showed a remarkable power of management and talent for originality.

★ ★ ★

IT must be added that he can and does command the respect and win the ascent of his opponents. In Parliament and outside, if he is not good fun, he is good value. He has a predisposition to search for the broad measure of agreement between parties which (if it can be found) may be essential to effective government in these days of an almost equally divided electorate.

If his oratory is colourless, his character is not; and those who have worked with him know that behind his poised and debonair appearance there often rage fierce and consuming fires.

One can never be quite sure of the mettle of a leader until he has led; and both the powers and the responsibilities of a British Prime Minister are infinitely greater of those of any departmental head. But training, knowledge, and courage are, in a high degree, the unquestionable assets of our new Prime Minister. He incarnates as well as any man the new Conservatism which provides Britain, almost alone among European countries, with a successful alternative to Socialism.

VICTORIA 2211
C.G.NORMAN & Co
LONDON DISTRIBUTORS 50 VAUXHALL BRIDGE RD. VICTORIA LONDON S.W.1
CITROEN
SALES – SERVICE
SPARE PARTS
REPLACEMENT UNITS
GUARANTEED USED CARS

The Daily Telegraph
and Morning Post
No.31,276 LONDON, TUESDAY, NOVEMBER 1, 1955
Printed in LONDON and MANCHESTER Price 2d.

TAYLOR'S
For TYPEWRITERS
ADDERS · CALCULATORS
Cash – Hire – or Hire Purchase
74 Chancery Lane (Holborn End) W.C.2
and at Maidenhead Tel: HOLborn 3793

PRINCESS MARGARET: NO MARRIAGE

CHURCH'S TEACHING & DUTY TO EMPIRE

PERSONAL MESSAGE: DECISION MADE ALONE

'UNFAILING DEVOTION' OF GROUP CAPT. TOWNSEND

The following personal message was issued by Princess Margaret from Clarence House at 7.21 last night:

"I would like it to be known that I have decided not to marry Group Capt. Peter Townsend.

"I have been aware that subject to my renouncing my rights of succession it might have been possible for me to contract a civil marriage, but mindful of the Church's teaching that Christian marriage is dissoluble and conscious of my duty to the Commonwealth, I have resolved to put these considerations before any others.

"I have reached this decision entirely alone and in doing so I have been strengthened by the unfailing support and devotion of Group Capt. Townsend. I am deeply grateful for the concern of all those who have constantly prayed for my happiness." The message was signed simply "Margaret."

GROUP CAPTAIN TWO HOURS AT CLARENCE HOUSE

Princess Margaret, who is third in successsion to the throne, was in Clarence House as her message was issued. She had returned during the morning from Uckfield, Sussex, where she and Group Capt. Townsend were the guests of Lord and Lady Rupert Nevill during the weekend.

Just over two hours later, at 6.17, he left alone. He returned to Lowndes Square and then drove back to Uckfield, at times reaching 65 m.p.h., arriving at 8 p.m. According to present plans, he would be returning to duty as Air Attache in Brussels on Monday of next week.

Both the Queen and Queen Elizabeth the Queen Mother had the text of Princess Margaret's personal message communicated to them before it was issued. Last evening the Queen Mother and Princess Margaret remained indoors at Clarence House, while the Queen and the Duke of Edinburgh attended the Royal Film Performance.

There is no question of cancelling public engagements. The first this week for Princess Margaret is to-morrow evening. She will attend the service of thanksgiving and rededication at St Paul's Cathedral to commemorate the 50th anniversary of Dr. Barnardo. On Thursday she will attend the evening presentation party at Buckingham Palace for Diplomatic Corps, and on Saturday and Sunday the annual Remembrance Day commemorations.

MEETINGS ALMOST EVERY DAY

Last night's announcement followed months of speculation which moved to a climax on Oct. 12, when Group Capt. Townsend, who will be 41 on Nov 22, returned to London from Brussels. He met Princess Margaret, who was 25 on Aug. 21, at Clarence House the next day.

They had been separated for two years and three months. Since their reunion, for which Princess Margaret travelled from Balmoral, they have seen each other almost every day, either at Clarence House or at the homes of friends.

The Group Captain had visited Clarence House five times, staying for two and a half hours on Oct 18. On no visit did he dine or lunch there, and the only member of the Royal family he met besides the Princess was the Queen Mother. At the time he was posted to Brussels, in July 1953, he had been chosen as Comptroller of the Queen Mother's Household.

The Princess and he have attended four private dinner parties in London. Their hosts were Mr. and Mrs. Mark Bonham Carter on Oct 17; Major and Mrs. John Wills on Oct 20; Mr. and Mrs. Michael Brand on Oct 21; and Mr. and Mrs. John Lowther on Oct 24.

TWO WEEK-ENDS IN COUNTRY

They have spent two week-ends as the guests of friends in the country. During the week-end of Oct 14-17 they were guests of Mrs. Wills at Allanbay, Binfield, near Wokingham, Berks. Mrs Wills is the daughter of the Queen Mother's sister, Lady Elphinstone. Last week-end their hosts were Lord and Lady Rupert Nevill, at Uckfield House, Sussex.

Group Captain Townsend reached the Lowndes Square flat of the Marquess of Abergavenny from Uckfield at 3 p.m. An hour later he drove in his green Renault to Clarence House.

IMMEDIATE RETURN TO UCKFIELD

When the Group Captain returned to Lowndes Square last evening he was pale and unsmiling as he got out of his car. Without going into the flat, he said that he was leaving for Uckfield immediately.

At 9 p.m. Group Capt. Townsend sent out the butler at Uckfield House with a message to reporters waiting at the gate with uniformed policemen. The message said:

"Group Capt. Townsend is not in a position to make any statement to-night. He is very distressed and will not be leaving the house. He will not be seeing anyone before 11 o'clock to-morrow morning."

Last Thursday Princess Margaret visited the Archbishop of Canterbury, Dr. Fisher, at Lambeth Palace. She stayed for nearly an hour. No statement about the visit was issued. At Lambeth Palace last night a spokesman said the Archbishop had no comment to make on Princess Margaret's announcement.

MORE FLEE TO WEST

From Our Own Correspondent

BONN, Monday.

The number of Soviet Zone refugees reaching West Berlin in October was 21,537, 3000 more than in September, and by far the highest figure since 1953, the year of the uprising.

SOUTH AFRICA ORDERS LOCOMOTIVES

From Our Own Correspondent

CAPE TOWN, Monday.

South African Railways have given the order for 23 Garrett-type locomotives worth £3 million to the firm of Beyer, Peacock, of Gorton, Manchester, announced the Minister of Transport, Mr. Schoeman, to-day. This has been made necessary because of trouble with 90 special condenser locomotives put into service recently.

They were built by the North British Locomotive Co. in collaboration with Henschels of Germany, at a cost of £72,000 each. A third of them are out of service and this has led to a serious traffic situation.

DECISION WAS MADE WITHOUT PRESSURE

PREMIER NOT ASKED FOR FORMAL ADVICE

By Our Political Correspondent

Princess Margaret has reached her decision without any form of political pressure having been brought to bear on any aspect of the matter.

The Prime Minister has made no representations to the Queen on the subject at any time, nor has he been asked to tender formal advice.

If the Princess's decision had been otherwise, political consequences would have been inevitable. These have been discussed informally among Ministers as a hypothetical problem.

At no time has there been formal consultation with Commonwealth Governments about the Princess's future. This necessity would have arisen only if she had made a different decision.

M.P.'S QUESTION

A question to the Prime Minister asking if he had contemplated legislation to amend the Royal Marriages Act, 1772, stands on the House of Commons Order Paper in the name of Col. Lipton (Soc., Brixton). Col. Lipton intends to persist with the question, but it is not likely to be reached.

He may make a further effort to raise the matter in the House, but the Speaker would rule out of order any discussion of the private affairs of the Royal family.

The Royal Marriages Act makes invalid the marriage of any member of the Royal family under the age of 25 without the Queen's consent. After the age of 25 such a marriage can be valid only if notice is given to the Privy Council and if there is no Parliamentary objection within 12 months.

STATEMENT ON U.S. RADIO

PROGRAMMES BROKEN

New York, Monday.

At least two New York radio stations broke into their regular programmes to-day to broadcast bulletins announcing Princess Margaret's decision. Television stations also interrupted their programmes.

Within minutes people began to telephone the British Consulate and Information Service here seeking confirmation. At United Nations headquarters the announcement became the chief topic of conversation. Bells attached to the news agency clanged throughout the Press section to draw attention to the news.

In scores of languages the news was repeated along the corridors and delegates from 60 nations met in groups to discuss the unexpected development. Though the delegations had been occupied with pressing international problems, Princess Margaret had been asked about in the lobbies for the past three weeks.

THE QUEEN AT FILM SHOW

PRINCESS ABSENT

Daily Telegraph Reporter

Film stars from five different countries were presented to the Queen when she attended the tenth Royal Film Performance at the Odeon, Leicester Square, last night.

A crowd of several thousand had braved a chill evening to greet Her Majesty. They lined the approaches to the cinema in ranks 15 deep.

Those who shouted "Where is Princess Margaret?" were disappointed. It was the first time she had not attended since the first Royal Film Performance in 1946.

The film chosen for last night's performance was an American one, "To Catch a Thief" starring Cary Grant and Grace Kelly. It was in aid of the Cinematograph Trade Benevolent Fund for which it raised about £30,000.

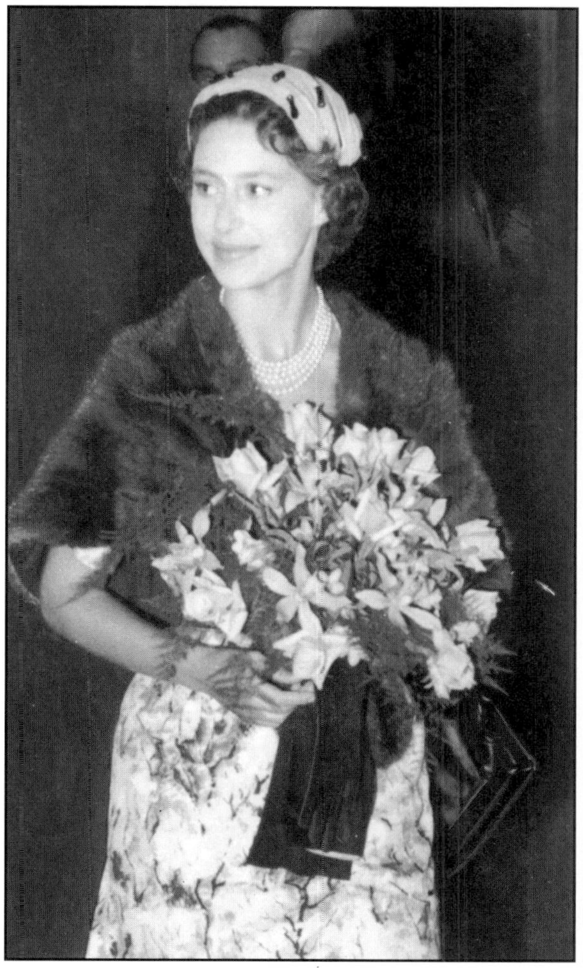

PRINCESS MARGARET

7 FIRMS CREATE FUND TO AID TEACHING OF SCIENCE

Daily Telegraph Reporter

Alarmed by the growing shortage of scientists, mathematicians and technologists in Britain, 17 major industrial organisations have established an industrial trust to assist the teaching of pure and applied science and mathematics in secondary schools.

More than £1,500,000 has already been guaranteed. The Trust, it is announced to-day, is to be known as the Industrial Fund for the Advancement of Scientific Education in Schools.

It is to be administered from 20 Savile Row by an executive committee of 13 prominent industrialists and educationalists.

The sponsoring companies plan to help independent and direct grant schools where facilities for teaching science subjects are "seriously inadequate through lack of capital resources". Public funds are available, the companies point out, for capital works at maintained schools.

CAPITAL GRANTS

The help will be in the form of capital grants towards building expansion, modernisation and equipment of science buildings. It will be available to schools in Britain, the Channel Islands and the Isle of Man.

The executive committee will adjudge and assess all applications. In arriving at decisions the committee will consider the volume and quality of the school's existing science teaching, the nature of the plans for improving it and steps which a school has taken to help itself.

On the committee are: Sir Wilfred Anson, 62, deputy chairman, Imperial Tobacco Co. Mr. R.A. Banks, personnel director, Imperial Chemical Industries; Sir Hugh Beaver, 65, managing director, Arthur Guinness, Son & Co. (chairman); Mr. E.H.O. Elkington, 64, director, Anglo-Iranian Oil Co.

Dr. Willis Jackson, 51, director of Research and Education, Metropolitan-Vickers Electrical Co.; Mr. W.E. Jenkins, managing director, Esso Petroleum Co.; Prof. Graham F. Mucklow, 61, Professor of Mechanical Engineering, Birmingham University; Mr. J.A. Oriel, President, Institution of Chemical Engineers.

Dr. F. Roffey; Dr. C.P. Snow, 50, Civil Service Commissioner; Prof. Sir Alexander Todd, 48, Professor of Organic Chemistry, Cambridge.

LD. DOUGLAS TO COMBINE B.E.A. POSITIONS

Daily Telegraph Reporter

The Ministry of Transport and Civil Aviation said last night that Mr. Boyd Carpenter, the Minister "understands that Lord Douglas of Kirtleside, chairman of British European Airways, is to combine temporarily his office with that of Chief Executive from Nov. 1."

Mr. Peter Masefield, present Chief Executive, is to join the Bristol Aeroplane Co. this month. There has been no serious suggestion of a successor to him in B.E.A.

It has recently seemed likely that no successor would be appointed, and that the board would be rearranged with the chairman combining the office of Chief Executive. This would be similar to the position on B.O.A.C., where Sir Miles Thomas, chairman, is also Chief Executive.

EXECUTIVE SOUGHT

The inclusion of the word "temporarily" in the announcement suggests that someone is being sought for the position.

Normally an announcement about the Chief Executive, who is appointed by the corporation, would be made by B.E.A., not by the Ministry.

In this case it was combined with a further announcement that Sir Arnold Overton, a part-time member of the B.E.A. board, will from today be a full-time member. During the illness of Sir John Keeling he is also to act as deputy chairman.

If suitable men are found for the position of deputy chairman of British Overseas Airways, and B.E.A.'s Chief Executive, the posts may be dispensed with, the work being undertaken by other members of the board.

MR. BUTLER HITS BACK AT MR. GAITSKELL

BUDGET CENSURE DEFEATED BY 329 TO 261

TALKS WITH T.U.C. TO-DAY

By Our Own Representative

WESTMINSTER, Monday.

Mr. Butler, Chancellor of the Exchequer, struck back vigorously at Mr. Gaitskell and other Opposition critics of his Autumn Budget when he spoke in the censure motion debate in the House of Commons to-night. The motion was defeated by 329 votes to 261, a Government majority of 68.

The Chancellor, describing Mr. Gaitskell's remarks on wage claims as "irresponsible" announced that the Trade Union Congress leaders had accepted an invitation to discuss the effects of the Budget with him, the Prime Minister and Sir Walter Monckton, Minister of Labour. They will meet to-morrow.

The censure motion charged the Government with incompetence, neglect and deceit. Mr. Butler seized on this and described the Socialists as "connoisseurs of incompetence".

SOCIALIST DELAY

1951 Crisis Recalled

He then revealed fully for the first time the extent of the crisis in 1951 when Mr. Gaitskell was Chancellor and "our life blood was being lost".

After two months' delay the only public measure announced was a saving of £40 million a year on cheese imports."So this marvellous roaring lion is a little mouse who can only gnaw at a piece of cheese."

Mr. Morrison, Deputy Leader of the Opposition, leading the attack, proposed selective import controls and price controls where necessary.

Winding up the debate, Sir Anthony Eden said it was absurd to pretend that the Budget proposals, though disagreeable, were harsh or cruel.

ANALYSIS OF VOTING

Our Political Correspondent writes:

The Government's majority in the censure division exceeded by four their paper majority of 64 over all other parties. Four Liberals voted with the Opposition. This means that there were three Socialist absentees.

TRIUMPH FOR CHANCELLOR

MR. MORRISON FAILS

By Our Own Representative

WESTMINSTER, Monday.

Mr. Butler's second-act appearance in the House of Commons debate this afternoon won him a resounding personal triumph. Mr. Morrison, who led for the Opposition, failed lamentably.

If the two debates had been written by a dramatist, the situation could hardly have been reversed more neatly. Mr. Morrison fluffed all his lines.

He was weak and hesitant, uncertain and unconvincing. It was as though he had unwillingly accepted a part he knew he could not play, and had gone on unrehearsed.

The Socialist benches lapsed from uneasiness to pure boredom. It was a pathetic failure. Here, some people felt, was a great performer who could never play Hamlet again.

SPARKLING REPLY

As Mr. Morrison's touch grew feebler, Conservative spirits rose. When the Chancellor got up to reply, the Government benches roared with acclamation, and when, with exemplary courtesy, he dismissed Mr. Morrison's speech as "thoughtful" they exulted.

It was Mr. Butler's turn to sparkle, and even the Socialists, Mr. Gaitskell prominent among them, enjoyed his best witticisms. But the ex-Chancellor was not let off easily.

Mr. Butler recalled, with the assurance of one who knows his part perfectly, the Socialist record in budgets. When he reached Mr. Gaitskell's own record in 1951, he had not been interrupted.

OVER 700 DEAD IN N. AFRICAN RIOTS

MOROCCO MASSACRE OF EUROPEANS

WOMEN AND CHILDREN AMONG VICTIMS

FIGHTING CONTINUES: MORE FRENCH TROOPS FLOWN IN

Nationalist rioting in Morocco and Algeria over the week-end cost at least 770 lives. Of these 528 were in Algeria, where the French yesterday claimed to have "stamped out" the insurrection.

Yesterday survivors related how tribesmen swept down on the Moroccan town of Oued Zem on Saturday and massacred 50 Europeans, includind women and children. It was one of the most savage events in French North African history, the Daily Telegraph special correspondent reported.

When cleared by the Foreign Legion after 5 ½ hours, the European quarter was in ruins and littered with mutilated victims. Yesterday the mining town of Khouribga, where the Oued Zem wounded were taken was also attacked and set on fire. The disorders were continuing last night.

From Paris last night 700 more troops were flown to Morocco. Earlier M. Faure, Prime Minister, said the riots followed "orders from abroad." It is thought he may have been referring to broadcasts in Arabic from Cairo. To-day talks open at Aix-les-Bains between French representatives and Moroccan leaders.

(August 22)

NEW ROAD CODE STARTS SAFETY DRIVE

A national road safety campaign starts to-day with the issue of two million copies of the Highway Code. The Code will be on sale at bookshops and bookstalls at 1d.

The five-colour booklet has 32 pages. It lays down in simple English, supported by illustrations, tenets of good road behaviour, including new rules which it is hoped all road users will observe at once.

Pedestrians are told to "be sensible about their right of way" on uncontrolled zebra crossings. Wait for a suitable gap in the traffic so that drivers have time to give way.

NEW CROSSING SIGNAL

Drivers giving way to pedestrians on zebra crossings are reminded to signal to other drivers their intention to slow down or stop. This signal is NOT an invitation to overtake.

When pulling up at the kerb, drivers are asked to give the signal meaning "I am ready to be overtaken" where appropriate. This will leave the slowing down signal to be used where the driver is not ready to be overtaken (as at zebra crossings).

(March 22)

TEDDY BOY 'WITH US ALWAYS'

The theory that Teddy boy fashions are due to the rising male birth rate, put forward in the current issue of Family Doctor, is discounted in an editorial in the Tailor and Cutter, which says: "The Teddy boy is with us in some strange shape or form, be he called Macaroni, knut, Johnny, spiv, lary boy, wide boy, Keelie or Charlie Farnes-Barnes.

"We do not deny that he dresses as smartly as he can in order to impress girls, but we reject the suggestion that in such behaviour there is something revolutionary."

(July 2)

18 NOBEL PRIZE WINNERS WARN WORLD

PERIL OF ATOM WAR

MAINAU, West Germany, Friday.

A group of 18 scientists who have won Nobel Prizes issued a warning to-day that the use of nuclear weapons might contaminate the world with radio activity and destroy whole nations. They came from six countries.

The scientists appealed to the world not to use modern weapons in war and to refrain from using force as the last means of politics. The appeal was issued at the end of their annual meeting.

It is to be sent to all Nobel prize-winners with a request for a signature.

It said: "We do not deny that perhaps peace is maintained in the world by this fear of the deadly weapons. Nevertheless, we deem it a delusion if Governments were to believe they could avoid a war for a long time by the fear of these weapons. Fear and tension have produced wars often before."

TRADITIONAL WEAPONS

"We also think it is a delusion to believe that small conflicts could in future always be decided by the traditional weapons. In extreme danger no nation will deny itself the use of any weapon that science and industry are able to produce."

In their appeal the scientists said that they had become the servants of science with enthusiasm. But they were "terrified to see that this science gives mankind instruments to destroy itself."

They said that the danger of radiation would menace neutrals as well as the warring Powers.

(July 16)

MRS. DALE'S DOG DEAD

By A Radio Correspondent

"Bo'sun", the 18-year-old mongrel dog of "Mrs. Dale's Diary," died on Wednesday. Listeners to the Diary yesterday heard Mrs. Dale say: "We are going to miss him terribly."

To-day he will be buried under an oak tree in the family's garden.

(February 18)

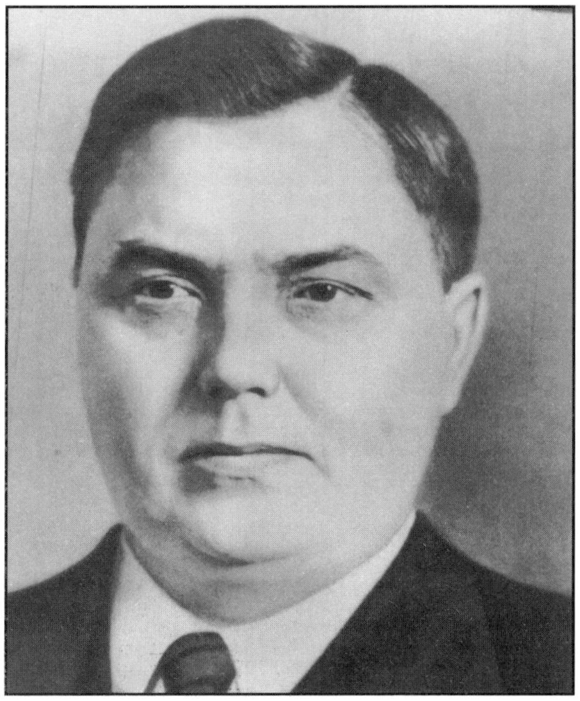

MR. GEORGI MALENKOV

MR. MALENKOV RESIGNS

POST TAKEN OVER BY MARSHAL BULGANIN

By David Floyd
Daily Telegraph Special Correspondent on Communist Affairs

Mr. Georgi Malenkov, 53, yesterday resigned his position as Prime Minister of the Soviet Union, which he assumed in March, 1953, after Mr. Stalin's death. Marshal Nikolai Bulganin, 59, hitherto Minister of Defence, was appointed in his place.

Mr. Malenkov submitted his resignation in a letter to the chairman of the joint session of the two houses of the Supreme Soviet in Moscow. The announcement came as a complete surprise to the many diplomats and Press correspondents in the public galleries who had attended the morning session expecting to hear a foreign policy statement.

As soon as the session opened Mr. Volkov, chairman, rose and read Mr. Malenkov's letter to the 1,347 deputies, who listened in silence. Then Mr. Puzanov, chairman of the Russian Federation, proposed briefly that Mr. Malenkov's resignation should be accepted and that he should be "released from his duties."

The deputies who voted Mr. Malenkov into power in March, 1953, unanimously voted him out. The session lasted only four minutes.

GUILT AND RESPONSIBILTY

The Soviet met again in the afternoon, when it appointed Marshal Bulganin Prime Minister and heard a long report on foreign affairs from Mr. Molotov, the Foreign Minister.

In his letter of "resignation" Mr. Malenkov gave as his reasons his lack of experience in administrative work and his "guilt and responsibility" for the failure of agricultural production. He indicated that he expected to be appointed to some other work and he promised that he would perform his duties "in the most conscientious manner."

(February 9)

CITY TO BE 'SMOKELESS'

OCTOBER ZONE ORDER

The City of London is to be a smokeless zone from Oct. 2. The Court of Common Council decided this at Guildhall yesterday.

No smoke may emit from any premises in a smokeless zone. Fires and furnaces are restricted to the use of approved smokeless fuels.

Mr. Stanley Cohen, presenting a committee report recommending a smokeless zone, said he had been given a Ministerial assurance that adequate supplies of smokeless fuel would be available.

An amendment, moved by Capt. Alfred Instone, that an inquiry should be held into the effects of smoke from Bankside power station was lost. Capt. Instone said the smoke was a danger to health and to buildings.

(March 4)

'SNOWMAN' TRACK SEEN BY BRITONS

From Our Own Correspondent
KHATMANDU, Thursday.

The British Merseyside expedition conquered 17 peaks in the Menlungtse range in its two months' stay. Mr. Alfred Gregory, the leader, said here to-day. The area was extensively surveyed and the maps would be given to the Royal Geographical Society.

The highest peak climbed was 22,000 ft, others were between 20,000 ft and 21,000 ft.

The Merseysiders saw old tracks of the Abominable Snowman at 18,000 ft. Mr. Gregory is flying to London from Calcutta on Saturday next. The other four members of the expedition will sail from Bombay in the first week in July.

(June 3)

SIR WINSTON DECIDES TO RETIRE

Sir Anthony Eden To Take Over

By Our Political Corrrespondent

Sir Winston Churchill has decided to retire from the Premiership in the near future. An announcement is likely before Parliament adjourns on April 7 for Easter and Sir Winston leaves for his holiday in Sicily.

Sir Anthony Eden will take over and will decide whether to hold a General Election as soon as possible or to wait until the autumn.

Well-informed Conservatives have always maintained that Sir Winston would give Sir Anthony the opportunity of six months in office before an election was necessary.

This pledge will be fulfilled, as an election need not take place before October or even spring next year. But Sir Anthony may well decide to dispense with the interval and proceed to the polls early in June, probably on June 16.

Undoubtedly one factor which has influenced Sir Winston in his decision is that the Russians have proved so intransigent that the likelihood of satisfactory high level talks has receded into the distant future.

CONTINUING AS M.P.

The announcement of his decision may be made after the dinner to the Queen and the Duke of Edinburgh at 10. Downing Street, arranged for a fortnight to-day. Sir Winston is expected to continue as a Member of Parliament.

Realisation that he intends to hand over to Sir Anthony will undoubtedly increase Conservative pressure for an early election. Many who were reluctant to appear to be taking advantage of the feud in the Labour party will agree that a change in the leadership of the Government is an appropriate occasion for an appeal to the country.

In particular, if the French ratify the Paris treaties a new diplomatic structure will be open. At the outset of this, a renewal of the Government mandate would be desirable.

The argument that six months in an electioneering atmosphere might do harm to foreign confidence in sterling would be strengthened by a change in the Premiership, which would be bound to stimulate overseas speculation about the election and its possible outcome.

DECISION BEFORE BUDGET

Conservatives hope for successes in the municipal elections, which conclude on May 14. This would give a good send-off to the campaign. But the decision between a June or October poll must be taken before Budget Day, April 19.

When Sir Anthony Eden becomes Prime Minister, there is little doubt that he will be succeeded at the Foreign Office by Mr. Macmillan, Minister of Defence. Few other changes are likely, for the time being at least.

(March 21)

PILTDOWN HOAX CONFIRMED

By Our Science Correspondent

An exhaustive re-examination of the "Piltdown remains" by 12 experts in various fields of research has "completely confirmed", the hypothesis of a hoax, and experimental work has shown that all the features of the Piltdown teeth and jawbone can be reproduced artifically. Findings are given in the latest bulletin of the Natural History Museum, published to-day.

Sir Gavin de Beer, director of the museum, writes in a foreword: "Not one of the Piltdown finds genuinely came from Piltdown." The remains, from which the experts of the time reconstructed the "Dawn Man," included part of a skull, a jawbone, a tooth and a number of crude tools of flint and bone.

Mr. Charles Dawson, a Sussex solicitor, now dead, took them to Sir Arthur Smith Woodward, keeper of the Department of Geology at the British Museum.

The report does not name the person believed to be responsible for the hoax, but it is no secret that those responsible for the report believe the man was Charles Dawson.

(January 21)

RUTH ELLIS IS SENTENCED TO DEATH

Life of Glamour and Jealousy

Daily Telegraph Reporter

Mrs Ruth Ellis, 28, a model and mother of two children, was sentenced to death by Mr. Justice Havers at the Old Bailey yesterday. It was the second day of her trial.

She was found guilty of murdering David Blakely, 25-year-old car racing driver, with whom she had been living. She had told the court that when she shot him outside a Hampstead public house she intended to kill him.

The Ruth Ellis trial will be remembered for two things, the speed with which it was conducted and the strange passion which Mrs. Ellis had for David Blakely, the man she murdered.

REVOLVER MYSTERY
Security For Debts

The murder investigations which exposed the secrets of her life failed to trace from where she got the revolver with which she committed the murder. It was a 0.38 Smith and Wesson of the type sent to Britain during the war under American lend-lease.

She claimed it was left with her, the six chambers loaded, by a man as security for debts in one of her bars about three years ago.

Ruth Ellis was born in Wales and her parents later moved to Manchester. After an elementary school education which she finished at the age of 14, she studied at a local drama school with the intention of becoming an actress, but gave this up when her family moved to London shortly after her 14th birthday.

She concentrated the whole of her interest in her life as a hostess. She met and married a dental surgeon in 1950 at Tonbridge, Kent. The marriage ended in the Divorce Court last February.

CAR ENTHUSIAST
Man's Racing Interests

As she built up her reputation as hostess, David Blakely was building up his life in car-racing. The son of a Sheffield doctor, he came of a good family and had a public school education at Shrewsbury.

At this stage the lives of attractive ash blonde Ruth Ellis and the athletic, ambitious young racing motorist crossed. To him she turned in the hope of gaining the security and the position she wanted.

At the time he was devoting his energies to assisting the designer, Anthony Findlater, to build the Emperor, a new challenger in the 1,500 c.c. racing car class.

FREQUENT QUARRELS
Stormy Relationship

They lived together in her flat over the club where she was now manageress but it was a stormy relationship. There were frequent arguments in which blows were struck and on one occasion a knife was used by her in a fight with Blakely.

She was earning £8 a week and commission on bar takings, but her tastes were expensive and her flat rent was £10 a week. The collection of expensive dresses and clothes that she required, she obtained as presents from men.

Her last attempt to keep Blakely and reach her ultimate goal of security and position was made three weeks before the murder. She started a six-weeks course at the school for deportment, poise and make-up near Oxford Street.

The course cost £20, but after starting it she realised she had lost Blakely. Then came the Easter week-end on which so much play was made by defence counsel at the trial.

Ruth Ellis who, friends said, could drink a bottle of Pernod a day without showing any effects, inwardly fumed and drank heavily all day. From the drawer in her dressing table she took the revolver, so long hidden, and went out.

(January 22)

CONSERVATIVES HAVE MAJORITY OF 59

NET GAIN OF 16 SEATS: TWO RESULTS TO COME

PREMIER THANKS NEW GENERATION

With the declaration of results in the General Election almost completed last night, the Conservative party increased its lead over all other parties to 59 and over the Socialists to 66. Two results were still to be announced .

Conservatives had a net gain of 16 seats, all from Labour. Socialists had won four from Conservatives.

All members of the Cabinet have been re-elected and Sir Anthony Eden's Government is free to continue in office without constitutional formality. The Prime Minister's first task will be to prepare a programme of legislation for the Queen's Speech at the State opening of Parliament on June 14.

Sir Anthony was given an ovation when he visited Conservative party headquarters yesterday. He paid tribute to the increased part played by the younger generation in the contest.

Mr. Morrison, Deputy Leader of the Opposition, said the Labour party had "lost the battle of marginal seats." It would have to make new approaches to party policy and ensure unity in its own ranks.

LARGER SHARE OF VOTES

The Socialists could not accuse their opponents this time of being returned on a minority vote. The total poll on 628 results was 76.82 per cent against 82.6 per cent in 1951.

Of this the Conservatives received 49.84 per cent. The Liberals secured 2.66 per cent. Aggregate votes for the main parties were:

	Gains	Losses
Conservatives	4	3
Labour	3	4
Liberals	-	-

There were many close contests and numerous recounts. In the new division of Glasgow Provan there were two recounts and the result was a majority of 180 for the Socialist. Another recount was at the new constituency of Baron's Court, won by a Socialist.

VICTORY "INEVITABLE"

A Conservative party spokesman said: "The result is inevitable - victory. The pattern is now shown to be consistent over the country with a swing of about two per cent in our favour."

Among notable changes were the defeat of two leading Bevanites. Mr. Michael Foot lost at Devonport to Miss Joan Vickers, Conservative Liberal-National, after a recount. Her majority was 100. This was a revised constituency. The other defeated Bevanite was Mr. Bing. He lost at Hornchurch to Mr. Godfrey William Langden.

The Foreign Secretary's son, Mr. Maurice Macmillan, gained the seat for the Conservatives at Halifax. He turned a Labour majority of 763 into a Conservative victory by 1,535. At Preston South, won by the Socialists in 1951 with a 16 majority, the Conservative won this time by 474.

At Bradford North, a revised division, Mr. Maurice Webb, a former Socialist Minister of Food, lost by 69 votes to a Conservative-National-Liberal, after a recount. He formerly stood for Bradford Central which has now disappeared.

(May 28)

State of Parties

The state of parties last night, excluding the Speaker, with results announced in 628 of the 630 constituencies was:

		At Dis- solution
Conservatives & Associates ...	343	322
Labour	277	293
Liberals	5	6
Others	2	3

Gains and losses in the divisions not affected by boundary changes were:

	Gains	Losses
Conservatives ...	11	1
Labour	1	10
Others	2	3

Gains and losses in the revised divisions on the basis of previous party holdings were:

	Gains	Losses
Conservatives ...	9	3
Labour	3	9

Two results - Argyll and Orkney & Shetland - will not be announced till to-day.

1954 HOUSING WAS POST-WAR RECORD

9 PER CENT INCREASE IN A YEAR

Daily Telegraph Reporter

A record in post-war house building was established in Britain last year. The number of permanent houses and flats completed was 347,605, an increase of 28,826, or nine per cent on the previous best in 1953.

Although it was 20,000 below the peak of pre-war days, the 1954 return, announced yesterday by the Minister of Housing and Local Government, was the fourth highest in any year. The total of permanent new homes provided since the end of the war is now 1,922,655.

A few months ago it was forecast that the 1954 total would reach 350,000. This was not achieved because bad weather impeded preliminary work during the summer and checked the completion rate in the last two months.

The number of houses completed in December was 30,662. This was a decrease of 2,843 or 8.5 per cent in December, 1953.

90,636 BUILT FOR SALE

The forecast that private builders now getting back into their stride would provide 90,000 homes for sale proved correct. The total for the year was 90,636.

This was 27,715 more than in 1953, an increase of 44 per cent. In 1953 the number of houses for sale was only 34,320.

There was a small reduction last year in the number of homes built for letting. The total was 256,969, a drop of 1,111 or 0.4 per cent.

Returns of homes under reconstruction also show a decline in those to let and an increase in those for sale.

	Dec. 1953	Dec. 1954	inc. or decrease
Letting	249,534	215,724	-34,110
Sale	59,608	75,753	+16,143
Total	309,442	291,477	-17,965

In Scotland, there was a drop in the number of houses completed during 1954. The total was 38,653 against 39,548 in 1953.

(February 4)

'BLACK BEAUTY' WAS A SUSPECT

DURBAN, Tuesday.

South African Customs men sent copies of "Black Beauty," Anna Sewell's novel about a horse, to the censors because they thought it had a suspicious title, it was disclosed here.

Also examined were a number of Enid Blyton's child books and a book called "Before We Go To Bed" - which the censors found was an anthology of bed-time prayers for children. The censors have banned 700 books so far this year.

(September 14)

AMNESTY OFFER TO MAU MAU TERRORISTS

NO PUNISHMENT FOR PAST CRIMES

From Our Own Correspondent

NAIROBI, Tuesday.

Sir Evelyn Baring, Governor of Kenya, to-day announced at a colourful baraza (tribal meeting) a new amnesty offer for Mau Mau terrorists. As he did so aircraft dropped leaflets in the forests and planes with loudspeakers broadcast the message.

The millions of yellow-paper leaflets printed in Kikuyu tell the terrorists that their last chance to save their lives is to surrender now. The oTer says: "You will not be hanged whatever you have done, if you com-n it no further acts of violence."

The Governor's speech to 11,000 Kikuyu men, women and children was received in complete silence. The Kikuyu Home Guard cheered and applauded as he left the platform.

Sir Evelyn Baring told the meeting that the terrorist morale had seriously deteriorated since the Army's big drive against the forest gangs known as Operation Hammer.

"END OF THEIR TETHER"

"We know that many terrorists feel they are reaching the end of their tether. We believe they are willing to give up the struggle, but are afraid of being hanged for past Mau Mau crimes."

He said he believed Mau Mau could be destroyed and added: "Signs of its destruction are now clearer than they have been at any time since the emergency started."

Sir Evelyn also announced amnesty terms for members of the Security Forces who may have committed offences. He said:

"The Government realising that for many months there was open violence and open fighting in the very heart of the reserves, and realising therefore the difficulty of supervision, has decided to bring no further prosecutions for offences committed by members of the security forces in the course of their services before to-day. But pending cases must go on."

PERIOD OF DETENTION

The new surrender offer to the terrorists guarantees that if they come in waving green branches they will not be prosecuted for terrorist offences they committed in the past, though they will be detained. But after to-day they will not be immune from prosecutions for any acts of violence committed in the future.

The authorities have promised fair treatment and proper feeding for those who surrender and say the

WRECKED MERCEDES BENZ AT LE MANS. The wreckage, still smouldering yesterday, of the Mercedes-Benz racing car which leapt a crash barrier and burst into flames in a crowded enclosure during the 24-hour race at Le Mans on Saturday.

LE MANS DEATH ROLL NOW 77

MERCEDES LEAPS INTO CROWD AT 150 m.p.h.

BRITAIN WINS RACE THAT BECAME GRIM FARCE

From W.A. McKenzie
Daily Telegraph Motoring Correspondent

LE MANS, Sunday.

Seventy-seven people, including 15 women and two children, lie dead here, and 77 are in hospital after the Le Mans road race, the most disastrous in the history of the sport. They were mown down yesterday by a Mercedes-Benz which leapt a barrier at about 150 m.p.h., somersaulting twice in a crowded enclosure.

The driver, Pierre Levegh, a veteran of 50 from Paris, was killed instantly. The race, which thus began in tragedy, continued for 22 hours more, a grim farce.

It came to an end at 4 p.m. to-day when Mike Hawthorn, Britain, won for Jaguars, for the third time in four years, at an average speed of 106,89 m.p.h., covering 2,565.5 miles in the 24-hour day and night contest but the spectators were too horrified to follow its fortunes. It was a farce, because the two remaining cars of the German team were withdrawn when they held a substantial lead, turning the winner's triumph into a glass victory.

The Mercedes withdrawal took place seven and a quarter hours after the disaster.

The makers explained that the decision was delayed so as to avoid a disorganised departure of spectators, which would have hampered rescue work.

period of their detention will depend on the Government's examination of each case.

The offer would not remain open indefinitely. The reverse side of each leaflet carries a safe conduct pass.

The amnesty offer to terrorists met with a mixed reception in Nairobi. Reaction ranged from bitter criticism to quiet optimism.

The most outspoken critic was Mr. Humphrey Slade, leader of the so-called moderate political group, who said he found it hard to express his horror and shame. He declared:

"This means that the men who have killed unarmed, inoffensive civilians by panga (knife) slashing, or strangling ropes or by slow torture, men who have disembowelled babies before their mother's eyes, men who have drunk blood and eaten the brains of their human victims are now assured they will not even be prosecuted, let alone hanged."

(January 19)

The same reason was given for the decision not to cancel the race.

(June 13)

MARILYN MONROE

STUDIO'S REPLY

The wish expressed by Marilyn Monroe, the actress, to make films based on "great literature" met with a less-than-lukewarm reception from Twentieth Century-Fox in Hollywood yesterday. A studio spokesman said: "Twentieth Century-Fox is very satisfied with both the artistic and financial results from the pictures in which Miss Monroe has appeared.

"These include: 'Gentlemen Prefer Blondes,' 'How to Marry a Millionaire,' and 'The Seven Year Itch'."

(January 10)

GREEN BELTS FOR ALL TOWNS

STEPS TO PREVENT URBAN SPRAWL

BAN ON NEW BUILDING IN RURAL ZONES

Daily Telegraph Reporter

Action was taken yesterday to stop the urban sprawl which threatens to spoil the countryside around many provincial towns. Mr. Sandys, Minister of Housing and Local Government, wrote to 140 local councils asking them to establish green belts similar to that round London.

Inside these belts there would be a general ban on further building. Small and large towns would have their rural areas protected in this way. The green belts, he says in his circular, are desirable to:

Check the further growth of a large built-up area;
Prevent neighbouring towns from merging into one another; and
Preserve the special character of the town.

Wherever practicable, the Minister recommends, the green belt should be "several miles wide." In the Greater London area provision has already been made in county plans for a band ranging from seven to 10 miles in depth.

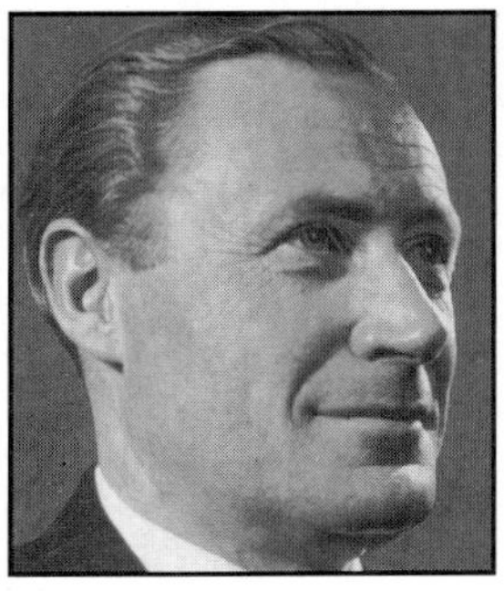

THE RT. HON. DUNCAN SANDYS, P.C., M.P.

Apart from some rounding-off of existing small towns and villages, no further urban expansion is to be allowed within it. A number of projects for housing estates and other developments in the belt have recently been rejected.

Now Mr. Sandys, as the Minister responsible for planning, has asked other towns in England and Wales to adopt this method. His letter has been sent to the planning authorities who approve or reject proposals for new building developments.

SKETCH PLANS SOUGHT

Proposed Boundaries

He draws their attention to "the importance of checking the unrestricted sprawl of the built-up areas and of safeguarding the surrounding countryside against further encroachment." He is satisfied that the only really effective way to achieve this is by the formal designation of clearly-defined green belts.

He asks them to submit as soon as possible sketch plans showing the approximate boundaries of the proposed belts. Informal talks with the Ministry, he suggests, might be helpful in preparing the proposals.

Eventually it would be necessary to amend the county development plan for each area for it to include the green belt. Detailed surveys would be needed to define precisely the boundaries.

"This procedure", the Minister acknowledges, "may take some time. Meanwhile it is desirable to prevent further deterioration in the position."

IMMEDIATE ACTION

Provisional Ban

Mr. Sandys therefore suggests that when the sketch plan has been submitted to him the planning authority should act on it forthwith. They would apply provisionally the ban on the construction of new buildings.

Inside a green belt, approval should not be given, except in special circumstances, for new building development or for change of use of existing premises for purposes other than those appropriate to a rural area. Existing villages should not be allowed to expand apart from a strictly limited amount of rounding-off or filling in.

(August 4)

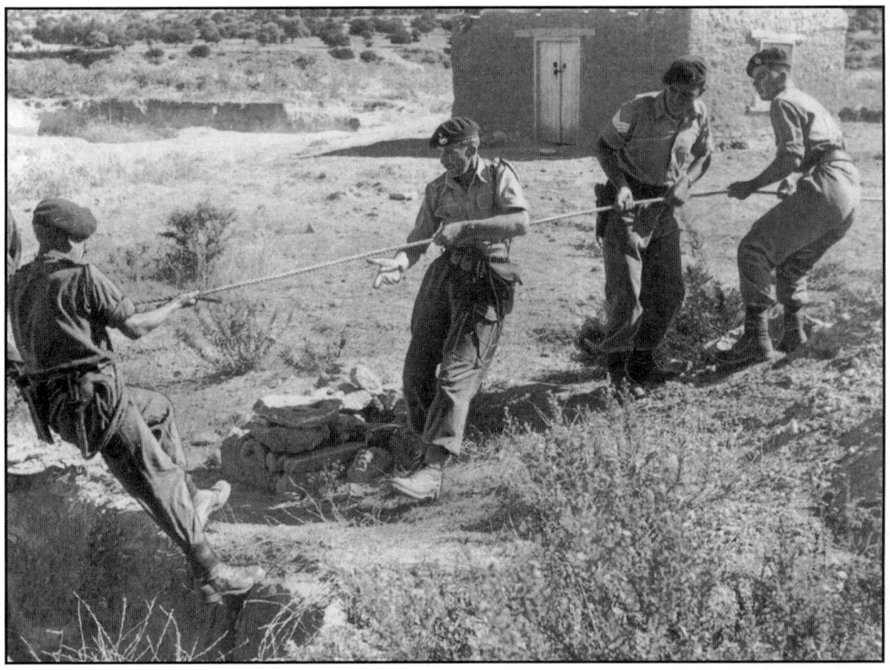

SEARCH FOR HIDDEN ARMS IN CYPRUS. Men of the 45 Royal Marine Commando hauling up one of the party which had been searching a disused well in Cyprus for hidden arms and ammunition. The arms were stolen from an Army store at Famagusta, after been taken from the Canal Zone.

MORE BRITISH TROOPS LAND AS TENSION RISES

SECURITY MEASURES REINFORCED

From Colin Reid
Daily Telegraph Special Correspondent

NICOSIA, Cyprus, Wednesday.

More than 600 men of No. 45 Royal Marine Commando were on their way from Malta to Cyprus to-day in three tank landing craft. At the same time 100 officers and men of the 1st Bn. the South Staffordshire Regiment were disembarking here from the Suez Canal Zone.

The Fleet carrier Ocean, 13,190 tons, is expected from Plymouth with military equipment, including troop-carrying vehicles but not tanks.

These moves to reinforce the public security organisation in the island coincide with increased tension between the Greek and Turkish-speaking sections of the population.

This tension was further heightened to-day by reports of riots, clashes and incidents in Istanbul, Smyrna and Salonika between Turks and Greeks over Cyprus, and of the Greek protest to the Turkish Government.

It was also announced that families of 15 Greek senior officers at the North Atlantic Treaty Organisation, South Europe Command, Smyrna, among those attacked, were to be evacuated from Turkey. This also deepened public feeling.

The newly arrived company of the South Staffordshire Regiment will be stationed at Troodos. This is the mountain resort where there is also a British Forces' holiday camp, near the summit of the Cyprian Olympus.

Agros, where the Cyprus Government imposed a week's curfew last month after arresting eight terrorists, and Amiandos, where masked men shot a police sergeant dead at his desk, are in the same area.

Two other companies of the 1st Bn. the South Staffordshires, who arrived here last month, are stationed at Nicosia. They are taking part in house-to-house searches and manning road blocks.

Leaflets being distributed here calling on Turkish Cypriots to unite in their own defence bear the name of a new Turkish underground organisation "Vulcano." The leaflets explain that the purpose of "Vulcano" is not to kill innocent people in a cowardly way.

But "any move against the Turkish community will be answered." "Eoka," the Greek underground movement, is now referring in its latest leaflets to the terrorism of last week-end as being only a taste of what is in store.

(September 8)

ARMED DETECTIVES FIND CACHE IN SHOP

NIGHT LONG WAIT FOR RETURN OF I.R.A. MEN

Daily Telegraph Reporters

All the arms and the remainder of the ammunition stolen by members of the Irish Republican Army from a Berkshire R.E.M.E. depot on Saturday were found by Scotland Yard yesterday in a derelict shop in Caledonian Road, Islington

A picked squad of 12 Special Branch detectives, armed with revolvers, had waited all night in the dark in rooms above the basement where the arms and ammunition were hidden. It was hoped that the I.R.A. men would return.

Others were standing by to give help if a shooting affray developed as was thought possible. When the police entered the basement they found an automatic pistol, cocked and ready for use, in an aclove by the stacked cases.

It had been decided when the detectives were allowed to move in that the members of the gang still at large had abandoned their haul because they realised that there was no longer any hope of getting out of London. Some of the weapons had been transferred to specially made wooden boxes which had been nailed down ready to be taken away. Others were only half packed as if the men had been disturbed.

A final check is being made by the War Office of the arms recovered. Some had already been found in a van stopped by police at the time of the Arborfield raid.

The police are satisfied that all the 67 guns and ammunition taken from the R.E.M.E. depot are now in their hands. Last night the arms were taken by van to Wokingham, Berks, police station.

The van was accompanied by patrol cars and six of the armed Special Branch men. The arms and the ammunition will be retained by the police until the conclusion of court proceedings against three men.

I.R.A GIVES ITS VERSION

The Irish Republican Army to-night in Dublin gave its version of the raid on Arborfield Depot. Ir came in the form of a communique signed by D. McDiarmid, Adjutant-General. It said:

"On Saturday a successful raid by a party of 10 volunteers was carried out on the Training Depot of No. 5 Bn R.E.M.E. at Arborfield, Berkshire. Entry to the camp was effected at 2 a.m. by the main entrance.

"Four men entered by the main barrier, passed the sentry and proceeded to the guardroom. Just as they entered the guardroom a further two men passed through the main barrier, seized the sentry and bundled him into the guardroom.

"The guard commander and the guard were then secured and bound and a new 'sentry' was posted at the main barrier dressed in the appropiate uniform. The remainder of the party then entered with transport.

SEARCH FOR KEYS

"The guardroom and the guard commander were searched for keys of the ammunition store and armoury. The keys were not in their usual place but were in possession of the armourer.

"Failing to find the keys, forcible entry was effected. The ammunition store was cleared and a quantity of selected weapons was taken from the armoury. The loaded vehicle then withdrew.

"A party of three including the 'sentry' remained behind to capture the four members of the picket returning to the guardroom from their two-hour beat of the camp at four a.m. and to ensure that no alarm was raised until the loaded vehicle had got clear away. This covering party withdrew at five a.m.

"All volunteers taking part in the operation have now been accounted for!"

(August 17)

ALL USE OF SALK VACCINE HALTED TEMPORARILY

Dr. Scheele, United States Surgeon-General, to-day requested that all inoculations with the Salk poliomyelitis vaccine be postponed till the vaccine already prepared or in its final stages of production had been re-tested. As fast as the vaccine was re-examined, it would be cleared for use on a "lot-by-lot" basis.

The first "re-appraised" batch would probably be available by the end of the week. There was no question of doubt as to the vaccine itself, Dr. Scheele said.

"In dealing with the lives of children it is impossible to be too cautious. But we have every faith that this vaccine - the brilliant achievement of an able scientist, Dr. Salk - is both safe and effective."

To-day's statement, which reveals that there have now been 52 cases of children developing the disease after inoculation - an increase of four - was prepared by a panel of experts who have been meeting for the past 10 days at the National Health Institute at Bethesda.

Dr. Scheele said that he wanted to assure "parents of all children who have received an injection of polio vaccine this spring that in the very best judgment of the Public Health Service they have no cause for alarm."

He pointed out that over five million children had been vaccinated with the Salk vaccine. To date there had been 50 cases of paralytic polio and two of non-paralytic polio among vaccinated children.

"SAFE AND EFFECTIVE"

In conclusion Dr. Scheele praised the work of Dr. Salk and stated: "His achievement is a milestone of medical progress. It promises a significant reduction in the occurrence of paralytic poliomyelitis.

"The public health service has every faith that within the ever narrowing limits of human fallibility the Salk vaccine is safe and effective."

(May 9)

EQUAL PAY BY INSTALMENTS

SIX-YEAR WAIT FOR WOMEN TEACHERS

By An Industrial Correspondent

The introduction by stages of equal pay for women teachers was recommended yesterday by the Burnham Main Committee and associated specialised committees. About 150,000 teachers are affected.

The recommendations follow the agreement between the Treasury and the Civil Service trade unions on equal pay for women Civil Servants.

Introduction of equal pay for teachers will be over the same period of six years. It will be made in seven instalments.

The proposals are subject to ratification by constituent associations and if approved by them to be submitted to the Minister of Education. If allowed the first instalment will be from May 1 and full equal pay should exist by April 1, 1961.

WELCOMED BY N.U.T.

Mr. Ronald Gould, general secretary of the National Union of Teachers, said last night: "Speaking on behalf of the 220,000 members of the union, which includes the vast majority of men and women in the profession, I welcome the decision of the committee. It will eliminate the discrimination which has existed against women.

"This is a historic day for the profession and especially for the union. It has been struggling to establish equality of treatment for men and women since 1919.

"The decision taken to-day is important. It makes a significant step towards placing teachers' salaries on a wholly professional basis."

"HIGHLY INDIGNANT"

The National Union of Women Teachers stated: "The union is highly indignant to learn that the representatives of teachers on the Burnham Committee have agreed to a scheme whereby women teachers will be expected to wait another six years before equal pay becomes operative."

(July 15)

SUBDUED OPENING BY RIVAL TV

'Shyness' Over Advertising

By L. Marsland Gander
Daily Telegraph Radio Correspondent

Commercial television, offering London viewers for the first time a choice of home pictures, last night made a subdued and dignified start, reminiscent of the B.B.C. senior service, when the Independent Television Authority opened its regular transmissions. It warmed up late in the evening.

George Formby was in rollicking form with his ukelele at the May Fair Hotel. He had to shout at noisy people attending a party there: "Shut up, you lot out there."

At the opening, the Hallé Orchestra played Elgar and there were speeches from Guildhall. A handicap for those who wanted to make a clear-cut choice was that the starting and finishing times of the individual rival items did not match exactly.

Associated Re-diffusion and the Associated Broadcasting Co., the two London commercial contractors, had joined forces for the evening. They were so shy of advertising that an hour elapsed before the first "commercial" appeared, an exhortation to buy toothpaste.

Though the programme then began to warm up, it did not become the hucksters' riot of vulgarity that opponents of commercial television had predicted.

LITTLE IMPACT

Rapid Announcements

I found the first advertisements disappointing. When they came at 8.13, in what was somewhat arbitrarily treated as a "natural break" in a variety programme, the "commercials" had a touch of anti-climax about them.

Jack Jackson, the compère, introduced them as "the moment you have all been waiting for." Three announcements followed one another in about two minutes, so rapidly that though watching intensely I found they made little impact.

The first was about a toothpaste and its delicious tingle. There was a lot of ice and snow and a glimpse of a rushing stream. I thought, then the picture of a girl somewhat needlessly scrubbing at immaculate teeth.

Then came a panel game parody which was rushed on, and Helene Cordet was seen easily picking on the solution of some unexplained riddle as a drinking chocolate. Finally a margarine held the screen.

Altogether during the evening 24 advertisers were represented. The picture quality was excellent. An attempt was made to force the pace of production but it did not succeed.

(September 23)

ACCOUNTANTS DENY COLOUR BAR

UNIVERSITY'S CHARGE

A suggestion that Midland chartered accountants operate a colour bar in refusing to accept coloured accountancy students as articled clerks was denied by an official of the Birmingham and District Society of Chartered Accountants yesterday. He added that accountants were restricted to a maximum of two articled clerks.

In his annual report Dr. Robert Aitken, Vice-Chancellor of Birmingham University, said the faculty of commerce was experiencing difficulty in placing coloured graduates in accountants' offices for training. "So far, its products have been welcome to accountants, with one exception, and have acquitted themselves well.

"This exception concerns coloured students from Africa. It seems that accountants in Birmingham and the Midlands have been so opposed to accepting them that some have had to return to Africa as graduates but without the professional qualifications they needed."

The official said: "The articles are usually arranged by a personal introduction of the prospective clerk to the principal, and in many firms the articles are pledged for a long period. Foreign students who come to Britain and go straight to university do not find the opportunities as easily as students who are resident in Britain; but there is no colour bar."

(February 11)

£212M. TO BE SPENT ON BETTER ROADS

PLANS FOR 2 NATIONAL MOTORWAYS

TOLLS MAY BE LEVIED: FLY-OVER CROSSINGS

MANY NEW BY-PASSES: DRIVE TO WIPE OUT BLACK SPOTS

Daily Telegraph Reporter

A national road building programme, involving a total expenditure of £212 million, was announced in the House of Commons yesterday by Mr. Boyd-Carpenter, Minister of Transport. The first stage of it, covering four years, will cost £147 million.

This instalment of the Government's plans to make the roads adequate for traffic needs will embrace bridge building, removal of black spots, trunk widening and scores of new by-passes. A start is being made this year.

In addition, towards the end of the four-year period work is expected to begin on a national motorway from London to Yorkshire, and later on a similar road from Birmingham to Preston. These will cost about £65 million.

For these roads, which would have fly-over crossings and junctions, and would be confined to motor traffic, the Government has in mind the levying of tolls "in suitable cases." But no decision has been made on this.

A Severn bridge is not included in the four-year plan. But a Firth of Forth crossing, either by bridge or tube on the river bed is likely. One estimate of the cost of tunnel on the river bed is £5½ million.

DARTFORD TUNNEL

Albert Bridge Rebuilding

The authorisation of £147 million will include major work such as:

Completion of the Dartford-Purfleet tunnel under the Thames to provide two traffic lanes. Passage will be subject to a toll, as in the case of the Mersey tunnel.

Reconstruction of Western Avenue to provide two traffic 30ft. carriageways between Park Royal station and Greenford Halt.

Rebuilding of the Albert Bridge, Chelsea.

Roundabouts at Elephant and Castle and the junction of Holborn and Kingsway.

TOLLS ATTACKED

"Burden on Industry"

In the opinion of the British Road Federation, the Government's whole scheme falls far short of the nation's urgent need. The Association stated last night: "The suggestion of tolls is scandalous.

"It is adding insult to injury to suggest that the first real roads to be built in Britain for motor transport should become an additional financial burden on trade and industry, and in turn on the entire community.

"The omission of any reference to the South Wales-Midlands motorways scheme, including the Severn bridge and tunnel, is astonishing, particularly in view of the fact that orders have already been made for 50 miles of motor-way in this scheme."

(February 3)

HUGHIE GREEN LOSES CASE

COSTS REACH £30,000

Hughie Green, the variety artist and producer, lost his conspiracy claim in the High Court yesterday.

After a 20-day hearing judgment with costs was entered for the B.B.C. and eight defendants.

Fourteen counsel, including seven Q.C.s., were retained. The costs will not be worked out for some time. They are estimated to be £30,000. The figure includes daily running charges of about £1,000.

Mr. Harold Brown, Q.C., for Mr. Green, asked for a stay of execution on costs pending a possible appeal. Opposing the application, Mr. T.G. Roche, Q.C., for Mr. Meehan, said he understood from the evidence that as soon as the case was over Mr. Green was going to leave the jurisdiction of the court.

(May 29)

PRIMATE FREED TO PLACATE PEASANTRY

HUNGARY MANOEUVRE

From Our Own Correspondent

VIENNA, Sunday.

Tactical moves in foreign and domestic policy are believed in Vienna to lie behind the Hungarian Government's decision to give provisional freedom to Cardinal Mindszenty, Primate of Hungary. He was sentenced to life imprisonment in February, 1949, on charges of "treason."

The decision was announced in a surprise communiqué from the Hungarian Ministry of Justice, broadcast by Radio Budapest last night. It said that in view of the Cardinal's age and state of health he had been permitted to "interrupt his prison term." He is 63.

The step was said to have been taken at the joint request of the Cardinal and the Hungarian Roman Catholic bench of bishops, who are now being allowed to choose a residence for him.

Inside Hungary the step has probably been aimed most of all at the peasantry, who are deeply religious and 65 per cent Roman Catholic. The timing here is also favourable because work on the Hungarian harvest has just started.

It is quite clear that this latest Communist retreat does not mean their attacks on religion as such will be relaxed. Indeed the latest evidence from Hungary shows that this ideological offensive has lately been redoubled.

(July 18)

U.S. TORNADOES IN PATH OF ATOMIC CLOUD

From Our Own Correspondent

NEW YORK, Friday.

Storms and tornadoes swept eastwards across Indiana, Ohio and Pennsylvania to-day. At least four people are missing, believed killed, and a trail was left of millions of pounds of damage to property. Winds of 98 m.p.h. were reported.

In their path came hail, lightning, thunder and rain. They tore off roofs and ripped down power lines.

GALES AFTER EXPLOSIONS

Though meteorologists insist that there is no connection with the atomic explosions in Nevada it is noted that the dust-storms, gales and tornadoes occurred soon after Monday's big explosion.

(March 12)

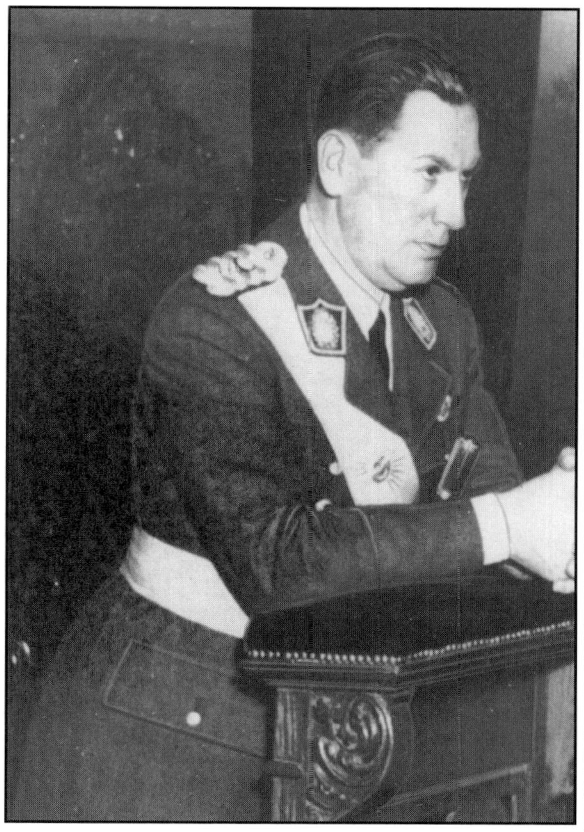

PRESIDENT PERON

PERON FORCED TO RESIGN

CEASE-FIRE ORDERED BY NEW JUNTA

As revolutionary forces extended their control over large areas of Argentina yesterday President Peron, 59, announced that he "insisted" on offering his resignation. He suggested that the Army was best qualified to take over control.

Gen. Lucero, Army Minister and Commander of the "Forces of Repression," who read the President's statement over the radio, later broadcast his own resignation. Before doing so he announced that Gen. Peron had authorised the creation of a military junta to negotiate peace.

Reports that Vice-President Teisaire and the entire Cabinet had also resigned were not immediately confirmed. But in a declaration late last night the new junta, announcing their readiness to open talks with the insurgents, stated:

In view of the resignation of his Excellency the President of the Republic and the decision of all other legal powers to accompany him in his determination, the Army has decided to take over the situation and invites the people to maintain calm in present circumstances.

The junta had earlier ordered Government troops to cease fire and called on the insurgents to do likewise. There followed an announcement over the State radio that it had been agreed to suspend fighting. Talks would open at midnight.

Late last night there was no news of Gen. Peron's whereabouts. Senor Chaves, Paraguayan Ambassador in Buenos Aires, denied that the President had taken refuge in his Embassy or had flown to Asuncion, Paraguay.

(September 20)

ENDING SCHOOLS SEGREGATION

SPEED IN U.S. URGED

WASHINGTON, Tuesday.

The United States Supreme Court to-day directed that segregation of white and Negro schoolchildren be ended as soon as feasible. A ruling read by Chief Justice Warren said that local conditions could be taken into account.

Lower courts could decide whether a prompt and reasonable start towards full compliance was being made by local authorities. Chief Justice Warren said the high tribunal expected full compliance with its decision as early as practicable.

Representatives of Southern States have argued before the Supreme Court against its ruling last year that segregation is unconstitutional. To-day the court upheld the validity of the decision.

COMMUNIST APPEAL

The Supreme Court agreed to-day to review next autumn the Communist party's appeal from lower court rulings upholding the constitutionality of the 1950 Internal Security Act.

(June 1)

PAKISTANI WOMEN PLAN TO STOP POLYGAMY

From Our Own Correspondent

KARACHI, Sunday.

The agitation among the Pakistani women against polygamy, precipitated by the second marriage of Mr. Mohammed Ali, the Prime Minister, is growing. A resistance plan of action has now been drawn up by the militant feminist organisation, the All-Pakistan Women's Association.

Punitive measures proposed include the social ostracism of erring husbands and second wives, as well as of the parents of the latter; spying on suspects, and, in extreme cases, direct action, like picketing.

The Association has set up a secret committee of vigilance, which is to enlist volunteers for watching erring or potentially erring husbands. Reports are to be passed on to wives and warnings sent to the parents of prospective second wives.

(May 9)

MR. PHILBY'S 'THIRD MAN' CHALLENGE TO M.P.

'Repeat Charge Outside and Produce Evidence': Friendship With Burgess

Daily Telegraph Reporter

Mr. Harold Philby, former First Secretary at the British Embassy in Washington, yesterday made a statement on his own position in the Maclean-Burgess affair. He challenged Lt.-Col. Lipton, Socialist M.P. for Brixton, to produce evidence to support his allegation of Mr. Philby's "dubious third man activities."

Mr. Macmillan, Foreign Secretary, said in the House of Commons debate on Monday that there was no reason to identify Mr. Philby with the "third man," if in fact there was one.

A slim, dark man of 43 with a quick smile and rapid nervous gestures, Mr. Philby held a Press conference that crowded his mother's Kensington flat. He gave a crisp "no comment" to dozens of questions.

He said that the Official Secrets Act, and concern for international problems of "great delicacy" raised by the case and for the efficiency of the security services prevented him from discussing the Maclean-Burgess affair.

M.P.'S QUESTION

"From a Safe Place"

His even good humour in answering or blocking questions gave way to a touch of anger as he said: "On Oct. 25, Col. Lipton, from a safe place sneaks into a supplementary question the charge that I was guilty of a crime for which the maximum penalty is 14 years or something of that order.

"He produced no shred of evidence to support that threat, under which I have now lived for 12 days.

"Last night in the House Col. Lipton again refused to produce evidence, refused to withdraw the charge and refused to repeat it outside the House. In justification of his refusal to repeat it outside the House, he indulged in the extraordinary verbal gymnastic of saying that even Mr. Philby has not asked him to do so.

"I suggest he repeats the charge outside the House and produces evidence or, if the evidence really is so secret, he should forward it, as he suggests, to a judicial member of the Privy Council and meanwhile withdraw the charge until the member has had a chance of examining the evidence and pronouncing upon it."

REQUEST TO RESIGN

"Imprudent Association"

Mr. Philby said his own political development had been unspectacular. He was a member of the Socialist Society at Cambridge. "I have never been a Communist, though I knew people who were Communist at Cambridge and for a year afterwards.

"The last time I spoke to a Communist, knowing he was one, was in 1934." He had always been "on the Left."

NO REPLY BY M.P.

"Statement in House"

Lt.-Col. Lipton did not reply to the challenge of Mr. Philby last night, but said: "I propose to make a statement in the House."

It is understood that Col. Lipton will seek the permission of the Speaker to make a personal statement. Such statements by leave of the Speaker are made immediately after questions in the House of Commons.

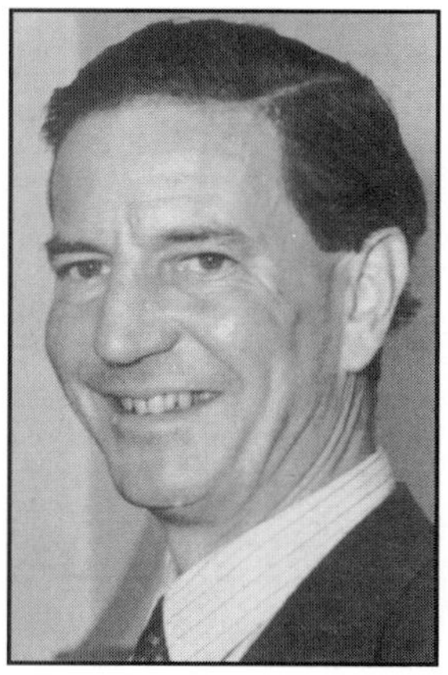

MR. H. A. R. PHILBY

(November 9)

NEW ATTACK ON HEIGHT RECORD

CANBERRA'S FLIGHT

The Canberra jet bomber which set up an altitude record of 63,668ft. in May, 1953, made another attempt on the record yesterday. The result will not be known until recording instruments have been studied.

Powered by two Bristol Olympus engines, the aircraft was piloted by Wing Cmdr. Walter Gibb, assistant chief test pilot of the Bristol Aeroplane Company. It took off from Filton and stayed in the air for about an hour. It carried observers of the Royal Aero Club and the Royal Aircraft Establishment. On landing films of instrument readings were taken away. From these, calculations will be made for confirmation of whether the record has been broken.

(August 30)

TITLE MAY GO INTO ABEYANCE

MOVE BY M.P.

Mr. Wedgwood Benn, 29, Socialist M.P. for Bristol South-East, yesterday signed an instrument of renunciation declaring his "irrevocable desire" to cease to be the heir to the "name, state, degree, style, dignity, title and honour" of Viscount Stansgate, his father, who is 77. His family support him.

But the renunciation has no validity until both Houses of Parliament have passed the Wedgwood Benn (Renunciation) Bill. This is a personal Bill to enable Mr. Wedgwood Benn to relinquish the title and thus remain an M.P. after the death of his father.

It is now proposed that the title shall be "deemed to go into abeyance" and shall remain in abeyance during the lifetime of Mr. Wedgwood Benn. When he dies, the title shall be fully restored and shall descend to the heir male next in succession.

(February 16)

FLEET-ST. STRIKE CALLED OFF

EMPLOYERS' ORIGINAL PAY OFFER ACCEPTED

FRESH NEGOTIATIONS WITHIN 8 WEEKS

STOPPAGE BY 700 COST £3m. AND MADE 23,000 WORKLESS

THE DAILY TELEGRAPH appears to-day for the first time since Friday, March 25. A strike of 700 electricians and maintenance engineers which stopped production of national daily, Sunday and evening papers, printed mainly in London, ended yesterday.

It was called off following a settlement on Tuesday night between the Newspaper Proprietors' Association, the Amalgamated Engineering Union and the Electrical Trades Union, whose district officials ordered the stoppage, and newspaper trade unions belonging to the Printing and Kindred Trades Federation, of which the E.T.U. and A.E.U. are not members.

Before the strike the two unions had demanded a wages increase of £2 18s 6d a week. The employers offered to consolidate a 23s cost-of-living bonus into the wage and give increases ranging between 9s and 12s. When those were rejected they proposed arbitration. The two unions rejected arbitration and ordered a stoppage.

After many talks, in which the Ministry of Labour and the Trades Union Congress were involved, the leaders of the A.E.U. and the E.T.U. decided on Tuesday to accept the offer of the N.P.A. pending further negotiations, which are to start within eight weeks.

The strike deprived the public of the main source of its news for 26 days, cost the industry £3 million, threw 23,000 other workers in newspaper offices, and workers in ancillary trades, out of employment, had serious repercussions in the City, in sport and entertainment and in many industries, and lost a total circulation of nearly 700 million.

(April 21)

100 HUNDRED YEARS ON

TO-DAY THE DAILY TELEGRAPH celebrates its hundredth birthday. It has to thank a host of readers who have already wished it many happy returns on an occasion notable alike in the life of individuals and of institutions. As the article on this page shows, there have been both peaks and valleys in its journey through a century, but the Centenary finds it upon a peak. For the fact the thoughts of all now associated with the paper turn in gratitude to the giants of the past.

It would be out of character to expatiate upon what THE DAILY TELEGRAPH tries to be and upon the causes which it tries to serve. Its news and views can be left to speak for themselves to-day and every day. EMERSON once said of a newspaper that it did "its best to make every square acre of land and sea give an account of itself at your breakfast table." That is not a bad ambition to cherish on a newspaper at such a milestone in its history.

(June 29)

THE BEACH NEAR JOSS BAY, North Foreland, where Green turned the carbine on himself after the shooting affray.

U.S. AIRMAN KILLS 3, WOUNDS NINE

CHASE ENDS IN DEATH ON KENTISH BEACH

Daily Telegraph Reporter

A gun battle on the beach near Broadstairs, Kent, in full view of holiday crowds, ended a shooting affray yesterday in which an American coloured airman killed three Servicemen, including an R.A.F. corporal, and wounded nine other people, mostly civilians.

The airman had gone berserk at the United Air Force base at Manston, near Ramsgate. Armed with a 0.45 Service revolver and an automatic carbine, he ran through the camp shooting into the huts and at cars.

He then commandeered a car by threatening the driver with the revolver. A widespread hunt led to the beach near Joss Bay, North Foreland, where the airman was cornered.

Holidaymakers took cover as bullets whined and ricochetted among the rocks and the others watched from the cliffs above. The battle lasted an hour. It ended with the man turning the carbine on himself. He was found dead among the rocks.

He was Napoleon Green, 21, whose home is in Chicago. He had hitherto had a good record, but had recently been charged with stealing a wallet.

He had denied the theft and a police inquiry was taking place at the base. It was likely that he would face a court martial.

Shortly before the shooting began, Green opened the door of a barrack hut. He startled the occupants by saying: "I am going to kill a couple of you."

The American Chargé d'Affaires, Mr. Butterworth last night expressed to Mr. Macmillan, Foreign Secretary, his "profound distress over the tragic occurrence at Manston R.A.F. base." He asked him to convey the United States Government's deep regret to the British Government, to the injured and to the families of the innocent victims.

(August 25)

BLIZZARD SWEEPS WEST COUNTRY

MAIN ROADS BLOCKED, CARS ABANDONED

The worst blizzard since 1947 swept the West Country yesterday. Last night snow blocked almost every main road west of a line from Exmouth to Taunton and frost made surfaces icy.

Dartmoor was isolated. Farmers spent hours digging sheep from 10-foot drifts. Using torches, they searched by night and rounded up missing stock. Moorland ponies were fed by the R.S.P.C.A. and wild red deer came down to the villages to forage.

Many moorland villages were isolated. Seventy vehicles were abandoned in Cornwall. Snowploughs rescued drivers and passengers in five-foot drifts on Bodmin Moor.

Heavy snowfalls were moving north last night. Falls were reported in the Midlands, Yorkshire, Lancashire, the Peak District and East Anglia. In Scotland pilots flying hay to drop to snowbound sheep radioed that thousands of animals were already dying.

Scotland had the lowest temperature recorded for 60 years. At Braemar it fell to 13 degs below zero, 45 degs of frost.

(February 24)

ELECTRICITY FROM 12 ATOM STATIONS

£300M. PLANS: FIRST IN ACTION BY 1960-61

By Leonard Bertin
Daily Telegraph Science Correspondent

A £300 million industrial atomic energy programme for the construction and the completion of 12 full-scale nuclear power stations within the next 10 years was announced in a White Paper on atomic energy published yesterday.

It is the first programme of its kind and size in the world.

The first two stations, each with two reactors, are to be started in mid-1957 and will be in operation by 1960-61, at a cost of £30-£35 million. Two further stations are to be started in 1958-59, in operation by 1963.

Building of four others is planned to start in 1960 and four more 18 months later. The programme is provisional. It is likely to be the subject to constant modification in the light of new knowledge.

The initial contribution of the new stations will be small, equivalent to about five million tons annually of coal.

This is only one quarter of the increased annual demand for electricity expected by 1965. Long before this initial programme is complete, however, work will have started on more powerful and more efficient reactors.

By 1975 these should be saving 40 million tons of coal a year.

Mr. Lloyd told a Press Conference afterwards that he regarded the statement he had made in the House of Commons as the most momentous any Minister of Fuel and Power had made. It offered the possibility of a "new industrial revolution," with continuing increase in productivity and in the standard of living in Britain.

NO DANGER

Sites Away from Towns

No sites have been chosen yet for the new stations. From a safety point of view there is no objection to siting the reactors near towns according to Sir Christopher Hinton, Director of the Atomic Energy Authority's Production and Power Division.

The types of pile to be used, he said yesterday, are inherently safe and could not blow up. Nevertheless, they will probably be sited away from centres of population to allay possible public anxiety.

TEDDY BOY SUIT TO ATTRACT A MATE

DOCTOR'S VIEW

Edwardian suits are the outcome of the increasing ratio of males to females. Another effect, from the same cause, is that girls are less particular about their dress.

These conclusions are drawn by Dr. J. MacAlister Brew, writing in the July issue of Family Doctor, published to-day by the British Medical Association. She is Education and Training Officer to the National Association of Mixed Clubs and Girls' Clubs.

She says that after the 1914-18 war there was a large surplus of women. To "guarantee pursuit" girls took great care in their adornment, while all the young male needed was to be clean, personable and manly.

MALE INCREASE

Now the situation had changed. In the marriageable age groups the sexes were about equal, but the total of males would increase while that of females would decrease.

"When any sex is outnumbered at the mating season, it will seek to attract by personal adornment. This is now finding expression at the adolescent level in terms of the Edwardian suit."

It would be a mistake to imagine it was merely the uniform of the young gangster. "There is no doubt that modern young women like the Edwardian fashion. The evidence is clear in any dance hall."

At inexpensive dance halls, for every girl wearing a pretty frock there was another in a sweater that might be more than a little grubby, wearing jeans or ballet slacks and with hair tied up in a horse's tail. When the girl was "able to pick and choose her partners she need not spend so much time on personal adornment."

QUARRELS FOSTERED

In the past some of the bitterest quarrels at youth clubs were between girls about boy friends. Now the quarrels broke out between the boys and some girls fostered them deliberately.

(June 28)   **(February 16)**

POET WALKS OUT DURING LUNCHEON SPEECH

LORD SAMUEL'S CRITICISM OF OBSCURE MODERN VERSE

Daily Telegraph Reporter

Mr. Stephen Spender, the poet, walked out of a Foyle's literary luncheon in London yesterday in the middle of a speech by Viscount Samuel criticising the obscurity of much modern verse.

Saying that it was largely the fault of the poets that poetry had received such scant recognition from the public between the wars and to a certain extent since, Lord Samuel condemned "this fashion of deliberate and perverse obscurity."

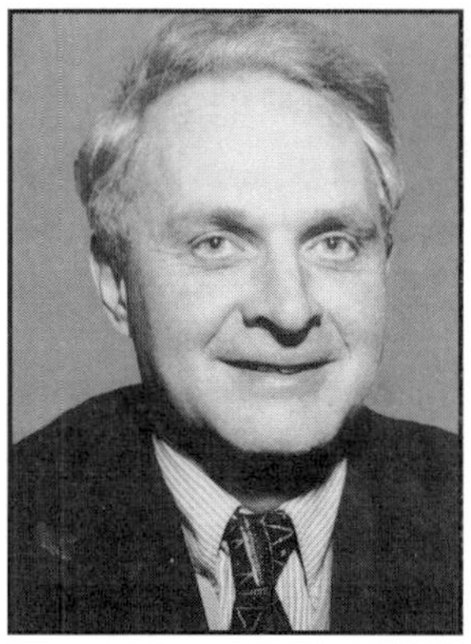

STEPHEN SPENDER

"On going through the anthologies of several years, I was appalled to find the degree to which this vice of obscurity was afflicting British poetry.

"I could give several examples, but I will only read one, and I will read it slowly so that you may appreciate whatever beauties it may have.

"It appeared in an anthology, I think for 1950 or a little earlier, and the title of it is "A Grief Ago." Lord Samuel then read the following lines:

A grief ago
She who was who I hold, the fate and flower
Or, water-lammed, from the scythe-sided thorn
Hell wind and sea.
A stem cementing, wrestled up the tower,
Rose maid and male
Or, masted venus, through the paddler's bowl
Sailed up the sun.

Lord Samuel did not name the author of the late Dylan Thomas.

"I AM GOING"

Top Table Departure

Before Lord Samuel had completed the quotation, Mr. Spender, sitting at the top table between Miss Rose Macaulay and Mr. John Neville, of the Old Vic, pushed back his chair. "I am going," he said to Miss Macaulay, and with that walked out through a door behind the top table.

Apparently unaware of the incident, Lord Samuel continued his speech. "That" he said, "was one of six or seven examples, each fully as incomprehensible as that one. I regret to say, reading the anthologies of the past two or three years, one finds many poems of such mystification.

"Self-conscious posturing," he added. "One finds tremendous intellectual effort. But one finds that the writer has not realised the distinction between having something to say and having to say something." He quoted the words of Keats: "If poetry comes not as naturally as leaves to a tree, it had better not come at all." [Letter to John Taylor in 1818.]

Later he said: "The author, I need not give his name, of that quite incomprehensible poem developed in later life into one who has written perhaps the finest poem of our time."

£250 PRIZE AWARD

Outstanding Work of 1954

Lord Samuel specifically excluded from his strictures the works of Mr. John Betjeman, to whom Mr. William Foyle presented his annual prize of £250 for the outstanding volume of poetry published in 1954.

His "A few late chrysanthemums," said Mr. Foyle, was unique in his experience in the book trade as a "best seller" which had actually been out of stock.

Accepting the cheque, Mr. Betjeman said: "I don't know who wrote the thing Lord Samuel read out."

MR. SPENDER EXPLAINS

Egg-Thrower Wanted

Mr. Spender said last night that he thought someone should have been permitted to throw an egg at Lord Samuel. "There was something quite false about sitting and listening to an attack on modern poetry at a luncheon given to honour a modern poet."

This was particularly so since Dylan Thomas some years ago had received a similar prize, and since John Betjeman was an admirer of Dylan Thomas. There should be more controversy in English art: we were too genteel, but attacks should be made on occasions when it was possible to answer back.

Although the Dylan Thomas poem quoted was obscure, it was also very beautiful. There were many occasions when phrases from it came into one's head. In any case, it was not fair to lift a piece out of context for criticism.

Mr. Spender emphasized that his walk-out was not meant as an insult to Foyle's. He thought their work was admirable and the prize for poetry a splendid thing.

He had left the luncheon as a "gesture" against Lord Samuel. He was sure no good would come of it, but he felt that gestures should sometimes be made, even though they might not be effective.

(March 12)

INDEPENDENCE FOR THE TATE

The Tate Gallery, it was announced in Parliament yesterday, is to become an independent institution on Monday. On that day the National Gallery and Tate Gallery Act comes into force.

This will make the Tate, for the first time since it was opened in 1897, independent of the National Gallery.

In a written reply, Mr. Brooke, Financial Secretary to the Treasury, states that Sir Winston Churchill proposes that the Tate's existing 10 trustees should continue in office until the expiry of their respective terms. They are:

SIR COLIN ANDERSON, whose term expires on May 30, 1959: MR. EDWARD BAWDEN, May 23, 1958; PROF. W. COLDSTREAM, March 31, 1955; MR. JOHN FREEMANTLE, May 20, 1960; PROF LAWRENCE GOWING, July 26, 1956; MR. HENRY MOORE, July 26, 1956; MR. JOHN PIPER, Nov 17, 1961; MR. PHILIP DENNIS PROCTOR, May 2, 1959; PROF. LIONEL ROBBINS, July 22, 1959; and SIR OSBERT SITWELL, May 23, 1958.

Sir John Rothenstein, Director of the Tate Gallery, now succeeds Sir Philip Hendy, Director of the National Gallery, as accounting officer for the vote of the Tate Gallery. He will be responsible to the trustees in financial matters as well as for day-to-day administration. Sir Philip thus ceases to be an ex-officio member of the Tate board.

(February 12)

DISNEY SPANIEL HEROINE

Walt Disney's new full-length cartoon, "Lady and the Tramp," based on the book by Ward Greene, and telling the story of a young female spaniel of aristocratic background bridges the social barrier to form a friendship with a young male mongrel from "the wrong side of the tracks" had its premiere in New York last night. Critics to-day were generally appreciative.

(June 25)

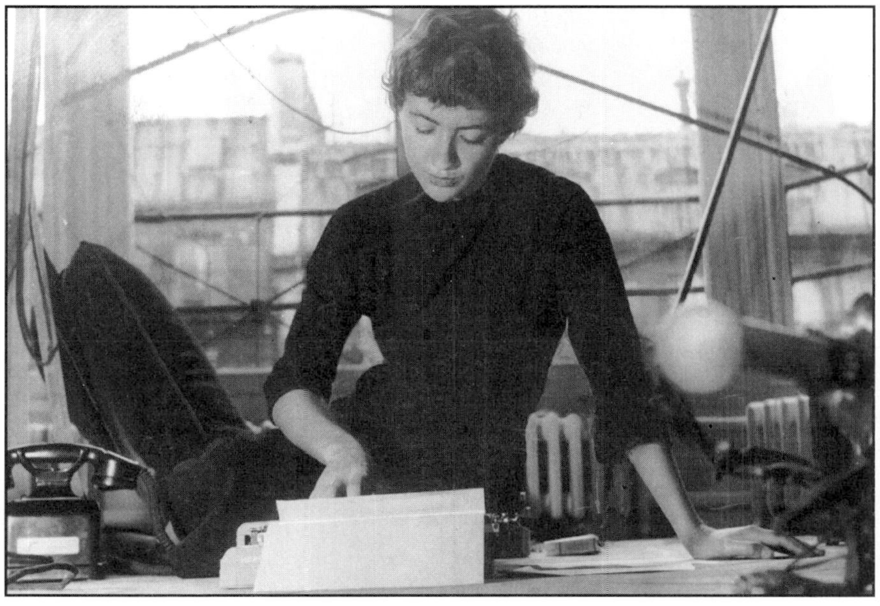

FRANÇOISE SAGAN, the author of "Bonjour Tristesse", which made her a best selling novelist at 18, is in London for two days as the guest of the publishers.

__*New Fiction*__

An 18-year-old French Girl Who is a Natural Novelist

By Peter Green

***Bonjour Tristesse.* By Françoise Sagan. (Murray. 7s 6d)**

Here is one recipe for a successful novel. It worked wonders in France and America, and will almost certainly do the same here. First be 18 years old. This will enable you to pass off your admirable emotional toughness as the precocity of adolescence.

Next, fail your Sorbonne exams but win the Grand Prix des Critiques with your first work, having written it in a month. Take a pen-name from Proust and a title from Eluard, admit to admiration for Cocteau and Sartre, and the thing is done.

Or is it? Françoise Sagan certainly has Gallic talent for displaying her wares to the best advantage (not a word about Colette's influence, for example); but she also happens to be a heaven-sent natural novelist. Her deft economy of technique will turn quinquagenarian professionals green with envy. Her detached capacity for character-exploration, shrewd and compassionate at once, is all the more remarkable for surviving the rigours of first-person narration.

"Bonjour Tristesse" deals with the Devil. This is the adolescent's Devil of arrogance and jealousy, that offers the power to hurt unsoftened by the understanding of maturity.

Cecile is a precocious girl, worshipping handsome Papa, amused by his scatter-brained mistresses, sun-bathing, flirting, day-dreaming through a Riviera summer. But the arrival of Anne - older, more formidable, with marriage in view - brings out Cecile's claws with tragic consequences.

Anne is certainly not an attractive person. She is cold, practical and bossy. In the end she brings disaster on her own head by shutting Cecile up with a volume of Bergson who is a heady philosopher for the young and miserable. Half-hysterical, half-hating herself, driven by a demon, Cecile begins to experiment with the raw materials of intrigue and jealousy.

So this is a tragedy: pathetic yet ruthless, with the peculiarly dry-eyed French clarity that enables the author to understand and pity not only for Cecile, but her gauche boyfriend; not only Papa, but his poor sun-peeled mistress; that invokes compassion even for Anne.

How easily this little masterpiece could have sunk into the egocentric maunderings of sensitive adolescence, and how triumphantly it avoids them! Irene Ash's translation matches the original; one need say no more.

(May 20)

In "THE QUIET AMERICAN" Graham Greene relinquishes the theme of his last two or three novels, which led to the exasperated comment that one would soon be unable to appreciate his work without having taken a degree in theology. As a result his grip is perceptibly loosened.

He is incapable of doing poor work, and the cessation of the accustomed sense of urgency is perhaps compensated for by easier and less exacting reading.

The setting of this novel is Vietnam, and the theme so far as there is one, is the ruinous damage that can be caused by idealism when ill-balanced and ill-informed. As the practical English newspaper correspondent, who tells the story, comments on the quiet American of the title: "I never knew a man who had better motives for all the trouble he caused."

Anyone who feels that Pyle, the American, is inconsistent to the point of unreality has a good deal to learn about Americans. Pyle is not a "typical American" - that anyway unrealistically hypothetical figure - but he is a brilliantly observed study of a particular type of American, in some ways admirable and often lovable, but also, being schooled by books and theories rather than life, often disastrous.

There is here much of Graham Greene's best writing, particularly in the quietly deliberate brutality of some of the descriptions, but also in the telling phrase that is much more than mere phrase-making, like "Sometimes she seemed invisible like peace." And both characters and setting are vivid.

(December 9)

FOOTLIGHTS COME TO LONDON

JONATHAN MILLER

When the Footlights revue "Between the Lines" was first produced at Cambridge a few weeks ago, my colleague Guy Ramsey drew attention in these columns to the outstanding talent of Jonathan Miller.

This comedian is now to be seen at the Scala, where this revue started a season last night, and I advise all connoisseurs of the comic not to let this opportunity pass of seeing an amateur in action who can compare with the best in the profession.

(June 29)

TITO GOBBI AT COVENT GARDEN

The revival of "Tosca" at Covent Garden last night had three Italian guest artists in the principal roles. Ferruccio Tagliavini sang Cavaradossi firmly, and with a certain dignity.

Renata Tebaldi was a queenly Tosca. Her tone was wonderfully free and open and her phrasing beautifully shaped at all times.

Dominating the performance was Tito Gobbi's Scarpia. This was no mere moustache-twirling villian or brutish Gestapo agent, but a man capable of noble things who had deliberately chosen evil, a man relishing his corruption.

Gobbi's fine, ripe voice curled luxuriously round Scarpia's music and with such a magnificent presence one would have easily understood Tosca had she succumbed to him.

(June 29)

OPERA MARRED BY OBSCURITY

'THE MIDSUMMER MARRIAGE'

By Martin Cooper

For all its strangeness, Michael Tippett's "The Midsummer Marriage" is not unique of its kind in the operatic repertory. The libretto by the composer is a drama of spiritual illumination - the initiation of two pairs of lovers into the mysteries of the Higher Thought.

The theme is thus the same as that of Mozart's "Magic Flute," with a vague Steiner or Jung philosophy replacing Freemasonary and an all-too-sensible businessman in the Queen of the Night's role.

In Mozart's opera we know that humanity, wisdom and virtue are the lovers' goal and we see, in sublime pantomine, how it is achieved.

In Tippett's libretto the goal is obscure and the means by which it is reached obscurer. Both are veiled in an extraordinary jumble of verbal images and stage mumbo jumbo, which includes a crystal-gazing medium and two transfigurations, one Greek and the other Hindu.

CONCISENESS LACKING

Tippett's music cannot, unfortunately, wholly redeem this hotchpotch. Although the score is complex in texture, the musical language is fundamentally simple and its effect on the ear often beautiful.

Much of the choral writing especially - and the chorus plays a very large part - is ingenious and refined, though it has not the dramatic conciseness needed in the opera house.

The chief musical weakness of the whole opera lies in the absence of strong characterisation. The worlds of Light and Darkness are not sufficiently differentiated, and the representatives of each are musically almost interchangeable. The monotony that results is only relieved by the extensive ballet.

The music for these highly esoteric dances is the best in the opera, but John Cranko's ingenious choreography only succeeds in underlining the rather pretentious symbolism of the underlying idea.

Barbara Hepworth's stage sets recalled those fashionable in Berlin some 30 years ago, effective in an austere and angular manner though not very practicable.

UGLY COSTUMES

The costumes on the other hand were depressingly ugly. But this was a small matter compared with what seemed a waste of much extraordinary vital and original music on an impossible libretto.

The performance of this difficult work was in many ways a triumph for Covent Garden. The orchestra under John Pritchard did full justice to Tippett's rhythmic volubility and the imaginative quality of his orchestration.

Joan Sutherland and Richard Lewis and Adele Leigh and John Lanigan were well cast as the lovers, and Oralia Dominguez and Otakar Kraus made the most of somewhat unrewarding parts.

(January 28)

PAUL SCOFIELD A HAMLET WITHOUT IRONY

SOLEMN PRODUCTION

By W.A. Darlington

Because of its spectacular pilgrimage behind the Iron Curtain, Peter Brook's "Hamlet" at the Phoenix had aroused great interest and high hopes. Hopes in the theatre are apt to run too high on these special occasions and so I found it last night.

Paul Scofield pleased the Russians as the Prince, but possibly the Russians did not know much of Hamlet lies in his gift of irony - a gift which Mr. Scofield appears not to value, for he made little attempt to achieve it.

Ernest Thesiger's Polonius, too, received high praise in Moscow, and deserved it so far as a beautifully spoken performance went. But has there ever before been a Polonius so solemn; or to put it another way, has Mr. Thesiger ever before played a part with so many comic possibilities and had so few laughs?

Of all great tragedies ever written, "Hamlet" most clearly demonstrates the difference between seriousness and solemnity. Mr. Brook, it seems, does not feel that way about it, and has influenced Mr. Scofield to forget that he once did.

VIGOUR AND PACE

I do not suggest that this is a bad Hamlet, only that it is not a particularly good one. It has an attractive masculine vigour which occasionally devolves into a meaningless vehemence.

It has pace, but this sometimes means that a line is spoken so quickly that it loses its ordinary emphasis without acquiring a new one. Emotionally, too, it is uneven.

Alec Clunes is a first rate Claudius, with no unevennesses at all. Diana Wynyard, on the other hand, makes surprisingly little of Gertrude, whom she endows with a core so hard that one cannot believe in her melting moments.

As for Mary Ure's Ophelia, this is a simple piece of miscasting. It really is not fair to an actress with so little experience to give her so difficult a part.

Mr. Brook handles his stage with his usual dexterity and Georges Wakhevitch's settings are at once imposing and simple. Though it misses special distinction this is not a production to be missed.

(December 9)

£350,000 PAID BY B.B.C. FOR EALING STUDIOS

Ealing Studios have been bought by the B.B.C. for £350,000. The studios will be used by the Corporation as a permanent home for its television service's film department and other developments.

Built in the 1930's, they cover about four acres and have a total area of 100,000 sq. ft. They include five stages and three projection theatres. A B.B.C. spokesman said last night that it would obtain vacant possession next year.

"We shall concentrate the film department which is scattered all over London."

"Our production of films has reached two million feet a year and we expect to expand with the advent of schools' television in 1957. There is also the possibility of a second television service."

Mr. Reginald Baker, chairman and managing director of Ealing Studios, said last night they were sold because the company thought it could work on a wider canvas in other places. "We shall decide within a few weeks where we shall go, but have found that owning studios is an onerous situation."

A protest against the sale is to be made by the Association of Cine Technicians. It has been campaigning during the last year against the encroachment of television into the film industry.

Mr. George Elvin, secretary of the association, said last night: "We shall ask the President of the Board of Trade to intervene to try to stop the sale."

(October 20)

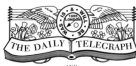

THE DAILY TELEGRAPH
AND
MORNING POST
DAILY TELEGRAPH - June 29, 1855
MORNING POST - November 2, 1772
[Amalgamated October 1, 1937.]
135, Fleet Street, London E.C.4.
Telephone: Central 4242.

PRINCESS MARGARET DECIDES

ALL will respect the motives which have led Princess MARGARET to decide against marrying Group Captain TOWNSEND. They include no element of selfishness - it would be quite alien to the Princess's character if she had been actuated by material considerations. It is, therefore, irrelevant that, if the marriage had taken place, she would undoubtedly have had to renounce the succession. Nor can reasons of State have influenced her, since there is no cause for her to contract such a marriage as would ensure the succession. The simple explanation, confirmed by the dignified statement which she issued last night, is that her own religious convictions caused her to conclude, in accordance with the tenents of the Church, of which she is a devout member, that marriage with a person whose divorced wife is still living would be wrong.

The decision has obviously been reached without promptings or pressure from any member of her family. The time taken to reach it is proof of that. For the duration of the period of suspense cannot have been welcome to the Royal family nor was it immune from some adverse comment by the public. Certainly both will be glad if it had been over sooner.

Ordinary people, it has been argued, are fully entitled to take as long as they like about agreeing whether to get married or not. That is true. But Princess MARGARET is not an ordinary person. The considerations which have now prevailed were not something new. They existed before, during and after the two years' separation; and with the best will in the world, it is impossible to lose the feeling that they could have been obeyed - or disregarded - to the great advantage of all concerned without so long a pause.

As for the conduct of the Press, the speculation and sensationalism indulged in by some of the newspapers was indeed nauseating. But it was quite futile to pretend that a matter which was engaging the interest of millions did not exist or that its outcome was of no more importance than that of an affair between any couple whose names had been linked. Factual notice of events was the only possible course to follow. Finally now that a decision has been reached upon grounds that, without impertinence, can be said to be convincing, it remains only to wish that Princess MARGARET may, in due course, find elsewhere that happiness which, both as a Princess and as a woman, she deserves.

(November 1)

COLONIAL IMMIGRANTS

No constructive suggestions appear to have been made to the Home Office yesterday by the deputation from Birmingham City Council which discussed the influx of West Indian immigrants. Last year nearly 900 immigrants a month arrived from the West Indies, making a total larger than the combined figures for the previous eight years. This year the 1954 figures may well be doubled. Economically the transfer of willing hands from a part of the Commonwealth where unemployment is severe to the United Kingdom, where there is in many areas a shortage of labour, is to be welcomed. Socially, on the other hand, an uncontrolled migration has created some difficulties which would become much graver if employment were to recede.

Basically the problem is not that the West Indians are coloured, but that they are strangers. Every wave of migration brings with it a certain percentage of undesirables, unemployables and unadaptables. Where foreigners are concerned, the Home Office can refuse admission to such people. Precisely the same rights to pick and choose and, on occasion, expel lie in the hands of colonial Governments when immigrants from the United Kingdom seek admission overseas. For the United Kingdom to exercise a reciprocal selection among colonial immigrants new legislation would be required.

It would, however, be hypocritical to pretend that no question of a psychological "colour bar" arises. Housing authorities and local trade union organisations would not be expressing so much alarm, were it not a fact that many theoretically liberal-minded persons feel a paradoxical social prejudice against what they consider the intrusion into their neighbourhood or their calling of people visibly of a different race.

This prejudice is logically untenable. No doubt some of the recent immigrants may be shirkers and some of them bad citizens. But investigation tends to show that the great majority are cheerful, friendly, hard-working folk.

(January 20)

MRS. RUTH ELLIS

ACCOMPANIED by the usual macabre incidents, the hanging of Mrs. RUTH ELLIS was yesterday carried out at Holloway Gaol. Outside the prison, drawn by motives too complex to analyse, stood the usual crowd, including women with prams. As the sinister notices announcing Mrs. ELLIS's death were pinned to the gate, the crowd surged forward, craning and jostling. These are the scenes which must make our present methods of exacting the supreme penalty repugnant to sensitive people.

The argument against capital punishment is another matter, and it is sufficient here to emphasize that the execution of Mrs. ELLIS neither strengthens nor weakens it in any way. This was not murder on the spur of the moment, but murder cold and premeditated. It was committed to the public danger; one innocent by-stander was maimed for life. We have no right even to assume gross provocation, since the only man who could have given it is dead and unable to defend himself. It was committed by a woman, certainly; but a woman capable of such a crime can hardly expect the leniency traditionally given to her sex. Whether capital punishment should be abolished or not is a subject of legitimate controversy; but certainly the execution of Mrs. ELLIS will not help those who urge it.

(July 14)

REVOLUTION ON THE AIR

The battle for Britain's eyes and ears will start tomorrow with London's first independent television programmes. The B.B.C. has already shown signs of a lively response. Its future may well depend on whether it thinks the mass audience is the only one worth having.

By Malcom Muggeridge

THE first intimation of being home again after a stay abroad is, to me, not the white cliffs of Dover; not the British Railways' ghastly turbot, not even the dear familiar sight of red buses racing valiantly away from waiting passengers. I know I am back in my native land when I hear again those unctuous, skimmed-milk B.B.C. voices pronouncing the news - only the faintest inflections permitted, as, for instance, a slight drop when death is involved, a slight slowing down and enriching when it is a question of the doings of the Royal family.

After to-morrow, when for the first time independent controlled television programmes will be put on the air, are there to be different voices or will I.T.A.-ese and B.B.C.-ese prove indistinguishable?

It has often been observed that the most usual consequence of a stormy matrimonial upheaval is for the parties concerned subsequently to team up with practically identical mates. Perhaps it is going to prove so now that our long enforced monogamy with the B.B.C. has been broken, and we are about to consort openly with these somewhat raffish, well-endowed programme companies licensed by the I.T.A. Where we looked for a mistress, shall we, perhaps, find but another wife?

Waiting And Seeing

WE can only wait and see, and we must wait for quite a while. Just as sedate a crocodile may well, in the first instance, emerge from Sir Kenneth Clark's academy as from Sir Ian Jacob's; but then, growing restless, or even desperate, what hand-turns, striptease, and other cheesecake items Sir Kenneth's might start doing!

I cannot but break off here to remark that for anyone engaged in the melancholy task of providing comic or light relief in this curious time the final closure on the controversy about whether independent television should be permitted at all is an appalling deprivation. What a rich and rare feast it has been! - those clerical dignitaries expending their episcopal fervour on television programmes they had never seen; those so sensitive politicans starting back like frightened fawns from the prospect of spoken advertisements assailing their delicate ears; Miss Popham's appointment to the I.T.A. Board of Governors; the appearance on the scene of Sir Robert Fraser, hotfoot from the Central Office of Information. Now, alas, the show is over, with only Dr. Hill left to spin out his harlequinade, alone on a stage that is littered and dark and desolate.

The B.B.C. has, in its own odd and portentous way, been engaged in the last nine months in rolling up its sleeves, bashing punch-balls, and generally getting into training for the coming struggle. Meetings have been held on august levels; policy decisions have been laboriously taken. The Director of the Spoken Word (when, oh when, will there be a Director of the Visual Image?) along with other eminent persons in the proliferating upper reaches of Broadcasting House, have all had their say. Now the big fight is to begin.

Opportunity Lost

WHAT shape is B.B.C. television in to wage it? Not too bad, I should say. Certainly better than might have been expected given its cumbersome, slow-moving procedure.

Ideally, of course, the B.B.C. should long ago have decided exactly what future sound broadcasting might be expected to have, and, on that basis, have consolidated - for instance, amalgamating the Home, Light and Third Programmes into one, which concentrated on features like music, news and a certain type of discussion, drama and story-telling not enhanced by visual presentation, and shaking all the superflux - money, programmes and personnel - in the direction of Lime Grove. Such an arrangement would have involved really popular sound programmes like "Any Questions?" being handed over to television, and Television News being detached from the sound radio news set-up, de-Holeised, and allowed to operate on its own, with ample budget and an exceptionally competent and energetic director. Also, funds would have thereby been available to buy cameras and other technical equipment now woefully lacking.

Instead, with that innate fatuity which dogs all human affairs, especially those in which the Government has a hand, B.B.C. sound radio and television have continued to compete right up to zero hour. It has been like those extraordinary departmental rows which took place during the war, when M.I. this and M.I. that fought one another with a ferocity and ingenuity which, pitted against the Abwehr, could not but have produced spectacular results.

Ins And Outs

AND what about the rival concern - the I.T.A. programme companies and their news service, of which Mr. Aidan Crawley, that unfortunate Harrovian who was born with a wooden spoon in his mouth, is editor-in-chief?

All that we know about them is that there has been a good deal of individual and financial coming and going. Figures like Mr. Wolfson, Mr. Maurice Winnick and Lord Kemsley have been in, and lo! were out; were back again and out again in a manner reminiscent of the great Major Salem. The result, in terms of actual television programmes, will begin to be apparent from to-morrow.

What can be said already with certainty is that the invigorating wind of competition has blown beneficially along the sultry corridors of Broadcasting House. A little pomposity, a little complacency, a little of that irritating sense of knowing what is good for us and the determination to administer it, have been blown away. The mere existence of alternative employment has proved highly advantageous to many a B.B.C. employee upon whom the Corporation has weighed heavily and long.

Salaries have had to be adjusted to bear some relation to competence and irreplaceability; ambition is less blocked than it was by a vast and impenetrable hierarchical structure. The B.B.C. climate, in short, has become more salubrious - sufficiently so to justify those who contended that its monopolistic position needed to be breached even if there were legitimate objections to the only means whereby this could, in present circumstances, be achieved.

Unlike the B.B.C, the I.T.A. programme companies are under the necessity of making a lot of money. They are heavily capitalised, and their running costs will be considerable. As numerous popular magazines and newspapers abundantly demonstrate, cupidity and eroticism provide the readiest means of attracting mass interest. Sir Kenneth Clark may well find that keeping bogus Rembrandts and Canalettos off the walls of the National Gallery was child's play compared with keeping gift schemes and leg shows off I.T.A. television programmes.

The B.B.C. has the immense advantage, because of its assured and fairly ample budget, of not being under the necessity to pursue a mass audience as an end in itself. If it uses this advantage to provide adult, sprightly and informative programmes, it will thrive. On the other hand, if it tries to compete with I.T.A. programmes on their, rather than its, terms, or alternatively, falls back discouraged on being even pretentious and anodyne than heretofore, it will assuredly fall on evil days.

Opiate Or Stimulant?

TELEVISION, far more than the hydrogen bomb (which will either blow us all up - a rather trivial matter), provides this age with a great challenge and a great opportunity.

It is capable, as many present programmes here and in the United States amply demonstrate, of ministering to mental vacuity and indolence, and thereby preparing the way for an ultimate collectivist servility and conformism.

At the same time, it is also capable of extending human understanding and enriching human life. It all depends how it is used - whether with timidity and a slavish surrender to base and fatuous, if not morbid, curiosity, or courageously and truthfully, to express and extend the dreams, intelligence and thought which are the only truly worthwhile things allowed to men.

Those superior individuals who shake their heads and regret that television was ever invented are as silly as the others who are content to stare at their television screen through the afternoon and evening hours irrespective of what may appear on it. The fact is that television is here to stay.

(September 21)

CAPITAL OF WALES

By Ronald Simmonds

CARDIFF is to be a capital at last. It is at once a monument to the enterprise of an ancient Scottish family and to the toil of thousands of Welsh miners - built of Portland stone, founded on coal.

It has broad avenues, dignity and civic pride. It has mean streets with shabbily-genteel faces, and more prosperity in its business houses than in the docks which gave it birth. Brooks and streams run clear into it from the surrounding hills, but the River Taff, which once carried salmon and trout, brings the black blood down from the wounded valleys to the sea.

The first coal came to Cardiff slowly, laboriously in pannier baskets on the backs of mules, down the valleys that radiate from the coastal plain. In 1766 the Norman Castle and its lands passed into the Bute family, the descendants of Scots kings. Thirty years later the first Bute enterprise which was to make Cardiff and its coal known all over the world, began with the opening of the Glamorgan Canal.

At the turn of the century 60 acres of Bute land near the Castle were purchased for £161,000. They called it Cathays Park and in it the city fathers built a poem in stone.

Now the avalanche of coal streaming down to the docks for export has dwindled. The historic docks Exchange is a place of ghosts. But paradoxically, as its coal trade has declined, Cardiff's standing has increased. In 1949 the City Council petitioned King George VI, in Welsh and English, for capital recognition. In 1951 the Council for Wales gave its support. The city was the headquarters of all Government departments, the home of Wales's National Museum and Britain's only Folk Museum. A national ballot showed overwhelming support for its claim.

It is a famous city that was a village on a cross-roads. It is an amalgam of Welsh, English, Irish, Scots, Jews and over 20 other nationalities. It is the church, the chapel, the synagogue and the mosque. In short, it is Cardiff.

(December 21)

'MO-PED' IS STAR OF CYCLE SHOW

BRITAIN ANSWERS FOREIGN CHALLENGE

By W.A. McKenzie
Daily Telegraph Motoring Correspondent

The 30th Cycle and Motor-Cycle Show at Earl's Court is dominated by the motor scooter and "mo-ped." The show will be opened to-day by Mr. Thorneycroft, President of the Board of Trade.

The "mo-ped" is a "baby" motor-cycle of up to 50 c.c. engine capacity assisted by pedals.

Over 30,000 motor scooters and "mo-peds" have been imported in one year. Now Britain has answered the challenge and is producing similar machines.

British "mo-peds" at the show number nine and Continental seven. They range in price from £40 to £80. Motor scooters range from rather less than £100 to £250.

The wave of interest in "mo-peds" had caused a big drop in the demand for motor-attached cycles. As a result, cycle manufacturers are turning their attention to the "mo-peds."

COMPANY'S PLANS

A case in point is the Hercules Cycle and Motor Co. They are the first of the leading cycle-makers to be showing a "motorised" product, the Grey Wolf, which is a 49 c.c. two-speed-gear "mo-ped" selling at £61 15s including £11 19s purchase tax. The company plans to make 500 a week, later 1,000.

Another new British "mo-ped" is shown by the Power-Pak Engineering Co., of Coventry. It is of 49 c.c., can cruise at 30 m.p.h., reach 40 m.p.h., and can cover 200 miles on a gallon of petrol.

The all-British Dayton Albatross motor scooter is shown. This is claimed to be a big advance on foreign scooters, and is appealing in design and finish.

Powered by a 225 c.c. engine, it is more powerful than most scooters. It is capable of 84 miles per gallon, with a cruising speed of 50 and a top speed of over 65 m.p.h.

An exhibit of special prestige value to the British industry is the world record-breaking Vincent 1,000 c.c. streamlined motor-cycle. This machine, in the hands of Russell Wright and Robert Burns, took the world's solo and sidecar records at 185 and 162 m.p.h., respectively, in New Zealand last July.

(November 12)

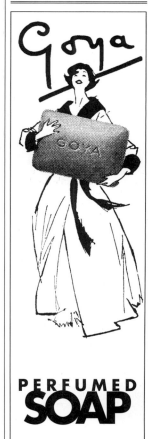

THE STORY'S THE THING

W.A. Darlington points to the cult of obscurity as the great fault of a group of contemporary British playwrights.

"Waiting For Godot," recently put on at the Arts Theatre, is as odd a piece of play writing as you could wish to see. It has no plot, no connected action, no clearly defined purpose, and only a vaguely suggested meaning.

It is superb as a serious frolic for highbrows; but in the regular workday theatre it has no conceivable place at all. No management would ask the ordinary playgoer to face it.

But in its deliberate formlessness and obscurity it merely carries to its logical extreme a fashion which is bedevilling the work of a whole group of our younger dramatists. They all love obscurity.

They seem to have taken for a motto the words of Claudio in "Measure for Measure":

I will encounter darkness as a bride
And hug it in my arms.

During the season just past two comedies were produced in the West End which were much above the ordinary level in the quality of their writing. Both failed badly with the public and were withdrawn with unhappy speed.

Owen Holder's "A Kind of Folly" was one, Denis Cannan's "Misery Me" was the other. To my mind, both these plays had all the ingredients of success, and might still have been drawing delighted audiences but for the extraordinary perfunctoriness with which both authors went about their job of story-telling.

AUTHORS IN REVOLT

This is a fundamental fault, but these two authors and others of the present generation - notably, Christopher Fry and John Whiting - seem unable to recognise it as such. The reason is easy to suggest.

All these authors are caught up in a reaction, so violent as to be almost a revolution, against the photographically exact naturalism of the pre-war theatre. One of the virtues of realists was clarity of exposition (which is another way of saying good story-telling) and consequently the new school of writers has no use for it. Not perceiving that it is in fact a universal virtue which the great dramatists (Shakespeare, Ibsen, Shaw in his best period, and all the rest of them) have always had, these young men have decided to throw the baby out with the bathwater, and now they are a baby short.

Their method is to raise the curtain in a confused first act, and in effect, to say to the audience: "Here are some people for you. Their relations with each other and the world are rather odd and I hope you'll find them amusing. Sort them out for yourselves."

POPULAR ART

But sorting things out for itself is just what a theatrical audience cannot be expected to do; it needs a dramatist to direct and control its perceptions. Drama is a popular art and the greater part of any theatrical audience simply want to be told a story.

They want to know as soon as possible who the characters are and what they are up to; and as soon as this information has been given they are ready to follow hopefully wherever the dramatist may choose to lead. But if the dramatist is one of the sort-it-out-for-yourselves school, the ordinary playgoer soon begins to be puzzled and upset.

Witty lines are spoken on the stage, and interesting ideas are put forward, but the audience responds half-heartedly because its attention is taken up with the attempt to "sort things out"; and the actors feel they are not getting across.

It should be made clear that it is only in the theatre, when spectators and actors are in direct emotional contact and the audience integrates itself into a single collective entity, that this early and swift clarification is necessary. A man reading the same story in a book, or encountering it in a cinema or on the radio or television, reacts as an individual, and is in no position to object if the author elects to tell his tale upside down or inside out.

I met a striking example of this recently. Dr. J. Bronowski's "The Face of Violence" had a great success on the radio, and the author left its form unchanged in a stage version which I saw produced by an amateur group.

For five out of its seven scenes we saw the chief character wandering the world looking for a man named Crump. What he wanted Crump for was the author's secret, and because we were not allowed to share it till the play was nearly over, we in the theatre audience grew more and more bored and resentful.

It would have been equally simple for Mr. Holder and Mr. Cannan, each of whom had a plot, to set their audiences' minds at rest with a few clear statements in their first acts.

EVEN "HAMLET"

Plot is paramount in the eyes of the ordinary playgoer - even where the play in question is a familiar classic.

I once went to a country town to see a special production of "Hamlet" and spent the night at the house of an old friend. Having a spare ticket, I asked my hostess, a woman who knows thoroughly her own honest mind, if she would care to come with me. She excused herself politely.

"I'm afraid "Hamlet" is not my favourite Shakespearean play," she said.

"Why, what's the matter with it?"

"I don't care for the story. He was such a silly young man."

(August 13)

'HORROR AND CONFUSION'

Lightning struck Royal Ascot yesterday when the crowd on the "popular" side of the course, opposite the Royal Box, were sheltering from a thunderstorm. The storm broke with tropical intensity, just before 4 p.m.

Many people in the Royal Enclosure saw the vivid flash at 4.10 p.m. It appeared first to strike the wire fence round No. 2 enclosure and then go to ground where a group of about 100 people were sheltering under the lee of a tea tent.

In the words of one witness "people were thrown around like nine-pins, and in a fraction of a second a fairly light-hearted scene became one of horror and confusion."

The woman who was killed, Mrs Barbara Batt, 28, of Caroline Street, Reading, went to the races with her husband, Mr. Ronald Batt, who was seriously injured and was taken to Heatherwood Hospital, Ascot.

(July 15)

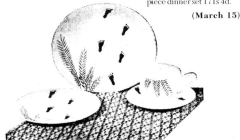

DIOR'S H-LINE HAS BECOME AN A-LINE

MOVEABLE BELT

From Winefride Jackson

PARIS, Tuesday.

If anyone thought that by ridiculing the flat-busted Dior line of last season they would drive him into designing a more natural line this spring they were wrong. True, at his opening show to-day he said it is now a freer line changing his "H" to "A."

This means that to make up for the cramping above you are allowed an easier waist and a more pyramid skirt line plus a "wandering" belt between mid-hip to under the bust.

But unless you are very slim I do not think you can achieve an elegant silhouette with this line. I wonder whether M. Dior noticed that scarcely a member of the audience was wearing his last season's "H-line" in its original conception.

My neighbours admitted to having bought such a dress. But she said she had thrown away the accompanying constricting corset under-bodice.

ONLY FOR THE YOUNG

The answer I think is that this is a line only for the young. Curiously enough I came out of this collection feeling the same cringing horror at my reasonably slim, but unconstricted figure, as I felt when as a young and developing girl the flat boyish look of the late Twenties was in.

I was desperately ashamed of my bust. It just shows how one's eye and artistic appreciation change.

What will the wholesalers who adapt these models for the stores take from this "A-line?" I think they will use the main silhouette of a gentle pyramid line.

They will keep the easily fitted waist, the wide shallow square neckline, the charming double-breasted summer suits and dress jackets that smooth out the bust line and the plain slim tunic dresses.

COLOURS MIXED

Fabrics for day are silk and wool mixtures with an alpaca surface, tweeds with a linen weave, a great deal of shantung for summer two-pieces, flower-printed silk organza for summer party dresses and a great deal of faille. Colours have never been so mixed as this season.

There is black, navy, clear light and dark brown for day; for evening all the pastel shades, Marie Antoinette blue, rose pink, a great deal of white, silver-grey mixed with pale gold, and peony red.

The hemline is still short, about three inches below the knee. In full skirted party dresses it actually appears shorter with the movement of the skirt.

With a softer and less constricted line Givenchy echoes Dior. The long, flat bodice line is achieved by a front panel which continues from the torso into the skirt for dresses, or the double-breasted hip-length semi-fitted jacket, both of which details smooth out the bust, but without constriction.

(February 2)

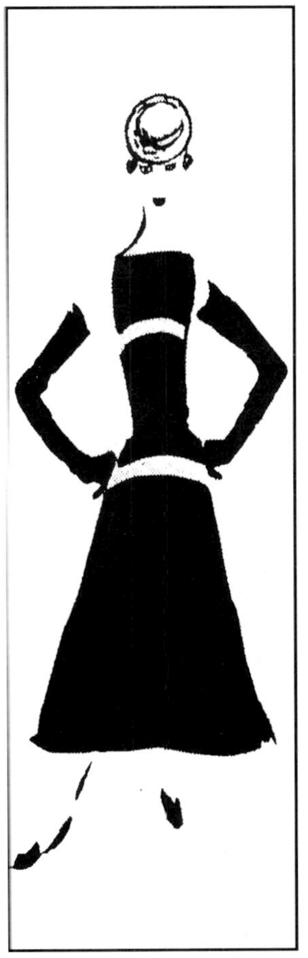

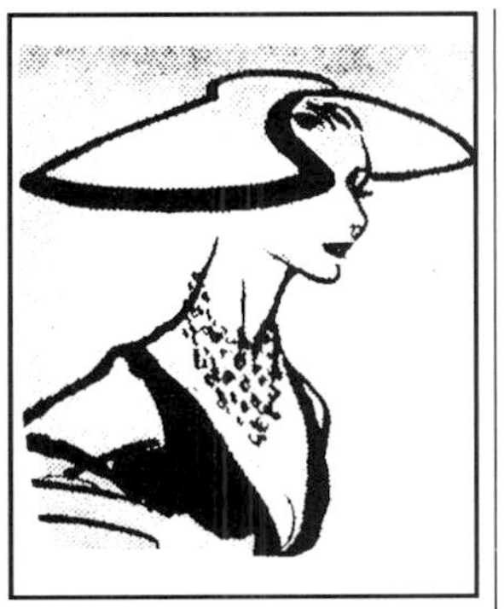

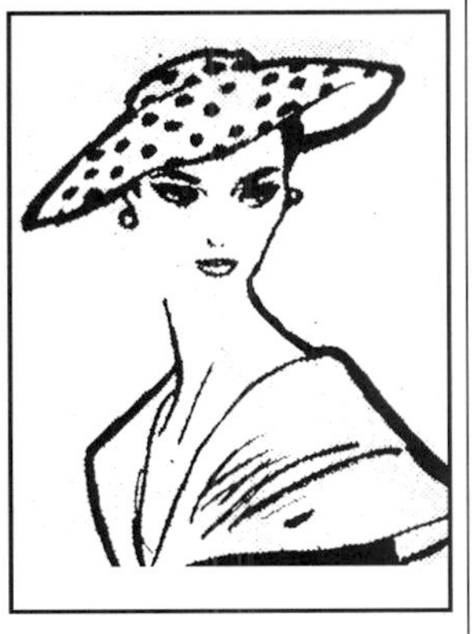

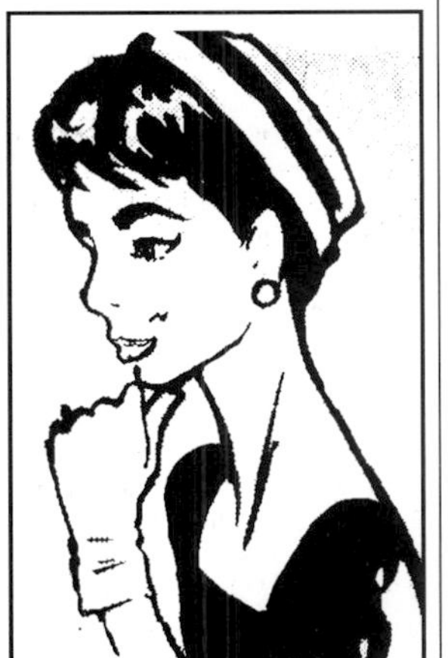

SKETCHES FROM PARIS. The new Dior "A-line" which allows an easier waist and a pyramid skirt-line, sketched in Paris yesterday by The Daily Telegraph fashion artist Beryl Hartland, according to Dior's ruling the dress-belt can be worn anywhere between the bust-line and the mid hip-line. She also sent her impressions, shown on the right, of a crescent-shaped picture hat covered in polka-dot silk by Balmain, and (below) the "Audrey Hepburn look" demonstrated by Givenchy with a chignon hat worn well back from a schoolboy fringe.

ALICE'S DODO AMONG THE STATE SCHOOLS

By Nicholas Bagnall

No one really likes examinations and the 11-plus exam, which decides to what kind of secondary school a child is suited, is probably the most unpopular of all. Like most of them, it quite often fails to spot talent, but the trouble is that no one has yet found a better alternative.

Some Socialists, however, think they know an easy way out of the difficulty. It is all so beautifully simple. "Abolish the exam," they say - which means, logically, putting all children over 11 in the same kind of school, whether they be dunces or scholars.

There are others ways of dispensing with the exam; for instance, the whole thing could be done by interview and personal recommendation. But Socialists, many of whom care little for the grammar schools whatever the method of entering them, evidently set no store by this notion. "We shall encourage," says the Labour party's manifesto, "comprehensive secondary schooling."

PARTY STRIFE

The comprehensive idea was inspired by Alice's Dodo (no connection with Miss Bacon), who, it will be remembered, awarded prizes to everybody after the Caucus-race. It has already been the subject of party-political strife within the Education Committee of the L.C.C., and even among Labour leaders themselves, and it is the greatest pity that Socialists should now have dragged it into a general election.

The idea, if it is to work properly, usually needs schools of 1,500 to 2,000 pupils each. Otherwise the "grammar school stream," as it is called will be little more than a trickle, and the school will remain merely a swollen secondary modern. But, despite this disadvantage, in certain conditions the experiment is worth making, if only because it makes easier the transfer of children from one "stream" to another.

It is clear, at any rate, that no conclusions can yet be drawn about its value. So much depends on the local conditions.

That is why Mr. Butler's Education Act of 1944 (which in most other respects the Socialists seem to have adopted as their own child) leaves local authorities considerate freedom in their choice of secondary school systems. The Act guards, in fact, the important principle that Plato was wrong (and so were Hitler and Stalin) when he thought that education should be exclusively the affair of the State, in this case, of the central government. It is always dangerous for anybody to pontificate about education, particularly for those in power.

The Socialist manifesto proposes to throw this principle overboard by pontificating on a thoroughly generous scale. Of the 11-plus exam, the manifesto says: "Local authorities will be asked to submit schemes for the abolition of the examination."

Why do Socialists want to impose a rigid pattern on local authorities, regardless (it seems) of regional variations of every possible kind, regardless of the traditions of the grammar schools, of the wishes, so far as can be judged, of the majority of teachers, and of the principles of the Education Act?

The idea pays lip-service to egalitarianism; but Nature is not a Socialist, and her inequalities will probably be even more in evidence in a comprehensive school than they are already under the present system, which ensures that those of more or less equal talent shall go to the school that suits them best.

(May 23)

WHO'S BEEN WALKING IN MY PORRIDGE?

Someone or something is at large in the design world. His inky black footprints have been left on mats and beach suits. Now they turn up on tableware.

The "Man Friday" earthenware set shown here is black & white, to match casseroles, which are black outside and white within.

In the shops at the end of March, a 21-piece tea set will cost 44s 1d, and a 38-piece dinner set 171s 4d.

(March 15)

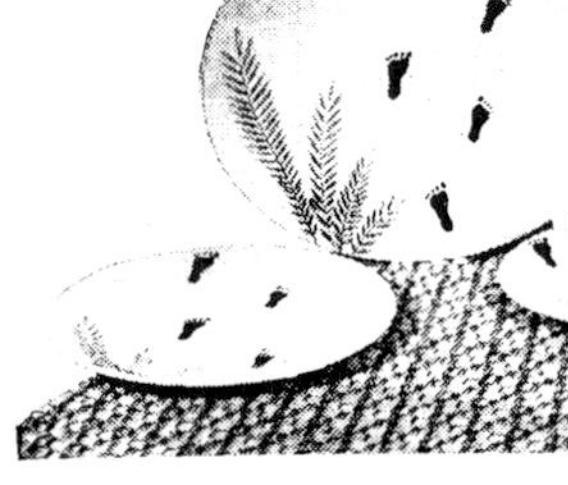

GAUNT LINE IN 'TOP TWELVE'S' NEW FASHIONS

SHIRT INSPIRATION

By Winefride Jackson

It is a long time since fashions have been so long, lean and lanky-looking as those launched yesterday by London's "Top Twelve" designers. At first sight it would seem that it is not so much necessary to diet as to starve.

In actual fact, the styles are not quite so difficult to wear as they appear at first glance.

The long torso bodice, finishing at mid-hip (favourite line so far) is fitted easily at the waist, which does at least make for a certain amount of comfort.

It is also a graceful line without undue emphasis on the bust, although there is no flattening process as in the "H" line. This long bodice also adds height.

Because the waist is no longer nipped in with a belt, the hips appear slimmer. For day wear all skirts have a slim silhouette with an occasional group of flat pleats at the back for easy movement.

At John Cavanagh's there was a complete absence of belts. Some dresses, in fact, are in one unbroken, slim line, their only decoration a stand-away roll collar.

One of his main inspirations is a man's shirt. Topcoats are in full length or three-quarter style and fall straight from gathers on the collar-bone seam with small side slits at the hem.

SLEEVES CUFFED

Jackets repeat the shirt line, except that they finish with a snug-fitting basque just below the natural waistline. All sleeves are set in at the normal shoulder level and the sleeves cuffed like a man's shirt.

Afternoon and evening dresses repeat the long torso line with the addition of fulness springing from the side at mid-hip and often with a lift to the hem in front.

Charles Creed also uses the casual shirt line for wool day dresses, and even for silk cocktail dresses. Town suits and coats are close-fitted and slim. Country suits are casual and loose-fitting.

Mattli's styles are a little softer and more rounded, and he particularly likes the three-quarter fitted coat with flared basque over a slim skirt. Coats are fuller, some even swagger, and bouffant evening dresses follow the lifted front hemline.

Worth's new designer, Hyde Clarke, follows the long-uncluttered bodice line to the hips, from which the skirt continues, slim for day and bouffant for evening.

Silk and wool mixtures, hessian for coats, ottoman, metal woven silks, fine silk taffeta and some lovely printed cottons are the outstanding fabrics.

Navy blue with white leads grey for day. There is repeated use of a lovely primrose yellow and cyclamen pink for evening.

(January 28)

SLIMMING CRAZE KILLED WOMAN

FORCIBLE FEEDING

The mother of a Coventry woman, Elsie May Collins, 29, told the North Warwickshire coroner, Mr. C.W. Iliffe, at the Coventry inquest yesterday that her daughter had never had a serious illness until 10 years ago. Then she started to go without food because of a "slimming craze which came over from America."

Mrs Elsie May Smith, the mother, said she did her best to make her daughter eat, but to no avail. Food packed for her to take to work she would throw away. She had been seen by the doctor, but normally if she knew the doctor was calling she would run away from the house. She had been forcibly fed when in hospital.

"She just could not make the break from the silly craze she had." On July 19 her daughter collapsed in the street and was taken to hospital. She was able to return home later, but became ill again, and died in hospital the next day.

Dr. W.C. MacCullagh Wilson said that the woman's body was emaciated, with a complete absence of fat. Death was due to malnutrition and exhaustion caused by a nervous disease brought on by the slimming.

The coroner recorded a verdict in accordance with the medical evidence.

(July 26)

THOMAS MANN, AUTHOR DEFIED NAZIS

DRIVEN INTO EXILE

The work of Thomas Mann, who has died aged 80, is assured a permanent place in literature by the great sweep of his imaginative powers, the precession of his writing, and his analytical approach to a number of problems which confront humanity.

He probed deeply into the antithesis of life and intellect, and, with acidity, into the position of the artist in the universal scheme.

While his writings betrayed considerable heart-searching, he rarely, if ever, offered any solution to the problems he propounded. The themes of decay and death attracted him, and featured prominently in much of his work, and many of his characters were notable for there abnormality.

Born in Lübeck in 1875 of an old Hanse family, Thomas Mann was the son of a merchant and senator, who died when his son was 15. Three years later the boy moved to Münich, where his mother had preceded him, and worked for a time in an insurance office. Quickly tiring of commercial life, he threw up his job to live in Rome, where he published his first novel.

MASTERPIECE AT 25

Some of his short stories had already attracted attention, but "Buddenbrooks", which appeared in 1901 when he was 25, was hailed as a masterpiece. Persecutor of many family sagas, it was largely autobiographical, and dealt with the decline, and the final dissolution, of a middle-class family. Its sale to date exceeds 1,200,000 copies.

Mann returned to Münich where he joined the staff of the satirical weekly Simplicissimus. "Death in Venice", considered by many as his most perfect work, appeared in 1912, and "The Magic Mountain", the scene of which was laid in a sanatorium for consumptives at Davos, in 1924. He was awarded the Nobel Prize for literature in 1929 and "Mario and the Magician" followed a year later.

Mann, who had been watching with growing alarm the rise of the Nazis, left Germany in 1933, the year Hitler became Chancellor. His outspoken condemnation of the new régime ended inevitably in the cancellation of his German citizenship and the withdrawal of his Bonn University degree, three years later.

There followed several years of restless wandering in France, Switzerland and Czechoslovakia, and a period of financial difficulty. He accepted the offer of Czechoslovakian citizenship made by President Benes, but had to flee when the country fell.

AMERICAN CITIZENSHIP

He became an American citizen in 1938, and was appointed Lecturer in Humanities at Princeton University. The first volume of "Joseph and his Brethren", an imposing and ambitious Biblical work, appeared in 1935, and was followed by two more.

In 1947, in the course of a visit to England, he expressed with emotion his admiration for Britain without whose unique resistance in 1940, he said, it was very doubtful if there would have been left any form of civilisation. In 1949 he visited Germany for the first time since his exile, to lecture in honour of the 200th anniversary of the birth of Goethe. He also lectured in London, and at Oxford, where he received an honorary degree of Doctor of Literature. In 1953 a Degree of Doctor of Letters was conferred on him at Cambridge.

Two of his latest works were "Doctor Faustus" a vast political and theological biography of a fictional German composer published in 1949 and "The Holy Sinner" a story of the Middle Ages, 1952. He left America, where, he said, life had become "too complicated" in 1952 to live in Switzerland near Lake Zurich.

Thomas Mann married in 1905, Miss Katja Pringsheim, who survives him, with two sons and three daughters. One daughter, Erika, is the wife of W.H. Auden, the poet.

(August 13)

Obituaries

PROF. ALBERT EINSTEIN

PROPHET OF THE ATOMIC AGE

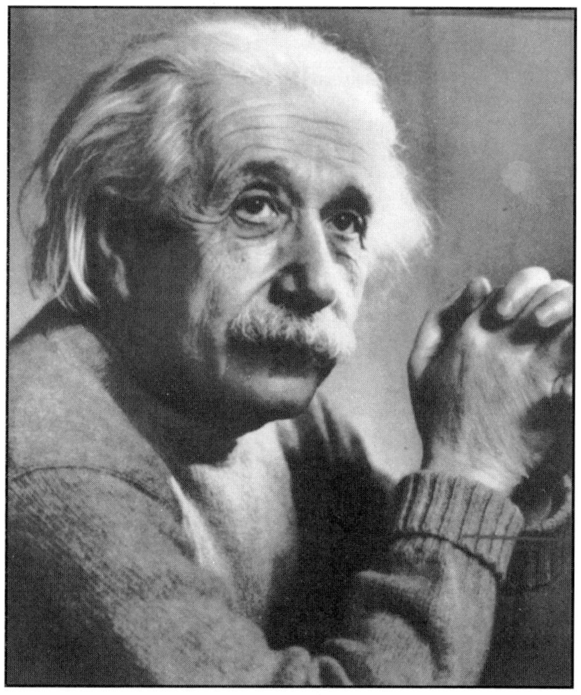

PROFESSOR ALBERT EINSTEIN

The death of Albert Einstein, originator of the theories of relativity, deprived the world of its greatest scientific intellect. He died, aged 76, at Princeton, New Jersey, on April 18.

Not since Newton has there been such a bold voyager on those "strange seas of thought" between physics and mathematics. His genius transformed modern science; though his theories were far beyond the layman's comprehension.He was, in a special sense, a prophet of the atomic age. His famous equation linking mass and energy pointed the way to the fission of uranium, and so to Hiroshima and Nagasaki. His letter in 1939 to President Roosevelt, saying that Germany was experimenting with the aim of producing an atomic bomb, led to the secret atomic bomb project in the United States.

Other scientists were behind the letter, but Einstein's prestige gave the necessary weight to their opinions. It has been suggested that he regretted the part he played. Some time after the defeat of Japan Einstein said he would have done nothing for the atomic bomb had he known that Germany would fail to discover the secret of its manufacture.

He denounced the Bikini experiments as for making insecurity abroad. In 1946 he led a scientists' campaign to tell the people of the dangers of an atomic war. Always a pacifist, he held that the only hope was the prevention of war by international action. These activities were a variation of his customary shunning of publicity, as his outspoken opposition to Communist - hunting among American scientists.

UNIFIED FIELD THEORY

Driven from Germany in 1933 because of Jewish birth and anti-Nazi opinions, he carried on his researches at the Institute of Advanced Studies in Princeton. In 1940 he became a naturalised American citizen.

In 1949 he put forward a "United Field Theory" in twenty typewritten pages, a third of them intricate mathematical equations. This theory, which still remains to be proved or disproved by experiment represents an attempt to explain the relationship of all physical laws, and in particular to find a mathematical link between gravitational effects on the one hand and those of electricity and magnetism on the other.

Asked once about his religious beliefs, he wrote: "I believe in Spinoza's God, who reveals himself in the orderly harmony of what exists: not with a God who concerns himself with the fates and actions of human beings."

Albert Einstein was born at Ulm, Germany. of Swabian Jewish parents. With them he spent his youth in various places - Münich, Milan, Zurich and Berne. Dreamy and different as a boy he confessed he was "extremely stupid" at learning by rote. He was an employee at the Swiss patent office in Berne, when in 1905 a "storm broke loose" in his mind.

In that year, at the age of 26, he produced three theories that were destined to shake the world. The best known of these was his "Special Theory of Relativity" which provided a relationship between matter and energy and showed the conditions under which one could be converted into the other.

His work in this, his "annus mirabilis," was destined to earn him a Nobel Prize 17 years later after observations of the 1919 solar eclipse had confirmed his prophecies about the "bending of light rays". At that time his relativity theories were still viewed with reserve.

After professorships at Prague and Zürich he was nominated to the Kaiser Wilhelm Academy for Research in Berlin just before the 1914-18 war. His anti-nationalist views brought unpopularity. After his rejection by Hitler's Germany other nations showered him with honours and offers of domicile. He was an ardent Zionist, but turned down an invitation to succeed Dr. Weizmann as President of Israel.

Einstein first married Mileva Marec, a Serbian student. They had two sons. The marriage was dissolved. In 1917 he married his cousin Elsa Einstein, a widow with two daughters. She died in 1936.

(April 21)

MR. CALOUSTE GULBENKIAN

OIL INDUSTRY'S MR. 'FIVE-PER-CENT'

Mr. Calouste Sarkis Gulbenkian, who has died in Lisbon aged 86, was reputed to be the world's wealthiest man. His personal fortune, most of which was derived from the oil industry, was estimated at £300 million.

In later life he lived quietly, shunning visitors and publicity. For several years he controlled his empire from the small but richly appointed Hotel Aviz in Lisbon.

Here he lived a strictly regulated life, with the expressed intention of living to be 106. His father, he claimed, died at 105. Included in his diet were whole raw carrots, which he once declared, he "chewed like a goat."

ART COLLECTOR

To the world outside he was best known as the owner of a matchless art collection. His mansion in Paris, which he visited rarely, housed superb paintings, porcelain, sculpture, furniture and tapestries.

He lent many of his finest pictures to the National Gallery for exhibition from 1936 to 1950. They were then lent to the American National Gallery in Washington for two years.

Born in Scutaru in 1869, of wealthy parent with oil interests in Asia Minor, he would, if he had followed his own inclination, have become a university professor.

At school in Istanbul and Marseilles, and at King's College, London, where he studied engineering, he showed an aptitude for physics and mathematics; he matriculated at the Ecole Normale Supérieure in Paris and devoted himself to astrophysics with the intention of becoming a lecturer.

BRITISH SUBJECT

But family pressure proved too strong, and he was sent to Baku to learn the oil business. He became a British subject in 1902, and by the time of the 1914-18 war had established an international reputation, he was consulted by the British, German and Turkish Governments.

After the break-up of the Ottoman Empire he mobilised the oil resources of the Near East. In London he met the late Sir Henry Deterding and together they set up the Royal Dutch Shell combine.

Mr. Gulbenkian became a master-manipulator in the world's markets and head of an involved international chain of holding companies and super-holding companies. His nickname, "Mr. Five-per-cent" originated in the extent of his interests in the Iraq Petroleum Corporation. His income from this was said to be £2,000 a day.

In 1951 Mr. Gulbenkian was stated to have made £500,000 in five minutes when some of his shares rose 10s. In the same year it was announced that he had been dismissed from his post as honorary commercial attaché to the Persian Legation in Paris on the grounds that he owned shares in the Anglo-Iranian Oil Company, now the British Oil Company.

SON'S CLAIM

His son, Mr. Nubar Gulbenkian, was dismissed from a similar post at the London Embassy. In 1940, Mr. Nubar Gulbenkian withdrew an action he had brought against his father claiming a share in the profits of the Iraq Petroleum Corporation Costs in the case reached £25,000.

Mr. Gulbenkian built, endowed and administered the American Orthodox Church in Kensington in memory of his father. He endowed the Lisbon Art Gallery with many treasures.

(July 21)

M.P. DETAINED IN WAR DIES

CAPT. A. H. M. RAMSAY

Capt. Archibald Henry Maule Ramsay, who died in London yesterday, aged 60, was Conservative M.P. for Peebles when he was detained under Defence Regulation 18b in May, 1940. He refused to resign his seat and resumed his Parliamentary activities after his release in 1944.

He represented Peebles from 1931 to 1945, but was "disowned" by the local Conservative Association in 1941. His views were strongly anti-Semitic and anti-Communist, and at the end of 1938 he formed the Right Club, an anti-Jewish organisation which included William Joyce ("Lord Haw Haw"), and other Nazi sympathizers.

He always repudiated suggestions of disloyalty. His arrest was considered by the Committee of Privileges, which decided it was not a breach of the privileges of the House. In 1941 Capt. Ramsay obtained judgment in a libel action against the New York Times on an article which alleged treasonable activity, but only .25d damages was awarded.

(March 12)

THEDA BARRA

The first of the famous "sirens" of the screen, Theda Barra, who has died in Hollywood, aged 63, was born Theodosia Goodman, of Cincinnati, Ohio. Between 1915 and 1919 she made about 40 films for the William Fox Film Company.

Theda Barra's screen name, which in the early days of the silent film industry became synonymous with the word "vamp", was evolved by her director Frank Powell. Her best-known parts included "Carmen" (1915), and Salome and Cleopatra (1917).

(August 21)

MISS ANNETTE MILLS

FAME WITH PUPPET VARIED CAREER

Daily Telegraph Reporter

Miss Annette Mills, who died in a London nursing home yesterday, aged 60, became famous as the human "partner" of Muffin the Mule, the television puppet. She was also a versatile and courageous figure in modern light entertainment.

Born in Chelsea, she was the daughter of a schoolmaster, and the elder sister of John Mills, the actor, who was at her bedside when she died. She trained as a concert pianist. Before graduating she turned to dancing.

She became the professional dancing partner of Robert Sielle, whom she later married. They introduced the Charleston to London, first to the Kit-Kat Club, and then to the Piccadilly Hotel, after noting its possibilities when danced as a solo in New York.

A few years later she brought "the Mooceni" a dance based on Zulu rhythms, to Britain after a South African tour.

WROTE "BOOMPS-A-DAISY'

It was on an African tour that Miss Mills broke her leg, and reverting to the piano, began to compose songs, many of them for revues and cabarets. She herself sang "Boomps-a-Daisy," her greatest success in this field.

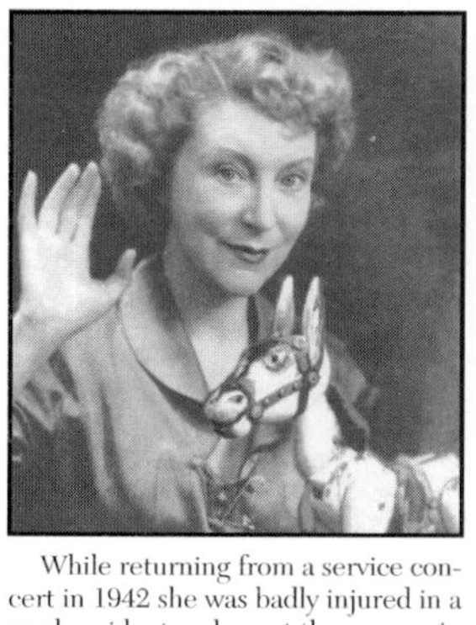

While returning from a service concert in 1942 she was badly injured in a road accident and spent three years in hospital. She began her association with Muffin the Mule when television restarted after the war.

Miss Mills had a nervous breakdown last November and since then had been under constant medical attention. She underwent an operation on Jan. 5.

Last night, McDonald Hobley, the television announcer, told Children's Hour listeners flowers were being sent to her family on their behalf.

Miss Mills marriage to Mr. Sielle was dissolved. Her only child, Mrs. David Blake, a daughter by an earlier marriage, survives her.

(January 11)

DEATH AT 41 OF CARMEN MIRANDA

BRAZILIAN STAR

Daily Telegraph Reporter

Carmen Miranda, who died in Los Angeles yesterday, was the volatile Brazilian film star who became the highest paid woman in America. She was 41.

Leaving her Brazilian convent school at 15 she became a radio singer in Rio de Janiero. Her metallic, lingering voice and overwhelming verve captured the imagination first of South America and later the world.

In 10 years she made more than 1,000 records and 50,000 copies of her most famous song, "I-yi-yi-yi" were sold in Brazil alone. Her migration to Hollywood coincided with the war and in a series of exotic musical extravaganzas she rapidly became one of the best loved and most mimicked of the Forces' entertainers.

Her war-time films included "Down Argentina Way", which introduced her to an astonished public. "That Night in Rio", "Springtime in the Rockies" and "Weekend in Havana". Their unblushing escapism and cult of energetic joy caught the prevailing mood. In 1945-46 Carmen became America's highest paid woman earning £50,364.

LONDON APPEARANCE

With her foot-high hat, covered in gleaming sequins and glass fruit, and violent limb contortions, she radiated physical exuberance. In 1948 she appeared at the London Palladium.

In 1947 she married Mr. David Sebastian, a Hollywood film producer. Complaining that the income tax authorities took most of her earnings, she cut down her films to one a year. Her latest "Scared Stiff" was seen in England two years ago.

She was born in Portugal, her stage name being a play on her real one, Maria do Carmen Miranda da Cunha. Her parents were well-born and opposed her stage aspirations but she took professional singing lessons and was soon established as a café entertainer.

(August 6)

FILM STAR KILLED

James Dean, 24, the successful star who scored a notable success in "East of Eden" was killed on Friday night when his sports car collided with another car near Hollywood.

(October 5)

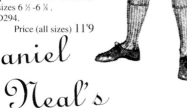

MR. L. S. AMERY

LIFE'S WORK IN EMPIRE CAUSE

Mr. L.S. Amery, who has died at the age of 81, was a life-long champion of the British Commonwealth. He never deviated from his profound inflexible belief that the future of the world depended largely on a virile, fully developed Empire.

His career was a triumph of temperament, training and industry, for he resembled little the conventional conception of a popular politician.

His voice was unmelodious, and his speeches were more factual than forensic. Yet in the course of his 24 years as Conservative M.P. for Sparbrook, Birmingham, he held many high offices, culminating in his term as a distinguished Secretary of State for India.

Courteous, courageous, conscientious and compulsive, Mr. Amery faced both personal and political tragedies with indomitable spirit.

HAD RESPECT OF ALL

In physical stature alone was he lower than the greatest of his contemporaries. Indeed, it has been said that if he had been half a head taller and if his speeches had been half an hour shorter, he would infallibly have been Prime Minister. He had the respect of all and the affection of many.

He firmly and courageously supported the causes of tariff reform and the rights of Ulster. Almost alone in his party, and indeed in the country, he criticised the "Geddes Axe," or economy measures, which followed the 1914-18 war.

But even a hostile House always gave him latitude, because of his transparent honesty and sincerity. This great Imperialist rose to almost sublime heights on two occasions when he uttered exclamations in the Commons which well exemplified his dery convictions.

To Arthur Greenwood, since then Deputy Leader of the Socialist party, he cried: "Speak for England!" on Sept. 2, 1939. In 1940 he expressed the mood of the House when he advised Mr. Neville Chamberlain, in the words of Cromwell, "In the name of God, go!"

GIFT FOR LANGUAGES

There were few countries, in and outside the Empire, with which he was not familiar, and he had an extraordinary facility for languages. This "most erudite statesman," as he was once called, could speak in more than a dozen foreign tongues, including Arabic.

He employed many of them to preach the gospel of Empire development and economic co-operation. For many years his hobby was mountaineering.

Leopold Stennett Amery was born on Nov. 22, 1873, at Gorakhpur, United Provinces, India. He was the son of an Indian Forestry Commission official, and was educated at Harrow, where he was once pushed into the swimming pool bath by a boy named Winston Churchill, and at Balliol College, Oxford.

From 1899-1909 he was a journalist, acting as war correspondent for the Times in South Africa, and later writing a history of that war. In 1902 he was also called to the Bar of the Inner Temple. He never practised, but this event showed the vast versatility of his erudition.

ELECTED M.P. IN 1911

His early attempts to enter Parliament met with failure. He unsuccessfully contested four by-elections between 1906 and 1910. In 1911 he was elected on Joseph Chamberlain's preferential Empire tariff platform.

In the early part of the 1914-18 war he served in Flanders and the Near East, but was recalled to become Assistant Secretary to the War Cabinet and Imperial War Cabinet in 1917.

He was Parliamentary and Financial Secretary for the Colonies from 1919-21 and served in similar capacity to the Admiralty in 1922-24, with which office he combined that of Secretary for the Dominions 1925-29. He lost his seat in the 1945 General Election.

He married in 1910 Miss Florence Greenwood, sister of the first Viscount Greenwood. Their companionship was long, gracious and tender. She survives him with one son, Mr. Julian Amery, Conservative M.P. for Preston North.

(September 11)

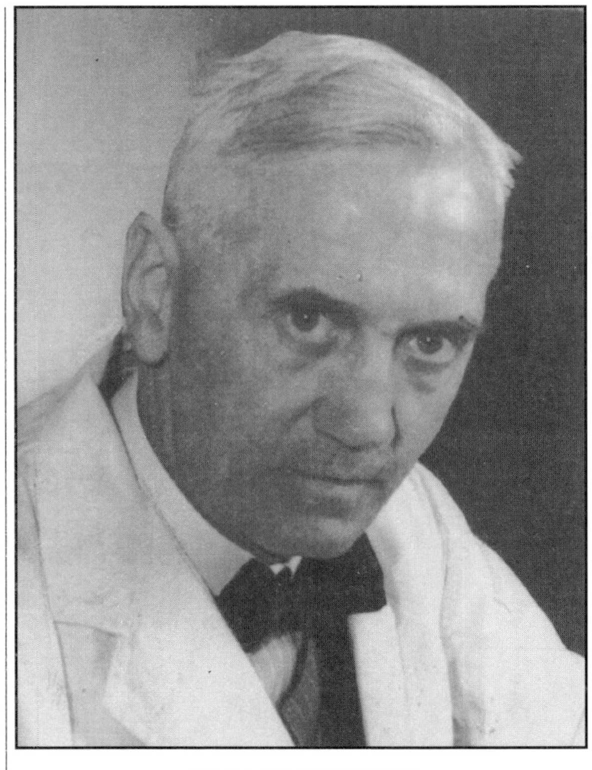

SIR ALEXANDER FLEMING

DISCOVERER OF PENICILLIN

SIR A. FLEMING

The discovery of penicillin by Sir Alexander Fleming, who has died at the age of 73, and its development into a most powerful agent against septic infections, ranks as one of the most important in the history of medical science. Penicillin has probably alleviated more suffering, and saved more lives than any other drug yet known.

Sir Alexander - then Professor - Fleming was pursuing bacteriological researches at St. Mary's Hospital, Paddington, when, in 1929, the accidental contamination by mould of a culture plate of bacteria aroused his interest.

He noticed that the mould appeared to be dissolving the colonies of staphylococci on the plate. Something in the mould, he deduced, was inhibiting the growth of the bacteria. He experimented with the cultivations of the mould on liquid broth.

He discovered, with some elation, that while non-poisonous and apparently harmless to white bloodcells, the mixture contained something definitely inimical to many of the most deadly microbes. The mould was identified as Penicillum notatum, and Fleming named the antibiotic it produced, penicillin.

MANY OBSTACLES

Several years elapsed before the great discovery could be put to use on the battlefields on the 1939-45 war. The production of penicillin in a more purer and concentrated form was accompanied by many obstacles.

By 1932 research workers had discovered how to grow the mould on a synthetic liquid medium and also how to pass it into ether. Unfortunately, destruction of the ether involved the disappearance of most of the penicillin. Disheartened, the researchers decided that the new antiseptic was too unstable to be practical.

It was not until 1938 that Sir Howard Florey and Dr. D.B.E. Chain, working at the Oxford school of Pathology with a considerable team of research workers, evolved satisfactory formulas for the production of the new antiseptic.

The next step was production to cope with war casualties. This was achieved by enlisting the aid of American commercial chemists. It remained a matter for regret with Sir Alexander that commercialisation of his product, which he gave freely to the world, involved payments to American chemists on all subsequent sales.

SON OF FARMER

Alexander Fleming, son of a farmer, was educated at Kilmarnock Academy, and he worked for five years in a London shipping office before entering St. Mary's Medical School.

Here he came under the wise direction of Sir Almroth Wright, the great bacteriologist. Under his instruction Fleming secured honours in every subject.

He served in the 1914-18 war, subsequently returning to St. Mary's, where in 1928 he was appointed Professor of the Medical School. Since 1948 he has been Professor of Bacteriology at London University.

He was knighted in 1944 and in 1945 he was awarded jointly with Sir Howard Florey and Dr. Chain the Nobel Prize for Medicine.

(March 12)

TEST CRICKETER OF GOLDEN ERA: LEN BRAUND

By C.B. Fry

Leonard Braund, the Somerset and England cricketer, who has died, aged 80, was one of the most valuable members of our Test elevens in what we now call the Golden Era. He was of the most remarkable value.

In the first place, he was an exceptionally fine leg break bowler, not a mere change bowler, but one who could start the bowling with a new ball, and keep an end for an hour and a half if necessary.

In class, he ranked along with such great leg bowlers as Grimmett and Mailey and in fact, was perhaps the nearest bowler of his kind we have had to Grimmett. In addition to that he was a good medium fast bowler, fit to go on second or third change in a Test match.

BIG SYDNEY STAND

But he had other merits. He was one of the best big-match batsmen England possessed, even in the days of McLaren and Jackson. In fact, there was no batsman on the England side so valuable to go in fifth or sixth wicket and put a stop to any failure to make runs.

When in Australia, 1903-4, with Sir Pelham Warner's team which brought back the Ashes, he shared in a tremendous partnership in the Sydney match with R.E. Foster. Foster made 287 and Braund collected 102 at the other end. It was a great partnership.

But there is more to be said about Braund, because he was in my opinion the best short slip I ever saw. The value of such bowlers as Statham and Tyson would be enhanced by about 15 per cent if we now had anyone like Braund in the slips. He used to pick up all sorts of catches, rather in the manner of a young lady gathering gooseberries, first on one side and then the other. He had a peculiar, delicate manner of pouching difficult catches with the tips of his fingers.

On one occasion he was fielding first slip when Clem Hill was batting at Edgbaston. The bowler was George Hirst.

CROSSED WICKET TO CATCH

Clem Hill played a perfectly timed glance to leg. But Braund, though at short slip, somehow succeeded in projecting himself quite amiably to the other side of the wicket, and Clem Hill was out. This is the most remarkable catch I ever saw in cricket.

But Braund had other titles to fame. One is that he formed one of the select band of England cricketers who were on the Surrey list but were not appreciated.

Besides him, there was R.E.S. Wyatt, A.E.R. Gilligan, and, will you believe it, Philip Mead, who after dismissal from the Surrey ground staff played for Hampshire and made 153 centuries.

BAD LUCK IN LIFE

On the whole, I am not sure that Braund's success for Somerset and England, after being allowed to drift away by Surrey, is not one of the bon mots of cricket history. Just fancy Leonard Braund, a truly great cricketer, being able to slip out of the Metropolitan area.

Leonard Braund had terrible bad luck in his life. He surmounted it with all the same curious, delicate equanimity with which he caught catches at short leg when he was supposed to be fielding at first slip.

He was one of those quite, unobtrusive but remarkably efficient cricketers, who succeeded in doing great performances, and yet avoiding the attentions of the boomster.

Between 1902 and 1907 he played 23 Tests, all but three of them against Australia. He joined Somerset in 1901 and quickly dominated the side by his forceful batting and clever bowling. In all first class cricket he scored 17,695 runs, took 1,101 wickets and held 508 catches.

He retired in 1920 and became an umpire. Late in life he had both legs amputated.

(December 24)

MAURICE UTRILLO

Maurice Utrillo, the French painter, who has died aged 71, brought remarkable feeling and perception to the studies of shabby streets, for which he was best known.

His youth was tempestuous. Born in Montmartre, which later was to provide him with the material for many of his paintings, he early succumbed to drink, and at 18 was admitted to hospital as a chronic alcoholic.

From then, until his marriage in 1936, he was a frequent inmate of hospitals and clinics. He once lived over a bistro and supplied the provider with paintings in return for drink. At another period his mother rationed him to one bottle of wine a picture, a manoeuvre which only led to a faster output.

After his marriage he lived quietly and abstemiously. In 1937 he brought a libel action against the Tate Gallery and a firm of catalogue publishers who, by a slip, had said that Utrillo had died from the effects of drink. The case was later settled.

T.W. Earp writes: Utrillo is best known as the painter of Montmartre, which he depicted with a haunting evocative magic. In luminous colour he imparted the time-corroded buildings and byways a perculiar vein of urban romance. Its appeal is the more nostalgic because of the changing aspect of the scenes he treated with sensitive but pronounced mastery.

(March 7)

LADY I. SACKVILLE

Lady Idina Sackville, who has died aged 62, was the daughter of the eighth Earl De La Warr. She had lived in Kenya since 1919, and left her farm at the start of the emergency to settle near Mombassa.

The first of her five marriages in 1913 to Capt. Euan Wallace, a former Minister of Transport was dissolved in 1919. The same year she married Capt. Charles Gordon, from whom she was granted a divorce in 1923.

In that year she married the 22nd Earl of Erroll, obtaining a divorce seven years later. Her fourth husband, in 1930, was Mr. Donald Carmichael-Haldeman, the marriage being dissolved in 1938, and in 1939 she married Flt. Lt. Vincent William Soltau.

(November 7)

PROF. JOSE ORTEGA Y GASSET

The anti-monarchial writings of Prof. José Orgeta y Gasset, the Spanish philosopher and the man of letters, who has died aged 72, contributed materially to the end of the Spanish Monarchy. But, paradoxically, he soon turned against the new régime, speaking of "the sour and gloomy race of the Republic."

A graduate of Madrid and Marburg Universities, he became a Professor of Metaphysics at Madrid in 1910. In 1930 he wrote an article in a Madrid newspaper entitled "The Monarchy must be Destroyed" which created a sensation in Spain.

His book "Invertebrate Spain" in 1923 summarised the Spanish political scene, but his reputation was founded largely on "The Revolt of the Masses" in 1930.

In this he traced the moral, political and religious degeneration of the world to the emergence of the "mass man", who has, he maintained, no ideals beyond those of material and economic well-being. He believed that whereas other civilisations were destroyed by barbarians from outside, our own would perish by reason of the barbarians within, the masses.

(October 12)

LONDON DAY BY DAY

Eden Leaves F. O. Woburn Open To Public

There was a sparse House on the evening of April 4 to hear Sir Anthony make his last speech as Foreign Secretary. It was on Britain's accession to the Turco-Iraki Pact.

In the course of a nimble and good natured debating performance he effectively defended Nuri es-Said, the Iraki Prime Minister, whom Mr. Crossman had earlier called "a stooge of the British".

Sir Anthony pointed out with some warmth that it was not a crime to be friendly to this country.

Then he hurried away to change for Sir Winston's dinner to the Queen at Number Ten. When next he entered the House it was as Prime Minister.

But Still Smoking

In Sir Anthony Eden we find one who has already served as Deputy Prime Minister since 1951. I do not know that he has had very much to do in that capacity: one might as well be a deputy volcano" - Lord Samuel in the House of Lords, the day after Sir Winston resigned.

Exodus On "Change"

On the Stock Exchange one evidence that a newspaper strike was in progress was a minor exodus into the basement at one o'clock.

For the first time since 1945 there was a reversion of the war-time practice of relaying the B.B.C. news in the Settling Room.

But the bookies have been hard hit. By the end of the first week of the strike the number of bets was down to "nearly nothing" - well below 5 per cent of normal.

Conditions improved slightly for the larger firms when they started issuing lists and giving an efficient telephone service. Each day an old and respected client used one such service.

She wanted to know each runner -an average of 120 a day - and jockey, and all the betting. She usually finished up with a half-crown bet. And she piled Pelion on Ossa by generally winning it.

Che Sarà Sarà

Nobody appreciates the fatalism of the Bedford family motto just now more than the Duke himself. "Che sarà sarà" (What will be will be) is an apt comment on the opening of the Woburn Abbey to the public to raise money for death duties.

He has made a good start. The Easter visitors totalled 21,600.

"I don't know what my grandfather would have said" he remarked to me after I had seen the swings and roundabouts. "He'd have spun around like a martini in a cocktail shaker."

It was the 11th Duke who had stocked the park with rare animals and birds visitors will now gaze at. The 12th demolished a Victorian wing on whose site Prof. Richardson, the P.R.A., has put a fine ornamental stairway.

Sullivan Orientalised

In Jordan the three Arab Legion bands are busy learning such bandstand favourites as "Rose Marie" and "The Pirates of Penzance".

All three are coming here this summer. Apart from such military events as the Royal Tournament and the Northern Command Tattoo, they have several purely civil engagements and will need a popular repertoire.

Col. Melville, the Arab Legion's liasion officer here, tells me the bands, which include bagpipes, are smart and efficient.

Sometimes they introduce an engaging "Oriental overtone" to their Western music. I hope they do the same with "The Pirates".

A Great English Painter

Nearly 250 paintings and drawings by Sir Alfred Munnings done during 60 years are on view at the Russel-Cotes Art Gallery in Bournemouth.

James Gunn, the well known portrait painter, who opened it on April 2, said there would be disappointment that such a remarkable exhibition had not been shown at the Royal Academy.

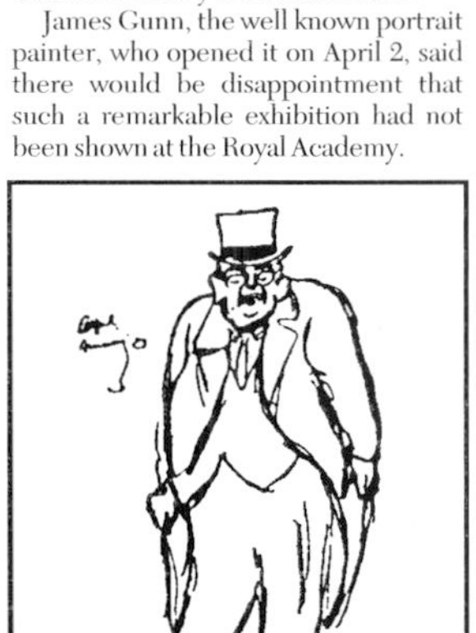

"A great artist and a master of his craft," was Mr. Gunn's appraisal of the P.P.R.A.

He knew the English countryside and he painted it, Mr. Gunn said, "for men of wit and sanity to appreciate in a world not quite sane."

Mr. Gunn also referred to a contemporary fashion which exalts the amateur and derides the craftsman. It came, he said, to us from a country "where art grows from disillusion and defeat."

Homage To Silence

Many tributes were apt to John W. Davis, who has died, when he was American Ambassador in London. The neatest, I think, described as his best speech one he never made.

He prepared it for a lunch in 1921 at the Mansion House at which the Prince of Wales gave an account of his visit to Canada.

The guests found the Prince's words both moving and amusing. Davis decided to pay him truly diplomatic compliment.

Discarding the notes of his own speech, he gave instead a two minute appreciation of the Prince's. Then he sat down. The applause was tremendous.

Eton History

I hear that Adrian Lyttelton, youngest son of Lord Chandos, formerly Oliver Lyttelton, has been awarded this year's Rosebery History Prize at Eton.

As an academic distinction it ranks second only to the Newcastle, a classical prize. It was awarded on three papers - Motley's "Dutch Republic", English history from 1870 to 1914 and a general paper.

Few families have such strong links with Eton, as the Lytteltons. Mostly they have been classics, and I believe Adrian is the first to win the Rosebery.

PETERBOROUGH

THREE CAPTAINS GIVE UP COUNTY CRICKET

Yardley's Distinguished Career As Player And Selector

By Michael Melford

The sadness that strikes most cricket watchers as a golden summer fades will be particularly acute in some counties this year as old friends of pre-war days pass from the active scene.

At Southend this week, N.W.D. Yardley leads Yorkshire for the last time in the championship. He will be ending at the age of 40 a full and distinguished career which has included the captaincy of Cambridge in 1938, of Yorkshire for eight seasons and of England in 14 of the 20 Test matches in which he played.

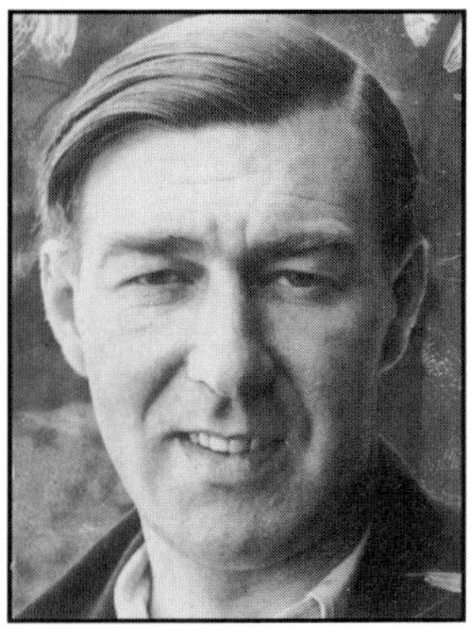

N. W. D. YARDLEY

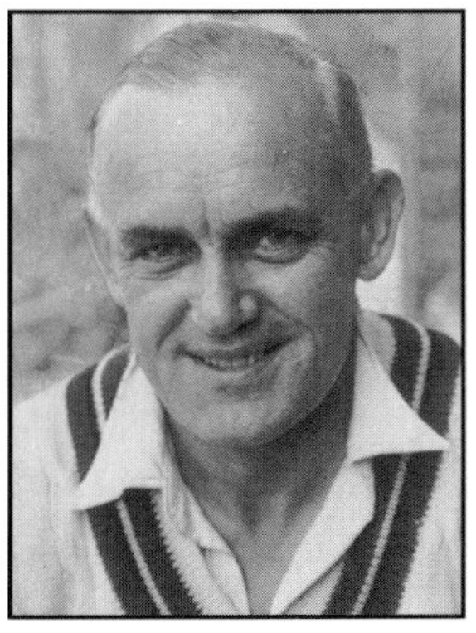

REG. PERKS

He has served for four years on selection committees, which is probably as severe a test of vitality as anything nowadays, for two years as chairman. There will be disappointment in many places outside Yorkshire if, as seems almost certain now, he cannot end by leading Yorkshire to the championship.

Another greatly respected county captain, Dollery, is leaving the stage while still at the height of his powers. The easy command and compactness about his batting has almost been depressing this summer in the way it has underlined the things still missing in the technique of many young players.

Perks steps down from the captaincy of Worcestershire, leaving behind all sorts of records concerning overs bowled and wickets taken. On his last matches will depend another record, for he needs only nine more wickets to reach 100 for the 16th season. No bowler of pace has ever done this before.

DOUBLE SUSSEX LOSS

Langridge and Cox

Nowhere is the sense of loss stronger than in Sussex where they will soon be saying good-bye to both Langridge and Cox.

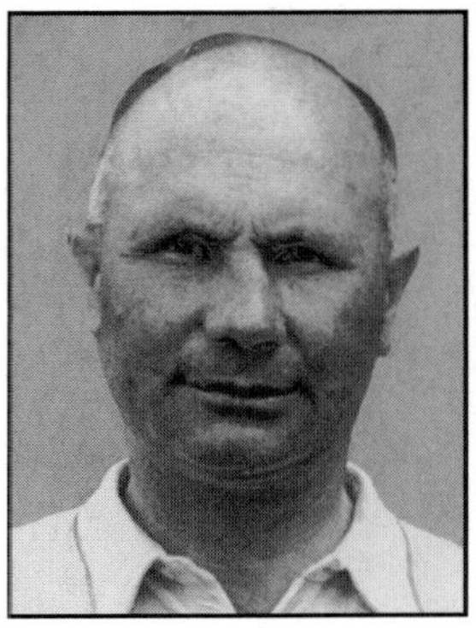

LANGRIDGE

John Langridge's name will stand long in the record books, not only of Sussex. One of the finest feats must be the slip-catching which within the last fortnight has taken him to join Tunnicliffe and Hammond, the only other fieldsmen ever to take over 50 catches in four separate seasons.

Hammond's last harvest was reaped at the age of 32, Tunnicliffe's at 38. Langridge has been performing his prodigies of eye and agility this year at 45.

He has made more runs for Sussex than anyone else (some 34,000) and more centuries (76). He has the best aggregate in a season for Sussex (2,850) and the most centuries (12). His opening stand of 490 against Middlesex in 1933 with Bowley – made in five hours 50 minutes - is still the third highest ever recorded in first-class cricket anywhere in the world.

TO COACH WINCHESTER

George Cox will be rembered not for the records but for the joyous bubbling gaiety which marks his cricket. Few batsmen of his time have given as much pleasure, though his runs were by no means reserved for festive occasions. For much of the last 10 years he has averaged around 100 against Yorkshire.

His reputation as a coach is worldwide already and it is a comfort that he is not to go to South Africa, where he has spent many winters, but to Winchester where he succeeds Bowley next month. Likewise it is good to know that Langridge is thinking of turning the aforementioned eye, if not agility, to the matter of umpiring.

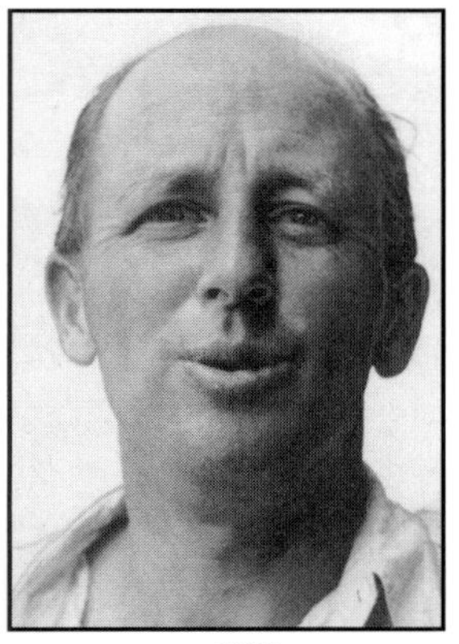

COX

The departure of these two marks the end of an era in Sussex cricket. Cox's service with Sussex overlapped that of his famous father, who first played for them at the turn of the century. There has been at least one Langridge in the side since 1924.

There is just a chance, however, that the Langridge link may soon be reforged. Richard, son of James, is a left-handed batsman, an off-spinner and a cricketer who at 16 carries hopes well outside the family circle.

John Langridge first played first class cricket in 1928, Cox in 1931. In their different ways they must surely through the years have covered all the cricketing virtues. In these lean years it is a shattering thought that neither ever played for England.

(August 22)

PLAYER STRUCK DEAD

From Our Own Correspondent

SYDNEY, Sunday.

A batsman was killed by lightning and the umpires and fieldsmen were struck to the ground in a thunderstorm during a cricket match at Frankstown, a suburb of Melbourne, yesterday. Four players were taken to hospital with burns and shock.

(October 3)

Holiday Soccer Highlights

MANCHESTER UNITED STILL LEAD BY 3 POINTS

Newcastle Scoring Outburst: Crowds Flock Back To League Games

By Frank Coles

Third and last day of the Christmas Soccer carnival brought some astonishing form upheavels yesterday.

Manchester United suffered their heaviest defeat of the season in losing 3-0 at Charlton. Luckily, their nearest rivals all faltered and they claim an overall lead of three points.

Erratic Blackpool dropped four of the six holiday points, but remain United's chief challengers.

Striking advancement has been made by Newcastle and Luton Town, now third on the list thanks to a double success over Sheffield United.

£12,000 FOR HOLDEN

Newcastle United, now sixth, were the only First Division side to gather the maximum six points. On Boxing Day they astonished the football world by routing Sunderland 6-1 at Roker Park and repeated the dose yesterday by winning at home 3-1.

Sunderland paid £12,000 on Boxing Day for the transfer of Holden, Burnley's centre-forward. He scored their only goal at Newcastle.

Newcastle ran up 14 goals in three Christmas games - nine against Sunderland. Keeble and Milburn eached netted five times.

A crowd of 61,040 assembled at St. James's Park yesterday, a figure narrowly beaten at Highbury, where 61,814 saw Arsenal and Wolves share the points for the second time in 24 hours.

STRANGE REVERSAL

There was a remarkable reversal of form in the matches between Birmingham and Everton. Birmingham won 6-2 on Boxing Day and yesterday Everton triumphed 5-1.

After losing five out of six games Bristol City returned to form with a 6-0 victory over Plymouth, to whom they lost 5-0 on Monday, and share second place in the Second Division with Swansea, two points behind Sheffield Wednesday.

In the Third Division (South) Leyton Orient lead Ipswich by one point, with Brighton and Torquay hard on their heels.

In spite of the rain over 965,000 watched yesterday's 45 League matches. The attendance over the three days was more than 2,500,000.

WON ALL, LOST ALL

The only clubs in addition to Newcastle to win all three holiday games were Nottingham Forest, Coventry and Workington. Seven teams, Sunderland, Bolton, Rotherham, Hull, Millwall, Carlisle and Wrexham, failed to make one point from their Christmas fixtures.

(December 28)

LAKER AND LOCK CLINCH RUBBER FOR ENGLAND

Waite Battles On In Vain After Early S. African Collapse

From E.W. Swanton

THE OVAL, Wednesday.

A swift, sad collapse that began just before one o'clock and was over almost on the hour decided the fifth Test to-day and established England as the winners of a close-fought and, after the first Test, an engaging and exciting rubber.

Waite played a very fine innings of 60, which, from the first stroke he played, must have suggested to every South African sympathiser present that the 244 which were required to win was not nearly so steep a mountain as the early successes of Laker and Lock had made it seem.

The game might have gone the other way just as the Lord's Test might have done, and just as England could have engineered draws both at Old Trafford and Headingley in spite of South Africa having had much the best of each match. The more one analyses the more it becomes clear that there is little between the two sides.

It was perhaps always probable that on a wicket on which the ball could be made to turn almost throughout England would be just the more likely to win. It should be mentioned, though, that the winning of the toss meant a good deal in this match and that England did have the better of the wicket.

MAY'S CONTRIBUTION

Again it was an innings of much character and the intensest sort of concentration by May that gave his bowlers their chance to do the job.

When compliments were being exchanged at the end to the edification of a very large crowd gathered in front of the pavilion, May said that he had learnt much during the series not least from the South Africans. That was a modest and proper admission from the youngest captain to have led England through a series in modern times.

It is to be hoped, though, that some other of the England batsmen have learnt something from this steadfast approach. Over the series May has averaged 72 for a total of 582 runs and in the course of history only two English Test captains have scored more: Hutton with 677 in West Indies last year, Hammond with something just over 600 in South Africa before the war. Whoever else has come well from the series May certainly has done so.

South Africa despatched the England 10 and 11 this morning before May could add substantially to the overnight score of 195 for 8. He had time to make one such drive over mid-on's head as many old cricketers were pining to see yesterday, not perhaps from May, who was constituting himself the strong spine of the innings, but from some of the middle-order batsmen. They under an earlier dispensation, would have met Tayfield's skilfully-flighted slow off-breaks by going to the pitch of the ball and hitting straight.

Nevertheless, whatever might be thought of much of the England batmanship, Tayfield's analysis represented an excellent piece of bowling and fittingly capped for him another successful Test series.

SPINNERS SOON ON

South Africa went in just before noon in search of the largest total of the match. The English fast bowlers did not greatly worry McGlew and Goddard, and it seemed that the deshining period was a mere prologue to the appearance of Lock and Laker.

However, with 18 scored, Goddard snicked Bailey clean and comfortably to Close at first slip and down went the catch.

After half an hour came Laker, ten minutes later, Lock, the latter from the Pavilion end with a breeze from mid-off which helped him to indip occasionally, just as Laker was apt now and then to float away.

The two had scarcely begun work together when there came South Africa's mauvais quart d'heure which all but signed and settled the verdict.

First Goddard went to play a square ball from Lock (over the wicket to the left-hander) which came far enough in to him to cramp the stroke and he was picked up easily at slip by Graveney.

Keith, another left-hander, lowed against a Lock well supplied with short-legs, and it was the most forward of them. May, who at the third clutch took a catch from a ball that did turn pretty sharply.

Whether or not it was this ball, allied with one or two more from Laker which pitched in the worn marks outside the leg stump and zipped sharply but harmlessly across towards the short-legs, that encouraged the South Africans to desperation, I do not know.

BALL TURNS

Wicket Not Wicked

At all events, the strokes played by both Endean and Mclean suggested that the wicket was truly wicked - which, in fact, it never was. The ball generally turned, as Tayfield had turned it yesterday, but it kept an even height and pace and neither Laker nor Lock could conjure anything out of the conditions that might not be met by a good eye, sound judgment and the use of the feet. Waite's lesson, however, lay ahead.

Endean swung at an off-break on the wicket, missed and was given out l.b.w. He seemed to be aiming a sweep and the ball appeared to pitch around the middle and leg.

If Endean miscalculated the risk he took with this stroke there was much less reason for McLean to do the same, for in his case the ball pitched a good deal further towards the off-side. McLean put his front leg out halfway and aimed his stroke to mid-wicket.

So many batsmen who should have known better had got out in this match aiming across the flight of the ball. Now this lapse of McLean's, and one can give it no other name, came as the climax of a period in which four wickets fell while the score was shunting forward by five miserable runs.

McGlew watched these things impassively, but his jaw seemed to be jutting further than ever down the crease as he and Waite proceeded to tide South Africa over any further trouble before lunch.

At 57 for four it seemed then up to these two or no one for the major effort. McGlew, with his tight forward stroke, was giving the spinners the very minimum scope, but after two runs had come in a tense quarter of an hour Lock made one hurry off somewhat quicker than the others and McGlew in his turn departed by that most unsatisfactory of verdicts l.b.w.

CHEETHAM BEATEN

Waite Enjoys Himself

Cheetham batted in company with Waite for nearly half an hour, durin g which Waite added 20 impeccable runs, driving through the covers and past mid-off when the ball was a full length and square cutting superbly when it dropped short.

Cheetham was slow to pick up the idea, but at length he missed an off-break on the back stroke and at quarter to three South Africa were 88 for six.

Was this the beginning of the end? Not quite, for Mansell now accompanied Waite for the best part of an hour and a half, defending sensibly and above all with a vertical bat while Waite continued apparently to enjoy himself.

England in this period failed to accept their one chance of disposing of Waite when he played outside an off-break from Laker and Spooner missed the difficult stumping.

May brought back Statham for Lock and Mansell forthwith cut him off the full blade of the bat to Ikin in the gully. Ikin almost held the hot chance but finally let it drop and it was after four o'clock before Mansell attempted to off-drive Lock, now from the Vauxhall end, and was taken in the covers.

(August 18)

HUTTON MADE M.C.C. MEMBER

LORD ALEXANDER NEW PRESIDENT

By E.W. Swanton

At the annual general meeting of M.C.C. at Lord's yesterday the President, Viscount Cobham, according to tradition nominated his successor. In naming Field-Marshal Lord Alexander of Tunis, Lord Cobham added to the list of holders of cricket's highest office a man of great renown whose earliest impact on the world was as a cricketer.

The older generation will recall how the Hon. R.H.L.G. Alexander was a central figure in perhaps the most exciting game ever played at Lord's: "Fowler's Match" wherein Eton beat Harrow by nine runs.

Alexander, when his turn came as No.11, could not pull the match out of the fire for Harrow though he took part in the last wicket stand that looked likely to do so.

The best contemporary evidence, however, suggests that the result would have been different if in the Eton last stand better use had been made of his leg-break bowling. He was a bowler and a very fine fielder as a schoolboy, a fact made easy to credit by his ability as a runner. Soon after leaving school Lord Alexander won the Irish mile.

Lord Alexander's accession follows the pattern whereby M.C.C. seek to avail themselves of distinguished men with a background not principally concerned with cricket affairs, who have nevertheless, a grasp of and affection for the game.

A new rule was passed covering the selection of professional cricketers the effect of which is that "in exceptional circumstances" the committee may elect before his retirement a man "who has throughout his career rendered outstanding service to the game, and to M.C.C. in particular." Hitherto elections have been made only after retirement.

At a committee meeting held immediately afterwards Len Hutton was duly elected a member under this rule.

DINNER TO HUTTON'S TEAM

M.C.C. have arranged a dinner to entertain the team that toured Australia and New Zealand. It will take place at the Dorchester Hotel on Monday, June 6. Members of the club can obtain details from the secretary.

This will be the first dinner of its kind since 1932-3 when M.C.C. entertained the winners of the Ashes. The successful teams of 1903-4 and 1911-12 were similarly honoured by M.C.C. and the 1928-29 team dined at the Mansion House as guests of the Lord Mayor.

Many no doubt will wish to mark by their presence their appreciation of the performance of the side in recovering so well from the disastrous first Test as to win the next three matches and the rubber.

(May 5)

(November 1)

OXFORD'S WILL TO ATTACK WINS AT TWICKENHAM

Just Result to Close and Exciting Match of Brilliant Passing

From E.W. Swanton

TWICKENHAM, Tuesday.

Oxford .... **9 pts** **Cambridge** **5**

The University Rugby match came back into its own this afternoon as a great sporting fixture. It was an admirable game from many points of view; it was full of incidents and variety, and its closeness, with one side always within striking distance of the other, kept a crowd in the region of 55,000, a total only once exceeded in the history of the match, in a perpetual roar and chatter of excitement.

The football was mostly pretty good, with many moments of real brilliance when Oxford were passing back and forth, through many hands, keeping the ball for what seemed minutes, probing for a way through the Cambridge defence. It was the persistent will to attack by Oxford which more than anything else, made the game such excellent entertainment.

This quality likewise will, I expect, have convinced all but the most purblind of Cambridge followers that there was full justice in the result.

Oxford won by a penalty goal and two tries to a goal, after Cambridge had opened the scoring and crossed over with a lead of five to three. Oxford went ahead at the start of the second half, and mid-way through it scored again.

Failure to convert meant, however, that Cambridge remained very much in the hunt, and when, directly after this fourth and last score, Fallon was helped off with damaged ribs, the seven Oxford forwards had all they could do to hold the strong and heavier Cambridge pack.

Oxford Hold Out

With Fallon back but little more than a brave passenger, functioning as an extra full back, Cambridge in the last moments mounted a series of dangerous attacks, in one of which Marques, supporting a strong run by Hodgson, hurled himself to within three of four yards from the line.

These were palpitating times for Oxford, but they survived them, and were back in safer territory when Mr. David's last whistle went.

The captains, Allaway and Clements, deserved many congratulations for having determined from the beginning of term to keep the emphasis on attack. It was Oxford's good fortune that they could call upon the experienced and talented Brace, and that they happened quickly upon the alliance of Brace and M.J.K. Smith at half back.

Clements had no such ready-made partnership at hand, and his side's potential was that much the weaker. Nevertheless, though Cambridge may have regrets there need be no reproaches. They were narrowly beaten by a very good side.

OXFORD SCRUMS

Cambridge Line-Outs

The game went pretty well according to forecast, with one exception to be mentioned later. Oxford won 26 scrummages to 19, eight times when Cambridge had the loose head. Raffle four times against the loose head outhooked Allaway.

In the line-out Cambridge got possession 39 times to 21, and these figures do not express what their line-out superiority meant to them, for Marques and the two Evans were getting the ball so cleanly, whereas Oxford won the ball, when they did only after a long maul by the end of which everyone was closely marked down.

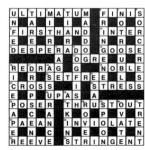

There were 10 penalties to Oxford from one of which they scored and had two other pots at goal. Cambridge had eight penalties, none of them within range. At this point, Mr. David comes in for a full share of praise for handling the game so firmly, and yet without obtrusion.

(December 7)

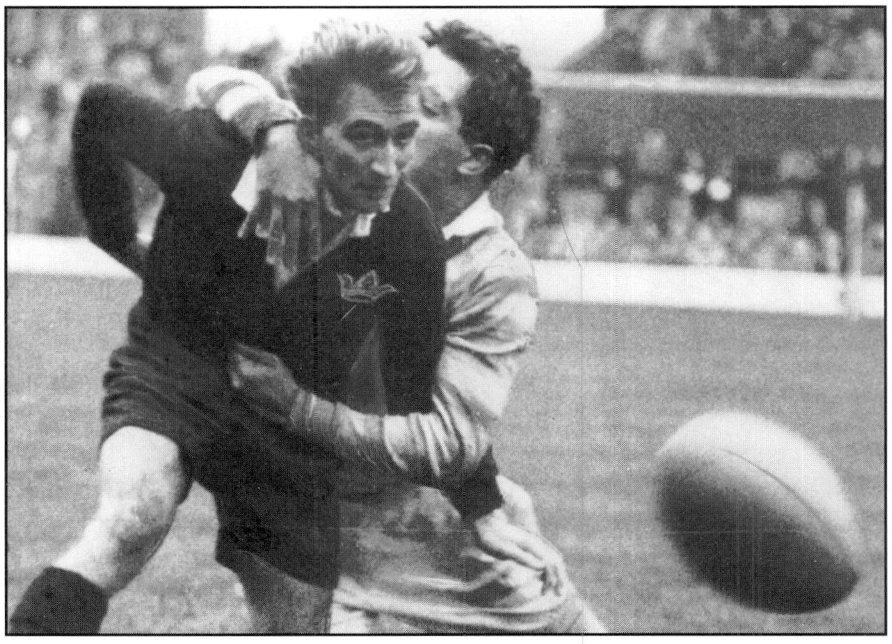

JUST IN TIME. D.O. Brace gets rid of the ball as he receives the full weight of a hurling tackle by J.W. Clements.

(Solution No. 9,349)

U	L	T	I	M	A	T	U	M		F	I	N	I	S
N		A		I		I		A		R		O		O
F	I	R	S	T	H	A	N	D		I	N	T	E	R
E		E		R		R		D		N		R		C
D	E	S	P	E	R	A	D	O		G	O	O	S	E
					A		O	G	R	E		U		R
R	E	D	R	A	G		G			N	O	B	L	E
I		R		S	E	T	F	R	E	E		L		S
C	R	O	S	S			I		S	T	R	E	S	S
E		P		U	P	A	S		A					
P	O	S	E	R		T	H	R	U	S	T	O	U	T
A		C		A		K		O		P		V		R
P	A	E	A	N		I	N	V	I	O	L	A	T	E
E		N		C		N		E		O		T		N
R	E	E	V	E		S	T	R	I	N	G	E	N	T

TRABERT EQUALS FEAT OF DONALD BUDGE

Women's Doubles Finals Will Be All-British Battle

From Lance Tingay

WIMBLEDON, Friday.

A RELENTLESS power player, who scarcely made a loose or thoughtless stroke from the start of things last Monday week, became men's singles champion here this afternoon. Tony Trabert, as expected, was the winner, the 12th American to take the crown, and in the final, watched by Princess Margaret and the Duchess of Kent, he overwhelmed Kurt Nielsen 6-3, 7-5, 6-1.

Great Britain have not, however, come so badly out of the Lawn Tennis Championships after all. The women's doubles finals to-morrow will be entirely British, Miss S. Bloomer and Miss P.E. Ward, against Miss A. Mortimer and Miss J.A. Shilcock.

A Wimbledon title has not been wholly British since 1937. The last all-British final was the men's doubles in 1936 and the last women's doubles exclusively British was 1929.

To bring about this happy state of affairs Miss Bloomer and Miss Ward in the semi-final to-day, reversed the result of the French Championship final by beating the Americans Mrs Beverly Fleitz and Miss Darlene Hard, 6-3, 9-7. Earlier in the curtain-raiser of the day, Miss Mortimer and Miss Shilcock beat the Australians, Miss F. Muller and Mrs. L.A. Hoad, 6-2, 6-1.

REAL CHAMPION

Hallmark of Calibre

It is a matter of record that since the abolition of the challenge round in 1922 only one man, Donald Budge, had become champion without losing a set. Trabert has equalled this feat. Not only did he not concede a set but he scarcely ever looked like doing so.

Trabert has become Wimbledon single's champion in about eight hours' total playing time. With Budge and Jack Kramer and Frank Sedgman it was much the same. They chopped down all opposition with the precision and vigour that is the hallmark of a real champions' calibre.

Trabert took 73 minutes on the Centre Court to-day to make himself the champion. There have been more adventurous finals fought out here and its excitement as a contest with uncertain issue was fleeting.

The winner was too good. Nielsen, who drew inspiration from the distinguished setting to bring Ken Rosewall down in the semi-final, was less inspired to-day. Even if he had been in better form I doubt whether Trabert would have been unduly troubled.

Surging Tide

His game, from start to finish, was like the surging of the tide. In attack he went on and on, always pressing, netwards. In recoiling against Nielsen's pressure weapons the sharp counter-thrust was always ready and even when such was obviously impossible he scampered to retrieve.

His precision and unity of purpose, his freedom from error, his lack of weakness (unless the common vulnerability to lob over the backhand shoulder to be reckoned as such) made him, so far as Nielsen was concerned, like a rock.

It was essentially a power game though some of his most damaging guns were muffled rather than loud. His service, for instance, was the kicking ball. Nielsen took one set and a half to get hold of this and always it gave Trabert time to stand dominantly at the net.

His backhand rolled out winning shots magnificently, but he was not without the gentler touch. The final winning shot was a lob, as good a hoisted shot as ever was, for it pitched within an inch of the baseline and had Nielsen entirely beaten.

NIELSEN'S WEAKNESS

Ineffective Volley

As for Nielsen, it can hardly be called a failure. It is true his service worked less well than sometimes and of the many points he gave away a high proportion came from an ineffective stroke of a forehand volley than was more than waist high.

He was, however, under such constant pressure that it is small wonder that he cracked. His purely defensive equipment was not able to cope with Trabert's guns and he did not try.

His counter-attack, with which he constantly persisted, proved ineffective. Trabert was always moving towards the ball and the general pattern of the contest was both men coming in towards the net. More volleys were played than ground shots.

Where Trabert had marked superiority was in the quality of service return. This factor alone marked him out among the majority of challengers at Wimbledon this year. It requires a delivery of special quality to induce a reply that lacked sting.

Ball Touches Hand

One small incident during the match gave the lawn tennis lawyers a talking point. In the fourth game of the first set Nielsen made a sweeping forehand passing shot that apparently touched the top of the post and was deflected into the court.

A seeming winner was given against Nielsen when the net-cord judge pointed out that it had touched his hand. No one would dispute the legal ruling, but Nielsen might well have asked what business the net-cord man had in not withdrawing his hand long before.

(July 2)

WEMBLEY LUCK CLINGS TO NEWCASTLE UNITED

Manchester City's Gallant 10-man Fight Against Adversity

By Frank Coles

Newcastle United.................. **3** **Manchester City** **1**

WITH the least notable of all the teams which have set up this magnificent unbeaten record of five Cup Final triumphs at Wembley since 1924, Newcastle United on Saturday beat Manchester City, the favourites, by 3-1.

That the win was well and truly deserved everyone among the 100,000 crowd (receipts £49,881) would agree. But the good luck which marked United's progress to the 1955 Final clung to them to the end of the story, a bitter end from the viewpoint of their rivals.

In 1952, the last time Newcastle were Cup winners, the task of mastering Arsenal by 1-0 became considerably less formidable when an unfortunate knee injury kept Barnes, the losers' right-back, off the field for more than hour.

But an almost unbelievable coincidence the incident was now reproduced in every particular, with the substitution of the name of Meadows, right-back for Manchester City, for Barnes.

Nineteen minutes after the start, and when Newcastle were prospering under the influence of a snap goal by Milburn 45 sec. from the kick-off, Meadows fell in agonising pain. He had wrenched the ligaments of his left knee and took no more part in the match.

UNHAPPY HISTORY

Repetition in Detail

Never has Cup Final history been repeated in such stark and unhappy detail. The accident which in the upshot handicapped the Manchester team fatality happened almost on the exact spot where Barnes went down three years earlier, also when tackling the left-winger Mitchell, and only four minutes sooner than in 1952.

Emulating Arsenal, Manchester City fought bravely to stave off the doom that seemed inevitable. With only three effective forwards they not only forced Newcastle back on their heels but actually seized the initiative with a display of quality football reaching Wembley's top level.

The roar which heralded Johnstone's equalising goal with a header half a minute before half-time was spontaneous tribute to as gallant a bid to overcome odds as any Cup Final has produced. But the immense strain it entailed had sapped City's stamina and the penalty had to be paid.

Eight minutes after the interval Spurdle, withdrawn from the right-wing to fill Meadow's place at back, made his first misjudgment of the ball's flight as it soared over from White, and Mitchell, the match winner, drove past Trautmann from a sharp angle.

Driven on by never-say-die attacking rallies headed by their wing-halves. Barnes and Paul (Barnes' long stride seemed to span the whole pitch), the City rallied once more, but six minutes later it was virtually all over. Mitchell again outwitted rather ill-at-ease Spurdle and the grateful Hannah, from close range, banged the winger's cross past the goalkeeper after he had partially cleared.

The goal tally would have been double but for the superb skill of Trautmann, the flaxen-haired German, whose saves all through the afternoon stamped him unmistakably as one of the finest world-class goalkeepers the game has ever known.

Johnstone's Contribution

Manchester had two more men of outstanding merit in addition to Trautmann. The energetic, buoyant Barnes refused to allow the state of the game or his side's overwhelming handicap to suppress him. He was splendidly seconded by the little Scot Johnstone, a brilliant dribbler who shared with Newcastle's Mitchell the forward honours of the day.

Everyone sympathised with Revie. The great playing-from-behind plan which was to put Newcastle strategically on the wrong foot failed to block them in the second half because Revie's aid was sorely needed in a defensive rather than in an attacking role.

(May 9)

UNBEATEN RIBOT WINS

By Hotspur

Ribot, unbeaten Italian three-year-old, won the £39,000 Prix de l'Arc de Triomphe at Longchamp yesterday, the second time since the war that an Italian-bred colt has taken the race. The other was Nuccio in 1952.

Ribot, bred by the late Signor F. Tesia and carrying the colours of the Marchese Incisa della Rochetta, was a convincing winner in the hands of veteran Italian rider E. Camici, who won the Ascot Gold Cup on Botticelli in the same colours.

Sad to relate, Elopement, the only English runner, and the Irish Hugh Lupus both failed badly. Zarathustra ran well for a long way, but finished in the ruck. Second place went to the St. Leger third, Beau Prince II, and the outsider Picounda was third.

Ribot, by the Goodwood Cup winner Tenerani, who now stands the National Stud, was taken out of the Italian classics because of an injury. His connections are hoping for a noteworthy double by winning the Champion Stakes at Newmarket on Thursday with Botticelli.

A record crowd of over 100,000 watched yesterday's race on going which was good, if on the soft side. The early leader was Mahan, followed by Zarathustra, Beau Prince II and Ribot. Coming down the hill Mahan, Ribot and Macip were the leaders, which with Picounda improving and Cordova making up ground on the outside.

Coming round the final bend into the straight Ribot took the lead followed by Beau Prince, and went on to win decisively by three lengths.

Picounda was a further two and a half lengths away, third, in front of Kurun (ridden by C. Smirke).

(October 10)

ROYAL WINNER DISQUALIFIED

The Princess Royal saw her three-year-old Va Presto defeat the joint St. Leger favourite, Acropolis, in the £2,300 Voltiguer Stakes to-day. Then she had the misfortune to lose the race on an objection by the stewards.

At York the stewards occupy a small stand looking straight down the course. It appears that A. Breasley, the rider of Va Presto, could not stop the Princess Royal's colt from hanging to its left in the final quarter of a mile, and interfering with Acropolis.

After hearing evidence from the jockeys concerned, they awarded the race to Acropolis, and Va Presto was disqualified. Acropolis is owned by Lady Irwin, who like the Princess Royal, lives in Yorkshire. It is leased by her to her grandmother, Alice, Countess of Derby.

(August 25)

MOSS WINS BRITISH GRAND PRIX BY ONE-FIFTH SECOND

150,000 AT The Daily Telegraph EVENT

From W.A. McKenzie
Daily Telegraph Motoring Correspondent
AINTREE, Liverpool, Sunday.

Watched by the greatest crowd ever at a motoring contest in this country, Britain's young racing champion, Stirling Moss, achieved the ambition of his life here yesterday. He won the British Grand Prix by a fifth of a second over Juan Fangio, the world champion.

The two silver-bullet Mercedes-Benz cars were followed over the finish line by another pair from the same "stable", the "Mercs" of Karl Kling and Pierre Taruffi. The German team won the first four places.

They were never seriously challenged. But for the rest of the field the Maseratis and the Ferraris from Italy, the Gordinis from France, and the Vanwalls, Connaughts and Cooper of Britain, it was a grim enough struggle.

Two drivers had to be replaced during the 270-mile contest, overcome by heat and strain. Only nine of the 24 starters finished, the remainder standing in the dead-car park, or on the circuit where they had "died".

ENCLOSURES FILLED

Grand National Beaten

The race, sponsored by THE DAILY TELEGRAPH, began with Aintree's grandstands and enclosures being filled by crowds approaching 150,000. Even the Grand National had never seen this multitude.

The county police force, engaged for traffic control, had to be augmented by 250 extra men. It was reported two hours before the race began that traffic formed a solid queue from Chester to Liverpool. Vehicles were taking between one and one and a half hours to transverse the two-and-a-half mile Mersey tunnel.

Over the crowd the sun blazed from a clear sky. Hundreds of high-masted flags of the nations, in honour of the foreign cars and drivers, completed the carnival scene, which had all the atmosphere of any grand prix on the Continent.

FANGIO TAKES THE LEAD

Moss Follows

At the "off", the field screamed away. Fangio took the lead, with Moss on his tail. Only the French ace, Jean Behra, in a Maserati separated them from their team mates, Kling and Taruffi. Two more Maseratis, the works car of Roberto Mieres and Luigi Musso followed Taruffi.

The best of the Ferraris, Eugenio Castellotti's, lay eighth. Its team fellows, driven by Maurice Trintignant and Britain's Mike Hawthorn, lay ninth and tenth.

The best Gordini, Robert Manzon's, was as far back as 12th. The best of the British cars, the Connaught of Tony Rolt, was 15th, with Harry Schell's Vanwall behind.

From the first lap the cars were in trouble. Andre Simon's Maserati came to the pits with a broken gear selector, and stayed there.

A lap later the superiority of Fangio and Moss was evident. Even Behra in the Maserati and Kling and Taruffi in "Mercs" were left behind.

MOSS DRAWS AHEAD

Gap Widens

On the third lap the crowd thrilled to see Moss, an imperturbable, white-helmeted figure, driving at arms length with a replica in style of the great Fangio, slipping past the world champion and then, yard by yard, widening the gap behind him.

By the fifth lap Behra, driving with every ounce of power extended, was 300 yards behind Fangio, with Moss 50 yards in the lead.

Four laps later Behra's Maserati began to pour smoke from its bonnet. It passed the grandstand but we did not see it again. It was the second casualty. An oil pipe had burst.

This put Kling in third place, three Mercedes-Benzes lying one, two, three. Only Mieres, in a Maserati, held Taruffi's Mercedes back from fourth place.

Castellotti's Ferrari came to the pits on the 11th lap to change plugs. Rolt's Connaught pulled in with a jammed throttle. Hermano da Silva Ramos stopped his Gordini to investigate lack of oil pressure. His team mate, Manzon, gave up at Bechers.

By now, with only 15 of the 90 laps covered, Moss and Fangio were handicapped by the necessity for overtaking the back markers, whose drivers, not expecting so soon to be "lapped", pulled over late.

By the 18th lap, Fangio passed Moss and took the lead again. The two were genuinely fighting, a luxury not always allowed to team-mates in the lead.

MOSS GOES FORWARD

Lead Kept Until End

Moss clung to Fangio's tail and on the 25th lap, rounding Tatts corner, he tried to pass. A third car, a back marker being lapped, complicated the manoeuvre, and Moss had to pull rein.

But the next lap he came round 50 yards in the lead. From then, until the finish, he never lost the lead.

(July 18)

WOMAN BEATS CHANNEL RECORD

Miss Florence Chadwick to-day beat her own women's Channel swimming record by completing the crossing to France in 14hr 9min. She came within three minutes of the men's record held by Bill Pickering, Britain.

The out-going tide repeatedly swept the 35-year-old Californian back, and the last 100 yards were the hardest. She seemed exhausted when she staggered ashore at Stangatte, near here, and embraced the few French spectators on the beach.

Plans for an immediate swim back to complete the double crossing were dropped. After only 12 minutes in France Miss Chadwick boarded one of the two boats which escorted her from Dover for the return trip.

(October 12)

OWNER SAW OAKS WIN IN DREAM

LADY ZIA WERNHER

Daily Telegraph Reporter

Nearly five months ago Lady Zia Wernher, owner and breeder of Meld, dreamed that her horse would win both the 1,000 Guineas and the Oaks. Her dream came true at Epsom yesterday when Meld, favourite after its Guineas success, easily won the Oaks with a prize of £14,078, beating Ark Royal by six lengths.

The Queen, accompanied by Queen Elizabeth the Queen Mother, Princes Margaret and other members of the Royal family, saw her horse, Belladonna, saddled for the big race. It finished last.

After leading Meld into the winners' enclosure, Lady Zia Wernher and her husband, Sir Harold Wernher, together with their trainer, Capt. C. Boyd-Rochfort were summoned to the Royal Box. The Queen congratulated them on their success.

Lady Zia said: "I have waited 27 years and have at last won two Classics in a season. In the dream I could see vividly my colours of green and yellow and told my husband what I had seen." She had £10 on her horse.

(May 28)

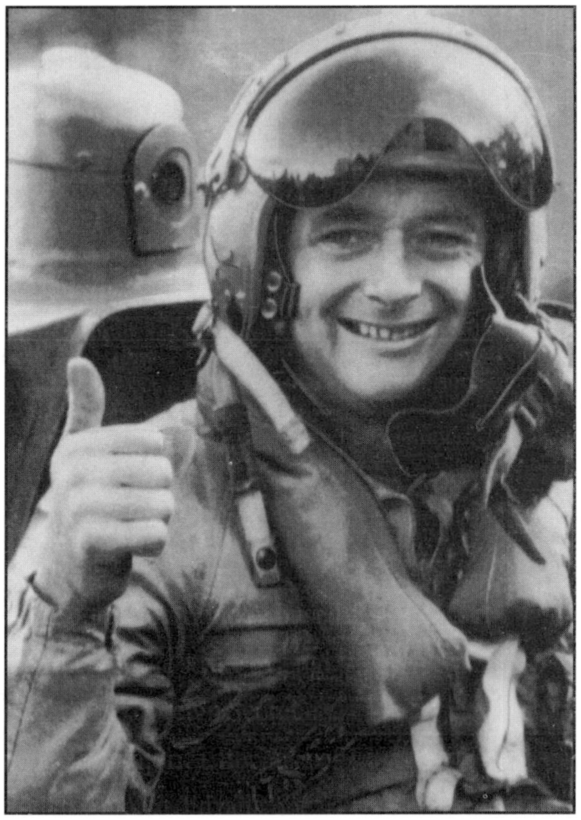

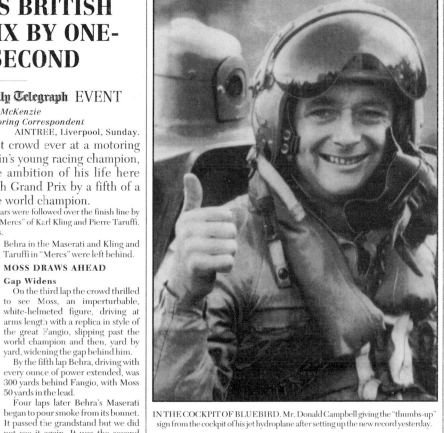

IN THE COCKPIT OF BLUEBIRD. Mr. Donald Campbell giving the "thumbs-up" sign from the cockpit of his jet hydroplane after setting up the new record yesterday.

CAMPBELL BREAKS HIS RECORD AT 216 m.p.h.

From our Special Correspondent
LAKE MEAD, Nevada, Wednesday.

In his jet-powered Bluebird, Mr. Donald Campbell to-day broke his own world water speed record by achieving an official average of 216.2 m.p.h. on two runs over a measured kilometre on the waters of Lake Mead.

His previous record was 202.32 m.p.h. on Ullswater, in July. His triumph to-day, with runs of 239.5 m.p.h. and 193 m.p.h., was achieved after more than a month of frustrating delays and difficulties, which included Bluebird's sinking on a test run on Oct. 16.

He said that at one point on his first run he was shooting along at something like 250 m.p.h. Mr. Kent Hitchcock, the referee, described this run as "fantastic".

On the return run Mr. Campbell encountered far more difficult conditions, with a stronger wind and the surface a little rough.

When the referee reported that after four verifications the average speed was 216.2 m.p.h., Mr. Campbell ordered all craft taking part in the operation to return to base slowly. Since he had a handsome margin there was no point in taking any further risks.

When it was suggested to him that he might try a third run to improve the average, he was heard to say over his radio: "Another run like that and I'd put it right in the drink."

SAVED BY HARNESS

Cheery Wave at End

Describing his return trip, Mr. Campbell said to me: "I was nearly thrown out. If it had not been for the harness I would have gone through the canopy. It was a terrific beating."

He waved to a cheery group of about 50 photographers, reporters and people who have been following his undertaking as he removed his yellow crash helmet, emergency breathing mask and wireless microphone and clambered out of the Bluebird's tiny cockpit at the dock.

After the second run he bought the boat back under her own power. Up to the knees in water he helped his crew with the beaching.

"Thank God I've done it," he said. "But I want to thank the five British chaps in my team who made it all possible. They have worked without sleep for long hours on end. They have been wonderful."

Bluebird's attempt to-day was delayed by sabotage. During the night thieves made off with nearly a mile of wire laid under the water along the shore of the lake to connect the timing devices at each end of the measured kilometre.

Mr. C. Richey, a superintendent of the National Park Service at the lake, told me that the culprits were probably youths who had already caused much trouble by stealing property and selling it.

(November 17)

TURPIN RETIRES

By Lainson Wood

Randolph Turpin fought his last fight last night at Harringay. It ended in the fourteen-round knock-out of the former world middleweight champion by Gordon Wallace, a former holder of the Canadian light heavyweight title.

Turpin had been nominated to fight Archie Moore for the world title at Earls Court in January. Now all those ambitious plans have been swept away.

Turpin was down twice against Wallace and almost out in the second round. His opponent took a count in the third, and then took Turpin with another right swing early in the fourth, which seemed to knock all the sense out of the Briton save the instinct to beat the count.

This he did on rubbery legs, with glassy eyes, to take another crude full swing smack on the chin. This bowled him down again, and this time, try as he would, he could not get into an upright position.

He was counted out in astonishing silence from the 10,000 spectators who soon made amends by their lapse of good manners by giving the Canadian a great ovation.

I would have liked in my heart to have joined them, but to my way of thinking Wallace showed nothing like championship form. He was a crude and inexperienced performer with no pretensions to any class whatsoever.

NO RECOVERY

Little Left

Turpin must take some credit for fighting through that ordeal as he did. But it is clear now that beyond his boxing instinct and the courage to fight on in adversity, Turpin has little left to recommend him. He clearly can no longer take a punch and recover fully from it in the required time.

After the fight Turpin announced his intention to retire. "I have had my last fight," he said. "I could see the punches coming, but I could not get out of the way."

(October 19)

PHIL DRAKE WINS DERBY FOR FRANCE

Late Run and Last-Minute Switch Beats 100-1 Chance

From Hotspur
EPSOM, Wednesday.

MME. SUZY VOLTERRA to-day became the third woman to win the Derby at Epsom. Her Phil Drake, 18th of 23 at Tattenham Corner, came with one of the most thrilling late runs in the history of the race to take the lead less than 100 yards from home from the rank outsider Panaslipper, and yet by 1.5 lengths.

The only two women owners previously to have won the Epsom Derby are Mrs. G.B. Miller with Mid-day Sun (1937) and Mrs. M. Glenister with Nimbus (1949). To-day's race reminded me of that first photo-finish Derby between Nimbus, the late M. Leon Volterra's Amour Drake, and the late Lord Derby's Swallow Tail six years ago.

Just as Phil Drake swooped from behind to-day, so in 1949 Rae Johnstone bought Amour Drake with a thrilling late challenge to Nimbus and Swallow Tail, who were battling for the lead. And just as Amour Drake was switched by Johnstone to the rails in the final furlong, so was Phil Drake in the same colours to-day.

The Irish-trained Panaslipper was in front with his race apparently won a furlong from home when he began to hang to his right. Palmer bought Phil Drake to challenge and had to make a split-second decision to go between Panaslipper and the far rails.

In Johnstone's case the Amour Drake switch unluckily failed. To-day it came off. It was history repeating itself - with a difference!

This was the first time a French woman has won the Derby, but the fourth French victory in the race since the war. Phil Drake's success follows that of Pearl Diver (1947), My Love (1948), and Galcador (1950).

PALMER'S FIRST

Man For The Big Race

Fred Palmer, who was winning the Derby for the first time, is English by blood but French by birth and domicile. His father has for many years been travelling head lad to the Chantilly trainer, Percy Carter. He is an Englishman and was born in Canterbury of a sea-going family.

The winning jockey was formerly the leading steeplechase jockey in France and is first jockey to Carter's stable. He has the reputation of being the man for the big occasion and has won the Grand Prix de Paris three times in the last five years - on Vieux Manoir (1950), Orfeo (1952) and Popof (1954).

(May 26)

No. 9349 ACROSS

1 Last terms able to make tum-tum all! (9)
6 The last word is wrong if backed (5)
9 Information of this sort should give one good grasp of the situation (5-4)
10 Starts to interrupt (5)
11 No doubt a slippery bad man, and half slides through trouble (9)
14 It inspired at least one army to take steps (5)
15 He was a horrid fellow, though royal and regimental (4)
16 A possibly annoying thing to pull along again (3,3)
19 Not one of the commoner coins (5)
20 Emancipate (3,4)
22 It can be a mark of affection (5)
23 If such a force were beheaded it might be attached to a head (6)
24 In botanical works it is not down to a tree (4)
26 The artist's answer to this one might not please the sitter (5)
27 Like the chin of the angry displaced person? (6,3)
32 Vocal praise for Apollo? (5)
33 Unbroken with the instrument whole inside (9)
34 Ruffled old magistrate? (5)
35 By no means lenient, and in the first place possibly blinding (9)

DOWN

1 Neglected state of those one should nourish? (5)
2 They can constitute a growing menace to food supplies (5)
3 In one way I term it a headpiece (5)
4 If this coronet lost its ego, its name would be royally Irish (5)
5 Its bark is certainly not worse than its bite (3,3)
6 A lock container with a ring in it (6,3)
7 One can see it is no foreign coin, without difficulty (2,7)
8 There'll be the devil to pay when she has to reckon with her master (9)
12 Anger is commonly a popular thing (4)
13 There were often barks at sea but not produced by this (7)
16 Is this used by artists because of it good grain? (4-5)
17 To discard part of the act would be something of a theatrical let-down (4-5)
18 Such confidence could deal U.S.S.R. an ace (9)
21 Rough as he was one might have a use for him (4)
25 Thomas had relations in the A.T.S. (6)
28 Places he knows may be all the world this beheaded (5)
29 Afternoon tea club? (5)
30 The shape of a vote (5)
31 This river would be split if beheaded (5)

(December 6)

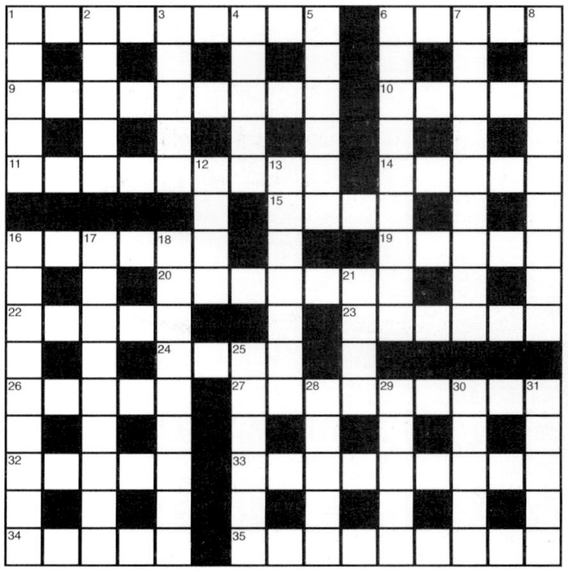

1956

The Daily Telegraph

The darkest year of the decade was dominated by two events in the autumn. Hungary and Poland sought to free themselves from Russian influence. Although the Poles gave way to Russian pressure, the Hungarians refused to bow to Moscow and the Hungarian "revolt" was crushed by Russian tanks. Thousands of Hungarians fled across the border to the West. Early in the year the Egyptian Government under President Nasser had nationalised the Suez Canal. After months of abortive negotiation, British and French forces joined the Israelis in invading Egypt by air, land and sea. After a few days, under United Nations pressure, a cease fire and a withdrawal was ordered and an international force was deployed to provide a buffer between Israel and Egypt.

The long-term effect of these two separate incidents was incalculable. Although Krushchev might in a monumental speech have denounced the Stalin myth and have made some overtures towards greater contact with the West, the split between the Communist and Western nations widened. In Britain the outrage at the events in Hungary led to the virtual dissolution of the Communist party, many of its most influential members resigning in protest. Western unity, too, was threatened by the Suez adventure when the United States refused to support the Anglo-French action, and in the eyes of the world the standing of Britain and France was much weakened by the ill-judged venture, the full nature of which was not to be made public for some years. The Suez affair caused several Conservative ministers to resign and left Anthony Eden a sick man at the end of the year.

In South Africa, 140 people were arrested on treason charges in a dawn swoop. President Eisenhower was re-elected but faced further problems over attempts to end segregation on buses and in schools by the Southern states. A Reverend Martin Luther King was fined for organising a boycott of racially segregated buses. The situation in Cyprus deteriorated after the exiling of the leaders of the Enosis (union with Greece) movement. The North African unrest continued and rising Arab nationalism led to the dismissal of Glubb Pasha as the commander of the Jordanian Frontier Force.

Britain saw the introduction of state gambling, a step regretted by some Church leaders, with the announcement of a monthly Premium Bond lottery. Parking meters installed in city centres would be patrolled by a new force of wardens. Rose Heilbron, QC, was appointed Recorder of Burnley, the first woman to hold this judicial post. A bill ending capital punishment was passed by the House of Commons on a free vote but was defeated in the House of Lords.

Cinemas were wrecked by crowds of youngsters cavorting to the music of Bill Haley and the Comets played in the film *Rock Around the Clock*. A new era in the theatre was presaged by the production at the Royal Court Theatre of John Osborne's *Look Back in Anger*, a play cautiously welcomed by *The Daily Telegraph* critic as being "of some power but uncertainly directed".

PRICE TWOPENCE

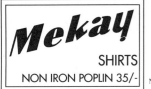

The Daily Telegraph

5 A.M.

No. 31,590 LONDON, MONDAY, NOVEMBER 5, 1956 — and Morning Post — Printed in LONDON and MANCHESTER

SOVIET TANKS CRUSH HUNGARIAN RISING

EISENHOWER APPEAL TO BULGANIN

'HELP... HELP ... HELP' CALL FROM BUDAPEST

U.N. ASSEMBLY DEMANDS TROOP WITHDRAWAL

The Soviet Army using its full weight of tanks, planes, artillery and infantrymen overran Hungary yesterday. Attacks on key points began before Sunday dawned and by noon, despite some heavy fighting, the Russians appeared to be in control.

An ultimatum was sent to Mr. Nagy, the new Prime Minister, calling on him to capitulate or Budapest would be bombed. Instead he broadcast an appeal "to the world" for help. But by 8.10 a.m. Radio Budapest was silenced, the last words heard being "Help Hungary... Help... Help... Help..."

President Eisenhower last night sent an urgent message to Marshal Bulganin, the Russian Prime Minister, expressing "shock and dismay" at the Russian attack. He asked the Marshal to withdraw the troops.

The United Nations General Assembly last night passed by an overwhelming majority an American resolution demanding the withdrawal of Russian troops and the entry of U.N. observers into Hungary. Earlier, in the Security Council, Russia vetoed an American motion to debate Hungary.

Mr. Nagy and his Ministers are believed to be under arrest. Moscow radio at lunch-time claimed that "the Hungarian counter-revolution has been crushed." It said that a "Revolutionary Workers' and Peasant Government" had been formed under Mr. Kadar, 44, a former Titoist, rehabilitated in 1954.

ATTACKS BEFORE DAWN

From Our Own Correspondent

VIENNA, Sunday.

A concentric attack by Russian tanks and artillery on Budapest began early this morning. About 1,000 tanks were believed to have been in action.

After heavy fighting with Hungarian army units dug in on the outskirts of the capital the first Soviet tanks entered Budapest soon after six a.m. The main centres of fighting were the Parliament Building, seat of the Nagy Government, and the Defence Ministry.

Russian troops took Parliament before 9 a.m. The fate of members of the Nagy Government assembled there is not known.

Earlier the Russians detained the Deputy Defence Minister Lt.-Col Pal Maleter, "hero of Budapest," who led the toughest rebel resistance group, and Gen. Kovacs, his Chief of Staff. They were in the middle of talks with Russian Army leaders about the withdrawal of Soviet troops from Hungary.

PREMIER'S APPEAL

4-Language Message

Mr. Nagy in an urgent appeal over Radio Budapest at 5.15 a.m. told his people and the world of the Russian attack. His words were repeated several times in Hungarian, German, French, English and Russian until the radio stations closed just before 9 a.m.

Telephone contact with Budapest was cut much earlier. About 11 a.m., the last teleprinter message was received. It ended with a frantic appeal to the West for help. The only link with the outside world since has been a small radio transmitter in the British Legation building.

The first Russian attacks were apparently made in the middle of the night in the east and southern Hungary. Heavy fighting was reported around the uranium mines of Pecs which were defended by Hungarian army and workers' units.

In Szolnok, 50 miles south-east of Budapest, a so-called "revolutionary peasant and workers' Government" was established under Janos Kadar, a Communist "Tito-ist" who only recently was rehabilitated.

He was also a member of the Nagy Government. Kadar denounced Mr. Nagy as a "tool of reactionaries" and asked the Soviet army for help."

U.N. CALL FOR OBSERVERS IN HUNGARY

From Our Own Correspondent

NEW YORK, Sunday.

An emergency session of the United Nations General Assembly to-night by 50 votes to 8, with 15 abstentions, adopted an American resolution calling on Russia to halt its armed attack on Hungary and "withdraw all its forces without delay."

The resolution also instructed Mr. Hammarskjoeld, the Secretary-General, to investigate the situation in Hungary with observers appointed by him. They would then report back as soon as possible on methods to end "the foreign intervention."

Mr. Sobolev, Russia, objected to the Assembly discussing the Hungarian situation. He said that to do so would be "a gross violation of Article II of the Charter... which prohibits the intervention of the organisation in the domestic affairs of member-States."

DEBATE "INVALID"

The appeal to the United Nations last week from Mr. Nagy, the deposed Hungarian Prime Minister, had been unconstitutional and was therefore invalid. The formation of the new Hungarian Cabinet had made the appeal invalid, and he therefore objected to any discussion of the matter at the United Nations, since the matter came under the jurisdiction of Hungary.

The Assembly agreed to debate the issue by 53 votes to eight, with seven abstentions.

All the Communist countries voted against debating the resolution. The Arab States, Egypt, Iraq, Libya, Saudi Arabia, the Lebanon, Syria nd Jordan abstained.

Mr. Lodge, United States, denounced Russia's "duplicity and double-dealing" in Hungary. He urged direct investigations by United Nations officials.

RUSSIAN GUNS & JETS BLAST BUDAPEST

REBEL WIRES REPORT AS FIGHT RAGES

VIENNA, Sunday.

An eye-witness account of the battle in Budapest to-day was tapped on a teleprinter by a Hungarian reporter as he sat in the office of the newspaper Szabad Nep. In the street below him Russian shells crashed.

"The people have just turned over a tram to use as a barricade near the buildings," he typed. "In the building, young people are making Molotov cocktails and hand grenades to fight the tanks.

"We are quiet, not afraid. Send the news to the public of the world and say it should condemn the aggressors. The fighting is very close now and we haven't enough tommy guns in the building. I don't know how long we can resist. We are fixing the hand grenades now.

"Heavy shells are exploding nearby. Above, jet planes are roaring but it doesn't matter."

JUMPING AT TANKS

Grenades Thrown Inside

8.30 a.m.: "At the moment there is silence. It may be the silence before the storm. We have almost no weapons only light machine-guns, Russian-made long rifles and some carbines. We haven't any kind of guns.

"People are jumping up at the tanks throwing hand grenades inside and then slamming the drivers' windows. The Hungarian people are not afraid of death. It is only a pity that we can't stand for long.

"A man just came in from the street. He said we should not think that because the street is empty the people have taken shelter. They are standing in the doorways waiting for the right moment.

"One Hungarian soldier was told by his mother as she said goodbye to him: 'Don't be a hero, but don't be cowardly either'.

HEAVY ARTILLERY

Tanks Get Nearer

A little later: "Now the firing is starting again. We are getting hits.

"The tanks are getting nearer and there is heavy artillery. We have just had a report that our unit is receiving reinforcements and ammunition. But it is still too little. It can't be allowed that people attack tanks with their bare hands.

"What is the United Nations doing? Give us a little encouragement."

There were between 200 and 250 people in the newspaper building with him, the reporter wrote. About 50 of them were women.

9 a.m.: "The tanks are coming nearer. Both radio stations are in rebel hands. They have been playing the Hungarian National Anthem.

"We will hold out to our last drop of blood. The Government has not done enough to give us arms. Downstairs there are men who have only one hand grenade."

At 9.15 the first Russian bombers were reported over Budapest.

MESSAGE SENT BY PRESIDENT

'SHOCK & DISMAY'

From Our Own Correspondent

WASHINGTON, Sunday.

President Eisenhower tonight sent an urgent personal message to Marshal Bulganin asking for the withdrawal of Russian troops from Hungary. Mr. Hagerty, White House spokesman, said the text of the message would not be published till agreement had been reached on the point with Russia.

Mr. Hagerty read a prepared statement announcing that a conference had been held at the White House to consider the ways and means available to the United States which would result in:

1 - The withdrawal of the Soviet troops from Hungary;

2 - Achieving for Hungary its own right of self-determination in the choice of its own Government.

EGYPT REPORTS ALLIES TRY TO LAND

FORCES ATTEMPTING TO DISEMBARK 'ENGAGED'

M. PINEAU FLIES TO LONDON

Anglo-French forces tried to disembark in Egypt yesterday and "were engaged," declared Mr. Omar Loufti, the Egyptian permanent representative at a special meeting of the United Nations General Assembly on the Middle East situation last night. He did not make it clear whether the landing to which he referred was a minor operation or a landing on a large scale.

Earlier in the day it was reported from Cyprus that British and French troops had begun embarking in a fleet of vessels.

There was intense activity at the island's ports, which were piled with stores, but military spokesmen declined to discuss plans for landings in the Suez Canal Zone. The distance to Port Said is about 230 miles.

The French Ministry of Defence last night imposed a black-out on news of the operations. British Seahawks blew up an Egyptian E-boat near Alexandria, set two others on fire and damaged a fourth.

Elsewhere the air assault switched from bombing to rocket and cannon attacks on radar installations, coastal and anti-aircraft batteries and a force of tanks. Egypt's Air Force "has ceased to exist," a communique said.

M. Pineau, French Foreign Minister, flew to London again last night with M. Bourges-Manoury, Minister of Defence. They were expected to discuss with Sir Anthony Eden a reply to the United Nations. A Cabinet meeting was called at 10 Downing Street, where Ministers had met twice during the day.

NOTE FROM RUSSIA

Russia yesterday delivered Notes to Britain and France protesting that their "blockade" of Mediterranean Powers contravened the 1888 Convention on free use of the Canal.

Iraq troops crossed into Jordan. Beirut radio said Saudi Arabian troops were moving to Jordan's border.

Israel said she would not agree to a United Nations police force in the Sinai peninsula, which her troops were stated to be occupying from the Suez Canal to the Gulf of Akaba.

Syria denied an Israeli claim that she planned to attack.

U.N. COMMAND LIKELY, SAYS Mr. ST. LAURENT

'WITHIN 48 HOURS'

From Eric Downton
Daily Telegraph Special Reporter

OTTAWA, Sunday.

Mr. St. Laurent, Canadian Prime Minister, said in a broadcast to-night that the Suez crisis had strained both the Western alliance and the bonds of the Commonwealth more than any event since the world war.

"But if we can use it as an opportunity to dissipate the black cloud which has hung over the Middle East for many years, the present dangers and strains may prove to have been a price worth paying."

The Canadian Government regretted that Britain and France, at a time when the Security Council was appraised of the matter, had felt it necessary to intervene with force on their own responsibility. It was also regretted that Israel used force against Egypt.

"ONLY FIRST STEP"

Mr. St. Laurent referred to the Canadian resolution urging a United Nations police force passed by the General Assembly early to-day. "We have strong reason to believe that a United States command will be established within the 48 hours set in the resolution. But that is only the first step towards a permanent settlement of Middle Eastern problems'.

LORRIES AND STORES LOADED

CYPRUS ACTIVITY

From Our Special Correspondent

NICOSIA, Sunday.

In a Cyprus port to-day I watched British and French troops embark. The harbour presented a scene of intense activity as men, vehicles and equipment arrived by road.

Many of the big assortment of vessels, including warships, were already loaded with Army lorries on their decks. Troops lining the rails of troopships watched with lively interest or lay sunbathing on the decks.

Aboard a British naval ship I talked with a number of officers and men, including some Reservist Sailors off duty who occupied themselves by reading, sunbathing and photographing one another.

REPORTS FOR M.P.s TO-DAY

PROROGATION DAY

By Our Political Correspondent

Following Saturday's emergency sitting of M.P.s a tense House of Commons will meet this afternoon. It will be the last sitting of the 1955-56 session.

After question time there will be a statement from Mr. Head, Minister of Defence, on the military situation in the Middle East and Mr. Selwyn Lloyd, Foreign Secretary, will follow with an account of the Russian coup in Hungary.

At about 5 p.m. Members will be called to the House of Lords to hear from the Lord Chancellor, Viscount Kilmuir, the Queen's commission proroguing Parliament. On their return the Speaker, Mr. W.S. Morrison, will report the Queen's Prorogation Speech.

TWO FRENCH MINISTERS AT DOWNING ST.

Russia Protests At 'Blockade'

By Michael Hilton
Daily Telegraph Diplomatic Correspondent

M. Pineau, French Foreign Minister, who was in London on Friday night for consultations with British Ministers, again flew over from Paris last night. He was accompanied by M. Bourges-Manoury, Minister of Defence.

The visit was at British suggestion. It is understood its main purpose was to discuss proposals before the United Nations formation of an international force.

Presence of the French Defence Minister suggeststhat the situation in Egypt was also discussed. The impression in London last night was that Anglo-French military operations there are still to go forward as planned.

The French Ministers left No. 10 at 11.43 p.m. Mr. Selywn Lloyd, the Foreign Secretary, left a few moments later.

"NO SECRETS"

Before driving off to return to Paris M. Pineau said that there were no secrets. Nothing had changed. He would be seeing the French Prime Minister before anything could be said on his talks with Sir Anthony.

Russia last night sent a Note to Britain and France claiming that the two countries had established a "naval blockade" of the shores of Egypt and of "a number of other Mediterranean States." The Note maintained that British and French naval commands had "closed" parts of the Eastern Mediterranean and Northern Red Sea merchant shipping.

It said: "The Soviet Government considers the above mentioned actions of Britain and France as an act of aggression affecting the interests not only of Egypt but also of other States."

CONTACT WITH EMBASSY

The Foreign Office said yesterday that the Swiss Legation in Cairo had reported that they had been able to make their first contact with the British Embassy since relations between Britain and Egypt were broken off. The Swiss reports said 100 members of the Embassy staff were concentrated in the Embassy premises.

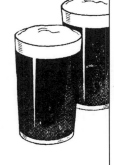

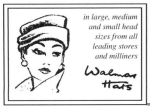

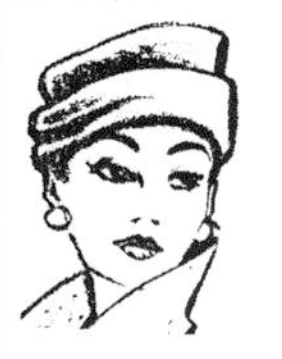
in large, medium
and small head
sizes from all
leading stores
and milliners
Walmar Hats

PRICE TWOPENCE

The Daily Telegraph

5 A.M.

No.31,586 LONDON, WEDNESDAY, OCTOBER 31, 1956 and Morning Post Printed in LONDON and MANCHESTER

For a drier dry Martini
PLYMOUTH GIN

BRITISH AND FRENCH MOVING ON SUEZ

ACTION SPEEDED UP: 2.30 a.m. REPORT

CAIRO REJECTS 12-HR. ULTIMATUM

FLEET SAILS EAST: TROOPS FLY FROM CYPRUS AT DAWN

It was understood in London at 2.30 this morning that British and French forces were moving to take up key positions at Port Said. Ismailia and Suez following the warning given to Egypt and Israel yesterday afternoon. This called on them to withdraw their military forces to a distance of 10 miles from the Suez Canal.

If the warning was disregarded or rejected these strategic points would be occupied. A 12-hour time limit set for replies was due to expire at 4.30 a.m.

But at 9.30 p.m. Col. Nasser announced that the warning was unacceptable in any circumstances. Israel accepted just before midnight, but only providing there was a positive reply from Egypt.

British Minister, after a midnight meeting, felt that in the light of these replies it was no longer necessary to wait for the time limit to expire. Action was sanctioned immediately so that the plan could be implemented as speedily as possible.

Yesterday a large British force, with an escort of warships, was sailing eastwards in the Mediterranean. At least four aircraft carriers were included in a combined force of British and French warships moving in the same direction. The Mediterranean Fleet cancelled its plans for exercises and also turned eastwards.

Throughout the day tanks, guns and heavy lorries moved to embarkation ports in Malta. Landing craft assembled in Valetta harbour with Royal Marine Commandos and infantry. From Cyprus, at dawn, transport planes were flying British and French troops to an unknown southerly destination.

270-218 VOTE FOR GOVERNMENT

Sir Anthony Eden announced the despatch of the warning in the House of Commons in the afternoon [Report - P13] after talks with M. Mollet, French Prime Minister, and M. Pineau, Foreign Minister, who made a hurried visit to London. He said the troops would act as a buffer between the belligerents and guarantee freedom of transport to ships.

He was asked by Mr. Gaitskell, Leader of the Opposition, for an assurance that no action would be taken until the Security Council, which was discussing the matter last night, had pronounced an opinion. Sir Anthony would give no such assurance.

In a debate which followed, the Socialists, acting on a decision taken at a meeting of their "Shadow Cabinet", decided to divide the House because the assurance was not forthcoming. This resulted in a vote of 270 to 218 for the Government, a majority of 52. At the request of the Opposition there will be another debate to-day.

U.S. AGAINST USE OF FORCE

Dr. Fawzi, Egypt's Foreign Minister, announced last night that he had sent a letter to the Security Council asking that the "threat of force by British and French Government to occupy Egyptian territory" should be considered immediately. The Council agreed to this.

A resolution introduced by the United States called on all United Nations members to refrain from the use of force and to refrain from giving aid to Israel as long as she refused to withdraw from Egyptian territory. Britain and France decided last night to veto this and also a Russian resolution calling for a cease-fire.

Commons Statement and Debate - P13; Egypt Has More Jets, Quiet On Jordan Border, Iraqi Division Ready and Cyprus Radio Taken Over - P7; Brief London Meeting and Mr. Eisenhower Cancels trip - P14; Editorial Comment - P6.

CONFUSED AND ANXIOUS DEBATE

OPPOSITION ANGER

By Our Special Correspondent
WESTMINISTER, Tuesday.

It was a confused and anxious debate on the Egypt-Israel situation in the House of Commons to-night. Opposition speakers buzzed with anger, but they could not make up their minds what they were angry about.

Apart from the figures of the division, a 270-218 defeat for the Socialists, it was an easy win for the Government. The Prime Minister who had had to speak from what might be called early dawn to dewy eve, carried his difficult bat.

Mr. Lloyd, Foreign Secretary fresh from the rigours of Security Council, wound up for the Government with pungency and vigour.

OPPORTUNITIES LOST

The Debate was divided, like all Gaul, into three parts. There was the Prime Minister's first statement, the inconclusive discussion which followed; and the final wind up.

Clumsiness and lack of statesmanship marked the resumption of the debate. Mr. Gaitskell threw away all the opportunities which he had tried to create for the Opposition earlier in the afternoon.

It was an occasion for showing both Parliament and the country that the Opposition was able to transcend pettiness. But the Socialist Leader niggled and haggled.

The debate opened in an atmosphere of tension and bewilderment, when the Prime Minister rose to make his first statement. The fight became violent, but it was a fight on the wrong terms, and in the wrong context.

When Sir Anthony rose, he spoke shortly, with the air of a man who has taken vital and exhausting decisions. Egypt and Israel had been asked to make a decision within 12 hours. If they did not comply, said the Prime Minister, "British and French forces will intervene in whatever strength may be necessary to secure compliance."

"INTERVENTION" CRUX

This was the crux of the debate. What did the Prime Minister mean by "intervene"? Against which side would the two powers "intervene"?

Sir Anthony had said that the Security Council had already been summoned to consider the issue. Did the British and French Governments propose to act before the Security Council had reached a decision?

These were the lines upon which Mr. Gaitskell, Leader of the Opposition, attacked the Government's decisions. But it was noticeable that most of the Opposition Front Bench sat silent.

SECOND EGYPT DEBATE

By Our Political Correspondent

There will be yet another debate in the Commons to-day on Egypt and the Middle East. The programme has been rearranged at the request of the Opposition.

The Socialists were to have moved a vote of censure on the Government for alleged "military weaknesses and administrative blunders in the Armed Forces."

They withdrew this motion to clear the way for another discussion on the Israel-Egypt problem as it will have developed by the time the House meets this afternoon. As happened to-day, the debate will take place on a procedural motion for the adjournment of the House. The line they will take will be determined at a meeting of the Parliamentary Labour Party this morning.

Three Socialist M.P.s were reported to have abstained from the debate last night. One of them, Mr. H. Lever (Cheetham), explained afterwards: "I deliberately abstained because I could not, by a vote, unequivocally support some of the statements made on my own side of the House."

Others who, though present in the Chamber, were reported not to have gone into the Opposition lobby were Sir Tom Brian (W. Nottingham) and Mr. Paget (Northampton). The three Liberals present supported the Government.

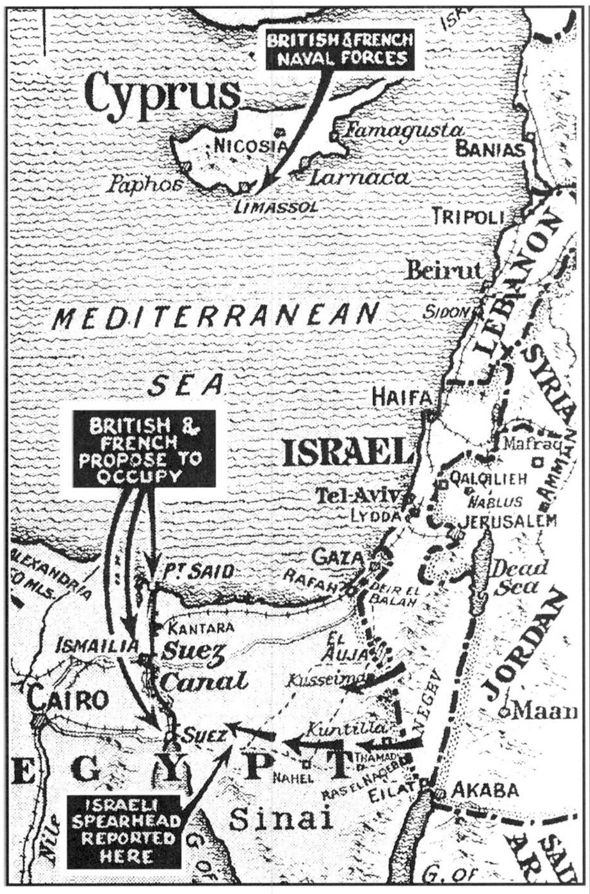
BRITISH & FRENCH NAVAL FORCES
Cyprus
NICOSIA
Famagusta
BANIAS
Paphos
Larnaca
LIMASSOL
TRIPOLI
Beirut
LEBANON
SIDON
MEDITERRANEAN
SEA
SYRIA
HAIFA
BRITISH & FRENCH PROPOSE TO OCCUPY
ISRAEL
Mafraq
QALQILIEH
AMMAN
NABLUS
Tel-Aviv
LYDDA
JERUSALEM
GAZA
Dead Sea
PT SAID
RAFAH
KANTARA
ISMAILIA
Suez Canal
EL AUJA
JORDAN
CAIRO
SUEZ
Kuntilla
NEGEV
Maan
E G Y P T
NAHEL
AKABA
ISRAELI SPEARHEAD REPORTED HERE
Sinai
EILAT

MAP showing Middle East States in relationship to the Suez Canal.

AIR RAID WARNING IN CAIRO: GUNFIRE HEARD

TANKS PASS THROUGH CITY

From Adrian Secker and D.J. Mossman
Daily Telegraph Special Correspondents
CAIRO, Tuesday.

Two air raid warnings sounded in Cairo this evening, and the city was plunged into darkness at a second's notice. Police in Jeeps with cowled headlamps patrolled the streets, stopping cars and ordering pedestrians to take cover.

After the "all clear" for the first alert, a practice, street lighting and advertising signs remained off. Traffic lights were also off and police directed traffic with lanterns.

Traffic was occasionally disrupted this morning by long military convoys of sand-coloured half-tracks, tanks on transporters and lorry loads of troops. Sporadic gunfire was heard during the afternoon.

Egyptian Army headquarters to-night announced that Egyptian forces repulsed an Israeli attack on outposts in the Kusselma area of the Sinai Peninsula. They destroyed "some" Israeli tanks and inflicted heavy losses.

AIR FIGHT CLAIM

7 Israeli Planes Down

The communiqué, the fifth to be issued Egyptian H.Q. since the Israeli attack, said Egyptian planes also shot down an Israeli Mystere jet fighter during a dog-fight over the battleground. Seven Israeli planes were shot down in the battle, the Egyptians said.

They claim they have lost no aircraft since the fighting began. The communiqué added: "Operations against enemy pockets scattered in the Sinai Peninsula are going on."

HIT CLAIMED ON BRITISH PLANE

EGYPT A.A. FIRE

CAIRO, Tuesday.

One of the two British Canberra jet bombers which flew over the Suez Canal area to-day was hit by Egyptian anti-aircraft fire, the Egyptian Middle East News Agency claimed to-night. The damaged jet landed in Jordan, the agency said.

The Egyptian Foreign Minister, Mr. Fawzi, protested to the British Ambassador, Sir Humphrey Trevelyan, to-night about the flight of the two Canberras over Egyptian territory.

ISRAELIS HEAR EDEN SPEECH IN BLACK-OUT

From John Whittles
Daily Telegraph Special Correspondent
JERUSALEM, ISRAEL, Wednesday.

The Israeli Foreign Office issued a statement at 1.25 a.m. local time (11.25 p.m. G.M.T.) accepting the British and French proposals for a cessation of hostilities and the withdrawal of troops from the Suez Canal. the statement said:

Israel indicates its willingness to take the necessary practical steps to this end. It is assumed that a positive response will have been forthcoming from the Egyptian side.

The significance of the final qualification was not entirely clear. Questioned after news of Sir Anthony Eden's speech in Parliament reached Jerusalem, Israeli Government Officials made no secret of the fact they were delighted and that the Anglo-French proposals would be accepted.

DOUBTS ABOUT U.S.

Reports of Colonel Nasser's rejection and Mr. Eisenhower's admonition caused a certain amount of consternation. Doubts were expressed whether, in the face of the American

(Continued on Back Page, Col. 5)

NEWMARKET CHOICE

In a high-class field for to-day's Cambridgeshire my selection is the five-year-old Swept, owned by Major T. Bardwell, an owner of many years' standing, and trained at Royston by W. Stephenson. Swept will be one of the few greys in the race.

BRITAIN AND FRANCE USE VETO TWICE

American & Soviet Resolutions

U.S. URGED BAN ON FORCE

From Our Own Correspondent
NEW YORK, Tuesday.

Britain and France to-night vetoed two resolutions before the Security Council. The first was proposed by the United States and the second by Russia.

The American-sponsored motion, designed to end fighting in the Sinai Peninsula, asked members of the Council to refrain from using force or the threat of force. The veto put a stamp on what was clearly a major breakdown in co-operation between Britain, France and the United States.

Voting on the U.S. resolution was: for, the United States, Soviet Union, Cuba, Peru, Iran, Nationalist China and Jugoslavia; against, Britain, France, Australia and Belgium abstained. Britain then used her veto for the first time in the history of the Security Council.

After the Council resumed its sitting for the third time in 12 hours Mr. Sobolev, the Soviet delegate, introduced this resolution:

The Security Council, noting that armed forces of Israel have penetrated deeply into Egyptian territory in violation of the armistice agreement between Egypt and Israel, expressing its grave concern at this violation of the armistice agreement, calls upon Israel immediately to withdraw its armed forces behind its established armistice lines.

Mr. Tsiang (China) proposed an amendment calling on both the Egyptian and Israeli forces to cease fire immediately. Mr. Sobolev accepted the amendment. The United States abstained from voting on the motion, which was vetoed.

MESSAGE FROM MR. EISENHOWER

'AVOID FORCE'

From Our Own Correspondent
WASHINGTON, Tuesday.

President Eisenhower this evening sent urgent personal messages to Sir Anthony Eden and M. Mollet, French Prime Minister, urging them not to use force in the Middle East crisis. This action was disclosed by the White House after the President had a telephone conference with Mr. Dulles.

He got in touch with Mr Dulles immediately on learning of Press reports that Britain and France had sent an "ultimatum" to Egypt and Israel. Mr. Dulles saw Mr. Alphand, French Ambassador, and Mr. Coulson, British Chargé d'Affaires, in the late afternoon to express United States concern over this new development.

PRESIDENT'S HOPE

Mr. Hagerty, White House Press Secretary, said that the President had expressed the hope in his messages that full opportunity would be given to the United Nations to settle the controversy by peaceful means.

Reading from a formal statement Mr. Hagerty said: "This Government continues to believe it is possible by such peaceful means to secure a solution which would restore the Armistice conditions between Egypt and Israel as well as to bring about a just settlement of the Suez Canal controversy."

He emphasised that the President had first heard of the so-called Anglo-French ultimatum through Press reports.

To-day's Weather

General Inference: An anticyclone off N.W. Scotland is intensifying and a cold N.E. wind covers most of British Isles. Cold in most districts.

London S.E. E. Central N. and N.E. England East Anglia E. Midlands Central S. and N.W. England West Midlands: Sunny periods. Perhaps showers. (42-47)

S.W. England all Wales: Perhaps showers. Mainly dry and sunny. (44-48)

Central S.W. W. and N.W. Scotland S.W. Scotland: Scattered showers. Some bright periods. (40-45)

E. and N.E. Scotland Orkney: Dry. Cloudy, but sunny intervals. (40-45)

THE 'STALIN MYTH' DENOUNCED

KHRUSCHEV ATTACKS TERROR REGIME

By David Floyd
Daily Telegraph Special Correspondent on Communist Affairs

According to reports yesterday from Bonn and Washington, Mr. Khruschev, Russian Communist party secretary, in a speech to a secret session of the party congress, accused Stalin of massacres and a reign of terror. The sole purpose of the speech was to destroy the "Stalin myth."

Mr. Khruschev, who is to visit Britain next month, went much further than any of the criticisms of Stalin made publicly at the congress. He appears to have attributed all the evils of the Soviet régime to the late dictator.

According to one account, the picture he painted was of a Stalin "not himself" in his late years and who through his career "had been subject to phobias about the supposed treachery of his associates."

The Moscow atmosphere in the late Stalin era as described by Mr. Khruschev was of a capital "ridden by plots, counter-plots and intrigue, in which no one knew who might be the next victim." Some delegates at the congress are reported to have shouted: "How did you stand it? Why didn't you kill him?"

Mr. Khruschev replied: "What could we do? There was a reign of terror. You just had to look at him wrongly and the next day you lost your head."

He said it had been thought wiser to break the story of the horror of the Stalin régime gradually to the people. Delegates are now said to be passing the substance of Mr. Khruschev's speech to the rank and file of the party and to the people.

The violence of the denunciation taken in the West to indicate that the wave of reaction against Stalin's method was much stronger than had been suspected. The dictator's successors have been forced to the conclusion that they must dissociate themselves entirely from Stalin and his ways if they are to retain power.

(March 17)

'DISC JOCKEYS' WEEK ON B.B.C.

In the week beginning Sunday, Dec. 9, about 1,600 gramophone records will be played to B.B.C. Light Programme listeners by an assortment of "Disc Jockeys." More than 15 hours will be devoted to them against the seven hours of a normal week.

Giving details of "The Record Week of 1956" Mr. R. Pelletier, controller, Light Programme, defended disc jockeys. Records, he said, were not "just slapped on."

Programmes ranging from advanced jazz, including "rock 'n' roll," Caruso, Elisabeth Schumann and Lotte Lehmann, will be presented by such personalities as Eamonn Andrews, Sam Costa and that pioneer of the broadcast turntable, Christopher Stone. There are no new names. During the week a number of the jockeys will also talk to their public.

Mr. Pelletier said it was not a question of saving money. Certain "riches of broadcasting" could be given by records that live broadcasting could not produce.

(October 24)

ORSON WELLES HURT

From Our Own Correspondent

Orson Welles, with one ankle broken and the other sprained, played "King Lear" in a wheel-chair here last night. He was in full costume and received a great ovation.

He broke the joint at a preview of the play at New York's City Centre Theatre, and at Thursday's opening he had it in a plaster cast. After this performance he fell and sprained the other ankle.

On Friday night he regaled the audience for an hour and a half with anecdotes and readings from the play. About a quarter of the audience left and demanded its money back. Yesterday's matinée was cancelled.

(January 16)

SIR B. DOCKER TO APPROACH SHAREHOLDERS

B.S.A. Voted 6-3 For Removel

BY Our City Editor

Sir Bernard Docker, who on Thursday was removed by his fellow directors from the board of the Birmingham Small Arms Company, has decided to approach the shareholders.

Before leaving London yesterday for a week-end in the country, he said: "I am going to the shareholders first. I think this is the best decision."

To call an extraordinary meeting of shareholders, Sir Bernard needs the support of 10 per cent of the shareholding, or more than 560,000 shares. The ordinary capital of B.S.A. is £5,630,344.

There are about 17,000 shareholders. Sir Bernard and Lady Docker hold about 100,000 Ordinary £1 shares. The Prudential Assurance Co. holds 260,000.

NAMES OF VOTERS

Cousin in Opposition

Mr. John Y. Sangster, the newly-appointed chairman of B.S.A., issued the following statement last night:

A statement appeared in some of this morning's newspapers attributed to Sir Bernard Docker that the board of the Birmingham Small Arms Co. Ltd. had passed a certain resolution affecting Sir Bernard's position by a narrow majority.

The resolution concerned was, in fact, passed by a majority of six votes in favour to three votes against. The directors who voted in favour were: Mr. Lewis Chapman, Mr. Noel H. Docker, Mr. James Leek, Mr. J.E. Rowe, Mr. John Y. Sangster, Sir Frank E. Smith.

The three directors who thus appear to have supported Sir Bernard are Sir Patrick Hannon, Mr. H.J.S. Moyses and Mr. H.P. Potts. Sir Patrick Hannon is deputy chairman of B.S.A. He holds 20 directorships, including some B.S.A. subsidiaries. He is also chairman of H.P. Sauce, Lea & Perrins and Norfolk Canners.

(June 2)

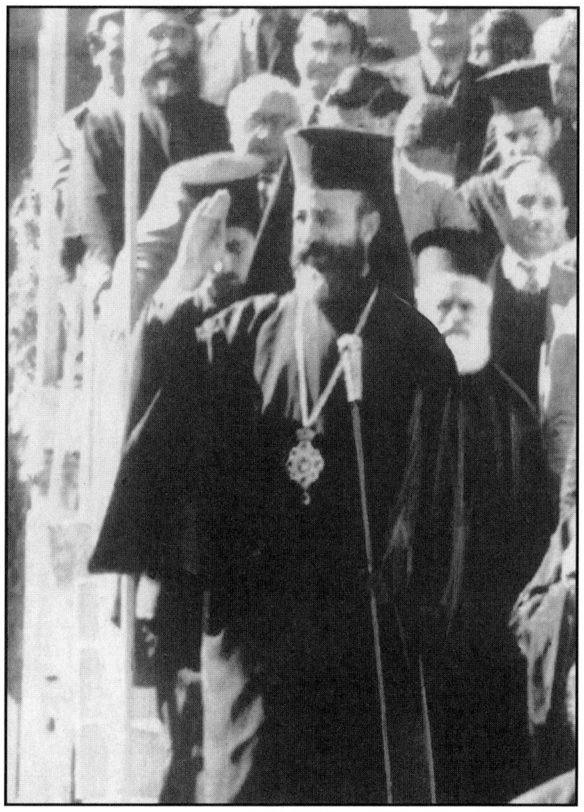

ARCHBISHOP MAKARIOS

TALKS AT NO. 10 ON GLUBB PASHA

DISMISSAL BY JORDAN 'A DEEP SHOCK'

By Our Diplomatic Correspondent

Lt.-Gen. J.B. Glubb, commander of Jordan's Arab Legion, was dismissed from his post under a decree published yesterday by King Hussein and told to leave the country at once. The General, better known as Glubb Pasha, is due to arrive with his family at London Airport at 5.40 p.m. to-day.

They will fly in on the regular airline from Cyprus, where they spent the night after their summary expulsion. Two other senior British officers, Brig. W. Hutton and Col. Sir Patrick Coghill, and several Arab officers were also dismissed. Brig. Raddy Innab was appointed to command the Legion.

Sir Anthony Eden is concerning himself personally with developments arising from the totally unexpected dismissal of Glubb Pasha, who is 58. The situation was discussed by the Prime Minister with the Defence Ministers and Chiefs of Staff at a meeting at 10, Downing Street yesterday.

A statement issued by the Foreign Office said the "abrupt dismissal" had come as "a deep shock." The Government was "deeply concerned at these developments and the possible consequences, internal and external to which they may lead." There will be an early statement to Parliament.

It seems clear that the decision to dismiss Gen. Glubb was taken personally by the 21-year-old King on his own initiative. There is no information in London about his motives.

It is probable that the King's action has been taken because he felt himself to be under extreme pressure to prove that he is an independent Arab ruler and not a "stooge" of the British. This pressure has come from Egypt.

(March 3)

SCHOOLS' FEES INCREASED

Boarding and tuition fees at the following schools have increased in the spring term:

BOARDING AND TUITION FEES	New £	Old £
Berkhamsted, Herts	285	252
Dartington Hall, Totnes	330	297
TUITION FEES		
City of London (Boys)	111	96
City of London (Girls)	83	70
Highgate	120	96
Lower School of John, Lyon, Harrow	96	78
Merchant Taylors' Rickmansworth	150	120
University College School, Hampstead (Sen)	126	111
University College School, Hampstead (Jun)	117	102
BOARDING FEES		
Taunton, Somerset	249	231
Westonbirt, Glos	315	285

(December 10)

A crowning achievment ...

Domecq's

DOUBLE CENTURY

"Double Century" is the sherry of all sherries. Some are too dry; some too sweet. "Double Century" is a sherry to suit all tastes, selected specially to celebrate the 200th birthday of the famous house of Pedro Domecq.

Try a glass to-day and see if you ever tasted such a lovely wine.

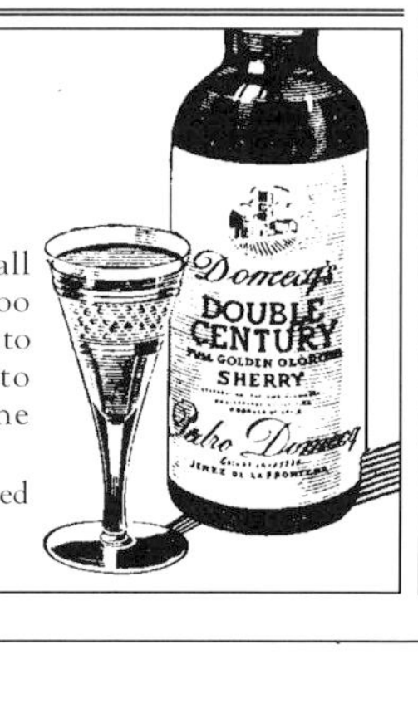
Domecq's
DOUBLE CENTURY
SHERRY

CYPRUS DEPORTS ENOSIS LEADERS

ARCHBISHOP FLOWN OUT SECRETLY

From Colin Reid
Daily Telegraph Special Correspondent

NICOSIA, Friday.

Archbishop Makarios, leader of the Union-with-Greece campaign, the Bishop of Kyrenia, second leading campaigner, and two other Greek Church priests were to-day deported by order of the Governor, Field Marshal Sir John Harding.

The Archbishop was politely intercepted when he reached the barrier of Nicosia's civil airport. There he intended joining a Greek airlines plane, in which he was to have flown to Athens to plan his next political moves in consultation with the Greek Government.

Instead he was conducted to an R.A.F. Hastings aircraft waiting at the far end of the runway. With the other three deportees he was then flown to "a destination which will be announced later."

Earlier to-day the tall black-bearded Archbishop, who is 42, had declared his intention to return from Athens to Nicosia in 10 days "if the British let me." Both he and the violently Anglophobe Bishop of Kyrenia, 47, have been hinting during the past few days at the possibility of their deportation.

A British communiqué this evening announced that all four priests were being deported under the Emergency Powers (Public Safety and Order) Regulations.

POLICE ESCORT

Joint Operation

The deportation operation went off quietly and without incident, in accordance with a plan prepared and carried out jointly by the Army and the police.

While waiting at the airport for the plane to depart the Archbishop chatted quietly to his companions. All four were apprehended within a few minutes. Three British policemen travelled as escorts in the plane.

Bishop Kyprianos Of Kyrenia was officially stated to have "repeatedly and publicly extolled terrorism, advocated bloodshed and incited the youth of Cyprus to violence."

The other two priests deported were:

Polycarpos Joannides, 52, the Bishop's secretary, described as having "supported and encouraged Bishop Kyprianos in extolling terrorism and advocating bloodshed": and

Papastavros Papagathangelou, 46, another priest, who was accused of exercising "the most pernicious influence on Greek Cypriot youths."

Troops entered the Archbishop's palace and grounds in Nicosia. Searches are now being carried out there and at the houses of the other three deportees.

Security forces at the Archbishop's palace have reported the discovery of an automatic pistol and magazines hidden under the robes of a priest.

The next senior dignitary in the Greek Church in Cyprus is the Bishop of Paphos, at present in Egypt. The temporary head therefore is the last remaining Biship, the Bishop of Kitium, whose See includes Limassol and Larnaca. He is a solid supporter of Makarios.

As the news spread shops and catering establishments in Nicosia began to close. Military vehicles were pelted and attempts were made to form crowds.

A curfew was put into force at Kyrenia, where the Bishop Kyprianos had been arrested in his palace.

Tension throughout the island tonight is unprecedented. Trade unions are believed to be organising a general strike.

Trunk telephone calls within the island and abroad have been prohibited, and a censorship has been imposed on telegrams to Greece.

(March 10)

NAVY GETS FIRST GUIDED MISSILE SHIP

With a form of ceremony introduced in the 18th century, the Navy's first experimental guided missile ship, the 8,580-ton Girdle Ness, was commissioned here this afternoon.

It was an historic occasion. Four hundred officers and men of her company paraded on the quay, and crowds of dockyard hands lining the decks and superstructure heard Capt. M.G. Greig say:

"This is one of the most important events in the Navy's history. In commissioning this ship we are inaugurating a new era."

At a Press conference held earlier on board he remarked that the design of guided missile ships to be ordered by the Navy would largely depend on the results of tests in the Girdle Ness.

Although this ship has arrived in service with no short cuts ("I believe we have not done at all badly," said Capt. Greig at the conference) she is not dissimilar to the Norton Sound, the United States Navy's first experimental guided missile ship.

The Norton Sound came into service two or three years ago. Guided missiles are already installed in a number of American warships.

It is likely that some time will elapse, before lessons learned from the Girdle Ness can be applied in new Royal Navy ships. The four big escort vessels for the Navy are to be ordered during the present financial year, but no date can yet be given for their being laid down.

(July 25)

SCHOOL BAN ON 'LOOKING LIKE LOLLOBRIGIDA'

A ban on boys without neckties and girls in low-neck blouses at Carr Lane Secondary School, Grimsby, was extended yesterday to a girl who arrived in a sweater with a low neckline. She is Ann Garrod, of Lichfield Road, Grimsby.

On arrival at school she had pinned the low neckline together just below the throat but was told to change at midday. When she returned to school she was still wearing the sweater, but she was allowed to stay.

Ann, who is the school's 150-yards sprint champion, said: "It is ridiculous: they want us to be old-fashioned. I am leaving school, in a month's time, and my mother does not object if I wear a sweater and make up to go to dances."

Mr. Stanley Hill, the headmaster, would not comment. Ald. W.J. Molson, chairman of the school governors, said: "We want everybody to know that we are going to support Mr. Hill right up to the hilt in this matter.

"SHEER AWKWARDNESS"

"The attitude of some of the parents is just sheer awkwardness, and it is only a few who are causing the trouble. We do not want our girls to come to school trying to look like Gina Lollobrigida, and we are not going to have it."

Ann's mother said: "It is all a bit of hooey. I have had seven children pass through the school and I have never heard anything like this before."

Keith Blakey, 14, who again arrived at school yesterday without a tie, despite having been sent home on several occasions, was again sent home. "I did not get beyond the gates," he said.

(June 14)

BIG FIGHT FIASCO

A capacity crowd stood up and booed for five minutes at Harringay Arena last night after Ezzard Charles, former world heavyweight champion, had been disqualified for holding in the second round of his fight with Dick Richardson, of Newport. The disturbance continued until the next bout was in progress.

(October 3)

PREMIER: TROOPS STAY TILL U.N. TAKES OVER

ASSEMBLY DEMAND FOR WITHDRAWQAL

64-NIL VOTE TO SET UP 'POLICE FORCE'

Questioned in the House of Commons last evening on British and French forces in the Suez Canal Zone, Sir Anthony Eden stated, "There is no question in our mind whatever of withdrawal by the United Kingdom or our Allies unless and until there is a United Nations force to take over from us."

A few hours later the United Nations General Assembly in New York endorsed an Afro-Asian resolution calling on Britain, France and Israel to withdraw their forces from Egyptian territory "immediately." Sir Pierson Dixon, Britain, had said the demand was unacceptable.

The Assembly voted 64 to nil to set up the international force. Mr. Lodge, United States, said his Government was ready to provide military transport planes "immediately" to move contingents to Egypt.

WARNING TO ISRAEL

Mr. Hammarskjoeld, Secretary-General, warned Britain and France early to-day that Israel's denunciation of her armistice agreement with Egypt could seriously complicate a settlement of the Middle East crisis. He had informed Israel that if she did not withdraw her troops he would raise the matter before the Assembly or the Security Council.

President Eisenhower appealed last night to Mr. Ben-Gurion, Israeli Prime Minister, to obey the United Nations resolution demanding a withdrawal. Egypt informed the General Assembly that failing an Anglo-French withdrawal the fight against their forces would continue.

(November 8)

PORT CALM, SAYS C.-IN-C.

From George Evans
Daily Telegraph Special Correspondent
NICOSIA, Wednesday.

The total Allied casualties in Egypt have been "just over 100 killed, and wounded." No breakdown of the figures as between British and French is available.

This was disclosed here to-day by Gen. Sir Charles Keightley, C.-in-C. Allied Forces. He flew to Port Said for a short visit this morning.

On his return he said: "I was able to assure myself that conditions generally in the town were calm, and everything possible was being done to restore things to normal."

The troops, both British and French, were in good spirits and were resting after a hard day yesterday. The operation to occupy the city had been carried out effectively, and Allied casualties were just over 100 killed and wounded.

"SOME DAMAGE"

Stubborn Fighting

"Some damage had been caused in the town, but this to a large extent resulted from the stubborn fighting of the Egyptians from house to house during the day."

Before the cease-fire became effective British paratroop patrols had reached a point on the causeway about a mile north of Kantara.

"There has been no fighting since the cease-fire became operative. But there was a case of looting by Egyptians this morning.

"There is no shortage of food or water. The French did a very good job in getting the waterworks intact quickly.

"The British and French fleets are standing by in the vicinity of Port Said, and are already at work clearing the ships sunk by the Egyptians in the port and entrance to the Canal."

Gen. Keightley's statement clears up a certain amount of confusion apparent here this morning. Reports had circulated that hostilities had been resumed, but an official spokesman said there was no knowledge of it.

"The Anglo-French forces stood fast when the cease-fire came into operation, and to my knowledge there has been no more shooting," I was told. It is not known whether the terms of the cease-fire preclude the landing of any more reinforcements, but troops were reported to have been disembarking at Port Said this morning.

It is probable, however, that these may have comprised the administrative tails of the units already there.

The most southerly British positions reached by paratroop patrols a mile north of Kantara indicate that about a quarter of the length of the Suez Canal is now in Allied hands. No official comment is available here on a French Defence Ministry statement this morning that Allied forces occupy "much of the Canal Zone."

(November 9)

ALLIES OCCUPY 'GREATER PART OF THE CANAL'

FRENCH SAY EGYPT LOST 95% OF PLANES

From Our Own Correspondent
PARIS, Tuesday.

French and British troops now occupy "the greater part of the length" of the Suez Canal, a French military spokesman declared to-night. In French military terminology the Canal is the stretch between Port Said and Ismailia and does not include the rest of the waterway.

He said that it was expected that about 95 per cent of the Egyptian Air force had been destroyed.

The Egyptian Navy had been seriously damaged and partially sunk. Egyptian land forces stationed on the sides of the Canal had either been destroyed or dispersed.

According to the spokesman, Anglo-French forces have captured Ismailia. Reports he had received indicated that the town, halfway along the Suez Canal, was taken at 7.0 p.m. The news had not yet been officially confirmed from Allied Headquarters in Cyprus.

Earlier the spokesman had said that Allied forces had obtained their objective, which was to re-establish a regime of international law in Egypt and to put a stop to the arbitrary action of a man who did not know how to respect the rights of others.

AIR FORCE MENACE

At the start of the operation the Egyptian Air force, in particular, had been a real danger. A modern fighter Air Force, with fast planes, had been stationed on airfields to the east and west of the Canal.

Therefore, during the first phase strategic operations had been undertaken, after unprecedented precautions had been adopted, to prevent loss of civilian life. Some bombing operations had been called off even when aircraft were in the air because of the civilians in the neighbourhood.

"Our troops during the engagements are showing extraordinary fighting spirit and this evening, despite the orders given by Nasser last night to prevent the approach of the British and French forces to the canal Zone, these same forces, after capturing Port Said and Port Fuad and passing El Kantara to the south, have continued to advance along the Canal, which they now occupy on the greater part of its length."

(November 7)

RESIGNATION OF SIR E. BOYLE

DISAGREEMENT WITH POLICY ON EGYPT

By Our Political Correspondent

It was announced from 10, Downing Street last night that Sir Edward Boyle, Economic Secretary to the Treasury, has resigned because of disagreement with the Government's policy in Egypt.

He is the second Minister to do so. The resignation of Mr. Nutting, Minister of State, Foreign Affairs, was offered on Oct. 31 and accepted by the Prime Minister last Saturday.

The Government are hoping that Sir Edward Boyle's resignation will be the last on this issue. The Cabinet remain firm, but no one can be certain that some other junior Ministers will not follow his example.

(November 9)

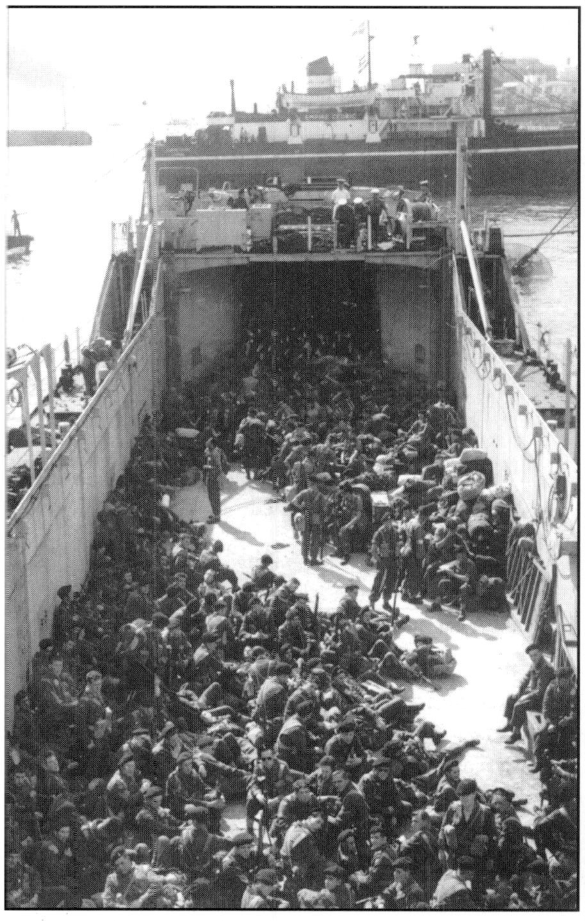

REINFORCEMENTS ARRIVE AT PORT SAID.
British troops waiting to be taken ashore from their landing craft. Essential supplies for the troops were taken by Valetta and Hastings aircraft of R.A.F. Transport Command from Cyprus.

LORDS' 238-95 VOTE TO KEEP HANGING

DEGREES OF MURDER URGED BY PRIMATE

The House of Lords last night, by 238 votes to 95, refused a second reading of Mr. Silverman's Bill for the abolition of the death penalty. This majority of 143 followed a speech by the Marquess of Salisbury, Lord President of the Council, which introduced a new possibility into the capital punishment controversy.

It is that the Government might introduce a Bill next session to amend the law of murder while retaining the death penalty. Such a Bill might be debated in the Commons alongside the Bill for abolition, which will be reintroduced next session under the Parliament Act.

Lord Salisbury gave no firm commitment that a Bill would be introduced. But he gave the assurance that such a possibility would receive serious consideration by the Cabinet.

Various suggestions were made during the debate that definite categories of murder to which the death penalty should apply should be considered. The Archbishop of Canterbury, Dr. Fisher, was one of the principal supporters of changes in the law to allow this.

NINE-HOUR DEBATE, 33 SPEECHES

Highlights of a nine-hour debate and 33 speeches were:

LORD GODDARD, the Lord Chief Justice: Why was it that ruffians who use razors, coshes, knuckledusters and broken bottles always stop short of murder? Fear of the rope was the great deterrent, though the time was ripe for amendment of the law on murder.

THE ARCHBISHOP OF CANTERBURY: If he voted for the Bill it would be in spite of those who mistakenly regarded the death penalty as un-Christian and wrong. He thought it should be kept for the murder of policemen and warders, premeditated and planned murders, murderers carrying arms and poisoners.

VISCOUNT SAMUEL: One execution might save 10 possible murders. The use of the Crown's Prerogative should be extended and restrictions on the Home Secretary concerning its use should be removed.

THE EARL OF MANSFIELD: The House should reject the Bill, but the Government should consult its sponsors and endeavour to get an agreed measure.

(July 11)

FIRST WOMAN RECORDER

MISS ROSE HEILBRON

Daily Telegraph Reporter

Miss Rose Heilbron, Q.C., who is 42, was appointed Recorder of Burnley yesterday, the first woman to hold such a post. Her appointment was one of three announced by the Lord Chancellor's office.

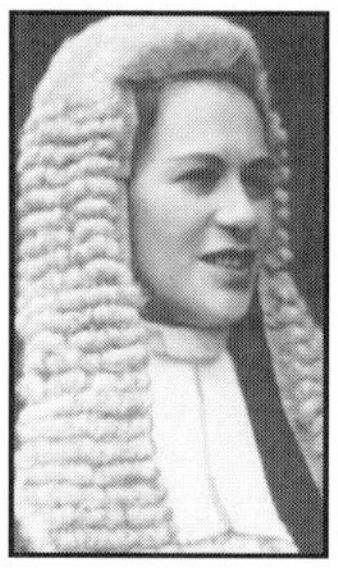

MISS R. HEILBRON

She was given the news when she telephoned her chambers in London after leaving the court room at Staffordshire Assizes. She was defending Freeman Reese, an American negro, accused of murdering a policeman at Burton-on-Trent in 1946.

Called to the Bar in 1939, she became one of the first two women to take silk in 1949. The other was Miss Helena Normanton.

Miss Heilbron is married to Dr. Nathaniel Burstein, an Irish-born surgeon. They have a daughter, Hilary, aged eight.

(November 27)

WEST GERMANY BANS THE 'GOOSE STEP'

RULES FOR FORCES

From Our Own Correspondent
BONN, Thursday.

Details of regulations for the West German armed forces, banning among other features of the former Wehrmacht the "goose step," were published by the Federal Defence Ministry to-day. Between 2,000 and 2,500 regulations are to be published during the rearmament period ending on Jan. 1, 1959.

During three months' basic training, Army recruits will undergo only 22 hours drill out of a total 484 hours, or five per cent, compared with 30 per cent before the war.

Punishment exercises with rifles, and drill with taut rifle slings, are banned with the "goose step." The "Present Arms," with loose rifle slings, will be practised only by units on direct instructions from the Defence Ministry.

"HARD" TRAINING

Attempts to evade anti-"parade ground" regulations are specifically forestalled by the instructions that only orders and commands as prescribed by the Defence Ministry will be employed. On the other hand, the regulations give warning that recruits' training will be "hard."

(February 24)

SPACE TRAVEL 'UTTER BILGE'

THE NEW ASTRONOMER ROYAL'S VIEWS

Talk about the future of interplanetary travel was described as "utter bilge" by Britain's new Astronomer Royal, Prof. Richard van der Riet Woolley, when he arrived at London Airport from Australia yesterday.

Prof. Wooley, who is 49, took up his new duties yesterday, on the retirement of Sir Harold Spencer Jones, to whom he was chief assistant at Greenwich 17 years ago. Since then he has been director of the Commonwealth Observatory at Mount Stromlo, Canberra.

Describing himself as a "straightforward scientist" he said: "I don't think anybody will ever put up enough money to do such a thing. It would be enormously expensive.

But if the next war could be won by the first chap getting to the moon and by that alone, some nation might put up the enormous amount required. I cannot give any idea how much it would cost, but it would be a very large sum indeed. It is all rather rot."

FLYING SAUCERS

He said he did not believe in flying saucers. "I have an amusing story about flying saucers. I was wakened up about 3 a.m. by the R.A.F., no less, who asked about an object at 3,000ft due west.

"I hopped out of bed and had a look, and then I missed my chance. I should have said 'Take off, boys, it's the Russians.' Instead I had to tell them it was the planet Mars."

Referring to his work in the Royal Observatory at Herstmonceux Castle, Sussex, Prof. Woolley said: "There was a time about 100 years ago when the English were pre-eminent among the world's astronomers, not only for theoretical work but for observing.

"There has been a tendency of late for this headquarters to be in California, but we hope to make some attempt to get England back to the fore in scientific astronomy and astro-physics.

"There is a new telescope, the Isaac Newton Memorial telescope, with a diameter of 90 inches. What we are interested in is the question of stars in relation to nuclear physics, and the interior of the stars. We have much work to do."

MR. KENNETH W. GATLAND, a member of the council of the British Interplanetary Society and one of Britain's leading authorities on space travel, commenting on Prof. Woolley's remarks, said: "Space travel is inevitable, it is bound to come as a follow-on of the exploration of the upper atmosphere with rockets and the launching of artificial satellites during the international geophysical year."

(January 3)

EX-M.P. MEETS BURGESS

'SOLITARY LIFE'

MOSCOW, Thursday.

Guy Burgess, former British diplomat, is working for a Russian foreign languages publishing house. This was disclosed in Moscow to-day by Mr. Tom Driberg, former Socialist M.P. for Maldon, Essex.

Mr. Driberg said he had seen Burgess constantly since he, Mr. Driberg, arrived in Russia a month ago. The firm for which he worked translated Soviet books into English and other languages.

"He still wears his Old Etonian tie," said Mr. Driberg, who is writing a book about him. Burgess lived in a three-room flat in the centre of Moscow and also had a country villa at his disposal.

He looked very well and seemed to be "well adjusted to his life in a Socialist State," Mr. Driberg added. He seems to live a quiet and fairly solitary life."

Burgess seemed to be a completely free agent. Normally he did not go to hotels frequented by correspondents as he did not want to see them.

He told Mr. Driberg there was no truth in reports of a rift between him and Donald Maclean, who went to Russia with him. They were getting on well together.

Mr. Driberg, who was unable to get in touch with Maclean, who is on holiday with his family, is returning to London to-morrow.

(September 14)

£1 PREMIUM BONDS TO WIN PRIZES UP TO £1,000

DRIVE TO CUT STATE SPENDING BY £100M.

2d ON CIGARETTES: PROFITS TAX UP: MORE FAMILY AID

Mr. MACMILLAN, Chancellor of the Exchequer, introducing his "Savings" Budget in the House of Commons yesterday announced:

A £1 PREMIUM BOND with tax-free prizes.

NEW SAVINGS CERTIFICATES and DEFENCE BONDS with higher interest rates.

EXEMPTION FROM INCOME TAX BUT NOT SURTAX on the first £15 of Post Office savings' interest.

STAMP DUTY reductions to make house purchase cheaper.

TAX RELIEF to self-employed people on premiums for retirement annuities.

AN INCREASE OF 2s A WEEK from 8s to 10s, in Family Allowance, for the third and subsequent children, with a raising of the age, at present 16, to which the allowance will continue if children remain at school or are apprenticed.

TOBACCO DUTY INCREASED

The Chancellor said all Government expenditure would be reviewed, civil and military, saving £100 million on this year's estimates. He then raised:

TOBACCO DUTY by 3s a lb, putting an extra 2d on a packet of 20 cigarettes, and

PROFITS TAX on undistributed profits from 2 ½ p.c. to 3 p.c. and on distributed profits from 27 ½ p.c. to 30 p.c.

Mr. Macmillan made no change in the Income Tax Rates or personal allowances. But he extended:

BRITISH WINE DUTY to include cider and perry (a drink made from pears) of 15 degs proof alcoholic strength; and

PURCHASE TAX to include shooting brake type motor vehicles.

£1,000 TAX FREE BOND PRIZES

Giving details of the new form of saving, the £1 Premium Bond, the Chancellor said: "This is not a pool or lottery where you spend your money. The investor is saving his money."

As long as the investor holds it, his reward instead of interest will be the chance of winning a prize in a draw to take place every three months. The annual prize fund will be equal to 4 p.c. of the bonds, prizes ranging from a few top prizes of £1,000 to a large number of smaller ones.

The bond holder will be able to get his £1 back on giving notice. There will be a limit, perhaps £250, on individual holdings. The scheme will begin later this year or early next.

(April 18)

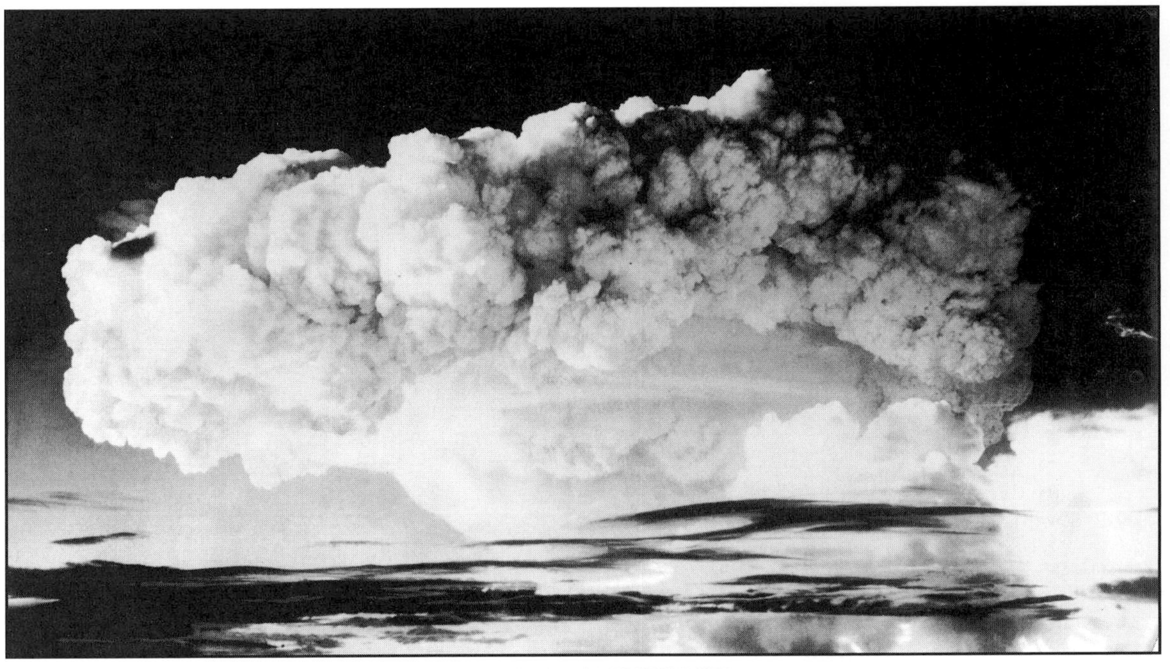

HYDROGEN BOMB DETONATED

H-BOMB DROPPED FROM U.S. JET

WEAPON DETONATED 10,000 FT. OVER BIKINI

From A Special Correspondent

ABOARD U.S.S. MOUNT MCKINLEY, off Bikini, Monday

The United States shortly before dawn to-day exploded its first plane-borne hydrogen bomb over Bikini atoll in the Pacific atomic proving grounds. The bomb was detonated precisely on schedule at 5.51 a.m. local time (6.51 p.m. Sunday B.S.T.).

The test shot, called "Cherokee," exploded well above the horizon at the planned altitude of 10,000 feet, or nearly two miles up. It was dropped by a B-52 jet bomber which immediately turned and fled to escape the blast.

From personal observation of past atomic explosions and comparisons with data released on earlier tests of hydrogen fusion devices the explosion this morning was the most stupendous ever released on earth. The fireball extended to a diameter of at least four miles and possibly larger, since part of it was hidden by cloud.

At a distance of 40 miles its luminosity exceeded 500 suns. Even 10 seconds after the burst I still found the light too intense for the naked eye. Only after a lapse of 15 seconds could I remove my high-density goggles - a time interval more than five times that required for direct observation of ordinary atom bomb explosions.

Indications are that it was not only the first airborne hydrogen bomb, but the first fully-fledged hydrogen fusion weapon, as distinct from the devices hitherto tested on towers.

About 13,500 persons, including 20 civil defence observers, watched the explosion. They saw a huge pink mushroom cloud edged with cerise and blue rise over the tiny target island of Namu on the north-west edge of the Bikini atoll.

PILLAR OF FIRE

The shock reached the fleet of observer ships some 40 miles away from the target two minutes 53 seconds after the explosion. Pressure from it lasted about 30 seconds, which was considered an unusually long time.

The giant fireball rose with a speed incredible to the eye. Behind it, after an interval of less than a second, there rose from the ground a colossal pillar of fire.

This pillar caught up with the base of the fireball and seemed to push it upward into the sky. For more than 20 seconds the fire pillar and the fireball kept climbing at incredible speed.

Then suddenly the pillar vanished behind clouds and the fireball dimmed into invisibility.

Less than half a minute had passed, but as far as human perception was concerned time had stopped. It was as though one was experiencing a nightmare with wide open eyes in broad daylight.

TOWERING CLOUD

Startling Spectacle

After the fireball there came what was probably the most startling and incredible phenomenon of all - a vast, unearthly cloud that kept climbing upward and upward, and spreading outward and outward, until it appeared as though it would envelop the entire earth.

For more than an hour the cloud kept growing in all directions. At first obscured somewhat by the grey clouds in front of it, it soon emerged in triumph from behind this puny, mundane obstacle.

Its iridescent mushroom of many colours from deep purple below to light orange and pink at the top, rose ever higher into the sky until it towered far above all its surroundings.

As I stood there watching in awe and wonder the sun rose to the right, and it seemed puny by comparison with what we had seen. Its first rays added a pinkish tint to the monster cloud to the West.

(May 21)

RAIL CHANGE TO 2ND CLASS

Daily Telegraph Reporter

Rail travellers were confronted with new signs at some booking offices yesterday, when Third Class officially disappeared from British Railways.

There are now only First and Second classes. The change was made to conform with the abolition of Third Class on railways in Western Europe.

There was little uniformity among London's main line termini yesterday. At Euston, where booking offices bore the "Second Class" sign, many travellers asked to be directed to the Third class office.

At Victoria suburban offices bore no sign at all but in the Kent Coast booking hall "Third Class" letters, cut out of metal, remained. Charing Cross compromised by retaining "Third Class" over office windows but displaying cards announcing the change.

BEST OF BOTH WORLDS

King's Cross was having the best of both worlds, all three classes being named. Over one booking office window a freshly painted "Third" sign was about to be replaced by an even more freshly painted "Second."

Fares in the newly designated Second Class accommodation will be those which otherwise would have been charged for Third Class. Only First Class compartments and coaches will have the class shown on the outside.

(June 4)

WARDENS FOR TRAFFIC DUTIES

PARKING METER SUPERVISION

A force of Traffic Wardens is to be formed to take over some of the duties of the police, if the Home Secretary agrees.

They would be non-uniformed patrols, enlisted from the ranks of ex-police officers, time-expired Servicemen and others who might welcome a part-time job to add to their pension.

They would not have police powers of arrest. But they would be able to call on a uniformed police constable to deal with any case which called for police authority.

This apart, it is thought that they would be able to enforce the law in most cases merely by admonishing offenders or pointing out the error they might be about to commit.

The idea is that of Mr. Watkinson, Minister of Transport, a keen motorist, and one of long experience. His new Road Traffic Act is about to come into force.

It is understood that local authorities would pay the wardens. The cost would be offset by any saving on local public services and earnings from parking meters, which might be about £35 per machine each year.

The new Road Traffic Act calls for a degree of surveillance by the police which, at their present strength, is impracticable.

The police forces are well under strength. Even at full strength they could not cope adequately with their primary function if they are to be responsible for enforcing all the provisions of the Act.

In particular, the projected car-parking regulations, under the new Act, make the Traffic Wardens force a necessity. Under these regulations roads would be classified into three groups.

There would be those in which no parking is permitted at all, those where parking for a limited period will be allowed, and where parking is to be controlled by parking meters, and roads where a car may be left all day, at a cost commensurate with charges in a public garage.

(August 30)

LEN HUTTON TO BE KNIGHTED

A viscountcy, two baronies, four baronetcies and 32 Knights Bachelor, apart from those for overseas territories, are created in the Queen's Birthday Honours announced to-day. Distinction is conferred on 2,000 people throughout the Commonwealth.

Len Hutton, first professional cricketer to be appointed captain of England, receives a Knighthood. He was born at Pudsey, Yorkshire, and celebrates his 40th birthday on June 23.

The new Viscount is Lord Cherwell, well known before his ennoblement in 1941 as Prof. F.A. Lindemann. He was personal scientific adviser to Sir Winston Churchill throughout the last war.

(May 31)

'ROCK & ROLL' CINEMAS CALL POLICE

YOUTHS EJECTED

Daily Telegraph Reporter

Police were called to five cinemas in London and surrounding districts last night to deal with excited young people creating disturbances during showings of the film "Rock Around The Clock." The film is based on "jive" music.

Teddy boys and girls started by clapping hands and banging their feet to the rhythm of the music. As the tempo grew faster they left their seats to dance in the gangways.

At the Gaumont, Chadwell Heath, Essex, 30 youths were ejected after scuffles. A policeman and several of the staff were hit. Seats were torn.

Later Edward Pillar, 17, of Lord Avenue, Ilford, Essex, was charged with assaulting a policeman. He will appear at Stratford to-day.

About 120 youths and girls jumped out of their seats at the Gaumont, West Ham, East London. Many protested at being ejected by police.

CHANTING AND DANCING

Crowds of Teddy boys and girls stood outside the Gaumont, Dagenham, Essex, hissing and booing as police ejected dancing and chanting youths.

Mr. E.C. Carter, cinema manager, said: "We all enjoyed the first performance. Rowdies and troublemakers turned up for the next show and we had to call in the police."

Crowds of girls and youths held up traffic in The Heathway, Dagenham. They were dispersed by police who had been dealing with troublemakers inside.

10 ARRESTED

Police were called to deal with a number of youths singing and dancing in the street after leaving the Gaumont, Twickenham, Middlesex. Later 10 youths were arrested and charged at Twickenham police station with using insulting words and behaviour. They will appear at Brentford to-day.

Last night's incidents brought to seven the number of times police had been called in the past fortnight to deal with young people excited after seeing the film. The other incidents were at Shepherd's Bush and Kilburn.

(September 5)

MOROCCO CROWDS CELEBRATE

From Our Own Correspondent

There was rejoicing all over Morocco this week-end at the declaration in Paris recognising the country as a sovereign Power. The declaration, signed by M. Pineau, French Foreign Minister, and Si Bekkai, Moroccan Prime Minister, stated that the country would have its own army and diplomacy.

A protocol to the statement said that France would assist Morocco in creating her army. The French representative in Morocco would have the title of High Commissioner.

(March 5)

MR. EISENHOWER RE-ELECTED

VICTORY CONCEDED BY MR.STEVENSON AT 6.15 A.M.

BIGGER MARGIN THAN 1952

From Our Own Correspondent

NEW YORK, Wednesday Morning.

With 47 per cent of the total vote counted it was certain at 6 a.m. G.M.T. to-day that Mr. Eisenhower had gained an even bigger victory in the American election than he did four years ago. Newspapers throughout the United States were saying in enormous headlines that he had won.

He had won or was leading in 42 States possessing a total electoral vote of 470, over 200 more than necessary for election. Mr. Stevenson, his Democratic opponent, was leading in only six States possessing a total of 61 electoral votes. At 6.15 a.m. G.M.T. he conceded victory to his rival for the second time.

The Democratic candidate could claim one minor consolation. In a surprisingly heavy turn out, he had received nearly 13 ½ million popular votes, compared with about 17 million for Mr. Eisenhower and that was by no means as big a margin as the tally of electoral votes indicated.

Mr. Eisenhower, on the other hand, was achieving something which the political prophets had not considered likely. He was carrying to victory a number of Republican senatorial candidates throughout the country whose chances had not been considered at all bright. On the Democratic side many senatorial candidates were running better than Mr. Stevenson.

NEW YORK WIN

See-saw Contest

In New York State Mr. Eisenhower swept to a tremendous victory, but it was a see-saw contest throughout the night for a senatorial seat made vacant by the retirement of Senator Lehman. Mr. Wagner, the Mayor, his Democratic would-be successor, appeared at 6 a.m. to have been defeated by his Republican challenger, Mr. Jacob Javits.

At 6 a.m. G.M.T. Mr. Eisenhower had won 16 States, giving him 166 of the majority of 266 electoral votes needed for victory. His opponent had only 39, having won four States.

The popular vote at 6 a.m. was

Eisenhower (Rep.) 15,599,491

Stevenson (Dem.) 11,897,033

(November 7)

NEGRO FINED IN BUS BOYCOTT

APPEAL LODGED BY MINISTER

From Our Own Correspondent

NEW YORK, Thursday.

The Rev. Martin Luther King, 27, Baptist Minister, first of 90 Negroes in Montgomery, Alabama, called for trial on charges of engaging in an illegal boycott of the local buses, was today found guilty and fined £178. Notice of appeal was given.

The solicitor for the prosecution then announced that the state had decided to postpone the trial of the 89 other Negroes pending the appeal. Under the Alabama anti-boycott law Judge Eugene Carter could have imposed a fine of £375.

He said he had decided on the lesser penalty because the evidence showed that Mr. King had appealed to his race to refrain from violence during the 17-week boycott.

Defence witnesses said that White bus drivers habitually referred to Negro passengers as "niggers." They also made Negroes stand while seats in the White section of the bus were empty, and also ordered Negroes to give up their seats to White passengers.

Mr. Robert Gaetz, 27, White pastor of an all-Negro church, said he had twice received threats because of his part in supporting the Negro boycott.

(March 23)

U.S. DOUBT ON SEGREGATION

POLICE TO DEFY BUSES RULING

From Our Own Correspondent

NEW YORK, Tuesday

Segregation of Negro passengers on buses in Montgomery, Alabama, ended to-day. It was a result of yesterday's Supreme Court decision that State laws requiring separate seating for white and Negro passengers were unconstitutional.

Many Montgomery Negroes, who for the past five months have been boycotting them, began to use the city's buses again this morning. The company which operates the buses announced it had "no choice" but to comply with the Supreme Court ruling.

(April 25)

YOUTH AWARD SPONSORED BY THE DUKE

SIR JOHN HUNT TO ADVISE AND ASSIST

Daily Telegraph Reporter

The Duke of Edinburgh has decided to sponsor an award for young people, initially confined to boys, to be known as "The Duke of Edinburgh's Award," it was announced last night.

Brig. Sir John Hunt, leader of the triumphant Everest expedition, will advise and assist in promoting the award. He is retiring from the Army, in which he is commander of a T.A. brigade, to take up the appointment.

Details of the award are being worked out with youth organisations and will be announced later. A provisional office has been taken in Piccadilly.

An announcement from the office yesterday said that in recent years many people had spoken to the Duke about the increasing need, under modern conditions, to provide further opportunities for young people between 15 and 18 to achieve a balanced development of character.

Emphasis had been given to the problem by the report "Citizens of Tomorrow," published recently by King George's Jubilee Trust.

SETTING UP STANDARDS

Since the autumn of 1954 the Duke had been considering this need "and the possibility of establishing certain standards, for progressive achievement, for which awards might be given." He consulted national voluntary youth organisations and others before deciding to offer his award for such achievements.

As a first step he accepted the offer of some organisations to conduct limited experiments in operating a scheme designed to carry out this purpose.

Other bodies might be invited to participate. The experiment was being financed as part of the Memorial to King George VI.

(February 28)

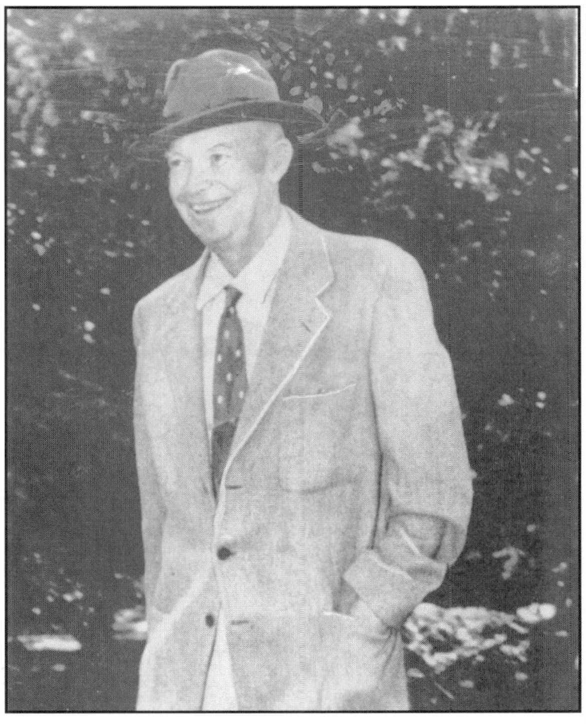

THE PRESIDENT steps out.

140 ARRESTED IN SOUTH AFRICAN 'TREASON' RAIDS

NATIVES' M.P. SEIZED: POLICE SEARCH SUSPECTS' HOMES

South African Air Force Dakotas were pressed into service to-day to fly to Johannesburg scores of Europeans, Africans and Indians arrested in Natal and Cape Town to-day on charges of high treason. Altogether 140 men and women were arrested in their homes at dawn.

Special aircraft from Pretoria arrived in Durban last night with a squad of detectives under the leadership of Col Prinsloo, head of South Africa's Special Branch. He personally directed the operations of more than 100 officers and detectives in raids in Durban and central Natal.

At sunrise detectives arrived at Stanger, Tongaat Verulam, Maritzburg, Ladysmith, Dundee and other points, and then spread out into the native areas. The arrested people were all brought before a magistrate in a specially constituted court and then flown to the Rand in three Dakotas.

FLOWN TO RAND

Wakened by Police

Nineteen men and women were arrested in Cape Town and were also flown in military aircraft to the Rand. Among them was Mr. L.B. Lee-Warden, M.P. for the Cape Western Area. He is one of South Africa's three M.P.s who represent natives.

Mr. Lee-Warden and others including a Cape Town lawyer, a surveyor and a former member of the Provincial council, were asleep when detectives arrived at their homes. Several of the houses were searched before the arrested men were taken off to court.

Prof. Mathews, acting principal of Fort Hare University, and Chief Albert John Luthuli were also among those arrested to-day. Both were remanded to Johannesburg.

A preparatory examination of allegations of high treason would begin in Johannesburg soon according to a statement made to-day by Mr. Swart, Minister of Justice.

(December 6)

U.S. REBUFF TO RUSSIA

The United States has suspended its exchange of visits programme with Russia to show disapproval of Soviet policy in Eastern Europe. Mr. Whitr, State Department spokesman, said to-day: "in view of recent developments the proposed exchanges have been suspended during a reappraisal of the programme." The suspension will work both ways.

The American Government will not sponsor Russian hroups' visits to the Ynited States nor American groups wishing to go to Russia. The suspension does not apply to satellite countries, nor to privately orhanised visits.

(December 4)

RAIL JOBS FOR WEST INDIANS

BARBADOS TRIP BY STAFF OFFICER

Daily Telegraph Reporter

The British Transport Commission is recruiting men in the West Indies for the railways. The target is 1,000 men for all grades of employment.

A Commission staff officer flew to Barbados on April 5 and is interviewing recruits. A spokesman for the Commission said in London yesterday that no arrangements were being made to bring them to Britain.

Those considered suitable are being advised to present themselves for employment when they arrive in England They will be offered the same conditions of employment as railway workers in this country"

This is the first time that large-scale recruiting has been undertaken in Barbados. British Railways last month began a three-month drive in Britain to obtain 20,000 workers.

Of 1,200 West Indians who arrived in England on Sunday, 120 had been recruited in the West Indies for London Transport. Two London Transport officials visited the islands seeking staff.

560 MORE ARRIVE

Overland from genoa

More West Indians seeking work in Britain landed yesterday at Folkestone from the Channel steamer Cote d'Azur, after travelling overland from Genoa to Calais. Two special trains took them to Victoria.

One of the party of 560, among whom was a good number of gaily dressed women, said:"None or us has a job yet. I am going to Nottingham, where some of my friends are."

(April 12)

SOVIET TROOPS WILL STAY IN POLAND

'CONTROL' PROVISION IN GOMULKA PACT

From A Special Correspondent

MOSCOW, Sunday.

Mr. Gomulka, rehabilitated Polish Communist leader, to-night signed an agreement with Russia allowing Soviet troops to remain in Poland "temporarily" and under Polish control.

Agreement was also reached on "the repatriation of Polish citizens and the release of persons detained in the Soviet Union." There was a reciprocal trade and cultural pact between the countries.

A joint communiqué, announcing the results of three-day talks at the Kremlin, was signed by Mr. Gomulka and Mr. Cyrankiewicz, Prime Minister, for Poland, and by Marshal Bulganin, Prime Minister, and Mr. Khruschev, Communist party leader, for Russia.

"MUTUAL CONFIDENCE"

Afterwards the Polish delegation left for home. The communiqué stated that the talks were conducted in a spirit of "cordiality, friendship, mutual confidence and sincerity."

Future relations between the countries would be based on "complete equality, respect for territorial integrity, national independence and sovereignty and non-interference in each other's internal affairs." The communiqué continued:

Both sides have discussed problems connected with the temporary stationing of Soviet troops in Polish territory. Until now agreed decisions have not been reached which could provide European States with sufficient guarantees against the rebirth of German militarism.

The constant objections by revanchist forces to the correct and existing frontiers between European States and, in the first place, to the established and existing Polish western frontier, also constitute a material reason hampering the normalisation of relations in Europe.

Both sides reached the conclusion that this state of affairs, as well as the existing international situation, continue to make the temporary presence of Soviet troops in Poland's territory necessary.

AGREEMENT ON DEBTS

Some Polish debts are cancelled under the agreement, especially those resulting from the Soviet extraction of reparations. New Soviet credits to Poland are to be made in the form of goods and loans.

(November 14)

G.M. FROGMAN MISSING AFTER TESTS

Daily Telegraph Reporter

Cdr. Lionel Kenneth Philip Crabb, 46, one of the Royal Navy's first frogmen in the war, is missing, presumed dead, after underwater trials in the Portsmouth area. It is understood that the accident was about a week ago.

A civilian diver employed by the Admiralty Research Laboratory at Teddington, Cdr. Crabb was in the R.N.V.R. Special Branch. He won the George Medal for searching the bottoms of ships for limpet mines.

As bomb disposal officer at Gibraltar in 1942 he found that Italian frogmen were entering the harbour to attack shipping. His men helped to clear Leghorn harbour of mines in 1943 and he persuaded captured Italian frogmen to clear Venice harbour.

AID TO SUBMARINES

In January, 1950, Cdr. Crabb tried to reach the men in the sunken submarine Truculent in the Thames estuary. He was in charge of the winch which lowered a television camera to identify the Affray, lost off Alderney in April, 1951.

He led the divers who searched Tobermory Bay in 1954 for a Spanish galleon believed to contain gold worth £3 million.

The closest secrecy was maintained at Portsmouth last night on how Cmdr. Crabb was lost. The Admiralty statement that he was missing presumed drowned means that the police in the Portsmouth area might not necessarily be informed of his death.

(April 30)

COMMUNISTS RESIGNING IN HUNDREDS

CHAOS IN PARTY OVER HUNGARY

By Hugh Chevins
Daily Telegraph Industrial Correspondent

The Communist party in Britain is in chaos if not in process of disintegration. Ordinary members are resigning in hundreds in all parts of the country. Leading figures, especially the full-time trade union officials, are throwing their membership cards away.

The reason is that although as "party-liners" they have previously obediently followed the frequent Kremlin somersaults, including the denunciation of Stalin, the recent brutalities of the Russian Army in Hungary have been too much for them to stomach.

It now seems that only the hard core of professional Communists and a few fellow-travellers are firm in their defence of the Kremlin policy of crushing the Hungarian patriots.

But even the Communist executive, in an attempt to stem the defections, has retreated strategically to the extent of calling a special national congress. It will "pronounce decisively on the various tendencies toward diminishing the role of the party or weakening its organisational principles which are showing themselves."

POLICY DISCREDITED

2 Major Resignations

This new move by the Communist leadership is in itself an indication of the turmoil inside the party. In nine area meetings during the last few days more than one-third of the 745 members represented has refused to support the party's policy on Hungary.

Such strength of opposition has hitherto been unknown in a party which prides itself on its discipline. It may be, of course, that in some cases Communists have decided, in view of their discredited position, that they should resume their old tactics of infiltration of other working-class organisations.

Yesterday Mr. J. Horner, secretary of the Fire Brigades Union, announced his resignation from the party. So did Mr. Alex Moffat, a prominent Scottish district official of the National Union of Mineworkers and brother of Mr. Abe Moffat, Communist President of the Scottish area of the union.

Mr. Horner, one of the few Communist general secretaries in the trade union movement, has been a member of the party for 10 years. He explained his resignation at a noisy meeting of union representatives in Newcastle on Tyne yesterday.

Striking a characteristic note of self-criticism, he said he had written to Mr. Collan, the Communist party secretary, saying: "I feel I have been responsible for propagating and defending policies which have produced this latest tragedy" - a reference to the situation in Hungary.

Mr. Horner continued in his letter: "You will take the view that I should remain in the party to seek to set right what is wrong. I can understand that point of view.

"Quite apart, however, from these political doubts and misgivings, my personal feelings on the events of the last six months make the course I am now following the only one open to me. I am doing what I must."

Later, Mr. Horner declined to make any statement about his future political activities. He said that events in Hungary were the "culminating point" in his decision to resign from the Communist party.

"NO CONFIDENCE" VOTE

Executives' Strike Call

Before he announced his decision, Mr. Horner was given a severe buffeting over the call of his union's executive to the Trades Union Congress General Council to order a general strike in protest against the British Government's action in the Suez Canal.

Mr. Alex Moffat, who has been a member of the Communist party for 32 years, said yesterday: "During internal discussions within the party on the international situation I have found myself so much in conflict with the policy, attitude and tactics of the leadership that I find it impossible in principle to continue membership of the party."

(November 9)

ALGIERS NIGHT OF UPROAR

MOB TRIES TO STORM PREMIER'S HOUSE

From John Wallis
Daily Telegraph Special Correspondent
ALGIERS, Monday.

Riots greeted M. Mollet, the French Prime Minister, when he arrived in Algiers from Paris to-day. Late to-night crowds of French settlers were demonstrating outside his official residence, although they had already forced the resignation of Gen. Catroux, newly-appointed Minister-Resident.

Several times they tried to storm their way in. They were held back by Republican Guards, experts in dealing with crowd disorders, who are part of the 15,000 security troops brought into the city to protect the Premier.

M. Mollet, who flew here to discuss the French Government's proposals for Algeria, and to install Gen. Catroux in office, made his way only with great difficulty through mobs of shouting demonstrators in the city's streets.

As soon as he arrived at the Government's Summer Palace here, pale, with his eyes streaming with tears from tear-gas bombs thrown by demonstrators, he telephoned to President Coty in Paris to tell him how he had been booed, hissed and pelted with tomatoes, stones and mud by a mob yelling: "To the gallows, Mollet, to the gallows."

Gen Catroux, who was with M. Coty when the telephone call was received, immediately offered his resignation for the third time. He said he did not wish to be the cause of public strife.

Mr. Mollet accepted it. He told reporters to-night that he did so to prevent further discord.

The French settlers felt that Gen. Catroux, who is 79, was too old for the post. They also accused him of being the "liquidator" of French interests in Indo-China, Syria and the Lebanon, and Morocco.

(February 7)

SERETSE GOING HOME AFTER 6 YEARS' EXILE

RETURN AS PRIVATE CITIZEN

Daily Telegraph Reporter

After spending six years in exile in England, Seretse Khama, 35, former Chief-designate of the Bamangwato tribe, is returning to Bechuanaland. He will make the journey home in two to three weeks' time.

He will go back as a private citizen but will be able to take some part in political life. He will be eligible for election as a member of an Advisory council which is to be established for the tribe.

At a later date, Seretse will be joined by Mrs. Ruth Khama, 32, his white wife and their two children, Jacqueline, aged six, and Seretse, three. The Khamas' five-bedroomed detached house in Croydon will be disposed of.

This new phase in a mixed marriage problem which has caused tribal disturbances and much political controversy came after Seretse had made an approach on his own initiative to the Commonwealth Relations Office. He suggested that he might return to the protectorate as a private person.

Announcing the Government's decision on this approach, the Commonwealth Office stated yesterday that the Earl of Home, Secretary for Commonwealth Relations, had at their request received both Seretse and his uncle, Tshekedi Khama. Tshekedi was on a visit to England from Bechuanaland.

Seretse and his uncle handed to Lord Home a document signed by both in which Seretse Khama formally renounced for himself and his children all claim to the chieftainship of the Bamangwato tribe, and Tshekedi Khama, who had previously renounced for himself and his children all claim to the chieftainship, re-affirmed his renunciation.

(September 27)

'KING OF THE TEDDY BOYS' GAOLED

Daily Telegraph Reporter

A self-styled "King of the Teddy Boys," about whom photographs and articles under his name appeared in a Sunday newspaper, was sent to prison for five years at the Old Bailey yesterday.

Judge Aarvold, passing sentence on Anthony Charles Reuter, 24, street trader, Westmoreland Road, Walworth, described him as "a weak and cowardly person" who had tried to hide his real character by displays of vanity, bullying and bluster.

Reuter was found guilty of wounding P.c. Anthony Still with intent to do him grievous bodily harm and of assaulting Miss Patricia O'Sullivan and Miss Georgina Doris Martin.

He was found not guilty of throwing an Army thunderflash at P.c.s Norman Muir and Roy Pugsley with intent to do them grievous bodily harm. He admitted an alternative charge of assaulting P.c. Muir.

(January 28)

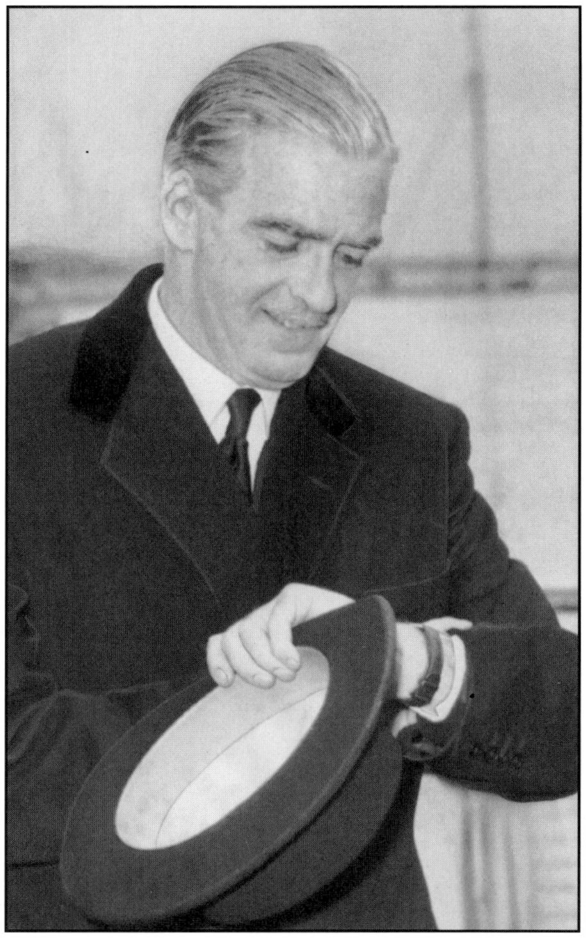

SIR ANTHONY EDEN, PRIME MINISTER.

BAN ON EXPORT AND IMPORT OF HEROIN

GOVERNMENT TO RESTRICT MANUFACTURE

Daily Telegraph Reporter

Export and import of the pain-killing drug heroin have been prohibited. Manufacture will be restricted to the quantities actually required for home medical consumption and scientific use.

These measures were announced in the House of Commons last night by Major Lloyd-George, Home Secretary. He said the ban on exports was effective from Jan. 1. The only exception would be small amounts needed for scientific purposes.

An announcement last April that manufacture and export of heroin would be banned after Dec. 31 led to criticism in both Houses of Parliament and by many doctors.

In the House of Lords Earl Jowitt, a former Lord Chancellor, questioned the powers of the Home Secretary to impose a ban. It was announced on Dec. 14 that licences for the manufacture of the drug would be issued for 1956.

Major Lloyd-George recalled yesterday that the original purpose of the ban had been to co-operate in the widespread international effort to help eliminate abuse of the drug.

12-MONTH LICENCES

Study of Substitutes

He pointed out, however, that the Government had been advised that it was not possible, under the present law, to prohibit manufacture. There were no legal obstacles to the ban on export and import.

Replying to Mr. Gaitskell, Leader of the Opposition, the Home Secretary said the licences ran for 12 months. Meanwhile, the feasibility of developing substitutes for the drug would be studied.

Socialists complained that the Government had been stampeded by a minority of doctors. Maj. Lloyd-George retorted that he was satisfied that its measures would fall in with the resolution of the United Nations Economic and Social Council.

Dr. Summerskill (Soc., Warrington) said that an individual could carry large quantities of heroin on his person and the Government's unfortunate compromise might produce a black market. The Home Secretary pointed to the strict control operated and added: "I do not know where the individual would get the large quantities."

He was not anxious to arouse great controversy over so difficult a matter. It was better for Britain to proceed in the hope that while substitutes were becoming better known, we should contribute to this world problem.

(January 27)

RAILWAYS TO RUN ON GRID POWER

The British Transport Commission has decided on "the bold step" of adopting a completely new system, with overhead wires taking current from the national grid, for its £185 million electrification plan for the railways. The decision was announced yesterday by Sir Brian Robertson, chairman of the Commission.

Britain will thus adopt a system which is common in other countries. The Commission believes that it will enable the electrification plan to be carried out quicker and more cheaply.

Sir Brian also announced a decision on the type of power brake for freight rolling stock. The vacuum continuous automatic brake, now used on all passenger coaches, is to be used for the 1,126,000 wagons, enabling goods trains to run at speeds of up to 60 m.p.h.

A survey of the Euston-Manchester-Liverpool line showed that adoption of the new system with alternating current would mean a saving of £5,800,000 compared with direct current and would cut operating costs on that route by £1 million a year.

NEW ERA

Minister's View

The decision on the new electrification system is subject to the approval of Mr. Watkinson, Minister of Transport.

(March 7)

PREMIER: SEVERE OVERSTRAIN

DOCTOR ORDERS AN IMMEDIATE REST

By Our Political Correspondent

A communiqué issued from 10, Downing Street at 11.45 last night, stated:

The Prime Minister is suffering from the effects of severe overstrain. On the advice of his doctors he has cancelled his immediate public engagements.

The official announcement followed a visit to 10, Downing Street during the evening by Sir Horace Evans, Sir Anthony Eden's personal physician.

For some time the Prime Minister's doctors have been urging on him the absolute necessity of seeking some rest and relief from his duties as soon as possible. The point has now evidently been reached where their advice can no longer be disregarded.

After the consultation the Prime Minister saw a number of his senior colleagues and told them that he had been advised to take an immediate and complete rest from his duties.

How long the rest is to last is not yet known, nor whether the Prime Minister will go into hospital. In the meantime, it was stated, he is remaining at 10 Downing Street.

Mr. Butler, Lord Privy Seal, will preside at Cabinet meetings in his absence, as he has done in the past. A meeting is likely to be held this morning. Sir Anthony Eden, who is 59, has been Prime Minister since April, 1955, when he succeeded Sir Winston Churchill.

(November 20)

LAST ALLIED TROOPS SAIL

From R.H.C. Steed and Ronald Payne
Daily Telegraph Special Correspondents
ABOARD H.M.S. MANXMAN, Sunday.

All Anglo-French land and naval forces withdrew from Port Said yesterday without loss. The operation was carried out with the same quiet efficiency, clockwork precision and success with which the men on the spot, from top to bottom, have accomplished all the tasks entrusted to them in this frustrating, ill-starred campaign.

All remained quiet in town until at last the squadron of tanks and the last few hundred men of the Royal Scots and the West Yorkshire Regt. began to leave. Then, as dusk fell, desultory shooting began from the Arab town a mile or two away.

This increased steadily until the sky was full of tracer bullets from automatic weapons. They were soaring into the air in the general direction of the landing stage.

Gen. Stockwell, the Allied C.-in-C., who with his Chief of Staff personally supervised the embarkation, left with the last party of troops. At the same time an assault craft carrying war correspondents also put off, leaving Brig. Grimshaw, commander of the 19th Brigade, with a few officers waiting on the quayside until the final moment.

CALM INACTIVITY

Myth Demolished

As we purred out to our warship, the distant wild firing increased and a couple of spent bullets hit the side of our craft. More splashed into the water.

At no time did the British troops or warships return any fire though they were ready to if necessary. This calm inactivity must have made it difficult even for the most credulous Port Said Arab to believe in the Nasser-created myth that the town was an "Egyptian Stalingrad" counter-attacking at last.

The Egyptian firing was ill directed and ineffective. But every precaution was taken. Deployed infantry covered the embarkation from behind piles of stone and shingle along the quayside with machine-guns and rifles at the ready.

Patrols advanced towards the Arab town as the firing increased, but were recalled to join the short columns marching up to the landing craft with full packs, one-man radio sets, machine-guns, mortars and ammunition boxes.

BAGPIPES SILENT

Discreet Withdrawal

Gen. Stockwell took the salute as each platoon turned sharp right through the iron gates and marched into the jaws of the waiting landing craft. At the head of each company of the Royal Scots pipers marched proudly, but with silent bagpipes. The order had gone out that our withdrawal was to be discreet and silent.

Everything was unhurried and orderly. There was an occasional observation expressing, tersely but simply, the pleasure at leaving Egypt.

At Port Fuad in the French sector the Second Colonial Parachute Regiment were the last to leave. They marched out proudly singing their paratroopers' hymn.

Earlier in the afternoon, United Nations troops had taken over the house near the waterfront which was used as headquarters by the British units. They posted armed guards on the roofs.

Here and there, an isolated blue helmet stood out along the barbed wire lanes. Occasionally we saw lorries or Jeeps carrying United Nations troops, Colombians, Swedes, Finns, Danes and Norwegians, on patrol.

As the landing craft reached a pontoon alongside the troopship Dunera Royal Scots pipers played the troops aboard amidst cheers from the warships' crews. The next item on the musical programme in the withdrawal was provided by Royal Marines in the headquarters ship Tyne which Gen. Stockwell and his staff had boarded.

One by one the troopships, landing ships and finally the warships slipped out into the night followed ineffectually by sporadic bursts of distant tracer bullets from the Arab town.

This was our last view of Port Said. Tracer in the night was a feature of local life with which we were already so familiar that we should have paid little attention to it except for the sake of the salvage ships.

They must have felt lonely there without us. But they had seemed in good spirit. "It's all right for some" bawled a bearded giant aboard one ship as we sailed.

(December 24)

£25,000 GRANTS BY ART FUNDS

BUYING PICTURES

Daily Telegraph Reporter

The National Art-Collections Fund gave £25,446 in the past year towards buying pictures and other works of art for public galleries and museums, says the report for 1955. The amount was over £5,000 more than in 1954.

The most expensive single item was "An old woman cooking eggs", by Velasquez, bought for £57,000 by The National Gallery of Scotland. The fund contributed £5,000.

Unusual activities by the fund included the purchase of "Portrait of Viscount Combermere", by Jivan Ram (Indian School), presented to the Barbados Museum. "View of London Road viaduct, Brighton, 1848," by T.H. Carmichael, was presented to The British Transport Commission.

(September 28)

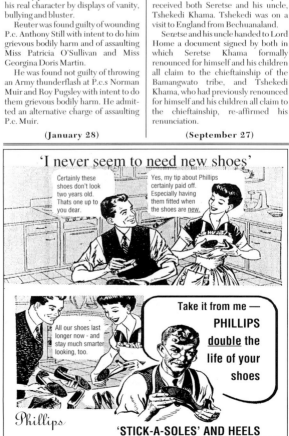

First Night

DEFT 'OTHELLO' BY OLD VIC

TOO SLY IAGO FROM JOHN NEVILLE

By W.A. Darlington

This notice of last night's "Othello" at the Old Vic inevitably has something of the nature of an interim report. Richard Burton and John Neville are alternating as Othello and Iago, and so the theatre-going experience of which I am now writing is still incomplete.

Mr. Burton led off as Othello, and gave a performance which was sometimes impressive and sometimes rather dull.

The best Othello I ever saw was Godfrey Tearle's at the Court in 1921 and there were moments when Mr. Burton's fine voice rang out in tones which seemed the very echo of Tearle's. But he lacked Tearle's power to make the poetry sing. I therefore found him moving only intermittently.

This Othello was a better soldier than he was a lover, for Mr. Burton's sense of authority never fails him.

SUSPICIOUS CHARACTER

Mr. Neville's Iago was never dull. It was incisive to a degree, and full of intelligence. But it lacked the bluff honesty of the perfect Iago.

I found myself reflecting that if I had been this man's commanding officer, I should have suspected him, for all his brisk orderly-room air of efficiency and his hail-fellow manners, of being a sly rascal.

Rosemary Harris is a charming but lightweight Desdemona. Wendy Hiller is forceful and down to earth as Emilia, and rises to a noble indignation in her last scene. Anthony White is a pleasant Cassio.

(February 22)

A STUDY OF AN EXHIBITIONIST

NEW AUTHOR'S PLAY

By Patrick Gibbs

John Osborne's "Look Back in Anger," seen at the Royal Court last night, is the first play to be given by the English Stage Company from a new author. It is a work of some power, uncertainly directed.

The leading character, a man of education living in poverty, would seem to be intended as a full-length study in resentment.

Something of a sadist and very much an exhibitionist, he has married above himself, apparently out of spite against middle-class respectability. His wife he lashes with a verbal fury that is often witty and always cruel.

It is not, however, resentment that is personified as much as self-pity and this causes the sympathy, which the author intends, to be withdrawn. When his wife left him, it seemed she was fortunate. When she returned to him in the end, a broken spirit, were we intended to cheer?

A similar uncertainty was present throughout all the deliberations in the squalid attic flat - a nondescript man and a girl-friend of the wife's who becomes, briefly, the husband's mistress, complete the audience for his passionate harangues on life and love.

What the hero's predicament was, apart from the hint that he was "born out of his time," I found difficult to decide. He was, perhaps, a character who should have gone to a psychiatrist rather than have come to a dramatist - not at any rate to one writing his first play.

Kenneth Haigh acted this part with great vocal abandon, as if it had no problems, not getting much sympathy for the fellow but making much of his literary jokes. Mary Ure played the wife with a compelling simplicity. Tony Richardson's production was forthright.

(May 9)

£116,000 FOR A CHRISTIE PLAY

By Our Film Correspondent

It was announced yesterday that the film rights of Agatha Christie's thriller, "The Witness for the Prosecution," have been bought by the American impresario, Gilbert Miller. The price, I understand, was £116,000.

(January 24)

Film Notes

MORE MIXED-UP KIDS

By Campbell Dixon

So the cynics had it wrong. It's not TV, but the movies, that have taken the place of entertainment.

Last week we had three horrifying pictures of the human rat-race under the Stars and Stripes. This week brings another socially-conscious drama from the West, and three stories of delinquency, cruelty and corruption from beyond the Iron Curtain, where entertainment is no laughing matter.

I must be a reactionary. I feel a sudden urge to see a gay, charming, socially-unconscious picture of a juvenile delinquent about the size and shape of Miss Grace Kelly.

Juveniles on Wheels

Incomparably the best of the quartet is Nicholas Ray's REBEL WITHOUT A CAUSE (London Pavilion).

In his new and more distinguished production poverty is not a factor, any more than it was in the case of Leopold and Loeb. His boys and girls come from comfortable homes; most of them own cars.

Does that, and their physical maturity, strike some readers as phoney? Well, education is compulsory in California up to the age of 18, and automobiles - 6m of them among as many adults - are taken much for granted.

What's wrong with these adolescents, then? Why do they feel that desperate need to prove their courage? We all know certain warrior races - the Spartans and Red Indians, for example - had harsh initiation tests.

Americans, however, are no more a military nation than we are; and, since psychology is much taught in American schools, one might expect the doubts to be resolved and the challenge to be laughed off as exhibitionism in poor taste.

"The Chicken Run"

But no. One of the high spots in Mr. Ray's film is a contest, brilliantly staged, called "The Chicken Run." Challenger and challenged race their stolen cars to the edge of a precipice and jump clear. He who jumps first is labelled "chicken." The other, in the film, gets caught and goes over the edge.

Something of the kind, Mr. Ray informs me, actually took place at Santa Monica. Should you be sceptical again, I can only quote a friend who was riding in a Hollywood cab when, to his alarm, it charged straight at an oncoming taxi. At the last second the other taxi swerved aside and all concerned escaped death by inches.

"Always knew that guy was yellow," confided my friend's driver out of the corner of his mouth.

Feverish Life

As a thriller, REBEL WITHOUT A CAUSE is first-rate; but it is much more. Mr. Ray brings his boys and girls to vivid, feverish life; and if their frustrations and fixations are a trifle over-simplified, if you feel at the end that you have been struggling painfully through a Freudian jungle in which the real delinquents are the parents, the characterisation is skilful and the direction and playing of many scenes quite superb.

Among several fine performances, one is unforgettable in its subtlety and strength, its power to suggest, buy a shrug, an awkward gesture, a hesitant word, an unexpectedly charming smile or suddenly unleashed fury, all the loneliness of the young, their dreams and agonised confusions. I have seen many interpretations of Hollywood's pet character, the mixed-up kid, which means anybody under 40. I still say this is a tour de force.

James Dean's performance has its own special pang when you remember that the most brilliant young discovery of the American stage and screen was recently killed, like one of these adolescents, in a car crash, through not through any fault of his own.

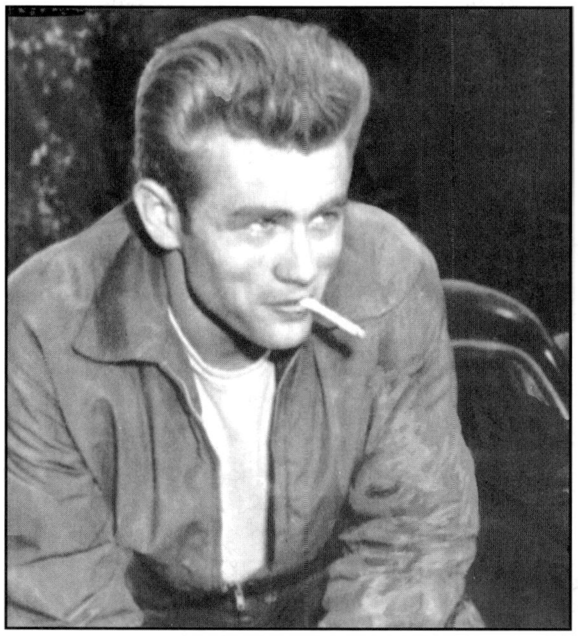

JAMES DEAN 'Rebel Without A Cause'

(January 21)

In *High Society* (Empire) Grace Kelly's last appearance on the screen? If so, her abdication is rather sad.

Where is another player as variously gifted - with youth, beauty, a talent seriously under-estimated by people who equate acting with pyrotechnics, and, rarest of all in a vulgar medium, the qualities of dignity and grace?

"HIGH SOCIETY" is a re-make of "Philadelphia Story". To provide opportunities for Bing Crosby and Louis Armstrong, a good many songs have been added, and the roles of journalist and photographer seem to have shrunk a little. Whether the music (such as it is) compensates for the loss of some of the wit (such as it was) is a matter of opinion.

This is no reflection on the great Satchmo. I had always supposed, by the way, that this was a title, royal or hierarchical - a variant, perhaps, of Sachem. But no - Mr. Armstrong, with a self-explanatory grin, tells us himself that it's simply an abbreviation of "Satchel-mouth."

Here the great man has little to do, but what he does he does superbly. Those rolling eyes radiating ecstasy and kindliness, those twin ivory keyboards, that wonderful gravel baritone, that golden trumpet capable of notes audible only to a dog - all this, though I'm normally allergic to jazz, I find quite electrifying.

Shoulders Up

Mr. Crosby, in contrast, is soothing, almost soporific. Once he does attempt a rock-'n'-roll song, but it must not be thought that, as a now solid citizen, he rocks or rolls in person. He just takes a firm stance and, without moving a muscle below the shoulders, produces a rhythmic flutter of the arms, like a butterfly with no place to go.

Between songs he is supposed to be infatuated with Miss Kelly, but his passions, as always, are tightreined. The most casual of all courtships has for climax the retirement of her stuffy fiancé and the appearance of Mr. Crosby, arrayed for nuptials in a natty blazer, pale blue slacks and the black-and-white shoes one associates rather with co-respondents.

Frank Sinatra makes his alcoholic love scene with Miss Kelly unexpectedly charming and has an amusing duet with Mr. Crosby. Celeste Holm reminds us that she has no superior in the art of putting over a line.

(December 15)

BOLSHOI GIVE SCINTILLATING 'SWAN LAKE'

A NOVEL STYLE

By A.V. Coton

The Bolshoi Theatre Ballet's version of "Swan Lake" at Covent Garden last night made quite clear that different versions of great ballets, conditioned by different cultural backgrounds, can exist.

Everything in style and mood throughout the four acts of this version differs from all others known here.

This choreography is based on the Gorsky version, the second Russian production after the original Petipa-Evanov work. There is the same general shape and duration of dancing to each familiar turn of plot, but choreographic structure is wholly novel to our eyes.

Generally the dances are simpler in shape, using fewer of the traditional steps, gestures and poses. But these elements are here assembled in different rhythms and stage patterns with a notable difference of dramatic and lyric effect.

FAIRY-TALE QUALITY

This Moscow "Swan Lake" is, to non-Russian eyes, quite fairy-tale in quality by the obvious simplicity of its story-telling and of its characterisation.

The décor of Versaladze has affinities with our dramatic theatre of the 1900s - naturalistic in style and with a colour range appropriate to respectable Academy painting of that day.

One of the company's younger talents, Nina Timofeyeva, appeared as Odette-Odile. Her interpretation in Act 2 seemed cool and remote some of the time, this sensation being sweepingly overridden by the passionate feeling she conveyed at the high dramatic moments.

Act 3, the ballroom scene, gave her occasion to scintillate in a choreography whose verve and brilliance are outstanding in comparison with any other production.

MASTERY OF STYLES

The *divertissement* dances here showed the Russians' unimpaired mastery of all kinds of dance styles of folk basis. In this act also Nikolai Fadeyechev as Siegfried showed his paces as a virtuoso in further novel and exciting choreography.

All through, the ballet seemed rather slower-paced than do other versions: the acting and miming were less obvious: more of the story's impact was carried through the actual dancing.

Possibly this modern version of a 19th-century success is too different - not inferior or superior - in expressive power compared with Western versions.

Some factor in the assembly of choreography, dancing, music and production does not come into perfect focus for the non-Russian eye.

(October 9)

Fiction

A MAJOR WORK OF FICTION

By Marghanita Laski

Anglo-Saxon Attitudes. By Angus Wilson (Secker & Warburg 15s.)

ANGUS WILSON'S deftly titled "Anglo-Saxon Attitudes" is a very good novel indeed. The development of craft and capacity as between this and his last novel, "Hemlock and After," is even greater than it was as between that book and the two volumes of short stories that preceded it.

Technically at least, it is now reasonable to assert that Mr. Wilson is our most accomplished contemporary novelist.

This last statement may, perhaps, provide something of an excuse for evading the reader's natural question: "But what is it about?" True, it would be difficult to say what "Our Mutual Friend" was about, or even, as Kipling's soldier found, "Pride and Prejudice."

But it is even harder to say what "Anglo-Saxon Attitudes" is about, because its function is rather to explore a situation than to tell a story. If we are to compare it with anything, a more valuable comparison than with novels of the past might be with Rosamund Lehmann's last book, "The Echoing Grove," where equally the author was concerned, by inter-weaving complexities, to create a many-dimensional pattern.

We can, of course, say what the situation is - if that helps. Gerald Middleton, an historian in his 60s, is involved in searching emotional decisions concerning both his relations with his family and a matter of professional integrity arising from an incident in which he was involved a generation earlier, the finding of a pagan fertility symbol in the grave of a seventh-century bishop.

How these situations, factual and emotional, are almost inextricably entwined, intimately explored, and finally unravelled, is a matter for marvelling admiration. Atmosphere, from ramshackle lodging-house to historical association, and whether known to the reader or not, is unmistakable right; wit, where appropriate, is beautifully edged; characters, more varied in scope that most modern novelists would attempt, are generally whole and capable of development.

Minor criticisms one could, of course, make, but on the occasion of this book's appearance it seems ungenerous and even niggling to carp. Here is a major novel of great technical efficiency that in a period of slipshod craftsmanship, of novels as short as a Victorian chapter, cannot fail to evoke delight for its triumph of skill.

The reviewer's task is to applaud its appearance and to indicate that here is a book of which critics will later have to make proportioned assessments in a wider context than this week's, this month's, and even this year's novels.

(May 18)

24-VOTE WIN BY W.H. AUDEN

Mr. W.H. Auden won a closely contested election for the Professorship of Poetry at Oxford yesterday with 216 votes and a majority of 24.

Sir HAROLD NICOLSON was second with 102. Mr. G. Wilson Knight, the Shakespearean scholar, came third with 91.

It is the first time an American, Mr. Auden having changed his nationality in 1946, has been elected to the Chair. He succeeds his friend and contemporary, Mr. C. Day Lewis.

The new Professor of Poetry will be expected to give one lecture a term for five years. His salary is £300 a year.

The result of the election was in doubt until the end of the last of the day's three voting periods. During the first period Sir Harold had a lead of two votes.

(February 10)

FESTIVAL HALL TRIBUTE

AUDIENCE CHEER COMPOSER

The whole Festival Hall audience rose cheering to its feet to greet Dr. Vaughan Williams at the close of the first London performance of his eighth symphony by Sir John Barbirolli and the Halle Orchestra last night - a tribute the more moving by its rarity.

Plainly this is a work whose construction has diverted the composer, and much of its lightweight enjoyment is passed easily to the listener.

The first movement is amusingly original in its discovery of what a pair of fourths can lead to. The wind scherzo is faintly pachydermatous but genuinely witty; and the string cavatina, for all its half-memories of earlier ruminative movements, is of great intrinsic beauty.

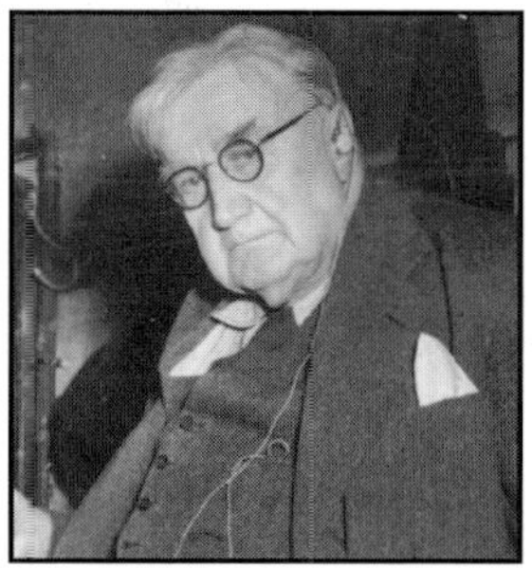

DR. VAUGHAN WILLIAMS

The worry is the finale, in which the composer indulges his relish for the percussion instruments, including that loathsome vibraphone. One cannot help feeling that some of its point is lost, and the symphony brought to an untidy end, when they consistently double the orchestra noisily instead of having distinctive music of their own.

But it is the happiness of this péché de vieillesse, flaws and all, that is the main impression and that gives such pleasure.

(May 15)

PICTURES BY 'YOUNG BRUTES'

SIR A. MUNNINGS STAYS AWAY

Daily Telegraph Reporter

Sir ALFRED MUNNINGS, who is 77 and a former President of the Royal Academy, yesterday said that the Academy's summer exhibition was the worst he had seen. It opens publicly on Saturday.

Because of his disapproval, Sir Alfred refused to attend the Academy banquet last night. "This is the first banquet I have missed since 1899," he said. "I am perfectly fit, but I just do not want to go."

He saw the exhibition on varnishing day last Saturday. Referring to the section of modern art, he said: Why does the Academy encourage this kind of nonsense? You get these kind of young brutes who want to knock you sky-high.

"These foolish things they are hanging. If they do not look out, they are going to abuse the fine premises they occupy. Reynolds and Gainsborough, they are the people who tried to paint.

"If you were a real painter, how would you feel having your picture next to one of these bits of nonsense? Any amount of good painting is rejected because of this stuff."

HE "IS A DARLING"

"We All Love Him"

Sir ALBERT RICHARDSON, President of the Royal Academy, when told of the criticism, accused Sir Alfred of committing a breach of etiquette by commenting on the exhibition before it was open to the public. "But Sir Alfred is a darling, a jolly good artist, and we all love him."

He laughed when I repeated Sir Alfred's comments. "If he looks on the Academy as the Augean stable, I can assure him there is some damned good marble under the dung.

"If he looks, he will find the marble there all right, and the marble is constant if the dung is transitory. After all, you are bound to find dung where there are horses." [Sir Alfred Munnings is famous for his horse paintings.]

"He had no right to insult his mother, because he has been tied to her apron strings for a good many years. We only regret that he is not coming to the banquet so that he could answer us in the appropriate language.

"The exhibition is a bit one and very representative. If he had gone round the galleries he could have seen works he could admire, including his own.

"Sir Alfred is a very good animal painter, but he is not in tune with the vigorous exhibition of to-day, which will be followed by something different next year, and the year after that. You cannot control it."

(May 3)

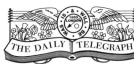

THE DAILY TELEGRAPH
AND
MORNING POST
DAILY TELEGRAPH - June 29, 1855
MORNING POST - November 2, 1772
[Amalgamated October 1, 1937.]
135, Fleet Street, London E.C.4.
Telephone: Central 4242.

MEN WHO CAME TO DINNER

It is a strange company that has been seen dancing to the rhythm of "Don't Let's Be Nasty to the Russians" since the notorious Labour party dinner. All that these Communists, Bevanites, Shinwellites, Liberals and - surprisingly enough - Conservatives have in common is that crude sense of opportunity that politicians call realism. this has driven them to harry Mr. Gaitskell and Mr. Brown with a charge of bad manners which, they hope, may turn out useful in some future party or general election. Yesterday they were encouraged by Marshal Bulganin, who said, in a speech marking his return from Britain, that only "the Labourites" tried to spoil the atmosphere of the visit. If that were true, it would be something to be ashamed of. As a matter of fact, representations on behalf of prisoners were not confined to the Socialist leaders, the only valid criticism of whose action is that so vastly important a topic should not have been made to seem the prerogative of one party.

It is curious, indeed alarming, how quickly controversy over this dinner party has got away from the main point. It is, surely, that Mr. Khruschev was prevented from finishing a tirade as abusive as his efforts in India, and was forced to answer a question about Social Democrats in prison which went to the heart of the difference between his world and ours. In other words, there was one protest in the name of truth and another in the name of freedom. The guest being the kind of man he is, it was necessary to heckle in the one case and to present a list in the other. Is it seriously argued that manners on this occasion should have come before morals? Should we really shed tears over Mr. Khruschev's obvious disappointment that British Communists will not easily be admitted into a Popular Front?

The Soviet leaders are, of course, trying to bring about the liquidation of the cold war at the lowest price they can get it for. They are, so to speak, in the market with minor political concessions. If few are asked for, few will be given. If it is sufficient to give a foot in Poland and an inch in Czechoslovakia in order to win the applause of Western opinion, then they will not give a yard anywhere. Their great wish is to settle down for the time being with the map of Europe as it is and the people on it as they are. It is therefore right and realistic that we should demand a price for peaceful co-existence; and that is what Mr. Gaitskell and Mr. Brown did.

(May 1)

A SIGH FOR SUEZ

Yesterday the last British soldier left Egypt. There was, we are told, no ceremony about the departure. Not a drum was heard, not a bugle note.

Useless though it may be to cry over spilt milk, we feel bound to put on record the feebleness of the reasons for and the frightfulness of the consequences of spilling any milk at all in this region. The evacuation of Suez was prompted by the practical argument that the base was useless in war, and by the political argument that Egypt must be kept friendly. In a major war, the base was no more useless than any other which might be subjected to nuclear attack, and certainly not more useless in that event than Cyprus. And there was one kind of store in it, already a bit cracked by Abadan and now further seriously damaged, in the shape of British prestige in the Middle East. As for Egypt's friendliness, it is enough to observe that Col. Nasser is to celebrate the evacuation by a display of the arms which he has obtained from Communist sources.

We have, it is believed, become wiser now, but not wise enough in time enough. It may be asked whether, without this scuttle, our oil supplies in the Middle East would have become so endangered as the Prime Minister says they are; whether problems in Cyprus and in North Africa would have been so acute; whether there would have been trouble in Jordan. Whatever be the answer, we have no reason to be proud today.

(June 14)

TALENT AND EMOTION

Above the din of the screaming maenads who yesterday welcomed Liberace to these shores, there rang out one clear voice of protest. Mr. John Marsh, Director of the Industrial Welfare Society, finds in the adulation accorded this new darling of television disturbing new evidence of an emptiness in peoples' lives that is increasingly filled by the second-rate. It is, of course, very tempting for educated people to find fault with the pleasures of the simple-minded. Few things are so difficult as to understand enthusiasms which one does not share. It is nothing new, therefore, to find the Mr. Marshes of this world wringing their hands over the Liberaces.

But there is to-day a new and more urgent cause for their alarm. Before the advent of television opportunities for giving vent to emotional infantilism were relatively limited. Now, however, every set owner can take a shot of this drug which, although harmless in small doses, cumulatively, night after night, will render the most stolid citizen moronic. Television, in short, tends to set up an inflationary pressure in popular entertainment: more and more fans chase less and less talent, a vicious spiral which ends with people swooning with enchantment for less and less reason.

(September 26)

BUDAPEST'S BATTLE IS OUTRIGHT CIVIL WAR

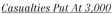

RUSSIAN TANKS BLOCK DANUBE BRIDGES

UNARMED CIVILIANS WERE MOWN DOWN IN STREETS

The following eye-witness despatch by
Gordon Shepherd
Daily Telegraph Special Correspondent,
from Hungary's isolated capital was brought out yesterday by an Austrian refugee who carried it across the frontier for safe transmission to London.

BUDAPEST, **Friday.**

Russian T.34 tanks and "loyal" Hungarian troops were still fighting in the streets of this shattered and sealed-off capital to-day to crush the great Budapest uprising. To judge from the fading scale of gunfire over the past 18 hours since my arrival here, the last defiant flickers of organised resistance are now being extinguished.

But the popular tumult in the capital is so intense that new slaughters can flare up in an instant out of the most harmless-looking street scene.

As this is being written, my hotel window is vibrating with the noise of tanks rumbling along the Danube embankment towards the southern end of the town. Heavy gunfire comes across the misty river from Csepel, where a pitched battle has been going on all night.

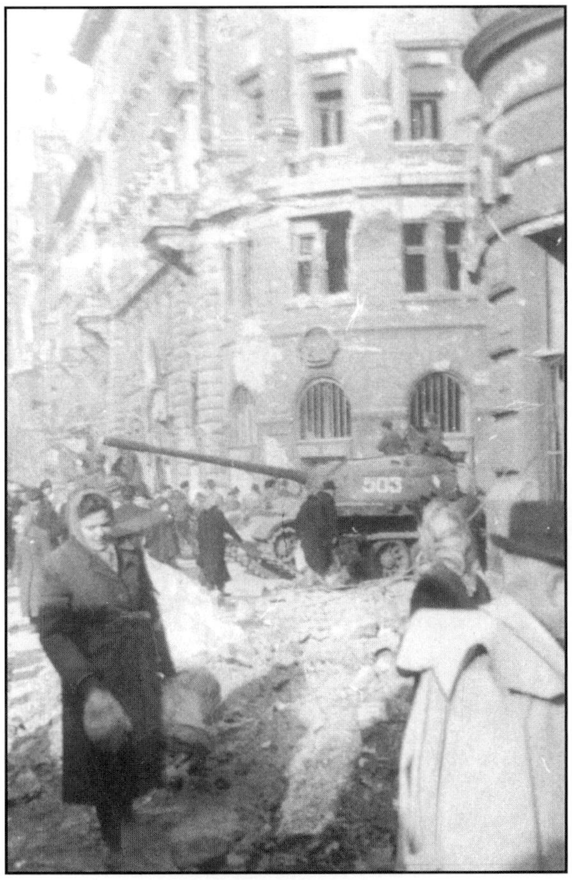

BUDAPEST AS IT IS TO-DAY. The after-effects of the Hungarian uprising are shown in this picture, received in London last night. While women pick their way through the rubble-strewn streets, Soviet tanks and troops maintain constant watch at every road junction.

This is no mere revolt of a disgruntled party junta. It is no mere demonstration which has got out of hand due to trigger-happy citizens.

It is an outright civil war in which the 90 per cent of Hungary's anti-Communists have struggled to express their hatred for the régime and its Russian protectors.

Casualties Put At 3,000

The number of dead and dying is impossible to estimate. One doctor assessed it for me at more than 3,000 killed and seriously wounded.

But he was judging only from the state of the Budapest hospitals. Every ward of these, he said, has been crammed since Wednesday with injured, lying sometimes two in a bed and one on the floor space between.

I drove slowly through the centre of the city soon after dawn to-day. It was like a front-line strongpoint in a major military campaign. Tanks blocked the main Danube bridges and covered all principal crossroads. Burnt-out lorries and cars lay on their sides in the street.

Broken glass glistened on the pavements and the smashed cable wires of the tram system trailed on the ground. From some blackened doors came that acrid war-time smell of debris mingled with spent gunfire and corpses.

It was last in the air of Budapest in 1944. On that occasion the Russian troops came as "liberators." Now hatred against them has provided the mainspring of the uprising and the popular fury which has kept it going for more than 72 hours.

OFFICERS GAVE REBELS ARMS
Barracks Seized

From what I have seen and been told already there is no doubt that the spearhead of the revolt was in units of the Hungarian Regular Army itself. The Kossuth Academy, the Hungarian officers' training school, went over en bloc to the rebels.

Other centres, like the Hadik barracks, were taken by force, but after half-hearted resistance. Several military commanders are said to have shown themselves "benevolently neutral" by taking no part but offering the rebels free pick of their arsenal. Three independent eye-witnesses told me how they had seen Hungarian officers distributing arms to the civilian demonstrators.

The rebels had also been in possession of some Soviet-type tanks, whose number is put conservatively at about a dozen. One which roared down the

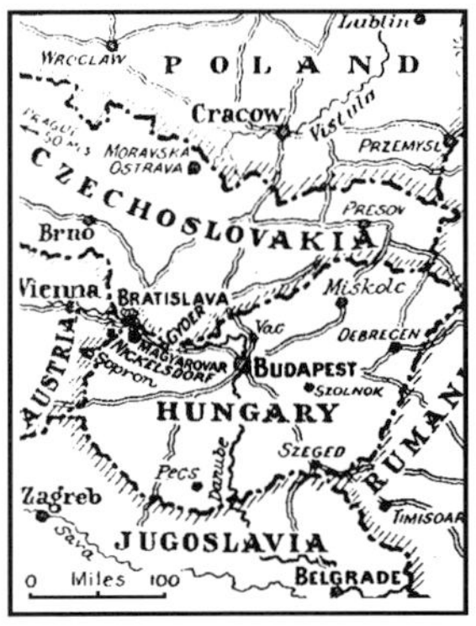

Danube embankment with its turrets open was piled high with civilians throwing out patriotic leaflets.

TANK INCIDENTS
Identification Problem

But all accounts of tank incidents are blurred by the problem of identification. The entire armoured element of one Soviet mechanised division, numbering more than 150 tanks, is thought to have been called in with other Russian troops.

In an attempt to disguise the detested Soviet present. Hungarian flags have been hung on many of their tanks. In other cases Hungarian tanks are filled with Russian crews.

The rebels seem to have only one clear way of identifying themselves. This is to fly Communist flags with the hammer and sickle slashed away to leave a ragged hole in the middle.

Reports that some Russian troops fraternised with the rebels and taught them how to fire from Soviet tanks are probably wishful thinking, arising from this identification muddle.

It seems fair to say that in some cases the Soviet troops appeared reluctant to carry out their unpleasant job. Yet in other cases their hastiness or wilful brutality have caused needless slaughter.

WOMEN MOWN DOWN
Tanks Opened Fire

One of the worst massacres of the last three days happened when Russian tanks opened fire without any clear reason on a crowd of passive and unarmed people in the Parliament Square yesterday. The total dead here alone is put at over 100.

Women and children were among the dozens mown down. Ambulances had removed the bodies when I drove by three hours later but some bloodstains were still on the pavement.

A few minutes later I witnessed a scene which showed well enough the part Hungarian army units are playing in the uprising. It took place in the army printing press in the Bajesy Bilinski Street.

This had been seized on Wednesday by the political police forces of the régime and had been recently retaken by military rebels. From the windows and balconies officers in uniform were hurling to cheering crowds below copies of a manifesto which had just been rolled off inside.

REBELS' DEMAND
End of Martial Law

It spoke in the name of the "Provisional Revolutionary Hungarian Government," and demanded the immediate end of martial law, the disarming of the political police, and Hungary's withdrawal from the Warsaw Pact under the terms of which Soviet troops are stationed in the country.

Neither this rebel leaflet, nor any other I have seen so far openly demands the end of any form of Communist rule in Hungary. This probably because the word Communism has lost here any specific meaning.

But the demand also printed on this sheet for "genuine democratic government" told its own language. So did the roars of assent from the crowd as they read the smeared and crumpled leaflets under the headlamps of cars.

This is the most impossible thing to convey out of the tragic Budapest scene yet the most important, the choking hate of the ordinary people against their present masters, and the Russians who protect them. For these three days and nights, under the cloak of a military revolt with which they are mostly unconnected, they have been able to give vent to this hate.

The worst side of this hatred is a still unshaken joy and hope at seeing anything Western. A dozen or more times driving around Budapest my car has been hemmed in by passers-by, shouting in English, German, or Hungarian "For God's sake tell the truth about these massacres," and "Do they know in the West what these Russians are doing?"

NO CONVOYS
Deserted Countryside

One man, thrusting an old Hungarian blade through the car window, cried, "This is our only weapon. When are you going to help us?"

My drive here from the Austrian frontier was across 100 miles of Hungarian countryside, strangely deserted except for a few troops. Until I got to within 50 miles of the capital none of these units was much above patrol strength, and there were no convoy movements on the road.

My document checks began only 12 miles inside Hungary, and continued at irregular intervals, sometimes by stray patrols, sometimes with regular roadblocks with barbed wire and machine-gun posts. Fortunately, no one could read my English passport.

It was only by describing myself as anything but a journalist that I got through to the capital. The most effective description was "delegate". This worked where "diplomat" failed.

Two colleagues and I were the first and only foreign correspondents to get into Budapest by any route since the fighting began.

PARTY'S DOUBT
On Future Hurried Reform

The political situation is still as confused as the military one. By reappointing Mr. Nagy as Prime Minister and making Mr. Kadar Secretary of the Communist party, the régime has used up the only two prominent Titoists.

In a desperate attempt to cling to power it has thus carried out in 48 hours reforms which were intended to be doled out over several weeks. They are up against a brick wall. There are no other "acceptable" Communists they can turn to and they dare not as yet consider seriously "multi-party rule."

(October 27)

Royal children share a lesson with twelve others
DANCING CLASS AT THE PALACE

Frilled Dresses, White Socks and Red Slippers For Girls
★
Dark Shorts And White Shirts for Boys

By Alice Hope

More and more mothers are following the example of the Queen and sending their children to dancing classes. It is fashionable now to start lessons at two years old, and many schools have long waiting lists.

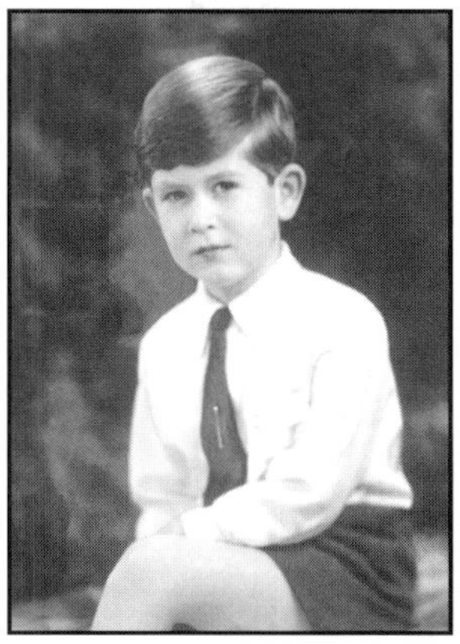

PRINCE CHARLES

The sound of a piano tinkling out simple rhythms, and perhaps a dance tune, in Buckingham Palace means that dancing lessons have started for the Duke of Cornwall and Princess Anne again.

Once a week Miss Marguerite Vacani and her niece, Miss Betty Vacani, drive up to the royal apartments in a taxi, wearing ballet length dance dresses and carrying their slippers in a case. At the same time come 12 children, some with nannies, some with their mothers to share the lesson.

SOMETIMES A BOW TIE

The girls wear frilled party dresses, short white socks, and often red dancing slippers. The boys have dark shorts and white shirts and the Duke of Cornwall sometimes has a smart bow tie.

Generally the lesson begins with the girls alone. For 20 minutes they learn ballet steps and the simple, classic postures. Then they are joined by the boys, and there are tap dances, Scottish reels and, finally, simple ballroom dances, with mothers and nannies watching.

The Duke of Cornwall is always very serious ('and SO intelligent," says Miss Vacani). He holds his sister firmly by her waist sash as they tread their solemn chassés.

EXTRA HELP

Miss Marguerite Vacani, who has been teaching Royal children to dance for generations, leaves the actual lessons now to her niece. But she guides the steps of the younger children when they falter and look appealingly round for extra help.

I spent an afternoon this week watching these famous Vacani lessons in Kensington , where other boys and girls receive the same tuition as the Royal children. "Now let's pretend we wear a crown," says Miss Betty; and up go the heads.

The famous wave that the Queen's children give to the public with so much poise was taught them at dancing classes. So was the Duke of Cornwall's grave low bow, and the quick little curtsy dropped by Princess Anne on the right occasions.

(July 18)

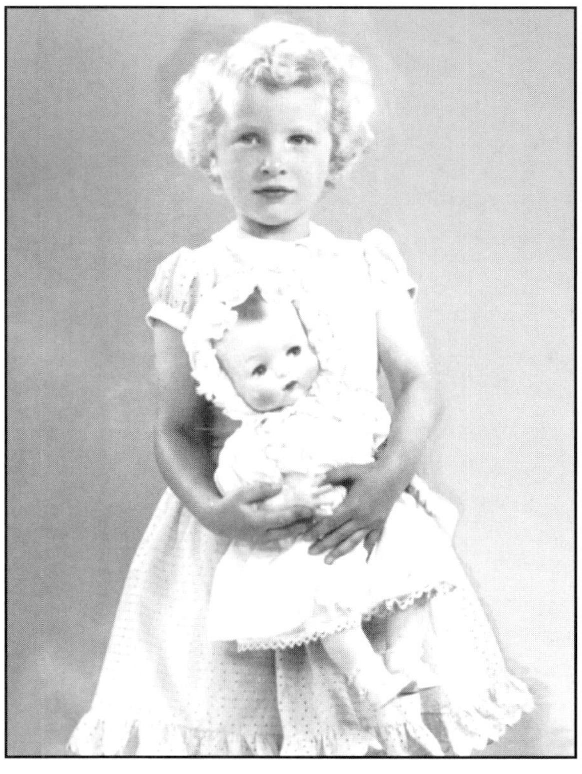

PRINCESS ANNE

GRACE KELLY BECOMES PRINCESS OF MONACO

From John Wallis
Daily Telegraph Special Correspondent
MONTE CARLO, Wednesday.

Miss Grace Kelly, the American film actress, became her Serene Highness Princess Grace of Monaco in the throne room of the Palace here at 11.30 a.m. to-day, when she and Prince Rainier III were proclaimed man and wife.

As the Judge conducting the civil marriage made the pronouncement Miss Kelly turned and smiled shyly and timidly at her mother and father. She will continue to be known as Miss Kelly for the next 24 hours, that is, until after the religious ceremony to-morrow which, as Roman Catholics, the Prince and Miss Kelly regard as the real marriage.

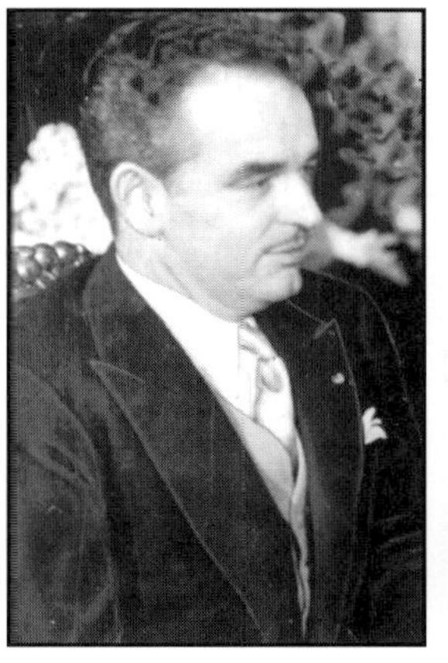

PRINCE RAINIER

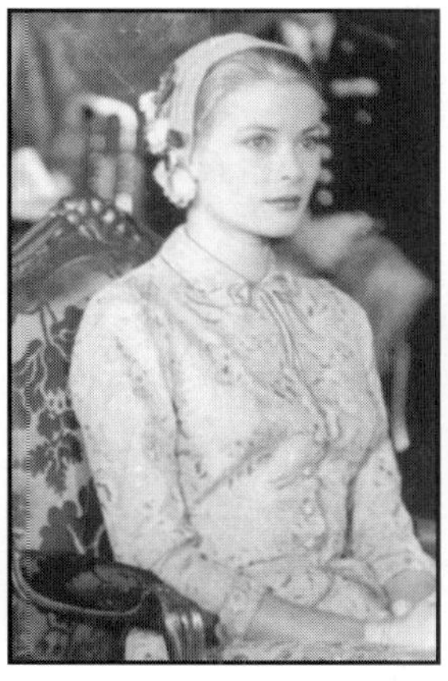

GRACE KELLY

The ceremony was repeated immediately afterwards for the benefit of the Metro-Goldwyn-Mayer cameras, who have exclusive film rights.

Miss Kelly, who is 26, was wearing a rose-beige dress of Alencon lace over a toning silk taffeta dress. Wisely, she did not repeat the error made on her arrival in the Principality, when she wore a huge hat. To-day she wore a small, close-fitting one.

She was obviously extremely nervous and tense as she took her place in one of the two red velvet chairs that had been placed in front of the throne on which the Princes of Monaco sit only on the day of their coronation.

TV ORDEAL

Prince's Discomfort

Prince Rainier, 32, wearing a black morning coat and grey striped trousers, then entered the room and smiled at Miss Kelly. But for the rest of the ceremony he sat gazing ahead, sometimes gnawing at the knuckles of his right index finger, a favourite gesture when he is disturbed.

He was obviously hot and ill at ease under the powerful television and cinema camera arc lights, which were placed far too near him. M. Marcel Portanier one of the senior Monaco Judges, then began the 40-minute ceremony.

Watching it were Mr. and Mrs. John Kelly of Philadelphia, the bride's parents; Prince Pierre of Monaco and Princess Charlotte, the bridegroom's parents; Monaco officials; personal guests and the representatives of 24 foreign nations.

Britain was represented by Major-Gen. Sir Guy Salisbury-Jones, Marshal of the Diplomatic Corps, and France by M. Francois Mitterrand, Minister of Justice.

(April 19)

MARILYN MONROE MARRIED

SURPRISE CEREMONY

Marilyn Monroe, film actress, and Mr. Arthur Miller, the playwright, were married in a surprise ceremony to-night at White Plains, New York. The wedding was held in a local court house, and the only witnesses were one of the bridegroom's cousins and his wife.

The newly-wed couple said afterwards that they planned a delayed honeymoon in England. Miss Monroe is due to fly there on July 13 to make a film with Sir Laurence Olivier.

One of Mr. Miller's friends said this evening he had received assurances from the State Department that they would let him have a passport. Only this afternoon Mr. Miller refused to say when or where the wedding would take place.

(June 20)

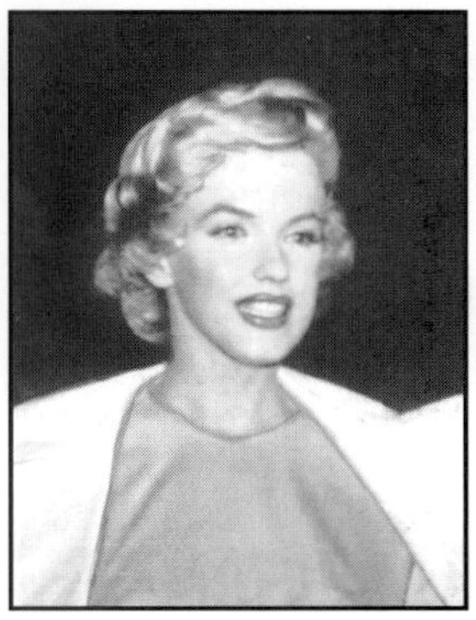

MARILYN MONROE

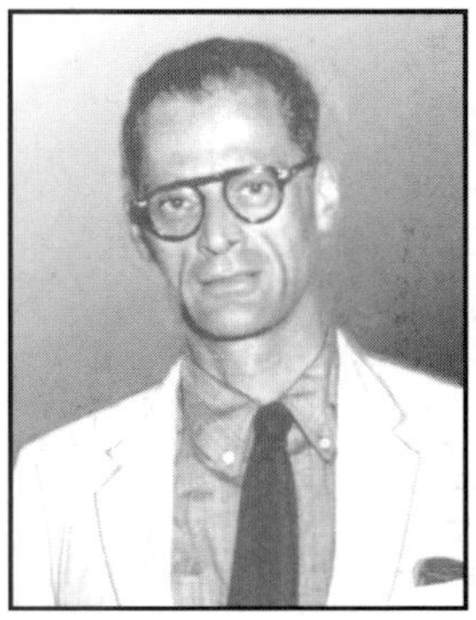

ARTHUR MILLER

HER COOKERY BOOK MAY STILL BE USED 100 YEARS FROM TO-DAY

"Cooking is an art; it demands hard and sometimes distasteful work, but on the whole it is the creative side that prevails."

By Winifrid Carr

"Flowers by Constance Spry " is to the English social scene what cream is to strawberries and mint sauce to lamb.

But there's much more to Mrs. Spry than being the world's most famous arranger of old-fashioned roses and cow parsley. In spite of the fact that hardly a single important occasion in British history in the past 20 years, from the Duke of Windsor's wedding to the Coronation of the Queen, has taken place without a background of her flower arrangements.

Fifteen months of travelling around the country with Mrs. Spry when she was one of the regular members of the Daily Telegraph Food and Cookery Brains Trust showed me what wide interests and a wise and perceptive personality she possesses. Her conversation brightened long train journeys. Her calmness before going on the stage to face large audiences of women waiting to ask awkward questions cured many a member of stage-fright.

And I was almost able to taste and smell the delicious-sounding dishes she described when answering questions on menu building.

Most of the time she was on our Food and Cookery panel, Mrs. Spry was also dealing with the proofs of a magnificently ambitious cookery book that she started to write seven years ago and which is published to-day. We had many tantalising glimpses of what was to come.

Humour and Sense

So that reading this book was for me like listening to Mrs. Spry again at our Brains Trusts. Her wholesome common sense about food and people shines through its 1,246 pages. What other cookery book writer would advise you: *"Never tolerate that nonsense about feed the brute; men are often more discriminating about food than women, and commensurately appreciative"*?

Writing about fish she is honest and amusing in saying: *"The distribution of fish in our country has its oddities. I am sure there are adequate.reasons for the fact that if one eats fish at the seaside more often than not it has had a look at London before being served up in its own home town again-misguided travel which may have broadened its mind but has not improved its quality as food."*

And when she introduces a chapter on ice-cream with the sentence: *"The first ice-cream I can remember was the delicious and utterly forbidden confection known as hokey-pokey"*, I am nostalgically carried back to my own young days in a.small Yorkshire town where the "hokey-pokey man" was one of the local characters.

Kitchen Party

Who else but Mrs. Spry would have thought of telling you how to weigh treacle when she gives you recipes for gingerbread? Or to give a kitchen party where the table is laid with copper dishes, wooden bowls and boards, clean nylon sieves, fireproof dishes and the centre-piece is a basket of fruit or a bowl of herbs?

The recipes take you from a boiled egg to a dinner party to please your husband's boss. And this is where Mrs. Spry "hands the cake" to her partner, Rosemary Hume. "She's a great cook, you know," she told me when I went down to her home in Windsor Forest this week. "Ninety per cent of the book's recipes are hers. I'm only a housewife cook, and all I know that's worth knowing I've learnt from her." That may be so, but I have a feeling that future generations of housewives will be "reaching for their Mrs. Spry."

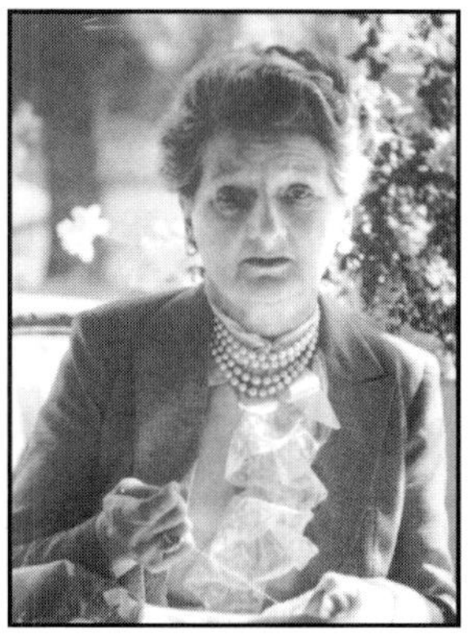

CONSTANCE SPRY

★

Taken from this wonderful cookery book is a recipe for a cool, refreshing first course for a summer luncheon. It can be prepared well in advance and is served in grapefruit shells.

Mint Ice

Allow half a grapefruit for each person. Prepare by cutting away membrane. Dust lightly with sugar and set aside to chill.

Boil 1pt of water, 4oz sugar and pared rind of 2 small lemons together for 5 minutes. Draw aside, add 1 large handful of mint leaves picked from the stalks, and infuse for 10 minutes. Strain, add juice of the 2 lemons. Colour with green colouring, cool and then freeze until firm. Serve a good spoonful in each grapefruit and sprinkle with chopped mint or crushed crystal- lised mint leaves.

(June 14)

FOOD EXPERT ON 'INVERTED SNOBBERY'

A form of inverted food snobbery leads some Hampstead and Chelsea intellectuals to a preference for tea and kippers. This was said by Prof. John Yudkin, Professor of Nutrition at London University, in a lecture reproduced in the Lancet.

An appreciable difference in the food habits of different social classes showed itself in a preference by the "so-called upper classes" for such things as brown bread, coffee and savouries. Such food as kippers and tripe were avoided.

"These preferences are not static, since they occur, or are cultivated, in those who are ambitious to move upwards in the social scale." The reverse was seen in Hampstead and Chelsea.

As the social scale was ascended, the range of foods eaten increased. It was difficult to get working-class people to try new foods. Trying them was almost a prerequisite of the socially superior.

"HARMFUL" FADS

While the present high demand for milk was partly due to propaganda, a greater part of the consumption was probably due to imposed State policy. Wealthy people, through taking up food fashions, often eventually had an adequate diet, but fads have proved harmful to people who have been duped.

Many people were convinced that fresh vegetables were nutritionally superior to canned ones and butter was nutritionally superior to margarine. "Neither of these statements is true."

Some women living alone and going out to work did not consider it worth while to cook a breakfast. They took sandwiches for lunch, and opened a tin of beans instead of cooking meat and vegetables for an evening meal.

(May 11)

Cheap flights open up Spain's Costa del Sol

Until now southern Spain and the northern tip of the magic African coast have been out of reach for the average holiday-maker. Andalusia was the playground for connoisseurs of Spain with powerful cars and plenty of time. Morocco was the winter resort of the leisured and wealthy.

This year the new cheap B.E.A. night flight to Gibraltar means that you can go to both areas for less than the journey to last year's most popular, and this year's most crowded Mediterranean island, Majorca.

It costs £42 19s return to fly to Palma, and only £37 for the night flight to Gibraltar. From there you can go by plane or boat to Tangier quite cheaply or take a bus to the many resorts on Spain's south-east coast.

Just over the frontier from Gibraltar, on the south-east coast of Spain, is a string of tiny fishing villages that sit in the sun on sandy beaches. The fishermen spread their nets to dry by day, and at night put out to sea to fish by lantern light. And apart from growing oranges, lemons, nectarines and sugar cane, that is all they have done on this stretch of the Spanish coast (the Costa del Sol as the travel agents call it) for generations - until a few years ago.

Then Torremolinos, one of the villages just outside the port of Malaga, began to be a fashionable holiday spot. Luxurious villas and smart hotels sprang up alongside the fishermen's cottages. The Costa del Sol is now on the holiday-maker's list, and Torremolinos, where three more new hotels and dozens of villas are being put up at this very moment, is the popular centre.

Twenty-five miles down the road towards Gibraltar is Marbella, a tiny village that is now what Torremolinos must have been 10 years ago.

It was in Marbella that I found the Mediterranean holiday hotel everyone dreams about. It is the Marbella Club, owned by a relative of Prince Rainier of Monaco. While I was there one of the suites was being prepared for the Prince and his bride. They are expected this week-end for a few days of their honeymoon.

The hotel, built like an elegant Spanish villa, is set in an olive grove and a garden that started out to be a formal one and has been taken over by enormous rose and geranium bushes, bougainvilleas and sweet-smelling herbs, all growing in a lavish southern way.

The villa houses a dining-room - but most people eat on the terrace - a smart bar and a sitting-room. The guest rooms are built along a patio like a row of cottages.

To get to the private beach you walk through the olive grove, which contains swimming pool, tennis court and miniature golf course, and is carpeted with special Mexican grass that stays green through the hottest summer.

To cap all this, the cost for two people is about 47s a day (25s for single room) with a 15 per cent service charge.

(May 19)

A.A. MILNE

A.A. Milne, who died yesterday at the age of 74, will live primarily as a writer for children. In the long sequence of volumes inspired by and written for his own son - the Christopher Robin of the "Pooh" books - he created a mythology: Pooh, the bear, Tigger the tiger, Eeyore the donkey, Kanga and her baby, Roo, the marsupials rank only just below Peter Pan and Alice as immortal characters.

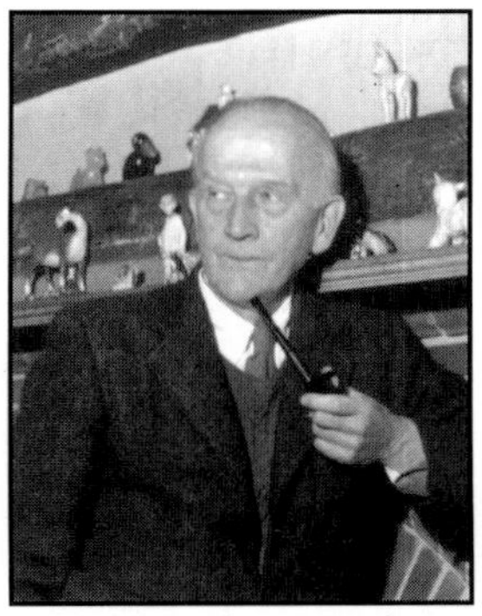

The Milne range was wide, and the Milne dexterity extraordinary. He wriote an admirable thriller in "The Red House Mystery"; he wrote a penetrating study of the perils of triumph, both on the conscious and the unconscious personality in "Success"; he displayed a unique combination of wistfulness and hilarity in "The Dover Road"; and "Mr. Pim Passes By" made him a fortune.

Only Milne had the vision, and the tenderness, properly to dramatise "Toad of Toad Hall", from Kenneth Graham's "The Wind in the Willows". And though he was a versifier rather than a poet, the quality of technical perfection never faltered. He would rhyme as trickily as Gilbert and juggle with metre like Guiterman.

It would be too much to claim he was an artist of genius: but as a talent he was at the top of the class. Especially in his children's books did he touch a chord to which adults could also vibrate in sympathy.

W.A. Darlington writes: My friendship with Alan Milne, which endured steadily in spite of his known dislike of critics, dates back 30 years and began with a public wrangle in the columns of The Daily Telegraph. At his suggestion we finished our argument over a cup of tea in his house.

But my admiration for his special gift of light humour had dated back many years further still, for in my day at Cambridge his name was one to conjure with. He had gone down a few years before and had almost immediately been taken on to the staff of Punch. He was a literary pioneer in those days, inventor of a new kind of irresponsible humour, expressed mainly in gay dialogue, which was later to become his strongest gift as a dramatist. He exercised an enormous influence on the younger generation of light writers in the years just before the first world war.

(February 1)

SIR GEORGE ALLEN

Sir Albert George Allen, who has died in London aged 68, was legal adviser to King Edward VIII at the time of his Abdication. Mr. Allen, as he then was, was the King's solicitor and during those days in 1936 was frequently at Fort Belvedere while the King made his final decision.

The following year he followed the Duke of Windsor to Castle Enzesfeld, in Austria, for conferences concerning financial provision for the Duke. He had acted for him subsequently.

Co-founder of the firm of Allen and Overy, Sir George was an expert on the commercial side of law. He was formerly chairman of Associated British Picture Corporation and was chairman of the Law Debenture Corporation and a director of other companies. He was knighted in the Queen's Birthday Honours, June, 1952.

(August 13)

MISTINGUETT, THE LEGEND

IDOL OF PARIS MUSIC-HALLS

The death in Paris yesterday of Mistinguett, a favourite of the Moulin Rouge and the Casino de Paris for more than half a century, closes a remarkable chapter in the history of the French music-hall. She was 82.

The idol of successive generations of Parisians, she had become something of a legend. Colette, the novelist, wrote of her: "Paris only hopes for one thing - an eternity of Mistinguett. She is national property."

Good-humoured controversy had raged round the subject of her age for many years. Mistinguett, who always protested vigorously at what she termed fiendish exaggerations, invariably flourished a birth certificate in her real name, Jeanne Bourjois, to prove that she had been born in 1888.

She was born of a family of upholsterers at Montmorency on April 17, 1873. Confusion over her age arose because of another woman named Jeanne Bourgeois who was born in 1888.

HER £100,000 LEGS

On one thing was there complete unanimity in Paris - the shapeliness of her legs. Described as "the most beautiful in the world", they were at one time reputed to be insured for £100,000.

Mistinguett's vitality contributed more than anything to her success: she was not good looking, and her voice was hoarse. But, whether she appeared as a penniless flower girl or in the dazzling ensembles beloved of Parisian audiences, she was always the darling of the boulevards and the despair of her rivals.

Her flower-girl characterisations had an authentic background; as a child she sold flowers outside the casino at Enghien.

She made her first appearance at the Casino de Paris shortly before 1895, and in December, 1911, she became the star of the Folies Bergère. Overnight, she and her partner, an unheard-of boy called Maurice Chevalier, became a sensation, especially in a dance act in which they ended up rolled together in a carpet.

During the first world war, she visited the front and rear areas to perform for the troops. She also presented a revue at the Folies Bergere with Chevalier, who had been released after 26 months as a prisoner of war.

LONDON PERFORMANCES

She visited London rarely. In 1947, on the first night of an engagement at the Casino Theatre, she broke down in the middle of a song, and had to be helped from the stage.

Among her most popular numbers were "Mon Homme", "C'est Paris" and "I Want to Find a Millionaire". While singing the last-named number she would descend from the stage and wander among the audience, bedecked in feathers, velvet and diamonds.

In 1950 she appeared in Rome and the following year at a New York night club. Early in 1953 it was announced that her legs were partially paralysed and she had cancelled plans to appear in a new show. She last visited London in 1954 to discuss the publication of her memoirs.

(January 6)

FRIEDA LAWRENCE

Mme. Frieda Lawrence Ravagli, who has died in New Mexico aged 77, was the widow of D.H. Lawrence, the novelist, who died in 1930. She married Angelino Ravagli, the Italian painter, in 1950.

German born, she was the daughter of Baron von Richtofen. She was the wife of Prof. Ernest Weekley, an authority on the English language, when in 1912 she first met Lawrence.

In her book, "Not I, But the Wind", published in 1935, she described their travels together on the continent, in Australia and New Mexico, and finally in France. They were married in 1914.

In February she presented in perpetuity to the University of New Mexico the ranch which Lawrence built with his own hands in the Rocky Mountains.

(August 13)

TRENCHARD THE INDOMITABLE

Man's conquest of the air produced no finer character

By George Fyfe

Marshal of the R.A.F. Viscount Trenchard, who died yesterday, aged 83, was beyond doubt one of the most remarkable men of his time.

To the last day of his life he was reverenced by all ranks, past and present, of the R.A.F. It is given to few men to stamp their name and personality on a great organisation, but this was achieved by Lord Trenchard who brought the love, care, and stimulus of a father to the force of which he was the indubitable progenitor.

It was he who, more than any other man, influenced the pattern of air warfare for the whole world. Indeed, his building of the R.A.F. was such a tremendous achievement that we are apt to forget he also spent five years in completely reorganising the Metropolitan Police Force.

Nothing daunted him, not even the affliction, terrible in so intensely active a man, of the almost total failure of his sight during the closing years of his life.

Trenchard was an imposing figure. Well over 6ft, broadly proportioned and of strong rugged features, he had jet black hair and clear steady eyes.

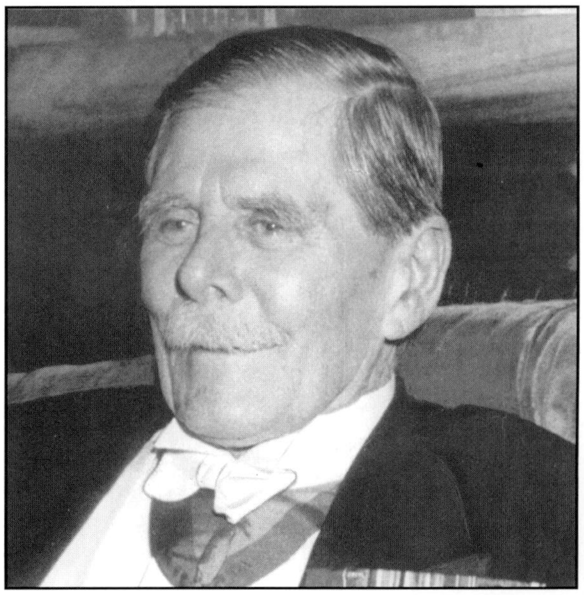

VISCOUNT TRENCHARD. Warmheartedness could not always be concealed.

His Human Side

His warmheartedness could not always be concealed. At one period during the 1914-18 war the Royal Flying corps had to suffer heavy casualties through the temporary superiority of German aircraft. Some pilots who arrived as urgent replacements for a hard-hit squadron broke under the strain.

They could not be blamed. They had been rushed into battle after a few hours' training in England. When all efforts to restore morale had failed, Trenchard arrived.

Despondently the young flying men watched as he silently inspected them and their equipment. Then, at lunch in the mess, they waited with dread for the "dressing-down" they expected to receive. The meal ended, and he rose. It was a tense moment, but instead of addressing them he walked slowly to the door. There he turned. "Well," he said simply, "you are good boys." That was all. Within a week the squadron was fighting again as efficiently as any on the Western Front.

Fame, when it came, was almost in the nature of a surprise. He achieved it after spending half his life - he was born on Feb. 3, 1873 - in diligently evading the limelight. He had preferred it that way from the time when, as a young regimental officer, he remained content with barrack-square duties in the tranquil conditions of the 1890s.

He went with his battalion to India, and from there to the South African war, in which he commanded units of irregulars. Instead of coming home at the end of hostilities, he stayed on for seven years with the West African Field Force.

He was nearly 40 before he returned as "a seasoned bush-wacker" (his own term). In 1912, when the Royal Flying Corps was being formed, he joined it with alacrity. Less than two years later the R.F.C. was fighting in France.

Trenchard was convinced that the aircraft must be primarily a weapon of offence, and in controlling the R.F.C. in the field he applied this policy rigorously. It entailed heavy casualties, but he never weakened in his views. Fighters must not wait for the enemy to appear; they had to go in search of him far behind the lines, and attack. Bombers must be employed to the fullest effect.

It was Trenchard's deep voice and explosive temperament that led to his being given the nickname of "Boom". When he was roused it often seemed as if his words, pouring from him in a torrent, could not keep pace with his thoughts.

Firm in Contention

No one could fight more doggedly for a policy, and he usually won, however strong the opposition. He once told me he had been involved during his career in no fewer than 23 official disputes.

The first of them, which occurred early in 1918, caused a first-class sensation. At a critical period of the war, and when he was at the height of his popularity, he abruptly resigned and asked to be transferred to the Army. He had found it impossible to reconcile his views as Chief of the Air Staff with those of the newly-appointed Air Minister, the late Viscount Rothermere.

There was nation-wide relief when, in the end, Trenchard accepted command of the Independent Air Force, which was being formed for the large-scale bombing of Berlin and other German centres. Immediately, however, he found himself in serious dispute with the French.

They flatly demanded that his force should be placed under the control of Marshal Foch. If not, they said, it would not be allowed to operate from any airfield in France.

Trenchard was in full agreement with the British Government's view that the demand could not be entertained. The disagreement had only just been settled when the Armistice was signed.

Post-War Task

After the war, as Chief of the Air Staff, he directed the formidable task of putting the new and traditionless Royal Air Force on as firm a basis as the two older Services. In the process he had to spend several years in overcoming determined opposition from the Admiralty and, to a lesser extent, the War Office. Both the Navy and Army wanted control of their own air forces. Trenchard masterly and unyielding, emerged triumphant from the long and acrimonious battle.

By 1930 he could regard his main work as completed. His active association with the R.A.F. came to an end, and he was created a baron. His leisure was short-lived. At the request of the government he became Commissioner of the Metropolitan Police at a particularly difficult time.

His major reforms included the inauguration of the radio-directed Flying Squad, the crime laboratories, and, biggest innovation of all, the establishment of a Police College at Hendon.

(February 11)

BERTOLT BRECHT

Regarded by many as Germany's most significant modern playwright, Bertolt Brecht, who has died in Berlin aged 58, was best known in Britain for "The Threepenny Opera". This version of "The Beggar's Opera" was produced in Berlin in 1928 and translated into 11 languages in the course of the next few years.

It was not till last February that it reached London, when it was presented at the Aldwych. It was taken off in May.

Disillusionment and cynicism, engendered by the social and moral chaos in Germany in the 1920s, were the keynotes of his work. He mocked sentiment, employed a brutal form of symbolism and preached militant revolution.

Born in Bavaria, he studied medicine and literature before his drama "Drums in the Night" attracted attention in Germany in 1922. A long-standing member of the Communist party, he aroused the hatred of the Nazis, who made hostile demonstrations at theatres where his work was staged.

When Hitler seized power Brecht went into exile, living in Russia, Sweden and the United States. He returned to East Germany in 1948.

His Berliner Ensemble, described as the most controversial theatre in Europe, is to open at the Palace Theatre next Monday week.

(August 16)

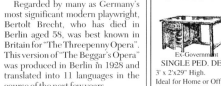

PRO-STALINIST AUTHOR DEAD

SUICIDE, SAYS MOSCOW

MOSCOW, Monday.

Alexander Fadeyev, the Russian author, foremost exponent of the Stalinist line for the isolation of Soviet literature from Western influence, committed suicide yesterday, Tass, the Soviet news agency, announced to-night. He was 55.

It was reliably reported that he shot himself in his apartment. The Tass announcement said Mr. Fadeyev suffered from chronic alcoholism and took his life "while in a state of grave mental depression".

His chronic alcoholism led to the "virtual cessation of his creative activity as a writer and of his public and social work. "The Soviet Government highly valued the services of A. Fadeyev and awarded him two Orders of Lenin as well as various medals."

ATTACK ON WEST

He caused a stir at the 1948 Left-Wing conference of intellectuals in Wroclaw, Poland, when he declared: "If hyenas could type and jackals could use fountain-pens, they would write like the poet T.S. Eliot and the playwrights Eugene O'Neill and Jean-Paul Sartre."

At the recent Communist party congress Mr. Fadeyev was demoted from full to candidate member of the central committee.

(May 15)

PRINCESS MARIE LOUISE

TIRELESS WORK FOR ART AND CHARITY

Princess Marie Louise, who has died aged 84, was our oldest Princess. She was the only surviving granddaughter of Queen Victoria.

Shrewd, conscientious and remarkably active, she earned more attention and affection in her old age than in her less publicised but equally busy youth. Throughout her life Princess Marie Louise was an indefatigable patron of the arts and a worker for charity.

Her erect and dignified figure and forthright speech will be missed at many functions associated with the Dockland Settlements, of which she was president, and the British Rheumatic Association. She will also be missed by numerous hospitals and clubs in which she took an untiring interest.

COUSIN OF GEORGE V

The younger daughter of Queen Victoria's third daughter, Princess Helena, and of Prince Christian of Schleswig-Holstein, she was born in 1872 and was a cousin of King George V. Her sister, Princess Helena Victoria, died in 1948.

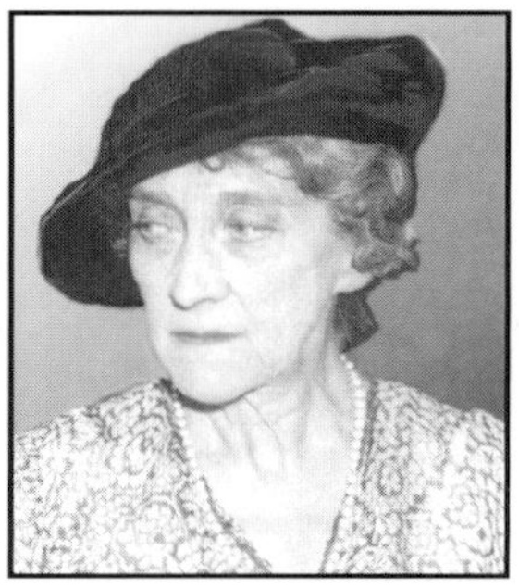

The two sisters lived together for nearly 50 years, until the death of Princess Helena. They shared a common interest in social welfare work and in the arts, particularly music and the opera.

Princess Louise succeeded her sister in 1948 as president of the Dockland Settlements, and in the same year became vice-president of the National Council of Y.M.C.A.s. She was the first woman to hold that office.

CHARITABLE OFFICES

She was for many years president of the Nursing, Midwifery and Public Health Exhibition. She was also president of the Friends of the Poor and of the Wandsworth Old People's Welfare Committee. Since 1926 she had been president of the Forum Club.

RACY MEMOIRS

An accomplished after-dinner speaker, never afraid to advance an opinion, she rarely used notes. Her memoirs, published in November proved to be a racy and fascinating volume.

(December 10)

SIR MAX BEERBOHM

SATIRIST WITH PEN & BRUSH

As a satirist with pen and brush, Sir Max Beerbohm, who has died aged 83, achieved a mastery in the Victorian and Edwardian eras which was unique. He excelled as a shrewd commentator on contemporary affairs and personalities.

Seldom bitter, and never, spiteful, he could yet invest his writings and caricatures with delightful irony. Unfortunately for many of a later generation who would have appreciated his subtle but audacious wit, he had lived in semi-retirement for many years.

His modish elegance was, he felt, ill suited to the changing times. Social turmoil was repugnant to him. Since 1910, with the exception of the two world wars, he had lived in a villa at Rapallo, on the Italian Riviera.

DRAWINGS WITHDRAWN

On his rare visits to London he generally brought a full portfolio, and his exhibitions were notable occasions to the selective. One of them, in 1923, caused a lively controversy which ended in the withdrawal of certain caricatures of the Royal family. A retrospective exhibition of his work was held in London in 1952.

Broadcasting in 1935, he described contemporary London as "a bright, cheerful, salubrious Hell ... cosmopolitanised, democratised, commercialised, mechanised, standardised, vulgarised." Max Beerbohm was the son of a London merchant of German parentage.

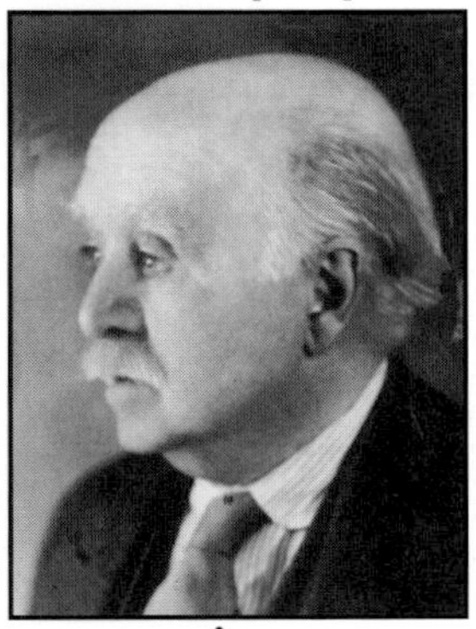

SIR MAX BEERBOHM

His half-brother was the late Sir Herbert Beerbohn Tree, the actor-manager. Max went to Charterhouse and then to Merton College, Oxford.

Even as an undergraduate he made himself known to the artistic world of the 'nineties. He was 20 when his first series of caricatures appeared in the Strand Magazine. Already he was making a reputation as a brilliant essayist.

SHAW'S APPRECIATION

His mischievous, elfin spirit was at home in the London of Whistler and Aubrey Beardsley, of Swinburne and George Moore. Shaw found him "spritely and incomparable", and these epithets proved adhesive. "The gods," declared Oscar Wilde, "have bestowed on Max the gift of eternal old age."

Even so, Max rejuvenated the art of caricature and rapidly became its brightest ornament. In the pages of the Yellow Book he broke through the cramping trimness of his predecessors. Like Beardsley in his influence - though unlike him in method - he abolished the "tight-lacing of the 'eighties".

As his technique matured he developed a remarkable gift of psychological portraiture, departing from actuality only the closer to approach truth. Much the same might be said of his exquisitely fashioned writings. "A Christmas Garland" is probably his finest book of parody, and "Zuleika Dobson" preserves some delightfully irreverent memories of Oxford.

LEISURELY WORKER

"Rossetti and his Circle" was considered a masterpiece, and "The Happy Hypocrite", a charming fantasy in miniature, was brought to the Theatre in 1936 by Clemence Dane and Richard Addinsell. These and other books appeared at intervals over a long period of time, for Max declined to work in a forcing-house atmosphere.

He was knighted in 1939. His acceptance of the honour provoked some bantering comment by his friends. Many years before he had predicted that the knighthood would become a penalty to be imposed on offenders.

(May 21)

SIR ALEXANDER KORDA DEAD

END OF ERA IN BRITISH FILMS

By Campbell Dixon

For British film production, the death of Sir Alexander Korda in London yesterday, at the age of 62, marks the end of an era. For those who have known him intimately for a quarter of a century, his death leaves the world a duller place.

What other man in his profession has been so many-sided? Alex, as he was called wherever two film men met, won fame as a producer of imagination and great daring.

Who else, in 1933, would have gambled his last penny on a cynical study of one of the most unsympathetic of monarchs, Henry VIII? As a director he was so brilliant that when "Marius" was shown in London 18 years after production, I had to include it among the best films of 1950.

Above all, Alex was a man of the world. He could be witty in six languages, and had directed films in them all. He loved rare books and antiques, and owned paintings by Renoir, Monet, Guardi, Canaletto and Belloto.

SIR WINSTON'S WORK

Distinguished Friends

His charm won him many distinguished friends: at one time or another dozens of them worked for him. For him, Sir Winston Churchill wrote a life of King George V (not produced). H.G. Wells put boyish enthusiasm into "Things to Come".

His players included Vivien Leigh, Merle Oberon, Robert Donat, Sir Laurence Olivier, Sir Ralph Richardson, Charles Laughton and Douglas Fairbanks, Sir Carol Reed, René Clair, Julien Duvivier, David Lean, Anatole Litvak. Powell and Pressburger and Launder and Gilliat were among his directors.

To write the music for :Things to Come" and "Richard III", he engaged Sir Arthur Bliss and Sir William Walton.

FAMILY HEAD AT 14

Became Schoolteacher

Korda was born in Hungary on Sept. 16, 1893, and on his father's death became the man of the family at 14. He taught in schools to keep his mother and two brothers, and managed to attend the Royal University in Budapest.

He became a journalist at 19 and, while still in his early 20s, resolved to make a film. He hired a shed on the outskirts of Budapest, wrote and directed the story, operated the camera and cut the film himself.

But he had setbacks. From Berlin, where he directed his first wife, Maria Korda, in "A Modern Dubarry" he went to Hollywood. Of several films he made there only "The Private Life of Helen of Troy" had much success. With 20 dollars in his pocket, he left America for Europe.

He was in Berlin, down to his last dollar, when Paramount invited him to direct European versions of Hollywood films. This brought him to Elstree. There he made "Service for Ladies", and gave to the British screen an atmosphere and wit that were quite new to it.

FAME OVERNIGHT

"Henry VIII" Acclaim

In the same year, 1932, London Film Productions was established. Two years later came "The Private Life of Henry VIII", and Korda was famous overnight. He built the great Denham studios (completed in 1936), and in 1935 bought an owner-producer share in United Artists with Chaplin, Mary Pickford and Samuel Goldwyn.

His productions during the next few years included two Wellsian fantasies, "Things To Come" and "The Man Who Could Work Miracles", that brilliant satire "The Ghost Goes West", "Rembrandt," The Scarlet Pimpernel", "The Four Feathers" and "The Thief of Baghdad".

But he had overspent and with the crisis of the early war years he lost control of Denham. In 1941-42 he was in Hollywood: "Lady Hamilton" was made there. But he never forgot he was now a British subject and faithfully remitted the film's large dollar earnings when many another would have

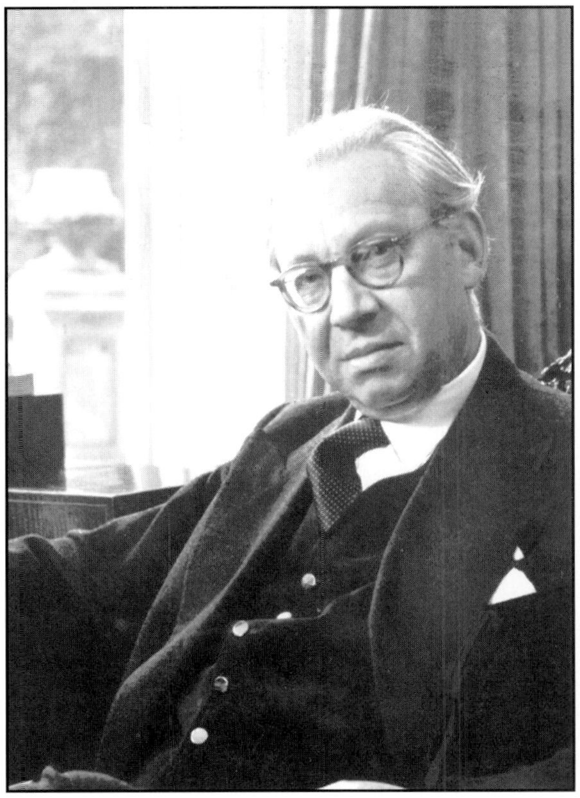

SIR ALEXANDER KORDA

invested them safely in the United States.

OLD FILMS' FORTUNE

Bought Back Rights

Korda, who had made a fortune by buying back from the Prudential Assurance Company the re-issue rights of his pre-war successes, took as offices four houses in Piccadilly (including the bombed No. 145, the residence of the then Duke and Duchess of York).

He started London Films on a new lease of life that was to give us among others, "An Ideal Husband", "Anna Karenina", and "Mine Own Executioner."

"Anna Karenina" and "Bonnie Prince Charlie", proved costly failures, however, and Korda put back into the business most of his private fortune - at one time estimated by him at £2 million.

British Lion, the company that distributed his films, went into liquidation in 1954. Korda's own company, London Films, remained active.

He was associated last year with the production of seven films, including "The Constant Husband", "Summer Madness", "The Deep Blue Sea", and (to end on a high note, as he would have wished), "Richard III. Korda, whose marriages to Maria Farkas and Merle Oberon were dissolved, married Miss Alexandra Boycun, a Canadian, in 1953, when she was 24. He leaves a son, Peter, by his first wife.

(January 24)

MR. WALTER DE LA MARE

THE 'LAUREATE OF DREAMLAND'

The poems of Mr. Walter de la Mare, who has died aged 83, were distinguished by a fanciful imagery and a delicacy of expression that early ensured him a high place in English literature.

At a time when many poets had abandoned both rhyme and rhythm, he clung, with overwhelming success, to a formalised traditional style.

One described as the "laureate of dreamland", he dealt chiefly in the eerie and the remote, but some of his loveliest work was written for, or about, children. He also wrote short stories, and a novel "The Return".

Huguenot on his father's side and Scottish on his mother's, he was born in Charlton, Kent, in 1873, and educated at St. Paul's Cathedral Choir School. At the age of 16 he was employed in the City office of an American oil company, where he remained for 18 years.

WORKS ON OFFICE PAPER

Favoured by a lenient employer who recognised the signs of genius, he is said to have devoted more of his time to his poetry than to business. Some of his earliest work was written on office notepaper.

His first book, which appeared when he was 30, was "Songs of Childhood". It was read and "found" by Andrew Lang. "Henry Brocken", a tale of the uncanny, followed.

In later years followed "Early One Morning", an anthology of childhood, "The Fleeting", "Poems for Children", and "On the Edge", a book of short stories. Other works were "Peacock Pie", "Bells and Grass", and "The Wind Blows Over".

COMPANION OF HONOUR

He was made a Companion of Honour in 1948, and a member of the Order of Merit in 1953. His "O Lovely England" won him the £250 William Foyle Prize for the best book of poetry published that year.

In 1955 he was elected honorary member of the American Academy of Arts and Letters. Two months ago the National Book League arranged an exhibition to commemorate his birthday.

For some time Mr. de la Mare had been confined to his 18th-century home in Twickenham. His wife, formerly Miss Constance Ingpen, died in 1943. They had two sons and two daughters. The elder son, Mr. Richard de la Mare, has published his father's poems for the past 30 years.

(June 23)

BATSMAN OF THE AUGUSTAN AGE

By Harry S. Altham
Treasurer, M.C.C.

Had Charles Fry, who has died aged 84, been born half a century later, he must surely have been for some years a focus for all the resources of modern sporting publicity. As a boy at Repton, he had, before he was 17, played for the Casuals in the F.A. Cup, had captained both cricket and football teams and had twice won the personal athletic trophy.

At Oxford he had set up a world record for the long jump; made a century in the University match, played four years against Cambridge in Association football and had been prevented only by injury from gaining still a fourth Blue as wing three-quarter in a very strong Oxford XV.

A few years later, in 1902, he played for Southampton against Sheffield United in the final of the F.A. Cup on a Saturday in April and on the following Monday made 82 runs at the Oval for London County against Surrey.

PARTNERED GRACE

Captained England

Most of these runs were made in partnership with W.G., with whom three years earlier he had opened the innings for England against Australia in what was his own first Test match and "the Old Man's" last. In 1912 he captained England to victory in the only Triangular Tournament ever played against Australia and South Africa.

These years have been called the Augustan age of English batting; certainly as a spectacle the game can never have been more worth watching; nor have there ever been, before or since, so many batsmen who could without serious criticism have been chosen to play for their country, or who, if they played and made runs, would have been more certain to give pleasure to those who watched them.

Among these Charles Fry was one

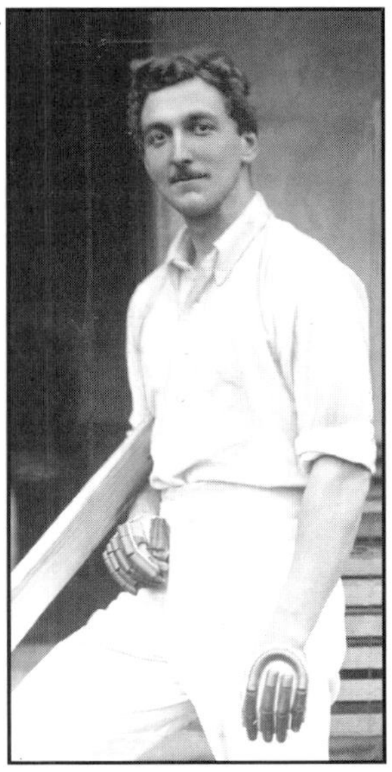

C.B.FRY

of the elect. He could not rank with his great friend "Ranji" for wizardry, with Jessop for sensation, or with MacLaren, Jackson, Spooner or Johnnie Tyldesley for ease and brilliance of stroke. But in the making of runs - after all the primary function of batting - and in making, on all wickets, the bowlers opposed to him look, to use a phrase of his own coining, "plainly playable," he could hold his own with any rival.

In all first-class matches he made over 30,000 runs with an average of over 50 and it must be remembered that he did not play so long or so regularly as many others. His greatest season was 1901, in which he scored 3,147 runs and made 13 hundreds, six of them in succession.

But Fry's athletic distinction, unparalleled in its versatility, reflected only one side of an astonishing endowment. Elected senior scholar at Wadham on a roll that included F.E. Smith, later Lord Birkenhead, he gained a first in Classical Moderations, though later a variety of distractions denied him similar distinction in "Greats".

After a short spell on the staff at Charterhouse he spent some years in Fleet Street, first as athletic editor to that admirable boys' magazine, the Captain, and later as creator, director and editor of C.B. Fry's Magazine.

In 1930 he initiated a new style in cricket reporting, in the form of a running commentary, which made him within a month the most eagerly read and most widely acclaimed of cricket journalists.

GREATEST WORK

Training Ship

But it was neither in his writing nor even in his athletic achievements that he found the chief interest of his own life and made the greatest contribution to the lives of others. In 1908, on the death of Charles Hoare, the banker who founded it, he took over, as an act of faith and in circumstances of great uncertainty and indeed hazard, the control of the training ship Mercury on the Hamble.

There, until his retirement a few years ago, and in perfect partnership with his wife, who died in 1946, he devoted all his great resources of mind and personality to developing its establishment and to the training of generations of boys for service in the Royal and Merchant Navies. He was an honorary captain in the Royal Naval Reserve.

(September 8)

MR. S.E.LINNIT

Mr. Sidney Edmonds Linnit, who began in the theatre as a call-boy and became Edgar Wallace's general manager, has died in London, aged 58. He was agent for a number of well-known actors.

(August 13)

ENGLISH COLTS ROUTED IN THE DERBY

Johnstone's Third Post-War Triumph on Lavandin: 30th Classic Win

From Hotspur

EPSOM, Wednesday.

For the first time since the Derby was founded in 1780 no English-trained horse finished in the first three to-day. The winner was the French-trained favourite Lavandin, the second the French-trained outsider Montaval, and the third the Irish-trained Roistar.

This was the fifth victory of a French colt in the Derby since the race returned to Epsom after the war, and the score is now only six-five in favour of England.

Lavandin belongs to M. Pierre Wertheimer, the Scent King of Europe, an owner for 48 years, and the winner of the 1,000 Guineas with Mesa exactly 21 years ago. Mesa was ridden, as was Lavandin to-day, by the imperturbable Australian, Rae Johnstone.

No other jockey of his generation has a record in big races comparable with Johnstone. It was his third victory in the Derby, and he already has three Oaks to his credit. His successes in the classic races of England, France and Ireland now number 30, a record which fills one with the greatest admiration.

Long Losing Run

Johnstone came to Epsom to-day with the record of having ridden over 50 consecutive losers in France, but that did not worry him in the least. In fact, he sat up chatting with a friend quite late last night and did not lose a wink of sleep in anticipation of riding the favourite.

He rode with supreme confidence, taking the lead from the fading Monterey just over a furlong from home after passing Tenarezae and Roistar, and riding as if he had something up his sleeve. In fact, he did not see Montaval coming with a desperate late run in the middle of the course.

MONTAVAL THRILL

Once Nearly on Knees

At the distance I thought Lavandin was going to win comfortably, but so fast did Montaval finish that he only went under by a neck after being almost on his knees on the approach to Tattenham Corner and swinging very wide as he came round it.

M. Wertheimer had never had a runner in the Derby before to-day in spite of his many years of ownership, but his colours have been known in England since Epinard won the Stewards Cup of 1923, and for a long time he had horses in training with the late Frank Hartigan.

It will be remembered that last year he won the King George VI and Queen Elizabeth Stakes at Ascot with Vimy and the Cheveley Park with Midget II.

(June 7)

WOMAN TRAINS WINNER OF 2,000 GUINEAS

RAN STABLE AFTER HUSBAND'S DEATH

From Hotspur

NEWMARKET, Wednesday.

For the first time in the history of English racing a woman has trained the winner of a Classic race.

Gilles de Retz, 50-1 winner of to-day's 2,000 Guineas, is trained in Steve Donoghue's old yard at Blewbury, Berks, by Mrs. Helen Johnson-Houghton, widow of Major Gordon Johnson-Houghton, who was killed while hunting four years ago.

Gilles de Retz is owned by Mr. Anthony Samuel, younger brother of Viscount Bearsted, who lives near Cobham, Surrey. It was his first big success, though Napoleon Bonaparte carried his colours in the Derby a few years ago.

Under Jockey Club rules no woman is allowed officially to hold a training licence. But Mrs. Johnson-Houghton decided after her husband's death to carry on his stable on a reduced scale.

MAN HOLDS LICENCE

The training licence is held by Mr. Charles Jerdein, who served his apprenticeship under Frank Cundell, a member of the well-known training family. Mr. Jerdein held a licence under National Hunt rules but had to give up after breaking his leg badly in riding "work".

Mrs. Houghton is the twin sister of Fulke Walwyn, who won the Grand National of 1936 on Reynoldstown, but had to give up race riding after fracturing his skull. Since his retirement from the Army he has been one of the leading National Hunt-trainers. He and his sister are 45.

Major Gordon Johnson-Houghton, but for his death, would certainly have been one of the biggest trainers in Britain by now. He made a speciality of buying horses in France, and Ma Soeur Anne, dam of to-day's winner, Gilles de Retz, was one of the horses he bought for Mr. Samuel in France.

A BIG PART

From his early days as a trainer in Cheshire before the war, Mrs. Johnson-Houghton, however, always took a big part in running the stable. She got it going again for her husband at Blewbury just before he was demobilised from the Cheshire Yeomanry at the end of the war.

Gilles de Retz was bred by Mr. Samuel at his Eveton Stud at Wroughton, Wilts. It is entered in the Derby, but before he runs in the Epsom Classic he will run in the Lingfield Derby Trial beforehand.

Bookmakers in London yesterday reported that they had "a very good race." William Hill said that it would have been a clean sweep if Gilles de Retz had not been heavily backed by "inspired money" before the Greenham Stakes at Newbury on April 13.

Those early backers secured odds of 33 to one. When the horse, carrying 9st 4lb. finished unplaced behind Ratification, carrying the same weight, he drifted in the betting.

(May 3)

<u>*Henley Royal Regatta*</u>

GRAND CUP TO GO ABROAD AGAIN

From B.C. Johnstone

HENLEY, Friday

Rarely can victory have been snatched more dramatically from the very jaws of defeat than it was by the French Army crew in the Grand Challenge Cup at the Royal Regatta here to-day.

On the second stroke of their race against Jesus College, Cambridge, the French stroke came off his shoe. By the time he had regained his position Jesus were three lengths to the good.

For a minute or two it seemed that Jesus conquerors of Leander yesterday must bring off another surprise. But the powerful French crew, rowing spendidly set about their apparently hopeless task with great determination and by Fawley had drawn level.

Slowly but surely the Frenchmen gained control and ran out worthy winners by 1½ lengths.

(July 7)

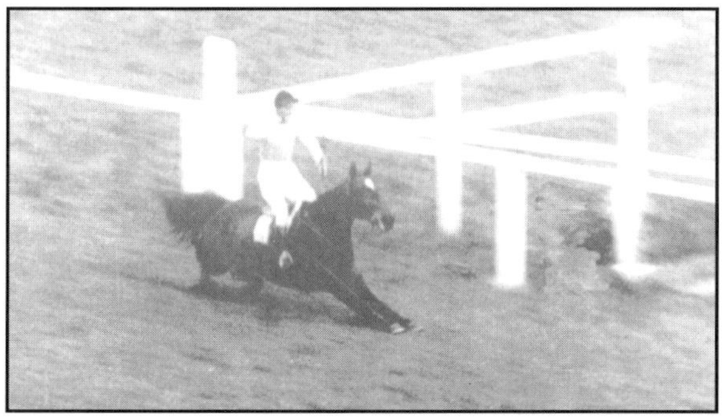

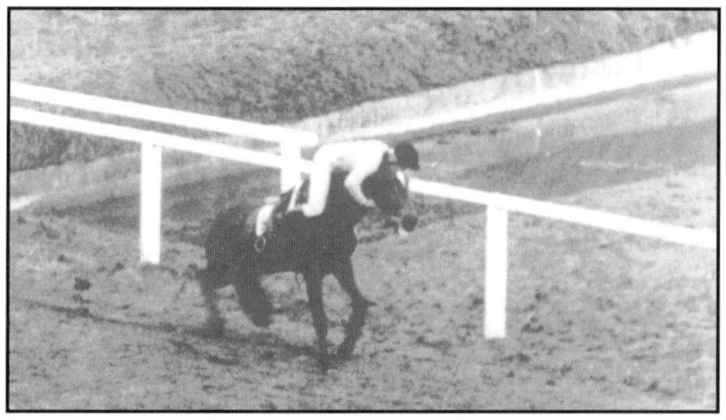

UNLUCKIEST NATIONAL LOSER OF ALL TIME

Royal 'Chaser, Out Clear, Stops 55 Yards from Winning Post

By Hotspur

WITH 55 yards to go and the Grand National at his mercy, Queen Elizabeth the Queen Mother's Devon Loch, clear of all opponents, stumbled, skidded, tried to keep his legs and stopped at Aintree on Saturday. It was, I think, the saddest and most dramatic event I have ever seen on a racecourse.

So E.S.B., ridden by D.V. Dick, strode on past him to win by 10 lengths from the mare Gentle Moya with the 1954 National winner, Royal Tan, a further 10 lengths away third.

It is unlikely that anyone will ever really know exactly what happened to Devon Loch. It was all over in a matter of seconds and occurred on the run-in from the last fence to the winning post, exactly opposite the water jump.

Some held that Devon Loch might have run into a patch of false-going. I do not think so. My impression was that the horse was in pain.

One of the racecourse vets who examined Devon Loch immediately after the race thought he might have had a sudden attack of cramp. Another felt his behaviour might have been due to a small blood clot in a hind leg.

The latter is known to cause paralysing pain and would explain the fact that Devon Loch appeared for a few moments to have no strength in his hind legs. Indeed, one's immediate reaction was that he had broken down.

PAST INCIDENTS

Unlucky Davy Jones

Though the result cannot show it this was in all but name Devon Loch's National and one cannot but feel extreme sympathy for his owner, his rider Dick Francis, and his trainer Peter Cazalet.

I can think of only two other National incidents of a comparable nature. One was in 1936 when Cazalet's great friend, the late Lord Mildmay, appeared to have the race won on Davy Jones two fences from home when the reins broke and the horse ran out; the other when Reavey took the wrong course from the last fence on Zalzia in 1948.

I shall long remember the picture of the Queen Mother, as E.S.B. was being led triumphantly in, going quietly towards the racecourse stables with a smile on her face, to see if her horse was all right.

A few minutes later, after the vets had examined Devon Loch, the Queen and the Queen Mother were congratulating Mr. and Mrs. Leonard Carver, owners of E.S.B., his rider Dick, and his trainer, Fred Rimell, on their victory. It was just as if nothing untoward had happened.

Though Devon Loch's fantastically bad luck blighted the race E.S.B.'s victory was that of a game, thoroughly exposed horse, now the winner of 17 chases out of the 56 races he has run.

(March 26)

MARCIANO HAS QUIT RING

WANTS MORE TIME WITH FAMILY

From Our Own Correspondent

NEW YORK, Friday

Rocky Marciano, world heavyweight champion, who has won all of his 49 professional fights - 43 by knockouts - announced his retirement here to-day.

The news was not altogether unexpected. Reports of his impending retirement have persisted since Marciano was in Rio de Janeiro on holiday recently.

"Before we went to Brazil I had spent only 150 days in the last four years with my wife," he told reporters.

"Those few days in my new home in Massachusetts in such a long time isn't right."

Marciano, who was the usual relaxed and amiable man he is when out of the ring, added: "Mary Ann (his only child), makes all the difference."

Reporters noted that Marciano was much heavier than when in trim. He agreed that he now weighed 15st 7lb - 2st higher than his fighting weight.

News of his retirement was actually given to the world by his wife. She telephoned the sports editor of a local paper in their home town of Brockton, Massachusetts, to say her husband had acceded to her "pleading and begging" with him to retire.

(April 28)

RETIREMENT WILL LEAVE GAP

By Lainson Wood

As the state of heavyweight boxing stands at the moment, Rocky Marciano might have continued to hold the championship for two or three years more.

At the same time his boxing abilities have never been really highly rated and in the next chapters of the heavyweight story he will add to the controversy as to who, of all the champions, was really the best.

(April 28)

REVIE MASTER MIND IN EPIC SCORING

Brazilians See Goals Recalling Hungary's Brilliance

By Frank Coles

Manchester City .... 3 **Birmingham City** 1

At last the F.A. Cup has been won by the brilliance of forward play as distinct from dour defence, and in accomplishing the feat Manchester City caused the greatest surprise since Portsmouth defeated Wolves in 1939.

Their three goals were of a standard unequalled at Wembley in a final tie and were comparable with Scotland's Wembley wizards of 1928 and the Hungarians' magic of 1953.

The result made history, as well as being a repetition of 22 years ago when Manchester city gained the first of their two Wembley wins only 12 months after being beaten there. They lost last year's Final to Newcastle by the same goal margin as on Saturday.

The new Soccer chapter tells an illustrious story of Lancashire supremacy. In lifting the Cup City have emulated United's triumph in the League and completed a unique Manchester double.

YEAR-OLD KNOWLEDGE

Worth a Goal Start

As I said on Saturday recent experience of Wembley's pitfalls is valued at a goal start. Again it was so, with Manchester City this time profiting to the letter from their 12-month-old knowledge. In 1955 Milburn put them behind straight from the kick-off. City now followed suit with a shock goal through Hayes in three minutes.

When Kinsey equalised with an in-off-the-post shot at the quarter-hour the Manchester players must have felt qualms about the ultimate outcome of their carefully-laid plot to strike swiftly.

My reaction was that Birmingham, with their trail of triumphs, would recover balance and break Manchester City's heart through the relentless power and efficiency of Boyd and his colleagues in defence.

At half-time, with the score 1-1 Birmingham were still very much in the game. No sign so far of the startling collapse that was to come; the ripping wide open of a system of defence so compactly built as to be considered well nigh invulnerable.

TWO SHINING LIGHTS

Revie and Johnstone

Why did this team of odds-on favourites falter and then flounder? Why did Trevor Smith, the most promising of our younger school of centre-halves, suddenly lose his told in the middle?

What had happened to Len Boyd's priceless gift of leadership which in the crises of earlier rounds had held his men together in an iron grip? What reduced Hall and Green, two accomplished backs, to Third Division level?

The answers are in two names: Don Revie and Bobby Johnstone.

These two international stars will remain the shining lights of the 1956 Final long after all else is forgotten except the result. Yet, right up to the morning of the match, neither was certain of his place in the side!

Revie was the grand master of ceremonies from the moment he made the superbly accurate crossfield sweep which split Birmingham's defence for the first goal in the third minute.

MASTERFUL FORWARD

Dictated The Pace

I have never seen a forward more masterful in the ebb and flow of battle. Revie dictated the pace. He spaced the match out like a champion boxer in a 15-rounds fight.

And Revie was brilliantly supported by his wing-halves, Barnes and Paul, in varying the tempo from short passing to the use of the telling long ball. It was a repetition of the Hungarian rhapsody.

I rate Manchester's goals, all three of them, on the same high plane as the scientific scoring of Puskas and company, with Revie adequately filling the rhythmic role of Hidegkuti, the first of the playing-from-behind centre-forwards.

Birmingham were bewildered by the variety of the feast the Manchester players set before the fascinated 100,000 crowd in the second-half. Boyd and his fellows were caught flat-footed and helpless in the last half hour of this football glory.

They had no answer to the moves and switches of Revie and Johnstone and let it not be forgotten by those who have disparaged Birmingham's forthright style they took the defeat like men.

Revie, as I have written, held the centre of the stage all through. Johnstone, brought into the attack in the unusual position of outside-right when Spurdie was declared unfit at the 11th hour, took a long time to settle.

He seemed unsure of his bandaged left knee through all but the last five minutes or so of the first half.

In that brief spell one noticed him often edging away from the wing to recover his confidence in the middle of the field. Revie or Hayes would switch outside and this manoeuvre was destined to pay handsome dividends.

DECISIVE BLOWS

2 Goals in 3 Minutes

The Birmingham goal had escaped more than once by a hair's breadth when, in the 66th minute, Manchester took the lead so well earned with a goal by cricketer Dyson, who snatched at his opportunity with a clean drive after perfect chessboard passing.

Unlucky Merrick and poor Birmingham! Before his fellow defenders could ensure him safe protection the goalkeeper was taking the ball out of the net for the second time in three minutes.

This third and decisive Manchester blow crowned Johnstone's day. The long down-the-middle move by which Birmingham were so often battled this time sprang from an accurate throw by Trautmann to Dyson.

When Dyson slipped the ball on to Johnstone a quick-as-lightning goal was a certainty if the little Scot kept his balance and his head. He did both and the shot slashed past Merrick.

Birmingham had shot their bolt and Manchester eased the pressure, but an injury to Trautmann led to the possibility of a dramatic climax.

TRAUTMANN HURT

Leivers a Sheet-anchor

With 15 minutes left Trautmann was knocked out in a collision and staggered about the goal area holding his neck in pain. He was in no state to repel an all-or-nothing Birmingham rally. That alarming situation never arose, however, and the Cup was worthily won.

(May 7)

TRAUTMANN'S NECK IS BROKEN

An X-ray examination yesterday showed that Bert Trautmann, Manchester City's German-born goalkeeper, broke his neck during the Cup Final against Birmingham City at Wembley last Saturday.

Trautmann, who had earlier seen his colleagues off on their tour of Germany, was detained in Manchester Royal Infirmary after being X-rayed. He was stated last night to be resting and comfortable.

(May 10)

Fourth Test Victory

LAKER TAKES 19 WICKETS FOR 90 RUNS

Australia Beaten by Innings and 170: Long McDonald-Craig Stand

From E.W. Swanton

OLD TRAFFORD, Tuesday.

For many nervous hours since last Friday evening it has seemed that England would be robbed of victory in the Fourth Test match. But Manchester expiated its sins of weather this afternoon, and it was in bright sunshine tempering the wind that the game ended in an innings win, which meant the safe-keeping of the Ashes until M.C.C. next sail in their defence two years from now.

The only proper formal announcement of the result is that J.C. Laker defeated Australia by an innings and 170 runs. Unprecedented things are always happening in cricket because it is so charmingly unpredictable a pastime. But now and then occurs something of which one feels certain there can be no repetition or bettering.

Laker followed his capture of nine first innings wickets with all 10 in the second. What is left in the vocabulary to describe and applaud such a tour de force? It is quite fabulous.

Once at Johannesburg on the mat, S.F. Barnes, still happily with us at a ripe 83, took 17 for 159. That analysis topped the list in Test matches until this evening - when Laker, wheeling relentlessly on, left the statistical gentry without another comparison to make or another record to be knocked down.

Hedley Verity took 15 for 104 after the thunderstorm at Lord's in '34. Wilfrid Rhodes, another old hero still listening to the play, even if he cannot now see it, got a like number at Melbourne half a century ago.

In the recent past, Alec Bedser got out 14 Australians for 90 at Trent Bridge on their last visit. Great figures. Great deeds.

But Laker in 51.2 overs has added a ten for 53 to his ten for 88 against this same Australian side for Surrey. And in this Test he has actually taken 19 for 90.

NON-STOP BOWLING

Always Attacking

Laker's first innings performance was phenomenal enough, but its merit was perhaps clouded by the deficiencies of the Australian batting, as also by the palaver over the condition of the wicket.

There was no room whatever for argument regarding his bowling today. He bowled 36 overs, practically non-stop except for the taking of the new ball, all the time attacking the stumps and compelling the batsman to play, never wilting or falling short in terms either of length or direction.

Nor was he mechanical. Each ball presented the batsman with a separate problem. Laker never let up and neither for an instant could his adversary.

Lock Toils On

It is, of course, scarcely less remarkable that while Laker was building up new heights of fame at one end Lock was toiling just as zealously, albeit fruitlessly, at the other. On a wicket on which one famous cricketer captured 19 wickets, the other, scarcely less successful and dangerous taking one day with another, in 69 overs had one for 106.

Of course if the gods had been kind Lock could have taken more. He was not, in cold fact, at his best.

Still, the comparison between the figures is in one sense unarguable evidence of Laker's great performance. If the wicket had been such a natural graveyard for batsmen it is inconceivable that Lock, even below his peak, even with the other arm tied to his side, would not have taken more than one wicket.

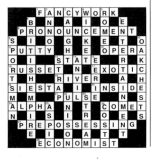

APPLAUD McDONALD

Kept the Balance

Applause for Laker, and applause also in a scarcely lesser strain for McDonald, who, in his long vigil, rose to the occasion for Australia and fought as hard as any man could do to win his side the respite of a draw.

So long as McDonald was in the odds were still fairly balanced. When he was beaten at last directly after tea the latter-end batsmen carried on in the same spirit, and there was a bare hour to go when Maddocks, the number eleven, played back and slightly across to Laker, fell leg-before and advanced up the wicket to shake the hero by the hand.

One of the Australian party summed up the day, as the crowd that massed round the pavilion dispersed, saying: "Well, it was a good scrap after all."

There was relief in his voice, just as there was jubilation in the surrounding English faces.

(August 1)

TEST AVERAGES

***ENGLAND* - Batting**

	Inns	N.O.	R.	H'est	Aver.
Rev. D.S. Sheppard	1	0	113	113	113.00
P.B.G. May	5	0	333	101	66.60
C. Washbrook	2	0	104	98	52.00
P.E. Richardson	6	0	293	104	48.83
M.C. Cowdrey	6	0	236	81	39.33
T.E. Bailey	5	1	117	33*	29.25
T.G. Evans	6	1	115	47	23.00
G.A.R. Lock	3	1	46	25*	23.00
T.W. Graveney	1	0	41	18	10.25
J.C. Laker	5	1	33	12	8.25
W. Watson	4	0	32	18	8.00
A.S. Oakman	2	0	14	10	7.00
D.J. Insole	1	0	5	5	5.00
F.S. Trueman	3	0	9	7	3.00

Also batted: R. Appleyard, 1*: J.B. Statham, 0*, 0*: O.J.H. Wardle, 0, 0: A.E. Moss played in First Test but did not bat. * Not out.

BOWLING

	O.	M.	R.	W.	Aver.
J.C. Laker	233.5	10	354	39	9.07
F.S. Trueman	74	13	184	9	20.44
G.A.R. Lock	194	94	271	12	22.58
R. Appleyard	30	10	49	2	24.50
T.E. Bailey	108.5	38	223	6	37.16
J.B. Statham	83	26	150	3	50.00
J.H. Wardle	27	9	59	1	59.00

Also bowled: T.W. Graveney 6-3-6-0: A.E. Moss 4-3-1-0: A.S. Oakman 8-3-21-0.

***AUSTRALIA* - Batting**

	Inns	N.O.	R	H'est	Aver.
J. Burke	8	1	262	65	37.42
C.C. McDonald	8	0	240	89	30.00
R. Benaud	7	0	168	97	24.00
I. Craig	2	0	46	38	23.00
G.R. Langley	3	2	21	14	21.00
R.N. Harvey	8	0	157	69	19.62
K.R. Miller	8	0	135	41	16.87
P. Burge	6	1	84	35*	16.80
K. Mackay	6	0	73	38	12.16
R.G. Archer	7	0	73	33	10.42
R.R. Lindwall	5	3	14	8	7.00
I. Johnson	7	1	39	17	6.50
I. Maddocks	4	0	6	4	1.50
P. Crawford	2	1	0	0*	0.00

A Davidson played in one match but did not bat.

BOWLING

	O.	M.	R.	W.	Aver.
K.R. Miller	143.1	34	320	16	20.00
A.K. Davidson	10	1	22	1	22.00
R.G. Archer	166.2	57	356	13	27.38
R.R. Lindwall	70.1	21	173	5	34.60
R. Benaud	144	46	299	3	37.37
K. Mackay	24	6	44	1	44.00
L.W. Johnson	106	23	268	6	44.66

Also bowled: J. Burke 4-2-6-0: P. Crawford 5-2-4-0.

(August 1)

(Solution No. 9620)

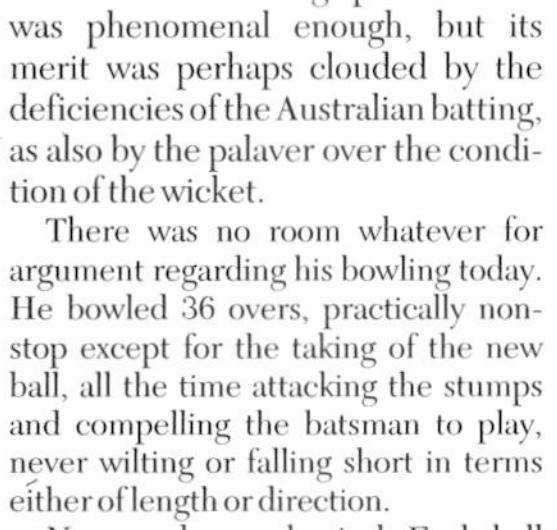

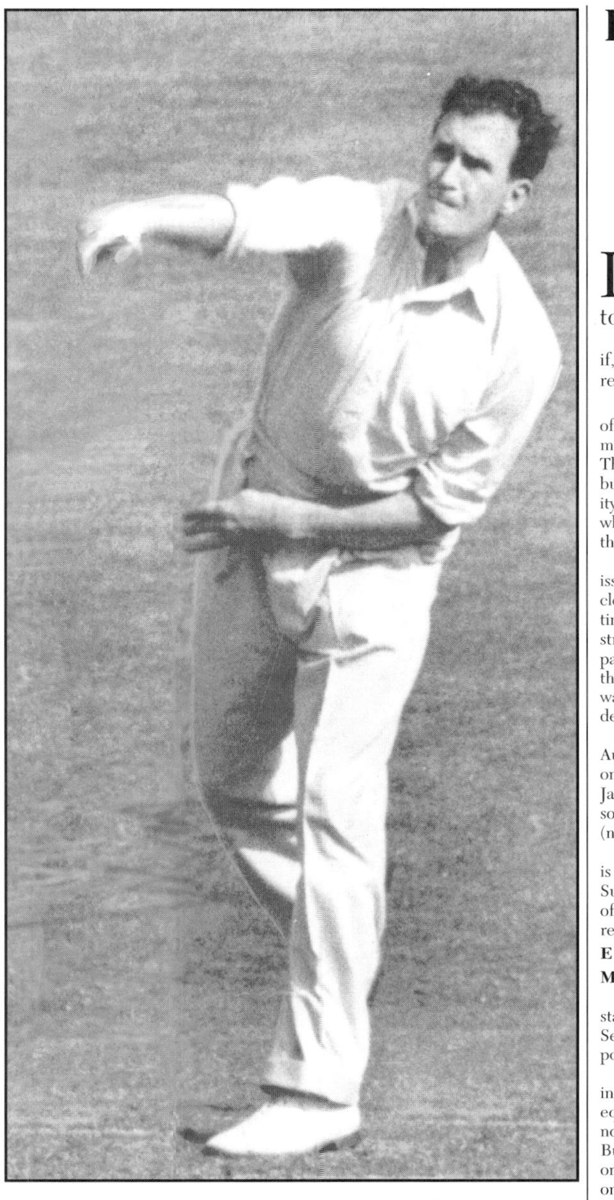

J. C. LAKER, whose nine wickets for 37 made cricket history.

HUTTON'S RETIREMENT IS GRIEVOUS LOSS

By E.W. Swanton

The cricket world had the most unwelcome possible news yesterday when L. Hutton announced his retirement from first-class play. Only the optimists, perhaps, were expecting him to take part, after the recent bulletins about his health in another Test rubber against Australia.

Speculation beforehand, however, scarcely blunts the shock of reality when the worst is known. The loss to English cricket is indeed a great one; more serious, of course, because of the lack of young professional batsmen of a stature comparable to that of Len Hutton and Denis Compton when they burst into the limelight more or less together 20 years ago.

Hutton, in publishing his decision, says he has taken it on medical advice, and mentions particularly the risks to his health attendant on playing six days a week. In this latter remark may be found, I think, the clue to his state of mind.

In an age when pressures on great sportsmen were less onerous he would probably have decided, in similar circumstances and with just on the right side of 40, to have had done with the burden of five-day Test cricket and to confine himself to a certain number of matches for Yorkshire.

That probably is what Hutton would have chosen now if he were not such a closely-prisoned victim of his fame. But in 1956 it would need only a hundred or two from him, coupled with the failure of one of England's opening pair in the first Test, to start up a loud cry for his return.

STRAIN OF CAPTAINCY

Indifferent Batting

The additional strain of the captaincy has already been responsible for his one and only indifferent Test series as a batsman.

Since he brought England to victory over Australia all else was naturally forgotten. But Hutton is predominantly a batsman, certainly one of the three greatest, in many views the very finest, since Hobbs.

To those who knew Hutton well, who were aware how the game monopolised his thoughts, and who realised the nervous effort involved in all he did, both as a player and as a captain, it seemed clear two years ago that he was being taxed beyond his strength.

Whether, if his responsibilities then had been lightened by the appointment to the captaincy in Australia of a younger man, he would now be looking forward to another series against the old enemy, whether in that case, with all the commotion such a decision would have caused, England would have brought home the Ashes, are imponderable questions which, however earnestly they continue to be discussed, can never be answered with any certainty.

QUIET DIGNITY

Always Conscientious

What is without doubt is that Hutton captained England with much tactical shrewdness, with the conscientiousness that has always been the prime key to his actions on the cricket field, and not least, with a quiet dignity that would have befitted any and all his predecessors.

One likes to think that the loss to the larger public will be a gain to many schoolboys and club cricketers who should have the chance for several years yet of appreciating his skill at close quarters, as fellow-players. Indeed I do not rule it out of all consideration that he may be persuaded after all to play a little more first-class cricket, if not this summer then next, when the Australians are safely back home and the cricket temperature is more nearly back to normal.

(January 18)

HOAD THE VICTOR IN RICH LAWN TENNIS FEAST

Triple Champion May Take Four Major Titles in One Year

From Lance Tingay

WIMBLEDON, Friday.

Lew Hoad beat Ken Rosewall 6-2, 4-6, 7-5, 6-4, to win the men's singles championship here to-day and to fulfil three-quarters of a major project.

The champion of Australia and France is now champion of Wimbledon, and if, as seems not unlikely, he goes on to gain American laurels he will equal the record of Donald Budge in taking all four major lawn tennis titles in one year.

Princess Margaret and the Duchess of Kent saw a worthy champion gain the most desired distinction in the game. There have been more exciting finals but none since the war where high quality of play has been so well sustained and where both winner and loser played to their best capacity.

In a rich lawn tennis feast, the basic issue between the two contestants was clear. Both were artists, but Hoad, befitting his burlier physique, piled his strokes with heavier touch, like the painter in oils who wields a knife rather than a brush. By comparison Rosewall was a water colourist, his effects more delicate and less permanent.

Hoad joined a not over-long list of Australian predecessors on the championship roll. Frank Sedgman in 1952, Jack Crawford in 1933, Gerald Patterson in 1922 and 1919, Norman Brookes (now Sir Norman) in 1914 and 1907.

It is tempting to question whether he is as great as they, but I hesitate to say. Such comparisons are made in the light of history rather than in the heat of current success.

ENIGMATIC CHAMPION

Many Minor Falls

Among post-war champions, Hoad stands well. Jack Kramer and Frank Sedgman certainly rank above him and possibly also Tony Trabert.

Hoad is an enigmatic champion, inconsistent, except in vital issues. If he equals Budge's famous record he will not do so with the same distinction, for Budge was immune from defeat, not only in the big events but also in lesser ones. Hoad has already suffered many a minor fall.

He is a player without half measures, an-all-or-nothing man. This accounts for his rather high proportion of errors which, some would say, marred his play.

Yet the number of mistakes must be balanced against his startling winners. It is significant that the only post-war final that can be compared with to-day's match in quality of performance is that of 1954, the year J. Drobny won.

Rosewall was also the losing finalist that year. His opposition has twice inspired a touch of greatness, a tribute to his own splendid qualities.

More than most finals it was curiously lacking in emotion. Whether the crowd was partisan it is hard to say, though possibly Rosewall, ranking as the underdog, had the more supporters. Yet there was not much on which to make a choice between one Australian or another, both of the same age, born and bred in nearby Sydney suburbs.

NO STRONG FEELING

Placid Contest

The players themselves, Hoad, fair hair short-cropped and with a solid, athletic frame, Rosewall, dark, strong-legged, but less robust above the waist, took the contest without strong feeling.

Just now and again, Hoad, bouncing a ball harder than usual, expressed mild annoyance at a stroke ill-executed, while Rosewall occasionally indicated fleeting despair when his shot went awry, but generally they took the ups and downs placidly.

The final lasted one hour and three-quarters. There was probably more wind than Rosewall liked, but apart from that conditions were ideal.

(July 7)

MISS FRY'S WIN HERALDS END OF AN ERA

By Lance Tingay

When, on Saturday, Miss Shirley Fry beat Miss Angela Buxton to become women's singles champion at Wimbledon, one had the feeling that here was the end of an era. The stimulation of having, for the first time since 1939, a British finalist did not survive many games of the match.

Miss Fry, who is 29 and a victor at her eighth attempt, belongs, albeit as one of the lesser rather than the greater to the school of magnificent American players who have dominated Wimbledon and the women's game generally both before and after the war.

With Miss Fry's well-merited success this era of unusual excellence has, I think, come to an end. It is possible that in the immediate future one will have to judge the women's game by less high standards: in women's doubles one already needs to do so.

NOT A VINTAGE YEAR

But Still Enthralling

As I wrote a week ago, it was not a vintage year in the Lawn Tennis Championships. Exciting, yes, and there was hardly a day without its remarkable upsets, but only the singles final and one or two other matches - Rosewall against Arthur Larsen, for instance, Wilson against Patty and, perhaps, Luis Ayala against Ulf Schmidt - produced strokes and shots of the highest calibre.

All years will not be great years and even a much less good meeting than this would still enthrall as does no other tournament in the world. And I would stress that Lew Hoad, the male champion who has emerged, as expected, is one who will stand high on any merit list of title-holders.

Miss Fry on Saturday beat Miss Buxton 6-3, 6-1 in 52 minutes to become the women's singles champion. To speak of it, as was done, as the poorest final ever played was rather less than fair.

There must be short memories, for, as recently as 1951 Miss Hart beat Miss Fry 6-1, 6-0, and Miss Fry was then so conscious of the occasion that she fell grievously below her standard.

(July 9)

PLAYERS BAN FLOODLIT & TV FOOTBALL

The Players' Union, which represents professional footballers, decided yesterday to place a ban on its members playing in matches which are televised unless they are paid fees and from taking part in floodlit games. The ban takes effect to-morrow week.

The union's management committee decided on this measure after an eight-hour meeting. Mr. C. Lloyd, secretary, said afterwards that they had considered a suggestion that professional footballers should stage a token strike on Good Friday. This proposal was thought too drastic at this time.

Mr. Lloyd said that the union had taken its step because the Football Association and the Football League had failed to implement the recommendations of a Ministry of Labour investigation committee in 1951, or to reach any satisfactory agreement on television and floodlight fees, provident fund and contract of service.

(March 5)

CAMBRIDGE WIN

Cambridge won the 102nd Boat Race on Saturday by 1 ¼ lengths in 18min 36sec, the fourth fastest time on record. Cambridge has now won 56 races and Oxford 45.

(March 26)

Olympic Games

BRASHER WAITS 3 HOURS FOR GOLD MEDAL

Appeal Against Disqualification Unanimously Upheld

From Michael Melford

MELBOURNE, Thursday.

CHRIS BRASHER will stand on the winners' rostrum to-morrow as the first Briton to win an individual Olympic running event since 1932 and as one of the most remarkable Olympic winners of all time.

Even without his disqualification for alleged interference with Ernst Larsen, of Norway, and the reinstatement which followed three agonising hours later, the story of his advance from third string to the world's best steeplechaser and Olympic record-holder is a classic of character and determination.

While the jury of appeal considered Brasher's protest against a decision which seemed grossly unjust at the time and turned out later to be based on no solid ground at all, one had time to think over his long career.

It reached its peak to-day at a time when those who ran under Brasher's presidency at Cambridge seven years ago have long put aside their running shoes.

FRIEND & PACEMAKER

Rarely a Winner

One thought of the resolute but far from brilliant runner who for years acted as friend and pace-maker to Bannister and Chataway, ran behind Disley and Shirley, scarcely ever won a race himself and had to work desperately hard to earn a place in the British team.

Then one thought of the new, rather incredible hopes which were born of his race at Geelong two weeks ago and of his own confidence these last few days against all previous form.

It seemed the most brutal trick of fate that any man should make this astonishing improvement at the age of 28, run the race of his life and then be disqualified.

One felt the same awful pang of unbelief as when Devon Loch slipped up at Aintree last spring.

However, as dusk fell, the Marquess of Exeter, chairman of the jury, which included another Briton Mr. D.T.P. Pain, an Italian, a Russian and a Czech, came out of the jury room and announced that the appeal had been unanimously upheld.

The jury decided that though Brasher and Larsen had come into contact this had not affected their running.

All was well and one regretted only that anyone should have to suffer such an unkind intrusion at this moment of triumph.

Some bumping in a field of 10 is inevitable and the jostling in this event was nothing compared with that which knocked over a German and passed unpunished in a 1,500 metres heat half an hour later.

MOVING UP

Trouble 350yds Out

The trouble occurred as Brasher made his effort approaching the third hurdle from home with 350 yards to go. Earlier he had lain seventh behind Larsen, who at one time led the field by 15 yards. He did not move up past Disley and Shirley into fourth place until three laps from home.

Ten yards still covered the field when with 600 to go the Russian, Rjichine, took up the running from Larsen, Rozsnyoi and Brasher. At the bell Shirley, after looking as comfortable as anyone, had gone and Disley was beginning to lose contact with the four leaders.

Brasher at this point seemed itching to make his run and was going well enough to stir wild hopes in British minds which have had their fill of disappointments since 1932.

MILD SCRIMMAGING

No Ground Lost

As the four approached the third hurdle out Brasher pulled out to pass Rozsnyoi. Larsen was on his outside and some mild scrimmaging took place from which nobody lost ground.

Brasher has made himself into a highly competent hurdler and as he cleared the obstacle and started up the back straight he was in front. In a few strides he was eight yards up and still gaining.

Over the next hurdle he went over the water, over the last hurdle and then, every British heart racing with him, up the run-in.

At last he was there, 15 yards ahead of Rozsnyoi. As he pulled up the plugging stride became a stagger and he collapsed on the grass.

(November 30)

PIRIE SMASHES WORLD 5,000 METRES RECORD

By Jack Crump

A.A.G. PIRIE, of South London Harriers, achieved the finest performance of his remarkable career when in a special 5,000 metres race at Bergen last night he smashed Hungarian Sandor Iharos's world record by the big margin of 3.8sec.

Pirie covered the distance in 13min 36.8sec and beat into second place the Russian champion and former world recordholder Vladimir Kuts, whose time of 13min 39.6sec was also inside the previous world's best.

Pirie's participation in the race was an almost casual, last-minute affair. He has been spending a holiday with friends in Norway. Before he left England he sought and received official permission to compete in Norway if the opportunity should present itself.

It certainly did. The Russian touring team, who have already competed in Oslo, were running in Bergen last evening and Pirie, who has long cherished the hope of meeting Kuts over 5,000 metres, seized the chance.

The race took place in drizzle on a heavy track for rain throughout the day had made it soft and spongy.

Pirie and Kuts ran together lap after lap, with Kuts always a yard or so ahead. Pirie tried to pass him several times, but Kuts would not allow him to until the last 300 yards.

Then came Pirie's final effort. A magnificent one it was as he made a devastating dash for the tape which Kuts was quite unable to match. Pirie, who won by about 20 yards, thus avenged the defeat he sustained from Kuts in the 10,000 metres race in the Great Britain v Russia match in Moscow last September.

(June 20)

Yachting

BOLERO WINS AT ITCHENOR

From our Yachting Correspondent

ITCHENOR, Sunday.

It is almost a tradition that the Itchenor Gallon race for International 14ft dinghies is sailed in a fresh breeze but to-day's race was an exception. At one stage the fleet of 37 was enveloped in thick mist which drifted in from the sea.

Near the finish, Mike Peacock, who had held on to a commanding lead for half the race in Surprise, was suddenly becalmed not far from the finish, while Stewart Morris, in his new boat Bolero, came running up and went through before Surprise could get going again.

Surprise took the lead on the first long beat down the Itchenor Channel to East Head, but at the Hayling mark she was 10 seconds astern of Conway. Then they disappeared in the mist in the long run up the Emsworth Channel.

On the next spinnaker run it took Bolero some time to shake Tornado off her weather, but when she did get clear she was making little impression on Surprise,.

Surprise was then forsaken by the wind and Bolero closed on her. Tornado, Otter, Gesture, Conway and Red Quill all ran up to them and it was anybody's race as they battled against the strong adverse current, short tacking in the slight and shifting wind. Stewart Morris sailed a fine defensive race to the finish.

(July 9)

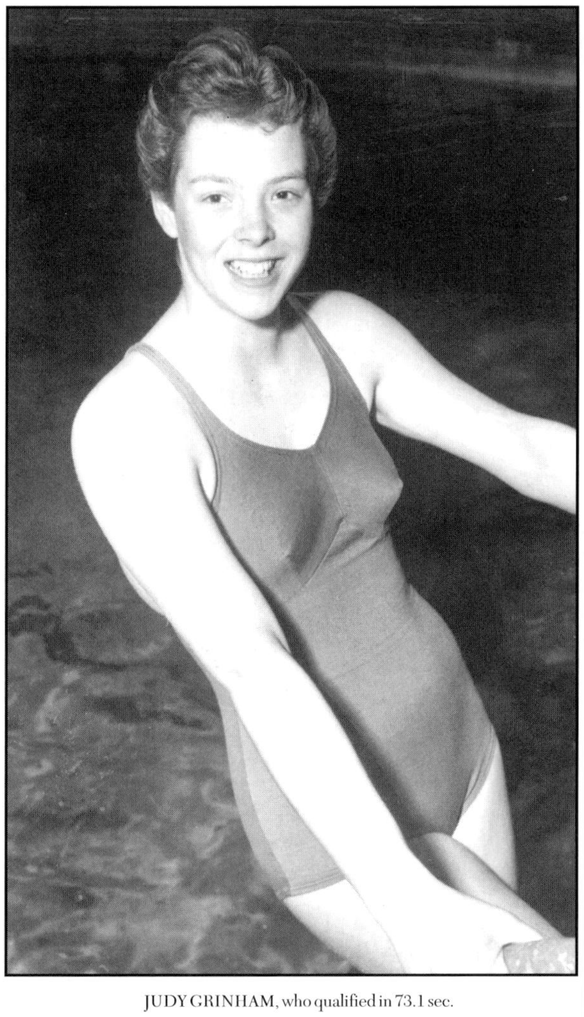

JUDY GRINHAM, who qualified in 73.1 sec.

MISS GRINHAM WINS GOLD MEDAL BY A TOUCH

Miss Edwards 3rd, Miss Hoyle 6th in Backstroke Final

From Ossian Goulding

MELBOURNE, Wednesday.

THE DUKE OF EDINBURGH was among the crowd which watched 17-year-old Judy Grinham, of Neasden, win a gold medal in the women's hundred metres back-stroke event in the new Olympic record time of one minute 12.9 seconds here to-night.

It was Britain's first Olympic swimming victory since Lucy Morton won the 200 metres breaststroke in Paris in 1924. Moreover, it came on a day when we won one silver and two bronze-medals for yachting.

Britain's young team of girl swimmers, none of the three over 17, will never want a closer, more thrilling finish than this.

Miss Grinham was clocked home in the same time as the silver medalist, 16-year-old Caren Cone, of the United States and won by the length of her fingers while Margaret Edwards of Heston, who won a bronze medal for Britain, was only one tenth of a second behind the American girl.

Britain's third contestant, Julie Hoyle, of Watford, taking part in her first international race, returned the fastest time of her life to take sixth place.

The electric time recorders in use at Melbourne's Olympic Pool showed that all eight finalists finished within one and one-tenth seconds of each other.

NERVOUS START

Left Trailing

It was obvious from the very start of the race that Miss Grinham was nervous and unsettled, for she was left trailing a bad last for the first half-length of the 50 metre race. She and Miss Edwards gradually drew up to the leaders but at the 50 metre mark it was Miss Hoyle who turned first.

Miss Grinham always swims a much stronger second length and sure enough she came ahead after the turn with Miss Edwards and Miss Cone neck and neck behind her.

Suddenly, 15 metres from home her usual sustained finishing sprint faltered and it looked as though she was spent. But she came again with a second magnificent burst of speed, hurling herself at the end of the bath to win by a touch.

CLOSE RIVALS

Rose to Occasion

Miss Grinham's only regret was that Miss Edwards had not succeeded in edging the American girl out of a silver medal, for the two British girls have swum together for years in close-fought rivalry, which has persisted even throughout the present games.

Since Miss Grinham won the British championship last September Miss Edwards has beaten her five times. ;But Miss Grinham has a reputation as a fighter who rises to the occasion, particularly at beg international events.

In the first preliminary heat she set a new Olympic record of 1 minute 13.1 seconds, only to see it beaten within half an hour by Miss Edwards with 1 minute 13 seconds.

To-day she settled the argument by reducing that record convincingly.

TRIUMPH OF WORK

Taught at Council Baths

The manager of the British team, Mr. Alfred Price, superintendent of Uxbridge Council Baths, said Britain's triumph was the result of two or three years of hard work - more work than the average swimmer ever dreams of.

All three girls, he said, had been taught swimming at their local council baths - Miss Grinham by Reg Laxton, professional at Hampstead and Seymour Hall Baths, Miss Edwards, who is still at grammar school, by George Fryer at Heston Baths, and Miss Hoyle, who returns to take up a job as a teacher at a physical training establishment, by Bill Juba, at Watford Baths.

"There is no easy road nowadays either to Olympic representation or to an Olympic medal," Mr. Price told me to-night. "It is work, work and more work, long after it has begun to hurt so much that you feel you cannot go on.

"But these girls have done it and are an example to British swimmers."

(December 6)

BRITISH RIDERS ROMP AWAY WITH TOP PRIZE

Weldon Gains Bronze Medal: Germany Second in Team Placings

From A Special Correspondent

STOCKHOLM, Thursday.

BRITAIN, as expected, won the three-day team event of the Equestrian Olympic Games, which finished here to-day. Germany were second, and Canada third.

Lt.-Col. Frank Weldon, on Kilbarry, best-placed Briton in the individual list, gained a bronze medal. He was third behind P. Kastenman, of Sweden, and A. Lütke-Westhues, a German.

Once the three British horses had trotted out sound before the veterinary surgeons this morning a British victory in the team event was a foregone conclusion.

The great issue was whether Weldon and Kilbarry could catch Kastenman and Ilsuster in the jumping phase. It was in the balance until the end.

TRICKY JUMP

The course of 12 jumps was one of the best I have seen. It made great demands on the horses' suppleness and obedience, especially the enclosed combination, Nos. 10 and 11, which necessitated a quick turn round in front of a fence and a jump out on the same side as the entry.

This caused surprisingly little trouble, although only a few, notably the German Otto Rothe with Sissi, accomplished it without a good deal of hard pulling on the bit.

The sixth fence, parallel bars 3ft 9in and 3ft 11in, a spread of 4ft 8in and no ground line, turned out to be a stiff one. It was knocked down by more than half the riders.

A measure of the testing nature of the course - and of the severity of the preceding endurance phase - is the fact that out of 38 starters, there was only one clear round - by K. Wagner and Prinzess of Germany.

Major L. Rook and Wild Venture came in first for England and a rather awkward round brought 10 faults (at No. 6) and 3.75 time faults.

NO CHANGE

When his turn came A.E. Hill took Countryman very carefully and looked like doing a clear round but he too was caught at No. 6 and also had a quarter time fault.

The two German horses, Sissi and Prinzess, had 10 faults between them so the Olympic team gold medal was ours. But all thoughts were on the three leading riders.

First came Kastenman and Muster for Sweden, leading with 46.53 pts. The first four jumps were faultless, then they blundered at the wall (No. 5); they recovered for No. 6 and were clear to the enclosure where the horse lost all impulsion and had the exit fence down.

Next to come were Lütke-Westhues and Trux von Kamax of Germany, second with 64.87.

They, too, failed at No. 5, and then at the water (No. 9) - again 20 faults, and the final score was 84.87.

GLOWING CHANCE

At last came Col. Weldon and Kilbarry with one of the greatest chances of an individual gold medal that he may ever have 0 but what a difficult one! The anxiety of the crowd could be felt as he started his round calmly enough.

Fences 1, 2 and 3 were cleared: there was a slight awkwardness at No. 4 but nothing touched; at 5 they were going beautifully; Kilbarry seemed to be easily over No. 6, but he hit the bar with his hind feet, lazily it fell and with it our hopes.

His faults were 20 and his final score 85.48 and the situation remained unchanged.

This was a great day for Britain.

(June 15)

No. 9620

ACROSS

1 Imaginary job which follows a pattern (5-4)
8 That which may be used for a name to bind together a declaration (13)
11 Whiting in oil, but not sold by a fishmonger (5)
12 A small work takes a long time to become a major one (5)
13 A condition in which prominent people may lie publicly (5)
16 Hardy lass returns after upsetting the old city, with a healthy colour (6)
17 Alien commonly regarded as glamorous (6)
18 It likes to run free but is averse to hill-climbing (5)
19 Seat is conveniently arranged for a nap (6)
20 Within the compass of the team which is batting? (6)
21 Peas, beans, &c but not cabbages although they have hearts (5)
24 A Greek letter (5)
26 The Commanding Officer (Meteorology) might observe it (5)
27 Pressing around a body of policemen giving a favourable impression (13)
28 Too much money, he says, is his major problem nowadays (9)

DOWN

2 Refusing word in any trouble (5)
3 Captured, but not taken on the hop? (6)
4 If it is sticky this one and several more may fall quite quickly (6)
5 The eternal city has nothing for a lover (5)
6 Territory, a stranger to nightfall? (7, 6)
7 "I rent men a tent" (anag.) (for a circus perhaps) (13)
9 He is expected to play the game and does (9)
10 A stock she orders which may be consigned to the attic (3, 6)
13 Back parts may be struck by this (5)
14 It is hard hit when strikers start work (5)
15 Exciting fear which is strange (5)
22 Certainly not harmony, but nevertheless complete agreement (6)
23 Go with it and you will eventually finish up in-deep waters (6)
25 A spice having no end of use in preparing game and poultry (5)
26 Scots are disturbed if these are high, so they say (5)

(October 21)

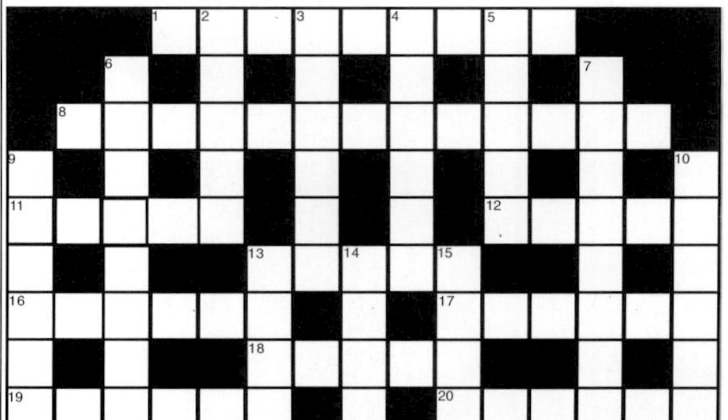

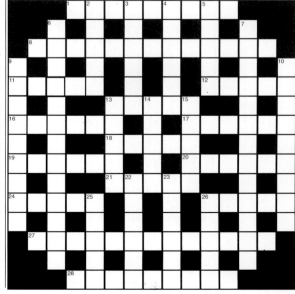

1957

After the traumas of the previous Autumn, a calmer year. Ill, and defeated by events, Anthony Eden resigned to be replaced by the urbane, unflappable figure of Harold Macmillan, ready to preside over an economic recovery and with the time to spend "the Glorious Twelfth" on the grouse moor. The creation of life peers and the admission of women to the House of Lords quietly found its way on to the statute book. The announcement was made that the call-up for National Service would be ended and that the last conscripts would have left the British services by 1962.

Social change was marked by the Queen's ending of the custom of presenting debutantes at court. A skyscraper beside Hyde Park was approved and the first park meters appeared in London streets. Old cars would be subject to a test for road worthiness. Sir John Wolfenden's Committee enquiring into homosexual offences and prostitution produced the report with its startling recommendation that homosexual relationships in private between consenting adults should be legalised. Lord Kilmuir, the Lord Chancellor, who earlier as Home Secretary had shown his unwillingness to countenance reform, announced firmly that the Government would take no immediate action. In a magisterial leader, The Daily Telegraph declared that "to the lay mind it seems clear that the law should provide against the possibility" that, if legalised, "homosexuality in any form .... would spread like an infection."

In Europe, Britain stood on the sidelines as the Treaty of Rome, the basis of the European Economic Community, was signed. The aged and ailing General Franco let it be known that, on his death or retirement from power, his country would revert to being a hereditary monarchy. The rows over the ending of segregation in schools in the United States boiled over into full scale rioting at Little Rock in Arkansas. In Ghana, as the Union Jack was lowered, signifying the end of British colonial rule, Dr. Nkrumah, the Prime Minister, trumpeted that "freedom had been redeemed."

As American rockets misfired, the Russians succeeded in launching the first artifical earth satellite, following his achievement a few weeks later by sending two dogs successfully into space. On the ground, the great Jodrell Bank radio telescope came into operation with future Sir Bernard Lovell prophesying that it would now be possible to reach the furtherest limits of the universe through its operation. While Dr. Albert Schweitzer warned of the danger to the world atmosphere of atomic testing, Britain's first nuclear power station at Sellafield was closed down because of an escape of atomic dust.

The musical world heard for the first time Sir William Walton's cello concerto but mourned the death of Sibelius and of the supreme conductor of his generation, Arturo Toscanini. The cinema lost its most illustrious "tough guy" when, early in the year, Humphrey Bogart died, to be followed a few months later by Oliver Hardy, the larger half of the comedy duo, Laurel and Hardy, who in the seemingly endless supply of short films always aspired to be tough but miserably failed. An 18-year-old Derek Jacobi played his first "Hamlet" at the Edinburgh Festival and the 17-year-old Jimmie Greaves scored a goal in his first football match for Chelsea.

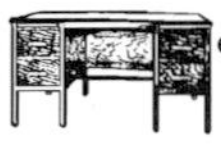

The Daily Telegraph 4 A.M.
and Morning Post
No. 31,927 LONDON, FRIDAY, DECEMBER 6, 1957
Printed in LONDON and MANCHESTER PRICE 2½d.

DEATH ROLL 92 IN RAIL DISASTER

ARMY WORK AVERTS BRIDGE CRASH

SIGNALLING WAS BY COLOUR LIGHTS

TRAIN MAY HAVE PASSED THREE WARNINGS IN FOG

The death roll in Wednesday night's London rush-hour disaster in thick fog, near Lewisham, had risen by last night to 92, a Southern Region spokesman said. The number of seriously injured was given as 110 and of slightly injured as 67.

All day yesterday rescue teams toiled in difficult conditions to free bodies in the wreckage of the coaches under the 500-ton collapsed fly-over bridge. It was feared last night that several dead were still in the wreck. The bridge dropped 8ft during the rescue work and was in danger of falling further, but Royal Engineers supported it with mobile piers and averted the danger.

Two senior Southern Region officials who called a Press conference at Waterloo yesterday, said that fog-signalmen were not provided in the crash area because the colour-light system operated there. Experience had shown that fog-signalmen were not necessary with colour-light signalling.

It was stated that if the signal system was working satisfactorily, the steam train from Cannon Street must have passed three signals giving warning of danger.

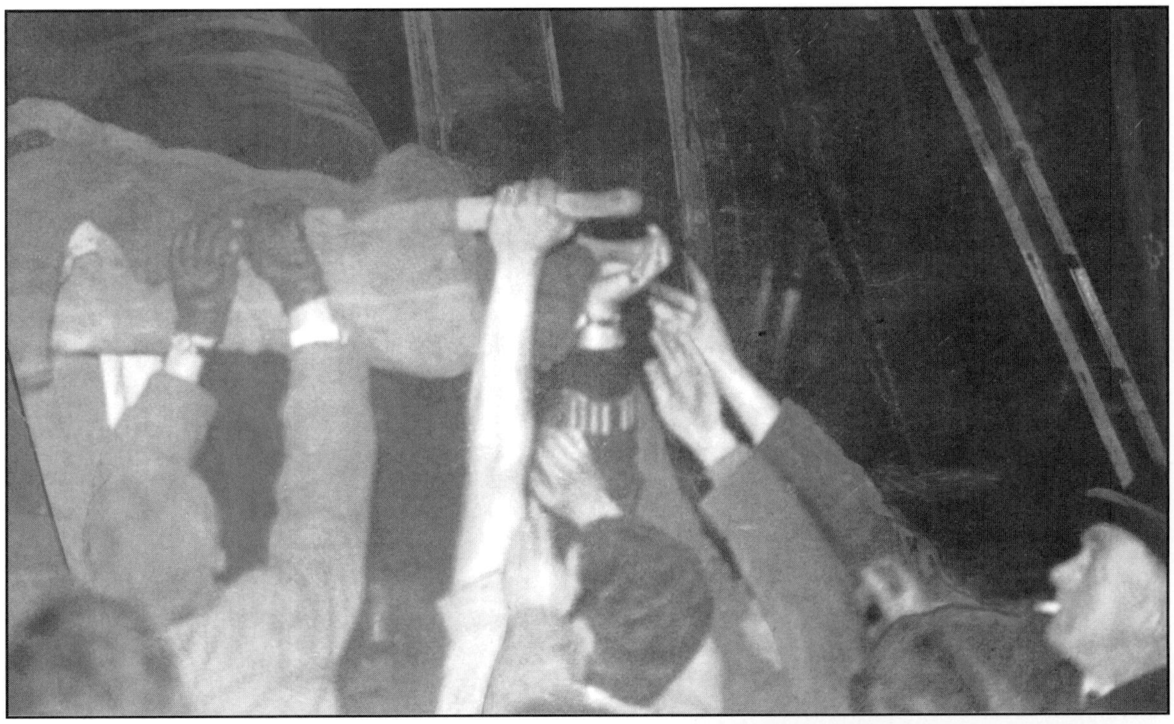

WILLING HANDS reaching up to lift an injured passenger on a stretcher from a wrecked coach after three trains were in collision in dense fog near St. John's Station, Lewisham, last evening. Firemen, police and people living near worked under floodlamps to free trapped victims. RIGHT: Police and other workers surveying in the glare of an arc light the twisted wreckage of coaches and bridge structure.

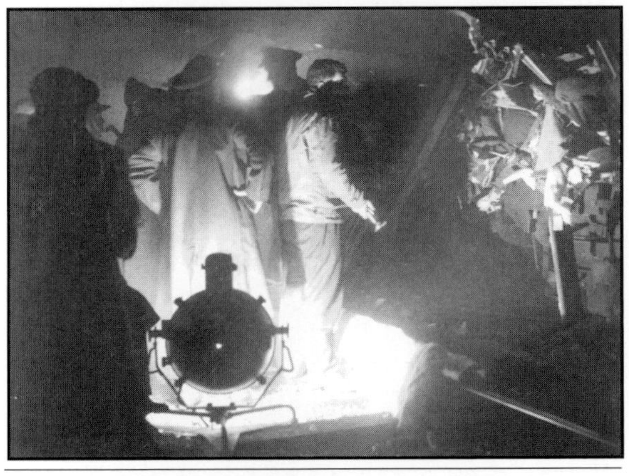

OFFICIAL DENIES 'SLIP-UP'

Daily Telegraph Reporter

Mr. S.A. Fitch, Chief Operating Superintendent, Southern Region, called a conference at Waterloo yesterday "to explain and to reassure the public about the signalling system in use at the scene of the disaster."

One point which, it was stated, emerged was that if the signal system was working satisfactorily on Wednesday night, the steam train from Cannon Street to Ramsgate must have passed three signals giving a warning of the danger ahead.

Fog-signalmen were not provided in the area because the colour-light signal system was in operation. "This is established practice." It was "extraordinarily doubtful" whether the presence of fog-signalmen would have increased the safety factor.

"FOG SERVICE"

Cut in Numbers

Railway experience had always shown that fog-signalmen were not necessary with colour-light signalling. He explained that the "fog service" which sometimes came into operation was merely a reduction in the number of trains running.

There were fog-signalmen out in the eastern section of the Southern Region on Wednesday night, but not in the colour-light areas. The "fog service" was not in operation, but the slowing down of trains by the fog brought about a reduction in the number of trains running within any one period.

Mr. Fitch did not agree that the introduction of "fog service" in this section would have prevented the accident. He denied that someone had "slipped up" in not ordering such a reduced service, adding: "The fog service is a planned, reduced service which needs a certain amount of notice."

He was accompanied by Mr. L. Boucher, Chief Signals Officer, Southern Region. Together they spent 45 minutes in answering dozens of questions from reporters, some of whom had arrived at Waterloo direct from the scene of the disaster.

"None of us had had much sleep or food," said Mr. Fitch. A Southern Region spokesman told me later that Mr. Fitch and Mr. Boucher had cancelled their meal break, long overdue, to call the conference.

1,000 TRAINS DAILY

System in Use 28 Years

The system in use in the area of the crash, said Mr. Fitch, was installed in 1929 and was one of the earliest in use in the region. "Well over 1,000 trains every day go through that area and have done so with perfect safety since 1929."

It was known as "four-aspect signalling" which told a driver or motorman:

1 - If he saw a red light he should stop;

2 - A single yellow light told him that the section was clear, but he must be prepared to find the next signal at red;

3 - Two yellow lights indicated that the next signal ahead was showing one yellow; and

4 - A green light.

"The lengths of the sections vary, but they always allow sufficient distance for trains at reasonable speeds to stop, even in bad fog conditions," said Mr. Fitch. The maximum permitted speed in that area was 45 m.p.h.

RANGE OF SIGHT

Overlap of Sections

Mr. Boucher said that the range at which a signal could be seen was greater than the length of the section. The electric train, the 5.18 p.m. from Charing Cross to Hayes, which left Charing Cross at 5.48 p.m, was stationary at the Parksbridge "home" signal.

The first warning signal the driver of the steam train would have seen was a double-yellow at New Cross. Four hundred and twenty yards further on he would meet a "single yellow" and 445 yards still further, a red signal.

This red signal was about 145 yards on the London side of the steel viaduct which collapsed when the steam train tender and coaches left the track and demolished its supports. The total distance, Mr. Boucher estimated, from the double-yellow to the stationary electric train was 1,237 yards.

Mr. Boucher said that if the signals were working properly the steam train driver would have encountered the St. John's downthrough intermediate signal at one yellow, and the St. John's inner home at red.

WAIT AT SIGNAL

Detonators "Not Needed"

If the steam train had then halted it would have been more than 400 yards from the Parksbridge signal, at which the electric train was waiting. This train was of 10 carriages, an approximate length of 200 yards, making a theoretical distance between the steam engine and the rear of the electric train of more than 200 yards.

Mr. Fitch said the electric train had been waiting at the signal for between eight and nine minutes. He was asked whether it was anyone's duty in those circumstances to put down detonators or otherwise warn following traffic. He replied that with colour-light signalling this was not required.

TRIBUNAL ASKS ABOUT GROUSE SHOOT

BANKER'S PARTY

Daily Telegraph Reporter

Mr. William Johnston Keswick, a member of the Court of the Bank of England, gave evidence yesterday before the Bank Rate Tribunal in London.

He described the circumstances in which he sent a telegram to a Hongkong firm on Sept. 17, advising them to sell gilt-edged securities. The Bank Rate was raised to seven per cent on Sept. 19.

Mr. Keswick said he sent the telegram in his capacity as a director of Matheson and Co. Matheson and Co. were London correspondents of Jardine, Matheson and Co., of Hongkong, who were general managers of a number of public and private companies in the Far East.

DIRECTOR'S "DREAD"

Future of Sterling

Mr. Keswick said that Mr. Hugh Barton, managing director of Jardine, Matheson, had a dread about the future of sterling and always wanted to get out of gilts. In August, he gave instructions on behalf of one of the companies in the group, to sell gilts to realise £100,000, and this was done.

A letter written by Mr. Barton on Sept. 3 was seen by Mr. Keswick on his return from a holiday in Scotland on Sept. 16. In this, Mr. Barton said he felt he ought to transfer some of his group's sterling assets to North America, and the telegram was sent in reply.

Mr. Keswick will continue his evidence to-day.

His brother, Mr. John Henry Keswick, who is not a member of the Court of the Bank of England, gave evidence earlier. He was asked by the Attorney-General, Sir Reginald Manningham-Buller, why he had not returned from Scotland before Sept 16, although he was expected earlier.

He replied: "I was playing truant. The office knew I was coming back. I had booked a series of sleepers, one night after the other."

He supported the telegram because he felt it was a correct telegram. He could not suggest what useful purpose was served by holding up its dispatch until he returned to London. He had not heard the possibility of a rise in the Bank Rate discussed at all.

SHOOTING PARTY

Minister a guest

Sir Reginald read a letter sent from Scotland by Mr. W.J. Keswick to Mr. J.H. Keswick. This named those in Mr. W.J. Keswick's shooting party. They included Mr. Nigel Birch. Economic Secretary to the Treasury.

TROOP COSTS IN GERMANY UNSOLVED

Little Headway At London Talk

By MICHAEL HILTON
Daily Telegraph Diplomatic Correspondent

Herr von Brentano, the West German Foreign Minister, left London last night after two-day talks with the Government. He said at a Press conference that Anglo-German relations were now "excellent." They had not been so good "for centuries."

A joint communiqué issued on the discussions contained no new information.

It is recorded that subjects covered had included the forthcoming N.A.T.O. meeting in Paris on Monday week, the European Free Trade Area, and "questions connected with the continued presence of the British forces in Germany."

On this last question, which involves payment for the cost of the British forces, it was admitted by spokesmen for both sides that there had been "no solution." The matter was now with the North Atlantic Treaty Organisation.

"NOT A WORD" ON ROCKETS

Herr von Brentano said the question of the stationing of rockets on German soil had not been discussed. In answer to a question, he said there had "not been a word" on this subject.

This must appear strange to many observers. The matter of whether American intermediate ballistic missiles are to be based in West Germany in future is one of the principal questions facing N.A.T.O.

The impression was strong in London last night that the Brentano visit has done little or nothing to bring new light to bear on the many problems now facing Western Europe and the United States in their relations with the Soviet bloc.

MR. JOHANNES VILJOEN

Mr. Johannes Viljoen, South African Minister of Education, Arts and Science, died yesterday in Pretoria, Reuter reported. He was 64.

MR. OLIVER HALL

Mr. Oliver Hall, R.A. the English landscape painter, died yesterday at his home near Ulverston, Lancs. He was 88.

'10,000 THINGS' COULD FAIL IN U.S. SATELLITE

LAUNCHING DELAY EXPLAINED

From Our Special Correspondent

CAPE CANAVERAL, Florida, Thursday.

Mr. George S. Trimble, the man in charge of manufacturing the United States Vanguard satellite rocket, said here to-day that the odds were the satellite would not be got into an orbit. Mr. Trimble is vice-president in charge of engineering at the Martin Company, leading contractor for the Vanguard.

He said the postponement in the firing yesterday "may run into days or weeks." Though separate parts of the three-stage Vanguard rocket had been flown before, the missile had never been flown in its complete form, he pointed out.

Speaking of the postponements, he said: "It is normal. There are 10,000 things that could go wrong." The whole Vanguard project, including test rockets and six launching vehicles, is costing, he said, about £28,500,000.

SERIES OF SETBACKS

The first United States attempt to launch a satellite was last night postponed after a cruelly disappointing procession of setbacks suffered during some 18 hours of firing preparations.

In spite of what Mr. Trimble said an announcement this afternoon stated that the satellite's carrier rocket was being prepared for a firing "during the daylight hours of Friday."

Cause of the postponement was not a major difficulty but a series of minor technical troubles, Mr. Walsh, deputy director of the project, said last night. The principal hitch was in a fuel valve.

Yesterday's discouraging result was a public demonstration of the fact that United States development of accurately guided long-range missiles is still below the level where a successful firing can be confidently predicted.

LIFE PEERS WILL NOT GET EXTRA PAY

BILL UNOPPOSED

By Our Political Correspondent

The Bill for the creation of life peers of both sexes was given an unopposed if unenthusiastic Second Reading in the House of Lords last night.

This was in spite of the deep disappointment voiced on both sides of the Chamber on hearing from Viscount Hailsham, Lord President of the Council, that the new class of peers would not be specially paid.

The Bill will not complete all its stages in the Lords before the end of January. It will then come to the Commons for Second Reading.

In the meantime it is expected that a Select Committee of the Lords will be framing new standing orders enabling hereditary peers to "opt out" of attending the House. A motion to this effect is to be moved on Tuesday by the Earl of Swinton.

The ultimate result may be a "working house" of 200 or 250 hereditary peers. The Government intends to bring this number up to about 300 by the creation from time to time of life peers of both sexes. It is possible that the first group will be named in the Birthday Honours next summer.

The Daily Telegraph

4 A.M.
No.31,874 LONDON, SATURDAY, OCTOBER 5, 1957 and Morning Post Printed in LONDON and MANCHESTER Price 2d.

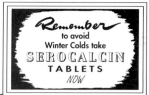

RUSSIA LAUNCHES EARTH SATELLITE

MIDNIGHT REPORT OF ROCKET TAKE-OFF

ROUND THE WORLD IN 105 MINUTES

SENDING RADIO SIGNALS AMATEURS CAN PICK UP

By Anthony Smith,
Daily Telegraph Science Correspondent

Russia has successfully launched the first artificial earth satellite. This news was announced just before midnight in a special statement by the Soviet News Agency, Tass. It said:

As the result of intensive work by the research institute and designing bureaux, the first earth satellite in the world has now been created. It was launched in Soviet Russia on Oct. 4.

This satellite is now revolving round the earth along an eliptic trajectory at a height of about 560 miles. It is travelling at a speed of more than 18,000 m.p.h. and takes 1 hour 45 minutes to make each revolution round the earth.

Two radio transmitters in the satellite are giving out continuous signals. They are operating at frequencies of 20,005 and 40,002 megacycles, or 16 and 17.5 metres respectively.

It is claimed that the transmission power is sufficient for the signals to be picked up by a large number of amateurs. The signals are in the nature of telegraph signals and last for about 0.3 sec.

They are followed by a pause of the same duration. The signals on one frequency are transmitted during the pause on the other frequency.

Reports will very quickly start coming in on the satellite's path. In spite of its speed and height it should be visible just before sunrise or just after sunset in those regions of the earth over which it will be passing.

Almost certainly it will not be visible with the naked eye. But a pair of binoculars or a small telescope should be enough.

185lb WEIGHT
Spherical Shape

The satellite, the first thing ever to be thrown up beyond the earth's atmosphere which will not immediately come down, is spherical. Its weight was given in the statement as 83.6 kilograms, or about 185lb.

This is much heavier than the first satellites which the Americans have planned to send up before the International Geophysical Year is finished.

Until reports come in from observers of the Soviet satellite's movements it will not be known how far out into space it will be travelling when furthest away from earth. The shape of the ellipse on which it travels depends on the angle and the speed at which it is travelling when the power is finally cut off.

The satellite is now travelling under its own momentum. It has been given an orbital velocity by the rockets which carried it up into space.

At such a speed, at least five miles a second, the centrifugal force flinging the rocket out into space is balanced by the gravitational force of the earth bringing it back again. The satellite is in fact a moon.

ARTIFICIAL MOON
Conditions the Same

The moons around some of the planets and the moon revolving round the earth are being influenced by exactly the same sort of conditions. But the Russian satellite is the first moon ever known to have been positioned artificially.

Although it will probably stay in its orbit and at roughly the same height for many days, it will not stay up there for ever. Space, even 560 miles away from the earth's surface, is not empty.

There are molecules up there, even though their density bears little relation to the density of molecules in the atmosphere we live in. But they will be sufficient to cause friction to the satellite, and it will inevitably slow down.

The gravitational pull will then exceed the centrifugal force and the satellite will be slowly dragged back to earth. As soon as it reaches the denser layers of the atmosphere it will break up, melt and be burnt up.

SIMILAR IN SIZE AND WEIGHT TO U.S. 'MOON'

From A Special Correspondent
WASHINGTON, Friday.

Statements by the Soviet delegate at the conference on rockets and satellites here this week convinced Western delegates that Russia was hurrying to complete a simply-designed satellite before the United States could do so.

Western specialists had the impression that Russia's satellite would be roughly the same size and weight as the American one. Its speed and expected shape of orbit were to be roughly the same The surface of the sphere would be mirror-like for maximum gleam in sunlight like the American.

It was believed that it would almost certainly be fired from a military installation, probably an inter-continental ballistic missile launching site. The launching vehicle was thought likely to be one of the Soviet missile rockets.

For this reason the entire programme was thought to be under close military control. This, in turn, might account for the secrecy surrounding the entire Soviet operation.

20-IN. DIAMETER

Directors of the American satellite programme said to-day that they would issue an alert before test firings this autumn which might hurl a miniature satellite into orbit. The first attempt to launch a full-fledged satellite is due early next spring. Its 20-in diameter would make it barely visible through binoculars.

The Russians have hinted that their satellite would not have the elaborate instrumentation comparable to that planned for the first American one. The American will contain devices to record virgin ultra violet light from the sun before the sun's filtration by the atmosphere.

U.S. CONGRATULATIONS
'It is Fantastic'

Dr. Lloyd Berkner, an American official of the International Geophysical Year, congratulated the Russians at a Soviet Embassy cocktail party in Washington yesterday held for those attending a special conference of the Geophysical Year. He said that American teams were being called into action to look for the Russian "moon".

Dr. Joseph Kaplan, chairman of the United States National Committee for the International Geophysical Year, said: "I hope they give us enough information so that our moon-watch teams can learn the scientific benefits."

Noting reports that the satellite was 23in across and weighed about 185lb. Dr. Kaplan said: "This is really fantastic. If they can launch that they can launch much heavier ones."

Pentagon officials were slow in reacting, saying that they wanted to check details of the Soviet report.

COURT ORDERS SECRET TRIAL FOR MR. DJILAS

ACCUSED PROTESTS: JUDGMENT TO-DAY

From Our Special Correspondent
SREMSKA MITROVICA, Jugoslavia, Friday.

Mr. Milovan Djilas, 46, the former Jugoslav communist leader, was tried in secret by the district court here to-day for "spreading hostile propaganda." He is accused of publishing abroad the book "The New Class" [extracts of which appeared in The Daily Telegraph in August].

The prosecutor, Mr. Ante Djukic, described the book to-day as being "vulgar, anti-Socialist and anti-Jugoslav propaganda."

This evening the trial ended after the final defence speeches and a word from Djilas himself. Judgment will be pronounced to-morrow at midday.

After the reading of the indictment the prosecutor proposed that the public and Press should be excluded from the hearing. Despite protests by the accused and his lawyer the court ruled that the trial should continue in secret.

Until this ruling there were not many more than 100 people in the court. Half of these were Jugoslav and foreign journalists.

The correspondent of the New York Times and the correspondent of the Corriere della Sera, as well as a correspondent of the United Press, did not receive permission to attend the trial. The court had stated that their attitude "was incorrect" when reporting on the Djilas case.

BROUGHT FROM PRISON
President Corrected

Exactly at 7 a.m. G.M.T. Mr. Djilas was led into the court-room. He had been brought from the prison here, where he is already serving a three-year sentence given last year for "hostile propaganda."

The president of the court, Mr. Nikalo Nickolin, then read the generalities about Mr. Djilas. When the president mentioned his national group and said "Montenegrin," Mr. Djilas corrected him and said: "Jugoslav."

After the president had asked those present to behave correctly the prosecutor read the long indictment. This emphasised that Mr. Djilas's activity was intended to threaten the Socialist basis of the Jugoslav state and the social order fixed by the constitution and to undermine Jugoslav interests abroad.

Accusing Mr. Djilas of slandering not only the leaders of the Jugoslav revolution but also all her fighters, the prosecutor pointed out that there was not a single institution or authority in Jugoslavia at which "the accused in his pamphlet did not throw mud."

The prosecutor quoted some passages from "The New Class" in which Mr. Djilas criticised particularly the Communist camp and the entire Jugoslav social system, as well as the system of workers' self-management and Jugoslav foreign policy.

He then asked for the trial to be held in secret "to secure public interest" and "to eliminate the possibility that material from the trial might be used for propaganda against the social system and against Jugoslav interests."

NO CHANGE IN CERTIFICATE

BRITANNIAS 312

The certificate of airworthiness of the Britannia 312 long-range airliner is not to be withdrawn or modified by the Air Registration Board despite the engine trouble which has beset the plane. An official of the board made this clear yesterday.

But the Ministry of Transport and Civil Aviation is passing on to operators of the plane advice by the Board that its use should be limited to crew training. British Overseas Airways and El Al, Israeli Airlines, are the only operators so far of Britannia 312s. They have one each which have been used only for training and proving flights.

Modifications devised by the Bristol Aeroplane Co. to overcome the trouble in the Proteus 755 engine are to be tested shortly and may later be incorporated in future engines for the Britannia.

THOUSANDS MARCH ON WARSAW PARTY H.Q.

STONES & TEAR GAS USED IN STREET BATTLE

From A Special Correspondent
WARSAW, Friday.

Police and students clashed again on the street of Warsaw to-night. Security chiefs, who were obviously nervous, threw a guard of several hundred Workers, militia around the headquarters of the ruling United Workers (Communist) party.

For the second successive night the police broke up demonstrations by firing tear-gas and beating students and others with rubber truncheons. What began last night as a protest against the closing of one newspaper was turning to-night into a general protest against police brutality and the suppression of free speech.

Among those injured to-night was Franco Fabiani, correspondent here of the Italian Communist paper Unita. He suffered two minor head wounds.

Fabiani was caught in crowds charged by the police after about 3,000 students had met and adopted a resolution protesting against both the closure of the newspaper Po Prostu and the "brutal interference" of the police in last night's meeting. An unknown number of persons have been injured.

REPORTED CASUALTIES
20 Treated at Hospital

One hospital reported treating 20 persons last night. Most of them suffered minor scalp wounds, but one student was said to have had his skull fractured and another his back broken. There is no way to confirm these reports immediately.

Ten policemen were also reported to have been injured last night by rocks thrown by students. The students answered the police with rocks again to-night. It was not known immediately whether there had been further police casualties.

To-night's trouble centred on the Polytechnic, the huge advanced technical school near the heart of Warsaw. It was at the Polytechnic that some of the student rallies were held last October in support of Mr. Gomulka and the reformation of political life here.

Mr. Gomulka was restored then as Communist First Secretary and became a national hero for his defiance of the Soviet Union's threat of armed intervention. If talk in the Warsaw street to-night was any criterion of the nation's feelings, the police measures of the last two days have cost him a considerable amount of this hero-worship.

CLASSES SUSPENDED
Broadcast Appeal

Even before to-night's meeting began the Ministry of Higher Education had ordered classes to be suspended to-morrow. It was assumed that the schools would be reopened as usual on Monday, but no one knew for sure.

(Continued on Back Page, Col. 4)

LABOUR PARTY DEFERS ACTION ON PRICES

From Our Industrial Correspondent
BRIGHTON, Friday.

Although the Conservative Government was berated in the final session of the Labour party conference here today for failing to reduce the cost of living, the Socialists were unable to produce an alternative policy.

Delegates were persuaded to wait until next year for Executive reports on economic planning and agriculture. A resolution from the National Union of Tailors and Garment Workers had urged the Executive to present a policy for the stabilising of prices and pegging profits.

Mr. Morgan Phillips, Secretary of the party, said food prices had risen by 45 per cent, under the Conservative Government and the value of the £ had dropped to 15s 9d. He nevertheless advised the delegates to remit the resolution to the Executive. They agreed.

COLONIES' RIGHTS

The Executive's Colonial policy was adopted. It asserted that every Colony, including the smallest, should have the right of self-determination and that the right of secession was inherent in the Commonwealth.

A proposal from the South Paddington local party that the next Labour Government should end "the exploitation by British capitalists of the resources of the colonies" by nationalising colonial, commercial and industrial concerns registered in Britain was rejected on Executive advice.

U.S. MISSILE HELP FOR BONN

TRAINING OF TROOPS

WASHINGTON, Friday.

Troops of the new West German Army will go to the United States early next year to be trained in handling American-built rocket missiles. They will receive their training at Fort Sill, Oklahoma.

They will be instructed in the use of the Honest John, Matador and Nike missiles. The Honest John is an Army short-range rocket for troop support.

The Matador is an Air Force tactical missile of sub-sonic speed with a range of several hundred miles. The Nike is an Army ground-to-air rocket and is at present the mainstay of America's anti-aircraft defence. A.P.

U.S. GOLFERS LEADING 3-1

RYDER CUP MATCH

Britain's professional golfers lost the foursomes 3-1 in the Ryder Cup match against the United States at Lindrick, Notts, yesterday. The British point was gained by the captain, Dai Rees, of South Herts, and Ken Bousfield, of Coombe Hill.

Max Faulkner and Harry Weetman, beaten in yesterday's foursomes, have been dropped from to-day's singles. Jack Burke, American captain has left himself out of to-day's matches.

BANK RATE: NEW CALL FOR 'LEAK' INQUIRY

Socialist Hint of 'Political Source'

PREMIER ASKS FOR EVIDENCE

By A Political Correspondent

A claim yesterday by Mr. Harold Wilson, Socialist "Shadow" Chancellor, to have received prima facie evidence suggesting that a "leak" of the intention to raise the Bank Rate from five to seven per cent. on Sept. 19 "emanated from a political source" received a prompt reply from the Prime Minister last night.

Mr. Macmillan, taking over the matter in the absence in his constituency of Mr. Enoch Powell, Financial Secretary to the Treasury, immediately offered, in a reply to Mr. Wilson, that any evidence made available to him would be referred to the Lord Chancellor, Viscount Kilmuir.

If Mr. Wilson agreed, the Lord Chancellor would be asked to report whether the new evidence offered sufficient grounds for further investigations. Mr. Wilson declined to make a statement for publication after receiving the contents of the Prime Minister's letter by telephone.

A first demand for an inquiry made on Sept. 24 was rejected by Mr. Powell on Sept 26 after consultation with the Prime Minister. Careful investigation had disclosed no evidence, either in the operations on the gilt-edged market or elsewhere to suggest a "leakage."

INDISCRETION HINT
Timely Intervention

Mr. Wilson's latest letter bore the suggestion on the possibility of Ministerial indiscretion. Obviously, it demanded serious attention. In the absence in Washington and Canada of Mr. Thorneycroft, Chancellor of the Exchequer, and of Mr. Powell, it was sent to the Prime Minister.

It was on the authority of the Prime Minister that the original refusal to set up an inquiry was made.

It is clear that the Prime Minister took the view that Mr. Wilson's letter cast suspicions upon Ministers which could not be left without immediate answer. His solution of offering the services of the Lord Chancellor, the chief law officer, was regarded last night as a swift and timely intervention.

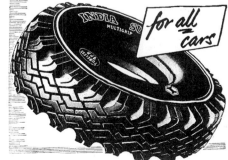

MR. MACMILLAN IS PRIME MINISTER

FIRST CABINET NAMES 'IN A FEW DAYS'

MR. BUTLER SAYS HE IS READY TO SERVE

By Our Political Correspondent

Mr. Macmillan is the new Prime Minister. He is 62 and had been Chancellor of the Exchequer since December 1955. The news of his appointment came in the following announcement from Buckingham Palace at 2.27 p.m. yesterday, 19½ hours after the resignation of Sir Anthony Eden:

The Queen received the Rt. Hon. Harold Macmillan, M.P., in audience this afternoon, and offered him the post of Prime Minister and First Lord of the Treasury. Mr. Macmillan accepted her Majesty's offer and kissed hands upon his appointment.

No immediate announcement of Ministerial changes was expected last night. In a message recorded for television, the new Prime Minister said he would present the list for the Queen's approval "in a few days." Meanwhile, all the Ministers of the Eden Government will carry on in their posts.

FIRST "CABINET-MAKING"

Soon after his return from the Palace, Mr. Butler, Lord Privy Seal, and the Marquess of Salisbury, Lord President of the Council, joined Mr. Macmillan at No. 11. They stayed with him for half an hour. It is assumed that this conference represented the first stage of "Cabinet-making."

Mr. Butler afterwards went to his own room in the Lord Privy Seal's office in Whitehall by way of an interior communicating corridor and remained there most of the afternoon and evening. He finally returned to Downing Street at about 8 p.m. and was seen to leave by the side entrance into Treasury Passage. This gave rise to unfounded speculation that he had spent 4 ½ hours with the Prime Minister.

As he left he was asked if he was going to co-operate with Mr. Macmillan. "If my services are of value," he replied, "they will be at his disposal. I have wished Mr. Macmillan the greatest possible success. That is what I feel."

The reference was to a prepared statement which Mr. Butler had read to reporters before entering 11, Downing Street. In this, after expressing his distress that Sir Anthony Eden's career should have been ended by ill-health, he said:

"His successor and I have worked closely together in times of exceptional national stress and for many years, and I wish Mr. Macmillan the greatest possible success."

No politician weighs his words with greater care than Mr. Butler. It was felt that he would not have used these phrases unless he was prepared to co-operate with Mr. Macmillan in the new Administration.

(January 11)

OXFORD CHAIR APPOINTMENT

MR. TREVOR-ROPER

Daily Telegraph Reporter

The Queen has approved the appointment of Mr. HUGH REDWALD TREVOR-ROPER as Regius Professor of Modern History in the University of Oxford, it is announced from 10, Downing Street. He succeeds Prof. Vivian Hunter Galbraith, who is retiring in September. Mr. Trevor-Roper, who is 43, wrote "The Last Days of Hitler." During his service as a British Intelligence officer he was responsible for investigation into Hitler's death and for the discovery of Hitler's certificate of marriage.

The appointment of Mr. Trevor-Roper ends speculation that has been rife in Oxford senior common rooms since it became known that Prof. Galbraith was to retire.

(June 6)

MLLE. SAGAN'S CAR CRASHES

NOVELIST IN COMA

From Our Own Correspondent

PARIS, Sunday.

Francoise Sagan, 22, the authoress of "Bonjour Tristesse" and "A Certain Smile" was seriously injured in a car accident near Fontainebleau this afternoon. The car she was driving overturned and the three other occupants were also hurt.

Later to-night it was stated that Mlle. Sagan was suffering from internal injuries. She had sunk into a coma and had been placed in an oxygen tent. There was no sign of her regaining consciousness.

According to the police the car somersaulted, bounced over a wide ditch and ended upside down in a field.

She had been spending the week-end at the home of Christian Dior, the fashion designer, who is at present in the United States.

(April 15)

LIFE PEERS & WOMEN FOR LORDS LIKELY

UPPER HOUSE'S REFORM DEBATE

PRINCESS IN GALLERY

By Our Own Representative

WESTMINSTER, Wednesday.

Princess Margaret paid an unexpected visit to the House of Lords to-day. She heard the peers give general approval to the Government's proposals for the creation of life peers and for the admission of women to the Upper House.

Doffing her fur coat and wearing a red dress, she took a seat in Black Rod's box alongside Lt.-Gen Sir Brian Horrocks. She stayed for almost an hour.

The Princess entered during the speech of octogenarian Viscount Samuel. She laughed heartily when Lord Samuel, speaking of the need for younger men in the House, said: "It is a mistake to suppose, as recent experience has shown, that every young peer is gifted with good sense, or even good manners."

LIMITED REFORM

Parties Must Agree

The limited reform was announced by the Earl of Home, Leader of the House. Emphasising the importance of gradualness in making constitutional changes, he declared that any more ambitious scheme of reform must depend on agreement between the parties of which there was no sign.

There must also be an assurance that it would be an improvement on the present system, which, however illogical it might be, did work.

The Opposition Leader, Viscount Alexander of Hillsborough, refused to pledge the Labour party to support the proposals, though he personally conceded that there was a case for both innovations.

The Marquess of Salisbury, powerful advocate of reform while he was Leader of the House, set the tone of many speeches when he congratulated the Government on its courage in grasping a nettle which had frightened successive Governments for the past 40 years.

"HALF A LOAF"

Accepted as First Stage

"But I regard this as only the first stage," he warned his ex-colleagues on the ministerial bench. He called the proposals "half a loaf", which was better than nothing, but said it was only as a first stage that he accepted them at all.

Reform of composition, he believed, would ultimately prove necessary. There should be greater financial assistance to peers than that recently announced by the Government.

Other aspects of reform emerged as the debate progressed. In a maiden speech, Viscount Ingleby suggested that every Member of Parliament should have a pension of £500 a year after 25 years service.

The Bishop of Chichester, Dr. Bell, urged that not only bishops but representatives of the Roman Catholic Church and other denominations should be made members of the House.

The debate continued late, and will be resumed to-morrow. Of the first score of speakers, not one seriously challenged the Government's proposals.

(October 31)

QUEEN AND PRINCE PHILIP IN ACCIDENT

The Lagonda car driven by Prince Philip in which he and the Queen were returning from London to Windsor yesterday afternoon was involved in a slight collision in Staines.

After being halted at a T-junction the car moved off. The car in front stopped and there was an impact.

There was no damage to the other car. The Lagonda suffered a broken offside headlamp. Nobody was hurt.

(June 2)

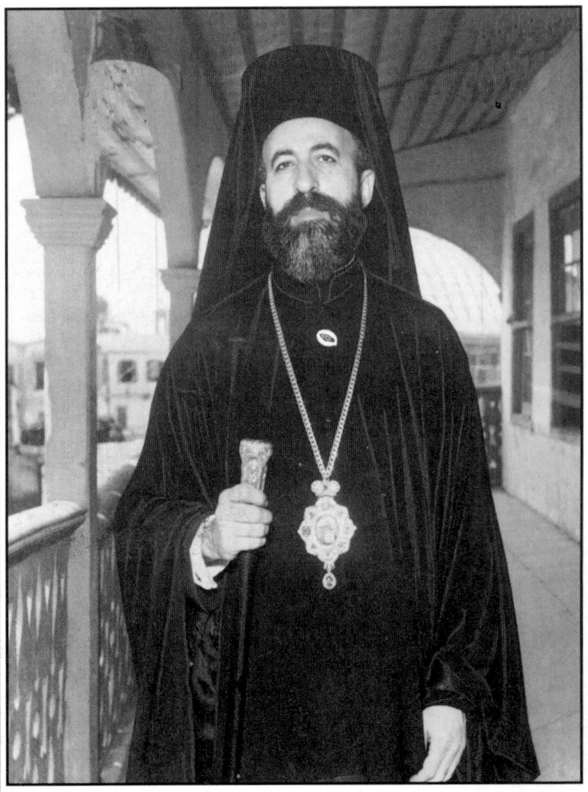

ARCHBISHOP MAKARIOS,
whose release from the Seychelles was announced yesterday.

CHURCH BELLS SIGNAL CYPRUS REJOICING

From Brian Wright
Daily Telegraph Special Correspondent

NICOSIA, Thursday.

A babel of bells and motor horns, crowds thronging the streets, and cheers for patrols of troops left little doubt about the way the ordinary people of Cyprus received the news of the release of Archbishop Makarios to-night.

I was here when the truce was declared by Eoka in August, but reaction then was nothing to compare with to-night's. Within minutes of the news being received bells of Greek churches all over the island began ringing.

Here in the capital these bells brought almost the whole Greek Cypriot population out of their houses, standing, laughing and cheering in the narrow streets and waving to every passing car. There were similar reports from other centres.

From Famagusta came the message: "The town is going mad." Soon after the news had been elaborated I saw a convoy of six taxis charging perilously through Nicosia streets, the drivers and passengers cheering and horns screaming incessantly.

YOUTHS PARADE

Less than two hours after the announcement, young Greek Cypriots, all of whom should have been in their homes under the curfew which is still in force, were parading the streets here with a Greek flag. They were shouting "Enosis."

Behind them followed a patrol of British military police, who made no attempt to interfere with the demonstration. They and the civil police had the greatest difficulty in keeping traffic moving.

(March 29)

POCKET MONEY UP FOR AGED

2s 6D A WEEK MORE

By Our Political Correspondent

Mr. Walker-Smith, Minister of Health, announced yesterday that pocket-money for old age pensioners in homes maintained by local authorities is to be increased from 7s 6d to 10s a week on Jan. 27. This is the date on which the retirement pension is to be raised by 10s.

Residents in old people's homes provided by local authorities under the National Assistance Act have to pay according to their means. In assessing their ability to pay the local authority must assume that they need for "personal requirements" a weekly sum prescribed by the Minister.

(November 27)

'ALARMING' DANGER OF ATOMIC TESTS

SCHWEITZER PLEA

OSLO, Tuesday.

Dr. Albert Schweitzer, 82, the French missionary doctor and musician, today gave a warning that radioactivity was a "catastrophe for the human race." Further nuclear weapon explosions would increase the danger of radiation to an alarming extent.

He appealed to public opinion everywhere to demand the stopping of nuclear tests. Dr. Schweitzer sent his script from his hospital in Lambarene, French Equatorial Africa, and it was broadcast to-day in Norwegian, French, German, English and Russian.

It was certain that radioactive clouds would constantly be carried by the winds around the globe, he said. Some of the dust, by its own weight, or brought down by rain, snow, mist and dew, would fall on the earth.

Reports of radioactive rainfall were coming from all parts of the world. In several places the water was unfit to drink.

ABSORBED IN FOOD

Wherever radioactive rainwater was found the soil was also radioactive. So, too, was vegetation and consequently meat and milk, and thus the radioactive elements were absorbed in the human body.

Japan was the only country where public opinion was demanding an end to nuclear tests. Britain, the United States and Russia had said they wanted to end them, but in these countries there was no public opinion asking for it.

Failure to consider the consequences would be a folly for which humanity would have to pay a terrible price. "We are committing this folly in thoughtlessness."

Greatest danger came from internal radiation, from drinking-water and animal and vegetable foodstuffs. Dr. Schweitzer described the blood and bone diseases caused by radioactivity.

DESCENDANTS THREATENED

Cells of the reproductive organs were particularly vulnerable. It was not only our own health, but that of our descendants which was threatened by the greatest and most terrible danger.

Statistics showed the higher percentage of still births and births of deformed children for doctors continually using X-ray apparatus. By the laws of genetics the damaging effects were cumulative and full results would appear only 100 or 200 years later.

(April 24)

QUEEN ENDS DEBUTANTES' PRESENTATION

AIM TO MEET MORE PEOPLE AT PALACE

Daily Telegraph Reporter

Royal presentation parties for debutantes will end after next year and instead the Queen will hold additional garden parties so that larger numbers may be invited to Buckingham Palace. The announcement was issued last night from the Lord Chamberlain's office.

A Buckingham Palace spokesman said: "The announcement means that the formal presentation party at Court for unmarried girls is finished. They will no longer get presented in that form, but they can be asked to attend a garden party."

While the holding of additional garden parties will enable more people to be invited, it will not necessarily mean that debutantes, who would otherwise have been presented under the existing arrangements, will in fact personally meet the Queen. Nor will the fact that they have received an invitation mean that they have been presented at Court.

Details of the arrangements for 1959 have not yet been completed but will be announced next year. Usually there are two garden parties and two presentation parties at Buckingham Palace each year and one of each in Scotland when the Queen goes to Holyrood House.

ADDING TO DUTIES

Review Three Years Ago

The new arrangements will add to the Queen's already onerous duties. A presentation party takes about one hour but a garden party generally lasts about two and a quarter hours and the new procedure may mean that two or three garden parties will be held.

I understand that the Queen began considering the question of ending the presentation parties three years ago. At that time the whole pattern of official entertaining was being reviewed.

One of the main reasons why she has decided to end the presentation parties is because they affect only a few people. The garden party enables more to be entertained.

This broadening of the invitation will also mean that more people from the Commonwealth, as well as in Britain, will be able to meet the Queen and Prince Philip.

The afternoon presentation party in its present form where every debutante makes her curtsy to the Queen goes back to 1951. But the first opportunities of the general public to meet their sovereign date back to the time of Queen Elizabeth I.

Then, she allowed the public access to the long galleries at Greenwich Palace while she walked to church. During her walk she would stop and talk with some of the people.

In the time of Queen Anne there were what was known as "drawing rooms." Paintings show these drawing rooms in the form of an assembly of people, mostly women in full evening dress with feathers in their hair and long white trains. The Sovereign used to mingle with her guests.

LEVEES FOR MEN

Evening Courts

About the same time the levee was held for men. This function was more popular during the reign of the early Georges and there is a mention of George II holding a levee at the same time as the Queen was holding a drawing room. History records both George II and his Queen holding a drawing room which was restricted to women.

Drawing rooms were held at Frequent intervals throughout the reign of Queen Victoria in both London and Scotland. In the reign of King Edward VII these entertainments moved from the afternoon to the evening and were called evening courts.

They continued from 1901 until 1939, King George VI holding them until the war started. Levees also continued until 1939.

(November 15)

RUSSIA'S NEW MOON WEIGHS HALF A TON

AIR-CONDITIONED CABIN: CODED RADIO SIGNALS

By Anthony Smith,
Daily Telegraph Science Correspondent

Another earth satellite was successfully launched by Russia yesterday. This second achievement completely eclipses the first, for the new satellite, weighing half a ton, is just over six times heavier than the first, which weighed 184lb, and includes an air-conditioned chamber containing a living dog.

Further information given in an announcement by Tass, the Soviet News Agency, said the new satellite "represents the last stage of the carrier rocket, and houses containers with scientific instruments and radio transmitters. The containers, with apparatus, weigh 508.3 kilograms (1,118lb). The satellite also carries a compartment with an experimental animal (a dog)."

Within the new device are instruments for studying solar radiation, cosmic rays, temperature and pressure. There is an air-conditioning system for the dog, with food and instruments so that its life may be studied.

As with the previous experiment there are two radio transmitters operating on frequencies of 40.002 and 20.005 megacycles (wavelengths of 7.5 and 15 metres respectively). But this time the shorter wavelength transmitter emits continuously, while the other transmits off and on every 0.3 seconds.

The satellite was launched, as before, at 65 degrees to the plane of the equator, and probably from the same point somewhere to the north of the Caspian Sea. The workers who made the second satellite have dedicated it to the 40th anniversary of the "Great October Socialist Revolution."

The dog, a husky, is "alive and apparently well," Moscow radio reported yesterday. She is understood to be Kudryavka, a dog which, it is claimed, has already made several rocket flights unharmed.

ROCKET "VETERAN"
Husky's Flights

Kudryavka, the first living animal to reach such a height has already been trained for such conditions, said Prof. Blagonravov, Soviet rockets expert. But he did not indicate whether there was any hope of her returning to earth.

Three weeks ago Prof. Prokrovsky said a satellite containing a dog would be launched and "would certainly have to be returned to earth for experiments with living organisms to be a success." But Prof. Boris Kukakin, speaking last night on Moscow radio, said the second satellite would remain in space "a significantly longer time than the first."

According to reports from Moscow, people in the streets are asking what provision has been made for the dog. Only the West German News Agency, quoting from an unnamed Russian scientist, has reported plans for the dog's safe return.

(November 4)

'BARKING AT THE MOON' BY BRITISH DOG-LOVERS

MOSCOW SCORNS PROTESTS

Moscow Radio last night poured scorn on British dog-lovers who had protested against the use of the dog Laika in the second satellite. It accused them of "barking at the moon,": Russia's artificial moon.

Their protests would be drowned in the laughter of millions, said the broadcast. It referred to deputations to the Russian Embassy in London and the call for a minute's silence.

In the broadcast, in Arabic, the radio said: "The British are known for their sense of humour and fondness for teasing. They have surpassed their American colleagues whose sense of humour has led them to name satellites which they have not yet launched, such as Vanguard, Jupiter and Thor.

"Some British societies for what is called kindness to animals protested against putting a live dog in Sputnik. They appealed to all humanitarians to express their anxiety, alarm and anger at the brutal and cruel action of Russian scientists.

"With regard to the Canine Defence League, we should like to ask them to define more precisely in their appeal what they want.

"In their letter to the Soviet Ambassador, the league said: 'What horror is induced in the mind of the dog can never be known, just as no explanation of the purpose of the journey can be made to her.'

"We do not know why these London dog-lovers experience such anxiety. They know the purpose of the journey of the experimental animal."

PEOPLE "SHAKEN"
League's Reply

Mr. R. Harvey Johns, Canine Defence League secretary, said last night: "We are not worried by the laughter. I think people have been a bit shaken by the whole thing.

"We feel that if man is going to explore unknown reaches it is perfectly reasonable for him to take dogs with him, as Arctic explorers do. But just to send the dog on its own is unfair." The league did not really know the purpose of the animal's journey.

(November 6)

B.B.C. FOOLS ABOUT WITH SPAGHETTI

APRIL 1 HOAX FILM

By L. Marsland Gander
Daily Telegraph Radio Correspondent

The B.B.C. made "April Fools" of many television viewers last night by showing a film apparently of spaghetti growing on trees. It was broadcast at the end of the "Panorama" programme with great seriousness and a commentary by Richard Dimbleby.

The film depicted women gathering the "crop" and laying it in receptacles. Then some peasants were seen eating it. The pictures were made by the B.B.C. in Switzerland.

Hundreds rang up Broadcasting House and Lime Grove studios seeking an explanation. There were so many calls that for a time the lines to the studios were blocked.

All the B.B.C. regional centres were also flooded with calls. Most viewers took the joke good-humouredly and expressed amusement but there were a minority who thought it was childish and irresponsible. Some contended that "April Fools" jokes ought to stop at noon in accordance with tradition.

Mr. Dimbleby, who spoke throughout with his usual solemnity, began by referring to the exceptionally mild winter which, he said, had resulted in the unusually heavy spaghetti crop.

(April 2)

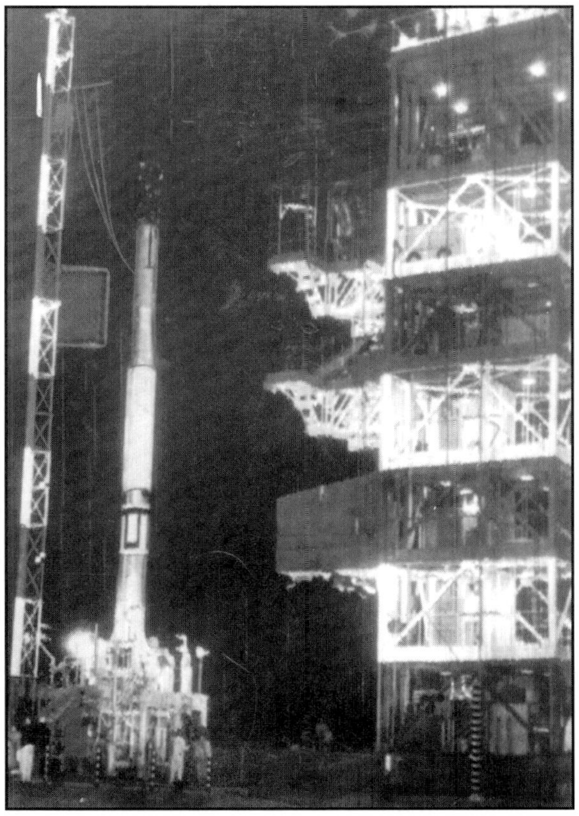

AMERICAN SATELLITE ROCKET BLOWS UP

VANGUARD WRECKED IN 100FT BALL OF FLAME

From Ian Ball,
Daily Telegraph Correspondent

CAPE CANAVERAL, Florida, Friday.

America's first attempt to launch an earth satellite ended to-day in utter failure. The 72-foot high Vanguard carrier rocket exploded on its launching stand here as the firing button was pushed at 11.45 a.m., Florida time (4.45 p.m. G.M.T.).

A ball of orange flame 100 feet in diameter enveloped the launching site and the 22,600lb rocket disintegrated. Within 30 seconds it was apparent to those watching that this first venture of the £39 million United States satellite project had ended in tragic and humiliating disaster.

The first and second stages of the Vanguard were destroyed. The third stage, containing the satellite, was thrown clear, and the satellite was found to be still transmitting when picked up.

There were no casualties. The first announcement from a Defence Department spokesman at the missile testing centre said that all officials and technicians were safe in their concrete blockhouse.

Several hours after the failure officials could not say what had caused it. Mr. Walsh, Deputy Director of Project Vanguard, an engineering specialist himself, gave to a hastily summoned Press conference here this afternoon his account of the accident.

"The rocket was ignited," he said. "It started leaving the launching stand and burned (under control) for about two seconds, whereupon something happened.

"We are not really sure what happened, but we lost thrust. The engine was firing, but the rocket fell back down and toppled over on the launching stand."

(December 7)

HEAVY SELLING ON WALL STREET

Failure of the American satellite rocket to get off the ground in Florida to-day caused heavy selling in missile shares on the New York Stock Exchange. There was some recovery later but an early flurry of selling orders made it necessary to suspend trading for an hour and a half in shares of the Martin Company which was supervising Operation Vanguard.

Boeing, North American and Douglas stocks lost up to two dollars after news of the failure had been received but they improved before the market closed. The general list was only mildly irregular.

(December 7)

CHOU'S UNITY MISSION TO MOSCOW

From A Special Correspondent

MOSCOW, Monday.

Chou En-lai, Communist Chinese Prime Minister, arrived here to-day for talks with the Soviet leaders. It was presumed the discussions would be aimed at strengthening the unity of the Communist world and at working out plans to meet critical international problems.

The economic and ideological crises, especially in Hungary and Poland, are expected to head the list of topics Chou will take up with the Soviet rulers. He will not only hear the Kremlin's version of the current situation, but will also see much for himself.

"ETERNAL" COMRADES

On arrival at the airport the Chinese Prime Minister stressed Communist China's friendship with the Soviet Union. He said the strengthening of those ties was "considered by us our highest international duty." Comradely relations between the two countries were "eternal and unbreakable."

Chou followed the Soviet line in attacking the new American policy for the Middle East. He said the fundamental fact of that policy was its aim to replace Britain and France with the United States in Middle Eastern affairs.

American policy, he said, also demonstrated that "the imperialists have not folded their arms."

(January 8)

LAST CALL-UP TO BE IN 1960

MANY SHIPS TO GO: NO MORE SUPERSONIC PLANES

By Our Political Correspondent

Britain is to make the biggest change in defence policy ever undertaken in normal times. The immediate effect is that the Chancellor will have to find about £79 million less for tax-borne defence expenditure in the Budget he presents next Tuesday.

There will be no further call-up after 1960. This means that the last National Serviceman will come out of the Forces at the end of 1962.

The combined male strength of the British Forces is to be reduced this year from 690,000 to 625,000. The aim is to stabilise on an all-Regular footing of 375,000 at the end of 1962.

These were the main points of the White Paper on Defence, issued yesterday. The savings have been obtained, apart from the reduction in the strength of the Forces, by cutting down on production and stores, and curtailing some research and development.

(April 5)

AGA KHAN IS SUCCEEDED BY GRANDSON AGED 20

KARIM, SON OF ALY, NOMINATED

From Our Own Correspondent

GENEVA, Friday.

Karim, elder son of Aly Khan, has succeeded his grandfather, the Aga Khan, as Imam of the 10 million Ismaili Moslems throughout the world. He will be known as Aga Khan IV. He is just 20.

This afternoon the Aga Khan's last will and testament was opened and read at a two-hour family meeting at the Villa Barakat at Versoix near here, where he died yesterday aged 79. Present were the Begum Aga Khan, the Aga Khan's two sons, Aly and Sadruddin, and Karim as well as Aly's other son, Amyn, aged 18. Amyn arrived here to-day from the United States where he is a student at Harvard. It had first been decided to keep the news secret until to-morrow but to-night Karim decided that it should be published immediately to satisfy the millions of Ismaili Moslems who were anxiously awaiting the news.

Karim and Amyn are the sons of Aly Khan's first marriage to the Hon. Mrs. Joan Guinness, a sister of Lord Churston, and formerly the wife of Mr. Loel Guinness. The marriage to Aly was dissolved in 1949.

FATHER OPENED WILL
Succession Revealed

Karim said to-night: "I learned the news of my succession this afternoon when my father opened the will at the villa. It was a complete surprise. None of us knew until my father made the announcement to the family."

"The first thing I did when I heard the news was to notify my mother," Karim said. Asked if he would keep his grandfather's racing stable, he replied with a laugh: "No comment."

Aly Khan said: "I am very pleased, and consider that my father's choice is a happy one."

Karim, who has travelled considerably, is an accomplished sportsman. One description of him has been that he is a handsome, younger edition of his father.

Much of his growing up has taken place in Europe and the United States, where he was at Harvard. His travels to various parts of the world were at the direction of the Aga Khan.

As a pupil at Switzerland's Le Rosey school, Karim was outstanding at tennis, ski-ing and his studies. He is a friend of the Duke of Kent, who also went to Le Rosey.

(July 13)

MONACO REJOICING AT ROYAL BIRTH

Princess Grace's daughter

From Ronald Payne,
Daily Telegraph Special Correspondent

MONTE CARLO, Wednesday.

"With us, give thanks to 'God and rejoice'"

These words ended a proclamation by Prince Rainier of Monaco which this morning announced the birth to his wife, Princess Grace, of a Princess who will be named Caroline Louise Marguerite.

The child was born at 9.27, local time, weighed 8lb 3oz and was said to have chestnut-brown hair and blue eyes. It was a natural birth, without anaesthetics, and two hours later doctors announced that Princess Grace, who is 27, and the baby were well.

Princess Grace, the former Hollywood film actress, and Prince Rainier were married on April 18 last year. The Prince is 33. His message to his people was broadcast by Radio Monte Carlo a few minutes after 11 o'clock this morning. At the same time a twin gun battery in the Fort Antoine high above the port began firing its 21 gun salute.

The guns brought the first news of the birth into most Monégasque homes. It was confirmed by the hooting of ships' sirens in the port and the ringing of carillons in churches throughout the principality.

Gun Jammed
Salute Interrupted

In the streets small groups of people gathered to count the explosions. After the 20th shot there was a long gap. In the heavy rain one of the guns had jammed.

The other artillery piece was mobilised for one round and the cannonade ended. "It's a girl, it's a princess" were the first shouts heard as the noise subsided.

At dawn this morning four doctors led by Dr. Emile Hervet, Paris gynaecologist, were summoned to Princess Grace. They took her to a specially prepared room in what was formerly her husband's office.

They watched the Prince's ensign with his coat of arms on a white background holsted over the crenallated tower. It flew against the grey sky as they shouted "Vive la Princess." Cars began to arrive with Monégasques and they were escorted by a motor-scooter posse of students.

Prince's Message
Affectionate Terms

A crowd gathered to read the parchment message. It was addressed in warmly affectionate language to "Monégasques and inhabitants of the principality." Under his elegant signature Rainier Prince of Monaco informed his subjects:

At 9.27 this 23rd of January, 1957, my well beloved wife gave birth to a princess who will be named Caroline Louise Marguerite. The Princess and the child are in good health. With us give thanks to God and rejoice".

Among the first ships in the harbour to dress overall with signal flags wee the yacht Christina of Mr. Onassis, the ship owner, and Prince Rainier's Deo Juvante.

Baby's Bouquet
Lilac, Tulips and Rose

Bouquets of flowers from municipal and State offices arrived with congratulatory messages. Among the early ones was a telegram from the Consular Corps, while President Coty of France also sent congratulations.

The first bouquet was of white lilac and tulips with a red rose in the centre. It was for the baby from the palace staff.

(January 24)

1,000 U.S. TROOPS CORDON SCHOOL

NINE NEGRO PUPILS ESCORTED TO CLASS

From Edwin Tetlow,
Daily Telegraph Special Correspondent

LITTLE ROCK, Arkansas, Wednesday.

More than 1,000 United States paratroopers in full battle-kit ringed Little Rock's yellow brick Central High School to-day while nine Negro children, three boys and six girls, were hurried inside. It was a sight which will live long in American history, and will be long discussed.

The end of racial segregation in American schools, ordered by the United States Supreme Court, had come at last to Little Rock. It did so in the form of a military operation, a melancholy affair carried out with brisk efficiency by troops with fixed bayonets and rifles at the ready.

Governors of the Southern States decided at their conference at Sea Island, Georgia, this afternoon to send a committee to Washington to confer with President Eisenhower on the withdrawal of troops from the Little Rock school "at the earliest possible moment."

They adopted a resolution declaring: "The situation in Little Rock is a matter of grave concern. It is imperative that a constructive solution be found." It was made clear that the use of Federal troops was regarded as a major threat to States' rights.

The soldiers, from the 101st Airborne Division, had been flown into the State of Arkansas. But they were brought to Little Rock in Army lorries and other vehicles. Those on duty were all white, although the division is "integrated," with Negroes and white men serving side by side.

A military spokesman told me frankly this morning that it had been decided that the use of Negro troops would have been "inadvisable."

But some Negroes were serving in the background as helpers in the regimental headquarters set up in the school gymnasium and in tents behind the school building.

ROADS BLOCKED

Radio Jeep Patrols

The school had been practically isolated by the troops, who were standing around its precincts only two or three yards apart. Road blocks barred every street access. A helicopter kept patrolling Army cars informed of the situation near the school.

Radio Jeeps were in constant rasping contact with a command car stationed in the sunshine in front of the main school entrance. Only people on business directly concerned with the day's events were allowed near, and even they were given brusque orders to keep to pavements and barrier lines.

More than 750 of the school's 2,000 white pupils stayed away to-day. Feeling against racial integration is still running high in the city.

FLAG CEREMONY

Troops Drive In

All was quiet, if ludicrously abnormal for half an hour after the classes began. The customary ceremony of raising the flag to the accompaniment of school bugles was observed, with the pupils standing to attention inside the school.

Troops guarding the area sprang to attention as the Stars and Stripes which had been drooping lifelessly at the foot of a long flagpole in the breeze-less heat was hoisted, and the school flag on another pole followed suit.

Then came action swift and spectacular. An olive-coloured Army command station-wagon, preceded by one car-load of troops and followed by another, swung round a corner at high speed and screeched to a standstill at a path leading round the big lawn to the steps of the main school entrance.

A score of paratroopers with their rifles and bayonets at the ready spilled out from the two cars. The tail-gate of the command car was lifted, and out scrambled the fine Negro pupils who had been enrolled weeks ago at the school.

The girls, in gaily-coloured blouses and skirts, were smiling. The boys wore T-shirts and light trousers. They did not seem to be taking the matter quite so lightly as the girls.

"THESE YANKEES"

Schoolgirl's Jibe

Paratroopers formed a screen round the children. In answer to officers' commands more soldiers who had been lined up in reserve on the lawn, joined their comrades on guard in the street.

There was no chance for any would-be demonstrators to get near. Quickly, but without unseemly haste the children went into the school.

(September 26)

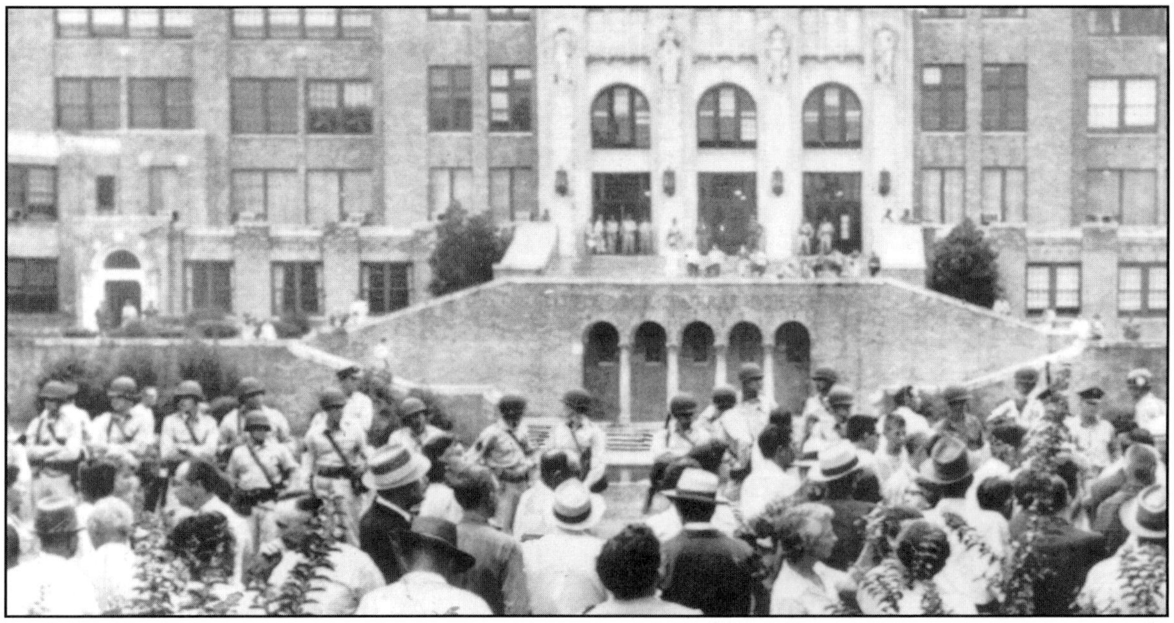

ARMED GUARD OUTSIDE AMERICAN SCHOOL. White people and students outside the Central High School in Little Rock, Arkansas, on Tuesday, when about 250 armed National Guardsmen cordoned the building. The militia were sent there on the instructions of Mr. Faubus, Governor of Arkansas, and as a result the School Board cancelled its planned integration of white and Negro pupils.

RENT BILL WILL BE IN FORCE ON JULY 6

By Our Political Correspondent

The Rent Bill, introduced in the House of Commons on Nov. 7 last, completed its final stage in Parliament to-night and is due to receive the Royal Assent in the House of Lords this evening. It will thus come into force on July 6.

From then on the Rent Acts will cease to apply to about 1,750,000 houses at present in owner-occupation which, if let unfurnished, would be subject to rent control. Houses which at any time fall vacant will also be freed from control.

The limits of rateable value above which the Rent Acts do not operate are lowered to £40 in the Metropolitan police district and Scotland, and £30 elsewhere. This will release from control about 800,000 houses now let at controlled rents, including 190,000 in London.

The tenants of those houses are protected by a "standstill" transition period of 15 months. This means that they will have security of tenure until Oct. 5, 1958.

Landlords must give at least six months' notice to quit. Even if this is served before the end of the ninth month it cannot take effect before the end of the 15th month.

During the transition period the landlord cannot raise the rent, except by negotiating with the tenant an agreement or lease lasting not less than three years. This is calculated to induce landlords to make reasonable proposals to their tenants, so as to benefit from a moderate increase in rent without waiting 15 months.

On the tenant's side the advantage of signing a new agreement will be to gain at least three years' security of tenure. It will be illegal for three years to demand premiums in respect of dwellings to be decontrolled.

A tenant who loses possession after decontrol will be able to claim compensation for improvements, adding to the value of the house, on which he has spent his own money.

(June 6)

DRIVERS SHY OF METERS

Daily Telegraph Reporter

Parking meters made an unobtrusive and not very auspicious entry into the West End yesterday. Fewer than 20 motorists used them.

Seven twin meters were installed in a bombed site park, operated by National Car Parks, off Great Cumberland Place, near Marble Arch. A sign on the side of each one said: "Two hours for 1s."

Occasionally pedestrians slipped into the park to examine the unfamiliar grey shapes, each about 4ft 6in high. But motorists were more wary. The meters were brought into use about midday, and attracted most customers during the afternoon. Last night, when I visited the park, only one of the 14 spaces was occupied.

The meter showed red, indicating that the owner of the grey Vauxhall had overstayed his leave. Outside, a few yards away, Great Cumberland Place and Seymour Street were crowded with parked cars.

(August 10)

TERRORIST BOOBY-TRAP KILLS ULSTER POLICEMAN

BOMB IN HOUSE: 20 MEN HELD

From Our Own Correspondent

BELFAST, Sunday.

After one of the most intensive terrorist attacks for years, Northern Ireland police to-night detained 20 men for questioning in their hunt for the anonymous telephone caller whose message sent a police sergeant to his death in a booby-trap last night.

The sergeant, Arthur J. Ovens, 43, of Coalisland, Co. Tyrone, died instantly. Both his legs were severed by an I.R.A. gelignite bomb placed behind a door in a disused farmhouse near Coalisland. Two constables and two soldiers were slightly injured.

Although hundreds of people were questioned throughout County Tyrone, no arrests were made. Fingerprints on telephone kiosks in the area were taken in an effort to trace the man who made the fatal call to "Coalisland 2."

HUSKY VOICE

"Four Men in House"

It was just before 11 o'clock last night when Sgt. Ovens, who was having a cup of tea, received the call. In a low husky voice the informant told him that four men were acting suspiciously in the old house at Kettle Lane, Brackaville.

Sgt. Ovens pressed him for his name but he would not divulge it. A search party of police and soldiers was organised and within half-an-hour the building was surrounded.

Sgt. Ovens called twice to the occupants to come out. But there was no reply although a light could be seen in one of the rooms.

He moved forward backed by other policemen and soldiers armed with Sten guns and called out "It is the police." There was no response.

He kicked the door and immediately there was a deafening explosion. He was thrown to the ground. Beside him lay two constables and two soldiers who escaped most of the blast and who suffered only minor abrasions.

HURLED 15ft

Grenades in Hands

One of them, Constable Mervyn Graham, said to me: "I was standing facing the building when Sgt. Ovens kicked the door. The explosion hurled me 15ft and I fell on my face.

"I had two grenades in my hands and it was fortunate they did not explode, otherwise the party would have been obliterated."

The other injured constable, Robert Porter, was released from hospital to-day. The two soldiers, Bombardier Michael Moss and Gunner Robert Baird are detained there.

A police spokesman said in Belfast that the gelignite charge was one of the most powerful used by the I.R.A. terrorists for some years.

"People in a village five miles from the farmhouse heard the explosion."

Sgt. Ovens, a native of County Fermanagh, had 22 years' service, and recently received the Long Service Medal. He leaves a wife and two daughters aged five and four.

(August 19)

U.S. BACKING FOR LONDON SKYSCRAPER

HOTEL PROJECT

Daily Telegraph Reporter

An American hotel group is backing a project for the construction in Park Lane, London of a skyscraper hotel with 700 bedrooms. The central feature would be a crescent-shaped tower of 34 storeys and a height of 378ft.

The highest bedroom would be on the 33rd floor. The top storey would be occupied by a roof restaurant and lounge. At present-day prices the cost of the building might be in the region of £4 million.

Its height would exceed that of the proposed Shell offices on the South Bank site, near Waterloo Station, which, with 25 storeys and a height of 340ft, was to be the tallest fully-occupied building in the capital. St. Paul's is 365ft to the top of the cross.

Application has been made to London County Council for planning approval of the hotel and the question is being considered by the town planning committee. I understand that the promoters are ready to go ahead with the scheme as soon as approval is given.

DOLLAR EARNER

Letter to L.C.C.

The importance of the proposed hotel as a dollar earner for Britain has been pointed out to the L.C.C. planning committee in a letter sent by the architects, Lewis Solomon, Son and Joseph, of London, on behalf of New City Properties.

The consent of the Capital Issues Committee had been obtained to the raising of part of the finance required for the scheme. This indicated that the venture "is recognised by the Treasury as being one of national importance." The application also had Board of Trade support.

The promoters considered that there was no other site in London which was so suitable. There was an urgent demand in London for high-class hotels. It was only a hotel of the nature and size contemplated which was capable of proving an economic proposition and an attraction to visitors.

(July 3)

ATOM DUST ESCAPES IN EXPLOSIVES PLANT

OPEN-AIR HAZARD WARNING

By Anthony Smith,
Daily Telegraph Science Correspondent

Both piles at the Windscale Atomic explosives factory near Sellafield, on the Cumberland coast, have been closed because it was discovered that some of the uranium cartridges in Pile No. 1 had become red hot and were oxidising. This reactor may not be working again for several months.

In a statement, the Atomic Energy Authority announced that there was no evidence that the trouble would be any hazard to the public. Some radio-active material had escaped up the chimney.

A small amount has been distributed over the works site. The greater part has been carried out to sea by the wind.

A spokesman for the authority said: "There has been no injury of any sort to any person. There is no danger of the reactor exploding."

It was reported later that, with the exception of the reactors themselves, the whole of the plant area was back to normal operation.

BAN ON TRAFFIC

Some Men Sent Home

Three thousand men work at the plant. Of these 250 had been sent home yesterday. They were from the chemical and process plant near the faulty reactor. Some men who were working at the Calder Hall power station nearby were also sent home "as a precautionary measure."

Those who stayed on at Windscale were advised not to spend any more time out in the open than was absolutely necessary. All roads to the plant were closed to traffic.

The second pile was closed down so that the workers from it could help to deal with the No. 1 reactor. No explanation was given yesterday for the accident.

Sir Leonard Owen, managing director of the authority's industrial group, said that the cause was not known. An inquiry was to be made.

PLUTONIUM OUTPUT

Explosives Ingredient

Mr. H.G. Davey is head of the Windscale factory which mainly produces plutonium for defence purposes. But no announcements were being made yesterday either by him or his staff on the significance of the accident.

Plutonium, an element not found in nature, is made from uranium and is the important ingredient in nuclear explosives. The first pile at the Windscale factory was started up in January, 1951.

The second started a few months later. The production from both of them mean that Windscale is this country's largest atomic explosives factory.

Yesterday the uranium was being cooled by cold water being poured on it. Normally the uranium is cooled by air, but as it had become over-heated further cooling by air would only have led to greater oxidisation.

(October 13)

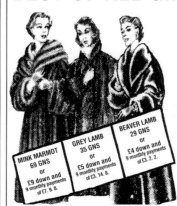

DR. ADAMS ACQUITTED OF WIDOW'S MURDER

No Action on Second Indictment: Bail Renewed on 16 Other Charges

Daily Telegraph Reporter

Dr. JOHN BODKIN ADAMS, 58, of Eastbourne was acquitted at the Old Bailey yesterday of the murder of Mrs. EDITH ALICE MORRELL, 81, a rich widow and his former patient. The jury of 10 men and two women gave their verdict, after an absence of 44 minutes, at noon on the 17th day of the trial.

The verdict was received in the crowded No. 1 court with little emotion. Dr. Adams, dressed in the same blue serge suit he had worn since the trial began, stood motionless, his hands resting by his sides, as the foreman uttered the words "Not Guilty."

The only outward signs of his feelings appeared to be a deep, almost inaudible sigh, and a slight flushing of his cheeks.

As he sat down on the oak chair in the dock, with three warders beside him, he heard Sir REGINALD MANNINGHAM-BULLER, Q.C., Attorney-General, say the Crown would not proceed on a further indictment charging him with the murder of Mrs. Gertrude Joyce Hullett.

Mr. Justice DEVLIN, looking straight at Dr. Adams, said: "John Bodkin Adams, you are now discharged." Dr. Adams stood up bowed low to the Judge and hurriedly left the dock, preceded by a warder.

After he had left, the Judge agreed to an application by Mr. GEOFFREY LAWRENCE, Q.C., for the defence, that Dr. Adams should be granted further bail on 16 charges under the Dangerous Drugs, Forgery and Cremation Acts. These charges stood adjourned at Eastbourne when Dr. Adams was charged with murder.

FAIR TRIAL

Reports and Rumours

The ATTORNEY-GENERAL said to the Judge: "I have given most anxious consideration to what course the Crown should pursue in relation to the further indictment charging Dr. Adams with the murder of Mrs Hullett.

"My learned friend [Mr. Lawrence] referred to the difficulty owing to the reports and rumours that were current in securing a fair trial in the case which has now been returned.

"One of my distinguished predecessors has said that the Attorney-General, when deciding whether a particular prosecution should be carried, has regard to a variety of considerations, all of them leading to the final question: would the prosecution be in the public interest, and included in that phrase, of course, are the interests of justice.

"My lord, one of the considerations I have felt it my duty to consider is that the publicity which has attended this trial would make it even more difficult to secure a fair trial of a further indictment.

"I have also taken into account the length of this trial, the ordeal which Dr. Adams has already undergone, and the fact that the case for the prosecution on this further indictment is based on evidence given before the Eastbourne magistrates, and depends in parts on the evidence of Dr. Ashby [a Crown witness] and very greatly on evidence not supported, as in Mrs. Morrell's case, by the admission of the administration of drugs.

"Having given the matter the best consideration I can, I have reached the conclusion that in all the circumstances the public interest does not require that Dr. Adams should undergo the ordeal of a further trial on a charge of murder, and therefore I enter a nolle prosequi [prosecution abandons its action] in relation to that indictment."

While the Attorney-General was speaking, Dr. Adams listened intently with his head inclined forwards. The Judge then said: "The result of that is that all further proceedings on the indictment are stayed, and there is no further action taken in this court." He discharged Dr. Adams.

LUNCH NEAR CELLS

Little Spoken

Before leaving the Old Bailey by car, after four months in custody, Dr. Adams had lunch in a reception room near the cells. He spoke little during the meal, but seemed relieved.

At Eastbourne many people waited outside his house. Inside Miss DOROTHY LAWRENCE, his receptionist, heard the news of his acquittal within minutes. She said: "I am delighted at the result. I never doubted it for a moment. The house is ready for the doctor if he decides to return to Eastbourne right away."

(April 10)

SOPRANO WINS SLIMMING CASE

From Our Own Correspondent

ROME, Wednesday.

Mme. Maria Meneghini Callas, the operatic soprano, has won her libel action in Milan against Prince Marcantonio Pacelli, a nephew of the pope. Prince Pacelli's spaghetti company published a series of large Italian magazine advertisements last year stating that the singer had slimmed by eating the company's special spaghetti.

Damages and costs were awarded to Mme. Callas. She said she had not eaten the spaghetti, although several cases of it were sent to her. The court ruled that the singer had not slimmed by eating the spaghetti and ordered the company to publish advertisements reporting the court's sentence.

(March 21)

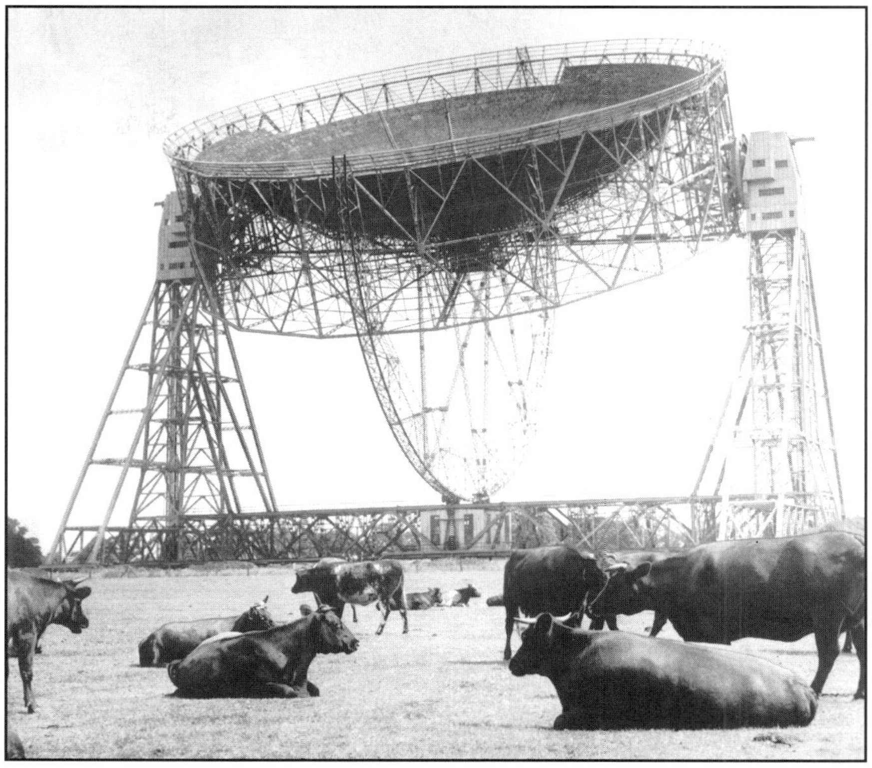

RADIO-TELESCOPE NEARS COMPLETION.
A general view of the radio-telescope for Manchester University, which is being built at Jodrell Bank, Cheshire.

'BAD LUCK IF WE COULD NOT REACH LIMITS OF UNIVERSE'

From Leonard Bertin,
Daily Telegraph Science Correspondent

JODRELL BANK, Near Crewe, Wednesday.

SCIENTISTS of Manchester University believe that they may eventually be able to solve the mystery of the creation of the Universe with their giant radio-telescope here. Prof. A.C.B. Lovell said this to-day.

Dr. Lovell is Professor of Radio Astronomy at Manchester. He said that with telescopes of this sort it was possible to reach further out into space than had ever been possible with optical telescopes.

He foresaw that it would be possible to obtain a picture of events a thousand million light years away or more. The radio waves that brought this picture would then have taken almost as long to reach us as the total suggested age of the universe.

"With this telescope it would be extremely bad luck if we could not reach the limits of the universe," he said.

Extent of The Universe

Prof. Lovell recalled that when the 100-inch Mount Wilson telescope in the United States started its work after the first world war astronomers believed that the entire universe was "contained within the confines of the Milky Way. This is only a few hundred thousand light years across."

To-day, for the first time since the great dish-shaped aerial took form, reporters were able to see it, virtually in its finished form. The term "unique" that was frequently applied to it to-day was, for once, justified.

Its bowl, 250ft in diameter, is three times bigger across than any other completely steerable telescope in the world. It has already become a focus of intense international scientific interest.

Its designer, Mr. H.C. Husband, said that the contractors who built it had performed a feat of structural engineering "rarely equalled, and never surpassed." The steel was fabricated and directed by United Steel Structural Company.

Weighs 2,000 Tons

Some idea of the problems involved may be gathered from the fact that the total weight of the movable structure, including the 700-ton bowl reflector, weighs 2,000 tons.

Yet, by pressing a button, it can be pointed in any direction, both vertically and horizontally, and can even be turned upside down. Once on a "target" electronic computers do all the calculations required to keep the aerial pointing at it, wherever it moves in the sky.

The telescope, which should be fully operational in October, will be equipped both as a passive receiver of radio waves emitted by celestial bodies like the stars, the sun, and distant nebulae, and also as a transmitter.

(June 27)

COMPULSORY TESTS IN 1958 FOR CARS OVER 10 YEARS OLD

By W.A. McKenzie,
Daily Telegraph Motoring Correspondent

Compulsory fitness tests for cars 10 years old or more will be started before next spring. Mr. Watkinson, Minister of Transport, will give full details of the plan in a White Paper early in 1958. The scheme is provided for in the Road Traffic Act, 1956.

The number of cars concerned is estimated at 1,618,000. In recent months many discussions have taken place between the Ministry of Transport and the retail motor industry. The chief problems to settle were:

1 - Laying down a standardised test to be applied by all officially appointed testing stations.

2 - Fixing a standardised charge for the test.

On the first problem the Ministry and the trade had to find a formula which represented a comprehensive vehicle test but which did not involve equipment not readily obtainable by garages.

EQUIPMENT PROBLEM

It was realised that motorists could not be expected to travel considerable distances to a testing station. Equipment involved would have to be such that even small country garages could install it.

Secondly there had to be agreement on a charge for testing which was not an unreasonable burden for the car owner, but which represented a fair return to the garage for the man-hours involved.

The two interests have been guided by the free experimental testing stations at Slough and Hendon, and by experimental schemes carried out by the trade at a charge in Bristol and Wolverhampton. The experiences of these stations varied considerably.

At Hendon the equipment and staff were on a standard higher than could be expected in the average garage testing station. But at Hendon there was a steady stream of applicants for the test which, had a charge been made, might well have shown a profit.

I am told, however, by a spokesman of the Motor Agents' Association that a special Ministry of Transport committee, on which the retail trade is represented, has made good progress recently and that these problems are expected to be settled by the autumn.

The expectation is that the test will occupy no more than 45 minutes on the average at a fixed charge of between 12s 6d and 15s.

(August 15)

ARTHUR MILLER FOUND GUILTY OF CONTEMPT

From Our Own Correspondent

WASHINGTON, Friday.

Arthur Miller, 41, playwright and husband of Marilyn Monroe, was convicted to-day of contempt of Congress.

The verdict was announced in a 15-page "opinion" by Federal Judge McLaughlin who presided without a jury at Miller's six-day trial. This ended a week ago.

The indictment was based on Miller's refusal to tell the House of Representatives Committee on un-American Activities the names of allegedly Communist writers with whom he attended five or six meetings in New York in 1947. When he appeared before the committee last June, Miller answered all questions about himself.

But he said his conscience would not permit him to give the names of others and bring possible trouble to them.

LINK WITH LEGISLATION

Judge McLaughlin ruled that the questions the House committee asked Miller could be related to legislation. In refusing to answer them Miller was therefore guilty of contempt.

Mr. Rauh, Miller's lawyer, had argued that the committee sought "to expose" the playwright and claimed that "exposure for exposure's sake" was illegal; that the questions he refused to answer had no reasonable connection with a passports inquiry; and that the Committee called Miller merely to capitalise on his approaching marriage to Miss Monroe.

(June 1)

MONARCHY TO RULE OVER SPAIN AFTER GEN. FRANCO

DON JUAN'S SON MAY BE KING

From Our Own Correspondent

MADRID, Monday.

The Spanish Parliament was told officially to-day that a traditional monarchy would rule over Spain on the death or withdrawal from power of Gen. Franco, the Head of State.

Señor Luis Carrero Blanco, Minister in charge of Gen. Franco's office, said: "Everyone asks what will happen when Gen. Franco is not with us. "When the Caudillo is not with us the destinies of Spain will be directed by a monarchy which will be neither liberal nor absolute, but a traditional, representative and Catholic monarchy. The person who embodies the monarchy will have to serve loyally the principles of the régime.

"The monarchy which replaces Gen. Franco cannot have the same powers as those held by Gen Franco, an exceptional man who won the [civil] war and reconquered Spain."

SKILFUL SPEECH

Reassuring Party

The Minister's statement was the strongest indication yet that Gen Franco is going ahead with his intention to hand over his succession to a member of the former Royal family. Gen. Franco, who is 64, has been in power for 20 years.

Prince Juan Carlos, 19, son of Don Juan, the claimant to the Spanish throne and grandson of the last monarch, King Alfonso, is expected to be the next King of Spain.

Señor Blanco is a friend and adviser of Gen. Franco in political and economic matters. When he made his announcement he was speaking in support of a Bill defining the limits of Ministerial and administrative responsibility.

His speech was skilfully directed towards enlisting the sympathies of the Falange party, which contains strongly anti-monarchist elements.

A commission of 37 members representing the Church, Industry and the Falange is now meeting to decide how Spain should be ruled after Gen. Franco's departure. It is expected to support a restoration of the monarchy.

(July 16)

WEST EUROPE UNITY PACTS SIGNED IN ROME

COMMON MARKET

From Our Own Correspondent

ROME, Monday.

Ministers of six Western European countries signed draft treaties here to-night for the setting up of a common market and an atomic energy pool. The participants are West Germany, France, Italy, Belgium, the Netherlands and Luxembourg.

The Common Market, an economic community of countries with a total population of 160 million, will be developed in stages over 15 years. Its basic aims are to allow the free movement of goods, manpower and money among the six member States, and to abolish Customs tariffs among them.

The treaties take the place of the abortive European Defence Community of three years ago. To become effective they must be ratified by the six Parliaments.

Despite opposition from industries in some countries and from agricultural interests in others, spokesmen of member States to-night expressed confidence that the treaties would be ratified before the end of the year. This would enable the Common Market and Euratom to come into being on Jan 1 next.

PALACE SIGNING

The signing took place in the Palazzo Senatorio, seat of the Mayor and Municipal Council on the Capitoline Hill. The signatories were Dr. ADENAUER, West German Chancellor; M. PINEAR, French Foreign Minister: M. SPAAK, Belgian Foreign Minister; M. BECK, Luxembourg, Foreign Minister; Mr. LUNS, Netherlands Foreign Minister; and Signor SEGNI, Italian Prime Minister.

Millions of viewers saw the ceremony in a Eurovision link-up. Bells rang out on the Capitoline Hill and seven million Italian school children were given a holiday to celebrate the signing.

Dr. ADENAUER described the occasion as an "historic moment." He pointed out that not all details of the treaties had found unanimous agreement everywhere, but "we must not fail to see the wood in looking for the trees.

"Only an ever closer union of our six States guarantees the survival of all of us, and safeguards our development in freedom and our social progress."

"WAY OF SURVIVAL"

Signor MARTINO said the signing "opens a new phase in our relations. We have chosen a way of survival knowing the efforts in store for us in the future.

"We must look ahead and realise that what we have forged to-night is no more than a tool for the creation of the greater moral and political solidarity of Europe. In the world of to-day Europe can only survive if it unites."

The ruling body of the Common Market will be a Council of Ministers, which will have to reach all major decisions either unanimously, giving the power of veto to every member, or by a majority of 12 votes. France, West Germany and Italy will have four votes each. Belgium and Holland will have two, and Luxembourg one.

The Euratom Treaty will provide for the free exchange of atomic information and for the common development of the European economy to meet the vast power of Russia and the United States.

(March 26)

GROUSE SEASON PROSPECT BEST SINCE WAR

Prospects for the grouse season which opens to-day, the "Glorious Twelfth," are reported to be better than for any year since the war. After the mild winter, moors are well-stocked with birds strong on the wing.

Gunsmiths have been busy, catering particularly for large numbers of transatlantic and Continental visitors. With cartridges at 57s per 100, about four times their pre-war cost, the demand is steadily increasing.

The Queen, with Prince Philip, now in residence at Balmoral, will again give a royal lead to the sport. The Queen has rented moors on the neighbouring estate of Invercauld.

There will be a number of private parties from Balmoral, among them those in which the Prime Minister will join. With Lady Dorothy Macmillan, he will be a guest of the Queen from Aug. 31 to Sept. 2.

(August 12)

12 DIE IN MILLE MIGLIA CRASH

RACING MARQUIS'S CAR PLUNGES INTO CROWD

From W.A. McKenzie
Daily Telegraph Motoring Correspondent
BRESCIA, Italy, Sunday.

A Ferrari car hurtled into spectators only 25 miles from the finish of Italy's Mille Miglia (1,000 mile) road race to-day, killing nine people. The driver, the wealthy Spanish sportsman the Marquis de Portago, who was 28, and his co-driver were also killed.

The co-driver was Mr. Edmund G. Nelson, 40, well-known American bob-sleigh racer. Among the dead, the police stated, were five children. One of 11 spectators taken to hospital died later, bringing the total toll to 12.

After many accidents to drivers and spectators and the lesson of the Le Mans disaster two years ago, when 82 people were killed, the fate of the Mille Miglia was in the balance. To-day's crash will almost certainly end the race, the last speed contest of the city-to-city type.

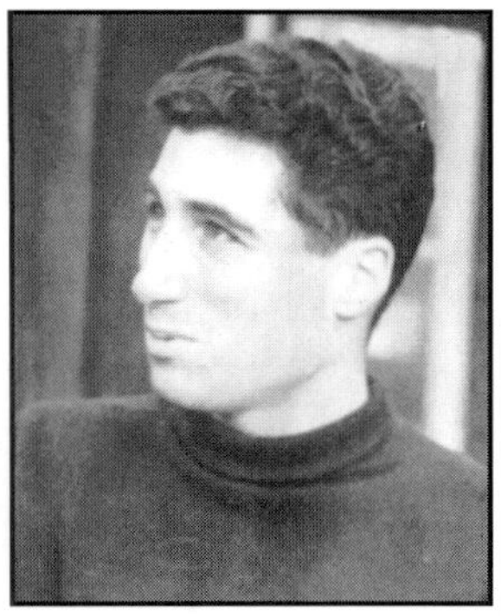

THE MARQUIS DE PORTAGO

ITALIAN WIN

Speeds up to 180 m.p.h.

The race, won by Piero Taruffi, of Italy, was run at the usual breakneck speed. He averaged 94.6 m.p.h. in his Ferrari for the whole 1,000 miles, which form a figure eight from Brescia in the north to Rome in the south, twice crossing the Apennines. Ferraris also took second and third places.

Taruffi, and others in the big sports car class, were motoring wherever possible at speeds up to 180 m.p.h. Round the course, massed 10 deep in places, were many millions of Italian men, women and children, often grouped in masses at the bends and corners.

On the straights where the cars were passing at over two miles a minute they formed massed lines converging into a solid block of humanity.

As a car swung into the narrowing channel of spectators, the crowd would fall back only to reform the moment it had passed. It was in such a scene that de Portago left the course.

CAR BOUNCED 15ft

Spectators Crushed

According to eye-witnesses the Marquis's car, which was lying in third place at the time, blew a front tyre between Goito and Guidizzolo, north of Mantua, on the way to the finish at Brescia. It swerved into a telegraph pole.

Then it bounced 15ft in the air and hit a group of three people, killing them immediately. Bouncing back on to the road, it rolled over several times crushing a group of people on the other side of the road. Six of them died on the spot.

When it left the road the car leapt a wide ditch filled with water, in which it ended up after somersaulting. People at once forced back spectators who crowded on to the road. As it happened, there were no cars immediately behind.

At Mantua, the last checkpoint, the Marquis had been told that Taruffi was leading. After a quick drink of orangeade he set off in pursuit.

One eye-witness estimated the car's speed at 125 miles an hour when the tyre burst with "a terrific explosion." A police officer said terrified spectators scattered and several were injured in the stampede. Another policeman described it as "a massacre."

The Marquis was well known as an amateur jockey, horse-owner and winter sports expert as well as a leading racing driver.

It was the worst crash since the 1955 disaster in the Le Mans Grand Prix. Thousands of troops and motorist volunteers had been placed along the route to-day to control the crowds as far as possible.

(May 13)

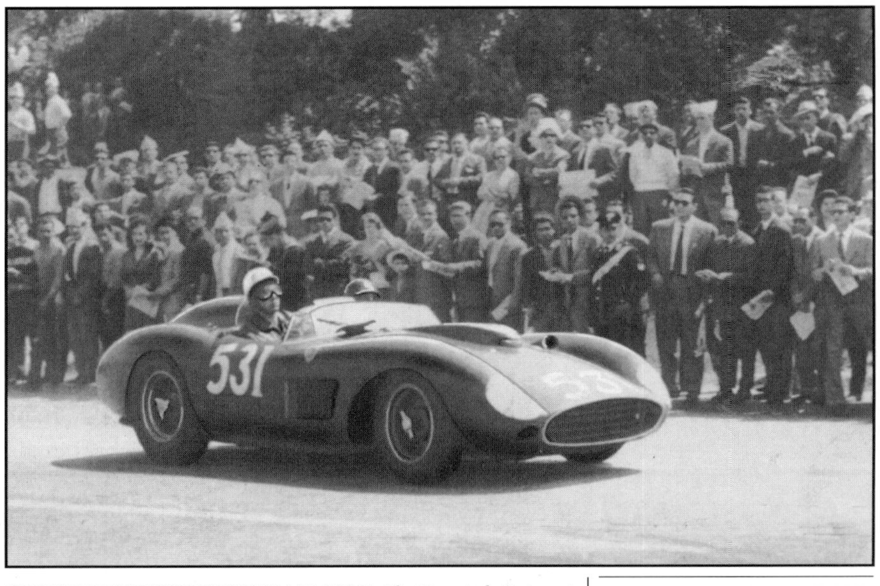

SPANISH DRIVER KILLED IN MILLE MIGLIA. The Marquis de Portago at speed in his Ferrari after driving past the check point in Rome while competing in the Mille Miglia yesterday. Later in the race one of his tyres burst and he left the road killing himself, the co-driver and ten spectators.

SIR J. HARDING QUITS CYPRUS NEXT MONTH

Field-Marshal Sir John Harding is to relinquish his post as Governor of Cyprus and to return to Britain on leave early next month. He will be succeeded by Sir Hugh Foot, Governor of Jamaica.

Sir Hugh will take up his new duties about Dec. 1. An official announcement made to-day is as forecast in THE DAILY TELEGRAPH last Saturday. Sir John is 61 and Sir Hugh 50.

A Colonial Office spokesman denied the change in Governors implied any change in British policy over Cyprus. Appointment of a civilian in the place of a soldier did not signify reduction in the island's strategic importance.

The Government is satisfied that the security organisation built up by Sir John is capable of dealing with all emergencies and that its efficiency will be maintained under its chief. Maj-Gen Kendrew, Director of Anti-Terrorist Operations.

Sir Hugh Foot's appointment as Governor of Jamaica began in April, 1951, and was renewed for two years in April, 1956. He was Colonial Secretary, Cyprus, from 1943 to 1945 including a period as Acting-Governor.

(October 22)

HUNGARIANS TO DIE

REVOLT LEADERS SENTENCED

From Our Own Correspondent
VIENNA, Monday.

Verdicts in the first show trial of "counter-revolutionaries" in the Hungarian uprising were announced to-day in a closely-guarded courtroom in Budapest. Three of the 11 accused were sentenced to death.

They included a woman medical student, of 25, Ilona Toth. She admitted killing a wounded political policeman last October by giving him petrol injections.

Main interest in the verdicts is in the remarkably light sentences passed on two leading intellectuals.

Gyula Obersovsky, who led the underground resistance even after the second Soviet attack against Budapest, was gaoled for three years. His colleague, Joszef Gali, a well-known dramatist, received one year and a £30 fine.

REGIME'S "MILDNESS"

Both faced charges of incitement to resist the Russian forces, for which the death penalty has frequently been applied in recent secret trials. This public display of "mildness" is thought to mark the reluctance of Mr. Kadar's Government to provoke a new wave of opposition among intellectuals.

There was a gasp from the 400 spectators as the woman presiding judge, Dr. Matild Toth, pronounced the death sentences. She gave warning that she would order the court to be cleared if there was the least disturbance.

The accused sat in two rows with policemen beside them. They answered their names smartly before the verdicts were given.

(April 9)

JELLYFISH "INVASION" OF SOUTH COAST BEACHES

LETHAL STING: WARNINGS TO BATHERS AND CHILDREN

Daily Telegraph Reporter

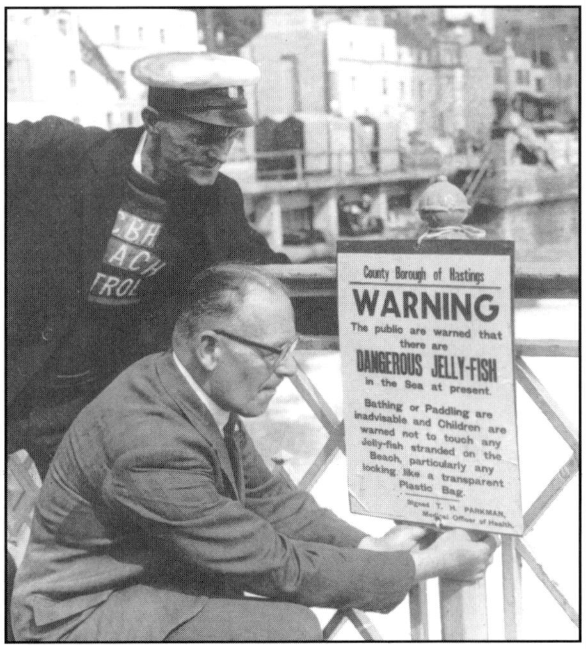

THREE SPECIMENS of the poisonous jellyfish. Known as "Portuguese Men o' War," they look rather like a transparent plastic bag.

Warnings to bathers and children playing on the beaches of the danger from the tropical blue jellyfish known as Portuguese Man o' War have been issued in resorts all along the South and South-East coast. The sting of these fish can be lethal.

Normally found around the Canary Islands, they have been brought to Britain by the prevailing winds. Previous big invasions of them were in 1954 and 1955. Before that they had not been here in numbers since about 1912.

Dr. D.P. Wilson, of the Marine Biological Laboratory, Plymouth, explained last night how jellyfish sting. They have a large number of microscopic capsules which shoot out poisoned threads when touched by fish or human skin.

"In the Portuguese Man o' War, the threads are longer than in most other jellyfish and they penetrate farther into the skin. Poisoning as a result is more severe."

DOCTOR'S WARNING

'Extremely Dangerous"

Reports of the "invasion" from various resorts last night were:

Hastings: Dr. T.H. Parkman borough medical officer, in an emergency statement to the Town Council, said: "These jellyfish are extremely dangerous, for they have a sting which can be lethal."

The first were found by a corporation employee, Charles Gearing, who destroyed them with a spade. The warning notices advise the public not to swim or paddle at present, and especially warn children not to pick up any jellyfish on the beach.

Bexhill: Gangs of men with buckets and spades searched the beach. Several of the fish were caught while crowds of holiday-makers looked on. Dog owners have been told to keep their pets away.

Hayling Island: The public health department set up a beach patrol, warning holidaymakers and particularly bathers. Police took specimens to all schools in the hope of putting children on guard.

(September 12)

MR. DE VALERA WINS

From Our Own Correspondent
DUBLIN, Thursday.

Mr. de Valera's Fianna Fail party, in opposition since 1954, has won, with 78 seats out of 147, a majority over all other parties in the Eire General Election. The previous Government was a Coalition led by Mr. Costello, Fine Gael party. The Daily reassembles on Wednesday week.

(March 8)

EARTHQUAKE HITS SAN FRANCISCO

From Our Own Correspondent
NEW YORK, Friday.

San Francisco had five earthquake shocks to-day. One, at 11.45 a.m. (7.45 p.m. G.M.T.) was the most violent the city has felt for 30 years. The fifth, again violent, came at 3.15 p.m. (10.45 p.m. G.M.T.)

"It felt just as heavy as the 1906 earthquake," said Mr. Paul O'Brian, a clerk in the United States Court of Appeals, speaking of the second quake. Mr. O'Brian remembers the disaster of that year which destroyed much of the city.

But Dr. Charles Richter, of the California Institute of Technology, Pasadena, challenged this. He said his instruments indicated a magnitude of 5.5 compared with 8.2 for the 1906 San Francisco earthquake, which killed more than 450 people.

20 WINDOWS BROKEN

No casualties have been reported in to-day's quake, other than about a dozen people bruised by being thrown about. But more than 50 small fires were started. Twenty plate glass windows were broken at the Golden Gate Bridge toll station.

In the centre of San Francisco the main movement was a zig-zag start. The climax was a see-sawing motion northward and southward which lasted about 30 seconds.

The fifth tremor was accompanied by a rumbling noise. It had an east-west motion.

BRIDGE TOWER SHOCK

John King, a painter working on the south tower of the Golden Gate Bridge, said: "I thought it was coming down. The tower shook like a tree in a gale. I ran off the bridge as fast as I could go."

Hundreds of office workers ran from the five-storey State Building. One man said it shook like a pendulum.

The California highway patrol reported that the earthquake washed out a large section of the coastal highway between Daly City and Sharps Park. A 400ft stretch of boulevard bordering Lake Merced cracked and crashed into the water.

(March 23)

AGREEMENT ON MOSCOW AIR TRIPS SIGNED

Daily Telegraph Reporter

A civil aviation agreement for regular air services between London and Moscow was signed in London yesterday by Britain and Russia. Either side can give six months' notice to end the agreement.

It is confined to the route via Copenhagen. Services will be operated by British European Airways and Aeroflot, the Russian airline.

The agreement will not operate until both countries are satisfied that the technical and commercial conditions for safe, economic and comfortable services exist. For this reason no date has been settled for them to start.

Under the agreement, if either country finds the noise of an aircraft excessive, suitable alterations must be made before it is used on the London-Moscow route.

(December 20)

2,000 A WEEK EMIGRATE TO COMMONWEALTH

AIM TO BENEFIT CHILDREN

Daily Telegraph Reporter

Despite full employment, the flow of skilled workers and their families from Britain to the Commonwealth shows no sign of abating. At least 2,000 a week are going to Rhodesia, Australia, Canada and New Zealand under assisted or free passage schemes, and hundreds travel independently.

At Rhodesia House an official gave a clear indication of the type of man now seeking a fresh start abroad. "Generally," he said, "he is a skilled man who has given the matter a lot of thought and shared the problem with his wife. Uppermost in his mind, often, is not so much his own future as the better prospects he foresees for his children."

Last year 9,640 left Britain for the Federation of Rhodesia and Nyasaland. This year the average so far has been about 900 a month. Almost all have assured jobs awaiting them.

HELP WITH FARES

Interest-free Loans

Their industrial history for 10 years is carefully vetted before they can qualify for an assisted passage. The money is lent to them interest-free, repayable over three years.

Young couples with children are encouraged. But they may have to wait if there are no vacancies in the particular industry in which the man works.

Every month a list is circulated of the jobs for which there are no vacancies and for which no entry permits can be given. It also draws attention to urgent requirements, such as six caterpillar mechanics, single men preferred, whose average earnings will be £100 to £120 a month in an area where accommodation with full board costs an average of £18 per month.

"There is no scope whatever for unskilled or semi-skilled persons," states the latest list.

WORK PLEDGE

Two-year Stay

Of about 1,000 a month going to New Zealand nearly half are given free passages. In return the emigrants undertake to stay two years in the employment for which they have been accepted.

Housing difficulties limit family groups to about half the total number emigrating after a strict "screening" procedure. The men represent a wide cross section of professions and skilled trades.

(August 6)

JOHN OSBORNE MARRIED

MISS MARY URE

Daily Telegraph Reporter

Mr. John Osborne, 27, author of "Look Back in Anger," left London Airport last night with Miss Mary Ure, 24-year-old actress, a few hours after they were married quietly by special licence at Chelsea Register Office.

When the couple were recognised at the airport Mr. Osborne, whose play won him the reputation of being an "angry young man," found he had to soothe an angry, and weeping young bride. "I hoped it was secret," he said.

Miss Ure refused to pose for photographers. Her eyes brimming with tears, she said: "My producer will be furious if he knows I am leaving the country. I am supposed to be at work again to-morrow morning." She is making the film "Windom's Way" at Pinewood.

Mr. Osborne tried to pacify her. "It's no good getting excited," he said, "It's too late now."

The wedding was attended by about two dozen close friends. The couple left on a flight to Nice but Mr. Osborne said they would move on elsewhere.

(May 12)

First Night

A FINE STUDY BY LAURENCE OLIVIER

'THE ENTERTAINER'

By W.A. Darlington

John Osborne is certainly a dramatist of great promise. He has the gift of conveying atmosphere, and - an actor himself - he can write parts for actors.

These important assets carry his new play "The Entertainer" at the Royal Court to what looks like a success on the scale of his "Look Back in Anger," for they give Laurence Olivier the chance for a tour de force of impersonation and disguise.

He plays Archie Rice, a third-rate music-hall comedian, a cocky, strutting, forcedly gay, lecherous and drunken fellow, who has the income-tax man on his heels and is a constant disappointment to his family.

Mr. Osborne, torn between the desire to write a play and the temptation to make Archie a star part, lets us see him on the stage in his deplorable little turn, and this gives Sir Laurence his chance to amaze us.

COMEDIAN'S TAP-DANCE

Completely unrecognisable, he sings and makes off-colour jokes into the "mike," he tap-dances with just the right air of confidence and the right lack (for Archie) of any remarkable skill. It is all brilliantly brought off.

However, it thrusts into the background the other elements of the play - Archie's home-life.

These were his relations with his second wife, the fate of a stepson who is captured and killed in Egypt, and the gradual widening of a rift with his daughter, whose growing social conscience disgusts her with what she takes to be her father's lack of heart.

These matters have so much potential interest that we are left regretting that we have not heard more about them.

Brenda de Banzie acts with great feeling as the wife, and was given a warm reception by last night's audience.

Dorothy Tutin, as the daughter, gives a curiously muted performance, for which indistinct speaking is chiefly to blame. Tony Richardson directs.

(April 11)

LEYTON BOYS PLAY 'HAMLET'

From W.A. Darlington

EDINBURGH, Thursday.

To-night, in the hall of the Edinburgh Academy, I have seen "Hamlet" vigorously acted by a company calling itself the Players of Leyton, with an 18-year-old schoolboy acting the Prince.

This organisation is in fact based at the Leyton High School for Boys in East London and consists of boys and old boys under the leadership of several masters, of whom one, B.G. Brown, is producer.

It has a formidable and varied record of achievement and is not by any means wedded to Shakespearean production - and this I think may well be a reason why it falls well below the best standard of school drama so far as verse-speaking is concerned.

WHISPER AND BELLOW

In most other respects its work deserves high praise. Its players tackle their parts with spirit and maintain an excellent pace. They have feeling for character and they speak their lines with intelligence.

But they seem to me to have the wrong line on Shakespeare. In the desire for speed they gabble the lines in a manner that deprives them of all their music.

Even Derek Jacobi, who is in some ways a remarkably interesting Hamlet, is culpable in this respect.

There must be a sincere tribute to the spirit and enthusiasm of this company whose members have contrived to raise the money for their Edinburgh venture out of their own pockets or by their own exertions.

(August 23)

3,000 CLAP A WELCOME TO BILL HALEY

FIRST LONDON SHOW

Bill Haley and his Comets, whose Rock 'n' Roll stage show closely resembles some sort of musical battering ram, last night launched the first assault of their British tour, at the Dominion Theatre, Tottenham Court Road, and won hands down.

The reception they received could only be described as rapturous. An audience of 3,000 cheered, sang, clapped in time to the music, and showed nothing more harmful than healthy enthusiasm.

It did not hesitate, either, to voice its disapproval because Haley's appearance lasted little more than half an hour in a variety bill of one and a half hours.

These Comets arm themselves with three loudspeakers, aimed, of course, at the audience. There is the rasping tenor saxophone, the familiar electric guitar and the heavy, infectious, unflagging off-beat, all of it by now the stock-in-trade of Rock 'n' Roll.

"SIMPLE AND EASY"

What is its appeal? Two young members of the audience, aged 15 and 16 and both from Hemel Hempstead, Herts, put it this way. "It's simple and easy to understand. It's got a beat and you can jive to it, and sing to it."

Haley, whose figures for sales of his records have reached the respectable little total of 22 million, says: "I'm really no ogre."

With that kiss-curl hanging limply over one eye how can we doubt him? In any event I enjoyed the fun of the Haley type of entertainment. Let no cat call me square. S.G.

(February 7)

'CATS' APPLAUD TOMMY STEELE

That present-day phenomenon, the Bermondsey Blonde, Tommy Steele headed the variety which opened at the Dominion, Tottenham Court Road, last night.

It may seem a far cry from the 12th century troubadour to Mr. Steele, but the connection is there, though he may appear to some to be no more than a crazy mixed-up minstrel with ants in his pants.

After 10 minutes of this entertainer, who followed closely on Freddie Ball, another instigator of Rock 'n' Roll, I was ready to cry "O, death, where is thy sting?" Yet honesty compels me to admit that the indescribable din let loose by these two turns caused - to put it mildly - something of a furore around me.

In the modern idiom, this was an evening out for the "cats." Personally I'll take the more soothing, more civilised caterwaulings of the four-legged kind. L.L.

(May 21)

SADLER'S WELLS GROUPS LINKED

The grant of a Royal Charter setting up a new Corporation with the title of "The Royal Ballet" was announced by Viscount Waverley, chairman of the Royal Opera House, Covent Garden, yesterday.

The new body will co-ordinate the activities of the Sadler's Wells Ballet at Covent Garden, the Sadler's Wells Theatre Ballet at Sadler's Wells, and the Ballet School at White Lodge, Richmond Park.

In future the senior company will head its posters "The Royal Ballet (formerly the Sadler's Wells Ballet at Covent Garden)"

The Corporation will be controlled by a board of not more than 18 governors and a council of 10, drawn from the board. Lord Waverley is chairman of both. All are unpaid.

The Queen has consented to be Patron, and Princess Margaret is the first President. The office of Vice-President, provided for in the Charter, is being left open for the present.

(January 17)

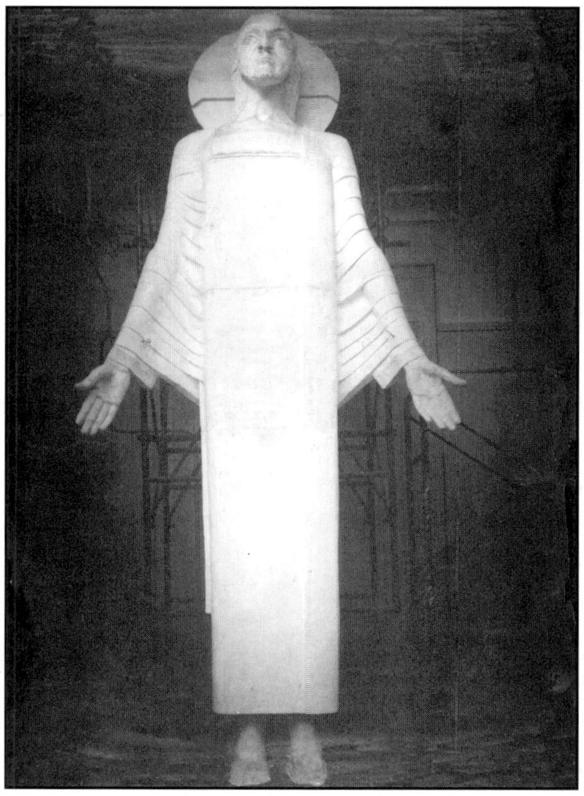

THE PLASTER CAST of Epstein's Christ in Majesty from Llandaff Cathedral now in the Epstein Exhibition at the Tate Gallery. It is 17.5 in high.

NEW WALTON WORK INTENSE AND EXCITING

CELLO CONCERTO

By Martin Cooper

The cello concerto heard for the first time in this country at the Festival Hall last night is Walton's first large-scale orchestral work since the violin concerto of 1939.

The reflective, melancholy vein, already strong in the viola concerto of 1929, has deepened and the purely lyrical is no longer inhibited by considerations of fashion or prestige. The rhythmic excitement remains though characterised by greater nervous intensity and less staying-power.

This is in accordance with a universally observable law by which we find, as we grow older, the delivery of our messages less urgent and the manner of their delivering more important. In fact, Walton at 55 has the courage and self-confidence to be wholly himself.

STRONGLY ATTRACTIVE

The result in this new concerto is extraordinarily attractive. The delicate, relaxed mood of the first movement, in which the solo part consists of an almost unbroken series of cantabile melodies, successfully defies convention with its natural, loosely-knit structure.

The following Allegro Appassionato gives the soloist a great amount of very fast, minutely splintered melodic material excessively difficult to articulate clearly against the orchestra.

The excitement is partly technical and partly rhythmic but the pace - possibly faster than the composer intended? - the concentration of thought and the distracting glitter of the orchestral writing made this the most difficult of the three movements to judge at a first hearing.

The final theme and variations form the heart of the work. Here Walton's characteristically elliptical harmony lends a very personal distinction to the lyrical mood, although the writing for the solo instrument in the second variation was one of the work's few disappointments.

MASTERLY CODA

The long coda, with its reminiscences from the first movement, provided one of those experiences hitherto associated almost exclusively with music of the past - the long, masterly and apparently effortless sustaining of mood throughout a slowly unravelling cadence.

The soloist was Gregor Platigorsky, for whom the work was written and the ease and refinement of his playing, his wide range of tone and obvious delight in Walton's singing style captivated the large audience. Sir Malcolm Sargent, who conducted the B.B.C. Symphony Orchestra, showed his accustomed instinctive understanding of Walton's music.

(February 14)

EPSTEIN CHRIST ON CATHEDRAL ARCH

ALUMINIUM FIGURE

Daily Telegraph Reporter

Drapes and scaffolding were removed yesterday from a statue which with its setting may cause yet another Epstein controversy. Since it left a London foundry Sir Jacob Epstein's "Majestas" a 16ft representation of "Christ in Majesty," has been carefully hidden from public sight.

For 10 months it lay in its crate while restoration work went on round it in the 12th century cathedral at Llandaff, Glamorgan. The cathedral was severely damaged in the war.

It now stands on the apex of a modern reinforced concrete arch spanning and dominating the nave. The statue is a frontal figure to a "block" which will contain a section of the organ for choir accompaniment.

The inclusion of the statue and arch in the work at Llandaff is part of a bold policy to find a place for contemporary expression in church architecture. Whatever are the reactions of the public to it, the few who saw it yesterday could not fail to be impressed by its power.

THEOLOGICAL CHALLENGE

The Dean, the Very Rev. Eryl S. Thomas, described the figure as "a theological challenge." He said: "Epstein has caught not only the majesty of God, but the mercy and serenity of the reigning Christ.

"Like the restorers of the last century who called in the Pre-Raphaelites, then under a cloud of suspicion for their so-called modern art, so in this century the Dean and Chapter have resisted every temptation to take refuge in a timid artistic traditionalism.

"If the church is to be a patron of the arts and true to her times she should build in the style and technique of the age, otherwise she is an anachronism and a museum piece."

The setting and design of the arch are the work of the cathedral architect, Mr. G.G. Pace, of York. Sir Jacob, now 76, has called his statue "My greatest act of faith." It took him 16 months to complete.

ONLY 7CWT

It has been cast in aluminium, has an unpolished surface, weighs only 7cwt, and cost £3,500. With the £4,000 arch it has been paid for from funds received from the War Damage commission.

The figure itself is elongated, giving the impression of suspension. The arms are slightly raised, palms outermost. The head is backed by a haloed cross.

Leaders of Church and State will see it to-morrow during a service of hallowing and dedication. Sir Jacob will be present.

(April 9)

ANATOMY OF COURAGE

By Campbell Dixon

If "heroism is the brilliant triumph of the soul over the flesh," as a Swiss has said, then Col. Nicholson, in **"The Bridge on the River Kwai"** (Plaza), is a hero. He is also alas, a fool - or rather, in the end a little mad.

David Lean's opening shot of half-starved men working on a jungle railway beside which stand rough crosses, establishes the background. When Col. Nicholson marches smartly into the Japanese prison camp at the head of his scarecrow battalion, watched cynically by an American, you also get the theme.

His insistence that war, like sport, has its rules, enrages Col. Saito, the ruthless Japanese commandant, and bewilders junior officers. When the prisoners are ordered to build a vital bridge, at a time when men in other fields are risking their lives in sabotage, he sees not the slightest objection. Doesn't the Geneva Convention permit prisoners to be worked?

But when his captor tells him that officers must work, too, the Colonel is outraged. Icily he produces a copy of the rules, and neither guns nor torture can shake him.

A Job for the Army

In the end, because the bridge is going badly and he needs more discipline and know-how, Salton gives way. Col. Nicholson responds by telling his officers that the troops need an objective, work they can be proud of, and, in a scene charged with irony, takes over the whole job.

The first thing he discovers is that the bridge is in the wrong place: the river-bed is too soft to take the weight of a train. Where most men would chortle with glee, the colonel is shocked by inefficiency. He moves the bridge to a better site, and induces officers and even partially disabled men to work as volunteers, all to the end that any unit he commands shall do a good job, reflecting credit on the British Army.

By this time, of course, you are beginning to suspect that though he would never ill-treat prisoners, because that sort of thing is expressly forbidden by the rules, Nicholson has much in common with Saito, whose dearest wishes - in fact, commands - are that the bridge shall be finished on time, and prisoners shall be happy in their work. Brave, narrow and rather stupid, he is the type of officer who has won many a decoration and lost many a battle.

If "The Bridge on the River Kwai" were concerned only with the rival officers and the peculiar anatomy of courage, it would still be interesting. As a classic of adventure, its appeal is even wider. The escape of the American, his dismay at finding himself with British Commandos ordered to destroy the bridge, the party's adventures on the forced march through the jungle - all this is the best thing of its kind since "North-West Passage."

All Madness

The climax is chilling in its suspense. As the hidden Commandos watch the bridge and wait for a troop train before blowing it, a brilliant coup is threatened by two disasters, one natural, the other psychological.

When the smoke has cleared, and the screaming has died away the Commandos' sole survivor limps away into the jungle. A weary British doctor is left to survey the wreckage and the dead, and pass his own judgment on the heroism and wastefulness of war: "Madness ... madness!"

The acting is very fine. Alec Guinness brilliantly suggests the fanatical streak latent in many conventional men; William Holden makes the American, with his cynical humour and reluctant heroism, typical of Everyman; and Jack Hawkins is at his best as the Commando leader.

Sessue Hayakawa, once a silent star in Hollywood, is a memorable Saito, and there are good performances by James Donald, Andre Morell, Geoffrey Horne, Peter Williams and a number of others, including a bevy of pretty Siamese girls serving as porters. The backgrounds - the film was shot in Ceylon - are magnificent.

(October 5)

Recent Fiction

SMALL-TOWN LIFE

By Peter Green

When an American author lifts the lid off small-town life, the resultant stink tends to breed royalties as well as scandal. **"Peyton Place"** (Muller, 16s) is no exception. In it Grace Metalious gives America the domestic low-down on Northern New England, rather in the manner of John O'Hara, and presto, sales boomed overnight.

With a population of 3,675, Peyton Place, in a few brief years, can run to patricide, suicide, technical incest and compassionate abortion, besides such lesser failings as D.T.'s voyeurism, illegitimate children and psychotic malingering. A young New York novelist refers to the place as "that charming snake-pit," and it isn't hard to see why.

Yet the fact remains that Mrs. Metalious has written a big, powerful, humane book which manages to absorb its own sensationalism. Her cross-section extends from the old families on Chestnut Street to the slum-dwellers in their filthy tar-paper shacks. The pattern of inter-dependence between them, moral as well as social, is clearly drawn, and the crabbed local rhythm caught to a nicety.

The ingredients are familiar enough - golden-hearted doctor, scheming mill-owner, stubborn teacher, blonde widow, several nasty accidents, and adolescent crises by the dozen. But Mrs. Metalious has a stubborn intellectual honesty which drives her clear of emotional clichés: somehow or other she batters her way to the truth time and again in prose as tough and cussed and indefatigable as a team of mules.

(May 3)

★

It is fascinating to compare Mr. Glyn's murderously U world with that which John Braine depicts in **"Room at the Top"** (Eyre & Spottiswoode, 15s). Joe Lampton is the archetypal local boy on the climb. He is as sensitive as a Geiger counter to the social nuances of clothes, cars, incomes and accents.

Here, too, the money-virus spreads poisonously, warping love and corrupting honesty. Joe graduates from the Town Hall to a cushy business job by putting Susan Brown in the family way. Her rich father offers to set them up together on one condition: that he ditches his middle-aged mistress (the one really engaging character in the book). He does, and she promptly commits suicide.

Joe is a really loathsome character: lecherous, vain, touchy, grossly materialistic. Mr. Braine intermittently enlists our sympathy for him with a disarming show of honesty: Joe is an inverted Jack Horner who pulls out his plum and tells what a bad boy he is - but keeps the plum.

Life, as we know, often follows just such a pattern: but in the last resort is this camera-like amorality enough by itself? There is no doubt about Mr. Braine's skill as a writer: his scabrous portrait of provincial snobbery is superb: his vision of lust is authentic sergeants' mess. But the spiritual nullity he displays leaves a vast void at his novel's heart.

(March 22)

★

Keith Waterhouse's **"There is a Happy Land"** (Michael Joseph, 12s 6d) shows Joe Lampton's world, as it were, in embryo. It is a child's-eye-view of life on a North Country corporation estate: the author evokes a rich grimy atmosphere of slag-heaps, schoolboy myth, back-street slang and fish-and-chips.

Tender and piquant at first, the novel bogs down for a while in its all too realistic inarticulateness. But Mr. Waterhouse throws a kind of clear, aching nostalgia over his grubby innocents which carries him through. At present he recalls Julian Maclaren-Ross; but with luck and perseverance he might become an English J.D. Salinger.

(March 22)

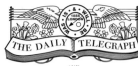

THE DAILY TELEGRAPH
AND
MORNING POST
DAILY TELEGRAPH - June 29, 1855
MORNING POST - November 2, 1772
[Amalgamated October 1, 1937.]
135, Fleet Street, London E.C.4.
Telephone: Central 4242.

S. AFRICA GOES IT ALONE

The "go it alone" is every sovereign nation's right, but there is a continually narrowing sphere in which it can be practicable or safe for any country. This is the harsh reality that confronts the South African Government as it pushes forward the policy of *apartheid*. The Government's juridical right to do so is indisputable. That is why the South African delegation walked out when the United Nations Assembly put this question on its agenda. That is why Britain has voted against its pretension to discuss the domestic affairs of a member nation. Nevertheless, the Assembly has, by a large majority, called on South Africa to "reconsider" the *apartheid* policy and to "co-operate in a constructive approach" to the racial question.

South Africa will, of course, ignore this interference, as she has done in the past. What she cannot indefinitely continue to ignore, save at her peril, is the increasing isolation into which she is being forced. The Afro-Asian-Communist entente is now strong enough to hale her repeatedly before the Assembly. Among other nations embarrassed abstention is likely to spread: and South Africa's loneliness will only be emphasised by the support she may still receive, on political or juridical grounds, from Powers with dependent territories on the continent. This would be regrettable at any time; it is profoundly disturbing at a moment when other events ought to be drawing South Africa closer to the free world.

The very sympathy between Communism and colour-conscious nationalism, which pillories her at the United Nations embodies a threat of economic, ideological and ultimately military penetration from the north. Egypt is the gateway to Africa, and Russia already has a foothold there. Manifestly, preparedness against such a threat must be conceived in terms of the defence of Africa as a whole, and that as a part of global defence. Yet the South African Government's domestic policies, however stoutly it may maintain that they are its own affair, must make it harder to form international partnerships for defence. The United States, because of the Negro vote, is bound to be inhibited from close association with a Government standing for *apartheid*.

The interdependence between Britain and South Africa is being newly demonstrated by the Union's active co-operation in re-routing shipping round the Cape, and will be illustrated again soon by the formal handing over of the Royal Navy base at Simonstown. The Commonwealth association is liberal enough to embrace another republic, if South Africa should choose to become one; and it can certainly survive such childish gestures as the banishing of the Union Jack, proposed by a private Bill which the South African Parliament debates today. What really strains the link between us is the feeling in this country that South Africa is in danger of compromising her own unity, morally as well as physically, by policies that set White against Black - and divide the Whites themselves through the attempts of the Afrikaaner Nationalists to whittle away the constitutional rights of the English-speaking citizens.

(February 1)

RATE REFORM

MR. BROOKE announced a major reform in local government finance yesterday. In the main it is wholly welcome. Instead of the present system by which local authority finance is supplemented from the national Treasury by grants of money tied to specific types of expenditure, the local authorities are to have block grants - fixed for several years at a time - which for the most part they will be free to spend as they like. These general grants, instead of comprising only one-sixth of the money paid to local authorities by the Treasury, are to rise to two-thirds. Local authorities, instead of being encouraged in extravagance as they are at the moment, will have a great incentive to economy: with a Treasury grant fixed over a number of years, any saving will accrue to the ratepayer.

In this general welcome for the Government's plans there must, however, be one reservation. The object is to increase the responsibility and therefore the status of local authorities by giving them greater control over their own expenditure. As a further step towards this the Government has decided to go some way towards restoring to the local authorities the rates which are withheld from them by the industrial derating of 1929: industry is to pay 50 per cent of its assessed rates instead of the present 25 per cent. There is very little actual money involved in this - probably not more than £15-20m. a year. But it must be emphasised that the object of doing this is purely to transfer revenue from the central Government to local government. There is no justification either in this itself, or in present circumstances, for increasing industrial taxation, as it were, on the side. Assurances should be sought from the Government, on the earliest possible occasion, that this is not its intention, and that when industrial re-rating takes effect an equal relief from national taxation will be forthcoming.

(February 13)

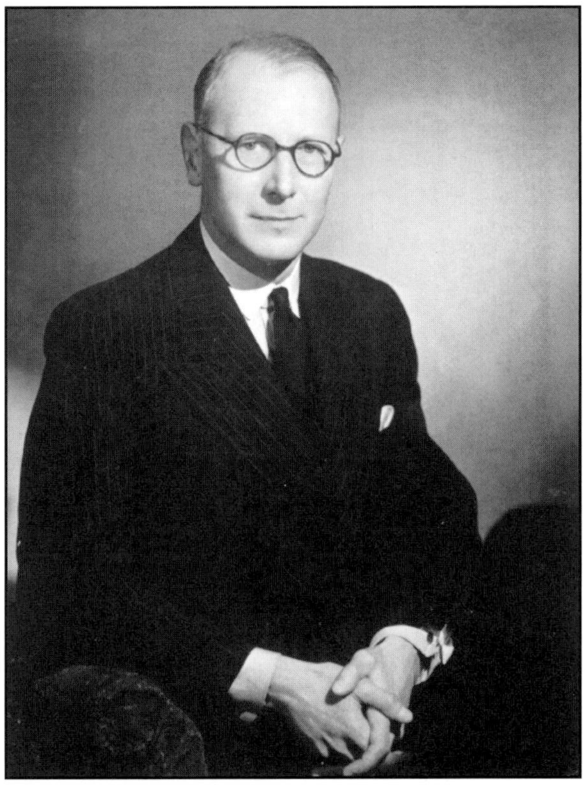

JOHN FREDERICK WOLFENDEN, CBE, MA. Vice-Chancellor of Reading University; Chairman Secondary Schools Examinations Council.

KEEPING VICE OFF STREETS

SIR J. WOLFENDEN EXPLAINS AIMS

Sir John Wolfenden, chairman of the Committee on Homosexual Offences and Prostitution, whose report was issued yesterday, said in a B.B.C. television interview last night: "We are concerned primarily with public order and not with private morality.

"We are not trying to abolish prostitution by law. We are saying that the purpose of the criminal law is to preserve public order and decency, to clean up the streets of London and the big towns.

"At present there are streets where, if I am walking with my 14 or 15-year-old daughter, I have to make a detour. We are trying to make it possible for ordinary men and women to go about the streets as they like."

EXAGGERATED TALK

The Committee had considered a suggestion of setting up licensed brothels but "turned it down flat." He added: "So far as our evidence went, we came to the conclusion that talk about organised vice has been exaggerated.

"There are men behind the women, but most of those associations are voluntary and are for mutual profit and, if you like, mutual support."

The recommendation that homosexuality between adult consenting males in private should be taken out of the criminal law would be a major change. We believe, rightly or wrongly, on the medical evidence we have had, that to permit adult males to behave in this way in private might itself be a protection of younger people."

Whatever happened to the recommendations, the committee's document was a contribution towards the ordinary person's understanding of complicated and rather difficult matters.

(September 5)

NO ACTION ON WOLFENDEN REPORT

The Lord Chancellor, Viscount Kilmuir, announced in the House of Lords this evening that the Government would not accept the Wolfenden Committee's recommendation to legalise homosexuality in private between consenting adults.

It did not believe, he said, that public opinion was with the Committee on this point. He stuck to this view although all five of the speeches he had heard before getting to his feet were on the side of the Committee.

(December 5)

GHANA'S FLAG FLIES IN PLACE OF UNION JACK

From R.H.C. Steed,
Daily Telegraph Commonwealth Affairs Correspondent

ACCRA, Wednesday.

The lowering of the Union Jack at midnight above the floodlit Parliament buildings here and its replacement by the flag of Ghana signified to jubilant crowds that a new, independent African nation had been born. This came as the climax to yesterday's anticipatory celebrations in which the participation of the Duchess of Kent, representing the Queen, symbolised Ghana's free entry into the Commonwealth.

While the crowds waited outside Parliament for the signal, Dr. Nkrumah, Prime Minister and "liberator," was making a policy speech. In this he stated the terms on which Ghana was entering the Commonwealth and emphasised her rights to be accepted as an equal in fact as well as in theory.

The Prime Minister announced the creation of Ministries of Foreign Affairs and Defence. He was assuming both posts himself in addition to that of Prime Minister.

The Government of Ghana has thus taken over the only two remaining powers which were entrusted to the British Governor under the previous régime.

Speaking in English, Dr. Nkrumah began with phrases that have been the staple of his political agitation over the past eight years.

"When the day dawns we shall have left behind us the chains of imperialism and colonialism which have hitherto bound us to Britain. By 12 o'clock midnight Ghana will have redeemed her lost freedom."

(March 6)

PUBLIC AND PRIVATE MORALITY

Sir John Wolfenden and his colleagues have taken three years to produce their Report on Homosexual Offences and Prostitution. This is by no means too long. There is only one thing to be said about the present system of laws prescribing penalties for various kinds of sexual misbehaviour, and that is that there is nothing systematic about it. It has grown up haphazardly and presents so many anomalies that reform is long overdue. Public opinion has for long held that in some respects these Statutes do not mete out an evenhanded justice, and that in others they are completely ineffective. Besides these questions of principle, there are others of fact. Between 1931 and 1955 the number of prosecutions for homosexual offences has risen from 390 to 2,504; those for prostitution offences from 1,303 to 11,916. It was quite time that the Government should take action, and the setting up of the WOLFENDEN Committee in August, 1954, was a necessary and satisfactory first step.

★

The Committee's findings, though necessarily controversial, are clear, conscientious and courageous. In particular, it has done a considerable service in its attempt to define the boundary between public and private morality. The Report states: "Unless a deliberate attempt is made by society, acting through the agency of the law, to equate the sphere of crime with that of sin, there must remain a realm of private morality and immorality which is, in brief and crude terms, not the law's business." These are useful and valid distinctions. In certain aspects of sexual morality, they are quite obvious. But it is far from easy to apply them where the social consequences of private acts are debatable.

★

This is the crux of the argument which will develop around the Committee's most controversial recommendation, that homosexual behaviour between consenting adults in private should no longer be a criminal offence. In reaching this conclusion, they have followed out a logical pattern. Their belief is that penalties should be retained for all forms of sexual conduct which involve assault, seduction of the young, or public indecency. They have taken great care to define, in this context, what would be meant by "adult," "consent," and "private." They have considered the present stringency of the law, the opportunities which it affords for blackmail, and the extraordinary divergence of police action. With one exception, they do not believe that the law as it stands is any real deterrent to homosexual behaviour. The exception, Mr. ADAIR, a former Procurator-Fiscal, has put the opposite case in his "reservation." Many will share his opinion that homosexuality in any form, if legalised, may spread like an infection. Medical opinion is divided, but to the lay mind it seems clear that the law should provide against the possibility.

★

On prostitution the Committee is agreed that the present system of 40s fines is absurd, though it admits that fining women off the streets may not fine them out of their profession. But some young girls might be prevented from entering a profession which now appears easy and lucrative - not least because of the exemption of its profits from income tax. Would this result in what might be described as a "MESSINA Brothers' Charter"? That would depend on whether it is possible to bring guilty landlords into the net of those deemed to be "living on the earnings of prostitution." Here the committee's logic seems to falter. It proposes that it should be an offence to let premises at exorbitant rents for the purposes of prostitution, but feels "that it would not be right to make the mere letting of premises to a prostitute an offence." Where is the line to be drawn?

★

Whatever doubts and hesitations may be expressed, the WOLFENDEN Committee has performed a singularly difficult task with dispassionate skill. These are not matters which should become subject to political passions - indeed, they are matters in which any kind of passion tends to darken counsel. As in the controversy on hanging, the Government of the day cannot abrogate its responsibility, and such a Report should at least give the Home Secretary material for a sensible Bill.

(September 5)

FILIGREE REPLACES THE CHUNKY LOOK ON JEWELLERY

Wonderful in design and value are the two gold mesh bracelets, each set with semi-precious stones, sketched below, while the third bracelet, in a delicate leaf design, is set with aquamarines and synthetic rubies. The brooch is in gold and studded with aquamarines.

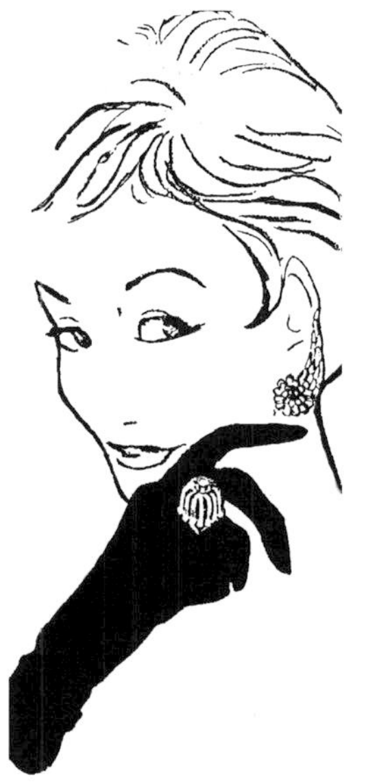

If you have always preferred real jewellery to costume jewellery, but winced at the price – well, here is your chance. Norman Hartnell has designed a lovely range of fine (9 carat) gold jewellery allied with semi-precious and synthetic-precious stones that will sell for the same price as good costume jewellery.

It is spectacular enough for anyone without being too extreme. Mr. Hartnell calls it "jewellery that will last."

He has introduced stones in wonderful modern colours like rose de France (a pale cyclamen) and African blue tourmaline (a gorgeous deep sea blue).

Out is the chunky look. Rings, clips, earrings and bracelets all have a decorative filigree quality. There is not a dangling earring among the lot; they all wing upwards following the line of the ear.

Prices range from £5 10s for a ring, to £30 for a glittering mesh bracelet, and the range will be in the London shops next month.

(September 19)

THE LONG SLIM LINE FROM PARIS

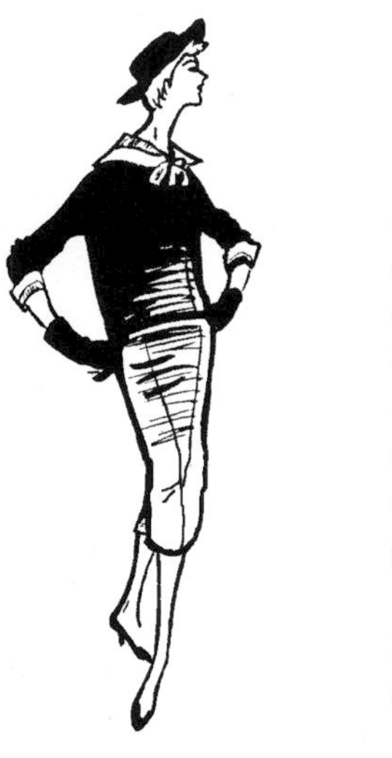

FROM the level of haute couture to the rails of ready-to-wear, the slim, easy-fitting line pervades Paris fashion. On the left, the black velvet tunic suit by Mme. Chanel has a casualness which should please the American market. The ensemble was admired last week by Juliette Greco, the young singer-actress.

(August 7)

THERE'S A CULINARY BATTLE RAGING IN BOLOGNA

NERINA V. CESARINA

Bologna, dominated by towers souring up against the deep blue sky, and where whole streets of medieval palaces slumber in the sun, is a centre of Italian gastronomy.

BERYL HARTAND made a detour on her way to Elba (this feature last week) and called on the city's two great women restaurateurs, whom she describes below.Among the ancient towers and terracotta buildings of Bologna a battle rages. It is a battle of pans and pastas; of sauces and secrets. On one side is large, motherly Signora Nerina, on the other large, volatile Signora Cesarina.

They are two of the top women cooks in Italy. Cooking is their whole life, and their restaurants are only a couple of streets apart.

(There are, of course, good men cooks in Bologna, too but to Nerina and Cesarina they just don't count.)

Keeping a jealous eye on each other, they both claim to serve the only real Bolognese food. Signora Nerina serves her tortellini (paper-thin squares of melting pasta stuffed with chicken and veal and twisted into a little coil around the tip of the finger) with her own special rich Bolognese sauce.

Signora Cesarina serves her tortellini tossed in a bubbling cream and cheese sauce of her own creation which has to be tasted to be believed.

The one thing they see eye-to-eye over is their opinion of men. Listen to what these two Queens of Cuisine say when I asked what they thought of men cooks.

Said Nerina: "Women are much better cooks than men. Men lack patience and easily become too self-satisfied, then their cooking deteriorates."

Flashed Cesarina: "I don't want men in my kitchen – they are not as clean as women."

Nerina, whose mother and grandmother both had a restaurant before her, has just moved into new, more sophisticated premises.

Cesarina prefers hers to stay small and personal, as it has for 30 years, where she serves food "that comes from the heart." I found her in a snowy apron with sleeves pushed up, hard at work at her great wooden board, deftly cutting tagliatelle into special widths for her regular customers: a shade of an inch narrower for the solicitor.

Her kitchen is small with not a scrap of plastic in sight. The tables and benches are of scrubbed wood.

Despite black brows and indomitable look, Cesarina mothers her customers as she bosses them, refuses to let smart Italian women diet, and completely spoils the men.

It is well worth a detour to Bologna to eat at either of these great restaurants and taste the mouth-watering specialities, cooked as they should be – tagliatelle with ham, lasagna verdi, tortellini and mortadella, not to mention the world-famous Bolognese sauce.

A "CHARMANTE GOURMETTE" IS MAKING HISTORY

Frances foremost connoisseur of food and wine dined with me on Sunday evening and my ideas of a gourmet were shattered. Insead of a portly avuncular gentleman I met a smart, good-lockng woman who conversed wittily and expertly about eating and drinking.

Madeleine Decure is making history in France. She is the first woman to be recognised as an authority in the masculine field of gastronomy and is tipped to succeed her late master, the fabulous Curnonsky, elected 'prince des gastronomes' 30 years ago by the great chefs of France.

"Britain is thought of in France as the country of mint sauce, heavy sweets, overcooked meat and excellent Scottish fish," she told me. "I wanted to come and find out the truth for myself."

I took her and her friends, also experts, to Curzon Street's show-piece oyster bar. Instantly charmed by the soft candlellight and mellow English oak, she kept to simple dishes "I mostly cook simply at home," she said. "and do not always order sauces in restaurants. They are not enjoyable unless absolutely faultless."

I am accustomed to the tourist's praise of succulent smoked salmon and grilled sole. But her admiration for grilled oysters with bacon warmed my heart and her enthusiasm for our everyday brown bread took me by surprise. "If only we had bread like this in Paris" she said. An eye-opener for our French-bread addicts.

But I was on the men's side when we discussed cooking and compared chefs with conductors of orchestras. "In grande cusine, I agree" she admitted " men may be masters of classical perfection, but they easily become its slaves. Women are less dogmatic about recipes and more receptive to new ideas." In fact it was her feminine curiosity about cooking in Britain that brought her here.

Gastronomic Map

Mlle. Decure presided over a dinner at Frunier's, organised by "Cuisine et Vins de France," a culinary magazine she runs in Paris. Fifty notable French and British gourmets had a meal which included sole grillée Milford Haven, Aylesbury duckling in oranges and curaçao. Cheddar soufflé and Irish coffee with cream and whisky ("I usually don't drink coffee, but adore tea without lemon or milk, just for its ownsake")

The occasion showed what French genius for cooking can do to our prime foods. Madeleine Decure's plan to make these gourmet dinners a regular monthly feature and to publish a regional gastromomic map of Britain is good news. Egon Ronay

(January 25)

GHANA COLOUR

WOMEN of Ghana who had taken to the westernised cotton dress have reverted to their traditional "kenti" as a mark of their national feelings at being given Independence, writes our special correspondent. It is a garment of three pieces - skirt, blouse and voluminous overwrap which goes high round the waist. It is handy, too, for carrying a baby slung in the small of its mother's back.

A number of men have also taken to national dress. Some look very handsome in a single piece of brilliantly coloured fabric wrapped round to leave one arm and one shoulder bare.

Wealthy Africans sometimes pay more than £100 for their gorgeously patterned fabrics.

(March 5)

'ENOUGH FOR 10 DAYS IN NEW YORK'

From Our Own Correspondent

NEW YORK, Tuesday.

To-day's announcement of a dollar allowance for British tourists is welcomed here not only as a step towards closer Anglo-American understanding, but also as a possible forerunner of greater relaxations in the rigid currency regulations imposed on sterling for so long.

The allowance was not altogether unexpected, because of recent reports of agitation in several quarters in London. But Britons should not think that free-spending holidays in America are now in store.

An allowance of $280 (£100) is just about enough to cover a comfortable stay of 10 days in New York City, with no extras such as travel, the purchase of gifts or more than a couple of visits to the theatre.

Visitors' needs and standards vary immensely, but the following figures will give an idea of the range of outlays to be expected in New York:

Hotel rooms: from $6 (about £2 2s) to $12 (£4 4s) a day; one day's meals from $5 (£1 16s) to $15 (£5 8s); theatre ticket from $1.50 (10s 9d) to $8 (£2 17s); cinema seats from 75 cents (6s) to $2.50 (18s); man's haircut from 75 cents (6s) to $2 (14s 4d); woman's hair wash and set from $3 (£1 1s) to $8 (£2 17d).

TIPPING EXPENSIVE

Visitors will find that tipping is an expensive part of their budget. The minimum reward for a minor service is 25 cents (1s 9d) and the tip on a restaurant bill ranges from 12 to 20 cents, according to circumstances.

Persons of extremely frugal tastes will be able to cut down considerably on many items. Anybody who is prepared to take quarters in one of the least fashionable neighbourhoods of the city will be able to find a room for about $20 (£7) a week.

(June 5)

OFF-SEASON BY SEA

By Our Shipping Correspondent

For the new British dollar tourists to America, the cheapest sea fare to New York is £129 return in the summer months and £114 off-season. To Montreal it is £136 return in the summer and £125 return in the winter.

(June 5)

IF YOU ARE BUILDING: OUTLOOK FOR THE 1957 HOME

ALICE HOPE VISITS A BRITISH STANDARDS HOUSE

The odds are fairly even between one big living room and a sitting room plus dining-room in this year's new houses. But there is one feature to which the Englishman and his wife cling through thick and thin - the coal fire.

To use gas or electricity instead would save pounds on the building cost, as well as giving extra floor space. "But they all want it and I don't blame them," says Mr. Ellis Berg, the man who is putting up thousands of moderately priced homes in the southern counties. Mr. Berg himself lives in a century-old country house.

One of his bungalows, which I visited near Portsmouth, has been equipped as the first British Standards home in the country. Drainpipes, guttering, plumbing, sanitary fittings, the cold-water storage system, electric wiring, door and window furniture, even the screws, all conform to the standard of efficiency laid down by the British Standards Institution. So does the furniture, refrigerator, linoleum, bedding and fire-guard.

Shoppers who want to make sure of their rights to well-made merchandise will soon be able to join a section of the Institution. For a subscription of 10s a year they will be supplied with free advice and free information on new standards.

(January 23)

20m PHONES ARE PLANNED

NATIONAL DIALLING

Daily Telegraph Reporter

The Post Office is planning for 20 million telephone subscribers, linked to 8,000 exchanges, with automatic trunk dialing. This dialling will start in Bristol in 1959, and the equipment will do the "thinking" required to route calls.

A new national telephone numbering scheme will be needed because of nation-wide dialling. Electronic exchanges, cheaper to house and maintain, will ultimately replace the present mechanical equipment.

(May 17)

LONDON DAY BY DAY

As odd as the virulence of the official Russian statement on Marshal Zhukov's disgrace is its timing.

Moscow does not, of course, explain why the Central Committee delayed the announcement of its decision. Yesterday's news of the second sputnik, though a useful diversion, is probably a mere coincidence.

A more likely link is with Mao Tse-tung, the Communist leader of China. He declared his intention to visit Moscow on the day Zhukov's dismissal from the Defence Ministry was briefly disclosed by Tass, the Russian news agency.

Mao's statement seems to have been as diplomatic as the lumbago which has prevented Marshal Tito from going to attend the Revolution anniversary.

The full attack on Zhukov came a few hours after Mao's arrival. In view of his known opposition to a revival of Stalinism, B. and K. may have thought it politic to have a prior word with him.

This theory is supported by the recent absence from public life of Mao's No. 2, Liu Shao-chi, a leading theorist of Chinese Communism.

He did not attend Mao's banquet for the Afghan Premier last week. Nor was he seen at other party occasions where normally his presence would be de rigueur.

But he was back in Peking to see Mao off. He is believed to have been to Moscow in advance of his master to discuss the new upheaval.

White Lines & Cat's Eyes

It is odd that the origin of white lines should be lost in the mists of the early 1920s. The A.A. can only state with confidence that it was then concerned with a proposal to paint white lines on certain Brighton roads.

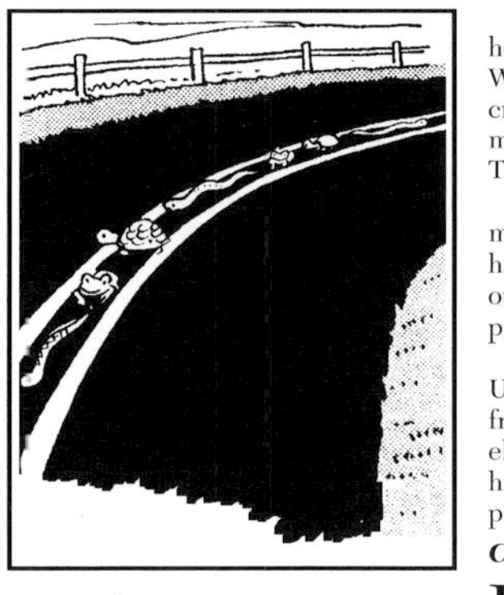

The Chief Constable was agreeable and the A.A. (then a relatively poor organisation) offered to defray the cost.

It seems well enough established that the development of double white lines began in France. Neither is there any doubt about the originator of cat's eyes, which in many ways are a greater boon to drivers. A certain Percy Shaw, who lived in the North of England, got the idea from tramlines. He found these helpful as pointers in foggy weather.

In 1933 the A.A. used its influence to promote Mr. Shaw's scheme.

Dexter's Dilemma

CAMBRIDGE's golf captain, E.R. Dexter, is among the 26 amateurs short-listed by the R. and A. yesterday for higher selection.

This will not make any easier the decision which I believe Dexter has decided to take at once on his own future. He has to resolve whether to concentrate on reaching the top flight of cricket or golf.

The R. and A's announcement means he is in the running for a place in the Walker Cup side. Last summer his cricket got him a place in two Gentlemen's sides and a summons to the Leeds Test. Injury caused him to refuse.

Both sports therefore offer him their most glittering prizes, but he cannot have both. Cricket and golf, unlike other games, are not seasonally complementary.

No other undergraduate at either University since the war has been confronted by the same dilemma. If Dexter elects cricket it can be made possible for him financially for a year or so. My own prediction is that he will plump for golf.

Christ Church Lobby -

LORD ADRIAN, Master of Trinity, is the only Cambridge man among the score of peers who have so far decided to speak in to-day's Lords debate on the Oxford road plan.

Perhaps he will draw their attention to the lesser but growing menace of traffic to the comparative calm of his own university.

Christ Church, which will suffer most of all Oxford colleges should the relief road bisect the Meadow, can muster a formidable lobby.

Lords Birkenhead, Conesford and Salisbury were undergraduates there. Lords Pakenham and Cherwell are Students, as the House calls its Fellows. All intend to speak.

The Duke's Sacrifice

During his recent State visit to Portugal with the Queen, the Duke of Edinburgh was given a pipe - 56 dozen bottles - of 1955 vintage port.

He has now decided to present it to the National Playing Fields Association to be auctioned. Mr. L.E. de Rouet, chairman of the Port Wine Trade Association, tells me that they will gladly bottle it and arrange for the sale.

Its market price is about 25s a bottle. Its origin, however, and the cause to which the proceeds will be devoted should ensure a total of more than £1,000.

Another source of revenue for the N.P.F.A. of which I have heard recently is a hat-trick tie made by Cassells, the Oxford tailors.

The Chinese were warned
Dexter has the choice

Sitter for Annigoni

Next to sit for Annigoni will be Tina Onassis, wife of the well-known Greek shipowner.

Mrs. Onassis first met Annigoni about a year ago when he painted her mother. He was impressed by her beauty and personality and agreed there and then to her request for a portrait.

Annigoni, I gather, always makes a point of seeing prospective clients before accepting a commission.

There is no actual waiting list of sitters but a few people have been waiting over a year, which means that this news about Mrs Onassis may well cause them to be piqued.

Now that Annigoni has decided not to return to England permanently, but "only from time to time," she will sit for him at his Florence studio in the near future.

Where to Die

The North Borneo News reports that "one of the most attractive features of Jesselton's new hospital is undoubtedly the mortuary, which is designed to resemble a very comfortable cottage." From a Board of Trade report.

PETERBOROUGH

Obituary

HUMPHREY BOGART

ONE OF SCREEN'S CHIEF 'TOUGH GUYS'

Humphrey DeForest Bogart, one of Hollywood's foremost screen "tough guys," died at his home in California yesterday from cancer. He was 56, and had been one of the screen colony's most popular and highly-paid stars for 20 years.

He starred in over 50 films and in 1951 was awarded an Oscar as best actor of the year for his part in "The African Queen." In this he played a dissolute river-boat captain whose brand of courage was entirely alien to the gangster type.

In 1935 Humphrey Bogart's feet were set on the ladder of success by Arthur Hopkins, who picked him for the tough, unemotional gangster role in the film version of "The Petrified Forest." Playing with him were Bette Davis and the late Leslie Howard. Humphrey Bogart had taken the part in the Broadway play.

Before this "Bogie," as he preferred to be called, had given up hope of becoming a screen-leading man. A slight lisp, the result of his lip being pierced by a splinter when he was in the United States Navy, was considered too great a handicap.

LISP AN ADVANTAGE

Later, as every cinema-goer knows, he turned that slight lisp, and the habit of pulling his lip back from his teeth in a blood-curdling snarl, to good effect. His most recent film was "The Harder They Fall," a boxing exposé.

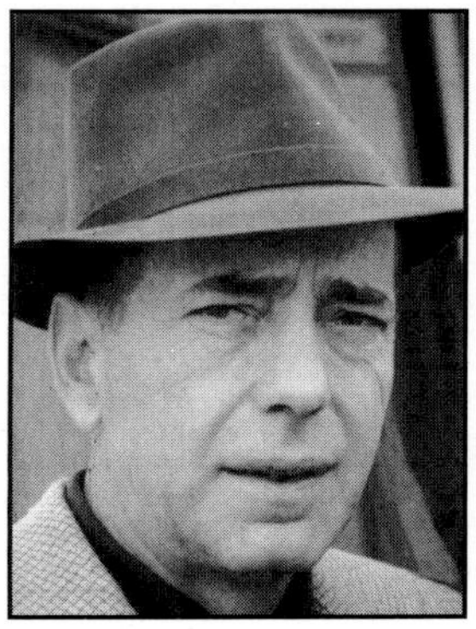

HUMPHREY BOGART

Others included "Casablanca," "The Desperate Hours", "We're No Angels," "The Barefoot Contessa," "The Left Hand of God," and "The Caine Mutiny". His fourth wife, Lauren Bacall, who survives him, played with him in Hemingway's "To Have and Have Not" and Chandler's "The Big Sleep."

They have two sons, Stephen, eight, and Leslie, four. Humphrey Bogart, who was the son of a New York doctor, had been inactive since a serious throat operation for cancer last March.

Though most people knew he was desperately ill he maintained his characteristically hard-bitten humour to the end. "Reports of my death are exaggerated," he said to questioning reporters.

He was particularly irate when a woman columnist said he had suffered a relapse and been removed to the eighth floor of the Los Angeles Memorial Hospital. "The fact that there is no such hospital did not bother me, but that eighth floor got me," he remarked.

NOT VERSATILE

CAMPBELL DIXON writes: Humphrey Bogart was not a versatile actor, but then, few of the biggest stars are. Their asset is personality.

The ravaged face, bitter brooding eyes and rasping voice, all the things that disqualified Bogart as a stock actor, made a tremendous impact in the right role. His deadpan face and lethal monotone were just what the public expected of a gunman, and having hit their fancy, he went on giving the same performance for 20 years.

Occasionally he did experiment, notably in John Huston's "The African Queen." His river-boat captain, which won him an Oscar, was toughly comic instead of just tough.

In private life Mr. Bogart took pride in unconventionality, was apt to be quarrelsome, and became involved in a series of nightclub and other brawls. One thing he never lacked was courage, especially in his long fatal illness, and the screen will be the drabber for his death.

(January 16)

SENATOR McCARTHY

WITCH-HUNT LEADER

Senator McCarthy, who has died aged 47, earned obloquy for five years as America's most implacable political witch-hunter. His name became synonymous with a form of interrogation which viciously resuscitated the victim's early discarded beliefs, and smoothly blanketed evidence of loyalty and integrity.

His malignant activities began in 1950. In that year he delivered his first broadside against the Truman administration, declaring it was riddled with Communists. Dean Acheson, then Secretary of State, was a particular target for his fulminations: to Mr. Acheson, he affixed the label "Red Dean."

To his supporters McCarthy appeared as "the greatest patriot since George Washington." There were early signs, however, that his methods, if not his objectives, were increasingly distasteful to a large section of the American public. It was widely appreciated that his "smear" tactics tainted the reputations of many innocent people.

Personal ambition played no small part in McCarthy's plans. He saw himself as the leader of the Republican Right wing, an eventual leader of the party, who would be hailed as a national hero, a Wisconsin St. George who had slain the dragon of Communism. But America sickened of the McCarthy technique, the hounding and branding which savoured too much of totalitarian methods.

Criticism of his methods as chairman of the Senate Investigation Sub-Committee came to a head in 1954, when a Senatorial Committee, after stormy scenes, rendered an adverse report on McCarthy. As a result, after a lengthy debate, remarkable for heated exchanges, the Senate condemned him for contempt and abuse, and for his defiant attitude.

PRESIDENT ATTACKED

Omitted from Invitations

A year later, in consequence of the Democratic victories in the elections for Congress, McCarthy relinquished his chairmanship of the sub-committee, and subsequently his power declined. He made several vituperative attacks on Mr. Eisenhower, who retaliated by deliberately omitting his name from invitations to White House receptions for members of Congress.

Joseph R. McCarthy had been a centre of acid controversy for a great deal of his political life. Born in Wisconsin, which State he was later to represent in the Senate, he was one of seven children. At 16 he left school to work on his father's farm, and three years later he went to work in a country store.

At 21 he entered high school, and finished a four-year course in a year by studying 16 subjects simultaneously. Later he studied engineering and law at Marquette University, and in the last war joined the Marines, went to the Pacific and, although an intelligence officer, insisted on serving as a tail-gunner on air bombing missions.

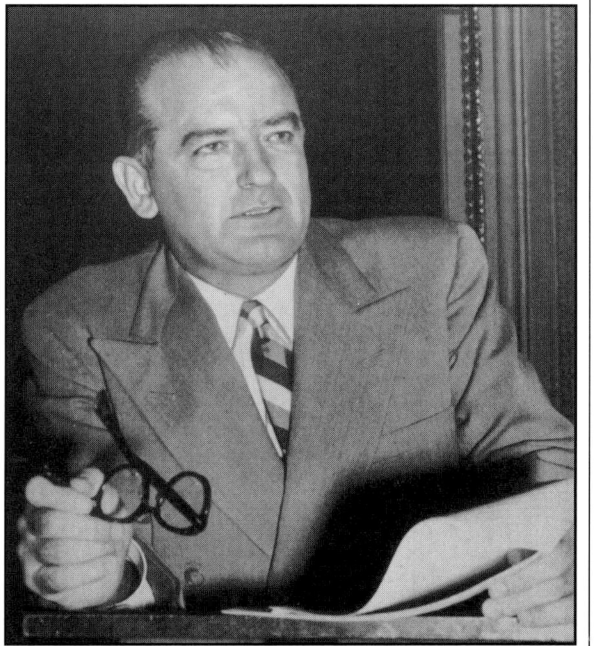

SENATOR JOSEPH McCARTHY

In 1946 he challenged the well-established Senator M. La Follette in a senatorial campaign as a Republican and won a surprising and easy victory. A judge at that time, he was subsequently rebuked by the State Supreme Court for not relinquishing office while conducting his campaign. He was also involved in income-tax disputes.

A payment he accepted for writing an article on housing for an advertising booklet was investigated by a Senate subcommittee. The firm who made the payment had subsequently gone bankrupt, owing the Government many millions of dollars. Senator McCarthy claimed that it was ethical for him to accept the payment as the firm was in a sound condition at the time he wrote the article.

ALGER HISS CASE

Anti-Communist Drive

Early in 1950 a federal court jury in New York convicted Alger Hiss, a former State Department official, of perjury: this verdict branded him in effect as a betrayer of State secrets to the Communists. Hiss was sentenced to five years' imprisonment, and the case provided McCarthy with the springboard for his anti-Communist campaign.

He promptly accused American diplomats of "selling out" China, Poland and other countries to Communism. A Senate sub-committee investigated the charges and denounced them as "perhaps the most nefarious campaign of half-truths and untruths in the history of this Republic."

McCarthy continued his accusations undaunted. He went so far, in the course of a speech in the Senate, as to link Gen. George Marshall, former Army Chief of Staff and author of the Marshall Plan, with what he described as a "conspiracy" aimed at weakening the United States and strengthening Russia. He subsequently published the speech in book form.

As chairman of the Senate Investigating Sub-Committee, Senator McCarthy employed methods considered by many inquisitorial; he became notorious for hectoring cross-examination and damaging innuendo. His activities reached a climax in his dispute with Service chiefs.

An Army dentist who was promoted and given an honourable discharge after displaying leftish tendencies led McCarthy to declare that the Army was "coddling" Communists. He summoned Gen. Zwicker, the dentist's Commanding Officer, told him he should be "removed from the Service," was "unfit to wear that uniform," and "lacked the brains of a five-year-old child." Mr. Stevens, Secretary of the Army at that time, angrily intervened and declared he would not permit loyal officers to be subjected to such treatment.

REBUFFED BY ARMY

Mr. Cohn and Pte. Schine

Senator McCarthy suffered a setback when an Army report was published that strongly suggested that his chief counsel, Mr. Cohn, was trying to secure preferential treatment in the Army for Pte. Schine, Mr. Cohn's former fellow-investigator.

In June 1955, McCarthy was severely rebuffed in the Senate. His motion that the United States should refuse to attend "summit" conferences with Russia was overwhelmingly defeated. This was the final blow to his ambitions; thereafter his activities were confined mostly to waspish ovations.

(May 3)

LORD CHERWELL

WAR-TIME ADVISER TO SIR WINSTON

The immense scientific knowledge of Viscount Cherwell, who had died aged 71, was twice enlisted in the nation's cause by Sir Winston Churchill.

Even before the war, when Sir Winston was in the wilderness, the two men had dourly co-operated. When Sir Winston became Prime Minister he appointed Professor Lindemann (as Lord Cherwell then was) his personal scientific adviser. The result was a notable contribution to Allied victory.

In October, 1951, Sir Winston charged him with the supervision of atomic energy research and production. From 1942-45 Lord Cherwell was Paymaster-General, a post to which he was again appointed in 1951. On the second occasion he declined to accept any salary.

He resigned his office as Paymaster-General in November, 1953, but assured Sir Winston Churchill that his services on scientific matters would always be at the disposal of the Prime Minister. In his letter accepting Lord Cherwell's resignation, Sir Winston praised the "wisdom of your counsel and the unstinted hard work you have contributed to our labours."

MEMOIRS TRIBUTE

Brilliant Team Work

To his ingenuity during the 1939-45 war Sir Winston has paid warm tribute in his memoirs. They had been friends since the 1914-18 war, in which, as an experimental pilot at the R.A.F. Farnborough station, Lindemann had deliberately plunged his machine into a spinning dive to prove a theory.

Their association between 1940 and 1945 was, in Sir Winston's words, "pleasant and fertile." Under Lord Cherwell's direction several brilliant teams worked on the problems presented by the new type of scientific warfare.

WARTIME PROJECTS

The Balloon Barrage

Under Lord Cherwell's broad direction a number of projects were started and brought to fruition that were to have considerable influence on subsequent operations.

Among these were the balloon barrage, counter measures to the German magnetic mine, the use of "window", that is aluminium foil strips, to baffle enemy anti-aircraft instruments, various scienfic aids to bombing, together with a method of confusing the navigational aids of enemy bombers over Britain.

He was only too glad of the opportunity to return to Oxford after the war ended. He took a great joy and pride in the introduction of new apparatus that would stimulate new lines of research and help to win from the Cavendish Laboratory in Cambridge some of the prestige that had been gained in the "Golden age" of nuclear physics in the thirties under figures like Lord Rutherford.

RETIRED LAST YEAR

Nicknamed "The Prof"

Born at Sidmouth, Lindemann was educated on the Continent. He took his PhD at Berlin University in 1911, and after studying radio-activity in Paris he became a lecturer at Chicago University.

He was Professor of Experimental Philosophy at Oxford from 1919 until 1956 when he retired. The nickname, "The Prof.", which he acquired there, clung to him throughout his life. In 1919 he was elected a Fellow of Wadham College and in 1921 became a Student of Christ Church.

In Nov., 1956, he was elected to an Honorary Fellowship at Wadham College.

In 1937, angered by Britain's lack of preparedness in the air, he unsuccessfully contested a by-election at Oxford University as an Independent Conservative.

Lord Cherwell was a bachelor. There is no heir to the Viscountcy.

GREAT INFLUENCE

Power to Guide Others

OUR SCIENCE CORRESPONDENT writes: A professor's position in a university, and the influence that he has on his own laboratory, normally depends on his achievements in his chosen field and on his power to guide others and inspire them to great work.

In Lord Cherwell's case the picture was complicated by his well-known friendship with Sir Winston Churchill.

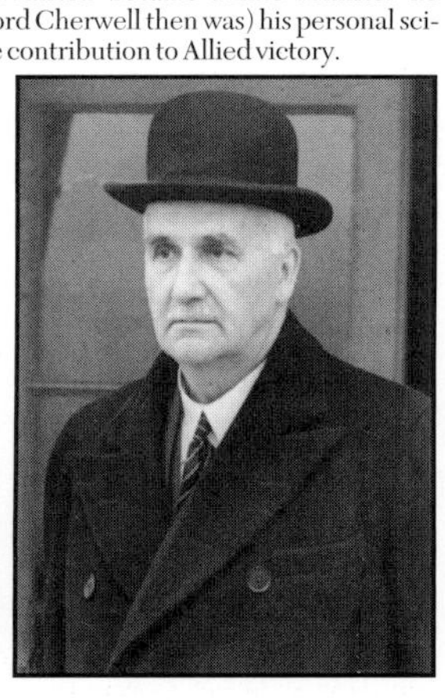

VISCOUNT CHERWELL, wartime scientific adviser to Sir Winston Churchill, who died at Oxford yesterday.

The aura that surrounded him was accentuated by his own shyness. Nevertheless, with people he knew and liked, both scientists and laymen, he was only too glad to expound freely.

The Clarendon Laboratory had many novel pieces of apparatus. Nothing seemed to give him greater pleasure than to take a layman round and explain the most complex experiments in simple language. It was this ability to reduce matters to first principles, both for the purposes of explanation and also for analysis, that no doubt endeared him to lay politicians with whom he had to deal.

Coupled with this was the fact that he often gave to people the feeling that they knew far more than they really did. He would go farther and seek their opinions on matters beyond their competence.

Nevertheless, Lord Cherwell, like everybody else, had his "blind spots." One of these led him to underestimate the work that had been done in the first few years by the Ministry of Supply in laying the foundations of our atomic energy project.

When he finally visited the plutonium factory at Windscale, in Cumberland, the progress that had been made surprised him.

(July 4)

ERIC COATES

MUSIC INSPIRED BY LONDON

Eric Coates, who has died aged 71, was one of the most popular British composers of light orchestral music.

Although he was born in Hucknall, Notts, much of his best creative work was inspired by London. From his "London Suite," written in 1933, the B.B.C. took the "Knightsbridge March" to act as part of the introduction to "In Town To-night." Mr. Coates also wrote the "Television March."

The son of a surgeon, he won a scholarship to the Royal Academy of Music in 1906, and for a time played the viola in a theatre orchestra for 15s a week. Subsequently he became principal viola player with the Queen's Hall Orchestra under the late Sir Henry Wood.

COMPOSED ON HORSE-BUS

He wrote his first best-seller, "Stonecracker John," in the course of a journey on top of a London horse-bus. One of his most delightful and widely known earlier suites was the "Miniature" Suite.

Among the most popular of his later works were "Sleepy Lagoon," "Calling All Workers" - the signature tune of the radio feature "Music While You Work" - "The Three Bears" and "Cinderella."

His autobiography, "Suite in Four Movements" (1953), is a delightful book full of amusing, well-told stories of musical life.

Mr. Coates married Miss Phyllis Black in 1913. She survives him, with a son.

(December 23)

ADML. BYRD DIES AGED 68

FIRST POLAR FLIGHTS

BOSTON, Mass.

Rear-Adml. Richard E. Byrd, first man to fly over both the North and South poles, died to-day. He was 68.

A pioneer explorer, he was named overall head of the United States Navy's operation "deep freeze" in Antarctica last year, but he had been ailing with a heart condition for several months. This prevented his assuming on-the-spot supervision of the expedition.

In 1926 he made an exploration flight over the North Pole. The following year he flew across the Atlantic with two other airmen, and in 1928 he flew over the South Pole for the first time.

He organised an expedition of ships and aircraft which left for its base on the ice at Little America, Antarctica, in the autumn of 1933, to map out the district and claim any uncharted lands for the United States. His departure was marked by a special issue of American stamps.

A series of mishaps culminated with Adml. Byrd crashing in a plane. He nearly died when he insisted on being left alone in a small hut near the Pole to make meteorological studies.- Reuter.

(March 12)

BENIAMINO GIGLI

SUPREME TENOR SINCE CARUSO

Beniamino Gigli, who has died aged 67, was widely regarded as the supreme tenor since Caruso. At the height of his career his income was reputed to be £50,000 a year.

In recent years, if his voice had lost some of its former remarkable range and power, he concealed the fact by his artistry. Few singers could attract audiences as large, or more enthusiastic, in England and on the Continent.

The son of a village shoemaker, he was born at Recanati, Italy, in 1890. As a child he sang in the village church choir, and to pay for his studies in Rome he worked as a chemist's assistant. He made his stage debut at Roviga, near Venice, in 1914, and then served for four years in the Italian Army.

His 12-year association with the Metropolitan Opera House, New York, which was to establish his world fame, began in 1920. He made his first appearance at Covent Garden in 1930 and sang in England for the last time in 1955.

He married Costanza Cerroni-Gigli, they had a son and a daughter.

MARTIN COOPER writes: Gigli was an inspired "natural" among singers who often silenced criticism of his defective style by the sheer beauty of his voice and the ease of his production.

One of the causes of his great popularity lay in the fact of his sharing the musical tastes of his most unsophisticated audiences. He made very little attempt to act a part on the stage and had, for an Italian, extraordinarily little natural dramatic ability.

But he had the gift of identifying himself with the lyrical characters who simply exist in and for their music, Cavaradossi, Pinkerton, Rodolfo or des Grieux. The naturalness and simplicity of his character, which might be guessed from his singing, found expression in his delightful autobiography.

Universally quoted as Caruso's successor, he himself leaves none able to command universal admiration in the great roles of the Italian repertory and, without any condescension, to fill the Albert Hall on a Sunday evening with a programme in which the inevitable "Mamma" would bring tears to all Italian and many English eyes by the sincerity of his pathos.

(December 2)

TOSCANINI

A CONDUCTOR OF ARDENT FIDELITY

Arturo Toscanini, who has died aged 89, was the greatest conductor of his generation. His name was familiar to millions with but a scant knowledge of music, and to most experts his interpretations were incomparable in their ardent, compelling fidelity.

He was born at Parma, Italy, in 1867, the son of a tailor who had fought for Garibaldi and remained a diehard Radical. Young Toscanini studied at the local conservatoire. He did not impress his instructors. Turning to orchestral playing, he became a 'cellist in an opera company.

In Rio de Janeiro, at the age of 19, he made his debut as a conductor. At a performance of "Aida" two conductors in succession were hissed by the audience. Eventually Toscanini, urged on by his colleagues, went to the desk. He conducted the opera from memory. At the end he received an ovation.

MATURED RAPIDLY

It was the first of a series which was to last a lifetime. Returning to Italy, he was appointed conductor at the Carignano Theatre. His powers matured rapidly, and many similar engagements followed.

Toscanini's work in Italy will always be associated with la Scala, Milan, where he was appointed conductor in 1898. Later he became musical director. In 1908 he was engaged by Gatti-Casazza at the Metropolitan Opera House, New York. He resigned in 1915, and after the 1914-18 war returned to La Scala as musical director.

In 1926 Toscanini first appeared as a guest conductor of the New York Philharmonic Orchestra. Two years later he became chief conductor of the newly formed Philharmonic-Symphony. From 1933 to 1936 he was musical director. By that time the world was his audience.

His first London appearance was in 1930, during a European tour with the Philharmonic-Symphony. He returned in 1935 and again in 1937, 1938, 1939 and 1952.

In 1930 and 1931 he conducted at the Wagner Festival in Bayreuth, being the first non-German to do so. But the Nazis' persecution of Jewish musicians incensed him, and in 1933 he refused to reappear.

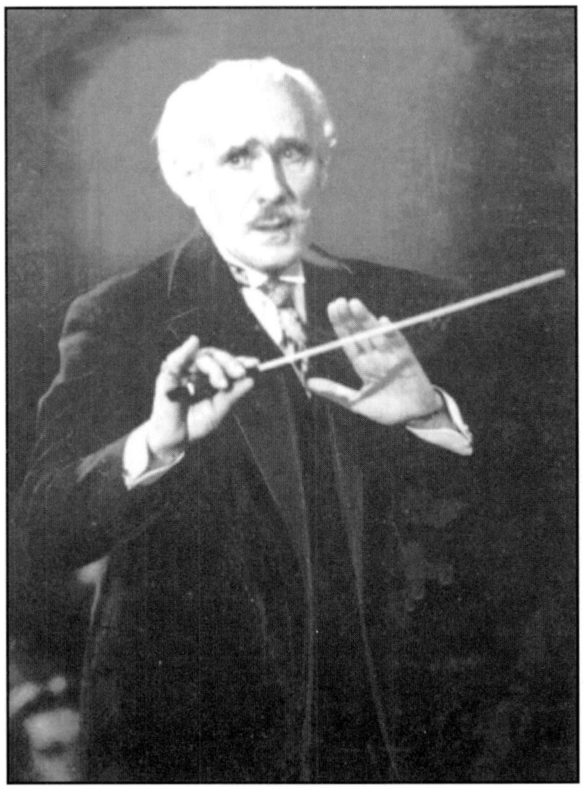

ARTURO TOSCANINI

CONTEMPT OF DICTATORS

Toscanini was too outspoken and fearless to conceal his contempt for dictators. Inevitably he clashed with the Fascists in Italy. Matters came to a head in 1938 when he refused to play the Blackshirts' anthem, "Giovanezza," on what he regarded as an unsuitable occasion.

He was publicly assaulted. From then on he lived mainly in the United States, where the National Broadcasting Company Symphony Orchestra had been specially created for him.

With the fall of Mussolini came insistent requests for Toscanini's return to Italy. At length he consented. On May 11, 1946, he was back at La Scala, inaugurating the restored theatre and triumphantly reviving its old glories.

London and Paris might have heard him again in the following month. But politics had not ceased to strike discords in his mind. The Council of Foreign Ministers awarded two Italian towns to France. Toscanini promptly cancelled his tour. He returned to New York and to his work with the N.B.C. orchestra.

LONDON OVATION

In 1949 he was nominated a Life Senator of the Italian Parliament in recognition of his achievements in music. In 1952 he was accorded an ovation when he gave two concerts in London - his first visit to Britain for 14 years.

He gave his last concert in April, 1954, conducting the N.B.C. Symphony Orchestra in New York, on the day his resignation was announced. He then returned to Italy, and the orchestra was disbanded.

His farewell operatic performance was at Carnegie Hall last January, when he conducted the last two acts of Verdi's "Masked Ball."

His wife, formerly Miss Carla De Martini, died in 1951. A son and two daughters survive.

(January 17)

DIOR A GREAT ARTIST OF FASHION

From Winefride Jackson
PARIS, Thursday.

At the moment it is almost impossible for me to think of future Paris dress collections without that benign figure of Christian Dior, who died early today in Italy, coming forth at the finale to receive the applause and embraces of the world's fashion writers.

This scene was never a set stage piece. It was a genuine appreciation of a great artist and to many the repeated triumph of a friend.

UNCANNY INSTINCT

Christian Dior had an uncanny instinct in timing the arrival of a new silhouette. Even though women at first said they would never wear the new line, whether the new look, the silhouettes that went through the alphabet, or his last creation which has become known as the sack, he knew that eventually they would come to it. They did, and they are now doing so with his new line.

Just now his compatriot designers are stunned with "this catastrophe to France."

No matter how badgered he was with calls upon his time for personal appearances or interviews, he gave of his best. His personal preference would have been for a quiet life among personal friends.

He had a great love of England and a tremendous admiration for the Queen and the Royal Family.

Much as one may dislike repeating personal remarks or compliments, I was very proud when one of his senior staff said to me to-day: "You know, M. Dior had a great regard for you. You were one of his friends he enjoyed meeting."

(October 25)

MISS DOROTHY SAYERS

CREATOR OF LORD PETER WIMSEY

Although Miss Dorothy Leigh Sayers, the author who has died aged 64, was most widely known as one of the handful of the most successful detective fiction writers, she wrote with equal fluency on theological matters, and also had completed a translation of Dante's "Divine Comedy."

Lord Peter Wimsey, the monocled detective whose insouciance was a trap for unwary criminals, was her most popular creation. She had written no novels for several years because of the income-tax liabilities they would have entailed.

Daughter of a minister, and a brilliant Somerville graduate, she taught modern languages at a Hull school for a time after leaving Oxford. Her first published work, several years before she turned to fiction, was a book of religious verse.

"Whose Body?" in which Wimsey made his bow, appeared in 1923 and made an immediate impression as the product of a thriller-writer with "class." With, among others, "Lord Peter Views the Body," 1928, "Five Red Herrings," 1931, and "The Nine Tailors," 1934, for which she undertook a course on bell-ringing, she firmly established herself as a notability, and sales of her books soared.

REMARKABLE DRAMA

"Busman's Honeymoon" in 1936 (in collaboration with M. St. Clare Byrne) was Miss Sayers's first appearance as dramatist. It was a play in which Wimsey featured. She demonstrated her adaptability in 1937 by writing for the Canterbury Festival "The Zeal of Thy House," a remarkable drama based on the life of the architect of Canterbury Cathedral.

"The Devil to Pay" was presented at Canterbury two years later and displayed imagination and intellectual power of a high order. Her series of radio plays, "The Man Born to be King," created in 1941 a controversy which raged for several months and was at its most intense in the correspondence columns of THE DAILY TELEGRAPH.

By putting words into the mouth of Christ other than those found in the Authorised Version, her critics claimed that she was guilty of blasphemy. Questions were asked in Parliament, and the B.B.C. Religious Advisory Committee was asked to reconsider the matter. But the committee, after carefully weighing the views of the objectors, decided unanimously in favour of the plays.

IRONIC THANKS

In a foreword to the book of the plays Miss Sayers ironically thanked the Lord's Day Observance Society and the Protestant Truth Society for their publicity work.

She married Capt. Atherton Fleming in 1926. He died in 1950.

GENIAL HUMANITY

Lord Peter's Magic

H.C. BAILEY writes: One of the most accomplished writers of the detective story has been lost by the death of Miss Dorothy L. Sayers. Her work was based on an imaginative power of uncommon originality.

Her Lord Peter Wimsey is devoid of the melodramatic atmosphere which surrounds many of the popular detectives and without any pretence to abnormal genius and scientific knowledge.

Lord Peter casts a fascinating atmosphere of mystery over rational plots and works his magic as an accomplished man of the world endowed with a capacity for divining obscure motives and plans

It is significant that a masterpiece among Miss Sayers's stories was called "The Cave of Ali Baba." She often mingled the fascination of The Arabian Nights with modern, matter-of-fact setting and a completely realistic background, keeping her highly-aristocratic detective a natural man and brother.

(December 19)

P. WYNDHAM LEWIS

MASTER OF PEN AND BRUSH

Percy Wyndham Lewis, who has died aged 72, was an intellectual so exceptionally gifted as to find outlets for his talents with both brush and pen.

He used them with equal facility and success in vigorous and aggressive fashion, delighting some and puzzling many. Always in both mediums, challenging and provocative, he inevitably attracted controversy.

Born in America of British parents, he went to Rugby and the Slade, whence a scholarship took him to the Continent. His first stories, published in 1909, aroused at once a lively interest. It was heightened by the publication of a rebellious periodical which he named, typically, Blast.

SERVED IN ARTILLERY

Service in the First World War, first in the Royal Artillery and later as a war artist, was followed by the publication of his first novel, "Tarr." It was hailed by his admirers as a major achievement.

It was followed by "The Art of Being Ruled," in 1926, a political treatise, and a year later came "The Lion and the Fox," on Shakespeare and Machiavelli. "The Apes of God," two autobiographical volumes, and "The Human Age", a trilogy, were among the many works in which he demonstrated his gifts for masterly prose, poetry, satire and devastating attack.

In recent years blindness had enforced his abandonment of painting and of his art criticism, but he continued his writing by using a dictating machine.

He married Miss Anne Hoskyns, who was the subject of some of his paintings, in 1929: she survives him.

DYNAMIC FIGURE

Led Vorticists

T.W. EARP writes: Until stricken with blindness in 1951, Wyndham Lewis had long been the most dynamic figure in contemporary British art. He first came into prominence in 1914, when he banded together and led a group of young fellow painters under the title of the Vorticist Group.

Their main purpose was to combat the Futurism of Marinetti, who was then exhibiting the works of his movement in London. This began a career of constant warfare waged by Lewis against opposing factions in art. He carried it on with a fire of mordant and extremely witty writings, but the example of his own work was his most forceful argument.

He was also a novelist, in whose "Childermass" many readers perceive an enduring quality. T.S. Eliot has called him "the most fascinating personality of our time." Of himself he wrote: "He is the Diogenes of our day."

(March 9)

OLIVER HARDY

Oliver Hardy, the American comedian, who has died aged 65, was associated with his English-born partner, Stan Laurel, for more than 30 years. Together they appeared in 200 films.

PATRICK GIBBS writes: Although Oliver Hardy was the dominant partner in the comic team of Laurel and Hardy, the large, eupeptic fellow to whom the insignificant Laurel was the foil, he did not contribute more to its success. They were complementary, and had the combination never been made, Hardy must have remained a small-part player little known.

As it was, his name became household property. In the 30's, we were never without a Laurel and Hardy film, and if these did not contribute to culture at least they provided much harmless fun.

The humour was simple. Hardy was the man to whom things happened. It was his ample face that received the custard pie, his equally ample posterior which hit the pavement after the inevitable slip on a banana skin.

(August 8)

KING HAAKON

NORWAY'S SYMBOL OF RESISTANCE

King Haakon VII of Norway, who has died at the age of 85, was the first King of an independent Norway for more than 500 years. The Queen and the Duke of Edinburgh paid a State visit to Oslo in 1955 to attend some of the celebrations arranged for the 50th anniversary of his coronation.

By his unwavering faith in the Allied cause and his firm belief in ultimate victory, during five years of exile in Britain, while his own land was overrun by the Germans, he became for his people the symbol of steadfast, unconquerable resistance, and a unifying figure in the struggle for freedom.

In 1940 he rejected all Hitler's demands for surrender and for the formation of a Government under the traitor Quisling. While it was possible to continue fighting in the field King Haakon shared the dangers and hardships of his troops. When retreat was made inevitable his person became the special target of the enemy. He was bombed from village to village.

Before he left Norway King Haakon demonstrated his faith in Britain by suggesting to Vice-Adml. J.G.P. Vivian that the whole of Norway's merchant fleet, the fourth largest in the world, should be requisitioned for the war effort.

QUEUED FOR BUSES

Familiar London Figure

Before many months had passed this fleet was to play a vital part in the Battle of the Atlantic, and in convoying supplies to Russia. King Haakon finally embarked for Britain, with the Crown Prince and his Ministers, from Tromsoe in the cruiser Devonshire, then the flagship of Adml. Sir John Cunningham, First Sea Lord, in 1940.

During the next five years King Haakon's sterling qualities endeared him to the hearts of the British people, and particularly to Londoners. This shy, tall and handsome monarch became a familiar figure in the streets of London. The fact that he often wore civilian clothes, frequently joined queues for buses, and as regularly "strap-hanged" in them, could not detract from his dignity, and certainly increased his popularity.

He was accorded a tremendous ovation from his people when he returned to Norway on June 7, 1945, a homecoming which completed a remarkable trinity of events in the history of Norway. On June 7, 1905, Norway became independent of Sweden, and it was on June 7, 1940, that King Haakon had sailed from Norway to continue the fight from Britain against his country's invaders.

(September 23)

SIBELIUS

FINNISH MASTER COMPOSER

Sibelius, the great Finnish composer, who has died at the age of 91, was venerated by his countrymen as a national hero. Granted a State annuity at 32, he was able from then on to concentrate upon creative work.

Yet he was 60, and his active phase was virtually over, by the time his fame was fully established abroad. He was the least derivative of modern composers. His music had a severe clarity, an austere reticence which seemed at times to approach an abrupt concision.

The elements were traditional: the employment highly personal. He made no use of folk-music, but all the world sensed the landscape of Finland in the noble breadth of his draughtsmanship and the delicate greys of his colouring.

LAST OF MASTERPIECES

These qualities are most notably present in the sombre orchestral legend, "The Swan of Tuonela," and in the grand and wintry tone-poem, "Tapiola," the last of his masterpieces. His originality has been somewhat obscured by the embarrassing popularity of "Valse Triste" and "Finlandia." The symphonies, for example, show a steady advance beyond traditional form, and the magnificent seventh is in one continuous movement.

(September 21)

MGR. R. KNOX

SCHOLAR, WRITER & BROADCASTER

Monsignor Ronald Knox who has died aged 69, has every claim to be the most distinguished convert to the Roman Catholic Church since Newman. Manning stands as his only possible rival.

But Manning was essentially an administrator, and although his ability won him the archbishopric of Westminster and a cardinal's hat, he lacked the sensitivity of Newman, the wit of Knox, and the wide humanism of both.

Knox was a great scholar, and his outstanding feat of scholarship was the new English version of the Bible, which he produced single-handed. It has been widely praised by critics of all denominations, although some have maintained that he failed in his search for that almost impossible will-o'-the-wisp "timeless English."

Ronnie Knox was born, as it were, in one purple, and died in another. He was a son of Dr. E.A. Knox, Bishop of Manchester from 1903 to 1921, and two of his grandfathers were Church of England divines. His elder brother, E.V. Knox, is a former editor of Punch.

WON SCHOLARSHIPS

Greek Verse at 10

He was born, therefore, into the tranquil circumstances of a late Victorian home, with its background of strong Anglican piety, family feeling, classical scholarship, and settled social conviction. Much of this he retained throughout his life.

At the age of 10 he was writing commendable Greek and Latin verse. In 1900 he won a scholarship to Eton, and subsequently at Balliol he won, in turn, the Hertford, Ireland, and Craven scholarships, and the Gaisford and Chancellor's Latin Verse prizes.

He was, in fact, the intellectual Marcellus of his year, and to classical triumphs he added those of pungent satire and lively dabate. In 1910 he took a First in Greats, and was elected Fellow of Trinity College, of which he became Chaplain after his ordination in the Church of England in 1912.

As a churchman, he was always in the van of high Anglicanism. He enjoyed twisting prelatical tails, and "Reunion All Round," which he wrote three years before his reception into the Roman Church, is still read and quoted, especially by those who now hold the views he then expressed.

"SPIRITUAL AENEID"

Range and Versatility

Like Newman, he found the decision to change his doctrinal allegiance unbearably painful, and like Newman, he was saddened by the reproaches of former friends. His "Apologia" was entitled "A Spiritual Aeneid," published in 1918.

More fortunate than Newman, his connection with Oxford was re-established 10 years later when he became Roman Catholic chaplain to the University. Trinity, which had "always been kind" to them both elected him an honorary Fellow in 1941, and Balliol paid him the same honour in 1953.

He remained at Oxford for 13 years, and all the time he was writing, broadcasting, and speaking at the Union. His range and versatility are exhibited in such works as "The Belief of Catholics" (1927), "Caliban in Grub Street" (1930), "Let Dons Delight" (1939) and his detective stories.

LISTENERS ALARMED

Sherlock Holmes Expert

One of his radio fantasies, which described an imaginary revolution in England in 1926, caused alarm among his listeners, many of whom failed to realise that the broadcast was not serious. His humour was always delicate, and he enjoyed the absurd, and the recondite. He was an authority on the mythology of Sherlock Holmes.

In 1939, three years after he had been appointed a domestic prelate, he retired to Aldenham Park, Lord Acton's estate at Bridgnorth, Shropshire. There he started work on his translation of the Bible, beginning with the New Testament, published in 1945.

(August 26)

Daily Telegraph and Morning Post, 1957

CROWD STORM PITCH TO ATTACK ITALIANS

No Referee, So World Cup Match Becomes (Officially) "Friendly"

From Donald Saunders

BELFAST, Wednesday.

Ireland ....2 Italy 2

The most disgusting exhibition of mob hooliganism ever to disgrace a British football ground occurred at Windsor Park here to-day at the end of the dirtiest, nastiest match I have seen.

As the teams were leaving the field of battle hundreds of the 40,000 angry spectators stormed over the 4ft wire netting fence surrounding the pitch and savagely attacked several Italian players.

They in turn were charged by a posse of 50 burly policemen and for a few minutes we watched the sort of battle we used to think took place only on South American grounds.

And all this came after what ironically was to have been a friendly match to replace the World Cup tie, postponed because the Hungarian referee did not arrive.

The explosion we had expected throughout the afternoon came when an Irish fanatic raced up and punched Rino Ferrari, the powerfully built French centre-half and club colleague of John Charles.

Meanwhile other mobs were attacking the Italian left-winger Montuori, centre-forward Bean and left-half Segato.

I saw Ireland's captain, Blanchflower, battling heroically to protect Montuori. Newcastle's hefty fullback McMichael went to Bean's aid and goalkeeper Gregg helped to scramble Segato to safety.

RIOT QUELLED

Off They Scuttle

Eventually the police regained control of a frightening situation. They marched off the apparent ringleaders while other shamefaced rioters scuttled away to the far corners of the ground.

Ferrario was carried by policemen into the dressing room where later he was fortunately found to have no more serious injuries than a bruised head and a cut under the chin.

When it was all over, Dr. Ottavio Barassi, president of the Italian Football Federation, showed remarkable control and told me quietly that his team would come back to Windsor Park in January for the postponed Cup-tie.

How I wish the Italians had been as eager to please earlier in the day. Had they shown such co-operation this morning their second journey and this afternoon's disgraceful scenes would have been avoided.

But the Italians adamantly refused to play the Cup-tie when they heard that Mr. Istvan Zsolt and his two linesmen were fogbound in London. Despite long discussions the Irish F.A. were unable to persuade the Italians to accept an Irish referee and linesmen.

But the blame does not rest only with the Italians. I think the Irish F.A., though admittedly faced with a delicate situation, might have handled things better.

Though the crowd's behaviour cannot possibly be excused it is not difficult to imagine their feelings. Many of them had taken a day off from work and had paid anything between 3s 6d and 30s to see the most important match Ireland had ever played.

Then at the last moment they were told that they would have to watch a game that meant absolutely nothing.

Their reaction was noisy and immediate. They booed, they stamped, they slow-clapped and they catcalled. Their angry growl increased as the players came on to the field and blotted out the band who bravely struggled through the Italian national anthem.

Wrongly the crowd decided to vent their feelings on the Italian players. This really led to the violent storm that followed.

The Italians, like so many continentals, disliked the Irishmen's shoulder-charging of goalkeeper Bugatti, which by British interpretation of the rules is perfectly fair. Every time the Italians protested they were loudly booed and they soon began to retaliate by hacking, tripping, pushing and elbowing their opponents.

One or two of the Irishmen occasionally hit back but on the whole I thought Blanchflower's men were very patient. So was the Irish referee, Mr. Tommy Mitchell.

ENOUGH OF IT

Italian Sent Off

But a minute from time Mr. Mitchell decided he had had enough of this fouling.

As Ireland's left-winger McParland went leaping over Bugatti, the Italian left-half, Chiapella deliberately kicked him, then jumped on to the back of centre-forward McAdams.

After a seething, fighting crowd of players had been separated, the referee sent Chiapella off.

Thus was the stage set for an ugly climax to a match best forgotten.

For what it matters, Italy took the lead in the 23rd minute through Ghiggia and Cush equalised four minutes later. In the 50th minute Montuori put Italy in front again but the determined little Cush once more levelled the scores on the hour.

(December 5)

CHELSEA DISCOVER YOUNG FORWARD STAR

By Frank Coles

Tottenham H..................1 Chelsea..................1

The first of the London derbies ended, like so many before it, in the draw which satisfies no-one. But if the main pattern was the same the match took one bright, unexpected turn.

Intense local rivalry, fanned by keenness to start the new season well, is not the ideal cradle for the birth of a star. Yet 17-year-old Jimmy Greaves, Chelsea's find at inside left, emerged from the ordeal of his first League test with a highly enhanced reputation.

Mr. Ted Drake has made a rare discovery in this young Londoner, who, with all the assurance of a veteran, slipped into the tempo of a battle waged to the last gasp before 52,580 roaring fans.

Greaves scored the goal which saved Chelsea their precious point five minutes from time, the perfect ending to a perfect debut. A calmly-taken chance, it stamped the newcomer as a prospect who in a year's time may be in line for the game's highest honours.

BIG REPUTATION

100 Goals Last Season

Greaves entered the White Hart Lane scene with a schoolboy's reputation of having scored more than 100 goals in minor football last season. His opportunities of putting Reynolds to the test in Spurs' goal were limited.

But who was not impressed by one super-confident second-half dribble which took him gliding past three challengers in six yards and ended in the goalkeeper diving to make a do-or-die save?

(August 26)

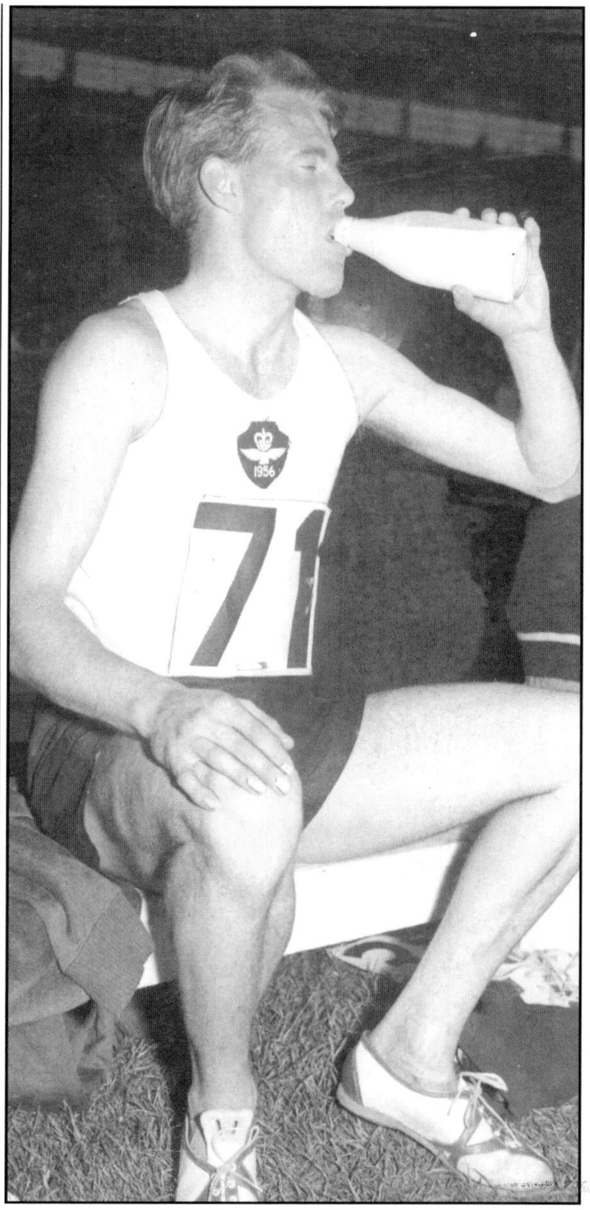

IBBOTSON'S WORLD RECORD MILE. Derek Ibbotson refreshing himself with a bottle of milk after his victory at White City Stadium last evening, when he ran the mile in 3min 57.2 sec, beating the world record by eight-tenths of a second.

Another Controversial Cup Final

England Should Join in Banning Charges on Goalkeeper

By Frank Coles

Aston Villa..................2 Manchester United..................1

Several important questions are posed by the most memorable Cup Final played at Wembley since the Stadium's 1923 invasion.

In the presence of the Queen, Prince Philip, the Prime Minister, and 100,000 spectators, Ray Wood, the Manchester United goalkeeper was knocked out in the sixth minute by an act which the referee penalised as a foul and was carried off on a stretcher to take very little further part in the match.

Surely it is up to referees on Soccer's Show Day, as, indeed, on all occasions, to let the assembled public realise that such incidents are not part and parcel of the game and are not covered merely by a routine free-kick.

Should not the offender in this conspicuous scene have been as conspicuously cautioned? McParland's offence was the use of excessive vigour in his charge on the goalkeeper.

The affair ruined the whole match and wrecked Manchester United's hopes of the Cup-League double, built up over a matter of 50 tense and trying matches, and left the Villa on a pedestal as the club with the greatest number of victories in the Cup Final.

TIME TO ACT

Remember Trautmann

Remembering that only last year a Cup Final goalkeeper, Trautmann, of Manchester City, suffered a broken neck at Wembley, is it not time that England and her sister countries withdrew from the attitude of "they are all out of step but us" and fall into line with foreign countries by prohibiting charges on the goalkeeper even if the space of restriction is only limited to the six yards goal area?

England have only to take the lead in the legislation chamber for this difficult and dangerous law to be altered and come rapidly into universal use. Then the many-sided problem of substitution of injured players will become far less pressing.

ANOTHER QUESTION

Wood's Recall

Manchester United have everyone's sympathy in getting so near but yet so far from the realisation of their magnificent challenge to overcome the 60 years' elusiveness of the double event. But there is another question to be asked:

Seeing that Wood, their injured goalkeeper, had resumed at outside-right early in the second half and was showing more and more that he was able to make a contribution to his team's fight back, how was it that it was not until eight minutes from the end when the margin had been reduced to 2-1, that he was recalled from outside-right to his proper position in goal?

This is not an easy question to answer as the critics in high places and elsewhere could not know the facts about his physical condition.

Matt Busby afterwards explained that Wood was suffering from blackouts. Of all injuries in football, remember, concussion is the most dangerous to handle.

(May 6)

IBBOTSON RUNS FASTEST MILE EVER

3min 57.2sec: FIRST FOUR BREAK 4min

Derek Ibbotson, of Huddersfield, Yorks, beat the world record for the mile at White City, London, last night, his time of 3min 57.2sec, clipping eight-tenths of a second off the record held by John Landy, of Australia. Ibbotson is 25.

The race was an international event. So fast was it run that the first four all clocked times under four minutes.

It was the first time that four men had beaten four minutes in the same race. Ibbotson passed the post 8 yards in front of Ron Delany of Ireland, the Olympic 1,500 metres Gold Medal winner, who had to be helped from the track.

Delany's time was 3min 58.8sec. Third was S. Jungwirth, the Czech, who recently beat the world 1,500 metres record. His time was 3min 59.1sec. Fourth was Ken Wood of Sheffield, in 3min 59.3sec.

Five British runners have now run a mile in under four minutes. They are Dr. Roger Bannister, C.J. Chataway, B. Hewson, Derek Ibbotson and K. Wood.

"SLOW" THIRD LAP

When asked if he thought the mile could be run faster, Ibbotson said: "It might be, but they do not use motor bikes yet." He thought that if the third lap, which took 64.2sec, had not been so slow, he might have won the race somewhere near 3min 55sec.

His wife, formerly Madeleine Wooller, who has run a mile in under five minutes, and five-week-old daughter Christine, were present at White City, and Ibbotson said that his little girl undoubtedly brought him luck.

She was born on the day that he broke the European record with 3min 58.4sec in Glasgow, and now she was present for the new world record. "I shall have to take her everywhere in future," Ibbotson said.

Ibbotson, who has now beaten four minutes three times, has one more aim in the immediate future. He said: "I want to break the world three-mile record." Only a week ago, on the same track, he set a new British record for the three miles with a time of 13min 20.8sec. The world record is 13min 14.2sec held by Iharos of Hungary.

DELANY'S COMMENT

Delany said afterwards: "It was a fabulous race and a pleasure as well as a privilege to run in it. I shall dream about it for years." It was his own personal best performance.

(July 20)

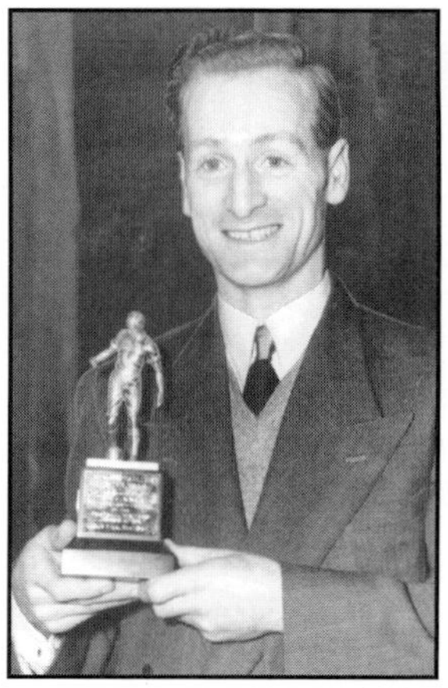

TOM FINNEY, the Preston and England centre-forward, who was yesterday elected "Footballer of the Year" by the Football Writers' Association, thus becoming the first player to win this honour for the second time. This picture shows him when he was chosen in 1954 as a winger.

This distinction crowns a wonderful week for Finney, who celebrates his 35th birthday to-morrow and leads the England attack against Scotland at Wembley on Saturday.

Holder of 63 England caps, Finney topped a very heavy poll to win his second trophy which he will receive at the Association's annual dinner in London on May 2. Duncan Edwards, John Charles, Roger Byrne and Stanley Matthews followed him in that order in the ballot.

(April 4)

MADRID RETAINS EUROPEAN CUP

MADRID, Thursday.

A disputed penalty goal played a major part in Real Madrid's 2-0 win over Florentina (Italy) here to-day in the final of the European Soccer Cup.

It was the first of the goals, scored by di Stefano, in the 24th minute of the second half, after Mateos, Madrid's inside-right, had been brought down by Orzan, the Florentina centre-half.

The Dutch referee, Leo Horn, whistled for a penalty but a linesman was flagging that the ball had previously gone out of play.

The second goal was scored by Gento in the 31st minute.

The result, enabling Madrid to retain the Cup, was a fair one. - Reuter.

(May 31)

ANGELINI WINS SWISS OPEN SCOTT THIRD

CRANS-SUR-SIERRE, Thursday.

Alfonso Angelini, of Turin, won the Swiss Open Golf Championship here to-day with a 72-holes aggregate of 270.

Flory Van Donck, of Belgium, was runner-up with 274, followed by Sid Scott (Carlisle), the British Ryder Cup international, with 275. British players Bernard Hunt (Hartsbourne C.C) and John Jacobs (Sandy Lodge) shared fourth place on the 275 mark.–Reuter.

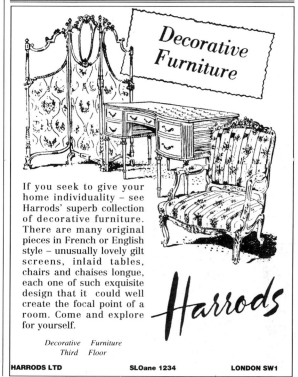

CREPELLO SEEMS ALL SET FOR TRIPLE CROWN

Piggott Times His Run to Perfection: French Colts Eclipsed

From Hotspur

EPSOM, Wednesday.

SIR VICTOR SASSOON'S Crepello (6-4) came home a clear winner of the Derby to-day from Ballymoss (33-1) and Pipe of Peace (100-8), and if all goes well with him, looks destined to be the first winner of the Triple Crown - 2,000 Guineas, Derby and St. Leger - since Bahram brought off the treble 22 years ago.

Only 14 horses have achieved such fame in the long history of English racing, beginning with West Australian 104 years ago. Diamond Jubilee was the first to land the treble in the 20th-century, and one hopes Crepello will be the seventh.

Diamond Jubilee, Rock Sand, Pommern, Gay Crusader, Gainsborough and Bahram reads the bare record. Blue Peter would probably have been in the list too if the war had not caused the abandonment of the 1939 St. Leger.

Crepello defeated the Irish-trained Ballymoss to-day by one and a half lengths, with Pipe of Peace a further length away third and Tempest fourth. For the fourth time since the war there was no French-trained runner in the first three.

Competently and cooly ridden by Lester Piggott, Crepello did an exceptionally good time - two minutes 35 2-5ths seconds, the fastest since Mahmoud set the record for the Derby with 2 minutes, 33 4-5ths seconds in 1936.

In winning the Derby with Crepello Sir Victor Sassoon was gaining his second success in the race as an owner and his first as a breeder. When Pinza won for him in 1953 he started joint favourite at 5-1. Crepello was the shortest-priced winning favourite since unbeaten Bahram.

Sir Victor has now won six classic races. The St. Leger alone has eluded him so far. The imperturbable Piggott has added a second Derby to his name, and Noel Murless, Crepello's trainer, has saddled his first Derby winner.

Throughout the last three furlongs of the race Crepello always looked like justifying the faith Murless has had in him since his early days.

(June 6)

DICK FRANCIS HAS RIDDEN HIS LAST RACE

DICK FRANCIS, one of the best steeplechase riders since the war - and one of the most courageous - has decided to retire from race-riding at the age of 36.

Francis, who rode as first jockey to Queen Elizabeth the Queen Mother, said yesterday: "It was a terrible decision to have to make, but I wanted to stop before I began going rapidly down the scale." He added that his decision was precipitated by the Queen Mother's Devon Loch, breaking down at Sandown and being taken out of training. "I had been looking forward to another ride on him in the Grand National," he said.

Francis's name will always be associated with Devon Loch, on whom he all but won last year's National. The horse's inexplicable mishap 50 yards from the post, with the race so nearly won, will remain one of the saddest and most tragic happenings in the history of 'chasing.

He had more than his fair share of falls in the last few seasons, but always made light of them.

Champion National Hunt rider in the 1953-54 season, Francis had his first ride as an amateur in October 1946, and turned professional 18 months later.

(January 31)

IRISH-TRAINED BALLYMOSS WINS ST. LEGER

From Hotspur

DONCASTER, Wednesday.

IRISH-TRAINED, American-owned Ballymoss, in spite of overnight rain considered prejudicial to his chances, won the St. Leger to-day on merit from Court Harwell, the favourite Brioche and Tempest. He is the first horse trained in Ireland to win the St.Leger since it was founded in 1776.

The race was yet another triumph for 40-year-old Vincent O-Brien, who, since he started training 13 years ago, has three Grand Nationals, three Cheltenham Gold Cups, three Champion Hurdles, three Irish Cesarewitches, two Irish Derbys, and now a St. Leger to his credit - a training record which for versatility has not been beaten in this century.

The first four in to-day's race were all bought at the Doncaster Yearling Sales two years ago - the winner, bred by Mr. Richard Ball in Co. Dublin, for 4,500 guineas; Court Harwell, bred by Sir Richard Sykes, for 5,000 guineas; Brioche, bred by the Duchess of Westminster, for only 2,700 guineas; and Tempest, bred by Mr. E Cooper Bland, for 13,000 guineas.

Ballymoss was only the eighth winner of the St. Leger in the last 30 years to have been bought at public auction. The others have all been home-bred. It is rather extraordinary that both Ballymoss and Court Harwell came under the hammer on the same day two years ago.

Ballymoss has been invited to run in the Washington International at Laurel Park, Maryland, on Nov. 11 and will probably be flown across the Atlantic to take part in it. Before going to the United States, if the going is on top of the ground, he may run in the Prix de l'Arc de Triomphe at Longchamp (Oct. 6).

Mr. McShain has an alternative runner in the Prix de l'Arc de Triomphe in the four-year-old filly Gladness which he bought shortly before she won at Ascot in July.

Mr. Richard Ball bought Ballymoss's dam, Indian Call, for only 15 guineas in 1939 from a batch of horses in training sent up by the late Lord Glanely.

Bargain Horse

She has certainly proved one of the greatest bloodstock bargains in the last 20 years, for she has already bred six winners and Mr. Ball may reasonably expect to get a good price for Ballymoss's sister who comes up for sale tomorrow morning.

Though Britt chose to ride Tenterhooks instead of Brioche this did not deter backers from making Brioche favourite and he was probably the unlucky horse of the race.

(September 12)

(Solution No. 9920)

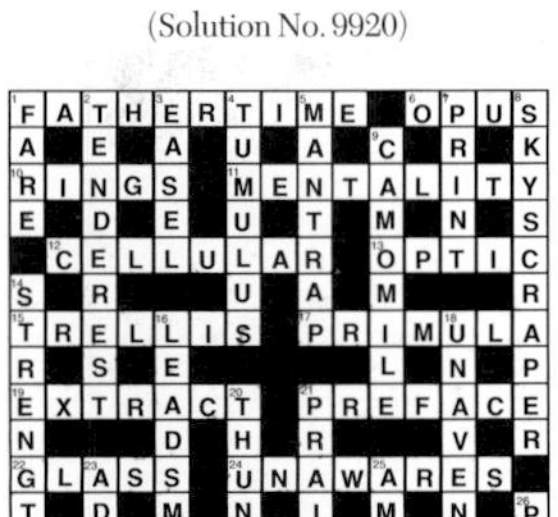

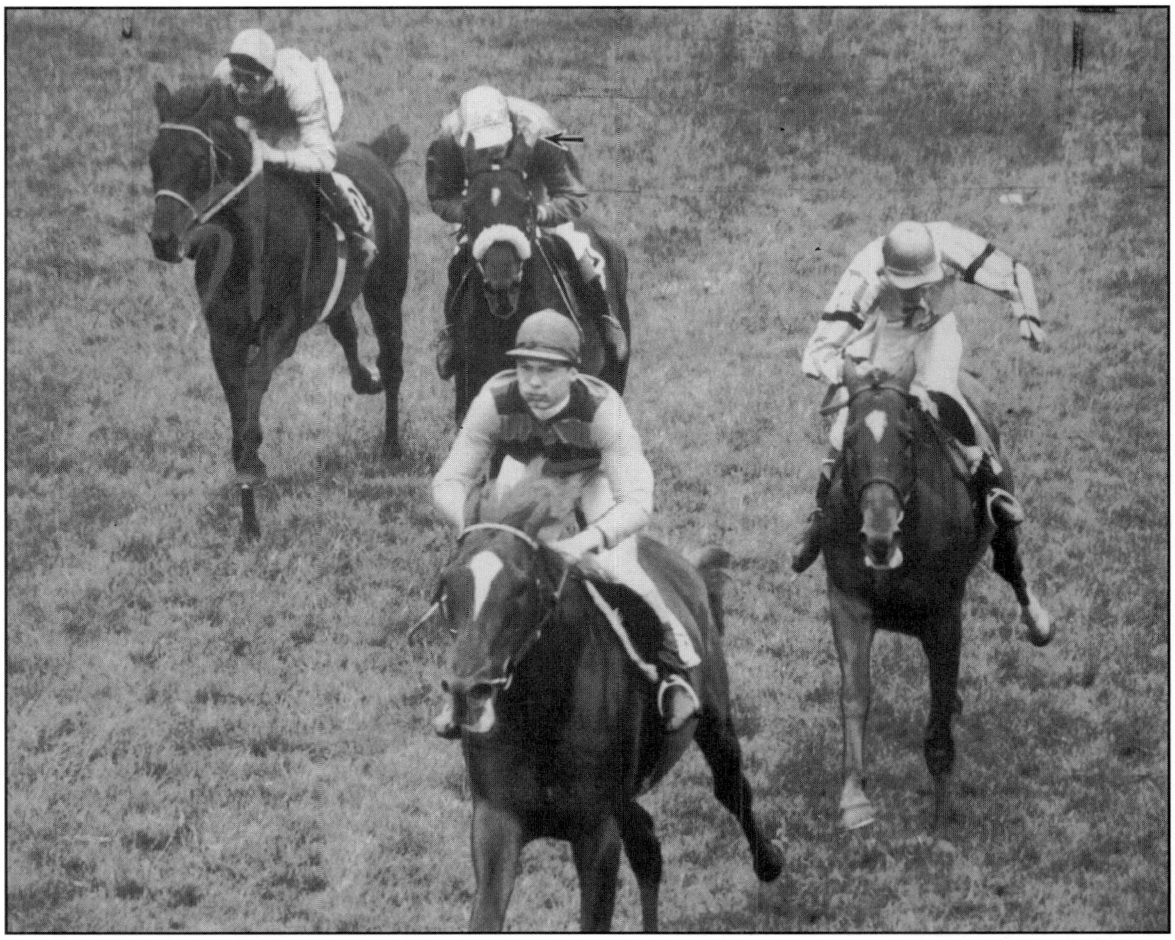

CREPELLO RIDDEN BY LESTER PIGGOTT, Winning the Derby from Ballymoss. The winning margin was a length and a half.

THIRD TIME LUCKY FOR GALLANT SUNDEW

Leads All The Way To Give Winter His First National Triumph

From Hotspur

AINTREE, Friday.

IT was third time lucky for Mr. and Mrs. Geoffrey Kohn, of Henley-in-Arden, Warwickshire, to-day when Sundew, a 20-1 chance, ridden by champion jockey Fred Winter, romped home an eight lengths' winner of the Grand National from Wyndburgh and the unconsidered Tiberetta.

Sundew was the third horse the Kohn's have purchased in Ireland with the sole object of winning the world's greatest steeplechase - Quite Naturally and Churchtown were the others - and he triumphed at the third attempt.

Mr. Kohn, a stockbroker, bought Sundew on the eve of the Grand National in 1955. The horse led approaching Becher's in that year but fell four fences from the finish. He tried again 12 months ago and came down at Becher's the second time round when lying second.

That he should succeed at the third attempt, and after making practically all the running, is the more credit to him. Yet when he was offered for sale at Newmarket in December there was not one bid! An attempt to sell him afterwards at £2,500 also produced no takers.

The winning owners have a farm adjoining the gallops of Sundew's trainer, Frank Hudson, and are friends and neighbours of Mr. and Mrs. L. Carver whose E.S.B. won the National last year. At one time they held a half-share in E.S.B. so were due for a change of luck.

Hudson, who deserves much of the credit for Sundew's success, is a Coventry man by birth and started as a stable lad with the late Mr. R. Reid Walker, of Shifnal.

SMALL STABLE AGAIN

Hudson's Distinction

Hudson has been a trainer for 30 years, and now has the distinction of having won, within a short period, the longest race on the flat - the Queen Alexandra Stakes with Bitter Sweet - and the longest steeplechase, the National. Sundew, strangely enough, is the only 'chaser in his 10-horse stable.

(March 30)

Badminton

DANISH WOMEN BEAT ENGLAND

By Lance Tingay

England's initial venture in the Uber Cup, the new women's badminton team championship of the world, was a failure at Wimbledon last night. Denmark won easily to qualify to meet Ireland in the European Zone final.

If one may venture a prediction, an ultimate tie between Denmark and the United States will settle the fate of the trophy. The Danes got the whiphand on England and did not let go.

Staying power had much to do with the Danes' success. This was clearly indicated in the singles, which resolved 2-1 to the visitors.

Mrs. W.C.E. Rogers won the opening game against the Danish champion, Miss T. Petersen, and appeared in command. Miss Petersen, trim and strong, set behind her what had been a bad spell and yielded an increasingly effective drop shot to win.

A not dissimilar pattern was set when Mrs. T. Ahm beat Mrs. E.J. Timperley. The English lead here did not extend to the first game but Mrs. Timperley was in fact three times within a stroke of taking it to 10-7.

Here the Danish resurgence and the power of an adroitly wielded drop shot was such that Mrs. Ahm went to victory without losing another point.

Young Miss H.M. Ward justified her selection as leader by beating Miss A Jacobsen in two close games.

(January 17)

Lawn Tennis Championships

MULLOY-PATTY HEROES OF LAST DAY

Crowd Acclaims Veteran Pair: Too Easy for Miss Gibson

By Lance Tingay

THE final tally in the Lawn Tennis Championships which ended at Wimbledon on Saturday was two titles to Miss Althea Gibson, who won the women's singles and doubles. Four Americans and two Australians have thus taken all the trophies.

This is a familiar post-war pattern, but what stood out on the last warm day of the meeting, when the Queen was in the Royal Box, and where normality was amusingly disturbed by the intrusion of an eccentric citizen exercising an ancient right to petition the reigning monarch, was not so much the efficient victory achieved by Miss Gibson as the exciting win by Mulloy and Patty in the men's doubles.

Miss Gibson's singles championship, noteworthy as the first achieved by a coloured player, I will comment on later. The crux of the last day was the inspiration found by Mulloy, now in his mid-forties, and his 33-year-old partner Budge Patty in becoming the first unseeded pair to win the men's doubles.

What would otherwise have been rather a humdrum conclusion to the championships was redeemed by the display of this near-veteran pair in bringing down the favourites, the leading Australian combination of Hoad and Fraser.

One cannot praise too highly the wise doubles craft shown by Mulloy, or the splendid forehand volleying of Patty.

VITAL STROKE

Return of Service

The vital stroke in doubles play is return of service. Here both Mulloy and Patty evinced a happy strength and in the end their joint efforts broke Hoad's sparkling individual skill and showed that this brilliant player lacked the capacity to carry along a partner less good than himself. Patty's success was warmly welcomed, too, for he has always been a favourite. His singles title was won in 1950, but in men's doubles he had never before progressed beyond the semi-final.

MISS GIBSON

Almost a Triple

Miss Gibson almost went through three events unbeaten. Her defeat in the last match of all, the mixed doubles, in which she and Fraser went down to Rose and Miss Hard, thwarted her from emulating the record last performed by a woman in 1951, when Miss Doris Hart wore the triple crown.

In the singles she won without losing a set to anyone. She was not even taken to advantage games, and the hardest contest for her was the opening match against the Hungarian, Mme. S. Kormoczky, who held her to 6-4, 6-4.

The final, in which she trounced Miss Hard, was more notable for its poverty than its riches. It was a long way short of being a regal duel - and even Miss Gibson, who won so easily, hardly put her best foot forward.

Farewell To Hoad

As for Wimbledon's outstanding hero, Lewis Hoad, singles winner for the second year and exponent of the most brilliant lawn tennis seen for many years in his breath-taking final on Friday, he will not be seen again as an amateur.

A prodigious player, Hoad! I doubt if it will be in the power of flesh and blood to hit the ball so hard and accurately as he did against Ashley Cooper.

(July 8)

Wimbledon Finals

MEN'S SINGLES

L.A. Hoad (Australia) bt A.J. Cooper (Australia), 6-2, 6-1, 6-2

WOMEN'S SINGLES

Miss A. Gibson (U.S.) bt Miss D.R. Hard (U.S.) 6-3, 6-2.

MEN'S DOUBLES

G. Mulloy, B. Patty (U.S.) bt N.A. Fraser and L.A. Hoad (Australia) 8-10,6-4, 6-4, 6-4.

WOMEN'S DOUBLES

Miss Gibson, Miss Hard (U.S.) bt Mrs. K. Hawtoh, Mrs. T.D. Long (Australia) 6-1, 6-2.

MIXED DOUBLES

M.G. Rose (Australia), Miss Hard (U.S.) bt N.A. Fraser (Australia), Miss Gibson (U.S.) 6-4, 7-5.

MEN'S PLATE

G.L. Forbes (S. Africa) bt A. Segal (S. Africa) 10-8, 11-13, 6-3.

WOMEN'S PLATE

Miss M. Hellyer (Australia) bt Miss R. Schuurman (S. Africa) 6-4, 6-4.

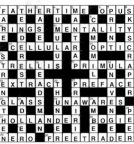

ENGLAND JUST FAIL TO WIN FABULOUS MATCH

West Indies Avoid Defeat by Matter of Minutes

From E.W. Swanton

EDGBASTON, Tuesday.

This has been a fabulous Test Match. Writing a few moments after watching Goddard and young Smith fighting for their lives against Laker and Lock, with the English fieldsmen clustered round them like bees round a honeypot (and with the steel calypso band performing with smiles of relief on their faces in front of the pavilion), I cannot summon the memory or the knowledge of any previous game wherein the fortunes have changed with such utter completeness from one side to the other.

At noon yesterday May and Cowdrey came together, as they did at Sydney three years ago, knowing that only a day-long stand or thereabouts could bring England back into the match. A day and a half later West Indies surveyed a scoreboard showing 62 for 7, thanking their stars for an escape from defeat which could surely be measured only in terms of minutes.

Laker and Lock did not have the sort of wicket to bowl on which filled the Australians with dread last summer. Each is a master of using what little help a wearing wicket affords. Indeed, they set the West Indies batsmen a testing problem enough.

The root of the collapse this evening was, however, psychological. The change in events, catastrophic from their angle combined with the long weary spell in the field, made them always likely victims. In such circumstances two hours and 40 minutes can seem an eternity.

DRAW FAIR RESULT

The scoresheet will make it seem that England declared too late and I believe they could have come in with complete safety half-an-hour earlier than they did, in fact when Cowdrey was out.

At this point West Indies could have been asked to bat for just over three hours, with 237 runs standing between themselves and victory. Yet in retrospect a draw seems perhaps the fairest answer, bearing in mind the various West Indian injuries which dislocated them so seriously at the crucial time.

For instance they bowled with the same ball for more than seven hours since they had no one left to use a new one. In any case no one who has any conception of the strain imposed by an innings of 10 hours will be disposed to blame May himself for not declaring earlier. With him I daresay times and figures were a blur in the mind.

EXEMPLARY INNINGS

May's batting, taking all the circumstances into consideration, deserves all the superlatives so sadly overworked which are part and parcel of a modern Test. It was an excellent innings from the technical viewpoint, an exemplary one in point of responsibility. This is the aspect, of course, which merits most praise.

George Geary at Charterhouse taught May the basic things of batsmanship and so made the sound foundations of his cricket. But the self-discipline which schools and directs his play is something he had to develop himself, albeit with the example of others to help.

Here the name that suggests itself naturally is Hutton, on whom May has based not only his batting on occasions, but to a considerable amount his uncompromising philosophy of Test cricket.

It may be added that only four Englishmen have played bigger Test innings than this 285: Hutton, Hammond, Sandham and R.E. Foster, the latter by two runs. As a captain's effort, needless to say, it stands alone.

As to Cowdrey's innings, it had all the attributes of his captain in an only slightly less degree. His qualities have been known and his potentialities realised ever since his notable exploits in Australia.

Now that this remarkable innings has come in a Test at home he must surely take the unquestioned place in the England side for which his talents qualify him.

(June 5)

Test Scoreboard

ENGLAND - First Innings

P.E. Richardson, c Walcott, b Ramadhin 47
D.B. Close, c Rohan Kanhai, b Gilchrist 15
D.J. Insole, b Ramadhin 20
P.B.H. May, c Weekes, b Ramadhin 30
M.C. Cowdrey, c Gilchrist, b Ramadhin 4
T.E. Bailey, b Ramadhin 1
G.A.R. Lock b Ramadhin 0
T.G. Evans, b Gilchrist 14
J.C. Laker, b Ramadhin 7
F.S. Trueman, not out 29
J.B. Statham, b Atkinson 13
Extras (b 3. lb 3) 6
Total 186

Fall of Wickets: 1-32, 2-61, 3-104, 4-115, 5-116, 6-118, 7-121, 8-130, 9-130, 10-186.

BOWLING

	O	M	R	W
Worrell	9	1	27	0
Gilchrist	27	4	74	2
Ramadhin	31	16	49	7
Atkinson	12.4	3	30	1

Second Innings

P.E. Richardson, c sub. b Ramadhin 34
D.B. Close, c Weekes, b Gilchrist 42
D.J. Insole, b Ramadhin 0
P.B.H. May, not out 285
M.C. Cowdrey, c sub. b Smith 154
T.G. Evans, not out 29
Extras (b 23, lb 16) 39
Total (4 wkts dec.) 583

Fall of Wickets: 1-63, 2-65, 3-113, 4-524.

BOWLING

	O	M	R	W
Gilchrist	26	2	67	1
Atkinson	72	29	137	0
Ramadhin	98	33	179	2
Sobers	30	4	77	0
Smith	26	4	72	1
Goddard	6	2	12	0

WEST INDIES - First Innings

B.R. Pairaudeau, b Trueman 1
Rohan Kanhai, lbw, b Statham 42
C.L. Walcott, c Evans, b Laker 90
E.D. Weekes, b Trueman 9
G. Sobers, c Bailey, b Statham 53
F.M. Worrell, b Statham 81
J.D. Goddard, c Lock, b Laker 24
D. Atkinson, c Statham, b Laker 1
S. Ramadhin, not out 5
R.L. Gilchrist, run out 0
Extras (b 1, lb 6) 7
Total 474

Fall of wickets: 1-4, 2-83, 3-120, 4-183, 5-197, 6-387, 7-466, 8-469, 9-474.

BOWLING

	O	M	R	W
Statham	39	4	114	3
Trueman	30	4	99	2
Bailey	34	11	80	0
Laker	54	17	119	4
Lock	34.4	15	33	0

Second Innings

B.H. Pairaudeau, b Trueman 7
Rohan Kanhai, c Close, b Trueman 1
G. Sobers, c Cowdrey, b Lock 14
E.D. Weekes, c Trueman, b Lock 33
F.M. Worrell, c May, b Lock 0
C.L. Walcott, c Lock, b Laker 1
O.G. Smith, lbw, b Laker 5
J.D. Goddard, not out 0
D. Atkinson, not out 4
Extras (b 7) 7
Total (7 wkts.) 72

Fall of wickets: 1-1, 2-9, 3-25, 4-27, 5-43, 6-66, 7-68.

BOWLING

	O	M	R	W
Statham	2	0	6	0
Trueman	5	3	7	2
Lock	27	19	31	3
Laker	24	20	13	2
Close	2	1	8	0

UMPIRES: C.S. Elliott and E. Davies.

(June 5)

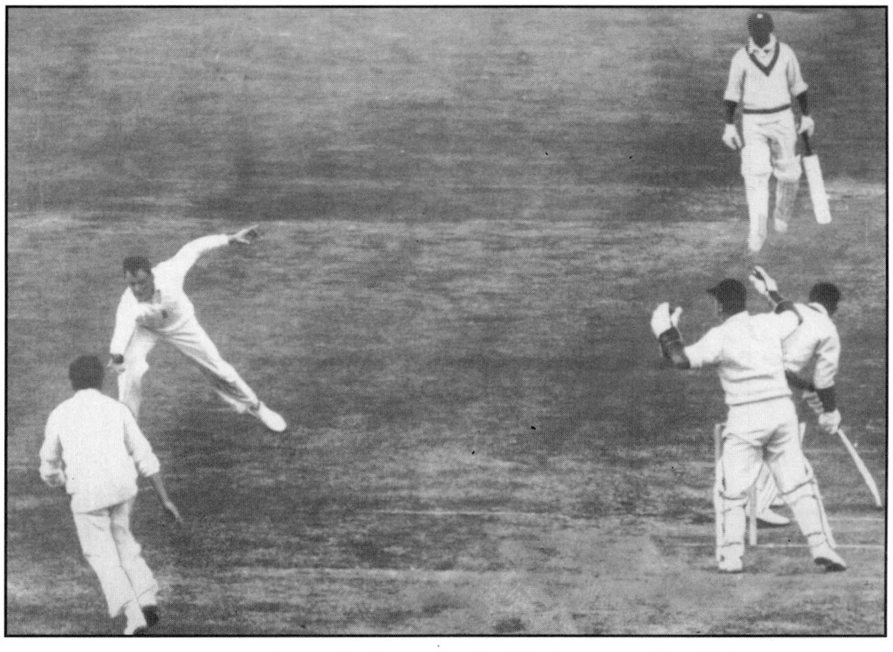

DOWN THEY GO. May takes a fine catch one-handed to dismiss Worrell for a "duck."

MIDDLESEX BEATEN BY 3 RUNS IN TENSE FINISH

From Michael Melford

PORTSMOUTH, Tuesday.

A great game of cricket fascinatingly poised throughout, ended after a tense and absorbing four hours' play here to-day, in victory for Hampshire by three runs.

Robertson and Edrich made substantial ground early on towards Middlesex's goal of 244. Compton fought for over two hours to take them a long way nearer, and Delisle took them to the brink of victory. But in the end the victor was Shackleton.

All day the match had fluctuated, a wicket falling every time Middlesex seemed to be forcing their way on top. Only when the eighth wicket fell, with 32 still needed, did Hampshire seem at last to have won control.

ACCURATE BOWLING

Delisle, however, was still there, having already struggled for nearly 2 ½ hours against the relentless accuracy of Shackleton and his sides, mostly as junior partner to Compton.

Now he opened out with much skill and resource, monopolised the strike successfully, and made all the next 20 runs. With 12 still needed, however, Hurst, who had been defending confidently when called upon, was magnificently caught low down at short-leg by Sainsbury, hurling himself to his right. It was a match-winning catch if ever there was one, and one which only a few of exceptional reactions could have caught.

With Angus in the runs trickled on, Angus contributing four - one off the inside edge, three from a lofted on-drive.

For the first four balls Eagar had nine men in a circle 10 yards in from the boundary, which to-day was not easily reached over a poppy outfield. Delisle made four unsuccessful passes.

For the last two balls Eagar had to split his forces to save both four and one, and off the last ball Delisle was encouraged to swing across the line. He had struck Shackleton's slower ball fairly well previously. Now, weary after three hours, he missed it, was hit on the front leg and lbw.

The Scoreboard

HAMPSHIRE - First Innings: 133 (Bennett 4-17, at 2.14 runs per over. Second Innings: 218 (Marshall 62: Compton 3-15).

MIDDLESEX - First Innings: 108 (Shackleton 5-31) at 2.20 runs per over.

Second Innings

Robertson, c Barnard, b Gray 49
Gale, c Harrison, b Shackleton 7
Edrich, c Barnard b Shackleton 50
Compton, b Shackleton 52
Titmus, b Shackleton 0
Delisle, lbw b Shackleton 50
Bennett c Harrison, b Heath 13
Melluish, b Heath 3
Warr, c Sainsbury b Shackleton 0
Hurst, c Sainsbry, b Heath 0
Angus, not out 4
Extras 12
Total 240

(May 22)

STIRLING MOSS DRIVES A VANWALL TO VICTORY

BRITISH GRAND PRIX RECORD

From W.A. McKenzie, Daily Telegraph Motoring Correspondent

LIVERPOOL, Sunday.

Stirling Moss achieved Britain's greatest motor-racing triumph for 34 years when, with a Vanwall car, he won the British Grand Prix on the three-mile Aintree road circuit yesterday.

It was the first time since the late Sir Henry Seagrave's victory in a Sunbeam in 1923 that a British car had won a major Grand Prix in the Championship series. Moss won at 86.2 m.p.h. and achieved a new lap record of 90.6 m.p.h.

This was not only the British, but also the European Grand Prix. The Vanwall, a private venture of Mr. Tony Vandervell, the industrialist, had won against the might of the full teams from the hitherto all-conquering Ferrari and Maserati factories of Italy.

He gained for Mr. Vandervell, as the car's entrant, 2,500gns and a £100 trophy for finishing in first place; £500 for the first British car: 200gns for the first car to reach a lap speed of 90 m.p.h., which had never been done before at Aintree, and 200gns for the lap speed record.

LIFE'S AMBITION

Championship Hope

"I have achieved one of my life's ambitions, to win a major Grand Prix in a British car," Moss said after the race. He has another ambition. It is to become world champion, a title no British driver has ever won, with a British car.

The win brought Moss up in the World Championship table from 20th place, with only one point, to second, behind Juan Fangio, last year's champion. Against the 25 points of Fangio, who gained none yesterday, Moss now has 10. He is two above Jean Behra of France, the previous runner-up to Fangio in the table.

FERRARIS MOVE UP

Gap Widened

Moss took the lead from Behra's Maserati half-way round the first lap. He held on in front with Behra never more than bare seconds behind, while a dog fight went on for third place between Tony Brooks (Vanwall), and Peter Collins and Mike Hawthorn (Ferraris).

Brooks, still suffering from leg injuries received at Le Mans last month, had soon to give way to the Ferraris, and Hawthorn passed Collins. But Moss widened the gap over Behra, who in turn was gradually leaving Hawthorn further behind.

By the 20th lap, Moss was 8.4 seconds in the lead, and the Vanwalls of Lewis-Evans, who had come up from 11th place on the first lap, and Tony Brooks were holding fifth and sixth places behind the two leading Ferraris. The crowd warmed to the prospects of a British victory.

(July 22)

PRINCE SCORES 6 GOALS AT POLO

Prince Philip scored six goals at Smith's Lawn, Windsor Great Park, yesterday when he played polo in two matches for two hours without a break. There was heavy rain.

The first three were scored as captain of the Welsh Guards, who won the Combermere Cup, by defeating Swallet House by four goals to three. The cup was presented to the Prince by the Queen.

Prince Philip's second match came when he volunteered to fill a gap in Windsor Park's side, who were a man short. They played Friar Park and the Prince again scored three goals. The final score was Windsor Park 8, Friar Park 2 ½

(May 13)

CAMBRIDGE SHOW GREAT RACING QUALITIES

By B.C. Johnstone

EXHIBITING really great racing qualities, Cambridge won the Boat Race of 1957 by two lengths in a time of 12mins 1sec, and defeated an eight which few expected to lose.

The sheer courage of the victors and their refusal to accept defeat made this an exciting occasion for the many thousands who had come down to the river on a gorgeous spring day to watch this essential item in the London calendar.

That Oxford were supremely fit cannot be denied and yet their inability to challenge Cambridge at critical stages can only be explained in exhaustion of some kind.

One must presume that they were mentally stale and in this state any weakness was sure to be accentuated. Barnard at No. 5 has always been a backward member of the crew and his failure to pull his weight must have slowed down both the striking weight and the pace of the Oxford boat. His appearance proclaimed him definitely off colour and he was certainly in no shape to give of his best.

Their long swing enabled them to exercise ceaseless pressure and make continual spurts which eventually proved the downfall of the Dark Blues.

Congratulations to the entire Cambridge crew must most certainly be shared, in full measure, by their coach, Mr. Derek Mays-Smith for the almost unique manner in which he brought them to their highest pitch of efficiency so rapidly and at the right moment.

The rate at which Cambridge were improving in the last day or two, in fact which was still noticeable in their outing at 10 a.m. on the morning of the races, led me to explain in my forecast the possibility of a surprise.

(April 1)

No. 9920

ACROSS

1 This old man would surely find a watch quite superfluous (6, 4)
6 A composer's work might well provide a dish, of course (4)
10 Bands that have been involved in many a fight (5)
11 Mind the L.T. any time it goes wrong (9)
12 Descriptive of some vital matter (such as prison?) (8)
13 Eye in a jocular kind of way (5)
15 Criss-cross effort put back badly in very French surroundings (7)
17 The plant that makes a suitable start for the formal garden (7)
19 Take out what was apparently once a large area (7)
21 It gives an introduction to walk around the little umpire (7)
22 A type of paper to look into? (5)
24 A war centre, taken by surprise (8)
27 He might, without offence, be called abroad a low fellow (9)
28 A morass that is found under many a B.R. engine (5)
29 A 'tyrant' always seen in fine robes (4)
30 Such a description would doubtless fit the smuggler (4-6)

DOWN

1 Good-bye being well off for food (4)
2 The offer is French and most susceptible to pressure (9)
3 A well-known supporter of an artist's work (5)
4 Those who raised it had heaps of grave intentions (7)
5 Part return, the man is starting to set a snare for you! (7)
7 This shop is suitable for the display of an engraver's work (5)
8 In which one might get a lift to high living (10)
9 Came around to moll, in a muddled way; altogether a tonic (8)
14 Make more powerful, even though at heart it's plainly n.g.! (10)
16 The same land is different and he sounds better away from land (8)
18 A feud will continue as long as one side feels this (9)
20 Flash follower, worth a clap! (7)
21 Plain expanse with an atmosphere of its own (7)
23 He has delivered many a sound blow in cradle-rocking (5)
25 Companion of the red, so be careful, fellow-travellers! (5)
26 If he had less on the result would be unequalled (4)

(October 9)

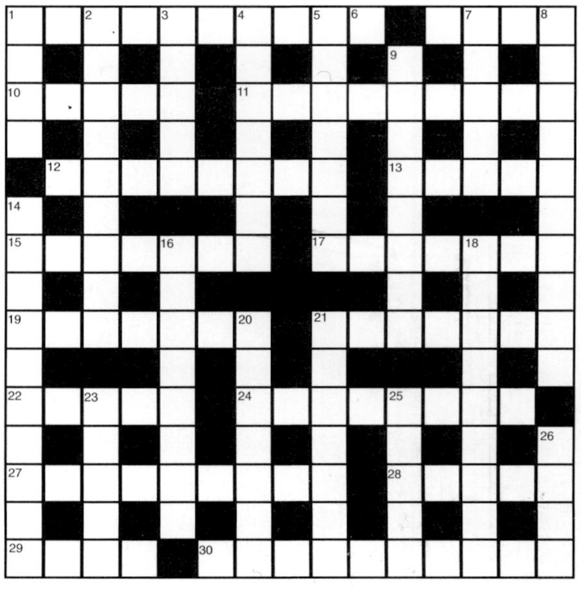

1958

General de Gaulle's year. With France in despair over the civil war in Algeria, in May he received the summons at his home at Colombe-les-Deux-Eglises to return from self imposed obscurity to lead his nation. By December the Fourth Republic was dead and de Gaulle was the first President of the Fifth Republic.

In September, Pope Pius XII, whom later generations were to reassess because of his accommodation with the dictators Hitler and Mussolini, died, and in his place was elected the first of the modern popes who was to break out from the confines of the Vatican. The new Pope immediately showed his individuality by choosing to be called John XXIII, a name once used by the dethroned schismatic Pope in the early 15th century.

The Middle East remained a cauldron. In Iraq, the young king Feisal and his chief minister were assassinated. The American marines landed in Lebanon to protect local interests while Egypt and Syria joined forces as the United Arab Republics under the joint leadership of President Nasser. In Cyprus the unrest continued as the cease-fire of the previous year was abrogated.

As rockets were fired into space, not always with great success, the anti-nuclear movement came into prominence. The first protest march set out from Trafalgar Square in London to wind its way to the Atomic Energy Establishment at Aldermaston. London and Nottingham experienced their first race riots.

The British economy was looking up, though the situation at the beginning of the year had caused Peter Thorneycroft, the Chancellor of the Exchequer, to resign over his collegues refusal to cut the defence estimates. Credit restrictions were relaxed. High-rise blocks of flats were being built.

There was still room for exploration on earth as Sir Vivian Fuchs completed the first crossing of the Antarctic continent. In a rather different sphere, for the first time in their own right, life peeresses took their seats in the House of Lords. On the same day a new Lord Chief Justice took over from the stern Lord Goddard. For the first time in 29 years a Liberal won a by-election seat in the House of Commons.

The sporting world was saddened by the crash of an aircraft carrying the Manchester United football team ("Bushby's Babes") home from a match in Germany.

Only three months later the team deprived of many of its best players, and with its goal keeper injured early in the game, gallantly but unsuccessfully sought to win the Cup Final.

But there was joy for the English cricketers in winning the test series against New Zealand and for the women's tennis team that re-captured the Whiteman Cup from the United States for the first time since 1930.

A British film, The Bridge over the River Kwai won seven oscars in the year when two of its brightest English-born stars, Ronald Coleman and Robert Donat died. The young Peter Hall took over as Director of the Shakespeare Memorial Theatre while a new playwright, Harold Pinter, was puzzling the critics in London. Within months of the first performance of his Ninth Symphony, Britain's greatest living composer, Ralph Vaughan Williams, was to die.

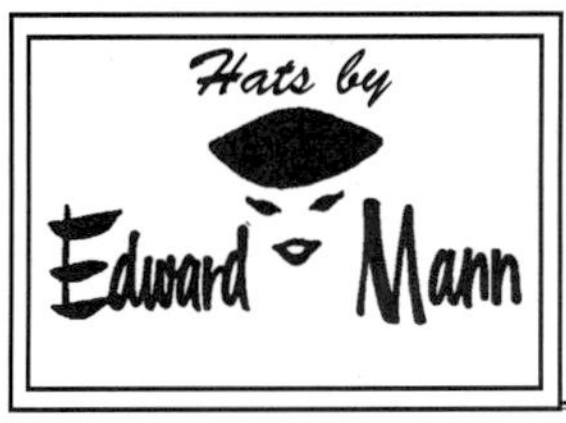
Hats by
Edward Mann

The Daily Telegraph

and Morning Post

No. 31,979 LONDON, FRIDAY, FEBRUARY 7, 1958 — Printed in LONDON and MANCHESTER Price 2½d.

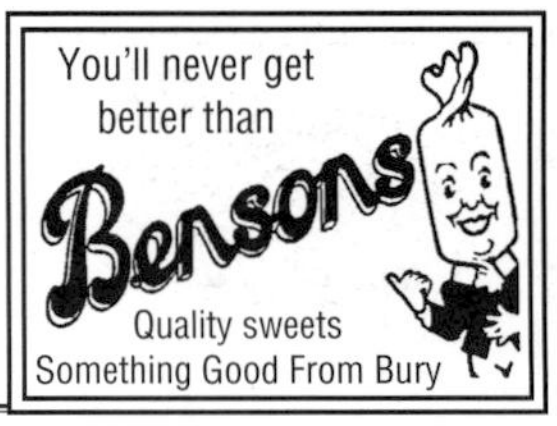
You'll never get
better than
Bensons
Quality sweets
Something Good From Bury

FOOTBALL PLANE CRASHES: 21 DEAD

MANCHESTER UNITED IN MUNICH DISASTER

THIRD ATTEMPT AT SNOWSTORM TAKE-OFF

SEVEN PLAYERS KILLED: MATT BUSHBY CRITICAL

From Percival Banyard and John Adams
Daily Telegraph Special Correspondents

Munich, Tuesday.

Seven players and three officals of Manchester United football team were among 21 people who lost their lives to-day when the British European Airways Elizabethan airliner bringing the team home from Belgrade crashed at Munich airport. Matt Bushby, the team manager, and eight players are in hospital. Bushby, who is also Scotland's World Cup team manager, has been put in an oxygen tent in a critical condition.

The plane, named Lord Burghley, was on charter. It crashed in a snowstorm while taking off, at the third attempt, late this afternoon. The Manchester United team were returning to Britain from Jugoslavia, where they had drawn 3-3 with the Red Star team in a European Cup match.

Of the 44 occupants of the plane, who included 11 sports writers, 20 were killed in the crash, and one, Frank Swift, former England goalkeeper, died in hospital. Swift was travelling as a guest of the Manchester United team.

Eye-witnesses at the airport said there was ice and snow on the runways. B.E.A confirmed in London that the plane first taxied out to take off, but returned.

The reason for the return was uncertain. Shortly afterwards it taxied out again and attempted to take off but again returned.

Describing the crash a B.E.A spokesman said: "The plane passed over the threshold of the runway and ran into a wooden fence. The port wing-tip hit a small building and the plane then caught fire."

Only one member of the crew of six was killed. He was the steward, W.T. Cable, 40, of Fanham Common, Bucks. He was married with one child.

Capt. J.G. Rayment, 36, the first officer, is seriously ill in hospital, but not on the danger list. He joined B.E.A in 1946 and has been flying Elizbethan aircraft since 1953. He is married with two children.

The other survivors among the crew members are Capt. J. Thain, 37, the pilot in charge of the aircraft, who is married with one child, G.W. Rogers, 35, Senior Radio Officer, of Harlington, Middlesex, married with one daughter; and two stewardesses, Rosemary Cheverton and Margaret Bellas.

A B.E.A spokesman said: "We understand that Capt. Thain and other members of the crew did a splendid job in fighting several small fires which followed the crash.

"They fought the flames with hand extinguishers and then apparently went into the aircraft to bring out as many passengers as they could."

CAUSE UNKNOWN

Full Inquiry

Mr Anthony Milward, B.E.A. chief executive, arrived at Munich's Reim airport to-night in a special Viscount airliner to investigate the crash. With him in the plane were Capt. W. Baillie, general flight manager, and Capt. James, flight operations director, and a number of engineering investigators.

At a conference held at the airport an hour after his arrival, Mr Milward said: "We do not know at this stage what caused the accident. There will be a full inquiry by German authorities and the B.E.A. investigating officials.

"The aircraft came from Belgrade this morning to Munich and had a normal flight. The plane refuelled at Munich. It went out for a take-off and the captain made two initial attempts to take off, but he was not satisfied with the power of the engines.

"He then came back to the tarmac and consulted with the B.E.A. station engineer. He was then completely satisfied after consultation, and he went out for his final take off . After that we don't know what happened, and we are not yet certain that the aircraft became fully airborne."

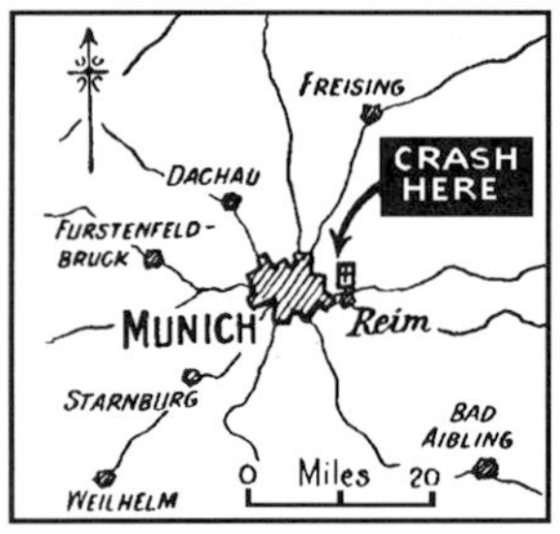
FREISING
CRASH HERE
DACHAU
FURSTENFELD-BRUCK
MUNICH
Reim
STARNBURG
BAD AIBLING
WEILHELM
0 Miles 20

FULL LIST OF DEAD

B.E.A. last night issued this complete list of the 21 dead in the crash:

Footballers: Eddie Colman, Roger Bryne, Mark Jones, Billy Whelan, Tommy Taylor, Geoff Bent, David Pegg.

Officals: T.H. Curry, trainer; H. Whalley, coach; Walter Crickmer, secretary.

Journalists: Tom Jackson, Manchester Evening News; Archie Ledbrooke, Daily Mirror; H.D. Davies, Manchester Guardian; Eric Thompson, Daily Mail; Henry Rose, Daily Express; George Follows, Daily Herald; Alf Clarke, Manchester Evening Chronicle.

Others: Frank Swift, former English international goalkeeper and guest of the team; B.P. Miklos, travel agent; W. Satinoff

Aircrew: W.T. Cable, steward.

MOTHER AND BABY ESCAPE

FAMILY OF ATTACHÉ

Daily Telegraph Reporter

Mrs. Vera Lukitch, who is reported to be one of the survivors, was flying back to Britain with her baby daughter, Vanessa, aged 22 months.

Mrs. Lukitch is the young wife of Mr. Veljko Lukitch, air attaché at the Jugoslav Embassy in London. The baby was also reported to have survived with slight injuries. Both were said to be in hospital.

Mrs. Lukitch travelld in the aircraft to Belgrade on Monday together with the Manchester team and two officials of the Jugoslav Embassy. She and her husband have been in London for about three years.

A spokesman at the Embassy said last night that she went to Belgrade to be re-united with her baby after an eight months' seperation. The child had been staying with relatives.

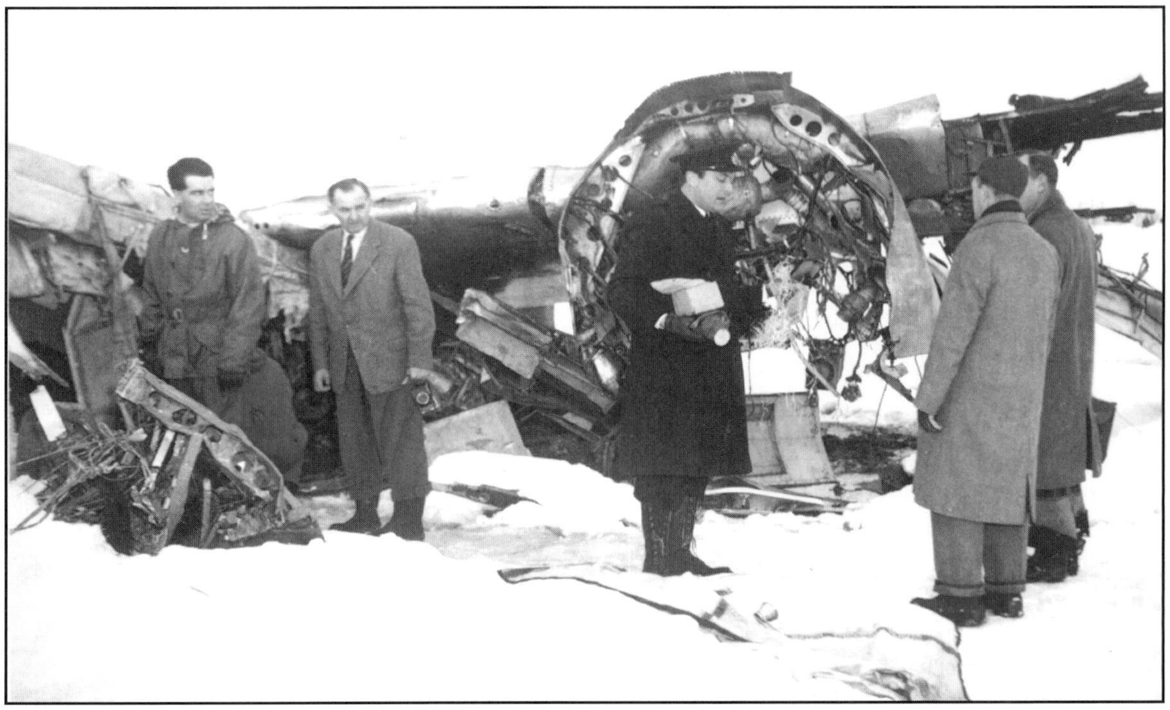

GERMAN OFFICIALS AT CRASH SCENE. Captain Hans Reichel (second from left) of the West German Federal Aviation Board, who is heading the German Mission inquiring into the Munich aircrash, and members of the Mission are shown inspecting the BEA Elizabethan wreckage at the Munich airport, Munich, Germany, February 8. Third from left is Herr Adolf Roth, British European Airways Station Manager in Munich.

AIRLINER ROSE A FEW FEET

WOODEN FENCE HIT AFTER TAKE-OFF

By Air Cmdre. L.G.S. Payne
Daily Telegraph Air Correspondent

According to information available last night, the British European Airways Ambassador (Elizabethan) was only a few feet off the ground when it crashed yesterday while taking off from Munich. It collided with a wooden fence and hit a small building with its wing tip.

Part of the aircraft and the building then caught fire. The aircraft previously taxied out to take off and then returned. The reason for this is still uncertain. Snow was fallling at the time. Take off accidents have been caused by troubles arising from ice formation.

FIRST FLEW IN 1947

The Ambassador, made by the Airspeed Division of the de Havilland Aircraft Company and called by the B.E.A. the Elizabethan, is powered by two Bristol Centaurus piston engines and was designed to accomadate about 47 passengers. The first prototype made its first flight on July 10 1947.

B.E.A. had a fleet of 20 Ambassadors. After the deliveries of Viscount 800s began, the Corporation announced, in March 1957, that it intended to sell its Ambassadors progressively. Five have already been sold.

One B.E.A. Ambassador made a crash landing on April 8 1955, in a field a few minutes after taking off from Dusseldorf. The accident is believed to have occurred after trouble in one engine.

None of the 47 passengers was injured. Four members of the crew were slightly hurt. B.E.A.'s fleet of Ambassadors now numbers 14.

QUEEN SENDS HER SYMPATHY

The Queen last night sent the following message to Mr Watkinson, Minister of Transport and Civil Aviation:

"I am deeply shocked to hear of the accident to the plane carrying members of the Manchester United Football Club and newspapermen back from Belgrade. Please convey my sympathy and that of my husband to the relatives of those who have been killed and of the injured."

The Queen's message to the Lord Mayor of Manchester read: "My husband and I have learned with great regret of the tradegy which will have caused so much grief to the citizens of Manchester."

In reply Ald Lever sent the following telegram: "I desire on behalf of the citizens of Manchester to thank her Majesty the Queen and his Royal Highness Prince Philip, Duke of Edinburgh, for their kind message of sympathy which is deeply appreciated and which will give so much comfort and strength to all concerned."

MANCHESTER STUNNED: TICKETS SALE STOPPED

Daily Telegraph Reporter

News of the air disaster, the worst in English football history, stunned Manchester. Crowds of supporters went to Manchester United ground at Old Trafford to seek the latest information.

Ald Lever, the Lord Mayor said: "I am deeply grieved to hear about this tragic accident and am sure that every one in the city and beyond will feel likewise. We are grief stricken."

Councillor Edward Reid, Mayor of Stratford, in which district the United 's ground is situated, cancelled all engagements. "The whole town mourns their loss as do thousands upon thousands of other people." he said. "Everyone is deeply shocked."

Some time after the news of the crash reached Old Trafford, some supporters who were queueing to buy tickets for the Fifth Round of the F.A. Cup against Sheffield Wednesday on Saturday week were told that the sale of tickets had been stopped.

EIGHTH YEAR

"Wonderful Planes"

Mr Anthony Milward, chief executive of B.E.A. said before leaving for Munich last night that the accident was the first fatal one involving an Elizabethan. "They are now in their eighth year of service with us and they have been wonderful planes.

"We know that their must have been some sort of engine trouble. The accident happened almost immediately after take off."

CLUB TOOK OUT £210,000 POLICY

HEAVY LIABILITIES

By Our Insurance Correspondent

The Elizabethan airliner was insured in London by Lloyds and the insurance companies for £150,000. The Manchester United club took out a £210,000 policy to cover 21 players and officials at £10,000 each.

Presumably at least some of the other passengers are also covered. Taking into consideration the the loss of the hull and claims under passengers' policies, the crash means a probable loss to the insurance companies and Lloyds of £500,000.

The automatic liability of British European Airways for passengers is governed by the provisions of the Warsaw Convention under which compensation is limited to £3,000 a seat. As a proposal to increase this to £6,000 has apparently not yet been generally ratified the lower limit is still applicable.

LIFE PEERAGES BILL OPPOSED

SOCIALISTS TABLE AMENDMENT

By Our Political Correspondent

To ensure that all shades of Socialist opinion on the Lords' reform are represented, Mr. Bevan as well as Mr. Gaitskell will contribute to the two-day debate on the Life Peerages Bill in the Commons next Wednesday and Thursday.

Because the Bill is confined to the creation of life peers of both sexes, thus enabling women to sit in the Lords for the first time, the Socialists do not intend to oppose the it outright. Instead last night they tabled a "reasonable amendment."

This suggests the Commons should decline to give a Second Reading to the Bill "which leaves the House of Lords overwhelmingly hereditary in character and with unimpaired powers to frustrate and obstruct the will of the representatives of the people."

JUNE 1 CLEAN AIR DAY

NO DARK SMOKE

By a Political Correspondent

The emission of dark smoke from chimneys will be an offence punishable by fines of up to £100 after June 1. An Order bringing in the remaining provisions of the Clean Air Act on that date was presented to Parliament yesterday.

The ban will apply to factories, shops, offices, ships and railway engines. House chimneys, although covered by the Order, rarely produce dark smoke, which is defined as shade two on the Ringelmann chart.

Failure to minimise grit and dust will also be an offence.

CABINET ANGRY AT BONN OFFER

SUPPORT COST CLAIM TO BE PRESSED

By Our Political Correspondent

Though West Germany's offer to deposit £100 million in London against future purchases of arms has not yet reached the British Government officially, it is thought to have been discussed at the Cabinet meeting yesterday.

Ministers made no attempt to conceal their indignation that this entirely separate proposal should be put forward as an acceptable alternative to a German contribution towards the cost of maintaining British forces in Germany.

It would not mitigate the burden on the British taxpayer of finding £40,000,000 to £45,000,000 in Deutschmarks to keep British troops on the Rhine for the next financial year.

Credit for this amount has been taken in the Defence Estimates for 1958-59. The Government is determined to obtain a substantial share of it from Germany with "no strings."

STILL HOPE OF SOLUTION

Hopes of a reasonable arrangement have not yet been abandoned. The Government is relying on Western European union and the N.A.T.O. Council to press its claim.

There is no question of Germany's ability to pay. But if Bonn remains adamant the withdrawal of a large proportion of Britain's forces from Germany will undoubtedly be considered.

The Cabinet meeting lasted more than two hours. It was learned afterwards that the White Paper on Defence will be published within the next week.

FOREIGN OFFICE MEETINGS

Our Diplomatic Correspondent writes: Sir Christopher Steel, British Ambassador to West Germany, had a meeting yesterday at the Foreign Office with Mr. Selwyn Lloyd, Foreign Secretary. He has come to London for consultations. Herr Herwardt, West German Ambassador in London went to the Foreign Office to see Sir Anthony Rumbold, Assistant Under-Secretary.

PRINCESS ARTHUR TAKEN ILL

PNEUMONIA ATTACK

Princess Arthur of Connaught is suffering from pneumonia. A bulletin issued last night from her London home said her condition showed a slight improvement over Wednesday.

The granddaughter of King Edward VII, the Princess is 17th in order of succession to the Throne. She is 66. Last August she was seriously ill with pneumonia.

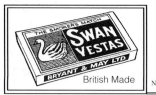

The Daily Telegraph

No. 32,077 LONDON, TUESDAY, JUNE 3, 1958
and Morning Post
Printed in LONDON and MANCHESTER Price 2½d.

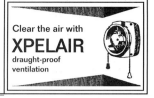

1A.M. VOTE ENDS FOURTH REPUBLIC

GEN. DE GAULLE GETS ALL HE SOUGHT

MAJORITY OF 187 FOR CONSTITUTION BILL

6 MONTHS' RULE BY DECREE: AUTUMN REFERENDUM

The French National Assembly at 1 a.m. to-day passed, by a substantial majority, a Bill for constitutional reform after Gen. de Gaulle had threatened to resign as Prime Minister. Its decision ended the Fourth Republic and completed Assembly action on the General's three-point emergency programme on which he insisted.

This included full powers to rule by decree in France for the next six months and special powers in Algeria. The Senate has also approved these measures and is expected to agree quickly to the reform Bill later to-day. The Government intends to hold a referendum on the Constitution in the early Autumn.

Voting by the Assembly on the three main issues was the following:

	For	Against	Majority
Constitutional Reform ...	350	163	187
Special Powers	322	232	90
Algeria emergency Powers	337	199	138

Last night the Assembly's Committee on Suffrage had amended the Constitution Bill, giving Deputies a bigger voice in the reforms proposed. Gen. de Gaulle, in a five minute speech, told the House that it would have to take the consequences, civil war, if he stepped down while Algeria and Corsica were in almost open revolt.

The General said it could not accept the hamstringing amendments proposed to his reform plan. If the debate dragged on, his Government "would have no purpose. It would not be possible for it to continue beyond to-night."

TALKS WITH SERVICE CHIEFS

France's leader all yesterday maintained a constant link with Parliament through his Cabinet Ministers, who reported to him at his hotel headquarters. He also saw Adml. Nomy, Chief of Naval Staff, Gen. Ely, former Chief of Staff of the Armed Forces, Gen. Gelee, Chief of Air Staff, and M. Gorse, French Ambassador to Tunisia.

Mr. Macmillan sent a message to Gen. de Gaulle expressing pleasure at the opportunity of renewing "our wartime friendship forged in those days when, as President of the National Liberation Committee, you led France to victory."

STRIKE CALLS FAIL

The situation throughout France was quiet, Communists' efforts to foment widespread strikes failing. The Tunisian Cabinet met when it discussed the coming to power of Gen. de Gaulle.

Already the General has sent friendly messages to the King of Morocco and to President Bourguiba of Tunisia. He expressed belief in the possibility of better and closer relations with North Africa.

Tunisia branded France as an "aggressor" before the United Nations Security Council and she asked the Council to ensure that French troops quit Tunisian terrority. The debate was adjourned until to-morrow.

Mr. Leon Delbecque, Vice-President of the Algiers Public Safety Committee, left Algeria for Paris yesterday. It is believed that he is to see Gen. de Gaulle to urge him to appoint M. Soustelle as Minister for Algeria.

THREAT OF RESIGNATION

From Our Own Correspondent

Paris, Tuesday morning.

At 1 a.m. this morning the French Assembly granted Gen. de Gaulle the right to present a revised Constitution to the people of France in a referendum without the previous consent of Parliament. They did so by 350 votes against 163.

He came down to the Assembly himself and threatened to resign unless it overruled the advice of its Universal Suffrage Committee on this point. He agreed that when framing the constitutional reform the Government should consult a special commission drawn from the standing committees of the Assembly.

Earlier in the day the General had been granted full powers to govern the country for six months without reference to Parliament. It can therefore be said that the Fourth Republic no longer exists.

SOCIALISTS SPLIT

Immediate Change

The General was assured of a three-fifths majority in favour of revising the crucial Article 90 of the Constitution when the dissident Socialists stated that they would abstain. This means that the Constitution will be changed immediately.

The Government, in consultation with Assembly committees, will carry out a complete revision on the lines laid down by the Bill. The new Constitution will be submitted to a referendum without the necessity of previously passing through Parliament.

In his winding-up speech Gen. de Gaulle recalled that if three-fifths of Parliament did not decide in favour this would make a first referendum necessary in the very near future. This would take place at a most unfortunate moment and create confusion.

ALGIERS ENVOY TO PLEAD FOR M. SOUSTELLE

POST AS MINISTER URGED

From John Wallis
Daily Telegraph Special Correspondent

Algiers, Monday.

Mr. Leon Delbecque, vice president of the Algerian Committee of Public Safety, left here to-day for Paris. It is presumed he is going to see Gen. de Gaulle to urge him to appoint M. Soustelle as Minister for Algeria.

It is clear that the Committee of Public Safety does not realise Gen. de Gaulle's intransigence and dislikes. The General is arriving here on Wednesday.

M. Soustelle said over the radio to-day concerning Gen. de Gaulle's visit that he had received a message from the General to ask the population to "remain calm." Later, after the broadcast, the Home Guards Vigilance Corps received orders from their district chiefs. They were told to calm the populace, with whom they are in constant contact.

It is believed here that feeling among the civilian European population is running very high on the subject of the future Minister for Algeria. For them, their hero, M. Soustelle, is the only possible choice.

BAN ON REPORTS

M. Lejeune's Post

Last night M. Neuwirth, spokesman for the Committee of Public Safety, formally banned any mention in the local press of Paris reports that M. Max Lejeune, Socialist former Minister for the Sahara, was to be appointed Minister for Algeria. The local press are also playing down M. Pflimlin and his speeches on negotiations with the rebels.

An extremely important declaration was made last night by M. Jacques Chevalier, Liberal mayor of Algiers. He came out for a Federal solution of the Algerian problem under Gen. de Gaulle.

SOUSTELLE STATEMENT

Integration Plea

"Integration in the Federal Republic would appear to give satisfaction to the aspirations and interests of everyone," M. Chevalier said. "It might perhaps even lead to the return into the great French body of certain elements which the instability of the system in the absence of coherent policy has forced away from us."

This was an obvious reference to Tunisia and Morocco. M. Chevalier's formula of integration in a Federal Republic differs sharply from M. Soustelle's declaration that there was "only one kind of Frenchman from Dunkirk to Tamanrasset, in the Sahara." This means assimilation.

The movement of May 13 had produced "positive and indisputable results in the way of bringing together Europeans and Moslems," M. Chevalier continued. The Europeans had abandoned in their enthusiasm a number of prejudices of which they were suspect.

The delicate question would be to give concrete values to the immense surge of generosity so that the undertakings solemnly sworn

(continued on back page, col 6.)

SHOOTING GOES ON IN LEBANON

THREE KILLED

From Our Special Correspondent

Beirut, Monday.

Beirut had another night of sporadic firing and bombing. Three people were killed and six wounded in fighting in a neighbouring town between security forces and rebels.

In Basta, the Moslem quarter of Beirut, mortar and automatic fire was exchanged. On the 22nd day of the rebellion, the beleaguered insurgents were apparently trying to bolster up their crumbling facade. It is considered here that their chance of a coup has nearly passed.

Now that the re-election of President Chamouno for a second term is almost out of the question, names of a possible successor are being whispered. One is that of Mr. Eddeh, a Christian Deputy of long experience.

PREMIER REJECTS NEW BUS TALKS

T.U.C. MEETING TO-MORROW: URGENT CALL TO MEMBERS

By Hugh Chevins
Daily Telegraph Industrial Correspondent

The Prime Minister yesterday told the Trade Union Congress that he saw no useful purpose in meeting them again that day to discuss the strike of 50,000 London busmen, now in its fifth week. A special meeting of the T.U.C. General Council has been called for to-morrow.

A measure of the importance which the T.U.C. attaches to this meeting is the urgent recall to London of its delegation of six, led by Sir Alfred Roberts, the textile workers' chief, who had gone to Geneva for the International Labour Organisation conference. All members of the General Council, wherever they may be, have been urged to do their utmost to attend.

A delegate conference of the busmen unanimously rejected the London Transport Executive's terms of settlement (L.T.E. statement, p9.). They decided to meet again after they had heard the result of the T.U.C. General Council deliberations tomorrow.

No further steps were taken to embroil the petrol lorry drivers and mates or the electrical power workers in the dispute.

The approach to the Prime Minister for another meeting with union leaders was made on the telephone by the T.U.C. special sub-committee who met him on Friday to discuss the strike situation.

STRIKE EXTENDED

Private Firm's Buses

While yesterday's talks were in progress, other moves were:

The first extension of the strike to a private firm occurred when a union official ordered employees of the Eastern National Omnibus Co. to withdraw the bus services which normally operate between Brentford, Romford and Wood Green and between Upminster and Romford.

The executive council of the Amalgamated Engineering Union decided to give £1,000 to the Transport and General Workers' Union in aid of the busmen.

REQUEST TO PREMIER

Downing Street Reply

As a result of the T.U.C. interview with the Prime Minister on Friday negotiations were reopened between Sir John Elliot, chairman, and other members of the London Transport Executive and Mr. Cousins, general secretary of the Transport and General Workers' Union and members of its negotiating committee.

The talks which took place on Saturday and Sunday failed. In consequence the T.U.C. special sub-committee met again yesterday and sought the further parleys with Mr. Macmillan.

A statement was received from 10 Downing Street, while the sub-committee was still meeting yesterday.

(continued on p9, col 4)

WAY OPEN FOR MEETING LATER THIS WEEK

By Our Political Correspondent

Mr. Macmillan's statement on the London bus strike yesterday is not to be interpreted, I understand, as a rebuff to the Trade Union Congress. Nor does it close the door on the possibility of a meeting before the Prime Minister leaves for the United States on Friday.

Mr. Macmillan took the view that it would be no avail to reopen discussions with the T.U.C. representatives until the result of the busmen's delegate conference was known. He may also have had in mind the fact that the T.U.C. General Council is due to meet to-morrow.

A meeting of the Cabinet, the first since Parliament rose for Whitsun, is also likely to-morrow. This will provide an opportunity for Ministers to discuss the bus dispute in the context of the general economic situation.

The Downing Street statement followed telephone conversations between T.U.C. officals and members of the Prime Minister's secretariat.

CZECHS FIRE ON GERMANS

Bonn, Monday.

Shots were exchanged between four West Germans and four Czechoslavak frontier policemen to-day in the mountains near Zwiesel in the Bavarian Forest.

One fell over 30 yards from the frontier, breaking a knuckle. The Czechs came over the frontier, handcuffed him and took him to a frontier post where they bandaged his hand. Later he escaped.

STABILITY CAN BRING TAX CUT

CHANCELLOR'S AIM

Daily Telegraph Reporter

Mr. Heathcoat Amory, Chancellor of the Exchequer, said at Weston-super-Mare last night: "Once we have dealt with inflation and stabilised the cost of living, then the way is open for further tax cuts.

"I cannot say more about that without disclosing my intentions for the next Budget." Mr. Amory was speaking in support of David Webster, the Conservative candidate in next week's by-election.

He said that if everyone behaved with restraint this year, particularly over wage claims, he believed there was a better chance of stabilising the cost of living than at any time since the war.

"A return of a Socialist Government at the present time or at any foreseeable time in the future, would mean a return to rapid inflation, a big rise in the cost of living and a tremendous increase in taxes."

16,000 NOW OUT IN LONDON DOCK STRIKE

FreshWarning On Food Danger

100 SHIPS HELD UP IN PORT

By Our Industrial Staff

Several hundred London dockers due to return yesterday from their annual holidays failed to report for work. Their absence brought the total of men on unofficial strike in the London docks to nearly 16,000.

One hundred ships, many of them with food cargoes and others part-loaded with exports, are held up in port. Another 15 have too few dockers working to enable them to load or discharge efficiently.

Mr. A. J. M. Crichton, chairman of the Port Employers in London, repeated a warning about the condition of 10,000 tons of foodstuffs lying in ships, on barges and on the wharves since the strike began more than two weeks ago.

He said that examination showed that 4,500 tons of butter was now "very soft" and 3,700 tons of cheese was "sweating badly." A quantity of yeast had been destroyed.

PORT POSITION

Onions in Jeopardy

Other cargoes in jeopardy included about 500 tons of potatoes and a quantity of bacon and fat. The position in the port last night was:

Docks	Men on Strike	Ships Idle	Ships Under-Manned
Upper Pool (including Tooley Street area)	3,377	9	-
London and St. Katherine's	3,663	34	-
Royal Group	5,294	32	10
W. India and Millwall	2,061	20	2
Surrey	2,042	5	3
Totals	15,347	100	15

This compares with Saturday's total of 15,499.

Apart from a "hard core" of dockers and cold store workers, mainly in the Tooley Street area, who have been on strike for more than a fortnight in support of the Smithfield Market workers, the dockers have stopped in protest against the use by the employers of unregistered labour.

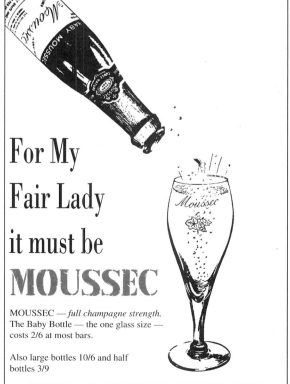

PATRIARCH OF VENICE ELECTED POPE AT 76

DECISION IN 12TH BALLOT: TITLE TO BE JOHN XXII

From Our Own Correspondent

ROME, Tuesday.

Cardinal ANGELO GIUSEPPE RONCALLI, Patriarch of Venice, who is 76, was elected the 263rd Pontiff of the Roman Catholic Church to-night. He will take the title of Pope John XXIII

The new Pontiff's first gesture was to resume a custom which had fallen into disuse. When he started to don the white papal robes in the vestry of the Sistine Chapel he placed his cardinal's purple skull-cap on the head of the Secretary of the Conclave, Mgr. di Jorio, thus signifying his intention of elevating him to the purple. Mgr. di Jorio, considered one of the ablest administrators of the Vatican, has been in charge of its financial affairs for several years and is well known as a financial expert.

A man of humble, almost peasant stock, the new Pope was born in the hamlet of Sotto il Monte, 30 miles east of Milan. His brothers still till a small plot of land there, and in recent years he has always gone there for his holidays.

The first announcement of Cardinal Roncalli's elevation was given at 5.08 this evening by a small puff of streaky yellow smoke from the top of the slender chimney emerging over the roof of the Sistine Chapel. The ballot papers which elected the new Pope on the 12th count of the conclave were being burnt.

The colour of a subsequent little puff of smoke continued to be dubious, but as the minutes went by without a further smoke signal uncertainty turned into certainty. Thousands of people began to converge on St. Peter's Square.

CARABINIERI BAND

Gay March Played

Fifty minutes later the band of the Italian Carabinieri, followed by a battalion of Italian grenadiers, marched into the square. While the band was still playing a gay march, the curtains were drawn behind the loggia just above the bronze doors of St. Peter, and the window was thrown open.

A golden crucifix and a little cluster of purple emerged on to the balcony and the proto-deacon of the College. Cardinal Canali made the announcement.

His voice broken by emotion Cardinal Canali, speaking in Latin, said to the world: "I have tidings of great joy. We have a Pope." He then gave the new Pontiff's name as a cardinal and the name he had decided to adopt as Pope, John XXIII.

The last Pope to bear that name reigned from 1313 to 1334. The history of the Church also records another John XXIII, from 1410 to 1415, but he was considered an anti-pope.

A thunderous cheer rose from the more than 300,000 people who were literally packed into the square. The window was then closed for a few minutes until members of the Papal Court emerged to drape it with a tapestry carrying the crest of the late Pius XII.

As the crowd waited tensely for the appearance of the new Pontiff a little white pigeon was caught in the beams of the searchlight trained on the basilica. It fluttered fearfully in front of the facade.

OPEN WINDOWS

Guards' Drawn Swords

After Cardinal Canali's announcement the great bronze bell of St. Peter's began to peal out the joyful news and was picked up by the bells of the 300 churches of Rome and on by those of every Roman Catholic church in the world.

(October 29)

TROOPS KILL EOKA AMBUSH CHIEF

From Brian Wright
Daily Telegraph Special Correspondent

NICOSIA, Wednesday

Kyriakos Matsis, 32, the most wanted Eoka leader after Col. Grivas, was killed by British troops this afternoon in the Kyrenia Range. Troops threw two hand grenades into his hiding place after he had shouted: "You will have to come and get me."

Matsis, an ambush expert, was found when security forces searched a house for arms in Kato Khikomo village. A private of the 1st Bn. Wiltshire Regt. prodded the tiled floor of the back parlour with his bayonet and it slipped between two tiles.

Investigation showed that it was an entrance to a hide-out. There was a shout from down below. Matsis said he would only come out shooting but there were two other men who wanted to surrender. These two crawled into the room.

When Matsis refused to give himself up after repeated orders by a security officer the grenades were thrown through the narrow entrance. Before his body was moved a German automatic weapon and a Sten gun could be seen by the light of a torch.

(November 20)

RELAXATION IN EXPORTS TO SOVIET BLOC

By a Political Correspondent

A major relaxation in the embargo on the export of goods to the Soviet bloc and China was announced yesterday. From to-day the control on the export of stategic goods by quantitative limitation will be discontinued.

The main list of goods completely banned is revised and reduced from 181 to 118 types Sir David Eccles, President of the Board of Trade, who announced the changes, described the operation as "cutting the list down to the bone."

The articles completely freed as a result of to-day's relaxation include:

Tankers, designed for 18 knots or less:
Fishing vessels, less than 17 knots:
Other vessels, less than 20 knots:
Floating docks"
All non-military vehicles:
Aircraft and aero-engines in normal civil use:
Most machine tools, except those used for making weapons:
All electrical generating machinery, except mobile generators of more than 5,000 KW:
Industrial diamonds and diamond tools:
All tyres for civilian use.
Petrol and lubricating oils.

A small number of goods have been added to the banned list. These are mainly used in electronics or the chemical industry and would be of potential military value. They include equipment designed to provide secrecy in communications.

Arms banned

Arms, munitions, military equipment and machinery continue to be generally banned. But the Board of Trade will consider applications for licenses to export small quantities of rifles, shotguns, carbines of pistols, for "sporting or ornamental purposes."

(August 15)

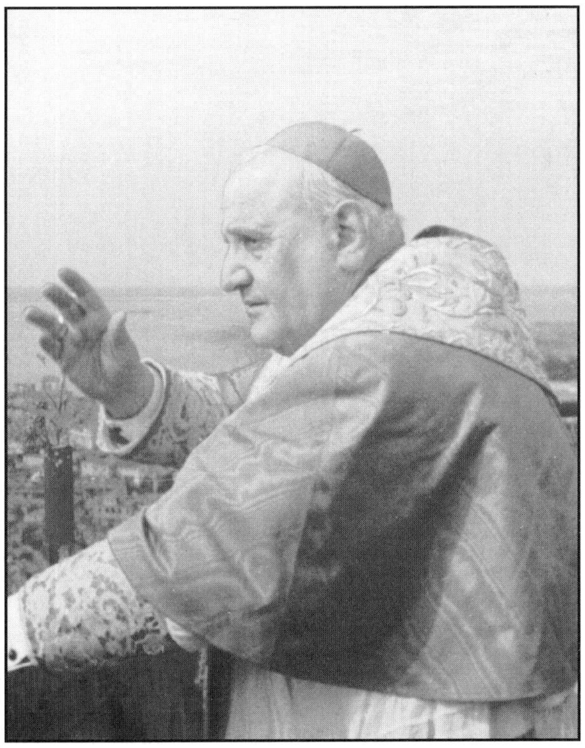

POPE JOHN XXIII blesses crowds in Vatican Square

SPENDOUR OF PAPAL CROWNING CEREMONY

HOMAGE AND THANKSGIVING BY 200,000 IN ST. PETER'S SQUARE

From Our Own Correspondent

ROME, Tuesday

In a four-and-a-half-hour ceremony of moving solemnity and antique splendour, John XXIII, 263rd legitimate Pope to mount the Pontifical Throne, was crowned to-day in the Basilica of St. Peter.

Following the awe-inspiring and protracted ritual of a Pontifical Mass, he was carried to the open loggia over the main entrance of the Basilica. The Triple Crown was placed upon his head before the eyes of 200,000 spectators who filled St. Peter's Square.

A roar of homage and thanksgiving rose from the throng as the Pope imparted his blessing. Urbi et Orbi.

Plenary Indulgence was accorded to Roman Catholics who attended, either within or in front of the Basilica. By a recent decree, this extends also to all those throughout the world who listened to today's ceremonies on radio or television.

Delegations from 59 nations, members of the Diplomatic Corps accredited to the Vatican, and their wives, and other guests of honour, began filling their allotted boxes at 8 a.m. One of the first delegation leaders to arrive was the Duke of Norfolk, representing the Queen.

Dressed in the scarlet and gold Coronation uniform of Earl Marshal of England, with white silk knee breeches and blue riband of the Garter, he took his seat in the front row, next to Prince Albert of Liege, brother of the King of the Belgians.

25,000 IN BASILICA

Crowds Wait from 6 a.m.

Before the ceremony began at 8.30, nearly 25,000 participants were crowded into every available space within the Basilica. Many ticket holders had arrived before 6 o'clock to secure seats at points of vantage. Those waiting in the square stood patiently in a slight drizzle.

As the Papal Procession began entering the Basilica, headed by Swiss Guards in polished breast plates and the scarlet, gold and blue uniforms designed by Michalangelo, the congregation rose with cries of enthusiasm. Women in black mantillas waved lace handkerchiefs, and shouts of "Long live the Pope!" were heard in many tongues from all parts of the Basilica.

SPLASH OF COLOUR

Japanese Costume

A particular splash of colour in the Dipomatic Gallery was provided by two Japanese women. They were wearing Japanese national costume with the black lace mantillas prescribed for Papal audiences.

Solemn though the cortege was the brilliant colours of many uniforms and vestments, and the splendour of gold and silver embroidery lent emphasis to the joyousness of the occasion. A scarlet-robed ecclesiastic carrying the Pontifical Tiara, and flanked by Swiss Guards, was among the first to enter.

Chaplains in violet soutanes, bishops in white mitres and robes decorated with silver, ecclesiastics in scarlet capes, and the College of Cardinals in cream coloured vestments heavy with gold embroidery, followed each other in measured procession.

Finally, amid renewed shouts of enthusiasm, the Pope was carried in by 12 bearers. He was seated in the Gestatorial Chair beneath a richly embroidered canopy.

He wore a gem-studded mitre and the ritual Falda, an ample white robe with full skirt and train. To right and left were members of the Noble Guard and Palatine Guard in gala uniform and immediately before the Chair came the Prince Assistant at the Pontifical Throne, Prince Giuseppe Colonna.

On either side of the Chair, red caped attendants carried the Fiabelli, enormous ostrich feather fans mounted on handles covered in crimson and gold.

(November 5)

SPUTNIK I ENDS SILENTLY

1,350 CIRCUITS

The time has now come to write the obituary of the first artificial earth satellite, launched by the Russians from a point north of the Caspian Sea in the evening of October 4. Tass, the Soviet News Agency, has not mentioned it for the last three days.

Astronomers predicted its end in the early days of the New Year. Tass's silence now is the same as its silence on the rocket carrier when that was plunging into the atmosphere.

Prof. A.C.B. Lovell, of Jodrell Bank, Cheshire, said last night that the last phase of the first satellite is likely to remain unknown unless observations are available elsewhere. Therefore one of the loudest bangs ever to be achieved in rocketry ends with one of the quietest of whimpers.

(January 3)

ICELAND CLAIMS NAVY SHIP 'USED FORCE'

GUNBOATS WERE KEPT OFF

The first day of Iceland's enforcement of a 12-mile fishing limit passed without clashes yesterday, although Reykjavik radio claimed the British frigate Palliser, 1,800 tons, used "force" to prevent Icelandic coastguard craft reaching British trawlers fishing inside the limit.

The radio said the Palliser "came steaming at great speed, with guns manned, and sailed between the coastguard and the poachers, so that the coastguard could not reach the trawlers." The Icelandic ships in other areas warned British trawlers by loud-hailer that they were infringing the limit.

Their numbers were taken and they were told that if caught inside the three-mile limit which Iceland claims as territorial waters, as opposed to the 12-mile fisheries limit, they would be arrested.

Mr. Gudmundsson, Icelandic Foreign Minister, announced last night that he had protested to Mr. Gilchrist, British Ambassador, against the sending of trawlers inside the 12-mile limit. He also accused Britain of using force and said he had instructed Iceland's N.A.T.O. representative to inform the N.A.T.O. Secretary-General.

(September 2)

FRIGATE PLAYS CAT-AND-MOUSE

GUNBOATS OUTPACED

From Guy Rais
Daily Telegraph Special Correspondent

REYKJAVIK, Monday

Strapped in the co-pilot's seat of a light twin-engined aircraft, I flew 150ft above the frigate H.M.S. Russell, 1,100 tons, as she steamed four miles off Iceland's west coast, keeping a vigilant eye on nine British trawlers defying Iceland's 12-mile fishing limit.

The trawlers, black smoke rising from their funnels, cast their nets about seven miles off Kopanes Point, an area near the western tip of Iceland dotted with fjords and deserted bays. As we circled low, I spotted two of Iceland's protection boats hovering by the Russell.

It was fascinating to watch the cat-and-mouse tactics of Russell's commander. By skilful manoeuvring and turning, the frigate never allowed the two smaller vessels to come between her and the flotilla of trawlers in the fishing lanes.

BUSY CREWS

Hungry Seagulls

As we flew over a scattered bunch of nine trawlers we could see the crews busying themselves with their nets. Hundreds of hungry seagulls surrounded the ships.

We banked sharply and headed for the frigate four miles off the rocky coast. I could see her name and her number, F 97. Moving slowly towards her was the Icelandic gunboat Odinn, 72 tons.

When the Odinn was less than 75 yards away she hove to. I could see her crew lean over the deck rail and exchange views with the British ratings. Almost immediately I spotted a second Icelandic ship, the Albert.

She appeared to have steamed out of a fjord and headed straight for the frigate. As she drew near the Russell quickly turned almost full circle to split up the two Icelandic ships.

The frigate's wake churned up the calm sea as she again turned sharply, preventing the two smaller vessels from slipping past her towards the trawlers fishing in the distance.

From my circle seat above it appeared as if the two Icelandic ships tried to break through but the frigate was too alert from them. I did not think, in view of previous statements, that they were there to make arrests.

Before my aircraft headed for Reykjavik, about 100 miles away, we headed once again for the trawlers. Their nets were down as they trawled unmolested for prime plaice and halibut in the grounds where they and their fathers before them have fished for more than a century.

(September 2)

PRINCE OF WALES IS HOME FOR HOLIDAYS

AN EARLY VISIT TO PRINCIPALITY

Daily Telegraph Reporter

Prince Charles, the Heir Apparent, who is aged nine, has been created Prince of Wales. This announcement was made by the Queen in a recorded message broadcast at the end of the Empire Games, at Cardiff, on Saturday.

The Prince of Wales yesterday was visited by his sister, Princess Anne, at Cheam School, at Headley, near Newbury, Berkshire, where he has been a pupil since September of last year. The school has now broken up for the summer holiday.

TOP IN GEOGRAPHY

Examination Results

Earlier the end of term examination results had been pinned up on the school notice board. The Prince of Wales had discovered he was top in geography and highly placed in French.

"The young Prince was very pleased with his results," a member of the school staff said. "There are 20 boys in his class, standard 2, and he got first place in geography with 70 marks out of 100. In French he had made excellent progress and gained 52 marks out of 100."

When the Prince and Princess Anne left the school in a black saloon car only a few villagers, standing in the rain, saw them go by. They drove to Windsor Castle for tea.

Later, the Prince and Princess Anne drove from Windsor and joined the Queen at Buckingham Palace. Princess Anne was smiling happily and the Prince of Wales waved as the car went quickly through the Palace gates.

PRAYER TO CHANGE

Order In Council

The Heir Apparent became Prince of Wales from the moment of the Queen's announcement. The creation entails the alteration of the form of prayer for the Royal Family. This will be made by an Order in Council.

Boys of Westminster School yesterday heard Prince Charles referred to as "Prince of Wales" during the prayers for the Royal Family at Westminster Abbey. They were attending morning service at the Abbey on their Election Sunday, the last Sunday of the summer term.

The Prince may visit Wales on Aug. 9. It was announced earlier this month that the Queen and Prince Philip, with the Royal children, would make a 12-day cruise up the West coast in the Royal yacht Britannia.

The cruise was to include a two-hour visit to Holyhead, Anglesey. Officials at Holyhead are making plans on the assumption that it will still take place.

Together with the title of Prince of Wales, the Prince will automatically assume the title of Earl of Chester. He also automatically becomes a Knight of the Garter, but he will not be invested or installed until he is grown up.

(July 28)

DANCE COLOUR BAR TIGHTENED

More powerful lighting is to be installed in the entrance of the Scala, the Wolverhampton ballroom, after a breach of its colour bar rule by an unknown Indian who got in undetected. Mr. Michael Wade, for the management, said yesterday: "This man will be the last Indian to dance at the Scala."

The case was brought to light by a woman who complained to him that she was asked to dance by an Indian. One of the staff said that some time after the man was admitted he was recognised as a coloured person in the bar.

(July 8)

IRAQI REVOLT: BRITISH EMBASSY SACKED

AMBASSADOR, STAFF & FAMILIES SAFE

A group of young Iraqi Army officers yesterday overthrew the pro-Western regime of King Feisal, head of the Arab Union with Jordan, and proclaimed a Republic, according to Baghdad radio. The King, who is 23, was stated to be a prisoner in his palace.

Gen. Nuri es-Said, 70, Prime Minister of the Arab Union, and his "master," the Crown Prince Abdul Illah, 44, had been killed and their bodies burnt, the radio claimed. There was some doubt about Gen. Nuri's fate, as a later report said only the Crown Prince had been killed.

Britain's Baghdad Embassy was set on fire and "virtually destroyed" by mobs, the Foreign Office stated. Confirming reports of the attack from Washington, Baghdad and Rome, it said Sir Michael Wright, the Ambassador, had reached an hotel after spending several hours in the ruins of his Embassy.

A report forwarded by Italy said all the Embassy staff and their families were believed safe. There was no confirmation that one person was shot. The staff radio operator went off the air at 9 a.m. after reporting the arrival of rioters.

All available Ministers were summoned by Mr. Macmillan to a special Cabinet meeting at 10, Downing Street last night to consider the Iraqi crisis. The meeting which followed a conference of senior Ministers, was adjourned after two hours and resumed at 11 p.m. for an hour. Mr. Selwyn Lloyd, Foreign Secretary, stayed on with the Prime Minister till 2.37 a.m.

(July 15)

U.S. MARINES LAND IN THE LEBANON

The first 1,700 of more than 5,000 Marines of the United States Sixth Fleet ordered into the Lebanon made an uneventful landing at Beirut yesterday. It was America's first direct military intervention in the Middle East.

Announcing the landings President Eisenhower stressed that the Marines had "not been sent as any act of war." They were going in conformity with the United Nations Charter, in response to an urgent appeal by President Chamoun to safeguard Lebabon's independence and American lives. They would withdraw as soon as the United Nations took adequate action.

(July 16)

BRITISH DEFENCE PRECAUTION

In London there was creat activity at 10, Downing Street. Service Ministers attended a Cabinet meeting. A statement issued by the Defence Ministry just before 5 p.m. said:

In view of the generally unsettled situation in the Middle East the Government have decided to take certain precautionary measures. These include the alerting of one infantry brigade in this country and of the Parachute Brigade and the 1st Guards Brigade in Cyprus, and the movement of reinforcements from Kenya to Aden and from Aden to the Persian Gulf.

(July 6)

ISRAELI ARMY CHIEF RESIGNS

GEN. MOSHE DAYAN

From Our Own Correspondent

JERUSALEM (Israel), Sunday.

Gen. Moshe Dayan, 43, Israeli Army Chief of Staff, to-day tendered his resignation to Mr. Ben-Gurion, the Prime Minister, who accepted it. Friends of the general said he wanted to continue his studies at a Hebrew university.

On Mr. Ben-Gurion's suggestion the Government approved the appointment of Gen. Haim Laskow, 39, as the new Chief of Staff. Gen. Laskow was born in Haifa of parents of Russian origin. He is known to his soldiers as a strict disciplinarian, a born fighter and a good organiser. He is one of the people closest to Mr. Ben-Gurion. Those who know him well say that even his professors at Oxford, where he took special courses a few years ago, remember him as seeking the military element in all his studies, including philosophy.

He served with the British Army during the war and reached the rank of major when in the Western Desert. In the Israeli Army he held a number of important positions, including Deputy chief of Staff. During the 1956 Sinai campaign he commanded the Armoured Corps and distinguished himself in the battle for the Gaza strip. He was later appointed chief of the southern Command.

(January 27)

ISRAEL GAOLS 8 POLICEMEN

43 ARABS KILLED

From Our Own Correspondent

JERUSALEM (Israel), Thursday

Eight Israeli Border Police were to-day sentenced to prison terms ranging from 17 years to seven years for their part in killing 43 Arabs near the village of Kafr Kassem on Oct. 29, 1956. They were found guilty of murder last Sunday.

On Oct. 29, 1956, the day Israeli forces invaded Egypt, a handful of men belonging to the frontier force was sent to enforce a curfew on the Arabs. Within an hour they shot dead the 43 men, women and children returning to their homes unaware of the curfew. Notice of appeal was given.

Capt. Malinka, commander of the battalion, who, to enforce the curfew, ordered his men to fire on villagers seen outside their homes after dark, received 17 years, the two next in command 15 years each, and the remaining five seven years.

(October 17)

1 ½ -MILE JAM ON MOTORWAY

So many motorists went for sightseeing drives along the new Preston by-pass yesterday that a queue of vehicles one and a half miles long formed at the northern end in the afternoon. After covering the first seven miles at 60 m.p.h., cars had to wait 30 minutes to get to Broughton.

(December 8)

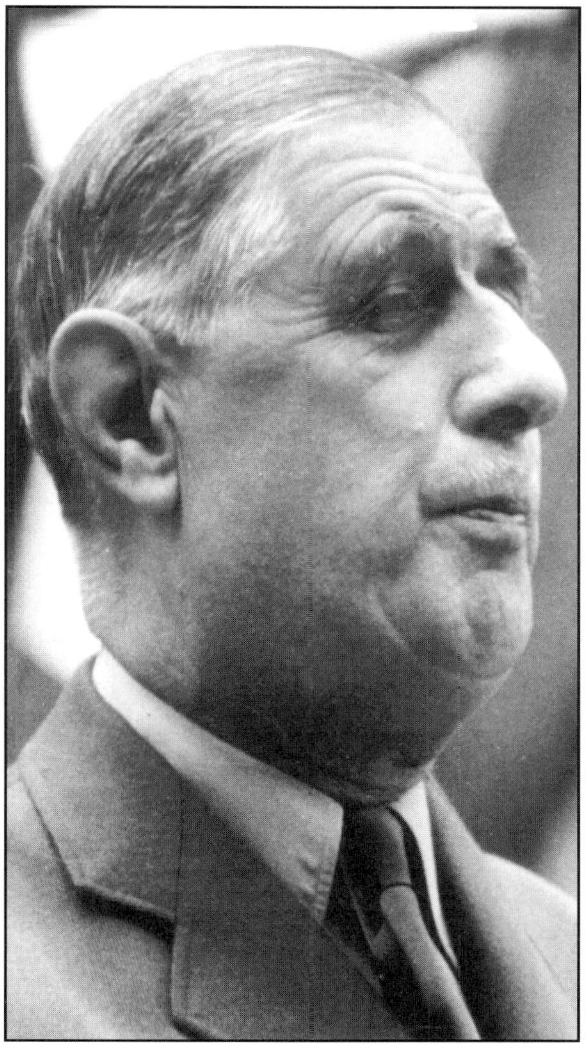

DE GAULLE INSTALLED AS PRESIDENT. Gen. de Gaulle speaking in the Elysée Palace in Paris yesterday after being proclaimed President of the Fifth Republic. he was wearing the Grand Collar of the Legion of Honour, with which every President is traditionally invested. Standing beside him was M. Coty, the outgoing President.

GEN. DE GAULLE IS PRESIDENT

From Our Own Correspondent

PARIS, Sunday.

Gen. de Gaulle was to-day elected the first President of France's Fifth Republic by an overwhelming majority of the 80,508 "grand electors." Under the new constitution this electoral college makes the choice by a secret ballot.

Long before the final figures were available, the outgoing President, M. Coty, telephoned his congratulations to the General at his home in Colombey-les-deux-Eglises. It was then already apparent that his victory was ensured.

Final returns, excluding 58 Polynesian votes not yet received, and with percentages for Metropolitan France, were:

	Votes	Percentages
GEN. DE GAULLE	62,338	77.50
M. MARRANE, Communist	10,354	13.4
M CHATELET, Radical-Soc.	6,722	8.46

Gen. de Gaulle secured 81.45 per cent. of the vote in Overseas Departments and 97.04 from members of the French Commity. He will continue as Prime Minister until Jan. 8, when President Coty, who received a great ovation outside the Opera on Friday, his last public official appearance, hands over.

The new President, who has been elected for seven years, will then, or shortly afterwards, appoint a Prime Minister. The name of Senator Michel Debre, 47, Minister of Justice, and for long a Gaullist, is being mentioned as his most likely choice.

OVERSEAS VOTE

Opponents' Failure

All Senators, Deputies, mayors and town and county councillors took part in the election. The de Gaulle vote was especially noticeable in the overseas possessions, where his two opponents failed in many places to get a single vote.

The figures show that while the Communists, backed by a few Socialists and Radicals, voted against the General, in the main the elected local government representatives of the Socialists, Radicals, Popular Republicans and others supported him.

(December 22)

UNITED ARABS ELECT NASSER

From Colin Reid

BEIRUT, Friday

Syrians and Egyptians of all classes and sympathies went through the motions of electing Col. Nasser President of the United Arab Republic of Egypt and Syria to-day.

One hour before polling closed in Syria to-night about 80 per cent of the "electorate" were announced to have exercised the "franchise". All pretence to the principle of secrecy was flouted.

In Damascus, President Kuwatly, of Syria, accompanied by Mr. Assali, his Prime Minister; Gen. Bizreh, Syrian C.-in-C.; Mr. Haurani, Speaker of the Syrian Parliament, and members of the Caninet went in procession to the Shahoor constituency polling booth. There they made speeches extolling Col. Nasser.

(February 22)

CHANCELLOR RESIGNS OVER ESTIMATES

INSISTENCE ON NOT A PENNY INCREASE

By Our Political Correspondent

Differences of opinion over the extent of cuts in Government expenditure have led to the resignations of Mr. Thorneycroft, Chancellor of the Exchequer, Mr. Birch, Economic Secretary to the Treasury, and Mr. Enoch Powell, Financial Secretary to the Treasury, it was announced from 10, Downing Street late last night.

The announcement came on the eve of Mr. Macmillan's departure for his Commonwealth tour. The differences proved irreconcilable at the long Cabinet meeting on Sunday night.

The Chancellor insisted that the estimates of Government expenditure for 1958-59 should not exceed by a single penny the amount actually spent in the current financial year. The rest of the Cabinet decided that they should be pruned to within one per cent. of the current total. This meant that the increase would be less than £50 million.

(January 7)

ALL ALGERIANS 'FULL FRENCHMEN NOW'

Gen. de Gaulle, in a frank speech to a vast, cheering concourse in Algiers last night, accepted integration and equal rights for Europeans and Moslems, men and women alike. "There are only Frenchmen, Frenchmen with full citizenship.

"Frenchmen, with one and the same rights. We will show within the next three months that all Frenchmen, including the 10 million of Algeria, will determine their own destiny. For these 10 million Frenchmen their votes will count exactly the same as those for all other Frenchmen in Metropolitan France."

He held out the prospect of an amnesty for rebels. "To these men I, de Gaulle, open the door of reconciliation."

He spoke from the balcony used three weeks ago to proclaim the movement that led to his being called to power. Earlier, after his arrival by air, he had been given a wildly enthusiastic welcome.

His car took an hour to complete a triumphal 15-mile drive from the airport to the beflagged city centre, where an immense crowd roared a greeting. Chants of "Soustelle" underlined the settlers' demand that the Algiers leader be given political office.

In New Delhi Mr. Nehru, Prime Minister, said India supported Algeria's struggle for independence.

(June 5)

BRIDGES LINK TALL FLATS WITH LIFTS

The East End of London, where extensive rebuilding is taking place, is to have homes of new design in a 16-storey cluster construction in Bethnal Green. Architects from seven countries, including Russia, have been to see it.

The building, which will contain 56 maisonnettes and eight bedsitting room flats, is being built in Claredale Street for Bethnal Green Borough council. It is in five sections.

There is an independent central core, 170ft high which has the staircase, two lifts, drying platforms and a refuse chute. Stretching out from the centre are four arms in the form of oblong blocks. These are 150ft high, 40ft long and 26ft wide.

At the end of each block there will be narrow bridges, giving the tenants access from the lifts to their homes. On the lower floor of the blocks each maisonnett will have a hall, and a living room and a kitchen leading to a private balcony. On the upper floor accommodation will consist of two double bedrooms and a bathroom.

The tenants will be people moved from slum clearance areas. Mr. Denys Lasdun, the architect of Fry, Drew, Drake and Lasdun, said to me yesterday that this had influenced his design.

"Each maisonnette has an individuality and a semi-detached feeling," he said. "This will be specially suitable for persons who are used to living in old two-storey houses. The design gives privacy and avoids a sense of living in a high, box-like building.

(August 5)

ALASKA THE 49TH STATE

VOTE BY SENATE

From Our Own Correspoondent

WASHINGTON, Monday.

The Senate to-night voted to make Alaska the 49th State of the American Union. The vote was 64 in favour and 20 against.

Acceptance of the Bill left only the requirement of Presidential approval and accceptance by Alaskans of the Bill's terms to extend the Union to a point 55 miles from Russian Siberia.

The Bill permits Alaska to take its place late this autumn or early winter as the first new State since the admission of Arizona and New Mexico in 1912. It has already been passed by the House of Representatives.

(July 1)

PRINCESS OPENS FIRST W. INDIES PARLIAMENT

From Alex Faulkner, Daily Telegraph Special Correspondent

PORT OF SPAIN, Trinidad, Tuesday.

Speaking with quiet dignity, Princess Margaret to-day inaugurated the first Federal Legislature of the West Indies in a ceremony here which she described as "a great political occasion." She said she had come to the inauguration by a Royal command from the Queen.

She spoke of the far-sighted men, both in the West Indies and in Britain, who for 10 years and more had accepted "the challenging vision of a West Indian Federation." This "dream of full West Indian nationhood within the Commonwealth" to-day became "a living reality."

"Your path may not be easy and you may have many obstacles to surmount, but at least you will know the burden you bear is an honourable one, for what you are seeking is the well-being of your fellow countrymen in the Caribbean. You will be watched with friendly sympathy by well-wishers in the United Kingdom' Commonwealth, and many other lands."

QUEENS MESSAGE

The Princess also read a message from the Queen in which she said: "On this happy day when the inauguration of this Legislature brings to completion the establishment of the Federation of the West Indies, I send warmest greetings to all my people in these territories."

(April 23)

MOTLEY 4,000 BEGIN H-BOMB PROCESSION

JIVE TO 'RED FLAG' IN CARNIVAL AIR

Daily Telegraph Reporter

Britain's anti-H-bomb brigade, a motley 4,000 yesterday began its 50-mile march from London to the Atomic Weapons Research Establishment at Aldermaston, Berks. It had the air of an Easter carnival although one of its leaders, Mr. Michael Foot, described it as "a crusade."

From Trafalgar Square to the first halt, the Albert Memorial, marchers were supposed to remain silent. But they laughed, talked and "skiffled" their way along.

At the memorial a group of bowler-hatted young men, with some girls, jived to the tune of the "Red Flag," which was played on a mouth organ. Communist party leaflets were handed to marchers as they slogged onward.

The leaflets stated: "The Communist party, which has itself taken part in many actions for peace, welcomes and supports these activities." The march organisers stressed that the event was "entirely non-political."

OVERNIGHT STOP

Halls and Houses

Last night at Hounslow, the first overnight stop, 500 people, including children, slept in halls and in private houses. They are starting out again this morning for Maidenhead.

The march began with a rally in Trafalgar Square. Police estimated the number there at 10,000.

Mr. Michael Foot, almost shouting into the five microphones before him, raised the loudest cheers, frightening away the pigeons, when he informed the rally:

"This can be the greatest march in English history. It can be the start of the greatest movement in British history. This is a crusade that we are going to win."

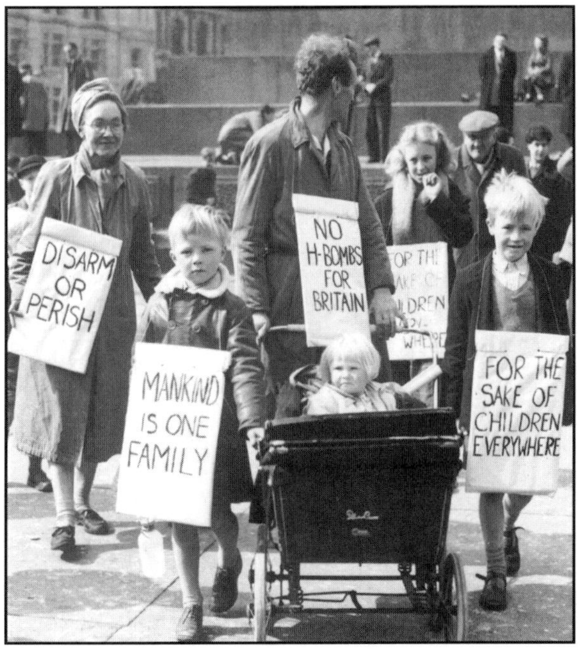

MR. AND MRS. CHRISTOPHER BAKER, from Cambridge, arrive at Trafalgar Square, London, to-day (Good Friday) with their children, carrying slogans protesting against the H-bomb.

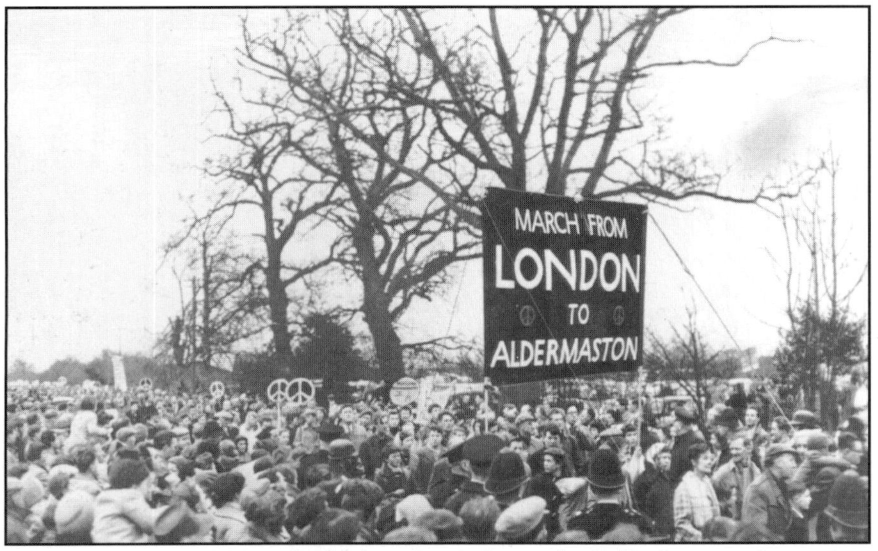

H-BOMB PROTEST MARCH. Some of the four thousand people who set out from Trafalgar Square yesterday to march to the Atomic Weapons Research Establishment at Aldermaston, Berks, passing Hyde Park Corner.

At 11.30 prompt the march began. Four thousand set out but by the time the marchers passed Turnham Green, the tea-time stop, the numbers were nearer 1,000.

Posters of all sorts were carried. In the fore were two road safety propagandists, whose placards declared: "Hiroshima, 1945: 160,000 casualties. Britain's roads, 1957: 273,858 casualties."

Other slogans read: "Disarm or die." "Make friends, not enemies." "Would you drop an H-bomb?" and, round one man's neck, "To be or not to be: that is the question."

A jazz band of six musicians blared out "The Saints Go Marching On" in front of a banner which said: "Let's get back to bows and arrows."

The marchers were a fantastically varied lot, in fantastically varied garb. Bearded old men; girls in slacks, high heels, and red, white and blue stockings; children in prams and push-chairs; and a boy of 17 in bare feet were among them.

The bare-footed boy, carrying a banner, is a pupil at Merchant Taylors'. He refused to give his name, saying that he had had several arguments with his headmaster about the H-bomb. "I am strongly against it," he informed me.

He said that he had very hard soles to his feet and he had bet a fellow pupil 5s he could march from Trafalgar Square to Hounslow without shoes or socks. "It's an easy way to make money."

One group of marchers, the Chingford Nuclear Disarmament Committee, from Essex, chanted: "One, two, three, four, what are we marching for? No H-bomb, no war." Another band, from a Highgate school, carried a poster, "Sixth-formers for peace."

EMBLAZONED VEHICLES

Rolls-Royce and Coach

In the convoy of 50 emblazoned vehicles following the march was a Rolls-Royce and a large blue motor coach which carried on its sides the words "Mothers of the world say abandon the H-bomb."

A number of dogs, as well as children, were in the march. Two men drove invalid cars bearing the legends, "Long live life," and "Bury the bomb before it buries you."

Two M.P.s Survive

At the Hounslow boundary, Socialist members of Heston and Isleworth Borough Council joined the procession as it made its way to Treaty Road.

Bands of new marchers, including members of the Amalgamated Engineering Union, joined in. By the time the procession arrived at its rallying point, the police estimated that there were 1,500 demonstrators.

Of the M.P.s who started the march, only two lasted the 11 miles to the first overnight stop. They were Mr. Baird, who is 51, and Mr. Allaun, 45.

(April 5)

ATLAS MISSILE BLOWS UP

An Atlas inter-continental ballistic missile was fired by the United States Air Force from the launching pad at Cape Canaveral, Florida, to-day. But it blew up after 2min 20sec soon after the powered phase of its flight had ended. The Air Force merely reported that "the cause of the malfunction is not available."

(February 21)

EGYPT AGREES TO PAY £29M TO SUEZ CANAL CO.

INSTALMENTS OVER SIX YEARS

From Our Own Correspondent

ROME, Tuesday.

Egypt, under an agreement initialled in Rome to-day, will pay shareholders of the Suez Canal Co. about £29 million in seven instalments over six years as compensation for the nationalisation of the Canal. The Egyptian delegation and company's representatives are to meet again in Cairo on May 17.

The final meeting between the parties before the signing of the preliminary agreement lasted only 40 minutes. The main points of the agreement are as follows:

1 - As a full and final settlement of the compensation due to shareholders and to holders of Founders' shares as a consequence of the nationalisation law, the Government of the United Arab Republic will make a payment equivalent to £E28,300,000 and will leave all the assets abroad to the stock-holders of the company.

2 - In consideration of the above, the shareholders will accept responsibility for all liability outside Egypt as of July 26, 1956, including liability for the service of the outstanding Debentures and for pensions.

3 - The Government of the United Arab Republic will continue to assume responsibility for all liabilities within Egypt as of July 26, 1956, including liability for pensions for those who are resident in Egypt.

The initial compensation payment will be £E5,300,000. This is constituted by Egypt's renouncing her claim to transit tolls for the Suez Canal collected in Paris and London since July 26, 1956, when Egypt nationalised the Canal.

(April 30)

PRESIDENT'S WARNING TO LITTLE ROCK

'MY FEELINGS ARE EXACTLY AS THEY WERE A YEAR AGO'

From Our Own Correspondent

WASHINGTON, Wednesday.

President Eisenhower left the distinct impression at his Press conference to-day that he would, if necessary, send back Federal troops to Little Rock to see that violence there did not prevent the Supreme Court's integration decisions from being carried out at the central high school.

Reading a statement, he said that "defiance" by a State of the Court's orders would present the most serious problem, and he added: "But there can be no equivocation as to the responsibility of the Federal Government in such an event.

"It is my hope," he said, "that each State will fulfil its obligation with a full realisation of the gravity of any other course. It cannot by action or deliberate failure to act permit violence to frustrate the preservation of individual rights as determined by free decree.

"My feelings are exactly as they were a year ago," he said. A year ago the President called out Federal troops and federlised the national guard (State militia) after Mr. Faubus, the Governor of Arkansas, had used Guardsmen to keep Negro children from entering the school.

BASIS OF FREEDOMS

Federal Court Decisions

"Each State owes to its inhabitants, to its sister States and to the Union the obligation to suppress unlawful forces. It cannot by action or deliberate failure to act permit violence to frustrate the preservation of individual rights as determined by a court decree," the statement added.

"The very basis of our individual rights and freedoms rests upon the certainty that the President and the executive branch of Government will support and ensure the carrying out of the decisions of the Federal courts.

"Every American must understand that if an individual, community or State is going successfully and continuously to defy the courts, then there is anarchy.

"I continue to insist that the common sense of the individual and his feeling of civic responsibility must eventually come into play if we are to solve this problem."

REPORTED DOUBTS

President's Insistence

Some reports had represented the President as having had doubts about the use of Federal troops, because their use had sharpened the lines of division in the south and, it was argued, had set back, rather than improved, the climate necessary for integration and equal civil rights between the White and Negro sections.

Mr. Eisenhower, however, insisted that the main responsibility for maintaining order, so that individual rights as determined by the courts could be enjoyed by all, rested with State Governments."

(August 21)

BIGGEST DEMOCRATIC WIN SINCE NEW DEAL DAYS

INCREASED CONTROL IN U.S.

From Our Own Correspondent

WASHINGTON, Wednesday.

Like one of those famous East coast hurricanes which sweep all before it, the Democratic party has won its biggest majorities in Congress since New Deal days in the 1930s and has increased its control of State governments.

But like the hurricanes, the Democratic sweep followed a zig-zag course which left Republican candidates unscathed in many unexpected places. With some contests still undecided, the Democrats appeared to have gained 14 seats in the Senate, 40 or more in the House of Representatives, and now hold their largest number of Governorships since 1936, with a net gain of four States.

For the first time in United States history President Eisenhower will be confronted for the third time in succession by a hostile Congress.

The Democratic Senate victory is so large that the party is assured of Senate control two years hence when one-third of the Senate faces election. They will then have 21 seats at stake to 11 Republicans, but 10 of these are in the South, where no Republican is likely to be elected.

At his Press conference to-day the President succinctly summed up yesterday's election results with the comment: "We did not get enough Republican votes."

(November 6)

HINDS ESCAPES FOR THE THIRD TIME

Daily Telegraph Reporter

Alfred George Hinds, 41, the Houdini of British gaols, made his third escape from custody yesterday. He scaled a 20ft wall at Chelmsford Prison, and was picked up by a waiting car outside.

It was 9.30 a.m. when Hinds, serving a sentence of 12 years' preventive detention, made his carefully-timed escape. With him went another prisoner, George Walkington, 38, of Dalston, who is serving an eight-year sentence. Both were still free early to-day.

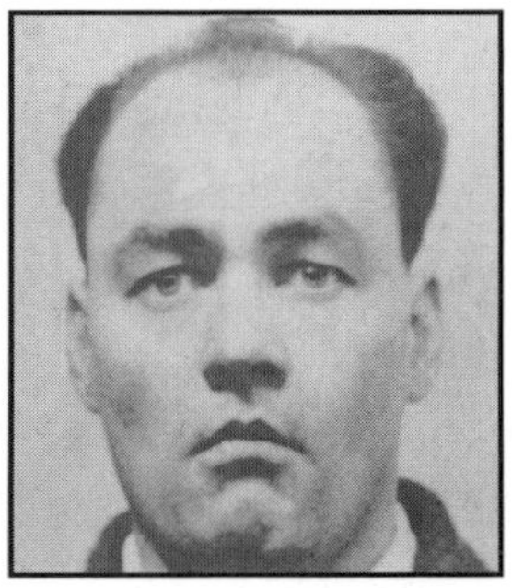

A. G. HINDS

Watch was being kept at seaports, airports and main railway stations.

The two escaped just after church service and during a recreational period. They got over the 20ft outside wall by climbing on to a low workshop inside the recreation ground and getting on to the wall.

They dropped to freedom into a narrow piece of waste ground separating the prison wall from the playground of Trinity Road Primary School. They dropped on to tall, soft grass and ran alongside the prison wall and into the cemetery of Holy Trinity Church.

Their 200-yard dash through the cemetery was screened from overlooking houses by shrubs and trees. As the two ran out of the cemetery into the main Trinity Road a car was waiting for them outside Holy Trinity Church.

It was immediately driven off at high speed, heading for the main A.12 road, affording them escape routes to the East coast, South coast and London. Hinds and his companion were seen as the car sped along to be peeling off their brown prison uniforms and changing into other clothing.

(June 2)

CREDIT SQUEEZE RELAXED

LIMIT IS ENDED ON BANK ADVANCES

By Our Political Correspondent

Mr. Heathcoat Amory, Chancellor of the Exchequer, announced in the House of Commons yesterday measures to relax the credit squeeze which has been in force for three years. The main points were:

From Aug 1, the banks will be under no obligation to restrict the total level of their advances;

From to-day, the limit of exemption from the control of the Capital Issues Committee, which has stood at £10,000 since March, 1956, is being raised to the original 1947 level of £50,000.

Instead of confining its consent to urgent transactions, the Committee will be free to assent to applications which anticipate future needs;

Bonus issues or capitalisation of reserves will be exempt from the Committee's control, but Treasury consent will be needed if they take the form of issues of redeemable securities.

A new scheme is to be introduced to control credit supplied through the banks. The Government has decided to abandon the method of making "official requests" to the banks to restrict total advances, on the ground that it hampers the efficient working of the banking system.

Instead, the Chancellor will retain control over bank credit by the normal machinery of interest rates and open market operations. This will be reinforced by a new scheme for "special deposits."

TEMPORARY MEASURE

Awaiting Inquiry Report

It will be a temporary measure pending any recommendations which may be made by the Radcliffe Committee. This is inquiring into the working of the monetary and credit system.

When it appears necessary to restrict the liquidity of the banking system and the banks' ability to extend credit, the Bank of England will call for special deposits to be made with them by the clearing and Scottish banks.

These deposits will not qualify for inclusion among the banks' liquid assets. They will carry interest based on the current Treasury Bill rate. The Bank of England's ability to call for them will operate as a general control of credit in much the same way as Bank rate.

Details of the scheme are given in an exchange of letters between the Chancellor and Mr. Cameron Cobbold, Governor of the Bank of England.

The new directive to the Capital Issues Committee is also set out in correspondence with its chairman, Lord Kennet. It is given legal force in the Control of Borrowing (Amendment) Order, 1958.

TREASURY CHECK

Preventing Tax Evasion

This makes clear that though it will now be lawful to raise up to £50,000 without Treasury consent, the Chancellor is tightening his control in some respects. By maintaining the Treasury check on issues involving redeemable securities, he will prevent operations designed to reduce tax liabilities.

He is also bringing within the control various transactions, exempt since April, 1955, which certain companies have been using to evade scrutiny by the Capital Issues Committee. A favourite device of this kind was to acquire, in consideration of an issue of shares, the assets of another company consisting largely of cash or securities that could be easily realised.

From now on this sort of transaction will be covered by statutory control. So will:

Transactions between associated companies;

Transactions by which the price of property or of an undertaking is left unpaid;

Issues of shares in settlement of existing indebtedness; and

Issues of securities otherwise than for securing a bank overdraft or refinancing a maturing loan.

The Capital Issues committee will no longer be concerned with the appropriateness of bank finance for capital purposes, it will leave to the discretion of the banks themselves the terms as to period and repayment of such advances.

The decision to relax the credit squeeze reflects the Government's view that internal inflationary pressure is easing off. At the same time it is conscious of the need to encourage greater use of industry's productive capacity.

(July 4)

QUEEN MAKES FIRST TRUNK

DIALLING CALL

Daily Telegraph Reporter

The Queen made history yesterday when she dialled an Edinburgh number on a telephone in Bristol to inaugurate the first stage of subscriber trunk dialling in Britain. The Postmaster-General, Mr. Marples, invited her at the Bristol telephone exchange to make the first call.

It was to the Lord Provost of Edinburgh, Mr. Johnson-Gilbert. The Queen dialled the number, 031 CAL 3636. After a brief conversation with the Lord Provost she turned a switch linking about 18,000 Bristol Central subscribers to the new service.

Mr. Marples presented her with the colonial blue telephone she had used. Her Majesty dialled another number before she left the Bristol exchange. This time it was a 999 call.

(December 6)

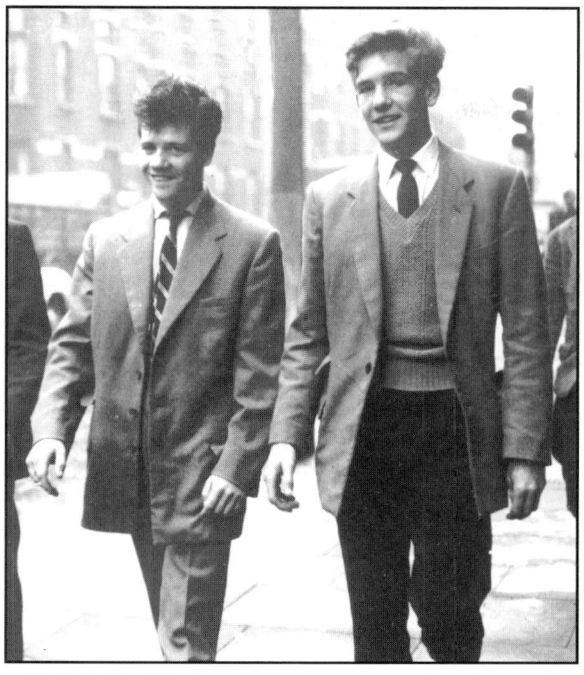

SOME OF THE MEN who were remanded at West London police Court last Monday after they had appeared on charges arising out of the disturbances in the Notting Hill race riots.

13 ARRESTS IN NOTTING HILL RACIAL FIGHTS

GANGS OF YOUTHS HURL MISSILES AT POLICE

Daily Telegraph Reporters

A white man was slashed across the neck and police cars hit by bricks thrown by crowds in racial disorders in Notting Hill last night. Thirteen people were detained at Notting Hill police station.

Eight were charged with using insulting behaviour, two with assaulting the police, and three with possessing offensive weapons. They will appear at West London court to-day.

At midnight one coloured and two white people had been taken to St. Charles's Hospital, Exmoor Street.

Hundreds of youths, many in teddy boy clothes, roamed streets in the Lancaster Road district, jeering whenever they saw a coloured person. Others, in bands 50 strong, waited outside houses in which Negroes live.

The streets swarmed with policemen and hundreds of people watched from their windows. Several families evacuated their homes, leaving coloured occupants in a state of siege.

MAN STABBED

Boy Hit With Bottle

The disturbances broke out afresh in the district, including Blechynden Street and Bramley Road, where racial clashes occurred during the week-end. Many police cars and vans went to the scene. More than 400 people were involved.

Police were jeered at by black and white youths and broken bottles were thrown. A fight broke out between 10 coloured people and seven whites. One man was stabbed in the shoulder.

An elderly woman was knocked over by the crowd. A boy of 10 was hit in the mouth with a broken bottle.

Earlier a gang of 100 youths armed with sticks, iron bars and knives gathered under the railway arches near Latimer Road Underground station.

VIOLENCE FLARES

Fighting Gangs

In tears, Mrs. Kathleen Harper, 23, of Latimer Road, Notting Hill, described how she saw her husband, Bert, a builder, slashed across the neck by a coloured man, making a 5in cut.

As mobs surged about roads and side streets in the Lancaster Road area ugly incidents and scuffles became more frequent. Again it was youths in their late teens who were to the fore, shouting insults at cruising police cars.

Fighting broke out again, with the police facing superior odds. I saw one officer fall to the ground with a punching, kicking youth. Before help could reach him he was surrounded by a knot of kicking, yelling young men.

Stones were thrown through shop windows. One police car, with a prisoner inside it, was the target for a glass bottle which splintered against its side. One man was pinned by police against a wall and the mob, screaming insults, threw bottles at them.

I watched a Jamaican woman attempt to pass a jeering crowd of 200 youths and teddy boys. Two police officers moved to her side to escort her to her house, through a window of which a bottle had just been thrown.

As she moved inside her gateway the crowd broke into a run as if to follow her. Another crowd of 300 youths and men came along chanting "Down with the dirty niggers."

One woman said to me: "We are scared to death. They say they are coming back to-morrow night. There will be a revolution between the blacks and whites here if something is not done."

Further fighting broke out again later at Latimer Road Underground station. Empty bottles from a milk float were used as missiles by the crowd.

Gradually, as more and more police arrived, the situation was brought under control. The big crowds were split up into smaller groups, which were then dispersed.

Earlier yesterday, after disorders among a crowd of 200 coloured and white people which went on from 11.30 on Saturday night till the early hours of yesterday, four were charged with obstructing the police.

(September 1)

JUDGE CHOSEN AS LORD CHIEF JUSTICE

LD. JUSTICE PARKER: LIFE BARONY

By Our Political Correspondent

Speculation over the new Lord Chief Justice ended last night with an announcement from 10, Downing Street, that the choice has fallen on Lord Justice Parker.

The choice, made on the recommendation of the Prime Minister, will be warmly approved by the legal profession. Lord Justice Parker was bracketed with Mr. Justice Devlin as having an outstanding claim to advancement.

It will also give great satisfaction to lawyers outside Parliament that Mr. Macmillan has followed the precedent set by Mr. Attlee, in the case of Lord Goddard, of making the appointment a non-political one.

(September 6)

LD. GODDARD RESIGNS HIS OFFICE

12 YEARS LORD CHIEF JUSTICE

Daily Telegraph Reporter

Lord Goddard, 81, Lord Chief Justice of England since 1946, has resigned his £10,000 a year post. An announcement from 10, Downing Street yesterday stated:

"It was confirmed at 10, Downing Street to-day that Lord Goddard having tendered his resignation as Lord chief Justice of England, the Queen has been graciously pleased to accept it. The resignation takes effect from Sept. 29."

The retirement of Lord Goddard has been forecast frequently, particularly in the last few months.

LAST DAY IN COURT

Busy Afternoon

At 3.29 yesterday afternoon, four hours after his resignation had been announced, Lord Goddard, in his crimson robes and his wig, rose from the chair of his Court of Criminal Appeal and stepped through the oak-panelled door to his private rooms for the last time.

Characteristically, Lord Goddard spent a busy three hours 49 minutes in the Court. He and Mr. Justice Cassels, another octogenarian, and Mr. Justice Ashworth, a young member of the Queen's Bench, dealt with five cases of criminal appeal and 25 appeal applications.

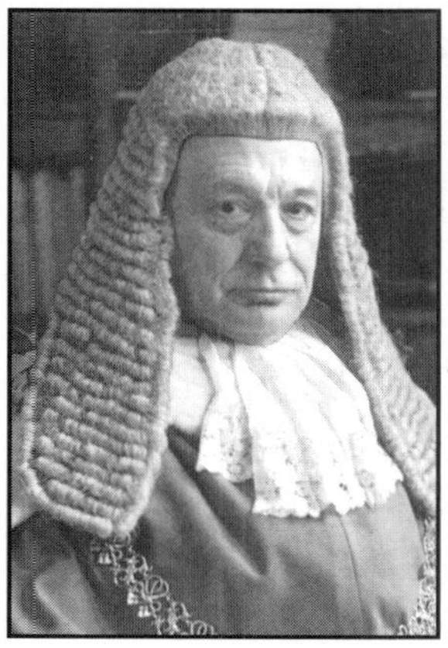

LORD GODDARD

Lord Goddard, looking as alert as ever and belying his 81 years, alternated from sternness to mercy as he dealt with the applications. His quality of mercy concerned a youth of 17 serving three years' Borstal for office breaking and larceny.

FAMOUS TRIALS

Sentenced Fuchs

Called to the Bar of the Inner Temple and Gray's Inn in 1899, Lord Goddard took silk in 1923. Recorderships at Poole, Bath and Plymouth took him to his appointment as a High Court Judge in 1932 and as a Lord Justice of Appeal in 1938.

In his long career he presided over many famous trials. They ranged from that of Thomas Ley, former Minister of Justice for New South Wales, convicted of the "chalk pit" murder of a hotel barman, to that of Klaus Fuchs whom he sentenced to 14 years' imprisonment for conveying atom secrets to Russia.

(April 21)

WELENSKY PARTY KEEPS CONTROL

SALISBURY, Southern Rhodesia.

The United Federal party, supporting independence within the Commonwealth, had won control of the Federal Parliament when counting in yesterday's General Election stopped at midnight.

At that time the United Federal party, which opposed the outgoing Government, led by Sir Roy Welensky, held 31 seats and the Dominion party five.

(November 13)

PRESLEY IN U.S. TANK UNIT

FEAR OF 'NOT DOING THE RIGHT THINGS'

From Our Special Correspondent

FRIEDBERG, near Frankfurt, Thursday

Pte. Elvis Presley, 23, American rock 'n' roll singer who has arrived in Germany to complete the last 16 months of his two years' military service, was to-day incorporated into the Third Armoured Division for general duties in a tank company.

The operation was completed here solemnly, unhurriedly and efficiently. It reflected credit on an Army prepared for all emergencies.

The "draftee" [National Serviceman], newly out from Texas, drew his European winter kit in the full glare of publicity. The Secretary of Defence himself, Mr. McElroy, would never have attracted so many newsreel and television cameras, but no one in the barracks expressed surprise.

At a Press conference, which lasted a full hour-and-a-half, the private behaved with an almost painful modesty. He spoke of his need to adjust himself to each new job in the Army.

EXPECTED "KIDDING"

"I expected a lot of kidding and harassment: I expected a hard time. But I find that if I do the same things as the others do I make a lot of friends."

He was asked why he appeared self-conscious. "I am not self-conscious," he replied earnestly. It is simply that I am not sure of myself. I am afraid of not doing the right things."

About music he had little to say. "I am not an expert on music: I don't even read it."

There were certain types of music, like progressive jazz, that he did not understand, but he was not going to "knock it" [complain about] for that reason. "Classical music is good for sending you to sleep."

"IF PEOPLE FORGET ..."

One question went right home. "Are you afraid," he was asked, "that people will forget you while you are in the Army?"

Pte. Presley smiled, disarmingly but confidently. "It makes you wonder," he said, "but, if people forget me I can't complain. I had it once."

(October 3)

PANDA JUMPS FOR FREEDOM

Daily Telegraph Reporter

Chi-Chi, the giant panda from China, nearly escaped yesterday during her first morning in the London Zoo, where she is staying for three weeks. She leapt the 3ft railing round her grass enclosure, scattering a crowd of delighted, squealing children.

Her owner, Mr. Heini Demmer, the Austrian animal trapper, vaulted the railing and caught her when she had gone about 20 yards. She was returned to her pit, from which she had been taken for the benefit of photographers, and given lumps of ice to cool her down.

Chi-Chi is about 20 months old, 4ft long and 3 ft high. Looking slightly rakish because of the black circles round her eyes, and with a thick woolly coat, she is like an outsize cuddly toy.

PLAYS LIKE A DOG

The panda is docile and affectionate with her owners, and plays with them like a dog. She also shows off by lying on her back with a bamboo shoot clutched in her forepaws or sits holding her toes with her forepaws.

Her pit has oak branches, brought from Whipsnade, and a large wooden tub for a bath. A canopy in the centre keeps off the sun.

Mr. Demmer is willing to sell Chi-Chi. Dr. H.G. Vevers, London Zoo assistant to the scientific director, was asked if he thought the Zoo might buy her and replied: "Yes, we would be very interested if she is a good draw."

(September 6)

LIBERAL IN AT TORRINGTON

FIRST BY-ELECTION SUCCESS FOR 29 YRS.

By Our Political Correspondent

The result of the Torrington by-election, declared yesterday after a recount, was a gain for the Liberal candidate by a majority of 219. The figures were:

MARK BONHAM CARTER (Lib.) 13,408
ANTHONY ROYLE (Nat. Lib. and Con.) 13,189
LEONARD LAMB (Soc.) 8,697
Liberal Majority 219

Of the electorate of 44,128, the high percentage of 79.98 went to the poll. This was 10.8 per cent. higher than in the General Election of 1955, when Mr. George Lambert, National Liberal Conservative, had a majority of 9,312 in a straight fight with the Socialist candidate. The by-election was caused by the succession of Mr. Lambert to the peerage on the death of his father, Viscount Lambert.

Mr. Bonham Carter polled 37.99 per cent. of the votes. The Government's share was 37.37 per cent., a fall of 27.68 per cent. compared with 1955. The Socialist vote dropped by 10.31 per cent. to 24.64 per cent. The number of Liberal M.P.s is now brought up to six.

The Liberal success is the first at a by-election for almost exactly 29 years, and is bound to give the party an even rosier view of its "revival." That the victory should have been won by a grandson of Mr. Asquith also helps to project past grandeur into future hopes.

The high poll indicates the intense interest aroused by the contest. It appears to dispose of any suggestion that the result is not a true reflection of political feeling at the moment, at any rate in the West Country.

MAJORITY REVERSED

Lessons of the Poll

But there is no doubt that the result can be regarded as a vote against Mr. Macmillan's Government rather than a vote for Liberalism. The real lesson is that a pro-Government majority of 8,916.

The turnover of votes has been by no means entirely at the expense of the Government. While the National Liberal-Conservative candidate's total fell by 6,935, Mr. Lamb's fell by 2,115. It is obvious that the electors of Torrington have even less confidence in the Socialists as an alternative Government than they had in 1955.

It also supports the belief that where a Liberal stands, at least in parts of the country with a strong Liberal tradition, he is liable to take one vote from the Socialist for every two he takes from the Conservative.

(March 29)

RECORD TRADE SURPLUS OF £334 MILLION

By Our City Editor

In the first half of this year Britain earned a surplus of £334 million in its current transactions with the rest of the world. This is a record figure, which compares with a surplus of £118 million in the first half of 1957.

This encouraging news of Britain's greatly-improved position in the field of overseas trade and finance is given in a White Paper issued by the Treasury yesterday. [Cmnd. 540, Stationery Office, 1s 3d.]

For the full 12 months to June 30, 1958, the current surplus works out at £488 million, the highest yearly figure achieved since balance of payments estimates were first officially prepared 10 years ago.

Between the first half of last year and the first six months of 1958 there is an improvement of £216 million. Of this £162 million is accounted for by Britain's better showing in the balance of visible trade. For the first time since the beginning of this century Britain has earned a visible trade surplus.

(October 14)

FIRST WOMAN BANK MANAGER

Miss Hilda Harding, who is 42, has been appointed Britain's first woman bank manager by Barclays Bank, which she joined 24 years ago as a shorthand typist. She will take over a branch which is to open next December at Hanover Street, Mayfair, and her chief clerk will be a woman.

About one-third of Barclays' employees are women, and several hold executive jobs. Mr. R.G. Thornton, general manager, said yesterday that the appointment of a woman branch manager was a further stage in the development of women's roles in banking.

(May 17)

MOTHERS AT WORK 'ENEMY' OF HOME LIFE

Whole-time employment for mothers was described yesterday by the Bishop of Woolwich, the Rt. Rev. R. W. Stannard, as an "enemy" of Christian family life.

"Far too many mothers of young families are doing whole-time jobs," the Bishop said. "How can there be home life when mother is too tired at the end of the day for either children or husband?

"There are twice as many women in whole-time employment as there were before the war, and half the women in industry to-day are married. Surely this is too high a price to pay for prosterity?"

(March 17)

KING LIGHTS 10FT FLAME AT BRUSSELS WORLD FAIR

Declaring open the Brussels International Exhibition to-day, King Baudouin of the Belgians said its aim was "to revive the atmosphere of collaboration and peace." Fifty-three countries and internatioanal organisations are represented.

In the Belgian Square, centre of the exhibition, the King pressed a button to kindle a 10ft high flame which will burn for the next six months. At the same time fountains by the hundred began to play. They will be illuminated at night.

Belgian political and civic leaders and members of diplomatic missions assembled at the reception hall to hear the King. He spoke in Flemish and French.

"The human race has entered a new era in its history," he said. "More than ever before civilisation appears to depend upon science." Two roads were now open. One led to an ever more dangerous armaments race.

"The other is the way which should make it possible, whatever the social, political or spiritual differences, to reach the understanding which alone is capable of bringing about true peace. The aim of this exhibition is to revive the atmosphere of collaboration and peace."

Technical progress was not enough. It must be accompanied by a parallel development of spiritual ideals and "our will to achieve together a constructive effort.

"Such is the great idea which inspired the Belgian people to invite the world to come together in the exhibition which we are inaugurating to-day. The greatest powers of the West and the East, all people, all races, are magnificently represented here."

(April 18)

HOUSE OF LORDS GREETS ITS PEERESSES

FIRST TWO ARE SWORN IN

FULL BENCHES FOR CEREMONY

By Our Own Representative

WESTMINSTER, Tuesday.

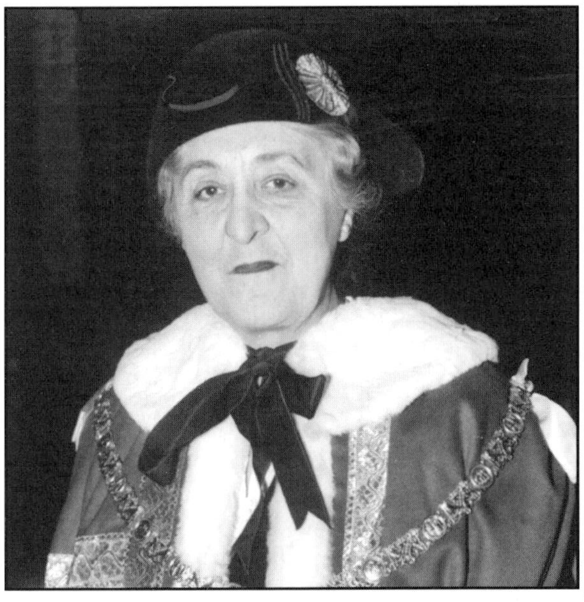

LADY SWANBOROUGH, better known as Stella Marchioness of Reading.

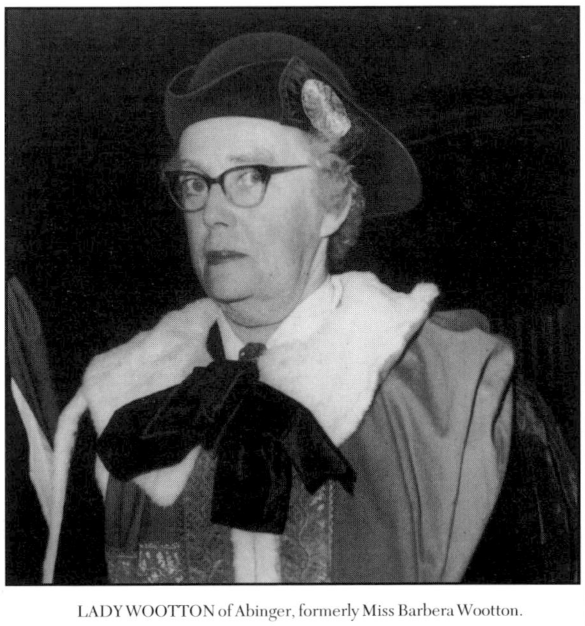

LADY WOOTTON of Abinger, formerly Miss Barbera Wootton.

For the first time in its 1,000-year history, a woman's foot trod the floor of the House of Lords during a sitting to-day. And for the first time, except for queens (and dare one say Miss Vivien Leigh?) feminine voices were heard in the Chamber.

They were those of two of the new life baronesses, Lady Swanborough, better known as Stella, Marchioness of Reading, and Lady Wootton of Abinger, who as Miss Barbara Wootton is widely known as a television personality.

With the new Lord Chief Justice, Lord Parker of Waddington, and three of the new life peers, they went through the ceremony of formal introduction to the House. Their reception was, by the restrained standards of the peers, almost emotional.

Even peers like the Earl of Glasgow, who opposed the admission of women when the Life Peerages Bill was before the House, sat back and beamed approvingly. To the champions of women's rights, like the veteran Suffragist, Lord Pethick-Lawrence, it was obviously a dream come true.

GOOD ATTENDANCE

Socialists Make Room

Few debates produce such a House as had mustered for this historic occasion. Behind the Earl of Home, Leader of the House, and his colleagues on the Ministerial bench 70 peers filled the Government benches.

Viscount Alexander of Hillsborough, Leader of the Opposition, and a score of his supporters vacated the front row on their side of the House to give more room for the ceremonial.

Octogenarian Viscount Samuel with half a dozen Liberal peers added their voices to the traditional welcoming rumble of "hear, hears."

In single file came a slow procession consisting of Black Rod, Lt.-Gen. Sir Brian Horrocks; Garter King of Arms, Sir George Bellew, in his gorgeous mediaeval tabard; the Earl Marshal, the Duke of Norfolk, and then Lady SWANBOROUGH, preceded and followed by her sponsors, Lord Burnham and Lord Chorley.

All were in robes of scarlet and miniver, Lady Swanborough's conspicuously new. On her greying hair she wore the tricorn hat, with a gold badge decoration on the left of it that has been specially designed for peeresses. Round her neck hung the chain and Grand Cross of the Order of the British Empire.

A neat figure, she seemed, as she was led to the Lord Chancellor to kneel and hand him her letters patent and her writ of summons. She performed this feat, which often causes much fumbling, with unaccustomed grace.

(October 22)

FIRST MAN ACROSS ANTARCTICA

From Ian Ball,
Daily Telegraph Special Correspondent

SCOTT BASE, Antarctica, Sunday.

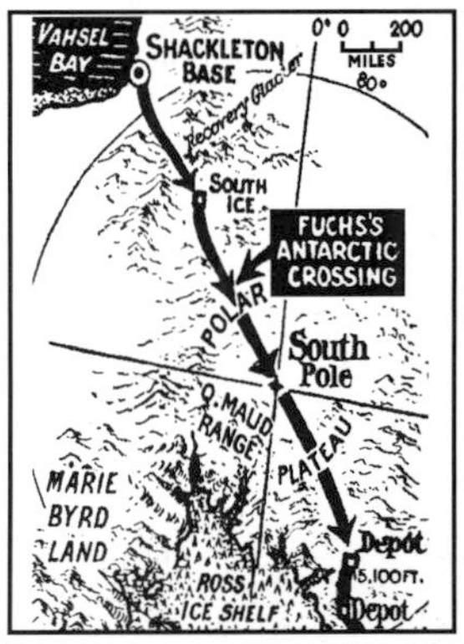

Dr. Fuchs and 10 members of the Commonwealth Transantarctic expedition reached Scott Base today, completing the first overland crossing of Antarctica. Their 2,150-mile trek began 99 days ago at Shackleton Base on the Weddell Sea coast.

It ended at 1.47 p.m. when four travel-scarred Sno-cats came to a halt on the bay ice about 100 yards beyond the edge of the Ross ice shelf.

Four hours and 43 minutes after the expedition's arrival Dr. Fuchs learned that the Queen had signified her intention of conferring a knighthood upon "Vivian Ernest Fuchs, Esq." The message was received in the radio room at Scott base just after six p.m.

At the time Dr. Fuchs was in the bathroom here shaving off his steel-grey beard and taking his first bath for more than three months. He was told about the knighthood when he had returned to the station's common room and had joined other members of the expedition.

CHEERS AND TOASTS

Congratulation to 'Bunny'

He had changed from his heavy trail clothes into Army trousers and a green tartan shirt and had just accepted a glass of beer when the message was handed to him. Dr. Fuchs read it to himself and then Sqdn. Ldr. John Lewis, R.A.F., the expedition's flight officer, made an announcement.

Dr. Fuchs stood in the centre of the group as the small room rang with three cheers and toasts were offered to "Sir Vivian." Immediately afterwards his colleagues were again calling him "Bunny," the nickname he has had since his school days.

"I am delighted by this honour, but at the same time slightly embarrassed that I have been singled out," he remarked later.

Never before had explorers in Antarctica been welcomed home from the trail with such gaiety and excitement. A 16-piece band played, Bright lights, orange and red signal flares and streamers traced a colourful welcome across the snow. There were about 100 Britons, Americans and New Zealanders to cheer the convoy in.

(March 3)

B.O.A.C. JET FOR ATLANTIC RUN

By An Air Correspondent

The new Vickers V.C.10 jet airliner is to be developed for British Overseas Airways Corporation as a London-New York non-stop plane as well as for the Commonwealth routes.

This was announced by Vickers-Armstrongs yesterday when a contract to supply 35 V.C. 10s costing £60 million to B.O.A.C. was signed in London. The Corporation has also taken an option on a further 20 planes. This is the largest single order for a British civil aircraft.

The first details of the V.C.10 were given by Sir George Edwards, managing director of Vickers-Armstrongs, and Mr. Basil Smallpiece, managing director of B.O.A.C., at a Press conference at London Airport. Carrying up to 152 passenger, it will be the largest British airliner ordered.

MORE ENGINE POWER

Developments in the design since B.O.A.C. said in May that they intended buying it, and increases in the power of the Rolls-Royce Conway jet engines it will use, have made the greater range possible.

The extended range means that a British jet airliner will be available to compete with the american Boeing 707 and Douglas DC-8 on the North Atlantic route. But the first 11 V.C.10s will not be delivered until 1963, about three years after the American types are due to go into service.

The V.C.10 is to be undertaken as a private venture involving an investment estimated at about £4 millions.

(January 15)

RECORD JAMS IN CENTRAL LONDON

By W.A. McKenzie,
Daily Telegraph Motoring Correspondent

Although not one bus was out of the 7,000 which ply in London, such was the volume of traffic on the first day of the strike that main thoroughfares at times reached saturation. It showed again that it is not the buses which create congestion in the centre.

In the morning rush hours the jams reached a new record. In the evening there was partial paralysis of home-bound traffic.

The situation over a wide area of the Metropolis was almost beyond the capacity of the streets and the ability of hundreds of police to cope with. The moral is that car traffic can be expected to double itself in London and every other major city in the next few years.

The volume began building up between 7.30 and 9.15 a.m. I motored from Inner London to Croydon, across the Western Avenue and the Great West road, then on to the Great North road and back to Marble Arch. I could average 25 m.p.h..

I saw no car displaying "free lift" on its windscreen. Pedestrians took little notice of passing cars. Here and there one or two stood at bus stops, but only twice did I see anyone accept a lift when approached by a motorist. Almost all cars carried only the driver.

At Marble Arch the density had thickened. Soon I was in a mass of traffic resembling an army division on the move.

(May 6)

BILLY WRIGHT WEDDING HALTS TRAFFIC

Thousands of people from the surrounding districts travelled by road and rail to Poole, Dorset, yesterday to see the "secret" wedding at the Register office there of Billy Wright, 34, England's football captain and Joy Beverley, 34, eldest of the Beverley Sisters, the singers.

Police, taken unawares, were unable to cope with the traffic despite a call for reinforcements. The main road was blocked with cars and buses.

People stood on walls, climbed fences and trees and sat on the roofs of cars. They sang "For they are jolly good fellows" and brandished football rattles.

Two firls fainted. Several others including one of the bride's sisters, Teddie Beverley, lost shoes in the jostling crowd.

(July 28)

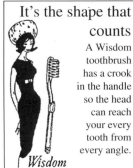

PETER HALL TO BE STRATFORD DIRECTOR

YOUNGEST HEAD

By Our Theatre Reporter

The governors of the Shakespeare Memorial Theatre, Stratford-on-Avon, will name the new Director in the next 10 days. He is expected to be Peter Hall, 27, probably the youngest man ever to be appointed to such a position.

The 17 members of the Executive Council have been considering three names. They have now reached the stage where a meeting, later this month, will place the final seal on the appointment, a remarkable one in the theatre world.

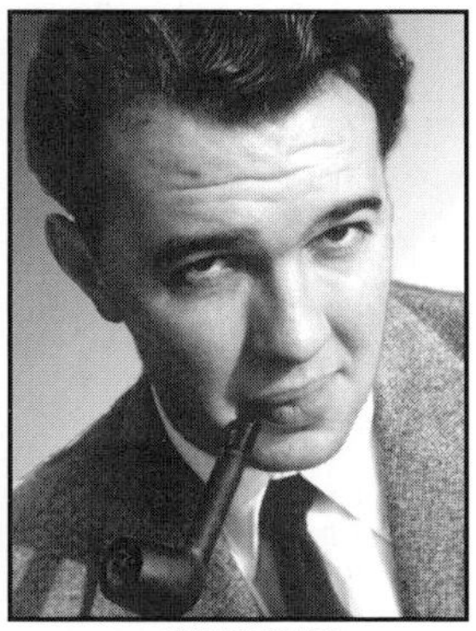

PETER HALL

Although neither the theatre nor Peter Hall would comment yesterday, his appointment is described as certain both in Stratford and the West End. He has directed three plays at Stratford since 1956 and, as Director of the current production of "Twelfth Night," will travel with the company on their visit to Russia next month.

The appointment as Director would date from April, 1960. The present Director, Glen Byam Shaw, who will be 54 next month was co-director with Anthony Quayle from 1953 to 1956 and has since been in sole charge. His total term in office of seven years is above the recent average.

In London Peter Hall said he could not comment at the moment and referred inquiries to Stratford. Theatre spokesmen there said no statement was possible, except that an announcement would be made before the end of the present season, on Nov. 29.

MANY PREMIERES

Peter Hall, husband of Leslie Caron, the actress and dancer, was Director of Productions at the Arts Theatre in January, 1955, at the age of 24, and remained until August, 1956. He has directed the English premieres of many important plays.

Stratford's new season, beginning next April, will be celebrated as the 10th in the Theatre's history. Glen Byam Shaw plans to make it a memorable one, with many visiting celebrities taking part.

Among those who may appear are Charles Laughton, as Flagstaff and Bottom; Paul Robeson, as Othello; Sir Laurence Olivier and Dame Edith Evans.

(November 14)

PASTERNAK REFUSES HIS NOBEL PRIZE

NEW RUSSIAN DRIVE TO FORCE HIM OUT

By David Floyd
Daily Telegraph Special Correspondent on Communist Affairs

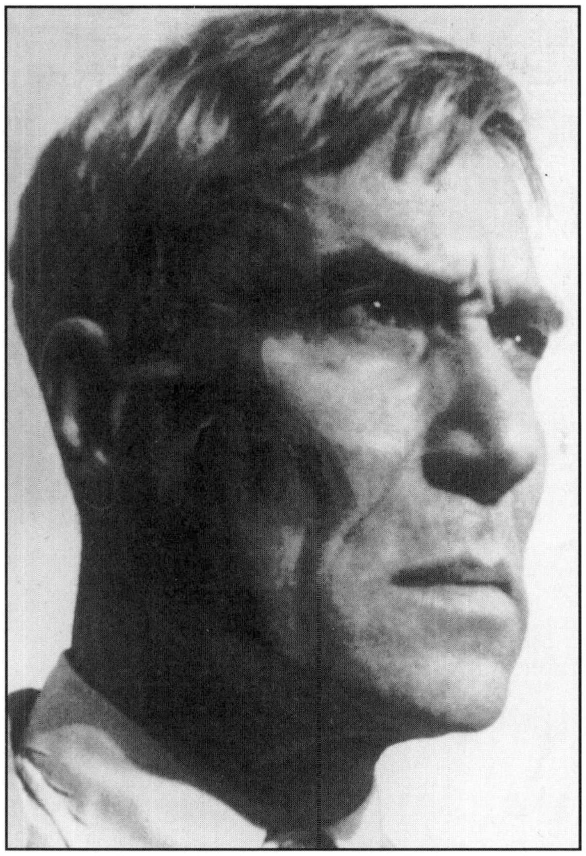

BORIS PASTERNAK

The Swedish Academy announced yesterday that it had received a telegram from the Russian author Boris Pasternak refusing the Nobel Prize for Literature awarded him last week.

He gave as his reason the manner in which the award had been interpreted "in the society to which I belong." The telegram, in French, concluded: "Please do not receive my voluntary rejection with displeasure."

When, four days ago, Pasternak cabled his acceptance of the prize, he described himself as "immensely grateful, touched, proud, astonished, abashed." He told reporters in Moscow that it was "a great joy" for him.

PARTY ATTACK

"Let Him Depart"

There was no certain indication from Moscow of what form of pressure had been brought to bear on him to make him change his mind. But there was clear evidence of a new campaign to force him to leave Russia for good.

Speaking in the presence of Mr. Khruschev, Prime Minister and party leader, at a Young Communist League rally in Moscow last night, Mr. Semichastny, the League's secretary and a top party official, said of Pasternak:

"Why should not this internal emigrant sample the air of capitalism, for which he has such a yearning? I am sure that public opinion here would welcome that.

"Let him become a real emigré and depart to the capitalist paradise. I am sure that neither public opinion nor the Government would put any obstacles in his way.

"On the contrary, they would feel that his departure from our country would freshen the atmosphere."

Mr. Semichastny's remarks were interrupted by applause from the delegates. Earlier he had likened Pasternak to a pig.

He added: "A pig never fouls the places where it eats and sleeps. No pig would do what Pasternak has done. He has fouled the place where he eats and thrown muck at those by whose labour he lives and breathes."

Pasternak's cottage near Moscow was said yesterday to have been put under police guard. He is no longer able to receive visitors.

It was reported that he had been told that if he left Russia he would not be allowed to return. This, it is thought, rather than any more direct pressure, may account for his refusal of the award.

SCIENTISTS' AWARD

Going To Stockholm

The Russian physicists, Dr. Cherenkov and Prof. Tamm, who were awarded the Nobel Prize for physics on Tuesday, announced yesterday that they would go to Stockholm to receive the award, "with great pleasure."

In a letter published in the Communist party newspaper Pravda a group of scientists contrasted the award with the one to Pasternak.

They said: "In the former case the decisive factor was the real scientific value of their work. In Pasternak's case specific reactionary political aims were of sole importance."

Dr. Oesterling, secretary of the Swedish Academy, said last night he had received Pasternak's statement with deep regret. "Behind it one senses a human tragedy which must move us all."

FIRST REFUSAL

Academy Discussion

He added that this was the first time the Nobel Prize for Literature had been refused. The academy would have to discuss the situation at its meeting to-day.

The last time any Nobel Prize was refused was when Hitler forced three German scientists to do so in 1938. This followed the award of the Peace Prize to Karl von Ossietsky, an anti-Nazi journalist, in 1935.

(October 30)

Recent Fiction

GRAHAM GREENE'S UNWILLING SPY

By Kenneth Young

***Our Man in Havana.* By Graham Greene.** (Heinemann. 15s)
***Balthazar.* By Lawrence Durrell.** (Faber, 15s)
***The Darling Buds of May.* By H.E. Bates.** (Michael Joseph. 12s 6d)

One fine morning in the "Gents" at Sloppy Joe's Bar, Mr. Wormold, agent in Cuba for "Phastkleaner" vacuum sweepers, is recruited into the British Secret Service and becomes "Our Man in Havana," or rather (SECURITY!) "59200 stroke five." From then on Graham Greene rips away in as comical, satirical atmospherical an "entertainment" as he has yet given us.

Wormold has been patriotically blackmailed into the job by "59200," who speaks commercial travellers' English ("take a pew, old man"), but he needs the money, for he has a beautiful and expensive young daughter. He is not, however, nature's gift to espionage, and he finds it easier to invent his reports and choose names for his imaginary sub-agents from a club membership list. His fictions impress the "Chief" in London, whose black monocle hides an innocent glass eye of baby blue.

The moral is not as one might suppose that - shades of Fuchs and Pontecorvo! - we need a new Secret Service, but that loyalty to a person, in this case the expensive daughter, is more important than loyalty "to organisations ... I don't think" (Wormold says) "that even my country means all that much. Would the world be in the mess it is if we were loyal to love and not to countries?"

Very subversive. But this is really no more than an amiable, dodgy tale with some cunning and colourful scenes and some odd characters. There is only a passing glimpse of Greene-esque harelips and cruel childhood; his obsession with dogmatic religion is not quite excluded, but it trips with gay insouciance from the lips of a cute young thing. Something nasty in the potting shed? Illusion, friends, pure illusion.

(October 10)

★ ★ ★

Lawrence Durrell looks upon the cosmos with a slight squint. The reason is that one eye is fixed on some ambivalent characters in modern Alexandrea, "impossible city of love and obscenity," while the other is turned inwards on a mental scene of almost geometrical complexity.

He seeks to align the outer with the inner - the cryptic, ironical novelist Purswarden with the psychological paradoxes of Dr. Georg Groddeck; the beautiful, tormented, bisexual Jewess Justine with the Tibetan mysticism of Mila Repa; the schoolboy talk and transvestist impulses of Bimbashi Scoble with the a l'outrance philosophy of Sade.

Happily, the alignment is always imperfect. In "Balthazar," as in "Justine," its predecessor in Mr. Durrell's projected quartet of novels, the filthy, fiery, swarming life so vividly presented is never entirely explained by the quicksilver intellect.

"Balthazar" is a "brief memorial to Alexandria," a "search for my proper self," "an investigation of modern love" - most essentially perhaps the latter, for it is an attempt of unparalleled acuity to get at the flavour of personality, and "Nothing except the act of physical love tells us this truth about one another." Sophisticated, Byzantine (the dry, perverse spirit of Cavafy hovers jocosely), Mr. Durrell's quartet is likely to be one of the greater eminences of mid-century fiction.

(April 11)

★ ★ ★

It would be possible to take "The Darling Buds of May," by H.E. Bates, simply as a comic story. This is its theme. A jolly old tax-dodger with a large family, a roll of banknotes and an untidy smallholding in Kent is visited by a young income tax inspector. He is wheedled into the family circle and given iced lollies, crisps, lashings of drink and a huge meal.

I said this novel could be taken simply as a comic story, because it will see so if you regard as comic a family which has a television set in every room, desecrates the countryside with bungalow and scrapheaps, and lives generously only so far as its own members and friends are concerned. I do not want to seem a prig and on the side of the tax inspector, but I do not really like the family life Mr. Bates so uproariously and vividly describes.

(July 18)

PRINCESS PRESENTS DUFF COOPER PRIZE

BETJEMAN POEMS

Princess Margaret visited the home of Lady Jones (Enid Bagnold, the novelist) in Hyde Park Gate yesterday to take part in an informal and friendly literary event. She presented the Duff Cooper Prize, a cheque for £150, to Mr. John Betjeman for his collected poems.

Presenting the award, Princess Margaret said she was sure Duff Cooper would have wholeheatedly endorsed the decision of the judges. It was a particular pleasure to her that this year's recipient of the prize should be "a friend of mine."

"It is not every author who can both instruct and entertain," said the Princess. "A careful study of Mr. Betjeman's work should enable us all, not only to explore every church in the country with appreciation, but also to move in society with greater confidence."

(December 19)

9th VAUGHAN WILLIAMS SYMPHONY

JOCOSE VITALITY

By Martin Cooper

It can safely be presumed that a composer who writes a symphony at the age of 85 does so for his own satisfaction and for no other reason.

Now, if ever, he can afford to pull a long nose at the so called rules, even if he obeys many of them from second nature.

It was in this spirit, to judge from his own jocose programme notes, that Dr. Vaughan Williams wrote his ninth symphony which had its first performance at the Festival Hall last night.

This is a bigger, generally more serious work than No. 8 and shows at least occasional affinities with two of the composer's finest creations - the sixth symphony (whose key of E minor it shares) and "Job."

NOTE OF FANTASY

There is a very personal note of fantasy in the orchestration, including a flugelhorn, whose mellifluous tone dominates much of the slow movement, and a choir of saxophones.

In the Scherzo - perhaps the most successful of the four movements - these announce a theme whose rhythm and shape recall "The Teddy Bears' Picnic" rather than Job's comforters, though honour is saved by their eventually uniting in a mock chorale.

Formally the music coheres by association and contrast (or is it sometimes the fashionable techniques of "alienation"?) rather than according to the textbook rules of symphonic development and its easy yet original sequence of thought and feeling must convince all but the pedant.

PROPHETIC GLIMPSES

There is certainly evidence of abounding vitality in each of the very different movements and both the first and last contain glimpses of the old prophetic manner. These are nonetheless impressive for being interspersed with excursions into a world of humour from which all sardonic feeling is absent.

Under Sir Malcolm Sargent the Royal Philharmonic Orchestra gave a lively and eloquent account of the new work.

(April 3)

CENSOR BARS BECKETT PLAY

Daily Telegraph Reporter

The Lord Chamberlain has refused a licence for public performance of "End Game," the latest play by Samuel Beckett, author of "Waiting for Godot," it was announced by the English Stage company yesterday.

The company had planned to produce it at the Royal Court Theatre this spring.

The principal objection by the censor is to a scene of about 30 lines in which three of the characters are seen in prayer. The official view is that this is blasphemous.

The play, with the scene in full, was seen at the Royal Court last April, when it had its world premiere there. It was then acted in French by Parisian players before an audience which included the French Ambassador. Its French title was "Fin de Partie."

AUTHOR'S OWN TRANSLATION

Mr. Beckett, a Dubliner and former secretary of James Joyce, who lives in Paris, translated the English version himself. He usually writes in French.

Mr. George Devine, the artistic director of the English Stage Company, flew to Paris to discuss the censor's objections to "End Game."

Mr. Beckett agreed to make four of the five alterations demanded by the censor before a licence could be a granted. But he refused to cut or alter the "prayer" scene. Discussions with the Lord Chamberlain's Office have extended over two months.

(February 10)

7 AWARDS FOR BRITISH FILM

'BRIDGE ON THE RIVER KWAI'

By Our Own Correspondent

Three of the Hollywood Academy's chief awards have been won by the British film "The Bridge on the River Kwai." It was voted the best picture of the year.

Alec Guinness receives the award for the best performance by a male star and David Lean for the best direction. In the absence of Mr. Guinness in England, Jean Simmons received the Oscar on his behalf.

Mr. Lean received his in person from Sophia Loren. He and Mr. Guiness had previously won the awards of New York film critics as well as those of the Directors' Guild.

"The Bridge on the River Kwai" also brought recognition to Pierre Boulle for his screen-play, to Malcolm Arnold for his scoring of the music, to Jack Hildyard for cinematography and to Peter Taylor for film editing.

BEST FEMALE STAR

The foot-high gold Oscar for the best performance by a female star went to Joanne Woodward for "The Three Faces of Eve."

Two other newcomers, the not-very-successful television comedian, Red Buttons, and the Japanese actress Myoshi Umeki, who played the doomed lovers in "Sayonara," were selected as the best supporting players of the year.

Other awards (all American) included:

Documentary: "Albert Schweitzer."
Cartoon: "Birds Anonymous.
Sound-recording: "Sayonara."
Story and screen-play: "Designing Woman," by George Wells
Costume: "Les Girls."
Special effects: "The Enemy Below."
Art direction: "Sayonara."
Jean Hersholt Humanitarian Award: Samuel Goldwyn

The presentations were watched on television by an audience estimated at 75 million.

(March 28)

MAD MEG AND LODGER

PLAY REVELS IN OBSCURITY

By W.A. Darlington

Disappointment was my lot at the Lyric, Hammersmith, last night.

As it chanced that "The Birthday Party," by Harold Pinter, was sandwiched between two sets of two visits to Sadler's Wells to see the Russians, I had looked forward to hearing some dialogue that I could understand.

But it turned out to be one of those plays in which an author wallows in symbols and revels in obscurity. Give me Russian every time.

The author never got down to earth long enough to explain what his play was about, so I can't tell you. But I can give you some sort of sketch of what happens, and to whom.

THWARTED MATERNITY?

To begin with there is Meg (Beatrix Lehmann), who lets lodgings in a seaside town. She is mad. Thwarted maternity is (I think) her trouble and it makes her go soppy over her unsavoury lodger, Stanley (Richard Pearson).

He is mad, too. He strangles people. And I think he must have strangled one person too many, because a couple of very sinister (and quite mad) characters arrive (John Slater and John Stratton), bent on - I suppose - vengeance.

There is also a mad girl (Wendy Hutchinson), nymphomania being her fancy.

The one sane character is Meg's husband (Willoughby Gray) but sanity does him no good. His is a deeply depressed little man, a deck-chair attendant by profession.

Oh well, I can give him one word of cheer. He might have been a dramatic critic, condemned to sit through plays like this.

(May 20)

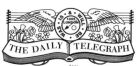

THE DAILY TELEGRAPH
AND
MORNING POST
DAILY TELEGRAPH - JUNE 29, 1855
MORNING POST - NOVEMBER 2, 1772
[Amalgamated October 1, 1937]
135 Fleet Street, London, E.C.4.
Telephone: 4242

OUR COLOUR PROBLEM

Disturbing as recent colour troubles in London and Nottingham certainly are, it would be foolish to exaggerate either their extent or their long-term implications. There is absolutely no comparison between what is happening here and developments in South Africa and the Southern States of America.

To pretend that our attitude represents moral superiority would be unduly complacent. It is largely a question of historical accident. They were faced with a colour problem at a time when all sorts of biological falsehoods were widely believed. Prejudices once adopted are difficult to escape. In a sense, therefore, they are prisoners of their past - a past which Britain was fortunate enough never to experience to anything like the same extent. We need not claim that our attitude is a moral virtue; but it should enable us to grapple with racial problems more rationally. To panic because a few Teddy-boy thugs pick on coloured men to vent their violence - if it were not coloured men it would be some other target - would be pitifully short-sighted. The police, backed by public opinion, and by a firm magistracy, should be able to put an end to these minuscule riots. So long as public opinion refuses to abdicate its reason, the problem will remain within bounds.

There is a further point of great importance. Much more effort needs to be made to ensure that coloured immigrants come as families, with a proper balance between men and women. For what most of us instinctively recoil from is miscegenation. Sexual suspicions are always potent sources of racial conflict. But such wise precautions are quite different from erecting a colour bar, for which in this country there is neither excuse nor need.

(September 2)

NOISY SCOOTER

CONSIDERABLE feeling has been stirred up among our readers in letters complaining about a new source of offensive and irritating noise. This time the complaints, which have in the past been directed in turn against motor horns and motor-cycles, are focused on the high-pitched sounds of the motor scooter. True, we have no technically definable limitation on exhaust noises as have, for example, Germany, Sweden and Switzerland. But because these countries are important markets for the sale of motor-cycles and scooters, most manufacturers, including the British, will tend to keep within the legal noise limit imposed abroad. There is a presumption that all up-to-date machines at least will satisfy the test of acceptable sound.

This does not dispose of the fact that all too many machines emit intolerable noises, whether as a result of defective exhausts or of deliberate interference by the owner anxious to make the machine sound more powerful than it is. Many people think the police should show more zeal in suppressing this sort of nuisance. But, setting aside these special cases, it is right to ask whether the resentment against the motor scooter in general is really substantiated; or whether it has been picked on for creating a new type of noise, to which we are unaccustomed.

(July 5)

PRINCE OF WALES

THE enthusiasm which greeted the QUEEN'S recorded announcement at the end of the Empire Games at Cardiff on Saturday is enough to justify the decision to revive the title of Prince of Wales now. There was nothing irregular in the postponement of Prince CHARLES'S appointment until he was old enough, as he now is, to have a vivid sense of the honour it bestows. It is equally sensible to put off the elaborate ceremony of investiture at Caernarvon - the resuscitation of which was one of the happier flights of LLOYD GEORGE'S Celtic imagination - until Prince CHARLES is old enough to bear the strain of such an occasion.

(July 28)

FAMILY PLANNING

We publish to-day an account of a report, drawn up for presentation to this summer's Lambeth Conference, which is, in every sense, a challenge both to the Christian intellect and to the Christian conscience. Backed by impressive technical studies, economic as well as theological, the authors present the problem of the world's population. Given that it must be morally wrong in principle to withhold from every-one whatever advances in medical science are available to anyone; and given that, in the under-developed countries, wealth does not and cannot advance at the same rate as population; is it, or is it not, a Christian duty to support control of the number of births, if necessary by contraception? The report answers that it is.

Its authors go much further than this. In a long forthright and honest chapter on sexual relations within marriage, they conclude not merely, as did the Lambeth Conference of 1930, that "though normally to be avoided, contraception can be justified by circumstances."

They suggest now that there are "very strong moral-theological grounds for regarding the responsible use of contraceptives by married persons as morally right."

In what may prove a classic of understatement, the authors admit that they do not expect their report to give satisfaction to all the Bishops attending the conference. But whatever its reception - and we hope it will be favourably received in its main outlines - the courage with which it has been written should go far to establish two points. The Anglican church is prepared to face the world's problems as they are and to think before making its moral pronouncements.

(April 7)

FORTY YEARS UNDER THE SOVIETS IN HUMAN TERMS

FALSEHOOD CAME TO STAY

By David Floyd

For the first time a great Russian writer has given an unbiased, uncensored picture of life in his own country since the Revolution. The publication to-day in English of Boris Pasternak's novel "Dr. Zhivago" is therefore a political as well as a literary event.

A few works by Russian authors, mostly in the earlier years of the régime - those of Ilf and Petrov, and of Zoschenko come to mind - have held one aspect or another of the Soviet system up to criticism or ridicule. Even during the brief and partial "thaw" that followed Stalin's death one or two braver spirits, unquenched by years of terror, made some outspoken comments on Soviet Communism.

But never since the régime was installed 40 years ago has there appeared a work attempting to sum up the whole significance of the Russian Revolution in human terms and to put it into its true place in Russian history. That was Boris Pasternak's aim in writing "Dr. Zhivago."

"You have the right to ask me whether I believe what I have written," he told a Western journalist who visited him in his home near Moscow. "My answer is yes. I have borne witness as an artist; I have written about the times I lived through." He wanted, he said, to provide a document of the age.

Unique Witness

On another occasion he said: "My novel is no political pamphlet. It is just the story of a man and his family whose fate it was to live in our momentous epoch." It is, indeed, no political tract, for or against the Soviet system, written by some outside "expert." It is the work of a man deeply imbued with the spirit of Russia, who has lived through all the terrifying events of the past 40 years, and who has yet managed to remain outside them and untouched by them.

As a witness Pasternak is unique, because the authenticity of his knowledge cannot be questioned and his judgments are made in terms of universal human values which everyone, in Russia and outside, can understand. It is as though Tolstoy had lived to witness and write about the Russian October and its aftermath.

The Revolution is no more than a vague backcloth to the novel, which is primarily concerned with the experiences of Dr. Zhivago, the disillusioned but romantic intellectual who in his detachment from the world around him parallels Pasternak himself. The comments on the régime and its works are therefore incidental to the story, but they are devastating when they come.

The whole of Stalin's years of economic terror is summed up in a few sentences about Bolshevik officials:

"How lucky to be so blind! To be able to talk of bread when it has long since vanished from the earth! Of propertied classes and speculators when they have long since been abolished by decree! Of peasants and villages when there aren't any peasants or villages in existence! Have they no memory? Don't they remember their own plans and measures?"

In as few words Zhivago summarises the effects of the Revolution on the Russian people:

"It was then that falsehood came to our Russian land. The great misfortunes, the root of all the evil to come was the loss of faith in the value of personal opinions. People imagined that it was out of date to follow their own moral sense, that they must all sing the same tune in chorus."

In the same way, with fierce strokes of his brush, Pasternak reveals the horrors of the concentration camps, the relief that came with the war with Hitler - which was "a breath of fresh air, an omen of deliverance, a purifying storm"; the hopes that followed the war - "a presage of freedom was in the air throughout those postwar years"; and the failure of those hopes to be fulfilled.

But what mattered for Zhivago, as for Pasternak himself, was the preservation of his own values and principles. It is because Zhivago succeeded, as Pasternak has also succeeded in this task that the book is not permitted to appear in Russia itself. The high priests of Soviet literature prefer to disclaim and ban a great work of art than to have their own hypocrisy and literary impotence revealed by its appearance.

Alive and Free

Alexei Surkov, the present dictator of the Moscow literary world, is reported to have said that to permit the publication of "Dr. Zhivago" would be tantamount to renouncing the whole Soviet régime. It was this, as much as his own personal hatred of Pasternak, that sent him rushing to Italy to try and prevent its publication there. It was this that prompted other efforts to stop the book from appearing in English.

But it has appeared, first in Italy and France, and now for the whole English-speaking world. And Pasternak is still alive and free.

He owed his survival under Stalin, who murdered so many of his contemporaries, to nothing but his great genius. It seems equally unlikely that Stalin's successors will want to destroy the author of the one genuine work of art to emerge from Russia in the past quarter of a century. It is even possible that Mr. Khruschev has in fact connived at the appearance of this book outside Russia, as a proof that everything has not been lost.

Nor is it still impossible that "Dr. Zhivago" will appear in Russia, even though in a slightly expurgated edition. If it did, that would offer genuine grounds for believing that the hopeful note on which it ends is justified and that something new is really stirring in Russia.

If, on the other hand, this great Russian novel does not appear in its native land, then all the talk of change in the Soviet world is empty. Freedom still remains a dream, even if, as Pasternak believes, it is a dream that will ultimately be realised.

(September 4)

REBEL WITH AN OBSCURE CAUSE

From Ian Ball

NEW YORK.

With a turbulent and bloody election behind them, Cubans are now waiting to see whether President Batista's successor, his protegé Dr. Rivero Aguero, intends to hold out an olive branch to the entrenched rebel forces of Fidel Castro, or employ harsher measures in an effort to flush them from their mountain strongholds.

For more than a year now there has been a stalemate. Castro's band of students and young plantation workers is far too small to conquer Cuba. But it is too mobile and too well hidden for the Cuban Army and Air Force to eliminate it.

Undoubtedly to a sizeable number of Cubans Castro has become the Robin Hood who symbolises the fight against corrupt government and suppression of civil liberties. His present hit-and-run tactics, guerrilla warfare and sabotage seem designed principally to keep the spirit of revolution alive in areas where the Government is vulnerable.

There are reported to be five separate bands of insurgents active in Cuba but behind each new rebel strike the hand of Castro is seen. His movement has been held responsible for the seizure in mid-air last Saturday of a Cuban Airlines Viscount which crash-landed on a beach in Oriente Province, with the loss of 17 lives, including four rebel gunmen.

There have been even bolder acts of defiance than this. The most daring, perhaps, was the capture of some 48 American Servicemen and civilians last summer by a rebel band led by Castro's brother Raul. They were held for up to three weeks as "international witnesses" to the use of American arms by the Batista Government against rebels and civilians.

Now Castro has served notice that he may be interested in capturing British subjects in Cuba as "international witnesses." The sale by Britain of a small number of jet planes for the Cuban Air Force has drawn angry threats of retaliation.

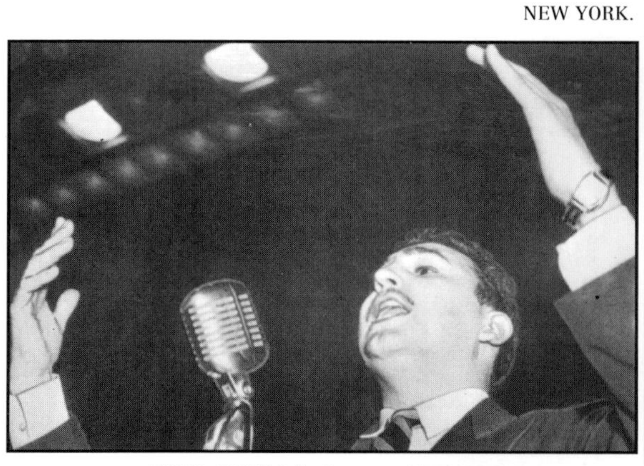

FIDEL CASTRO, fund raising in NEW YORK.

Castro's anti-British campaign has not yet materialised. In rebel-held territories there are no large British properties. In the capital, however, where student groups inspired by Castro's insurrection have been carrying out sabotage and nuisance raids against the Government there are important British interests.

Although he has been in hiding now for several years, a good deal is known about Fidel Castro the man and the methods of his 26th of July movement, the first unsuccessful uprising in Santiago five years ago. But the movement's aims remain obscure.

Journalists and photographers have had little difficulty in reaching him. Castro is a strapping six-footer, 32 years old. He has an ascetic face, framed now by a bushy black beard. Most of those who have met him came away with the impression of a man sincerely devoted to the cause of Cuban nationalism, but with a strong streak of personal ambition. He has issued vague economic proclamations.

His puritanism is reflected in the manner in which he operates his rebel band, and in many of his pronouncements. The legalised gambling in Havana and resorts elsewhere in Cuba is a sore point with him.

He seems now to have a smoothly operating supply line for obtaining arms and ammunition, much of it ferried from Florida in fishing boats. Who pays remains largely a mystery.

Dr. Carlos Prio Socarras, who headed a constitutional but corrupt Government until he was ousted by Batista in 1952 is said to have contributed heavily to Castro's movement from his exile in Miami. Strangely, Castro has been able to make such deals without losing his appeal. In the two years since his original band of 82 seasick soldiers landed on a beach in Oriente Province and were all but wiped out. Castro has mustered some 4,000 devoted followers.

(November 7)

COMPLAINT BY MR. MUGGERIDGE 'UNJUSTIFIED'

PRESS COUNCIL VIEW

The Press council issued last night a statement on its quarterly meeting in London on Tuesday at which it examined a complaint by Mr. Malcolm Muggeridge against the editors of the People and the Sunday Express.

The complaint was in respect of articles published in these papers on Oct. 13 giving extracts from Mr. Muggeridge's article, "Does England really need a Queen?" which appeared in the Saturday Evening Post on Oct. 19.

Mr. Muggeridge claimed that the accounts in the two Sunday papers were "inaccurate, distorted and altogether gave a completely misleading impression of what I had written." The Press Council examined copies of the full text of Mr. Muggeridge's article, the summaries which appeared in the People and the Sunday Express and statements made by the editors of the two papers.

HONEST IMPRESSION

Right to Put Case

The Council decided that Mr. Muggeridge had not justified his accusation, although it regretted that neither newspaper saw fit to quote anything that Mr. Muggeridge wrote to the credit of the Royal family and the Monarchy.

It recognised that Mr. Muggeridge's long analytical article would cause different impressions in the minds of different people according to how they viewed the Monarchy and the criticism made against it.

The Council believed the impression of the article conveyed by the two Sunday papers was honestly held and the papers had a right to put their case that the article contained a number of unfair, untimely and wounding disparagements of the Royal family.

That these occurred in the course of an article much of which was reasonably argued did not affect the point that the disparagements and the gratuitous warning based on the fate of the Russian Imperial family were offensive.

"MISQUOTATIONS"

Palace Life Comment

The Council said Mr. Muggeridge had called attention to two alleged misquotations of what he wrote.

He said: "There are those who find the ostentation of life at Windsor and Buckingham Palace little to their taste." The Sunday Express put it in this way:

"He (Mr. Muggeridge) says she (the Queen) leads an ostentatious and tasteless life at Buckingham Palace and Windsor Castle."

The Press council did not consider this an accurate condensation since

1.-It attributed to Mr. Muggeridge an opinion he reported as that of other people, and

2.-What is not to the taste of some people is not necessarily tasteless, in the broad sense.

But if Mr. Muggeridge put some opinions in the mouths of unnamed persons he could not be absolved from all responsibility for disseminating them.

The Council said Mr. Muggeridge further complained that whereas he describes King George VI's Christmas broadcasts as "funereal in tone," the People reported him as saying they were "funereal." It did not think this version did any injustice, since in the context "funereal" could mean only "funereal in tone or character."

Some compliments were paid to King George VI, but these did not affect the sting in the phrase quoted.

The Press Council did not think the considerable misfortunes of which Mr. Muggeridge had complained were due to the alleged "gross falsification" but were the outcome of the disparagements which he deliberately put in his article.

Mr. Muggeridge was dismissed as a columnist on the Sunday Dispatch after writing only one article. He is now employed as a columnist on the Sunday Pictorial.

"Woolly" Finding

Commenting last night on the Press Council's statement, Mr. Muggeridge said the finding "came as no surprise." He added: "It is woolly, inconclusive, feeble and mistaken."

(January 23)

THESE DEBS WILL MAKE HISTORY AS WELL AS CURTSIES

By FELICIA LAMB

They Learn to Cook, too

Cooking as well as curtsy classes are part of the debutante's training. Above, a class at Mme. Boue's finishing school in Paris, which several British girls have just left to attend this week's presentation parties at the Palace. Right are pictured some of the girls who are going to be presented.

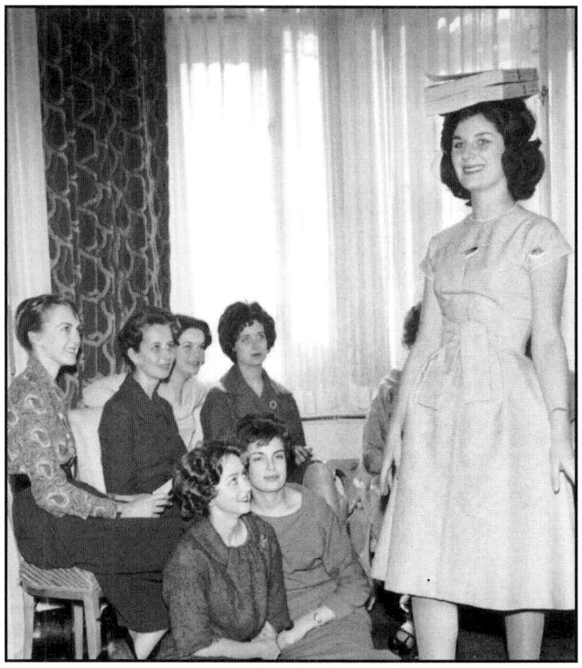

DEBUTANTES practise "poise" for the Debutante Dress Show at the Berkeley Hotel.

The girls going to Buckingham Palace this afternoon will make history as well as their curtsies. To-day, tomorrow and Thursday see the last debutantes' presentation parties at the Palace.

The girls themselves will not realise what a difference this has made to the atmosphere of the season. But the young men, the regular escorts who turn out summer after summer, will realise just what a whirl it is.

One hundred and eighteen dances have been announced so far, and more are being fixed every day. There isn't even the customary break in August - festivities continue, except that the parties in that month are all in the country.

All Rather Expensive

It may seem that the young men are in for a summer of high life without having to pay for it. But one said to me, "I can't afford to go to more than one dance a week. Clean shirt and waistcoat, probably a taxi from the dinner party to the dance and if you are not careful one of the girls says, 'Do let's leave this dreary dance and go to a night club.' Even if you manage to avoid this, somebody's mother is sure to say, 'Can I trust you to see Susan home if I go now?' - and that means another taxi chugging all the way to furthest Kensington."

Reliving Old Splendour

Londonderry House will relive its splendid days again when the Dowager Lady Londonderry will give a ball there for her granddaughter, the **Hon. Camilla Jessel,** Clandon Park, near Guildford, the home of the Onslow family, will see the coming-out of **Lady Theresa Onslow,** whose great-aunt, the Countess of Iveahg, is giving a dance for her and her cousin, the Hon. Eliza Guinness.

At Melford Hall, a lovely Tudor house in Suffolk, **Miss Elizabeth Hyde Parker,** whose family has lived there for centuries, will come out. The Countess of Devon is giving a dance for **Lady Katherine Courtenay** at Powderham Castle, near Exeter; and there are many more from Northumberland and Norfolk, to co. Tyrone. The young men think it well worth saving for the fare to see these great houses as they were at the peak of their history.

(March 18)

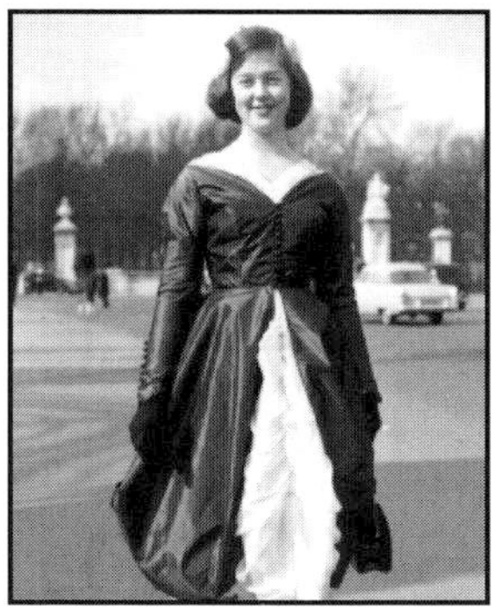

JULIA CHATTERTON at Buckingham Palace for the Presentation Party.

FOOD, DANCING AND 2 SHOWS

LONDON'S NEW ENTERTAINMENT

By Our Theatre Reporter

A mile of multi-coloured neon and fluorescent lighting, two large cockatoos in a cage and a mile and a third of thick Wilton carpet were among the visible signs yesterday of what £250,000 can do to establish a new form of entertainment, and yet thrust a once-renowned theatre even further into the past.

Charles Forte, Bernard Delfont and Robert Nesbitt announced details of their latest venture, "The Talk of the Town," which has replaced the old London Hippodrome. "The Talk of the Town" will open on Sept. 11 and will be "the most modern theatre-restaurant in the world."

The theatre-restaurant will hold just under 700 people, will be open from 7.30 p.m. to 2.30 a.m., will stage two different shows nightly, and will offer food, dancing and entertainment for 42s 6d. At the same time, anyone wishing to spend £5 or more will not be shown the door.

ETRUSCAN VASE RECALLED

After the 4ft-high illuminated letters outside, and the cockatoos inside, the most striking impression is the colour scheme of terracotta, black and gold. The terracotta is repeated in innumerable shades on the walls, carpets, chairs and curtains, recalling, as Mr. Nesbitt, the theatrical producer, put it, the colour on an Etruscan vase.

Mr. Nesbitt was asked what sort of entertainment would be staged. He replied: "With Mr. Delfont and myself connected with it you can be sure it will not be a concert party. It will be glamorous, colourful, vivid, but not French in any sense."

Did that mean no nudes? "It certainly does." Mr. Delfont, the impresario, took up the description. "We anticipate that each show will run a minimum of a year. The food service will be suspended while the show is on."

London, said Mr. Forte, required a place like this, particularly for the tourists who, after Buckingham Palace and the Tower, would want entertainment. Bookings for tables had already been received.

(August 20)

'FLARE LINE' NOW IN MEN'S FASHIONS

Daily Telegraph Reporter

The arbiters of men's fashion have abandoned this year the innocuous "trends" and "styles" designed to woo the retiring male from the kind of suit he has worn for the last 20 years. For the first time men's fashions have a Line.

It is called the Flare Line. This is the masculine version of the fashionable "trapeze" line, the 1958 "must" for women.

About 500 members of the tailoring and allied trades from this country and abroad had a pre-view of it in London last night. They were attending a show put on by the Men's Fashion Council and the International Wool Secretariat.

SINGLE SLEEVE BUTTON

They saw jackets and coats which flared prominently at the back, sleeves with an outward flare at the wrists, secured with only one button. Trousers flared from the knees to 19 inches at the ankles.

There were innovations in materials, too. Although the bulk of them were quiet in tone, there were a few which, recommended for country wear, would be dubbed by the conservative "loud" or perhaps even "bookmaker style."

One lounge suit was greeted with guffaws even by these innovators of the trade. It was of blue worsted with the kind of wide stripe seldom seen outside the chorus line of musical comedy.

(May 20)

MINIATURES AND BUBBLE CARS

Devotees of miniature and bubble cars will find some new examples at the Show.

The 4-wheeled **Messerschmitt,** the TG 500, will be there offering motoring at the lowest cost, but a very different kind of motoring from that provided by its predecessor, the KR200. It will seat two or three persons, and can reach 90 m.p.h. (Price £554, including tax.)

The makers claim that the centre of gravity is so low that the car cannot be overturned. The driver sits along in front and one or two passengers behind. This provides balanced weight distribution and prevents drift and sway.

The car's fuel consumption is said to be 52 m.p.g., with a 500 c.c. twin-cylinder, two-stroke engine.

The **Isetta** is represented by several models, among them the little 300 c.c. coupe (£350, including tax) and a 4-seater 600 (£676, including tax). The 300 c.c. models are being built at Brighton, but the larger model is available only from Germany. The Smith electro-magnetic automatic clutch is featured on one of the small Isettas as an optional extra.

(October 22)

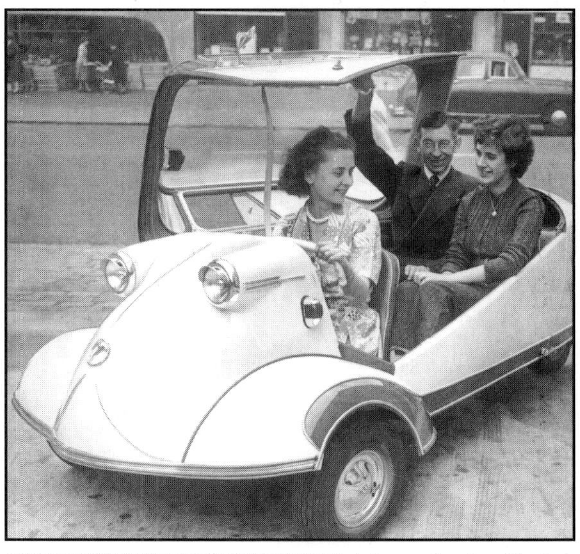

NEW MESSERSCHMITT CABIN SCOOTER. An improved version of the German cabin scooter which can now carry two people in the back seat. Powered by an air-cooled two-stroke engine, it can attain a maximum speed of over 60 m.p.h. Petrol consumption is in the region of 100 miles per gallon.

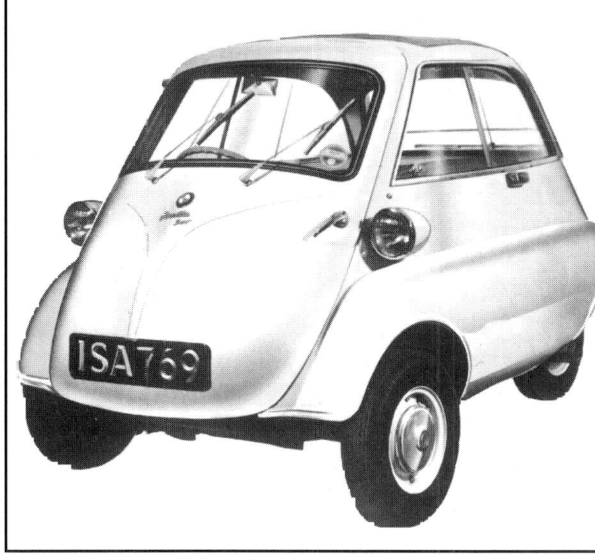

BRITISH-BUILT B.M.W. ISETTA makes its debut. Illustrated is the standard model of the British-built B.M.W. Isetta which is being shown for the first time at the Geneva Motor Show this week.

LONDON DAY BY DAY

Gatwick's opening by the Queen yesterday was a severely simple affair. It was faultlessly staged but at no moment set the pulses racing.

You can do splendid things with a river, ships, roads, horses and troops. But a modern airport - and Gatwick is the last word - simply defies the English genius for ceremonial.

Assembled and seated in the grey dining room, with its sibilant air-conditioning, we were begged not to rise and peer at the Queen's arrival by air on the adjacent apron. Though, possibly, this was the symbolic act of inauguration.

We waited, obediently, until she entered and mounted a little platform with the Bishop of Kingston and the Minister of Transport for brief speeches and the unveiling of a plaque.

Magnificent Bishop

The Bishop was magnificently attired with a stole and mitre of many colours, which attracted much attention. I understand that his sister is a needlewoman of resource.

She had worked the episcopal robes with coloured threads to give the effect of stained glass fragments.

Like the airport, his crook was strictly functional, straight from a shepherd's hands.

This and some of the Queen's words reminded us that this modern creation of glass, steel and concrete has risen over some highly disputed acres of English countryside.

Gatwick will be a joy to travellers, but a 7,000ft runway is not won from this island without sacrifices - as the Queen, countrywoman as well as air traveller, showed awareness.

It is, we are told, the first airport in the world to combine air, rail and road transport in one unit. This felicitous trinity was reflected in yesterday's company.

Forster, Homer, Islam

Octogenerian Mr. E.M. Forster the novelist, is enjoying his trip to the Aegean on one of the archeological cruises.

Yesterday, I hear he was vigorously going round the ruins of Troy in cap, raincoat and yellow scarf, distinguishing level six of Homeric fame from the other levels uncovered.

He took in his stride the 20-mile ride in an Anatolian bus of no mean order, rattling through villages of peasants and veiled women on donkeys.

The day before he was to be seen listening to the strange Islamic sounds in the beautiful Blue Mosque at Istanbul.

At Bursa in Asia Minor Mr. Forster was in high good-humour despite heavy rain that made mosque-going a penance.

English Stage Co. Act 2

The English Stage Co. is celebrating its second birthday to-night at the Royal Court Theatre with "A Resounding Tinkle."

But the man who made possible those astonishing 24 months in which three of their plays were successfully transferred to the West End and four were presented in New York will miss the fun. He and his wife are in Cannes.

I refer to Neville Blond, the industrialist and one-time E.M. Trade Adviser in Washington. Under his chairmanship the venture has thrived beyond everybody's wildest hopes.

He provided the first £5,000 himself. Working in close co-operation with Joseph Hodgkinson drama director of the Arts Council, he also achieved remarkable State backing.

His council has never lacked enthusiasm. Mr. Blond would call it "disciplined enthusiasm."

Artistic Rarity

Mr. Humphrey Brooke tells me that although Mr. John Merton's portrait of Lady Dalkeith is the first picture to receive an "A" (accepted) from the selection committee of the Royal Academy since he became secretary in 1951 a drawing has done so.

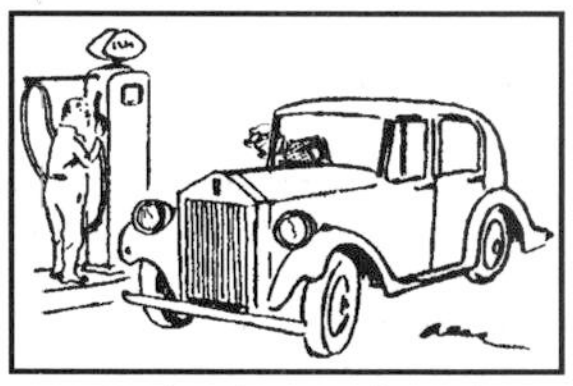

"Road worthiness test? Never! I'll have her put down first!'

This was a small sketch of Oxford by Sir Muirhead Bone. It was submitted in 1953, the year he died.

Almost all works sent in receive an "X" (rejected) or "D" (doubtful). A "D" from the selection committee does not commit the hanging committee and only about half of those so designated appear in the Summer Exhibition.

Even Academicians have to go through the mill. There is no certainty that their works will be hung.

15th Winner

John Lawrence, who writes racing articles for The Daily Telegraph under the pen-name of Marlborough had his 15th steeplechase winner this year when he rode Gaillac at Sandown yesterday. This is a high figure for an amateur.

On the second, beaten only by a neck in a close finish, was Arthur Freeman who rode the winner of the National Mr. What, on Saturday.

Gaillac was Lawrence's fifth win in his last nine rides and his fourth in four this year on horses trained by Kent Cundell. Three of the latter have been on Gaillac.

To-day at Cheltenham he rides Flaming East, on which he won the £2,000 Imperial Cup at Sandown 10 days ago.

Michelin for 1958

I have just received the 1958 number of the Michelin France Guide, an invaluable companion for anyone motoring, or simply travelling, in France.

Michelin's compendium includes practically everything in France to interest the visitor - its cathedrals, its old towns, its beauty spots and so on.

Functional v Ceremonial Voyage to Troy

To the epicure a feature of Michelin is always his grading of restaurants. Three stars indicate one of the best tables in France and worth a special journey.

Of these there are only 11 in the whole country, Paris having four - Maxim's, Tour d'Argent, Grand Vefour and Laperouse. You must expect a meal at all of these, except Maxim's, to cost you more than 2,000 francs.

Escaping the Strand

While new water mains are laid in the Strand westbound traffic alone may use the street. Traffic going east to the City is diverted along the Victoria Embankment.

After two mornings of this my reaction yesterday was one of delight. With the exception of Waterloo Bridge and its no less unlovely neighbour, the Bankside power station, one's new morning vista is charming.

Not only does one have a splendid vision of St. Paul's hanging above the river as St. Peter's hangs above Rome. One is also spared the Strand. It was once written:

"The Strand utterly unmans me, leaving me with only two sensations: (1) a regret that I have made such a mess of my life. (2) a craving for alcohol."

Sir Max Beerbohm was the author.

Too Much to Believe

A young couple watching the film "The Ten Commandments" were much impressed by the spectacular effects.

When the Red Sea parted they could hardly contain themselves. As the pillar of fire came down the girl whispered to her companion: "I wonder who thought of that?"

"No idea," was the reply. "But it's too far-fetched for me."

PETERBOROUGH

Obituary

PIUS XII SPENT HIS LIFE WORKING FOR PEACE

By Martin Moore

The 19 years' pontificate of Pius XII spanned a period in which the greatest of wars was succeeded by ideological conflict on no less vast a scale. In him Roman Catholicism had a leader able to take the measure of these events.

No man who could have been elected to St. Peter's throne in 1939 was better fitted by training, diplomatic experience and temperament to guide the Church through these critical years. Succeeding to the measure of temporal power which the Papacy had regained 10 years earlier, he sought to give it an international influence on affairs parallel to the spiritual universality which the Church claims.

For five centuries the College of Cardinals has been predominantly Italian; election of an Italian Pope had become automatic. Because of the appointments made by Pius XII - including that of the first Chinese Cardinal - the College which will now choose his successor contains a large majority of non-Italians.

FAMILY TRADITION

Service To Holy See

Born in Rome on March 2, 1876, Eugenio Pacelli inherited a family tradition of service to the Holy See. His father was dean of the Consistorial Advocates at the Vatican; his grandfather had been Under-Secretary of the Interior to Pius IX.

Young Pacelli had no doubt of his vocation nor, as he soon showed, of the sphere in which he believed he could best serve the Church. In 1901, only two years after his ordination, he entered the Papal Secretariat of State as an apprentice, becoming at the same time professor of Diplomacy and International Law in the Academy of Noble Ecclesiastics.

Working under two prelates of wide vision, Cardinals Merry del Val and Gasparri, he also cultivated friendships among the foreign community outside the Vatican. His ascetic, aristocratic figure became familiar at their social gatherings, and especially in the English drawing-rooms of Rome.

To these associations he largely owed his remarkable linguistic fluency; he spoke five languages - besides his own and Latin - well enough to converse and broadcast in them.

Pacelli's first important appointment was in 1913, as Secretary for Extraordinary Ecclesiastical Affairs. The following year he became Under-Secretary of State, under Gasparri.

In this capacity he helped to draw up the peace proposals by which Benedict XV tried to end the first World War in 1917. The Pope chose Pacelli as his envoy to the Kaiser, appointing him Nuncio at Munich - Bavaria being then virtually an independent Kingdom within the Reich.

NUNCIO IN GERMANY

Concordat With the Nazis

In 1920 he was appointed first Nuncio to the new German Republic. Long-drawn diplomatic negotiations occupied the next nine years, resulting in a Concordat between the Holy See and Bavaria, followed and superseded by a similar treaty with the German Republic in 1929.

This task accomplished, he was recalled to Rome by Pius XI, with whom he had formed a close friendship while the future Pope was Nuncio in Warsaw. He made Pacelli a cardinal in December, and a few weeks later, in February, 1930, appointed him Secretary of State in succession to Gasparri.

His first task as Secretary of State was to work out the detailed application of the Lateran Treaty just concluded between the Holy See and Fascist Italy. In 1933 he negotiated with Germany a new Concordat by which he hoped to safeguard the liberties of the Church under Nazism.

No cardinal stood closer to the Pope, who, in 1935, had made him Cardinal Camerlengo, to which office the administration of the Church would pass during an interregnum.

But this did not mark Pacelli as a likely successor; indeed, tradition seemed to make him an improbable choice. No Secretary of State had ever become Pope, nor, for more than a century, had any cardinal of the Curia, the central Government of the Church.

Yet, when Pius XI died early in 1939, Pacelli was elected on the third ballot; so clearly did his character and abilities mark him as the man best fitted to lead the Church in that period of gathering crisis.

Taking the title of Pius XII, the new Pontiff made earnest private efforts to prevent the war. When it came he did all he could to mitigate its brutalities and to open the way for peace. In his first Christmas allocution to the cardinals he laid down the principles of a just peace, including the right of all nations to independence.

The later years of Pius XII's reign were saddened by a persecution of Christians which he has likened to that of Nero, by the arrest and imprisonment of Roman Catholic prelates in Eastern Europe and brutal assaults upon missionaries in China.

Denunciation of the Communist creed has been a continually recurring theme in his speeches, and the rallying of the Church against it the purpose which inspired the great gatherings of the Holy Year in 1950.

The most travelled Pope was also the most accessible to pilgrims from every part of the world, as well as to non-Catholic visitors. Last year he gave audience to nearly a million people and made 132 speeches in seven languages.

DYNAMIC SPEECHES

Echoes Round the World

Besides the simple and devout who daily thronged to receive the apostolic blessing, he met the members of every professional or specialist international gathering held in Rome.

These audiences were not merely formal solemnities - the Pope's addresses were dynamic contributions to the subjects that had brought his listeners together. It was then that he made the speeches, often acutely controversial, that attracted notice all over the world and echoed long in debate.

In applying the criteria of Roman Catholic doctrine to modern problems Pius XII never spoke only in generalities, but to experts in their own terms - yet always with a directness and simplicity intelligible by everyone. Nuclear energy and warfare, radio and television, films, fashions, migration, the impact of automation on the individual worker - these were among the subjects of recent addresses.

To specialised branches of medicine he repeatedly turned, making clear the Church's attitude to birth-control, painless childbirth, artificial insemination, psychiatry, euthanasia and the use of drugs in incurable illness.

VISION AND ENERGY

His Wide Knowledge

If his personal spirituality affected all who came near him, those who heard him speak or only read what he had said were no less impressed by the Pope's extraordinary range of knowledge, and those who worked with him by the phenomenal energy animating his frail body.

The man who felt himself sustained by a personal vision of Christ (as he allowed the Vatican to make known three years ago) was the same who controlled every detail of the Church's vast machinery of government, and yet found time to keep in touch with the questions that were agitating the world outside it.

"Let us enjoy the Papacy," said Leo X, the Medici Pope. If Pius XII had formulated a worldly ideal of office it might have been, "Let us energise the Papacy." That indeed he has achieved, through a combination of spiritual force with intellectual grasp and diplomatic skill.

(October 9)

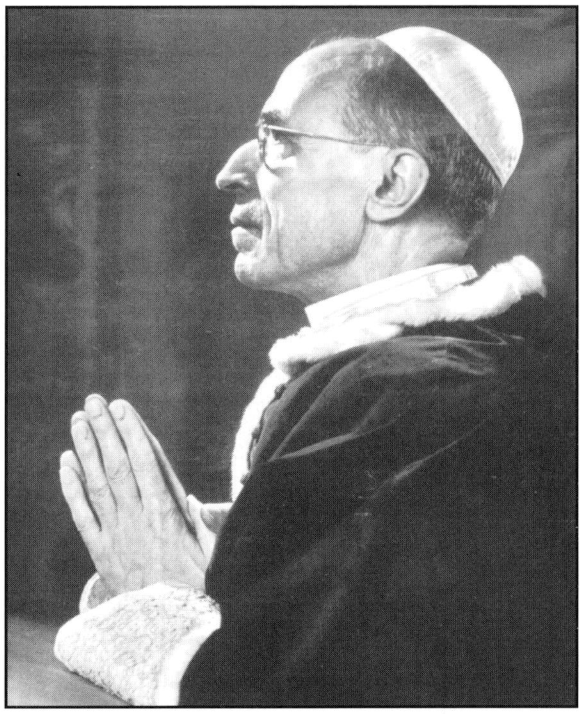

POPE PIUS XII

DR. R. VAUGHAN WILLIAMS

FAME AT 35 AFTER FESTIVAL PIECE

Dr. Ralph Vaughan Williams, the composer, who has died aged 85, received the Order of Merit in 1935. Born the son of a clergyman, at Down Ampney, Glos, he was educated at Charterhouse, and Trinity college, Cambridge. He later attended the Royal College of Music.

His development was anything but precocious, and among his generation - which was exceptionally brilliant - at the R.C.M. he was not at first expected to attain pre-eminence.

Not hard-pressed for money, he went abroad for experience. He was 35 before the world in general came to know him through the effect made at the Leeds Festival in 1907 by his noble "Toward the Unknown Region."

In the 1914-18 war Vaughan Williams served in the R.A.M.C. as a private, and later gained a commission in the Royal Artillery. Before he left the Army he was appointed a professor at the Royal College of Music.

His first wife, formerly Miss Adeline Fisher, died in 1951. Two years later he married Mrs. Ursula Wood, a widow, who survives him.

(August 27)

CONDUCTORS PAY TRIBUTE

'BELOVED GENIUS'

Among the many tributes paid to Dr. Vaughan Williams yesterday were:

Sir John Barbirolli, conductor of the Hallé Orchestra: "I think the loss is incalculable because he was undoubtedly the greatest living composer of our time, especially since the passing of Sibelius. Up to then we had two greatest living composers.

"As time passes the loss will become greater and greater. He was the beloved genius of our music because it could only have been given to few men and only the greatest geniuses to touch the hearts and minds of our fellows at so many points as he did."

Sir Malcolm Sargent, the conductor: "It is terrible that, within a year, the two greatest figures living in music today, Sibelius and Vaughan Williams, should both have passed away. Music is very much the poorer for their going."

Sir Adrian Boult, the conductor: "Vaughan Williams has been, in every sense, the leader of British music for many years. The wideness of scope of his output and its wonderful consistent quality have been a constant inspiration and have done everything to win the proud place which British minsic now holds in world opinion."

(August 27)

DAME C. PANKHURST

SUFFRAGETTE AND EVANGELIST

Dame Christabel Pankhurst, who has died in Los Angeles aged 77, was one of three militant suffragettes whose names were synonymous with the movement in the early part of the century; the others were her mother, Emmeline, and her sister Sylvia.

Christabel's influence was largely responsible for the founding in 1903 by Mrs. Pankhurst of the Women's Social and Political Union.

This was the organisation which for years conducted the vigorous campaign of window-breaking and arson which led to the imprisonment of many of its members, and to their hunger-strikes in prison.

With Annie Kenney, Christabel attended the first meeting in 1905 at which militant action resulted in a prison sentence. Ejected from the hall in Manchester where Sir Edward Grey was speaking the two women addressed crowds in the street and were arrested for obstruction.

Annie Kenney was sentenced to a fine of 5s or three days' imprisonment, and Christabel to 10s or one week. Both promptly elected to go to gaol, to serve the first of several sentences in the cause of women's suffrage.

In 1912, hearing that detectives were on the way with a warrant for her arrest, Christabel eluded them and escaped to France.

On the outbreak of war in 1914 she declared a truce in the Pankhursts' campaign so that suffragettes could devote their energies to war work.

She was made a Dame Commander of the Order of the British Empire in recognition of her political and social services, in 1936.

(February 15)

HENRY FARMAN

The name of Henry Farman, who has died aged 84, is associated in the history of flying with those of the Wright Brothers and Louis Bleriot.

The last of three famous brothers ,Henry Farman first flew in a heavier-than-air machine in 1907, after winning a reputation as a cycle and motor-racer.

In 1908 he established two records by making the first circular flight of a mile at a height of 25ft, and by flying 17 ½ miles across country from one town to another. In the course of the second flight he also broke the world's speed record, flying at 47 m.p.h

He founded an aircraft factory which manufactured military machines, some of which were employed by the Royal Naval Air Service in the 1914-18 war. Several of his patents were embodied in the engines of British machines which flew in the 1939-45 war.

(July 11)

DR. MARIE STOPES

PIONEER'S CAREER OF CONTROVERSY

Dr. Marie Stopes, who has died aged 78, was a talented pioneer woman scientist who became a happy wife and mother. But she aroused a storm of protest in 1918 and succeeding years by her books on birth control.

"Married Love," the first of her works to offend the susceptibilities of church and social authorities, led not only to heated controversy, but to several court actions. Bans were applied in Ireland and New York.

An American publisher was fined £50 in 1921 on the grounds that the book was obscene, although it was later freely published in a modified form. Dr. Stopes was awarded £100 in a libel action she brought against Dr. Halliday Sutherland, who accused her of "exposing the poor to experiment," but the House of Lords allowed his appeal.

The late Mr. H.A. Gwynne, then editor of the Morning Post, sued Dr. Stopes for libel in 1928 and was awarded £200 damages. She appealed and conducted her own case, but the appeal was dismissed.

PROTEST MEETINGS

Indignation meetings were held in many parts of the country, a furious controversy raged in the correspondence columns of newspapers, and advertisements for her books were rejected by various publications. Some branches of the British Medical Association cancelled lectures she was to have given.

Despite this, or because of it, "Married Love" sold more than 750,000 copies and was translated into a dozen languages. It was followed by, among others, "Radiant Motherhood," "Sex and the Young," and "Enduring Passion." She also had a propaganda play produced, "Our Ostriches."

The daughter of an anthropologist, Marie Stopes studies science at the North London Collegiate School with such success that she was able, when the teacher fell ill, to take over the class. She even privately taught chemistry to her biology teacher.

BOTANIST AND GEOLOGIST

She later achieved a reputation as a botanist and geologist, and became an expert on coal-formation. In 1904 she was appointed to the science staff of Manchester University, the first woman to hold such a post there. She also lectured at University College, London.

Among the things she advocated at various times were bare feet for children and the reduction of the legal age for marriage for girls to 15; she argued on biological, not economic, grounds. In December last she was taken ill in Germany. She later claimed to have been a victim of "radio-activity in the atmosphere."

She married the late Mr. H.V. Roe, the aircraft pioneer. With him she established in Holloway in 1921 the first birth-control clinic. They had two sons.

(October 3)

PROF. G.E. MOORE

Prof. George Edward Moore, the distinguished philosopher, who has died aged 84, was Professor of Philosophy at Cambridge University from 1925 until his retirement in 1939. The O.M. was bestowed on him in 1951.

Born in Upper Norwood, the son of a doctor, he went from Dulwich College to Trinity College, Cambridge, where he secured firsts in classics and moral science, and was Craven university scholar in 1895. A Fellow of Trinity 1898-1904, he was appointed Lecturer in Moral Science at the University in 1911.

He exercised great influence on British and American philosophic thought in the early years of the century. "States of mind," he considered, are all-important. In ethics he propounded the doctrine that "good" is indefinable, and not a mere description of fact.

He elaborated his theories in "Principia Ethica," published in 1903. "Ethics," 1912, and "Philosophical Studies," 1922. All three works provided material for stimulating controversy. From 1921-1947 Prof. Moore was editor of Mind.

(October 25)

MR. RONALD COLMAN

ROMANTIC HERO WHO REMAINED ENGLISH

Ronald Colman, the actor, who has died aged 67, never gave up his British nationality, although his greatest successes were gained in America. He was born in Richmond, Surrey, and made his first professional stage appearance in London in 1916.

He went with the London Scottish to France in 1914 and was awarded the Mons Star with bar on being invalided out of the Army in 1916. Between 1916 and 1919 he made his British stage and screen debut. In 1920 he went to New York and then to Hollywood.

He was chosen to play the lead opposite Lillian Gish in "The White Sister," and went on to become one of the few Hollywood stars to survive the advent of talking pictures. His complete "Englishness" and his fine speaking voice made him the hero of many films.

Ronald Colman's most popular successes include early versions of "Beau Geste" and "A Tale of Two Cities"; the "Bulldog Drummond" series; "Clive of India"; "Prisoner of Zenda" with Douglas Fairbanks, Jnr., "Lost Horizon"; "The Light That Failed" and "Random Harvest."

GAINED OSCAR

In 1947 he was awarded an Oscar for his performance in "A Double Life." His last appearances, except in television films, were brief roles in Michael Todd's "Around the World in 80 Days" and "The Story of Mankind," shown in London last November.

His first marriage to Thelma Ray, the actress, was dissolved in 1935. Three years later he married Miss Benita Hume, at a ranch in California. He is survived by his widow and one daughter.

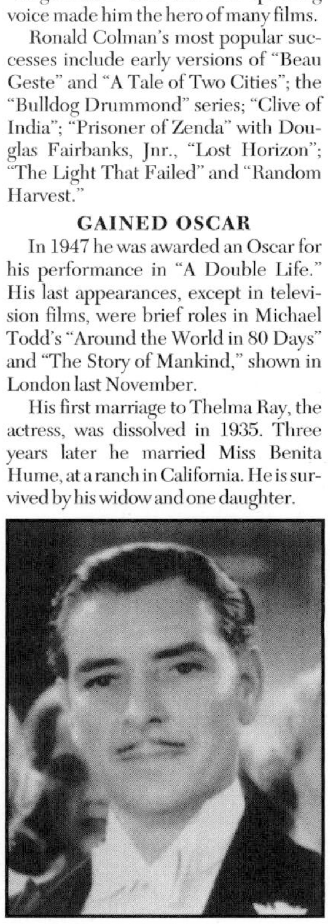

SUPERB POLISH

The Screen's Need

CAMPBELL DIXON writes: One of the most curious documents in the history of the film industry, worth a place in any museum, is a card once shown to me by a British producer. It recorded a screen test of a British actor who made no great stir in a few plays, including one talked about by everybody but seen by few, Brieux's "Damaged Goods."

The verdict was a rejection, the reason: "Does not photograph well." The name was Ronald Colman.

Eventually, of course, he was given his chance by Hollywood in "The White Sister." The rest is history.

NO TOUCH OF SCANDAL

Mr. Colman was one of the most charming and best-loved of all film stars, and none kept his following longer or set a better example in private life. Socially, he was Hollywood's uncrowned king, unspotted by scandal, unspoiled by success.

I wish I could say that he was also a great actor, but the fact is that, except for more ambitious performances in a "Tale of Two Cities" and "A Double Life," he was content to display an easy competence and superb polish.

His very good looks may have been a handicap. They typed him always as romantic lead, often in parts he felt so little that he would play love scenes with hardly a glance at the lovely ladies he was supposed to adore.

All the same, with his chivalrous bearing and air of distinction, he gave the screen something it badly needed, something no other actor, except Clive Brook, could supply.

Though there have been many actors more powerful and more profound, few won so much affection and admiration as a man. Sorrow at his death will be all the greater because he has no successor.

(May 20)

Obituary

KING FEISAL

BRITISH INFLUENCE ON CHILDHOOD

King Feisal II of Iraq, whose murder in the Iraqi revolt is now confirmed, was 23. He was enthroned in 1953 at the age of 18.

Previously, for 14 years his country had been under a Regency, that of his uncle Abdul Illah, who also died in the rebellion. Feisal's father, King Ghazi, died in 1939 from injuries sustained when, driving his own car, he crashed into an electric power standard near his palace.

The only son of King Ghazi and the late Queen Aliyah, Feisal ibn Ghazi ibn Feisal el Hashim was a member of the Hashemite family which claims descent from Mohammed. Born in Baghdad, he was a great-grandson of the first King of Hejaz, grandson of King Feisal I, and a cousin of King Hussein of Jordon.

BRITISH INFLUENCE

British influence on his childhood was strong. He had an English nurse and a Scottish governess, and at the age of 12 came to a preparatory school near Salisbury. Two years later he went to Harrow, where his father had been educated, and took a lively interest not only in his studies but also in sports. Arab tutors came with him from Iraq to teach him Middle Eastern history, and Turkish and Kurdish.

His mother died while he was at Harrow. He left the school in 1952 and toured the United States with his uncle, the Regent Emir Abdul Illah, paying a State visit to Britain shortly afterwards. He was a guest at Balmoral.

On May 2, 1953, he was installed as King; on the same day his cousin Hussein ascended the throne of Jordan. Wearing the uniform of a field-marshal, Feisal was acclaimed with enthusiasm by thousands of his subjects as he drove to take the oath of allegiance to the Constitution.

Travel occupied much of the young King's time during the early part of his reign. He paid visits to Pakistan, London, Jordan, the Lebanon, Rurkey and Spain.

ASSURANCE TO M.P.s

His country became a founder-member of the Baghdad Pact, largely due to the efforts of his Prime Minister, Gen. Nuri es-Said, also murdered by the rebels. On a second State visit to England, the King assured M.P.s at a reception that Britain and Iraq stood together in the Middle East.

He was dining with Sir Anthony Eden in July, 1956, when news reached London that Nasser had nationalised the Suez Canal. On his return home he attended conferences with King Saud of Saudi-Arabia, with Nasser and with the King of Syria.

British and French intervention in Egypt was followed by more discussions, in which King Hussein of Jordan joined. Solidarity with Egypt was the keynote of subsequent joint pronouncements.

(July 21)

TYRONE POWER

Tyrone Power, who has died in Madrid at the age of 45, was one of the few American film stars to spring from purely theatrical stock.

He made his debut at the age of seven in a mission play, but worked as an assistant in a music-hall before he appeared professionally with his father in "The Merchant of Venice."

His father died while filming in Hollywood and for several years Tyrone Power played in the theatre. He had appeared in Broadway productions with Katherine Cornell before accepting a contract with 20th Century-Fox in 1936.

33 PICTURES IN 16 YEARS

For them he appeared in 33 pictures in 16 years. Among the best-known of his earlier films were "The Mark of Zorro," "Blood and Sand," and "Lloyds of London."

After service with the United States Marines in the Second World War he resumed his film career. Included in his more recent productions were "The Eddie Duchin Story," "Seven Waves Away," and "Witness for the Prosecution."

He was married three times. His first marriage, to the actress Annabella, was disolved in 1948, and his second, to Linda Christian, the actress, by whom he had two daughters, in 1955. In May he married Mrs. Deborah Minardos.

(November 17)

D.R. JARDINE DIES AT 57

CENTRAL FIGURE IN BODYLINE TESTS

By Michael Melford

Douglas Robert Jardine, who has died aged 57, captained England in the "bodyline" Test series in Australia in 1932-33.

The general public will remember him mostly for his share in that England victory, for his austere approach and his uncompromising use of the fast bowling of Larwood and Voce, but he was also a cricketer of outstanding ability, the leading amateur batsman of his day. He made 35 centuries in first class cricket.

Jardine evolved the bodyline policy himself and in Larwood had the perfect instrument to implement it. He did not himself agree that short bowling at the body constituted physical intimidation of the batsman. In a book later he described such charges as "stupid and patently untruthful."

When he himself was confronted with it he did not flinch. One of his most famous innings was his 127 for England at Old Trafford in 1933 against the West Indian fast bowlers, Constantine and Martindale.

However, the later matches of the 1932-33 tour were played in an atmosphere of unparalleled tension and hostility which induced a series of cables between the Australian Board of Control and M.C.C.

CONFIDENCE OF M.C.C.

The first Australian cable stated that bodyline bowling had assumed such proportions that physical defence of the body was becoming the first consideration. M.C.C. replied that they had all confidence in Jardine.

They confirmed their confidence not only by appointing him captain in India but by congratulating him when he returned from Australia on his able and determined captaincy.

In time, however, official and public opinion began to change until bodyline was generally accepted as having been a pernicious influence on the game.

The son of M.R. Jardine of Oxford University and Middlesex, Jardine was one of the few Scots to reach the highest class of cricket. Born in Bombay, he was educated at Winchester, where he was three years in the XI, and at Oxford University.

Six feet tall and strong of wrist and forearm, he was a graceful, thoroughly sound batsman, particularly fluent on the off-side.

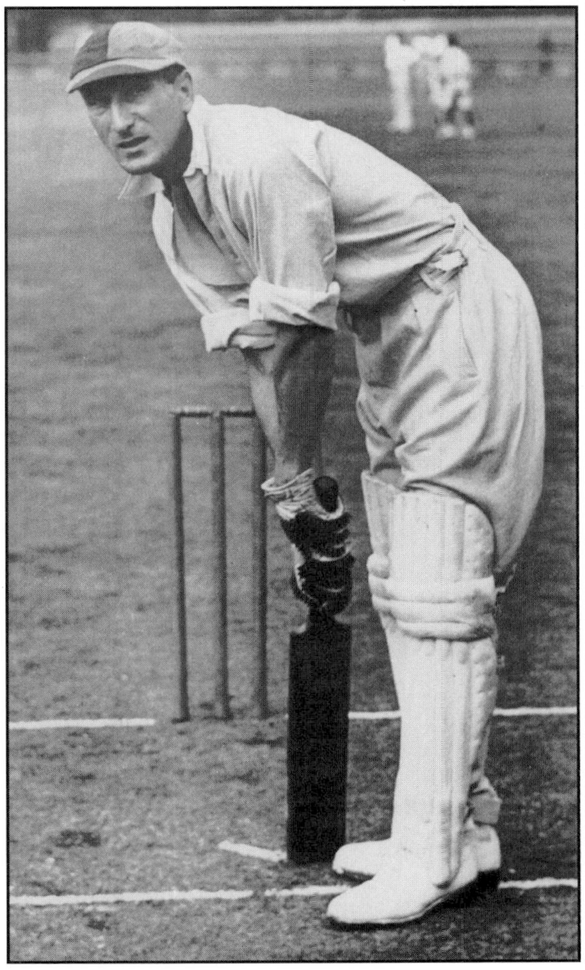

WON BLUE AT OXFORD

He won his Blue at Oxford as a Freshman in 1920 and played against Cambridge in 1921 and 1923. A knee injury kept him out of the side in 1922.

After he began to play for Surrey, Jardine improved steadily and played for England for the first time against West Indies in 1928. In all, he played 22 times, the last 11 times as captain.

In Australia in 1928-29 he averaged 61, scoring centuries in his first three matches, but in the next two English seasons played little first-class cricket.

The M.C.C. team which Jardine led in Australia in 1932-33 curbed Bradman at the height of his power, played some of the best cricket ever shown by a touring side and won the series 4-1.

Yet the bitterness surrounding the tour robbed the victory of much of its sweetness.

Jardine returned to England a figure of controversy. He had succeeded P.G.H. Fender as captain of Surrey in 1932 and he led them again in 1933. But while in India next winter captaining another M.C.C. side he resigned and dropped out of first-class cricket.

Jardine was a barrister and a director of several companies. He was taken ill with a tropical fever while visiting Salisbury, Southern Rhodesia, to inspect land he owned there.

He married in 1934, Miss M.I. Peat who survives him with a son and three daughters.

(June 20)

DAME ROSE MACAULAY

Dame Rose Macaulay, who died yesterday, aged 77, had written since 1906 more than 30 books, 22 of them novels. "The Towers of Trebizond" won for her in 1956 the James Tait Black Memorial Prize.

She was the daughter of Mr. G.C. Macaulay, lecturer in English Literature at Cambridge University, who was a grandson of Aulay Macaulay, uncle of the historian.

In 1955 she became the first woman member of the Council of the Royal Literary Fund. She was created a Dame of the British Empire in the New Year honours.

BRILLIANT TALKER

Deeply Religious

Eric Gillett writes: Admirers who read her books and listened to her on the air must have sensed that behind the wit, precision and beauty of her writing and talk, there lay an extraordinary personality, charitable and tolerant of all that was genuine and sincere, a brilliant and very modest talker, and a sworn foe to humbugs, pretension and every kind of evil.

She disliked the act and not the person for she was deeply religious. She was also altogether fearless.

About everything that concerned herself she was reticent. She once told me that in her fiction, the only autobiographical allusions she had allowed herself were five lines in "And No Man's Wit," but she said it with a twinkle.

Rose Macaulay received most applause for her scintillating satirical

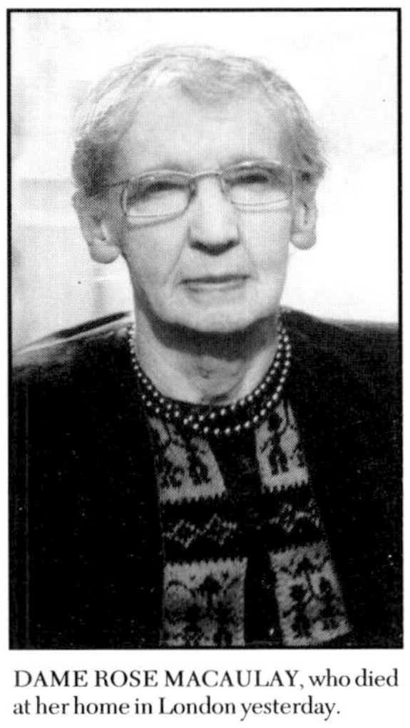

DAME ROSE MACAULAY, who died at her home in London yesterday.

novels, "Potterism," "Crewe Train," "Keeping Up Appearances" and "Told by an Idiot." She had a warm corner in her heart for "They Were Defeated," in which she introduced Robert Herrick.

I remember how vigorously she defended it when I said I preferred her other novels, above all, "The World My Wilderness," with its sympathy for the young orphans of the war, and "The Towers of Trebizond," full of wit and wisdom and extravagant humour.

Among her other books "Some Religious Elements in English Literature" and the superb "Pleasure of Ruins" will be read for a long time to come.

(October 31)

PETER COLLINS

DRIVER HAILED AS FUTURE CHAMPION

Peter Collins, who has died aged 27 after a motor race accident, was regarded as second to Stirling Moss as a Grand Prix driver. Before the race at Nurburgring in which he was killed, he was lying third in the world championships.

In February, 1957, he left the Aston Martin sports car team to join the Ferrari Grand Prix team. He drove under Fangio, the world champion.

Two months after he joined Ferrari, he drove to victory in the Syracuse Formula I Grand Prix in record time. He followed this success with a win in the Naples Grand Prix.

Later the same year he won the Venezuelan Grand Prix. This year he was victorious in the Buenos Aires "1,000 kilometres" race, the Sebring endurance race at Florida, and the British Grand Prix at Silverstone last month.

He married the American actress, Louise Cordier, in February last year.

Quiet, modest, with a ready smile, he was more often near the leader in big races than in the lead itself. But he had many notable victories in Britain and abroad. In his last big triumph, in the British Grand Prix at Silverstone in July, he led from start to finish.

Contemporary with Stirling Moss and Mike Hawthorn, he started racing seven or eight years ago. But he came into the limelight when he began to drive for Mr. David Brown in the Aston Martin team, taking part in the most important sports car races in the world, Le Mans.

(October 4)

ROBERT DONAT

CAREER WAS MARRED BY ILL-HEALTH

The death of Robert Donat, the actor, at the age of 53, followed closely on his last return to acting. For five weeks, in April and May, he played a Chinese mandarin in the film "The Inn of the Sixth Happiness" with Ingrid Bergman.

He was attended by a nurse at the studios and an air conditioner was installed in his dressing room. The set was closed to visitors while he appeared. As soon as the film was completed he went into hospital "for rest and observation."

Donat was born at Withington, Manchester, and made his stage debut at the Prince of Wales's Theatre, Birmingham, in July, 1921, as Lucius in "Julius Caesar." He played in repertory in Birmingham, Manchester, Wakefield, Huddersfield, Liverpool and Camabridge before his first appearance in the West End, at the Ambassadors, in 1930.

ACADEMY AWARD

His first big London part was that of Dunois, in Shaw's "St. Joan" in 1931. In 1939 he won an Academy award for his most famous role, that of the schoolmaster in the film "Goodbye Mr. Chips." Other film successes included "The Count of Monte Cristo," "The 39 Steps," "The Winslow Boy" and, in 1951, "The Magic Box."

Mr. Donat's first marriage, in 1929, to Ella Annesley Voysey, by whom there were two sons and a daughter, was dissolved. Later he married Renee Asherson, the actress, and they separated two years ago.

GREAT BUT UNLUCKY

£40,000 Film Fees

CAMPBELL DIXON writes: Robert Donat was one of the greatest actors of his generation, and probably the most unlucky. The gods gave him every grace and every gift but one, good health.

He was still only in his thirties, with the stage and film worlds at his feet, and producers begging for his services at fees of £40,000 a film, when he was condemned by asthma to long periods of suffering and inaction.

Even when in apparently normal health he was reluctant to accept a role really worthy of his talent and personality: there was also the risk of his breaking down during the run of the play or the shooting of the film.

Radio scripts had to be reduced to a series of short speeches to give him a chance to get his breath. His part in his last film was completed at the cost of desperate effort that possibly shortened his life.

(June 10)

IMRE NAGY

Imre Nagy, Hungarian Prime Minister during the rebellion against the Russians, who has been executed, was a Communist whose nationalism frequently gave rise to misgivings in Moscow. He was 62.

Replacing Rakosi as Prime Minister, he pursued a "Malenkov course," giving consumer goods preference over the development of heavy industry, encouraging private traders, and permitting peasants to contract out of collective farms.

Reported seriously ill with thrombosis in 1955, he was dismissed from the Communist party.

Whilst living in retirement he acquired considerable popular sympathy, and in August of 1956 Rakosi's successor as First Secretary, Geroe, hinted that his readmission to the party might be considered; it was in fact granted in October.

Nagy's final rise and fall were both swift and tragic. On Oct. 23, a wave of nationalist rebellion against the old leadership broke out. Yielding to popular pressure, Geroe on the following day restored Nagy to the Premiership and Politburo.

But meanwhile an appeal had been made, in Nagy's name, to Soviet troops to come to the Government's aid against the rebels. Nagy subsequently vehemently denied being responsible for this appeal (which may indeed have been the defeated Geroe's parting shot).

(June 17)

MISS YVONNE ARNAUD

CHILDISH 'DARE' LED TO STAGE CAREER

Miss Yvonne Arnaud, who has died aged 62, delighted theatregoers for nearly 50 years with her squeaky voice, ineradicable French accent and air of irrepressible naughtiness. Born in Bordeaux, she studied originally for the concert platform, and in 1905 won the first prize for pianoforte at the Paris Conservatoire.

She toured many countries as a child pianist. Throughout her life she remained a talented musician, appearing with notable orchestras on many occasions.

She made her debut as Princess Mathilde in "The Quaker Girl" at the Adelphi in 1911, because of a childish "dare" with her cousin. She was then 15, and had gone with him to see "The Count of Luxembourg."

Watching the artists, she declared she could act as well as they. Challenged by her cousin, she called on George Edwardes the next morning. She wrote him a note in French because her English was inadequate, and, to her surprise, secured a part.

EARLY ILLNESS

Although her debut was cut short by illness, it was the forerunner of a string of successes which endeared her to Londoners. Among them were "Tons of Money" in 1922, "A Cuckoo in the Nest," 1925; "And So To Bed," 1926; "Canaries Sometimes Sing," 1929; and "The Improper Duchess," 1931.

Her more recent plays included "Love for Love," 1943, "Travellers' Joy," 1948, and "Dear Charles," 1952. Her last play "The Big Tickle" at the Duke of York's in May, was not a success, despite her own personal triumph.

She married Mr. Hugh McLellan in 1920.

(September 22)

SIR WILLIAM BURRELL

Sir William Burrell, who has died aged 96, was a Scottish shipowner who gave his native city of Glasgow a £1,500,000 art collection. He also gave £450,000 to provide a building for it.

The gift was made in 1944. He died without seeing his dream of a gallery for the collection realised.

As the man who had done most for Glasgow in the previous three years he was awarded in 1947 the St. Mungo prize of £1,000. The Burrell collection includes paintings, tapestries, furniture, porcelain, silver and glass.

Sir William insisted that the gallery to house the collection should be situated 16 miles outside Glasgow. He feared the effect of the city's atmosphere on the tapestries.

SEARCH FOR SITE

Since 1944 several sites suitable for the new art gallery have been explored by Glasgow Corporation but none has yet been found. Part of the collection is on show at the Kelvingrove Art Galleries.

An earlier gift he made to Glasgow was a collection of oil paintings, watercolours and drawings in 1925. In 1944 he was given the Freedom of Glasgow.

Sir William, the son of a ship-owner, was knighted in 1927. He was a former member of Glasgow Corporation and a Trustee of the National Gallery.

His home, Hutton Castle, Berwickshire, was richly furnished with tapestries, panels and other art objects. He was a J.P. of Berwickshire. He married in 1901 Constance Mary Lockhart, daughter of James L. Mitchell. His wife survives him with one daughter.

Discerning Collector

TERENCE MULLALY writes: Sir William Burrell was among the most discerning collectors of his generation. His tastes were catholic.

The particular importance of the bequest was that it was made to a gallery outside London. At a time when pictures and works of art have more and more tended to be centralised in London, Sir William set a precedent that in recent years has been particularly followed in a few, but not many instances, and which many would like to see followed.

(March 31)

LOFTHOUSE GOAL RENEWS OLD CONTROVERSY

Charging The goalkeeper Should Be Restricted: Out-of-Date Britain

By Frank Coles

Bolton Wanderers.........2 Manchester United.........0

The 1958 Cup Final may have been one of the poorest seen at Wembley, but it should have far-reaching consequences. Here we are again with a goalkeeping controversy on our hands.

Was Lofthouse's charge on Gregg, which accompanied Bolton's second goal, legitimate? Even among neutral observers some say "Yes" and some say "No."

Did Lofthouse head the ball over the goal line before his forward rush bundled Gregg into the net?

LOFTHOUSE GOAL RENEWS

What was the point of impact - shoulder, as required by law, or, as I think, chest and body?

Was the goalkeeper holding the ball when Lofthouse charged him or, as it appeared to me, was he merely reaching for it and perhaps touching it with the tips of his fingers?

The answer to all these questions and to the everlasting clamour and contention surrounding such goals is that our law is out of date. British football is now practically alone in the world in allowing charges on the goalkeeper. They are all out of step but us!

MUCH ARGUMENT

In Consecutive Years

So we have a charge on the goalkeeper creating argument in consecutive Cup Finals with, strangely enough, Manchester United the victims in each case.

Fortunately this year's affair did not decide the game. It had less effect on the result than the memorable incident of last year which is now generally accepted in the football world as having cost Manchester United the Cup-League double.

This time Bolton won with a goal to spare and no one questioned their right to victory.

What a red-letter day this was for 32-year-old Bolton-born Nathaniel Lofthouse, scorer of the two goals by which his beloved Wanderers beat United and so took the Cup back to Bolton for the fourth time after a break of 29 years.

No player, and I include Stanley Matthews, has ever been granted by the gods a more appropriate or better-deserved reward for years of devoted service as a one-club man - he joined the Wanderers from school in 1943 and made his League debut when 15 - than this laughing cavalier.

Bold and fearless and, considering his build, one of the quickest centre-forwards England has ever honoured, he has scored more than 350 goals in League football and Wembley has formed the background of some of his greatest successes in the international field.

But it was Vienna and not Wembley which was the scene of his most famous goal six years ago. The score was 2-2 and Austria, all out for the kill, were besieging the England citadel in the dying minutes of a thrilling struggle.

Suddenly the ball came out of a ruck of players massed in the penalty area to Lofthouse, a lone white-shirted figure on the halfway line.

Off in a flash, he outraced the Austrian right-back, collided with the goalkeeper as he ran out to challenge and landed his shot in the net for a fantastic winner.

The same courage, the same opportunism, served Lofthouse again in the third minute of the latest Wembley Final. Left unmarked by a Manchester United defence all at sixes and sevens, he side-footed the ball past the sprawling Gregg and netted the all-important first goal.

CONFIDENCE SHAKEN

All Sixes and Sevens

Saturday's 100,000 crowd very soon realised that this vital goal had mortally shaken the confidence and the craft out of United.

All sixes and sevens! That aptly describes the disappointing attempts of the Manchester men to collect their thoughts and overcome Cup Final nerves in the next 20 minutes or so. Alarming and unexpected flaws were exposed in United's makeup from goalkeeper to outside-left.

Then nearing the half-hour, I thought I sensed the start of a genuine fight-back. The inside-forward machine of Taylor, Charlton and Viollet suddenly slipped into gear and - there was Dennis Viollet face to face with the glittering chance of an open goal.

Unluckily for United and disastrously for Viollet he shot over the crossbar and the glaring miss haunted him for the rest of the afternoon.

Before half-time, however, United forced Bolton to concede two more scoring openings and Hopkinson showed exactly why he will be England's goalkeeper in the World Cup matches in Sweden by making two glorious chearances. His full-length save from a Charlton rocket was a masterpiece.

So to the interval, the magnificent marching of the massed bands of the Royal Marines, and the growing certainty in the minds of all those present that this 1958 Final was going to be written off as one of the dullest and drabbest of all time.

But Wembley drama was as usual just round the corner. Only eight minutes of the second half had gone when the industrious Charlton again shot brilliantly.

With the goalkeeper beaten the ball crashed against the far post and ricocheted like lightning across the face of the goal into Hopkinson's grateful arms. It was nevertheless a very slick save.

And there is the kernel of the whole contest. Faulty goalkeeping by Gregg, the hero of Wembley when Northern Ireland beat England there in November, really gave Bolton their precious lead, whereas brilliant work by Hopkinson at the other end alone, prevented a Manchester equaliser and recovery.

It was one of the poorest Finals because Bolton's early goal undermined the confidence of these inexperienced Manchester players and the second goal after 55 minutes killed the match stone dead.

MUNICH AFTERMATH

No Settled Attack

But after all haven't we expected too much of United? Eight stars and three officials perished at Munich, others were injured. Since then the hurriedly remodelled United team has played two or three matches a week in order to complete their interrupted programme.

In attack they have had no settled line - change and change and change. Wear and tear has shattered the buoyancy of the men who filled the gaps, and weakness on the wings ramained an unsolved problem.

On Saturday it was a team in which Viollet and Taylor struggled to wriggle through the middle reaches and only succeeded in running themselves into tangles. Left along therefore to lead, inspire and really mount the attacks was 20-year old Charlton, the man for whom every onlooker must have had sympathy. It was Charlton who forced Hopkinson to that great first-half save and Charlton again who hit the post so unluckily eight minutes after the interval.

Bolton W: Hopkinson, Hartle, Banks, Hannin, Higgins, Edwards, (B), Birch, Stevens, Lofthouse, Parry, Holden.

Manchester U: Gregg, Foulkes, Greaves, Goodwin, Cope, Crowther, Dawson, Taylor, Charlton, Viollet, Webster.

Referee: J.V. Sherlock (Sheffield)

(May 5)

Show Jumping

MISS SMYTHE FAILS IN HAMBURG

HAMBURG, Sunday.

Miss Pat Smythe was unplaced on her two horses, Mr. Pollard and Flanagan, in the German show jumping Derby here to-day.

The event was won for the fourth time by Fritz Thiedemann, of Germany, on Finale.

(July 14)

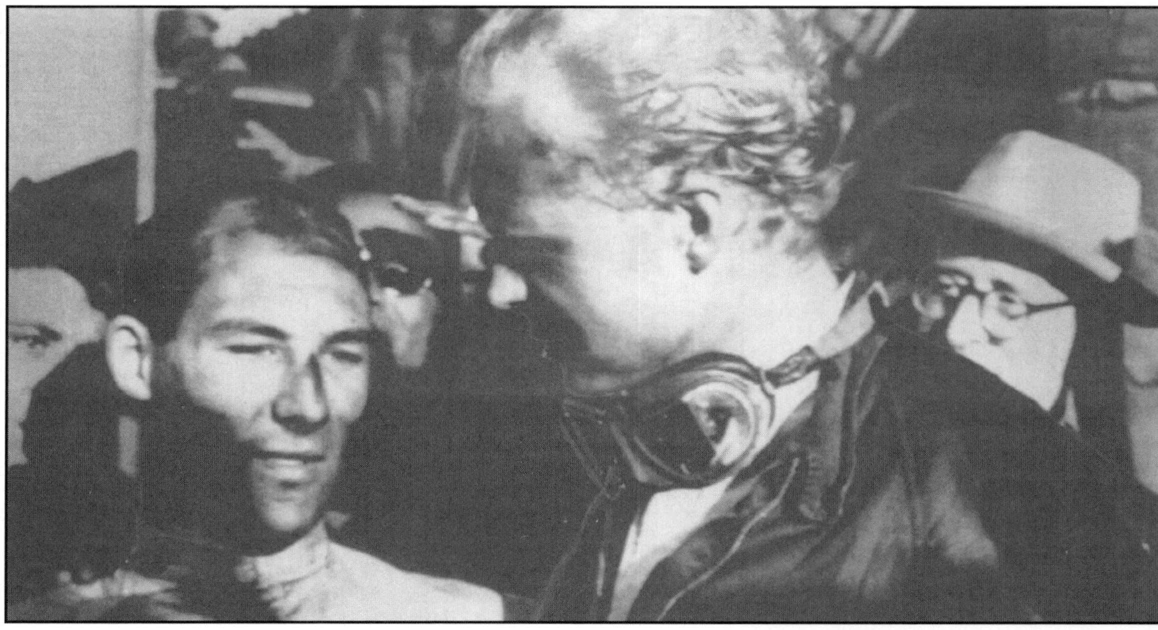

WORLD MOTOR RACING CHAMPION. Mike Hawthorn (Right), being congratilated by Stirling Moss at Casablanca yesterday on becoming the first British racing driver to win the World Championship. Stirling Moss had just won the Grand Prix of Morocco, but Hawthorn finished in second place, which gave him the necessary points to secure the title.

MOSS WINS BUT HAWTHORN CHAMPION BY ONE POINT

VANWALL GET MAKER'S PRIZE

From W.A. McKENZIE,
Daily Telegraph Motoring Correspondent

CASABLANCA, Sunday.

Stirling Moss, of Tring, Herts, to-day won the Morocco Grand Prix in a British Vanwall at a record speed of 116.2 m.p.h. His close rival for many years, Mike Hawthorn, of Farnham, finished second in a Ferrari, but won the 1958 World championship by one point.

He is the first British driver to get the title since it was instituted in 1950. Fangio, previous champion, retired this year.

The manufacturers' world championship goes to Mr. Tony Vandervell, maker of the Vanwall cars, which have won six Grands Prix this year.

Stuart Lewis-Evans, of Welling, Kent, in a Vanwall, crashed and his car went up in flames. Lewis-Evans, who is 28 was taken to hospital by helicopter with serious burns.

MAKING SURE

Temptation Avoided

Hawthorn could have lost the championship to Moss had he failed to finish within the first three places. He appeared to be making sure of the title, ignoring the temptation to fight out the race with the Vanwall.

But he had to be careful not to fall too far behind and lose second or third place. He came 84 seconds behind Moss.

It was obvious from the start that the two were out to win the championship. But their tactics were very different.

Moss was eight points down on Hawthorn before to-day's race, the last this season counting for the championship.

ONE MORE POINT

Lap Record Needed

To win the championship Moss would have had to finish first, scoring eight points, record the fastest lap, worth one point and Hawthorn would have had to be fourth or worse.

Moss went flat out from the fall of the flag, taking the lead on the second lap. He had the race to lose if the car "blew up."

But he had a chance of the world championship if he stayed in front. He not only led from the seond lap to the finish, but topped the lap speed record, too.

(October 20)

THOMSON IS ARTIST IN ALL CONDITIONS

By Leonard Crawley

PETER THOMSON, of Australia, won the Open Golf Championship at Royal Lytham St. Annes on Saturday for the fourth time in five years. In the play-off against D.C. Thomas, the 23-year-old Sudbury professional, he won by four strokes.

Thomson's record in the Open over the last eight years if judged by continuity alone, is incomparably greater than any other players - Henry Cotton, who retains much of his old skill, included.

In terms of hard figures, from 1951 Thomson's record reads fifth equal, second, second equal, first, first, first, second, and now first again.

There will no doubt be those who subscribe to the view that much has gone out of the game in recent years and that golf is now just a question of mechanisation.

I would not argue with them, but if that is really so there can be no sort of reason why with a little enterprise we should not mechanise other British professionals to help Thomas - the only young golfer since the war to make his presence felt in championship play.

But Thomson has proved himself a real artist under all conditions in the British Isles, and whatever his plans for the future his record will stand in this period like that of the Coldstream Guards' "Nulli secundus."

By his tremendous skill and charming deportment he has endeared himself to the British public, calling to mind the great names of Vardon, Braid and John Henry Taylor, who were the first to teach us that a game like golf, with its unlimited opportunities for taking advantage of its intricate rules, should always be played fairly and squarely by professional players.

Thomson played eight rounds in all last week over one of the greatest seaside courses in 24 under fours. Thomas held on to the bitter end, their scores being:

Thomson 63 + 77-66 + 72 + 67 +
73-68 + 71

Thomas 70 = 70-70 + 68 + 69 +
71-69 + 74

BRIGHT FUTURE

When He Masters Putting

For a young man of 23 such figures proclaim Thomas as the best young British professional of our time. He is superbly built and immensely strong.

He is essentially a great driver, and so soon as he finds the recipe for really effective putting he will take the majority of first prizes on the professional tournament circuit in this country.

To have hung on to Thomson for 135 holes was a really tremendous performance and we look forward to his winning the Open several times in years to come.

(July 9)

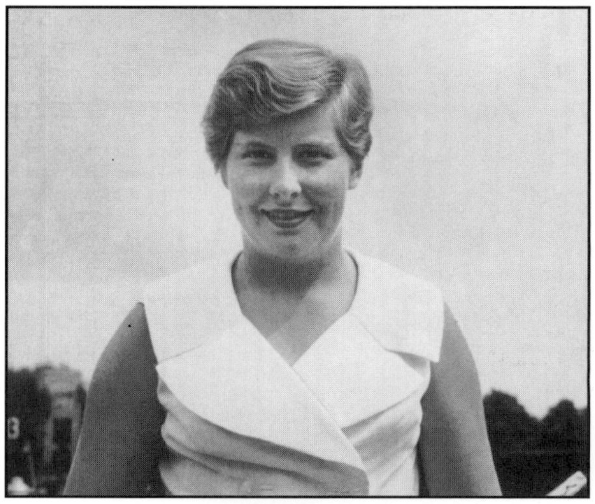

CHRISTINE TRUMAN

MISS TRUMAN'S COURAGE TURNS THE TIDE

Wightman Cup Returns to Britain After 28 Years, 21 Defeats

By Lance Tingay

After 28 years and 21 consecutive defeats, the Wightman Cup has returned to Great Britain. The final tally at Wimbledon after Saturday's play was: Britain 4, United States 3.

Twenty minutes past six is the time that will be remembered, for at that moment the 19-year-old Midlander, Miss Ann Haydon, hit a cross-court volley against Miss Mimi Arnold to ensure her team's victory.

When later, after the Duchess of Kent had given the Cup to the British captain, Mrs. Mary Halford, there was a loud cheer as Miss Christine Truman was presented to the Duchess, and no wonder!

There have been few team contests when victory was furthered more by such a fine and individual effort as that of this shy, 17-year-old Woodford girl. Her exciting, tremendous win over the Champion of Wimbledon, the commanding Miss Althea Gibson, a match I make no apology for having written off as belonging to America, turned what seemed a lost contest into one that could be won.

One can hardly not be jubilant. Yet I would pay tribute to the sporting way in which the Americans took defeat, to which they are unaccustomed.

British jubilation at success must be tempered to some degree because it was achieved on American weakness. The United States team was not of the calibre of former years, and I wonder how it came about that Miss Hopps was not originally selected, and how, having been brought in at the last moment, not then given a singles position.

Yet the fact remains that the key to victory was turned on America's strongest point, Miss Gibson. Miss Truman, winner of two singles and one double, and beaten by no one, did it.

DECIDING MATCH

Nervous Duel

It was a splendid moment for the British game, but serious business still lay ahead. Miss Haydon had to achieve her decisive win.

Most took it for granted she would, but the resistance of Miss Arnold was mettlesome, and there were some anxious British moments before the win was taken.

Complete Details

(British names first)

SINGLES

Miss S.J. Bloomer lost to Miss A Gibson
3-6, 4-6

Miss C.C. Truman bt Mrs D. Knode
6-4, 6-4

Miss Bloomer lost to Mrs. Knode
4-6, 2-6

Miss Truman bt Miss Gibson
2-6, 6-3, 6-4

Miss A.S. Haydon bt Miss M. Arnold
6-3, 5-7, 6-3

DOUBLES

Miss Bloomer & Miss Truman bt Mrs Knode & Miss K Fageros
6-2, 6-3

Miss J.A. Shilcock & Miss P.E. Ward lost to Miss Gibson & Miss J. Hopps
4-6, 6-3, 3-6.

(June 16)

MATCH AND SERIES GO TO ENGLAND

Margin Overwhelming, but N. Zealand Hold Out Until Mid-afternoon

From E.W. Swanton

HEADINGLEY, Tuesday.

ENGLAND won the third Test, and with it the series, here this afternoon, as they were virtually certain to do. But New Zealand batted with a purpose that was good to see, and despite losing Sutcliffe to the second ball of the day, kept England in the field until four o'clock.

With the warmth and sunshine there came a fresh resolution and confidence into New Zealand's cricket. They are aware of their limitations acutely enough, of course, but it may be hoped that the days of demoralisation are over, and that their luck may turn with the weather.

England's margin was an innings and 71 runs, and they lost only two wickets in the innings. One has to go back a very long way to find a series won by such margins as this.

Lock to-day was the more effective of the two spinners, and his analysis is as good as anything he has returned in Test cricket.

There was little indication from the early play that New Zealand's resistance would endure very long - except that Reid was clearly utterly determined to lead his team's resistance if he could.

Sutcliffe was lbw playing back to an off-break from the second ball of the day, a decision which looked clear enough to all who were looking in at their television sets. So Playle began his vigil, watched and encouraged by his captain at the other end.

Both Lock and Laker got a good deal of turn, and while the ball often hung, Lock occasionally straightened quite quickly. Playle hung on at first by his eyebrows, while Reid's defensive skill was stretched to the limit.

The wicket was a curious one, conditioned of course by the abnormal weather. Though by now quite dry, it was not hard, the artificial drying, as I mentioned before the game started, having disturbed the top soil. The spin bit, but as often as not the ball dug in and came slowly off. The speed bowlers found it completely lifeless.

By five minutes past 12, England had Reid's wicket, caught at

PITCH LACKS PACE

Now there remained MacGibbon, the 19-year-olds Playle and Sparling, and the New Zealand tail. Small wonder that cricketers and journalists began to think about convenient ways and times to get to to-morrow's appointments.

MacGibbon had other ideas though while Playle, having existed so far by the simple expedient of playing forward, with bat and pad together, and either stunning the ball or letting the spin take it on to the front leg, saw no reason to change his tactics.

They might not have worked so well if there had been more bounce in the wicket, or if it had had more pace. As it was, however close the short-legs crept forward, however close Bailey or Milton, or Trueman stood at old-fashioned point, the ball never carried to them.

MacGibbon used his reach to play forward, which he did almost exclusively. But when the ball was right up to him he swung the bat and hit it hard. One or two of his off-drives were good strokes in any company, and when Lock pitched the ball up on his legs he clumped it hard square-legwards, several times for four.

Then, after lunch, Playle and Sparling stayed together for 80 minutes. The cricket now was inevitably very slow, but it was defensive with a purpose, and the Leeds crowd are not the last people to appreciate the virtues of that.

Sparling, as in the first innings, made a good impression, while Playle once or twice trusted himself to go through with an off-drive, and sent the ball sweetly past the covers.

May took the new ball, and when that had failed, called for drinks.

Bailey was belatedly tried. But the partnership was broken at last by Laker, and in a way which, with due respect to that paramount technician, might, it seemed, have been exploited earlier.

Over after over one saw Laker bowling, now round, now over the wicket, and, whichever way it was, turning all six.

Sometimes he had a gully as well as his short-leg squad,but not a slip. Now at last he posted a slip, and appeared to be inducing Playle to play inside a straight one, assuming the turn. Playle did so, and was bowled, and soon afterwards the same sort of ball, going on with the arm, had Cave caught at slip.

With Petrie playing on, all was now virtually over, and Sparling, finally chancing his arm, gave a running catch to mid-off.

(July 9)

Test Scoreboard

NEW ZEALAND - First Innings

L.S.M. Miller, c Smith, b Laker 26
J.W. D'Arcy, c Smith, b Trueman.....11
N.S. Harford, c Cowdrey, b Laker..... 0
B. Sutcliffe, b Laker 6
J.R. Reid, b Lock 3
W.R. Playle, c Milton, b Lock............0
A.R. MacGibbon, b Laker..................3
J.T. Sparling, not ou9
E.C. Petrie, c Cowdrey, b Lock..........5
H.B. Cave, c Milton, b Laker.............2
J.A. Hays, c Evans, b Lock.................1
Extras (lb 1) 1
Total...67
Fall of wickets: 1-37, 2-37, 3-37, 4-40, 5-46, 6-46, 7-49, 8-59, 9-66

BOWLING

	O	M	R	W
Trueman	11	5	18	1
Loader	5	2	10	0
Bailey	3	0	7	0
Laker	22	11	17	5
Lock	18.1	13	14	4

Second Innings

J.W. D'Arcy, b Lock..........................6
L.S.M. Miller, lbw, b Lock 18
N.S. Harford, lbw, b Lock 0
B Sutcliffe, lbw, b Lock......................0
J.R. Reid, c Trueman, b Laker..........13
AW.R. Playle, b Laker 18
A.R. MacGibbon, lbw, b Lock..........39
J.T. Sparling c May, b Lock..............18
E.C. Petrie, b Lock 3
H.B. Cave, c Cowdrey, b Laker 2
J. Hayes, not out................................0
Extras (b 6, lb 6) 12
Total 129
Fall of wickets: 1-23, 2-23, 3-24, 4-32, 5-42, 6-88, 7-121, 8-124, 9-129.

BOWLING

	O	M	R	W
Trueman	14	6	22	0
Loader	13	7	14	0
Lock	35.2	20	51	7
Laker	36	23	27	3
Bailey	3	2	3	0

ENGLAND - First Innings

M.J.K. Smith, c Reid, b MacGibbon...3
C.A. Milton, not out........................104
T.W. Graveney, c & b Sparling 31
P.B.H. May, not out.........................113
Extras (b 5, lb 8, w 1, nb 2)................16
Total (2 wkts. dec.)...................267
Did not bat: T.E. Bailey, M.C. Cowdrey, J.C. Laker, P.J. Loader, T.G. Evans, G.A.R. Lock, F.S. Trueman.
Fall of wickets: 1-7, 2-73.

BOWLING

	O	M	R	W
Hayes	13	4	30	0
MacGibbon	27	8	47	1
Reid	27	7	54	0
Sparling	23	2	78	1
Cave	13	4	42	0

Umpires: F.S. Lee and J.S. Buller.

(Solution No. 10,257)

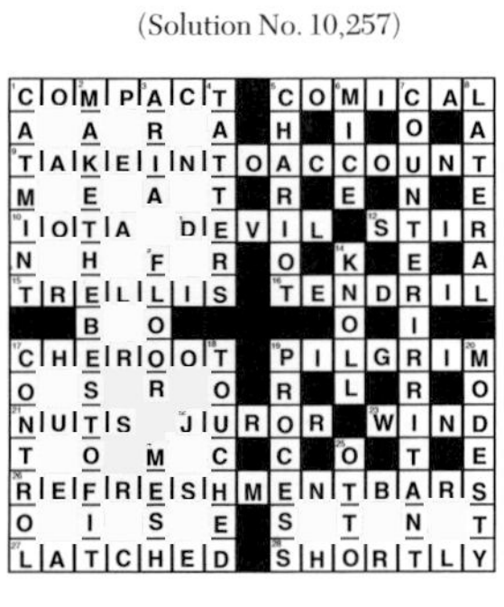

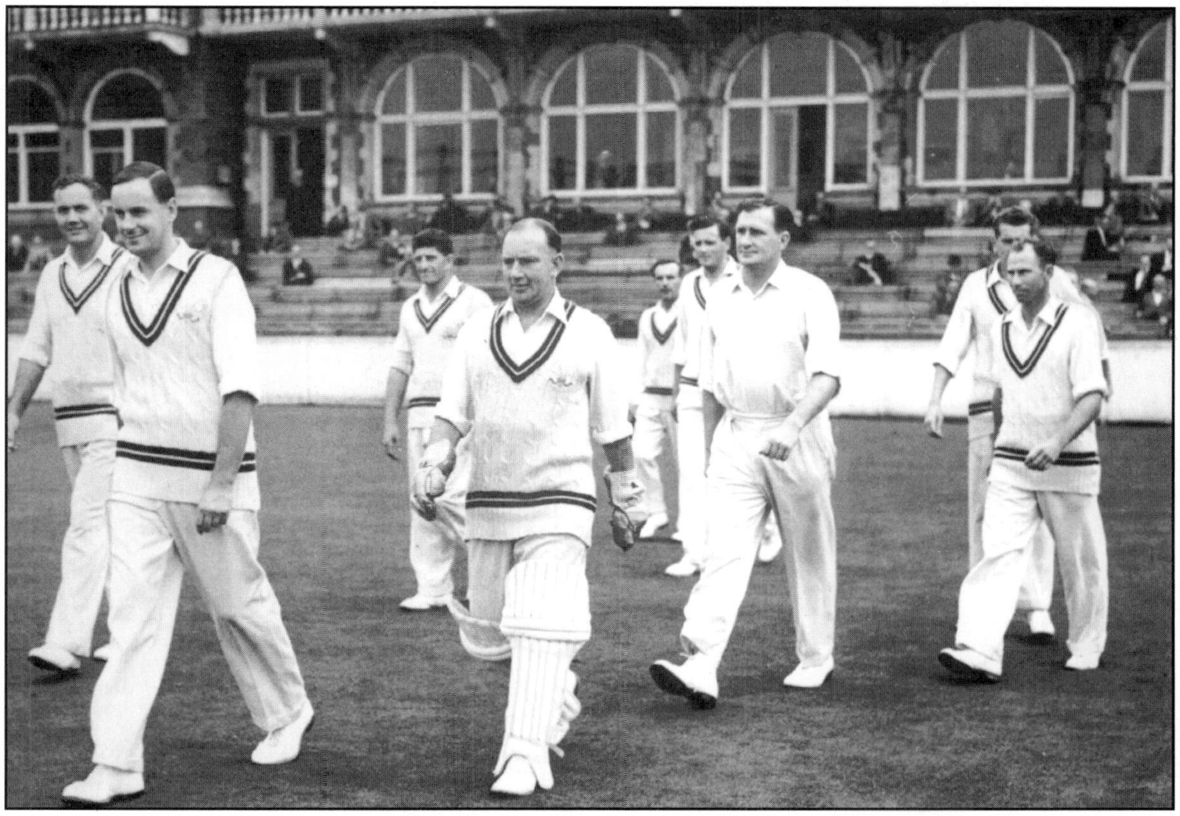

CHAMPIONS AGAIN. Surrey were already county cricket champions of 1958 when this photograph of the team going out to field against Somerset was taken at the Oval yesterday. From left to right: Eric Bedser, May (capt.), Barrington, McIntyre, Constable, Gibson, Laker, Loader, Fletcher and Lock. The "missing" man, Stewart, can just be seen behind Loader.

SURREY CHAMPIONS SEVEN YEARS IN SUCCESSION

Longest Run in History of Cricket: Handicaps Overcome

By E.W. Swanton

The summer of 1958 will be recalled as among the most liquid and gloomy within memory; but it will be notable at least for one thing - the victory yet again of Surrey, under P.B.H. May, in the County Championship.

For this win by Surrey is their seventh in a row, and therein they have written a new page of history. Since the Championship was begun in the early 1870s no county has had such a run.

Between 1930 and 1946 Yorkshire won eight years out of 10. In the last century Surrey in nine years had seven outright wins, and once shared the title. Those distant feats are the nearest approach to what Surrey have achieved in the 1950s.

It is not easy to find anything new to write in praise of Surrey. The foundation of their strength lies in the bowling, and once more they have won despite the frequent absences of Laker, Lock and Loader, in addition to the captain, during Test matches.

Here, too, they were additionally handicapped by the serious illness of Alec Bedser, which kept him off the field altogether until July, and forced Surrey to nurse him to a considerable extent after that.

Bedser has had his days of success, and he has been of great value as leader when May was otherwise engaged. But the number of times Surrey have been at completely full strength has been small.

Perhaps the main difference between the present Surrey and that of the W.S. Surridge days has lain in the greater attraction of the batting. In the Championship sense Surrey are not a formidable batting side: nor have they been since the cycle started in '52.

But May, of course, is a host in himself, and he nowadays sees a fast batting rate as a tactical end, apart from the concrete value of the bonus points. These they have picked up, time after time, as a matter of course.

That Surrey are far and away the strongest side goes without question. Yet at the start of August Hampshire were well in the lead. Since the Bank Holiday matches they have failed on the wet wickets, whereas Surrey have been in their element.

McIntyre, I think, should be mentioned specially in this connection. He has come in in several recent games when runs were needed against the clock, and hait extremely well. His wicketkeeping has been as reliable as ever, and once again Stewart, Barrington and Lock have set a high standard of catching close to the wicket.

(August 30)

REMARKABLE INNINGS BY 21-YEAR-OLD SOBERS

By Michael Melford

GARFIELD SOBER'S 365 not out for the West Indies against Pakistan at Kingston, Jamaica, seems to have been a remarkable innings in a remarkable context.

Not only was this vast score his first innings of over 100 in a Test match, but it precipitated a unique scene when he made the single to pass Sir Leonard Hutton's Test record of 364.

The crowd of 20,000 in Sabina Park swarmed on to the field and the West Indies having declared at the useful total of 790-3, carried the hero to the pavilion.

SECOND IN SERIES

The tall, left-handed Sobers batted from soon after tea on Thursday until Saturday evening 10 hours 8 min, or three hours less than Hutton. At 21 he is seven months younger than Hutton was in 1938.

The innings seems to have been attended inevitably by a perfect wicket, and also by a Pakistan attack seriously weakened by injury.

The extent of the Pakistanis' misfortunes can be estimated from the bowling analysis. Of the regular bowlers, only the medium-paced Fazal, and the fast-medium Khan escaped injury, and they bowled 139 overs between them.

Kardar's 37 overs were bowled with a fractured finger against doctor's orders. The injuries to Mahmood Hussain and Ghani have put them out for the rest of the tour. Negotiations are going on for replacements.

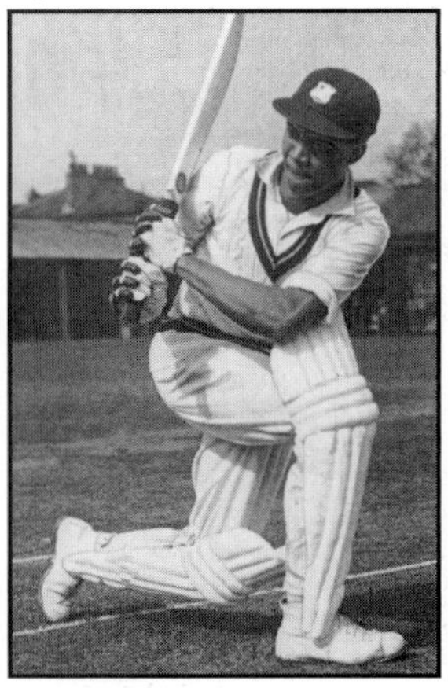

Though this is Sobers's first Test century, his achievement will be no surprise to the many in England who saw him making large scores last summer, particularly in May, who enjoyed his elegant driving, admired his resolution when pinned down by the best bowling, and reckoned him no doubt a great batsman in the making.

(March 3)

ELLIOTT RUNS FASTEST MILE IN 3 MIN. 54.5 SEC.

By Jack Crump

Herbert Elliott, the 20-year-old Australian, set up a world mile record of 3min. 54.5sec., and Elliott finished 15 yd. ahead of his fellow-Australian Mervyn Lincoln.

Elliott knocked 2.7sec. off the previous world's best recorded time set up by D. G. Ibbotson at the White City which is still awaiting official recognition.

The first four in the race were:

H. Elliott, Australia 3min 54.5sec
M. Lincoln, Australia ..3min 55.9sec
R. Delany, Ireland.......3min 57.5sec
M.G. Halberg,
New Zealand.......3min 57.5sec.

FAST PACE

Crowd's Inspiration

Albert Thomas, a third Australian, ensured a fast pace from the start by covering the first quarter mile in 58 seconds. He reached the half-mile post in 1min. 58sec. He finished in 3min. 58.6sec.

Lincoln, who had run on Thomas's heels for much of the second lap, took the lead in the third lap with Elliott just behind him. The enthusiasm of the Irish crowd certainly seemed to inspire the runners.

Just after the three-quarter mile mark, reached in 2min. 59sec. with Lincoln in the lead, Elliott made his effort and went smoothly to the front. From then on it became a one-man race.

He finished 15 yards ahead of Lincoln. The Irish runner Delany just managed to beat Murray Halberg of New Zealand for third place.

It had been considered that the limit for the one mile was likely to be 3min. 55sec. But Elliott's time clearly establishes him as the greatest miler of all time.

Lincoln, who finished second and who has been a keen rival of Elliott for a long time, must consider himself unfortunate in finishing only second in the wonderful time of 3min 55.9 sec, while Delany and Halberg have both set up the fastest times of their career.

Elliott has made quite a habit of running sub-four-minute miles in the last two years. His previous best times were 3min 57.8sec and 3min 57.9sec.

The present officially ratified world record is the 3min 58sec achieved by John Landy of Australia. There is little doubt that Ibbotson's time of 3min 57.2sec will be ratified in Stockholm later this month.

(August 7)

World Cup Soccer

BRAZIL REAL CHAMPIONS

STOCKHOLM, Sunday

Sweden......2 Brazil......5

Brazil won the World Cup for the first time here to-day when they beat Sweden in the final with a brilliant exhibition of fast, artistic football.

To-day's final opened encouragingly for Sweden when Leidholm scored in the fourth minute. Brazil soon struck back with a goal by Vava in the eighth minute and they took the lead in the 32nd minute with a replica of the first goal.

Though a goal down at the interval, the Swedes were not out of the game and their attack still looked dangerous. But the Brazilians kept a firm grip on the match-winning wingers, Skoglund and Hamrin, and went further ahead with a great goal by Pele, the inside-left.

He lobbed the ball over the Swedish centre-half before breasting it down and hitting it on the half-volley. This came after nine minutes of the second half, and 13 minutes later Zagallo cut in to score the fourth.

Sweden got their second goal through centre-forward Simonsson in the 79th minute, but just before the final whistle Pele headed in a fifth for Brazil.

(June 30)

BALLYMOSS ROMPS HOME IN LONGCHAMP MUD

Lands £37,925 Prize and Brings Winning Total to £98,650

From Hotspur

LONGCHAMP, Sunday.

BALLYMOSS, with conditions all against him, stormed home in the Longchamp mud to win the Prix de l'Arc de Triomphe clearly on merit to-day by two lengths from the French-trained Fric, with another French horse, Cherasco, a further two and a half lengths away third.

The colt thus becomes the biggest money-spinner ever trained in the British Isles. To-day's race was worth £37,925 to the winner, and in England, France and Ireland Ballymoss has now won £98,650 in prize money thus surpassing the records set up by Tulyar in 1951-52 by £22,233.

If Ballymoss, as is expected, goes to America to run in the Washington International at Laurel Park, Maryland, next month and is successful he will have won more in stake money than any European horse in the history of racing. At present Ribot, winner of the Prix de l'Arc de Triomphe in 1955 and 1956 and of the King George VI and Queen Elizabeth II Stakes in 1956 holds the record.

Mr. J McShain, American owner of Ballymoss, did not see his four-year-old win to-day as he is in the United States. The race was another triumph for his Irish trainer Vincent O'Brien who has had a staggering run of successes this season with Ballymoss and the Ascot Gold Cup winner Gladness.

It is the first time since the victory of the Aga Khan's Migoli in 1948 that a horse of British blood has won the Prix de l'Arc de Triomphe and it is the first time in the history of the race that an Irish-trained runner has been successful.

RAIN PELTS DOWN

Just Before the Race

It rained hard at Longchamp in the early hours yesterday but the course dries quickly and before the first race this afternoon it seemed that the going would be reasonable. It was coming down in buckets as the horses paraded for the big race, however, and there was talk that O'Brien was considering withdrawing Ballymoss at the last moment.

Fortunately, O'Brien wisely decided to let his four-year-old take his chance and as usual the colt was completely unconcerned, both in the parade ring and in the parade in front of the stands.

NEARLY POCKETED

Then Goes Through

Coming to the final bend Nogaro still led with Fric just behind him on the rails and Ballymoss close up. I thought that Breasley was likely to be pocketed, but he was able to switch Ballymoss round Nogaro and Fric on the final bend and take the lead.

I believe Bella Paola was interfered with at this stage, but I doubt if it made any difference to the result, for Ballymoss was going exceptionally well and with more than a furlong to go took a clear lead from Fric with Cherasco now making up ground from behind.

Strongly ridden, Ballymoss ran on well in the final furlong and won easily from Fric, with Cherasco third, the fill V.I.P. courth, Malefaim fifth and Scot, who was outpaced in the last half-mile just behind.

(October 4)

LEADING JOCKEYS

	1st	2nd	3rd	Unp	Tot
D. Smith	142	110	101	339	692
A. Breasley	129	107	77	254	567
E. Mercer	115	90	81	259	546
E. Hide	108	98	80	288	574
J. Mercer	80	72	55	228	435
L. Piggott	80	73	61	274	488
W.H. Carr	69	81	72	232	454
E. Larkin	68	52	54	207	381
A.J. Russell	53	39	32	165	289
E. Smith	50	47	44	273	414
S. Clayton	47	52	54	274	427
E. Butt	47	39	38	183	307
J. Sime	47	48	40	205	340

KERSTIN LANDS GOLD CUP FOR THE NORTH

For the second time a mare won the Cheltenham Gold Cup to-day when Kerstin, owned by Mr. G.H. Moore, a retired Northumbrian businessman, trained by C. Bewicke in Northumberland and ridden by S. Hayhurst, also a Northumbrian, got the better of a long duel with Polar Flight by half a length.

Both Mandarin and Linwell, first and second favourites, made mistakes and got rid of their riders at the 13th fence, and the finish concerned only the first two. Gay Donald, the old man of the party, was a bad third.

Kerstin, a thoroughly game and consistent staying mare, was bred in Ireland by Mr. Con Burke, a Tipperary farmer, and, curiously, she is closely related on her dam's side to last year's winner, Linwell.

Bewicke bought her as an unbroken four-year-old for Mr. Moore from Mr. C.J. Powell, of Tipperary. Mr. Moore has had other good winners in Newberry and Vindicated, who is a full-brother to Kerstin.

Miss Kilcash, the dam of Kerstin, is also the dam of Bridge of Honour, one of the best jumpers that Bewicke has trained.

The Gold Cup was Kerstin's 10th victory. Last year she won only once but was placed in five other races including her second to Linwell in the Gold Cup, so that if luck was on her side to-day she certainly deserved it.

She never made a mistake throughout, and though one or two of her opponents might have beaten her for finishing speed if all had remained standing, quite rightly it is jumping which counts, or rather should count, in steeplechasing, and Kerstin was a most worthy winner.

The only other mare to have won the Gold Cup was Ballinode, successful in 1925 when the race was run for the seond time.

TRIUMPH FOR TRAINER

Bewicke, besides being a most successful trainer, is a fine player of ball games. As a boy he played cricket for Eton and later squash rackets for Northumberland. He is a great-nephew of Percy Bewicke, an leading trainer of a past era, and set up at his home in Northumberland soon after the war.

(March 14)

104th Boat Race

CAMBRIDGE WERE NEVER IN DANGER OF DEFEAT

By A. T. M. Durand

Cambridge won the 104th Boat Race on Saturday the official verdict being 3 ½ lengths. Their time, 18min 15 sec, has only twice been bettered. They led from the first stroke, and from then to the finish were never in real danger of defeat.

Cambridge deserve all credit for their victory. Technically they were a good crew, and in spite of severe setbacks caused by illness their coach, Mr. Harold Rickett, brought them to the stakeboat at the very peak of their form.

(April 7)

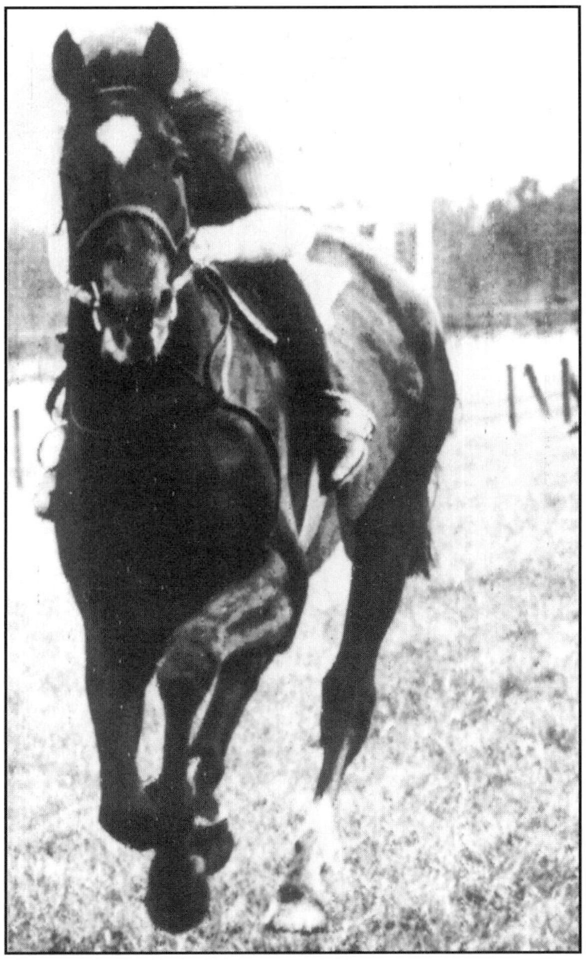

270 GNS. YEARLING LANDS £20,000 DERBY PRIZE

Hard Ridden Storms Home by Five Lengths: French Eclipsed

From Hotspur

EPSOM, Wednesday.

For the first time since the success of Orby in 1907 an Irish-trained horse won the Derby to-day, when Hard Ridden belied his name to win unextended in the hands of the irrepressible C. Smirke. Bought for only 270 guineas as a yearling by Sir Victor Sassoon, Hard Ridden is certainly the cheapest Derby winner bought at public auction this century. The value to the winner to-day was £20,036.

He won by five long lengths from the Irish-trained rank outsider Paddy's Point with Nagami third on merit after a rough passage and the French, for a change, out of the money.

Sir Victor Sassoon, a great supporter of racing for 40 years, first won the Derby in 1953 with Pinza, which he bought as a yearling from the late Fred Darling. He won it last year with Crepello, of his own breeding, and now joins the late Aga Khan as the only other owner to have won the race in successive years in this century.

Although Sir Victor never had any luck in a Derby before the war he won two Irish Derbys with Phideas and Museum, both trained over there by Jack rogers.

After buying Hard Ridden as a yearling in Dublin in September, 1956, he decided for old time's sake to send the colt to be trained at The Curragh by Rogers's 33-year-old grandson Mickie, son of another well-known trainer, Darby Rogers.

A GOOD START

Paddy's Point Last Away

There was no delay at all at the start, and the well-backed horses all got off, the last to leave the gate being Paddy's Point who lost about three lengths. The running was made by Midlander with Guersillus, Amerigo, Noelor II and Bald Eagle among those well placed.

Soon after reaching the top of the hill Midlander fell back beaten, and Hide, lying second on Guersillus, found himself in front much sooner than he had planned. The pace at this stage seemed slower than usual in a Derby, and Guersillus was galloping well within himself and going well.

As they came down the hill to Tattenham Corner Guersillus led from Amerigo and Bald Eagle, with Arctic Gittell and the blinkered Boccaccio just behind Guersillus, and Nagami, Noelor and Currito in the third rank.

Mahu, Alberta Blue and Paddy's Point all took the Corner wide, but Smirke was to be seen waiting for an opening just behind Noelor, with Wallaby and Miner's Lamp badly placed near the tail of the field.

Soon after rounding Tattenham Corner, Guersillus and Amerigo were the clear leaders with Amerigo, I thought, going very well and looking the possible winner.

Bald Eagle was soon beaten, and then with nearly two furlongs still to go, Smirke, who had switched Hard Ridden to the inside of Nagami, came bursting through on the rails.

He quickly had Guersillus and Amerigo beaten, and in the final furlong drew clear of these two tiring colts. As Amerigo fell back a row of horses closed with Guersillus, and Paddy's Point, finishing strongly on the outside, passed him a hundred yards from home and at the winning post was one and a half lengths in front of the third, Nagami.

Baroco II was fourth, Guersillus fifth, Miner's Lamp and Alberta Blue equal sixth and Noelor eighth. Less than a couple of lengths covered the third and the eighth.

SCRAMBLE AT CORNER

Wallaby Nearly Down

Although the riders of Nagami, Baroco, Miner's Lamp, Alberta Blue and Noelor may not have had much luck in running - and Longden, on Alberta Blue, certainly came very wide at Tattemham Corner - I feel sure it did not affect the result. Hard Ridden won without being hard ridden.

(June 5)

COOPER STEPS IN LINE FOR WORLD TITLE

Henry Cooper, the Bellingham heavyweight we all once thought was on the way out, is this morning within reach of a world title fight with Floyd Patterson.

At Wembley Pool last night Cooper fought his best and bravest fight to outpoint Zora Folley, of New Orleans, rated the No. 2 contender. It was close, desperately close. Indeed, if Mr. Tommy Little had held up Folley's hand at the end I would have had no big quarrel to pick with him.

At the end of 10 rounds I shall remember for a long time I made Cooper just one-quarter of a point in front.

Mr. Little must have thought the margin was wider, because he had no hesitation in holding Cooper's hand aloft as the crowd stamped cheered and roared their approval.

But how disappointed Swift must have been. In the third round the fight looked to be in Folley's pocket, for after two comparatively quiet rounds the tall, handsome American suddenly seemed to move into top gear. For three minutes he looked wonderful.

Long straight lefts smashed into Cooper's face, opening an old wound above his left eye and splitting his left eyelid. Then chopping rights crashed on to Cooper's jaw.

As Cooper was beaten to the boards for a count of eight I thought: "This is going to be another British disaster".

But somehow Cooper hung out for the rest of the round and tottered off to his corner for attention to that damaged eye.

Cooper's seconds worked swiftly and expertly between rounds and out came the young Londoner looking only slightly the worse for wear.

But two more solid, chopping rights made him sag. I thought he would go down again.

Then suddenly, bravely, and at that time we thought desperately, Cooper began to fight back.

A right thump to Folley's right temple and a left hook to the body followed immediately. We saw then that this American could be hurt.

Cooper saw it too. In he went, smashing a left and right that momentarily had Folley flustered.

He kept the American off balance with stabbing left jabs to the face that eventually brought blood pouring from Folley's nose.

But every so often Cooper would also bring that right over, and sometimes he followed it with a thumping solid left hook into Folley's ribs for good measure.

The American now looked like an ordinary fighter. Cooper in fact had begun to cut him down to size.

The stream of left jabs that pierced his defence clearly irritated Folley and once or twice he tried to bull his way and sweep Cooper out of the ring.

As a result, he was warned several times for the careless use of his head, a failing which earned the crowd's disapproval too when blood again began to flow down Cooper's left cheek.

Level Pegging

Cooper then seemed to remember his bad eye and faltered sufficiently for the American to snatch the round.

So as they came up for the last round I made them dead level. Both seemed to realise that there was little between them. They hammered viciously away at each other, Cooper countering the American's short rights to the head with stiff left jabs, an occasional hook and a hard right cross.

So intent was Cooper on his job that he was still trying to get through his opponent's guard after the bell had brought a memorable battle to an end. I thought Cooper had done just enough work in that last round to win it. But it was indeed very close.

(October 15)

No. 10,257 ACROSS

1 It is carried by women, but mutual agreement (7)
5 Funny that the 6 down dealt with by the farmer's wife should be in the fuel! (7)
9 Reckon it's what the auditor must do to every item (4, 4, 7)
10 A little matter of nine returned letters (4)
11 Even if beheaded he is still as bad as ever (5)
12 Mostly it's the wrong way to use a spoon (4)
15 The habit of climbing it is naturally growing ... (7)
16 ... this often being used to gain a hold (7)
17 A welcome gift to take to a brave fellow in hospital? (7)
19 One of those who told tales on the way? (7)
21 When threadbare they can serve no useful turn (4)
22 The twelfth man who can prevent the eleven from effecting the dismissal of anyone? (5)
23 Do a turn and gain quite a lot (4)
26 "Fresh batsmen err" (anag.) (and duck herein to console themselves!) (11, 4)
27 Not open to cheat with change in signs of money (7)
28 Without undue delay, in brief (7)

DOWN

1 A plant that is a pet money-maker (7)
2 Ideal advice on how to treat the inevitable (4, 3, 4, 2, 2)
3 Ventilate a return to the air (4)
4 Women at work maybe, but not with rags (7)
5 Scotch a riot in which the northerner doesn't take part (7)
6 They have been used in atomic experiments (4)
7 Does it describe reaction to asperityr between shop assistant and customer? (7, 8)
8 All rate as a side reference (7)
13 Vanquish, giving you a walk-over (5)
14 No great eminence, though mostly a reminder of Cromwell (5)
17 The man in it works to rule (7)
18 Scarcely handled, but nevertheless moved (7)
19 What a carry-on this entails! (7)
20 My set do arrange for retirement (7)
24 It can show its bigness in letting the little ones go (4)
25 Palindromic perfume (4)

(November 10)

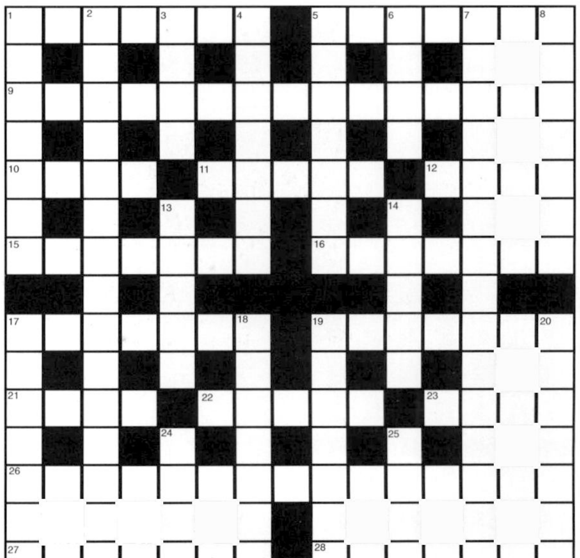

1959

So the decade ended on an up. Certainly not all the problems with which the Fifties began had been solved. The Cold War remained chilly, but Mr. Krushchev during the year came to the United States. His chief complaint during the visit was that he was not allowed to tour Disneyland. The old Cold War warrior, John Foster Dulles, dies. The state of emergency in Kenya ended and agreement over the future of Cyprus was reached. Before the end of the year Archbishop Makarios became president. The seemingly impossible-to-resolve clash in Algeria which brought General de Gaulle back to power looked as if it was coming to some sort of conclusion by the offer of self-determination to the local people.

A Russian rocket landed on the moon while another circled behind it and for the first time people on earth were able to see the dark side of the moon. Sad to say, it proved to be rather dull. An American rocket carried two monkeys on a brief trip into space and brought them back alive, though one was to die a few days later. The British invention, the hovercraft, made its way on its cushion of air for the first time in public over the waters of the Solent.

In Britain cuts in taxes and freedom from constraints in the borrowing of capital brought the promise of a boom in consumer spending presided over by a benevolent and optimistic Prime Minister in Harold Macmillan, the first British politician truly to master the art of appearing on television. In the autumn general election , he was returned with an increased majority. Meanwhile, the Labour Party looked as if it was about to tear itself apart at its annual conference over its nationalisation programme. While Sunday drivers sampled the pleasures of the new motorway, British rail announced its plan to close branch lines all over the country. But after 50 years London was to have its first new tube, the Victoria line.

As the bill, sponsored by Roy Jenkins, to amend the obscenity laws slowly made its way through Parliament, the literary world, as well as the political one, was divided over the merits of Vladimir Nabokov's *Lolita. The Daily Telegraph's* reviewer thought very little of it. Though it caused very little stir at the time, a young singer called Buddy Holly was killed in an air crash. Much more notice was taken of the death of the filmstar tenor Mario Lanza. The art world lost the sculptor Jacob Epstein and two painters of very different schools, Alfred Munnings, former President of the Royal Academy, and Stanley Spencer, while the best-known architect of the day, Frank Lloyd Wright, also died.

Her husband's involvement in the tangled politics of Panama landed Margot Fonteyn briefly in what *The Daily Telegraph* correspondent described as "common gaol" in Panama City while in London the flamboyant pianist Liberace picked up handsome libel damages from a British newspaper. The House of Christian Dior announced that skirts were to rise above the knee. Could it be that the Sixties were about to swing?

The Daily Telegraph 4 A.M.
and Morning Post
No. 32,339 LONDON, WEDNESDAY, APRIL 8, 1959
Printed in LONDON and MANCHESTER Price 2 ½d.

9d. OFF INCOME TAX: PURCHASE TAX DOWN

ALL-ROUND CUTS: 2d. A PINT OFF BEER

POST-WAR CREDITS SOONER: 2 ½ % INTEREST

INVESTMENT ALLOWANCES AGAIN: AID FOR LORRIES

PENSIONS REVIEW PLEDGE

MR. HEATHCOTE AMORY, Chancellor of the Exchequer, introducing his second Budget in the House of Commons yesterday, proposed tax reliefs totalling £295 million this year and £360 million in a full year. Chief changes were:

INCOME TAX: Standard rate reduced by 9d to 7s 9d in the pound; the lower rates on earned income each cut by 6d;to 1s 9d on the first £60 after allowances, to 4s 3d on the next £150, and to 6s 3d on the next £150.

Rebates on the first pay day after June 7 will be about £15,000,000. For the most part they will take the form of a cut in the P.A.Y.E. deduction, although for some there will be a repayment.

PURCHASE TAX: From to-day the 60 p.c. rate is cut to 50 p.c.; 30 p.c. to 25 p.c.; 15 p.c. to 12 ½ p.c. Commercial vehicle chassis (30 p.c.) and replacement television tubes (60 p.c.) to be freed.

BEER: Duty down by 2d a pint from opening time to-day.

POST-WAR CREDITS: Qualifying age for payment cut by two years to 63 for men and 58 for women. Credits of holders who have died are payable forthwith to beneficiaries. Interest of 2 ½ p.c. added to credits not released by next Oct. 1.

INVESTMENT ALLOWANCES: Restoration of investment allowances to industry and an extension to agriculture.

PAY RESTRAINT VITAL

The Chancellor said if progress were to continue in keeping living costs stable everything depended on the restraint shown this year in pay negotiations.

Speaking of pensioners, formerly employed in the public service and Service pensioners, he said: "We should take another look at their position and see what additional help can be given. I am inviting representatives of local authorities to consult at once and I hope we can put proposals for legislation before the House in a few weeks".

CHEAPER MOTOR CARS

Goods affected by the purchase tax changes include:

Cut from 60 to 50 p.c.: Motor cars, television sets, radios, gramophone records, cosmetics and perfumery. An average family car will be about £50 cheaper.

Cut from 30 p.c. to 25 p.c.: Refrigerators, vacuum cleaners, washing machines, furs (other than rabbit skin, lamb or sheepskin), jewellery and imitation jewellery, clocks, watches, motor cycles, cameras, sports goods, toys.

Cut from 15 p.c. to 12 ½ p.c.: Floor coverings, carpets, ironmongery and kitchenware.

No change in 5 p.c. rate: Clothes (except children's), furniture, rabbit skin, lamb and sheepskin.

POST-WAR CREDITS: In future credits still outstanding will be paid on the death of the holder. Compound interest of 2 ½ p.c. a year tax free will be added to credits becoming eligible on or after Oct. 1, 1959. Interest is payable when credits are released.

TWO SLOGANS FOR HISTORIC BUDGET

QUIET RECEPTION FOR CHANCELLOR

By Our Special Correspondent

WESTMINSTER, Tuesday.

"Ninepence off the income tax" will probably compete with "twopence off the beer" as the slogan which will give an historical stamp to the Budget which the Chancellor, Mr. Heathcote Amory, introduced in the House of Commons to-night.

Rarely has a Chancellor made so important and far-reaching a series of proposals to Parliament. Rarely, too, has his speech been so quietly received.

The Chamber of the House was filled to capacity. So were the galleries which M.P.s use when they cannot find a seat downstairs.

The Peers' and the Speaker's Galleries were equally full. When the Chancellor rose, 10 minutes before the expected time, there were only five empty seats in the generous provision made, upstairs and downstairs, by those who organise accommodation in the Palace of Westminster.

PAST AND FUTURE

Milk, Honey and Rum

Mr. Heathcote Amory was not in his best form. He seemed to be tired, and from time to time took a sip from a glass which was understood to contain a mixture of milk, honey and rum.

The early part of his task, as the House well knew, had to consist of a review of the past economic situation, an assessment of the present, and a prognostication of the future. That is something which all who listen to Budget debates have to bear with equanimity, and interpret according to their several capacities.

But the Chancellor began by sounding a note which discounted past achievements and looked forward to the challenge of present opportunities. He told the House that complacency would be an utterly misleading recipe for the future.

BEST CUT SINCE CROMWELL

2d OFF PINT TO-DAY

Daily Telegraph Reporter

The Brewers' Society said last night that the twopence reduction for a pint of beer would take effect from opening time this morning. A spokesman said: "I think since the time of Cromwell or Charles III, when beer tax was first imposed, there has never before been a reduction of 2d a pint."

The last reduction to be made was in 1949. Duty was reduced by 21s a bulk barrel of 36 gallons, giving a reduction of one penny a pint.

While London and most of the rest of the country had to wait for cheaper beer, 800 public houses controlled by Newcastle Breweries gave the benefit to their customers last night. Col. George Brown, director of Newcastle Breweries, said: "We are highly delighted to hear of any reduction in the 'purchase tax' on beer."

BIG SAVINGS BY STAMP DUTY CUT

SEA INSURANCE

Daily Telegraph Reporter

The abolition of the special stamp duty on sea insurance will be of particular benefit to shippers who handle their own insurances on consignments. Non-marine policies bear a duty of 6d, and sea insurances will be reduced to this fixed rate.

A spokesman for the Institute of London Underwriters said last night the relief would mean "an awful lot of saving."

SINGLE PERSONS

Income £	Old Tax £ s	New Tax £ s	Income £	Old Tax £ s	New Tax £ s
200	1 15	1 07	2,000	541 12	493 00
225	3 18	3 01	2,500	736 17	693 14
250	6 02	4 15	3,000	984 13	906 18
300	14 13	12 06	4,000	1,490 04	1,383 06
350	23 18	20 11	5,000	2,092 15	1,952 10
400	33 02	28 17	6,000	2,745 10	2,571 19
500	55 10	49 05	7,000	3,448 06	3,241 08
600	81 15	73 11	8,000	4,151 01	3,910 17
700	111 17	101 04	9,000	4,903 17	4,630 06
800	144 18	131 07	10,000	5,639 05	5,352 02
900	178 00	161 10	20,000	14,684 05	14,002 02
1,000	211 01	191 12	50,000	42,434 05	40,627 02
1,250	293 13	266 19	100,000	88,634 05	85,002 02
1,300	376 06	342 06			

MARRIED COUPLES — WITHOUT CHILDREN

Income £	Old Tax £ s	New Tax £ s	Income £	Old Tax £ s	New Tax £ s
350	3 12	2 16	3,000	929 13	855 13
400	9 07	7 12	4,000	1,430 04	1,327 01
500	27 17	24 02	5,000	2,027 15	1,891 05
600	48 00	42 06	6,000	2,675 10	2,505 14
700	74 05	66 12	7,000	3,373 06	3,170 03
800	102 08	92 12	8,000	4,076 01	3,839 12
900	135 10	122 15	9,000	4,823 17	4,554 01
1,000	168 11	152 17	10,000	5,579 05	5,275 17
1,250	251 03	228 04	20,000	14,591 15	13,913 07
1,500	333 16	303 11	50,000	42,341 15	40,538 07
2,000	499 02	454 05	100,000	88,951 15	84,913 07
2,500	704 07	644 19			

MARRIED COUPLES — WITH 1 CHILD

Income	One child not over 11		One child over 11, but not over 16		One child over 16	
	Old Tax £ s	New Tax £ s	Old Tax £ s	New Tax £ s	Old Tax £ s	New Tax £ s
500	5 10	4 05	2 13	2 01	-	-
600	22 11	19 08	16 12	14 02	10 14	8 15
700	41 01	35 18	35 02	30 12	29 03	25 06
800	66 15	59 13	58 06	51 17	49 17	44 01
900	93 00	84 00	84 11	76 03	76 02	68 07
1,000	126 01	114 02	115 08	104 09	104 16	94 15
1,250	208 13	189 09	198 01	179 15	187 08	170 02
1,500	291 06	264 16	280 14	255 02	270 01	245 01
2,000	456 12	415 10	445 19	405 16	435 07	396 03
2,500	651 17	596 04	638 15	584 00	625 12	571 16
3,000	874 13	804 08	860 18	791 12	847 03	778 15
4,000	1,370 04	1,270 16	1,355 04	1,256 14	1,340 04	1,242 13
5,000	1,962 15	1,830 00	1,946 10	1,814 14	1,930 05	1,799 08
6,000	2,605 10	2,439 09	2,588 00	2,422 18	2,570 10	2,406 07
7,000	3,298 06	3,098 18	3,279 11	3,081 02	3,260 06	3,063 05
8,000	4,001 01	3,768 07	3,982 06	3,750 11	3,963 11	3,732 14
9,000	4,743 17	4,477 16	4,723 17	4,458 15	4,703 17	4,439 13
10,000	5,499 05	5,199 12	5,479 05	5,180 11	5,459 05	5,161 00
20,000	14,499 05	13,824 12	14,476 02	13,802 08	14,453 00	13,780 05
50,000	42,249 05	40,449 12	42,226 02	40,427 08	42,203 00	40,405 05
100,000	88,499 05	84,824 12	88,476 02	84,802 08	88,453 00	84,780 05

OVER 1m. TO GET POST-WAR CREDITS EARLY

AVERAGE £50 EACH

Daily Telegraph Reporter

It is calculated that about 4,400,000 holders of post-war credits, or their beneficiaries, will be paid out this year on the new grounds of lower age qualification, death, or hardship. This represents an average payment of about £50.

Those credits not eligible for repayment by Oct. 1 will carry tax-free interest at 2 ½ per cent. compounded until the beginning of the month in which repayment is made. Claims on hardship grounds will be considered from:

1. People who, for a continuous period of 12 weeks ended yesterday had been receiving National Assistance.
2. Those named in a register of blind persons kept by local authorities, but excluding the partially blind.
3. Those receiving constant attendance allowances or unemployability supplements mainly due to war or industrial injuries or industrial diseases.

STATUTORY ORDER SOUGHT

The Chancellor said he also intended to seek powers to permit repayment by Statutory Order. If later on in the year financial and economic circumstances were such as to justify going further, he would then be able to make a proposal to that effect.

Amounts due to building societies would also carry interest from Oct. 1 at 2 ½ per cent. tax free. He hoped forms would be available in a months' time and the Inland Revenue would begin to make repayments early in June.

He described his proposals as a comprehensive attack on the post-war credit scheme, "I hope that apart from the difficult cases, the bulk of the repayments can be made by the end of August."

All credits now belonging to the beneficiaries of holders who have died are to be paid forthwith and in the future, credits still outstanding will be repaid on the death of the holder. This will cost £34 m. this year.

£310m. PAID SO FAR

Nearly 12 million were due to claim their credits when they reached pensionable age. Five million others or their beneficiaries have been paid £310 million of the £765 million credited under the scheme which was introduced in 1941.

About £25 million has been set against tax arrears. Of the £430 million outstanding, credits vary between a few pounds and £325.

£50 OFF £750 CAR: HELP FOR ALL ROAD USERS

BUS OPERATORS' BIG SAVING

By W. A. McKenzie
Daily Telegraph Motoring Correspondent

Motorists and road transport users were jubilant at the cuts in the Budget affecting almost every road user. The average family car will be about £50 cheaper, and the cuts will make for reductions in every aspect of transport cost, and so help to cut the cost of living.

Transport costs of raw materials, and of delivery of the finished products, including door-to-door deliveries, will be reduced. Bus and coach passengers may benefit from the changes. The Chancellor announced, in all, four tax reductions which will save money to motorists, commercial vehicle users and operators of public service vehicles.

They were:

1. Purchase tax on cars is to be reduced from 60 per cent. on the ad valorem, or factory, price to 50 per cent.
2. Purchase tax on commercial vehicle chassis (there was no tax on the rest of the vehicle) to be abolished.
3. Excise duty on buses and coaches to be reduced to about one-third of the present rate, with a minimum tax of £12.
4. Duty on heavy oils used in road vehicles to be abolished when used in a subsidiary engine mounted on a vehicle. (Vehicles which use the roads to an extent which make them licensable as road vehicles will have to use dutiable oils.)

£750 MOTOR-CAR

New Price About £707

New Car Prices will have to wait for Board of Trade reckoning. Exact figures cannot be given at this stage. Purchase tax is a percentage on the manufacturer's price, which is not disclosed; not on the basic price.

But a car with a basic price of £500 was liable for a purchase tax of £250 1s 7d, making the total price approximately £750. Now the tax will be some £207, and the total price £707. Examples of approximate reductions are:

	Price Old £	s	New £	s
Austin A.35	570		538	
Austin A.55	848		802	
Ford Zephyr	916		866	
Hillmann Minx	795		750	
Jaguar 3.4 litre	1,672		1,581	
Rolls-Royce standard saloon	5,694		5,387	
Standard Vanguard	1,044		986	
Vauxhall Velox	983	17	929	
Vauxhall Victor	758	17	716	10

Imported cars into Britain will benefit more than British ones. This is because the tax is levied on the total sum of the manufacturer's price and the import duty.

The Italian fiat 600, one of the most successful Continental cars in any overseas market, now selling at £649, will come down to £613, a reduction of £36.

REFRIGERATORS AND WASHER PRICES DOWN

Daily Telegraph Reporter

Electrical goods and appliances will fall appreciably in price as a result of the purchase tax cut from 30 to 25 per cent.

A well-known retail firm gave these examples which will come into effect immediately:

	Old Price £ s d	New Price £ s d
Vacuum Cleaner	28.9.7	27.12.6
Refrigerator (2 ½ cubic ft.)	49.7.0	47.17.5
Refrigerator (3 ½ cubic ft)	63.3.8	61.5.9
Refrigerator (5 cubic ft)	99.13.5	96.13.7

Fridgidaire last night announced reductions ranging from five to two guineas on their refrigerators.

The retail price of furniture is unaffected because no change has been made in the 5 per cent. purchase tax rate at present imposed. But carpets and floor coverings will cost slightly less. The tax on these has been reduced from 15 to 12 ½ per cent.

JEWELLERY TAX CUT

The tax on all jewellery drops from 30 per cent. to 25 per cent. Mr. H. Southam, Director of the British Jewellers' Association, said that only about 2 ½ % of this was likely "to be reflected in prices paid by the public." The profit margin allowed for retailers was based on the cost price without the tax.

Among articles affected by the reduction in purchase tax from 60 to 50 per cent. are radio and television sets, records, cosmetics and perfumery.

The 30 per cent. to 25 per cent. reduction also affects furs (other than rabbit skin, lamb or sheepskin, which remain unchanged at 5 per cent.), clocks, watches, cycles and motor-assisted cycles, sports goods, toys and cameras, and musical instruments.

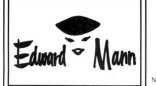

Edward Mann

The Daily Telegraph

4 A.M.
No. 32,300 LONDON, FRIDAY, FEBRUARY 20, 1959 — and Morning Post — Printed in LONDON and MANCHESTER Price 2½d.

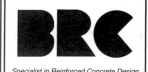

BRC
Specialist in Reinforced Concrete Design & Suppliers of Reinforcement

3 PREMIERS SIGN PACT FOR CYPRUS PEACE

CEREMONY IN CLINIC SICK ROOM

MAKARIOS DROPS HIS OBJECTIONS

'NEW CHAPTER': EARLY RETURN TO ISLAND

Britain, Greece and Turkey last evening ended nearly four years of conflict over Cyprus by initialling an agreement in Room 325 at the London Clinic occupied by Mr. Menderes, Turkish Prime Minister. Accord came after a day of tense conference in which Archbishop Makarios withdrew objections to the Zurich plan for independence.

Mr. Menderes, still suffering from the efects of Tuesday's plane crash, received Mr. Macmillan and Mr. Karamanlis, Greek Prime Minister, in pyjamas.

Announcing in the House of Commons agreements among the three Governments and the Cyprus communities, Mr. Macmillan said they took full account of Cypriot rights. They also represented "a fair and honourable compromise between the interests of Greece and Turkey."

BASES GUARANTEE

The friendship and alliance between these two countries, "so essential to all of us," had been re-established, and Britain had been guaranteed the facilities needed for her strategic obligations. "Our requirements have been fully met," Archbishop Makarios had accepted the accord "both in the letter and the spirit."

The Prime Minister said this "victory for reason and co-operation" would involve the release of detainees and the terms for an amnesty and the return of exiles. If desired, continued association with the Commonwealth would be sympathetically considered. Texts of the agreement would be presented in a White Paper on Monday.

MR. GAITSKELL REBUKED

Mr. Gaitskell, Leader of the Opposition, said they had heard the announcement with "great satisfaction and relief." When he went on to give credit to the Government for "eating so many words," Mr. Macmillan replied that Mr. Gaitskell "never has been and never will be able to rise to the level of great events."

Last night the Archbishop, who said he would be returning to Cyprus "in a few days," stated: "This day a new chapter opens up for the people of Cyprus." His acceptance of the proposals, which led to final successful talks at Lancaster House, had been reluctantly supported by his delegation.

CLINIC PEACE ASSEMBLY

By Our Diplomatic Staff

In dressing gown and pyjamas, Mr. Menderes, the Turkish Prime Minister, received the Prime Ministers of Britain and Greece in his room at the London Clinic for the initialling of the Cyprus agreement.

It was an almost theatrical moment concluding an era which reached the peak of drama when Mr. Menderes escaped from the wrecked Viscount airliner on Tuesday evening.

Room 325 in the Clinic was typical of one in almost any nursing home in Britain. Clinically adequate with its bed, bedside table and easy chair, it had none of the diplomatic grandeur with which the initialling of such a document is usually surrounded.

HOSPITAL PEN

10-Minute Proceedings

An ordinary hospital pen, which will almost certainly be preserved by the Clinic, served all three Ministers for their signatures. There were about ten people in the room and the whole proceedings lasted not more than 10 minutes.

Mr. Zorlu, the Turkish Foreign Minister, was the first arrival, and gave Mr. Menderes first news of complete agreement. He was followed closely by Mr. Esenhal, of the Turkish Foreign Ministry, who is also one of the survivors of the crash.

Mr. Macmillan and Mr. Karamanlis arrived together and both Dr. Kutchuk, the Turkish Cypriot leader and Archbishop Makarios also went to the Clinic. Neither went into the room for the initialling of the documents. They had already intimated their agreement with the proceedings.

When the other Ministers had gone, Mr. Menderes remained alone in the third floor room. His secretary, Mr. Fenmen, said afterwards: "I was present at the signing. The atmosphere among the three Prime Ministers was more than friendly. It was motherly."

According to another member of his staff, Mr. Menderes is recovering "fairly well" from the effects of the crash. But he is still subject to doctors' orders and was unable to take part in any celebrations at this important milestone on the road to peace in Cyprus.

Since Mr. Menderes has not been told when he will be allowed to leave the Clinic, no firm date for his return to Turkey has been arranged. According to a Turkish spokesman last night, he is expected to remain at the Clinic for "a few days more," presumably to make sure he is fully fit for his return home.

SILVER LINING TO DEBATE

FOREIGN AFFAIRS OVERSHADOWED

By Our Special Correspondent

WESTMINSTER, Thursday.

Cyprus loomed like a cloud over the opening of a debate on foreign affairs in the House of Commons tonight. Members were anxiously awaiting the statement from the Prime Minister, and wondering how far the cloud would prove to be silver-lined.

This reduced the House's immediate interest in Mr. Macmillan's forthcoming visit to Moscow and in the future of Germany. Rarely has so important a debate begun with such a poor attendance.

Members thronged into the Chamber for the Prime Minister's statement, which was due at 7 o'clock. The Conservative benches were quickly filled, but large gaps remained on the Opposition side.

Finally Mr. Macmillan entered in a burst of Government cheers, accompanied by Selwyn Lloyd, Foreign Secretary, and Mr. Lennox-Boyd, Colonial Secretary.

NO DEFEATS

Socialists Jeer

The Prime Minister was heard almost in silence. From time to time, a murmur of applause came from Conservatives, indicative more of thankfulness than of triumph.

Socialists started to jeer as he paid tribute to the patience and skill of the Foreign and Colonial Secretaries in the Cyprus negotiations. But their cries were drowned by loud Government cheers.

It had been a victory for reason and for co-operation, said the Prime Minister. Socialists shouted "Ho! Ho!" as he concluded that no party to it had suffered a defeat.

Mr. Gaitskell, for the Opposition, accepted the Prime Minister's statement "with great satisfaction and relief."

MR. KARAMANLIS WARNS EOKA MAN

INCIDENT IN HOTEL

By a Diplomatic Correspondent

Mr. Karamanlis, the Greek Prime Minister, administered a sharp rebuke last night to a member of the Eoka terrorist organisation who said he intended to carry on the struggle for Enosis. The incident occurred in Mr. Karamanlis's hotel when a man, who is not a member of the Cypriot delegation, was introduced to him.

Expressing his satisfaction at the outcome of the London conference, the Eoka man showed the Prime Minister the scars of three wounds he had suffered in the campaign. "I shall resume the struggle at a more appropriate time," he said.

Mr. Karamanlis drew himself up, and in the sharpest of tones warned him to drop all such thoughts unless he wanted to destroy his country. "You will do better to dedicate yourself to building the new State," he said, turning on his heel.

MR. BUTLER TO BE IN CHARGE

By Our Political Correspondent

Mr. Butler, Lord Privy Seal, Home Secretary, and leader of the House of Commons, will be in charge of the Government during the absence of the Prime Minister in Russia from tomorrow until Tuesday week. It was announced from 10, Downing Street after a Cabinet meeting yesterday that Mr. Macmillan had asked him to take charge.

The statement added: "Mr. Butler will preside at Cabinet meetings called during this period".

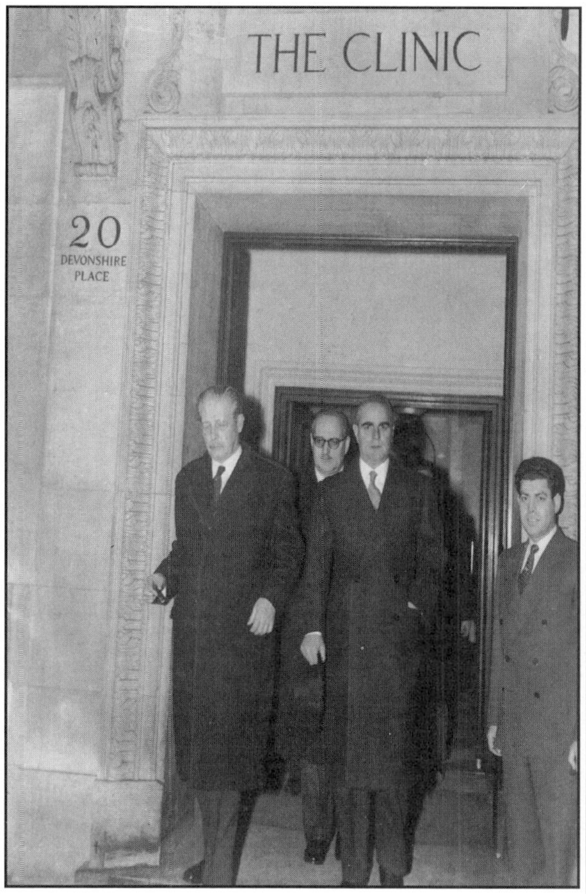
THE CLINIC
20
DEVONSHIRE
PLACE

AT THE LONDON CLINIC. Accompanied by Mr. Karamanlis, Greek Prime Minister, Mr. Macmillan is seen leaving the London Clinic last evening after calling to see Mr. Menderes. The Turkish Prime Minister was taken there after the Viscount airliner crash.

ARCHBISHOP'S 'NIGHT OF PRAYER & REFLECTION'

RELUCTANT ASSENT TO PLAN

By Our Diplomatic Staff

The story of the historic conference which gave independence to Cyprus is one of three days of intense and relentless pressure on Archbishop Makarios to accept a plan on which he and his 30-odd advisers have serious objections and misgivings.

The Archbishop, who is confidently expected by his delegation to become the first President of the new State, still thinks many of the provisions in the plan are both unfair to the Greek-Cypriot majority, and unworkable.

He told his colleagues at an 8.00 a.m. meeting in a London hotel yesterday that he hopes that as the plan is brought into operation modifications will be agreed to suit the circumstances.

It was at this meeting, after the crucial night session of the conference at Lancaster House that he announced his decision to acquiesce in the proposed settlement. He said he had reached his decision after "a night's prayer and reflection on the agonising dilemma" which faced him.

TWO APPEALS

Unity and Co-operation

The factors which had weighed most heavily in his meditation had been the "interests of the Cypriot people" and the involvement of the Greek Government by its agreement with Turkey and Britain.

He made two appeals to the Greek Cypriot leaders: to work for the unity of the Cypriot people and to co-operate sincerely with the Turkish population in putting the plan into effect.

BRITAIN SENDS ARMS TO IRAQ

By a Diplomatic Correspondent

Britain has met Iraqi requests for arms since the revolution last July, a Foreign Office spokesman said yesterday. The supplies were sent by bilateral agreement, not under the terms of the Baghdad Pact, membership of which has not been confirmed by the new Iraqi regime.

There had been several requests for arms, some dated before the revolution. "They were mainly for logistic support of British arms already possessed by the Iraqi army," added the spokesman.

THE SPEAKER TO RETIRE

HEALTH REASONS FOR DECISION

By Our Political Correspondent

The Speaker of the House of Commons, Mr. W. Morrison, is to retire at the end of the present Parliament. This decision, made known yesterday by Mr. Morrison, was received with surprise and regret on both sides of the House.

It has been taken on medical advice. The Speaker's doctors have told him he would be unwise to take on another Parliamentary term. Though as he said, he is "sound in wind and limb" for a man of his age, which is 65, he has been having increasing difficulty with his hearing.

The Speaker has a salary of £5,000, with a house in the Palace of Westminster and £750 as M.P. On retirement he is usually voted a pension of £4,000 and raised to the House of Lords with a viscountcy.

DOCTORS' ADVICE

Mr. Morrison, who had represented Cirencester and Tewkesbury, Glos, since 1929, told the House he had decided with regret that he should not offer himself as a candidate at the next General Election.

"I have recently undergone a very thorough medical examination and my advisers, in whom I have full confidence, told me I would be unwise to undertake the work of another Parliament."

ANTI-LABOUR AGREEMENT IS ENDED

MOVE BY BOLTON CONSERVATIVES

LIBERAL SEAT TO BE FOUGHT

An anti-Socialist Parliamentary electoral pact between Conservatives and Liberals at Bolton has come to an end. The executive council of the town's West Conservative Association decided by a 2-1 majority not to continue the agreement, it was announced yesterday.

Under the agreement, Liberals have supported a Conservative candidate in Bolton East and Conservatives have given reciprocal aid to a Liberal in the West division. The pact has been in force for two General Elections and each time the Socialist candidates in both divisions have been defeated.

One reason for the decision is the Liberal intervention at Parliamentary by-election for Conservative held seats. Mr. Arthur Holt, Liberal M.P. for Bolton West, hasn been strongly criticised in local Conservative circles for aiding Mr. Ludovic Kennedy at Rochdale.

IN TOWN'S INTERESTS

Conservative View

Mr. William G Morris, a vice chairman of Bolton West Conservative Association, said last night that it had been decided the time had come when they should offer the Conservatives of the West division a Conservative candidate at the next General Election.

"We feel it is in the interests of Bolton and the country that there should be a Conservative M.P. in Bolton West." The necessary machinery has been set in motion to select a candidate.

There was no official statement released from Bolton Liberal Association.

STEADY GAIN IN POPULARITY

M.P.'S CHANCES

By Our Political Correspondent

Mr. Holt, Liberal M.P. for the West division, took the news calmly. It was not unexpected, as it had been obvious for some time that many people in the Conservative party organisation, particularly the women workers, were keen to have a candidate of their own.

He will stand again, and his chance of holding the seat should not be dismissed as entirely negligible. In the last three-cornered fight in Bolton East, in 1950, the Socialists had a majority of 3,709 over the Conservatives. Mr. Holt, a newcomer, polled 8,647 votes.

Since winning the West seat in 1951', with the benefit of the pact, he has gained steadily in popularity. It is possible that a substantial number of Conservative voters disapproving of the decision to end the pact will continue to vote for him as the best hope of keeping the Socialists out.

If Mr. Holt's chances are slim, those of Mr. Philip Bell Q.C., Conservative member of Bolton East, seem even slimmer. When he won the seat in 1951 his majority was only 355, and it was calculated that about 6,000 of his votes came from Liberals.

HUDDERSFIELD SEAT

Liberals' Confidence

If the Huddersfield Conservatives also abrogate their local understanding, the Liberals consider that their M.P., Mr. Donald, Wade will have at least an even chance of holding Huddersfield West. The constituency has a strong Liberal tradition.

The arrangements at both Bolton and Huddersfield were strictly local. It has always been denied there was any national understanding.

General Election, Huddersfield West.
D.W. Wade (L) 24,345: J.F. Drabble Q.C. (soc) 16,418: L maj. 7,927

CASTRO IS GIVEN RECOGNITION

CUBAN VICTOR DUE IN HAVANA TO-DAY

From Edwin Tetlow
Daily Telegraph Special Correspondent

HAVANA, Wednesday.

Britain decided to-night to recognise the revolutionary Cuban Government put in power by Dr. Fidel Castro. On instructions from London Mr. Fordham, British Ambassador, delivered a Note advising the Government of the step.

The Note was accepted by the Chief of Protocol, as Señor Roberto Agramonte, Minister for Foreign Affairs was not available. Britain's action has added a new element of piquancy to relations between the two countries. Dr. Castro and his rebels,who are due in Havana to-morrow, are still aggrieved over the British sale of Sea Furies and tanks to the now defeated dictator, Gen. Batista.

He might order some temporary measure to mark official displeasure with Britain as a gesture to the new-found pride of Cubans. But Dr. Castro is not expected to declare the British Ambassador persona non grata or order confiscation of British property.

One forecast is that he might send a Note formally protesting against the arms deals and asking Britain not to interfere again in such a manner in the affairs of Cuba.

VICTOR'S ADVANCE

Crowds Weep and pray

Meanwhile Dr. Castro is at last approaching Havana and is receiving a welcome unprecedented in Cuba's turbulent history. Men as well as women wept and knelt in prayer in the streets as their bearded liberator rode by.

This victorious rebel seems unique among historical figures in this island for his moral purity and his sense of destiny as a liberator. If he can hold this standard Cubans will surely have cause to honour him.

Forgotten for a while were the worries harboured by some about the machinations of the Communists. There are said to be many within the higher ranks of his movement.

Gone, too, were the fears that traditional Latin American politics might ensnare and corrupt him. To-day he was a conquering Caesar, the idol of millions.

Havana and its people were in their most inviting mood. They offered a strange contrast to the perils, privations and plain cruelties and stupidities seen here in the past weeks.

MINOR GROUPS

Pressure Likely

When Dr. Castro and his provisional régime settle down to shaping Cuba's future they will hardly find themselves in a dictatorial position. Several smaller movements which fought with the rebels will make their presence felt.

Cuba's gambling industry is to be reorganised. It provides high revenue to Havana, gives employment to several thousand Cubans, and is a powerful magnet for rich American tourists.

Dr. Castro has said that he does not intend to be "puritanical." Apparently five leading hotels in Havana will run casinos, but public gambling will not be legal anywhere else.

At one of these hotels George Raft, the film-star, is stage manager. In this way it is hoped to cater profitably to tourists and Cubans who can afford the fabulously high prices charged at these hotels.

(January 8)

230 STATIONS MAY BE SHUT

BRITISH RAILWAYS SUBMIT PLANS

Daily Telegraph Reporter

Proposals for the closing of 230 stations throughout the country have been submitted by British Railways to the Central Transport Consultative Committee, it was stated by the British Transport Commission last night. It is possible that all 230 stations may be closed within the next 12 months.

A British Transport Commission spokesman said that the committee, at its discretion, would give details of the stations affected. Ample time would be allowed for any complaints and grievances to be aired and possible public inquiries to be arranged. The proposals affect small stations, junctions and halts.

The stations affected are in all four regions of British Railways. It is understood that officials of the railway unions have been informed of the potential closings.

A Midland Region spokesman said that a constant review of the running costs of small stations and halts was being carried out. Those found to be running at a heavy loss might well be marked for closure.

UNION CONCERN

Mr. W. Robinson, secretary, Preston No 1 branch of the National Union of Railwaymen, said: "We are greatly concerned by the proposals, but have no definite information on what is to happen. The management have said they are prepared to consider any proposals we may have to make concerning staff."

Officials of the various unions had held meetings with representatives of British Railways and feared that some 600 men might lose their jobs if stations in Lancashire, Cumberland and Westmoreland were closed. The unions had been told that not even the introduction of diesel trains could save certain lines.

He said the lines involved were: Preston to Crossens on the Southport line (13 miles); Blackburn to Hellifield (24 miles); Chorley to Blackburn (10 miles); Ulverston to Lakeside (8 miles); Workington to Penrith (31 miles) and Kirkby Stephen to Teaby (12 miles) and Penrith. Individual stations on other lines were also involved.

(May 8)

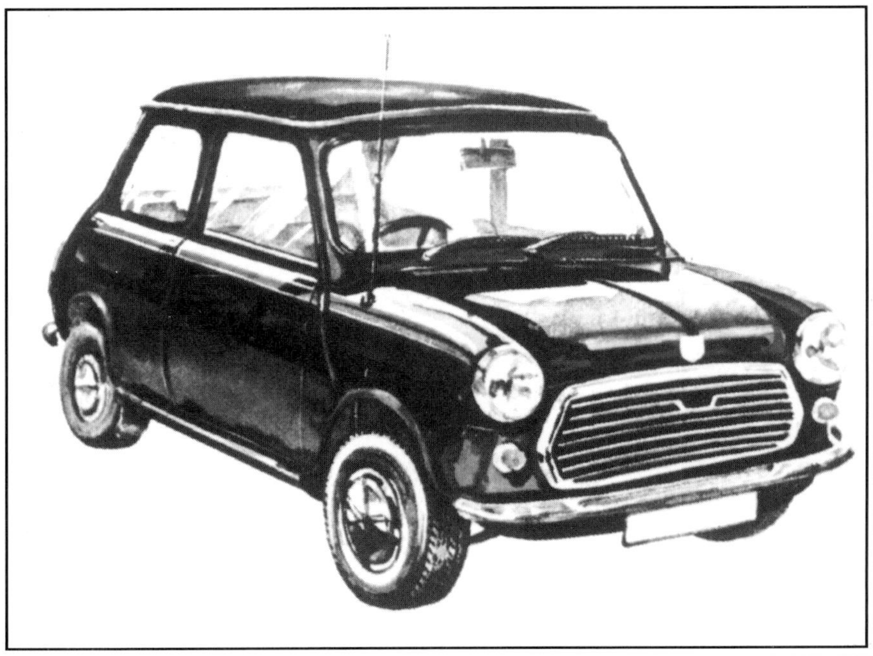

THE MORRIS MINI-CAR.

One view of the British Motor Corporation's "people's car," details of which will be announced to-morrow week and for which tens of thousands of economy motorists have been waiting. An Austin mini-car of similar specifications but with a slightly different front treatment will also be launched.

It can be seen that a large proportion of the wheel base is devoted to body space. It has small wheels and the equipment is austere. But the car is a full four-seater, with two doors and a trend towards the Italian styling which has influenced all recent B.M.C. cars.

The mini-car's 8-h.p. engine will be set diagonally in the chassis to keep the floor low, and will give a maximum speed of more than 70 m.p.h., but because of the low overall weight of the car, petrol consumption will be as low as 55 m.p.g. The price of the car is expected to be just over £500, including purchase tax.

(March 16)

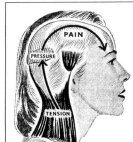

RUSSIANS SHOW MOON SECRETS

PICTURES WERE SENT 300,000 MILES BY LUNIK III

By Anthony Smith
Daily Telegraph Science Correspondent

The Russians last night issued the first pictures of the far side of the moon, which is never seen from the earth. They were taken from Lunik III, the rocket which circled the moon, on Oct. 7, developed automatically aboard the rocket and transmitted by radio to the earth 300,000 miles away.

They show that the far side of the moon has fewer landmarks than the visible side. But it contains a large "sea" about 185 miles in diameter, which the Russians have named the Sea of Moscow.

The pictures were shown briefly on the Russian television service's midnight news bulletin. They were released soon after and sent on to London by radio.

They are thus appearing in the West on the same day that they are first being published in Russian newspapers. A special committee of the Soviet Academy of Sciences has been set up to name the new features now seen.

Prof. Alexander Mikhailov, chairman of the Astronomical Council of the Academy of Sciences, said over Moscow Radio last night that a remarkable thing about the photographs was that the moon's unseen part "is considerably more monotonous than the side turned towards the earth. It contains fewer seas and fewer contrasts.

"Astronomers and geologists are thus faced with an exciting problem: To explain this phenomenom which, beyond any doubt, is associated with the question of the origin of the moon's relief. The photographs will be minutely studied to bring out all relevant details."

EIGHT FEATURES

Definite Findings

The Russians named eight features whch they said were definitely established. In the Sea of Moscow a large bay was gven the name Astronaughts' Bay.

A crater some 60 miles across, with a hill in the centre, seen in the southern hemisphere, was named after Prof. Konstanin Tsiolkovsky, a Soviet rocket pioneer who died in 1935. The Russians say he was the first man to propose multi-stage rockets to go beyond the Earth's atmosphere.

Another crater was named after Prof. Frederic Joliot-Curie, the French Physicist, who died in August last year. He was at one time president of the World Peace Council and was regarded in the West as a Communist. Mikhail Lomonosov, the fisherman's son who founded the Russian Academy of Sciences in the 18th century, had another crater named after him. He died in 1765. The crater lies to the north of the lunar equator, almost on the border of the visible and invisible portions of the moon.

MOUNTAIN RANGE

"Sea of Dreams"

A mountain range south of the Lomonosov crater, nearer to the equatorial regions, will be known as the Sovietsky Mountains. A sea near the border of the invisible part of the moon will be known as the Sea of Dreams.

Giving details of how the pictures were obtained, Tass said the camera was switched on by remote control from the Earth at 3.30 a.m. G.M.T. on Oct 7. This time was chosen so that Lunik III would then be between the sun and the moon and about 70 per cent of the moon's unknown surface would be lit up by the sun.

Lunik III was then about 40,000 miles away from the moon. There was an orientation system aboard. This made sure that the lenses of the camera were directed towards the moon when the camera was in action.

The Russians were certainly adept in triggering the camera at the right time. Not only is it a full moon from the camera's point of view, and therefore well lit up, but there is the convenient old slice with which to make comparisons.

Due to the fact that the moon is not quite constant in showing us only one face, and does enable us to see a total of 59 per cent. of the moon's surface, there was only 41 per cent. that was never seen. The Russian photograph, even though it includes the old slice, must show very nearly all of this unknown 41 per cent.

STILL IN ORBIT

300,000 Miles Away

Meanwhile Lunik III continues on its widely eliptical orbit. Having come back to the vicinity of the Earth once since its launching, it is now over 300,000 miles away from us again.

Now it has been given a life of half a year which will bring it down next April. During that time it will girdle the Earth 11 or 12 times, and will then burn up in the Earth's atmosphere.

(October 27)

DOCTORS AIM AT BANKS OF HUMAN 'SPARE PARTS'

By John Prince
Daily Telegraph Health Services Correspondent

Banks for human "spare parts" are the new aim of the famous team of heart operation specialists at the London Postgraduate Medical School, Hammersmith Hospital. They hope to make possible the repair or replacement of diseased organs such as the kidneys and liver.

The new techniques will involve modifications of the heart-lung machine invented by Dr. Denis Mulrose. This takes over the heart's function and enables the surgeon to operate on a stilled and bloodless organ.

News of the new projects was given yesterday by Prof. Ian Aird, Director of the Surgical Unit at the Postgraduate School. He was speaking at the opening, by Sir James Paterson Ross, president of the Royal College of Surgeons, of new laboratories costing £135,000.

The team hope to develop a medical workshop where a diseased organ can be left for repair or replacement. This will involve setting up banks for the storage of "spares," organs removed from people killed in, say, road accidents, or dying of some disease which did not affect the organ wanted.

"Both the Americans and the Russians," said Prof. Aird, "can keep an organ alive for eight to 10 days, occasionally. If we could do it for two to three weeks it would be very valuable."

"REJECTED ORGANS"

Transplantation Problems

One important future project would be the transplantation of organs. At present transplanted organs were rejected by the animal into which they were placed, and the barrier appeared to be insoluble. Work would also be carried out on replacing parts of the body by tubes.

Dr. Melrose said he hoped to have the extension of the heart-lung machine working on a kidney by the middle of next year. They were encouraged by successful work they saw on their recent visit to Moscow.

The transplantation difficulty had been overcome with blood, bone, skin and the cornea, but nowhere had it been possible yet to transplant a complete organ, save in the case of identical twins. "The actual transferring of a kidney has been done. The next thing to be overcome is the technical problem of storing these organs.

"WE SHALL HAVE TO BUILD A BANK."

Both Prof. Aird and Dr. Melrose emphasised the importance of experimental surgery on animals. Prof. Aird said he was not allowed, by law, to show the animal kennels.

(June 23)

FILTER TIPS ARE MORE POPULAR

TOBACCO SALES UP

A striking increase in the smoking of filter-tipped cigarettes in Britain was revealed yesterday in figures published by the Tobacco Manufacturers' Standing Committee. The amount rose to 18,200,000lb last year compared with 10,100,000lb in 1957.

An increase in tobacco consumption, from 256,000,000 lb to 260,800,000lb would seem to indicate that public statements linking lung cancer with tobacco smoking have had no effect on tobacco sales. But they may be influencing smoking habits.

Matching the increase in the choice of filter-tipped cigarettes is a drop in the consumption of non-tipped cigarettes from 211,200,000lb in 1957 to 206,900,000lb in 1958. Tobacco smoked in the pipe showed a slight drop from 19,600,000lb to 19 ,000,000 lb. Tobacco smoked in hand-rolled cigarettes rose from 13,200,000lb to 14,600,000lb.

A new development is the fact that about 25,000 women now "roll their own." Cigars and snuff show a small but steady increase in popularity. Women, whose cigarette smoking more than doubled between 1939 and 1945, appear to have settled down to a steady average of 3.3lb a head annually.

(May 25)

CHURCH SELLS A SUBURB

More than £300,000 has been realised by the Church Commissioners from the sale of the freehold of Hampstead Garden Suburb. The Commissioners drew about £16,000 a year from houses paying ground rents.

The new owners are the lessees, Suburb Leaseholds and Hampstead Garden Suburb Trust. The Commissioners are to reinvest the proceeds of the sale in office and commercial blocks with short leases, so the income can be increased.

The land at Hampstead, which the Commissioners had owned for many years, was held by the lessees on a 999-year lease.

(February 23)

KHRUSCHEV TALKS OF GOING HOME

'END BAITING' ADVICE BY WASHINGTON

From Ian Ball and Vincent Ryder
Daily Telegraph special Correspondents

Aboard the Khruschev train to SAN FRANCISCO, Sunday.

The American public to-day gave Mr. Khruschev a show of warmth for the first time on his tour and the Soviet leader was a happier man than yesterday when he had threatened in Los Angeles to fly home to Russia.

The threat of returning to Russia came at a banquet after Mr. Norris Poulson, the Mayor, had recalled Mr. Khruschev's phrase: "We will bury you."

Earlier the Russian leader protested that he was prevented, on security grounds, from visiting Disneyland, the amusement park. But to-day was different.

When his train drew into Santa Barbara, a city of 55,000 people, Mr. Khruschev was met by clapping and some friendly greetings.

He spent about ten minutes shaking hands with several hundred people and meeting the Mayor, Mr. Edward Abbott.

"My mission is for peace," he said repeatedly. "The people are wonderful. The people are for peace." Mr. Abbott understood the meaning of friendship far better than Mr. Poulson.

NEARLY A RIOT

Guards Powerless

There was nearly a riot when Mr. Khruschev, unable to move forward against the crowd barrier and in danger of being knocked off his feet, tried to return to his carriage. By now he was completely surrounded and unable to move.

He spotted a nine-year-old girl who was in danger of being trampled under foot, and he bent down to fondle her long brunette pigtails. The child looked up at him in wonder.

American and Russian security agents remained powerless in the face of the crowd, which was determined to get to Mr. Khruschev to shake his hands and pat him on the back. Obviously delighted by his reception, Mr. Khrushev said: "Well, I have seen some real Americans at last and it seems to me they are as good and kind as our Soviet people."

"HOUSE ARREST"

Chance to Meet People

He then unexpectedly walked informally through the 18 coaches of the train exchanging remarks with more than 350 Western and Russian correspondents and cameramen. He was asked about the Santa Barbara greeting.

"It was a relief to get away from house arrest and have a chance to meet the people and talk to some of them."

Mr. Khrushev was asked if last night's threat, perhaps only a rhetorical flourish, to fly home if there was any more of what he considered discourtesy from his local hosts, was meant literally.

"I thought perhaps, judging by my reception in Los Angeles, that I had become a burden to my hosts. We are guests and as guests must be a burden to our guests.

"A good guest is one who knows the right time to leave. It is always better to leave five minutes before the host asks you to go."

Mr. Cabot Lodge, American Ambassador to the United Nations, and Mr. Khrushev's official escort on the tour, interjected: "As a host I can say we are delighted to have you here. There is no need for anyone to talk of leaving."

The subject came up again. "Why should I go home?" said Mr. Khrushev. "I saw a little girl waving to me at Santa Barbara, waving to Communism. Her mother probably told her I am one of the men on whom depends war or peace. So why should I go home?"

Asked about a dancing scene from the film "Can Can," which he saw being made at Hollywood yesterday, Mr. Khruschev said: "The dancing was immoral and tasteless. That is a pornographic film that won't be allowed in Russia."

(September 21)

ANTARTIC AS WORLD'S CONTINENT OF PEACE

12 NATIONS SIGN TREATY

From Our Own Correspondent

WASHINGTON, Tuesday.

Twelve nations, including Russia, to-day signed a treaty to preserve the Antarctic for peaceful exploration for at least 30 years. The continent of five million square miles will be kept free of military bases.

After the ceremony of signing, Mr. Herter, United States Secretary of State, read a message from President Eisenhower who described the treaty as "a significant advance towards the goal of a peaceful world with justice." The agreement was of great importance to the world.

"It should be an inspiring example of what can be accomplished by international co-operation in the field of science and in the pursuit of peace." Antarctica would be a laboratory for co-operative scientific research.

In addition to Britain, the United States and Russia, the treaty nations are Argentina, Australia, Belgium, Chile, France, Japan, New Zealand, Norway and South Africa. The document was drafted in English, French, Russian and Spanish.

INSPECTION SYSTEM

Nation's Freedom

The most interesting feature of the 14-article treaty is its inspection system. Any member nation may send observers to "all areas of Antarctica" at any time to see that no military equipment is being sent there.

Previous inspection systems such as that to supervise the Korean armistice and the Suez settlement were far more elaborate.

Before the conference started seven weeks ago it had been suggested that Russia's anticipated agreement to the Antarctica inspection system might provide a pattern for Russian agreement to other inspection systems. But to-day American Government officals gave a warning against hoping that a similar inspection plan could be adopted in any test ban agreement or general disarmament agreement.

The treaty will not become effective until it has been ratified by all 12 signatories. A consultative committee will meet in Canberra two months after the treaty becomes effective and at suitable intervals thereafter to recommend measures to participating parties.

RUSSIAN ATTITUDE

"Favourable Conditions"

The Russian representative attributed the success of the conference to favourable conditions under which it was held, promoted to a large extent by Mr. Khruschev's visit to the United States. He said:

"This favourable atmosphere contributed to the successful termination of the work of the conference and had a positive influence on the results."

(December 2)

UNIVERSITY POPULATION DOUBLED SINCE 1939

110,000 STUDENTS BY 1961, SAYS REPORT: BIG SWING TO SCIENCE

The total number of full-time University students in England, Scotland and Wales is expected to rise to at least 110,000 by 1962. The present University population is about 100,000, double the figure for 1938-39.

After the war, the peak reached under pressure of ex-Service demand was 85,421 in 1949-50 and the lowest point reached after that demand had worked itself out was 80,602 in 1953-54.

Since then, there has been a progressive increase, states a report published yesterday by the University Grants Committee. In 1957-58, the year which the document reviews, the university population was 95,442.

"The main reason for this increase is the tendency since the war for pupils to remain at school to the age of 17 and over and to qualify for admission to universities'.

It was evident from statistics collected in October, 1958, that this trend was continuing. Of 95,442 students in 1957-58, 75.3 per cent. were men and 24.7 per cent. were women. There has been little change in these proportions since 1938-39.

STUDENT MOBILITY

25,174 in Residence

During the term, 25,174 students lived in colleges or halls of residence, 46,237 in lodgings, and 24,031 at home. "The decline in the percentage of students living at home is the out-standing feature," the report comments, "This increase in student mobility is mainly the result of a more liberal attitude by award-making bodies."

Full-time students, other than those doing advanced work, were distributed among subject groups as follows: arts 34,206; pure science 17,853; technology 11,943; medicine 11,728; dentistry 2,828; agriculture 1,675; veterinary science 1,139.

Of all full-time students, 43.1 per cent were studying arts subjects, including social studies and a teaching training course. The remaining 56.9 per cent. were studying pure, or applied science.

Evidence of a swing from arts to science was clearly seen in the number of new entrants. "Over the last four years the increases in pure science and technology have been proportionately twice as great as in arts." the report states. New entrants admitted in 1957-8 numbered 27,676. Over half were aged 19 and over.

HIGHER INCOME

Parliamentary Grants

On the financial side, the recurrent income of the universities and university colleges for 1957-8 amounted to £49,418,302, an increase of £7,762,693 over the income for the previous year. Recurrent expenditure, apart from allocations to reserves, was £48,335,053 as compared with £41,509,703 for the previous year

(September 5)

£100,000 OFFER TO YORK

ROWNTREE TRUST

York Academic Trust, which may apply next year for the establishment of a university in York, has received its first offer of financial help. It has been made by the Joseph Rowntree Memorial Trust.

The Memorial Trust welcomes the possibility of a York University. It is prepared to contemplate a contribution of £100,000 at the rate of £10,000 a year "to assist in a general way in its establishment."

It is also ready to give "substantial additional support" for social science. The Memorial Trust, one of the charitable foundations set up by Joseph Rowntree early this century, has wide interests in the investigation of social conditions, and in the development of social science.

(September 5)

MR. CARLETON GREENE TO BE HEAD OF B.B.C.

By a Television and Radio Correspondent

Sir Ian Jacob, Director General of the B.B.C. since 1952, will retire at the end of the year. He will be succeeded by Mr. Hugh Carleton Greene, a brother of the novelist, Graham Greene.

Last night Sir Ian who is 59, said: "I think I shall find other things to do, but I am not in a position to say anything about them at the moment. They might be business things."

He was retiring because after seven years and having reached his present age he thought it was time to retire.

Mr. Greene. who is 48, joined the Berlin staff of The Daily Telegraph in 1934. In May. 1939, as its chief correspondent there, he was expelled from Germany as a reprisal for the expulsion of a German correspondent from London.

Between July, 1940, and October of that year he was in the R.A.F. before going to the B.B.C. as head of the German service. In January, 1949, he was appointed head of East European services. He became Controller of Overseas services in November, 1954.

For the past year he has been Director of News and Current Affairs, being responsible for all current affairs. both on sound and television.

Mr. Greene said last night that he had nothing to say at present regarding any changes of innovations in B.B.C.'s sound and television programmes. He had been on holiday and had only just heard of his appointment.

The B.B.C. refused to disclose Mr. Greene's salary, as Director General, but it is reputed to be about £8,000 plus expenses.

(July 21)

VICTORIA TUBE TO COST £50m.

Daily Telegraph Reporter

The first Underground railway to be built in London since 1907 will run as straight as possible between stations and, unlike existing lines in Central London, will not follow roadways. This was stated last night by Mr. Frank Turner, 47, Principal New Works Assistant to London Transport.

Mr. Turner, who was speaking at the Institution of Civil Engineers, has worked on the proposed line since 1953. He said it would run 11 ½ miles from Victoria to Walthamstow through part of the West End. It would cost about £50 million without rolling stock and work would start when financial approval was received.

The practice of following roads kept down the cost of buying easements under private porperty. It also meant longer tunnels, often with sharp curves which made speed restrictions necessary.

The effect of tunnelling had recently increased and it was cheaper to drive a tunnel as straight as possible.

(February 4)

POSTAL CODE FOR NORWICH

By Our Philatelic Correspondent

As part of the Post Office mechanisation programme to cut wage costs, reduce the dull, monotonous and heavy manual work, and speed the mails, the public is to be asked to use postal codes to aid high speed automatic sorting.

Everyone in and around the city will be given a postal code and asked to use it as the last line of their postal address, said Mr. Marples, Post Master-General at Norwich yesterday. The people would be the first in the world to use a postal code in this way.

(July 25)

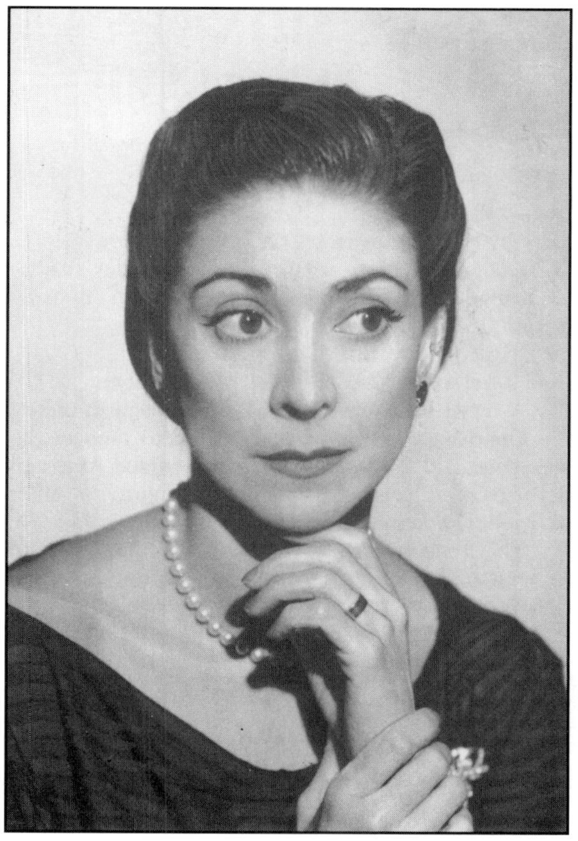

DAME MARGOT FONTEYN

DAME MARGOT IN PANAMA GAOL

from Vincent Ryder
Daily Telegraph special Correspondent

PANAMA CITY, Tuesday.

Dame Margot Fonteyn, 39, the ballerina, was to-day being held incommunicado in the common gaol here. Her husband, Dr. Roberto Arias, 40, former Panamanian Ambassador in London, is being hunted by National Guards in the hills around his country estate near Santa Clara, 75 miles from Panama City.

Sir Ian Henderson, British Ambassador, after trying all day to get permission to see the ballerina, was late to-night promised that the Foreign Ministry "would do its best to arrange a visit within a few hours." A member of the Arias family said: "She is being held as a hostage."

Her arrest at midnight added one more touch of melodrama to the bizarre story of a revolutionary "plot" that the people here are following with dispassionate interest.

After playing hide-and-seek with Government authorities off the Pearl Islands, Dame Margot slipped ashore at dawn yesterday in the family fishing launch while her husband and about 15 men made for the Santa Clara district in the shrimp boat Elaine.

She was in hiding in Panama City in the home of a widow of her husband's brother, Anthony, when the District Attorney last night issued a warrant for her arrest.

A few hours later she telephoned a message to Señor Hector Valdes, chief of the secret police. This is a force which combines security work with general criminal investigation.

INVITED TO HOUSE

National Guard Arrive

He invited Dame Margot to his home for a talk on her activities in Panama. Wearing a flared white summer frock, she drove up to his elegant home in the most fashionable district of the city just before midnight.

On the way her blue saloon car went past the H.Q. of the National Guard without being stopped.

Dame Margot had been in conversation with Señor Valdes for a short while when six National Guards sped in a car along the main thoroughfare and came to a halt outside the secret police chief's home.

They took her off, according to one version, on the pretext of a meeting with the District Attorney at the city prison.

There Dame Margot was escorted to a simple cell set apart from the quarters that are filled with drunks, petty thieves and other minor criminals

A few hours later Sir Ian drove up to the tall iron gates in the 25ft wall. He was allowed inside to talk to officials, but was refused permission to see Dame Margot.

By personal telephone calls and visits to officials by other members of the Embassy he persisted in his efforts throughout to-day. The promise by the Deputy Foreign Minister that he would do his best to arrange a visit came after the British Embassy has expressed growing concern at the delay in obtainting access to Dame Margot.

Cut off from the outside world Dame Margot remains in her clean, but bleak cell. It is 12ft long by 8ft wide and is furnished with an army type of cot and a chair.

FOOD PARCELS

Help from Family

From her barred window she can look down on the ornate front garden decorated, rather pointedly, with an outdated naval gun aimed directly at the front gate.

Only at noon were members of the family of Dame Margot's husband allowed to send in food parcels to relieve her of the necessity of taking the standard diet of dry bread, bean soup, scraps of meat and black coffee. It is understood a change of clothing and personal articles were also delivered.

Col. Bolivar Vallarino, head of the National Guard, a plump and amiable man, said to me in his office: "She is getting every consideration she deserves."

During the afternoon Señor Alvarado went to the prison to question Dame Margot. He drove from his modest office in a collection of old government buildings on the steamy waterfront, distinguished chiefly by the unpainted woodwork and patched plaster of the exterior and the noise of small boys hawking chewing gum and sweets up and down the stone stairs inside.

(April 22)

MR. BEVAN SAVES MR. GAITSKELL

TIGHTROPE ACT ON NATIONALISATION

From our Political Correspondent

BLACKPOOL, Sunday.

After two days of virulent argument on nationalisation, during which he was as good as told he should have been addressing a Conservative conference, Mr. Gaitskell was still leader of the Labour party when he left Blackpool to-night.

That simple fact is worth recording, because the continuance of his leadership was seriously in doubt for nearly 24 hours after he had delivered his personal credo on the principles and aims of British democratic Socialism.

If Mr. Gaitskell was honest with himself on the journey back to London, he must have been conscious that what rescued him from having to decide whether to resign was the closing speech of Mr. Bevan.

This was a masterly display of what Mr. Bevan would, no doubt, call funambulism. For 35 minutes the Deputy Leader balanced himself on a verbal tightrope which purported to bridge the awesome gap within the party.

The big surprise in the election of a new National Executive was the defeat of Mr. Ian Mikardo, who was to have been the next party chairman. He was narrowly beaten by Mr. Anthony Wedgwood Benn, M.P. for Bristol S.E.

(November 30)

TWO SIDES IN CONFLICT

OWNERSHIP ISSUE

On one side during the conference conflict over nationalisation were the fundamentalists who passionately believed with Mrs. Barbara Castle, party chairman, that "common ownership of the means of production distribution and exchange" should remain Labour's basic principle, and who equated it with more and more nationalisation.

On the other stood the pragmatists, prepared to believe with Mr. Gaitskell that nationalisation was not an end in itself, and that defeat in a third successive election was a warning of its unpopularity which, if ignored, could condemn the party to many years in the wilderness of Opposition.

With consummate skill, Mr. Bevan chose as his tightrope a single quotation from one of his own speeches, years ago, with which both Mrs. Castle and Mr. Gaitskell had sought to buttress their respective cases. This was his belief that Socialism in a modern society meant " the conquest of the commanding heights of the economy."

(November 30)

WORLD'S FASTEST

A speed equal to twice that of sound, about 1,300 m.p.h. has been reached a number of times by the English Electric Lightning jet fighter.

The company claimed yesterday that the plane was the fastest twin-engined all-weather fighter in full production anywhere. Single and two-seat versions are being produced for the R.A.F.

Mr. R. P.Beamont, the English Electric chief test pilot, said that the speed was reached at about 35,000ft in level flight during test flights over the Irish Sea.

(January 7)

CREW BLAMES ALBATROSS

STRIKE BEGINS AS BIRD DIES IN SHIP

More than 50 officers and members of the crew of the cargo liner Calpean Star, 14,232 tons, staged a sit-down strike aboard the ship at Liverpool yesterday. Between the decks, an albatross, bird of ill omen to seafarers, lay dead in its cage.

The crew complained of misfortunes during the voyage. The albatross, captured in Bird Island, South Georgia, was being taken to a zoo in Germany.

(July 7)

LIBERACE GETS £8,000 DAMAGES

Daily Telegraph Reporter

In an unremarkably sober suit, Liberace listened without expression in the High Court yesterday afternoon as he heard the jury decide his libel case against the Daily Mirror and Mr. William Connor (Cassandra), and award hin £8,000 damages. A stay of execution was granted pending an appeal.

The damages were awarded over an article published in the Daily Mirror of Sept. 26. 1956. Daily Mirror Newspapers Ltd. and Mr. Connor were given judgment, with costs, in respect of a second article published on Oct. 18, 1956.

Mr. Justice Salmon, who said he had received that morning a "sinister" letter which he intended to send to the Director of Public Prosecutions, put five questions to the jury. These were the questions and the answers given:

1- *Do the words complained of in the defendants publication of Sept 26, 1956, in the ordinary and natural meaning mean that the plaintiff is a homosexual?- Yes.*

2 - *Without this meaning are the words complained of*

(A) True in so far as they are statements of fact?- No.

(B) Fair comment in so far as they are expressions of opinion? -No

3 - *Damages, if any for the publication of Sept. 26.1956? - £8,000*

If the answers to Questions 1 and 2 are in favour of the plaintiff, how much of the damages are attributable to the imputation of homosexuality? - £2,000

4 - *Were the words in the defendants' publication of Oct 18, 1956 fair comment? - Case not proved*

5 - *Damages in respect of publication? - No answer.*

PHONE CALL TO "MOM"

Hand-clapping Crowds

After fighting his way through hand-clapping back-slapping crowds outside the Law Courts, Liberace hurried to his hotel and booked a long distance call to America. He wanted to tell "Mom" the result.

(June 18)

HIRE-PURCHASE DEBT RECORD

YEAR'S RISE £260M.

By Our City Staff

Britain's hire-purchase debt rose another £37 million, or about 5 p.c. in June to a new record, according to Board of Trade estimates. At the end of the month the total was about £763 million, or £260 million higher than a year earlier.

The June rise compares with increases of £33 million in May and £27 million in April. Durable household goods accounted for about a third of the June increase and motor vehicles for probably most of the balance.

Total hire-purchase contracts for motor vehicles in July were 167,217 against 167,919 in June and 127,708 in July last year. According to Hire-Purchase Information new cars accounted for 13,675 contracts and used cars for 76,190.

In both cases the figures are slightly down on June but show a considerable rise on July last year.

(August 5)

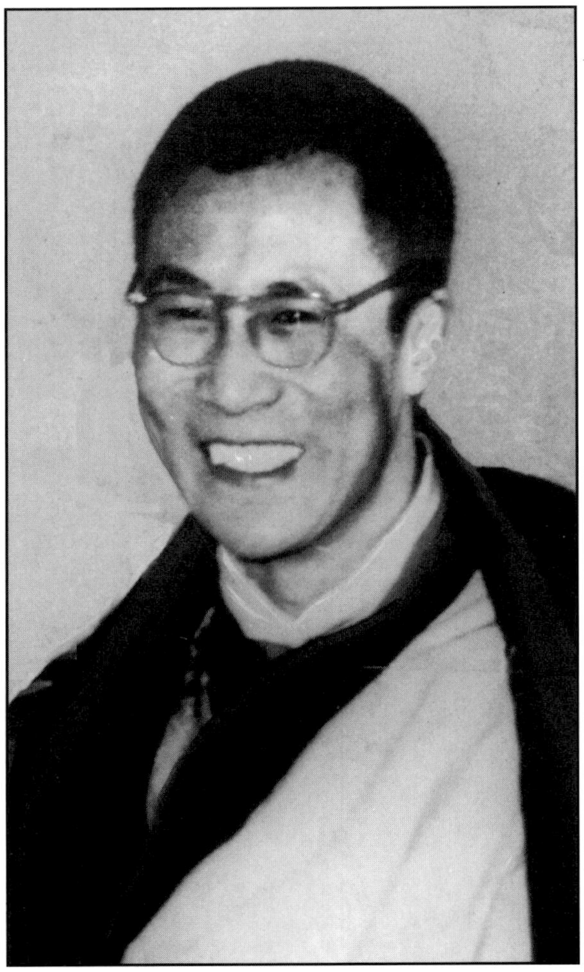

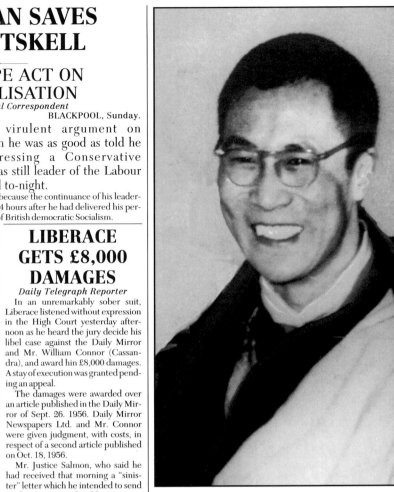

SELF-DETERMINATION OFFER TO ALGERIANS

FROM OUR OWN CORRESPONDENT

PARIS, Wednesday.

In his eagerly-awaited declaration to-night President de Gaulle solemnly offered all Algerians the right to choose the political future of their country. But before France could allow such a choice the country would have to be pacified.

"I consider it necessary that recourse to self-determination be here and now proclained," he said in his statement, which was televised and broadcast. In the name of France and the Republic he would ask Algerians what they wanted, as their "definitive political status."

He also asked all Frenchmen to endorse this choice. Speaking slowly and firmly, the President added that he would arrange the date for the constitutional vote.

THREE COURSES OPEN

Constitutional Choice

The President outlined the three possible results of a constitutional consultation in Algeria. He said it might produce:

- Secession from France:
- Complete identification with France; or
- Government of Algerians by Algerians, in association with France.

He made it clear that he thought the last possibility by far the most desirable. It would mean that the Algerian Government of Algeria would be supported by France and would exist in close union with her ecomically, educationally and in matters of defence and foreign affairs.

(September 17)

BANK ORDERS COMPUTER

To enable its West End branches to deal with a larger number of accounts, Barclays Bank has ordered a £125,000 Emidec 1100 electronic data processing system. It is scheduled for delivery by the manufacturers in mid-1961.

The bank's staff organisations have been assured that the computer's installation will not entail any foreseeable redundancy. It will enable more accounts to be kept at each branch.

(August 5)

ARCHBISHOP TO BE CYPRUS PRESIDENT

From Brian Wright, Daily Telegraph Special Correspondent

NICOSIA. Monday.

A roar from thousands of people to-night greeted the announcement that Archbishop Makarios had secured election as first President of the Republic of Cyprus. The Republic comes into being in February.

An incredibly slow count had delayed declaration of the result.

The final count was:

Archbishop Makarios	144,501
Mr. John Clerides	72,490

Mr. Clerides, a Q.C. and former member of the Legislative Assembly, was supported by the newly formed Democratic Union and the Communists. During the afternoon the Archbishop appealed for the result to be received with "calm and dignity."

But his supporters, confident of victory by early evening, began their celebrations. They arranged a mock funeral in Metaxas Square for the Democratic Union. The Square was crowded with people chanting the name of the Archbishop, letting off fireworks and sounding motor horns.

TRIBUTE TO EOKA

"Heroes of Liberty"

The vast throng moved down to the Archbishopric as the moment for the declaration drew near. Although he knew hinself to be the winner the Archbishop waited until the final count was known before he appeared on a balcony.

He paid tribute to the "heroes and martyrs" of the struggle for liberation and made particular mention of Eoka fighters and their leader, Grivas, to whom he referred by his code name of Dighenis.

(December 15)

DALAI LAMA IS SAFE IN INDIA

NEW DELHI, Thursday.

The Dalai Lama has crossed safely into India and will be granted asylum by the Indian Government, it was announced in diplomatic quarters here to-night. It was believed that Mr. Nehru, Indian Prime Minister, felt bound to give at least temporary refuge to the Tibetan leader.

Mr. Nehru to-day called a "top secret" meeting of the parliamentary group of his Congress party. It was understood that Tibet was discussed. An Indian External Affairs Ministry spokesman said no permits would be issued to correspondents to visit the North East Frontier Agency. This includes the area between South East Tibet and Assam, where the Dalai Lama was reported to have entered India.

Earlier to-day Peking radio said the Tibetan leader had entered India two days ago. Indian authorities at Tawang and news agency correspondents had gone to meet him.

Tawang, 18 miles south of the Tibetan border, is about 200 miles south of Lhasa.

The Dalai Lama, who is 25, left Lhasa on March 17, a week after the Tibetan revolt began and two days before the Communist Chinese garrison in the capital was attacked. The Chinese said he was "blatantly abducted" by the anti-Communist rebels.

This charge was repeated in today's Peking radio report, which gave no details of the Dalai Lama's mode of arrival in India, but said he was still "under duress" at the hands of the rebels.

CARAVAN ROUTE

Rebel-held Territory

For the past fortnight there has been no reliable clue to the Tibetan leader's whereabouts. The Chinese claim that he had been carried off against his will was countered by Tibetans in India, who asserted that he was fleeing to safety through a net of 50,000 Communist Chinese troops.

To reach the border at Tawang he must have crossed a 14,000ft high pass on the main caravan route from the Tibetan town of Tsona Dong. This area had been reported to be in the hands of the Khama rebels.

(April 3)

NOBEL PEACE PRIZE FOR BRITISH M.P.

From our own Correspondent

OSLO, Thursday.

The British Labour M.P., Mr. P.J. Noel-Baker, Derby South, has been awarded this year's Nobel Peace Prize, the Nobel Committee of the Norwegian Parliament announced to-day, Mr. Noel-Baker is 70.

The announcement described him as the "British politician and author of books on disarmament and the League of Nations." The prize consists of a cheque for about £15,300, a gold medal and an illuminated address.

Mr. Noel-Baker has informed the committee he will come to Oslo for the presentation ceremony. This will take place at the University on Dec. 10, the anniversary of the death of the founder, Alfred Nobel.

NO REASON GIVEN

According to custom the committee gave no reason for the award. The committee chairman usually explains the reason at the presentation ceremony.

Son of a Canadian-born Quaker and holder of several Ministerial posts in the post-war Labour Government, Mr. Noel-Baker is the eighth Briton to receive the prize. The last one was Mr. Lester Pearson, former Canadian Secretary of State for External Affairs.

(November 6)

DUTY-FREE LIQUOR AT TWO AIRPORTS

FOREIGN FLLGHTS

Daily Telegraph Reporter

Duty-Free bottles of wines and spirits will soon be on sale to travellers leaving Prestwick and Renfrew Airports for overseas. The drinks can only be delivered as passengers board their aircraft.

Customs and Excise approval has been given to Mr. Walter Harris, a Glasgow businessman, He already has shops at Prestwick, Renfrew and London Airports where tourists can buy a wide range of export goods free of purchase tax.

An application for similar drinks facilities from London Airport, with the biggest tally of overseas air departures, is inevitable. Such a service has been commonplace for years in many international airports.

WHISKY AT 21S A BOTTLE

In the overseas-bound and transit lounges at Prestwick, Britain's second biggest point of air departure and the departure lounge at Renfrew, Glasgow's airport, passengers with foreign destinations will be able to buy a bottle of whisky for 21s and sometimes less.

Mr. Harris has had to satisfy the Ministry of Aviation and the Customs and Excise about the "security" aspect of his scheme. The premises on which the sales are made and the liquor stored have to be scrutinised to make sure that no duty-free stocks reach the public at home.

SPECIALLY MARKED

A Customs and Excise official said: "These packaged bottles, specially marked, must be handed to the passenger as he boards the aircraft and are marked 'not for consumption on the voyage.'

"They must be handed to him at the foot of the steps to the aircraft, not in any through-the-Customs or transit lounge where he may be resting or where he may have ordered the liquor or paid for it."

At many of the big international airports abroad, in a passengers lounge where no visitors can officially gain access, air travellers, who have passed through Customs, find shops where they can spend to their hearts' content in any currency on local liquor and other products. They can often buy whisky and other British products at a personal discount to bring home as gifts.

In Britain, similar possibilities of earning foreign tourist currency are limited by the premises where the goods concerned can be shown, stored and secured against reaching an illicit home trade.

(November 18)

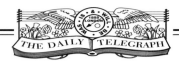

WAS · IS · & · WILL BE
1855 LONDON
THE DAILY TELEGRAPH

AND
MORNING POST
DAILY TELEGRAPH - - - JUNE 29, 1855
MORNING POST - - - NOVEMBER 2, 1772
[Amalgamated October 1, 1937]

135 FLEET STREET, LONDON, E.C.4.
TELEPHONE: FLEET STREET 4242

BORROWING AND SPENDING

Not getting and spending, but borrowing and spending: many people might think that this would be Wordsworth's view of the modern way of laying ourselves waste - and a worse one at that. Indeed, by themselves, some of the figures for the debts that people have been incurring can be made to look like a regular profligate's progress. During the 12 months up to the end of June, £270m. has been borrowed for hire purchase, more than half as much again as the total debt a year ago. Over roughly the same period the banks have lent an extra £160m. on personal and professional accounts, again increasing the total debt by a half. It can even be represented - and sometimes is - that the Government is the worst offender of all.

These fears cannot be dismissed out of hand. When borrowing becomes so much part of everyday life, some individuals can only too easily commit themselves too far. But the kind of figures given above present a picture which is both partial and incomplete. As many people must know, hire purchase debt here is not nearly so extensive as it is in some other countries, notably the United States. What is more important, the rise in borrowing during the past 12 months has been accompanied by an equally spectacular increase in the willingness to save. If anything, savings have been growing the faster. Since April, for example, savings through the National Savings movement have been rising at an annual rate nearly £250m. *above* that of the same time in 1958.

To organise this simultaneous increase in savings and in borrowing, and to match the amounts, is the essential object of the Government's monetary management. The right rate of interest plays a part; probably much more important is the stability of prices. Too much saving can contribute to the kind of disaster we experienced before the war.

Too much borrowing ensures inflation. By borrowing out of saving comes, not waste, but a full use of a country's resources.

(August 5)

CRIME IN LONDON

London's "crime sheet," presented yesterday by the Commissioner of Police, is the longest and blackest on record. The number of indictable offences rose last year by no less than one-fifth, and every class of serious crime shared in the increase. There were more crimes of violence, more robberies, and increases in housebreaking and burglary in every month of the year. A striking index of what this means in terms of merely material loss is that nearly £8m. worth of property was stolen. The fact that only one-third of it was recovered, if not necessarily a fair measure of police efficiency, does indicate the degree to which criminals may conclude that "crime pays."

But it is in human terms that the record is most disquieting. As might be expected, more people of every age-group were arrested, but once again the most serious increase of crime has been among young. Why is it that so large a proportion of these operate in gangs? Possibly there may be some significance in the parallel growth of what the Commissioner calls "vicious hooliganism" and the spread of the milk and coffee bar as a national institution. Everyone must have noticed how these harmless institutions are more likely to be beset by young thugs than are the old-fashioned pubs. This, however, is only a minor puzzle within the baffling problem of why crime continued to increase while poverty - once almost universally adduced as its chief cause - has almost disappeared. Nor, apparently, have "progressive" methods of dealing with the criminal done anything to stop him from pursuing his course, and others from following.

(July 23)

GRIVAS GIVES IN

Col. Grivas's last leaflet puts it beyond doubt that he supports the London agreement on Cyprus, and Archbishop Makarios's subscription to it. This is the end of Eoka. It will also be a great relief to the minds of all three Governments which initialled the London agreement, and to that of Sir Hugh Foot, whose responsibilities as Governor have not yet ended. Until yesterday the terrorist leader had not declared himself. Murder might have continued, in spite of the Greek Government's wise acceptance of the solution offered at Zurich and confirmed in London.

But Col. Grivas, whose enigmatic personality has for so long excited speculation - there are still those who do not believe that he exists - seems determined to falsify historical parallels. His conscience, it appears, is calm. He has done his duty. He has decided not to take part in politics, either in Cyprus or in Greece. Instead of a paean of war he proclaims "harmony, unity and love." It might be the last speech of some silver-haired democrat, retiring to pass an honoured old age in his quiet country cottage. Within the next day or two, no doubt, we shall hear of his departure for Rhodes or for Greece. It will be the end of a blood-stained chapter, and graves in Cyprus remain to mark it.

(March 10)

CHANNEL TUNNEL

Survey work on the Channel Tunnel project, restarted in 1958, is being carried one stage further. The idea of effortless non-stop journeys to the Continent was mooted nearly a century ago. But it has still to be established whether an under-water tunnel is a practical engineering proposition. Conclusive evidence may not, however, be lacking much longer.

The results of last year's electronic soundings appear largely to substantiate what the French surveyors proposed in 1873. Now, however, it is hoped by borings into the sea-bed to confirm the 1958 survey and thereby find a route to the Continent along a water-tight, fault free layer of chalk thick enough to ensure safe tunnelling. In that event, the Channel project would cease to be an engineers' pipe-dream.

That is perhaps precisely the point at which the real argument about the tunnel would seem to begin. Needless to say, circumstances and opinions have changed more than once since the project was first mooted.

Traditional objections raised by the spectre of foreign troops debouching at Dover have come to be modified. For a time and this coincided with the revival of the project in 1957 under new and powerful sponsorship - it seemed that the tunnel might well fit in with the economic strategy of a European Free Trade area. That argument no longer stands. What remains is the consideration of a vastly expensive project when our investment resources are already fully taxed. Indeed, spaceships may well appear before Channel trains.

(April 4)

PHONES IN CARS LIKELY SOON

RADIO SYSTEM

Post Office engineers are working towards providing a service which will enable motorists to telephone numbers all over Britain from their cars. Mr. Marples, Postmaster-General, is expected to make a statement on the scheme to Parliament at the first opportunity.

The initial area of the scheme will probably be bounded by Liverpool, Manchester and Preston. Communication will be by very high frequency radio and motorists will probably rent telephones in the way ordinary instruments are rented.

(August 28)

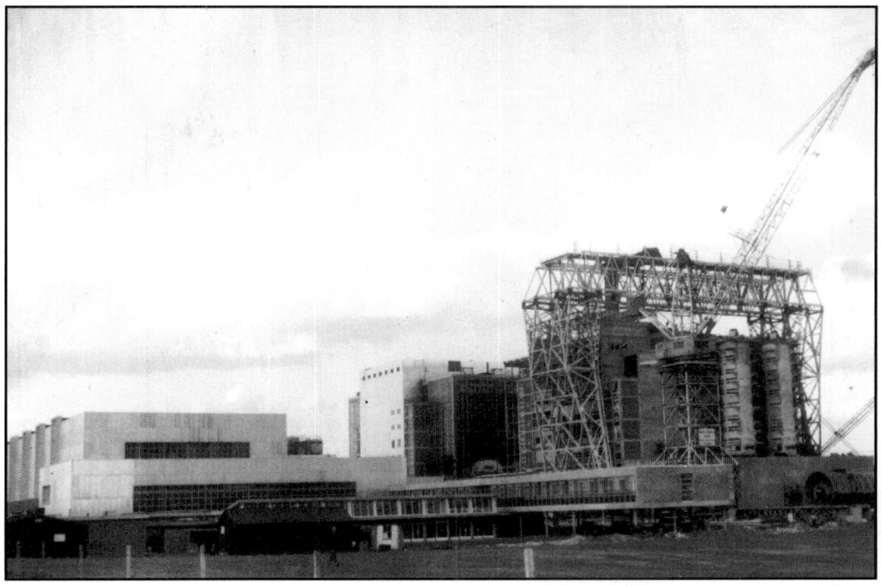

BRADWELL NUCLEAR POWER STATION

'DEPLORABLE BUILDING STANDARDS'

Concern over the "deplorably low standards" of many new buildings and the threat to the countryside of projects such as nuclear power stations was voiced by the Royal Fine Art Commission in its 16th annual report, published yesterday.

The report said that the building of nuclear power stations in practice meant building on what remained of unspoiled coastline. With the growth of industrial development there would be fewer areas of unspoilt natural beauty and it was therefore "fair to ask that the authorities should take the greatest care before siting nuclear power stations in them.

Legislation to create green belts and build new towns did not seem to have checked the spread of the suburbs into the country. Extensive redevelopment on the centre of cities seemed to be chiefly concentrated on new office and commercial buildings in small central areas.

In the past many a striking architectural conception had arisen from the ingenuity and daring of an architect overcoming difficulties. "To-day, it seems to us, the dominating consideration in the instructions given to the architect is all too often simply the desire for the largest area of lettable floor space consistent with planning procedure in small and restricted sites.

"This is not the way to produce fine urban architecture. Much of the drabness and mediocrity of many buildings put up in the centre of big cities spring from the restricted site and opportunities given to the architect."

The Commission thought redevelopment should depend on comprehensive planning of far larger areas than were usually the subject of present schemes. In most cities fair-sized inner rings of property, more or less obsolete, could be more intensively developed. This would make it possible to loosen the stanglehold on the present central areas and might at the same time provide a new pattern for urban living.

"LITTLE GUIDANCE"

Master-plan Needed

The need for concentrating very large administrative staffs in central areas was often greatly exaggerated partly due to "a mistaken sense of prestige."

"It is not enough to invite private developers to submit their own schemes with little guidance from the planning authority and then to accept the highest bid, whatever architecture may happen to have been included. Without such a master-plan the outlook for London and other large cities is indeed a poor one."

The Commission re-affirmed its opposition to high buildings on the fringes of city parks. Residential town squares should also be protected from the intrusion of giant blocks of flats or offices.

The report stated that the Commission saw something like 100 designs for new buildings annually. Only a very small proportion of designs were submitted to them.

Many comparatively small building schemes were still being carried out without the help of qualified architects. "much of it of a deplorably low standard. We have no doubt that the measure of architectural control exercised by the planning authorities must continue."

In civic building, competitions should be more widely used.

MOTORWAY DESIGN

Landscape Architect

Other points from the report include:

Motorways: The Commission doubted whether the high standard of engineering would be matched by skill in fitting the new roads into the landscape. It strongly urged that a landscape architect be appointed to work closely from the outset with the engineers.

(December 19)

LONDON DAY BY DAY

The Queen's Decision on Lord Alexander's O.M. Jane and John Still Most Popular Names.

No award in the whole Honours List is likely to give such wide spread pleasure as Lord Alexander's appointment to the Order of Merit.

In recent months the dust raised by the squabbles of more junior field marshals has tended to obscure his name. It now emerges with greater honour than ever.

The London Gazette gives no indication of whether Lord Alexander will receive the military or the civil insignia of the order. The former has two gold swords between the arms of the cross.

Since the order was founded in 1902 I can think of no other member whose award might have been for either. As a soldier he was Supreme Allied Commander in the Mediterranean. Then he won civil fame as Governor-general of Canada.

The decision rests with the Queen and will probably not be known until the Field Marshal goes to the Palace after her return from Sandringham.

Kokoschka, Etc.

Among the recognition of the arts, I dare say that Oskar Kokoschka's name will puzzle a good many to whom he is not even a name.

This Czech painter acquired British nationality after fleeing to England in 1938. In Central Europe he ranks among the greatest of contemporary artists. Making him a C.B.E. is an imaginative gesture.

Alec Guinness's knighthood, Sir Kenneth Clark's C.H. and Rebecca West's D.B.E. are self-explanatory, but one of the O.B.E.s deserves a reference.

This is Tom Goff, the harpsichord maker, whose fine craftsmanship I have

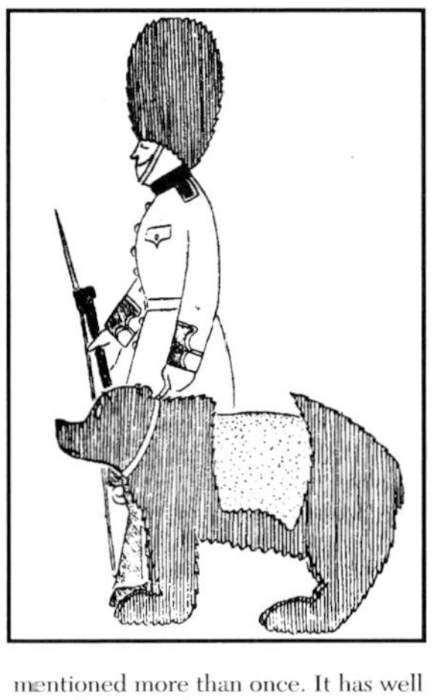

mentioned more than once. It has well earned its reward.

Lucullus /Ascendant

Yesterday's annual lunch in London of the Royal Society of Health, I felt, placed its hosts in something of a dilemma.

There was manifestly a desire to do honour to the Minister of Health, Mr. Derek Walker-Smith, the principal guest, and to provide a lunch worthy of the occasion.

There was also, I supposed, a need to recognise the Society's prime objective-the promotion of health and to provide the sort of lunch which might widely be regarded as the exemplar of meals for ensuring *mens sana in corpore sano.*

Tens of thousands of very heavy mid-day feeders will learn with pleasure that our menu included hare soup, lobster paté, roast duck and a chestnut sweet, all promoted by a succession of full-bodied wines.

Eton's Film Award

I hear that the British Film Institute has made a special award to the Eton College Film Unit for its production entitled "Manhunt."

A master, Mr Giles St. Aubyn, supervises the unit. But much of the technical work and all the acting parts are undertaken by boys.

The script of "Manhunt" was written by Tristam Powell when a boy at Eton two years ago. It is based on part of "A Question of Upbringing," the novel written by his father, Anthony Powell.

Nothing to Fear in W.I.

I was surprised to hear at a lunch Hedges and Butler gave yesterday that many people are afraid to ask in Regent Street for a single bottle of wine, particularly if it costs less than 10s.

This is rather hard on reputable wine merchants who are doing their best to unearth good wines at a moderate price. Such as the 1958 Muscadet, Château de la Bijdière, served yesterday with the *moules gratinées.* Its price is 8s. 9d.

Mr Thavenot, the firm's managing director, was put on to this crisp Loire wine when he was in Bordeaux and has shipped between 20 and 30 hogsheads.

Wine-drinkers now beginning to stock up for Christmas have a choice of at least 40 wines under 10s, including a Chilean import which is one of the few remaining from pre-phylloxera vines.

Poet's Workshop

For the centenary of the most famous of all translations - barring the English title - "The Romance of the Rubaiyat" enables us to appreciate the infinite pains taken by Edward Fitz Gerald over his masterpiece.

Prof. Arberry's book shows us how Edward Cowell, who was FitzGerald's Persian teacher, helped his pupil. It was Cowell who, as the Professor says, elucidated a passage which led to the most famous stanza of the Rubaiyat:

Here with a Loaf of Bead
beneath the Bough,
A Flask of Wine; a Book of
Verse - and Thou
Beside me singing in the
Wilderness-
And Wilderness is Paradise enow.

It all turned on a difficult phrase, "tungi mai-yi la'l." Tung means a bottle of wine, Cowell declared, and from that hint the stanza grew.

Names - 1958

My annual counting of the names appearing in The Daily Telegraph birth notices - the largest collection of any national newspaper - again shows John (496) and Jane (509) as the most popular. John is head of the list for the fifth year running and Jane for the fourth.

Second and third in the girls' list are again Elizabeth (327) and Mary (325). Richard (290) takes David's (289) place as second by a very short head.

Some of the erstwhile popular manes have almost disappeared. Isobel (2), Olive (2), Sylvia (3), Irene (5), Muriel (6), Jean (27), Adam (16), Leonard (4), and Malcolm (18) are all sparsely represented.

PETERBOROUGH

IT'S BACK TO PRE-SACK DAYS

LOVELY FABRICS: CONE SKIRTS

By Winefride Jackson

As I sit on my little gold chair in the fashion salons I keep rubbing my eyes, not only to keep awake after nearly four weeks of looking at nearly 10,000 garments, but at the brilliantly simple idea of bringing back the female shape.

First Italy did it; then Paris; now London.

They say that simplicity is the essence of genius. In that case, designers can pat themselves on the back this season. They are greater than they think.

The last laugh, however, is with women who have clung to their pre-sack clothes. They can go right on wearing them, unless they are tempted by the new fabrics.

For the fabrics this season are very lovely, from the new open-weave wools to gossamer silks and chiffons.

A new trend is to use pastel leather belts with silk and chiffon summer dresses. Owen Hyde Clarke at Worth shapes them to follow the line of intricately draped skirts accentuating the curve of waist and hips.

The whole theme of this collection is intricate drapery that can only be done with infinite care.

Short Jackets

Suit and dress jackets are short, but not absurdly so. They usually reach to the hipbone. For summer, the dress bodice of a two-piece is frequently embroidered, making it suitable for cocktail or dinner wear.

John Cavanagh's collarless cardigan suits with softly broadened shoulders are some of the most effortless and elegant I have seen, even in Paris, in pastel hopsack weave wools, including a very springlike cowslip yellow. Just to look at them makes one feel that winter is over.

As a change from "walking pleats," slim skirts flare to a gentle width at the hem in a slim cone.

One might have been at the Chelsea Flower Show, so great was the number of life-size floral printed silks in vivid colours for cocktail and evening dresses. Always the skirts were full, with the fullness invariably drawn through and over the waistline to the back.

On Cavanagh's very décolleté grand evening dresses, I liked the way he bowed to modesty with a slit over-bodice that can best be described as "bust blinkers."

Easy to Wear

"Restful elegance" was the keynote of the Lachasse collection. In other words no restriction of movement with full flaring skirt, to coats, easy-waisted jackets and slim skirts with walking room afforded by back pleating.

Slim town dresses are topped with short matador cape-jackets or coats lined with brilliantly - coloured screen - printed silks to match the dress. Pleating is used from shoulder to hem on leather belted cocktail dresses and Grecian drapery adds a long flowing line to evening dresses.

"Normal and formal," says Norman Hartnell of his collection. This is an under-statement of his very lovely clothes in which the fabrics are always shown to the full advantage.

With tongue very much in cheek he named an eye-catching blue wool ensemble "I Want to Be Alone." Not for long I would say.

The basic cardigan suit (there are quite a number in the collection) was topped by a loose collarless ⅞ths coat and over this a beaver-lined blue wool stole. When the coat is removed the stole is worn with the suit, fur side uppermost, one of the most practical and attractive ideas I have seen at any collection.

At first, large Quaker collars on afternoon dresses seem unpractical for wear under a coat until you see that the accompanying coat is collarless, and the dress collar worn outside.

Norman Hartnell also turned his attention to something new in mink - three shades, from blonde to dark brown, in one stole.

Navy blue with white accessories is the answer to a spring ensemble if you are afraid of the now popular greens and apricot. Hartnell had many navy blue models in silk, lace and, for late day, white spotted navy net.

Perhaps because he has been immersed in Royal Tour clothes (last touches were still being put to those for the Duchess of Kent's visit to South America), we were treated to a galaxy with embroidery and given their final dignity with mannequins wearing a tiara.

(February 5)

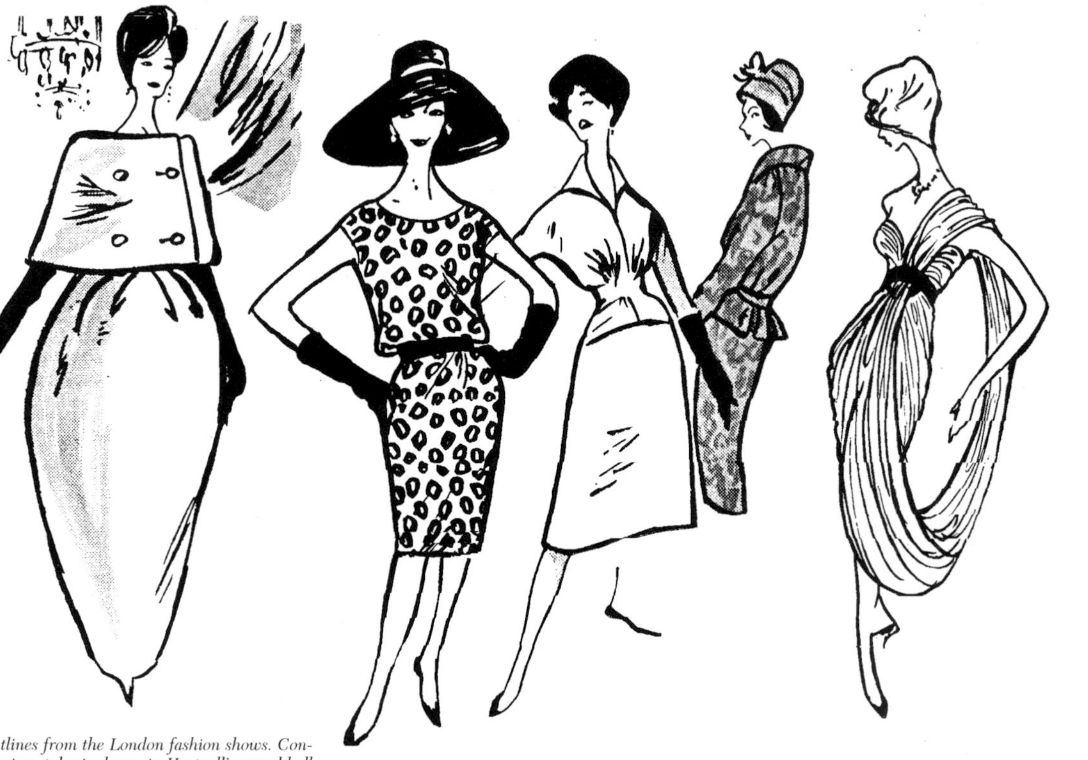

More outlines from the London fashion shows. Contrast in evening styles is shown in Hartnell's grand ball dress silhouette with melon-shaped bouffant skirt (note the enormous shoulder cape instead of a stole) on left, with the Grecian drapery used by Worth on far right. The printed dress with bolero front and the suit with frilled back peplum are from John Cavanagh. Centre sketch shows the easy and shapely silhouette by Lachasse.

Sketched by Hartland

28s 1d A HEAD WEEKLY SPENT ON FOOD FOR THE HOME

Average domestic food expenditure in 1957 was 28s 1d a head each week, compared with 27s 3d in 1956, says the report for 1957 of the National Food Survey Committee. It is published to-day. The rise of 10d, or three per cent, was the smallest annual increase recorded by the survey since 1950.

Liquid milk accounted for 3¼d of the increase and bread for 2¾d - in each case wholly because of higher prices. Beef and veal contributed 2¼d and fresh fruit 1½d, partly because of increased purchases.

The only change in expenditure exceeding a penny was a fall of 2d on eggs. This was due to lower prices.

This relatively small annual gain marked a significant slowing down from the steady gain recorded between 1953 and 1956.

Developments in technology and distribution, a widening range of new foods and new packaging methods all contributed to changes in relative prices of different foods and consumer preference.

Since 1955 there had been some movement in demand from such staple commodities as bread, flour, potatoes, fresh fish, bacon, pork, mutton and preserves to what the report describes as "convenience" foods, requiring less time and labour in preparation.

But in spite of these developments the continued stability of British spending habits between broad groups of commodities was evidenced by the fact that in the autumn and winter quarters from October, 1957, to March, 1958 18 per cent of the total domestic expenditure on food was devoted to milk, cheese and eggs, 32 per cent to meat and fish, 16 per cent, to fruit and vegetables, 26 per cent to cereals, fats, sugar and preserves and eight per cent to all other foods. This compared with 18, 30,14, 27 and 11 per cent respectively for the corresponding period in 1936-37

In a chapter on household diets of social classes, the report says that all income groups spent more per head on food than in 1956, with the exception of the under £7 a week group (without other earners in the family).

(Domestic Food Consumption and Expenditure 1957, Annual Report of National Food Survey Committee Stationery Office 8s 6d.)

(August 28)

DIOR SKIRT TO BE ABOVE KNEE

Yves St. Laurent, the young designer for the house of Dior said to-day, 24 hours before his fashions are presented, that they will bring a new "new look" which will make women show their kneecap. Not since the late Christian Dior dropped skirts to near the ankle in 1947 has such a drastic change been made.

Almost every other Paris dressmaker who has shown his fashions so far has favoured the longer skirt. "skirts will be above the kneecap," said M. St. Laurent.

"The waist will be at its place and the bust will be honoured." The same applied to the hips. Shoulders would be narrow and collars small. – B.U.P.

(July 3)

WHEN THE FAMILY GROWS, THIS HOUSE GROWS, TOO

An experimental house just built and furnished at Hampton Hill, near Kingston, is so designed that when the family grows, the house grows too. It will cost around £4,000.

The ground floor plan comprises the living-room, dining room, kitchen, bathroom and two bedrooms - a complete house on a single floor. Upstairs, the first floor is boarded and ready to expand into the completed house - another two bedrooms, bathroom and a family recreation room.

A large family can have a teenagers' or hobbies room on the first floor, leaving the downstairs living-room for more formal use and furnishing, OR

A middle-aged couple who prefer to live on one floor will be able to accommodate a married son or daughter upstairs, OR

The newly-married couple who can't afford the initial outlay for a large house can move in and convert the top floor later.

(September 22)

ALLERGY-FREE STORE

New York has the first allergy-free store to help clients suffering from hay-fever, asthma etc. Fitted with micronaire which purifies the air, it is claimed that New York's one million hay fever sufferers will find relief there for the next six weeks, until the first frost.

(June 15)

THE ROAD TO THE RIVER KWAI

Holiday travel may not yet reach as far as the River Kwai, but Princess Alexandra is due to go there when she visits the war graves at Kanchanaburi during her visit to Siam on her way home from Australia.

Many people make the car trip to Kanchanaburi, some to see the war graves and others to search for the famous bridge on the River Kwai. It is only 92 miles from Bangkok and the excellent road is full of interest.

At Nakorn Prathom, the first town of any importance, I wandered around the ancient wat (temple) and admired the great Cedt, a large and impressive pagoda-like structure. A few miles farther on is the turning off for Hua Hin, where the Siamese Royal family spend the hot months. Soon after this junction the road starts to run parallel to the River Kwai, and here the surrounding country is like parkland, filled with fruit trees, vegetables and various crops.

I passed many villages along this tree-lined section of the road, each with its own wat and school. I wondered where all the small children could possibly live.

Markets along the road were selling pineapples, bananas and other fruits very cheaply. I turned off the main road down a lane which led to the river. As I was enjoying my fruit in a cool spot, a few peasants wandered up. First they stood a little distance away, curious but friendly.

Then they advanced a few steps nearer. Neither of us new the other's language, but we seemed to be able to say a lot with gestures.

I left them regretfully to hurry on to Kanchanaburi. I by-passed the town and drove straight to the cemetery, at whose gates the metalled road ends abruptly. It is a wide expanse of ground, peaceful and well-kept. Each grave is marked with a white cross on which are recorded the soldier's name, date of birth and death, and his regiment.

There are British, Australian, New Zealand and Dutch soldiers buried here; and the charming and knowlegeable superintendent pointed out one large mausoleum where Chinese who worked on the Siam "Death Valley" were buried after dying during an epidemic.

With its roses, jasmin, gardenias and exotic tropical plants, the cemetery is a really beautiful place. Relatives and friends of those who lie here can rest assured that it is a fitting memorial.

(June 15)

DR. LEAKEY SHOWS SKULL OF 'EARLIEST KNOWN' MAN

The skull of what is claimed to be the earliest known type of man, who lived in what is now Tanganyika between 600,000 and a million years ago, was shown to a scientific audience for the first time in London last evening.

Dr. L.S. G. Leakey, Curator of the Corydon museum, Nairobi whose wife found the skull by accident on July 17 said he had since found on the same spot a tibia, or leg bone, which made possible a conjectural reconstruction of the appearance of this link between the African near-men and true man.

Zinjanthropus Boise, as Dr. Leakey christened his find, in honour of Mr. Charles Boise, the London businessman who has supported the excavations, was probably less than 5ft tall. He had practically no forehead and an astonishing long face.

He was bull-necked, but walked more completely erect than do many people to-day. His chest was thick and his collar bones enormous, but his limbs were slender. Having no weapons, he would depend for his safety on his agility and fleetness.

HALF-SIZE BRAIN

Probably he was one of a large family living beside a lake full of fish and crocodiles. It is likely he was at the stage of changing from a vegetarian to a carnivorous diet, for though he was incapable of hunting the gigantic creatures whose remains have been found on the same level, he ate smaller animals, such as frogs, rats and snakes, which he could catch with his hands.

He was probably a youth of about 18. His brain was less than half the size of modern man. His tools, of the crudest kind, were of stone brought from miles away.

After his death his family, probably a large one, left him. In later years the lake repeatedly flooded the site and sediment descending on his bones solidified into stone.

It was beneath 22ft of rock, overlaid in its turn by deposits of other material and volcanic lava that Dr. Leakey and his wife excavated his remains, his tools and the remnants of his food.

ASSEMBLED FROM 450 PIECES

The strange, dark-brown skull assembled by Dr. and Mrs. Leakey from 450 pieces, was inspected by archaeologists and anthropologists invited to it at the British Academy.

The audience marvelled at the enormous size of the palate and teeth compared with those of a present-day African. But there were no dissentient voices when Dr. Leakey gave his conclusions that this was a creature much closer to true man than any earlier discoveries.

(October 8)

YOUTHS WITH £5 A WEEK TO SPEND

DRESS MAIN ITEM

After meeting obligations to the State and parents, youths and young men between the ages of 15 and 24 have on an average about £5 a week to spend as they choose. The average young woman is left with about £3 a week.

In all, Britain's 4,200,000 young workers in this group have roughly £17 million a week to dispose of at their own discretion. These are conclusions reached in a survey of their spending habits.

It has been made by Dr. Mark Abrams, a market research specialist. The results are given in a paper "The Teenage Consumer," published by London Press Exchange.

This large sum is spent mainly on dressing up to impress others of a similar age. It is used to buy goods which "form the nexus of teenage gregariousness outside the home."

Their purchases account for at least 25 per cent of all consumer expenditure on bicycles and motor-cycles, on records and record players and the cinema and other entertainments. In confectionery, soft drinks, footwear, women's clothing, recreational and sports goods and cosmetics, they account for between 15 and 25 per cent of the national total.

WORKING CLASS MARKET

Dr. Abrams estimates that at least 647 per cent of all spending in this age group is in male hands. The market is almost entirely working class.

Sixty per cent of all young people visit the cinema once or more a week against only 13 per cent of the rest of the adult population. But the 15-24 age group watches less television.

Of all those with multi-channel sets, 67 per cent watch I.T.A. programmes for five nights a week or more. Among their elders the frequency is as high as 80 per cent.

He points out that between now and 1969 this age group will increase in Britain by 20 per cent.

(August 1)

DOMINATION OF 'MODERNS' AT ACADEMY

Daily Telegraph Reporter

The experiment of mixing the "advanced" school of art with traditional styles, begun last year at the Royal Academy Summer Exhibition, has evidently come to stay. The same method of hanging has been adopted, with lively and colourful effect at this year's Exhibition, which will be open to the public from to-morrow.

"Moderns" which, two years ago, would have been grouped together in what some critics cuttingly described as the "kitchen sink" or "horror" galleries now hang boldly throughout the exhibition. They present a series of striking contrasts. In some cases they dominate the surrounding paintings.

Sir Charles Wheeler, president of the Royal Academy, said yesterday in justification of the continuation of the experiment: "We are trying to get the best value out of each picture by showing them in contrast.

"All the great works of art over the centuries have been what may be called 'quiet' pictures. I think quiet paintings are seen to advantage alongside contrasting styles."

64 PEOPLE IN PAINTING

The traditional place of honour in Gallery III this year is occupied by A.R. Thomson's painting, "Commemorative Dinner of the Royal Air Force, Bentley Priory, 1st April, 1958."

The dinner was attended by the Queen and other members of the Royal Family. Every one of the 64 people in the painting, from the Queen to the waiters, gave a sitting to the artist. The Queen appears in several paintings, including William Roberts' "Trooping the Colour."

Directly opposite this picture is the 15ft by 10ft painting of a group of artists by John Bratby, the newly elected Associate of the Royal Academy. Mr. Bratby applied his oil direct from the tubes. In places, it is nearly an inch thick.

Sir Winston Churchill has two paintings in the exhibition this year. One, simply entitled "Fruit Study," shows a melon, apples, grapes and a peach in a table bowl. This appears in the main gallery. The other, in Gallery XI, is a sunny landscape painted from above Cannes.

(May 1)

PERRY COMO SIGNS £9m. TV CONTRACT

Perry Como, the singer, to-day signed a contract with a cheese firm under which he will receive £8,928,000 for television programmes over the next two years. It was claimed to be the largest individual fee ever paid any performer in television, on the stage or in films.

Como's personal company, Roncom Incorporated, will produce 104 weekly shows, and he will be given complete autonomy in deciding what form the shows take. The contract specifies that Como must star in 66 colour television programmes.

The television industry was keenly studying to-day many unique aspects of the contract. For instance, the sponsor has agreed to a "pension" provision which will start at the end of the two-year period and run for 10 years. Como will be paid what is described only as a "six-figure (dollar) salary" for activity "in areas unrelated to television."

"LARGE" ANNUITIES

He is also to receive stock options in the sponsor's company, a typical incentive to recruit, or retain, key executives. In case of accident, or death, Como's wife and their three children will be protected with "large" annuities for life.

The sum paid to the singer is to cover all costs of production, including guest stars, and television time. His personal income from the contract cannot be accurately estimated, Como's agent said to-day, because so many variable cost factors are involved in producing television shows.

(March 6)

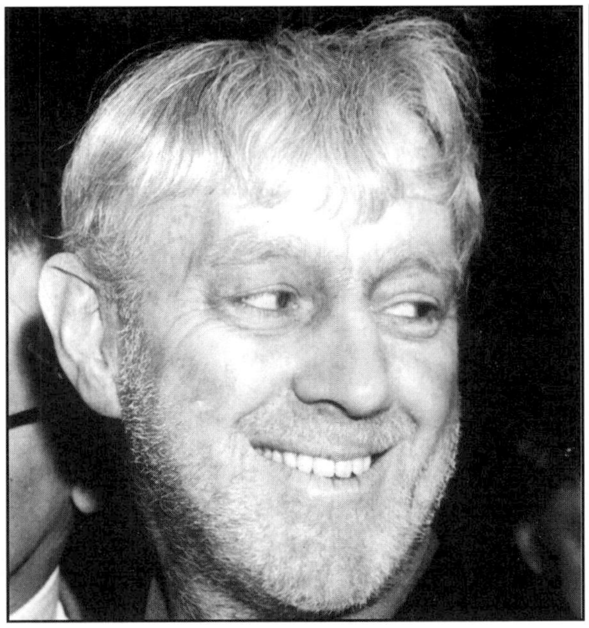

ALEC GUINNESS

SUPERB 30 min CHARIOT RACE IN 'BEN-HUR'

By Campbell Dixon

METRO-GOLDWYN-MAYER bet over £5 million on the chariot race in "Ben-Hur". With luck they should double their money.

This is not merely because the race itself is the most thrilling spectacle ever brought to the screen, but because it is also the climax to a wonderful story of its kind, magnificently told.

"Ben-Hur" is not a film for the high-brow or the militant atheist. Its elements are of the simplest, basic kind - love and hatred, courage in the face of suffering and intolerable oppression, faith rewarded by the Saviour on the Cross.

Such themes are deathless, and when the construction is as sound as Wallace's the fantastic success of the book, play and silent film is perhaps not so surprising after all. It is one of those stories, like "Les Miserables" and "A Tale of Two Cities," that will always strike a responsive chord in humanity's heart.

GIGANTIC SCALE

Many fans still remember Fred Niblo's silent version (1926). They need have no fear of anticlimax. M.G.M. have thrown into the new film famous stars, 452 players of speaking parts, 25,000 extras, colossal sets and the thrilling pageantry of sea battle and chariot race, all shown in colour on gigantic screen with stereophonic sound.

The chariot race is brutal but superb. Pilate gives the signal, nine four-horse teams race off, and then it's every man for himself, with Messala wrecking his rivals, chariots turning over, attendants dragging off the dead and injured, and the villainous Roman lashing his horses and his Jewish rival, as they round corners on one wheel and thunder neck and neck down the straight.

With the lining up of the starters, shots of the vast arena and the howling crowd and the race itself, this sequence lasts half-an-hour. It left me exhausted and limp.

Perhaps I should add that, according to the producers, no man or horse was seriously injured. I must accept their word, merely remarking that this is not the least miraculous feature of the production.

PATHOS ACHIEVED

If I have emphasised spectacle that's because "Ben-Hur" is famous for it. The fact is, however, that William Wyler, the director, has taken great trouble with atmosphere, characterisation and incident, and often achieves a moving pathos.

The dialogue - mostly, according to the director, by Christopher Fry, who is not credited on the screen - is literate and effective, in sharp contrast with that of other American ventures into antiquity.

The acting, too, makes the old version a little hammy. Charlton Heston, who looks as if he might well have lasted three years as a galley-slave, convinces you of Ben Hur's tenacity, loyalty and love of family.

Stephen Boyd gives his best performance as Messala, Jack Hawkins is a finely Roman Tribune and Hugh Griffith, Sam Jaffe and Finlay Currie do well in character roles.

(December 15)

ALEC GUINNESS BRINGS ARTIST TO LIFE

FINE COMEDY

By Campbell Dixon

"The Horse's Mouth," this year's choice for the Royal film performance before Queen Elizabeth the Queen Mother at the Empire Theatre last night, is one of the best and most intelligent comedies I have seen for years.

This should not be surprising. Alec Guinness not only plays Joyce Cary's eccentric painter, Gulley Jimson, but adapted the novel himself, and Ronald Neame is just the director to make the best of it.

All the same, there is so much cant about art, and the artist is so often presented in an atmosphere of bogus religiosity, that it is a relief to see one presented as a bit of a genius and more than a bit of a rascal.

Cary's Gulley Jimson is dirty, dishonest and abysmally poor. He borrows and sponges and never passes a telephone booth without hopefully pressing button B. He pockets anything he finds loose, and never tells the truth where a lie will serve.

ARTIST-REPROBATE

On the screen he lacks some of the book's exuberant wit - there was a deal too much of it, anyway. But the essential character is there.

Moving at a fast toddle from gaol to pub. from a "studio" in a barge to the homes of the rich he is trying to exploit, always sacrificing expediency to his fierce and mocking integrity when it comes to Art, the old reprobate springs to life. We accept the artist while we laugh at the charlatan.

Brilliant character drawing is accompanied by plenty of comic action. Having no sense of shame and only one principle - that the world owes him a living and is much behind with its payments - Jimson is never at a loss for a confidence trick.

He rings up collectors pretending to be the President of the Royal Academy; he takes possession of a flat while the owner is abroad; he pawns the furniture and with a clear conscience deducts the receipts from the £5,000 owed to him for a gigantic mural that the owner knows nothing about.

MOVING CLIMAX

He is a brilliant starter but a poor stayer. All his plans end in disasters both ludicrous and moving, and it is with mixed emotions that we part from him, in a scene devised for the film, floating down the Thames on a barge he leaves destiny to steer.

The role is rich in opportunities, and Alec Guinness takes them all. Supporting parts are well played by Kay Walsh, Renee Houston, Mike Morgan, Ernest Thesiger, Robert Coote, Arthur Macrae, Veronica Turleigh, Michael Gough, Reginald Beckwith and a number of others. John Bratby supplied the paintings.

"The Horse's Mouth" begins its public run at the Gaumont, Haymarket, to-day.

(February 5)

Recent Fiction

WHY ORCHIDS FOR LOLITA?

Lolita. By Vladimir Nabokov.
(Weidenfeld & Nicolson, 21s)

Henderson the Rain King. By Saul Bellow.
(Weidenfeld & Nicolson. 16s)

Memento Mori. By Muriel Spark.
(Magmillan, 15s)

Absolute Beginners. By Colin MacInnes.
(MacGibbon & Kee. 15s)

Miguel Street. By V.S. Naipaul.
(Deutsch. 15s)

Heralded by several years' free gossip-column publicity, damned unseen by censorious moralists, and carrying a sheaf of tributes from high-minded admirers such as Graham Greene, Taylor Caldwell and James M. Cain, "Lolita" at last makes her bow before an English audience. I can only report that at least one first-nighter all but fell asleep from sheer stupefied boredom.

I find the furore this novel has generated quite inexplicable. An English critic has praised it for a style "of startling beauty and originality"; in fact it is a mannered piece of *fin de siècle* flummery - coy, tedious and over-decorated. An American critic, Prof. Lionel Trilling, says it is about love: in fact it is the record of a devouring and obsessional perversion, meaningless outside its physical context.

For the benefit of such readers as still have no knowledge of the somewhat rudimentary plot, a few details may be in order. The whole novel is concerned with the compulsive pursuit of a 12-year-old "nymphet" (to use the author's own inimitable term) by the narrator, Humbert, an Americanised European intellectual. Like anyone with an overwhelming obsession, poor skittish Humbert is the most pulverising bore.

Nothing really exists for this drooling egghead apart from Lolita. He rhapsodises over her bodily charms like a third-rate Baudelaire. In meticulous detail and at inordinate length he chronicles their erotic progress together from motel to motel. He knows perfectly well she is a boring, vapid little slouch, yet he still attempts, with references to Petrarch and Dante, to convince the reader (if not himself) that his perverted itch is really true love after all.

"Sex", Humbert pronounces at one point, "is but the ancilla of art." Despite his Yellow Book aestheticism, one can't help feeling he got it the wrong way round. It is for sexual gratification, not love, that Humbert, poor dear, marries Lolita's mother and all but murders her, it is for motives of sexual jealousy that he actually shoots the playwright who cuts him out with the wretched nymphet herself.

Anyone who proclaims this novel a splendid satire on American education, holiday camps, &c., is being a little disingenuous, to say the least of it. The novel records, clinically, the progress of a distasteful but by no means uncommon perversion: there will always be Lolitas as well as Humberts. Its very accuracy makes for tedium: it is dull rather than urticant. But let us hear no more high flown stuff about Mr. Nabokov having written a great work of art. His theme is unlikely to corrupt; his manner almost certain to anaesthetise.

P.G.

(November 6)

Rippling with energy, sizzling with invention; comic as Quixote, pathetic as man, mutable as life: it is difficult to avoid superlatives about **"Henderson the Rain King."** But I shall try.

Saul Bellow, who wrote "The Adventures of Augie March" and became the pet of the American intellectuals, stacks and packs his novels, loads every rift with ore. So that Henderson is not just an eccentric American who has inherited three million dollars, a tough cookie, a drunken rogue elephant too big and too *désorienté* for society to contain.

Henderson is what Americans call "the mostest." He is all heroes to all readers - or tries to be - and he is an allegory of man. In fact he is too much to be true. I suspect Mr. Bellow's literary exuberance carried him away. I wonder, even, whether this is quite the novel he meant to write, for deep down there is an uneasy, obsessive, almost maniacal note. These are among the reasons why "Henderson the Rain King", despite its constant brilliance, is not a great novel.

K.Y.

(May 29)

★ ★ ★

Youth in our time gets rather more than its fair share of fictional attention: and many readers will be pleased to know that not one of "Memento Mori's" main characters, from Dame Lettie to the "grannies" of the geriatric ward is under 65; even the envious, malign, blackmailing housekeeper, Mrs. Pettigrew, who is still capable of attracting the spry, 80-year-old Godfrey, is in her seventies.

Muriel Spark's novel is, in fact, a bizarre, half-Gothic study in gerontology, a sort of contemporary Dance of Death executed to the intermittent ringing of the telephone and the voice which says: "Remember you must die."

But the frivolities of old age as well as its creaking, physical horrors are part of the picture; and Miss Spark offers a remarkable collection of characters - Charmian, the novelist enjoying a period revival: the aged sociologist assembling data about the aged; the poet with his passion for examining the cremated ashes of his former mistress.

"Memento Mori" is perhaps a *tour de force*, but it is unforgettable.

K.Y.

(March 20

★ ★ ★

The wild-life in "Absolute Beginners," by Colin MacInnes, is home-bred. The cubs are teenagers in London - not of the "Ted" class exactly, but not models of decorum from a "square's" point of view. This spokesman, himself on the brink of adulthood, looks back wistfully to the days:

"when the kids discovered that, for the first time since centuries of king-dom-come, they'd money, which hitherto had always been denied to us at the best time in life to use it ... and also before the newspapers and telly got hold of this teenage fable and prostituted it..."

He is a photographer ("street, holiday, park, studio, artistic poses and from time to time, when I can find a client, pornographic") hovering on the fringe of and sometimes engaged in a miscellany of nefarious activities; a son at odds with his mother and brother but kind to his dear old dad; a wised-up-youth, concientiously tough but over anxious to prove that he has a heart. He might be more successful in retaining the interest of the readers he initially attracts if he did not depend upon their being "cool cats" who are "hep" enough to "dig" him all through. As it is, he may give them, the feeling that they are being jostled about in a frowsty and hostile crowd from which they must slip away at the earliest opportunity.

It will be a pity if they do, because this novel, which ends with a racial riot at Notting Hill, offers every now and then as true a picture of superannuated juvenile existential expressionists as we are likely to get. If only we could be sure that we shall get no more!

D.G.

(September 4)

★ ★ ★

From Cape Town to Port of Spain, Trinidad, where V.S. Naipaul is still doing a brisk trade showing us how quaint, funny and lovable are what Gwyn Thomas would call the voters up and down **"Miguel Street."** This time he has abandoned continuous narrative altogether (it was never his strongest suit), and produced a series of loosely linked sketches, which still aren't quite real short stories. Like his own Mr. Popo, the carpenter, Mr. Naipaul might well retort: "Ha, boy! That's the question. I making the thing without a name."

P.G.

(August 8)

A PROMISING DRAMATIST IN THE MAKING

By W.A. Darlington

It is a highly unusual feat for any dramatist under 30 to write a successful play. It is a practically unprecedented achievement for anybody under 20 to write a play worth professional production, let alone one worth a transfer to the West End after a try-out elsewhere.

Let us therefore be in no doubt at all that when the curtain fell last night at Wyndham's after the presentation of Shelagh Delaney's "A Taste Of Honey," in the Theatre Workshop production from Stratford, a remarkable page of theatre history had been written.

It may also turn out in the future that a notable new dramatist has been started on her career; but to be sure of that we shall have to have more evidence than this one play can provide.

Meanwhile, we have to acclaim a remarkable piece of "slice of life" recording. The characters are transferred from the dingy purlieus of Salford to the stage with startling vitality.

No. Miss Delaney is not yet a dramatist, but I think she will be, for she shows a theatre sense upon which Joan Littlewood has seized in her swift and amusingly stylised production.

(February 11)

MME. CALLAS IS GIVEN OVATION

Maria Callas, the operatic soprano, made her first impact on a British concert audience at the Royal Festival Hall last night. She was given a tremendous reception and took 12 curtain calls at the end of her performance.

The performance started 12 minutes late. This delay was put down to the fact that the house was full to capacity and it took some time for the audience to assemble.

The dramatic highlight of the first part of the programme came when Mme. Callas as Ophelia in the aria from Ambroise Thomas's "Hamlet" thrust back the shoulder straps of her dress in a fine frenzy. She wore a gown of sage green silk with a sash and draperies of deep pink and pale blue satin.

(September 24)

MR. ONASSIS IN PARIS

From Our Own Correspondent

PARIS, Wednesday.

Mr. Onassis, the shipowner, flew to Paris from Nice today and disappeared from Orly Airport in a van belonging to his company before anyone had time to ask questions about his relationship with Maria Callas. Before leaving Nice he again denied rumours of a divorce from his wife. "There is nothing in it," he said.

(September 24)

THE MERMAID THEATRE OPENS

By Our Theatre Reporter

The Mermaid Theatre, a full-blooded enterprise which began as a dream of one man, Bernard Miles, many years ago, was opened by the Lord Mayor of London, Sir Harold Gillett, at Puddle Dock, Blackfriars, last night.

He described it as a "wonderful concept of enormous courage and enormous enterprise," and added "I think I can speak for the City when I say that we will do all we can to make this theatre a lasting success."

Trumpets sounded a flourish, the audience of celebrities applauded, and we were all left in no doubt that this was a moment of true theatrical history. This was the first new theatre in London for nearly 30 years, and the first in the City for nearly 300 years.

(May 8)

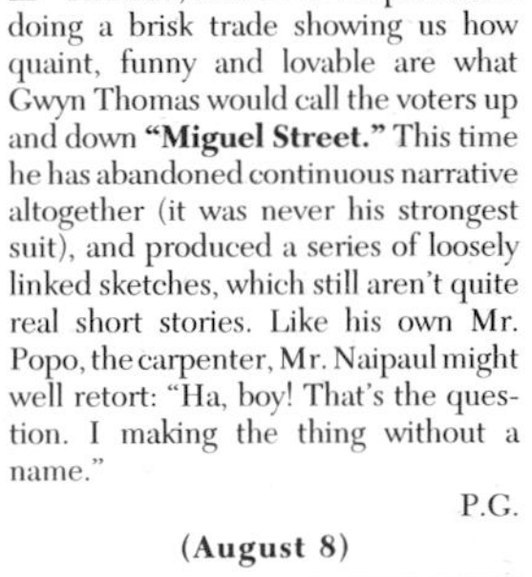

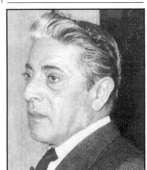

EARL OF HALIFAX

In the evening of his life the Earl of Halifax, who has just died aged 78, took so little part in public affairs that it is easy to forget his eminence in earlier years. He was actually some people's candidate for the succession to Mr. Neville Chamberlain as Prime Minister in May, 1940.

Being one of the most modest, as well as the most charming, of men, he would probably have never considered himself for such a post at such a time, unless convinced that it was his duty. It was indeed his fate to find that his counsel and actions, though always supremely conscientious, sometimes seemed singularly ill-advised.

His only unchallenged success, curiously enough, was as Ambassador to Washington during the war years. There his patent sincerity and patient dignity overcame his association in the public mind - only too truly, as the Foreign Office papers since published show - with the spirit of Munich.

Conciliation at great, though not at any cost was ingrained in his character. This led to what were considered at the time remarkable successes when he had to deal with a rather similar character in Mr. Gandhi during his five years' Viceroyalty of India. But as Foreign Secretary from 1938 to 1940 he was too good a man to deal with essentially amoral men like Hitler and his cronies.

IDEAL FAMILY LIFE

Moral Background

He was first elected to Parliament in 1910, but really did not become known outside his Yorkshire circle until he returned to Westminster in 1918 from four years' service with the Yorkshire Dragoons. Angular, gaunt, with a damaged hand enclosed in a black glove, he was a distinct and distinguished personality, with a scholastic background of Eton, Christ Church and a Fellowship of all souls, and the moral background of an ideal family life and of a father who evoked in him the deepest affection and respect.

His debut as a Minister was swift but modest. Nobody in those days - more's the pity - could really make a mark at the Board of Education or the Ministry of Agriculture. It therefore surprised everybody except his intimates when he was chosen to be Viceroy of India in 1926.

It was a most critical moment. As has not been unknown on a smaller scale elsewhere, the always latent conflict between the colonial Power and local nationalist aspirations had reached what seemed to be an impasse. A lot of nonsense has been talked on both sides about it, but it was not between "do nothings" and "give everythings." The real issues were the speed at which advance towards self-government, to which the British Government had been pledged for a generation, should take place; and whether it should take the form of provincial autonomy or something bigger.

KINDRED SPIRIT

Mr. Gandhi's Recognition

Mr. Gandhi, the mystic and idealist, who had emerged as the inventor of the policy of "peaceful non-co-operation," was in gaol for one of those deliberate breaches of the law which were part of his method. Lord Irwin (as Edward Wood had by that time been created) saw no future in cat-and-mouse strategy. He brought Mr. Gandhi out of prison, recognised in him and was recognised by him as a kindred spirit; and arranged a Round Table Conference in London, from which emerged a new Government of India Bill.

The scheme actually worked in a reasonably peaceful atmosphere for some years. Whether or not it was a good scheme, there is little doubt that it would never have been conceived or worked at all without Lord Irwin. With these laurels, as most people thought them, on his brow, he found himself on his return to British politics in the position of an Elder Statesman.

That has its disadvantages. An Elder Statesman who has become elderly on one road is expected to be able to travel equally successfully on any other - even the roughest track. In particular, it is not unknown for such a person to make a mess of foreign affairs - the late Lord Simon is one example. Halifax was another, but it must in fairness be added that Mr. Chamberlain was largely his own Foreign Secretary.

(December 24)

JOHN FOSTER DULLES

STORM-CENTRE OF AMERICAN FOREIGN POLICY

MR. JOHN FOSTER DULLES, who died yesterday aged 71, had been American Secretary of State since Mr. Eisenhower first became President. Previously, under America's bi-partisan foreign policy, he had assisted Mr. Truman as an adviser.

Wryly described on one occasion as America's "most misguided missile," he succeeded often in mystifying and exasperating his country's allies by his indecision and contradictory assertions. On the other hand, none doubted his integrity, his almost passionate sincerity and his unfailing courage. The world watched with admiration and warm sympathy his long and dogged fight against the cancer which finally killed him.

One facet of Mr. Dulles's crowded political career that proved particularly irritating at times even to those who admired him most was a garrulity that led inevitably to misinterpretation, angry expostulation and semi-retraction. Among his most controversial pronouncements were his threat to France of "agonising reappraisal" of America's attitude to that country if she persisted in opposing Germany's entry into N.A.T.O. and his advocacy of "massive retaliation," in certain circumstances, against China.

His assertion, in an article in the American magazine Life, that the United States had on three occasions been on the brink of war with China caused international dismay.

HIS VACILLATIONS

Suez Emergency

But his vacillations reached their climax, at least so far as Britain was concerned, with the Suez emergency. His angry denunciations of Nasser, and other statements, inspired the belief in Britain and France that America was prepared to give them support.

His conception at the London conferences of a Canal Users' Association was gladly accepted until he made it abundantly clear in subsequent speeches that America would do little or nothing to ensure that the Association would prove efficacious.

To the astonishment and anger of his allies, he said quite bluntly that America had no commitments in the Suez area, and added some comments on colonialism that caused additional resentment. The opinion that "we had been sold down the Canal" was widespread in Britain.

Mr. Dulles entered office after apparently well fitting himself for the position of America's chief diplomat by long training in international affairs. A highly-paid lawyer, an authority on international cases, and a prominent writer on world affairs, he had been an adviser on foreign policy to several Secretaries of State of opposing political persuasions. For nearly four decades he had represented the United States at international conferences.

In 1945 he played a part in the formation of the United Nations as an adviser, appointed by President Roosevelt, to the American delegation. Mr. Truman offered him the appointment of America's first postwar Ambassador to Japan, but he declined it.

One of his most notable achievements was the preparation of the Japanese Peace Treaty, which he described as "a peace of reconciliation." He also negotiated three Pacific security pacts.

Mr. Dulles remained in the State Department until early in 1952, when he cut away from the Truman administration in order to have a free hand in election year to attack those of its foreign policies with which he disagreed. He objected chiefly to the policy of "containment" of Russia which he assailed as inadequate and generally defensive. He had long advocated an "ultimatum" policy toward the Soviet Union, maintaining that America should warn the Kremlin that any aggression, such as the Korean war, would bring Russia into conflict with American strength.

MISSION IN 1917

Panama Canal

Mr. Dulles, who was born on Feb. 25, 1888, was only 29 when President Woodrow Wilson assigned him his first diplomatic mission. That was in 1917 after the United States had broken relations with Germany. To protect the Panama Canal against attack, he was sent as a special representative of the State Department to Central America and successfully negotiated with the republics concerned to achieve that end.

He wrote two books. The first "The Church" exerted a strong influence on his life. In 1940, before the United States entered the war, the Federal Council of Churches of Christ in America formed the Commission on a just and Durable Peace and named Mr. Dulles as its chairman. It was one of several of his activities in the international religious field.

Married in 1912, Mr. Dulles was the father of two sons and a daughter.

(May 25)

HEITOR VILLA-LOBOS DIES

BRAZILIAN MUSICIAN

Heitor Villa-Lobos, the Brazilian conductor-composer, died on Tuesday in the city of his birth, Rio de Janeiro. He was 72. His early years were spent learning various instruments, chiefly the cello.

JOHN WARRACK writes: No man has ever done more, single handed, for his country's music than Villa-Lobos. Before him Brazil was musically stagnant, though not, as he was to prove, infertile. With equal enthusiasm he travelled, composed music for strange instruments, directed his own conservatoire, wrote forceful educational treatises and conducted choirs of 40,000.

He produced over 2,000 works in every conceivable musical form and in a number not previously conceived.

(November 19)

SIR STANLEY SPENCER

A CONTROVERSIAL FIGURE IN ART

Sir Stanley Spencer, who has died aged 68, was the centre of controversy in the artistic world for many years. Many of his paintings on religious themes were among the best known of our times.

Born at Cookham, Berks, in 1891, he was the seventh son of a professor of music. He studied at the Slade School of Art. His painting of the "Resurrection," exhibited at the 1950 Royal Academy, began a fierce controversy.

In the same year he made his peace with the Academy after a 15-year quarrel. He had resigned as an A.R.A. in 1935 after two of his pictures had been rejected. But in his later years few questioned the authenticity of his insight. He was knighted last June.

CHAPEL MURALS

He lived practically all his life in his native Cookham and in 1923 began perhaps his most famous work, the mural paintings for a memorial chapel at Burghclere, Hants.

The 16 panels depict the daily life of a solider. He had served as a private in Macedonia in the 1914-18 war.

His outstanding works include "Christ Bearing the Cross," which shows the procession to Cavalry passing his Cookham home, "Christ Preaching at Cookham Regatta" and "The Nativity."

In May, 1958, an exhibition of his pictures was held at Cookham Vicarage. A large sum was raised for the parish church restoration fund.

Many examples of his work are in public galleries all over Britain, America and the Commonwealth. He was twice married. His first wife died in 1950.

(December 15)

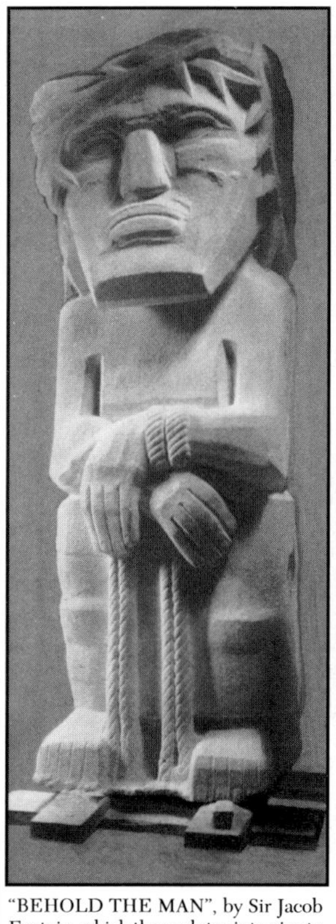

"BEHOLD THE MAN", by Sir Jacob Epstein, which the sculptor is to give to Selby Abbey, Yorks.

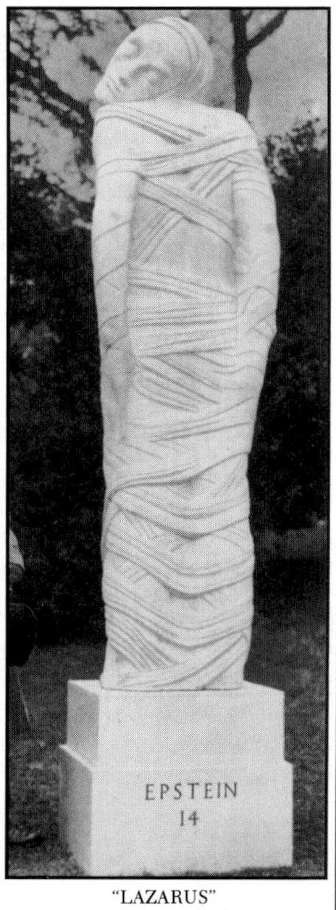

"LAZARUS" in Battersea Park

SIR JACOB EPSTEIN

MANY DISPUTES OVER SCULPTURES

The many controversies inspired by the work of Sir Jacob Epstein, who has died aged 78, failed to prevent him from establishing himself as one of the foremost sculptors of the day.

Indeed many of the severest critics of his bold experiments in "neo-barbarism" were prepared to enthuse over the consummate artistry of most of his bronzes.

The controversy over his "Ecce Homo" ("Behold the Man"), the statue of Christ created in 1933, continued until a few weeks ago. After Sir Jacob offered it to Selby Abbey 434 parishioners objected to it being placed there, calling it "too modernistic." Sir Jacob was "not particularly disappointed" when in July a Consistory Court refused to allow the statue to be installed.

NATURALISED BRITON

Born in New York on Nov. 10, 1880, of Russian-Polish parents, he left America at an early age and studied on the continent. He finally settled in London and adopted British nationality.

His first commission for an architect, 18 figures for a building in Agar Street, Strand, then used by the British Medical Association, aroused a storm of criticism that continued for months. The nudity of the figures led to many heated accusations of vulgarity from churchmen, journalists and members of the public.

STATUES DEFENDED

This controversy broke out again in 1935, although on different grounds. The Southern Rhodesian Government, which had taken over the building, proposed to remove the statues on the grounds of their "unsuitability."

Fellow-artists, not all of whom approved the works, rushed to defend what they considered an affront to art as a whole. The dispute led to the resignation of Sickert from the Royal Academy, and the withdrawal by Epstein from the Academy nominations.

Although the statues were reprieved then, it was not long before they made their presence felt again. A head dropping off one of them on to the foot of a passer-by led to a decision to remove the heads and other projecting parts.

MEMORIAL DISFIGURED

In 1925 London displayed its continued reluctance to accept his standards by raising a chorus of protest at his conception of Rima on the memorial to W.H. Hudson in Hyde Park. This was disfigured on several occasions by paint, and was once tarred and feathered.

Criticisms of his "Madonna and Child," a bronze group now in the Tate Gallery, were mild compared to the outburst which greeted "Adam" which was taken on tour on the Continent and in America.

His "Genesis" and "Consummatum Est," a massive, recumbent figure of Christ after death, aroused further protests. "Night" and "Day," two statues on the London Transport headquarters in Broadway, Westminster, suffered several disfigurements from tar and oily substances.

BUSTS ADMIRED

But his bronze busts, many of them of children, including his own, were almost always the subject of unanimous admiration. "Lucifer," a large bronze winged figure, was considered by many to be one of his major, and least controversial, pieces.

He was created a K.B.E. in 1954. His first wife, formerly Miss Margaret Dunlop, died in 1947. A son and daughter survive. In 1955 Sir Jacob married Mrs. Kathleen Garman.

ABUSED BY PHILISTINE

Creative Figure

TERENCE MULLALY writes: Epstein's death robs us of one of the really creative figures of this century. There was a greatness about the man that was reflected in his eyes, in his hands and in the best of his work.

Throughout his life he was fated to be abused by the philistine and to be pursued by shrill vituperation as violent as it was unintelligent. The abuse hurled at him over the decades will come to be seen as a manifestation of one of the least favourable aspects of the British character.

Not that everything that Epstein produced was good. Indeed, his interest in Primitive and Pre-Columbian art at times led him to introduce into his own work distortions that seem more striking than rewarding.

BRILLIANT WORK

Yet whatever the man did he was passionately sincere. Always he remained an example to his critics and his finest work is heartful and technically brilliantly accomplished.

In fact he ranks among the outstanding portrait sculptors of all time. In head after head he mirrored the qualities of some of the most remarkable men and women of our age. He was a superb craftsman, a brilliant psychologist and a compassionate interpreter.

Posterity's most vivid impressions of men like Sir Winston Churchill, Nehru, T.S. Eliot and Einstein will be derived from Epstein.

(August 22)

ERROL FLYNN

COSTUME ACTOR OF MANY PARTS

ERROL FLYNN, the film actor who has died in Vancouver at the age of 50, excelled in the portrayal of colourful extroverts, preferably in costume.

Admired by many filmgoers in several countries, he figured frequently in newspaper reports. His critics averted that his private personality differed but little from his film one.

Born at Hobart, Tasmania, he served as a patrol officer in New Guinea before beginning his acting career in England. He appeared with a Northampton repertory company and at the Malvern Festival.

In 1935 he went to Holywood. He quickly established himself as a popular favourite in such films as "Captain Blood," "Sea Hawk" and "Adventures of Robin Hood."

BURMA ROLE

Comments on fighting

In his role in "Objective Burma," he appeared to fight the war with Japan almost single-handed. This aroused a good deal of comment.

He became a naturalised American citizen in 1942. In recent years he had figured in a series of court cases, including one of attacking two girls, aged 16 and 17, of which he was acquitted.

On several occasions he was involved in restaurant and night-club brawls with prominent Hollywood and New York personalities. "The rest of my life," he said jokingly a few weeks ago, "will be devoted to women and litigation."

He married three times. His marriages to Lily Damita, a French film actress, and Nora Eddington ended in divorce. He married Patrice Wymore, the actress, in 1950.

PROFESSOR'S SON

Dashing and Reckless

CAMPBELL DIXON writes: Son of a slight, sedate professor of zoology at London University, Errol Flynn was everything that fans expected of a film star, tall, handsome, dashing, reckless and unconventional.

Sensational newspapers printed so many stories of his romances, drinking and general wildness that he was assumed to be just another Hollywood playboy.

This did him an injustice. It is true he was reckless, that he found pretty girls as irresistible as they found him, and that he drank far more than was good for him.

But this was only half the picture. Well over six feet tall, with a powerful physique, chiselled features and a charming voice, he was one of the most attractive fellows you could wish to meet, and one of the most amusing. He had a lively wit, was a brilliant raconteur and, unless provoked, bubbled with high spirits and good will.

About his work he was always modest. If his looks and physique generally condemned him to play dashing officers and adventurers, he cheerfully did his best with them, and his best was very good indeed.

(October 16)

RAYMOND CHANDLER

Raymond Chandler, who has died aged 70, was once a Bloomsbury poet and essayist. Late in life he achieved fame as the creator of "tough" private detectives. Although he did not turn to writing fiction until he was in the middle forties he was said to be earning £35,000 a year.

Born in Chicago, Raymond Thornton Chandler was educated at private schools in France and Germany and at Dulwich College. While living in London which he spoke of as his "second home" he contributed articles, verse and essays to newspapers and magazines.

Returning to the United States after the 1914-18 war, in which he served with the Canadian Expeditionary Force and the R.A.F., he found fame with his mystery novels. But although he was able to spend £100 a week he was never a prolific writer. He published only seven novels featuring his private detective Philip Marlow in 26 years' writing.

Many of his novels were made into films. In 1934 "The Long Goodbye" was chosen as the best mystery book of the year by the Mystery Writers of America. His last detective novel "Playback" was published last year.

(March 27)

CECIL B. DEMILLE

DIRECTOR WHO PUT HOLLYWOOD ON MAP

Cecil Blount DeMille, who has died aged 77, was the acknowledged master of the film epic. Born at Ashfield, Massachusetts, he was the son of Henry Churchill DeMille, who collaborated on plays with David Belasco.

CAMPBELL DIXON writes: Cecil B. DeMille stood for everything the world long associated with Hollywood, sensation, hokum, sex and popular religion. If not actually the founder of Hollywood (early American films were made in New York or Florida), he was the man who put Hollywood on the map.

That was in 1913. Sam Goldwyn and Jesse Lasky had raised 20,000 dollars and sent him West with the vague order to shoot "The Squaw Man," starring Dustin Farnum, at Flagstaff, Arizona. He wired back: "Flagstaff no good for our purpose.

"Have proceeded to California. Want authority to rent barn in place called Hollywood for 75 dollars a month."

After a sharp argument with Lasky Goldwyn cautiously wired back: "Authorise you to rent barn but on month-to-month basis. Don't make any long-term commitments."

TRIO WON FAME

Flair for Showmanship

"The Squaw Man" was a hit, proving the new team's theory that if the public would pay to see shorts, they would pay more to see longer stories giving room for characterisation, atmosphere and the building up of suspense.

First together, then separately as temperaments asserted themselves, the trio went on to win fame and millions, in DeMille's case through a long series of spectacles and adaptations of stage successes such as his brother's play, "The Warrens of Virginia."

In "The Warrens" he showed invention as well as his flair for showmanship. Films were then made in the open air by sunlight. "The Warrens", shot with a velvet backdrop, was the first ever to have interior night scenes without sunlight blazing in incongruously through doors and windows.

PRICE RAISED

"Rembrandt Lighting"

He was also the first director to vary lighting by using sunlight reflectors. But his ingenuity was not always appreciated and once provoked a crisis with his backers.

(January 22)

MARIO LANZA

MARIO LANZA, the American tenor who died yesterday in Rome after a heart attack at the age of 38, had a brief but phenomenally successful career.

Born in New York, his real name was Alfred Arnold Cocozza. In his youth he worked as a piano shifter.

He served in the United States Army from 1942-45, and afterwards appeared in radio shows and made concert tours. In 1948 he made his operatic debut in New Orleans in "Madame Butterfly."

CAMPBELL DIXON writes: Young though Mario Lanza was, his death comes as no great surprise. A sufferer from both temperamental and physical weaknesses, he shocked his Hollywood employers by demanding £357,000 a picture, and he had no sooner made a success than his screen career was threatened by a tendency to put on weight.

Severe dieting lowered his resistance and he became a victim to all manner of illnesses, including phlebitis and septicaemia. As a result, for the last two or three years, his managers had found it difficult to plan concert tours or films.

Mr. Lanza had a fine robust tenor, extremely effective both in opera and "pop" numbers. As an actor his range was limited.

His voice was heard to advantage in "The Great Caruso," where he played a greater tenor with a similar inability to act, and more recently in "For the First time," a pleasant romance of a tenor and a deaf girl, in which his singing of "La donna e mobile," "O sole Mio" and "Come prima" delighted his admirers.

(October 8)

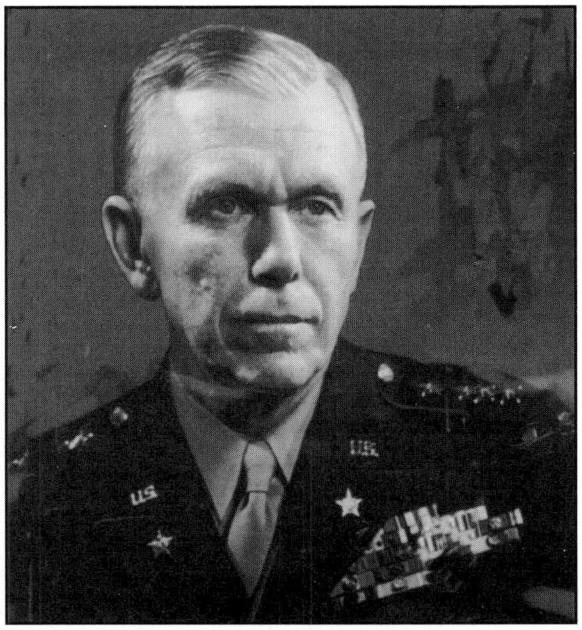

GEN. GEORGE MARSHALL

STEADY CHAMPION OF AID TO WESTERN EUROPE.

BY the death of Gen. Marshall, at the age of 78, the United States has lost one of the most eminent soldier-statesmen in its history. To Mr. Truman, who leaned heavily on him for military advice, he was "the greatest living American."

Both as Secretary of State from 1947 to 1949, and of Defence from September, 1950, until Sept. 12, 1951, when he resigned "for very personal reasons," he was the symbol of his country's new leadership in world politics.

As the author of the Marshall Plan and the sponsor of the European Recovery Programme, he dominated international relations as no man had done since Woodrow Wilson. As Chief of Staff of the United States Army throughout the late war he was one of the principal architects of victory.

In 1953 he was awarded the Nobel Peace Prize. Accepting it in Oslo, he called for a spiritual regeneration of mankind.

SPECIAL ENVOY

Task in China

When he retired from the War Department, in November, 1945, it was assumed that his active career had ended. He himself desired nothing but the peace and quietness of retirement. "What I wanted most," he said, "was to go and fix things up at Leesburg," his country residence in Virginia. He longed to return to his reading, his fishing, his vegetable gardening.

In a week, on Nov. 27, 1945, he was appointed as President Truman's special envoy to China. There, with the personal rank of ambassador, he spent 13 months attempting to mediate in the civil war between Nationalists and Communists.

His mission was a failure. In a personal statement, on Jan. 7, 1947, he declared that "extremist elements" on both sides had frustrated his efforts. He had found the Communists "irreconcilable," the Nationalists "reactionary."

On the same day came the surprise announcement that he would succeed Mr. Byrnes as Secretary of State. He was the first professional soldier to be appointed to the post, and the fourth person to hold it within 26 months.

HIDDEN DEPTHS

Talent for Friendship

But apart from his China mission, he had no experience of diplomacy as such. Many people wondered if he was equal to the new task and all its complexities. Those who wondered were those who did not know him.

For George Catlett Marshall was a great military strategist with a keen eye for political implications. He possessed the rare quality of being able to transfer his imaginative insight from the realm of war to that of high policy. He was a man of hidden depths.

His austere aloofness repelled intimacy. Yet he had an unusual talent for friendship. Witness his warm personal relations with Mr. Bernard Baruch and with the late Field-Marshal Sir John Dill, former C.I.G.S. and later British representative on the Joint Chiefs of Staff in Washington.

The story of Marshall's term of office as Secretary of State falls into several sub-divisions, each marking a definite phase of the "cold war" between Communism and the Western democracies.

On Feb. 27, 1947, while Marshall was "cramming" for the Moscow conference on the German and Austrian treaties, London sent a Note to Washington. It stated that Britain was no longer able to continue her aid to Greece and Turkey.

The result was the Truman Doctrine, enunciated by the President in a speech largely written by Marshall. The American people assumed the burden to the tune of £100 million, and warned the Kremlin of their willingness to help free peoples "against aggressive movements that seek to impose on them totalitarian regimes."

HOPE FOR EUROPE

U.S. Policy Reversed

Two months later, on June 5, he stood under the elms of the Harvard Yard, the recipient of an honorary degree. Quietly, almost casually, he said that if the nations of Europe would agree on their economic needs, the United States would underwrite their recovery.

In one matter-of-fact sentence he had made a pronouncement more momentous than that of Monroe. He had reversed the historic trend of American foreign policy, placed the Truman Doctrine on a Continental scale, and brought hope to a distracted Europe.

At the same time he had seized the initiative from Russia. The violence of Moscow's reaction was the measure of his potential success.

Inevitably, the Marshall Plan tended to overshadow his work in other respects. On Palestine, for example, the American abandonment of partition and advocacy of a United Nations trusteeship was at first attributed to President Truman. But Marshall frankly admitted that he had advised this change of policy.

The diplomacy of 1948 was dominated by the Berlin blockade. On July 21 Marshall warned Moscow that the United States would not be intimidated. He would use "every possible resource" of negotiation. "But," he declared, "I repeat that we are not going to be coerced."

The magnitude of Marshall's wartime achievement is now a matter of history. In 1939 the United States Army numbered 200,000. On the day of Pearl Harbour it numbered 1,500,000. In May, 1945, when Germany surrendered, America had under arms 8,300,000 men, of whom more than four million were serving overseas.

It was Marshall who planned and coordinated this enormous effort. Even apart from his country's woeful lack of preparedness, he had many obstacles to overcome.

(October 17)

MIKE HAWTHORN

CHAMPION DRIVER AT AGE OF 29

Mike Hawthorn, who was killed yesterday in a road accident, had many escapes on the race-track during his spectacular progress to the forefront of British drivers.

World champion at the age of 29, Hawthorn announced in December his retirement from Grand Prix racing. In a Ferrari he won the title at Casablanca last year by a single point after coming second to his friend and rival, Stirling Moss, in the Morocco Grand Prix.

In eight years as a race driver Hawthorn won prize-money estimated at £40,000. In the course of collecting it he suffered mishaps which included:

The collapse of a rear spring at Goodwood which threw him out of the car at more than 100 m.p.h.

Failure of brakes at Aintree which sent him careering into a ploughed field.

A collision with two other cars while racing in Sicily as a result of which his car burst into flames. He was badly burned and spent several weeks in hospital.

Hawthorn was deeply saddened by the death of his friend and fellow driver, Peter Collins, in the German Grand Prix in August last year. Hawthorn, driving in the race, saw Collins hit a bank and turn over. Many felt that the loss of his friend was a factor in Hawthorn's decision to retire.

PERSONAL POPULARITY

Tall fair and genial, Hawthorn was immensely popular with his fellow-drivers. His father, Mr. Leslie Hawthorn, himself a racing driver, bought him a motor-cycle while he was still at Ardingly College. By the age of 18 he had won a cup.

By 1950 he owned his first sports car, a 1934 1,100 c.c. Riley "Ulster Imp," and drove it successfully in speed trials. In 1952 he leaped into prominence by beating the great Argentine driver, Juan Fangio, at Goodwood.

Hawthorn drove B.R.M. cars for a time, but in 1956 signed for Ferrari, the Italian firm, and by victories in race after race in many parts of the world established himself as a fearless and first-class driver.

(January 23)

SIR HENRY TIZARD

Sir Henry Tizard, who has died at his home near Fareham, Hants, aged 74, was principal scientific adviser to the Government from 1946-52. He was chairman of the Advisory Council on Scientific Policy, and the Defence Research Policy Committee.

His pre-1939 research on defence against aerial attack qualified him as one of the original "backroom boys," or "Boffins." The development of the Spitfire and the Hurricane, and of radar, owed a great deal to his enthusiasm, drive, and immense scientific knowledge.

He was chairman of the committee set up by the Air Ministry to study defence the year Hitler seized power. By Easter, 1939, a chain of radar stations, at which a 24-hour watch was maintained, had been established along the East Coast. They played a vital part in the Battle of Britain.

FIGHTER PILOT

In the 1914-18 war he transferred from the royal Artillery to the Royal Flying corps, where, as a fighter pilot, he applied scientific principles to his combats. For as long as possible before engaging he would make copious notes on the behaviour and performance of the enemy machines. He ended the war as Assistant Controller of Aerial Experiment and Research.

Henry Thomas Tizard was appointed a lecturer on natural science at Oriel College, Oxford, in 1911. From 1927-29 he was Permanent Secretary to the Department of Scientific and Industrial Research.

Rector of the Imperial College of Science and Technology from 1929-42, he was created a K.C.B. in 1937. From 1941-43 he was a member of the Council of the Ministry of Aircraft Production, and an additional member of the Air Council.

In 1947 he was appointed chairman of the Committee on Industrial Productivity, and of the Advisory Committee on Scientific Policy. A Fellow of the Royal Society, he was president of the British Association in 1948

(October 10)

FRANK LLOYD WRIGHT

PIONEER AMONG ARCHITECTS

Mr. Frank Lloyd Wright, who has died aged 89, was a pioneer of modern architecture, whose name was familiar throughout the world. An American of Welsh Nonconformist stock, he had for many years exerted a powerful influence on design.

His methods, which included the study of the nature of available materials, and designs which harmonised with the land beneath and around the buildings, were greeted initially with derision. On the prairies he built low houses with long horizontal roof-lines.

Some of his churches resembled country clubs. One spectacular dwelling near Pittsburgh was poised above a waterfall.

"TEA-TRAY" HOTEL

His best-known building was the Imperial Hotel, Tokyo. Designed to withstand earthquake shocks, it was his first ambitious use of the cantilever principle. Each concrete floor slab rested on a central support like, in his own words, a tea-tray balanced on a waiter's fingers. In the great earthquake of 1923 the hotel was almost alone in escaping destruction.

He lived to see many of his innovations become standard practice. In 1941 he was awarded the Royal Gold Medal for Architecture of the Royal Institute of British Architects. In 1948 he received the Gold Medal of the American Institute of Architects.

There is only one example of his work in New York, the Solomon R. Guggenheim Museum in Fifth Avenue. This, which included a "pudding-basin" gallery, is regarded as one of the most revolutionary and controversial buildings in the city.

In 1956 he drafted plans for a 510-storey, one-mile-high office building for Chicago's lake-front. It was to be by far the world's tallest building. He later suggested that a sky-scraper of similar height would solve New York's housing and traffic problems.

(April 10)

KAY KENDALL

Miss KAY KENDALL, the actress, who has died aged 32, was granddaughter of Marie Kendall, the old-time variety star.

Her first important film role was given her when she was 18, by Wesley Ruggles, the Hollywood director. She starred opposite Sid Field in the musical "London Town."

It was not an outstanding debut, but numerous film parts followed. She scored her first success in the British comedy "Genevieve." Miss Kendall later appeared in "Doctor in the House" and "The Constant Husband." Apart from "Genevieve," her most notable films were "Les Girls," which was chosen for the Royal Film Performance in 1957, and "The Reluctant Debutante," in which she appeared opposite her husband, Rex Harrison, the actor.

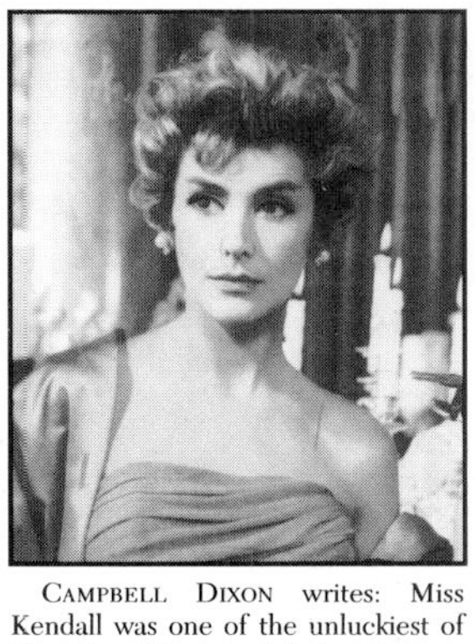

CAMPBELL DIXON writes: Miss Kendall was one of the unluckiest of film stars. She was tried early in a British musical, "London Town," that brought nobody any kudos, and as a result of its failure it was some years before she had another opportunity.

By the time "Genevieve" came along she had learned her trade and her performance lifted her into the front rank of British comediennes.

Miss Kendall was that rare creature, a comedienne of elegance and beauty. Under the direction of Lubitsch she might long have been one of the screen's biggest stars.

(August 7)

SIR ALFRED MUNNINGS

TRADITIONAL ART CHAMPION

PRESIDENT of the Royal Academy (1944 to 1949) Sir Alfred Munnings, who has died aged 80, was all his life a forceful champion of the traditional school of thought in art.

His tempestuous comments on the work of some of his contemporaries rarely failed to stimulate controversy, in which he delighted, and his most bitter opponent could accuse him of neither complacency nor insincerity.

Born at Mendham, Suffolk, where his family had farmed for centuries, it was natural that he should specialise in the painting of horses and of the English countryside. From the age of 10, armed with pencil and sketch-pad, he became a familiar sight in the Suffolk lanes in the intervals of his education at Framingham College, and at Norwich School of Art.

Success came to him early, with the acceptance, when he was 18, of two pictures by the Royal Institute of Painters in Watercolours.

In 1898 he had two oils accepted by the Royal Academy, and with the proceeds from the sale of these and other pictures he bought a disused carpenter's shop, which he converted into a studio. This he shared with a mare which acted as his model.

In the 1914-18 war he painted 45 war pictures for the Canadian Government while attached to a cavalry brigade in France. He was elected a full Royal Academician in 1925.

BOYCOTT OF OWN WORKS

In 1939 he boycotted an exhibition of his works in Norwich because he disapproved of the selection. Knighted in 1944, he broke all records in 1947 for a one-man exhibition which he held at the Leicester Galleries, by selling pictures for more than £20,000.

The work of Mr. Henry Moore, the sculptor, was a favourite target of Sir Alfred. In 1951 he accused Leeds City Council of "the most awful blunder" in installing a statue by Moore in a public park. "I hope the people of Leeds will rise up in their fury and have the thing thrown out," said Sir Alfred.

TERENCE MULLALY writes: The death of Sir Alfred Munnings removes from the scene a lively controversialist and an artist who has had many admirers. As long as the Englishman continues to love horses his work will be in demand.

For many years his race course scenes and his other paintings of horses have always been among the first pictures to sell at the Royal Academy. Their popularity has been even more convincingly evinced by their performance in the sale rooms.

In fact only a few years after being painted, pictures by him have sold at auction for considerably more than he charged for them.

But posterity will, I am sure, recognise that Munnings was in no sense an outstanding artist. He has frequently been bracketed with Stubbs. Yet the comparison is a sourly superficial one.

(July 18)

LOU COSTELLO DIES AT 53

HOLLYWOOD, Tuesday.

Lou Costello, the fat clown of the Abbott and Costello comedy team, died in Hollywood to-day of a heart attack. He was 53.

Abbott and Costello were among the "Top 10" box office favourites for 10 years in Hollywood. - B.U.P.

(March 4)

BILLY MAYERL

At Beaconsfield, Bucks, aged 56. Pianist known to millions of radio listeners: began studying serious music at Trinity College of Music but became pianist in East End cinema at 50s a week to help support his family; at 18 was pianist with Savoy Havana band at £30 a week; composed over 1,000 pieces.

(March 27)

BOBBY CHARLTON WRECKS DISAPPOINTING SCOTS

ENGLAND FORWARDS MOVE WELL BUT LACK SHOOTING POWER

By Donald Saunders

Bobby Charlton came of age at Wembley Stadium on Saturday. With the instinctive timing of a great showman, this Soccer prodigy from Manchester United chose English football's historic headquarters to demonstrate that he is ready to take his place among the honoured names of Britain's national winter game.

Here were artistry, authority, audacity and that indefinable quality that separates the many good players from the few really great ones.

For Charlton it was a notable triumph, a victory for character as well as skill. Perhaps, too, it was a triumph for the selectors.

Last summer they drew, deservedly I think, a barrage of criticism for omitting Charlton from the World Cup team while the rest of the Soccer world loudly recommended his inclusion.

The selectors were big enough to change their minds when Charlton, showing commendable strength of character, overcame his bitter disappointment, rolled up his sleeves and forced them again to take notice of him.

And it may well be that by making Charlton fight his way back the selectors have helped him become a better footballer.

MORE MATURE

Controlled Game

Certainly this young man is to-day a more mature player than he was a year ago. I had seen him play many fine games for Manchester United and for England's senior and intermediate teams. But never had I seen him so completely control a match as he did on Saturday. And this, it should be remembered, was the annual show-piece of the Home International Championship.

Every time Charlton moved on to the ball danger threatened Scotland and the pulse of the crowd quickened.

He seemed to be everywhere, finding an unexpected opening for his colleagues, bursting through the astonished Scottish defence like an impatient motorist accelerating away from the lights or moving instinctively on to that patch of turf where the ball was next due to arrive.

Moreover, Charlton was the only forward on either side who brought along his shooting boots.

GALLANT EVANS

Agile Brown

Indeed, without Charlton, this game would have been memorable only for the gallant stand of Bobby Evans, Scotland's defiant centre-half, and the triumphal departure of Billy Wright astride the shoulders of two teammates at the conclusion of his 100th international.

It was a match that fascinated me for 20 minutes, held my attention less surely for another half an hour and finally left me vaguely disappointed.

The Scots failed entirely to find the form expected of them. Their defence was sound, thanks principally to Evans, and the agile Brown, but their forwards rarely moved as a unit and seldom seriously troubled England's defence.

Ultimately the match became a battle of wits between England's attack and the Scottish defence. For much of the afternoon those England forwards seemed to be moving forward neatly, at times brilliantly, like pawns on a chess board.

How England's manager, Mr. Walter Winterbottom, and the selectors must have smiled when they saw Charlton, Haynes and Broadbent quickly form a co-operative movement that Docherty and David Mackay could never disrupt.

They must, too, have been happy to note the confidence and skill with which Holden strode through his first international.

SHOOTING PROBLEM

Not Satisfied Yet

But Mr. Winterbottom, wisely, is not yet satisfied. "We still have a long way to go." he said. "Our finishing needs to be a little snappier."

Perhaps Mr. Winterbottom remembers that 12 months ago England easily defeated a Scottish side not greatly inferior to Saturday's and a few weeks later were themselves thrashed 5-0 by Jugoslavia.

I do not think he need fear a repetition of that humiliation when England take on the world champions, Brazil, in Rio de Janeiro, next month.

Wembley Result

ENGLAND..............................**1**
Charlton (61 minutes).
SCOTLAND..............................**0**

Half-time 0-0. Attendance 100,000
Receipts £49,840.

ENGLAND

Hopkinson (Bolton)
Howe (West Bromwich), **Shaw, G.** (Sheffield United);
Clayton R. (Blackburn), **Wright** (Wolverhampton), **Flowers** (Wolverhampton);
Douglas (Blackburn), **Broadbent** (Wolverhampton), **Charlton** (Manchester United), **Haynes** (Fulham), **Holden** (Bolton).

SCOTLAND

Brown (Dundee);
McKay (Celtic), **Caldow** (Rangers);
Docherty (Arsenal), **Evans** (Celtic), **Mackay** (Tottenham Hotspur);
Leggat (Fulham), **Collins** (Everton), **Herd** (Arsenal), **Dick** (West Ham), **Ormond** (Hibernian).
Referee: **J. Campos** (Portugal).

But there is no doubt at all that England must solve their shooting problem before they can really expect to overcome the Brazilians.

The plain fact is that England's inside-trio frequently threw the Scots into confusion with delightful moves and then found no one in the middle to complete the job.

There is not now much time left for experiment before the South American tour begins. But were the selectors to be bold they could attempt to solve the problem by bringing in an orthodox centre-forward such as Brian Clough, switching Holden to the right-wing and giving Charlton a roving commission as nominal outside-left.

Charlton did much of his most effective work at Wembley on and from the left flank, while Holden often wandered over to the right touchline, already occupied by the out-of-form Douglas.

Possibly we should have seen more goals on Saturday had not Broadbent been over-cautious in the 19th minute. Following a perfect pass from Charlton, Holden crossed the ball into the penalty area, where Broadbent hesitated just long enough to give Brown time to turn his shot aside.

Had the ball gone into the net then, the Scottish defence might well have capitulated. Instead, we had to wait until the 60th minute for England to score the goal they had so often threatened.

GLORIOUS GOAL

And what a glorious goal it was. Haynes began the move with a neat pass to Broadbent, who switched the ball out to Douglas near the corner-flag.

Douglas curled a centre into the penalty area and there was Charlton, flinging himself upwards and forwards to head the ball down past the astonished Brown.

Several times thereafter England almost increased their slender lead. Broadbent shot just wide, and Brown brilliantly turned a screaming shot from Charlton round the post and later dived bravely to grab the ball from Charlton's toe.

But the goal England needed for safety would not come. Thus Scotland were in the hunt with a chance right to the end. Indeed they almost snatched an unwarranted draw when Hopkinson failed to cut off Docherty's free kick and saw Herds' shot hit Leggatt before bouncing off the post out of play.

This narrow squeak may encourage England to remember in future that goals play an extremely important part in football matches.

(April 12)

<u>*Wimbledon Lawn Tennis*</u>

NEW CHAPTER OPENED IN S. AMERICA'S HISTORY

By Lance Tingay

The 1959 Lawn Tennis Championships, which ended at Wimbledon on Saturday, will stand bolder in the annals of the game than was expected by those who forecast an undistinguished meeting.

Not only did it produce two very good singles winners, but the emergence of A. Olmedo, a Peruvian, and Miss Maria Bueno, a Brazilian, as champions, emphasised a shift from the Australian-United States lawn tennis axis.

South America have produced notable players before, the Argentino, E. Morea, the Brazilian, A Vieira, the still prominent Chilean, L. Ayala, and best of all, the professional F. Segura, of Equador. Among women players I can think only of the Chilean, Miss Anita Lizana.

Yet even among those aware of the growing strength of Latin-American nations, who would have been bold enough to declare the time would come when South America would claim both the singles champions at Wimbledon? Very few, I am sure. A new page in the history of lawn tennis has been turned.

SPELL BROKEN

Fraser Wins at Last

The doubles followed more expected courses.

The solid but not very imaginative expertise of Australians dominated the men's events where, in the final, N.A. Fraser at last broke the spell of being often a finalist and never a winner by taking the title with R. Emerson against their compatriots, R. Mark and R. Laver.

The women's doubles did not surprise those who had seen the American national meeting last year. What Miss Jeanne Arth and Miss Darlene Hard did at Boston, they capably repeated at Wimbledon and will obviously constitute a bulwark in the American effort to win back the Wightman Cup at Pittsburgh in August.

As for the mixed, the one event left in serious lawn tennis where participants seem able to play a relaxed happy game, this meted out lawn tennis justice by giving Laver, with Miss Hard, a title he deserved as a triple finalist.

This was in some degree Laver's Wimbledon, for this 20-year-old Queenslander came through everything and raised himself from being workaday in world-class standards to somewhere near the top.

ESTONIAN SUCCESS

One British Victory

In a minor sense it was a Russian Wimbledon as well. The Estonian, T. Leius, won the junior boys' event, a fine performance for a tyro.

The only British success, alas, was the women's consolation singles. Mrs. Shirley Brasner won that.

The great success of the 19-year-old Miss Bueno brought a chorus of "I told you so." It was obvious in Rome early last year, when she had her first European success, that a potentially splendid player had arrived.

Wimbledon Finals

MEN'S SINGLES

A. Olmedo (U.S.) bt R Laver (Australia) 6-4, 6-3, 6-4.

WOMEN'S SINGLES

Miss M. Bueno (Brazil) bt Miss D. Hard (U.S.) 6-4, 6-3.

MEN'S DOUBLES

R. Emerson and N.A. Fraser (Australia) bt R. Laver and R. Mark (Australia) 8-6, 6-3, 14-16, 9-7.

WOMEN'S DOUBLES

Miss J Arth and Miss D.R. Hard (U.S.) bt Mrs. J.G. Fleitz (U.S.) and Miss M. Bueno (Brazil) 2-6, 6-2, 6-3

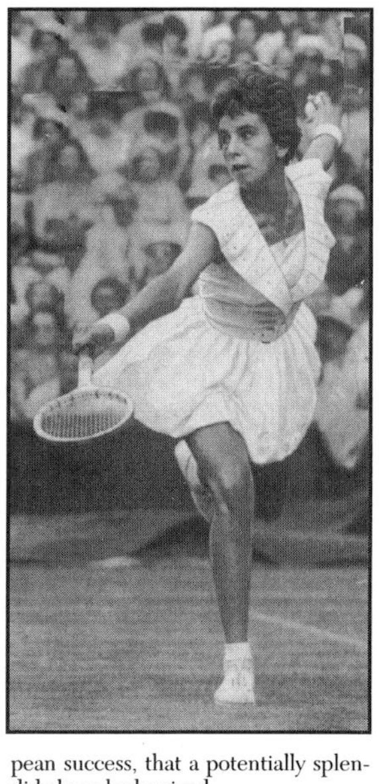

While many have talent it was clear that Miss Bueno, slight and trim, had genius. Her fluency and penetration of shot, produced from easy grace, is effortlessly brought about.

Timing, not muscle power, is her secret and that is something that can never be taught. For more than a year she proved a wayward genius, but this time she shed her errancy in the course of the early season.

(July 6)

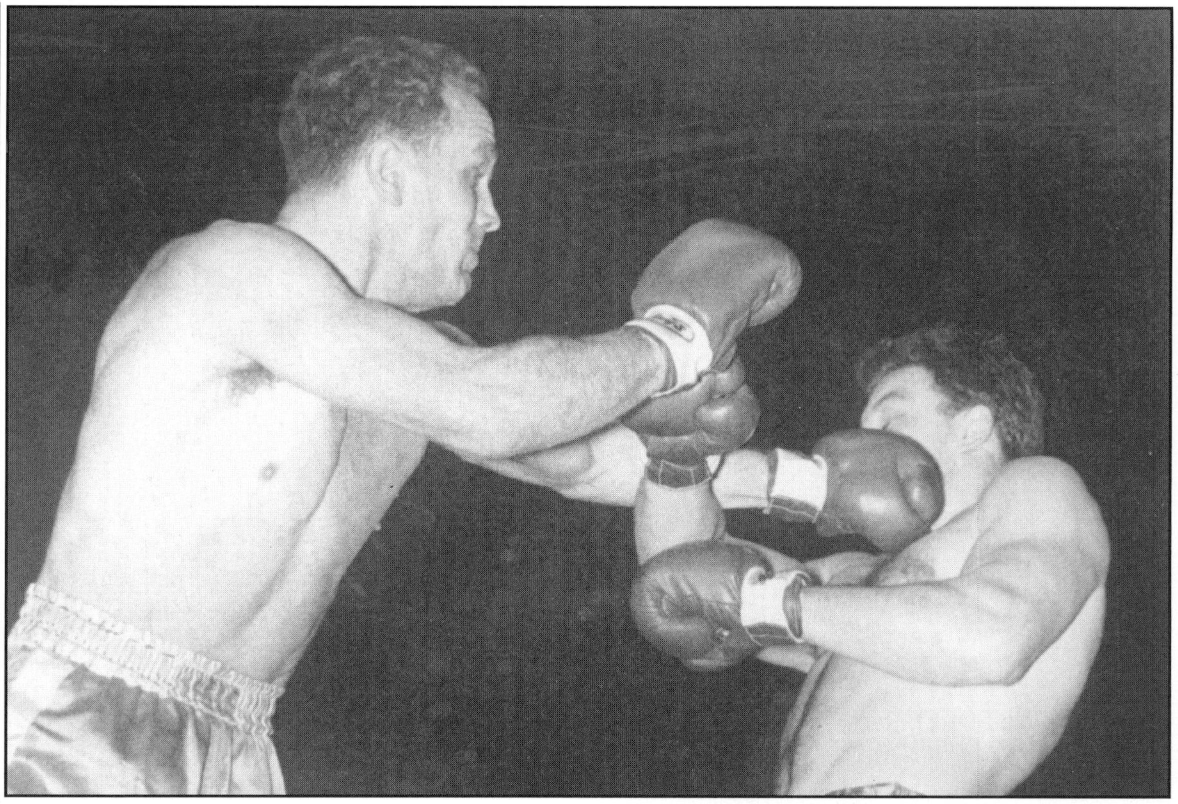

PUSHING HIM BACK. Henry Cooper's left to Brian London's face sends the champion back on his heels.

COOPER THRASHES LONDON FOR THE TITLE

COMPLETE TRIUMPH FOR MAN WHO NEVER GAVE UP HOPE

By Donald Saunders

Henry Cooper, the young man from Bellingham, who tried, tried and tried again, is the new British and Empire heavyweight champion. He earned those proud titles at Earls Court last night after outboxing and outpunching Brian London over 15 of the most bitterly contested rounds I have ever watched.

At the end of a contest that must surely consolidate Britain's new-found prestige among world heavyweights, both warriors looked as though they had been fighting with meat axes.

Cooper was bleeding from cuts above and below his left eye and from a gash over his right eye. London's right eye was a grotesque sight - a mere slit of bruised and bleeding flesh. Both men were almost too weary to stand.

For Cooper this victory is the climax of a story as full of ups and downs as the most imaginative boxing fiction ever written.

FOURTH ATTEMPT

Full of Courage

A few months ago his future as a heavyweight looked like being confined to the smaller halls of Britain.Three times he had tried to win a title - from Joe Erskine, Joe Bygraves and Ingemar Johansson. Each time he had met with humiliating defeat.

Last September this courageous young man was given another chance - in a British title eliminator against the tough, hard-punching Welshman, Dick Richardson. Cooper got up off the floor that night to win a memorable victory.

A month later he again hauled himself from the canvas and went on to outpoint the American, Zora Folley.

Again last night Cooper had to overcome adversity that would have defeated many a lesser man before he received the award that had so long eluded him.

BRUISING SIX ROUNDS

Cooper Worried

After six rounds of bruising fighting it looked as though London was going to keep his title and that Cooper was going to suffer the fate many had predicted for him - a summary defeat caused by eye injuries.

The tender skin round Cooper's eyes had already begun to show signs of wear and tear. His left eyebrow had been grazed in the fourth round and was bleeding freely by the sixth.

By the seventh the wound had worsened and Cooper was further handicapped by another, deeper cut under the same eye.

At the end of the seventh, the referee, Mr. Ike Powell, went over to Cooper's corner and asked him if everything was all right. Bravely Cooper replied "Yes, I'm all right."

Then back he went into battle. Mercilessly the now supremely confident London hammered him around the ring, throwing punches from all angles with those long, well-muscled arms.

Though he still could not keep out London, he did at least succeed in jolting him frequently with left jabs to the face. At first the blows seemed a mere annoyance to London, but slowly they began to show their effect.

London was no longer barging in with quite the same fury, nor was he showing his opponent the contempt that had been plain earlier on.

Then, in the 10th round, Cooper at last saw blood trickling from the champion's right eyebrow. Immediately he made that wound the target for his copybook left jabs. And Cooper's aim was so much more accurate than London's had been.

Punch after punch ripped through London's guard and widened the gash. But whereas Cooper's seconds had skilfully succeeded in stanching the blood - at least from the cut under his left eye - London's corner was powerless to stop the flow that handicapped the champion.

Boxing on with confidence, Cooper's grip on the fight grew tighter. The only question left to be answered was whether the champion still had the power to pull the fight out of the fire with one big punch.

Soon he knew he hadn't. Cooper's other eye was cut, but even that could not rekindle the fire in London's weary fists.

He was so bewildered at the end of the 14th round that he attempted to hold aloft Cooper's hand in token of victory.

Only when he returned to his corner did he discover that three long minutes remained. Bravely and wearily he heaved himself out of his stool for the 15th time and went forward gamely, wearily and bleeding to what he knew was inevitable defeat.

(January 13)

AUSTRALIA REGAIN ASHES

DEFENSIVE ENGLAND'S TEAM WILL BE DIFFICULT TO RESHAPE

From E.W. Swanton

ADELAIDE, Thursday.

Australia won the Fourth Test match here this evening by 10 wickets with an hour and a quarter to spare and so retrieved the Ashes which they had surrendered at the less beauteous Oval at Kennington five and a half years ago.

There was a time to-day, during which Graveney and Tyson were holding up a rather weary Australian attack, when it seemed that England might achieve the minor satisfaction of another drawn game. The Australian bowling, after three full days in the field, had lost its bite, though the fielding still sparkled.

However Benaud at last broke a stand that had lasted an hour and a quarter into the afternoon and there the resistance ended.

It is said that when the manager of the American Davis Cup team in Australia, Perry T. Jones, was trying to get wise to this cricket game he was moved to inquire; "What precisely is an ash?"

I do not suppose his guide enjoyed the task of answering the question any more than I relish having to account for the present result.

It is not so much that England have lost as that they have not succeeded in any one of the four Tests in playing the cricket of which they were capable. I felt and wrote before the tour started that the odds were somewhat against them. But if anyone had said they were due to win the toss four times running I would certainly not have supposed they would have gone down 3-0 with one game drawn.

KEEN AND HAPPY

Well-Knit Team

The first comment to be made obviously is that Australia have well earned their success. While England's strength at first was commonly over-estimated that of Australia was under-valued by people who kept thinking back to the abnormal conditions at home in '56.

A much better gauge was the Australian Tour of South Africa during which the younger men matured and grew in confidence. As they were enthused there by Craig so they have been knit together and kept keen and happy here by his successor, Benaud.

The fact is that these two have restored to Australian cricket the determination and enthusiasm which had been sapped during the five-year period of defeat. I happened to note two very small incidents illustrative of the Australian attitude during the game just ended.

During the long Australian first-wicket stand the number ten batsman with the temperature over the hundred mark, was having a protracted and thorough innings in the nets. His name? Linwall, aged 37, playing in his 56th Test match.

If, as I believe, M.C.C. were inclined to take their practice lightly early in the tour that aspect of preparation has been rectified some time since.

DIFFERENT APPROACH

Attack or Defence

But one of the contrasts between the two sides has been the difference in approach between one, most of whose members are, in the cricket sense, still coming up, and another, of whom more than half have left most of their Test cricket behind them.

The Australian batting and fielding have been very much better and the excellence of most of the English bowling has not compensated for the disparity. Technically Australia have looked the better and tactically they have not been nearly so quick to go back on to the defensive.

(February 6)

The Scoreboard

AUSTRALIA - First Innings

C.C. McDonald, b Trueman 170
J.W. Burke, c Cowdrey, b Bailey ..66
R.N. Harvey, run out 41
N. O'Neill, b Statham 56
L. Favell, b Statham........................4
K. Mackay, c Evans, b Statham.......4
R. Benaud, b Trueman 46
A.K. Davidson, c Bailey, b Tyson..43
A.W. Grout, lbw, b Trueman..........9
R.R. Lindwall, b Trueman............19
G. Rorke, not out 2
Extras (b 2, lb 8, nb 2, w 4).............16
Total 476

FALL OF WICKETS: 1-171, 2-276, 3-286, 4-294, 5-369, 6-388, 7-407, 8-445, 9-473

BOWLING

	O	M	R	W
Statham	22	0	83	3
Trueman	30.1	6	90	4
Tyson	28	1	100	1
Bailey	22	2	91	1
Lock	26	0	96	0

Second Innings

J.W. Burke, not out 16
L. Favell, not out...........................15
Extras..............................(b 4, lb 1)5
Total ....(no wicket) 36

BOWLING

	O	M	R	W
Statham	4	0	11	0
Trueman	3	1	3	0
Lock	2	0	8	0
Cowdrey	1.3	0	9	0

ENGLAND - First Innings

P.E. Richardson, lbw, b Lindwall...4
T.E. Bailey, b Davidson..................4
P.B.H. May, b Benaud..................37
M.C. Cowdrey, b Rorke 84
T.W. Graveney, c Benaud, b Rorke 41
W. Watson, b Rorke......................25
F.S. Trueman, c Grout, b Benaud ..0
G.A.R. Lock, c Grout, b Benaud.....2
F.H. Tyson, c and b Benaud 0
T.G. Evans, c Burke, b Benaud 4
J.B. Statham, not out 36
Extras (lb 2, nb 1)...........................3
Total 240

FALL OF WICKETS: 1-7, 2-11, 3-74, 4-170, 5-172, 6-180, 7-184, 8-184, 9-188.

BOWLING

	O	M	R	W
Davidson	12	0	49	1
Lindwall	15	0	66	1
Rorke	18.1	7	23	3
Benaud	27	6	91	5
O'Neill	2	1	8	0

Second Innings

P.E. Richardson, lbw, b Benaud...43
W. Watson, c Favell, b Benaud.....40
P.B.H. May, lbw, b Rorke.............59
M.C. Cowdrey, b Lindwall 8
T.W. Graveney, not out 53
T.E. Bailey, c Grout, b Lindwall 6
F.S. Trueman, c Grout, b Davidson0
G.A.R. Lock, b Rorke 9
F.H. Tyson, c Grout, b Benaud 33
J.B. Statham, c O'Neill, b Benaud ..2
T.G. Evans, c Benaud, b Davidson .0
Extras (b 5, lb 5, w 3, nb 4).............17
Total 270

FALL OF WICKETS: 1-89, 2-110, 3-125, 4-177, 5-198, 6-199, 7-222, 8-268, 9-270.

BOWLING

	O	M	R	W
Lindwall	26	5	70	2
Rorke	34	7	78	2
Benaud	29	10	82	4
Davidson	8.3	3	17	2
Burke	4	2	6	0

FIRST, Brisbane, Australia won by 8 wkts. SECOND, Melbourne, Australia won by 8 wkts. THIRD, Sydney, drawn FIFTH, Melbourne, Feb. 13-19.

(February 6)

(Solution No. 10,333)

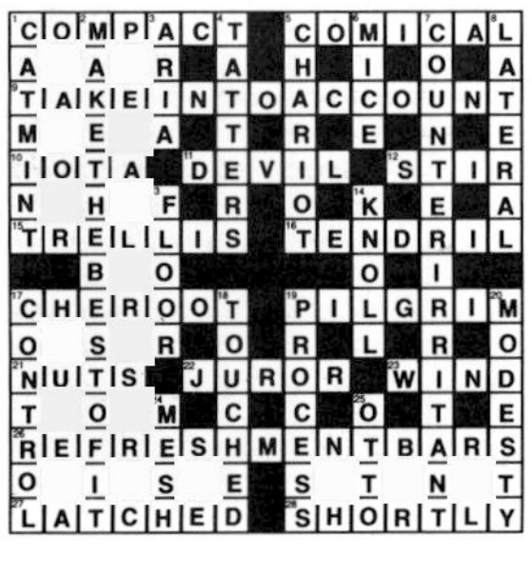

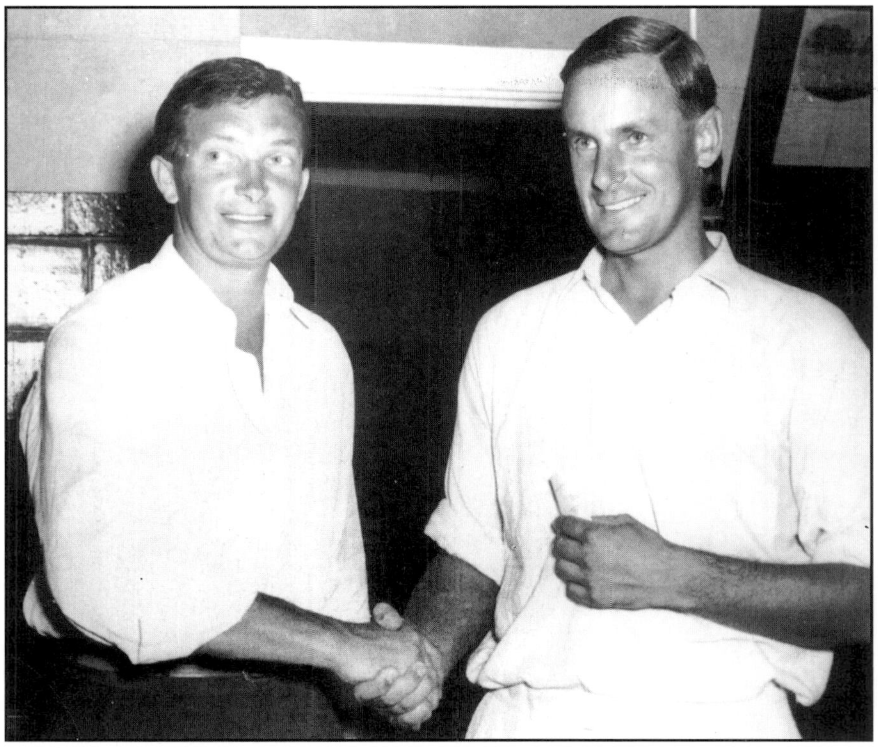

ENGLAND CAPTAIN Peter May (right) congratulates Australian Captain Richie Benaud in Adelaide, after Australia had won the fourth test and the ashes by 10 wickets

YORKSHIRE CHAMPIONS AFTER 13 YEARS

From E.W. Swanton

HOVE, Tuesday.

YORKSHIRE won the Championship here this afternoon thanks to two innings of exemplary hitting, each in its way a model, by Stott and Padgett. In 61 minutes they scored 141 together, starting at 40 for two and taking their side to the brink of victory.

Needing 215 in a shade under 1¾ hours Yorkshire got them for five wickets with seven minutes to spare. Thus they put themselves beyond the reach of Surrey, Gloucestershire and Warwickshire, and the prize is theirs at last, for the first time, apart from one tie, since 1946.

Yorkshire have never before gone for 13 years in the wilderness, just as no side had won seven times in a row, as Surrey have. I dare say that when the disappointment has worn off at the Oval, a feeling of some relief at the easing of the tension may follow.

Surrey have fought as hard as ever this summer in the modern tradition inspired by W.S. Surridge. But P.B.H. May's absence was too much of a handicap. In the minds of most people it will seem all to the good that the Championship has changed hands at last.

A more detailed analysis can await a calmer moment when the last games are finished on Saturday. For the moment it is enough to congratulate Yorkshire with all possible warmth, and in particular their captain Burnet.

When the unhappy domestic events of last summer are brought to mind to-day's victory will seem all the sweeter to him. From 11th to the top is quite a feat!

(September 2)

Women's Athletics

FASTEST 100yd BY MISS HYMAN

By Jack Crump

SURPRISE in the first day's programme of the Women's Amateur Athletic Association Championships at Motspur Park yesterday was the defeat of the holder of the 100 yards, Miss Madeleine Weston, in the semi-final.

Miss Western was beaten by inches by a Dutch competitor, J. Bijleveld, a member of the small Dutch team who were managed by the former Olympic champion Mrs. F. Blankers-Koen. Miss Weston, however, will have an opportunity of retaining her title to-day, for she qualified for the final, in the same time as the Dutch girl, 11.1sec.

The other semi-final produced faster running, Miss Dorothy Hyman winning in 11 sec. To-day's final should be an excellent race with Miss Hyman, who seems to be in particularly good form, slightly favoured to win.

After being eliminated from the 100 yards Miss Carole Quinton, holder of the 80 metres hurdles title, hurdled stylishly to win her heat in 11.1sec, improving the English native record (of which she is a joint holder) by one-tenth of a second.

There should also be an excellent final of the 880 yards in which there will be six girls who have run for Britain in international competition. The fastest in the heats was Miss Diane Leather with 2min 13.2sec. Other qualifiers include the holder, Miss Joy Jordan, and Miss Madeleine Ibbotson.

(July 5)

WEAK OXFORD OVERWHELMED

By Arthurian

Newport ... 35pts. Oxford Univ.... 8

Another splendid display by Newport at Rodney Parade yesterday earned them a decisive victory over a weak Oxford University side by four goals and five tries to a goal and a penalty goal.

Oxford had no answer to the speed and penetration of the Welsh club. A noteworthy feature of the game was that of the nine tries scored by Newport, only one was by a forward.

For long periods the Oxford pack contested the issue vigorously. They out-hooked Newport in the set scrums and they did well in the lineouts until the closing stages, with Higham, Bos and Bouwer, all jumping high against Newport's star men Lewis, Herrera and Davidge.

In the open, it was different story. Here Oxford were far too slow and Newport's rhythm quickly led to a fast build-up of points, and the issue was never in doubt after 20 minutes.

Even with England player Phillips in the centre, Oxford showed little thrust and what they did offer was ruthlessly smothered by Newport's fast and forceful covering.

(February 6)

Squash Rackets

BROOMFIELD CRUSHES PARTIDGE

KILLING SKILL

By Lance Tingay

The progress of N.H.R.A. Broomfield in the Amateur Squash Rackets Championship at the Royal Automobile Club yesterday was all one could expect from a defending title holder and favourite.

He took up a third-round place with dashing verve, killing skill and in the minimum of time. This forthright progress was made to the discomfiture of J.R. Partridge, of Surrey.

One hardly expected so good a player to be dismissed with the loss of a mere couple of points, but Partridge found no way of averting the punishing power of Broomfield's low hitting and spectators had hardly settled to the contest before it was over.

In contrast to Broomfield's lightning display, the top seed of a year ago, D.B. Hughes, now seeded No. 5, crept through to his last-16 place. He and C.P. Sharman, of Sussex, had a curious encounter.

Its oddity was in the fact that Hughes, still not himself after a recent illness, played with the conservation of energy necessarily uppermost in his mind, while Sharman, in an effort to hold his own against a more accomplished shotmaker than himself, relied extensively on the lob and slowing-down tactics.

In the end the ability of Hughes to produce winning shots gained him a halting victory.

MEDWAY HURT

Lethal Follow-Through

The ever-present occupational risk of squash was unhappily confirmed when M.P. Medway, of Middlesex, had his face cut from a backhand follow-through by the Egyptian, T. Shafik. As far as it went Medway was leading, but his first game advantage of 3-love did him small good since the match came to its gory finish at that stage.

The unlucky Medway was taken to hospital for treatment. The last 16 survivors include H.E. Truman, a brother of Miss Christine Truman, who had made firm progress in squash in the last couple of seasons.

Truman had a fine win yesterday over T. Pickering, a useful Yorkshireman. Truman maintained a solid game, gave little away and generally maintained a fast winning pace.

Truman now meets the fourth seed, the Scottish No. 1, M.A. Oddy, semi-finalist a year ago. Like Broomfield, Oddy is playing with consistent pace-making pressure betokening peak form, and the evidence of it yesterday was a one-sided win over G.D. Roynon, of Oxfordshire, who was allowed only a small share of the play.

(January 3)

MOSS WINS ITALIAN GRAND PRIX

BRABHAM IN THIRD PLACE

From W.A. McKenzie, Daily Telegraph Motoring Correspondent

MONZA, Sunday

STIRLING MOSS of Britain, driving a British Cooper, won the Grand Prix of Italy here to-day on the tremendously fast Monza road circuit. His victory transformed his chance of becoming World Champion driver this year.

There is only one more championship race to go, at Sebring in Florida. It will decide the championship between Jack Brabham, Australia, who finished third in a Cooper here to-day, Moss and Tony Brooks, the Manchester dental surgeon, who failed to finish to-day.

Moss had this morning only 17 points against Brabham's 27, and Brooks's 23. Brabham now has four more for his third place, a total of 31. But Moss, getting eight points for his victory to-day, is only 5 ½ points behind, with a total of 25 ½.

Yet only a week or two ago he had not won a Grand Prix this year, and despaired of getting anywhere in the picture. He began to pick up when he won the Portuguese Grand Prix. To-day he won the 257 mile event at an average speed of 124.38 m.p.h.

RECORD BROKEN

American Second

Several times he broke the lap speed record for the circuit, raising it to 127 m.p.h. But Phil Hill, the American, driving a Ferrari, who finished second, raised it to 128 m.p.h. Hill now has 19 points towards the championship.

Moss, driving a privately owned Cooper, entered by Rob Walker, took the lead at the start. But Hill was on his tail and passed him on the second lap. Moss regained the lead at once, but when Hill repassed him on the fifth lap he decided to sit behind and let the American make the pace.

It was a duel between the two right to the end, with never more than a few car lengths between them until the halfway stops for fuel and a change of tyres. After that Moss regained the lead, piling on speed and drawing away to win by a handsome 47.7secs.

Never out of the picture, however, were half a dozen other cars, Coopers and Ferraris. Any of them were potential winners if the two battling cars in the lead had failed.

The B.R.M.s were running strongly but always behind this string, and the Aston Martins never found any real speed. Seven of the 22 starters retired.

CLUTCH FAILURE

Out on First Lap

Tony Brooks's Ferrari was out on the first lap with clutch failure. Graham Hill's Lotus retired on the second lap. Innes Ireland's Lotus followed suit after 15 laps.

Jack Fairman, whose Cooper-Maserati was in and out of the pits with trouble, gave up after 19 laps. Bruce McLaren, whose Cooper was lying eighth most of its race stopped with mechanical trouble, and was abandoned on the course after 23 laps, and Roy Salvadori, whose Aston Martin had been lying well back, was out of the race after 45 laps.

The speed of the race, which covered 72 laps in the heat of Italy and on a somewhat rough surface, was killing. By 10 laps the race average was around 124 m.p.h. and steadily it went up till the refuelling stops.

RESULTS WERE:

1. Stirling Moss (Cooper) 2hr 4min 05.4sec;
2. Phil Hill (Ferrari), 2-4-52.1;
3. Jack Brabham (Cooper), 2-9-17.9;
4. Dan Gurney (Ferrari), 2-5-25;
5. C.B. Allison (Ferrari), 2-4-18 (one lap short);
6. Olivier Gerdeblen (Ferrari), 2-5-37.9 (one lap short);
7. Harry Schell (B.R.M.) 2-4-15.8 (two laps short);
8. Jonkim Bonnier (B.R.M.), 3-1-17.5 (two laps short).

(September 14)

PARTHIA AND FIDALGO SHATTER THE FRENCH

Boyd-Rochfort Achieves Ambition: Carr Beats His son-in-Law

From Hotspur

EPSOM, Wednesday.

FATHER and son-in-law fought out the finish of the Derby to-day, 42-year-old Harry Carr on Parthia defeating his 24-year-old son-in-law Joe Mercer on Fidalgo by one and a half lengths after a tense duel over the final three furlongs. Unlucky Shantung, badly baulked in running, came from last at Tattenham Corner to finish third. It was Carr's 13th ride in the Derby and his first success.

The race was a most satisfactory one for British breeding. Parthia is owned and was bred by Sir Humphrey de Trafford, and is closely related on his dam's side to the 1958 St. Leger winner Alcide, who would probably have won last year's Derby but for meeting with a mishap shortly before the race.

Sir Humphrey de Trafford has been a strong supporter of English racing since he rode as an amateur as a young man. It was his first success in the Derby, and a success long overdue for his trainer, Capt. C. Boyd-Rochfort, who now has all five classic races to his credit and has won practically every big race worth winning.

Carr, previously second in the Derby on Prince Simon and Aureole, has won four of the five classic races for Boyd-Rochfort's stable - the St. Leger with Meld and Alcide and the 1,000 Guineas and the Oaks with Meld. He was also second in the 2,000 Guineas on Prince Simon.

PERFECT DAY

Immense Crowd

The weather was perfect. The sun shone, there was a cooling breeze and the Downs held an immense crowd.

There was no delay at the start, which was a good one, and the first to show in front were Saint Crespin, Princillon, Lindrick and Rousseau's Dream. Shantung was among those caught flat-footed and was slow to find his stride.

Nobody seemed keen to make the running, and as a result the mediocre Rousseau's Dream went to the front after a furlong with Josephus and Lindrick just behind, Fidalgo lying fourth, and Arvak, Saint Crespin, Parthia and Above Suspicion well placed.

The pace after three furlongs seemed definitely on the slow side for a Derby. Probably as a result of this there was a good deal of bunching as the course begins to swing to the left.

It was at this point that Piggott sent Carnoustie for an opening and badly interfered with Above Suspicion. Moore, on Princillon, had to snatch up his colt. Palmer and Shantung had been making up ground on the inside, which was asking for trouble, for a colt well back at the top of the hill and racing near the rails is unlikely to have a clear run.

Palmer was tracking Princillon, when the latter was snatched up, and he could not prevent Shantung striking into him. Shantung fell back quickly and at the top of the hill was last. His rider, feeling that the colt had broken down, was on the point of pulling him up altogether when he began to go better again.

DOWN THE HILL

Shantung Well Last

Meanwhile, as the field began the long run down to Tattenham Corner the four leaders - Rousseau's Dream, Josephus, Lindrick and Fidalgo - were clear of the others and led round the Corner, with Arvak, Parthia, Saint Crespin, Princillon, the improving Carnoustie and Thymus all within hail. Shantung was a long way last, even behind that mediocre pair Beau Tudor and Barbary Pirate.

Fidalgo was going easily and well, and at this point I thought he was certain to go near winning. Soon after turning into the straight Mercer brought Fidalgo out to make sure of a clear run, and with three furlongs to go he had taken up the running and gone over to the rails. He held a clear lead, and looked the probable winner.

Carr, however, had been biding his time on Parthia, and a quarter of a mile from home he joined Fidalgo.

For the next furlong it was difficult to say which of the two would gain the day, but Parthia gradually began to wear down his rival and in the last furlong went clear to win by one and a half lengths.

Shantung, coming with a long run on the outside, passed horse after horse in the straight and snatched third place on the post from Saint Crespin. He never looked like getting to Parthia and Fidalgo, but from the amount of ground he made up in the last half mile it is reasonable to think he would have come very near winning with a clear run.

Nevertheless, it is not fair to Parthia to take from him any of the honour and glory. If Palmer, on Shantung, had got to Parthia a furlong from home Parthia might well have pulled out more. That, at any rate, is Carr's opinion.

(June 4)

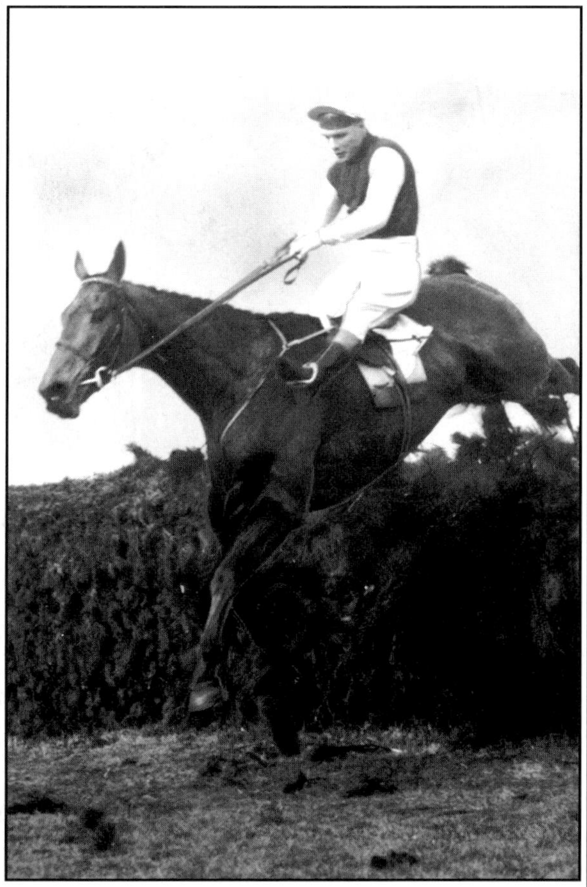

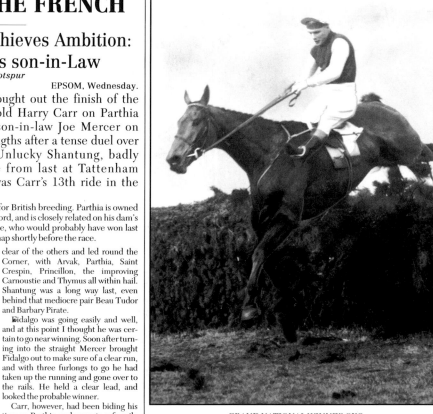

GRAND NATIONAL WINNER OXO.

OXO & SCUDAMORE HOLD ON TO WIN NATIONAL

By Hotspur

WILLIE STEPHENSON, son of a Durham farmer and formerly a competent flat-race jockey, became the third trainer to saddle both a Derby and a Grand National winner when Oxo, in the colours of Bedfordshire farmer Mr. J.E. Bigg, won the National on Saturday from the proven Aintree horses Wyndburgh, Mr. What, and the gallant mare Tiberetta. Eight years ago Stephenson trained Arctic Prince to win the Derby for Mr. J. McGrath.

Stephenson was formerly apprenticed to the late Major Vandy Beatty and gained his first big success at 14 when Niantic dead-heated with Medal in the 1927 Cambridgeshire. He now joins the late Dick Dawson, of Whatcombe, and George Blackwell as trainers both of a Derby and a National winner.

WONDERFUL MARE

Tiberetta's Last Race

Oxo, running at Aintree for the first time, won from Wyndburgh, Mr. What and Tiberetta. The first three live to fight another day, but Mr. Edward Courage, owner, breeder and trainer of Tiberetta, tells me that his great-hearted mare has run her last race and will now go to stud. What a wonderful career she has had!

She has run 68 times and has never fallen, though she has twice got rid of her rider. As winner of the Grand Sefton and third, second and fourth in the National in successive years, her name will be remembered for many seasons to come.

Although the going was perfect on Saturday, only four of the 34 finished. Becher's claiming the majority of the fallers - eight first time round, six the second. Most of the grief there on the first circuit was caused by two of the early leaders falling and bringing down several of those following, including Done Up.

UNLUCKY BROOKSHAW

Rides Without Stirrups

It was at Becher's the second time that Tim Brookshaw, riding Wyndburgh, broke a stirrup, kicking his foot out of the other iron to give him better balance for the rest of the race. In spite of his rider's great handicap, Wyndburgh was beaten by only one and a half lengths and would probably have won in another hundred yards - a great performance.

Both Brookshaw and Michael Scudamore, who rode Oxo, are sons of farmers from near the Welsh border. Scudamore has twice gone near winning the National before, for he was second on Legal Joy in 1952, and on Irish Lizard in 1954. His victory was therefore thoroughly well deserved.

(March 23)

PIGGOTT ACCUSED BY U.S. TURF WRITER

LESTER PIGGOTT, suspended by the Nottingham stewards last night for "rough riding" on Astrador, and in trouble at Chantilly on Sunday has also come in for searing criticism from a leading American racing journalist, Frank Talmadge Phelps, because of his conduct at Laurel Park last year.

Phelps, in the new edition of the Bloodstock Breeders' Review, says: "Had American riders conducted themselves as Piggott and the Russian Kovalev did at the start of the Washington International, they would have been suspended on the spot.

"Yet there is nothing American officials can do to jockeys in the United States for this one race once they return thereafter to their own countries.

"Some form of international sporting agreement is badly needed to enable suspensions or fines assessed in one country, because of careless or unsporting conduct, to be enforced in all racing countries. Otherwise, there will always be a few visitors who, feeling themselves beyond the reach of discipline in another jurisdiction, may be tempted to take undue advantage of the situation."

WALK-UP FIASCO

Seven False Starts

According to Phelps, Piggott behaved badly at the "walk-up" start, used for this race because visiting horses are not used to the American-type starting gate. There were seven false starts. The chief offenders were Escribane, from Venezuela, the Russian horse Zaryad, ridden by Kovalev, and the German Derby winner Orsini II, ridden by Piggott.

Phelps says: "Orsini kicked and stomped about and his jockey appeared unable or unwilling to control him. Finally the German colt was removed from the next-to-inside post position and placed on the extreme outside, where he could do less damage with his lashing heels - but every time the starter looked away Piggott tried to edge towards the inside.

"Victor Kovalev on Zaryad repeatedly tried to beat the start and seemed unable to understand the instructions of a Russian-speaking assistant starter, who at last grasped the reins to keep the Russian colt in line. When the field finally managed an official start, Zaryad was left at the post."

The whole race was covered by the film patrol, which probably the visiting jockeys did not realise until later. At any rate the Russian delegation protested after the race, Kovalev saying that Zaryad's reins had been held too long at the start. When the films failed to substantiate this charge the entire Soviet group denied that it had ever been made!

It will be recalled that the English-bred American-owned winner Tudor Era was disqualified, after a thorough investigation of the film, in favour of the second, Sailor's Guide, also of English blood but foaled in Australia.

(June 9)

Winter Sports

MITCHELL LEADS

From T.D. Richardson

ST. MORITZ, Thursday.

Flt. Lt. C.N.C. Mitchell of Britain and the fine young Swiss rider R. Kuderli had a neck-and-neck struggle for supremacy during the first day's racing of the Cresta Run world championship for the Cartier Cup from Junction to-day.

Mitchell gained a lead of one-tenth of a second on the day with a total of 134.8 sec. The crack Italian N. Bibbia lay third with 135.6 sec.

(February 6)

THE COURAGE AND SKILL OF MANNY MERCER

Tragic End of a Great Jockey and Natural Horseman

By Marlborough

A TRAGIC shadow was cast at Ascot on Saturday over the entire fabric of British racing. From Worcester to Hamilton Park, from Newmarket to Malton, tens of thousands of men and women heard with incredulous dismay that Manny Mercer was dead.

To many thousands more who had never seen him in the flesh, this cheerful, smiling little man had long been a familiar, much-respected friend. Only a name in their morning papers, perhaps, but a name that could be trusted day in, day out, to do a difficult job as well as any man.

It is 12 years now since a tiny 17-year-old apprentice won the Lincolnshire Handicap on a rank outsider called Jockey Treble.

Many apprentices win big handicaps and are praised to the skies for a while, but most of them discover all too soon that dash and nerve by themselves have never made a top-class jockey.

GIFTED RIDER

True Horseman

But in the years that followed that far-off day at Lincoln it quickly became evident that there was much more to Manny Mercer than just the courage that goes with youth.

When they were first apprenticed neither Manny nor his younger brother, Joe, had any kind of riding experience. What they did have, however, was far more important - that magical natural sympathy which makes big horses run for little boys as they never will for stronger but less gifted men.

One had only to watch Mercer cantering to the post - as he was when tragedy overtook him on Saturday - to know that this was that precious rarity, a horseman as well as a jockey.

The angle of the body, the easy confident length of rein and the horse itself obviously at peace with the world - these were the trademarks of Manny Mercer, and few men now riding have brought them to such perfection.

Strong in a finish, nerveless in a big field, and capable of fitting his tactics to the special needs of the hour, he had craved himself a secure niche very close to the top of the tree and would no doubt have retained it for many years to come.

LIKED AND RESPECTED

Blow to Racing World

Mercer was riding lately at the very height of his powers. He had ridden 15 winners in the 10 racing days before his death and had reached his century for the season, for the fourth year running, on Friday afternoon.

As a man I did not know him well, but to those that did perhaps his greatest qualities were loyalty and the unquenchable cheerfulness that turns disaster into a joke and shares success with all the world.

Now he is gone, and the sympathy of all goes out to the family he left behind. In the weighing room, on the racecourse itself and on the training gallops he knew so well, he will be long and sorely missed.

Great jockeys are rare enough, but those that command and keep the respect and liking of the entire racing world must in their way be great men as well. Manny Mercer was one of these.

(October 17)

No. 10,333

ACROSS

5 Sleeve-end about to be removed (3, 3)
8 Cook might use it when her work becomes a strain (8)
9 Many such are famous, but the best-known, perhaps, is unknown (7)
10 Such a beast is up in arms (7)
11 Rub out a doctor, but provide an opening for the big guns (9)
13 Island returned to a mutinous spot in Denmark (8)
14 Not down on the ballot paper? (6)
17 Draw it too tight and you will choke (3)
19 How singular! (3)
20 What the home-sick soldier wants to a point, and the loafer who wants a rise (6)
23 O dry rain would be quite out of it (8)
26 Fourteen points for nothing? It's worked by chisellers! (9)
28 Where in S. America one might otherwise distinguish people from Denmark (5)
29 Gestures that may call for upward movements of hands? (7)
30 Purchase made by the first woman in possibly regal surroundings (8)
31 It's made in collision (6)

DOWN

1 Hardly - well, hardly plentiful (6)
2 Look quickly to catch it (7)
3 How motorists travel, neat, reorganised, and in a body (9)
4 The crossword compiler really leads a dog's life! (6)
5 Does he carry off the debate? (8)
6 They are no holiday, but agreeable people come to them (5)
7 Someone's sole support? (8)
12 They may be over-age for household management (3)
15 They cling to one single idea (9)
16 Sounds as if it weaves an atmosphere about the old home? (8)
18 One relies on it without reason (8)
21 Students looking up to him might get his consent (3)
22 The group caught sight of a revolutionary woodcutter (4-3)
24 An aspect of the Pavlov theory that is coming back (6)
25 These just don't argue (3-3)
27 In turning over an area of land I may dig it up (5)

(February 9)

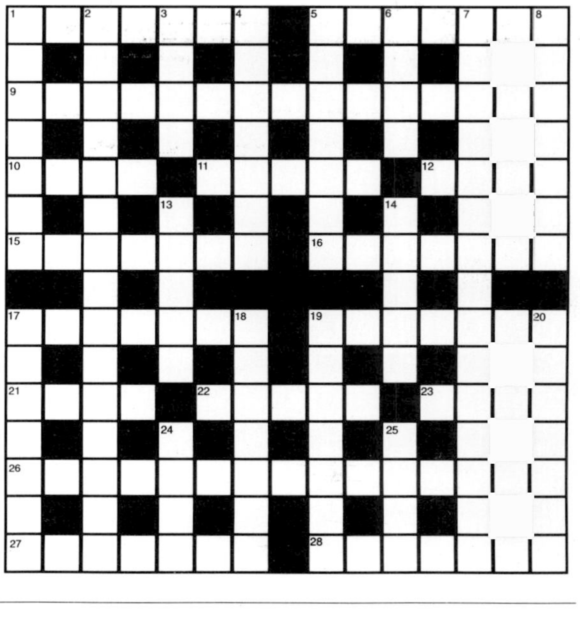

THEMES

of the

DECADE

A DECADE OF THE ARTS

The Fifties was a decade of transition, bounded at one end by the violent upheaval of the Second World War and at the other by the cultural revolution of the 1960s. But predominant in all the arts were certain common themes and moods: the importance of realism, a pervasive feeling of alienation and the resumption of the interrupted rise of modernism and its explicit rejection of the rules, order and conventions that had characterised 19th-century art.

The suppression of artistic freedom in totalitarian Europe during the 1930s and the war had led to the rise of America as the dominant force in painting. From America came Abstract Expressionism (Jackson Pollock, William de Kooning, Mark Rothko), bold, aggressive and in its own words 'extremist' art. In Europe many of the old heroes of Modernism survived, and it was an exhibition of work by Picasso and Matisse in England immediately after the war that stimulated a growth of Modernism in British art. The respected Victor Pasmore abandoned representation for abstraction in his work. The leading sculptors of the day, Barbara Hepworth and Henry Moore, both produced important abstract works.

British Neo-Romanticism, inspired by the war (John Minton, Keith Vaughan, John Piper) was overtaken not only by Modernism but also by 'kitchen sink' realism (John Bratby, Edward Middleditch, Jack Smith), its key characteristics provincialism, grime and everyday life. For many artists the 1950s were an age of anxiety. There is pain, loneliness and disorientation in Francis Bacon's grotesquely distorted subjects and in the twisted, fragile, vulnerable

BARBARA HEPWORTH

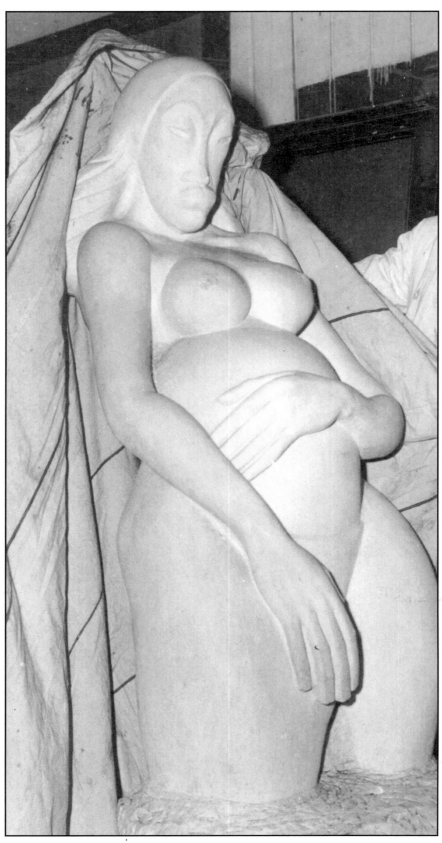

EPSTEIN'S "GENESIS": The much discussed figure of "Pregnant Woman".

figures sculpted by Lynn Chadwick and Reg Butler. Lucian Freud's nudes are slabs of meat, joylessly and dispassionately observed.

Some of the gloom was dispelled in the mid-50s when Jasper Johns and Robert Rauschenberg pioneered Pop Art, described by one critic as youthful, transient, cheap, witty, sexy, gimmicky and glamorous. In its love of bright colours, popular culture and sex, in its irreverent humour and classlessness, it looked forward to the cultural explosion of the 60s.

The style in which architects chose to rebuild after the wholesale wartime destruction was Modernism. Utopian in aspiration, utilitarian in conception, its characterising features were abstraction, functionalism and severe geometricality. Le Corbusier's Unité d'Habitation, Marseilles (1952), a monumental 17-storey apartment block, and the twin glass towers of Mies van der Rohe's Lake Shore Drive Apartments, Chicago (1951) set the pattern. Blocks of flats everywhere from New York to Tokyo, from Brasilia to Bethnal Green were identically constructed as faceless, featureless blocks. New public buildings (UNESCO Headquarters, Paris, 1958), commercial buildings (Pirelli Tower, Milan, 1959), churches, cultural centres, railway stations, universities, throughout the Fifties emerged as anonymous glass turrets, with no sense of either individual or national identity. Massive totalitarian constructions devoid of life or soul, they unwittingly embodied the sense of alienation recognisable in other areas of the arts. The English version of this international style was justly dubbed 'The New Brutalism' on the appearance of the Smithsons' Hunstanton School (1954).

The war had given a boost to nationalism in music and after the war the old giants of the English Musical Renaissance (Walton, Vaughan, Williams, Bliss), who had responded to the need to express the national identity in music, continued to work in a distinctively English idiom. Similarly in the USSR Prokofiev, Shostakovich and Kachaturian produced music that was distinctively Russian. The 'great white hope' of British music in these years was Benjamin Britten, who produced operas for the Festival of Britain (*Billy Budd*) and the coronation (*Gloriana*). But in music too, experimentation, abstraction and modernism (atonal music, serialism, electronic music) were making great strides, particularly among younger composers (Pierre Boulez, Karlheinz Stockhausen, Milton Babbitt). They served merely to increase the reputation of classical music for inaccessibility. The Russians brought classical ballet to a thrilling peak and the tours of the West by the Bolshoi and Kirov Ballets in the 1950s dazzled audiences. Western choreographers like George Balanchine, Martha Graham and John Cranko responded by developing a self-consciously Modern Ballet, emphasising abstract music, disjointed movement and overt sexuality.

Perhaps the most far-reaching musical development of the decade was the rise of rock n' roll. Loud, throbbing and overly sexy, it was distinctively youth music and for the first time decisively divided the generations musically. Hip-swivelling, greased-haired Elvis Presley became a worldwide musical idol, inspiring English analogues in Cliff Richard and Tommy Steele.

A VIEW OF A POWER STATION, showing two boilers already in position.

The most influential movement is post-war world cinema was Italian neo-realism, in particular the work of Roberto Rossellini and Vittorio de Sica, who made films without stars, no real locations and telling stories of ordinary people. Realism and naturalism became the battle cries of younger film-makers and in the later 1950s both Britain and France experienced a 'New Wave' in film-making. Its leading lights, Jean-Luc Godard, François Truffaut and Claude Chabrol in France and Karel Reisz, Tony Richardson and Lindsay Anderson in Britain, rejected the formality, structure and middle-class ethos of the older generation epitomised by directors like Marcel Carné, Julien Duvivier, Carol Reed and David Lean and made films dealing realistically with working class life, youth and sexuality.

But cinema was badly hit by the rise of television. 1946 was the peak year of cinema-going in Britain (1,635 million attendances). The audience thereafter declined

ELVIS PRESLEY

drastically, down by two thirds by 1960. The great British film studios like Ealing, home of the Ealing comedies, and Lime Grove, home of the Gainsborough melodramas, were sold to BBC-TV. To lure audiences from their televisions, cinema developed gimmicks like 3-D and Cinemascope and produced

BEAUTIFUL ITALIAN STAR GINA LOLLOGRIGIDA as she appears in the Romulus-Santana comedy-adventire, "Beat the Devil"

expensive epics (*The Ten Commandments, Around the World in 80 Days, War and Peace, Ben Hur*). Hollywood, however, continued to produce stars capable of attracting younger film-goers (James Dean, Marilyn Monroe, Marlon Brandon) and the old masters were producing some of their best work, notably Alfred Hitchcock (*Rear Window, Vertigo, Strangers on a Train*) and John Ford (*The Sun Shines Bright, The Quiet Man, The Searchers*). But an international 'art house' film culture was growing, producing new cinematic heroes for the young

FRANCIS BACON by Lucian Freud (1952)

cineastes in all countries; the Pole Andrzej Wajda (*Ashes and Diamonds*), the Swede Ingmar Bergman (*Seventh Soul*), the Japanese Akira Kurosawa (*Seven Samurai*), the Frenchman Jacques Tati (*Les Vacances de Monsieur Hulot*) and the Indian Satyajit Ray (*Pather Panachali*).

In British and French theatre the older generation of masters of the 'well-made play' (Noel Coward, Terence Rattigan, Jean Anouilh, Jean Giraudoux) continued to work and there was a brief flowering of poetic drama (Christopher Fry, T. S. Eliot). But a new mood of realism, psychological investigation and relevance gripped the theatre. Its standardbearer in America was Arthur Miller (*The Crucible, Death of a Salesman, A View from the Bridge*), though his popularity was equalled by the more extravagantly theatrical Tennessee Williams (*The Rose Tattoo, Suddenly Last Summer*). 'Method' acting too developed in the USA,

emphasising the search for motivation over the more traditional training based on direction and technique. From France came Existentialist drama (Sartre) and Absurdism (Beckett, Ionesco), both of which underlined the essential meaningless of life. Then in 1956 John Osborne's *Look Back in Anger* exploded onto the English stage and the 'angry young men' of the theatre came along with the New Wave directors in the cinema and the 'kitchen sink' realists in painting to symbolise the youthful discontent with the status quo that was to fuel the Sixties cultural revolution.

By the end of the 1950s, the developments in cinema, theatre, painting and music were all pointing to the emergence of a new and different cultural scene. But Agatha Christie's *The Mousetrap*, which opened in 1952, continued to run - and is still running, a symbol of the tenacious survival of older entertainment values.

A DECADE OF SCIENCE

The Fifties was one of the most exciting scientific decades since the start of the century. It started with three promising steps in "artificial intelligence," the art of teaching computers to "think" like humans, an ability that will one day enable machines and people to colonise the universe as partners.

Claude Shannon built a chess-playing machine in 1950. Its play was far inferior to the chess computers found in today's electronic toyshops, but it was the first time that a non-human learned to play this most complex of games.

A draughts-playing computer was even more impressive. A. L. Samuel of IBM built such a device that consistently defeated its own creator, overturning the ancient belief that machines would never be more than obedient slaves. Also in 1950, the British mathematician Alan Turing published his famous "test" by which humans could determine by conversations with a machine whether it was truly "intelligent". By 2000, he prophesied, a machine will have passed that test. We shall see.

Or will we even see the year 2000? After 1952, some people were less sure. That year saw the explosion of the first hydrogen bomb on Bikini Atoll in the Pacific. Within a year, the Russians had let off a hydrogen bomb of their own. In 1958, the American nuclear submarine Nautilus, with the capacity to launch nuclear missile-tipped rockets, sailed under the North Pole icecap. As Isaac Asimov put it, "the world descended further into the abyss of fear, from which it has not yet emerged."

But there was rapid progress in more peaceful technologies. The first electric power from atomic fission was produced in 1951. The transistor, the precursor to the silicon chip which is the heart of today's computers, was invented in 1953 by William Shockley and John Bardeen. Spray cans, whose gas emissions were later to threaten the Earth's ozone layers, were invented by Robert Abplanalp in the same year; and liquid-free photocopying, known as Xeroxing after the Greek word xerography of "dry writing", was perfected for office use by Chester Carlson in 1958.

There were great leaps in medicine. In 1951, an electron microscope was used in University College, London, to examine human brain cells. In the following year, Robert Wilkins introduced tranquilliser pills and Gregory Pincus invented another kind of pill,

BRITAIN'S FIRST H-BOMB TEST.
One of a series of official pictures of Britain's nuclear test explosion on May 15 in the Christmas Island area of the Pacific.

the oral contraceptive, which encouraged women's liberation by making sex possible without fear of pregnancy.

John Gibbon built a heart-lung machine for coronary by-pass operations in 1953. The first successful kidney transplant was performed in 1954, when the first contact lenses were put to use. Jonas Salk and Albert Sabin perfected the polio vaccine in 1957, the year that Clarence Lillehei's heart pace-maker was inserted under the skin of a patient's chest.

An achievement in biology caused a still greater sensation. In 1953, Francis Crick and James Watson cracked the "genetic code." They succeeded in analysing the structure of DNA, a spiral-shaped substance which forms the core of life itself.

This work, which won both men Nobel prizes, is now the basis for the vast and growing genetic engineering industry, in which new and, one hopes, benign life-forms can be made in laboratories for a host of medical and agricultural uses.

Not all science was so Earthbound. The astronomer Jan Oort transformed our staid vision of the

PROFESSOR WILLIAM SHOCKLEY, the American physicist who holds a key part in the invention of the transistor.

Sun's planetary system in 1950 when he explained the continual appearances of comets. He suggested that beyond Pluto, normally the most distant planet, there is an unimaginably large source of such icy, rocky objects. The now widely-accepted Oort Cloud is believed to consist of a gigantic cloud of some 100,000 million comets that stretch in distance towards the nearest star.

The diameter of Pluto was first measured at 3,600 miles by Gerard Kuiper also in 1950, and its six-day rotation five years later (although discovery of its giant moon Charon would have to wait another 28 years). Seth Nicholson found Ananke, a 12th moon of Jupiter in 1952 - NASA's Voyager space probes were later to find many more. William Morgan discovered the Catharine wheel-like structure of our Milky Way galaxy in 1951, and four years later Viktor Ambartsumian found that whole galaxies elsewhere in the universe sometimes explode cataclysmically.

Even the Sun itself was demonstrated to be a violently energetic body. In 1959 Eugene Parker discovered the "wind from the Sun", a stream of atomic particles that pours continuously from the Sun into space at millions of miles per hour. Today, space scientists plan to exploit this wind by building spacecraft with giant sails.

The year 1957 saw one of the most important events in the history of man. The Soviet Union launched Sputnik I, the first Earth-orbiting space satellite. President

A FULL-SCALE DUPLICATE OF THE RUSSIAN SPUTNIK II

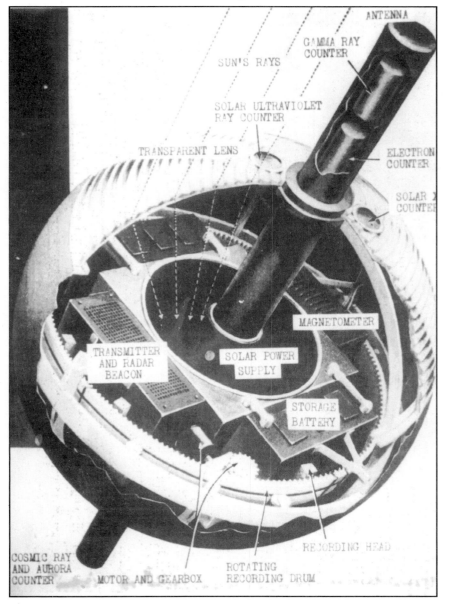

ANTENNA

GAMMA RAY COUNTER

SUN'S RAYS

SOLAR ULTRAVIOLET RAY COUNTER

TRANSPARENT LENS

ELECTRON COUNTER

SOLAR X COUNTER

MAGNETOMETER

TRANSMITTER AND RADAR BEACON

SOLAR POWER SUPPLY

STORAGE BATTERY

COSMIC RAY AND AURORA COUNTER

MOTOR AND GEARBOX

RECORDING HEAD

ROTATING RECORDING DRUM

Eisenhower was at first complacent about this tremendous feat which horrified and astounded American scientists and engineers. The "Russians have put a small ball up in the air," he declared inaccurately. "That doesn't raise my apprehensions one iota."

But within a year he had changed his mind. He created NASA, the National Space and Aeronautics Administration, to organise America's long-range exploration of the Moon and planets.

The East-West space race was now on. In 1959, Russia sent the Lunik

THIS IS AN ARTIST'S IMPRESSION of Sputnik I, with its new companion in globe-circling space, Sputnik II, which whirls in a higher orbit. Sputnik I travels around the earth once in 96.2 minutes while Sputnik II takes 103.7 minutes, on account of the higher altitude.

probes to explore the Moon, the third of which sent back spectacular pictures of its mountainous far side. The Americans, after a series of explosions on the launch-pad, orbited Vanguard I, an unmanned probe that measured the Earth's shape more accurately than ever before.

The stage was now set for a human adventure that may have no end. As the decade closed, the Russians were preparing to launch their first cosmonaut, and the Americans drew plans to land people on the Moon. No one dreamed that the coming Moon race would transform the world's communications and production by introducing miniaturised electronics and desktop computers.

A DECADE OF FASHION

The Fifties, in fashion, were the last time a girl wanted to look like her mother. The great sweeping democratic youthquake of the Sixties was totally unthought of, and meanwhile it was white gloves, hats, neat little suits, respectful nods to the great designers whose work, with luck and effort, might be copied exactly. The very idea of looking round London for bright young design talent was shocking. Fleets of British manufacturers and their sketchers and cutters descended on the Italian and French couture collections twice each year in a sort of reverent pilgrimage, eager to get the newest look from the tabernacles there. In lots of ways it was all quite restful, as structured societies often are. Fashion inspiration came, of course, "from those foreign fellas" and later in the decade, with the rise of Chanel and Galitzine, from those ladies who understood what a woman wanted.

The dates for inspiration were carved in stone: we trekked to Italy and to Paris on virtually the same days each January and July, making the next season's hotel reservations as a matter of course on departure from the eight-day orgy of fashion shows. Paris couture was rigid with rules: no

A HARTNELL LINE-UP: The late Sir Norman hartnell hosting his own show of lavish evening dresses in 1953, the year he made the Queen's Coronation Gown.

ASCOT: One of the ensembles seen in the sunshine of Hunt Cup Day.
A swathed white dress by Hartnell.

photographers were allowed in to the shows, only sketchers (The *Daily Telegraph* at this time and for long after enjoyed the talents of fashion artist Beryl Hartland). The great fear was that if photographers published their work instantly, alongside the writer's review of the collection, the copyists would work from that and demur at paying the whacking entrance fee demanded to see the collection in person.

So one could stroll round the cafés after every show and see intense-looking fashion manufacturers from many lands giving the hot news to their acolytes. "Look, Manny, you do the sleeves like this" - a quick sketch on a café's paper tablecloth - "and then he puts a neckline like so . . and of course you've got to find some pale pink gaberdine, God knows where . . Go to it, boy."

Fashion photographers were there, but hovering until nightfall when they could actually get at the clothes (which all day long had been available to the big store buyers for real pounds-and-shillings business). Many a taxi chugged through the Paris night bearing a Balmain ballgown, chosen by a fashion editor as the garment for her magazine's cover picture, en route to a photographer's rented studio where at midnight someone like Alec

Murray or John Antill waited with model girls, hairdressers and make-up artists. It was agony to stay in the same hotel as these dear folk, and I moved away several times as models discovered my quiet gem: they chattered merrily as sparrows at midnight as they prepared for their all-night work before the camera.

Exactly one month after the collections the pictures were, in great formality, allowed to be published. Backgrounds in these were immensely important: the spearing cypresses of Florence, the fountains of Versailles - whatever said "We're abroad, this is the real stuff." The *Daily Telegraph* for years bought the poetic and flavourful photographs of Regina Relang, a quiet, immaculately tailored Munich photographer whose work was sold by agents all over Europe and America.

Industrial giants such as ICI and British Nylon Spinners were present at the couture collections as well, backing the designers' use of their inventive new weaves of nylon or Terylene as good props for publicity. Their free pictures were a real help to the hard-up editor with little to spend on her fashion pages.

Parties! Everybody gave parties. I remember one glorious starlit summer evening when ICI gave a midnight supper in a Florence hotel

garden, and all the fashion world guests dressed to the nines, coming straight from the usual evening shows in the Palazzo Pitti. Designer Ken Scott once showed his entire collection in a circus ring off the Appian Way in Rome, bands, animals and popcorn rampant. Roberta di Camerino's were perhaps most lavish: she treated the world fashion press to two days and two nights in Venice, putting us all up at the Excelsior Lido, chartering gondolas to sweep us over to her private island for a fashion show in her barn, wine bottles and fruit stands set up amongst the wild grasses and grazing donkeys.

All of us wanted, of course, to be first to show the new lines and The *Daily Telegraph* sparred with the best of them. London manufacturers like Polly Peck and Frederick Starke would buy a toile (a muslin copy of the couture dress) and copy it exactly at a realistic price. One could buy, as I did, a beautifully made black crepe cocktail dress, a dead ringer for Guy Laroche, for £14.

Meanwhile, back at the ranch, we had our own couture designers - a round dozen of them - and news of their fashion shows was so hot it made page one of the evening papers. I rushed, for my pre-*Telegraph* job on the *Star* (evening sister of the *News Chronicle*) to phone booths in Shepherds Market where ladies of the evening beat angrily on the doors while I dictated what Hartnell had just shown us.

Norman Hartnell, who of course had made the Queen's wedding dress and coronation gown, was the first of the London Incorporated Society of Fashion Designers to go wholesale and ready-to-wear. (He had designed Utility clothes during the war). Soon many of the others followed, and the ordinary woman (whoever she might be) could buy, for example, a suit manufactured by Reldan from couturier Digby Morton's design for around £12. Waiting in the wings were two of Britain's glories Jean Muir and Mary Quant, both to make their impact in the Sixties. But in the late Fifties Jean Muir's wool jersey shift dresses for Jane & Jane, before she launched her own label, were sensational buys at around £12 and I still have several.

Hair was pageboy, quietly unremarkable, and usually squashed anyhow by the hats we always wore as we covered fashion collections. Vidal Sassoon with his triangular cut was waiting offstage in the East End. Most fashion writers encountered each other under the hairdryers at André Bernard. Gloves were as vital as well-polished shoes: we bought both on our forays to Florence and Rome.

Separates dawned, and a few enterprising stores opened departments especially for them. Enid Chanelle won fame and a fortune with her chain of Maryon shops selling angora jersey shirt-neck dresses at £3. We bought them in every colour. The great boutique

KENNETH MICHAEK CLARK, 17, leaving the shop of his Petticoat Lane tailor wearing the outfit for which he has just paid £15, 18s.

COUNTESS BUNNY ESTERHAZY in a white spotted navy silk dress with an Alice band of white flowers, and Miss Florence Harcourt-Smith in a grey and white surah silk suit with a frilled pancake hat of white crin.

avalanche was just around the corner, Woollands was the much-loved news-making fashion store, with its 21 Shop and 31 Shop.

Swirling skirts, tiny tight-belted waists of the 1947 Dior New Look still dominated the early part of the Fifties. Schoolgirls wore these long full skirts in poodle cloth, with tight black polo neck sweaters tucked in (a glance at Paris Existentialist all-black fashion as typified by Juliette Greco and denizens of the Deux Magots café). Brigitte Bardot's enchanting pink and white gingham wedding dress put Paris couturier Jacques Esterel on the map and brought fresh air to a stuffy scene. Down in Florence, Emilio Pucci dazzled with his glorious colour prints, exhilarating especially to a British public not long freed from the drab tyranny of clothing coupons.

Chanel made her historic comeback from Swiss exile to Paris in 1954 to mixed reviews (many

hated her apparently casual jersey cardigan suits). St. Laurent, a gangling, timid youth of 21, was appointed Christian Dior's successor, and was later sacked from the classic house for his brave introduction of black leather Beat and Street fashion. And Balenciaga, the greatest cutter of them all, came out (at the same moment as Italy's Marucelli - which was first?) with the sack dress, loathed by most men, but women found it a relaxing pleasure to wear. Valentino entered the world stage in Florence at the close of the decade and a handsome young man called Givenchy dressed gamine Audrey Hepburn in slender black sheath dresses, and he's still doing it! We all starched our crinoline petticoats in the bathtub, wore matching sets of jewellery. Hotel ballrooms, and airlines too, shrieked and forbade our spike heels which punched floors in beautiful parquet and fuselage.

Genteel was the norm in the London scene. No model girl showed up for a photo session without having her hair done (at her own time and expense) first. She often went on to marry a lord or a cabinet minister. (Bronwen Pugh, Shirley Worthington and Anne Gunning spring to mind). Dulcet tones prevailed - the Cockney kid, photographer David Bailey, the enchanting Twiggy and followers, came later, in the next decade.

It was a working world without today's helpers and acolytes. The fashion writer was expected to fetch and carry the clothes, iron them, pin the model girls into them, provide the accessories, fold up and return the clothes to the store or manufacturer, noting of course prices, colours and when and where the fashions were available for the readers to buy. Incidentally, almost as an afterthought, of course she wrote the article to accompany these pictures - the job she thought she'd been hired for in the first place.

Royal fashion excited interest, it seems odd to recall. We were all terribly correct about reporting it. Sacred and secret as the recipe for Chartreuse was the information on what the Queen might wear on each day of a tour overseas. Nothing was revealed to us until she actually put it on her back! We used to gather at the end of the day in Hartnell's salon awaiting the revelation: this morning in Canada she wore the

A face of the Fifties

blue and yes, here are sketches of it we can show you at last! One bolted down to the newspaper office in Fleet Street to get sketch and story into that night's edition.

In a sense it was all calm-before-storm. The fashion excitements of the Sixties changed the way we worked, changed the way women wanted to look, brought new freedoms, defiance, craziness. Suddenly everything was possible. The Fifties were the last tranquil time.

A DECADE OF CRIME

BIG BEN showing dimly through the fog.

CHRISTIE, the murderer – a police picture issued in 1953.

MR. JUSTICE FINNEMORE¹ who is hearing the Christie murder case at the Old Bailey.

The 1950's, when London was still a prey to devastating fogs, began ignominiously for the guardians of the British legal system with two infamous and starkly contrasting miscarriages of justice. Barely had the new decade been ushered in when, early in January 1950, the wretched Timothy Evans, a simple and illiterate Welsh van driver, was convicted and sentenced to death for the murder by strangulation of his wife and baby daughter in the squalid west London flat in which they had lived. Evans, a troubled, neurotic man, confessed to the crimes under intensive police interrogation and his later protestations of innocence at the Old Bailey were ignored. He was hanged on March 9, 1950.

Three years later the real murderer was exposed when a new tenant at the same flat found to his horror that a number of women's bodies had been entombed under floorboards and inside a cupboard which had been papered over. Six bodies in all were discovered at 10 Rillington Place and the former owner of the premises John Reginald Halliday Christie, a violent and sinister sexual inadequate, confessed to the murders, including that of Mrs. Evans, who had been his tenant at Rillington Place along with her husband Timothy. The odious Christie was hanged at Pentonville in July 1953 but, inexplicably, an official inquiry into the case found that Evans had been fairly convicted of double murder - a transparent case of the legal establishment refusing doggedly to own up to its mistakes.

The second miscarriage, equally grotesque but for quite different reasons, concerned the case of Brian Donald Hume, a former airman and racketeer who was acquitted in 1950 of murdering a car dealer and receiver of stolen goods named Stanley Setty. Setty's dismembered body, wrapped in a collection of grisly bundles, had been scattered across the Essex mud flats around Tillingham from a light aircraft. After a retrial, Hume, who admitted having disposed of the body, was found not guilty of murder and sentenced to 12 years as an accessory. On his release in 1958, realising he could not be tried again for the same crime, he promptly confessed to the murder through the columns of the *Sunday Pictorial* newspaper.

Hume was eventually committed to Broadmoor for life but not before killing again. After emigrating to Switzerland he robbed a bank and shot a taxi-driver while escaping. He was convicted of murder, subsequently judged to be insane and returned to Britain. Both cases dominated public attention for several years and led to the realisation that the criminal justice system, revered throughout the world for its fairness and thoroughness, was fallible after all.

With international drug smuggling in its infancy, computer fraud still the stuff of futuristic fiction, sophisticated armed robbers generally thin on the ground and serious public disorder restricted to the occasional bank holiday scrummage on a south coast beach, crime headlines in the 1950's were made largely by murders, still relatively rare in Britain. But it was also the decade which saw the genesis of the Cold War, communist witch-hunts and "reds under the bed" scares. Special Branch and military intelligence were detailed to uncover a deeply buried seam of treachery within the Western intelligence community but ultimately failed to bring the principals to justice.

Their most blatant and embarrassing failure was the inability to prevent the defection of Guy Burgess and Donald Maclean to Russia in 1951. Before breaking cover and fleeing, they betrayed almost the entire British espionage network in Europe. After their highly-publicised flight, the authorities were still unable to expose their two main co-conspirators. Kim Philby and Anthony Blunt continued to undermine British intelligence work until they were identified in

DONALD HUME

DONALD MACLEAN, the British Diplomat who vanished in 1951 with Guy Burgess.

1963 and 1964 respectively. Even then Philby seemed to have little difficulty in escaping across the Iron Curtain and Blunt not only avoided arrest but was later knighted for his services to the art world.

There were, of course, some successes against the enemy within during the 1950's. In 1950 Klaus Fuchs, a government scientist at Harwell, was jailed for 14 years for passing atomic secrets to the Soviets and in the US, Ethel and Julius Rosenberg were executed by electric chair for the same offence. The information provided by Fuchs was said to have allowed the Soviet Union to bring its nuclear weapons programme forward by five years.

The decade also saw the beginning of the end for capital punishment in Britain, although it was not finally abolished until the next decade. No case speeded the reform process more than that of Ruth Ellis, the last woman to be hanged in this country. An obsessively jealous nightclub hostess and call-girl, the 28-year-old Ellis shot her charming but faithless boyfriend David Blakely in full public view outside a public house in Hampstead in 1955, shortly after miscarrying his child. It was a classic crime of passion and an offence which today would probably carry a medium-term prison sentence for manslaughter. Ruth Ellis was hanged at Holloway prison on July 13, 1955.

Three years earlier the murder of a policeman also led to a court case which prompted an outcry from the abolition movement. On November 2, 1952, Christopher Craig, 16 and Derek Bentley, 19

HOUSE OF MURDERS. The front view of the house in Rillington Place, Notting Hill, London, scene of the Christie murders.

were seen entering a London warehouse. When confronted by police on the warehouse roof, Bentley quickly surrendered but Craig continued shouting defiance and brandishing a pistol. In the ensuing struggle he shot dead a police constable before jumping 30 feet from the roof in an apparent suicide bid which he survived.

At the Old Bailey trial, much was made of Bentley, while already in police custody, having shouted to

Craig: "Let him have it Chris." The prosecution took this as an incitement to shoot, the defence as a plea to Craig to give up the gun. Bentley, illiterate and educationally subnormal, although not in possession of a firearm and already under arrest at the time of the killing, was convicted and sentenced to death for murder. Craig was also convicted but was too young to hang. He was detained at Her Majesty's Pleasure.

The campaign for a posthumous pardon for Bentley continues to this day.

Large scale organised crime was still regarded in Britain as a foreign problem. Scotland Yard believed Mafia-style organisations could not operate successfully on their ground but towards the end of the decade a pair of East End twins were beginning to create a criminal empire based on murder and intimidation which would soon shock the police out of any complacency. Both moderately successful amateur boxers, the twins were starting to realise how much money there was in a different type of brutality. But it would be another decade before the names of Ronald and Reginald Kray would be etched indelibly in the annals of criminal history.

JULIUS AND ETHEL ROSENBERG sentenced to death as atom spies. President Eisenhower refused them executive clemency on February 11, 1953, saying they had been accorded "the full measure of Justice."

THE FESTIVAL OF BRITAIN

THE SYMBOL OF THE FESTIVAL OF BRITAIN, 1951, designed by Abram Games, F.I.S.A.

The idea was born in the cold Spring of 1947 at a time when industry was almost at a standstill and coal shortages meant that chilly householders were only allowed to use electric fires for a few hours a day. In the darkness of the immediately post-war world, this was a shout of defiance. Britain would celebrate the centenary of the 1851 Exhibition, that proud statement of the nation's status as the leader of the industrial world, with a Festival proclaiming that, however much it had been battered and impoverished by the Second World War, it was still a great nation.

To many, this seemed an impossible dream, an absurd waste of money, but it caught the imagination of Herbert Morrison, the Deputy Prime Minister in the 1945 Labour Government. He persuaded his Cabinet colleagues to vote £11.5 million for the project and appointed Gerald Barry, the editor of the *News Chronicle*, who had floated the idea in his newspaper, to be the Festival's director general.

The 1851 Festival had been sited on 19 acres of Hyde Park, its central feature being Paxton's Crystal Palace. Its successor, on Morrison's insistence, since he was himself a South Londoner whose power base had been for many years County Hall, was destined for a former area of slum houses that had been almost entirely destroyed in the London blitz on the south bank of the Thames between Westminster and Waterloo bridges. Though at 27 acres it was larger in area than the 1851 site, it was hemmed in and awkwardly divided by the unsightly Hungerford railway bridge.

Barry recruited Hugh Casson to lead a team of young architects to create something exciting on these gloomy surroundings. Clearly, there was no possibility of another Crystal Palace: a series of pavilions were produced to house the different themes of the exhibition (The Land of Britain, Power and Production, Sea and Ships, British Tradition and so on) to be dominated by Ralph Tubb's 365ft diameter circular Dome of Discovery built of aluminium and supported by 48 tubular struts. To provide a special distinction, a competition was held to select a crowning glory for the site. This was won by the architectural team of Powell and Moya with the skylon, a thin pencil-like shape, 290ft high, which when lit up at night appeared to float above the dome and the lesser pavilions. To the critics of the Festival, and there were many of them, this seemingly purposeless "folly" represented the futility of the whole enterprise. But to others, myself among them, there was something magical about the London night with the skylon floating there, that has never been recaptured since.

Sculptors, like Henry Moore and Reg Butler, were commissioned to produce work. The idea of a cultural centre on the South Bank was mooted. The Royal Festival Hall, much derided at the time for its aircraft-hanger like appearance, though highly praised for its acoustics, was actually built. A foundation stone for a national theatre to be constructed hard by, was laid though the actual theatre was built in the 1960's, a short distance away.

Barry was an ideas man, less adept at following them through than dreaming them up, and, though he had picked a bright team, featuring unlikely talents like Gerard Hoffnung and Laurie Lee, there was never quite the follow-through there should have been. Strikes and bad weather bedevilled the building of the exhibition which was scarcely finished for the May opening. The ideas of the commercial exhibitors did not always chime well with those of the architects and decorators. Perhaps the full-size statue of the White knight from Alice in Wonderland which dominated one pavilion expressed best the slightly schizophrenic atmosphere of the enterprise.

Nevertheless, some eight million people visited the South Bank site during the summer of its existence. Then it was dismantled, the great dome cut up for scrap, many of the exhibits being packed aboard an old

WITH THE FRAMEWORK now finished, the Skylon, symbol of the Festival of Britain on the South Bank, takes on a pointer appearance.

liner, the Campania, to be toured round the coasts of Britain while others were taken by train for display in provincial cities.

It must not be thought that the South Bank comprised the whole Festival. The arts were represented in London theatres by the Oliviers performing Shakespeare's *Antony and Cleopatra* in repertory with Shaw's *Caesar and Cleopatra*, while John Gielgud presented *The Winter's Tale* and at Stratford-upon-Avon a series of Shakespeare's history plays were staged. Benjamin Britten's opera, *Billy Budd*, was specially commissioned and performed. Music festivals and art exhibitions were held in many parts of the country.

The most popular of all the entertainments provided were the Pleasure Gardens in Battersea Park, a brave attempt to create an equivalent of Tivoli at Copenhagen in a London setting. Like so much of the festival, it was uncertain of its purpose and hard commercial interests jockeyed for attention with the ideas of Barry's team. A fantastic miniature railway designed by the artist Rowland Emmett sat oddly beside a conventional big dipper. The imaginative illuminated walk which threaded through the tops of the park trees did not entirely match the candy-floss atmosphere below. The one undoubted success was the Guinness Clock, a wonder

of the advertising man's art and ingenuity, which displayed its mechanical charms every quarter hour. There were stages for ballet performances and concerts, but, while the fun fair continued when the rest of the Festival was just a memory, the concept of a pleasure garden never really took shape. The wrong place, perhaps.

When all was done and the Royal Festival Hall remained as the sole reminder of a brightly decorated site, what was the legacy? The immediate one was of a feeling of well-being. At one time, it looked as if the Festival would never take place, but it did, and the majority of the millions who visited it did have a feeling that Britain could be colourful again.

A number of architects and designers had used the Festival as a show case. Later, the cynics were to say that ill-constructed tower blocks were the most obvious architectural aftermath. (Indeed, the building of the Lansbury Estate in East London did form part of the 1951 Festival enterprise). But so did much more imaginative work. Institutions like the Design Centre and the growth of London and other cities as tourist attractions could be traced back to the Festival. Above all, it made a nation look forward and outward with some hope at a time when it badly need such a fillip.

PREHISTORIC MONSTER IN THE FESTIVAL DOME.
One of the features of the Dome of Discovery at the Festival.

FOUNTAINS PLAY as the Royal Family tour the South Bank Festival of Britain Exhibition after its opening to-day.

I was not around for the first half of the Fifties, arriving four years after the Festival of Britain, two years after the coronation, a few hours too late to be a contemporary of James Dean. I was completely self-absorbed throughout the second half. But though I missed the decade on its first showing, I was able to catch up with it when it came around again twenty years later.

For British art students in the Seventies, particularly students of design, the 50's were ripe for revival: a lost world of exhuberance, optimism and good ghastly taste.

The catalogue of an exhibition devoted to the Festival of Britain, "A tonic to the Nation," was an essential text for the avant-garde art student, as was Revis Hillier's book "Austerity/Binge", about the design boom that followed the war years. "Kitsch" became a term of approbation. Art nouveau and psychedelic posters were replaced by wire-and-coloured-ball wall plaques in the shape of artist's palettes. Baggy flared trousers and batik skirts went to Oxfam and drainpipes and ultra-bold frocks came out. At dinner parties, food was served on surviving examples of Ridgeway Potteries' "Homemaker" crockery, with its transfer-print design of Kitsch utensils, kidney-shaped coffee tables, potted plants and palette-shaped leaves, all jauntily collaged on a background of primitive stripes.

The Fifties, we half-understood, was a time when anything had seemed possible. A proliferation of inventive scientists and designers had set about creating the future. Hand in hand, they were developing new modes of transport, leisure-making home appliances, and all those wall plaques and furnishing fabrics inspired by molecular-structure models and microphotography. A booming economy and an egalitarian education system meant that everyone, or at least everyone's children, had a ticket to the party.

And then something must have gone wrong, or so it seemed from the perspective of the Student Union bar two decades later. The Fifties had promised *life* and *style*, long before the two were welded

Dressed-up as "Teds", Pete Murray, Freddie Mills and Josephine Douglas.

together into a single dreary word. The Seventies seemed to offer not much of either.

But of course history does not divide neatly by ten. The art students of twenty years ago who scoured the charity shops for "very Fifties" knick knackery were themselves a very Fifties, an essentially Fifties invention:

rebellious youth. Some of us were even teenagers, another Fifties coinage. The Seventies were in many respects our parents' Fifties dreams come true, so naturally we found fault with it on principal.

Rebellious teenagers, original mid-Fifties models British-style, were typified by a young man in parody Edwardian gear - draped jacket, crepe-soled shoes - and young woman in a delinquent dress and Yardley make-up. He, more often than she, was incited by Bill Haley singing "Rock Around the Clock" to riot in the aisles of the local cinema. Haley, like the disc jockeys who appeared in his wake on the television sets which half the country had bought in time for the coronation, was an ageing, avuncular figure from an earlier, country-and-western tradition. But an era has to start somewhere, and there were soon plenty of sneering youths - Presley, and the home-grown Wilde, Fury, Storm, Eager, and so on through the thesaurus of sexual depravity - to develop the theme.

It was all pretty theoretical at first, that depravity, or so the participants' children are now told. Pre-Sixties, girls were expected to say no and boys to respect them for it when they did. Instead, the newly defined teenager, loaded with cash from part-time or full-time jobs or both, was provided with newly-marketed distractions: clubs, coffee-bars, milk-bars, records, fashions, exploitation films to replace the Ealing comedies that had been killed by TV.

Parents despaired. They had

THE NEW ZODIAC:
"The distinctive styling of the new Zodiac and the superlative luxury of its appointment are everything the most discerning motorist could wish for."

TIES' CHILD

Tim Rostron

"The Edwardian"

A Fifties' interior with television set.

The "teenage look"

mapped out a future for their children, a life style, that the older generation could only hope to get started. They imagined a future where "frozen food" would be more than a matter of a bag of peas in the frosty ice-cream compartment of the few fridges in private homes.

There would be carpets covering the whole floor, in place of rugs and lino. The memory of the rubbish shown at the Festival of Britain - a showplace for frustrated old Forties designers - would be wiped out by the coming wave of clean and elegant Scandinavian styling.

One day, perhaps, we would have big, powerful cars like the American models, and more long, straight roads to accommodate them. Cheap jet travel might bring the new resorts on the Mediterranean coast as close as the converted barracks of Butlins. Machines would take half the burden at the workplace, and help with the housework in the modern new homes in the modern new towns.

It was there for the taking, so long as you had enough GCEs to get a decent job. "Homemaker" crockery, I now notice, is popping up in the catalogues of up market auctioneers. I know where it has come from. Art students started selling it off in the mid-Seventies, when Rotten, Vicious and crew came along, in their draped jackets and crepe-soled shoes and with their catchphrase, "I'm bored". Their parents may never have had it so good, but their children had never known it any different.

INDEX

a = column 1   b = column 2   c = column 3   d = column 4   e = column 5   f = column 6